The Mammals of Virginia

The Mammals of Virginia

by

Donald W. Linzey
Wytheville Community College
Wytheville, Virginia

The McDonald & Woodward Publishing Company
Blacksburg, Virginia
1998

The McDonald & Woodward Publishing Company
P. O. Box 10308, Blacksburg, Virginia 24062

The Mammals of Virginia

Composition by Rowan Mountain, Inc., Blacksburg, Virginia
Printed in the United States of America by McNaughton & Gunn, Inc., Saline, Michigan.

04 03 02 01 00 99 98 10 9 8 7 6 5 4 3 2 1

First printing August 1998

Library of Congress Cataloging-in-Publication Data

Linzey, Donald W.
The mammals of Virginia / by Donald W. Linzey.
p. cm.
Includes bibliographical references (p.) and index.
ISBN 0-939923-36-X (cloth) : $59.95
1. Mammals—Virginia. I. Title.
QL719.V5L56
599.09755—dc20 94-25288
CIP

To Nellie
My constant companion and faithful friend

Table of Contents

Appendixes

References and Index

Preface

This book is a personal expression of an abiding interest in mammals that has stimulated almost four decades of research on mammals in the southeastern United States. It is designed and intended for use by persons with a wide variety of backgrounds. Students of mammalogy and vertebrate biology, sportsmen, game biologists and wildlife management specialists, public health workers, mammalogists engaged in research on a given species or group of species, and individuals simply with an interest in mammals can all find valuable and useful information in this book. Although written primarily about the mammals of Virginia, the information included applies to mammals found in much of the surrounding region.

While the literature of mammalogy is extensive, it is not readily available to the average individual or even to the serious researcher who does not have access to a large research library. For this reason, I have included pertinent references throughout the text. Technical terms have been kept to a minimum; in some instances, however, their usage is unavoidable. For this reason, a glossary of such terms has been included.

In compiling information for this most comprehensive work on Virginia mammals to be published in more than fifty years, astounding gaps in knowledge were discovered. Although field studies in recent years have contributed much data about the biology of Virginia's mammals, many aspects of the life history and distribution of even the commonest species are still unknown. It is my hope that this compilation, by revealing these gaps, will stimulate future research on the mammals of Virginia. I urge anyone who has specimens or significant information relevant to the mammals of Virginia to contact me at: 1418 Nellies Cave Road, Blacksburg, Virginia 24060.

No present-day volume on mammals would be complete without acknowledging the fact that many populations of mammals have changed considerably since the influence of humans became established in North America. Some mammal species have benefitted from, or adapted to, man's activities and have increased and extended their ranges and numbers as the region's natural biota and ecological structure have been altered and the land settled by increasing numbers of humans. Such has been the case with the white-tailed deer, eastern cottontail, red fox, gray fox, raccoon, woodchuck, and cotton rat. In the case of the deer, overpopulation has resulted, with the numbers of animals sometimes exceeding the capacity of the land to support them.

On the other hand, some mammal species have been virtually extirpated in many areas through direct reductions by hunting, trapping, and poisoning, as well as indirectly by habitat destruction. Hopefully, we are approaching an enlightened age in which mammalian species will no longer be generally bountied and persecuted. However, the destruction of habitat, which is more detrimental than direct persecution to most biotic populations in the long run, continues, seemingly unabated. Practices detrimental to wildlife include the filling of coastal marshes, channelization of streams, flooding of wildlife habitat by impoundments, conversion of land to agricultural uses, strip mining, and, in some cases, inappropriate forest management. These activities, together with urban encroachment, continue to deplete the amount and quality of living space available to our native mammals.

The ranges of all mammal species are continuously changing — some only slightly, others drastically — results of either climatic changes or man's activities. New species may find conditions suitable and move into the state. Others may no longer be able to find suitable habitat within the state and be lost from Virginia's fauna.

For many people, a glimpse of a wild animal in its native habitat is an occasion rare enough to be long remembered. While a visit to a zoo can be highly instructive, it rarely serves to foster a true appreciation for the biology of a wild species and its place in the natural world. This situation bestows upon naturalists the responsibility to educate others about the lives and habits of our native biota in the hope that such enlightenment will lead to a greater appreciation of native species and a desire for their preservation. Such a hope has been uppermost in my mind as I prepared this book.

Donald W. Linzey
Department of Biology
Wytheville Community College
Wytheville, Virginia 24382

Acknowledgements

This book has been in preparation for the past 18 years. During this period, many individuals have assisted me in a variety of ways.

The following 84 individuals either searched their collections and forwarded data, loaned specimens for verification of taxonomic identification, permitted access to the mammal collections under their care, or provided data in some other way.

Fred J. Alsop, III, East Tennessee State University, Johnson City, Tennessee; Ronald E. Barry, Jr., Frostburg State University, Frostburg, Maryland; Rollin Bauer, Charles M. Dardia, and Kevin J. McGowan, Cornell University, Ithaca, New York; George D. Baumgardner, Texas A and M University, College Station, Texas; Michael D. Bay, Averett College, Danville, Virginia; Janet K. Braun, Oklahoma Museum of Natural History, University of Oklahoma, Norman, Oklahoma; Walter Bulmer, Northern Virginia Community College, Annandale, Virginia; Jerry R. Choate, Museum of the High Plains, Fort Hays State University, Hays, Kansas; Mary K. Clark, North Carolina State Museum of Natural Sciences, Raleigh, North Carolina; Jack A. Cranford, Matt Barnes, and Llyn Sharp, Virginia Polytechnic Institute and State University, Blacksburg, Virginia; Ted Daeschler, The Academy of Natural Sciences of Philadelphia, Philadelphia, Pennsylvania; Jack Dubois, Manitoba Museum of Man and Nature, Winnipeg, Manitoba; Robert E. Dubos, University of Connecticut, Storrs, Connecticut; Carl H. Ernst, George Mason University, Fairfax, Virginia; Linda Fink, Sweetbriar College, Sweetbriar, Virginia; Robert D. Fisher, National Museum of Natural History, Washington, D. C; William L. Gannon, Museum of Southwestern Biology, University of New Mexico, Albuquerque, New Mexico; Sarah B. George, Natural History Museum of Los Angeles County, Los Angeles, California; Eugene Gourley, Radford University, Radford, Virginia; Nancy Groseclose, Emory and Henry College, Emory, Virginia; Gene Grubitz, Roanoke College, Salem, Virginia; Paula M. Guthrie, Vertebrate Museum, Humboldt State University, Arcata, California; Michael J. Harvey, Tennessee Technological University, Cookeville, Tennessee; Michael S. Hensley, Bridgewater College, Bridgewater, Virginia; Gene K. Hess, Delaware Museum of Natural History, Wilmington, Delaware; David Huckaby, California State University, Long Beach, California; Robin Hughes and Tim Cutter, Virginia Living Museum, Newport News, Virginia; Michael L. Kennedy, Memphis State University, Memphis, Tennessee; Gordon L. Kirkland, Shippensburg University, Shippensburg, Pennsylvania; Allen Kurta, Eastern Michigan University, Ypsilanti, Michigan; John Leffler, Ferrum College, Ferrum, Virginia; William Z. Lidicker, Jr., Museum of Vertebrate Zoology, University of California, Berkeley, California; Robin Lillie, Museum of Natural History, University of Iowa, Iowa City, Iowa; David Lintz, Strecker Museum, Baylor University, Waco, Texas; Timothy O. Matson, Cleveland Museum of Natural History, Cleveland, Ohio;

Gregory J. McConnell, Emory and Henry College, Emory, Virginia; J. Kelly McCoy, Oklahoma State University, Stillwater, Oklahoma; V. Rick McDaniel, Arkansas State University, State University, Arkansas; M. Elizabeth McGhee, University of Georgia, Athens, Georgia; Robert McKinney, Mount Rogers National Recreation Area, Jefferson National Forest, Marion, Virginia; Suzanne B. McLaren and Duane Schlitter, Carnegie Museum of Natural History, Pittsburgh, Pennsylvania; Nancy Moncrief, Virginia Museum of Natural History, Martinsville, Virginia; Musser, Guy and Wolfgang Fuchs, American Museum of Natural History, New York, New York; Philip Myers, Museum of Zoology, University of Michigan, Ann Arbor, Michigan; James R. Northern, University of California, Los Angeles, California; Douglas Ogle, Virginia Highlands Community College, Abingdon, Virginia; John F. Pagels, Virginia Commonwealth University, Richmond, Virginia; Bruce D. Patterson, Field Museum of Natural History, Chicago, Illinois; Matthew C. Perry, Patuxent Wildlife Research Center, United States Fish and Wildlife Service, Laurel, Maryland; Ralph Peters, Lynchburg College, Lynchburg, Virginia; Yar Petryszyn, University of Arizona, Tuscon, Arizona; J. Dan Pittillo, Western Carolina University, Cullowhee, North Carolina; Charles W. Potter, Smithsonian Institution, Washington, D. C; James R. Purdue, Illinois State Museum, Springfield, Illinois; David L. Reed and Mark S. Hafner, Museum of Natural Science, Louisiana State University, Baton Rouge, Louisiana; Rick Reynolds, Endangered Species Biologist, Virginia Department of Game and Inland Fisheries, Verona, Virginia; Robert K. Rose, Old Dominion University, Norfolk, Virginia; Maria E. Rutzmoser, Museum of Comparative Zoology, Harvard University, Cambridge, Massachusetts; Paul W. Sattler, Liberty University, Lynchburg, Virginia; Douglas H. Shedd, Randolph-Macon Woman's College, Lynchburg, Virginia; Aine Shiozaki, Museum of Natural History, University of Illinois, Urbana, Illinois; Robert S. Sikes, James F. Bell Museum of Natural History, University of Minnesota, Minneapolis, Minnesota; Robert Simpson, Lord Fairfax Community College, Middletown, Virginia; Donald A. Smith, Carleton University, Ottawa, Ontario; Betsy Stinson, Wildlife Biologist Supervisor, Virginia Department of Game and Inland Fisheries, Blacksburg, Virginia; W. Mark Swingle, Stranding Program Coordinator, Virginia Marine Science Museum, Virginia Beach, Virginia; M. Pete Thompson, Eastern Kentucky University, Richmond, Kentucky; Robert M. Timm, Museum of Natural History, University of Kansas, Lawrence, Kansas; Wayne VanDevender, Appalachian State University, Boone, North Carolina; Ron Vasile, The Chicago Academy of Sciences, Chicago, Illinois; John O. Whitaker, Jr., Indiana State University, Terre Haute, Indiana; Paul Whitehead, Peabody Museum of Natural History, Yale University, New Haven, Connecticut; Shirley Whitt, Lynchburg College, Lynchburg, Virginia; Laurie Wilkins, Florida Museum of Natural History, University of Florida, Gainesville, Florida; Susan M. Woodward, Royal Ontario Museum, Toronto, Ontario; Shi-Kuei Wu and David J. Holton, University of Colorado Museum, University of Colorado, Boulder, Colorado.

In addition, the following 124 individuals, schools, and museums indicated that, as of 1992, they either had no specimens of Virginia mammals in their collections or that they did not maintain collections of mammals: Laura Abraczinskas, Michigan State University, The Museum, East Lansing, Michigan; David D. Adams, Kentucky State University, Frankfort, Kentucky; Steve Adams, Dabney S. Lancaster Community College, Clifton Forge, Virginia; Delise Alison, McGill University, Redpath Museum, Montreal, Quebec; Ticul Alvarez S, Escuela Nacional de Ciencias Biologicas, Instituto Politecnico Nacional, Mexico, DF; David Archibald, San Diego State University, San Diego, California; Peter V. August, University of Rhode Island, Kingston, Rhode Island; Donald Baird, Princeton University, Museum of Natural History, Princeton, New Jersey; David Baron, Saskatchewan Museum of Natural History, Regina, Saskatchewan; M. Barton, Centre College, Danville, Kentucky; Billy Batts, Longwood College, Farmville, Virginia; Thomas S. Baur, Virginia Military Institute, Lexington, Virginia; Lawrence E. Bayless, Concord College, Athens, West Virginia; Tom Bennett, Bellarmine College, Louisville, Kentucky; Joy E. Berg, Jefferson National Forest, Roanoke, Virginia; Charles E. Bland, East Carolina University, Greenville, North Carolina; Elizabeth Blatt, Science Museum of Virginia, Richmond, Virginia; Jack Brooks, College of William and Mary, Williamsburg, Virginia; John Brushaber, Asbury College, Wilmore, Kentucky; R. J. Cannings, University of British Columbia, Vancouver, British Columbia; Angelo Capparella, Illinois State University, Normal, Illinois; W. Buddie Chandler, George Washington National Forest, Staunton, Virginia; Robin Rich Coates, Eastern Shore Community College, Melfa, Virginia; Ronald E. Cole, University of California-Davis, Museum of Wildlife and Fisheries Biology, Davis, California; Paul W. Collins, Santa Barbara Museum of Natural History, Santa Barbara, California; Harold N. Cones, Christopher Newport University, Newport News, Virginia; Joseph A. Cook, University of Alaska Museum, Fairbanks, Alaska; Dan Covington, Union College, Barbourville, Kentucky; Curtis W. Cox, Southwest Virginia Community College, Richlands, Virginia; Bruce S. Cushing, Middle Tennessee State University, Murfreesboro, Tennessee; Scott Cutler, Museum of Northern Arizona, Flagstaff, Arizona; Michael J. Davis, George Washington National Forest, Hot Springs, Virginia; Wayne H. Davis, University of Kentucky, Lexington, Kentucky; Rafael O. de SB, University of Richmond, Richmond, Virginia; Department of Biology, Alice Lloyd College, Pippa Passes, Kentucky; Charles L. Douglas, University of Nevada, Las Vegas, Nevada; Ruth Douglas, Piedmont Virginia Community College, Charlottesville, Virginia; Steve D. Earhart, Campbell University, Buies Creek, North Carolina; George A. Feldhamer, Southern Illinois University, Carbondale, Illinois; John W. Fern, Thomas Moore College, Crestview Hills, Kentucky; Sandy Florence, Jefferson National Forest, Wytheville, Virginia; Kenneth N. Geluso, University of Nebraska, Omaha, Nebraska; A. L. Gennaro, Eastern New Mexico University, Natural History Museum, Portales, New Mexico; Andrew G. Gluesenkamp, University of California, Davis, California; Robert E. Goodwin, Colgate University, Hamilton, New York; Bob Gordon, West Liberty State College, West Liberty, West Virginia; Steven E. Hardin, Spalding University, Louisville, Kentucky; Edward G. Haverlack, George Washington National Forest, Covington, Virginia; Bruce J. Hayward, Western New Mexico University, Silver City, New Mexico; Cleve Hickman, Washington and Lee University, Lexington, Virginia; Mary Etta Hight, Marshall University, Huntington, West Virginia; Mark Holmgren, University of California-Santa Barbara, Vertebrate Museum, Santa Barbara, California; Ellen Holtman, Virginia Western Community College, Roanoke, Virginia; Herbert W. House, Elon College, Elon College, North Carolina; Howard E. Hunt, Louisiana Tech University, Ruston, Louisiana; Frances James, Florida State University, Tallahassee, Florida; Frederick J. Jannett, Jr., Science Museum of Minnesota, Saint Paul, Minnesota; Cheri Jones, Mississippi Museum of Natural Science, Jackson, Mississippi; Cheri A. Jones, Denver Museum of Natural History, Denver, Colorado; Stephen R. Karr, Carson-Newman College, Jefferson City, Tennessee; Verne Keifer, Virginia Wesleyan College, Norfolk, Virginia; Michael H. Kesner, Indiana University of Pennsylvania, Indiana, Pennsylvania; Kerry S. Kilburn, West Virginia State College, Institute, West Virginia; Rick Kopp, Georgetown College, Georgetown, Kentucky; Thomas E. Labedz, University of Nebraska State Museum, Lincoln, Nebraska; Al Lavergne, Jefferson National Forest, Flatwoods Civilian Conservation Center, Coeburn, Virginia; Donald W. Linzey, Wytheville Community College, Wytheville, Virginia; Jeffrey B. Llewellyn, Brevard College, Brevard, North Carolina; Nancy G. Makin, Germanna Community College, Locust Grove, Virginia; Donald F. McAlpine, The New Brunswick Museum, Saint John, New Brunswick; Nancy L. McCartney, University of Arkansas, Fayetteville, Arkansas; Thomas M. McGrath, Central Virginia Community College, Lynchburg, Virginia; Les Meade, Morehead State University, Morehead, Kentucky; Albert G. Mehring, The State Museum of Pennsylvania, Harrisburg, Pennsylvania; Sharon Mohney, Jefferson National Forest, Buena Vista, Virginia; B. L. Monroe, University of Louisville, Louisville, Kentucky; Montshire Museum, Norwich, Vermont; Henry B. Mushins, University of South Florida, Tampa, Florida; Joseph B. Myers, Norfolk State University, Norfolk, Virginia; David Nagorsen, Royal British Columbia Museum, Victoria, British Columbia; Nevada State Museum, Carson City, Nevada; Anne W. Nielsen, Blue Ridge Community College, Weyers Cave, Virginia; Steven M.

Norris, Arizona State University, Tempe, Arizona; David F. Oetinger, Kentucky Wesleyan College, Owensboro, Kentucky; Charles A. Owens, King College, Bristol, Tennessee; Roger A. Powell, North Carolina State University, Raleigh, North Carolina; Sandie Purick, Grayson Highlands State Park, Mouth of Wilson, Virginia; Dennis C. Quinlan, West Virginia University, Morgantown, West Virginia; Robert F. Randall, Bluefield College, Bluefield, Virginia; Cynthia E. Rebar, Murray State University, Murray, Kentucky; W. Roberts, Rappahannock Community College, Glenns, Virginia; W. E. Roberts, University of Alberta, Edmonton, Alberta; Franklin Robinson, Mountain Empire Community College, Big Stone Gap, Virginia; A. Roest, California Polytechnic State University, San Luis Obispo, California; Beth A. Schramm, Southern Virginia College for Women, Buena Vista, Virginia; Catherine Seibert, Montana State University, Bozeman, Montana; Herb Shadowen, Western Kentucky University, Bowling Green, Kentucky; John Sharp, John Tyler Community College, Chester, Virginia; Russell E. Shea, Randolph-Macon College, Ashland, Virginia; Howard Shellhammer, San Jose State University, San Jose, California; Shaukat M. Siddiqi, Virginia State University, Petersburg, Virginia; Terry Slater, George Washington National Forest, Bridgewater, Virginia; David H. Snyder, Austin Peay State University, Clarksville, Tennessee; L. F. Southard, Virginia Department of Forestry, Charlottesville, Virginia; J. M. Spencer, Thomas Nelson Community College, Hampton, Virginia; Frederick B. Stangl, Midwestern State University, Wichita Falls, Texas; David W. Steadman, New York State Museum, Albany, New York; Gerald E. Svendsen, Ohio University, Athens, Ohio; Joe H. Taft, Bays Mountain Park, Kingsport, Tennessee; Richard S. Teitz, Dartmouth College, Hanover, New Hampshire; Ralph L. Thompson, Berea College, Berea, Kentucky; G. S. Trelawny, James Madison University, Harrisonburg, Virginia; Philip Unitt, San Diego Natural History Museum, San Diego, California; University of Maryland, College Park, Maryland; K. Verghese, Southside Virginia Community College, Alberta, Virginia; Stephen H. Vessey, Bowling Green State University, Bowling Green, Ohio; Jerry W. Warner, Northern Kentucky University, Highland Heights, Kentucky; William David Webster, University of North Carolina, Wilmington, North Carolina; Gordon K. Weddle, Campbellsville College, Campbellsville, Kentucky; Peter D. Weigl, Wake Forest University, Winston-Salem, North Carolina; Charlie White, New River Community College, Dublin, Virginia; Joseph J. Whittaker, North Carolina Agricultural and Technical State University, Greensboro, North Carolina; Erik K. Wright, University of Missouri, Museum of Zoology, Columbia, Missouri; Philip L. Wright, University of Montana, Missoula, Montana; Bruce A. Wunder, Colorado State University, Fort Collins, Colorado; R. H. Yahner, Pennsylvania State University, University Park, Pennsylvania.

All drawings appearing in this book are by Robert Turner. Mammal skulls used for illustration were obtained from a variety of sources including the National Museum of Natural History in Washington, D. C.; the North Carolina State Museum of Natural Sciences in Raleigh, North Carolina; the Virginia-Maryland College of Veterinary Medicine in Blacksburg, Virginia; The Virginia Museum of Natural History at Virginia Tech in Blacksburg, Virginia; the Animal Damage Control Office of the United States Department of Agriculture in Blacksburg, Virginia; and from the author's private collection.

Many photographers have graciously agreed to allow their photographs to be used in this book. Their names appear in the Credits for Color Plates, Appendix IV. In addition, I would like to express my appreciation to Don Wick for allowing access to the photographic files of the Tennessee Wildlife Resources Agency in Nashville, Tennessee; to Lisa Morgan for providing access to the United States Fish and Wildlife Service Audiovisual Library in Washington, D. C.; to Rick Lewis for providing access to the National Park Service Photographic Library in Washington, D. C.; and to Mrs. Roger Barbour of Lexington, Kentucky, for graciously permitting use of her husband's photographs.

The resources of the Wytheville Community College library were used extensively. My thanks are extended to Anna Ray Roberts, George Mattis, Jr., and Brenda King, without whose help the acquisition of vital data would have been considerably more difficult.

Other individuals who assisted in some way include Bill Bassinger, Steve Croy, Mike Fies, Robert Fisher, Larry Freeman, Tammy Hall, Suzanne Jenkins, Rick Reynolds, Tom Tomsa, Merlin Tuttle, and Mack Walls.

My sincerest appreciation is expressed to James L. Wolfe and the late William J. Hamilton, Jr., who read early versions of the complete manuscript, and to John O. Whitaker, Jr., who reviewed the entire final manuscript and range maps. Each of these individuals offered valuable comments. I also wish to thank the following individuals for reviewing sections of the manuscript and offering constructive suggestions: Robert L. Downing, United States Fish and Wildlife Service (retired), Clemson, South Carolina; Michael J. Harvey, Tennessee Technological University, Cookeville, Tennessee; Ronald R. Keiper, Pennsylvania State University, Mont Alto Campus, Mont Alto, Pennsylvania; James N. Layne, Archbold Biological Station, Lake Placid, Florida; and Peter D. Weigl, Wake Forest University, Winston-Salem, North Carolina.

The monumental task of typing and revising early versions of the manuscript was superbly supervised and handled by Pamela Aliff. Her expertise with the computer and her dedication to her work were invaluable contributions to the preparation of this book. Tammy Hall assisted in revising early versions of the manuscript. Final versions of the tables as well as final revisions of the manuscript were competently prepared by Andrea Deel. Christy Brecht assisted in preparing the index.

Finally, I thank my wife, Nita, for putting up with the many mammal skins and skulls and the piles of books, reprints, correspondence, and manuscript sections that cluttered several rooms of our home for varying periods of time. Her understanding and patience made possible the completion of this book.

Introduction

Introduction

Mammals are a diverse and fascinating group within the Animal Kingdom. They inhabit all regions of the world from the tropics to the poles, excepting only the interior surfaces of the Antarctic and Arctic.

Mammals, along with some marine organisms known as lancelets and tunicates, as well as fishes, amphibians, reptiles, and birds, belong to a major group of animals classified as the phylum Chordata, all of whom possess a dorsal, hollow nerve chord. At some point during their lives, all chordates pass through a stage where they possess at least rudimentary gill slits and a notochord. The subphylum Vertebrata comprises the fishes, amphibians, reptiles, birds, and mammals, all of whom possess a vertebral column composed of individual vertebrae.

Characteristics of Mammals

Mammals can be distinguished from other vertebrates by two main external features. The word "mammal" is derived from the Latin word *mamma,* meaning breast. Breasts, or mammary glands, are typical of female mammals. The milk that they secrete provides nourishment for the young during their early development. The second external distinguishing characteristic of mammals is the presence of hair during at least some part of their lifetime. In addition to these obvious external characters, mammals also possess a number of unique internal structures, such as three bones, or ossicles, in the middle ear; a lower jaw, or mandible, of only one bone, the dentary; and a temporal-dentary type of jaw articulation. Together with the birds, mammals have a four-chambered heart and are warm-blooded, maintaining a relatively high, constant body temperature (i.e., they are homeothermic).

Various aspects of mammalian biology will be covered below, where appropriate, in individual species accounts. Several key topics covering some generalizations of mammalian biology are presented here to serve as an introduction to the more detailed discussions that follow.

Hair and Pelage

The bodies of most mammals are covered by hair. The typical pelage (fur) of mammals consists of the underfur and guard hairs. The *underfur* consists of a layer of soft hairs which lie next to the skin, while the *guard hairs* are longer and coarser. The underfur serves to insulate the body against extreme heat or extreme cold, while the guard hairs protect the skin and body from such things as briers and thorns. Many marine species have lost most of their hair secondarily — that is, through continuing evolution — except for a few whiskers, or vibrissae.

Hair contains various kinds and amounts of pigments. Individual hairs may be white, gold, tan, black, or many other colors, but together they combine to give the pelage a brownish, golden, whitish, blackish, or grizzled appearance. Some individuals have little or no pigment. They are light-colored or white. Individuals with no pigment have white fur and pink eyes and are referred to as *albinos.* Individuals that are completely black are referred to as being *melanistic.* Hairs are periodically replaced by new ones, a process known as *molting.* The sexes are similar in appearance in most mammals.

Teeth

Mammals generally possess two sets of teeth during their lifetime — *deciduous* (milk) teeth and *permanent* teeth. The teeth are divided into four types from front to back: *incisors, canines, premolars,* and *molars.* Dentition consisting of different types of teeth used for different purposes is referred to as *heterodont dentition.* Incisors are chisel-shaped, sharp-edged, and specialized for cutting and/or gnawing. Canines, which are best developed in the carnivores, are used for piercing skin and tearing flesh. Premolars and molars *(cheek teeth)* are used mainly for grinding food. An exception to this pattern is that the fourth upper premolar and first lower molar of most carnivores have developed into specialized teeth for cracking bones and shearing tendons and are known as the *carnassial teeth.*

While all members of a species typically have the same number, kinds, and arrangements of teeth, not all species of mammals have all four types of teeth. Rabbits, hares, and rodents, for example, lack canine teeth. A relatively long space *(diastema)* exists between the incisors and the premolars in these forms. Many ungulates lack upper incisors and upper canines, their place being occupied instead by a callous pad.

The distribution, kinds, and numbers of teeth typical of any given species are expressed as a *dental formula.* The dental formula of a striped skunk, for example, is: 3/3, 1/1, 3/3, 1/2 = 34. Each of the four types of teeth are separated by a comma, with the teeth of the maxillary, or "upper jaw," being written above those of the mandible, or "lower jaw." Thus, the adult striped skunk has 3 incisors, 1 canine, 3 premolars, and 1 molar on each side of its upper jaw and 3 incisors, 1 canine, 3 premolars, and 2 molars on each side of its lower jaw. Each side of the mouth contains 17 teeth, while the entire mouth contains 17 x 2, or 34, teeth. All dental formulas given here are for adult animals.

Locomotion

Methods of locomotion typical among mammals vary considerably. Some mammals, such as the bear and raccoon, place the entire lower surface of each *manus,* or forefoot, and *pes,* or hindfoot, on the ground each time they take a step. This is a primitive means of walking; animals that possess it are said to have a *plantigrade,* or flat-footed, means of locomotion. Humans, although bipedal, are also plantigrade. A more advanced form of walking, where the weight of the animal is borne on the ends of the "knuckles," is found in such animals as the bobcat, mountain lion, and dogs. These mammals exhibit a *digitigrade* form of walking. They have more spring in their walk and usually more speed than is characteristic of plantigrade species. They also walk more quietly and are better balanced. The most specialized means of locomotion is found in the hoofed mammals, where the entire weight of the animal is borne on the nails (hooves) of only one, two, or three toes on each foot. This method of locomotion is termed *unguligrade.* It is a modification of the lower limbs for fleet-footedness and occurs in species such as the deer, antelope, and horse.

Reproduction

Some mammals (e.g., mouse, rat) have young several times a year, while others (e.g., bat) have young only once or even only once every other year (e.g., black bear). Generally, the smaller mammals, which have a shorter life span and are preyed upon by many generally larger species, are the more prolific, while the larger mammals normally have only one or two litters per year. Bats, which normally have a single annual litter, are an exception because even though small, they are long-lived.

Most mammals bear living young; that is, they are *viviparous.* The *ovum,* or egg, is fertilized in the anterior portion of the oviduct. Fertilization usually occurs shortly after mating, but many bats mate in fall and can store the sperm within their reproductive tracts for extended periods. Fertilization does not take place until spring. This process is called *delayed fertilization.* The resulting zygote then travels down the oviduct and becomes implanted in the wall of the uterus. Implantation usually occurs shortly after the zygote reaches the uterus, but in some forms (e.g., otter, weasel, bear) it is delayed for periods of six to nine months, a process called *delayed implantation.* Mammalian embryos receive their nourishment through an *umbilical cord* which connects the embryo with the *placenta.* The length of time that the embryo remains within the uterus is known as the *gestation period.* Gestation may range from 12.5 days, as in opossums, to 22 months, as in elephants. The process of delayed implantation results in an extended gestation period.

The condition of newborn mammals varies widely. In some groups (e.g., marsupials), the young are born in a very immature condition. Following birth, they immediately climb into the *marsupium,* or pouch, on the female's abdomen, attach themselves to a teat, and continue their development. The young of most other species of mammals (e.g., mouse, squirrel) are born in a more fully developed form but without hair or teeth and with their eyes and ears sealed. These young remain helpless for varying periods, depending upon their species, and are wholly dependent upon their mother or parents for food, shelter, and care. Such mammals are referred to as *altricial.* On the other hand, the young of yet other mammals (e.g., white-tailed deer, beaver) are born fully covered with hair, with their eyes and ears open, and are able to stand and walk about shortly after birth. Such mammals are referred to as *precocial.*

Longevity

The life span of wild mammals in Virginia varies from less than one year (most rodents) to 20 or more years (some bats, black bear). Mammals in captivity generally survive longer than their wild counterparts because they receive regular and better food and are protected from parasites, predators, and adverse weather conditions.

Habitats

Mammals may live on land *(terrestrial)* or in the water *(aquatic).* Those mammals that live on land may be surface-dwellers (e.g., deer), or they may be *aerial* (e.g., bat), *arboreal* (e.g., gray squirrel, flying squirrel), or *fossorial* (e.g., mole). Each has evolved specialized anatomical features in order to adapt to its mode of existence. Such features include the specialized structure of the bat forelimb to better support the wing, the palmate forefeet of the mole for efficient digging, and the broad membrane *(patagium)* between the wrists and ankles of flying squirrels to provide a broader surface for gliding.

Freshwater inhabitants such as beaver and otter spend some time on land, while some marine species such as the dolphin and whale spend their entire lives in the water. These forms may possess such structural adaptations as webbing between the toes, paddlelike limbs, and a dorso-ventrally flattened tail.

Some mammals live in restricted ecological habitats (e.g. jumping mouse, cave-dwelling bats), while others can adapt to many types of situations and may range from coastal marshes to the mountains (e.g., foxes, raccoon).

Home Range

Most mammals live within, and are quite familiar with, an irregularly circumscribed area known as their *home range.* Within this area are located the homesite, food, water, and all other resources upon which an individual depends for survival. Home ranges are not static but change in response to variations in environmental parameters such as population density, food availability, flooding, season of the year, and other factors. The home ranges of two or more individuals of a species may overlap each other and, if a portion of the home range is defended, it is known as the *territory.* Not all species are territorial; some are social and live in colonies or herds.

Food

Mammals may be categorized as *insectivorous* (insect-eating), *carnivorous* (meat-eating), *herbivorous* (plant-eating), *granivorous* (seed-eating), or *omnivorous* (feeding on both plant and animal matter). Within each category, the food of most species is determined partly by the seasonal availability of food items and partly by choice. Many species remain active throughout the year. During the warmer months, food is generally more plentiful than during the colder winter months. Some mammals store food in caches for use during the winter. Others store food in the form of body fat. During the colder winter months, some of these mammals (e.g. chipmunk, gray squirrel, bear) become inactive for varying periods, while others (e.g., bats, woodchuck, jumping mouse) enter a deep sleep known as *hibernation* that is characterized by lowered metabolism, lowered heartbeat, and lowered respiration rate. Hibernation allows a species to survive during an unfavorable period of the year in a given area.

Predation

Many smaller mammals are preyed on by other animals, including snakes, large turtles, birds of prey, and other mammals. This is particularly true of rodents (mice, rats, etc.) which are important links in the food chains and food webs.

A food web is an intricate network of plants and organisms which are dependent on each other for survival. Two major trophic levels exist — producers and consumers. Green plants form the broad base of all food webs. Plants are *producers* since they convert inorganic materials (carbon dioxide and water) into organic materials by utilizing the energy of sunlight in the process of photosynthesis. Those mammals that feed directly on plants (e.g., rabbits, voles, deer) are known as *primary consumers.* Primary consumers are always fewer in number and possess less biomass than producers. *Secondary consumers* feed on primary consumers. Secondary consumers are always fewer in number and possess less biomass than primary consumers. A *tertiary consumer* level may be present in some food webs. Predatory species are secondary or tertiary consumers.

Classification of Mammals

The classification of organisms serves several purposes. It is a means by which organisms can be differentiated, particularly wide-ranging forms that may be found in regions around the world. It permits persons in other parts of the same country as well as in other countries to identify a specific animal. For example, in various parts of the United States, the mountain lion is known as a puma, panther, painter, catamount, and cougar. In Central and South America the animal may be known as the Mexican lion, leopardo, Leon, or *chim blea.* The scientific name of the mountain lion, however, is the same worldwide — *Puma concolor.*

Phylogenetic classifications permit the grouping of forms based on their relationship. Forms that are most closely related are grouped together, whereas more distantly related forms are placed in separate groupings. For example, the mountain lion and bobcat are closely related; thus, both are classified in the same family, Felidae. The bobcat is more distantly related to the wolf, *Canis;* thus, it is placed in a different family.

All mammals are classified in the Kingdom **Animalia**, the phylum **Chordata**, the subphylum **Vertebrata**, the superclass **Tetrapoda**, and the class **Mammalia**. The class **Mammalia** is composed of two subclasses — **Theria** and **Prototheria**. The subclass Prototheria includes the egg-laying monotremes (duck-billed platypus and echidna) of Australia and New Zealand. All other living mammals are classified in the subclass Theria. Members of the subclass Theria are viviparous mammals whose young are retained, at least for a portion of their development, within the reproductive tract of the female. This subclass is divided into two infraclasses — **Metatheria** and **Eutheria**.

Infraclass Metatheria

Mammals in the infraclass Metatheria differ from those in the only other living infraclass — the infraclass Eutheria — by the presence of epipubic bones and by having the placenta either incomplete or absent. An external abdominal pouch, the marsupium, may be well developed, rudimentary, or absent. If present, such a pouch encloses the teats and serves as a pocket in which the young are carried. The duplex female reproductive tract consists of a double vagina and two uteri. The posterior ends of the uteri are fused medially. At this point, a third canal, the birth canal or median vagina, develops at the time of parturition and opens into the urogenital sinus independently of the already existing lateral vaginae. Uterine development is brief in these mammals, and the young are born at a very incomplete stage of development.

The skull of marsupials has a relatively small braincase and a correspondingly small brain.

Infraclass Eutheria

The infraclass Eutheria comprises the true placental mammals. Members of this infraclass have a well developed placenta and have neither a marsupium nor epipubic bones. In addition, few species possess more than 44 teeth.

Each kind of mammal is further classified into an order, a family, a genus, a species, and in some instances, a subspecies. For example, the complete classification of the golden mouse would be as follows:

Kingdom — Animalia
Phylum — Chordata
Subphylum — Vertebrata
Superclass — Tetrapoda
Class — Mammalia
Subclass — Theria
Infraclass — Eutheria
Order — Rodentia
Family — Muridae
Genus — *Ochrotomys*
Species — *nuttalli*
Subspecies — *aureolus*

The mountain lion, however, would be classified in the following manner:

Kingdom — Animalia
Phylum — Chordata
Subphylum — Vertebrata
Superclass — Tetrapoda
Class — Mammalia
Subclass — Theria
Infraclass — Eutheria
Order — Carnivora
Family — Felidae
Genus — *Puma*
Species — *concolor*
Subspecies — *couguar*

History of Mammal Investigations in Virginia

The earliest reference to mammals in Virginia was by Thomas Hariot, who visited America in 1585 and conducted natural history explorations from the Roanoke Colony in what is now eastern North Carolina. Hariot was the first to describe the natural characteristics of what is today eastern North America, writing on the Indians, plants, and wildlife (Hariot, 1588). In his account of Virginia, Hariot enumerated among the beasts "Deare," "Conies" [rabbits], "Saquenúckot, and Maquówoc, two kinds of small beasts greater then conies which are very good meat," "Squirels," and "Beares" and added:

> *I have the names of eight and twenty severall sorts of beasts which I have heard of to be here and there dispersed in the coutrie, especially in the maine: of which there are only twelve kinds that we have yet discovered, and of those that be good meat we know only them before mentioned. The inhabitants sometime kil the Lyon and eat him: and we sometime as they came to our hands of the Wolves or wolvish Dogges.*

The 12 mammals were the black bear, gray squirrel, rabbit, otter, opossum, raccoon, civet cat or skunk, "Lyon" or panther, wolf, marten, deer, and porpoise. Although the porpoise was listed under the fish, the illustration clearly showed that Hariot was referring to the mammal. Hariot was the first to distinguish the American from the European deer, noting that the former have longer tails "and the snags of their hornes looke backward." John White, a companion of Hariot, completed a series of 112 watercolor paintings of the people, plants, and animals of the new colonies. Dr. E. E. Hale examined these paintings in the British Museum and reported on their condition (Hale, 1860).

George Percy was the next to record observations of Virginia's mammals. In 1606, he noted many "Squirels" and "Conies" along the James River near the present city of Williamsburg. In describing the area, he stated:

> *In this Countrey I have seene many great and large Medowes having excellent good pasture for any Cattle. There is also great store of Deere both Red and Fallow. There are Beares, Foxes, Otters, Bevers, Muskats, and wild beasts unknowne* (Tyler, 1907).

Some "Otters, Beavers, Martins, Luswarts [lynx], and sables" were found along the Potomac River above the present site of Washington, DC, by Captain John Smith and his men during their exploration of that region in 1608 (Barbour, 1969).

In a *True Declaration of the Estate of the Colonie in Virginia*, printed in 1610, we read:

> *The Beasts of the Countrie, as Deere, red, and fallow, do answere in multitude (people for people considered) to our proportion of Oxen, which appeareth by these experiences. First the people of the Countrie are apparelled in the skinnes of these beasts; Next, hard by the fort, two hundred in one heard have been usually observed. Further, our men have seen 4000. of these skins pyled up in one wardrobe of*

Powhaton; *Lastly, infinite store have been presented to* Captaine Newport *upon sundry occurrents: such a plentie of Cattell, as all the Spaniards found not in the whole kingdome of* Mexico, *when all their presents were but hennes, and ginycocks, and the bread of Maize, and Cently. There are* Arocouns, *and* Apossouns, *in shape like to pigges, shrouded in hollow roots of trees; There are Hares and Conies, and other beasts proper to the Countrie in plentifull manner* (Force, 1836–1846).

Goode (1886) stated:

The State papers of Great Britain contain many entries of interest to naturalists. King James I was an enthusiastic collector. December 15, 1609, Lord Southampton wrote to Lord Salisbury that he had told the King of the Virginia squirrels brought into England, which were said to fly. The King very earnestly asked if none were provided for him — whether Salisbury had none for him — and said he was sure Salisbury would get him one." In the Domestic Correspondence of Charles I "is a note of one Jeremy Blackman's charge, in all 20 pounds, for transporting four deer from Virginia, including corn and a place made of wood for them to lie in.

In 1611, Captain Samuel Argall traveled to the head of the Potomac River, and:

then marching into the Country, he found great store of Beasts as big as Kine, of which, they killed two, and found them to be good and wholesome meat, and yet easie to be killed being but heavy, and slow Creatures (Purchas, 1625).

Most later authors have considered the word "Beasts" to be buffalo. However, Clarke (1670) understood it to mean elk.

In 1612, Captain John Smith wrote *A map of Virginia. With a description of the country, commodities, people, government and religion.* This work contained accounts of 18 kinds of mammals plus a drawing of a porpoise which was listed as a fish. The mammals included the deer, gray squirrel, flying squirrel, opossum, muskrat (*mussascus*), hare, bear, beaver, raccoon (*aroughcun*), otter, fox, marten, polecat, wolf, weasel, mink, wildcat (*vetchunquoyes*), and rat. He was the first to describe the raccoon, muskrat, and flying squirrel. He stated:

There is a beast they call Aroughcun *(raccoon), much like a badger, but useth to live on trees, as Squirrels doe. Their Squirrels some are neare as great as our smallest sort of wilde Rabbits, some blackish or blacke and white, but the most are gray.*

A small beast they have, they call Assapanick *but we call them flying squirrels, because spreading their legs, and so stretching the largenesse of their skins that they have bin seene to fly 30 or 40 yards. An* Opassom *hath a head like a* Swine, *and a taile like a* Rat, *and is of the bignes of a Cat. Under her belly shee hath a bagge, wherein shee lodgeth, carrieth, and sucketh her young.* Mussascus, *is a beast of the forme and nature of our water* Rats, *but many of them smell exceeding strongly of muske.*

The Historie of Travell into Virginia Britania by William Strachey (1612) discusses 21 species of Virginia mammals, many of his data from the writings of Captain John Smith. Smith stated "Martins, Powlecats, weessels and Minkes we know they have, because we have seen many of their skinnes." Strachey wrote "Martins, polecatts, weesells, and monkeys we knowe they have, because we have seene many of their skynns." The term "monkey" may refer either to the raccoon or to some of the larger species of squirrels. The 21 mammals listed include "red" and "fallow" deer, raccoon, squirrel, flying squirrel, opossum, muskrat, hare, bear, beaver, otter, lion, wild cat, fox, wolf, marten, polecat, weasel, porpoise, and seal.

In 1613, Alexander Whitaker, who was minister to the colony of Virginia, wrote to a friend in London:

Amongst the Beasts in Virginia, there are two kinds most strange. One of them is the Female Possowne, *which hath a bag under her belly, out of which she will let forth her young ones, and take them in again at her pleasure. The other is the flying* Squerril, *which, by the help of certain broad flaps of Skin, growing on each side of her fore-legs, will fly from one tree to another at twenty or thirty paces distance, and more if she have the benefit of a little puff of Wind* (Clarke, 1670).

Ralph Hamor, secretary of the colony, wrote his *True Discourse on the Present Estate of Virginia* in 1615. He noted that:

The Land is stored with plenty and variety of

wilde beasts, Lions, Bears, Deere of all sorts . . . Beavers, Otters, Foxes, Racounes, almost as big as a Fox, as good meat as a lamb, hares, wild Cats, muske rats, Squirills flying, and other of three or foure sorts, Apossumes, of the bignesse and likenesse of a Pigge, of a moneth ould, a beast of as strange as incredible nature, she hath commonly seaven yong ones, sometimes more and sometimes lesse which at her pleasure till they be a moneth olde or more she taketh up into her belly, and putteth forth againe withour hurt to her selfe or them.

In addition, he stated:

Of each of these beasts, the Lion excepted, my selfe have many times eaten, and can testifie that they are not onely tastefull, but also wholesome and nourishing foode.

Samuel Purchas (1625) briefly summarized some of the larger forms comprising the mammalian fauna. He stated:

The chiefe beasts of Virginia are Beares, lesse then those in other places, Deare like ours, Aroughcun *much like a Badger, but living on trees like a Squirrell. Squirrells, as big as Rabbets, and other flying Squirrels, called* Assapanick, *which spreading out their legges and skinnes seeme to flie thirtie or fortie yards at a time. The* Ouassom *hath a head like a Swine, a taile like a Rat, as bigge as a Cat, and hath under her belly a bagge wherein shee carryeth he yong. Their Dogges barke not, their Wolves are not much bigger then our Foxes, their Foxes are like our silver-haired Conies, and smaell not like ours.*

He also noted that in 1613 the adventurers discovered in Virginia "a slow kinde of cattell as bigge as kine which were good meate."

In June, 1631, Henry Fleet ascended the Potomac to the region of the Little Falls above the present site of Georgetown in the District of Columbia. He noted that the woods abounded with deer, buffalo, and bear. A list of the more common plants and animals of Virginia was prepared for Governor Berkeley in 1649 (Force, 1838; Ewan and Ewan, 1970). Brief descriptions were given for only a few of the more unique mammals. Wodenoth (1649) and Bullock (1649) listed approximately 20 kinds of mammals known from Virginia.

On the map of Virginia and Maryland so carefully drawn by Augustine Herrman in 1650, the area near the Dismal Swamp is described as follows:

The Land between James River and Roanoke River is for the most part Low Suncken Swampy Land not well passable but with great difficulty. And herein harbours Tiggers Bears and other Devouring Creatures.

Between 1650 and 1674 several expeditions were organized to explore the regions west of the Blue Ridge Mountains. These expeditions were summarized by Alvord and Bidgood (1912) in *The First Explorations of the Trans-Alleghany Regions by the Virginians, 1650-1674.* An 11-day expedition in 1650 covered the area from Fort Henry (now Petersburg) to Clarksville in Mecklenburg County. Only brief references to mammals are contained in the accounts of this journey.

John Lederer, a German, arrived in Jamestown in 1668. During 1669 and 1670 he led three expeditions to what is now western Virginia. While traveling near the York River in eastern Virginia in March, 1669, he recorded an account of a wild cat seizing a deer and noted:

This creature is something bigger than our English fox, of a reddish grey colour, and in figure every way agreeing with an ordinary cat; fierce, ravenous and cunning: for finding the deer (upon which they delight most to prey) too swift for them, they watch upon branches of trees, and as they walk or feed under, jump down upon them (Lederer, 1672).

On March 15, 1669, near the Rappahannock River, Lederer observed:

Great herds of red and fallow deer [probably elk and white-tailed deer] *I daily saw feeding; and on the hill-sides, bears crashing mast like swine. Small leopards I have seen in the woods, but never any lions, though their skins are much worn by the Indians. The wolves in these parts are so ravenous, that I often in the night feared my horse would be devoured by them, they would gather up and howl so close round about him, though tethr'd to the same tree at whose foot I my self and the Indians lay: but the fires which we made, I suppose, scared them from worrying us all. Beaver and otter I met with at every river that I passed; and the woods are full of grey foxes* (Alvord and Bidgood, 1912).

During his third expedition, in August,

1670, Lederer recorded "vast herds of red and fallow deer" near the headwaters of the Rappahannock River. Concerning the deer, he stated:

To heighten the beauty of these parts, the first springs of most of those great rivers which run into the Atlantick ocean, or Cheseapeack bay, do here break out, and in various branches interlace the flowry meads, whose luxurious herbage invites numerous herds of red deer (for their unusual largeness improperly termed elks by ignorant people) to feed. The right elk, though very common in New Scotland, Canada, and those northern parts, is never seen on this side of the continent: for that which the Virginians call elks, does not at all differ from the red deer of Europe, but in his dimensions, which are far greater; but yet the elk in bigness does as far exceed them: their heads, or horns, are not very different; but the neck of the elk is so short, that it hardly separates the head from the shoulders; which is the reason that they cannot feed upon the level ground but by falling on their knees, though their heads be a yard long: therefore they commonly either brouse upon trees, or standing up to the belly in ponds or rivers feed upon the banks: their cingles or tails are hardly three inches long (Alvord and Bidgood, 1912).

John Banister, a clergyman of the Church of England, emigrated to Virginia before 1668 and spent much time studying the natural history of coastal Virginia. In 1670, he noted the bartering of "furs of Beaver, Otter, Fox, Cat, Raccoon, and Deer-Skins." He stated:

We have here also (besides our Tame Breed of Cows Horses and Hoggs) Bears Panthers, Elks Possums, a sort of Creature with a false belly, into which it receives its young when in danger; it hangs by its Tayl, and is frequently shown in England for a Sight. Three sorts of Squirrels, Hedge Conies and other Quadruped Inhabitants of ye Woods.

Expeditions by Batts, Woods, and Fallam in 1671 and by Needham and Arthur in 1673 recorded little information about mammals (Alvord and Bidgood, 1912). The Reverend John Clayton, rector of Crofton at Wakefield in Yorkshire, visited Virginia in 1685. In 1688, he submitted a letter to the Royal Society which was published in three parts in the *Philosophical Transactions* (Clayton, 1693; 1694). His annotated list of the reptiles, birds, and mammals of the colony was the most complete up to that time. He listed 18 kinds of native mammals including elk, deer, raccoon, opossum, hare, fox squirrel, flying squirrel, ground squirrel, muskrat, two kinds of bats, lion, bear, several kinds of wild cats and polecats, beaver, wolf, and fox. Several mammals were discussed by Thomas Glover in his "Account of Virginia" published in 1676.

In 1694, William Byrd took a female opossum to England. This animal furnished the materials for the first dissertation on the anatomy of the marsupials (Tyson, 1698; Goode, 1886).

Beverley's *History* of 1705 (Wright, 1947) noted that beavers, otters, muskrat, mink, and many other wild creatures were common in the coastal marshes, swamps, and savannas. He stated that the Inner Lands have:

an Infinity of small Birds, as well as Deer, Hairs, Foxes, Raccoons, Squirrels, Possums. And upon the Frontier Plantations, they meet with Bears, Panthers, Wild-Cats, Elks, Buffaloes, and Wild Hogs, which yield Pleasure, as well as Profit to the Sports-man.

He also noted the presence of whales and porpoises. An expedition under the command of Captain Henry Batt set out about 1665 from Appomattox. Within seven days they reached the foothills of the Blue Ridge. Beverley stated that:

they found large level Plains, and fine Savanna's, *Three or Four Miles wide, in which were an infinite Quantity of Turkies, Deer, Elks and Buffaloes, so gentle and undisturbed, that they had no Fear at the Appearance of the Men: But wou'd suffer them to come almost within Reach of their Hands.*

Beverley also noted that: "Hoggs swarm like Vermine upon the Earth. . . . The Hogs run where they list, and find their own Support in the Woods, without any Care of the Owner."

Alexander Spotswood led an expedition to the Shenandoah Valley in 1716. In the meadows bordering the Shenandoah River they found "herds of buffalo and elk feeding like cattle in a pasture" (Bruce, 1924). Mark Catesby lived in Virginia from 1712 to 1719, collecting and painting many of the plants and animals. He listed 30 native and five domestic species of mammals from Virginia (Catesby, 1754).

William Byrd's *History of the Dividing Line betwixt Virginia and North Carolina* (1728) lists the following species encountered by the surveying party: opossum, rabbit, four kinds of squirrels, beaver, muskrat, rats and mice, raccoon, bear, fox, otter, mink, lynx, wild cat, polecat, panther, two kinds of seals, dolphin, bottlenosed whale, buffalo, deer, and elk. In William Byrd's *Histories of the Dividing line betwixt Virginia and North Carolina* (Boyd, 1929), observations on 13 mammals are recorded. William Byrd's *Natural History of Virginia*, originally published in German in 1733, includes 28 native and five domestic species of mammals (Beatty and Mulloy, 1940).

Salmon's (1736–1738) discussion of Virginia mammals is an extensive quotation of John Clayton's letter of 1688. No new information is included.

John Mitchell, a physician who lived and practiced medicine in Urbanna, Virginia, for over 40 years was interested in studies of natural history. In 1738, he wrote a *Dissertation upon the Elements of Botany and Zoology* of Virginia (Mitchell, 1748). Although not a major contribution to the listing of Virginia's mammals, it does contain the names of some of the larger and more easily observed species. Goode (1886) stated that Mitchell appeared to have been engaged in physiological studies on the opossum in 1743.

In a letter dated March 21, 1739, John Clayton, a botanist living in Gloucester County, wrote:

To satisfie the Gentlemen you mention who is so desirous of Knowing the diversion of hunting and shooting here and the several sorts of game pray give my service to him and tell him, that we have all the tame domestick beasts and fowls that you have in England, and great variety of wild ones as Deer in great pleanty, Bears, Buffaloes, Wolves, Foxes, Panthers, wild Cats, Elks, Hares (smaller than any of y's which run in holes in the earth and hollow trees when pressed by the dogs, and are much like w't you call in England bush Rabbits), Squirrels 3 or 4 sorts, Raccoons, Oppossums, Beavers, Otters, muskrats, Pole cats, minks and there has been two Porcupines killed here but they are very scarce.

. . . the bears, Panthers, Buffaloes and Elks and wild Cats are only to be found among the mountains and desert parts of the countrey where there are as yet but few inhabitants and the hunting there is very toilsome and laborious and sometimes dangerous. Yet the Common Sort of People who live among the Mountains kill great Quantitys of Bears every year; but the greatest destruction of 'em is made in the beginning of the Winter when the bears lay themselves to sleep in the caves and holes among rocks of the mountains at w'ch time the people go to the mouth of the Cave w'th their guns loaded and shoot 'em as they lye in their dens (Anonymous, 1899).

Although Peter Kalm traveled in North America from 1748 to 1751, it is unclear whether the nine or ten mammal species mentioned in his accounts from Virginia actually were observed there (Kalm, 1772; Benson, 1937).

Dr. Thomas Walker traveled from Albemarle County, Virginia, to Kentucky and back between March and July, 1750. "We killed on the Journey 13 Buffaloes, 8 Elks, 53 Bears, 20 Deer, 4 Wild Geese, about 150 Turkeys, besides small game" (Hulbert, 1903; Summers, 1929). Daniel Boone frequently traveled through Virginia from 1750 to 1780. His accounts, primarily of the larger furbearers, are contained in numerous journals and books (see Thwaites, 1916; Bakeless, 1939).

Andrew Burnaby visited Virginia during 1759 and 1760. "Of quadrupeds there are various kinds; squirrels of four or five different species, opossums, raccoons, foxes, beavers, and deer; and in the dosorts and uninhabited parts, wolves, bears, panthers, elks or moose-deer, buffaloes, mountain-cats, and various other sorts" (Burnaby, 1775). He also mentioned ground and flying squirrels and the polecat or skunk.

John Forster summarized the findings of several early naturalists and in 1771 published *A Catalogue of the Animals of North America*, with many references to Virginia mammals. A somewhat similar synthesis of all known publications on explorations was published in 12 volumes in 1819 by John Pinkerton. The section on Virginia in the last volume (pages 564–620) reviewed previous papers but added nothing new concerning the state's mammals.

Thomas Jefferson's *Notes on the State of Vir-*

ginia (1787; Peden, 1955) was the most important scientific work published to that time in America. Jefferson discussed the topography, natural history, and natural resources of Virginia, and included a section comparing the quadrupeds of America and Europe. Although he obviously drew upon some of his own observations of Virginia's mammals and may have utilized weights of some species taken in Virginia, he added little new information about these species.

Benjamin Barton's *Notes on the Animals of North America* (1792) provided useful information on the early ranges and distributions of several species, including the elk, buffalo, woodchuck, fox squirrel, and red squirrel. Richard Harlan's *Fauna Americana* (1825), John Godman's *American Natural History: Mastology* (1826), and Audubon and Bachman's *Viviparous Quadrupeds of North America* (1846-1854) contained several references to Virginia mammals.

Kercheval, in his *History of the Valley of Virginia*, first published in 1833, noted: "Much the greater part of the country between what is called the Little North Mountain and the Shenandoah River, at the first settling of the Valley was one vast prairie, and like the rich prairies of the west, afforded the finest possible pasturage for wild animals. The country abounded in the larger kinds of game. The buffalo, elk, deer, bear, panther, wild cat, wolf, fox, beaver, otter, and all other kinds of animals, wild fowl, etc., common to forest countries, were abundantly plenty." He further commented: "The sheep and hogs were devoured by the wolves, panthers and bears." In addition to the above mammals, Kercheval also made mention of the muskrat, squirrel, raccoon, groundhog, and polecat (Kercheval, 1925).

A number of Virginia's mammalian species were included in Baird's "Report of the Pacific Railway and Mexican Boundary Survey Expedition" which was contained in his *Mammals of North America* (1859). Thomas Whitehead's *Hand-Book* of Virginia (1893) treated groups of small mammals, such as mice and rats, but not individual species. Vernon Bailey's two papers on the mammals of the District of Columbia (1896a, 1923) listed 38 and 41 species, respectively. Many of the species he listed are also found in Virginia. In a later paper entitled "Mammals of the Vicinity of Washington," Bailey (1926) stated:

> *Two hundred years ago the country now occupied by Washington and the District of Columbia was real wilderness, teeming with game animals, large and small. There were buffaloes, elk, deer, bears, panthers, wolves, beavers and martens, which have since disappeared before the advance of civilization, but most of the smaller quadrupeds of that day are still to be found here in more or less reduced abundance.*

A survey of the Dismal Swamp by Charles Stansbury (1925) resulted in a listing of 29 mammals plus eight others whose occurrence was deemed likely. A three-day study of the mammals of Bath and Highland counties was conducted by Vernon Bailey and W. B. Bell during April, 1929. They discussed the occurrence of 34 species in general terms, but no specimens were taken or examined (Bailey, 1929).

During the 1930s, the first two attempts by zoologists to treat systematically all of the mammals of the state were undertaken. A thesis by Margaret Slaughter entitled "The Wild Mammals of Virginia" (1934), completed at the University of Richmond, listed 66 species. In 1938, Clyde Patton completed a thesis entitled "A Preliminary Distributional List of the Mammals of Virginia" in which he included 106 species and subspecies (Patton, 1938b). In 1940, John Lewis published his annotated "List of Mammals of Amelia County, Virginia." This list included 33 species and subspecies.

The years 1946 and 1947 saw the appearance of the only two books published to date on the mammals of the state. *The Mammals of Virginia* by John W. Bailey (1946) included sections on the history of mammalogy in Virginia as well as a list of the fossil mammals from Virginia. His species accounts covered all of the native terrestrial and marine forms as well as the domestic species in the state. An extensive bibliography was included. *Wild Mammals of Virginia* by Charles Handley, Jr., and Clyde Patton (1947) was published by the Virginia Commission of Game and Inland Fisheries. All native species were discussed and their ranges were mapped.

Since 1947, the only systematic study of mammals covering the entire state has been a thesis on rare and endangered species in Virginia by W. P. Russ (1973). However, a great number of papers have been published dealing with the distribution, ecology, life history, physiology, and other characteristics of individual species. These are listed in the Bibliography. Also, many theses concerning the biology and/or management of particular species of Virginia's mammals have been written by graduate students at Virginia's colleges and universities. These also are listed in the Bibliography.

The proceedings of a Symposium on the Great Dismal Swamp was published in 1979. These proceedings included Handley's historical account of mammal investigations in this unique area (Handley, 1979a).

In May, 1978, a Symposium on Endangered and Threatened Plants and Animals of Virginia was held at Virginia Polytechnic Institute and State University. The proceedings of this symposium (Linzey, 1979) contain the species accounts and recommendations of the more than 200 biologists who participated in this meeting. In the preface of the proceedings, Linzey wrote:

> *It is becoming increasingly important that the flora and fauna vulnerable to extinction or extirpation be identified. Knowledge of their distribution, habitat and biology is essential for assessing environmental quality and for land-use planning by various organizations and agencies. Furthermore, by identifying those forms about which little is known, it is hoped that significant future research efforts may be directed towards these results.*

A second symposium on Virginia's endangered species was held in 1989 (Terwilliger, 1991). In his chapter on mammals, Handley (1991) stated: "Many, if not most, of the recommendations and concerns of the 1978 symposium have been addressed. The result is a leap in knowledge of natural history greater than anything that ever preceded it in Virginia."

Although those individuals who have contributed so much to the increase in knowledge about Virginia's mammals during the past two decades are too numerous to mention here, their contributions are recognized and discussed throughout the text and are listed in the Bibliography. A few, however, do deserve special mention at this time. Dr. Charles O. Handley, Jr., National Museum of Natural History, has done more to advance knowledge of Virginia's mammals during the past 50 years than any other individual. He has taught, conducted field studies, done taxonomic research, chaired the Mammal Committee for both endangered species symposia, lectured, and published. His contributions to mammalogy in Virginia are immeasurable. Other mammalogists who have made significant contributions to mammal distribution, taxonomy, and biology during the past decade include Jack Cranford, Virginia Polytechnic Institute and State University; Virginia (Tipton) Dalton, University of Arizona; Donald Linzey, Wytheville Community College; John Pagels, Virginia Commonwealth University; Charles Potter, National Museum of Natural History; Robert Rose, Old Dominion University; Jerry Wolff, Oregon State University and Environmental Protection Agency; and John Baker, Michael Fies, and Joe Coggin of the Virginia Department of Game and Inland Fisheries. Most of these individuals are currently involved in continuing studies of Virginia's mammals.

Physiographic Regions of Virginia

Virginia is located midway along the east coast of the United States.

In latitude, the state reaches from 36° 30'N along its southern border to about 39° 30'N at its northernmost point. Roughly triangular in shape, Virginia encompasses some 102,830 square kilometers. The greatest north-south distance is approximately 320 kilometers, the maximum east-west extent about 640 kilometers (Woodward and Hoffman, 1991).

Five major physiographic provinces occur in Virginia. From east to west they are the Coastal Plain, Piedmont, Blue Ridge, Ridge and Valley, and Appalachian Plateau provinces (Figure 1).

The Coastal Plain Province (or Tidewater region) is a low, relatively flat region deeply penetrated by the sea. It consists primarily of sands, gravels, and clays. The larger rivers draining the region include the Potomac, Rappahannock, York, and James. The province extends westward to the fall line, an area where the low, relatively flat recent sedimentary deposits of the coastal plain meet the mass of old, hard, rolling crystalline rocks that form outcrops over most of the rest of Virginia. The fall line creates on all the rivers that cross it a zone of rapids that limit the inland penetration of ocean tides and brackish water. It separates two areas of different geological ages and textures; thus, these areas possess different landforms and soils. Pines are common over much of the coastal plain. Swamp forests of bald cypress, tupelo, red maple, and black gum are found along the rivers and in the Great Dismal Swamp.

The Piedmont Province is generally a low, rolling plateau that slopes gently eastward until its hard crystalline rocks descend deep under the sediments of the coastal plain at the fall line. Its gently rolling uplands provide a gradual transition between the flatter coastal plain and the mountains. The western portion of the Piedmont Province, however, is characterized by a series of hills and ridges that make that portion considerably more hilly than the eastern and central portions. Oaks and hickories are the predominant trees in the northern portion of this province with pines becoming more abundant south of the James River.

West of the Piedmont stands the majestic Blue Ridge Province, composed of sharp peaks and broad, rolling ridge crests. The crest of the Blue Ridge gradually rises in elevation from north to south. The portion northeast of Roanoke consists of an irregular mountain ridge that ranges from a single ridge with a width of less than 3.2 km to a complex group of ridges with an overall width of 16 to 19 km. Elevations range up to almost 1,220 m above sea level. Southwest of Roanoke, the Blue Ridge Province is a slightly to highly dissected upland that ranges up to nearly 113 km in width. Here it begins a steady increase in height and width which culminates in western North Carolina with many peaks reaching elevations of more than 1830 m above sea level. In Vir-

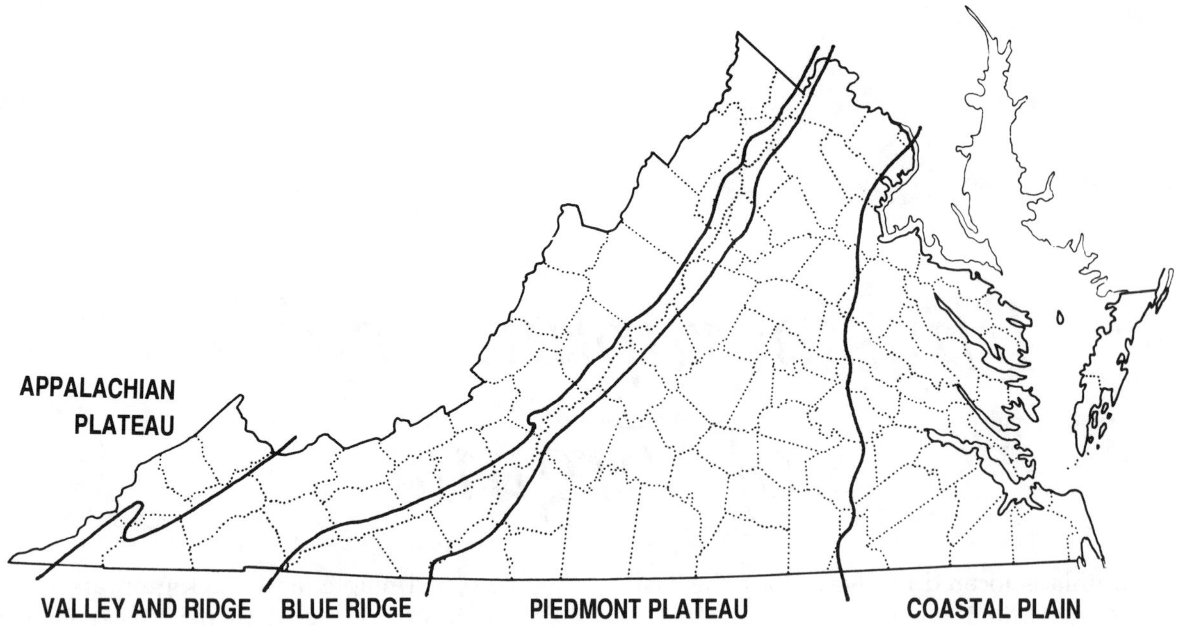

Figure 1. Physiographic provinces of Virginia.

ginia, this province culminates in an elevated plateau almost 915 m above sea level from which arise the tallest and most scenic mountains in Virginia — White Top and Mount Rogers with peak elevations at 1,682 m and 1,746 m above sea level, respectively. These mountains, with their stands of red spruce (White Top), Fraser fir (Mount Rogers), and northern hardwood forests, provide habitat for a number of vertebrates with northern affinities. Among the mammals, these include the northern flying squirrel, the red-backed vole, and the bog lemming. Major rivers draining the Blue Ridge include the Potomac, Shenandoah, James, Staunton, and New.

The Ridge and Valley Province consists of two quite different subregions. A broad, undulating plain lies immediately west of the Blue Ridge. This valley, known as the Great Valley, ranges in width from about 48 km in northern Virginia to less than 1.5 km near Buchanan. The Great Valley forms a zoogeographic barrier to the dispersal and distribution of some animal species, but acts as a dispersal corridor for others. In some areas, the valley narrows and forms high-elevation "land-bridges" connecting the Blue Ridge with the Alleghany Mountains to the west. Such constricted areas occur near Buchanan, Wytheville, and Marion. The Piedmont is connected to the Great Valley via the Potomac, James, and Roanoke water gaps. Oak, hickory, and formerly American chestnut, are the dominant forest trees.

Along the western edge of the Great Valley the terrain changes abruptly into a series of alternating ridges and valleys. The valleys range in width from approximately 24 to 56 km. Elevations exceed 1,220 m (4,000 ft) above sea level at several points (Beartown Mountain, 1,435 m; Elliotts Knob, 1,360 m; Reddish Knob, 1,341 m; Sounding Knob, 1,339 m; and others). Numerous water gaps break through the parallel ridges. Oak-hickory forests are predominant. Formerly, American chestnut was an important member of this forest type.

The Appalachian Plateau Province is a low plateau with rolling hills and valleys. It gradually slopes downward to the Kentucky state line. Coal beds are abundant. Major drainage is by means of the westward-flowing Big Sandy and Cumberland rivers which flow westward, draining eventually into the Ohio River. Beech, maple, hemlock, oaks, tulip trees, buckeyes, hickories, ashes, and magnolias characterize the forest vegetation of Virginia's westernmost province.

The average annual precipitation for Virginia ranges from approximately 89 to 127 cm.

Areas of heaviest rainfall are found in western Lee County and in the vicinity of the Dismal Swamp. The southeastern portion of the state receives an average of less than 25 cm of snow per year, while the areas of maximum snowfall include the central Blue Ridge, the Burkes Garden region, and the Mount Rogers area.

A more extensive discussion of the physiographic regions and climate of Virginia may be found in Fenneman (1938); Hoffman (1979); and Woodward and Hoffman (1991).

Species Accounts

Species Accounts

An individual species account has been prepared for each of the 114 species of mammals currently or previously inhabiting Virginia. Information for each species is presented in a standardized format incorporating a systematic description of 11 parameters of life history, as described below. If no data are available for one or some of these parameters for a given species, the pertinent section has been omitted. Classification generally follows that of Nowak (1991). Scientific and vernacular names follow Jones et al. (1997).

The life history parameters given for each species include the following:

Description. A qualitative description of the adult of both sexes together with a range of typical measurements and weights. A brief description of the skull is also included.

Distribution. A description of the current distribution of each species in North America, the past and present distribution in Virginia and, where appropriate, surrounding states. Maps depict the current North American range of each species as well as its range in Virginia.

Habitat. A short description of the principal habitat types in which the species has been found.

Habits. A variety of behavioral and ecological information which helps to characterize the species in question. Information may include activity patterns, sociability, movements within the home range, denning habits, relationships with other species, economic importance, and notes about the voice and the primary senses. Unique abilities are given special attention.

Food. The food habits of the species with primary emphasis on studies in Virginia. When data from Virginia are unavailable, preference is given, in order, to information from surrounding states, the southeastern United States, and elsewhere in the United States.

Reproduction and Development. The breeding season, gestation period, and litter size, with primary emphasis on data from studies in Virginia, and secondarily, from studies in surrounding states, the southeastern United States, and elsewhere in the United States. Information about the growth and development of the young is also summarized.

Longevity. The life span of the species and, where available, data concerning the longest-lived individuals.

Pelage Variations. A review of molting patterns and albinistic, erythristic, and melanistic individuals from Virginia.

Parasites and Disease. A review of parasites and disease recorded specifically in mammals in Virginia. Scientific names of parasites presented in this section are those given in the original reference.

Predation. Specific instances of predation within Virginia along with a list of potential predators.

Geographic Variation. A list of geographic variants currently described as subspecies, with discussion of their morphological differences. The approximate ranges of these geographic variants are delineated by broken lines on the range maps. Ranges of biological subspecies are shown on range maps with solid lines.

Subspecies are recognized on the basis of criteria for a biological subspecies concept presented by Whitaker (1970). That concept recognizes the interruption of gene flow as the first and basic criterion for recognizing subspecies. The introduction of a primary isolating mechanism represents the first step in speciation and recognizes the subspecies as an evolutionary unit rather than as simply a geographic variation. Thus, the biological subspecies is defined as a population or group of populations separated from other such populations by the existence of some factor which has stopped or significantly reduced gene flow but in which individuals from different groups potentially can interbreed — that is, secondary isolating mechanisms have not formed completely (Whitaker, 1970). The second criterion is that after a primary isolating mechanism is in effect, the results of evolution must be observable, i.e., the population or populations must have evolved in different directions and morphological or other recognizable taxonomic designation of differences must have formed. In cases where the biological subspecies differs from that of the geographic variants, the earliest recognized subspecific name has been chosen.

Location of Specimens. Each museum, college, university, or private collection known to contain one or more specimens from Virginia is listed. Acronyms for mammal collections cited by Yates et al. (1987) are given in Table 1.

Key to the Orders of Virginia Mammals

1a Animal with four feet with claws 2

1b Animal with flippers, wings, or hooves 6

2a Canine teeth absent, leaving wide diastema between incisors and cheek teeth; incisors chisellike 3

2b No diastema between incisors and cheek teeth; incisors not chisellike 4

3a Ear longer than tail; hind foot with four claws; side of rostrum extensively fenestrated; two pairs of incisors in upper jaw, the second pair reduced and located directly behind first pair . . . . . Lagomorpha page 95

3b Ear shorter than tail; hind foot with five claws; side of rostrum not extensively fenestrated; only one pair of incisors in upper jaw . . . . . Rodentia page 111

4a Eyes inconspicuous; snout flexible and protruding beyond mouth; canine teeth neither longer nor noticeably different from adjoining teeth; skull small, narrow, and pointed; skull length of adult less than 44 mm . . . . . Insectivora page 33

4b Eyes well-developed; snout not flexible and not protruding beyond mouth; canine teeth prominent and longer than cheek teeth or incisors; skull length of adult greater than 44 mm 5

5a Five upper incisors on each side; innermost toe of hind foot thumblike, opposable, and without a claw; tail prehensile; female with external abdominal pouch in which young are carried . . . . . Didelphimorphia page 27

5b Three upper incisors on each side; innermost toe of hind foot not opposable; female without pouch . . . . . Carnivora page 219

6a Forearm modified as wing; incisors of upper jaw separated by emargination of anterior portion of palate . . . . . Chiroptera page 57

6b No wings; incisors and palate not as above 7

7a Hind limbs absent externally 8

7b Hind limbs present; toes modified into hooves 9

8a Forelimbs modified into flippers; blowhole (nostrils) on top of head . . . . . Cetacea page 195

8b Forelimbs modified into flippers; no blowhole on top of head . . . . . Sirenia page 275

Key to the Orders of Virginia Mammals (continued)

9a Axis of foot passing between almost equally developed third and fourth digits .... Artiodactyla page 283

9a Axis of foot passing through third digit .... Perissodactyla page 279

Opossums

The opossums are contained within the order Didelphimorphia, the characteristics of which are the same as for the infraclass Metatheria, the marsupials. Marsupials occur primarily in South America and the Australian region. Especially the Australian forms have undergone extensive adaptive radiation. The few progenitor groups present there have adapted to many diverse life styles.

Opossums (Family Didelphidae)

All living members of the family Didelphidae are confined to North, Central, and South America, although fossils representing this family are known from Europe. They are primarily nocturnal animals, and most are either arboreal or terrestrial. Each front foot has five claw-bearing toes, while each hind foot has four claw-bearing toes and a thumblike, clawless hallux, or big toe, which opposes the other digits. The snout is long and pointed, and the tail is usually prehensile and is used for grasping. The abdominal pouch, well developed in some genera but rudimentary in others, is lined with soft fur and contains the mammae. The degree of development of the pouch varies considerably with the breeding condition of the animal.

The skull has a large preorbital region, large zygomatic arches, a prominent median sagittal crest, and a small braincase.

Genus *Didelphis*

Dentition: 5/4, 1/1, 3/3, 4/4 = 50

Virginia Opossum
Didelphis virginiana Kerr

Description. The opossum (Plate 1) is the only representative of its family in North America. It is a medium-sized mammal with long, rather coarse, grayish-white fur. The general coloration is a result of the guard hairs, which are white, and the underfur, which consists of pure white hairs tipped with black. These animals have sharp, slender muzzles; large, thin, leathery, naked ears; an opposable hallux; and a long, grasping, scaly, sparsely haired tail. The nose is pink, the eyes are black, and the ears are bluish-black to black with some individuals having a pinkish or whitish ear margin. The legs are relatively short. Locomotion is plantigrade. The proximal portion of the tail is black, with the remainder being yellowish-white to pink. Females have a well developed marsupium in which the mammae are located. The usual number of teats is 13, 12 in a circle with one in the center, although all may not be functional. Records exist of females with as few as 11 or as many as 17 teats. The male reproductive organ is forked, while the female reproductive system consists of paired vaginae and paired uteri. Adult opossums are approximately 600 to 875 mm long, including a tail 275 to 350 mm long. Adults usually weigh between 1.3 and 4.5 kg, although specimens weighing

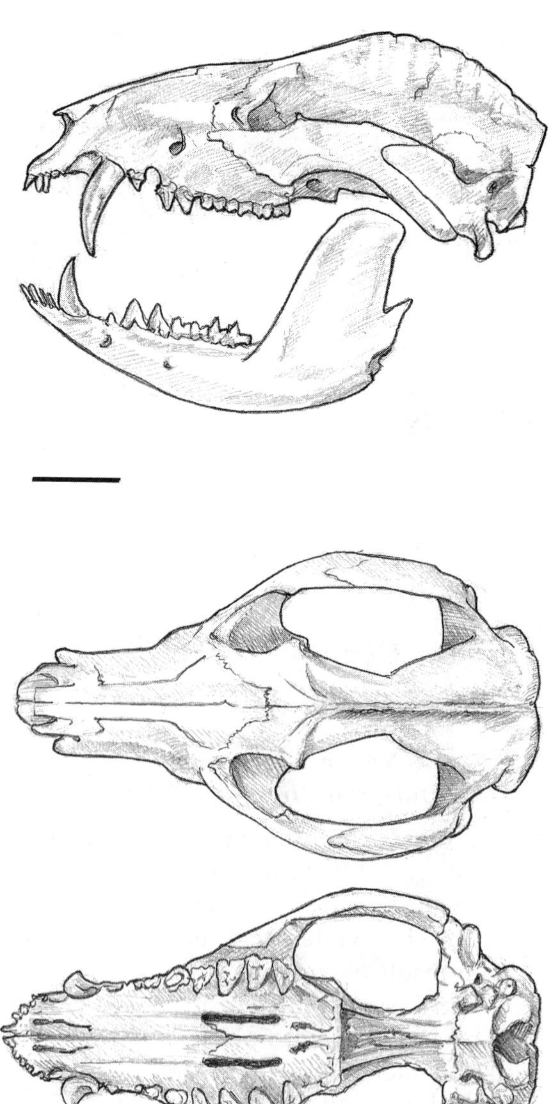

Figure 2. *Didelphis virginiana:* Left lateral view of skull and mandible, and dorsal and ventral view of skull. Scale bar = 20 mm.

as much as 6.3 kg have been reported in Virginia (Shaffer, 1948b).

The opossum possesses 50 heterodont teeth, more than any other mammal in Virginia. The braincase is extremely small relative to the body, the nasal bones are broadly expanded posteriorly, postorbital processes are present, a definite interorbital constriction is present, sagittal and occipital crests are prominent in adults, and the angle of the lower jaw is turned inward (Figure 2).

Distribution. Opossums have been remarkably successful in terms of distribution and abundance. They range from Costa Rica north through Mexico and the central and eastern half of the United States to southeastern Canada. They are most abundant in the south, but a northward range expansion has occurred in historic times (Gardner, 1982). Barring a change in the climate such as global warming, further expansion to the north seems unlikely considering that individuals presently surviving northern winters often show effects of frostbite on the ears, toes, and tail. This species has been introduced and has become established in California, Oregon, Washington, and southern British Columbia.

The opossum is one of the most common and generally distributed mammals throughout the state (Figure 3).

Comparative data on the wild fur catch and values of the opossum from 1981 to 1987 in Virginia are presented in tables 2 and 3. During this period, the number of opossums purchased by fur dealers ranged from approximately 7,300 in 1985–1986 to over 18,800 in 1982–1983. The average price per pelt in 1986–1987 was $1.57.

Habitat. The opossum prefers low, damp, wooded areas along streams, around lakes, and in swamps. Farming areas having hedgerows and small, wooded streams are preferred over densely forested upland areas.

Habits. The biology of the opossum has been discussed by McManus (1974) and Hunsaker (1977). Opossums are shy and secretive and generally den and feed alone but are tolerant of neighboring individuals. Family groups break up rapidly following weaning (80 to 100 days of age).

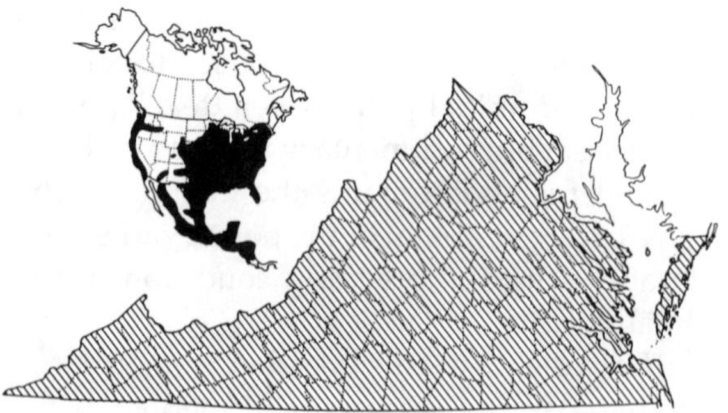

Figure 3. *Didelphis virginiana:* Range in Virginia and North America.

No home range data are available for Virginia, but data from other areas suggest that the size of home ranges may vary considerably. Some studies have concluded that opossums are more or less nomadic. Studies in Texas and Maryland have shown that at least 50 percent of the individuals in a given area are wanderers. Holmes (1991), however, cited studies refuting the notion that opossums are nomadic. Overlapping home ranges and recent evidence showing a well developed system of chemical communication suggest that opossums have higher rates of encounter with conspecifics than previously has been suspected.

In Maryland, Llewellyn and Dale (1964) noted that opossums range over long, narrow areas rather than circular ones and that this general shape was probably a result of the ranges being associated with stream courses. The average length of home ranges for 25 opossums was approximately 0.9 km. Radio-tagged male opossums in Wisconsin had average home ranges of 108 ha for males and 51 ha for females, (Gillette, 1980). Nightly foraging ranges for males averaged 946 m from their den, while those for females averaged 413 m. Adult males changed home ranges gradually through a series of shifts. Adult females in the study almost always had pouch young when they dispersed, which explains in part how the opossum can expand its range or repopulate depleted areas rapidly. Home ranges overlap broadly, and there is no evidence of territoriality. Stout and Sonenshine (1974) recorded an annual average density of two opossums per 41 ha in Virginia.

These mammals are abroad throughout the year but may hole up during cold periods. They are active mainly after dark and seek protective cover during the day and for nest sites. Opossum den sites include hollow trees, fallen logs, brush piles, and ground burrows. The nest is located in the den and is composed almost entirely of leaves. Smith (1941) reported the following observations on nest-building behavior and the transport of nesting materials by a half-grown opossum:

> *The animal came out of a hole in the ground about eight feet from where I stood and proceeded to select small mouthfuls of two or three leaves each. The leaves were taken out of the mouth with the forepaws and passed back along the abdomen to a position in front of the thighs. There they remained momentarily while the front feet were placed on the ground and the hind feet were brought up to take them and slide them along the tail into a loop in that member, which is ordinarily thought of as a means of support by suspension but which in this case was sustaining the hind quarters above the ground while the hind feet were being used to place the leaves in the loop.*
>
> *About six or eight mouthfuls were handled in this way. The action was rapid, and the leaves were in almost continuous motion from the time they were picked up from the ground until they came to rest in the coil of the tail. After the loop was filled, the opossum chose a last mouthful and, with its tail extended almost horizontally except for the loop which held the bundle of leaves, proceeded into the hole in the ground.*
>
> *Soon the animal returned, and when it first came up the tail was nearly straight with the end dragging on the ground. When the first leaves were picked up, the loop was formed in the tail, and the process of gathering a bundle of leaves was repeated. The opossum made four trips in about ten minutes.*

Opossums readily climb, using their prehensile tail extensively for balance and support. They are not aquatic, but can swim with ease and dive readily.

These mammals are probably best known for their death feigning act known as "playing 'possum." This phenomenon, which apparently has survival value, has been compared to fainting or temporary paralysis. It seems to be a reaction controlled by the nervous system and probably is not deliberate and willful. During death feigning, Gabrielsen and Smith (1985) recorded a heart rate decrease of 46 percent and a respiratory rate reduction of 30 percent from pre-stimulation values.

Although recovery is often slow, the opossum may suddenly come out of its coma and administer a severe injury with its sharp teeth and front claws. The opossum apparently maintains some level of sensory awareness during death feigning. Studies by Sentell and Compton (1987) showed that recovery from death feigning occurs sooner when the aggressor leaves the area (average of 3.25 minutes) than when the aggressor remains nearby (average of 14.24 minutes). No differences between males and females were observed in the length of death feigning.

Food. The opossum has often been called a scavenger and is widely believed to subsist largely on garbage. This notion has been fostered by the frequency of its appearance about human habitations. Although the diet of the opossum does include many foods that might not be considered natural to the diet of a wild creature, food studies by several investigators have disclosed that its feeding habits are not unlike those of other predatory mammals of comparable size.

The opossum is omnivorous, eating a wide variety of foods but preferring animal matter during all seasons. A Maryland study revealed a diet composed of 14 percent plant material and 86 percent animal material (Llewellyn and Uhler, 1952). Dewberries, blackberries, persimmons, pokeberries, wild grapes, and apples were the principal plant foods consumed. Insects formed one-third of the yearly intake of animal food. Beetles were the most frequently consumed insect, followed by crickets, grasshoppers, and hemipterans. Snails, millipedes, crayfish, rodents, shrews, birds, snakes, frogs, and salamanders formed the remaining animal food. Similar studies in other states showed that over three-fourths of the volume of opossum's food usually consists of animal matter. In Virginia, a southeastern shrew was recovered from the stomach of an opossum taken in Augusta County (Bruce, 1937). In Amelia County, opossums have been observed eating large, globular mushrooms during winter, and a large individual consumed a 3-foot 8-inch black racer (Lewis, 1940).

Reproduction and Development. Radio-tracking data suggest that mating is promiscuous or polygynous with females being seasonally polyestrous (Holmes, 1991). In Virginia, the reproductive season probably extends from late January to midsummer. In Maryland, opossums begin to breed in early February, and young are found in the pouch until August (Llewellyn and Dale, 1964). In West Virginia, Barbour (1951b) recorded estimated birth dates for four litters as February 9, 12, 17, and 20. Stout and Sonenshine (1974) recorded pouch young once in March, four times in June, three times in July, and once in August in Virginia. A female with 11 young was recorded on March 16 (VPI-W). Two litters are usually produced each year. Individual females may vary as much as two to three weeks in the time of breeding, and varying weather conditions from year to year may hasten or delay the onset of the breeding season. Peak periods of breeding appear to occur from late January through late March and from mid-May to early July. The female mates for the second time at about the time of weaning of the first litter. By September all young have usually been weaned.

The gestation of 12 to 13 days is the shortest of any American mammal. Litters may contain as many as 18 young, but usually about seven survive the period of pouch life. Average litter size (pouch young) has ranged from 6.8 to 8.9. Stout and Sonenshine (1974) recorded litters of six, seven, and nine young in Virginia. Llewellyn and Dale (1964) noted that, due to juvenile mortality, the production of young per female would be between 4.0 and 5.4 animals.

Unlike the embryos of higher mammals, those of opossums do not develop a placenta, nor do they become embedded in the uterine wall. Instead, the embryonic chorion and its many blood vessels lie in close contact with the tissues of the mother in one of many folds in the wrinkled wall of the uterus. The developing embryo is nourished and has its wastes eliminated by diffusion and osmosis between the blood vessels in the chorion and those in the uterine walls.

A newborn opossum weighs approximately 0.16 g and has an average crown-rump length of 14 mm (McManus, 1974). It is about the size of a small navy bean. The hind legs are small and weak, but the front legs are well developed, and the fingers are equipped with sharp, deciduous claws, which drop off some time after the animal reaches the pouch. At birth, the young ascend into the marsupium, climbing the mother's hair in a hand-over-hand swimming motion. Unassisted by the mother, each newborn opossum attaches its mouth to one of the teats, which expands in its mouth so that the young is well attached. During the first week after birth, the weight of the young increases tenfold. The young remain firmly attached to the nipple (Plate 2) until about 60 days of age. The pouch young breathe and rebreathe air that contains 8 to 20 times the normal content of carbon dioxide. The eyes open between 58 and 72 days of age.

Approximately two months following their birth, the young opossums begin to leave the pouch but remain near the mother for an additional three to four weeks, at which time the litter begins to break up and disperse. During this time, the young frequently travel on the back of the female. Weaning usually occurs between 80 and 100 days of age. Opossums reach sexual maturity at approximately eight months of age, but females do not breed until the first estrus the following year.

Longevity. Petrides (1949) computed an average life expectancy of 1.33 years with a 4.8-year turnover in population. Holmes (1991) reported that wild opossums in Virginia surviving to breeding age live an average of 17 months with yearling females constituting most of the breeding population. Known aged individuals have lived approximately three years in the wild. Captive opossums have lived over seven years.

Pelage Variations. Regional variation in color occurs, northern opossums often being paler than southern individuals. Albino opossums have been taken on several occasions. Dark and even black animals are occasionally reported. One taken in Brunswick County, Virginia (Lewis, 1940) was solid black except for a sprinkling of white hairs.

Parasites and Disease. The following parasites and disease organisms have been recorded from opossums in Virginia by Hasseltine (1929); Dickerson (1930); Emmons (1950); Yager et al. (1953); Emmons et al. (1955); Holloway and Dowler (1963); Sonenshine, Lamb, and Anastos (1965); Holloway (1966); Bozeman et al. (1967); Solomon and Warner (1969); Sonenshine and Levy (1971); Sonenshine and Stout (1971); Jones (1978); Eckerlin (1983); and Snyder et al. (1991): **Fungus** *(Histoplasma capsulatum);* Bacteria *(Leptospira ballum, Rickettsia rickettsii);* **Acanthocephala** (unidentified immature specimens); **Trematoda** (flukes) *(Brachylaema virginianum, Harmostomum opisthotrias);* **Cestoda** (tapeworms) *(Mesocestoides corti);* **Nematoda** (roundworms) *(Capillaria didelphis, Cruzia americana,* "filarial" nematode, *Longistriata didelphis, Trichinella spiralis, Turgida (Physaloptera) turgida);* **Siphonaptera** (fleas) *(Cediopsylla simplex, Ceratophyllus fasciatus, Ctenocephalides felis, Orchopeas howardii);* **Acarina** (ticks and mites) *(Amblyomma americanum, Dermacentor variabilis, Ixodes cookei, Ixodes scapularis,* unidentified immature mites).

Jones et al. (1978a) recorded positive titers for tularemia. Since 1961, rabies has been confirmed in six opossums from Arlington, Fairfax, Loudoun, Prince William, and Wise counties (see tables 5 and 6).

Opossums in North America have some interesting parasites of their own, although ectoparasites associated with other animal hosts often infest these marsupials on a temporary basis. Information on diseases affecting this species has been summarized by Barr (1963) and Potkay (1970). Opossums are known to be naturally infected with, among others, Chagas' disease, histoplasmosis, tularemia, and leptospirosis.

Predation. Great horned owls, carnivorous mammals including dogs, and man are probably the chief predators. Automobiles are responsible for the deaths of many opossums. They are frequently killed on the road where they are scavenging on road kills. In the South, opossums are hunted and trapped for both their fur and their meat.

Geographic Variation. The subspecies occurring in Virginia is *Didelphis virginiana virginiana* Kerr.

Location of Specimens. AMNH, ANSP, BCV, CM, CU, CUC, EHC, GMU, LC, LFCC, LU, MCZ, MVZ, NVCC, PWRC, RMWC, RU, SNP, UMMZ, USNM, VCU, VLM, VMNH, VPISU, VPI-W.

Insectivores

The insectivores, order Insectivora, constitute a group of mammals that is difficult to characterize because of its diversity. Many features of insectivores are present in other groups, and no single characteristic typifies the order. Insectivores are generally small mammals having an elongated head, often with a movable snout projecting well beyond the jaw. They have very small eyes and small ears. The teeth are not well differentiated into incisors, canines, and molars. Five toes are usually present on each foot, and the first digit is not opposable in either the fore or hind foot. These mammals utilize plantigrade locomotion. Insectivores possess a primitive brain. The skull is usually broad and flat with the braincase only slightly elevated above the face line. The zygomatic arches are often reduced and may be entirely absent. Prominent scent glands occur in most species. These primitive mammals are predominantly insectivorous or carnivorous.

The order Insectivora is represented in Virginia by two families.

1a Forefeet less than twice as wide as hind feet and not modified for digging; eyes small but visible; pinnae present; total teeth 30 to 32 (9 or 10 on each side above and 6 on each side below); teeth tipped with chestnut; zygomatic arch absent.
Shrews .... Soricidae

1b Forefeet more than twice as wide as hind feet and modified for digging; eyes hidden; pinnae absent; total teeth 36 or 44 (10 or 11 on each side above and 8 or 11 on each side below); teeth not chestnut-tipped; zygomatic arch present.
Moles .... Talpidae

Shrews
(Family Soricidae)

The family Soricidae includes the smallest mammals. The medial incisors of both upper and lower jaws are greatly enlarged and specialized into a pincer-type apparatus. The incisors are followed by a series of three to five simple pointed teeth, the unicuspids, and a series of sharply pointed molariform teeth. The skull is triangular and lacks zygomatic arches and tympanic bullae. The eyes are very small, often partly hidden in the fur, and probably capable of only limited vision. Hearing and smell, however, are acute. Pinnae are present but may be reduced and hidden by the fur. The nose is long and tapers to a sharp point. The brain is small.

Members of this family possess a gland along each side of their body. The hairs surrounding the gland are kept stained and greasy by its secretion, which apparently is the source of the specific musky odor characteristic of these mammals. This odor may function as a pheromone to attract members of the same species. It may also be used to establish territories. A ventral gland is also present in *Blarina.*

Most shrews inhabit moist areas. Because of their small size and large surface-to-body ratio, temperature and evaporation may be of more importance in governing the distribution of shrews than of most other mammals.

Shrews are active during all seasons. They are not strictly nocturnal or diurnal but are active throughout most of the day, with scattered short periods of rest. Although the majority are terrestrial, some shrews are highly aquatic, and many will use burrows while foraging. Shrews undoubtedly spend a great percentage of their time searching for food, since they have an extremely rapid metabolic rate and normally require 50 percent or more of their own weight in food every 24 hours.

Shrews are extremely nervous; when frightened, their heart may beat 1,200 times per minute, and they often die of fright from loud noises, even from thunder. The average breathing rate of captive short-tailed shrews at rest is about 168 breaths per minute, while the average heart rate is about 750 beats per minute when active (Doremus, 1965).

Shrews are relatively vocal and include a variety of shrill chirps, buzzes, clicks, and twitters in their repertoire. French (1980a) reported a "birdlike series of very soft chirps" from *Sorex longirostris.* Many of these sounds are beyond the range of human hearing. Shrews of the genus *Sorex* and *Blarina,* like bats, use their high-pitched voices to echolocate objects in their paths (Gould, Negus, and Novick, 1964; Buchler, 1976; Tomasi, 1979). A description of these sounds and their behavioral significance can be found in Gould (1969).

The family Soricidae is divided into two subfamilies, with all North American shrews in the subfamily Soricinae. Members of this subfamily are commonly referred to as red-toothed shrews because of the red or chestnut pigments on the tips of their teeth.

Key to Species of Soricidae

1a Tail at least approaching length of head and body; ears visible; one incisor on each side of lower jaw
.... 2

1b Tail much shorter than head and body; ears hidden in fur; two incisors on each side of lower jaw
.... 7

2a All five unicuspids visible in lateral view
.... 3

2b Only three unicuspids visible in lateral view; third and fifth unicuspids minute
.... *Sorex (Microsorex) hoyi*

3a Total length greater than 140 mm; hind foot 18 mm or more and distinctly fringed with hair
.... *Sorex palustris*

3b Total length less than 140 mm; hind foot less than 18 mm and lacking fringe of hair
.... 4

4a Tail more than 50 mm long; posterior border of infraorbital foramen lying behind space between first and second upper molars
.... *Sorex dispar*

4b Tail less than 50 mm long; posterior border of infraorbital foramen even with or anterior to space between first and second upper molars
.... 5

5a Total length greater than 100 mm
.... *Sorex fumeus*

5b Total length less than 100 mm
.... 6

6a Rostrum long and narrow; third upper unicuspid not smaller then fourth upper unicuspid; inner ridge of upper unicuspids with pigment
.... *Sorex cinereus*

6b Rostrum short and wider; third upper unicuspid usually smaller than fourth upper unicuspid; inner ridge of upper unicuspids lacking pigment
.... *Sorex longirostris*

7a Incisors 4/2; five unicuspids with four visible from the side; first four unicuspids in two pairs with fifth minute; total teeth 32
.... 8

7b Incisors 3/2; four unicuspids with three visible from the side; unicuspids never in two pairs and with fourth always smallest and wedged between third unicuspid and first

large cheek tooth; total teeth 30
. . . . *Cryptotis parva*

8a Total length usually greater than 105 mm; hind foot usually greater than 14 mm
. . . . *Blarina brevicauda*

8b Total length usually less than 105 mm; hind foot usually less than 14 mm
. . . .*Blarina carolinensis*

Genus *Sorex*

Dentition: 3/1, 1/1, 3/1, 3/3 = 32

Masked Shrew
Sorex cinereus Kerr

Description. The masked shrew (Plate 3) has a sharp conical snout and minute eyes and ranges in color from dark brown to grayish-brown on the back with pale gray underparts. It is very similar to *Sorex longirostris* and *Sorex hoyi,* but differs from the former in having a longer, more narrow rostrum and by having pigment on the inner ridges of the upper unicuspids. It also has a larger and somewhat furrier tail. It differs from the pygmy shrew in having all four of the unicuspids about equal in size. Females have six mammae. The tail is relatively long and is indistinctly bicolor. Adults are generally 85 to 100 mm long, including a 30 to 40 mm tail. These shrews usually weigh between 3 and 7 g.

The skull is relatively weak and teardrop-shaped with a narrow rostrum. The pincerlike incisor teeth are tipped with red. The fourth unicuspid is usually smaller than the third unicuspid (Figure 4).

Distribution. The masked shrew ranges from Alaska and Canada south through the Rocky Mountains to New Mexico and through the Appalachian Mountains to western North Carolina. In the southern Appalachians it has been recorded at elevations between 885 and 1921 m.

This shrew occurs in northern and western Virginia (Figure 5). The status of one subspecies *(Sorex cinereus fontinalis),* known only from specimens taken in 1938 from Arlington County by Bray (1939), was listed as threatened in Virginia by Handley (1979b). This geographic variant was subsequently deleted from

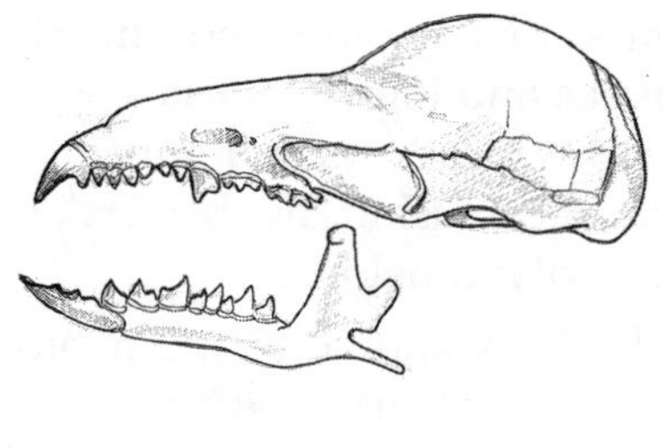

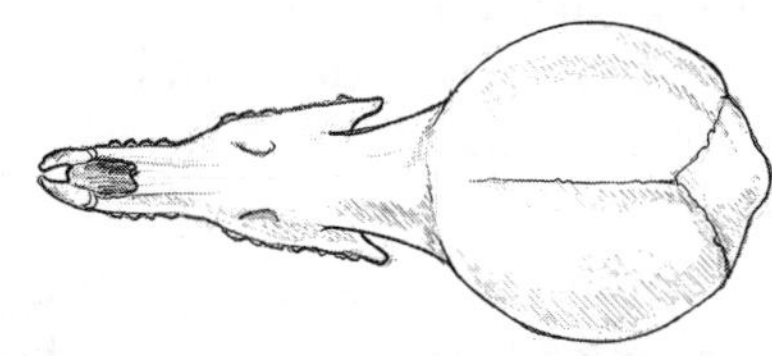

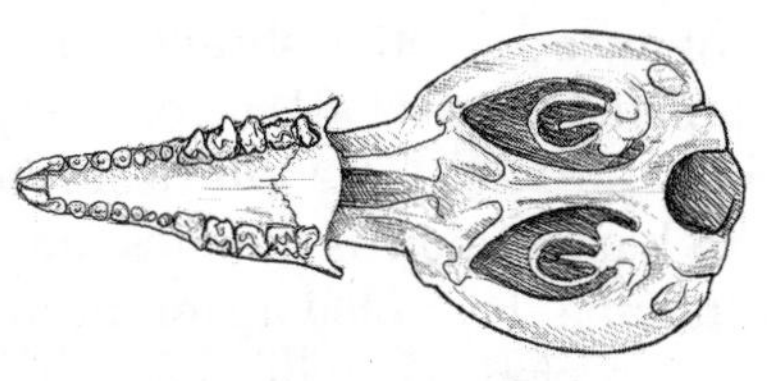

Figure 4. *Sorex cinereus*: Left lateral view of skull and mandible, and dorsal and ventral view of skull. Scale bar = 10 mm.

Virginia's taxa (Handley, 1982). Handley (1991) stated:

> *One of Bray's specimens (USNM 267569) was found in the National Museum of Natural History. It proved to be not* Sorex cinereus fontinalis *but* Sorex longirostris longirostris *Bachman, a shrew that is common and widespread in northern Virginia* (Handley, 1982).

Since there are no verified records, Handley assumed this subspecies is not present in Virginia.

Habitat. Masked shrews are found in a variety

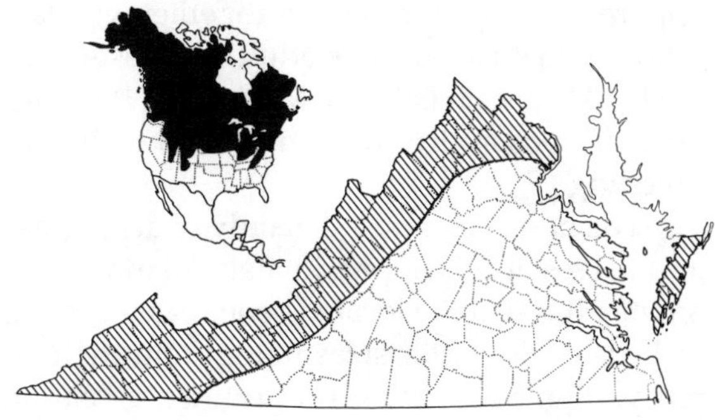

Figure 5. *Sorex cinereus:* Range in Virginia and North America.

of habitats, but are most commonly found among rocks and logs in moist woods as well as in marshy meadows and sphagnum bogs. They have, on occasion, also been taken in relatively dry upland fields.

Habits. Little is known of the habits of this shrew. It commonly uses the runways and burrows of meadow mice and other small mammals. It is active both day and night during all seasons of the year and is able to swim well. The senses of sight, hearing, and touch are probably well developed, but the sense of smell appears poor.

Food. A voracious eater, the masked shrew consumes a variety of foods including beetles, crickets, bugs, caterpillars, worms, and spiders. The flesh of mice and other shrews is occasionally consumed. French (1984) recorded spiders, Lepidoptera larvae, Coleoptera larvae and adults, and harvestmen as the most important foods in Indiana. He noted a significant overlap in dietary preferences with *Sorex longirostris.* Also in Indiana, Whitaker and Cudmore (1987) reported spiders, insect larvae, beetles, earthworms, and centipedes forming the greatest volume of the diet. Vispo (1988) reported sciarid and chironomid (Diptera) larvae in the diet of this shrew in North Carolina. Ryan (1986) reported ants forming 50 percent of the prey items in Michigan along with other Hymenoptera, Arachnida, Coleoptera, and lepidopterous larvae. Prey less than 5 mm in body length seemed to be preferred. A high degree of dietary overlap occurred with *Sorex hoyi.*

Reproduction and Development. Little is known of the breeding habits, but the breeding season may extend from March to September with as many as three litters being produced in a single season. The presence of six apparently immature shrews together with lactation in just two of nine adult females in August at Mountain Lake led Moore (1949) to suggest the possibility of a midsummer lull in breeding.

The nest is composed mainly of dead grass and leaves and is approximately 75 mm in diameter. It is usually located beneath a log, rock, or brush pile. Litter sizes range from three to ten young. Short (1961a) estimated gestation at 22 days and nursing at 21 days. The male may stay with the female before pregnancy and during the early development of the young. Young shrews are usually able to survive on their own when 20 to 25 days of age and reach sexual maturity in 20 to 26 weeks.

Longevity. Masked shrews probably do not survive more than two years in the wild.

Parasites. The following parasites have been recorded from masked shrews in Virginia by Moore (1949) and Solomon and Handley (1971): **Nematoda** (roundworms) *(Capillaria hepatica);* **Siphonaptera** (fleas) *(Ctenophthalmus pseudagyrtes, Doratopsylla blarinae);* **Acarina** (ticks) *(Ixodes* sp., probably *angustus*); **Acarina** (mites) *(Eulaelaps* sp., *Euschongastia blarinae, Gymnolaelaps* sp., *Haemogamasus sternalis, Hydrogamasus* sp., hypopial stages of Listrophoridae, Laelaptidae nymphs).

Predation. Owls are probably the main predators, although hawks, snakes, and carnivorous mammals also prey on these shrews.

Geographic Variation. The subspecies occurring in Virginia is *Sorex cinereus cinereus* Kerr.

Location of Specimens. BCV, DMNH, DWL, FSM, GMU, HSU, LACM, LFCC, LU, MVZ, RMWC, RU, SNP, SUVM, UFMNH, UMMZ, USNM, VCU, VPISU.

Southeastern Shrew
Sorex longirostris Bachman

Description. The upperparts of the body of the southeastern shrew (Plate 4) are reddish-brown, and the underparts are grayish. It has a long, indistinctly bicolor tail. The sexes are similar in color. Females have six mammae. Adults are generally between 72 and 108 mm long, including a 25 to 40 mm tail. These tiny mammals usually weigh between 3.3 and 5.6 g.

The skull is relatively short and broad, as compared to *Sorex cinereus.* The first and second unicuspids are about equal in size; the third and fourth are decidedly smaller than the first and second; and the fifth unicuspid is minute (Figure 6).

Distribution and Status. The southeastern shrew inhabits the southeastern United States from central Florida, Louisiana, and Arkansas north to Indiana, Illinois, Kentucky, and southern Maryland.

The southeastern shrew occurs throughout most of Virginia (Figure 7). A geographic variant, *Sorex longirostris fisheri,* has been classified officially as threatened federally and in Virginia

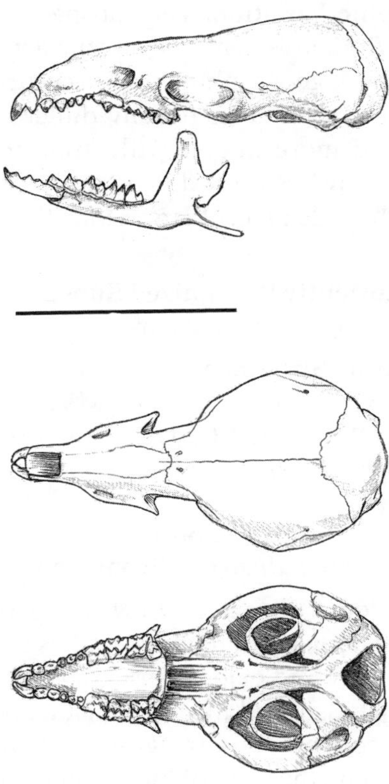

Figure 6. *Sorex longirostris*: Left lateral view of skull and mandible, and dorsal and ventral view of skull. Scale bar = 10 mm.

(Handley, 1979b; 1991). It was only thought to occur in the Dismal Swamp area in southeastern Virginia, but Rose, 1983; Rose et al., 1987; and Moncrief et al., 1996 have shown it to be broadly distributed in suitable coastal plain habitat in both Virginia and North Carolina.

The relatively few records of this species may indicate that populations are small and widely scattered, but the fact that they are common at certain localities suggests that mousetraps may not be too effective for this species. Pitfall traps have proven most successful for small shrews (Rose, 1983; Rose et al., 1987; Pagels, 1987; Pagels et al., 1982; and Pagels and Handley, 1989). A two year study employing pitfall traps in Virginia, for example, yielded 73 specimens (Pagels and Handley, 1989).

Habitat. Previous captures throughout the southeastern United States indicate that this species inhabits mostly moist situations in woods or fields on comparatively high ground. In Virginia, it occurs in a variety of habitats from fields to forest. Most individuals in Virginia have been taken in disturbed habitat such as cultivated fields, abandoned fields, thickets of saplings and shrubs, and young forest (Pagels et al., 1982). A dense ground cover of honeysuckle, grasses, sedges, or herbs is usually present. Pagels et al. (1982) found no evident preference for upland or lowland sites, dryness or moisture, type of old-field, or type of young forest. Pagels and Handley (1989) noted: "In the lowlands this shrew was caught with similar frequency in all habitats. In the mountains, however, it was caught more often in fields and field-forest edges than in forest."

In Amelia and Brunswick counties, Lewis (1943) recorded seven of eight shrews in dense cover of either prostrate honeysuckle or tall sedges and grasses. Four were taken within 12 m of water. Only three were taken in woods. In Chesterfield County, Peacock (1967) took one individual in a damp weedy ditch between corn rows. In the Dismal Swamp this shrew has been found at the edge of canebrakes and around rotting logs on drier ground in thickets of myrtle, blackberry, poison ivy, and holly. A specimen from Hanover County was taken in a relatively dry forest-old field ecotone with an understory of honeysuckle mats (Stout, 1967).

Sorex longirostris and *Sorex cinereus* have never been taken together in Virginia. Pagels and Handley (1989) considered these two species to exhibit contiguous allopatry. They stated:

> Sorex cinereus *is common at high elevations, and we found that its lowest elevational limits (between 442 and 594 m) approximated the highest elevations at which the southeastern shrew was collected (457 to 610 m). Mean elevations of captures of the two species were 823 m versus 155 m.*

Rose (1983) and Handley (1991) believe

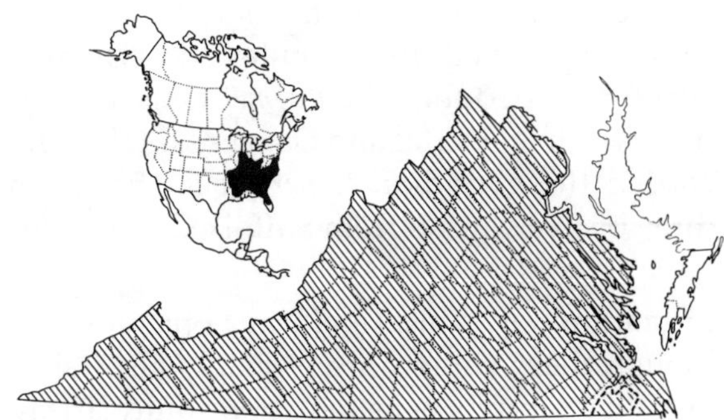

Figure 7. *Sorex longirostris:* Range in Virginia and North America.

that interbreeding between *Sorex longirostris longirostris* and *Sorex longirostris fisheri* is occurring around the periphery of the Great Dismal Swamp. As parts of the historical Swamp have been drained for development, the smaller upland geographic variant *Sorex longirostris longirostris* has invaded the drained ares and interbred with the larger form, *Sorex longirostris fisheri*.

Habits. The habits of this shrew presumably are similar to those of *Sorex cinereus.* French (1980a) reported population densities of 30 to 44 individuals per hectare.

Food. In Indiana, Whitaker and Mumford (1972) found the five most common foods, by volume, to be spiders, lepidopterous larvae, slugs and snails, vegetation, and centipedes. French (1984), also in Indiana, recorded spiders, lepidopterous larvae, Gryllidae, Coleoptera adults, and harvestmen as the most important foods. A significant overlap in foods with *Sorex cinereus* was observed. Whitaker and Cudmore (1987) reported spiders, insect larvae and pupae, beetles, centipedes, and crickets (Gryllidae) as major food items.

Reproduction and Development. The normal litter size is four or five, with the first litter usually being born in April. One or more additional litters may be born throughout the summer. A litter of five young was found in the Dismal Swamp in May, 1905 (Hollister, 1911a). French (1980b) compiled data from a six state region and reported a mean litter size of 3.9 with a range from one to six. Nests consisting of masses of cut leaves have been found inside rotting logs and in cavities beneath the bark of fallen trees. French (1980b) noted that most individuals probably survive only one winter.

Parasites. The chigger *Euschongastia blarinae* has been recorded from this species in Giles County by Farrell (1956). Smiley and Whitaker (1979) recorded the mite *Pygmephorus horridus* from Virginia. Hertel and Duszynski (1987) recorded the coccidian *Eimeria palustris* from three of five shrews from Suffolk County, Virginia.

Predation. Owls are significant predators, although these shrews are probably also taken by other carnivores as the opportunity arises. One southeastern shrew was found in the stomach of an opossum in Augusta County (Bruce, 1937).

Geographic Variation. The subspecies occurring in Virginia is *Sorex longirostris longirostris* Bachman. A geographic variant occurring in the Dismal Swamp "is usually duller in color above and more tinged with drab or wood brown below" (Rose and Padgett, 1991). It averages about 20 percent larger than the upland form.

Other Currently Recognized Subspecies. *Sorex longirostris fisheri* Merriam.

Location of Specimens. AMNH, CM, DWL, GMU, ISUVC, LFCC, MSB, MVZ, NCSM, NVCC, ODU, RMWC, UGAMNH, USNM, VCU, VPISU, VPI-W.

Water Shrew
Sorex palustris (Richardson)

Description. The water shrew (Plate 5) is the largest eastern long-tailed shrew. It is blackish-gray dorsally and pale to dark gray below. The feet are whitish, and the tail is distinctly bicolored. A conspicuous fringe of stiff hairs is present along the sides of the feet and toes. The third and fourth hind toes are joined for slightly more than half of their length by a thin web. Females possess six mammae. Adult water shrews are usually between 135 and 165 mm long, including a 60 to 75 mm tail. They usually weigh between 9 and 14 g.

The rostrum of the skull is relatively short and only slightly curved ventrally at its anterior end. A total of 32 teeth are present. Five unicuspids are present in each side of the upper jaw with the fourth unicuspid being larger than the third (Figure 8).

Distribution. The range of the water shrew extends across Canada from Labrador and Nova Scotia to southeastern Alaska. The range extends south in the Appalachian Mountains to Tennessee and North Carolina, in the Rocky Mountains to Utah and New Mexico, and in the Sierra Nevada to California.

This shrew was first taken in Virginia along Back Creek in northwestern Bath County. It has since been recorded from four additional localities in Bath and Highland counties (Figure 9) (Pagels and Tate, 1976; Pagels, 1987). It is listed as endangered in Virginia (Handley, 1979b, 1991). Handley (1991) noted:

Populations of the water shrew in the Southern Appalachians are relicts of the last Ice Age.

Because of climatic warming and retreat of the water shrew's preferred boreal habitats to higher elevations, populations of this mammal in the southern mountains must have been declining for thousands of years. Turn-of-the-century logging accelerated the demise.

Habitat. The water shrew inhabits the banks of rocky, rapidly running, cold mountain streams in the southern Appalachians, where rhododendron and yellow birch are usually the dominant vegetation. Occasionally, they may be found in marshes, bogs, and along lakes and ponds. The Bath County specimens were taken in or near a small rocky stream in a narrow, steep-sided valley in beech-yellow birch-sugar maple forest (Pagels and Tate, 1976).

Habits. The dense fur and large, hair-fringed feet and toes make the water shrew well adapted for swimming, and it readily takes to the water. It can swim, dive, float, run along the bottom of a pond or creek, and actually run upon the surface of the water for some distance (Jackson, 1961). It has most often been taken on stream banks or on rocks in streams, although occasionally it has been captured in can traps dug into willow thickets near streams

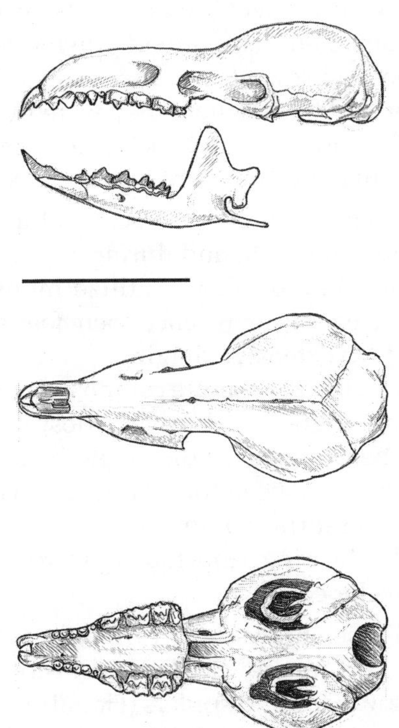

Figure 8. *Sorex palustris:* Left lateral view of skull and mandible, and dorsal and ventral view of skull. Scale bar = 10 mm.

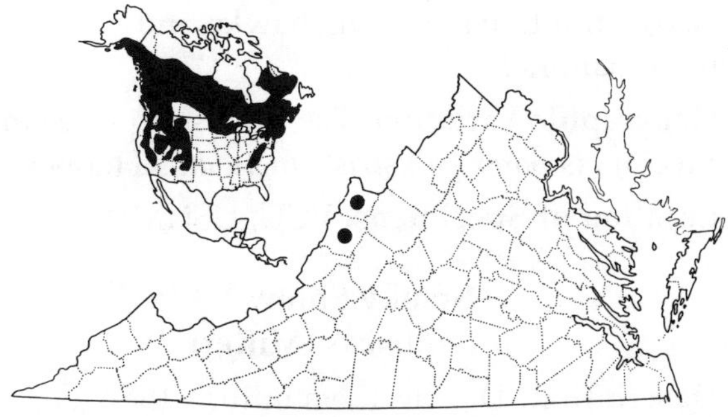

Figure 9. *Sorex palustris:* Range in Virginia and North America.

(Handley, 1979b). Kellogg (1937) in West Virginia noted that a water shrew dived into a stream like a little muskrat, looked like a little silver streak when it swam submerged, and attempted to hide under the banks of the stream.

These shrews are active during all seasons. They are primarily nocturnal, although occasionally an individual may be active during the day.

Nests are usually constructed in tunnels and in or under hollow logs (Beneski and Stinson, 1987). A nest of this species measuring about 10 cm in diameter was found in a beaver lodge in New Hampshire (Siegler, 1956).

Food. Water shrews feed primarily on small aquatic organisms that they capture while swimming in the water. Both Conaway (1952) and Linzey and Linzey (1973) recorded aquatic organisms in 49 percent of the stomachs analyzed. Conaway and Pfitzer (1952) and Whitaker et al. (1975) recorded caddis flies, stoneflies, and mayflies as the most frequent food items. Beneski and Stinson (1987) noted the presence of small fish and other animals along with the fungus *Endogone* and some plant material.

Reproduction. A female taken April 20 in North Carolina contained five embryos (Whitaker et al., 1975). Asdell (1964) recorded five to seven embryos from this species. Data from the western United States have revealed the presence of pregnant and lactating females from March through August.

Longevity. Conaway (1952) estimated that maximum age in the wild would not exceed 18 months.

Predation. This species is preyed upon by largemouth bass (Hodgson, 1986) and probably also by trout, snakes, owls, hawks, and carnivorous mammals.

Geographic Variation. The only subspecies in Virginia is *Sorex palustris punctulatus* Hooper.

Location of Specimens. VCU, USNM.

Smoky Shrew
Sorex fumeus (Miller)

Description. During the summer, the smoky shrew (Plate 6) is a medium-sized, uniformly dull brownish shrew. Its uniform coloration helps to distinguish it from the masked shrew, *Sorex cinereus*, which is dark brown or brownish gray above with paler gray or silvery underparts. During the winter, the smoky shrew's pelage is grayish. The tail is darker above than beneath and is sparsely haired. Females possess six mammae. Adult smoky shrews are usually between 100 and 125 mm long, including a 37 to 50 mm tail. They weigh between 5.5 and 9.2 g.

The skull is relatively broad and short with a broad interorbital region. The infraorbital foramen is large. This shrew possesses 32 teeth with the third unicuspid larger than the fourth (Figure 10).

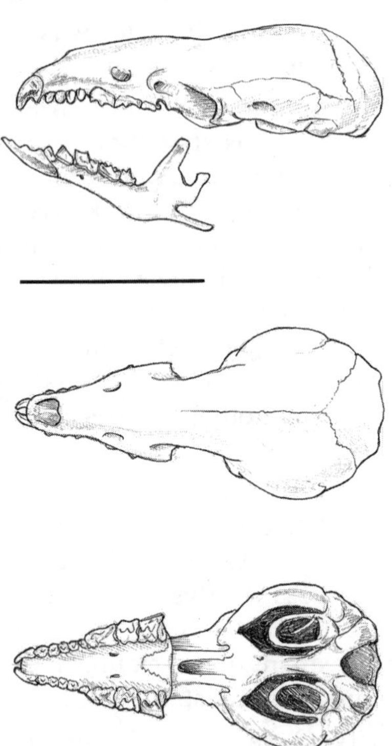

Figure 10. *Sorex fumeus:* Left lateral view of skull and mandible, and dorsal and ventral view of skull. Scale bar = 10 mm.

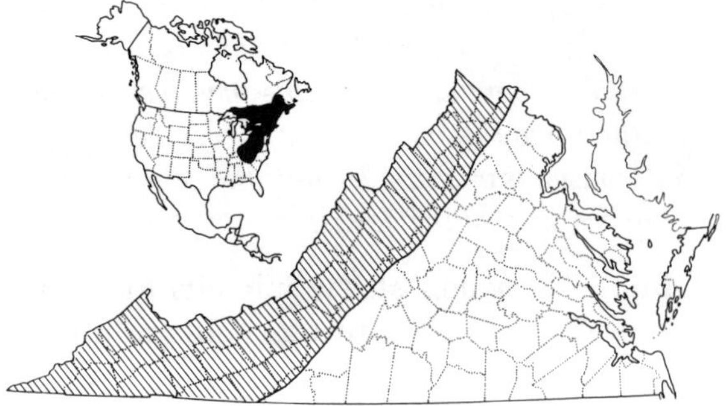

Figure 11. *Sorex fumeus:* Range in Virginia and North America.

Distribution. The smoky shrew is primarily a northern and mountain species and is found throughout the northeastern United States and adjacent Canada, south in the Appalachian Mountains to northern Georgia, and west to central Ohio and Kentucky.

In Virginia, this shrew has been taken only in the western portion of the state at elevations above 610 m (Figure 11).

Habitat. These shrews are most abundant in cool, damp woodlands with a deep layer of leaf mold on the ground. Hemlock and spruce forests as well as deciduous forests of maple, beech, birch, and oak provide preferred habitat. These shrews have also been taken in swamps and bogs, where they were living beneath the moss-covered rocks, logs, and root systems that are abundant in such areas.

Habits. Smoky shrews are active at all hours of the day and night and during all seasons of the year. They primarily utilize mouse and mole burrow systems since their feet are not adapted for extensive digging.

Baseball-size nests are composed primarily of shredded grass and leaves. Most nests are located beneath logs, stumps, old boards, and rocks, and have been found as much as 48 cm beneath the surface of the ground.

Sight, hearing, and touch are reasonably well developed.

Food. These shrews feed primarily upon insects, insect larvae, earthworms, centipedes, snails, sowbugs, and spiders (Hamilton, 1940a; Linzey and Linzey, 1968; Whitaker et al., 1975; Whitaker and Cudmore, 1987). Salamander, bird, and mammal remains have also been identified in analyses of stomach contents.

Reproduction. The breeding season probably extends from early spring to fall with a gestation of about 20 days. As many as eight young have been recorded. Most litters contain five or six young, each weighing approximately 0.14 g. A female containing five embryos has been recorded from Giles County, Virginia. In Harlan County, Kentucky, males in breeding condition were taken in June and July, and a lactating female was recorded in June (Barbour, 1951a). A lactating female was recorded in West Virginia on August 21 (Barbour, 1951b). Two or three litters may be produced annually (Owen, 1984).

Longevity. Most smoky shrews probably live about 12 months, although a very few may survive as long as two years. Hamilton (1940a) estimated the maximum life span at 14 to 17 months.

Parasites. The nematode *Capillaria hepatica* has been reported from this species in Virginia (Solomon and Handley, 1971).

Predation. Snakes, birds of prey, and carnivorous mammals are probable predators.

Geographic Variation. The subspecies occurring in Virginia is *Sorex fumeus fumeus* (Miller).

Location of Specimens. AMNH, BCV, CHAS, DWL, FSM, HSU, LFCC, NVCC, RU, SNP, SUVM, UGAMNH, UMMZ, USNM, VCU, VPISU, VPI-W.

Long-Tailed Shrew
Sorex dispar Batchelder

Description. The long-tailed, or rock, shrew (Plate 7) is a medium-sized shrew with slate-gray pelage. The underparts may be slightly paler than the back. The long, thick, sparsely haired tail is only slightly bicolor, being blackish above and only slightly paler below. The feet are whitish. Females possess six mammae. Adult long-tailed shrews range in length from 110 to 132 mm, including a 50 to 59 mm tail. They weigh approximately 4 to 8 g.

The smooth skull is long, narrow, and moderately flattened. The third unicuspid is about equal to the fourth in size. The skull contains 32 teeth (Figure 12).

Distribution. The long-tailed shrew inhabits the mountains from New Brunswick south to Tennessee and North Carolina, but is seldom seen. It is endemic to the Appalachian Mountains.

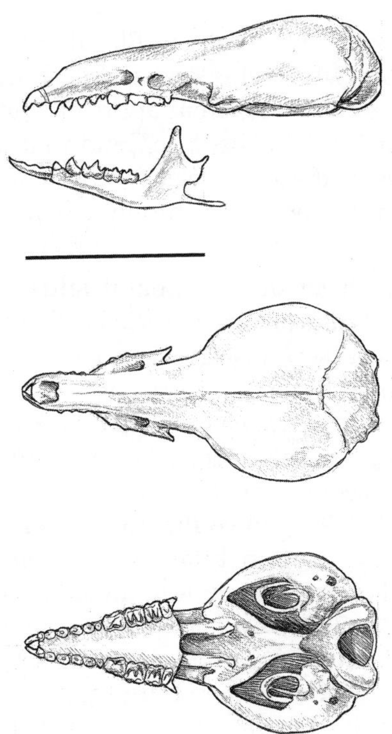

Figure 12. *Sorex dispar:* Left lateral view of skull and mandible, and dorsal and ventral view of skull. Scale bar = 10 mm.

The first specimens reported from Virginia were taken in Giles County by Handley (1956) and Holloway (1957b). It is restricted to western Virginia (Figure 13). This species was classified as of special concern in Virginia (Handley, 1979b), but was deleted from the list of Virginia's vulnerable mammals in 1989 after it was shown to be more common and widespread than formerly believed (Handley, 1991).

The long-tailed shrew was known from only five localities in Virginia in 1978. Subsequent pitfall trapping by Pagels (1987) added

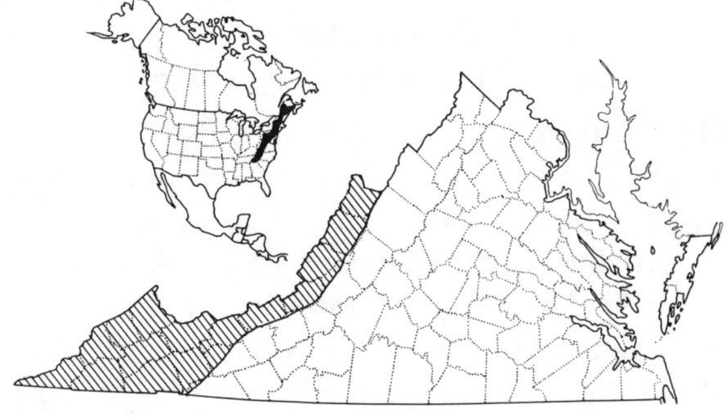

Figure 13. *Sorex dispar:* Range in Virginia and North America.

an additional five localities. Elevations in Virginia from which the long-tailed shrew has been recorded range from approximately 503 m to over 1,600 m. The Wise County site at 503 m represents the lowest elevation at which this species has been taken throughout its entire range.

Habitat. These shrews inhabit talus slopes, cool, moist cliffs or rock slides in northern hardwood or conifer forests (Handley, 1979b). They live in the subterranean tunnels that occur naturally in the rocky crevices between boulders. They have also been taken beneath moss-covered logs in damp coniferous forests.

Pagels (1987) noted that this shrew is very specialized in its habitat requirements. He stated: "Forests with talus as an obvious component characterize all new sites except that in Smyth County which is a disturbed seep area along a roadside. Scattered large boulders there add to the horizontal features of the habitat."

Habits. Practically nothing is known about the habits of this species. Its habits are probably most similar to those of *Sorex fumeus.*

Food. Centipedes, insects, spiders, and beetles have been reported from stomach analyses of this species (Condor, 1960; Richmond and Grimm, 1950; Conaway and Pfitzer, 1952).

Reproduction. Pregnant and lactating females have been recorded from Virginia and Tennessee from May through mid-August. Embryo counts have ranged from three to five. Males in breeding condition have been taken from March through July (Handley, 1979b).

Geographic Variation. The subspecies in Virginia is *Sorex dispar dispar* (Batchelder).

Location of Specimens. DWL, NVCC, RC, UMMZ, USNM, VCU.

Pygmy Shrew
Sorex (Microsorex) hoyi (Baird)

Description. The pygmy shrew (Plate 8) is the smallest mammal in Virginia. It is also the smallest mammal in North America and among the smallest in the world by weight. Adults are between 70 and 85 mm long, including a 25 to 30 mm tail. They weigh between 2.0 and 4.0 g, about the same as a dime. The fur is grayish-brown above and grayish below. The tail is indistinctly bicolored.

The skull is relatively flat and narrow with a short, broad rostrum. All five unicuspids are present, but the third and fifth are minute and are scarcely, if at all, visible in lateral view. They can be seen by looking at the inside of the tooth row. The skull contains 32 teeth (Figure 14).

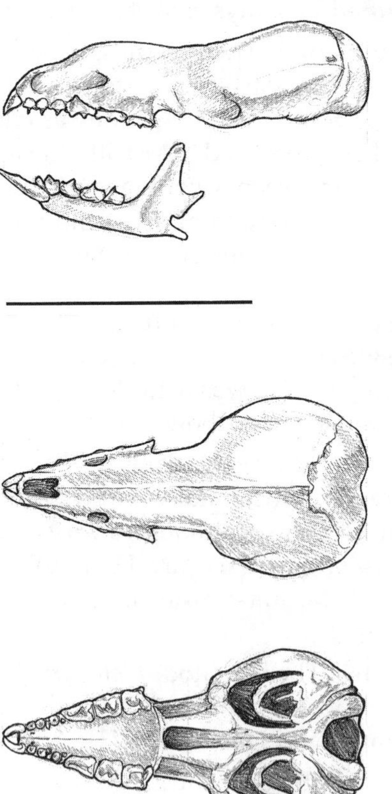

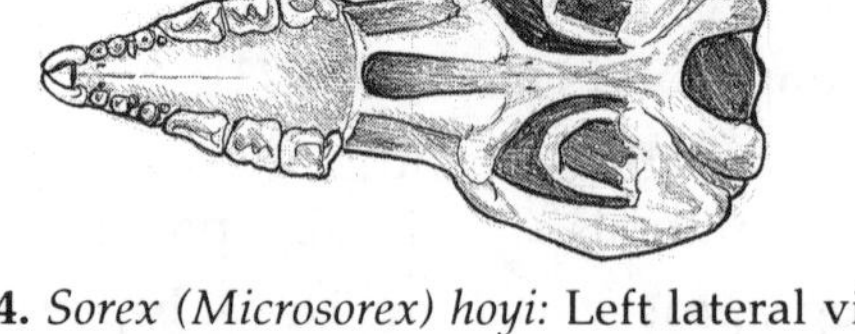

Figure 14. *Sorex (Microsorex) hoyi:* Left lateral view of skull and mandible, and dorsal and ventral view of skull. Scale bar = 10 mm.

Distribution. The pygmy shrew ranges from the Gaspé Peninsula across Canada to Alaska and south to northeastern Washington, northwestern Montana, Iowa, southern Wisconsin, and Ohio. The range includes New England and extends southward along the Allegheny-Appalachian mountain chain into northern Georgia (Long, 1974). An apparently isolated population exists in the central Rocky Mountains of southcentral Wyoming and Colorado.

This shrew occurs statewide in Virginia (Figure 15). In 1978, on the basis of eight known specimens from Virginia, one of which was later reidentified as a juvenile *Sorex longirostris* (Pagels and Handley, 1989), this species was classified as of special concern in Virginia (Handley, 1979b). Extensive pitfall trapping throughout the state from 1983 to 1985 by

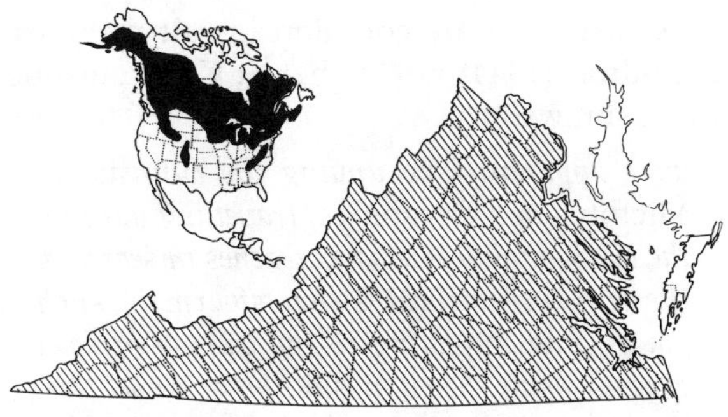

Figure 15. *Sorex (Microsorex) hoyi:* Range in Virginia and North America.

Pagels (1987) has shown this shrew to be widely distributed geographically in a variety of habitats ranging in elevation from 18 m to over 1,219 m. It has the greatest distribution (elevation, longitude, and latitude) of any Virginia shrew (Erdle and Pagels, 1995). The pygmy shrew was removed from Virginia's list of vulnerable mammals in 1989 (Handley, 1991).

Habitat. Handley (1979b) noted that most pygmy shrews from Virginia and Maryland came from well-drained sites — slopes or tops of ridges or banks above streams, in or under decaying logs or in deep leaf litter in hardwood forest with little or no underbrush.

Pagels (1987) recorded this species from a:

> *broad expanse of cover types, ranging from a fence row situation with grasses, goldenrod,* Solidago, *and blackberry,* Rubus, *as the predominant vegetation to a northern mixed forest of yellow birch,* Betula lutea, *red spruce,* Picea rubens, *and scattered hemlock,* Tsuga canadensis. *Four of the 14 specimens caught were in old field and edge situations. In general, these individuals were under dense vines like Japanese honeysuckle,* Lonicera japonica, *which usually offers 100 percent cover to small mammals. Those specimens taken in forested situations, 10 of 14, were generally taken under or beside rotting logs or stumps. Seven of the 10 forested sites were mixed forests with hemlock as the prevalent evergreen at six of those.*

Habits. These shrews are active both day and night during all seasons. Runways often lead beneath logs and old stumps.

Food. Miller (1964) recorded lepidopterous larvae, coleopteran larvae and adults, dipteran adults, and other unidentified insects from stomachs of this species in Vermont. Ryan (1986) reported ants forming 46 percent of the volume of prey items in Michigan with other Hymenoptera, Arachnida, Coleoptera, and lepidopterous larvae making up the remainder of the diet. Prey less than 5 mm in body length seemed to be preferred. A high degree of dietary overlap occurred with *Sorex cinereus.* Whitaker and Cudmore (1987) examined 63 stomachs from south-central Indiana and reported insect larvae, spiders, beetles, centipedes, ants, flies, and crickets forming the largest percentage, by volume, of food.

Reproduction. A male from Prince Edward County had enlarged testes and was presumably in breeding condition on July 26 (Handley, 1979b). Elsewhere, Long (1972) recorded one lactating and one probably lactating female, respectively, on July 2 and June 13.

Geographic Variation. The only subspecies in Virginia is *Sorex hoyi winnemana* Preble. See Diersing (1980) for discussion of taxonomy involving *Sorex* and *Microsorex*, and George (1988) who examined the systematic relationships of 26 species of *Sorex* using allozyme electrophoresis.

Location of Specimens. BCV, CM, GMU, GWNF, KU, LU, USNM, VCU, VPISU.

Genus *Cryptotis*

Dentition: 3/2, 1/0, 2/1, 3/3 = 30

Least Shrew
Cryptotis parva (Say)

Description. The least shrew (Plate 9) is the smallest of the three short-tailed shrews in Virginia. The upperparts are dark grayish-brown, while the underparts are somewhat paler. The least shrew looks like a smaller brown version of *Blarina.* Females have six mammae. These tiny shrews are about 75 mm long, including their 12 to 19 mm tail. They weigh 2.8 to 5.7 g.

Four unicuspids are present, but only three are visible from the side. The unicuspids are never in two pairs. The fourth is always smallest and is wedged between the third unicuspid and the first large cheek tooth (Figure 16).

Distribution. The least shrew is found throughout the eastern United States south of a line from central New York to central South Dakota, western Nebraska, and eastern Colorado and

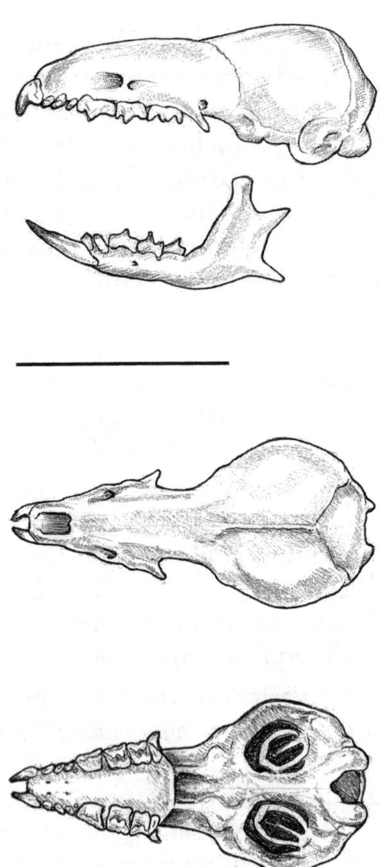

Figure 16. *Cryptotis parva:* Left lateral view of skull and mandible, and dorsal and ventral view of skull. Scale bar = 10 mm.

west through Kansas, Oklahoma, and Texas to New Mexico. The range extends south through Mexico to Costa Rica.

This species occurs statewide in Virginia (Figure 17). Paradiso (1969) reported that it was one of the two most common small mammals on Assateague Island, and Hamilton (1944) reported they were fairly numerous on the tidewater flats and offshore islands near Cape Charles and at Chincoteague. Pagels (1991) recorded this shrew from Whitetop Mountain in Grayson County at an elevation of 1,524 m, the highest elevation recorded for this species in the United States.

These small mammals are undoubtedly more abundant than the number of specimens in collections would indicate, possibly due to ineffective trapping techniques. Owl pellets from numerous states have revealed large numbers of *Cryptotis* skulls.

Habitat. This shrew, unlike most species, prefers dry, open, grassy fields. Along the Atlantic Coast, they are common in salt marshes. Hamilton (1944) noted that at Chincoteague these shrews:

> *were apparently occupying the runways of* Microtus *and* Oryzomys, *travelling out into the black muddy tidewater reaches in search of the tiny invertebrates that swarm in such places, and retreating to the canopy of dead grasses about the clumps of the grounsel tree,* Baccharis halimifolia, *and the marsh elder,* Iva frutescens, *as the tide covered these feeding areas.*

On Assateague Island, this species was relatively common at open sites in the shrub-marsh edge habitat as well as in open microhabitats of the dune grassland area (Cranford and Maly, 1990). Pagels (1991) recorded this species on Whitetop Mountain in a red spruce *(Picea rubens)* forest with scattered northern hardwood trees, a very unusual habitat for this species.

Habits. Little is known about these shrews. They may be active at any hour, but the peak of activity is at night. The home range is probably small, perhaps as little as a fraction of an acre. They use the runways of mice and rats and the tunnels of moles, or they construct their own tunnels, which are characteristically wider than high. Least shrews apparently have little use of their eyes, but they depend on their ears and nose in locating prey, and also the well developed tactile sense in their sensitive snout and vibrissae.

Nests have been described as rather compact structures of dried, shredded grass and leaves, roughly globular in shape, with an entrance on the side. Hamilton (1944) found a nest of shredded marsh grass, smaller than a base-

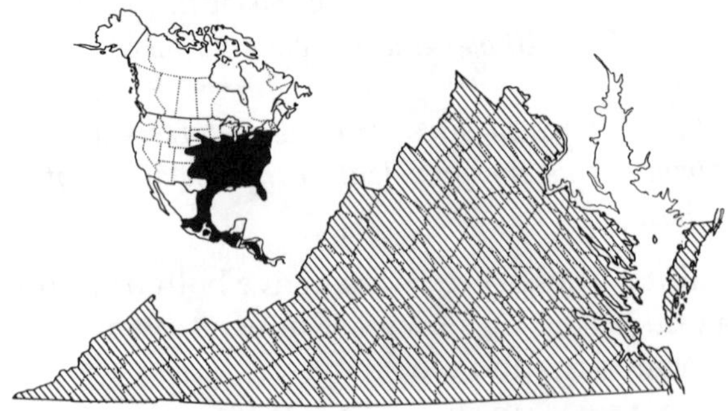

Figure 17. *Cryptotis parva:* Range in Virginia and North America.

ball and flattened above, at Chincoteague. Nests have been located at the bases of trees and beneath rocks, pieces of tin, boards, and logs.

Unlike most shrews, this species is often gregarious. Nests containing as many as 31 individuals have been reported. Approximately 25 least shrews were found in a leaf nest beneath a log in April in Virginia (Jackson, 1961). It has been suggested that this behavior may serve as a heat conservation measure.

In east Tennessee, Howell (1954) found that the home range of one female trapped nine times was 0.23 ha, while a male trapped five times ranged over 0.17 ha.

The breathing rate of a resting animal is about 170 times per minute (Moore, 1943). These shrews sleep very soundly.

Food. Besides his reference to these shrews feeding on tiny invertebrates on Chincoteague Island, Hamilton (1944) recorded evidence of this species feeding on the snail *Melampus lineatus*. The most common foods of these shrews in Indiana were lepidopterous larvae, earthworms, spiders, internal organs of orthopterans, and beetle larvae (Whitaker and Mumford, 1972). These made up 47.2 percent of the total volume of food. The authors noted that *Cryptotis* apparently opens up larger insects and eats the internal organs since 9.4 percent of the total food volume consisted of internal organs of orthopterans and beetle larvae. Detailed accounts of the feeding behavior of this species have been presented by Moore (1943) and Hamilton (1944).

Least shrews have enormous appetites. In captivity, individuals have been known to eat more than their weight in food each day, but under natural conditions the intake of food is probably considerably less. This large intake is necessary to supply the energy for their nearly continuous activity. The rate of digestion is extremely rapid; chitin from insect food took only 95 minutes to pass through the digestive tract and appear in the feces (Hamilton, 1944).

Food hoarding has been reported in this species by Formanowicz et al. (1989). Females killed and hoarded more prey than males. Larger prey was cached nearer the nest and smaller prey farther from the nest.

Reproduction and Development. Brimley (1923) recorded pregnant females in February, May, and September in North Carolina, and Hamilton (1944) took a pregnant female on July 1 at Chincoteague that gave birth to six young on July 5. In other areas, breeding extends from February to November. The gestation period is 21 to 23 days with litter size generally ranging from three to six. Four to five litters may be produced annually. At birth, the young are pink, blind, naked, and weigh about 0.6 g. The eyes open at about 10 days of age. Least shrews are weaned after 21 days. Details of growth and development are described by several authors (Hamilton, 1944; Broadbooks, 1952; Walker, 1954; and Conaway, 1958). Female least shrews may begin breeding at three months of age.

Longevity. Captive shrews have lived two years.

Predation. Jackson et al. (1976) recorded this species in barn owl pellets in Chesterfield County. Least shrews formed 26 percent of the total catch of barn owls in Prince William County (Deibler, 1988). Mitchell and Beck (1992) reported its capture by a free-ranging domestic cat in New Kent County. Remains of these shrews have also been recorded from rough-legged hawks; great horned, barred, and short-eared owl pellets; bobcats; foxes; spotted skunks; and snakes.

Geographic Variation. The subspecies in Virginia is *Cryptotis parva parva* (Say).

Location of Specimens. AMNH, BCV, CM, CU, DMNH, GMU, ISUVC, LFCC, MVZ, NCSM, NVCC, ODU, SBC, SUVM, SNP, UCONN, UMMZ, USNM, VCU, VMNH, VPISU, VPI-W.

Genus *Blarina*

Dentition: 4/2, 1/0, 2/1, 3/3 = 32

Northern Short-Tailed Shrew
Blarina brevicauda (Say)

Description. In overall length, the northern short-tailed shrew (Plate 10) is the second largest of the nine species of shrews found in Virginia. By weight, however, it is the heaviest. The pelage of both sexes is uniformly slate gray with slightly paler underparts; it is short, dense, and velvety. The tail is short and covered with hair. The eyes are minute, and the ears are so small that they are hidden in the fur. Females have six mammae. Adult northern short-tailed shrews are usually 105 to 138 mm in length,

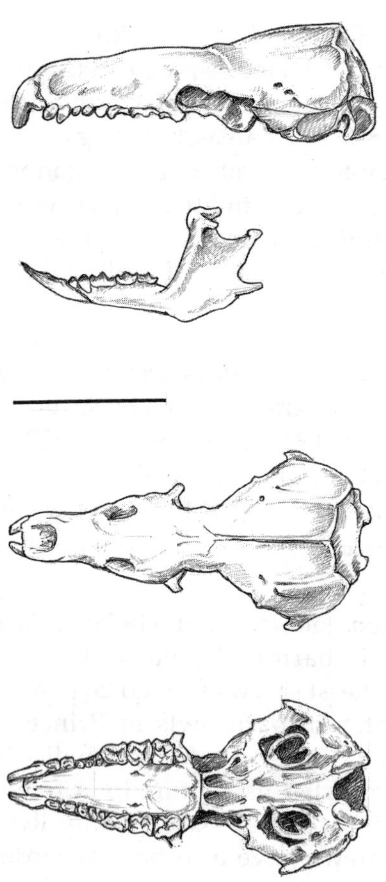

Figure 18. *Blarina brevicauda:* Left lateral view of skull and mandible, and dorsal and ventral view of skull. Scale bar = 10 mm.

including their stubby 18 to 30 mm tail. They weigh between 14 and 28 g.

The skull is relatively robust and has prominent ridges and crests. As in all Virginia shrews, the zygomatic arches are incomplete, and all of the teeth are tipped with chestnut. The 32 teeth include five pairs of unicuspids. When viewed from the side, the unicuspid teeth are in two pairs — a large pair in front with a smaller pair behind. The fifth unicuspid is so small that it is not apparent from a side view (Figure 18).

Distribution. The northern short-tailed shrew inhabits the forests and grasslands of the eastern half of the United States and adjacent Canada south to Georgia and Alabama. The range extends west to Saskatchewan, North Dakota and central Nebraska.

This shrew occurs statewide in Virginia (Figure 19).

Habitat. Northern short-tailed shrews may occupy a wide variety of habitats but are found most commonly in moist woodlands bordering swamps, marshes, bogs and streams. They have also been taken in fields, thickets, and even in pine woods.

Habits. Although this shrew can be found abroad at any hour, it is most active at night. One study found that the short-tailed shrew had about 11 active periods in 24 hours with a major peak occurring during darkness. Much of the daytime is spent in a burrow, a hollow log, or a stump. The shrews make shallow runways beneath the surface litter and also use the burrows and runways of other animals. Individuals are generally solitary, only allowing the approach of the opposite sex during the mating season.

No information exists concerning the home range of this species in Virginia, but studies in other areas have revealed an average home range size of about 0.2 ha, varying somewhat on food availability and population density.

The nest is constructed mainly of dry leaves and grasses and is approximately 13 to 20 cm in diameter. Nests are commonly placed beneath logs, stumps, rocks, and debris.

These shrews have poor eyesight, but this is compensated for by their ability to detect sounds and vibrations. Tactile stimuli are received via the vibrissae and snout. These shrews have large olfactory lobes of the brain in association with their highly developed sense of smell. They are able to distinguish such things as healthy from unhealthy sawfly cocoons by olfaction (Holling, 1958). Carson et al. (1994) examined the ultrastructure of the olfactory epithelium.

Tomasi (1979) concluded that the primary

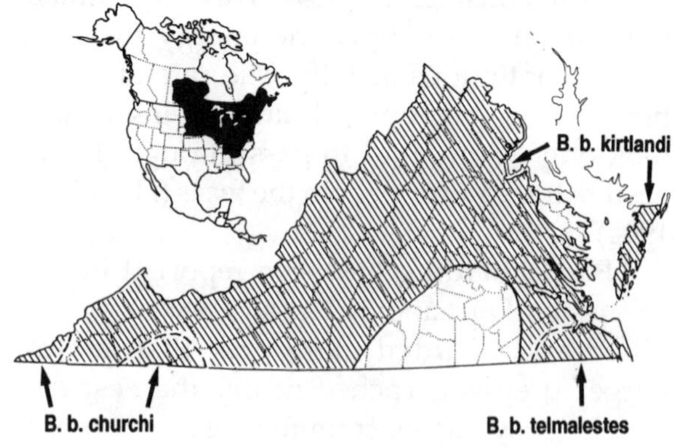

Figure 19. *Blarina brevicauda:* Range in Virginia and North America.

usage of echolocation in *Blarina* was for exploration of the environment.

Echolocation seems to be best suited for exploring the tunnel ahead, investigating side tunnels, searching for cover when above ground, and avoiding obstacles when in a hurry. The detection distance is too short to be of much use in predator detection....Olfaction is probably more important for this purpose (Tomasi, 1979).

Pagels and French (1987) reported that animals trapped in discarded bottles can be a source of information about small mammal distribution data in Virginia. A total of 378 soricids were recorded at 64 different sites. Approximately 85 percent of all shrews found in bottles were species of *Blarina*. The species and number of individuals included *Sorex cinereus* (3); *Sorex longirostris* (8); *Sorex fumeus* (18); *Blarina brevicauda* (183); *Blarina carolinensis* (144); and *Cryptotis parva* (22).

Food. Stomach analyses of 17 short-tailed shrews from the Great Smoky Mountains National Park in Tennessee and North Carolina revealed major food items to be millipedes, insects and insect larvae, snails or slugs, and earthworms. A fungus, *Endogone* sp., composed 4.9 percent of the total volume of food (Linzey and Linzey, 1973). Major food items in Indiana were earthworms, insect larvae, beetles, slugs and snails, and centipedes (Whitaker and Cudmore, 1987). Studies of food habits of *Blarina* from widely separated areas indicate that the diet is fairly similar regardless of geographic location. Eadie (1944) reported that 56 percent of 200 winter scats from a region of high *Microtus* concentration in New York contained mouse remains. Reports of predation by this shrew on shrews of the genus *Sorex* have also been recorded.

The short-tailed shrew has an enormous appetite and may consume the equivalent of its own weight in food per day, although on the average captive shrews eat about half that amount.

Several instances of food storage by these shrews have been reported. Several investigators have noted finding stores of snail shells during the winter. Audubon and Bachman (1851) stated:

We observed in the sides of one of these galleries a small cavity, containing a hoard of coleopterous insects, principally of the rare species Scarabeus tityrus, *fully the size of the animal itself; some of them were nearly consumed, and the rest mutilated, although some still living.*

Robinson and Brodie (1982) reported in a laboratory study that 86.6 percent of captured prey was cached, 9.4 percent was consumed immediately, and 3.9 percent was left where it was killed. Shrews usually ate the first prey captured but normally cached subsequent prey. They defecated and possibly urinated on edible cached prey. They returned and consumed the marked prey, suggesting that marking may help in its location. Shrews were also observed consuming prey cached by conspecifics. Numerous prey items were cached together in sites used as nests as well as in sites used solely for storage.

The short-tailed shrew, the male duck-billed platypus, and the echidna are the only mammals equipped with poison glands. In the shrew, the poison is produced by the submaxillary glands and is present in the saliva. Studies by Martin (1981) indicated that the venom (or saliva) acted as a slow poison as well as an immobilizing agent on insects. Immobilized insects remained alive for three to five days, thus allowing *Blarina* to exploit a sudden abundance of insects and extend the availability of fresh, non-decomposing food. It has also been suggested that this salivary secretion may aid in protein digestion. Mice and rabbits injected with a submaxillary gland secretion exhibited a local reaction, lowering of the blood pressure, slowing of the heart, and inhibition of respiration (Pearson, 1942). When injected intravenously, only one-fourth of the total secretion obtainable from a single shrew was a lethal dosage for a 2.7 kg rabbit (Pearson, 1956). Few records are available concerning the effect of this poison on man, although the bite may cause considerable discomfort and has been known to produce local swelling (Maynard, 1889; Krosch, 1973). Other persons may be bitten and suffer no reaction (Whitaker, personal communication).

Experiments involving dietary toxicity and residue relationships of DDT, dieldrin, and eldrin were reported by Blus (1978). In comparison to other mammals, short-tailed shrews were not unusually sensitive on the basis of two-week feeding tests. The influence of age and sex on toxicity was frequently more important than body weight.

Reproduction and Development. Female shrews may have several litters of three to nine young per year. Studies by Pearson (1944) have shown that female *Blarina* do not ovulate spontaneously, but that release of the egg from the ovary occurs only after repeated matings. The gestation period is between 18 and 21 days. The female may be bred again while still nursing.

Reproductively active individuals can be found during most months in Virginia. Peaks of breeding often occur during spring and autumn, with a reduction in midsummer, but in West Virginia and Kentucky, breeding males and lactating females have been recorded during June, July, and August.

Newborn short-tailed shrews are pink and naked and have their eyes and ears sealed. At about four weeks of age they are weaned and independent. Some early-born shrews breed late the same summer, while later-born ones breed the following spring. Male short-tailed shrews are capable of breeding at about seven weeks of age and perhaps earlier.

Longevity. Studies indicate that the maximum age for wild *Blarina* is probably about 20 months. Few individuals survive their second winter. Manville (1949) recorded two individuals surviving for 12 months in Michigan, while Getz (1989) recorded nine shrews surviving 12 months and one for 16 months in Illinois. Captives have lived up to 33 months (George, et al., 1986).

Pelage Variations. Molting in this species has been described by Hamilton (1940b) and Findley and Jones (1956). The post-juvenile molt usually begins in the head region and proceeds caudad on both dorsal and ventral surfaces. In second year females, the summer pelage appears first on the head region and proceeds posteriorly. In second year males, the molt is irregular. In the fall, new winter pelage appears first on the posterior part of the body and proceeds cephalad.

Ernst (1994) reported a full albino adult taken in Fairfax County in 1985. Moncrief and Anderson (1997) reported a partial albino from Henry County.

Parasites. The nematode *Capillaria hepatica* and the flea *Doratopsylla blarinae* have been recorded from this species in Virginia by Jordan (1928) and Solomon and Handley (1971). Smiley and Whitaker (1979) recorded the mites *Pygmephorus whitakeri, Pygmephorus horridus, Pygmephorus designatus, Pygmephorus hastatus, Pygmephorus hamiltoni,* and *Pygmephorus faini.* The mite *Haemogamasus liponyssoides* was reported by Williams et al. (1978). The coleopteran *Leptinus orientamericanus* was recorded by Eckerlin and Painter (1991). The flea *Ctenophthalmus pseudagyrtes* was recorded by Painter and Eckerlin (1993) from Westmoreland County.

Predation. Snakes, hawks, owls, weasels, foxes, bobcats, and other predators including largemouth bass (Hodgson, 1986) have been known to kill these shrews. In Maryland, Llewellyn and Uhler (1952) noted that more shrews were eaten by house cats than by any other predator. Because of their musky odor, some individuals that are killed may not be eaten. Rageot (1957) recorded this species in the stomach of a copperhead and in barred owl pellets in the Dismal Swamp. Jackson, Pagels, and Trumbo (1976) took this species from barn owl pellets in Chesterfield County. Mitchell and Beck (1992) reported the capture of these shrews by free-ranging domestic cats in Henrico County.

Geographic Variation. The subspecies occurring in Virginia is *Blarina brevicauda brevicauda* (Say). Three geographic variants occur in the state. One occurs throughout most of western and northern Virginia except for the high mountains in Washington, Smyth, Grayson, Wythe, and Lee counties. Its range includes the Eastern Shore. A larger, whiter-toothed form inhabits the extreme southeastern portion of the state, including the Dismal Swamp, and has been found as far west as Southampton County, where it intergrades with the brown-toothed variant. The largest short-tailed shrew in Virginia has been recorded from the higher elevations, including Whitetop Mountain, in Washington, Smyth, Grayson, Wythe, and Lee counties. It is darker and has less glossy fur than the western and northern variant.

Other Currently Recognized Subspecies. *Blarina brevicauda kirtlandi* Bole and Moulthrop; *Blarina brevicauda telmalestes* Merriam; *Blarina brevicauda churchi* Bole and Moulthrop.

Location of Specimens. AEL, AMNH, ASU,

ASUMZ, BCV, BRP, CHAS, CM, CSULB, CU, CUC, DMNH, DWL, EHC, EKU, FSM, GMU, HSU, ISM, ISUVC, KU, LACM, LC, LFCC, LSUMZ, LU, MCZ, MHP, MMMN, MSUMZ, MVZ, NCSM, NVCC, RMWC, RU, SBC, SNP, SUVM, TTU, UA, UCM, UCONN, UGAMNH, UIMNH, UMMZ, USNM, VCU, VHCC, VMNH, VPISU, VPI-W, YPM.

Southern Short-Tailed Shrew
Blarina carolinensis (Bachman)

Description. The southern short-tailed shrew (Plate 11) is a smaller, darker relative of the short-tailed shrew. The uniform slaty-black pelage is glossy and velvety. The underparts are slightly paler. The tail is short and covered with hair. Females have six mammae. Adult southern short-tailed shrews are usually between 85 and 105 mm in total length, including a 15 to 23 mm tail. They weigh between 6 and 12 g. This species was formerly considered a subspecies of *Blarina brevicauda* (Handley, 1979b; Tate et al., 1980).

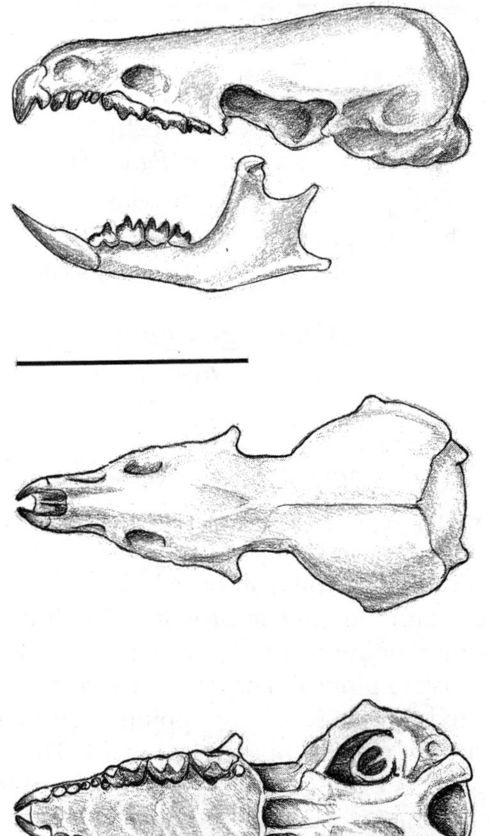

Figure 20. *Blarina carolinensis:* Left lateral view of skull and mandible, and dorsal and ventral view of skull. Scale bar = 10 mm.

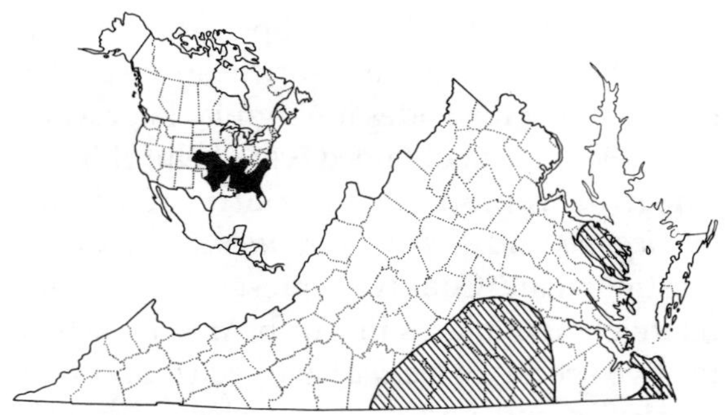

Figure 21. *Blarina carolinensis:* Range in Virginia and North America.

The skull is smaller (total length less than 20 mm) and less massive but otherwise similar to the skull of *Blarina brevicauda*. The zygomatic arches are incomplete. All teeth are tipped with chestnut. When viewed from the side, the five unicuspids are in two pairs with the fifth unicuspid usually not being visible from the outside (Figure 20).

Distribution. This species occurs from southern Maryland south through Florida. The range extends west of the Appalachian Mountains to Arkansas, Oklahoma, Kansas, and eastern Colorado and north into Nebraska, Iowa, and Illinois.

In Virginia, Handley (1979b) noted that the southern short-tailed shrew has a discontinuous distribution in the Coastal Plain and lower Piedmont, with numerous isolated populations (Figure 21). Although *Blarina brevicauda* and *Blarina carolinensis* usually have mutually exclusive ranges, and are contiguously allopatric in most of the central to eastern portions of North America where their ranges meet, Handley found them together in the Northern Neck of Virginia, and Erdle and Pagels (1995) captured them at the same site in the Great Dismal Swamp. Handley noted that the southern short-tailed shrew occurs near the southern and eastern margins of the Dismal Swamp but probably not actually within it. Tate et al. (1980) found no evidence of intergradation or hybridization and concluded that the two shrews represent distinct species.

Habitat. Southern short-tailed shrews are most frequently found in moist woodlands and fields.

Habits. Probably similar to the short-tailed

shrew *(Blarina brevicauda)*. Species of *Blarina* were the most abundant soricid in discarded bottles along roadsides in Virginia (Pagels and Tate, 1987). Data obtained were helpful in delineating regions of sympatry of *Blarina brevicauda* and *Blarina carolinensis*. A site in Westmoreland County "represents one of the relatively few places in North America where the two species of *Blarina* have been found sympatrically and here, both species were even found in a single bottle" (Pagels and Tate, 1987).

Food. Predominant foods in South Carolina, both in terms of volume and frequency of occurrence, were slugs and snails (Mollusca), the fungus *Endogone*, earthworms (Annelida), and beetle (Coleoptera) adults and larvae (Whitaker et al., 1994).

Reproduction and Development. Probably similar to the short-tailed shrew, *Blarina brevicauda*.

Predation. Snakes, hawks, owls, and various carnivorous mammals probably prey on this shrew.

Geographic Variation. The subspecies occurring in Virginia is *Blarina carolinensis carolinensis* (Bachman).

Location of Specimens. CM, CMNH, CU, DMNH, ISUVC, LFCC, MVZ, NCSM, ODU, UMMZ, USNM, VCU, VPISU, VPI-W.

Moles (Family Talpidae)

Moles are fossorial mammals, highly specialized for subterranean life. Their robust bodies are covered by dense, soft, silky, grayish-brown pelage. The fur lies equally well when brushed either forward or backward, and this facilitates movement in either direction in the mole's underground burrows. They have a long, slender skull with complete but weak zygomatic arches. The shoulder girdle is greatly enlarged, with the muscles of the shoulders and forelimbs being enlarged and powerful. The forelegs are short with the front feet being greatly enlarged for digging. The forefeet are broader than long, and the palms face outward. The claws on the forefeet are broad and flat, while those of the hind feet are relatively short and weak. The tiny, degenerate eyes are concealed in the fur and are covered by fused eyelids. External ears (pinnae) are absent.

Nearly all species of moles construct elaborate tunnel systems and spend most of their time underground. In the star-nosed mole, *Condylura cristata*, some of the burrows have underwater openings to accommodate this mole's semiaquatic habits. Moles may be active at any hour of the day and night and neither hibernate nor aestivate. Their diet consists primarily of earthworms and other invertebrates. Like shrews, moles are voracious eaters.

North American moles consist of two subfamilies — the Condylurinae including only *Condylura* and the Scalopinae containing the other four genera (Yates and Greenbaum, 1982).

Key to Species of Talpidae

1a End of snout with a fringe of fleshy processes; third incisor resembling a canine
 .... *Condylura cristata*

1b End of snout without a fringe of fleshy processes; third incisor not resembling a canine
 2

2a Tail densely haired; 11 teeth in each half of upper jaw; total teeth 44
 .... *Parascalops breweri*

2b Tail sparsely haired; 10 teeth in each half of upper jaw; total teeth 36
 .... *Scalopus aquaticus*

Genus *Scalopus*

Dentition: 3/2, 1/0, 3/3, 3/3 = 36

Eastern Mole
Scalopus aquaticus (Linnaeus)

Description. Oil glands occurring on the head, chin, wrist, and belly of the eastern mole (Plate 12) produce brownish or yellowish secretions that stain the grayish-brown fur with varying degrees of intensity. The face, feet, and tail are whitish or pinkish. The tail is short and sparsely haired. The nose is long, pointed, and naked, with the nostrils opening upward. The external ear is evident only as a small opening beneath the fur. The toes of both the forefeet and the hind feet are webbed. Females have six mammae. Adults are usually between 135 and 200 mm long, including a 22 to 40 mm tail. They weigh up to 140 g.

The skull of the eastern mole is triangular in outline, pointed in front and broadest near

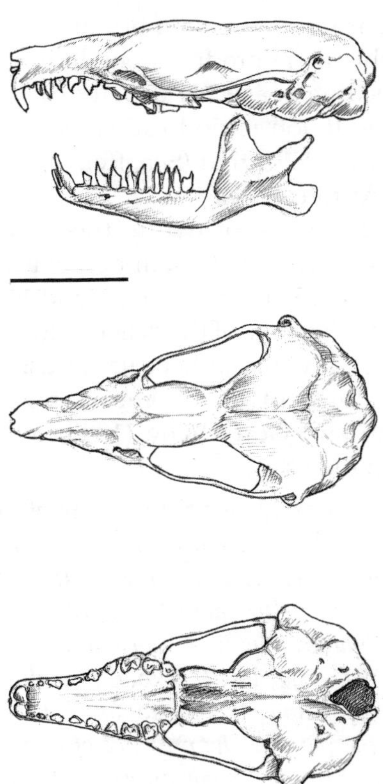

Figure 22. *Scalopus aquaticus:* Left lateral view of skull and mandible, and dorsal and ventral view of skull. Scale bar = 10 mm.

the back. The skull contains 36 teeth. The cheek teeth have sharp pointed cusps adapted for crushing invertebrate prey (Figure 22).

Distribution. This species occurs in suitable habitat throughout much of the eastern United States. It ranges from southern Ontario, southeastern Wyoming, Minnesota, Michigan, and Massachusetts south to southern Florida, the Gulf Coast, and west to western Texas and northern Mexico.

In Virginia, the eastern mole occurs statewide up to an elevation of approximately 610 m (Figure 23).

Habitat. Moist, sandy or loamy soil is preferred by this mole, and it occurs in meadows, gardens, cultivated fields, river bottoms, mountain slopes, and both coniferous and hardwood forests.

Habits. Arlton (1936) showed that there were three main periods of activity — 2 to 6 A.M., 10 A.M. to 2 P.M., and 9 to 11 P.M., while Harvey (1967) reported that moles were most active from 9 A.M. to 3 P.M. and from 11 P.M. to 3 A.M. The latter study reported two periods of inactivity — one from 4 to 7 A.M. and one from 6 to 9 P.M. Moles in Kentucky spend 37 percent of their time in their nests.

Eastern moles work at two levels. Temporary, or feeding, tunnels are constructed barely beneath the surface but at a uniform depth. These tunnels are built by the mole during its search for food, with construction concentrated mainly at times when the ground is relatively soft such as during the spring months and after precipitation. These tunnels vary in length, with some reaching 335 m or more. Tunnel construction leaves characteristic ridges that serve as the main indication of a mole's presence in a given area. Mounds of earth, or molehills, are formed much less commonly by the eastern mole than by other species of moles.

Arlton (1936) described the digging behavior of a male placed on the ground:

> *The fore feet are placed close to the snout and the earth is pushed aside. The snout becomes active, not in boring or shoving the earth aside, but in discovering a suitable spot to place the fore feet for the next side-stroke. In a few seconds the mole is half buried. Then the animal twists the anterior half of its body, turning on its side, and pushes the soil upward with its fore feet. In this way are made the conspicuous ridges commonly called surface tunnels.*

The lower-level tunnels are located from 20 to 60 cm beneath the surface. These lower tunnels constitute the mole's living quarters and serve as a retreat during dry or cold weather. A large chamber in the deeper runways serves as a retreat and as a nest site for the young.

Schwartz and Schwartz (1959) noted that the digging of surface tunnels occurs at a rate of about 0.3 m per minute while deeper excavation occurs at approximately 3.5 to 4.5 m per

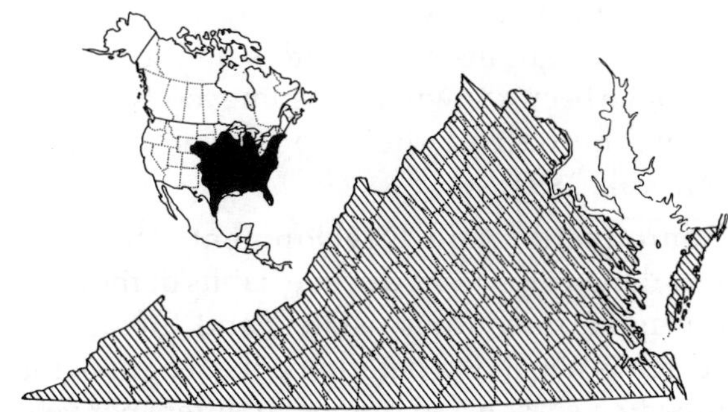

Figure 23. *Scalopus aquaticus:* Range in Virginia and North America.

hour, including stops for rest and food. One individual dug more than 31 m of shallow tunnels in one day (Walker, 1964). Burrow systems may cover an area as large as 3,540 m^2. Harvey (1976) recorded an average home range among males of 1.09 ha. Home ranges of females were considerably smaller. Home range size increased as the length of study time increased, and there appeared to be a high degree of overlapping of home ranges.

Their eyes are essentially nonfunctional, and moles depend on hearing and touch to perceive their surroundings. The snout and tail are well developed tactile organs, aiding the mole in backward and forward movements.

Moles breathe rapidly, respiring between 40 and 42 times a minute. Tests have shown that they have a very high metabolism, and this is reflected by their general nervous disposition and high consumption of food.

Moles have a distinctive, strong, musky odor that may have some communication significance, particularly during the breeding season. In addition, the musky odor makes them undesirable as a food item for most other animals.

Although the ridges caused by the tunneling activity of these moles are not appreciated by most homeowners, their destruction of injurious insect larvae is exceedingly beneficial.

Food. The diet of this mole is primarily earthworms, insect larvae, and insects. Some vegetable matter is eaten occasionally. Calhoun (1941) found that 72 percent of the food of the eastern mole at Reelfoot Lake, Tennessee, consisted of insects and insect larvae, with plants making up the rest of the diet.

Moles capture and kill active prey by crushing it with their front feet against the sides of the tunnel or by throwing loose soil on it and then biting the prey.

Moles are insatiable eaters and in captivity have been known to consume food equal to over one-half of their body weight daily (Nowak, 1991).

Reproduction and Development. There are few data on the reproductive habits of the eastern mole in southern states, and further research is needed to determine the length of the breeding season and number of litters per year in the South. Females with embryos have been recorded in March, April, May, and June in North Carolina. In more northern parts of its range, this mole produces one litter per year. The breeding season is usually early spring with a gestation period estimated to be four (Conaway, 1959), five (Scheffer, 1909), or six weeks (Arlton, 1936).

Litters consist of two to five young. The young are born in a globular nest of leaves and grass about 15 cm in diameter and is located in a chamber in one of the deeper runways. The nest is usually placed beneath a bush, stump, or boulder and has several approaches. Hartman and Gottschang (1983) noted that newborn moles:

> *were naked except for the presence of numerous short vibrissae. Vibrissae were arranged in nine rows on either side of the snout extending from the tip of the snout to almost the dorsal-ventral plane of the eyes. Vibrissae on the lower jaw were arranged in three rows extending from the anterior tip of the jaw to not quite the corner of the mouth. The presence of vibrissae at birth suggests the importance of tactile perception to the animals.*

Young males grow rapidly and leave the nest when approximately four weeks of age. They begin breeding during the spring following their birth.

Longevity. Several moles, adults when first captured, lived in the field for periods up to 36 months in Kentucky, and several were still alive and healthy at the end of the study (Harvey, 1967).

Pelage Variations. An albino specimen has been recorded from Montgomery County (VPI-W).

Parasites. The flea *Ctenophthalmus pseudagyrtes* and the coleopteran *Leptinus orientamericanus* have been recorded from this species in Virginia (Fox, 1968; Eckerlin and Painter,1991).

Predation. Few animals prey on moles because of their subterranean habits and musky odor. Snakes, owls, and foxes are probably their main predators. Remains of two moles were recovered from barn owl pellets in Chesterfield County (Jackson, Pagels, and Trumbo, 1976). Mitchell and Beck (1992) reported captures of this mole by free-ranging domestic cats in New Kent and Henrico counties.

Geographic Variation. *Scalopus aquaticus aquaticus* (Linnaeus) is the only subspecies that occurs in Virginia.

Location of Specimens. AMNH, BCV, CM, CMNH, DMNH, GMU, HSU, LFCC, LSUMZ, LU, MCZ, MVZ, NCSM, NVCC, ODU, OSU, OU, RC, RU, SNP, UMMZ, USNM, VCU, VHCC, VPISU, VPI-W.

Genus *Parascalops*

Dentition: 3/3, 1/1, 4/4, 3/3 = 44

Hairy-Tailed Mole
Parascalops breweri (Bachman)

Description. The robust blackish hairy-tailed mole (Plate 13) is the smallest of Virginia's moles. The shiny, dark fur together with the densely haired, very short tail will immediately identify this species. The fusiform body, flattened head, minute eyes, and the absence of external ears are reflections of the fossorial habits of this mammal. The nostrils are lateral and crescent-shaped. The front feet are as broad as they are long. Females posses eight mammae. Adult moles are between 135 and 176 mm in total length, including a 25 to 35 mm tail. They weigh between 40 and 65 g.

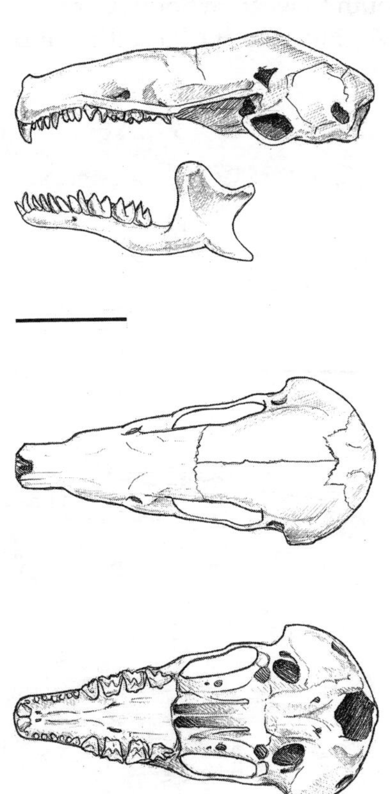

Figure 24. *Parascalops breweri:* Left lateral view of skull and mandible, and dorsal and ventral view of skull. Scale bar = 10 mm.

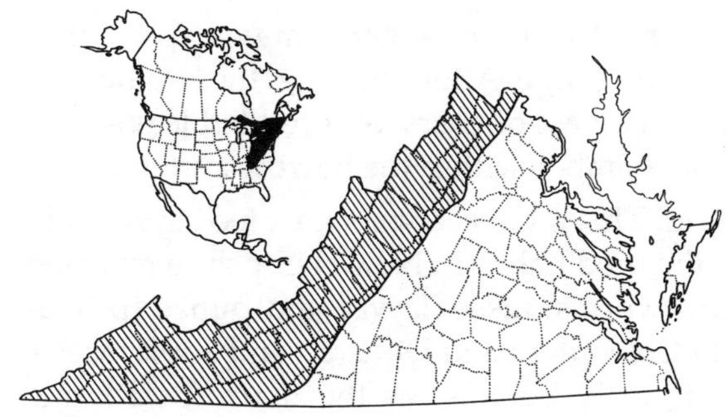

Figure 25. *Parascalops breweri:* Range in Virginia and North America.

The rostrum is slender. There are 44 teeth which, along with the star-nosed mole, is more than any other terrestrial mammal in Virginia, except the opossum (Figure 24).

Distribution. The hairy-tailed mole ranges from southern Quebec and Ontario south through the New England states to central Ohio, eastern Tennessee and western North Carolina.

In Virginia this species is restricted to the western portion of the state (Figure 25). It has been recorded at elevations ranging from 915 to 1,678 m.

Habitat. Well-drained areas with sandy loam soil supporting a good cover of vegetation are preferred. Unlike the star-nosed mole, this species is not found in low, wet areas.

Habits. Like other moles, *Parascalops* digs both a system of surface tunnels and a system of deep tunnels. The spherical nests are generally in the deeper tunnels and are composed of coarsely shredded deciduous leaves. Some tunnels have been actively used for eight years or more by successive generations. Average home range size is approximately 0.1 ha.

Hairy-tailed moles are active throughout the year, although during the colder season most activity is confined to the deep tunnel system. They are active at all hours of the day and night.

Because of the extreme specialization of the front limbs, the hairy-tailed mole, like most other moles, is awkward when above ground. An individual was observed to move 4.6 m in 30 seconds on the hard surface of a dirt road. This slow rate probably represented its top speed.

In the spring when males move about in

search of a mate, several may appear in a female's range. After breeding, the female constructs a nest of coarsely shredded leaves in a nest chamber within the burrow system.

Food. This mole is a voracious feeder. A study of the food habits in New Hampshire revealed earthworms, insect larvae and pupae (primarily Coleoptera and Diptera), and adult insects (primarily beetles) as the main food items (Eadie, 1939). In West Virginia, Brooks (1923) found evidence that *Parascalops* removed the larvae and pupae from nests of ground-nesting wasps. Jensen (1986) found little evidence that surface tunnels acted as pitfall traps for invertebrates.

These moles may forage above ground at night. Moles in captivity have been recorded as eating between three and four times their weight in food daily (Fay, 1954). Studies by Jensen (1983), however, found no evidence for an unusually high rate of metabolism, although at times they may become hyperactive and expend a great deal of energy.

Reproduction and Development. Mating normally occurs in early spring with females producing their single annual litter following a four to six week gestation period. Usual litter size is four or five. Newborn young are naked except for short vibrissae on the snout and facial hairs near the eyes and on the lips. The skin is whitish and wrinkled. They remain in the nest for about four weeks. They are sexually mature when 10 months of age (Eadie, 1939; Connor, 1960; Hallett, 1978).

Longevity. Hairy-tailed moles have a life span of four to five years.

Predation. Since moles spend most of their time underground, they have relatively few enemies. Snakes, carnivorous mammals, and man are their main predators. A food habits study of snakes in the George Washington National Forest revealed the presence of hairy-tailed moles in three copperheads (Saylor, 1938).

Location of Specimens. BCV, CUC, DWL, FSM, ISM, ODU, UMMZ, USNM, VMNH, VPISU, VPI-W.

Genus *Condylura*

Dentition: 3/3, 1/1, 4/4, 3/3 = 44

Star-Nosed Mole
Condylura cristata (Linnaeus)

Description. This blackish-brown to nearly black mammal has a unique nose ring of 22 fleshy rays. The long, hairy tail is covered with coarse, blackish hairs and is constricted near the base. The palms of the front feet are as broad as long. The eyes are very small. Females possess eight mammae. Adult star-nosed moles (Plate 14) are between 160 and 210 mm long, including a 60 to 90 mm tail. They weigh between 30 and 75 g.

The skull contains 44 teeth. The first upper incisors are large, recurved, and project anteriorly (Figure 26).

Distribution. This species ranges from Labrador, New Brunswick, Quebec, and Ontario south to central Ohio, Indiana, Minnesota, and South Dakota. Along the Atlantic Coast, the range extends to southeastern Georgia, while in the Appalachian Mountains the range extends south to western South Carolina.

In Virginia, the star-nosed mole has been

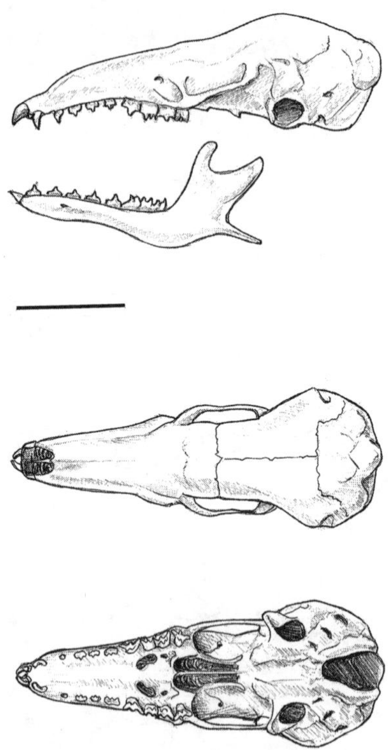

Figure 26. *Condylura cristata:* Left lateral view of skull and mandible, and dorsal and ventral view of skull. Scale bar = 10 mm.

recorded most commonly in the eastern portion of the state (Figure 27). However, individuals have also been taken in Warren, Greene, Loudoun, Highland, Cumberland, Patrick, and Russell counties. It has been reported but not collected from Wythe County.

Habitat. Unlike our other two moles, the star-nosed mole prefers low, wet areas. Wet meadows, marshes, and low wet ground near lakes and streams provides ideal habitat.

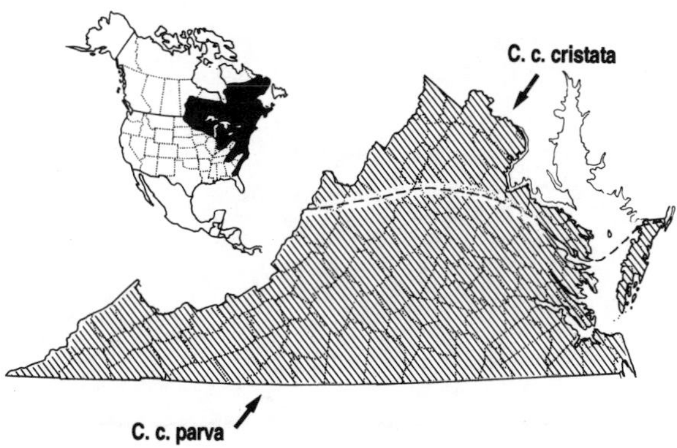

Figure 27. *Condylura cristata:* Range in Virginia and North America.

Habits. Like our other moles, this species constructs underground tunnel systems. However, the tunnels are irregular and crooked with surface ridges appearing and disappearing. Most of the underground tunnels are not visible as ridges on the surface of the ground. Unlike those of the other moles, some of the tunnels lead directly into water. This mole is an expert swimmer and has often been taken in minnow traps and muskrat traps. Waterways, rather than burrows, seem to be used more frequently during the winter months.

This mole is active both day and night. It generally spends more time on the surface of the ground than do the other species. Its nest of grass, straw, and leaves is usually constructed near the surface in soft earth, compost and manure piles, under stumps and logs, and in rotten trees. The nest is approximately 20 cm in diameter.

Sight and smell are poorly developed, while the sense of hearing is more acute than in other moles. The sense of touch is very well developed. Gould et al. (1993) presented evidence suggesting that the fleshy nose rays might serve as an electrosensory organ that would allow prey detection beyond the range of the body surface and considerably increase foraging efficiency.

The peculiar enlargement of the tail in this species has often been noted. It has been suggested that tails swollen with fatty tissue may act as a temporary reservoir for energy useful during the breeding season (Eadie and Hamilton, 1956).

Food. No data are available for this species in Virginia. In an examination of 107 stomachs from New York, Hamilton (1931) found a large preponderance of aquatic organisms. Aquatic annelids and aquatic insects constituted more than 65 percent of the total volume of food, while terrestrial annelids made up only 9.8 percent of the diet. Rust (1966) examined eight stomachs from Wisconsin and recorded, by volume, terrestrial earthworms, 84 percent; slugs, aquatic annelids, caddis worms, and midge larvae, 7.6 percent; organic material, 2.1 percent; and mineral matter, 6.3 percent. Crustaceans and small fish may also be taken.

The highly sensitive fleshy processes on the nose (star) are used in detecting potential food items. This highly mobile appendage is richly supplied with nerves and blood vessels. The rays are in constant motion when the animal is searching for food, except for the two median upper ones, which are held rigidly forward. The tentacles "feel" for prey as the mole hunts near or in the bottom sediment of streams (Pagels, 1986). The tentacles are drawn firmly together while the animal eats. Gould et al. (1993) correlated movements of the rays with the use of electroreception to detect prey. If verified by future studies, this would represent the first evidence of prey detection by electroreception in a placental mammal. The anatomy of the nasal rays has been discussed by Van Vleck (1965).

Reproduction and Development. Females usually produce their single annual litter during May and June after a gestation period of about 45 days. The three to seven young are blind and naked at birth. The eyes are visible as dark swellings beneath the skin, and there is no evidence of external ears. Young moles grow rapidly and are able to leave the nest when approximately three weeks of age. They are sexually mature at 10 months.

Parasites. The coleopteran *Leptinus orientamericanus* has been recorded from this species in Virginia (Eckerlin and Painter, 1991).

Predation. Snakes, hawks, owls, and carnivorous mammals such as skunks are the major predators of the star-nosed mole.

Geographic Variation. The subspecies occurring in Virginia is *Condylura cristata cristata* (Linnaeus). A geographic variant inhabits the southern three-fourths of the state.

Other Currently Recognized Subspecies. *Condylura cristata parva* Paradiso.

Location of Specimens. BCV, CM, GMU, HSU, LFCC, ODU, SBC, USNM, VPISU, VPI-W.

Bats

Bats, those mammals represented by the order Chiroptera, are unique among mammals in that their specialized forelimbs are modified for true flight. In fact, the word *chiroptera* means "winged hand." Bats comprise a large and widely distributed group with most of the nearly 1,000 living species being found in the tropics. Sixteen species of bats have been recorded in Virginia. Thus, bats comprise 20 percent of the 80 species of terrestrial mammals presently occurring in the state.

Most bats have small eyes, large ears, and a peculiar fleshy outgrowth of the ear canal known as the tragus projecting upward in front of the pinna. The tragus is thought to serve a sensory function. Other characteristics relating primarily to their capability for flight include greatly elongated fingers, a keeled sternum, a well developed pectoral girdle and collarbone, and fusion of some vertebrae. Flight membranes connect the body with the wings, legs, and tail. The knees are directed outward and backward because of the rotation of the leg to support the wing membranes. Unlike birds, bats use both legs and wings during flight.

The flight membranes are actually extensions of the skin of the back and belly. They are elastic and consist of two thin layers of skin with no flesh between and only a small amount of connective tissue, including blood vessels and nerves. The thumb projects forward from the front bend of the wing. It possesses a sharp hooked claw, as does each of the toes of the hind foot.

The membrane extending from the tail to the hind legs is known as the interfemoral membrane. It is partially supported by the calcar, a cartilaginous projection of the calcaneum, or ankle bone. The calcar often possesses a "keel".

Most bats become active near dusk and are active through much of the night. Contrary to popular opinion, bats can see well, but vision is not important in nighttime navigation. Rather they have echolocation, similar to radar. They emit ultrasonic calls far above the range of human hearing that are reflected from objects ahead of them. They hear the echoes and are thus able to avoid obstacles or to find food in total darkness. Each time a call is given, a minute muscle in the bat's ear contracts momentarily preventing the bat from hearing its own call, which might interfere with reception of the echo. Bats are unable to echolocate when their ears are plugged. Fenton and Bell (1981) were able to distinguish different species by differences in the structure of their echolocation calls.

The mechanism used by bats is similar to radar, used for the same purpose. Radar employs electromagnetic waves, whereas bats use ultrasonic sonar. The range of frequency employed by bats is between 25 and 75 kHz but is most commonly around 50 kHz. A human ear can rarely hear up to 20 kHz. When cruising on a relatively straight course, big brown bats produce about 10 pulses each second, each pulse being only about 1/200 of a second in length. These pulses are increased in rate as objects are approached. During pursuit of prey they may reach 200 per second (feeding buzzes) for short periods (Pierce and Griffin, 1938; Griffin, 1953, 1958). Simmons, Howell, and Suga (1975) reported on the kinds of information conveyed by echoes of the bat's sonar sounds. Sonar permits bats to determine the size, shape, distance, direction, and motion of objects by sensing the way they modify the sonar signals reflected back to the bat.

Bats can detect and intercept flying insects by echolocation, without use of vision or passive hearing of insect flight sounds (Griffin, Webster, and Michael, 1960). Further studies on little brown myotis have shown that they are able to discriminate between small moving targets by echolocation (Griffin, Friend, and Webster, 1965). During feeding maneuvers, the tail and wing membranes are used to capture and restrain prey. The tail membrane is formed into a pouch to intercept insects, and the head is bent forward to take the insect. Some insects may be taken from the wing by mouth. The wings may also be used to convey an insect to the pouched tail membrane.

Many bats have a well developed homing tendency, their success depending on a number of variables, such as age and sex of the bat, distance displaced, familiarity with the territory, season, whether released individually or in a group, and direction of release. It is not clear whether the mechanism is due to some innate homing device or navigational abilities such as many species must possess for migration, or whether it is due to random wandering. Previous work in the field of bat homing has been summarized by Fenton, Racey, and Rayner (1987).

The ability of bats to navigate during short flights and in long-distance homing or migration has been the subject of a number of studies. The discovery of echolocation in bats and finding that obstruction of vision had little effect on homing ability at distances of 8 to 97 kilometers (Mueller and Emlen, 1957) led to the belief that the system was used to the exclusion of other senses. However, Davis, Herreid, and Short (1962) have pointed out that bats flying at high altitudes during long flights would be too high to echolocate from the earth's surface, vegetation, or other structures. Indiana bats *(Myotis sodalis)* with normal vision were better at homing than blinded or blindfolded bats (Barbour, Davis, and Hassell, 1966; Davis and Barbour, 1970). This suggests that vision may contribute to navigational ability, or, as has been suggested by Mueller (1968), elimination of vision may result in diurnal flight and increased predation. In experiments with the southeastern bat *(Myotis austroriparius)*, Layne (1967) compared the ability of normal bats, bats with earplugs, and blindfolded individuals to reorient when displaced from the home cave during daylight from distances of 60 to 150 m. Fewer bats lacking hearing ability returned to the cave than normal bats, while none of the blindfolded individuals was able to return. *Myotis lucifugus* and *Myotis septentrionalis* were able to return home from a distance of 51.5 km without vision, but no deafened individuals found their way back (Stones and Branick, 1969).

Bats may seek shelter in a variety of places such as caves, crevices, or buildings, or they may roost in a tree. During the winter in temperate climates, bats either hibernate, migrate, or both. Some bats, such as *Lasionycteris*, move south and then hibernate. Hibernation may be sporadic or of short duration in the southern states. A hibernating bat's metabolism is greatly reduced, and oxygen consumption is only about a hundredth of the normal active rate. Individuals awaken periodically and may become quite active during these arousal periods. Intervals between arousals average about once every two weeks during the winter although the intervals vary greatly, often being shorter towards the beginning and end of hibernation (Whitaker, personal communication). Flights within and between caves are not unusual. When sleeping during the day, many bats become semitorpid. During this time the body temperature approximates that of the surrounding air, but it rises as the bats awaken. When asleep, a bat's oxygen consumption may be only a tenth of the active rate (Pearson, 1947).

Populations of bats hibernating in caves often contain a preponderance of males, although there is an apparent decrease in the percentage of males of several species the farther south one goes. The sex ratio at birth, however, is known to be equal. One theory to explain this phenomenon has been that female bats experience a higher mortality rate, especially during the first year. Observations on hibernating *Myotis lucifugus* indicate that males prefer a cooler location than females. Davis (1959) suggested that the sex ratio may reflect the severity of the winter. In mild winters, females would be in the caves and males would select colder outside locations, but the harsher the winter, the more males that would overwinter in the cave. His hypothesis would explain the extremely high percentages of males reported in the far northern populations where climatic conditions are more severe than in the south. In a study of *Myotis velifer* in Texas, Tinkle and Milstead (1960) found the sex ratios were nearly equal in caves in the late fall. Then there was a steady decline in the percentage of males and an increase in the percentage of females throughout the winter until the bats left the cave in late winter and early spring. They postulated that this was due to a greater immigration of females than males into the cave throughout the winter. These southern data further corroborate Davis's theory.

Mating in most hibernating species of North American bats occurs in the fall, presumably much of it from late August through October during the time of swarming at cave entrances. The spermatozoa are stored in the uterus and/or oviducts of the female during the winter until ovulation occurs in the spring after arousal from hibernation. At that time the stored sperm supposedly fertilize ova released from the ovaries. The element zinc, which is involved in regulating the maturation, metabolism, and motility of spermatozoa, may be important in sperm storage in hibernating bats (Crichton et al., 1982). A second mating may occur in the spring.

Females of most species of bats have one or two young per year, although those of the eastern red bat *(Lasiurus borealis)* (Plate 15) usually have three or four. Female lasiurine bats possess four mammae; all other Virginia bats have just two mammae. Bats ranging in age up to 30 years have been recorded in the wild; hence their low reproductive rate is compensated for by longevity and low predation. Details of parturition in bats are discussed by Wimsatt (1960). A number of reports of young bats being transported by a flying female are contained in the literature. While the transportation of young within the roost or from one roost to another often occurs, a close examination of these reports reveals that in a majority of cases the bats were disturbed before the observation (Davis, 1970). Statements in the literature to the contrary, females of most species do not routinely carry the young while foraging.

In a study of postnatal growth rates in *Eptesicus*, Burnett and Kunz (1982) stated:

> *For many temperate zone bats, the period of greatest mortality probably occurs between the time of departure from maternity roosts in late summer and the end of hibernation* (Beer, 1955; Brenner, 1968; Humphrey and Cope, 1976; Tuttle, 1976). *Juveniles with inadequate energy reserves to sustain the rigors of migration and hibernation are the most likely to succumb. This creates a powerful selective pressure for rapid postnatal growth and accumulation of fat. Deferment of reproduction until their second year, at least among some female bats in the temperate zone, emphasizes the importance of autumn fat stores. Deferred reproductive maturity may reflect the necessity of individuals with low fat levels to allocate most of their energy reserves to maintenance and survival during their first winter and spring. To be adaptive, the gain in residual reproductive value achieved by this tactic must be greater than the fitness lost by not reproducing the first year* (Pianka, 1976). . . . *Furthermore, autumn mating and delayed fertilization, typical of temperate zone bats* (Wimsatt, 1969), *may also be an adaptation for maximizing growth. This unusual reproductive strategy allows gestation to begin immediately following emergence from hibernation in spring providing maximum time for juveniles to grow and deposit fat reserves before entering hibernation in autumn.*

Although bats in other parts of the world may feed on fruit, fish, or even blood, most North American species and all of those in Virginia are insectivorous.

Bats are capable of transmitting two diseases to humans — rabies (tables 4, 5 and 6) and histoplasmosis, the latter a disease caused by inhaling dust that contains contaminated spores. Tuttle (1988) stated: "Less than a half of 1 percent of bats contract rabies, a frequency no higher than that seen in many other animals. Like others, they die quickly, but unlike even dogs and cats, rabid bats seldom become aggressive." Bats don't go mad and attack when they get rabies; they just lie in one place. They usually have "dumb rabies" and should not be picked up.

Although it is unusual for humans to contract rabies from infected bats (about ten people have ever died in North America from bat rabies (Whitaker, personal communication)), persons handling them should be aware of this possibility. Although rabies is usually transmitted via the bite of an infected animal, experiments by Constantine (1967) in caves where the air was saturated with vapors created by millions of Brazilian free-tailed bats *(Tadarida brasiliensis)* have shown that the rabies virus is capable of aerosol (through the air) transmission. Rabies was first found in a bat in the United States in 1953 when a Florida yellow bat *(Lasiurus intermedius)* was killed after having bitten a seven-year-old boy (Venters, Hoffert, Scatterday, and Hardy, 1954). Table 2 presents data on rabies in bats in the United States during the period 1980–1993. Tables 3 and 4 present similar data for Virginia for the period 1951–1994. An average of 11 bats are reported rabid in Virginia each year (Jenkins, 1994).

For various reasons, many bat populations have declined alarmingly in recent years. Part of the blame has been attributed to the use of DDT and other organochlorine insecticides (Reidinger, 1972; Clark, 1981, 1988). Bats, being insectivorous, acquire insecticide dosages through their food in the same manner as birds. Since insecticide residues accumulate primarily in fatty tissues, bats drawing on stored fat during hibernation may receive lethal dosages. Long-term effects may include impairment of reproductive ability. Other major factors negatively affecting bat populations have been persecution by man, loss of habitat, disturbance of caves, and, in the case of some species, overcollecting or overdisturbing by scientists. Vigorous conservation measures are necessary to save some of our bat species from extinction.

The order Chiroptera is divided into two suborders: Megachiroptera and Microchiroptera. The megachiropterans rely primarily on vision. They have large eyes and do not use echolocation; this group contains a single tropical family whose members are generally referred to as flying foxes. The suborder Microchiroptera includes the remaining tropical and temperate families. Three families occur in the United States — the leaf-nosed bats (Phyllostomatidae), free-tailed bats (Molossidae), and vespertilionid bats (Vespertilionidae). Only members of the family Vespertilionidae have been verified to occur in Virginia. Two Mexican free-tailed bats *(Tadarida brasiliensis)* were reportedly captured and examined at the Mountain Lake Biological Station during the fall of 1994 (Cranford and Fortune, 1994). Since the individuals were released and no photographs or other documentation exists to support their occurrence in the state, this species is not considered to be a verified member of the mammalian fauna of Virginia.

Vespertilionid Bats (Family Vespertilionidae)

The Vespertilionidae is the largest bat family and is found throughout most of the world. One member, genus *Myotis*, has been said to have the widest natural distribution of any genus of nonmarine mammal. Six of the 15 bat species found in Virginia belong to this genus.

Vespertilionid bats are small- to medium-sized and lack distinctive facial features often found in other bat families. External characteristics include a well-developed tragus and ears that are not united by a fold over the forehead. The wide interfemoral membrane is attached to the tail nearly to its tip. The third finger has two bony phalanges.

Key to Species of Vespertilionidae

1a One or two small teeth in space immediately behind the upper canine; total teeth 34 or more
.... 2

1b Tooth immediately behind canine large; total teeth less than 34
.... 10

2a Two small teeth in space behind canine *(Myotis)*
.... 3

2b One small tooth in space behind canine
.... 7

3a Wing membrane attached at tarsus; dorsal fur uniform in color rather than being dark at base
.... *Myotis grisescens*

3b Wing membrane attached to side of foot; dorsal fur dark at base
.... 4

4a Calcar keeled
.... 5

4b Calcar unkeeled
.... 6

5a Dorsal pelage fine, fluffy, and often slightly tricolored (black at base, grayish in middle, cinnamon brown tip); hind foot more than 9 mm; hairs on toes do not extend beyond tips of toes; no facial mask
.... *Myotis sodalis*

5b Very tiny species; dorsal pelage long, silky and yellowish; hind foot less than 9 mm; black facial mask
.... *Myotis leibii*

6a Dorsal fur dense, woolly; sagittal crest usually present in adults
.... *Myotis austroriparius*

6b Dorsal fur normal, silky; no sagittal crest
.... 7

7a Ear reaches noticeably beyond nose when laid forward; tragus long and narrow and tapers to slender point
.... *Myotis septentrionalis*

7b Ear barely reaches tip of nose when laid forward; tragus medium, erect, and tapers to rounded tip
.... *Myotis lucifugus*

8a Total teeth 34; fur tricolored (dark at base, lighter in middle, dark tip); forearm reddish
.... *Pipistrellus subflavus*

8b Total teeth 36; fur not tricolored; forearm not reddish
.... 9

9a Skull flattened; ears less than 25 mm in length; tragus short; dorsal hairs tipped with white; interfemoral membrane sparsely haired on basal half of dorsal surface
.... *Lasionycteris noctivagans*

9b Skull highly arched; ears more than 25 mm in length and joined across head; tragus long; dorsal hairs not tipped with white; interfemoral membrane naked
.... 10

10a Belly washed with white; belly hairs black at base with white tips; accessory cusp often present on first incisor
.... *Corynorhinus rafinesquii*

10b Belly brownish or buffy; belly hairs grayish-brown at base with buff or brownish tips; no accessory cusp on first incisor
.... *Corynorhinus townsendii*

11a Color uniformly dull brown
.... 12

11b Color varied; yellowish, orange, red, mahogany brown, or with white-tipped fur
.... 13

12a Size small; forearm less than 40 mm; one upper incisor; total teeth 30
.... *Nycticeius humeralis*

12b Size large; forearm more than 40 mm; two upper incisors; total teeth 32
.... *Eptesicus fuscus*

13a Forearm more than 45 mm
.... 14

13b Forearm less than 45 mm
.... 15

14a Total teeth 32; dorsal hairs yellowish-brown tipped with white, giving a distinct frosted appearance
.... *Lasiurus cinereus*

14b Total teeth 30; fur yellowish-brown but not tipped with white
.... *Lasiurus intermedius*

15a Color red, orange, or yellowish
.... *Lasiurus borealis*

15b Color mahogany brown
.... *Lasiurus seminolus*

Genus *Myotis*

Dentition: 2/3, 1/1, 3/3, 3/3 = 38

Little Brown Myotis
Myotis lucifugus (LeConte)

Description. The pelage of the little brown myotis (Plate 16), a medium-sized bat, varies considerably in color but is brownish, with the underparts gray washed with buff or whitish. The hairs on the back have long glossy tips that give the pelage a metallic sheen. The ears, wings, and tail membranes are dark brown and have little or no hair. The generic name *Myotis* means "mouse ear." The ear reaches barely to the tip of the nose when laid forward. The tragus is of medium length (about 7 mm), erect, and tapers to a rounded tip. Hairs on the hind foot extend beyond the toes, and the calcar is usually unkeeled, although occasionally a slight keel may be present. Females have two mammae. Adults are approximately 75 to 98 mm long, including a tail 30 to 45 mm long. The forearm is about 38 mm long. Weight averages between 7 and 10 g.

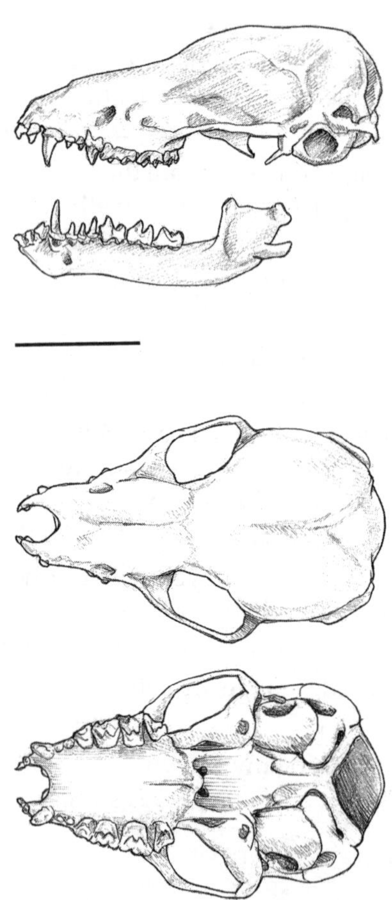

Figure 28. *Myotis lucifugus:* Left lateral view of skull and mandible, and dorsal and ventral view of skull. Scale bar = 5 mm.

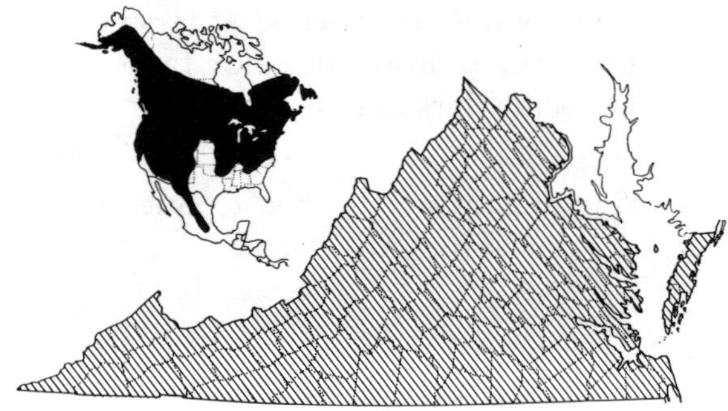

Figure 29. *Myotis lucifugus:* Range in Virginia and North America.

The skull is small with a gradually rising forehead and a broad brain case. This species possesses 38 teeth, including two upper incisors on each side and two tiny premolars directly behind the canine (Figure 28).

Distribution. The little brown myotis is found from Alaska across Canada and the United States as far south as southern California, Arizona, New Mexico, southeastern Oklahoma, northern Alabama, and northern Georgia. Specimens from coastal Georgia once thought to be *Myotis lucifugus* have been reidentified as *Myotis austroriparius* (Davis and Rippy, 1968).

This species is found throughout Virginia except in the southeastern portion of the state. It is one of the most common bats in the state (Figure 29). Dalton (1987) reported that this species accounted for 67 percent of the total bats counted in a 10-year survey of hibernating bats in Virginia caves.

Habitat. These colonial bats usually inhabit caves and abandoned mines in the winter. They hang isolated or in small groups of 25 or 30. During the summer they are most often found in buildings, towers, hollow trees, under the loose bark of trees, in crevices of cliffs, beneath bridges, and other similar areas. Females most often form maternity colonies in manmade structures.

Habits. These bats become active at dusk, first going to a stream to drink, then feeding for an hour or two before returning to roost. They may hang in an alternate or "night" roost during part of the night. Intermittent forays by some individuals occur throughout the night. There is another feeding period early in the morning, and by sunrise all of the bats have returned to their daytime roosts.

Bats do not soar like birds but continually beat their wings while flying. Flight speeds of little brown myotis tested over an open field averaged 20.4 km per hour. Their flight is often erratic as they rapidly change course to follow insects or avoid obstacles in their path. These bats apparently are able to swim if necessary.

The little brown myotis exhibits a marked homing tendency. Two (2.7 percent) of 77 banded bats in Ohio were recovered after being released at a distance of 141 km (Smith and Hale, 1953, Cockrum. 1956). Two (2.7 percent) of 74 banded individuals released as far as 108 km away from their point of capture returned to their original roost in New England (Hitchcock and Reynolds, 1942). Marked bats have been collected in the same cave for three different years, and about 40 percent of the bats banded in one cave were retaken in the same cave the following winter (Schwartz and Schwartz, 1981).

Little brown myotis hibernate in caves or mines during the colder winter months, and they may travel several hundred kilometers to find a suitable location. During studies of these bats in Indiana and Kentucky, fall migrations up to 454 km were recorded. Winter movements from one cave to another involved distances up to 219 km. During hibernation, little brown myotis hang upside down from the walls and ceilings of caves and mines in locations where the temperature normally remains several degrees above freezing. They may hang alone or in clusters of up to 50 individuals. The body temperature of a hibernating bat approximates that of the surrounding air. The heartbeat and breathing rates become slower. The bat enters a deep sleep which is usually broken by occasional periods of activity. The store of body fat, gradually accumulated during late summer, is the source of energy during this time. The periodic activity may be initiated by the reduction of body fat, the decrease in body fluids, the accumulation of urine in the bladder, or warm weather.

Hibernating bats arouse periodically during winter; these arousals are thought to be the main drain on their limited fat reserves. The number of arousals and the subsequent energy cost may be the key factors in determining the energy expenditures of hibernators during winter. For a 6.58 g *Myotis lucifugus,* Thomas et al. (1990) calculated that warming from 5°C to 37°C required the metabolism of 14.5 mg of fat. During the warming phase, heat is generated by brown adipose tissue, the liver, and muscles. Based on a hibernation period of 193 days in the Quebec-Ontario region of Canada, little brown myotis arouse about 15 times and require 1,618.5 mg of fat to cover arousal costs. This fat reserve represents 29.3 percent of the bat's live mass at the start of hibernation. These data are confirmed by an earlier study by Fenton (1970) who found that little brown myotis in Ontario lost 25 percent of their mass during hibernation.

It has long been believed that bats may be more sensitive to organochlorine insecticides than other mammals. Studies at the Patuxent Wildlife Research Center have revealed that adult little brown myotis are many times more sensitive to organochlorines than are laboratory rats and mice (Clark and Prouty, 1984; Clark, 1986, 1987). Juvenile bats were more sensitive than adult bats. Organochlorine residues in bats from Maryland and West Virginia have been reported by Clark and Prouty (1976). High levels of polychlorinated biphenyls (PCB) have been implicated in stillbirths among little brown myotis in Maryland (Clark and Krynitsky, 1978).

Lead concentrations ranging from 11 to 29 ppm have been recorded in this species near a major highway in Maryland (Clark, 1979). An average of 2.38 ppm of lead was recorded for embryos.

Food. These bats are almost entirely insectivorous and are very efficient feeders. They may fill their stomachs in less than one hour after emerging from their roost and may empty their digestive tracts two or more times during a single night's foraging (Buchler, 1975). While studying the feeding efficiency of bats, Gould (1955) concluded that under favorable conditions these bats theoretically captured insects at a rate of approximately 1.0 g/hr. Since the insects captured by this species were found to weigh between 0.2 and 15 mg, Gould conservatively estimated that if the 1-g/hr catch consisted on the average of insects weighing 2 mg, this would amount to 500 insects captured per hour, or approximately one every seven seconds.

No food data are available for little brown myotis in Virginia. A Maryland study, however, identified Coleoptera, Lepidoptera, and Diptera as major food items occurring in more than 50 percent of the samples (Griffith and Gates, 1985). Other prey included Hymenoptera, Homoptera, and Neuroptera. Preferred foods from other areas have included beetles, caddis flies, moths, leafhoppers and plant hoppers, ichneumon flies, and flies. Included in the food were such nonflying forms as beetle larvae and crickets.

Little brown myotis may consume between one-third and one-half of their body weight in food in one night. Favorite feeding areas are around lights where insects may congregate and over watercourses.

Reproduction and Development. Ovulation and fertilization in this species occur in the spring and both fall and spring breeding may occur. Usually only a single young is born in early summer after an estimated gestation of 50 to 60 days. In Pennsylvania, Mohr (1933) found young born as early as June 17. Several pregnant females were taken as late as July 16. Females remain reproductively active for many years. Records from a maternity colony in Massachusetts demonstrated that females 9 to 12 years old had newborn young or were nursing (Hall, Cloutier, and Griffin, 1957).

Prenatal stages of development and bone formation were studied by Adams (1992). Postnatal growth and a quantitative method of age determination, based on measurements of the forearm and digital epiphyseal cartilages, have been discussed by Kunz and Anthony (1982). The wings, ears, legs, tail, and interfemoral membrane of newborn bats are nearly black, but the trunk and head are flesh-colored and covered by fine silky hair. The eyes are closed at birth but open in two to three days. The young congregate in groups soon after birth and are left in the roost during the mother's foraging flights. They are able to fly when three to four weeks of age and become sexually mature when about one year old.

Immature bats of all species can readily be distinguished from adults by holding the wing membrane up to the light. The animal is fully adult if the phalanges meet as knobs, whereas the bat is immature if the phalanges gradually widen at their junction with each other.

Longevity. Keen and Hitchcock (1980) recorded two males that were recaptured in Ontario 29 and 30 years after they had been banded. Tuttle (personal communication, November 12, 1992) stated that one of these bats was subsequently recorded 32 years after banding. This represents the record for longevity of any bat. Griffin and Hitchcock (1965) reported two 24-year-old females in Vermont. There is also a record of an individual that reached 20.5 years (Hall, Cloutier, and Griffin, 1957). Cockrum (1956) cited reports of little brown myotis living as long as 12, and possibly 14, years, and the files of the US Fish and Wildlife Service through 1966 recorded 76 *Myotis lucifugus* living to ages of 10 years or more (Paradiso and Greenhall, 1967). The average life expectancy is about two years (Humphrey, 1971).

Parasites. The mite *Spinturnix americanus* has been recorded from a female taken from Covington, Virginia (Rudnick, 1960).

Predation. These bats have been observed being captured by American kestrels and sharp-shinned hawks. A bat abroad during daylight in Vermont was attacked by red-winged blackbirds, apparently in defense of their territory. Mink have been observed preying extensively on these bats in a Kentucky cave.

Geographic Variation. The subspecies in Virginia is *Myotis lucifugus lucifugus* (LeConte).

Location of Specimens. BCV, CM, CUC, DWL, FSM, GMU, LC, LFCC, LU, LSUMZ, MVZ, NVCC, SNP, SUVM, UGAMNH, UMMZ, USNM, VCU, VHCC, VPISU, VPI-W.

Southeastern Myotis
Myotis austroriparius (Rhoads)

Description. The southeastern myotis (Plate 17) is similar in appearance to *Myotis lucifugus* but can be distinguished by its somewhat shorter, thick, woolly fur. The dorsal pelage varies from grayish-brown to orange-brown; the underparts are dull buff. Hairs are uniform in coloration with little or no contrast between the base and the tip of the hair. Toes possess long hairs extending beyond the tips of the claws. The calcar is unkeeled. These bats range between 77 and 97 mm in total length, including a 26 to 44 mm tail. The forearm is between 33 and 40 mm. Individuals weigh 5 to 8 g.

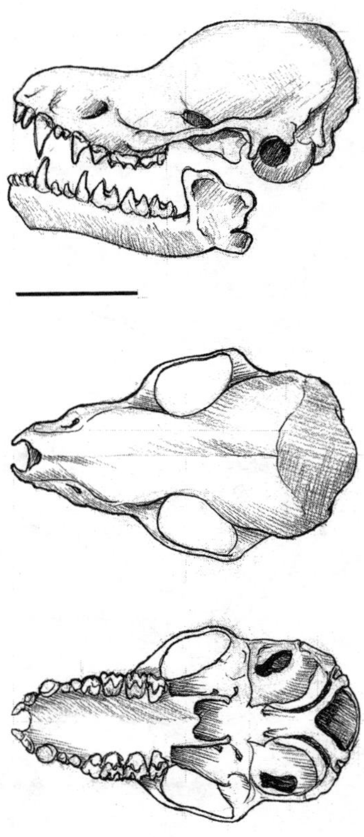

Figure 30. *Myotis austroriparius:* Left lateral view of skull and mandible, and dorsal and ventral view of skull. Scale bar = 5 mm.

The slender skull possesses a well-inflated braincase and a complete sagittal crest. A total of 38 teeth are present (Figure 30).

Distribution. The range of the southeastern myotis extends from southeastern Virginia south to Florida, west to eastern Texas and Oklahoma, and north to southern Illinois and Indiana.

This species was first discovered in Virginia in 1996 (Anonymous, 1996; Hobson, personal communication, 1996, in press, 1997). The two known sites are along the Blackwater River near Zuni, Virginia (Figure 31). One site is in The Nature Conservancy's Blackwater River Preserve.

Habitat. In many parts of its range, this species normally utilizes caves as summer roosting sites. Hollow trees, buildings, caves, mines, and boathouses serve as favored winter roosts. Roost sites are always near rivers or other permanent bodies of water.

Habits. These bats emerge late in the evening and forage over ponds and along streams. They fly close to the surface of the water when foraging (Barbour and Davis, 1969). In northern portions of its range, these bats may hibernate for as long as 6 or 7 months (Jones and Manning, 1989). They may hibernate in clusters ranging up to 100 individuals on the walls and ceilings of caves. Single bats may also wedge themselves into crevices in the ceilings of caves. In southern areas, these bats may remain active year-round. Lowery (1974) found that when the temperature dropped below 40°F, these bats became semitorpid, but as warmer temperatures returned, they resumed their normal foraging activities. Other bats sharing the same roosts with *Myotis austroriparius* include *Myotis lucifugus, Pipistrellus subflavus,* and *Plecotus rafinesquii.*

Bats of the genus *Myotis* do not exhibit territoriality, but they do maintain a definite, large home range (Rice, 1957). Juveniles have a tendency to wander, but adults exhibit a strong tendency to remain in or return to the same cave. In homing experiments conducted in Florida, Rice (1957) recorded a 20 percent (18 of 80 bats released) return of bats released 29 km from their site of capture and an 8 percent (8 of 100 bats released) return of bats released 72 km from their site of capture. No returns were recorded for bats released 174 and 287 km away.

Food. The diet consists predominately of insects. Mosquitos formed a staple in the diet of this species in Florida (Zinn and Humphrey, 1983).

Reproduction and Development. Mating usually takes place during the fall, with sperm being stored in the uterus of the female through winter (delayed fertilization). Ovulation and fertilization occur in early spring. Nursery colo-

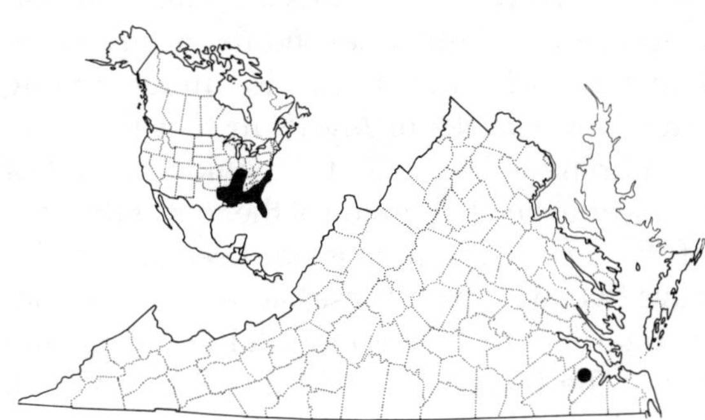

Figure 31. *Myotis austroriparius:* Range in Virginia and North America.

nies of hundreds or thousands of individuals form in the spring. These colonies are composed almost exclusively of adult females and their young. Males are solitary or form small groups during spring and early summer, but may join colonies of females and young during the summer (Jones and Manning, 1989).

Myotis austroriparius is the only North American form of *Myotis* which normally gives birth to two young. Barbour and Davis (1969) reported that 90 percent of the births are twins. Births usually occur in April or May. At birth, the mostly blackish young are naked except for a few vibrissae and a few hairs on the legs. Their ears and eyes are closed. Young bats begin to fly in 4 to 5 weeks and, shortly thereafter, they join the summer colony.

On August 8, 1996, a maternity colony was located in a black gum tree in Virginia. A total of 372 bats were counted as they emerged from a hole at the base of the tree between 8 and 11 PM. This represents the only known locality of a maternity colony in Virginia and one of the largest known maternity colonies outside of a cave anywhere in the range of the species (The Nature Conservancy, 1996).

Predation. Rice (1957) recorded rat snakes, corn snakes, opossums, owls, and cockroaches as predators in Florida caves.

Geographic Variation. The subspecies in Virginia is *Myotis austroriparius austroriparius* Rhoads.

Location of Specimens. USNM, VCU.

Gray Myotis
Myotis grisescens A. H. Howell

Description. The pelage of this medium-sized species (Plate 18) has the individual hairs of the upperparts uniform dusky or russet from base to tip. The underparts are paler. The ear reaches to or slightly beyond the nostril when laid forward. This species is unique among American species of *Myotis* in that the wing membrane is inserted at the ankle instead of being attached to the side of the foot at the base of the toes. The calcar is not keeled. Females have two mammae. These bats are 75 to 95 mm in total length, including a tail 32 to 44 mm long. The forearm is between 40 and 45 mm long. Individuals weigh 6 to 10 g.

The skulls of all *Myotis* are very similar. All have 38 teeth with two teeth in the "space" behind each canine tooth (Figure 32).

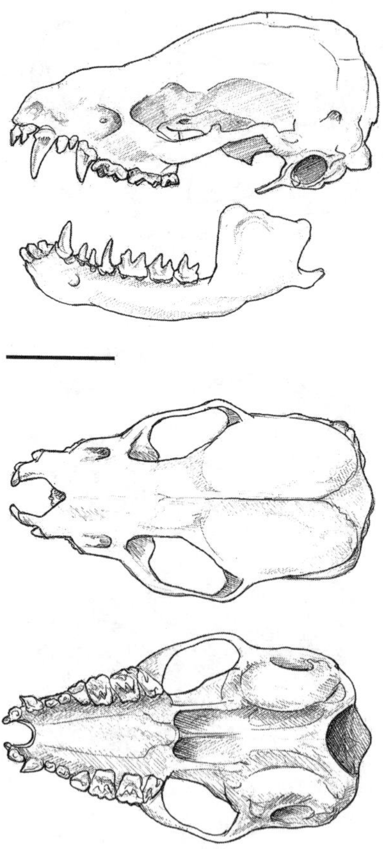

Figure 32. *Myotis grisescens:* Left lateral view of skull and mandible, and dorsal and ventral view of skull. Scale bar = 5 mm.

Distribution. The gray myotis is found from southwestern Virginia, Kentucky, southern Illinois, and Missouri south to northern Florida and west to northeastern Oklahoma and southeastern Kansas.

Gray bats are true cave bats; they hibernate in huge numbers in a few caves in winter and spread out and form smaller maternity colonies in summer. Bats covering a fairly wide geographic area in summer congregate into single cave systems in winter (Hall and Wilson, 1966). Moreover, such populations may be quite distinct from populations in other areas using a different cave as a winter retreat. Such wintering caves have been discovered in Missouri, Tennessee, Kentucky, Alabama, and Arkansas, and it is apparent that eight major caves may shelter 95 percent of the species during winter (Harvey, 1992). The gray myotis is federally endangered partly because such concentrations render the gray myotis population highly vulnerable since the destruction or disturbance of only a few caves could cause severe reductions in its numbers. Furthermore, the summer populations, even though dispersed, are also vulnerable because this species is highly intolerant to disturbance.

Dalton and Handley (1991a) stated:

Females are the first to migrate, in early September, to winter hibernacula. They are followed by juveniles and males in mid-October (Tuttle, 1976a). *Some colonies migrate as far as 500 kilometers. Nearly all gray myotis hibernate in only five caves in the southeastern United States* (Tuttle, 1975). *These caves are typically deep pits that trap cold air. The bats form tight clusters (sometimes layered) of up to several thousand individuals. Preferred hibernation temperatures range from 7°C to 10°C (45 to 50°F). Females emerge first from hibernation in early April, followed by yearlings and then males* (Tuttle, 1976a).

Concerning the decline of the population of this species (now estimated to number over 1,500,000), Harvey (1992) stated:

Estimates based on guano and ceiling stain have indicated an 89 percent decline in Kentucky, a 72 to 81 percent decline in Missouri, a 61 percent decline in Arkansas, and a 76 percent decline in Tennessee and Alabama.

According to Dalton and Handley (1991a) this species has been found in only four caves in Virginia (Figure 33). All have been summer populations of males and transients numbering 4,000 to 8,000 individuals. However, approximately 20,000 gray myotis were observed in a Scott County cave in May 1992. At about the same time approximately 1,900 other individuals migrated through four other caves in the same area (Annual Report Summary 1992).

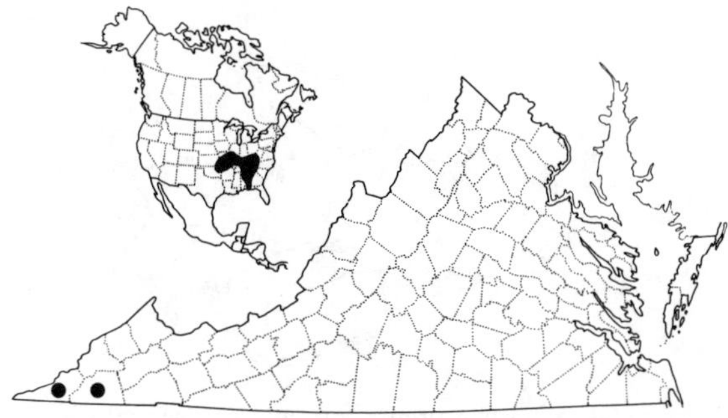

Figure 33. *Myotis grisescens:* Range in Virginia and North America.

One maternity colony is known to exist in Virginia in Washington County (Leffler and Terwilliger, 1991). Its size has steadily increased from 1,084 in bats 1990 to 2,150 in 1991 to 3,827 in 1992. The other two major summer colonies contained bats in May 1992, but were totally abandoned during the summer months (Annual Report Summary 1992). This species is endangered in Virginia as well as throughout its entire range (Handley, 1979b; 1991).

Habitat. The gray myotis is a true cave-dwelling bat. Large colonies of these bats occupy caves, both winter and summer, and they are seldom found far from these retreats.

Habits. Howell (1921) reported these bats hanging from the ceiling of a cave in Alabama in one compact mass covering three or four square feet and several bats deep. During mid-June the bats were observed coming out of this cave about 7 P.M.; they swarmed out in large numbers, feeding at the mouth of the cave and among the trees on the river bank.

Sealander and Young (1955) reported on two clusters of hibernating gray myotis in Arkansas in which males outnumbered females by 21 to 0 and 31 to 1. Other investigators also have reported that populations of bats hibernating in caves contain a much higher number of males than females.

The flight speed of the gray myotis measured under natural conditions in a cave in Tennessee was 6.91 km/hr (Kennedy and Best, 1972). Tuttle and Robertson (1969) recorded a summer movement of 209 km by a nonreproductive female across the Appalachian Mountains from Tennessee to North Carolina, suggesting "that the mountains may not be of primary importance in limiting the eastern dispersal of the gray bat".

Food. These bats feed mainly on flying insects. Studies in Missouri and Indiana showed the diet to consist of adult mayflies, dipterans, and beetles (Tuttle, 1976, LaVal and LaVal, 1980; Brack, 1985). In Kentucky, beetles, caddisflies, flies, and moths occurred at the highest percent volumes (Lacki, et al., 1995). Three beetle families (Carabidae, Chrysomelidae, and Scarabeidae) were common in the diet, but mayflies were not observed in fecal samples.

Data obtained from gray myotis in Missouri by the Patuxent Wildlife Research Center were the first to link observed field mortality directly to insecticide residues that resulted from routine pest control practices (Clark et al., 1978). The source was aldrin (the parent compound of dieldrin) applied to the soil to control cutworms in corn. Although the use of aldrin was cancelled in 1974, dieldrin is highly persistent in soils where aldrin was applied. Some bats contained as much as 10 ppm of dieldrin in their brains and over 1,300 ppm in their lipid tissues. Lethal brain concentration has been determined to be approximately 2.7 ppm (Clark et al., 1978). Such levels are known to be lethal in a variety of bird and mammal species. Milk from dead bats contained dieldrin residues as high as 89 ppm (Clawson and Clark, 1989). Residues of heptachlor and/or chlordane have also been reported in this species in Missouri (Clark et al., 1983a; 1983b).

Reproduction and Development. Males and non-breeding females segregate from pregnant females which are found in maternity colonies. Maternity colonies may consist of hundreds or thousands of individuals. Gray bats prefer caves that are warmer (14°C to 25°C) (58°F to 77°F) or those with rooms or ceilings capable of trapping the body heat from the clustered bats (Harvey, 1992). They also prefer caves with much water. Fewer than five percent of available caves are suitable for maternity colonies.

Most individuals probably mate in the fall shortly after arriving at their hibernation caves. Males continue to remain active for several weeks, but females enter hibernation immediately after mating (Harvey, 1992). Ovulation occurs in the spring with a single young normally born from May to early June. At birth the baby weighs about a third as much as the mother. During a visit to Indian Cave, Grainger County, Tennessee, between June 26 and July 1, Mohr (1933) found a large nursery colony of *Myotis grisescens*. The young ranged in age up to three weeks, and the smallest immature bat was hairless and weighed less than 0.1 oz (2.5 g). The young begin flying and are able to provide for themselves when about three weeks old. Females are sexually mature at two years of age (Guthrie, 1933).

Longevity. Kunz (1982) recorded a gray myotis that lived to a minimum age of 16.5 years. Tuttle (personal communication, November 12, 1992) reported an unpublished record of approximately 18 years.

Pelage Variations. There are apparently two pelage phases in this species; the gray phase is the common form, while russet-colored individuals have also been reported.

Location of Specimens. No specimens from Virginia are known to exist in collections.

Northern Myotis
Myotis septentrionalis (Trouessart)

Description. In coloration and size, the northern myotis (Plate 19) is similar to the little brown myotis, but has duller pelage and larger ears, which when laid forward usually extend 4 to 5 mm beyond the tip of the nose. The tragus is long and narrow, tapers to a slender point, and is often somewhat curved. The wing attaches along the side of the foot, reaching to the base of the toes. The fourth and fifth fingers are approximately equal in length. The calcar is not keeled. Females have two mammae. Adults average 75 to 100 mm in length,

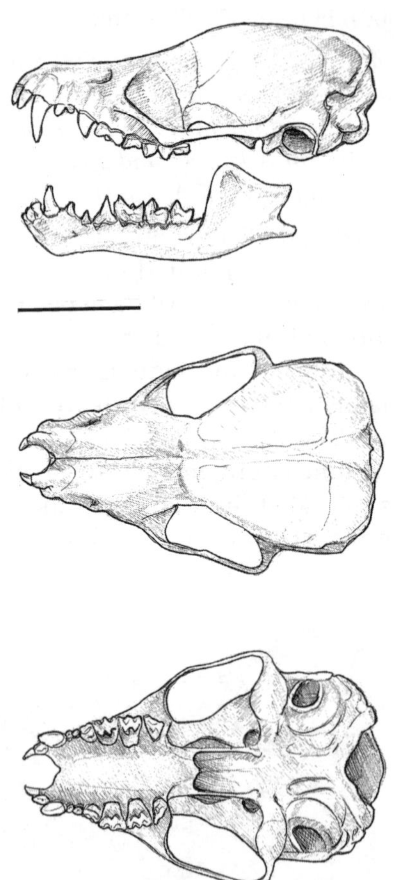

Figure 34. *Myotis septentrionalis:* Left lateral view of skull and mandible, and dorsal and ventral view of skull. Scale bar = 5 mm.

including a tail 36 to 45 mm long. These bats weigh 5 to 10 g, and their forearm is 35 to 40 mm long.

The skull is small and slender and closely resembles the skull of *Myotis lucifugus*. A total of 38 teeth are present (Figure 34).

Distribution. The northern myotis is found from Newfoundland, Nova Scotia, Quebec, and Ontario south to northern Florida and southern Arkansas and west to northeastern Oklahoma, eastern Wyoming, and eastern Montana.

The northern myotis is uncommon throughout Virginia (Figure 35). Handley (1979b) noted, however, that in certain caves this species comprises 35 to 50 percent of late-summer populations of *Myotis*. Dalton (1987), in a 10-year study of hibernating bats in Virginia, found this species to be the least abundant with only 20 individuals occurring in a few caves in seven counties. Since these bats are known to seek out cracks and crevices in cave walls and are difficult to locate, they may be more abundant than surveys indicate.

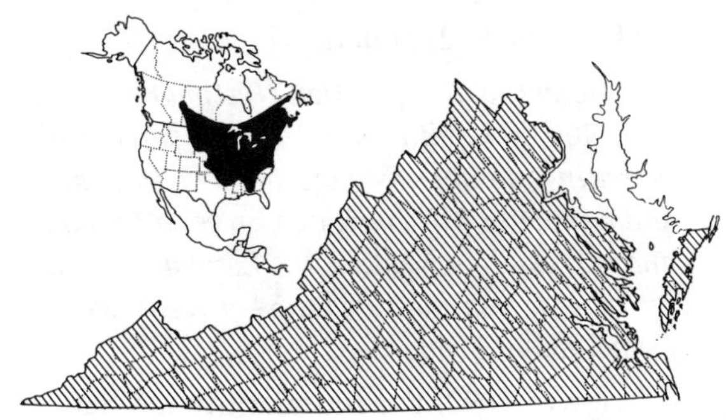

Figure 35. *Myotis septentrionalis:* Range in Virginia and North America.

Habitat. These bats may be found in caves, mines, buildings, hollow trees, under loose bark, behind shutters, and other similar retreats.

Habits. This species is less common in most collections than other species of *Myotis* mainly because it tends to roost singly or in small colonies, although concentrations of as many as 350 bats have occasionally been reported during winter in New England. Individuals have been found hanging in the midst of clusters of other bats such as the little brown myotis. Northern myotis have been found to experience average winter weight losses of between 41 and 43 percent (Fitch, 1966).

Griffin (1940) recorded one individual of this species that was banded in hibernation and recovered two months later in hibernation at a second locality 89 km away. Whitaker (personal communication) recorded this species flying all winter in Indiana.

Food. Foraging occurs just after dusk and also before dawn. In Maryland, the most important prey orders were Lepidoptera, Coleoptera, Neuroptera, and Diptera (Griffiths and Gates, 1985). LaVal et al. (1977) noted that in Missouri these bats foraged primarily in hillside and ridge forests rather than in riparian and floodplain forests. Most activity was concentrated in areas under the forest canopy and just above shrub level. Assassin bugs, leafhoppers, moths, caddis flies, mayflies, and ichneumon flies have been recorded as food items in New York and Indiana.

Reproduction and Development. Most breeding presumably occurs in fall with the sperm being stored in the uterus until fertilization occurs in the spring. Hamilton (1943) noted that this species, which appears to breed outside of caves, has a single young that is born somewhat later than those of other bats. He recorded females with large embryos in late June and early July in New York and concluded that parturition must take place there in July. A female captured in a mist net in Missouri gave birth to a single young on June 5 (Easterla, 1968).

Maternity colonies with up to 30 individuals have been reported. They have been discovered beneath loose tree bark and wooden shingles and in a barn.

Longevity. An individual banded in Massachusetts in 1937 was found dead in the same mine in 1956, indicating a minimum age of 18.5 years (Hall, Cloutier, and Griffin, 1957).

Location of Specimens. AMNH, CSULB, SNP, UCONN, USNM, VCU, VPISU.

Indiana Myotis
Myotis sodalis Miller and Allen

Description. The color of the pelage of the Indiana myotis (Plate 20) is distinctive. The hairs of the upper surface are somewhat tricolored, but the bands may not be sharply delineated. Each hair is black at the base, has a middle grayish band, and a cinnamon-brown tip. The ventral hairs are gray at the base, have gray-

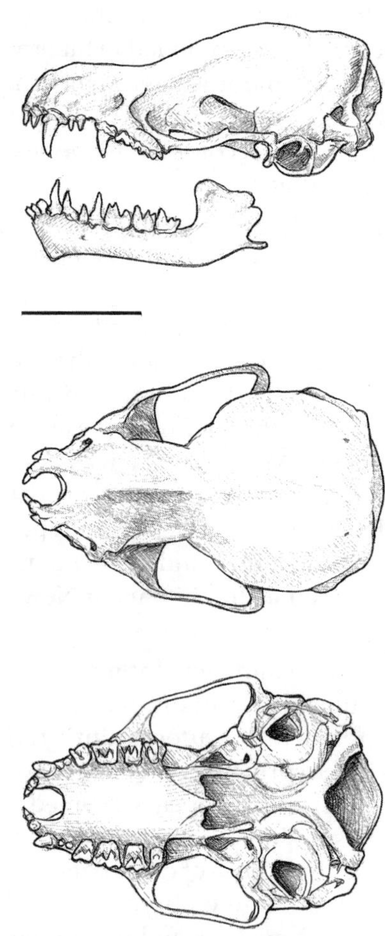

Figure 36. *Myotis sodalis:* Left lateral view of skull and mandible, and dorsal and ventral view of skull. Scale bar = 5 mm.

ish-white tips, and are tinged with cinnamon-brown. Overall coloration is pinkish-white below and dull chestnut-gray above. The ear reaches the nostril when laid forward. The tragus is rather short and blunt, very similar to that of the little brown bat. Wing membranes and ears are blackish-brown. The calcar is keeled. Hairs on the toes, unlike those of *Myotis lucifugus*, are short, barely reaching the base of the claw. Like other *Myotis*, females of this species have two mammae.

Overall length of adult Indiana myotis ranges from 69 to 95 mm, including a tail 25 to 45 mm long. The forearm is 35 to 40 mm long. Individuals weigh 4 to 8 g.

In general, the skull closely resembles the skull of the little brown myotis (Figure 36).

The Indiana myotis was not described as a distinct species until 1928. Before that time it was confused in collections with *Myotis lucifugus*, to which it bears a strong resemblance.

Distribution. This bat originally inhabited the eastern United States from central Vermont south along the Appalachian chain to northwestern Florida and west to southwestern Wisconsin and northeastern Oklahoma. Its distribution is associated with major cave regions. However, this species has shown a drastic decrease in population since 1950, and it is scarce in some parts of its range. Greenhall (1973) stated:

> *At present the species has a fairly restricted geographic range; 90 percent of the known population is found in two caves in Kentucky, and in a cave and a mine in Missouri. The other 10 percent occurs in groups varying from about twelve individuals to a few thousand in several dozen caves and mines in Illinois and Indiana. A total estimate of the present population of Indiana bats is believed to be about 500,000, and the cave areas of these states are thought to be the center of abundance.*

Harvey (1992) stated:

> *The present total population is estimated at less than 400,000, with more than 85 percent hibernating at only seven locations — two caves and a mine in Missouri, two caves in Indiana, and two caves in Kentucky....Estimates at major hibernacula indicated a 34 percent decline from 1983 to 1989.*

Prior to 1992, the Indiana myotis had not been recorded in Virginia during the summer. A study was begun in June, 1992, to locate the summer habitat and within one month this species was found in Lee and Highland counties (Annual Report Summary 1992). During the winter, however, it hibernates in limestone caves in the western part of the state. It had been reported from caves in Alleghany, Bath, Giles, Lee, Shenandoah, Montgomery, Bland, Botetourt, and Wise counties in 1978 (Tipton, Tipton, and Handley, 1979), but recent evidence (Dalton, 1987) indicates its presence in only eight caves in five counties (Bath, Bland, Lee, Tazewell, and Wise) (Figure 37). Two caves had about 1,000 bats each, two had about 250 each, and four had less than 10 bats each. During the winter of 1989–1990, the Virginia Department of Game and Inland Fisheries checked 15 caves for endangered species of bats. A total of 312

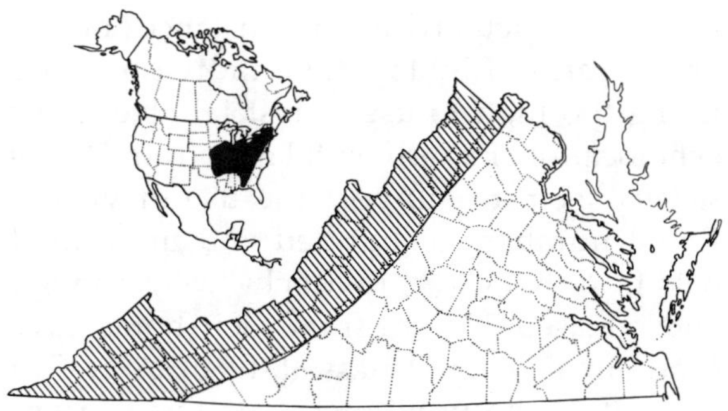

Figure 37. *Myotis sodalis:* Range in Virginia and North America.

Indiana myotis were found in seven of the caves (Nongame Summary EW-2-2, 1989/90). Hobson and Holland (1995) reported 10 known hibernacula in Virginia accounting for 2,500 individuals.

The fact that winter populations are concentrated to such a degree places the species in a vulnerable position. Disturbance or destruction of cave habitat, natural hazards such as flooding of caves, and vandalism are very real threats to its survival, particularly in privately owned caves. It is fortunate that the large population inhabiting Mammoth Cave National Park is given protection from human intervention.

The Indiana myotis is officially on the list of endangered Virginia mammals (Handley, 1979b; 1991) as well as being on the list of federally endangered native mammals compiled by the United States Fish and Wildlife Service's Office of Endangered Species and International Activities.

Mohr (1972) noted that Indiana myotis had disappeared from some previously inhabited caves and that they were virtually gone from the northeastern United States. Engel et al. (1975) recorded a 71.5 percent decline over the last 15 years in Indiana, Illinois, and Kentucky. This decline has been attributed to such factors as flooding, pesticide poisoning, and human disturbance.

British and American studies have shown a relationship between pesticides and a decline in populations of other species of *Myotis*. It is possible that pesticides may be a contributing cause of the decline of the Indiana myotis.

Habitat. All specimens from Virginia have been taken in caves, where the bats often gather into great masses on the walls and ceilings. In other parts of its range, occasional individuals have been found in or on buildings.

These bats congregate and hibernate in sites with very precise atmospheric conditions. Temperature seems to be the most important factor, with midwinter cave temperatures averaging between 3°C and 6°C (37°F and 43°F). Relative humidity is high, ranging from 66 percent to 95 percent with an average of 87 percent throughout the year (Greenhall, 1973). Such conditions are found in only a few caves and are restricted to a rather limited zone often near the cave's entrance. In addition, actual hibernation sites are precisely chosen and large clusters of bats form each year in exactly the same place.

Habits. The earliest comprehensive study of *Myotis sodalis* was carried out between 1956 and 1960 by Hall (1962). This species has been of interest to biologists because of the specialized conditions that it requires for roosting, and because its summer habits long remained a mystery. Most specimens, both in Virginia and throughout its range, have been collected from hibernating colonies. In fact, of 1,235 specimens examined in collections by Hall (1962), only 56 were taken during the summer. The first maternity colony of this species was found by Humphrey, Richter, and Cope (1977). A nursery population of approximately 50 individuals roosted beneath the loose bark of a dead tree and in the bark crevices of a living shagbark hickory tree. A number of maternity colonies have since been found in both riparian and non-riparian zones. It is apparent that individuals of this species are highly dispersed in the summer, in sharp contrast to the large aggregations found in winter. Summer colonies consist of about 30 to 80 individuals.

In hibernation, this species usually forms large, tight, compact clusters of 500 to 1,000 individuals. Hall (1962) calculated sex ratios in 15 caves in six states and found that approximately equal numbers of both sexes were usually present.

A winter colony of approximately 100,000 *Myotis sodalis* in Bat Cave, Carter Caves State Park, Kentucky, begins to disperse in late March, and the cave is vacant by early May. Banding studies in Kentucky have shown that after leaving their winter quarters, the females and nearly all the males move northward and occupy Indiana, the western half of Ohio, and southern Michigan. They return to their winter quarters from September to November (Barbour and Davis, 1969).

Spring and autumn swarming behavior has been discussed by Cope and Humphrey (1977). Fall swarming occurs as bats arrive at their winter roosts. Large numbers of bats fly in and out of cave entrances from dusk to dawn. Few roost in the cave during the day, although all will roost in the cave during the winter. Autumn swarming apparently serves as a means of bringing widely dispersed individuals together for breeding. Many of the bats engage in copulation during this time; a few will copulate in the spring following emergence from hibernation.

Banding studies have shown movements of these bats ranging up to 217 and 229 km during periods from 12 to 35 months. Indiana myotis banded during Hall's (1962) study often moved considerable distances, the longest being a movement of 515 km from northern Illinois to central Kentucky from one winter to the next. In Virginia, one individual carrying a radio transmitter moved 16 km southwest from the cave in which it was originally captured. It remained in the area for approximately three weeks foraging on an upland slope in a mature hardwood forest with several other Indiana myotis. It roosted beneath the bark of a mature shagbark hickory. It was recorded in the vicinity of a nearby stream on only two or three occasions during this time (Leffler, personal communication, 1995; Hobson and Holland, 1995).

The Indiana myotis has considerable homing ability. Up to 67 percent of bats released 322 km from the point of capture have returned successfully (Hassell and Harvey, 1965). In view of the large areas covered by these bats in their wanderings, it is possible that the reason they are able to home so readily is that they are familiar with the territory.

Myotis sodalis has been the subject of a number of experiments designed to test navigational and homing ability of blinded versus nonblinded bats (Griffin, 1970). Since the discovery of echolocation in bats, it has been postulated that this radarlike system dominates other senses during nocturnal flights. Others have speculated that vision is still needed, particularly in long-distance homing or migration flights where individuals are flying too high to use terrestrial objects for echolocation. Experimental data from *Myotis sodalis* seem to support the use of vision. Equal numbers of blinded and unblinded bats from Bat Cave, Kentucky, were banded and released 322 km from their home cave (Barbour, Davis and Hassell, 1966). Sixty-five percent of the unblinded bats were recaptured at Bat Cave within approximately two and one-half months. None of the blinded bats returned.

Average flight speed of *Myotis sodalis* clocked in a cave was 17.4 km/hr, while in an open field individuals averaged 20.1 km/hr (Patterson and Hardin, 1969).

Food. Whitaker (1972) recorded the following food items from four Indiana myotis in Indiana: ichneumon flies, leafhoppers, and beetles, including scarabaeid and snout beetles. Moths, flies, beetles, and other insects were identified by Belwood (1979) and Brack and LaVal (1985).

Foraging by the nursery population studied by Humphrey, Richter, and Cope (1977) ranged from 2 to 30 m high near the foliage of riparian and floodplain trees along 0.82 km of creek. The feeding rate ranged from 7.9 to 17.0 attempted insect captures per minute.

Reproduction and Development. No data on reproduction and development in Indiana myotis are available from Virginia. At Bat Cave in Kentucky, most breeding in this species occurs in early October during the night. By day, the sexes are segregated within the cave. The young bats are born from about mid-June to mid-July with each female giving birth to a single young. Between birth and weaning, the young bats experienced an 8 percent mortality. The young bats require from four to six weeks to begin flying and feeding on their own.

Longevity. LaVal and LaVal (1980) recorded one bat recovered 20 years after being banded as an adult of unknown age. The bat-banding files of the US Fish and Wildlife Service recorded a male *Myotis sodalis* from Kentucky that lived to a minimum age of 13 years, 10 months, as well as eight Indiana myotis that were at least 10 years old (Paradiso and Greenhall, 1967). Mohr (1953) recorded an Indiana myotis at least 10 years old.

Predation. Indiana myotis are captured by snakes and probably by birds of prey when the opportunity arises. Predation by mink and a pilot blacksnake have been recorded in Kentucky caves.

Location of Specimens. CM, USNM, VPI-W.

Small-Footed Myotis
Myotis leibii (Audubon and Bachman)

Description. The small-footed myotis (Plate 21) is the smallest member of the genus *Myotis* in North America. The fur is long, silky, and tan to golden brown above. A distinct black mask is present across the face. The ears are black, and a strongly keeled calcar is present. The only other myotis in Virginia with a keeled calcar is *Myotis sodalis*. The tiny feet average only 7 to 8 mm in length, thus making this the only myotis in Virginia with a hind foot less than 9 mm long. Females have two mammae. Adults average 72 to 83 mm in length, including a tail 29 to 36 mm long. They weigh between 3 and 9 g, and their forearm is 30 to 36 mm long.

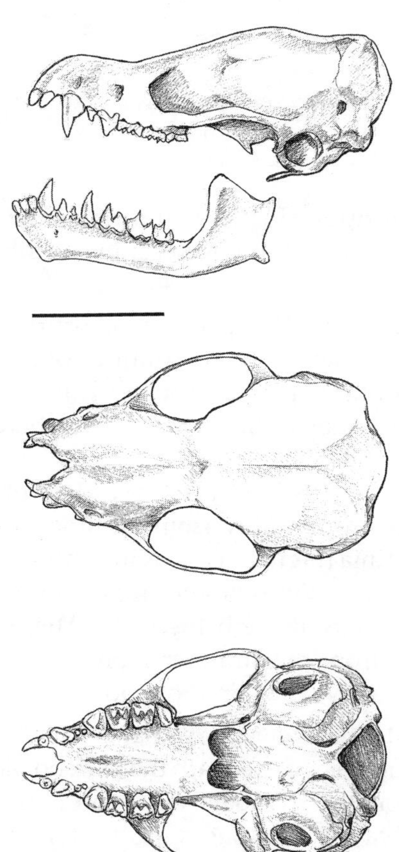

Figure 38. *Myotis leibii:* Left lateral view of skull and mandible, and dorsal and ventral view of skull. Scale bar = 5 mm.

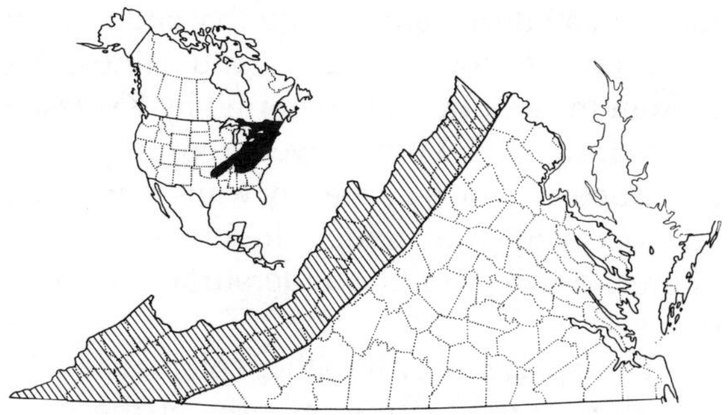

Figure 39. *Myotis leibii:* Range in Virginia and North America.

The skull is flattened and contains 38 teeth (Figure 38).

Distribution. The eastern small-footed myotis ranges throughout the northeastern United States, south in the Appalachian Mountains to northern Georgia and west to eastern Oklahoma. Western populations formerly thought to be this species are now considered a separate species, *Myotis ciliolabrum* (Harvey, 1992).

Handley and Patton (1947) noted that this species had not been recorded in Virginia but that it should be sought during the winter in caves in heavily forested sections of the mountains. Specimens have since been recorded from five localities in Highland, Bath, and Giles counties (Johnson, 1950). Handley (1979b) noted that this bat comprises approximately 15 percent of the late-summer populations of *Myotis* in Virginia caves (Figure 39). Dalton (1987) recorded this species hibernating in 10 caves in Virginia.

Habitat. Forested areas are the preferred habitat of this species. Individuals have been most commonly found in caves and mine tunnels, although some have been taken in rock crevices, in expansion joints beneath highway bridges, and in buildings.

In Virginia, Hobson and Holland (1995) recorded a foraging habitat of approximately 625 ha for a radio-tagged male. The habitat consisted of a mature oak-hickory mixed deciduous forest with a conifer component. When foraging, the bat flew in an elliptical pattern at canopy height.

Habits. This bat is one of the few species that sometimes roosts on the ground. Barbour and Davis (1974) reported individuals beneath rocks on a hillside and in a quarry and among rocks on the floors of caves and mines. Although most of the bats reported by Krutzsch (1966) from West Virginia were roosting either in the open on the passageway walls or in small crevices, some were under tilted rocks in areas of breakdown or on the undersurface of rocks on the cave floor.

This species may be either colonial or solitary during the warmer months of the year. Hibernating individuals may either form groups of several dozen bats or they may hibernate individually.

Paradiso (1969) noted that roosting eastern small-footed myotis can be identified by the fact that their arms are extended about 30 degrees from the vertical, whereas the arms in most other bats hang parallel to their body.

Food. The eastern small-footed myotis probably feeds heavily on small flies and moths, but no data are available.

Reproduction and Development. Little is known concerning reproduction in this species. Apparently a single young is produced. Nursery colonies of 12 to 20 bats have been reported.

Longevity. A 12-year-old specimen has been recorded (Hitchcock, 1965; Kunz, 1982).

Location of Specimens. LFCC, USNM.

Genus *Lasionycteris*

Dentition: 2/3, 1/1, 2/3, 3/3 = 36

Silver-Haired Bat
Lasionycteris noctivagans (LeConte)

Description. The moderate-sized silver-haired bat (Plate 22) has dark brownish-black fur. Many of the hairs on the back and interfemoral membrane are tipped with silvery-white. The underparts are paler and less silvery. The ears are short and nearly as broad as they are long. When laid forward, the ears barely reach the nostrils. The basal half of the dorsal surface of the interfemoral membrane is sparsely furred. The tragus is short, straight, and bluntly rounded. The calcar is not keeled. Females have two mammae. Adult silver-haired bats are about 100 to 108 mm long, including a tail 30 to 42 mm long. The forearm ranges between 37 and 44 mm in length. Adults weigh between 6 and 14 g.

The skull is elongate and flattened. There are two upper incisors and one small tooth immediately behind each canine. A total of 36 teeth are present (Figure 40).

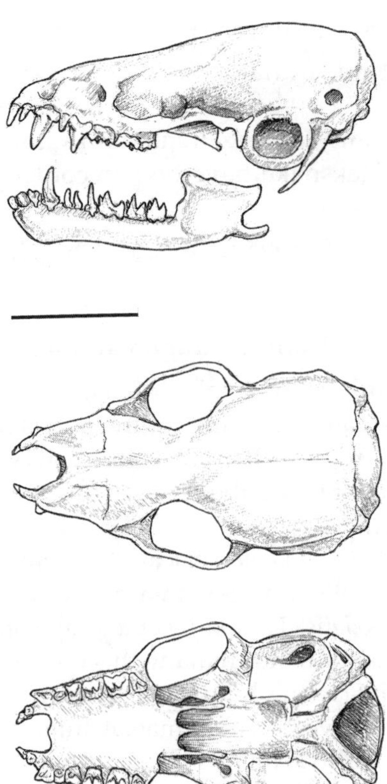

Figure 40. *Lasionycterus noctivagans:* Left lateral view of skull and mandible, and dorsal and ventral view of skull. Scale bar = 5 mm.

Distribution. This species ranges from southern Alaska and Canada south throughout the United States to Bermuda and northeastern Mexico. It may be taken rarely anywhere in the United States.

Individuals have been recorded from September through May from localities throughout Virginia (Figure 41). This indicates that they hibernate in Virginia and areas to the South, and migrate through the state. There are no records from the summer months, indicating that they give birth in more northern areas.

Habitat. The silver-haired bat is usually found in hollow trees or beneath the bark on old trees. Occasional individuals are found in buildings and in caves. This bat is most often observed flying about trees and tall shrubs that border streams and lakes.

Habits. The silver-haired bat is usually a solitary bat but may be found in small groups of

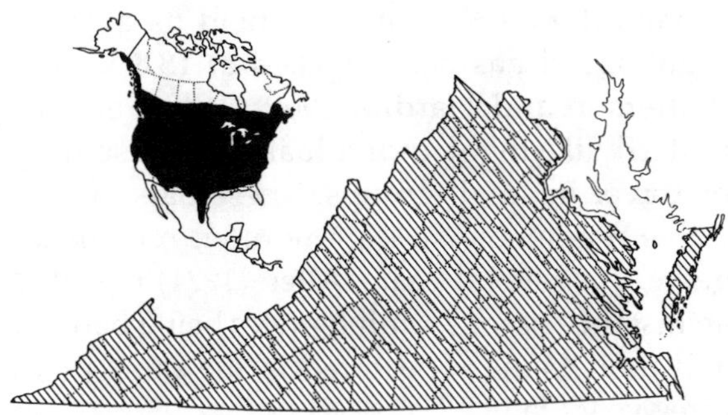

Figure 41. *Lasionycterus noctivagans:* Range in Virginia and North America.

two to six individuals. This crevice-dwelling species often seeks out narrow crevices in tree trunks as daytime roosting sites.

This is a migratory bat with most individuals breeding in the northern part of the United States and Canada and then migrating southward in fall. In the cooler portions of the winter range, the silver-haired bat hibernates during colder months, seeking shelter in buildings, crevices of trees or rocks, or in other protected locations. They apparently make long journeys over the ocean since there have been observations from vessels up to 805 km from the nearest land (Griffin, 1940). Silver-haired bats have also been recorded in Bermuda (Allen, 1923).

Homing in bats is well-known, but there is only one record of homing in *Lasionycteris*. Of three bats captured in New Mexico, banded, and released 172 km from the capture site, one returned within 18 days (Davis and Hardin, 1967).

This species can often be recognized in flight by its slow and erratic course. Silver-haired bats are early fliers, beginning their activity in late afternoon or early evening.

Food. Caddis flies, stable flies, fly larvae, and scarabaeid beetles have been reported as food of this species.

Reproduction and Development. *Lasionycteris* is not known to breed in the southern United States. In northern areas female silver-haired bats may form small maternity colonies in hollow trees in spring and summer (Parsons et al., 1986). Females usually produce either one or two young in late June or early July, although a female with two well developed embryos was recorded on August 7 in Saskatchewan (Parsons et al., 1986). Parturition in this species has been described by Kurta and Stewart (1990). Newborn young are pinkish with mottled tan and black wings. They are nearly naked and blind. The young cling to the breast of their mother or stay in the roost while she forages until about three weeks of age, at which time they are strong enough to follow her on her nightly flights for food.

Longevity. A 12-year-old individual was reported from Alberta (Schowalter et al., 1978).

Parasites. The fluke *Urotrematulum attenuatum* has been recorded from this species in Virginia (Eckerlin, 1988).

Predation. No instances of predation have been recorded in Virginia, although in other areas these bats have been eaten by predatory birds and skunks.

Location of Specimens. AMNH, BCV, CM, DWL, ETSU, GMU, NVCC, ODU, USNM, VCU, VPI-W.

Genus *Pipistrellus*

Dentition: 2/3, 1/1, 2/2, 3/3 = 34

Eastern Pipistrelle
Pipistrellus subflavus (F. Cuvier)

Description. The eastern pipistrelle (Plate 23) is the smallest bat in the eastern United States. Adults are generally light reddish-brown above and slightly paler below. Juveniles are grayer. The individual hairs on the dorsal surface are tricolored, slate gray at their base, then yellowish-brown almost to the tips, which are dark brown. Long guard hairs are completely reddish-brown. A distinctive characteristic of these bats is that the skin covering the forearms is reddish in color. The basal third of the interfemoral membrane is sparsely furred on its dorsal surface. The ears are distinctly longer than broad and taper to a narrowly rounded tip. When laid forward, the ear reaches slightly beyond the tip of the nose. The tragus is nearly straight with a bluntly rounded tip and is about half the length of the ear. The calcar is longer than the tibia and is not distinctly keeled. Females have two mammae. These small bats are 75 to 95 mm long, including the 32 to 46 mm long tail. The forearm is 31 to 35 mm long. Eastern pipistrelles weigh between 3 to 6 g.

The skull is very small but arched. There is one tiny tooth immediately behind each canine (Figure 42).

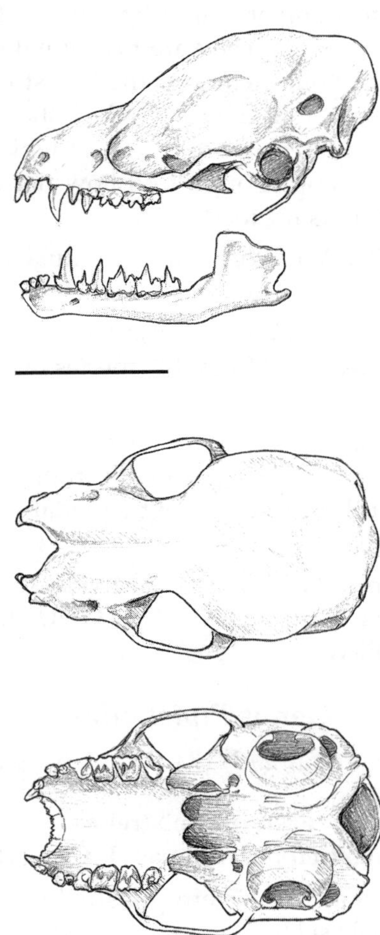

Figure 42. *Pipistrellus subflavus:* Left lateral view of skull and mandible, and dorsal and ventral view of skull. Scale bar = 5 mm.

Distribution. This bat ranges throughout the eastern United States west to central Minnesota, western Oklahoma, and central Texas. The range extends south through eastern Mexico to Guatemala and Belize.

The eastern pipistrelle has been recorded throughout Virginia (Figure 43), but is apparently more common west of the Blue Ridge than in the Coastal Plain and Piedmont portions of the state. Dalton (1987) found this to be the most widely distributed and the second most abundant species during a 10-year study of hibernating bats in Virginia.

Habitat. These bats hibernate in caves and in crevices in rocks. Their maternity colonies during the warmer months of the year are usually in buildings and in hollow trees. Pipistrelles frequently inhabit Spanish moss in areas where this plant is abundant.

Habits. The eastern pipistrelle is an early evening flier. Over an open field its average flight speed has been clocked at 18.8 km/hr (Patterson and Hardin, 1969). It has erratic, butterflylike flight. Individuals may be solitary or travel in small groups. These bats are sociable mammals, and a few often remain together for several years. Allen (1921) reported an instance of four adult females being banded and three being recaptured in the same place three years later.

During the winter, these bats hibernate in caves or mines. Dalton (1987) stated that this is Virginia's "least specialized cave bat in as much as it is found in a wider range of temperature, humidity, and cave configuration than any other bat in Virginia." Pipistrelles do not move about in their winter quarters as much as some other cave bats do. If the cave is moist, water collects on the bats until they often become covered with little droplets and look white in the flashlight beam.

Davis (1959; 1966) recorded males comprising 69.5 to 85.1 percent of the individuals of this species hibernating in caves in West Virginia. Males in this population apparently experienced a markedly higher rate of survival than females. The sex ratio of summer populations, however, showed a much lower percentage of males. Davis also noted that the percentage of females hibernating in caves increases as one goes southward, suggesting that perhaps females spend the winter farther south than do males. Of 281 pipistrelles examined in a cave in northeastern Alabama, 71 percent were males. In a cave in southwestern Georgia, the sexes were about equal. Furthermore, the winter climate of a region seemed an important factor, since the more severe the winter, the higher the percentage of males winter-

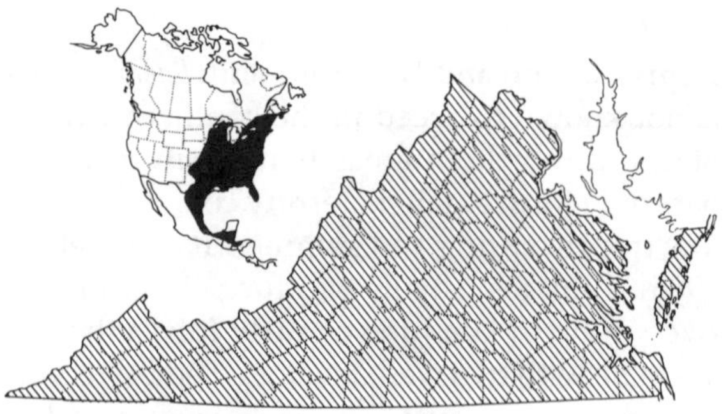

Figure 43. *Pipistrellus subflavus:* Range in Virginia and North America.

ing in the caves. He concluded, therefore, that the disproportionate sex ratios among hibernating pipistrelles seemed to be due to a combination of a difference in survival rate of the sexes and the probable wintering of large numbers of females outside the caves. Sealander and Young (1955) banded 468 pipistrelles in an Arkansas cave, of which 70 percent were males.

This species has been reported to return to its original roost from distances of 129 and 137 km (Rysgaard, 1942; Griffin, 1940).

Organochlorine residues have been reported from this species in Maryland and West Virginia by Clark and Prouty (1976).

Food. Feeding is usually at treetop level or along watercourses. A Maryland study found Coleoptera, Homoptera, Hymenoptera, Lepidoptera, and Diptera in more than 40 percent of the samples (Griffith and Gates, 1985). Insects fed upon in other parts of the range have included leafhoppers, plant hoppers, beetles, flies, moths, and flying ants (Ross, 1967; Barbour and Davis, 1969; Whitaker, 1972).

Hamilton (1930) examined individuals of this species 15 to 20 minutes after they first appeared in the evening and found their stomachs already filled with small insect remains. He suggested that these bats may make two foraging flights, one in early evening and another around midnight or early morning. Gould (1955) recorded 1.4 and 1.7 g of insects in two of these bats weighing 5.3 and 6.7 g, respectively, after 30 minutes of feeding time.

Reproduction and Development. Mating in eastern pipistrelles may occur intermittently throughout the winter in southern portions of their range. Elsewhere, this species has two mating periods per year — one in the fall probably involving individuals over one year old, and a second in the spring which includes yearlings (Nowak, 1991). Females usually give birth to two young from May to July. Small maternity colonies (12 to 25 individuals) have been discovered in buildings. Two females, each containing two well-developed embryos, were recorded on June 21 and June 22 in Amelia County, Virginia (Lewis, 1940).

Newborn young are blind, naked, and relatively large. The combined weight of a litter may be approximately one-fifth the weight of the mother. By about three weeks of age, the young are able to fly.

Males store spermatozoa in tubules of the testes and in the epididymis throughout hibernation during which time the testes are involuted but accessory gland activity is maintained (Krutzsch and Crichton, 1986).

Longevity. The oldest known eastern pipistrelle lived to a minimum age of 14.8 years (Walley and Jarvis, 1971). Other records of long-lived individuals include 13 years, 11 years and 3 months, and 10 years (Paradiso and Greenhall, 1967).

Pelage Variations. There is wide individual variation in pelage color. Specimens ranging from albinistic to reddish (erythristic) or very dark (approaching melanism) have been reported.

Parasites and Disease. This species has tested positive for rabies in Virginia (Evans and Pagels, 1987).

Predation. Both the hoary bat and the leopard frog are known predators.

Geographic Variation. The subspecies in Virginia is *Pipistrellus subflavus subflavus* (F. Cuvier).

Location of Specimens. AMNH, ANSP, BCV, CM, CU, CUC, DWL, FSM, GMU, LACM, LC, LFCC, MCZ, MVZ, NCSM, NVCC, ODU, RC, RMWC, UCONN, UMMZ, USNM, VCU, VPISU, VPI-W.

Genus *Eptesicus*

Dentition: 2/3, 1/1, 1/2, 3/3 = 32

Big Brown Bat
Eptesicus fuscus (Beauvois)

Description. The big brown bat (Plate 24) can be distinguished from all other bats in Virginia by its long, uniformly dark brown fur and by its large size. The fur of the ventral surface is paler. The sexes are similar. The ears are short, broad, and rounded and reach barely to the nostrils when laid forward. The tragus is short, blunt, and directed slightly forward. The ears and membranes are blackish. The top of the interfemoral membrane is naked except for a sprinkling of hairs on the basal fourth. A keeled calcar is present. Females have two mammae. These large bats are 94 to 130 mm in length, including a tail 35 to 52 mm long. The forearm is about 45 to 50 mm long and these bats weigh 14 to 21 g.

Big brown bats have a heavily built skull with a relatively broad rostrum. The skull has

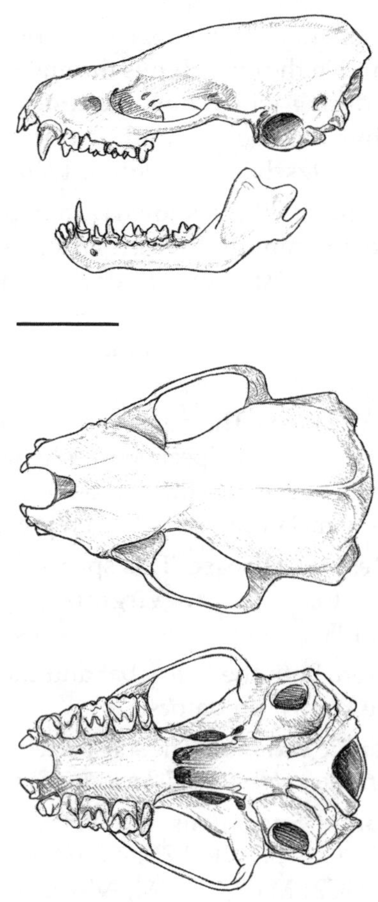

Figure 44. *Eptesicus fuscus:* Left lateral view of skull and mandible, and dorsal and ventral view of skull. Scale bar = 5 mm.

a nearly straight dorsal profile. The two upper incisors are well developed with the inner incisor being larger than the outer. There are only four upper molariform teeth. The first is enlarged; thus there is no "space" behind the canine (Figure 44).

Distribution. The big brown bat ranges from northern South America throughout Central America, Mexico, and the United States into Canada.

This species occurs statewide in Virginia (Figure 45). It appears to be more common in the western part of the state. Dalton (1987) recorded this species hibernating in 39 caves in 15 Virginia counties.

Habitat. Big brown bats have wide habitat preferences and have been found in buildings, caves, and hollow trees. Willingness to coexist with man is a characteristic trait.

Although a few individuals overwinter in caves, most big brown bats hibernate in buildings. It is the only northern species to do so. In summer, maternity colonies are almost always found concealed around buildings such as barns, churches, houses, and old stores, either in the attic, in some dark corner under the eaves, or behind a shutter. Occasionally they will use a large hollow tree, which was probably their original habitat.

Habits. In summer, female and baby big brown bats are found in maternity colonies of about 30 to 600 bats. Males are found singly or in small clusters, often in the same or nearby buildings.

Favorite hunting grounds of this species are cultivated fields, particularly cornfields, well surrounded by trees. Usually the first thing a big brown bat does upon leaving its resting place in the evening is to get a drink by scooping up water from a stream, lake, or pond. Their strong flight is marked by sudden and frequent changes in direction. They maintain a fairly steady flying height of 6 to 9 m above the ground. Under natural conditions, the flight speed of *Eptesicus fuscus* has been clocked at an average of 33.5 km/hr (Patterson and Hardin, 1969).

This species undoubtedly does not hibernate for sustained periods in the southern part of the United States and probably remains active throughout the winter. Even in northern areas where hibernation occurs, this hardy bat enters hibernation later and becomes active earlier than most cave-dwelling species. Comprehensive studies of big brown bat populations in areas where sustained hibernation occurs have been carried out by Phillips (1966) and Whitaker and Gummer (1992). There are frequent periods of activity during which these

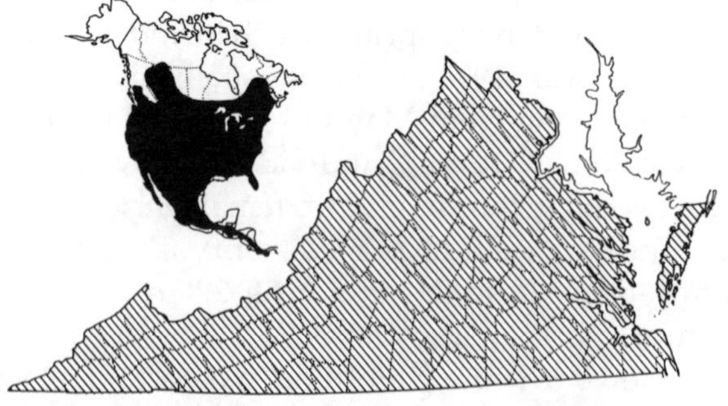

Figure 45. *Eptesicus fuscus:* Range in Virginia and North America.

bats move about within their roost or fly between roosts. Movement between roosts are probably beneficial in making them familiar with other roosts. This is probably evolutionarily beneficial as they have a place to go if their hibernacula suddenly disappears (burns down, torn down, abandoned by people, heat turned off, etc.).

An extensive study of this species in Minnesota and Wisconsin by Beer (1955) revealed that these bats do not normally travel great distances. Maximum distances of 53 km for summer and 98 km for winter movements were found. Most of the movements during both winter and summer were within a 16 km radius of the point of banding.

This species apparently has the ability to home from unfamiliar territory over distances greater than those covered by its normal movements. Seven of 155 bats captured in Cincinnati, Ohio, and released 725 km to the north returned home within a month (Smith and Goodpaster, 1958). These authors also noted the return home of 2 of 18 individuals captured in Cincinnati 15 days earlier and released 547 km to the southwest. Davis (1966) reported an 85 percent return rate for bats released 400 km north of their roost, but only a 6 percent return rate for those released 400 km south. Bats returned home in four to six days. Other homing records involve distances of 193 km (Davis and Cockrum, 1963) and 153 km (Hall and Davis, 1958).

Audiograms of *Eptesicus fuscus* reveal two distinct regions of maximum hearing sensitivity, in the region of 1 kHz and in the region of 10 to 60 kHz. Ultrasonic sounds produced in the range of 20 to 100 kHz are used for sonar. Those in the range of 10 to 30 kHz are used for communication with other bats. Poussin and Simmons (1982) stated:

> *There is no evidence to indicate that sounds in the frequency region near 1 kHz are used for either of these functions, so the low-frequency hearing sensitivity of this bat must be to detect and process sounds from other sources in the environment.*

Brigham et al. (1989) and Masters et al. (1991) found significant intraspecific variation in the echolocation calls of this species.

It is reasonable to expect that bats, being insectivores, might be adversely affected by the use of the long-lived chlorinated hydrocarbon insecticides. Experiments testing insecticide toxicity to bats have involved *Eptesicus fuscus* (Luckens and Davis, 1964, 1965; Clark and Lamont, 1976; Clark, 1978). Lethal dosages of endrin and dieldrin were about the same in the big brown bat as in the laboratory rat. However, *Eptesicus fuscus* was found to be far more sensitive to DDT than any other species of mammal yet tested. Reidinger (1972) analyzed insecticide residues in the bodies of *Eptesicus fuscus* from Arizona and concluded that these chemicals were directly or indirectly responsible for population declines.

Lead concentrations ranging between 20 and 90 ppm were recorded near a major highway in Maryland (Clark, 1979). Males had significantly more lead than females. Lead in embryos averaged 0.16 ppm.

Food. Big brown bats forage for food over cultivated fields and meadows in rural areas, while streetlights provide a productive hunting ground in cities. Coleopterans and hemipterans occurred in more than 70 percent of adult males examined in a Maryland study (Griffith and Gates, 1985). Studies from West Virginia, Ohio, Kansas, and Indiana also revealed that beetles are a major food source. Particularly favored were scarabaeid beetles, click beetles, ground beetles, and cucumber beetles. Other important foods included flies, stinkbugs, ants, katydids, ichneumon flies, moths, stone flies, mayflies, leafhoppers, crickets, assassin bugs, and caddis flies. Whitaker (1972) reviewed food studies of this species in other parts of the country.

Gould (1955) recorded an adult big brown bat feeding at an average rate of 2.7 g per hour, while 10 young bats averaged between 0.3 and 2.1 g per hour.

Reproduction and Development. Mating may occur in both fall and spring, although fertilization of the egg does not occur until spring. A large male collected on August 26 in Amelia County, Virginia, had enlarged testes (Lewis, 1940). Asdell (1946) has shown that the spermatozoa of this species can remain viable in the uterus of the female for periods of 140 to 150 days. Gestation is approximately two months, with the young usually being born in early June.

In Pennsylvania and Ohio, maternity colonies are formed in April and May and disperse in late July and August (Brenner, 1968). In Indiana, dispersal occurs from August to early November (Whitaker, personal communication). The usual number of young per litter in the eastern United States is two, whereas it is one in the west.

Gates (1937) noted that a colony of 10 female big brown bats in Louisiana gave birth to their young within a period of 48 hours. He stated:

> *This record furnishes evidence that all the females in this colony must have ovulated within a short time of each other, probably not more than 48 hours apart. It is hardly likely that any causative agent other than the environment would have induced ovulation almost simultaneously among all these females. This record also tends to support the theory that spring copulations are not necessary for fertilization, for it is rather beyond the range of possibility that all these bats would have copulated within such a short time. The most plausible explanation seems to be that as a result of fall copulations sperm had been stored in the uterus and oviduct, and that upon favorable spring conditions, ovulation had taken place with resulting fertilization, the same conditions affecting all females in the locality similarly, and eventually producing more or less simultaneous parturition.*

Growth and development of *Eptesicus* has been described by Davis, Barbour, and Hassell (1968) and Kunz (1974). Postnatal growth rates were determined by Burnett and Kunz (1982). Average weight at birth is 3 to 4 g and growth is very rapid, adult size being attained by about 10 weeks. Bats in one colony were known to retrieve young that had fallen and occasionally transported them from roost to roost. The young are weaned and able to fly when approximately three weeks old.

Organochlorine residues have been reported in adult female big brown bats in Maryland and West Virginia by Clark and Lamont, 1976a; 1976b) and Clark and Prouty (1976). Both PCB and DDE were present in all litters as a result of placental transfer. Concentrations of PCB were significantly greater in litters with dead young than in litters where both young were born alive. Even greater amounts of DDE and PCB were found to be transferred to young by lactation and nursing than by placental transfer.

Longevity. Big brown bats apparently have a high potential longevity. There are a number of records of these bats living to at least nine years of age, and the oldest individual on record attained an age of at least 19 years (Paradiso and Greenhall, 1967; Kunz, 1982). Also, the bat-banding files of the US Fish and Wildlife Service contain records of 21 *Eptesicus fuscus* that lived 10 years or more (Paradiso and Greenhall, 1967).

Parasites and Disease. Rabies has been reported from this species in Virginia (Enright, 1962; Evans and Pagels, 1987).

Predation. Big brown bats have been preyed on by snakes, American kestrels, peregrine falcons, owls, rats, weasels, and cats.

Geographic Variation. One subspecies of the big brown bat, *Eptesicus fuscus fuscus* (Palisot de Beauvois), occurs in Virginia.

Location of Specimens. BCV, CM, DMNH, DWL, FSM, GMU, LACM, LFCC, LSUMZ, LU, MVZ, NVCC, ODU, QM, RC, RMWC, SUVM, UCONN, UGAMNH, UMMZ, USNM, VCU, VHCC, VMNH, VPISU, VPI-W.

Genus *Nycticeius*

Dentition: 1/3, 1/1, 1/2, 3/3 = 30

Evening Bat
Nycticeius humeralis (Rafinesque)

Description. The evening bat (Plate 25) is smaller than, but very much resembles, *Eptesicus*. It also somewhat resembles *Myotis*. It can be distinguished from *Eptesicus* by its much smaller size (forearm about 38 mm rather than 45 or more in *Eptesicus*), and from *Myotis* by its first molar tooth being enlarged. Thus, there is no "space" behind the canine. *Myotis* has two tiny teeth in the "space" immediately behind the canine. Also, *Nyticeius* further differs from both *Eptesicus* and *Myotis* by having one rather than two incisors on each side. *Nycticeius* has a short, curved, blunt tragus. The individual hairs of the back are black at the base. The underparts are paler. The ears are thick and rounded, and both the ears and membranes are black and generally naked, although in some individuals hairs may be present on the extreme proximal portion of the interfemoral membrane. The calcar is not keeled. Adult evening bats are 75 to 100 mm long, including a tail 30 to 38 mm long. The forearm is approximately 38 mm long. These nondescript bats usually weigh 7 to 10 g.

The skull is short, low, and broad with a nearly straight dorsal profile. The evening bat and the yellow bat are the only species in Virginia that possess 30 teeth (Figure 46).

Distribution. The evening bat is essentially a southern species but is found throughout much of the eastern United States north to Pennsylvania and southern Michigan, west to eastern Nebraska and central Oklahoma, and south through central and southern Texas into northeastern Mexico. It is quite rare in many northern areas.

The evening bat is found at lower elevations in Virginia (Figure 47). It has not been recorded from the mountains.

Habitat. This species establishes maternity colonies in buildings and probably also in hollow trees.

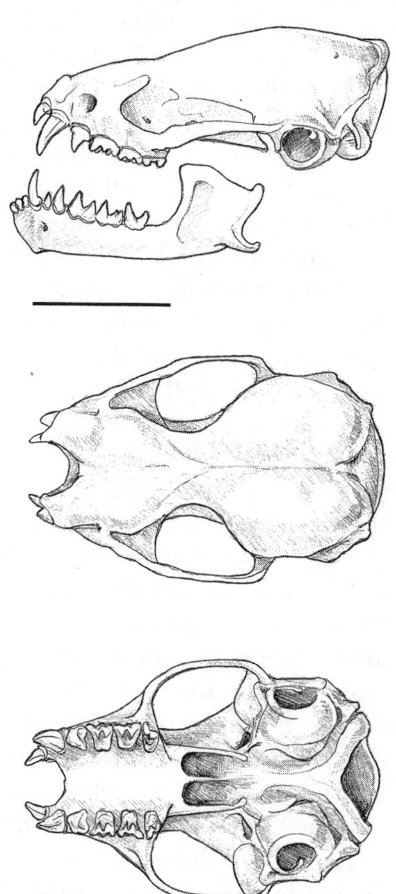

Figure 46. *Nycticeius humeralis:* Left lateral view of skull and mandible, and dorsal and ventral view of skull. Scale bar = 5 mm.

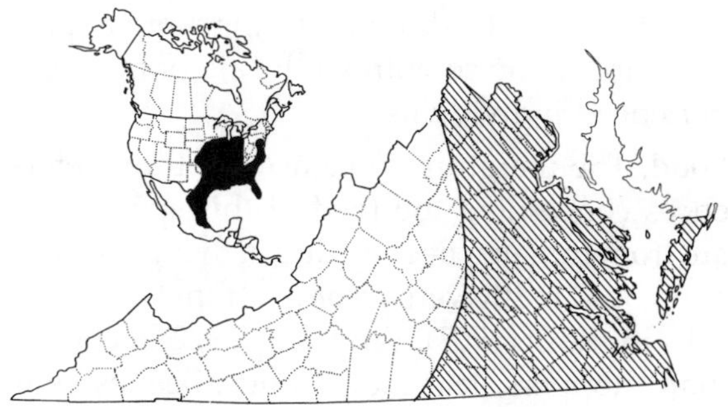

Figure 47. *Nycticeius humeralis:* Range in Virginia and North America.

Habits. Little is known about the habits of this southern species. During the breeding season, females form into colonies while males apparently remain solitary. Of 148 bats taken from an attic in Alabama in May (Linzey, 1970), 56 were adult breeding females, 39 were young females, and 53 were young males. All of the young bats were young of the year. Linzey (1970) also recorded 22 adult females, 23 young females, and 17 young males in a sample from another large Alabama colony.

The evening bat leaves its roost near dusk. Individuals begin flying at a height of 12 to 23 m, but as darkness falls they come much lower to the ground. These bats have a slow and steady flight.

Nycticeius is generally referred to as being migratory, although little information is available about its movements. Humphrey and Cope (1968) reported southward movements of three banded bats of 177 km, 193 km, and 301 km during July and August. They suggested that these movements may have represented the beginning of fall migration. Watkins (1969) reported an additional recovery 547 km south of another banding site. Humphrey and Cope also noticed autumn population declines at a nursery colony in Indiana with 89 percent of the colony having dispersed by late September. Spring arrivals at this colony began in early May, and the population was complete by the end of the month. Adults and immatures from this same colony were used in homing experiments (Cope and Humphrey, 1967). Individuals released at points 61 and 155 km away from the colony were able to return home. Moreover, since immatures were released at a different time than adults, those returning were apparently able to do so without the aid of more experienced individuals.

Food. The literature contains only three references concerning the food of this species; all are from Indiana. Beetles, flies, a flying ant, and a cercopid moth were recorded from two stomachs by Ross (1967). Whitaker (1972) recorded plant hoppers, leaf-footed bugs, beetles, and moths from two additional stomachs. Beetles, moths and leafhoppers were the major foods identified from guano of a maternity colony (Whitaker and Clem, 1992). The spotted cucumber beetle *(Diabrotica undecimpunctata)* was the species eaten in greatest quantity, comprising 14.2 percent of the total volume.

Reproduction and Development. Mating probably occurs in late summer and early fall, with the sperm stored in the uterus of the female during the winter. Ovulation and fertilization occur in the spring. All females in any one colony apparently ovulate within a relatively few days or even hours of each other, probably in response to an environmental cue, perhaps to a change in temperature. The two young are usually born during May or June. In northern Georgia, Baker (1965) found that female bats arrived at the nursery colony about the second week of April and the majority had departed by late August.

In a study by Jones (1967), 14 females gave birth to 12 females and 16 males between May 25 and June 4. All but two litters were born between 1 and 4 P.M. Newborn bats were pink, except for slight dark pigmentation on the feet, membranes, tips of the ears, and lips. Vibrissae were present on the lips, and a few hairs occurred on the feet and on the top of the head and shoulders. Weight at birth averaged 2 g. The eyes opened at 18 to 24 hours following birth, and the pinnae, which were folded over at birth, became erect when the bats were 24 to 36 hours old. By 9 days of age, the young were completely furred. Well-coordinated flight was possible at about three weeks, and bats accepted solid food between three and four weeks. Growth was extremely rapid, and by 30 days of age the forearm had nearly attained adult size.

Longevity. The average life span in the wild is probably about two years, although there are records of some individuals surviving for over five years (Watkins, 1972).

Predation. No data are available from Virginia. Snakes, cats, and raccoons may occasionally capture one, but as with other bats, there are probably no major predators.

Geographic Variation. The subspecies in Virginia is *Nyticeius humeralis humeralis* (Rafinesque).

Location of Specimens. AMNH, CM, DMNH, NVCC, USNM, VCU, VPI-W.

Genus *Lasiurus*

Dentition: 1/3, 1/1, 1/2 *(Lasiurus intermedius)*
or
2/2 (all other *Lasiurus*), 3/3 = 30 or 32

Eastern Red Bat
Lasiurus borealis (Müller)

Description. The moderate-sized eastern red bat (Plate 26) is one of the most attractive species of bats inhabiting Virginia, and it is one of the very few bats (or mammals, for that matter) in which the sexes are contrastingly colored. The fur of the male is generally a bright rusty-red with the guard hairs tipped with white, thus producing a slight frosted effect. Females normally have a dull buff-chestnut coat with considerable white frosting. There is much variation in the intensity of the reddish color, which may range in different individuals from bright rusty-red to almost pinkish-yellow; the amount of frosting also varies. Individual hairs are dark at the base. Both males and females have a yellowish-white patch on the front of each shoulder. The dorsal surface of the interfemoral membrane is thickly furred, but the ventral surface is only sparsely furred. The basal two-thirds of the ears are densely furred, and the fur extends outward from the body toward the elbow on both surfaces of the wing membranes. On the undersurface the furring extends along the forearm to the wrist and partway down the fingers. The third, fourth, and fifth fingers are progressively shorter. The ears are short, broad, and rounded, and when laid forward they reach slightly more than halfway from the angle of the mouth to the nostril. The tragus is triangular, being broadest at its base. The calcar is keeled.

Unlike most other species, female lasiurine bats have four mammae. Average length of adults is between 92 and 122 mm, including a tail 38 to 63 mm long. The furry forearm is 38 to 42 mm long, and weight varies from 6 to 14 g.

The skull of this species has a broad rostrum and flaring zygomatic arches. It is short and rather heavily built, with a nearly straight dorsal profile. A small but pronounced ridge is present above the lacrimal bones. There are 32 teeth including one tiny tooth in the "space" behind each canine (Figure 48).

The generic name *Lasiurus* is derived from two Greek words meaning "hairy tail." The specific name *borealis* is from a Latin word meaning "northern" (Shump and Shump, 1982a).

Distribution. The eastern red bat is found from northern Mexico and the eastern and central United States to southern Canada. Its range extends westward to southwestern New Mexico, eastern Colorado, western North Dakota and southwestern Alberta. It is absent from the Florida peninsula (Harvey, 1992). Individuals have been observed several hundred miles at sea and on the island of Bermuda.

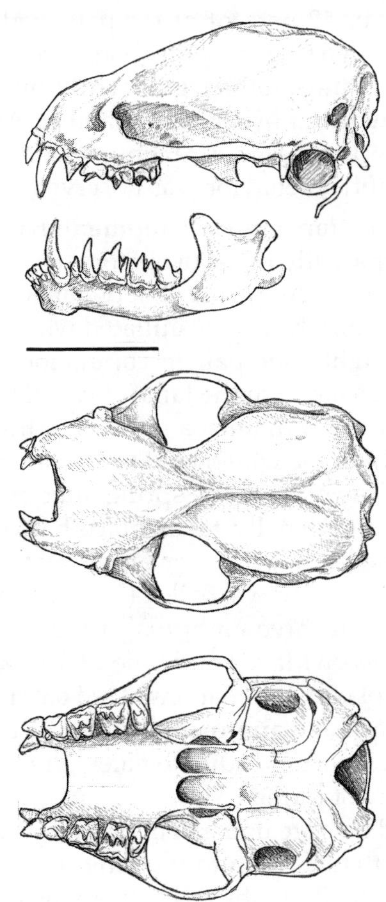

Figure 48. *Lasiurus borealis:* Left lateral view of skull and mandible, and dorsal and ventral view of skull. Scale bar = 5 mm.

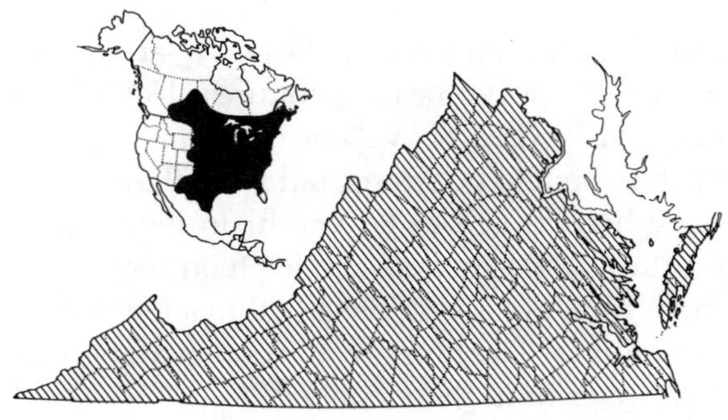

Figure 49. *Lasiurus borealis:* Range in Virginia and North America.

In Virginia, the red bat occurs statewide (Figure 49).

Habitat. This species roosts in trees. Thus, it is found most commonly in deciduous forests, open woodlands, and orchards. Individuals have been found concealed in masses of leaves within a few feet of the ground, as well as in clumps of Spanish moss. During the day they often hang by one foot and appear similar to a dead leaf. Roosting sites in the vicinity of water seem to be preferred. There have been a few reports of this bat occurring in caves, but this is very unusual.

Habits. During the summer red bats are solitary and usually roost in trees and shrubs. Mumford (1973) estimated the population density at one per ha in Indiana and one per 0.4 ha in Iowa.

Schwartz and Schwartz (1959) made an intriguing notation about the habits of this species:

> *The frequent recovery of mummified carcasses and skeletal remains from certain limestone caves indicates that these tree-dwelling bats may select caves as places to die, but why they do is not known.*

Barbour and Davis (1969) suggested that the bats presumably became lost in caves.

Red bats normally become active in early evening, although individuals have been observed in flight and feeding during the daylight hours. Lewis (1940) noted that in Amelia County they have been collected during every month of the year and that they fly at dusk in winter whenever the temperature is 13°C (55°F) or above. Red bats have long narrow wings that enable them to be strong and swift fliers. They have been timed at 64 km/hr in level flight (Tuttle, 1988). Their search for food may carry them from great heights to within a few feet of the ground. They forage most often along watercourses or in the vicinity of trees.

This is the best-known migratory species of bat in the United States, and its winter range extends over roughly the southern half of the country. It apparently is a normal occurrence for these bats to spend the winter as far north as West Virginia and Ohio. Tuttle (1988) noted:

> *Few have been found in hibernation, but available observations indicate a preference for tree hollows. They respond to subfreezing temperatures by increasing their metabolism just enough to maintain body temperature above the critical lower limit of 23°F (-5°C).*

In Missouri, wintering red bats leave their hibernating quarters as early as mid-March, but the northward migration occurs later in the spring. Hence, red bats not only migrate but also hibernate in some areas, adjusting their metabolism to ambient conditions. They are able to tolerate wide temperature fluctuations, and undoubtedly, the well-furred condition of their bodies, especially the furred membrane which they wrap around themselves, contributes to survival during extremely cold weather.

These bats begin moving to more southern areas as early as August, and from December to March they are more abundant in the southern part of the United States than during any other season of the year. Their migration is probably mainly nocturnal, although some have been observed migrating during the day. Groups of up to 100 have been sighted. They are sometimes found in caves during the winter.

Economically, this bat is one of our truly beneficial mammals since it is entirely an insect eater and does not annoy humans by roosting in houses and other buildings.

Brigham et al. (1989) found significant intraspecific variation and some intraindividual differences in echolocation calls of this species.

Food. Red bats emerge early in the evening to forage and tend to cover the same territory each evening. They are often attracted to insects swarming around city streetlights, and the presence of grasshoppers in the stomachs of these bats suggests that they may obtain some food from the ground. Lewis (1940) noted that in late summer and early fall in Amelia County red bats often congregated in large numbers at dusk about cribs that contained old corn to feed on the *Angomous* grain moths. Investigations of food habits dealing with red bats from widely separated geographic areas have all shown that beetles, plant hoppers, leafhoppers, and moths are their predominant foods. Other foods include ants and flies. Moths and flies constituted over 90% of the volume of food of winter-foraging bats in Virginia (Whitaker, Jr. et al., 1997).

Marked bats foraging around lights foraged for an average of 113.1 minutes per night, attacked an insect every 30 seconds, and captured, on average, 40 percent of the insects they attacked (Hickey and Fenton, 1990). This translated to a nightly food consumption of 6.2 g of insects, or 42 percent of the bats' body mass. They tended to select large (body length greater than 10 mm) moths significantly more often than predicted by their availability. Although intraspecific chases were common, no evidence of territorial behavior was observed.

Reproduction and Development. Eastern red bats apparently mate just before or during fall migration in August and September. Copulation apparently may be initiated while the bats are in flight. One pair in copulation was observed on a pier in the James River (Dearborn, 1946). The spermatozoa survive in the uterus throughout the winter, and fertilization apparently takes place in the spring after ovulation. Parturition usually takes place between late May and early July after an estimated gestation of 80 to 90 days. Bailey (1923) recorded females with three embryos in the District of Columbia on May 11 and June 23. Unlike many species of bats, populations of red bats in breeding areas have approximately equal numbers of adult males and adult females. Nursery colonies are not formed.

Red bats are unusual in that they normally give birth to three or four young. The lasiurine bats, particularly the red bat, are the only bats known that normally have three or four young per litter. Some litters may contain two or even five young. Cockrum (1955) reported that the average number of embryos per female was three, while Harvey (1992) reported an average litter size of 2.3.

The young are born completely hairless, with eyes closed, and weigh about 0.5 g each. During their first three or four weeks of life, the young bats cling to the fur of their mother while roosting, mainly with their hind feet but also with their teeth and thumb claws. It is commonly stated that the mother carries the young while foraging until their combined weight is so great that the female becomes unable to fly with them. Davis (1970) pointed out that most records of females "flying" with young are reports of grounded individuals that may have been disturbed, taking off before having the opportunity to dislodge the young. He noted, however, that females may transport the young, one or two at a time, from roost to roost. Of 100 netted red bats, some were pregnant and many were lactating, but none were carrying young. Barbour and Davis (1969) estimated that young red bats fly at three to four weeks and are weaned at five to six weeks of age.

Differences in pelage color between males and females is more pronounced in the young than in the adults. The pelage of young males has been described as being bright red, while that of females is gray with only a trace of red.

Longevity. Jackson (1961) noted that the normal life span of this species was probably near five years with a potential longevity of near 12 years. As of 1966, the bat-banding files of the US Fish and Wildlife Service contained no recovery records for the red bat (Paradiso and Greenhall, 1967). This is probably because red bats are solitary and are less frequently encountered and banded. It has also been suggested that the life span of this migratory species may be shorter than that of hibernating cave bats.

Parasites and Disease. This species has tested positive for rabies in Virginia (Prior, 1969; Prior and Giles, 1974; Evans and Pagels, 1987).

Predation. Horsley (1991) reported the capture of a red bat by a blue jay in North Carolina. Animals known to have preyed on red bats elsewhere in their range include hawks, falcons, owls, opossums, and domestic cats.

Geographic Variation. The subspecies in Virginia is *Lasiurus borealis borealis* (Müller).

Location of Specimens. AMNH, ANSP, CM, CUC, DMNH, DWL, GMU, LFCC, LU, MVZ, NVCC, ODU, SNP, UMMZ, USNM, VCU, VMNH, VPISU, VPI-W.

Seminole Bat
Lasiurus seminolus (Rhoads)

Description. The Seminole bat (Plate 27) is quite similar to the eastern red bat in all characters except color. It is usually a rich mahogany-brown throughout with less of a frosty overcast. The throat and chest are whitish. The interfemoral membrane usually is dark chestnut-brown. The calcar is keeled. Females have four mammae. Adults are normally between 92 and 120 mm in length, including a 38 to 63 mm tail. The forearm is between 38 and 42 mm long. These bats weigh 7 to 14 g.

The skull of this species is similar to that of the red bat. There are 32 teeth (Figure 50).

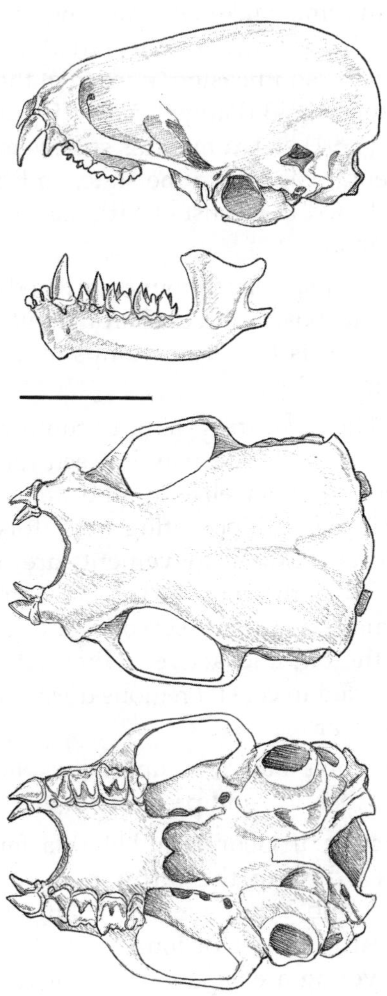

Figure 50. *Lasiurus seminolus:* Left lateral view of skull and mandible, and dorsal and ventral view of skull. Scale bar = 5 mm.

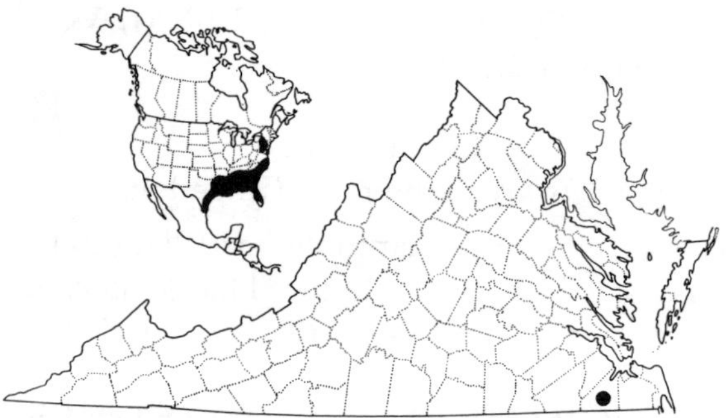

Figure 51. *Lasiurus seminolus:* Range in Virginia and North America.

Distribution. The seminole bat ranges from southeastern Virginia south along the Atlantic Coast to Florida and west to eastern Mexico. Several isolated records exist north of this range in Pennsylvania and New York (Hall, 1981).

The only record of this species in Virginia is an adult female taken on Washington Ditch at Lake Drummond in the Great Dismal Swamp in the southeastern portion of the state on October 6, 1983 (Padgett, 1987) (Figure 51). Handley (1991) stated that this species may be an accidental vagrant in the state, and thus it is not included in the list of Virginia's vulnerable mammals.

Habitat. This species is found in wooded areas where it roosts in trees. Throughout much of its range it is found in clumps of Spanish moss (Harvey, 1992).

Habits. These solitary bats become active shortly after dusk and may be seen foraging over open water as well as around streetlights.

This is a non-hibernating migratory bat, although its seasonal movements are not as pronounced as those of the red bat. Seminole bats do make a definite seasonal shift southward in the fall and active individuals have been observed in coastal regions during warm days in winter.

Food. Seminole bats feed upon crickets, true bugs, flies, beetles, and probably moths.

Reproduction. In Georgia and Florida, females give birth during the latter part of May (Hamilton and Whitaker, 1973). Litters normally consist of three or four young (average 3.3). The young are capable of flying at three to four weeks of age.

Location of Specimen. USNM.

Hoary Bat
Lasiurus cinereus (Beauvois)

Description. The general coloration of the large hoary bat (Plate 28) is a mixture of yellowish-brown, deep brown, and white. The hairs on the dorsal surface are mostly tipped with silvery-white, which give this bat a distinct silver frosting; the resulting hoary appearance is the source of this bat's common name. The fur is long, very fine, and dense. The forearm has a distinct patch of fur near its base. The ear is relatively broad and rounded with the margin of the ear conspicuously rimmed with dark brown or blackish-brown. The outer side of the ear is densely furred to near the tip while the inner side contains a conspicuous patch of yellowish fur anteriorly. The tragus is rather large, heavy, and triangular with a broad base. The dorsal surface of the feet and of the interfemoral membrane are densely furred. The body fur extends outward to the elbow on the upper surface of the wing. On the lower wing surface the fur extends along the forearm to the wrist and partway down the fingers.

The keeled calcar is twice as long as the foot and somewhat shorter than the free border of the interfemoral membrane. As in the red bat, the third, fourth, and fifth fingers are progressively shorter. Females have four mammae. These large bats are usually between 130 and 150 mm long, including a 50 to 63 mm tail. The forearm is about 50 mm in length. Hoary bats usually weigh between 21 and 40 g.

The skull is relatively broad and heavy with flaring zygomatic arches. The braincase is large, and the rostrum is short and broad. In general appearance, it closely resembles the skull of the red bat, although somewhat larger in overall size. There are 32 teeth (Figure 52).

The specific name *cinereus* means "grayish" or "ash" colored, referring to the white-tipped, frosty hair coloring (Shump and Shump, 1982b).

Distribution. The hoary bat ranges from southern Mexico throughout most of the United States and into Canada. It is apparently uncommon in the southern part of the United States and is absent from peninsular Florida. Like the silver-haired and red bats, this species apparently wanders quite widely on migration, since it has been recorded in Bermuda. It is the only land mammal endemic to Hawaii (Harvey, 1992).

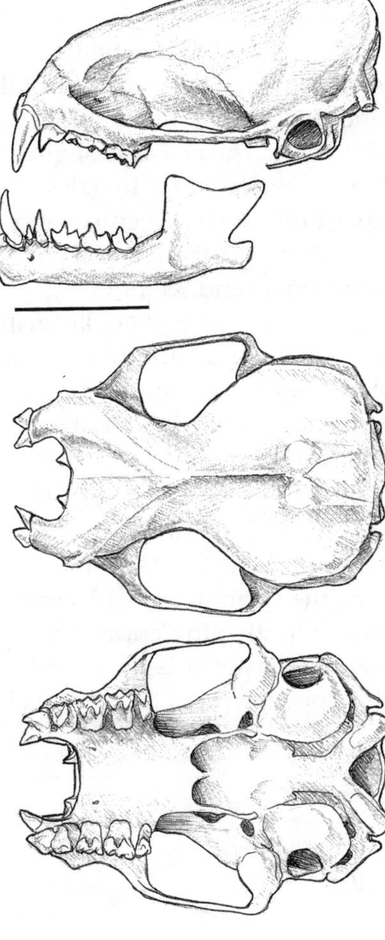

Figure 52. *Lasiurus cinereus:* Left lateral view of skull and mandible, and dorsal and ventral view of skull. Scale bar = 5 mm.

This solitary tree bat probably occurs throughout Virginia (Figure 53).

Habitat. The hoary bat often roosts in coniferous trees and is usually found hanging from a branch of a pine, spruce, or hemlock tree. Occasionally, an individual may be found in a deciduous tree or in a clump of Spanish moss. This species is not ordinarily found in caves, rock crevices, or inside buildings.

Habits. The hoary bat, like the red bat, is solitary, and most individuals migrate south to the southern United States, Mexico, and possibly into northern South America for the winter. Occasionally individuals are found during the winter months hibernating in their summer range (Findley and Jones, 1964; Whitaker, 1967). The summer months are generally spent in the regions of northern coniferous forest in the northern portion of the United States and Canada.

Findley and Jones (1964) mapped the distributional records of this species by month. In North America, they found that females apparently migrate northward earlier than males and occupy a summering ground in the northern United States and Canada where the young are born. Males are essentially all found in the southwestern United States. Fall migration appears to begin in August. Females fly to the Southwest and migrate with the males to Baja California and Central America. Mating occurs at this time. Both spring and fall migratory waves have been noted.

The hoary bat is usually the last bat to appear in the evening, generally leaving its roost well after sundown. These bats are strong and rapid fliers and are usually active throughout the night. They are not as common as the red bat, and thus relatively few data are available concerning them.

Food. Hoary bats feed primarily on moths. Hamilton (1943) noted that because of its size, the hoary bat can conquer larger nocturnal insects, but it does not ignore smaller prey. Food items recorded from hoary bats include moths, stinkbugs, mosquitoes, muscoid flies, flying ants, termites, grasshoppers, and various types of beetles. Bishop (1947) found a hoary bat feeding on an eastern pipistrelle in New York, and Orr (1950) observed one pursuing a small bat in California.

Reproduction and Development. Hoary bats mate during late summer and usually produce a litter of two young during June. Nursery colonies are not formed; hoary bats are solitary. Parturition usually takes place in the bat's summer range, although I recorded a female and two nursing young on June 22 in southern Ala-

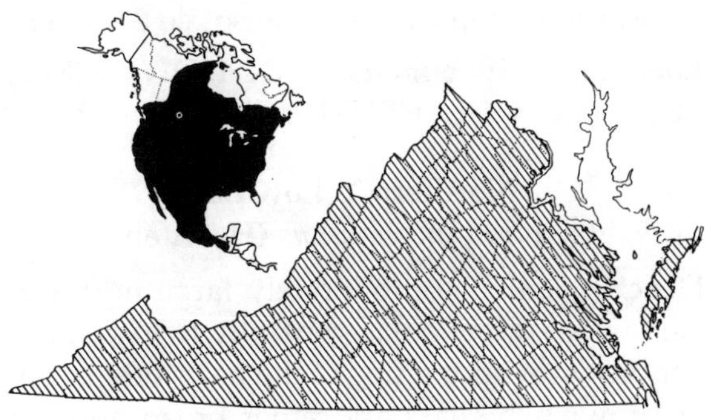

Figure 53. *Lasiurus cinereus:* Range in Virginia and North America.

bama. Gestation is about 90 days.

Tuttle (1988) noted:

> *In areas of low disturbance, mother hoary bats are quite loyal to particular roost sites. During three years of investigation in Wisconsin, I observed a mother return to exactly the same place under a blue spruce branch to rear her young each spring.*

Details of the birth and development of this species have been recorded by Bogan (1972). Newborn young are hairless except for fine silvery-gray hair on the dorsum of the head, shoulders, uropatagium and feet. Their eyes are closed, and they weigh approximately 4 g. The eyes open between 10 and 12 days of age. By three weeks of age, the young resemble adults in pelage color. Like the red bat, this species has been said to carry the young routinely on foraging flights. Females transport the young from roost to roost when necessary, but they most likely do not accompany her while she is feeding.

Koehler and Barclay (1988) found that the degree of call variation within and between family units was relatively high in this solitary species, and calls produced by different young could not be differentiated. This differs from some colonial species such as *Myotis lucifugus* in which each young bat has a distinctive vocal signature that allows auditory discrimination between calling young.

Longevity. Jackson (1961) noted that this species probably has a life expectancy of at least six to seven years and a potential longevity of 12 or 14 years.

Predation. Individuals have been taken by birds of prey and snakes in other states.

Geographic Variation. The subspecies in Virginia is *Lasiurus cinereus cinereus* (Palisot de Beavois).

Location of Specimens. AMNH, DWL, GMU, LC, NVCC, ODU, USNM, VCU.

Northern Yellow Bat
Lasiurus intermedius (H. Allen)

Description. The moderately large northern yellow bat (Plate 29) is generally light yellowish-brown with the tips of the hairs often gray or brown. The ears are rather broad and are more pointed than the ears of other lasiurine bats. The tragus is broad at its base and tapers toward the tip. The membranes range in color from brown to black with fur present on the dorsal surface of the basal half of the interfemoral membrane. The underside of the wing membranes is sparsely furred along the forearm to the wrist. The calcar is slightly keeled. Like other lasiurine bats, females have four mammae. Adults are between 115 and 125 mm in length, including a 48 to 52 mm tail. The forearm is between 45 and 55 mm long.

The skull is similar to other lasiurine skulls in that it is broad and short. Both sagittal and lambdoidal crests are present. It differs from other lasiurines primarily in that it has a total of 30 teeth instead of 32, lacking the tiny tooth behind the upper canine (Figure 54).

Distribution. The yellow bat occurs in the southeastern United States from New Jersey south along the Atlantic and Gulf coasts to eastern Texas and south into Central America. Only one individual has ever been recorded in Virginia. This specimen was taken at Willoughby

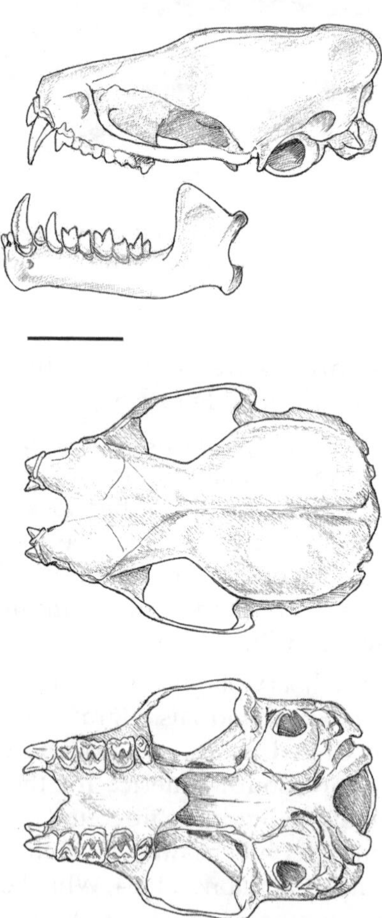

Figure 54. *Lasiurus intermedius:* Left lateral view of skull and mandible, and dorsal and ventral view of skull. Scale bar = 5 mm.

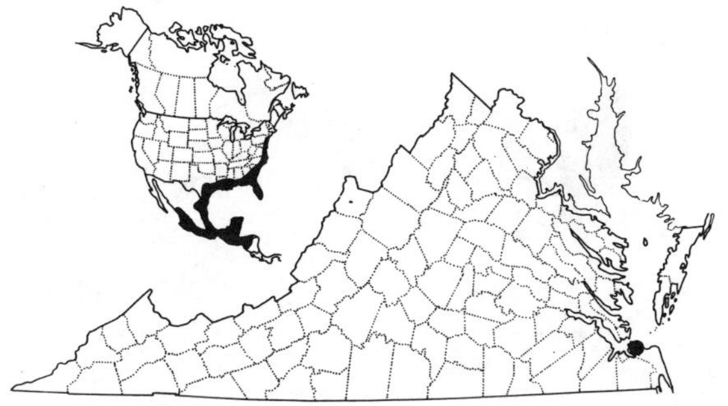

Figure 55. *Lasiurus intermedius:* Range in Virginia and North America.

Beach near Norfolk in May, 1954 (Rageot, 1955) (Figure 55). No specimens have been recorded between Norfolk, Virginia, and the coast of central South Carolina (Webster et al., 1985).

Habitat. The yellow bat is closely associated with Spanish moss. Females roost and bear their young in clumps of this moss.

Habits. The habits of the yellow bat in Florida, where it is relatively abundant, have been studied by Jennings (1958). Elsewhere, little is known about its biology. In Florida, these bats forage over grassy areas such as airports, open pastures, golf courses, and lake edges. When feeding, they fly between 4.5 and 6 m above the ground.

Although adults roost singly, there is a tendency for a number of them to roost in the same vicinity.

Food. Sherman (1939) listed true bugs, damselflies, flies, beetles, and winged ants as food items of the yellow bat.

Reproduction and Development. Mating in this species usually takes place in the fall with parturition occurring during May and June. In Florida, Sherman (1945) found male yellow bats in breeding condition from early September until mid-February. Between two and three young comprise a normal litter. Another Florida study revealed an average of 3.5 embryos per pregnant female, although it was estimated that the average number surviving to flight age was 2.8 per litter (Jennings, 1958). The single specimen known from Virginia contained three embryos, each of which measured 12 mm in total length. The sexes are apparently segregated in spring and early summer, when the females are pregnant or the young are small.

Geographic Variation. The subspecies occurring in Virginia is *Lasiurus intermedius floridanus* (H. Allen).

Location of Specimens. USNM.

Genus *Corynorhinus*

Dentition: 2/3, 1/1, 2/3, 3/3 = 36

Townsend's (Western) Big-Eared Bat
Corynorhinus townsendii (Cooper)

Description. Big-eared bats are medium-sized bats and are easily distinguished from other species by their very large ears and prominent lumps near the nose. The ears are over 25 mm high and are joined across the forehead. The overall dorsal coloration of the western big-eared bat (Plate 30) is dark brown with the underparts buff- or pale-brown. The bases of the ventral hairs are grayish-brown. The tail membrane is naked. Adults range from 97 to 112 mm in total length, including a tail 40 to 54 mm long. The forearm is 42 to 47 mm long. The weight is 9 to 11 g.

The skull is slender and highly arched. Two incisors are present, and the first premolar is reduced forming a "space" as in *Pipistrellus* and *Lasionycteris.* These bats possess a total of 36 teeth (Figure 56).

The only other bat in Virginia that could be confused with this species is Rafinesque's big-eared bat *(Corynorhinus rafinesquii).* The main distinguishing characteristics are the color of the underparts and the presence or absence of a cusp on the first incisor. In Rafinesque's big-eared bat the basal portions of the belly hairs are black and have white tips, and an accessory cusp is usually present, whereas in Townsend's big-eared bat the bases of the hairs are grayish-brown and have buff or brownish tips. The incisor lacks a cusp. Thus, the eastern species has a whitish belly, and the western species has a brownish belly.

Distribution. This species ranges throughout most of the western United States into southwestern Canada and the Mexican Highlands. The range extends eastward in a fragmented band through Oklahoma, Kansas, Missouri, Kentucky, West Virginia, western Maryland, and western Virginia.

In Virginia, this bat was known historically from five caves in Bath, Highland, Rockingham, and Tazewell counties (Figure 57), all at elevations above 458 m. Approximately 100 individuals were in the Tazewell County cave in 1977–1978 (Handley, Tipton and Tipton, 1979b).

During a 10-year investigation of hibernating bats, however, no big-eared bats were found in the original caves (Dalton, 1987), but four other caves in Bland, Highland, and Tazewell counties contained a total of 2,000 hibernating individuals with approximately 99 percent of the population hibernating in a single cave. One large cluster in this cave consisted of approximately 1,100 individuals. Dalton (1987) noted that this species has a more restricted distribution than any other Virginia cave bat. During the winter of 1989–1990, a survey by the Virginia Department of Game and Inland Fisheries found 2,015 big-eared bats in 7 of 15 caves that were checked (Nongame Summary EW-2-2, 1989/90). A 1992 survey of a wintering Highland County population and a summer survey of the only known maternity colony revealed that both remained stable from previous surveys. Over 200 big-eared bats were confirmed to be using the major hibernaculum as a summer roost as well (Annual Report Summary 1992).

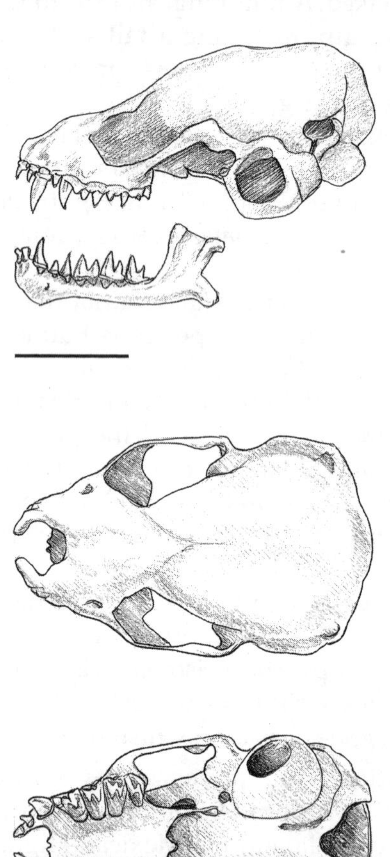

Figure 56. *Corynorhinus townsendii:* Left lateral view of skull and mandible, and dorsal and ventral view of skull. Scale bar = 5 mm.

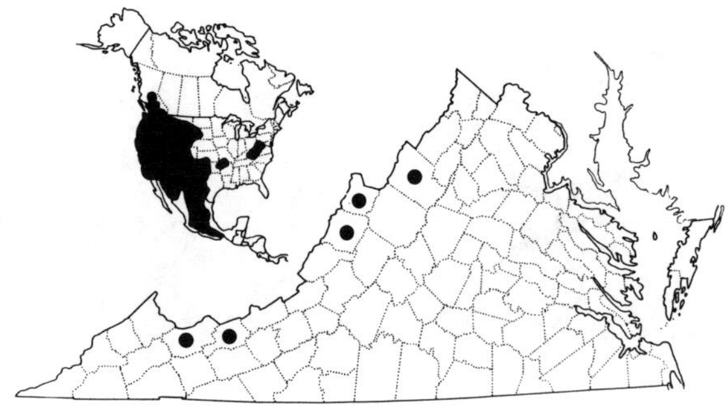

Figure 57. *Corynorhinus townsendii:* Range in Virginia and North America.

Corynorhinus townsendii virginianus has been classified as endangered in Virginia (Handley, 1979b; 1991) as well as throughout its entire range by the US Fish and Wildlife Service because it is restricted to a very small area for reproduction and hibernation, the total population is small, the population in some areas is decreasing, and the populations are extremely intolerant of being disturbed. Dalton (1987) and Handley (1991) noted that the total population for the subspecies in West Virginia, Virginia, Kentucky, and North Carolina is estimated to be about 10,000 bats. The population in caves in Virginia is stable (Dalton, 1987).

Habitat. Townsend's big-eared bat is a true cave bat and is usually found only in caves.

Habits. Handley, Tipton, and Tipton (1979b) stated:

> *Summer roosts usually contain maternity colonies of females and young; males are mostly solitary at that season. Maternity colonies seem to require warm caves. In contrast, winter roost sites are often near cave entrances or in passageways where there is considerable air movement. Temperature in these sites sometimes is lower than will be tolerated by other cave bats. Apparently* Plecotus townsendii *requires unusually low temperatures for successful hibernation. Solitary individuals and small clusters are the rule in hibernating* Plecotus townsendii, *although tight clusters of up to a hun-*

dred or more individuals of both sexes are occasionally encountered. The solitary bat protects itself from air temperature variations by wrapping its wings and interfemoral membrane over its underparts and coiling its ears against the sides of its neck. Bats in clusters fold their wings against their sides and may keep their ears extended except at very low temperatures.

These bats are not migratory. The longest recorded movement is only 64 km.

Adam et al. (1994) recorded average male foraging areas of 87.4 ha and average female foraging areas of 121.9 ha in Kentucky. Female foraging areas were larger in August when young bats began flying than they were in May. Big-eared bats foraged primarily in forest habitat along cliffs within 8.4 km of their roost.

Food. Big-eared bats are lepidopterous feeders. The food habits of a maternity colony in Virginia were determined by analyzing fecal pellets (Dalton et al., 1986). Moths (Lepidoptera) formed over 90 percent of the diet with beetles (Coleoptera) a distant second. Small quantities of Diptera, Hymenoptera, Homoptera, Neuroptera, Trichoptera, and Plecoptera were also identified. Similar results were reported from three maternity colonies in West Virginia (Sample and Whitmore, 1993). Hamilton (1943) reported that all specimens he examined contained only the remains of moths. Moths have been reported as a major dietary item of the species in several western states.

Reproduction and Development. These bats inhabit caves year-round with females moving to warmer maternity caves during April (Dalton, 1987). Only one maternity cave is known in Virginia.

Tipton (1984) recorded the following behavior of a maternity colony:

A maternity cave was monitored every weekend in 1983 from mid-March through early October. The bats began arriving in mid-March in small numbers and occupied the entrance areas of the passages. During the rest of March and through the middle of April, they were in torpor in the late afternoon. However, at the end of April, they moved to the "maternity site" and were awake and active during the daytime. It was a surprise to later discover the bats in locations other than the "maternity site" during the latter part of May, the entire month of June, and the beginning of July. They were wide awake during the daylight hours when they were checked in these other locations in the side passages. By the end of July, the bats had moved from the side passages and back into the main part of the cave again. They did not occupy the side passages for the rest of the season through October 8.

Mohr (1933) recorded females with young approximately 65 mm long from Burke's Garden, Tazewell County, Virginia, on June 26. Sperm are stored in the mostly dormant females until ovulation occurs in February, March, or April. During April and May females gather in warm caves to form maternity colonies where the single young is born around mid-June (Dalton and Handley, 1991b). Gestation is between 56 and 100 days depending on the mother's body temperature.

Newborn bats are pink and naked and have their eyes sealed. By the fourth day the body is covered with short gray hair. By seven days, the large ears assume an erect position and shortly thereafter the eyes open. Growth is rapid, and within about 30 days the young bats are almost full grown. They begin to fly in about three weeks and are weaned at about seven to eight weeks of age.

Longevity. Paradiso and Greenhall (1967) calculated the maximum longevity in this species to be 16 years, 5 months based on recoveries of banded bats in California. Kunz (1982) recorded 16.4 years as the maximum longevity for Townsend's big-eared bat.

Predation. Clark et al. (1990) reported a big-eared bat being eaten by an eastern wood rat *(Neotoma floridana)* in Oklahoma.

Geographic Variation. The subspecies in Virginia is *Corynorhinus townsendii virginianus* Handley.

Location of Specimens. FSM, LACM, MVZ, USNM.

Rafinesque's (Eastern) Big-Eared Bat
Corynorhinus rafinesquii (Lesson)

Description. Rafinesque's big-eared bat (Plate 31) is very similar in appearance to Townsend's big-eared bat. The large ears, which are joined at their base, measure more than 25 mm in length. The tragus is long and slender. The large glandular mass present between each eye and

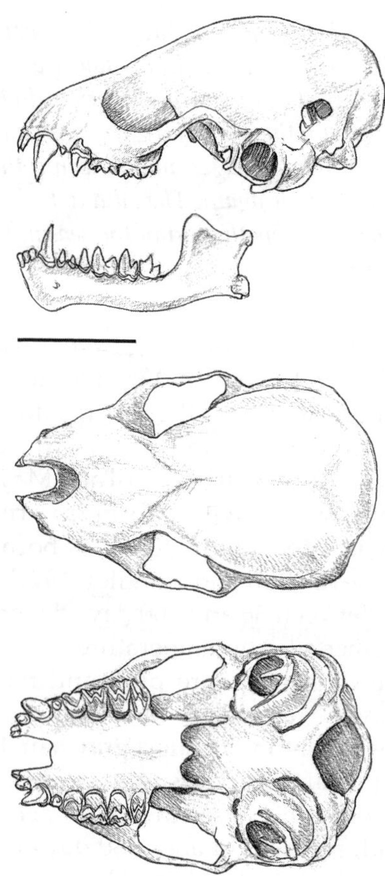

Figure 58. *Corynorhinus rafinesquii:* Left lateral view of skull and mandible, and dorsal and ventral view of skull. Scale bar = 5 mm.

nostril has given rise to the common name "lump-nosed bat" for both species of big-eared bat. *Corynorhinus rafinesquii* differs from *Corynorhinus townsendii* in having a white rather than buffy belly and by having cusps on the first upper incisors. The interfemoral membrane and the wings are unfurred. The calcar is not keeled. Adults average 92 to 106 mm in total length, including a tail 41 to 54 mm long. The forearm is 41 to 46 mm long. Rafinesque's big-eared bats usually weigh 6 to 10 g.

The skull of this species is slender and highly arched. A total of 36 teeth are present with two upper incisors, a "space" behind the upper canine containing one tiny premolar, and with the first upper incisors being bicuspid (Figure 58).

Distribution. This species is restricted to the southeastern United States. It ranges from southeastern Virginia, southern Illinois, central Indiana, and Ohio south to the Gulf Coast and from the Atlantic Ocean west to Missouri, eastern Oklahoma, and eastern Texas. It occurs only very sparingly in Illinois, Indiana, and Ohio.

Corynorhinus rafinesquii is known from five sites in southeastern Virginia (Handley and Schwab, 1991) (Figure 59). It was first recorded in June, 1897; a second specimen was not reported until 1978. Other specimens were taken in 1983, 1989, and 1991. Concerning a geographic variant, Handley and Schwab (1991) stated: "The subspecies *Plecotus [Corynorhinus] rafinesquii* has not been found in Virginia, but has occurred nearby in West Virginia (Frum, 1948), Kentucky (Barbour and Davis, 1974), Tennessee (Handley, 1959), and western North Carolina (Clark, 1987). M. D. Tuttle (pers. comm.) found a large nursery colony 8.0 km east-southeast of Kyles Ford, Hancock County, Tennessee, close to the Virginia-Tennessee boundary."

The geographic variant inhabiting Virginia has been classified as endangered, while the variant noted above as occuring in West Virginia, Kentucky, Tennessee and North Carolina has been classified as status undetermined in Virginia (Handley, 1991).

Habitat. Rafinesque's big-eared bat inhabits the forested regions of the South. Individuals are often found in buildings, attics, hollow trees, mines, and caves. They prefer buildings that are mostly unoccupied and partially lighted. The specimen reported from Virginia in 1897 was found roosting in a small hollow cypress snag in Lake Drummond. In 1991, a big-eared bat was found in an abandoned farmhouse in Sussex County, Virginia. An abandoned opened cistern was used as a roosting site by these bats in winter in Tennessee.

Habits. These bats do not migrate. They are permanent residents throughout their range.

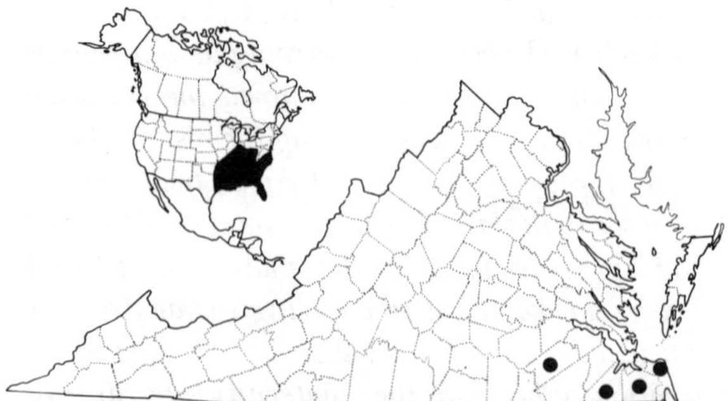

Figure 59. *Corynorhinus rafinesquii:* Range in Virginia and North America.

They usually roost singly rather than in clusters. Colonies range in size from several animals to approximately 100 individuals. Throughout a portion of their range they hibernate during the colder months of the year. When they are resting, their big ears are coiled backward in a spiral and folded against the body. The sexes are together in late summer and fall and at the same roosts in winter but are separate in spring and early summer. They leave their roost well after dark and return before dawn. They have not been observed feeding. Their flight is slow, and they can hover in one place.

Food. This species probably feeds predominantly on moths.

Reproduction and Development. Mating is in the fall and winter, and sperm is stored in the uterus until early spring when ovulation and fertilization take place. Pregnant females congregate in groups isolated from the males before the birth of their single young. Gestation of Rafinesque's big-eared bat is not known, although that of Townsend's big-eared bat varies from 56 to 100 days. Parturition in this species probably occurs in late May or June. Nursery colonies rarely exceed 10 to 20 adult females with young. Newborn bats are pink and hairless and have their eyes closed. The young bat remains with the female until it is weaned at approximately two months of age, only being separated from her while she forages for food. The young reach full size and assume their adult pelage by August or early September (Handley, 1959). A female probably bears her first young at one year of age.

Longevity. The bat-banding files of the US Fish and Wildlife Service record a female big-eared bat that lived to a minimum age of 10 years, 1 month (Paradiso and Greenhall, 1967; Kunz, 1982).

Predation. No instances of predation have been recorded in Virginia, although these bats may be occasionally fed upon by various predators on a chance basis.

Geographic Variation. The subspecies occurring in Virginia is *Corynorhinus rafinesquii rafinesquii* (Lesson).

Location of Specimens. USNM.

Rabbits, Hares, and Pikas

The order Lagomorpha comprises the rabbits, hares and pikas. The rabbits and hares have short tails and long ears, while the pikas lack an external tail and are short-eared. Rabbits and hares occupy a wide variety of habitats and are nearly worldwide in distribution. Pikas are found only in the mountains of western North America, in Siberia, and in the Himalayan region.

Lagomorphs were long considered to be members of the order Rodentia because of their chisellike incisors, lack of canine teeth, and the presence of a diastema. Because they have two pairs of upper incisors, they were placed in a separate suborder (Duplicidentata) from the true rodents, which, with a single pair of upper incisors, were placed in the suborder Simplicidentata. Many other characters also separate the two groups, and mammalogists now consider them to be distinct orders. It is generally accepted that the resemblances between lagomorphs and rodents are results of convergence rather than of close taxonomic relationship. There is some indication that lagomorphs are more closely related to hooved animals than to rodents.

As indicated above, members of this order do not have canine teeth; rather, the incisors and molariform teeth are separated by a wide space, or diastema. At birth, lagomorphs have three pairs of upper incisors, but the outer on each side is soon lost. In adults, the second pair of incisors is small, nearly circular, lacks cutting edges, and is set directly behind (not beside) the first functional pair. Each of the anterior upper incisors possesses a longitudinal groove on its anterior face. As in rodents, incisors grow throughout life, but unlike rodents, they are covered both anteriorly and posteriorly by enamel. In rodents, the enamel is restricted to the anterior face.

The distance between the tooth rows of the lower jaws is less than that between the tooth rows of the upper jaws, so that only one pair of upper and lower tooth rows is opposable at the same time. The motion of the jaws in mastication is lateral, unlike the rotary jaw movement of rodents. The incisive foramina are long and wide and are joined posteriorly, terminating at the level of the anterior cheek teeth. The palate is short and does not extend to the end of the tooth row.

The two main lower leg bones, the tibia and fibula, are fused for more than half their length, and the fibula articulates with the calcaneum in the ankle. The forelimbs have five digits, while the hind limbs may have four or five.

The diet of lagomorphs is restricted to vegetation. Two types of fecal pellets are expelled — brown pellets and greenish pellets. The reingestion of partially digested vegetation from the greenish pellets is common; this practice is known as coprophagy. It allows the animals to spend relatively little time exposed to predators while in the field actually feeding. They consume green vegetation rapidly and then make optimum use of it in the safety of their brushpile or burrow. It is somewhat analogous to cud-chewing in ruminant animals. These pellets have a high protein content and contain large amounts of B vitamins produced by intestinal bacteria (Hansen and Flinders, 1969).

The order Lagomorpha contains two families — the Ochotonidae, which includes the pikas, and the Leporidae, which includes the rabbits and hares. Only the family Leporidae is represented in Virginia.

Rabbits and Hares (Family Leporidae)

Members of the family Leporidae are familiar mammals. Their long hind limbs, oversized feet, furry tails, and long ears are well-recognized characteristics. Each of the limbs has five clawed digits, but the first digit is very small. The soles of the feet are covered with hair. A sensory pad, usually hidden by hair-covered folds of skin, is located at the entrance of each nostril, and a Y-shaped naked groove extends from the upper lip to and around the nose. The upper lip is divided. Female leporids are usually larger than males.

The skull is arched and elongated. It has a broad rostrum and is slightly constricted between the orbits. The long, narrow supraorbital processes always project posteriorly and sometimes anteriorly; they are close to the cranium or fused with it. An interparietal bone is distinct by being set off with sutures in rabbits *(Sylvilagus)* and indistinct in hares *(Lepus)*. Auditory bullae are small and not inflated. The bones at the side of the rostrum (maxillae) are riddled with openings (fenestrae), which serve to lighten the skull. The incisors are separated from the mouth cavity by lip folds that have a fine velvety covering.

The terms rabbit and hare are often mistakenly interchanged. The cottontail, marsh, swamp, and other true rabbits belong to the genus *Sylvilagus*, and they prefer habitats with plenty of cover. Young cottontails are born in a well-defined nest. At birth they are altricial, i.e., they are blind, naked, have undeveloped ears, and are helpless. Baby hares, however are precocial, i.e., they are well developed at birth and are able to scamper from danger. Hares belong to the genus *Lepus*. They are bigger than rabbits, have longer hind legs developed for leaping, and longer, broader ears. They favor wide-open spaces. Hares have longer gestation periods than rabbits. The female hare rarely constructs a nest for her young which, at birth, are furred and have their eyes and ears open. They are able to move about on their own shortly after birth. Both the snowshoe hare of the North and the jackrabbit of the West are classified as hares.

Leporids are prolific breeders, a fact popularized by the phrase "multiply like rabbits." Reproductive efficiency is increased by a phenomenon known as induced ovulation. Female rabbits normally ovulate only after copulation has occurred, a system that ensures optimum fertilization of ova.

Rabbits and hares are crepuscular, active mainly near dusk and dawn. They are not physically capable of defending themselves against predators and, instead, rely on a keen sense of hearing and smell, and the use of burrows or speed and agility to escape danger. At high speeds, lagomorph limbs function as digitigrade appendages, but when moving slowly the entire foot makes contact with the ground (plantigrade).

Virginia is inhabited by three kinds of rabbits and two kinds of hares: rabbits are the marsh rabbit, the eastern cottontail, and the Appalachian cottontail; hares are the snowshoe hare, and the black-tailed jackrabbit.

Key to Species of Leporidae

1a Interparietal bone distinct, not fused with parietals; hind foot less than 105 mm
.... 2

1b Interparietal bone fused with parietals; hind foot more than 105 mm
.... 4

2a Posterior supraorbital process joined to cranium along most or all of its length; underside of tail brown or gray
.... *Sylvilagus palustris*

2b Posterior supraorbital process only partly fused to cranium or not contacting cranium at all except possibly at very tip; underside of tail white
.... 3

3a Posterior supraorbital process partly fused with cranium, anterior exten-

sion of supraorbital process well developed; auditory bullae moderate; no black patch on top of head
. . . . *Sylvilagus floridanus*

3b Posterior supraorbital process usually not in contact with cranium, except possibly at very tip; anterior extension of supraorbital process absent or nearly so; auditory bullae small; narrow black patch on top of head between ears
. . . . *Sylvilagus obscurus*

4a Tail with black median stripe extending onto back
. . . . *Lepus californicus*

4b Tail without black median stripe
. . . . *Lepus americanus*

Genus *Sylvilagus*

Dentition: 2/1, 0/0, 3/2, 3/3 = 28

Marsh Rabbit
Sylvilagus palustris (Bachman)

Description. Marsh rabbits (Plate 32) have coarse blackish-brown or reddish-brown fur. The nape of the neck is somewhat reddish. The feet appear relatively small and slender because of the absence of the heavy covering of hair found in other species of *Sylvilagus* in Virginia. The feet are orangish above and darker below with long prominent claws. The ears are broad and relatively short in comparison with other leporids. The brownish tail is small and inconspicuous and is dingy gray or buff below. Although similar in appearance to the eastern cottontail, the marsh rabbit can be distinguished by the lack of white fur on the very short tail. The underparts are grayish, bordered along the flanks and side with buff. The throat is also buff. Adult marsh rabbits are between 350 and 440 mm long, including a tail 40 to 51 mm long. They weigh between 0.9 and 1.6 kg.

The braincase is broad and rounded. The anterior and posterior supraorbital processes are joined to the braincase along most or all of their length. Moderate-sized auditory bullae are present (Figure 60).

Distribution. The marsh rabbit is restricted to the southeastern United States. It is found along the Coastal Plain from the eastern side of Mobile Bay, Alabama, to southeastern Virginia, including most of peninsular Florida.

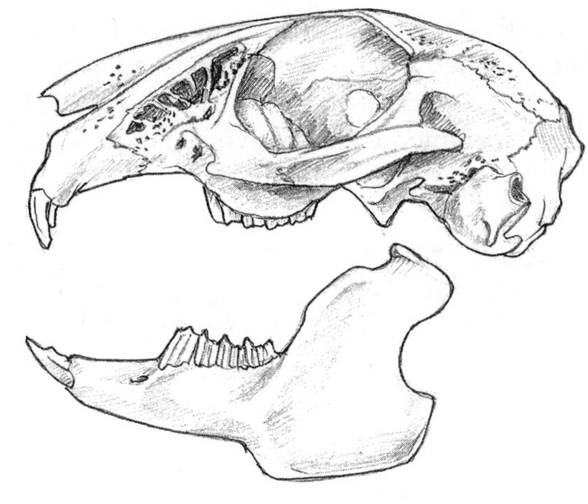

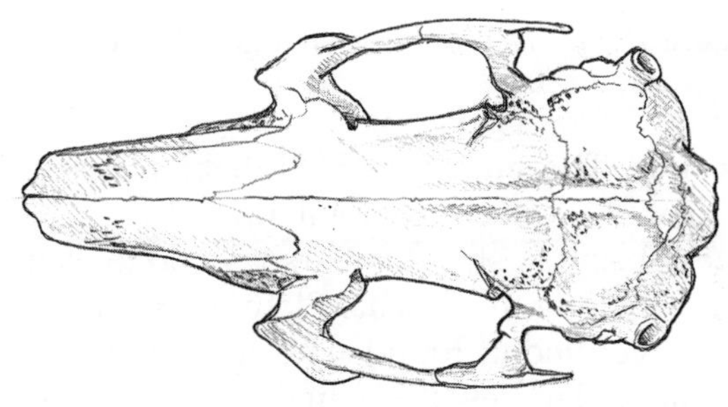

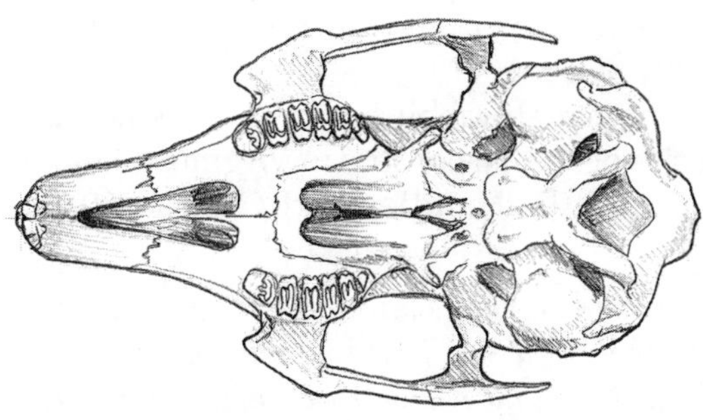

Figure 60. *Sylvilagus palustris:* Left lateral view of skull and mandible, and dorsal and ventral view of skull. Scale bar = 20 mm.

The marsh rabbit is found only in the extreme southeastern portion of Virginia, south of the James River and west to Surry and Greensville counties (Padgett, 1989; Fies and Handley, 1991). Specimens have been taken from Surry County and from the cities of Virginia Beach, Chesapeake, and Suffolk (Figure 61). Areas such as the Great Dismal Swamp, Hog Island, North Landing, and the islands in Back Bay have yielded specimens and/or reports (Payne, 1975; Handley and Gordon, 1979a). Bailey (1946) reported its occurrence from Pope's Creek in Westmoreland County, but no specimen exists for verification of this record.

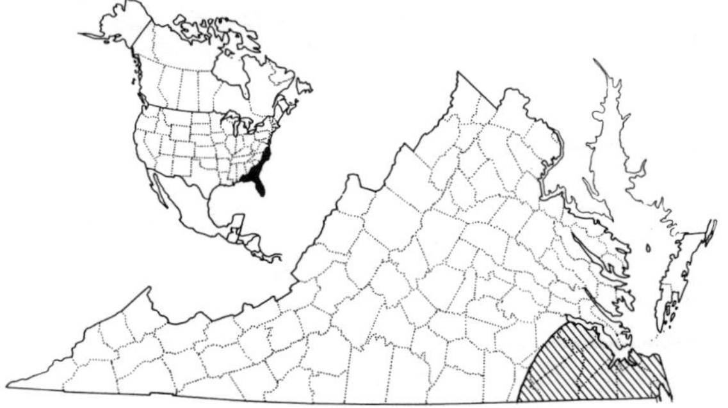

Figure 61. *Sylvilagus palustris:* Range in Virginia and North America.

Habitat. The marsh rabbit inhabits densely vegetated swamps, bottomlands, hammocks, brackish and freshwater marshes, and lowland thickets along the Coastal Plain. In Virginia, it is most commonly found in freshwater marshes (Fies and Handley, 1991). In Georgia, Tomkins (1955) noted that when the salinity increases beyond a certain point, the number of rabbits decreases. It is doubtful if any are found in strictly salt marsh.

The marsh rabbit has been classified as a species of special concern in Virginia (Handley, 1979b; 1991). Handley and Gordon (1979a) stated:

> *The marsh rabbit is uncommon to occasionally common in a small area in southeastern Virginia. It is at the northern edge of its range here. There is* **Special Concern** *for it because of its limited range and because of its ecological preference for relatively undisturbed marshes, an ever-shrinking environment. In Virginia it is considered to be a game mammal (lumped with cottontails and hares in the game regulations as a "rabbit"), but it probably is subject to very little hunting pressure.*

Habits. Marsh rabbits usually remain in their well-hidden form during the day and feed during late evening and throughout most of the night.

Some marsh rabbits take to the water readily and swim easily and swiftly, while others usually remain on land. They almost never leave the cover of the swamps. If they are driven out by fire or dogs, they seek the nearest thicket or take refuge in a hollow log or tree. Their short legs prevent them from attaining much speed; when pursued they depend upon their doubling and twisting movements to escape.

This species seldom uses burrows. Its forms and nests are located in broomsedge, in thickets, beneath fallen logs and limbs, or in other concealed locations. The form is usually oval and is approximately 30 cm long and 23 cm across. Forms may be utilized for varying periods of time.

Home ranges of marsh rabbits are usually not greater than 275 m in extent. On Hog Island, Payne (1975) recorded an average distance between captures of approximately 100 m for males and 75 m for females (range 31 to 183 m). Droppings of the marsh rabbit may be grouped in one small spot on a log or stump, or they may be scattered along the log. In grassy or marshy areas, or along the edges the droppings are usually deposited in piles containing 40 to 100 or more pellets. Scattered pellets may also be found at random.

The marsh rabbit perceives movements very well and has a keen sense of hearing.

Food. The food habits of the marsh rabbit have not been extensively studied. In Virginia, Fishel and McCravy (1988) found them feeding almost exclusively on rushes in the winter, on grass shoots in the spring, and on emergent vegetation in the summer. Audubon and Bachman (1846) observed marsh rabbits feeding on various grasses, sassafras shoots, pond rice, bulbs of wild potato, and the atamasco lily. They also feed upon reeds and amaryllis. Blair (1936) recorded captive marsh rabbits feeding on herbaceous plants such as centella *(Centella repanda)*, marsh pennywort (*Hydrocotyle* sp.), cattail *(Typha latifolia)*, and rushes *(Juncus effusus)*. They also ate leaves and twigs from 18 species of trees, shrubs, and woody vines as well as the seeds and fruits from a variety of plants. Wild rabbits fed on *Centella, Smilax,* tupelo seeds, and the bark of the groundsel tree. Blair (1936) recorded a daily food consumption averaging 28.9 percent of the weight of the rabbits.

Reproduction and Development. In Virginia, the marsh rabbit probably breeds in late winter, in early spring, and possibly again in the fall. In Georgia and Florida, specific records of breeding have been noted in February, March, April, and May. Gestation has been estimated to be between 30 and 37 days (Holler and Conaway, 1979). The usual litter size is apparently three to five (Harper, 1927).

Tomkins (1935) reported:

> *The nest was about fourteen inches across and perhaps eight inches deep. It was composed of the softer grass blades mixed with quantities of rabbit fur, and was floored with an inch or more of the same material. Placed among burnt sedges about one foot vertically and thirty feet horizontally from normal high water mark, it was easily located by the rabbit fur, and could be seen (when one knew where to look) at least fifty feet away. Had the sedge not been burned it would not have been visible ten feet away. The nest had been occupied long enough to be dilapidated, and the alarmed young went in or out through the side.*

Parasites. Botfly (*Cuterebra* sp.) infections were found on Hog Island in Surry County by Jacobson, McGinnes, and Catts (1978).

Predation. Predation by great horned owls, barred owls, barn owls, marsh hawks, red-tailed hawks, bald eagles, water moccasins, diamondback rattlesnakes, and alligators have been reported. Foxes, weasels, and mink also prey on this species. Hunters undoubtedly take a number of these rabbits each year.

Geographic Variation. The subspecies occurring in Virginia is *Sylvilagus palustris palustris* (Bachman).

Location of Specimens. AMNH, DMNH, MVZ, ODU, USNM, VPISU, VPI-W.

Eastern Cottontail
Sylvilagus floridanus (Allen)

Description. The eastern cottontail (Plate 33) is a medium-sized rabbit with long ears, large hind legs and feet, smaller front legs and feet, and soft fur. It is the only lagomorph in Virignia in which the nape of the neck is rusty. The upperparts vary from reddish-brown to grayish-brown sprinkled with black. A prominent gray flank patch is usually present. The ears are dark grayish-tan bordered with black. The underparts are grayish-white except for a brownish chest. The short, fluffy tail is brownish above and white below. Because the tail is usually turned upward when the rabbit runs, the white part is the most conspicuous and is the source of the common name, cottontail. The tops of the hind feet are tan to whitish. Five toes are present on the forefeet, four on the hind feet. Females possess four pairs of mammae. Adult cottontails attain a length of 320 to 500 mm, including a tail 40 to 75 mm long. They nor-

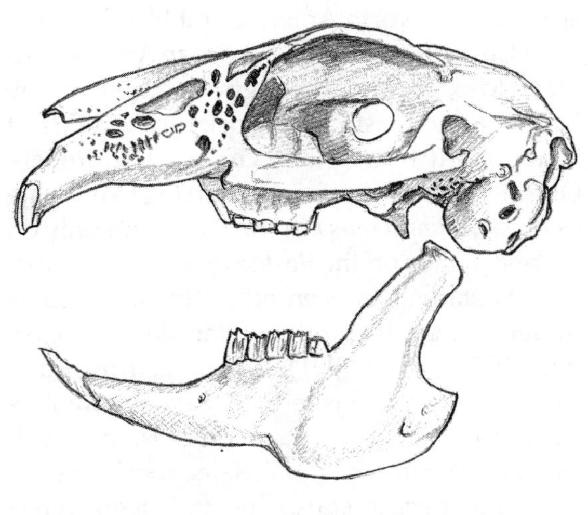

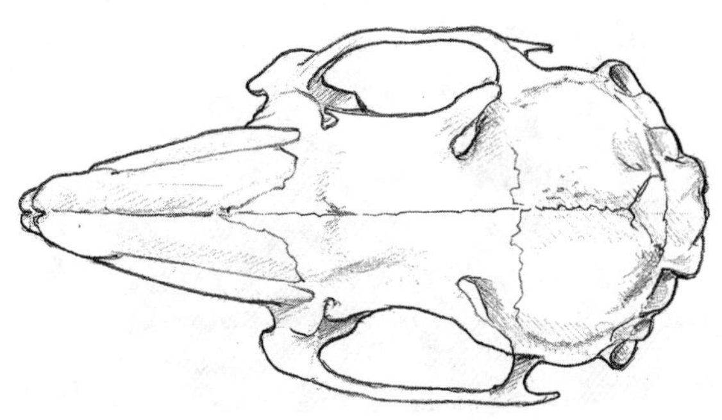

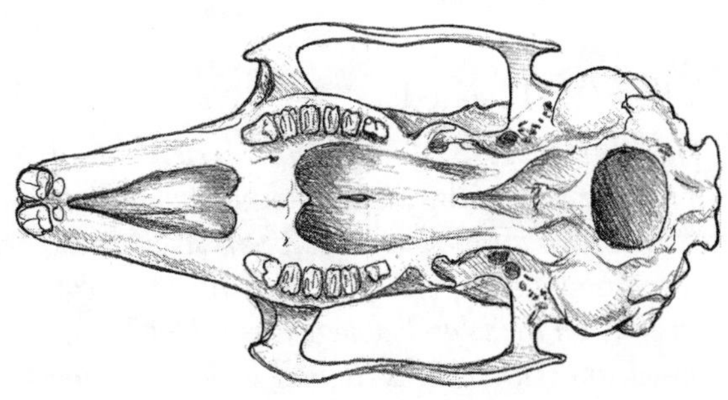

Figure 62. *Sylvilagus floridanus:* Left lateral view of skull and mandible, and dorsal and ventral view of skull. Scale bar = 20 mm.

mally weigh between 0.9 and 1.8 kg.

A small anterior extension of the supraorbital process is usually present. The posterior extension of the supraorbital process is long and broad and may be partly fused with the cranium, forming slitlike openings when viewed from above. Moderate-sized auditory bullae are present (Figure 62).

Distribution. The eastern cottontail rabbit is the most common and geographically widespread of all North American rabbits. It occurs from Costa Rica through Mexico to Arizona and New Mexico and throughout most of the United States east of the Rocky Mountains. It is abundant throughout Virginia (Figure 63). One of the two subspecies occurring in the state (*Sylvilagus floridanus hitchensi*) is found only on barrier islands off the Eastern Shore of Virginia, and its status has been officially classified as undetermined in Virginia (Handley and Gordon, 1979b; Fies, 1991). It has been recorded from Smiths and Fishermans islands. Rabbits have also been observed on other islands such as Hog, Parramore, and Assateague; however, their subspecific status has not been determined.

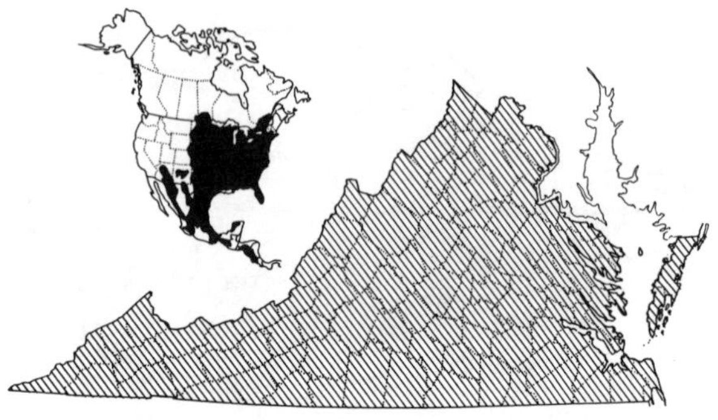

Figure 63. *Sylvilagus floridanus:* Range in Virginia and North America.

Fies (1991) stated:

The eastern cottontail of the barrier island, Sylvilagus floridanus hitchensi, *may well be extinct. No specimens have been taken in 80 years, and at the present time there are no cottontails on the islands where this rabbit is supposed to occur. This cottontail was vulnerable to storm tides, the introduction of exotic cottontails, and predation.*

Habitat. Cottontails live chiefly in old fields, brushy clearings, weed patches, brier patches, hedgerows, and along woodland borders. They may be found in orchards, gardens and cultivated fields, particularly if patches or borders of weeds, tall grasses, or brush are nearby. Conversion of cottontail habitat into pine forest and pastureland has reduced the capacity of such areas to sustain rabbit populations. On the barrier islands the subspecies *Sylvilagus floridanus hitchensi* lives "in grassy areas behind dunes, in marsh edges, thickets of myrtle and poison ivy, and to a lesser extent in scrubby pine forest or in mixed deciduous and pine forest" (Handley and Gordon, 1979b).

Habits. Eastern cottontails are chiefly nocturnal, leaving their forms with the approach of dusk and remaining active until late morning. Most of the daylight hours are spent in a burrow, in a form amid dense vegetation, or in the shelter of a brush pile. Most species of cottontails do not construct their own burrows, but, instead, occupy burrows made by other animals, particularly the woodchuck.

Locomotion is usually by short jumps or hops, although faster progress may be made by longer leaps. Cottontails may attain a speed of about 29 km per hour, although this cannot be maintained for more than 0.8 km. Cottontails depend more on ducking and dodging than upon speed to escape their enemies and will often travel in a circuitous route and return to near their starting place, a practice capitalized on by the hunter with a dog who places himself near the point the rabbit was "started". Eastern cottontails do not take to water readily, but they can swim if necessary.

The cottontail is solitary. Seldom are two or more found together, except for the young and during mating season. A complete account of the social behavior of these rabbits can be found in Marsden and Holler (1964). The home range size varies from a fraction of a hectare up to 9.4 ha, although Haugen (1942) suggested that breeding males may range across an area of 41 ha or more. In general, males range more widely than females. In Pennsylvania, home ranges of males were significantly larger than those of females for all seasons except winter. Median home ranges of males were 3.2, 7.2, 7.8, and 3.1 ha during winter, spring, summer, and fall, respectively; those of females were 2.1, 2.8, 2.4, and 1.5 ha (Althoff and Storm, 1989).

Although homing ability has been the subject of much study in bats, relatively little is known about this behavior in other mammals. A cottontail trapped in a clover field in Alabama was marked and released in an enclosure 3.75 km north of the capture site. It is not known when the rabbit escaped from the enclosure, but it was recaptured in the clover field 331 days after its original capture. In order to return home, it had to cross a highway, pasture, orchard, and cultivated fields (Hill, 1967).

Hearing is acute, and cottontails can move their ears at will to catch sounds from various directions. Their sight is excellent.

Food. Cottontails are herbivorous and eat many kinds of vegetation, their choice depending on the seasonal availability of the plants. Foods include grass, clover, cultivated and wild flowers, and many types of cultivated crops. The list of plant items eaten is nearly endless. During the winter months they feed upon twigs and bark and may girdle fruit trees and ornamental shrubs. Rabbit cuttings are easily identified because they are made at a sharp 45 angle from the vertical axis, which looks like they had been cut with pruning shears. Deer cuttings are pulled off, leaving a ragged edge.

Reproduction and Development. Some breeding may occur during all but the coldest months, but most breeding in Virginia is from mid-February to mid-August. During this period each female usually produces several litters. Mating occurs immediately following birth.

The basic mechanism controlling the onset of breeding, particularly in the male, is daylength (Bissonette, 1938). However, the frequency and extent of late-winter periods of warm and cold temperatures result in some variation in the onset of breeding from year to year (Hill, 1972; Pelton and Provost, 1972). Colder than normal temperatures delay breeding, while warmer temperatures result in earlier breeding.

Courtship and mating behavior of the cottontail have been described by Ecke (1955). The gestation is 26 to 28 days. Although there is a record of as many as 12 young, the usual litter ranges from two to six. Llewellyn and Handley (1945) recorded an average of 4.7 embryos in 21 females in Virginia. Resorption of embryos during gestation is not uncommon. A female may be bred again before her young are a day old. Shortly before the litter arrives, the female cottontail digs a nest cavity in the ground about 15 to 18 cm long, 13 cm wide, and 8 to 10 cm deep. This depression is usually hidden by tall grass or bushes. The nest, or form, is lined with grass and tufts of fur pulled from the female's body. Although it is commonly believed that the nest is lined with fur from the female's abdomen, Casteel (1966) observed that hair was pulled from "almost every part of their body they could reach, except the abdomen." There is some evidence that more than one female cottontail may utilize a single nest.

The location and density of nesting sites varies. The following approximate acres per nest for different types of cover were found in Pennsylvania:

Unkept orchard	1.5	Fencerow	10.9
Young pine plantation	2.0	Fallow field	13.0
Hayfield	7.0	Woods	13.5
Roadside	8.6	Pasture	14.0

Some studies on cottontails have indicated that litter size increased with latitude (Lord, 1960; Barkalow, 1962; Evans et al., 1965), while others have shown that soil pH or other factors related to soil fertility, with its effect on food quality, is a more important factor in producing larger litters (Williams and Caskey, 1965:, Hill, 1972). Hill (1972) noted that the average sizes of second litters were largest, third litters were intermediate, and first litters were smallest. He suggested that the reason for this may be that vegetative quality was highest during April and May, resulting in the largest litters of the year.

Newborn cottontails are pink, blind, and helpless (Rongstad, 1969). They are 100 to 125 mm long and weigh about 28 g. The female normally visits the nest only near dawn to nurse the young. During the day she keeps her distance so that attention will not be drawn to the nest. When the female leaves the nest, she covers the young with grass and fur for warmth, and she scratches leaves over the nest to hide it.

Young cottontails are well-furred in a week, open their eyes between six and nine days, and leave their nests at about two weeks of age. The structure and location of cottontail nests expose the young to many hazards. Cold may kill nesting cottontails and a variety of predators may find them, although they give off almost no odor. Others may drown, be burned, or be killed by farming or gardening operations.

Most cottontails breed for the first time in the spring following their birth, but in some southern states over half the females from early litters give birth by late August. The extent of breeding by young-of-the-year is apparently significantly influenced by the extent of early breeding by the adult population, which is in turn influenced by late-winter temperatures.

Longevity. Of the cottontails that survive nesting, approximately 80 percent will die before they are a year old and few live to be two. Majors (1955) reported that only 12 percent of 24 males and 28 percent of 18 females were recaptured after one year. Hill (1968) calculated average longevity at 1.3 years. There are reports of marked wild individuals reaching five and seven years of age (Linduska, 1947; Cornwell, 1966) and a captive cottontail was still living at 9 years and 8 months (Lord, 1961b).

Pelage Variations. A full-grown albino cottontail was taken and photographed in Bedford County, Virginia (Anonymous, 1949f).

Parasites and Disease. The following parasites have been recorded from the eastern cottontail in Virginia by Jordan (1928); Alicata (1929); Kohls (1940); Bell and Chalgren (1943); Llewellyn (1943); Llewellyn and Handley (1945); Erickson (1947); Handley and Patton (1947); Nelson (1950); Parker et al. (1947); McGinnes (1957; 1958; 1964a; 1964b); Holloway (1959); Shirai et al. (1961); Bellig (1962); Sonenshine, Lamb, and Anastos (1965); Holliman (1966); Holloway (1966); Sonenshine, Atwood, and Lamb (1966); Bozeman et al. (1967); Fox (1968); Sonenshine and Stout (1970); Jacobson (1973); Jacobson and Kirkpatrick (1974); Jacobson, Kirkpatrick, and Holliman (1974); Jacobson and McGinnes (1975); Nettles et al. (1975) Jacobson et al. (1976); Crum and Prestwood (1977); Jacobson, Kirkpatrick, and McGinnes (1978); Jacobson, McGinnes, and Catts (1978); Jones (1978); Garrett and Sonenshine (1979); Andrews et al. (1980); and Eckerlin (1993a): **Viruses and Bacteria** (Shope's fibroma virus, *Francisella tularensis, Rickettsia rickettsii);* **Protozoa** *(Eimeria* spp., *Sarcocystis leporum, Trypanosoma lewisi);* **Trematoda** (flukes) *(Hasstilesia tricolor);* **Cestoda** (tapeworms) *Cittotaenia variabilis, Raillietina salmoni, Taenia pisiformis);* **Nematoda** (roundworms) *(Baylisascaris procyonis = Ascaris columnaris, Dermatoxys veligera, Dirofilaria scapiceps, Longistriata noviberiae, Obeliscoides cuniculi, Passalarus nonanulatus, Trihostrongylus affinis, Trichostrongylus calcaratus, Trichurus leporis);* **Siphonaptera** (fleas) *(Cediopsylla simplex, Ctenocephalides canis, Ctenocephalides felis, Ctenophthalmus pseudagyrtes, Nosopsyllus fasciatus, Odontopsyllus multispinosus, Orchopeas howardi, Orchopeas leucopus;* **Acarina** (ticks) *(Amblyomma americanum, Dermacentor variabilis, Haemaphysalis leporispalustris, Ixodes dentatus);* **Acarina** (mites) *(Eutrombicula alfreddugesi, Neotrombicula whartoni, Trombicula microti);* and **Diptera** *(Cuterebra buccata).*

Tularemia, also known as rabbit fever and deerfly fever, is an infectious disease caused by a bacterium, *Francisella (Pasturella) tularensis.* Rabbits of the genus *Sylvilagus* are the principal source of tularemia. Other vectors responsible for transmitting the disease to man include hares, ticks, deerflies, fleas, cats, dogs, and squirrels. Tularemia has been reported throughout North America, Europe, Russia, and Japan. It has been reported in every state in the United States. Tularemia is not a major disease in Virginia, but its occurrence is frequent enough to cause considerable fear among hunters and persons handling wild rabbits. During the period 1928–1948 in Virginia, 1,240 cases were reported of which 120 were fatal. The greatest number of tularemia cases (144) were reported in 1938 (Roper, 1948). McGinnes (1964a) noted that Virginia ranked fifth in the United States with 1,401 cases between 1924 and 1949. Parker et al. (1952) reported strains of Rocky Mountain spotted fever and tularemia from ticks taken from Prince George, Sussex, and Frederick counties. During the period 1945–1955, 450 cases were reported in humans. Between 1955 and 1959, 85 percent of Virginia's counties reported one or more cases of tularemia. Between January, 1972, and December, 1986, 58 cases of tularemia were reported in Virginia, 29 of which were confirmed (Puscheck, 1987). From January, 1987, through June, 1992, a total of 11 cases have been reported (S. Jenkins, personal communication).

Data from the 1972–1986 tularemia study showed that 40 percent (23 cases) were reported during the summer months of June, July, and August and 33 percent (19 cases) were reported during September, October, and November. Summertime cases tended to be tick-associated, while fall and winter cases tended to be rabbit- and squirrel-associated. Most cases occurred in the northwestern and central regions of the state (Puscheck, 1987).

A person may become infected by handling the flesh of infected animals or by being bitten by deerflies or ticks which have ingested blood from infected rabbits. Any break in the skin is an open door for tularemia germs if the rabbit is diseased. The mortality rate in cottontails is 100 percent. The incubation period of the disease in humans is three to four days. Symptoms include a pimplelike swelling where the organism entered the skin, inflammation and enlargement of the lymph glands, fever, chills, aching, and prostration. The duration of the illness may be from three weeks to much longer; it is fatal in a small percentage of cases. Sick-looking rabbits should be avoided, and meat of wild rabbits should be thoroughly cooked. Hunters and food preparators should wear gloves when skinning or handling animals. Most rabbit livers are spotted to some extent; many fine white spots of pinhead size are an indication of tularemia, but a few large spots are not. The large spots are indicative of larval tapeworms which are present in most cottontails.

Since 1961, rabies has been confirmed in 6 rabbits, one each from Bland, Carroll, Fairfax, Prince William, Washington, and Wythe counties (see tables 5 and 6).

Predation. Rabbits have a multitude of enemies. Predators such as skunks, opossums, weasels, mink, raccoons, foxes, snakes, crows, hawks, and owls often prey on nestling cottontails. Adult rabbits are taken by foxes, mink, weasels, hawks, and owls and often fall victim to automobiles. Lewis (1940) noted that in Amelia County the eastern cottontail was the staple article of diet for foxes and that it formed 90 percent or more of the food of the great horned owl. Blem and Pagels (1973) and Jackson, Pagels, and Trumbo (1976) recorded this species from barn owl pellets in Northampton and Chesterfield counties. Mitchell and Beck (1992) recorded the capture of this species by free-ranging domestic cats in New Kent County.

Geographic Variation. Two subspecies of eastern cottontail inhabit Virginia. *Sylvilagus floridanus floridanus* (Allen), occurs statewide. The subspecies name herein is *floridanus* since no primary isolating mechanism exists between the forms *floridanus* and *mallurus*. A slightly darker variant inhabits the southwesternmost counties from Wythe, Smyth, and Tazewell counties westward. An insular subspecies, *Sylvilagus floridanus hitchensi* Mearns, is found on Smiths Island and Fishermans Island. The dorsum is pale yellowish-brown with no black or rufous streaking and the backs of the legs are dark chestnut.

In 1985 the Commission of Game and Inland Fisheries issued a permit to the Pittsylvania County Administrator "to purchase 105 dozen cottontail rabbits from the State of Kansas for immediate release in Pittsylvania County, Virginia." Four geographic variants inhabit Kansas. When contact was made with William Sleeper, County Administrator, on October 2, 1992, he informed me that permission had been given for four consecutive years to import the rabbits, but the supplier in Kansas could never fill the order. Thus, no rabbits were actually released in Pittsylvania County.

Location of Specimens. AEL, AMNH, BCV, CM, CUC, DMNH, EHC, GMU, IOWA, LC, LFCC, LU, MCZ, MVZ, NVCC, ODU, PWRC, RC, RMWC, SNP, UCM, UGAMNH, UMMZ, USNM, VCU, VHCC, VPISU, VPI-W.

Appalachian Cottontail
Sylvilagus obscurus Chapman

The Appalachian cottontail (Plate 34) was formerly classified as *Sylvilagus transitionalis* and was known as the New England cottontail. Multivariate statistical analyses of 19 cranial and toothrow measurements and the fact that previous investigations had revealed two discrete karyotypes (2N = 46; 2N = 52) led to the naming of this new species (Chapman et al., 1992).

Description. This moderate-sized species closely resembles the eastern cottontail. It differs only in the slightly smaller size, shorter ears, greater amount of black on the back, and certain skull features. The upperparts are reddish-brown during the summer and reddish-gray in winter, with the back overlaid with a blackish wash giving a finely streaked, rather than a grizzled, effect. A narrow black patch is

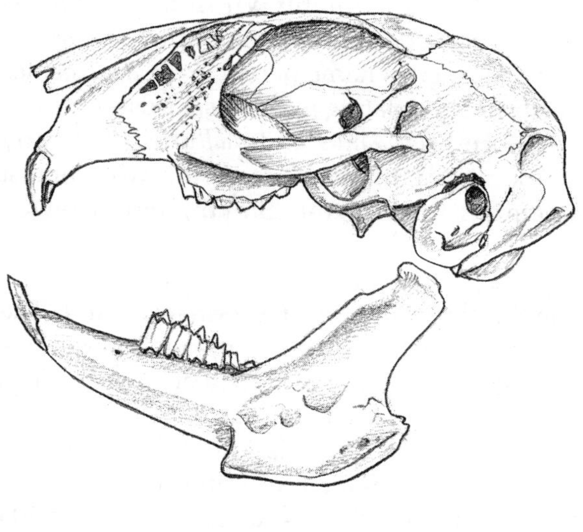

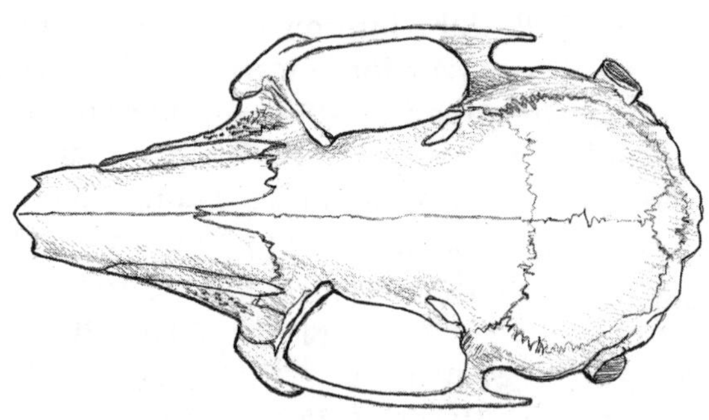

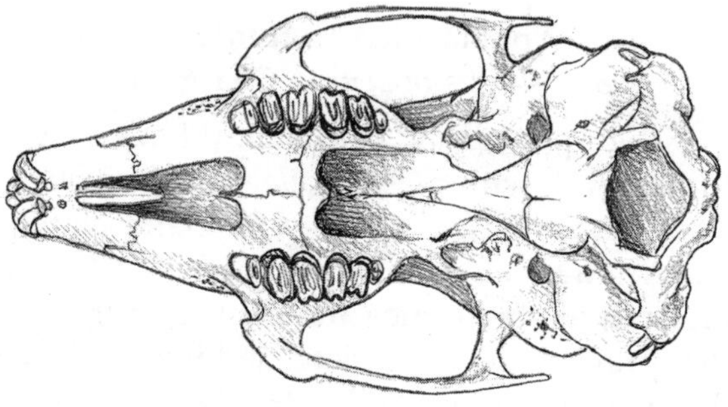

Figure 64. *Sylvilagus obscurus:* Left lateral view of skull and mandible, and dorsal and ventral view of skull. Scale bar = 20 mm.

present on the top of the head between the ears, and the anterior outer edges of the ears are bordered with black. The rufous or rusty nape patch characteristic of the eastern cottontail is lacking. Adult Appalachian cottontails are 350 to 450 mm long, including a 40 to 52 mm tail. They weigh between 0.9 and 1.5 kg.

The skull of this species is smaller and more delicate than that of the eastern cottontail and possesses markedly smaller auditory bullae. The supraorbital process decreases in width anteriorly and ends against the skull with no anterior process or notch. The posterior extension of the supraorbital process tapers throughout its length and usually does not touch the skull, although the very tip occasionally may be in contact (Figure 64).

Distribution. The Appalachian cottontail is a forest-dwelling rabbit that occurs:

> *only within the Appalachian Mountain chain, its marginal plateau and mountain balds from the Hudson River southwest through Pennsylvania, Maryland, West Virginia, Virginia, Tennessee, North Carolina, South Carolina, Georgia, and Alabama* (Chapman et al., 1992).

This species is never very abundant and is considered rare over most of its range. Because of its close resemblance to the eastern cottontail, distinguishing between the two requires critical examination of individuals.

Concerning its distribution in Virginia, Handley (1991) stated:

> Sylvilagus transitionalis [Sylvilagus obscurus] *was poorly known in Virginia in 1978. Specimens had been taken in forested areas above 600 m asl at widely scattered localities in eight counties between the northern Blue Ridge and the far southwestern part of the state. In the absence of persuasive local data, we were swayed by the studies of Chapman and Morgan (1973) in West Virginia and Maryland to believe that* Sylvilagus transitionalis *might be declining in Virginia because the species seemed to be declining over a wide area from West Virginia to Appalachian* (Handley and Gordon, 1979)....*Handley and Gordon (1979) recommended that high priority should be given to the study of the status of* Sylvilagus transitionalis *in Virginia. Consequently the Virginia Department of Game and Inland Fisheries conducted a two-year study of* Sylvilagus transitionalis (Fies and Coggin, 1985). *Two hundred cottontails were collected above 610 m asl in western Virginia. Seventy of these, from 17 of the 19 counties sampled, proved to be* Sylvilagus transitionalis. *This extends to 23 the number of counties in Virginia known to be inhabited by* Sylvilagus transitionalis.

Handley and Gordon (1979c) noted that although most southern records are from high elevations, the presence of extensive forest without significant openings may be a more important limiting factor than elevation. In Virginia, this species has been taken at elevations as low as 458 m in Dickenson County. Blymyer (1976a) recorded these rabbits between 549 and 653 m on Sinking Creek Mountain in Craig County. Approximately 90 percent of the cottontails taken between 573 and 604 m were *Sylvilagus obscurus.* Chapman and Paradiso (1972) reported a specimen from 412 m in Garrett County, Maryland.

The Appalachian cottontail was listed as status undetermined in 1978 but was deleted from the list of Virginia's vulnerable mammals in 1989 (Handley, 1991). The known range of this species in Virginia is shown in Figure 65.

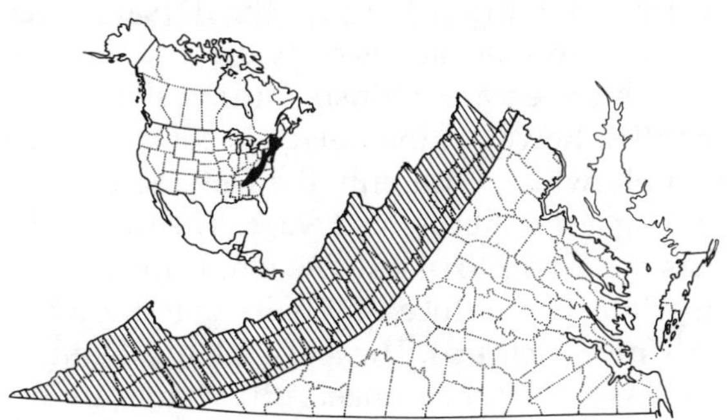

Figure 65. *Sylvilagus obscurus:* Range in Virginia and North America.

Studies in Maryland and West Virginia have shown that originally *Sylvilagus floridanus* and *Sylvilagus obscurus* were ecologically segregated (Chapman and Morgan, 1973; Chapman, Harman, and Samuel, 1977). Clearing the land for agricultural use has reduced habitat suitable for the Appalachian cottontail, while creating and improving habitat for the eastern cottontail. The eastern cottontail outcompetes the smaller and less aggressive Appalachian cottontail and displaces it on cleared and cultivated land. The eastern cottontail is abundant and spreading, while in Maryland and West Virginia the Appalachian cottontail has suffered a decline in distribution and abundance because of the loss of deep woods.

Handley (1991) noted that "massive stocking with exotic midwestern cottontails to temporarily improve hunting in the eastern states" has also proven detrimental to *Sylvilagus transitionalis [Sylvilagus obscurus].* Fortunately, Virginia cottontails have been minimally disturbed by such stocking.

Fies and Coggin (1985) stated:

> *Areas that were suited for* S. transitionalis [Sylvilagus obscurus] *may have been colonized by* S. floridanus *after the land was cleared for agriculture. Other areas, however, are probably being recolonized by* S. transitionalis *as farmland is abandoned and old fields are reforested. Since most of the habitats preferred by Appalachian cottontails are remote and at high elevations, we suspect that the populations of* S. transitionalis *in Virginia have remained relatively stable for at least 50 years.*

Records of this species from the District of Columbia and Alexandria (Nelson, 1909) were later shown to be invalid by Bailey (1923). Two of the specimens were erroneously included under this species, while the Alexandria record, which was based on a specimen purchased by Bailey, was later determined to have probably come from West Virginia.

Habitat. The Appalachian cottontail inhabits woods, shrubby areas, and brushy areas, preferring thicker wooded cover than the eastern cottontail. In Virginia, it has been found most often in mixed yellow birch-red maple forest, with glades of red spruce and rhododendron and small irregular shrubby openings. It has also been taken in and near areas of hemlock and rhododendron in oak-hickory forest (Handley and Gordon, 1979c).

Habits. The Appalachian cottontail is one of the most secretive and least known members of the genus *Sylvilagus.* Hamilton (1943) noted that the habits and behavior of this species do not differ from those of the eastern cottontail. He noted that they become active and begin feeding as dusk approaches and that they are particularly active during the hours immediately after sunset. Home range varies from 0.2 to 0.7 ha (Dalke, 1937).

Pringle (1960) found that New England cottontails *(Sylvilagus transitionalis)* emitted a characteristic type of call when disturbed which he described as a series of "ticks," sometimes a combined "tick-squeak". Eastern cottontails were never heard making such sounds.

Ruedas et al. (1989) examined chromosomal variation in this species from several states, including Virginia. Their data showed that *Sylvilagus transitionalis [obscurus]* from Virginia and West Virginia has 2N = 46 karyotypes.

Food. Dalke (1937) reported that 56 percent of the diet of New England cottontails during the summer in Connecticut consisted of grasses and clovers, 20 percent of herbaceous and shrubby plants including fruits and seeds, and 24 percent of herbage, twigs, buds, seeds, and fruit pulp. Autumn and winter foods included many of the common shrubby and herbaceous plants.

Reproduction and Development. Bailey (1946) stated that Appalachian cottontails in Virginia produced three or four litters per year beginning in April and May. Litter size was between four and eight, and the young were weaned at three to four weeks of age.

In western Maryland and West Virginia, the breeding season extends from early March to early September with the peak of reproductive activity between March and July. The gestation period is believed to be 28 days. Average litter size was 3.6, with first litters averaging smaller than succeeding ones (Chapman, 1975; Chapman et al., 1977).

Tefft and Chapman (1983) recorded a female in western Maryland that gave birth to litters on April 11, May 9, and June 6. The three litters contained 15 young. Crown-rump measurements averaged 73.8 mm. By seven days of age, they were able to stand on their feet and their eyes were from half to nearly fully open. By 10 days the eyes were fully open and the young were able to sit rabbit-like. By 16 days, they were completely independent of the nest and could run and hop quickly.

Nests may be located in either wooded or open areas. In Connecticut, Dalke (1937) reported that "43 percent were in brush, 25 percent in woods, 16 percent in hayfields, and 16 percent in grasslands other than hayfields." The usual nest consists of a depression approximately 10 cm deep and 13 cm wide. Nests in the open were lined and capped with fur and grass, which in turn, were covered by leaves and twigs. Nests were constructed at night (Dalke, 1942).

Parasites. The nematode *Dermatoxys veliger* was recorded from this species in Giles County, Virginia (Holloway, 1966). The ticks *Haemaphysalis leporis-palustris* and *Ixodes dentatus* have been recorded by Sonenshine, Lamb, and Anastos (1965). The botfly (*Cuterebra* sp.) has been reported from this species in Giles County by Jacobson, McGinnes, and Catts (1978).

Predation. Appalachian cottontails are probably preyed upon by many of the same predators as the eastern cottontail.

Location of Specimens. AEL, BCV, CM, FSM, PWRC, SNP, UMMZ, USNM, VCU, VPI-W.

Genus *Lepus*

Dentition: 2/1, 0/0, 3/2, 3/3 = 28

Snowshoe Hare
Lepus americanus Erxleben

Description. The snowshoe hare (Plate 35) is the only lagomorph in Virginia that is brown in summer and white in winter. During the warmer months of the year the dorsal pelage of the snowshoe hare is rusty brown. The chin and abdomen are whitish. During the winter months, however, the pelage becomes almost entirely white, with only the feet and ears retaining a slight brownish wash. The tips of the ears are dusky to black. The white appearance in winter is produced by hairs that are white only near their tips. The feet are large. Females possess 8 to 10 mammae. Adult hares are between 375 and 550 mm in total length, including a tail 40 to 65 mm long. The ears are 90 to 100 mm long, while the hind foot averages between 130 and 155 mm. Adults weigh between 0.9 and 2.3 kg.

The braincase is depressed posteriorly. The tips of the anterior and posterior supraorbital processes are not in contact with the cranium. The interparietal bone is fused with the parietals (Figure 66).

Distribution. This species is found south of the tundra in northern Alaska and Canada, south to the northern conterminous United States. In the western United States, the range continues south in the mountains to California, Nevada, Utah, Colorado, and New Mexico. In the eastern United States, the range extends southward in the Appalachian Mountains to eastern Tennessee.

DeKay (1842) stated that the snowshoe hare had been found on one of the highest mountains in the northern part of Virginia. Audubon and Bachman (1846) noted:

Mr. Doughty informed us that he had procured a specimen on the Alleghany Mountains in the Northern part of Virginia, Lat. 40° 29', where it had never before been observed by the inhabitants. On seeking for it afterwards in the locality from which he obtained it, we were unsuccessful, and we are inclined to believe that it is only occasionally that some straggler wanders so far South among these mountains, and that its Southern limit may be set down at about 41.

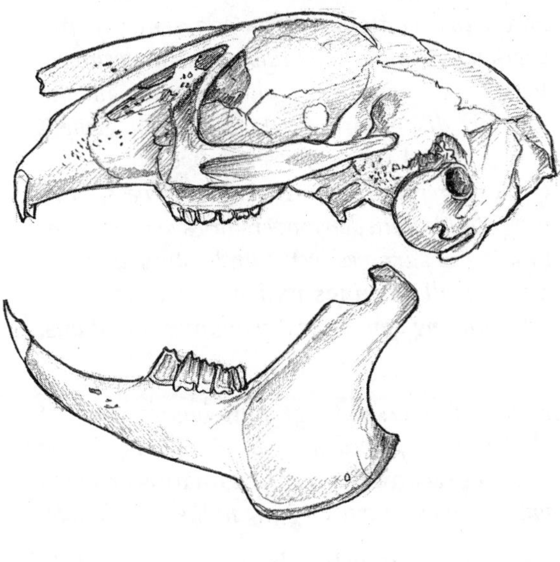

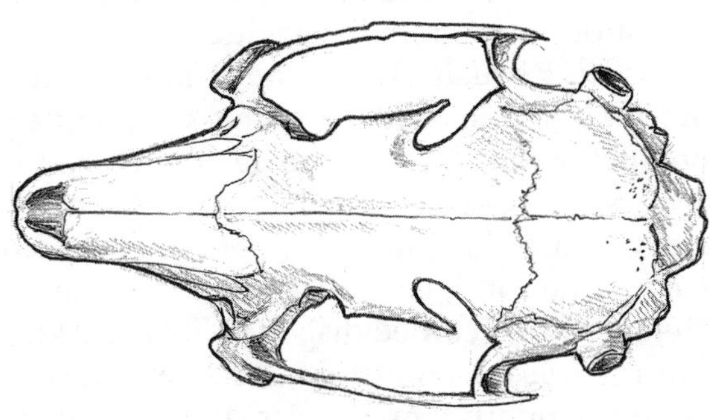

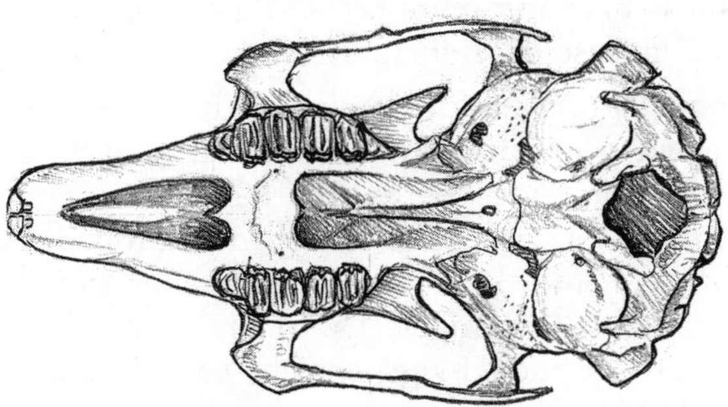

Figure 66. *Lepus americanus:* Left lateral view of skull and mandible, and dorsal and ventral view of skull. Scale bar = 20 mm.

Lee (1987) recorded notes from William Fisher in 1895 who stated that the range "extends along the Alleghany range into Virginia." Bangs (1895) also stated that its range extended down the Alleghanies to Virginia and North Carolina. Brimley (1905) noted that it "occurs in the Alleghanies as far south as Virginia."

The native geographic variant, *Lepus americanus virginianus,* has been officially classified as endangered in Virginia (Handley, 1979b; 1991). The known range of this species in Virginia is shown in Figure 67. Handley (1991) stated:

Before logging from 1890 to 1910 destroyed most red spruce forests in Virginia, the snowshoe hare probably was widespread in the western part of the state. By 1978, hare populations were estimated to number only dozens, or perhaps hundreds, of individuals. These populations inhabited 50 to 60 square kilometers where red spruce survived in northwestern Highland County contiguous with snowshoe hare range in West Virginia.

During the 1960s and 1970s, the fragile residual population was stressed by repeated introductions of exotic taxa, primarily Lepus americanus struthopus *from New Brunswick. Luckily, the native genotype survived these introductions, while the exotic taxon seems to have disappeared without leaving a trace.*

Hunting was permitted until 1990 . . . and the season on hares was closed. By then the population had dwindled to no more than a few dozen hares in a 25 square kilometer area (M. L. Fies, personal communication).

Fies (1991) stated: "*Lepus americanus virginianus* is known in Virginia only from three sites in northwestern Highland County. Reports from elsewhere in the Alleghanies and in the Blue Ridge are unverified."

Introductions of nonnative snowshoe hares occurred in 1961 on Laurel Fork in Highland County (50 hares), between 1972 and 1974 at several localities in Giles and Bland counties (257 hares), in 1973 on private property in Grayson County (24 hares), and again in Highland County in 1978 (158 hares). These releases were probably the variant identified as *Lepus*

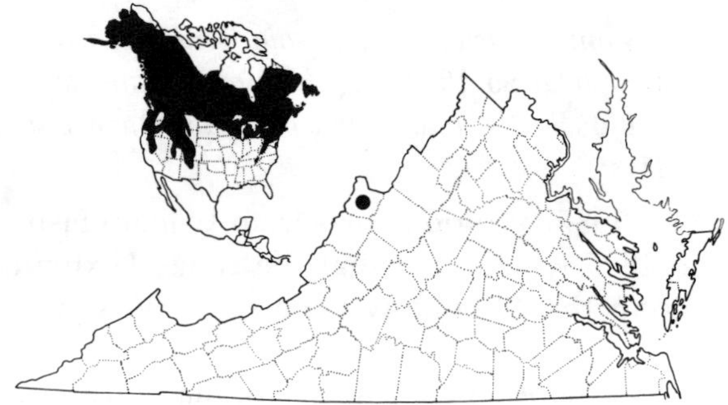

Figure 67. *Lepus americanus:* Range in Virginia and North America.

americanus struthopus and were obtained from New Brunswick (Fies, 1990). The history and details of these introductions are given by August (1974a; 1974b), Lowman (1975), and Handley (1979b; 1991). Handley (1991) stated: "Predictably and fortunately, the introductions of *Lepus americanus struthopus* failed. Today there is no trace of this subspecies in Virginia or West Virginia."

Beginning in January, 1989, the Virginia Department of Game and Inland Fisheries began a restocking program using native hares trapped in neighboring West Virginia (Fies, 1990). Captured animals were released into suitable habitat on George Washington National Forest. All were equipped with radio collars in order to monitor their movements. Twenty-six hares were trapped and relocated to the Laurel Fork area of Highland County (Fies, 1992). Twenty-four hares survived an average of 23.8 days post-release. The primary causes of mortality were predation by bobcats and by other unknown predators.

Habitat. In Virginia, the range of the snowshoe hare coincided rather closely with the range of red spruce *(Picea rubens).* Most areas containing spruce, however, have been clear-cut, cleared, and burned, and only a few small stands survive today. In Highland County, the snowshoe hare survives "in a high, cold area of second growth yellow birch-red maple forest, with scattered spruce thickets, extensive tangles of Rhododendron, thick brush, patches of bog and marsh, and small openings with brambles, mountain laurel, and scrubby yellow birch" (Handley, 1979b).

The presence of adequate understory cover is a critical attribute of snowshoe hare habitat. In Virginia, mountain laurel provides most of this. Fies (1991) stated:

Loss of habitat due to even-age succession of forests is the primary threat to remaining populations of snowshoe hares in Virginia. In recent years, absence of timber harvesting has resulted in loss of second growth forest and its cover. The overstory canopy of forest that once had thick stands of mountain laurel has closed to the point that the understory is thinning out. Forest that contained hares as recently as five years ago is now unsuitable and unoccupied. Very few areas with adequate cover remain and they are disappearing....Habitat management is urgent and critical for snowshoe hare in Virginia. Carefully planned timber harvest, thinning stands with dense overstories where mountain laurel survives in the understory, and creating small openings in dense cover for summer foraging would greatly improve conditions.

Handley (1991) noted:

Even with a crash program to improve habitat to the quality needed by hares, it may be too late. Lepus americanus virginianus *probably will disappear from Virginia in the next decade.*

Habits. The snowshoe hare is nocturnal, foraging from dusk to dawn with periods of greatest activity at dusk and dawn. During daylight, snowshoe hares remain secluded beneath shrubs and brush. Throughout most of its range, this species undergoes marked population fluctuations on the average of once every 10 years. The average home range is approximately 5 to 10 ha, although movements of as much as 1.6 km have been recorded. August (1974a; 1974b) recorded dispersals up to 7.2 km from the release points for hares introduced into Giles County, Virginia. Fies (1992) recorded an average home range of 78.9 ha for eight hares surviving more than 30 days following their release in Highland County.

Food. During summer, snowshoe hares feed on a variety of succulent vegetation including grasses, legumes, herbs, and the tender parts of woody plants such as rhododendron, red spruce, hemlock, mountain laurel, blackberry, beech, birch, and maple. During the winter they browse on buds, twigs, and the bark of many kinds of trees. Brooks (1955) noted that wherever southern highbush cranberry *(Vaccinium erythrocarpum)* occurs, it appears to be the favorite food plant, and that it appears to be the key plant in maintaining sizable populations of hares in West Virginia. Occasionally, hares may feed on carrion. Snowshoe hares are coprophagous, ingesting fecal pellets to extract additional nutrients.

Reproduction and Development. Snowshoe hares usually produce two to four litters each containing two to four young between April and August. Gestation is approximately 36 to 37 days, with the female becoming impregnated within a day after giving birth. The female does not construct a nest for her precocial young, which are fully furred and have their eyes open at birth. When 10 to 12 days of age, they begin feeding on grasses, although weaning does not take place until they are four to six weeks of age. Both males and females become sexually mature in their second year (Godin, 1977).

Longevity. Wild hares may live as long as four to five years, although captive individuals have lived up to eight years. Fies (1991) noted that "most hares do not live more than two years."

Parasites. August (1974a) recorded the following parasites from animals that died during shipment from Canada to Virginia: **Protozoa** (protozoans) *(Dirofilaria scapiceps);* **Cestoda** (tapeworms) *(Taenia cysticem);* and **Nematoda** (roundworms) *(Obeliscoides cuniculi, Protostrongylus scapiceps, Trichostrongylus* spp., *Trichuris leporis).*

Geographic Variation. The subspecies in Virginia is *Lepus americanus americanus* Erxleben.

Location of Specimens. USNM, VPI-W.

Black-Tailed Jackrabbit
Lepus californicus Gray

Description. The introduced black-tailed jackrabbit (Plate 36) has grayish-brown fur and large, black-tipped ears. This is in contrast to the snowshoe hare which is brown in summer and white in winter. A black middorsal stripe is present on the top of the jackrabbit's tail and extends onto the base of the rump. The snowshoe hare lacks a black stripe on the tail. Females possess six mammae. Adult jackrabbits are between 475 and 600 mm long, including a tail 75 to 100 mm long. The hind foot varies from 115 to 140 mm in length. Adult jackrabbits weigh between 1.3 and 3.2 kg.

The upper outline of the rostrum and frontal region of the skull is distinctly curved. The postorbital process touches the skull at its posterior tip, enclosing a large oval foramen (Figure 68).

Distribution. This is the most abundant and widespread species of jackrabbit, ranging over most of the western United States and Mexico. It has been successfully introduced into several localities including Massachusetts, Kentucky,

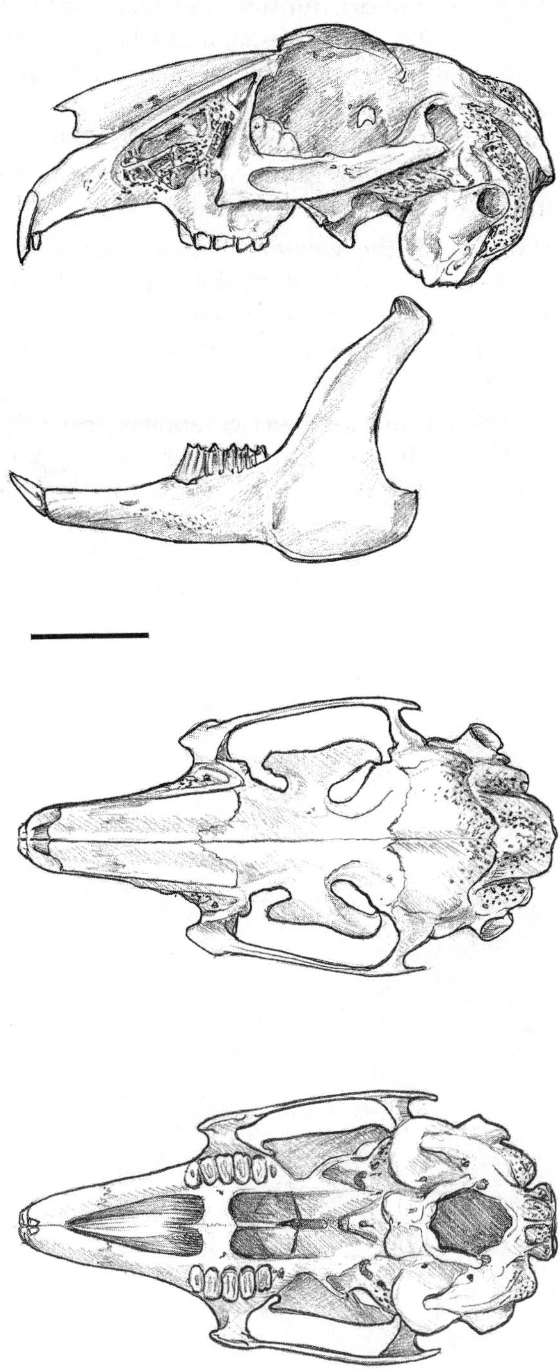

Figure 68. *Lepus californicus:* Left lateral view of skull and mandible, and dorsal and ventral view of skull. Scale bar = 20 mm.

Florida, and Virginia.

In Virginia, jackrabbits were reportedly released by sportsmen in Loudoun and Prince William counties (Anonymous, 1950h). In addition, six adult and two young jackrabbits from Kansas were released on Cobb Island in Northampton County by Harvey L. Bowen of Willis Wharf. This introduction was for the purpose of sport hunting and took place in about 1960 (Clapp, Weske, and Clapp, 1976). Since that time a breeding population has become established on Cobb Island, and individuals have been observed on Little Cobb Island to the south, Rogue and Hog islands to the north, and Castle Ridge to the west.

Habitat. In the western United States, the black-tailed jackrabbit inhabits the grasslands and open, sparsely vegetated deserts. In Virginia, it has adapted to the stabilized dunes and beach grass.

Habits. The black-tailed jackrabbit is primarily nocturnal. It spends the daylight hours partially concealed in a clump of grass or near the base of a tree. It is able to run at speeds up to 56 km per hour, and can leap 6 m at a jump if in a hurry. They swim well.

Food. A variety of green vegetation makes up the diet of the black-tailed jackrabbit. During the summer, fresh and herbaceous plants provide the major food, while in winter jackrabbits feed primarily on woody and dried herbaceous vegetation. Coprophagy, or reingestion of green fecal pellets, occurs in this species.

Reproduction and Development. In the western United States, breeding in the black-tailed jackrabbit occurs from December to September. A litter, usually consisting of two to four young, is born after an average gestation period of 40 to 43 days (Dunn et al., 1982). At birth, young jackrabbits are fully furred and have their eyes open.

Geographic Variation. The subspecies in Virginia is *Lepus californicus californicus* Gray.

Location of Specimens. USNM.

Rodents

The order Rodentia, the rodents, contains a large group of small to medium-sized mammals readily recognizable by their chisellike incisor teeth that are specialized for gnawing. Only four incisors are present, two in the upper jaw and two in the lower, and they grow continuously throughout life. Enamel is restricted to the anterior face of the incisor teeth. The softer dentine of the back of the tooth wears more rapidly than does the hard enamel; thus a sharp, chisellike cutting edge is maintained. There is no nerve in the tooth except at the growing base. Canine teeth are absent. A diastema separates the premolars from the incisors. The grinding surface of the cheek teeth have many peculiar patterns produced by the soft dentine and hard enamel arranged in various ways. The arrangement is constant for the different groups of rodents and is a basis for much of their classification. In some rodents, such as the Sigmodontinae, the molars are rooted and cusped and, once fully developed, cease growing. In the Arvicolinae (the microtines), the molars are open at the base, grow throughout life, and have crowns which form a complicated pattern of loops and triangles. A fold of velvety or furred skin is present between the incisors and the rest of the mouth.

The rodent's lower jaw is somewhat loosely articulated to the skull, thus allowing for an anteroposterior as well as a rotary, side-to-side movement of the jaw. When the jaw shifts forward to engage the incisors, the cheek teeth disengage. When the jaw shifts backwards to the cheek teeth for crushing or grinding food, the incisors are disengaged. In addition, the lower tooth rows are closer together than the uppers, and only the teeth of one side can be fully occluded at any given time. Thus, rodents chew with a side-to-side or slightly rotary motion of the lower jaw. Some rodents have either internal or external cheek pouches that open near the angle of the mouth. Rodents are primarily herbivorous, although animal foods contribute significantly to the diets of some species.

Rodent life-styles are highly variable. Most are active throughout the year, although summer or winter periods of inactivity (aestivation or hibernation) occur in many species. Rodents may be terrestrial, fossorial, arboreal, or semiaquatic. In addition, some forms can glide. Rodents walk on the entire foot or hand (plantigrade). Most species have four toes on their front feet and five toes on their hind feet.

Members of the order Rodentia are distributed nearly worldwide and comprise approximately 40 percent of the named species of mammals in the world. Living rodents are believed to exceed all other living mammals combined in actual numbers. Many of them serve as a source of food for predators. This order also contains some of the most economically important furbearers. The quest for furs, especially beaver, provided incentive for early exploration of the western United States and Canada.

The order Rodentia can be subdivided into two suborders based on the arrangement of the masseter (jaw) muscle: Sciurognathi (squirrel-like and mouse-like rodents), which encompasses the squirrels, woodchuck, chipmunks, beaver, muskrat, and most of the mice and rats; and Hystricognathi (porcupine-like rodents), which includes porcupines and the South American rodents such as the nutria (Nowak, 1991). Some researchers, however, do not believe that this classification reflects the true relationships among rodents (Nowak, 1991).

Chipmunks, Woodchucks, and Squirrels (Family Sciuridae)

Members of the family Sciuridae have evolved in several directions and have become adapted to living under a wide range of conditions. They are found throughout most of the tropical and temperate regions of the world. This family contains the tree squirrels, flying squirrels, ground squirrels, prairie dogs, marmots, and chipmunks. Most members of this family are diurnal with the exception of the nocturnal flying squirrels.

These mammals have rather large eyes and a well-haired tail. The limbs have four toes on the front feet and five toes on the hind feet. Internal cheek pouches are present in chipmunks.

Sciurids are characterized by a small infraorbital canal through which the masseter (jaw) muscle does not pass. Prominent postorbital processes are present. Two premolars develop in the upper jaw. The first one is shed at maturity in some forms so that either four or five molariform (premolar and molar) teeth may be present in the upper jaw. Four molariform teeth are present in the lower jaw. The molariform teeth are rooted and are usually low-crowned. Auditory bullae are present and prominent.

This family is divided into two subfamilies — the typical ground and tree-living forms, Sciurinae; and the flying squirrels, Petauristinae.

Key to Species of Sciuridae

1a Body skin forming lateral gliding membrane between fore and hind limbs
.... 2

1b No gliding membrane present
.... 3

2a Size smaller; hind foot less than 33 mm; belly hairs totally white
.... *Glaucomys volans*

2b Size larger; hind foot more than 33 mm; bases of belly hairs usually grayish at the base
.... *Glaucomys sabrinus*

3a Infraorbital opening a foramen rather than a canal; body with five blackish and four pale longitudinal stripes; cheek pouches present
.... *Tamias striatus*

3b Infraorbital opening a canal; no longitudinal stripes; cheek pouches absent
.... 4

4a Tail short, flattened, less than one-quarter of total length; incisors white; top of skull flattened; postorbital processes broad and nearly at right angles to skull
.... *Marmota monax*

4b Tail bushy, more than one-quarter of total length; incisors yellow or orange; top of skull convex; postorbital processes not at right angles to skull
.... 5

5a Anterior border of orbit ventrally opposite first large molariform teeth; total length less than 400 mm
.... *Tamiasciurus hudsonicus*

5b Anterior border of orbit ventrally opposite second large molariform teeth; total length more than 400 mm
.... 6

6a Total teeth 20; four molariform teeth in upper jaw; belly tawny; tail hairs yellow-tipped
.... *Sciurus niger*

6b Total teeth 22; five molariform teeth in upper jaw with first reduced in size; belly white, often streaked with brown; tail hairs white-tipped or silvery
.... *Sciurus carolinensis*

Genus *Tamias*

Dentition: 1/1, 0/0, 1/1, 3/3 = 20

Eastern Chipmunk
Tamias striatus (Linnaeus)

Description. The eastern chipmunk (Plate 37) is a small, fairly stout-bodied, terrestrial squirrel with conspicuous dorsal stripes, a flattened and hairy tail, and large, well developed, internal cheek pouches. The overall dorsal coloration is tawny or reddish-brown with the shoulders tending toward grayish and the rump toward reddish. Five conspicuous dark dorsal stripes are present. The middorsal dark stripe is bordered by fur similar to the general body color. On each side, a broad whitish longitudinal stripe is bordered by two dark stripes. Two buff stripes are present on each side of the face above and below the eyes. The ears are prominent and rounded. The tail is well-furred but not bushy. The underparts are white. Females possess eight mammae. Adult eastern chipmunks are usually between 220 and 255 mm in total length, including a tail 75 to 100 mm long. They normally weigh between 70 and 140 g.

The Cherokee Indians have an interesting legend accounting for the chipmunk's stripes, as related by Chamberlain (1963):

> *After man had invented weapons, and began to hunt and kill the animals, birds, etc., the latter held a grand council to decide how to retaliate. After considerable discussion, it was determined that each of the creatures in question should visit upon man some disease or sickness; and this is why mankind is now subject to such afflictions. One alone, of all the animals, said he had no quarrel with man, and spoke against the retaliation proposed. This was the little ground-squirrel, whose action so incensed the other animals that they fell upon him and sought to tear him to pieces. He escaped, however, but bears the marks of the struggle to this very day.*

The skull is fairly long, flat, and narrow with rather weak zygomatic arches. Postorbital processes are broad at their bases and rather short. The infraorbital foramina are large and rounded. Auditory bullae are inflated. The upper incisors are short, moderately stout, and but slightly recurved (Figure 69).

Distribution. The eastern chipmunk inhabits the forests of eastern North America west to northeastern Louisiana, eastern Oklahoma, eastern Kansas, eastern Iowa, and eastern North Dakota. These animals range throughout the eastern United States north of a line from eastern Louisiana to central North Carolina, but south to western Florida. Their range extends northward into central Canada.

In Virginia, chipmunks are common and have been taken in most areas of the state, although they are uncommon in many of the coastal counties (Figure 70).

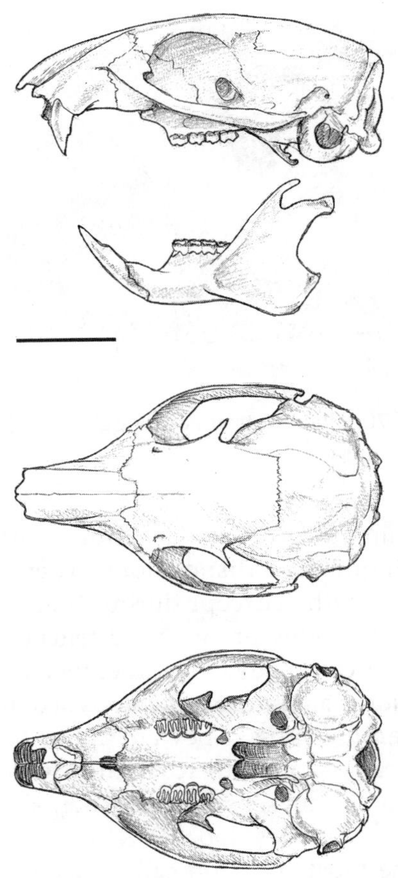

Figure 69. *Tamias striatus:* Left lateral view of skull and mandible, and dorsal and ventral view of skull. Scale bar = 10 mm.

Habitat. Chipmunks live in deciduous forests and brushy areas, especially near broken rocky ground, stone fences, and fallen logs.

Habits. The eastern chipmunk belongs to a group of squirrels that spend most of their existence on the ground rather than in trees. They can climb well, however, and occasionally they do climb up stumps or trees to feed or to es-

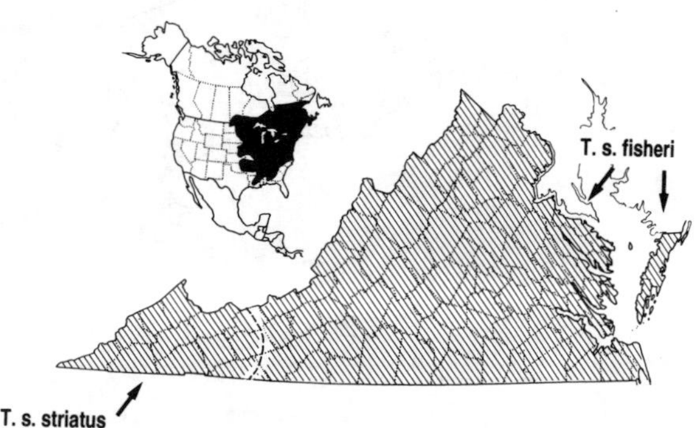

Figure 70. *Tamias striatus:* Range in Virginia and North America.

cape an enemy.

Chipmunks are solitary, diurnal mammals with inquisitive dispositions. They are not found together except during breeding and when the young are with the female. Family groups occasionally overwinter together. Their behavior is a mixture of nervous activity, curiosity, and shyness. They are apt to linger on the verge of safety to scold and chatter at an intruder. Their senses of hearing, sight, and smell are well developed.

The most common call or "song" of the chipmunk is a loud "chip" or "chuck" which may continue for several minutes without ceasing. This appears to be a mild warning to other chipmunks that danger may be near. Two other calls are a soft "cuck-cuck" which may also be repeated for several minutes but which does not arouse the neighboring chipmunks, and a combination of a loud chip with a trill — "chip-p-r-r-r-r-r." This latter call is an alarm and is usually accompanied by twitches of the tail and jerks of the body.

Chipmunks dig their own burrows, which may extend nine or more meters. Tunnels go straight down, then turn laterally. There is no mound of loosened soil at the entrance since the chipmunk either packs the earth as it goes or moves it several feet away from the entrance. A large living chamber that may be 30 cm or more in diameter is located within the burrow and normally contains a nest of dry plant material along with stored nuts and seeds. Other small "side pockets" are located at intervals along the passage. The intricacies of chipmunk burrow construction have been described by Panuska and Wade (1956) and Thomas (1974).

Seasonal activity patterns of the chipmunk seem to be a subject of controversy. There is quite clearly a period of relative inactivity during the summer months, although the causes of this lull have not been fully explained (Dunford, 1972). It is likely that more time is spent in the burrow when temperatures rise, and activity above ground is much less conspicuous than during spring or fall.

Although chipmunks enter into a deep hibernation, they do not store fat as other hibernators do and, thus, must awaken and feed at intervals. Active chipmunks have been observed in both northern and southern states during the winter. I have observed active animals in Blacksburg, Virginia, at temperatures as low as -9°C (15°F) and with 75 mm of snow on the ground. In more northern latitudes, chipmunks apparently have a fairly deep winter sleep, while in more southern areas they enter a torpid state during severe winter weather and then become active and can be seen above ground in midwinter when the weather is good.

Some chipmunks apparently subsist during the winter on food they have stored in their underground burrows. Audubon and Bachman (1851) described a chipmunk burrow and its inhabitants excavated in January, probably in New York State. The tunnel was located beneath 20 cm of leaves and 13 cm of snow.

> *The hole descended at first almost perpendicularly for about three feet. It then continued with one or two windings, rising a little nearer the surface until it had advanced about 8 feet, when we came to a large nest made of oak leaves and dried grasses. Here lay, snugly covered, three Chipping Squirrels. Another was subsequently dug from one of the small lateral galleries, to which it had evidently retreated to avoid us. They were not dormant, and seemed ready to bite when taken in hand; but they were not very active, and appeared somewhat sluggish and benumbed, which we conjectured was owing to their being exposed to sudden cold from our having opened their burrow.*
>
> *There was about a gill of wheat and buckwheat in the nest; but in the galleries we afterwards dug out, we obtained about a quart of the beaked hazel nut* (Corylus rostrata), *nearly a peck of acorns, some grains of Indian corn, about two quarts of buckwheat, and a very small quantity of grass seeds.*

The home range of this species ranges from about 0.10 to over 1.2 ha, probably depending upon the quality of the habitat and population density. Chipmunks prefer open-understory and closed-overstory habitats (Bowers, 1995). Analyses within individual home ranges by Bowers (1995) revealed more discriminating use of microhabitat at greater distances from their burrows than at closer distances. Home ranges overlap broadly, and only the portion that includes the burrow is defended against other chipmunks. The owner of the burrow is dominant only in his own territory. One chipmunk will enter the territory of another if tempted by an especially desirable food, but at the risk of being abruptly put to rout. Such territorial behavior apparently ensures adequate burrow spacing (Dunford, 1970). Chipmunks displaced from their normal home range exhibit homing ability over short distances, probably wandering at random until familiar territory is reached. Yerger (1953) recorded population densities ranging from 0.3 to 37.6 per ha. Jackson (1961) stated that population density averaged 5 to 10 per ha.

The chipmunk is not voluntarily a swimmer, but it can swim when occasion demands. Some wild individuals may become quite trusting of humans, even to the extent of accepting food from the hand.

Food. The chipmunk is chiefly a vegetarian and feeds mainly on the seeds (including nuts) of woody plants. Corn, wheat, the seeds of weedy plants, and berries are also eaten. The eastern chipmunk also has been known to eat earthworms, snails, insects, insect larvae, frogs, salamanders, small snakes, birds, bird eggs, and mice. In Virginia, chipmunks have been observed robbing a junco nest and capturing a young robin (Hostetter, 1939).

Storage of food is one of the chief daily activities of this species during the summer and fall with most foraging occurring during early morning and late afternoon. The large, internal cheek pouches greatly assist in transporting food to its underground storage chambers or to cache sites under bushes, in hollow logs, or beneath rocks. The pouches open between the lips and the molars and extend backward along the cheek and neck beneath the outer skin. When filled, each can be as large as the head. Food is placed in the cheek pouches by the forefeet and later is squeezed out by a forward motion of the feet. The cheek pouches of a chipmunk in New York were found to contain as many as 32 beechnuts.

Reproduction and Development. Eastern chipmunks produce litters in early spring and in midsummer, although it is not clear whether an individual female produces two litters in one year. After a gestation of about 31 days, a litter of two to eight (usually three to five) is born in a grass-lined chamber in the burrow system. A lactating female has been recorded from Montgomery County, Virginia, as late as October 26.

Newborn chipmunks are naked, have their eyes closed, and weigh about 3 g. The lateral stripes begin to show by the sixth day. The lower incisors erupt when the young are about one week old. The ears open and the upper incisors appear between 22 and 26 days (Allen, 1938). The eyes open in 30 to 31 days, and the young chipmunks venture from the burrow for the first time at five or six weeks of age. They are probably weaned before they are 40 days old. They are sexually mature at approximately three months, but most individuals do not breed for the first time until they are one year old (Yerger, 1955).

Longevity. The life span in the wild is probably between two and four years, although some have lived at least into year eight (Tryon and Snyder, 1973). In captivity, they have been known to live five to eight years (Godin, 1977).

Pelage Variations. Melanistic and albinistic individuals are rare but have been reported in other parts of the range. Information on molting in the chipmunk has been provided by Yerger (1955).

Parasites. The tick *Dermacentor variabilis* has been recorded from this species in Hanover County, Virginia, by Sonenshine, Atwood, and Lamb (1966). Hensley (1976b, 1978) reported botfly larvae, tentatively identified as *Cuterebra emasculator,* in 3 of 32 chipmunks in western Virginia. Holloway (1956b) recorded the acanthocephalan *Moniliformis clarki* from this species at Mountain Lake in Giles County, Virginia. Eckerlin and Painter (1994) recorded the louse *Hoplopleura erratica* from one of 26 chipmunks in northern Virginia, and Eckerlin and Painter (1995) recorded the giant flea *Tamiophila* *grandis* from two chipmunks from Burkes Garden in Tazewell County. Both represent new state records for Virginia.

Predation. The chipmunk may be preyed on by hawks, owls, weasels, mink, foxes, cats, opossums, and various kinds of snakes. Mitchell and Beck (1992) recorded its capture by free-ranging domestic cats in Henrico County, Virginia. Predation in Clarke County, Virginia by red-tailed *(Buteo jamaicensis)* and marsh *(Circus cyaneus)* hawks was reported by Bowers (1995).

Geographic Variation. The subspecies in Virginia is *Tamias striatus striatus* (Linnaeus). A dark form occurs in the southwesternmost counties. The head and rump are dark auburn, the sides of the body and face are deep cinnamon-buff, and the white dorsal stripes are washed with buff. A paler form with a much more grayish dorsum occurs throughout the remainder of the state.

Other Currently Recognized Subspecies. *Tamias striatus fisheri* (A. H. Howell)

Location of Specimens. AMNH, BCV, CAS, CHAS, CM, CU, CUC, DMNH, DWL, EHC, EKU, FSM, GMU, HSU, ISUVC, KU, LACM, LC, LFCC, LSUMZ, LU, MCZ, MSB, MVZ, NCSM, NVCC, ODU, OU, RC, RMWC, RU, SNP, SUVM, UCLA, UCM, UGAMNH, UMMZ, USNM, VCU, VHCC, VMNH, VPISU, VPI-W.

Genus *Marmota*

Dentition: 1/1, 0/0, 2/1, 3/3 = 22

Woodchuck
Marmota monax (Linnaeus)

Description. The woodchuck (Plate 38), also known as groundhog and whistle-pig, is the largest member of the family Sciuridae in Virginia. The specific epithet, *monax,* is an American Indian word meaning "the digger." The long, coarse pelage is yellowish-brown to brown and has a grizzled, or slightly frosted, appearance because of the intermixture of whitish, buff, or cinnamon-colored hairs. The softer underfur is dark gray at the base, but tipped with ocher or cinnamon. Whitish or buff areas are present on the sides of the face, nose, lips, and chin. The forelegs are overlaid with deep reddish-colored hairs, and the feet are dark brown to black. The well-haired, flattened tail varies from black to dark brown. The underparts vary from whitish-buff to brownish with the bases of the hairs blackish-brown.

These large, short-legged, terrestrial mammals have a heavyset body and a short tail. The head is broad and short, the nose is blunt, and the ears are low and rounded. The eyes are small. The thumb is small and rudimentary with a flat nail, but the remaining four claws on each front foot are strong and adapted for digging. The hind feet possess five clawed toes. The posterior pad on the sole of the hind foot is oval and is located near the middle of the sole. Females possess eight mammae. The head and body of adult woodchucks is normally between 550 and 675 mm long; the tail is usually between 100 and 175 mm in length. Adults generally weigh between 2.25 and 4.50 kg.

The braincase is broad and the zygomatic arches are wide-spreading. The interorbital region is much wider than the postorbital region. Postorbital processes are broad and are nearly at right angles to the long axis of the skull. The incisive foramina are normally widest posteriorly and narrowest anteriorly. The heavy incisors are pale yellow or ivory-colored on their front surfaces (Figure 71).

Distribution. The woodchuck is found from central Alabama and southeastern Oklahoma northward east of the central grasslands into Canada and westward nearly across Canada north of the grasslands. Clearing of dense forests has benefited the woodchuck, and the range of this species has increased since North America was first settled by Europeans.

In Virginia, the woodchuck occurs throughout the state except in the extreme southeastern portion (Figure 72).

Habitat. Woodchucks prefer the edges of brushy woodland, especially near open fields along streams or lake banks, fence rows, or railroad and highway rights-of-way. They may also be found in clearings, pastures, meadows, and grainfields, especially near the crest or top of a hill.

Habits. Woodchucks are diurnal and retire into their burrows at night. They are most active in early morning and late afternoon. As few as three of 24 hours may be spent outside of the burrow. Woodchucks dig their own burrows, each of which usually has one to five openings

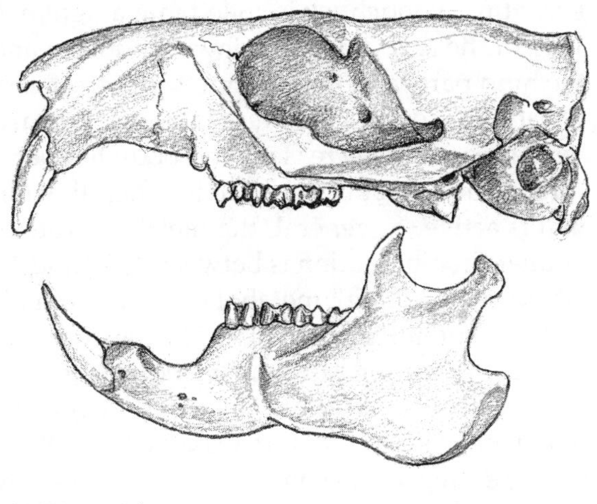

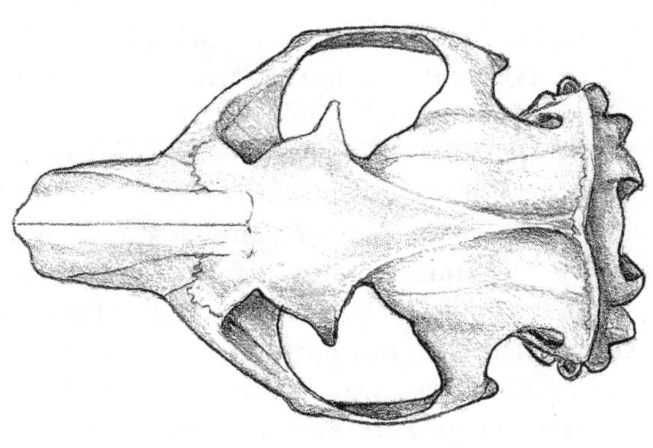

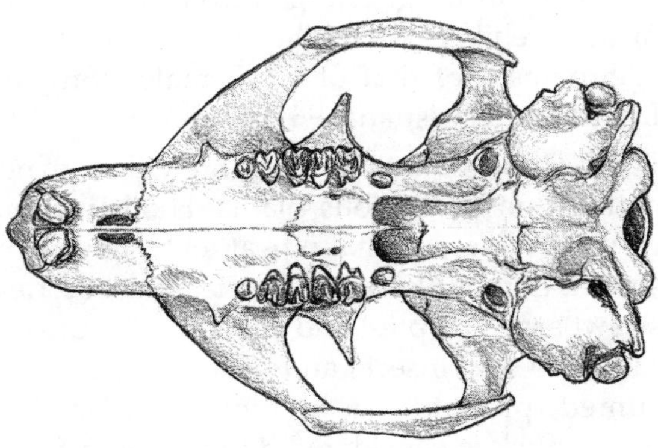

Figure 71. *Marmota monax:* Left lateral view of skull and mandible, and dorsal and ventral view of skull. Scale bar = 20 mm.

to the surface. The main entrance is marked by a pile of dirt, and fresh dirt on the mound signifies that the burrow is occupied. Entrances to "plunge holes," used for a quick exit from the ground surface, are usually well concealed and lack dirt mounds. Burrows may be up to 1.8 m deep and 7.5 to 9 m long. Offshoots of the main tunnel may contain nesting or hibernating chambers, while other branches may end in a chamber used for deposition of feces and urine. Feces may also be buried in the mound of dirt near the main entrance. Such "fertilizer" promotes plant growth, and vegetation may be higher and greener around a 'chuck hole.

Woodchucks are not sociable mammals, and usually only one adult is found in a burrow. Many other kinds of mammals utilize woodchuck burrows that have been abandoned or those in which an oblivious woodchuck may be hibernating. A reduction in the number of woodchucks often results in the lowering of the cottontail population, since these rabbits may be heavily dependent on woodchuck burrows. Other animals that may use a woodchuck burrow temporarily include skunks, foxes, opossums, raccoons, chipmunks, weasels, shrews, and various kinds of mice (Grizzell, 1955; Schmeltz and Whitaker, 1977). One den examined by Grizzell (1955) contained a dead rabbit and a short-tailed shrew *(Blarina brevicauda)* that had been feeding on the rabbit. Three snakes and a salamander were found in the surrounding soil. There is even an intriguing account of two woodchuck burrows that were used concurrently by fox and woodchuck families, each occupying separate nest chambers in the burrow system (Merriam, 1963).

Woodchucks occasionally climb into shrubs and small trees to feed, to sun themselves, or to escape an enemy. They have been observed sunning themselves 1.2 to 2.4 m above the ground on leaning trees and fence posts. Most of their activity, however, is confined to the ground. They walk with a waddling gait, oc-

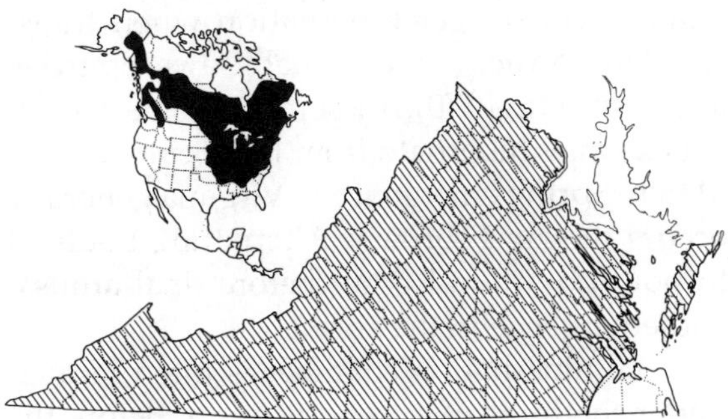

Figure 72. *Marmota monax:* Range in Virginia and North America.

casionally pausing to nibble vegetation or to rise on their haunches to glance around. Their eyesight is excellent, and their strength, tenacity, and vitality are remarkable. Woodchucks have been known to swim for considerable distances.

The average home range varies somewhat with the season, depending on availability of food near the burrow. The range is normally rather limited, within 60 to 90 m of the home burrow, although some may occasionally wander 180 to 240 m away. Hamilton (1934) stated that rufescent woodchucks "commonly travel a hundred yards from the den and may go an eighth of a mile when suitable food plants are not readily available." As Twichell (1939) pointed out, however, a woodchuck may never go far from its own den, but it may have several dens and thus be able to travel a considerable distance while always being near a place of refuge. These mammals are not migratory. Scent marking by muzzle rubbing is primarily used to advertise the occupation of a burrow (Ouellet and Ferron, 1988).

When startled, a woodchuck will usually utter a loud, shrill whistle. Alarm or fear is also expressed by grinding its teeth, and pleasure may be indicated by a low grunt or bark. Woodchuck vocalizations have been analyzed by Lloyd (1972).

Woodchucks are well-known hibernators. By the end of summer, most woodchucks have become very fat. The fat is metabolized during the winter and early spring and is necessary to sustain this species during its long period of hibernation, the length of which varies depending upon the length and severity of the winter. Entrance into hibernation is apparently caused by decreasing daylength. Research has demonstrated that blood from a hibernating animal will trigger hibernation when transfused into an active individual (Dawe, Spurrier, and Armour, 1970). In some regions woodchucks may hibernate from late September to March. Spring emergence in Virginia generally occurs during February. Alternating bouts of torpor and arousal occur before final arousal and emergence in the spring.

The hibernation chamber is often located under the roots of a tree or stump. Before the woodchuck goes to sleep, the hibernating chamber is isolated from the rest of the burrow by plugging the entrance with dirt. A hibernating woodchuck is coiled into a tight ball with the head resting on its lower abdomen and the hind parts and tail wrapped over the head. During this deep sleep, respiration and heartbeat are greatly decreased, and body temperature is considerably lower than when the animal is active. In general, the metabolic rate of animals in hibernation is between 1/30 and 1/100 of the "resting" metabolic rate of animals in the homoiothermic state. During hibernation, the breathing rate may be reduced to only one breath every five or six minutes, while the woodchuck's heartbeats may be as few as three beats per minute, in contrast to the normal rate of 80 to 95 beats per minute. Rectal temperature generally ranges between 6°C and 17°C during hibernation but may reach a low of 3°C (38°F). Normal summer readings range between 35°C and 40°C (95°F – 102°F).

Adult male woodchucks emerge from hibernation before the immature animals and the adult females. In Pennsylvania, loss of weight during hibernation ranged from 12.3 percent for young males to 29 percent for adult females. All woodchucks, but particularly adult males, continued to lose weight for some time after hibernation, presumably because of the absence of green food and the stress of reproductive activities. Total losses during the period of decline in weight ranged from 20.4 percent of the prehibernal weight of young males to 37.5 percent of that of adult males (Snyder, Davis, and Christian, 1961).

Food. These rodents subsist largely, though not entirely, on herbaceous plants. Foods include clover, grasses, alfalfa, wheat, oats, hay, corn, soybeans, pumpkins, raspberries, blackberries, strawberries, apples, and cherries. On rare occasions a few insects and snails may be consumed, probably as incidental items. The woodchuck is considered a nuisance to farmers not only because of what it eats but also because its large burrows may endanger livestock and machinery. The fact that it provides homes for "more desirable" species is perhaps redeeming.

Reproduction and Development. Woodchucks produce one litter annually, which normally consists of three to five young but may range from two to nine (Hamilton, 1934; Ferron and Ouellet, 1991). Breeding occurs shortly after the animals have emerged from hibernation in early spring. Gestation is 31 or 32 days. The young are born in an underground nesting chamber lined with such vegetable material as dried leaves, grasses, and weed stalks.

A study of this species in Virginia revealed that (1) it has a relatively short breeding season; (2) the reproductive activity of females is completed early in the year; (3) less than half of the yearling females examined ovulated; and (4) spermatogenesis was not evident in more than half of the yearling males examined (Ruckel et al., 1976).

At birth, the young are naked, blind, and helpless (Hamilton, 1934; Ferron and Ouellet, 1991). They weigh about 25 g. The eyes open between 20 and 26 days. Weaning occurs between four and five weeks of age, and the young are first seen outside the burrow at six to seven weeks of age. The young may remain with the female until midsummer, at which time each young digs its own burrow nearby. By fall, they are ready to disperse and find territories of their own. They may be sexually mature at one year but usually do not breed until they are two years old.

Longevity. Woodchucks in the wild have been known to live five to six years. In captivity, individuals have lived as long as nine years and eight months (Mann, 1930; Flower, 1931).

Pelage Variations. A pure white woodchuck was taken near Massanetta Springs in Rockingham County (Anonymous, 1953j). Molting in this species has been discussed by Davis (1966).

Parasites. The bacteria *Escherichia coli* and *Staphylococcus* have been recorded from woodchucks in Virginia (Virginia Wildlife Investigations Annual Report 1983–84, p. 141). Sonenshine, Lamb, and Anastos (1965), Jones (1978), Sonenshine and Stout (1971), and Sonenshine and Turner (1988) recorded the ticks *Dermacentor variabilis, Ixodes cookei,* and *Amblyomma americanum* from this species in Virginia. The nematode *Baylisascaris procyonis* was recorded from the state by Jacobson et al. (1976). *Histoplasma capsulatum* has been recorded by Emmons et al. (1955). Since 1961, rabies has been confirmed in 29 woodchucks in Virginia (see Tables 4 and 5 in the gray fox account).

Predation. Woodchucks are well protected by their alertness and their burrows. Some are taken, however, by birds of prey, dogs, bobcats, bears, foxes, weasels, and rattlesnakes, as well as by man. Many are killed by automobiles. I have eaten woodchuck and found it highly palatable.

Geographic Variation. The subspecies occurring in Virginia is *Marmota monax monax* (Linnaeus).

Location of Specimens. AMNH, AV, BCV, CM, CUC, EHC, FSM, GMU, HSU, KU, LC, LFCC, LU, MCZ, NCSM, NVCC, ODU, RMWC, RU, SNP, UCM, UCONN, UGAMNH, USNM, VCU, VLM, VPISU, VPI-W.

Genus *Sciurus*

Dentition: 1/1, 0/0, 1–2/1, 3/3 = 20 or 22

Eastern Gray Squirrel
Sciurus carolinensis Gmelin

Description. The eastern gray squirrel (Plate 39), a medium-sized tree squirrel, is generally gray above, with the head, midback, sides, and upper surfaces of the feet washed with yellowish-brown. In Virginia, it is most similar to the fox squirrel *(Sciurus niger)* from which it can be separated by the silvery-gray rather than yellowish or tawny underparts and tail. There is a white or off-white ring around the eye and white on the backs of the prominent ears. Grays predominate on the outer surfaces of the legs and feet, while the chin and underparts are usually whitish or silvery-gray. The hairs of the tail are banded blackish and tan, then tipped with white. The body fur is short, but the hairs of the tail are very long, giving the tail a bushy appearance. The sexes are colored alike, but the young tend to be grayer than adults. Cheek pouches are absent. Eight mammae are present in females. The head and body of adult gray squirrels is usually between 400 and 550 mm long; the tail is between 170 and 255 mm in length. Adult squirrels usually weigh between 360 and 650 g.

The skull is moderately long and broad. The rostrum is somewhat short and only slightly narrowed anteriorly. The front surface of the long and moderately heavy incisors is deep orange. Five molariform teeth are present in each side of the upper jaw of which the first, a premolar, is very small. Fox squirrels have four molariform teeth (Figure 73).

Distribution. The eastern gray squirrel inhab-

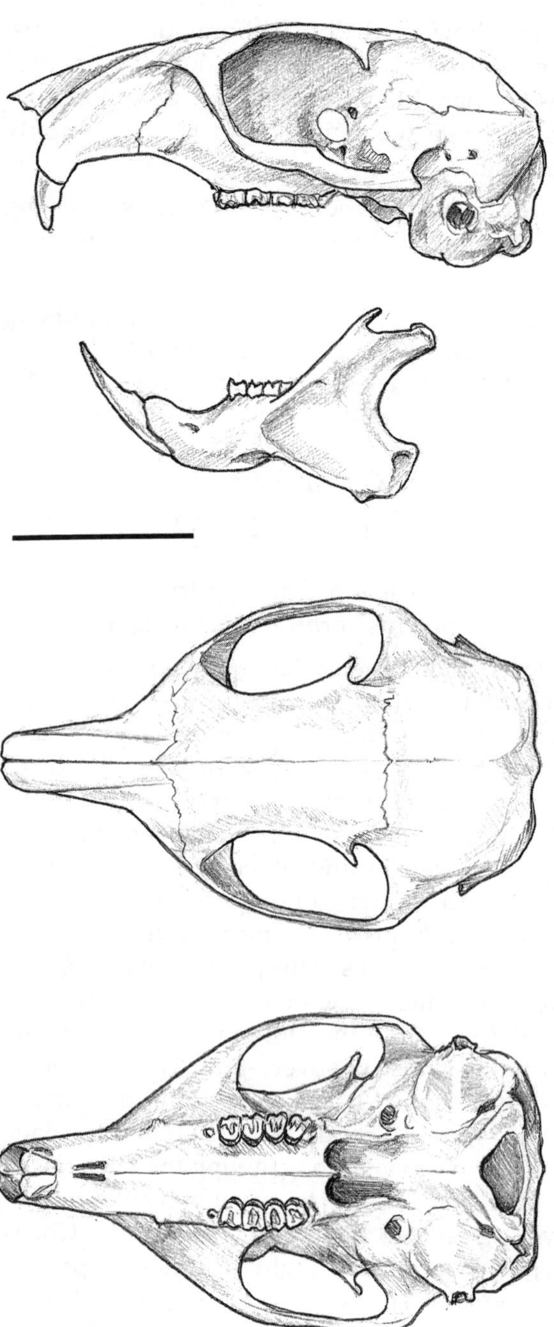

Figure 73. *Sciurus carolinensis:* Left lateral view of skull and mandible, and dorsal and ventral view of skull. Scale bar = 20 mm.

its the forests of eastern North America, extending westward from the Atlantic Ocean to the Great Plains and eastern Texas and south from southern Canada to the Gulf Coast. Its distribution is closely correlated with the distribution of the eastern hardwood trees, especially oak, hickory, and formerly chestnut. This squirrel is common throughout Virginia (Figure 74). These familiar mammals are extremely valuable members of our fauna, not only for their aesthetic appeal and tree-planting habit but also because of their status as a valuable game species.

Habitat. Gray squirrels occupy dense hardwood and mixed coniferous-hardwood forests, especially in ravines, slopes, and river bottoms. The twentieth-century gray squirrel is also an urban park dweller.

Habitats with trees suitable for dens are especially attractive to gray squirrels. In some areas, they are less abundant than in former times because of certain forestry practices such as removal of old trees and replacement of deciduous hardwood trees by even-aged pine stands. Overcutting lowland hardwood forests severely reduces squirrel populations. Other factors that have often been detrimental to gray squirrels include agriculture, fire, and grazing.

Habits. Gray squirrels are the most familiar tree squirrels in America. They are highly arboreal, usually living most of their lives in and around one nest tree and, in some areas, seldom traveling farther than 180 m from home in any one season. However, as different sources of food become available during the growing season, they may shift their home range one or more times and range over as much as an 8-km^2 area. Home ranges from different areas vary from 0.5 to over 20 ha, but are usually less than 5 ha (Don, 1983; Flyger and Gates, 1982). These differences are probably due to variations in habitat characteristics and population densities. Flyger (1960) reported an average male home range of 0.8 ha in Maryland and a female home range of 0.5 ha. Cordes and Barkalow (1973)

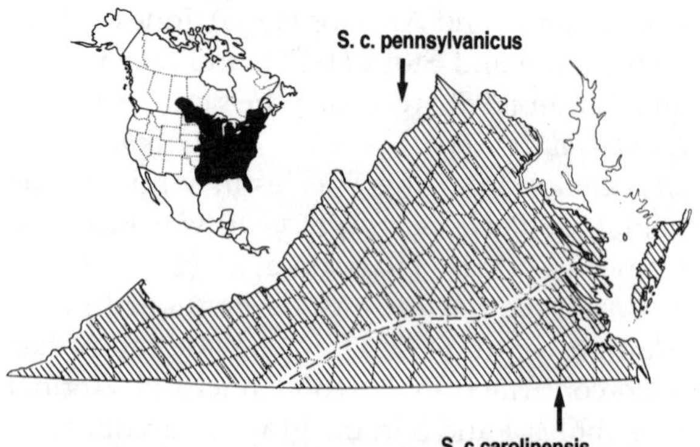

Figure 74. *Sciurus carolinensis:* Range in Virginia and North America.

reported an average home range of 0.7 ha, while Hougart (1975), using radiotelemetry, reported 1.8 ha. Home ranges are largest in spring and summer. Gray squirrels displaced from their homesite have been known to return from distances up to nearly 4.8 km (Hungerford and Wilder, 1941).

Population densities ranging from 0.5 to more than 20 per ha have been reported (Uhlig, 1955a; Flyger, 1959; Barkalow et al., 1970; Manski et al., 1981). In continuous woodlands in North Carolina, Barkalow et al. (1970) recorded densities usually less than 3 per ha. Densities in urban parks, however, may exceed 21 per ha (Manski et al., 1981).

Sometimes because of a failure of the nut crop or pressure from a high population, gray squirrels emigrate. Such movements were quite extensive in former times but are less so now. The stories of such emigrations told by pioneers and homesteaders of a hundred years ago seem almost incredible (Seton, 1920; Gurnell, 1987). According to these accounts, the great gray squirrel emigrations involved hundreds of thousands of animals. They seemed possessed with an unswerving desire to travel in a straight line. They crossed open prairies, climbed mountain crags, and swam roaring torrents. The bodies of hundreds of dead squirrels were strewn over the countryside or floated in streams, grim testimonials to the determination of the travelers.

Gray squirrels build a bulky nest of leaves and twigs in the crotch of a limb or else choose a hollow in some rotted trunk. Leaf nests may be constructed at any season when needed by a squirrel, but it is thought that the majority of leaf nests are built by young squirrels shortly after leaving the home nest and are extensively used during the summer months (Uhlig, 1956). A three-month-old squirrel which I raised constructed a large leaf nest in an oak tree. The ground beneath the tree became littered with cuttings, indicating that much potential nest material was either dropped or discarded. Dens in tree holes are superior to leaf nests in protecting squirrels from weather, natural enemies, and man.

Gray squirrels are diurnal. They do not hibernate but are active all year. They exit from their nests at first light of early morning. Their daily activity reaches a peak just before and after sunrise and again in late afternoon. The middle of the day finds them resting in the nest or sunning on a tree limb, although they are more apt to be active in the middle of the day on cool or cloudy days or late in the season. At dusk, they retire to their nests for the night. They are busiest during the fall when the nut crop is ripening and are least likely to be abroad during unusually cold weather, heavy rains, or high winds.

Gray squirrels are excellent climbers and can ascend to the top of a 24-meter-high tree in less than 20 seconds. They jump from limb to limb and tree to tree, lie flat on their abdomen on top of a limb (or on the ground) for concealment and for keeping cool in hot weather. They can hang by their hind claws head downward, and descend head downward almost as rapidly as they ascend. Their habit of descending a tree trunk in a head downward position led northern Indians to call the gray squirrel *adjidaumo,* meaning "head foremost," a name immortalized in Longfellow's *Song of Hiawatha.*

When traveling fast, gray squirrels make long leaps up to 1.5 m in length, and travel for short distances at rates up to about 24 km per hr. In trees, they may jump as much as 1.8 m from branch to branch on the same level and leap for 4.5 or more m downward.

The tail of a gray squirrel is a most versatile possession. It serves as a balancing agent as the squirrel performs its arboreal feats of agility, it may function as a sunshade, or it may be wrapped around the body for warmth. In a display of squirrel "language" for the benefit of an enemy, the tail is flicked rapidly from side to side.

Compared to most mammals gray squirrels are noisy and have a large vocabulary. One of the common calls is a "chur-r-r – chur-r-r – chur-r-r" given repeatedly and rapidly. This expresses excitement and is a warning to other squirrels. Nasal throaty grunts, purrs, or chattering of the teeth are given when one squirrel approaches another or when a person comes near a squirrel. These sounds may express affection or resentment. A rapid series of rasping "barking" notes — "quack-quack-quack-quaaaaaaa" — is given by both sexes when startled or irritated and also during the breeding season. Gray squirrel vocalizations and their significance have been discussed by

Bakken (1959); Flyger and Gates (1982); and Koprowski (1994).

Gray squirrels are gregarious and often congregate in considerable numbers. They are extremely alert and seem always to be totally "tuned in" to their surroundings. The senses of touch, sight, hearing, smell, and taste are all well developed (Koprowski, 1994).

Squirrels captured as adults often fare badly in captivity, a large percentage apparently going into shock as a result of confinement. With diligence, orphaned gray squirrels can be raised on a diet of milk, sugar, vitamins, and baby cereal. When young, they can be charming and affectionate pets. At about two months of age, their natural instinct to gnaw on anything and everything soon banishes them from the household. If released at an early age, they seem to adapt successfully to the natural world, while at the same time maintaining their association with humans. A female squirrel, born in September and raised by us, was released in November. She remained near the house and in a small adjacent wooded area. The following September, after several weeks of absence, she was noted to be lactating. Before and after this time, she remained quite tame, even occasionally entering the house of her own free will to doze in her favorite spot atop the living room draperies.

Food. The food of the gray squirrel is extremely varied, but a relatively few species of plants provide the important year-round staples. These are oaks and hickories of several species, black gum, and beech. The acorns, nuts, buds, and fruits of these trees are supplemented by those of other plants at various times of the year. Some woodlands may have one or two staple food items but lack enough variety to maintain sizable squirrel populations.

Acorns, other nuts, and fungi are the main foods in late summer, fall, and winter. Late winter is the most critical time for squirrels because much of the nut crop may be depleted and new spring growth may not have proceeded far. Stored nuts, as well as bark, immature buds, twigs, and waste corn tide squirrels over this difficult period. In early spring the buds, seeds, tender twigs, and flowers of elms, oaks, maples, and other trees are fed upon. Roots of herbs are dug and eaten. From about mid-May through summer, maple seeds, fruits, mushrooms, and corn in the milk stage are important in the diet. Insects and insect larvae may at times be important, and they form a significant part of the food of juvenile squirrels during late spring and summer. Eggs and young birds may be eaten occasionally. Bones such as the shed antlers of deer and turtle shells may be gnawed, and cattle salt blocks and soil are licked on occasion. These animal foods and soil are especially sought by breeding females and presumably are essential sources of calcium, phosphorus, and other mineral salts.

Nuts are usually buried singly. A small hole is dug, the nut is deposited and quickly covered over. After patting down the soil, the squirrel may rearrange or replace dry leaves or other debris over the site. Stored nuts have no particular ownership, and the members of a squirrel community share each other's efforts. The general position of stored food is probably located to a limited degree by a sense of memory, but many squirrels may just return to favorable areas. The actual position of individual nuts is located by a keen sense of smell. Nuts are more easily detected in moist soil than in dry soil. Many buried nuts are not recovered, and a large percentage of them sprout and eventually become trees.

An average gray squirrel consumes about two pounds of food a week. Ready access to water is an important part of optimum habitat. Gray squirrels are amazingly persistent in gaining access to bird feeders and hence are disliked by many householders. A pole-mounted feeder, equipped with a metal baffle and placed away from low-limbed trees, will usually foil the intruder.

Reproduction and Development. Virginia's gray squirrels have two main breeding periods each year, although a few litters are produced practically every month. The early mating season extends from January to early March with the litters born from February to April. Summer breeding is from late May to August with young produced from July to September (Kirkpatrick et al., 1976; Peery, 1948). Breeding and parturition occur slightly later in the mountains than in the Piedmont and Coastal Plain regions of the state. Cowles, Kirkpatrick, and Newell (1977) recorded pregnant gray squirrels during February, March, July, August, and September in Montgomery County, Virginia. Gestation is about 44 or 45 days. Data from Virginia, West Virginia, and other states suggest that gray squirrels average slightly more than one litter per year (Mosby, 1968b).

Average litter size in Virginia averages about 2.5 young, although litters consist of one to six young (Cross, 1946). The winter-spring litter is slightly smaller than the summer litter (Coggin, 1973). The young are cared for entirely by the female who may move them to a different location if the nest is disturbed.

Growth and development of young gray squirrels has been described by Shorten (1951) and Uhlig (1955). At birth the hairless young have their eyes and ears closed. They weigh about 14 g. By about three weeks, the dorsal body surface is haired, the lower incisors are appearing, and the ears begin to open. Most squirrels open their eyes at about 35 days, although there is considerable variation. The young come out of the nest for the first time when six to seven weeks old. At eight weeks they are half grown, fully furred, and have a bushy tail. Weaning occurs between 6 and 10 weeks, and the young gradually become self-sustaining. Young gray squirrels remain in family groups for four to five months. The litter born in the spring often remains with the female until summer, and the young born in late summer occasionally stay with the female during the winter.

Female gray squirrels typically produce their first litter when approximately one year old. Occasionally, however, some have produced young in the wild at less than 10 months of age. Such records are reviewed by Smith and Barkalow (1967), who also reported on precocious breeding in North Carolina. Included in their report are data for one female that bred when approximately 124 days old, the earliest age at which a wild female gray squirrel is known to have bred successfully.

Longevity. Although gray squirrels rarely live more than six years in the wild, Barkalow and Soots (1975) have recorded life spans up to 12.5 years in a natural population. Individuals in captivity have lived up to 15 years and 1 month (Mitchell, 1911).

Pelage Variations. Melanism and albinism, both partial and complete, are fairly often seen in this species. Baldwin (1969) reported a population of white (not albino) squirrels at Chickahominy Park Campground in James City County, Virginia. Published records of albino squirrels exist for Rockbridge County (Anonymous, 1949t) and Charles City County (Anonymous, 1950f). Melanistic specimens exist from Virginia Beach (VPISU) and Fairfax County (GMU). Bailey (1923) noted that black individuals had been introduced and liberated in the National Zoological Park and that they were evidently increasing, spreading, and breeding true to color. He stated:

> *Mr. N. Hollister, Superintendent of the Park, on March 11, 1919, contributed the following note: 'Two shipments of black squirrels have been received from Ontario and liberated in the Park. The first shipment of ten was from Rondeau Provincial Park, Morpeth, Ontario, May 18, 1906; and these squirrels were immediately liberated in the northwestern part of the Zoo where they were very much at home. They have since been constantly in the Park, especially from the vicinity of the great flight cage to the Klingle Valley, and they have spread northward to Cleveland Park and nearly to Chevy Chase. During the winter of 1919 two appeared near the Park Office and they are now frequently seen in the vicinity.'*

Innes and Lavigne (1979) reported that melanistic squirrels in winter pelage had significantly lower heat losses and lower basal metabolic rates than normal colored gray squirrels at ambient temperatures between -20°C and 25°C. Thus, melanistic squirrels appear to have a lower energy cost for existence during winter than do gray polymorphs. No differences were observed between color polymorphs in summer pelage.

Spring and fall molts in gray squirrels have been described by Sharp (1958).

Parasites and Disease. The following parasites have been recorded from this species in Virginia by Schwartz (1928); Shipley (1941); Cross (1942); Lucker (1943); Sonenshine, Lamb, and Anastos (1965); Hanson (1966); Lichtenfels (1970); Parker (1968; 1971); Parker and Holliman (1971a; 1971b); Sonenshine and Stout (1971); Davidson and Calpin (1976); Eckerlin (1985, 1992); Painter and Eckerlin (1993); and Guerrero (1994): **Protozoa** (protozoans) *(Eimeria wongi, Eimeria ontarioensis, Hepatozoon griseisciuri, Giardia* sp.*)*; **Nematoda** (roundworms)

(Ascaris lumbricoides, Bohmiella wilsoni, Capillaria americana, Citellinema bifurcatum, Contracaecum sp., *Enterobius sciuri, Gongylonema pulchrum, Heligmodendrium hassalli, Pterygodermatites parkeri, Rictularia coloradensis, Sciurodendrium gardneri, Strongyloides robustus, Syphacia thompsoni, Trichostrongylus calcaratus);* **Cestoda** (flukes) *Catenotaenia dendritica, Hymenolepis diminuta, Mesocestoides corti);* **Siphonaptera** (fleas) *(Orchopeas howardi);* **Anoplura** (lice) *(Bruelia rotundata, Enderleinellus longiceps, Hoplopleura sciuricola, Neohaematopinus sciuri);* **Acarina** (ticks) *(Amblyomma americanum, Dermacentor variabilis, Ixodes marxi);* **Acarina** (mites) *(Androlaelaps casalis, Echinolaelaps* sp., *Haemogamasus* sp., *Haemogamasus ambulans, Haemogamasus reidi, Hirstionyssus = Echinonyssus* sp., Trombiculidae sp.*);* and **Diptera** (flies) *(Cuterebra* sp., Simulidae sp.).

To the hunter, the most familiar gray squirrel parasite is the larvae of the botfly, *Cuterebra*. Botflies parasitize gray squirrels in late summer and early fall. The larvae, known colloquially as "wolves" or "warbles," remain in the squirrel until September or October when they emerge and enter the ground to pupate. Although the presence of these larvae do not affect the quality of the meat, squirrels with "wolves" are often discarded by the hunter.

Mange, or scabies, caused by the mange mite, can be a serious disease affecting squirrel populations. As in domestic animals, it causes loss of hair, exposing the squirrel to the elements in a weakened condition.

Schwartz (1928) recorded larval tapeworms in this species, while Herman and Reilly (1955) noted a gray squirrel from Lexington, Virginia, that contained numerous nodules on the skin of the extremities, head, and abdomen. Since 1961, rabies has been confirmed in only two squirrels in Virginia, one each from Tazewell and Wythe counties (tables 5 and 6).

Predation. Gray squirrels are preyed on by carnivorous mammals such as raccoons, weasels, foxes, and mink, as well as birds and snakes. Mitchell and Beck (1992) recorded the capture of this species by free-ranging domestic cats in New Kent and Henrico counties. Humans are the chief enemy of the gray squirrel.

Geographic Variation. The subspecies in Virginia is *Sciurus carolinensis carolinensis* Gmelin. One geographic variant has been identified in Virginia. It inhabits northern and western Virginia as well as the northern portion of the Piedmont Plateau south to Patrick, Pittsylvania, and Charlotte counties.

Other Currently Recognized Subspecies. *Sciurus carolinensis pennsylvanicus* Ord.

Location of Specimens. AEL, AMNH, ANSP, ASUMZ, AV, BCV, CHAS, CM, CSULB, CU, CUC, DMNH, FMNH, HSU, LC, LFCC, LU, MCZ, MSB, MVZ, NCSM, NVCC, ODU, OU, RC, RMWC, RU, SBC, SNP, SUVM, UA, UCM, UMMZ, USNM, VCU, VHCC, VMNH, VPISU, VPI-W.

Eastern Fox Squirrel
Sciurus niger (Linnaeus)

Description. The eastern fox squirrel (Plate 40) is the largest tree squirrel in the western hemisphere. It resembles the common gray squirrel but can be distinguished by its larger size, its squarish facial profile, and its normally orange or yellow underparts and tail.

The fur of the fox squirrel is coarse and highly variable in coloration. Three basic color phases exist — gray, red or buff, and black — although intergradations between them commonly occur. Most squirrels have varying amounts of black across the face and crown of the head and distinctive white noses, ears, and paws. Fox squirrels exhibiting the gray phase are buff gray on the dorsum with black-tipped hairs. The dorsal surface of the tail is colored the same as the back except that the longer hairs are black with creamy white tips. Like the nose and ears, the feet and toes are cream to buff. The underparts are yellowish-white with the underside of the tail reddish-buff, particularly at its base. The reddish or buff phase is a mixture of black and tawny or rusty brown above. The tail, both above and below, is much brighter and is bordered with orange-yellow. The underparts and feet are ochraceous orange. The black, or melanistic, phase is black throughout except for the nose, lips, and ears, which are creamy white. Female fox squirrels possess eight mammae. Fox squirrels are considerably bigger and heavier than gray squirrels. Adult fox squirrels are usually between 475 and 700 mm long, including a 250 to 390 mm tail. They weigh between 0.6 and 1.5 kg.

The braincase of this species is depressed posteriorly. Distinct interorbital notches and postorbital processes are present. The small infraorbital foramen forms a canal. Four molariform teeth, consisting of one premolar and three molars, all about the same size, are present in each side of the upper jaw and serve to distinguish the skull of this species from that of the gray squirrel (Figure 75).

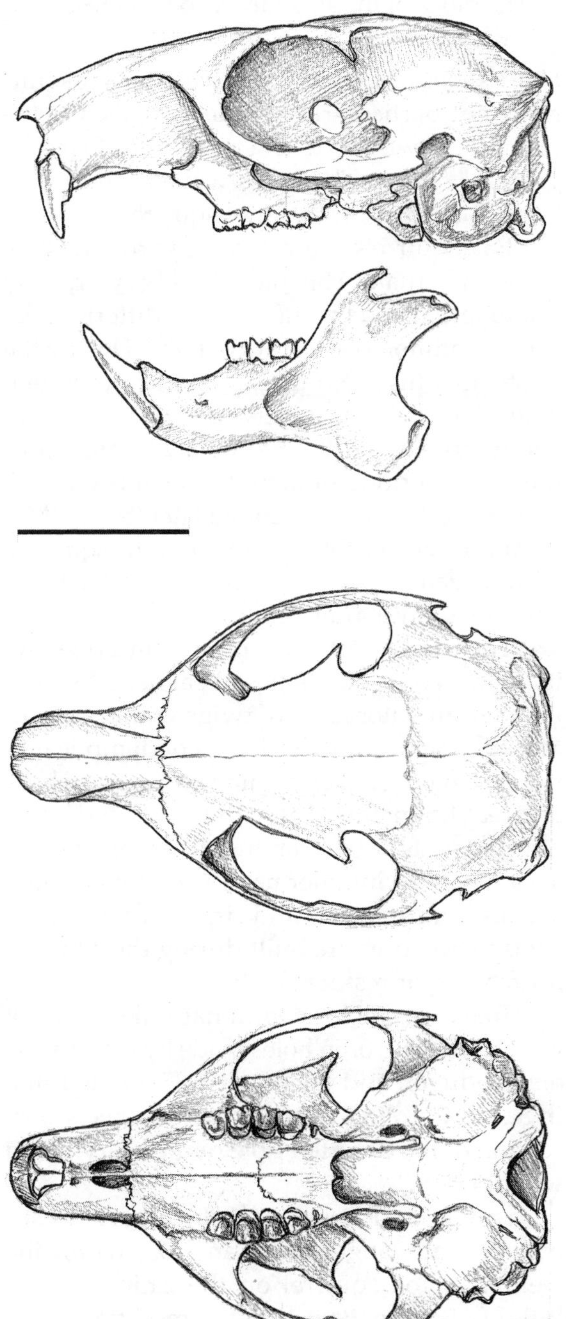

Figure 75. *Sciurus niger:* Left lateral view of skull and mandible, and dorsal and ventral view of skull. Scale bar = 20 mm.

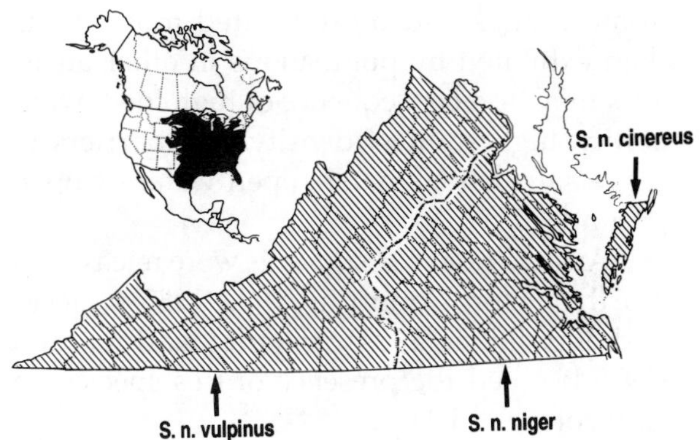

Figure 76. *Sciurus niger:* Range in Virginia and North America.

Distribution. The fox squirrel is found in the forests of eastern North America from southwestern New York and southern Pennsylvania to the Gulf Coast, west through most of Texas and Oklahoma, eastern Colorado, Kansas, Nebraska, and North Dakota, and north into Minnesota, Wisconsin, and Michigan. It has been introduced into California and other western states.

Three geographic variants of fox squirrel inhabit Virginia (Figure 76). One form is relatively common in most counties west of the Blue Ridge mountains (Fies, 1993). Low populations probably exist in most counties bordering the Blue Ridge mountains on the east and in a number of piedmont counties. Ernst (1994), who recorded a specimen from Fairfax County taken in October, 1973, stated that no other individuals have been seen in Fairfax or its immediate vicinity since the early 1970s.

A second, known as the Delmarva fox squirrel, is found on the eastern shore of Maryland in very low numbers. It apparently formerly inhabited Accomack and Northampton counties in Virginia, and has been successfully reintroduced onto the Chincoteague National Wildlife Refuge and Assateague Island in Accomack County. Thirty squirrels were released in Virginia during the period 1968–1971, giving rise to a self-sustaining population (Dueser and Terwilliger, 1987). The population is relatively stable (Dueser and Handley, 1991). The history of this population was detailed by Handley and Gordon (1979d) and Dueser and Terwilliger (1987). A two year study of the population and habitat dynamics of this population was completed in June, 1991 (Terwilliger, 1991b). Results of this study showed smaller home ranges and more limited movements than exhibited by populations in other areas. This may be a consequence of high food availability, high squirrel density, and barriers to dispersal such as marsh, open water or open ground.

An additional 24 squirrels were released in Northampton County in 1982–1983 (Dueser and Terwilliger, 1987). Handley and Gordon (1979d) noted the presence of this species on Chincoteague Island.

A third form which may have once occurred throughout southern Virginia now occurs only in small isolated populations in the southeastern portion of the state. These squirrels are multicolored or black and are very rare. In the early 1900s, this squirrel was supposedly common throughout southeastern Virginia, but by 1945 it was found only in Chesterfield and Prince George counties where it was rare (Handley and Patton, 1947). Currently, only two populations are known — one in Amelia County and the other in Surry County (Dueser and Handley, 1991). The Surry population is threatened by habitat destruction in the form of encroaching clearcuts.

Two of the three variants occurring in Virginia have been classified as endangered in the state (Handley 1979b; 1991) and one — the Delmarva fox squirrel — is considered endangered throughout its range by the US Fish and Wildlife Service. Dueser and Terwilliger (1987) noted that endemic populations of the Delmarva fox squirrel now occupy less than 10 percent of the historic range. The decline in numbers and suitable range has been attributed primarily to habitat destruction (Taylor, 1976; 1979). Nesting sites, especially tree cavities and natural hollows, are scarce in today's relatively young forests.

Habitat. Fox squirrels prefer higher ground and larger trees than gray squirrels. Open, mature stands of pine or mixed stands of pine, oak, hickory, and sweetgum are ideal. Suitable areas have a minimum of underbrush. Fox squirrels forage and pass through the cutover areas and young growth preferred by gray squirrels, but they do not live there permanently.

In regard to the Delmarva fox squirrel, Dueser and Handley (1991) stated:

On Assateague Island, this squirrel is most abundant in open stands of loblolly pine with sparse undergrowth (B. J. Larson, pers. comm.). It is found most often in open park-like forests of mature loblolly pine and oak or in mixed stands of pine, beech, and sweetgum (Dueser et al., 1988). *Both upland and bottomland forests are occupied.*

The Amelia County population inhabits a 500 ha block of mature hardwoods (Dueser and Handley, 1991).

Habits. Because of its large size, the fox squirrel is not particularly nimble in trees. On the ground, however, it is a relatively fast and graceful runner. The tail is waved rather than being flicked, as in the gray squirrel.

Fox squirrels are active year round; they do not hibernate. Their activity is governed by photoperiod and the influence of differing seasonal conditions (Weigl et al., 1989). During the winter months in North Carolina, squirrels generally left their nests between 9 and 11 A.M. and returned by 4 P.M. From May through July, however, periods of activity generally began earlier (7 to 9 A.M.) and ended later (5 to 6 P.M.). In August and early September, some squirrels became active as early as 6 A.M. and activity continued until after sunset.

The winter nest may either be in a tree cavity or in an outside leaf nest. Leaf nests for winter have an outer layer of twigs with leaves attached, a series of inner layers of damp leaves pressed together, then a lining of shredded bark and leaf fragments. These bulky but well-constructed nests are substantial structures and last several years. Summer nests used for denning are also substantial, and, in addition, many flimsy structures are built during the summer for feeding or resting shelters.

Tree dens are located in natural cavities of large dead trees or in holes made by woodpeckers. Audubon and Bachman (1851) noted that in South Carolina the fox squirrel "takes possession of the deserted hole of the ivory-billed woodpecker."

Larson and Dueser (1990) reported estimated home ranges of 1.4 and 12.8 ha for the Delmarva fox squirrel on the Chincoteague Wildlife Refuge. Based on the modified minimum area method, Larson (1990) calculated an average home range of 2.5 ha for females and 6.1 ha for males on the Refuge. In North Carolina, Weigl et al. (1989) used radiotelemetry to record home ranges of 26.6 ha for males and 17.2 ha for females using the minimum convex polygon method, and 43.7 ha for males and 25.0 ha for females using the 95% ellipse method of calculation. Seasonal ranges varied with food availability. Using radiotelemetry, Donohoe and Beal (1972) found that fox squirrel ranges in Ohio averaged 11.5 ha with individual range size varying from 3.0 to 31.8 ha. Individuals may normally travel up to 1.6 km from their den. During autumn dispersal, some tagged squirrels have moved from 1.6 km to 22.5 km from their previous home, with 64.4 km a known maximum (Allen, 1943).

The maximum speed of a fox squirrel on the ground is approximately 29 km per hour. They have been known to swim for 1.5 to 3 km in smooth water, but they have more aversion to entering water than do gray squirrels. Fox squirrels emit a variety of sounds including barks, chatter-barks, tooth chatters, grunts, squeals, whines, and screams.

Although fox squirrels are somewhat solitary in habits, they do tend to colonize and more than one fox squirrel may be found in the same nest. Population density is typically less than five per ha (Weigl et al., 1989).

Seton (1953) noted the following interesting behavior:

> *Arlington Cemetery had always been a haven of Fox-squirrels. About 20 years ago, they had increased to surprising numbers. Then, one day, they seemed to be possessed of a migration craze; they all set out eastward. At once, they were met by the broad Potomac; but plunged in, swimming away toward Analostan Island, the nearest wooded tract. Here many of them stayed; but many moved on, and were lost sight of. They still frequent Arlington Cemetery.*

Food. The food of fox squirrels consists of acorns, hickory nuts, insects, buds, twigs, bark, berries, fruits, corn, various other nuts, seeds, and mushrooms. Green and mature pinecones are staple foods in some areas. A Missouri study found that these squirrels consumed 109 identified plant foods throughout the year, 18 of which ranked as principal items of diet and accounted for 82.4 percent of all foods eaten (Korschgen, 1981). Collectively, hickories of seven species provided the foods selected most often and in the greatest amount (29.3 percent). Oaks of 11 species accounted for 22.9 percent of important year-round foods. There is apparently little or no difference between the food preferences of gray and fox squirrels but use of foods reflects differences in habitats and foraging behavior (Weigl et al., 1989). Competition for food may occur in some areas (Flyger and Smith, 1980). Bird nests are robbed occasionally, and in the spring, the sap and tender inner bark of trees is sometimes heavily utilized.

Much food is hoarded by placing items in separate holes in leaf mold or soil, where they are sought in time of need. Experiments on caching and food recovery have shown that between 33 percent and 99 percent of buried nuts are subsequently recovered, and that smell is the major sense used in discovering caches (Cahalane, 1942; Stapanian and Smith, 1984).

Reproduction and Development. Most mating takes place during late winter and early summer. Weigl et al. (1989) found no evidence of more than one litter per female per year in North Carolina. Female fox squirrels born in the spring first breed late the following winter; those born in summer breed the following spring or summer. Gestation is about 45 days, with the majority of young born during either February and March or August and September. Litters range from one to six, with two to four young being most common. Litter size averages 2.5 in eastern North Carolina (Weigl et al., 1989) and 2.25 on Maryland's Eastern Shore (Lustig and Flyger, 1976).

The development of fox squirrels has been described by Brown and Yeager (1945). Young at birth are naked and pink, have their eyes closed, and weigh about 14 g. As with other tree squirrels, the development of the young is slow. They have a fine hair coat in 10 days. Their eyes open at about four weeks of age. They are able to eat solid food when about eight weeks old and soon thereafter are independent.

Longevity. Marked fox squirrels in Illinois have lived to an age of 12.6 years under natural conditions (Koprowski et al., 1988). Thirteen years is the record life span in captivity (Flyger and Gates, 1982).

Pelage Variations. Partial albinos have been recorded from Charles City County (VPISU) and Bland County (VPI-W).

Parasites and Disease. Jones (1978) recorded the bacterium *Francisella tularensis* from two

Delmarva fox squirrels from the Chincoteague National Wildlife Refuge in 1977. Coccidian oocysts (Eimeria sp.) and four nematodes (*Strongyloides robustus, Heligmodendrium hassalli, Trichostrongylus calcaratus,* and *Dipetalonema interstitium*) were recorded from squirrels on Chincoteague by Eckerlin (1993b).

Predation. Fox squirrels, especially nestlings, may occasionally be taken by predatory birds, mammals, and some snakes. Humans using guns and automobiles are probably the chief enemy of adult fox squirrels.

Geographic Variation. The subspecies in Virginia is *Sciurus niger niger* Linnaeus. Two variants have also been identified.

Bailey (1923) noted that fox squirrels, some of which may be of southern forms, have been liberated at various times in the Zoological Park and have been observed from time to time during the past few years in Cleveland Park and adjoining wooded sections. Mr. N. Hollister, superintendent of the Park, reports importations of seven from Wichita, Kansas, in 1899; of one from South Carolina, in 1902; of eight from Arion, Iowa, in 1903; of one from Richmond, Virginia, in 1904; and one from Columbia, Tennessee, in 1916.

Other Currently Recognized Subspecies. *Sciurus niger vulpinus* Gmelin; *Sciurus niger cinereus* Linnaeus.

Location of Specimens. AMNH, ANSP, BCV, CUC, DMNH, EHC, GMU, HSU, KU, LFCC, LU, MCZ, NVCC, RU, USNM, VCU, VHCC, VMNH, VPISU, VPI-W, WL.

Genus *Tamiasciurus*

Dentition: 1/1, 0/0, 2/1 or 1/1, 3/3 = 20 or 22

Red Squirrel
Tamiasciurus hudsonicus (Erxleben)

Description. The red squirrel (Plate 41), which is also known as the mountain boomer, pine squirrel, and fairy-diddle, is a small tree squirrel about midway between a chipmunk and a gray squirrel in size. The upperparts are reddish-gray and the underparts are whitish. The dorsal pelage is most reddish along the middorsum. A conspicuous black stripe is present along the side of the body when the squirrel is in its summer pelage. Ear tufts are present in winter. Females possess eight mammae. Adult red squirrels are usually between 250 and 350 mm long, including a bushy tail 100 to 150 mm. Adults normally weigh between 200 and 250 g.

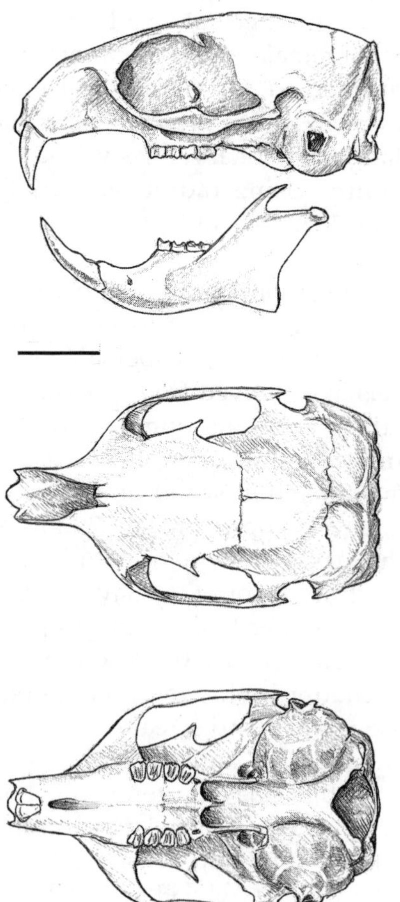

Figure 77. *Tamiasciurus hudsonicus:* Left lateral view of skull and mandible, and dorsal and ventral view of skull. Scale bar = 10 mm.

The top of the skull is relatively flat and the postorbital processes are short. The anterior upper premolar may be small and nonfunctional and covered by the crown of the last premolar, or it may be absent entirely (Figure 77).

Distribution. The red squirrel occurs throughout Alaska and Canada north to the limits of tree growth. The range extends southeastward east of the central grasslands to Virginia and south along the Appalachian Mountains to North Carolina, South Carolina, and Tennessee. In the West, the range extends southward along the Rocky Mountains to southern Arizona and New Mexico.

The red squirrel is found primarily in the western and northern portions of Virginia (Figure 78).

Habitat. This squirrel typically inhabits coniferous woodlands in the north and in high-elevation mountainous areas, but it is also found in mixed stands of conifers and hardwoods.

Habits. The solitary red squirrel is active during all months of the year. Most of its activity takes place during daylight hours. The nest, constructed of shredded bark, soft dry grasses, and other vegetation, is usually located in a natural tree cavity or a woodpecker hole. Leaf nests in trees and ground nests in old rotten stumps, log piles, or stone walls may also be utilized.

Red squirrels occupy home ranges of 1.3 to 1.5 ha for males and females respectively (Davis, 1969). Both sexes defend territories of 0.2 to 1.2 ha (Smith, 1965).

Red squirrels have five common vocalizations (Smith, 1978). Four of these — the rattle, the screech, the growl, and the buzz — are used during aggressive interactions and territorial defense, while the chirp indicates the presence of a potential predator. The often repeated "tscher-r-r-r-r" chatter is a familiar sound in areas occupied by these squirrels. It sometimes serves as a warning to another squirrel that an area is already occupied. Red squirrels act as forest sentinels and when an intruder is present, their chattering alerts not only other red squirrels but many other forest inhabitants as well.

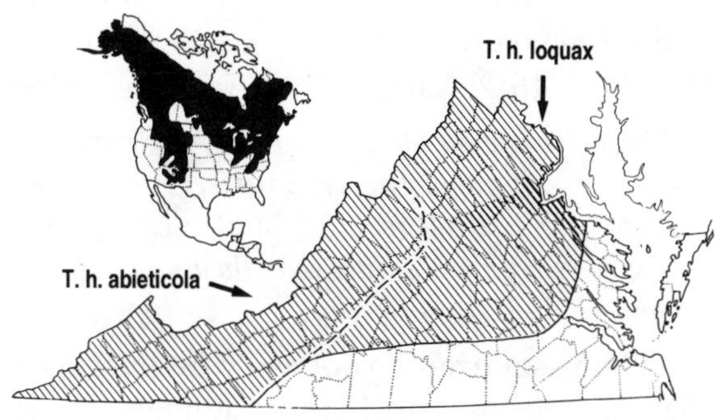

Figure 78. *Tamiasciurus hudsonicus:* Range in Virginia and North America.

Food. Many different food items are consumed by red squirrels. These include various kinds of seeds and nuts; fungi; mushrooms (sometimes including deadly poisonous ones); buds; catkins; and fruits such as blackberries and blueberries. Occasionally red squirrels raid bird nests and eat the eggs or nestling birds. Snails and insects, including many that are tree pests, also form part of the diet.

Red squirrels are either tolerant or immune to mushroom poison (Klugh, 1927). The many species of mushrooms that are eaten, both fresh and after being dried and stored, include the poisonous amanitas.

Red squirrels store large quantities of food, chiefly the seeds of conifers, nuts, and mushrooms. During late summer and autumn, the main activity of this species is the storage of food. It also stores food temporarily at all seasons of the year.

Reproduction and Development. Red squirrels breed during the spring and summer and may have two litters annually. Gestation is 32 to 38 days (Lair, 1985). Between two and seven young usually comprise a litter. Newborn red squirrels are pink, hairless, and blind. By two weeks, the fur has a reddish tinge and at about four weeks, the eyes open. Baby red squirrels first venture out of their nest when they are about one-third grown.

Longevity. Some individuals may live as long as nine years (Crandall, 1964).

Parasites. The flea *Orchopeas wickhami* has been recorded from this species in Virginia (Fox, 1968).

Predation. These squirrels are known to be preyed upon by rattlesnakes (Linzey and Linzey, 1971; Linzey, 1995b). Other snakes, birds of prey, foxes, fishers, weasels, and bobcats undoubtedly also prey on this species.

Geographic Variation. The subspecies in Virginia is *Tamiasciurus hudsonicus hudsonicus* (Erxleben). One variant inhabits the western portion of the state, while the other is found in the remaining portion of the state occupied by this species.

Other Currently Recognized Subspecies. *Tamiasciurus hudsonicus abieticola* A. H. Howell; *Tamiasciurus hudsonicus loquax* (Bangs).

Location of Specimens. AMNH, BCV, CHAS, CM, CUC, DMNH, DWL, EKU, GMU, IOWA, LFCC, LSUMZ, LU, MCZ, MVZ, NVCC, SNP, TTU, UCLA, USNM, VPISU, VPI-W.

Genus *Glaucomys*

Dentition: 1/1, 0/0, 2/1, 3/3 = 22

Southern Flying Squirrel
Glaucomys volans (Linnaeus)

Description. Flying squirrels are small nocturnal tree squirrels with large eyes and a broad, flattened, well-furred tail. Their most obvious general characteristic is a loose fold of furred skin that connects the front and hind limbs from the wrists to the ankles. The dense, soft, fine, glossy fur is generally brownish above, with black at the base of each hair. The hairs of the underparts are whitish or cream to their base. Black hairs ring the eyes and extend along the edges of the membranes. Each front foot possesses four sharp, curved claws, and each hind foot five such claws. The eyes are black but at night will shine red by the light of a flashlight. Females posses eight mammae. Adult southern flying squirrels (Plate 42) are usually between 200 and 265 mm in total length, including a tail 85 to 115 mm long. Adults normally weigh between 45 and 85 g.

The skull is rounded, comparatively small, and lightly built. The infraorbital foramen is oval and vertical. Postorbital processes are present, broad at their bases and tapering abruptly to a point. The rostrum is short (Figure 79).

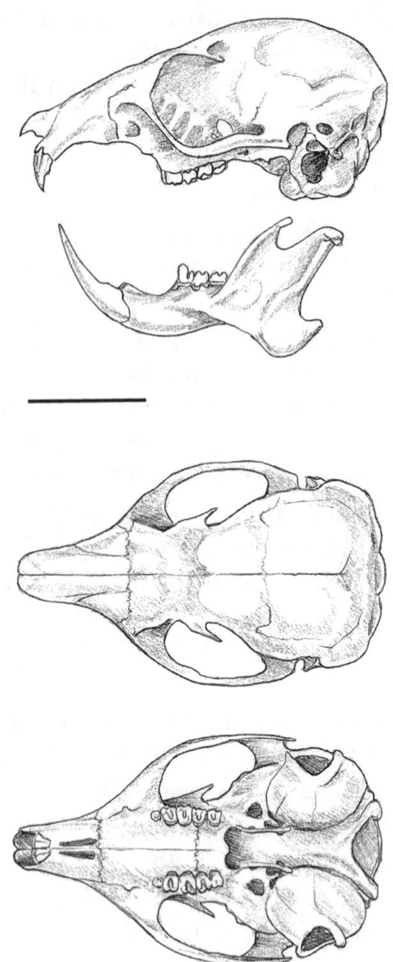

Figure 79. *Glaucomys volans:* Left lateral view of skull and mandible, and dorsal and ventral view of skull. Scale bar = 10 mm.

Distribution. The southern flying squirrel inhabits the forests of the eastern United States north to New Brunswick and Nova Scotia and west to the Great Plains.

This species occurs throughout Virginia (Figure 80). Although it is common in most areas of the state, many persons are unaware of its presence because of its nocturnal habits.

Habitat. The southern flying squirrel prefers dense, mature hardwood forests with large trees. It is found, however, in areas of mixed hardwoods and pine and around some residential areas, particularly where large trees abound. Although hollow stumps or trees are preferred homesites, leaf nests are sometimes constructed. The removal of dead trees from timber stands tends to limit the number of available nesting sites. These squirrels may also take up residence in birdhouses, particularly purple martin and bluebird houses, and they will occasionally move into human dwellings.

Habits. In 1612, Captain John Smith recorded:

> *A Small beaste they have, they call* Assapanick, *but we call them flying Squirrels, because spreading their legs, and so stretching the largenesse of their skins, that they have beene seene to fly 30 or 40 yeards.*

Flying squirrels do not really fly, they glide. (Bats are the only true flying mammals.) When the squirrel launches itself into the air, it spreads its legs, thus drawing taut the folded layer of loose skin along each side of the body. Cartilaginous spurlike supports at the wrists make it possible for the animal to extend the skin fold beyond the outstretched legs. When outstretched, this supports the body of the squirrel as it glides in a downward course from tree to tree. The usual gliding distance is six to nine m. However, glides of over 45 m from an

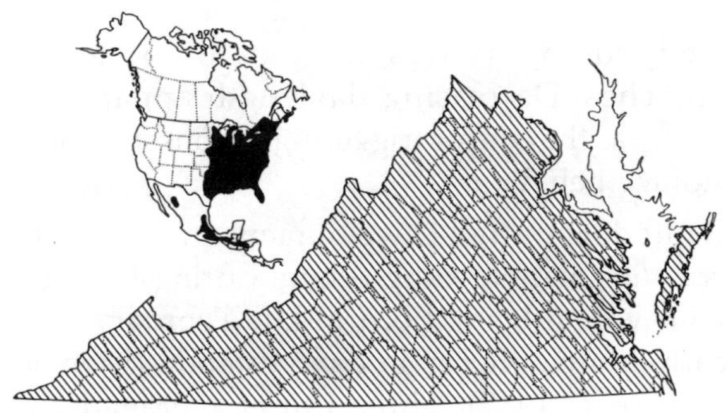

Figure 80. *Glaucomys volans:* Range in Virginia and North America.

18-m elevation have been recorded, as have turns of 90 degrees.

Before taking off, flying squirrels usually sway their head and body from side to side as far as possible several times — evidently a range-finding maneuver. They also gather their legs under them for as strong a leap as possible. They land with an audible thump, and then climb to a higher point and glide again. Their driving power is really the pull of gravity, aided by the muscular effort the squirrel makes when it leaps from a high position. By varying the tension on its membranes and by altering the position of its tail, the flying squirrel can control its direction and speed to some extent. Before landing, the squirrel checks its speed by manipulating its tail and comes to rest head up on the trunk of a tree.

Flying squirrels are the only members of the family Sciuridae in North America that are primarily nocturnal, and their large eyes are modified for seeing in dim light. They are highly specialized for an arboreal existence, leaping from tree to tree in the dark forest as the true squirrels do in the daytime. Without their sharp vision and their ability to control their flight, they could hardly do this, since they cannot see their landing point clearly until they are quite close to it. Although these squirrels spend the majority of their lives in the trees, they descend to the ground to forage, especially when the nut crop falls in autumn.

During the night it is possible to detect the presence of flying squirrels by listening for their faint squeaking notes. These notes are similar to the chipping of a small bird.

Sollberger (1940) found that these squirrels emerged from their nests "while there was still sufficient daylight to barely see them at a distance of twenty feet." None were heard, however, until it was completely dark, and the squirrels were continually active from the time they arose to just before daylight. Experiments monitoring the activity of flying squirrels have shown that intensity of activity is correlated with temperature; in winter, squirrels remained in their nests, coming out only for short periods after dusk and just before dawn (Muul, 1968).

The flying squirrel is usually a sociable mammal, several sharing a crowded nest during the day. These groups may be family clans or just neighbors. On cold nights in Virginia, Sawyer and Rose (1985) recorded up to 11 squirrels huddled in one nest box. Weigl (personal communication, 1995) and Linzey (1995a) recorded as many as 26 in one nest in North Carolina.

In central Virginia, Sonenshine et al. (1979) recorded densities ranging from 3.0 to 13.8 per ha, while Sawyer and Rose (1985) recorded peak densities of 38.4 per ha and 36.09 per ha in southeastern Virginia. Studies elsewhere in the range of this species have reported population densities ranging from approximately 2.5 to 12.4 per ha.

Dens may be in deserted woodpecker holes, in natural cavities, or in outside spherical nests. Although flying squirrels will adopt nests of other species, they apparently also build their own. Nests are constructed of shredded bark, dry leaves, moss, feathers, fur, or other soft material. Outside nests apparently are rarely found in northern latitudes. Nests have also been found below ground level under root systems of trees.

Flying squirrels do not hibernate, although long periods of cold or wet weather make them inactive. At such times, several will gather together to afford one another protection from the low temperatures. They may remain inactive for several weeks at a time. Twenty-six were found in one hollow chestnut tree in Tennessee (Linzey and Linzey, 1971; Linzey, 1995b).

Average home range size in Maryland varies between 1.89 and 1.95 ha for females and between 2.45 and 3.49 ha for males (Gilmore and Gates, 1985; Bendel and Gates, 1987). Sollberger (1943) and Muul (1968) suggested that territoriality was restricted to defense of brood nest trees by breeding females. Madden

(1974), however, recorded evidence of adult females defending their entire home range, whereas males were not territorial.

Flying squirrels may range a mile or more from their homesite, although their normal range is usually considerably less. Sawyer and Rose (1985) found that squirrels in Virginia returned home "with great frequency from distances up to 1000 m. None of the six squirrels released 1600 m away returned home." One marked southern flying squirrel was released over 1.6 km from its point of capture in Wisconsin and was recaptured at the original site six days later (McCabe, 1947). Depending on the route covered, this squirrel would have had to descend to the ground and cross treeless terrain for either 76 m or 0.4 km.

The senses of sight, hearing, and touch are very acute. Flying squirrels have long been favored pets of rural youngsters, as they are easily tamed and adapt well to captivity.

Food. Conner (1960) examined 15 flying squirrels taken between February and October in New York. Plant food accounted for 78 percent of the total volume and included mast and fungi with lesser amounts of buds and lichens. Animal food comprised 22 percent of the total volume and consisted of insects and other invertebrates.

A study on the Coastal Plain of South Carolina found that starch grains and seed coat parts of acorns were the more prevalent foods (Harlow, 1990). Major foods recorded were acorns, pine seeds, American holly fruit, tree moss, fungal spores, and hickory seeds. Animal matter consisted exclusively of insects and occurred in 11 percent of the samples but constituted less than 1 percent of the food volume.

Calhoun (1941) noted that flying squirrels are more carnivorous than tree squirrels, and food of animal origin predominates during the summer months. Flying squirrels are frequently attracted to lights at night where they find abundant moths and other night-flying insects. Much foraging is also done on the ground at night. In the winter and early spring, they feed on the buds, catkins, and shoots of trees. Flying squirrels will feed on dead carcasses, and occasionally they will kill and eat sleeping birds and bird eggs. These squirrels also feed on lichens and fungi. Nuts and other foods are cached in leaf litter on the ground, wedged in cavities in trees or between branches. Decreasing daylength apparently serves as the cue for triggering the onset of food storage behavior.

Reproduction and Development. In southeastern Virginia, breeding occurs during January with young being born in late February and early March after a 40 day gestation (Sawyer and Rose, 1985). Three litters averaged 1.7 young. Sonenshine et al. (1979) reported two peaks of reproduction in central Virginia – one in late summer and early fall, the second in spring. Nestlings were found as early as March. Lewis (1940) stated that mating apparently occurred in December in Amelia County, Virginia, since males collected on December 8 and 16 were in breeding condition.

At high elevations in Virginia, 24 of 29 litters were produced in the spring with the remainder being born in late summer. Average litter size was 2.7 (Fies and Pagels, 1988).

Gilmore and Gates (1985) recorded an average litter size of 2.54 in Maryland with autumn litters being larger than spring litters. In Tennessee, Pitts (1991) recorded a bimodal breeding season with litters being born from January 15 to March 6 and again from August 8 to October. Spring-born litters averaged 2.4 young (range 2 to 3), while fall-born litters averaged 4.0 (range 3 to 5). Barbour (1951b) recorded females containing three and four embryos between July 21 and 27 in West Virginia. Young squirrels were found during March, April, and September in North Carolina (Brimley, 1923). Sollberger (1943) noted that in New York and Pennsylvania there was one mating in late February or early March and another in July.

Muul (1969) stated that the annual minimum photoperiod may trigger reproductive activity and the annual maximum photoperiod may produce the postreproductive regression of the gonads. He found that gonadal development was independent of temperature cues.

Female squirrels become highly territorial as parturition nears and will not tolerate other adults in the vicinity. Information on the growth and development of this species in the northern portion of its range is provided by Sollberger (1943) and Muul (1970) and in the south by Linzey and Linzey (1979). Newborn southern flying squirrels are essentially hairless and pink, have their eyes and ears sealed, and weigh between 3 and 5 g. Their eyes open between 26 and 28 days of age, and they are weaned between six and eight weeks. The young squirrels make short glides when about eight weeks old. The family may stay together until near the time of birth of the next litter. Giacolone-Madden (1976) noted that wild populations of summer-born animals may produce litters the following spring at six to eight months of age, but usually these squirrels first mate at 11 to 12 months of age. Sonenshine et al. (1979) reported 94.2 percent of females in central Virginia became pregnant within six to eight months after birth, at the next breeding season following their birth. The oldest female to bear young was three years and eight months old.

Female flying squirrels will go to great lengths to retrieve their young. While studying golden mice in the Great Smoky Mountains National Park, North Carolina, my wife and I investigated a leaf nest placed in the fork of a tree limb about 8 to 10 feet above the ground. The nest contained four young squirrels that were fully haired but did not have their eyes open. Since the nest had been dislodged during our investigation, it was deposited in a box which was placed on a nearby dirt road. While we were pondering what to do with the young squirrels, the female appeared at the edge of the road and, with no hesitation, hopped into the box, picked up a baby, and carried it off. As we watched from a short distance, she returned for each of the babies. So intent was she, that we were able to take several photographs at close range. She apparently had an alternate nest site, as she made at least two long glides following exactly the same route each time. Others have also reported this strong propensity for retrieving the young. There are reports of females climbing up the pants-leg of an observer to remove the babies from his hand and even removing young from a pocket. This behavior is most intense when the young are very small and diminishes as they approach weaning age.

Longevity. Southern flying squirrels have a probable life expectancy in the wild of between three and five years (Sollberger, 1943). One lived 13 years in captivity (Burt, 1957). Sonenshine et al. (1979) reported spring-born squirrels disappeared from the population within 5.5 months, and two-thirds within seven months. For the fall-born squirrels, the same rate of disappearance occurred within five and eight months.

Parasites. The following parasites have been recorded from this species in Virginia by Price (1928); Keegan (1951); Sonenshine, Atwood, and Lamb (1966); Fox (1968); Redington (1970); Painter and Eckerlin (1984, 1987); and Eckerlin and Painter (1986): **Nematoda** (roundworms) *(Syphacia thompsoni;* **Siphonaptera** (fleas) *(Conorhinopsylla stanfordi, Epitedia faceta, Opisodasys pseudarctomys, Orchopeas howardii, Orchopeas leucopus, Orchopeas wickhami);* **Acarina** (ticks) *(Dermacentor variabilis);* and **Acarina** (mites) *(Euhaemogamasus ambulans, Haemogamasus reidi).*

Painter and Eckerlin (1987) reported that over 60 percent of the flying squirrels taken from nest boxes were infested with fleas.

Predation. Flying squirrels are preyed on by bobcats, domestic cats, owls, and snakes. Cahalane (1947) noted that flying squirrel remains were more numerous than any other prey at two raven's nests near Lexington, Virginia. Mitchell and Beck (1992) recorded the capture of this species by free-ranging domestic cats in Henrico County, Virginia.

Geographic Variation. The subspecies in Virginia is *Glaucomys volans volans* (Linnaeus).

Location of Specimens. AMNH, BCV, CM, CMNH, CUC, DMNH, EKU, FSM, GMU, HSU, LC, LFCC, LU, MCZ, MVZ, NVCC, ODU, RMWC, RU, SNP, SUVM, UCLA, UCM, UGAMNH, UMMZ, USNM, VCU, VLM, VPISU, VPI-W.

Northern Flying Squirrel
Glaucomys sabrinus (Shaw)

Description. Except for its larger size, the northern flying squirrel (Plate 43) is very similar in appearance to the southern flying squirrel. The upperparts are brownish, and the underparts are grayish. The main distinguishing pelage characteristic is the fact that the bases of the belly hairs are often grayish on the northern flying squirrel, in contrast to the totally white belly hairs of the southern flying squirrel. The long densely-furred tail has a dorsoventrally flattened appearance. Females possess eight mammae. Adult northern flying squirrels are usually between 255 and 275 mm in total length, including a tail 100 to 130 mm long. Adults generally weigh between 95 and 140 g. In Virginia, Reynolds and Fies (1993) recorded a mean body weight of 109.8 g (range 93–126) for adult males and 120.6 g (range 98–141) for adult females.

The rounded skull is larger (total length more than 36 mm) than, but otherwise similar to, that of *Glaucomys volans*. Broad-based postorbital processes taper abruptly to a point. Intraorbital foramina are oval and vertical. The rostrum is short (Figure 81).

Distribution. This forest-inhabiting squirrel ranges from eastern Alaska and Canada south through New England and the Great Lakes region. The range continues south along the Appalachian Mountains to western North Carolina and eastern Tennessee, but south of Pennsylvania, it exists only in isolated, relict populations. In the western United States, the range extends southward in the mountains to southern California and Utah.

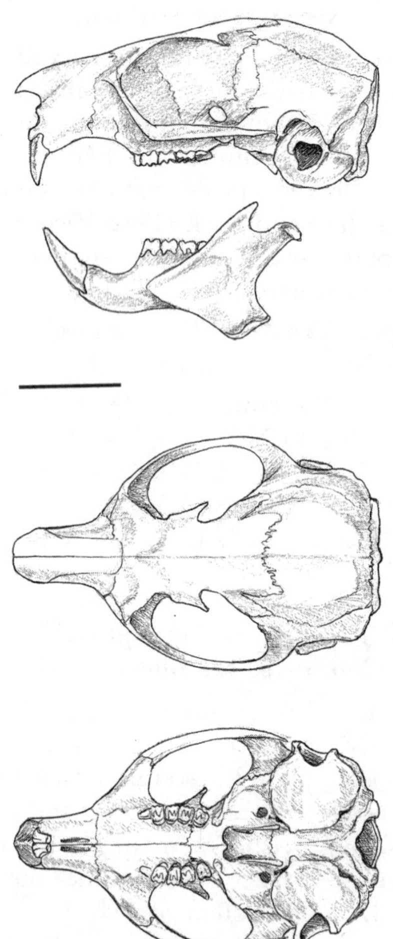

Figure 81. *Glaucomys sabrinus:* Left lateral view of skull and mandible, and dorsal and ventral view of skull. Scale bar = 10 mm.

The northern flying squirrel is designated as endangered in Virginia (Handley, 1979b; 1991). Prior to 1979, it had been recorded on only two occasions from the upper slopes of Whitetop Mountain in Smyth County. It has now been recorded from five localities in three counties (Figure 82). Handley (1979b) noted that the numbers and range of this species in the southern Appalachians has probably been shrinking as climate and habitat have changed since the Pleistocene. The range has also been reduced by timber harvesting and fire. The northern flying squirrel is now probably on the verge of extirpation in Virginia.

An intensive study of this species in the southern Appalachians was begun in 1979 (Linzey, 1983). Only 27 specimens of *Glaucomys sabrinus* from seven sites in the southern Appalachians were known to exist in university and museum collections. A total of 490 nest boxes were erected at elevations above 1,220 m at 35 sites in Maryland, Virginia, West Virginia, North Carolina, and Tennessee. A pair of adult northern flying squirrels occupied one of these boxes on Mount Mitchell in North Carolina — the first specimens seen on Mount Mitchell in more than 30 years and an adult female was marked and released along the Highland Scenic Parkway in West Virginia. Six other high elevation areas in Virginia — Allegheny Mountain, Mountain Lake, Whitetop Mountain, Mount Rogers, Pine Mountain, and Beartown (Russell County) — were included in the study (total of 198 nest boxes), but no specimens were obtained (Linzey, 1983). It was recommended that the Appalachian variants be listed as federally endangered, and this listing became official on July 1, 1985.

Beginning in 1985, the Virginia Department of Game and Inland Fisheries has erected 339 nest boxes in Virginia (Fies and Pagels, 1988). By December, 1989, northern flying squirrels had been recorded at five localities in Grayson, Smyth, and Highland counties in Virginia (Handley, 1991). As of December, 1994, a total of 75 northern flying squirrels had been captured and tagged.

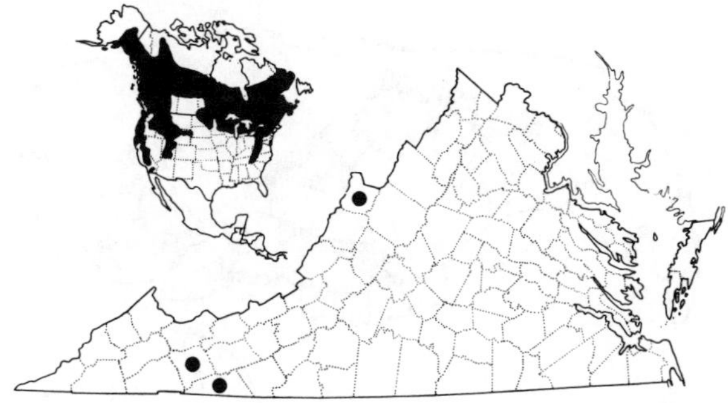

Figure 82. *Glaucomys sabrinus:* Range in Virginia and North America.

Habitat. This species is found primarily in spruce-fir forests and in mixed conifer-northern hardwood forests. Handley (1953a) stated that this squirrel is "irregularly distributed at high elevations in the spruce and balsam cloud forests of the southern Appalachian Mountains." The first individual ever taken in the Great Smoky Mountains National Park, however, was found in a deciduous forest, "at least seven airline miles from the nearest spruce and fir" (Handley, 1953a). Five sites in Grayson and Highland counties had a mean elevation of 1,354 m (1,097 to 1,615 m) (Pagels et al., 1990).

Habits. Weigl (1977) studied the interactions of northern and southern flying squirrels in North Carolina. He found that the smaller southern flying squirrel was more aggressive than the larger northern flying squirrel and that when the ranges of the two species overlap, the northern flying squirrel may be displaced. Handley (1979b) noted that the southern flying squirrel now occurs to the tops of the highest mountains in Virginia and occupies the best remnants of habitat suitable for the northern flying squirrel. Weigl also recorded evidence of a nematode parasite (*Strongyloides* sp.) of *Glaucomys volans* that is lethal or debilitating when transferred to *Glaucomys sabrinus.*

Temperature telemetry studies have yielded home ranges with a radius of 100 to 150 m in North Carolina and a radius of 125 to 200 m in Pennsylvania (Weigl, 1974). A telemetric monitoring study in West Virginia showed an average home range of 5.2 ha but with a core-activity area of 1.0 ha (Urban, 1988). Activity was found to be negatively correlated with moonlight. Population density ranges from 0.3 to 10 animals per ha (Jackson, 1961; Wells-Gosling and Heaney, 1984).

Food. Grimm and Whitebread (1952) noted that the principal foods were probably acorns, beechnuts, cherry pits, and the seeds of various coniferous trees. Weigl (1977), however, believed the northern flying squirrel to be more omnivorous than its southern relative, feeding mostly on hypogenous fungi, lichens, and mushrooms supplemented with seeds, buds, fruit, staminate cones, meat, and arthropods.

Reproduction and Development. Nests are composed primarily of shredded yellow birch bark, moss, and grass. Litters of two to five young are usually produced in spring and midsummer following a gestation period of 30 to 37 days (Asdell, 1964; Muul, 1969; Godin, 1977). Litters in Virginia average 2.3 young (range 1–3) (Reynolds and Fies, 1993). The estimated birth date of a litter observed on March 22, 1988, represents the earliest known record of litter production in the southern Appalachians (Fies and Pagels, 1988). Newborn squirrels are approximately 70 mm long and weigh 5 to 6 g. The eyes open at about 31 or 32 days, by which time the young are fully furred and their locomotion and coordination are well developed.

Parasites. Pagels et al. (1990) recorded the nematodes *Syphacia thompsoni, Strongyloides robustus,* and *Citellinema bifurcatum* from northern flying squirrels from Highland and Grayson counties, Virginia.

Longevity. Most squirrels probably survive less than four years in the wild (Jackson, 1961). An adult female in Virginia was at least two years old when last captured (Fies and Pagels, 1988).

Predation. Snakes, hawks, owls, bobcats, domestic cats, and weasels, are probably the major predators of the northern flying squirrel.

Geographic Variation. The subspecies in Virginia is *Glaucomys sabrinus fuscus* Miller.

Location of Specimens. NVCC, USNM, VCU.

Beaver
(Family Castoridae)

Beavers are large rodents with distinctive features that relate to their semiaquatic existence. The caudal vertebrae are flattened, as is the broad, scaly tail. The dense pelage acts as insulation in icy water. The hind feet are webbed and locomotion on land is plantigrade.

This family, which includes a single genus, once inhabited most of the forested regions of the Northern Hemisphere. These animals still range over many parts of North America. In some areas their numbers are not as great as in former times, but in other areas they are abundant.

Genus *Castor*

Dentition: 1/1, 0/0, 1/1, 3/3 = 20

American Beaver
Castor canadensis Kuhl

Description. The American beaver (Plate 44) is the largest rodent in the Northern Hemisphere and one of the largest in the world. Beavers are stocky mammals with scaly, nearly naked, horizontally flattened, paddle-shaped tails and webbed hind feet. The dense pelage consists of fine, short underfur overlaid with long, coarse, shiny guard hairs. The coat is brown to blackish-brown, becoming slightly lighter on the underparts. The tail and feet are black.

The ears are short and black and are set far back on the broad, rounded head. The small ears, like the nose, are equipped with valves that shut when the animal is underwater. Each front foot possesses five strong digging claws. Each large, fully webbed hind foot also has five clawed toes. The claws of the two inner toes are highly modified and are apparently used by the beaver as a comb for grooming and removal of ectoparasites. Female beavers possess four mammae. Adult beavers generally are between 900 and 1,200 mm in total length. This includes a tail which is 150 mm wide and 225 to 300 mm long. A full-grown beaver normally weighs from 13.5 to 22.5 kg. If exceptionally large, however, they may weigh closer to 40 kg. Wass (1972) reported individuals weighing 18.8 kg and 21.6 kg from Gloucester and York counties, Virginia, respectively. Howle (1915) reported a beaver from the James River that weighed 30.1 kg.

The skull is massive, has a narrow braincase, and lacks postorbital processes. The small infraorbital canal opens on the side of the broad rostrum anterior to the zygomatic arch. The incisors are heavy, broad, and dark orange-chestnut on their anterior surface. They continue to grow throughout the life of the animal. The high-crowned cheek teeth, however, do not grow throughout life (Figure 83).

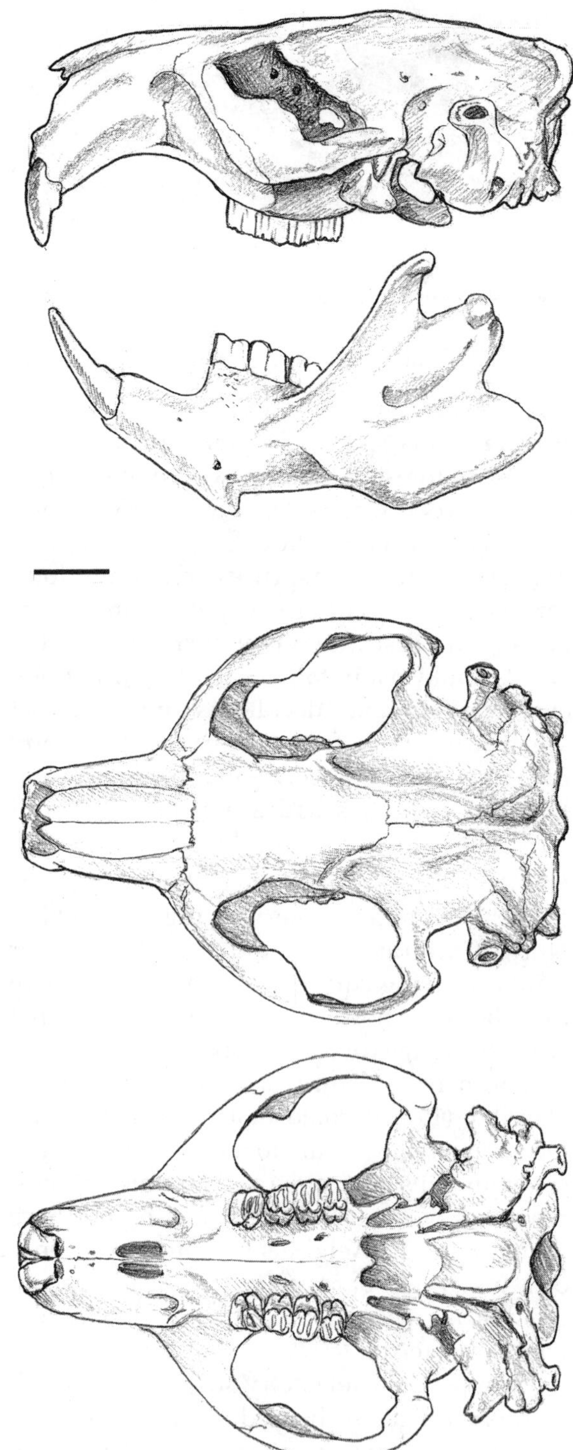

Figure 83. *Castor canadensis:* Left lateral view of skull and mandible, and dorsal and ventral view of skull. Scale bar = 20 mm.

Distribution. Beavers formerly ranged along streams and lakes throughout most of North America from Alaska to Labrador and south to the Rio Grande. They have been extirpated over much of their former range primarily as a result of overtrapping, but the species has been successfully reintroduced in many places, and populations are increasing. In some areas, beaver are so abundant they are considered a nuisance because of timberland and cropland flooding caused by their dams.

Handley (1979b) chronicled the decline and subsequent reestablishment of beavers in Virginia. Beavers once occurred abundantly throughout the state. In fact, they were the most important furbearing mammal of colonial America. Unfortunately, beavers continued to be trapped until the last one had been caught. Their extirpation from Virginia occurred between 1885 and 1911. Between 1932 and 1938 the Virginia Game Commission purchased 35 beavers from Pennsylvania, New York, New Hampshire, Maine, and Michigan and released them in nine counties in Virginia — Augusta, Dinwiddie, Goochland, Giles, Chesterfield, Cumberland, Prince George, Montgomery, and Craig (Blackwell, 1948). These beavers established themselves, bred, and began increasing. Beginning in 1943, surplus beavers were redistributed to new areas. The first trapping season since the restocking was in February, 1953. Trapping was permitted in five counties, and 30 beavers were trapped (Engle, 1954b). During the winter of 1986–1987 a total of 7,828 beaver pelts were tagged in Virginia, the last year that tagging prior to sale by the trapper and hunter was required by law. A summary of beaver tagging data for the period 1976–1987 is presented in Table 7. Comparative data on the wildfur catch from 1981 to 1987 is shown in Table 2. Virginia's total estimated fur value for 1986–1987 is given in Table 3. The range of this species is given in Figure 84.

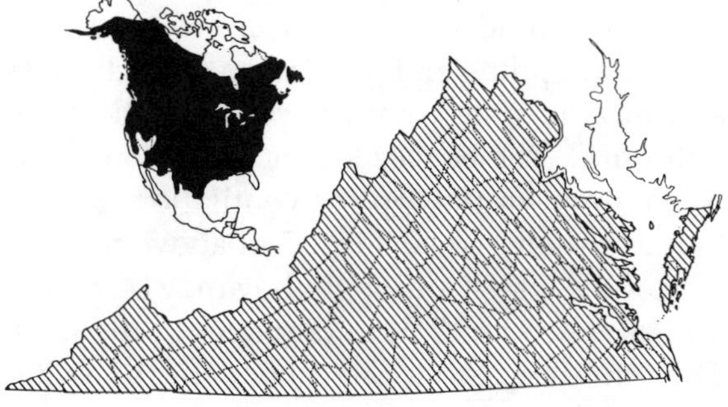

Figure 84. *Castor canadensis:* Range in Virginia and North America.

Habitat. Beavers are found mainly along streams, although they also are found in swamps and lakes wherever sufficient food is available and the terrain is suitable for the construction of a dam and the subsequent formation of a pond.

Habits. Beaver signs include the familiar dams, lodges, canals, and tree cuttings. Probably the most interesting of the beavers' works are their dams. The beavers select a slow meandering stream which usually passes through a flat, moist, wooded valley. There they construct a dam to make certain they have plenty of water of adequate depth close to their home. They will get that water even it they have to block shallow streams and brooks and turn them into ponds.

In 1679, John Bannister discussed the habits of the beaver in Virginia. He stated:

> *They cohabit and build themselves houses on the Banks of Creeks dividing them into partitions into some of which the water flows, which by building a damm below they keep at a stay tho' the Current rise. There is one among them the Indians call Perecue, ye Overseer of ye Gange, whose care it is to see his hands mind their Work, which is falling of Saplings, these they hale joyntly to their house or dam the Overseer walking with them, and biting or lashing forward with his Tayl, those that keep not up and bear their equal weight* (Ewan and Ewan, 1970).

All members of a beaver colony join in building and maintaining a dam. A foundation is made of mud and stones, then any available material is used in making the dam. Logs, dead limbs, bushes, and trees cut from along the stream are placed in position butt end upstream, across the stream, and mud, leaves, and other debris are added to give strength to the framework and to plug holes. With its powerful, orangish, chisellike incisor teeth, a beaver can fell a tree 10 cm thick in 15 minutes. While the majority of trees cut are under 15 cm in diameter, there is a report of beavers felling a tree 5 feet, 7 inches in diameter and 110 feet tall (Hatt, 1944). In cutting a tree, a beaver uses its upper front teeth for leverage, the cutting action being by the lower ones only. There is no control over which direction the tree will fall. A series of measurements of beaver cuttings used in dams showed that trees of larger diameter were cut into shorter lengths (Shadle, 1954). The longest piece handled was a 627 cm sugar maple, 5.49 cm in diameter at the base.

The beaver also takes advantage of natural obstacles such as logs, trees, boulders, and low banks to help retard the flow of water. Any debris floated downstream collects against the dam, presenting added material without much effort on the part of the beaver. Any breaks that occur in a dam are quickly repaired. There is usually one master dam that impounds the stream or floods the surrounding swamp and there are often smaller dams below and/or above the master dam. If the beaver colony abandons the site or is exterminated, the pond gradually fills in and is revegetated, ultimately resulting in a semiaquatic or dry-land condition known as a beaver "meadow."

Beaver dams will stand for many years. There are beaver dams over 90 m wide that contain an estimated 100 tons of construction material. The record dam is believed to be one that was built in Montana and measured 653 m in length. Most dams do not approach these dimensions, however. The average dam is not more than 1.2 to 1.5 m high, though it may be 75 m or more wide.

Beaver canals are still more remarkable, not only because they may extend over 300 m and are often branched or forked, but because of their locks. The lock is made by raising a low dam that causes the water level to rise. The logs must be dragged over the dam. Beaver canals are made for much the same purpose as our canals — for the transportation of freight too heavy to drag overland to the place where the animal is preparing its food pile, lodge, or pond. The beaver expends considerable effort in the construction of its canals and in keeping them in repair. They are about 0.6 or 0.9 m wide, with about 45 cm of water throughout.

One fortunate result of the beaver's work is that water is conserved. Water stored behind dams during rains is available during periods of drought. A discernible rise in the water table occurs in the vicinity of beaver impoundments (Arner et al., 1969), and conditions may actually be improved for some trees such as cypress and tupelo gum. There are many places in the western states where farmers depend on the beaver for their water supply in the irrigation of their crops. Likewise, these structures help to control floods. Beaver ponds provide quiet water for deer and many other animals, they supply moisture for trees and vegetation, they are valuable as forest-fire guards, and they make excellent breeding places for fish, amphibians, and many types of waterfowl and other birds. Beaver ponds contain a higher concentration of nutrients than the feeder streams and can support larger populations of warmwater fishes.

In some places, however, beaver damage woodlands and highways by flooding, cutting timber, damaging streamside crops, and creating undesirably high temperatures in trout streams. Many timbermen become alarmed about beaver damage to their trees, and indeed damage to timber in some parts of Virginia may be substantial. However, most beaver-damaged areas are vegetated by inferior and second-growth hardwoods. Echternach and Rose (1987) found the most heavily used trees at study sites in eastern Virginia were viburnum, alder, ironwood, bayberry, tulip poplar, and dogwood. These trees generally are of low economic value relative to pine and other species of hardwoods. Propagation of trees suitable to conditions around impoundments would restore such areas to productivity. If necessary, the water level of a beaver pond can be lowered by inserting a perforated pipe through the dam, a solution that may afford an agreeable compromise between the desires of man and beaver. Generally speaking, even in settled areas, the presence of beavers in small numbers is desirable.

The beaver is chiefly nocturnal, spending the daylight hours in a lodge or bank burrow. An interesting account of daily activity and behavior of beavers was presented by Tevis (1950). Beaver houses or lodges are usually built in the open expanse of the pond or lake. They are dome-shaped and are formed by a haphazard piling and interlacing of thick sticks and heavier poles that are plastered together with mud. The beaver leaves a small air hole, or chimney, in the top for ventilation. Beaver lodges usually rise 0.9 to 1.5 m above the surface of the water, although they may be higher and as much as 12 m in diameter at the base. The entrances are located beneath the water level, and a crude platform in the center of the pile is used for a place to rest. This arrangement affords the beaver excellent protection from enemies. Bank burrows, which are most common in the Piedmont areas of the state, are dug into stream banks, under tree roots, and other suitable spots. The entrances are well below the surface of the water, with the main tunnels slanting upwards and inland to bring their upper reaches well above the surrounding water level.

On the surface of the water, beavers can swim at the rate of 3.2 km per hour, propelling themselves with their webbed feet. The flat tail acts both as a rudder and as a warning signal. By turning the tail at an angle, the beaver can set its course direct for its objective instead of being forced to travel in a more or less circular route by the unbalanced load of timber it often carries. When alarmed, the beaver slaps the water with its tail as it dives, making a loud noise and a sizable splash. This warning signal alerts other beavers to danger, usually causing them to swim to areas of deeper water.

The beaver carries branches and limbs in its open mouth beneath the surface of the water. Certain anatomical features associated with the mouth block the passage of water to the lungs, enabling the beaver to use the teeth freely and hold objects with them when it is submerged. The lips can be drawn in behind the front teeth and sealed together. Also, the epiglottis is placed above the soft palate, and the middorsal surface of the tongue is elevated and shaped to fit against the ventral surface of the palate (Coles, 1970). Its large lungs and liver enable the beaver to carry a considerable amount of air and oxygen-rich blood for its extended stays under the water. During dives, the heartbeat decreases markedly, and the flow of blood through the brain is increased while the flow through the muscles is diminished (Irving and Orr, 1935; Irving, 1937). The beaver's speed underwater and its lung capacity are truly remarkable; it is able to cover 0.4 km in 15 minutes without coming up for air.

Both male and female beavers possess paired anal scent glands known as "castors." These glands are largest in male beavers, and their secretion is known as castoreum, a bitter, orange-brown, pungent oil that is used in the manufacture of perfume and as scent for traps. This secretion is deposited on scent mounds, small piles of mud, grass, sticks, or stones shoved together by the beaver. Such scent mounds are not easily found, but they are a characteristic and dependable sign which a keen nose can detect by the musky odor. Since scent mounds are usually located near the edge of a colony's territory, it is thought that they serve to indicate to wandering beavers that the territory is already occupied. This marking system appears to be a mechanism of self-regulation that limits the population before food becomes a major limiting factor (Aleksiuk, 1968).

Movements of resident beavers are restricted to the home pond and as much of the surrounding woodland as is needed to provide trees for construction and food. The average beaver colony includes 2.5 to 4.0 ha of water, with a land range of rarely more than 275 to 365 m. Dispersing young or emigrating adults in search of a new home, however, may cover considerable distances. Studies of tagged beavers have shown that such movements are usually under 12.9 km. However, one beaver in Alaska traveled at least 242 km and probably in excess of 322 km from the original capture point (Libby, 1957).

Although the beaver's eyesight is not exceptional, its senses of hearing, smell, and touch are excellent. Its vocal repertoire, which has been studied by Novakowski (1969), includes grunts, nasal sounds, hisses, and whines.

Food. Beavers feed mainly on the bark and adjacent outer layers (cambium) of deciduous trees. Favored foods include aspen, cottonwood, birch, willow, hackberry, alder, sweet gum, magnolia, maple, and dogwood. They occasionally damage pine. During spring and summer, beavers also eat other vegetable matter such as the roots of aquatic plants, grass, and some agricultural crops such as corn. In Virginia, Wass (1972) noted that sweet gum, pine, and red cedar are preferred foods. Echternach (1981) recorded the main foods in James City County, Virginia, as bayberry *(Myrica cerifera)*, tulip poplar *(Liriodendron tulipifera)*, dogwood *(Cornus florida)*, pine *(Pinus virginiana* and *Pinus taeda)*, beech *(Fagus grandifolia)*, and red maple *(Acer rubrum)*.

In areas where freezing winter temperatures are the norm, the beaver busily spends the fall months caching branches in the mud at the bottom of the pond. This is its winter food supply. It cuts the branches into lengths that it can easily manipulate and stores them beneath the frozen surface where it can reach them in a quick swim from its lodge.

During winter, the beaver can also draw upon fat reserves from storage depots in various parts of the body. The tail serves as one of the main fat storage depots, reaching a maximum level in early winter and being depleted by spring.

Reproduction and Development. Beavers are monogamous, and normally a male and female are mated for life. The main mating season in Virginia begins in January and extends through late February, with most kits born in May and June. Gestation is approximately 107 days. Females apparently breed for the first time during the third winter after their birth. Most studies report average litter sizes of between three and four young, although up to nine young have been recorded. In Pennsylvania, Brenner (1964) recorded an average of 5.50 embryos (range one to nine) per pregnant female and 5.04 embryos per female in which complete or partial resorption of litters occurred. Resorption of embryos occurred in 16.7 percent of the pregnant females examined. Adult females produced larger potential litters than did two-year-old animals.

A kit at birth is about 375 mm long, has a flat tail 90 mm long, weighs 0.2 to 0.6 kg, has its eyes open, and is covered with soft fur. The incisor teeth of a newborn beaver are well developed and ready to erupt and are covered with a thin layer of tissue.

The young mature slowly. In spite of the fact that they learn to swim when a month old and are weaned after six weeks, they remain under their parents' care for about two years. Thus, a typical beaver colony may consist of the parents, kits, and yearlings. The young may weigh approximately 6.75 kg when six months old. Both father and mother are devoted parents and spend much time training and instructing the young. Sexual maturity is usually attained during the beaver's second winter.

Before the birth of the next litter, the two-year-old beavers are either driven out or voluntarily leave the colony to establish their own residence. The male also seeks quarters elsewhere at the time of parturition, returning when the kits are about a month old. Beavers begin to breed when 1.5 to 2 years old.

Longevity. The life span of beavers in the wild is approximately 10 to 12 years, and some marked individuals are known to have lived more than 15 years (Rawley, 1954). The record longevity in captivity is 19 years, while wild individuals, aged by degree of dental development, have been found to be 20.5 to 21 years old (Larson, 1967), and possibly 24 years old (Brown, 1979).

Parasites. Since 1961, rabies has been confirmed in three beavers from Fairfax, Middlesex and Shenandoah counties in Virginia (tables 5 and 6).

Predation. Because of their size and habits, beavers have few enemies. Dogs, foxes, bobcats, and otters may occasionally kill a young beaver. Elsewhere, such animals as wolves, fishers, lynx, and wolverines have been known to attack beavers. By far the most significant predator of beaver has been, and continues to be, humans.

Geographic Variation. The subspecies in Virginia is *Castor canadensis canadensis* Kuhl. Two variants of beaver occur in the state. One form inhabits the mountains, the northern Piedmont, and the Coastal Plain. A second variant has been identified in the Dan and Roanoke River drainages in southcentral Virginia.

Location of Specimens. GMU, GWNF, MCZ, LFCC, LU, SNP, USNM, VCU, VHCC, VLM, VPI-W.

Murid Rats and Mice (Family Muridae)

This family includes a great number and variety of species and represents the largest family of mammals. These animals are found throughout most of the world, being absent only from Australia, Ireland, Iceland, and the Antarctic. There is considerable controversy regarding the interrelationships and the classification of this group of rodents (Nowak, 1990). Many authorities have divided this family into two families – the Cricetidae, or New World rats and mice, and the Muridae, or Old World rats and mice. Others feel that the differences between the families Cricetidae and Muridae are not sufficient to warrant familial distinction. This taxonomic controversy is beyond the purvue of this book. Thus, these rodents will be classified in a single family, Muridae, which has three North American subfamilies — Murinae, Sigmodontinae, and Arvicolinae.

The subfamilies Sigmodontinae and Arvicolinae are composed of New World genera; the subfamily Murinae includes the Old World rats and mice. In general, members of the subfamilies Sigmodontinae and Murinae have large ears, large eyes and long tails, while members of the subfamily Arvicolinae have small ears, small eyes, and short tails. Murinae differ from sigmodontinae primarily in having three rows of cusps on the molar teeth rather than two. The hind feet of murids always have five toes, while the forefeet have four or five. Virginia is inhabited by 17 species of murid rodents, which range in size from the 10 g eastern harvest mouse *(Reithrodontomys humulis)* to the 1.5 kg muskrat *(Ondatra zibethicus)*.

The skulls have an infraorbital canal that has a rounded upper portion through which passes a part of the masseter (jaw) muscle. The narrow, V-shaped lower portion of this canal transmits a nerve. Postorbital processes are always absent. The upper molar teeth are either flat-crowned or have rows of tubercles on their cutting surfaces. The molar teeth of sigmodontid rodents do not continue to grow throughout life as do those of most arvicolinid rodents.

The majority of murid rodents are terrestrial, but some are semiaquatic, semiarboreal, or fossorial. Most are nocturnal, although some are active during the day. None is known to hibernate, although several are known to experience daily torpor due primarily to low temperatures and/or food scarcity.

Members of this family are characterized by diverse food habits, but most are essentially omnivorous. They form an important link in the food web, as they often constitute the bulk of the diet of some of the larger predators.

Some species exhibit remarkable fluctuations in population size that are cyclic in nature. Such fluctuations, in turn, affect the numbers of carnivores. The reproductive rate is generally high, while the life span is short. Inevitably, some of these species come into conflict with man, while at least one, the muskrat, is a valued furbearer.

Key to Species of Muridae

1a Cheek teeth flat-crowned or with cusps, except in very old individuals where cusps may be worn flat and are outlined with an even rim of enamel; cheek teeth rooted
. . . . 2

1b Cheek teeth flat-crowned, without cusps, and with crowns having a prismatic pattern of dentine (loops and triangles) surrounded by angular rims of enamel; cheek teeth usually rootless (Subfamily Microtinae)
. . . . 12

2a Cheek teeth flat-crowned or with two rows of tubercles (cusps) (Subfamily Sigmodontinae)
. . . . 3

2b Cheek teeth with three rows of tubercles (cusps) (Subfamily Murinae)
. . . . 10

3a Upper incisors grooved on anterior surface; size small, resembles house mouse
. . . . *Reithrodontomys humulis*

3b Upper incisors without grooves; size larger
. . . . 4

4a Supraorbital ridges present; zygomatic plate cut back above giving infraorbital canal an emarginate dorsal border
. . . . 5

4b Supraorbital ridges absent; infraorbital canal not emarginate dorsally
. . . . 7

5a Total length 325 mm or more; supraorbital ridges not prominent; frontal region concave; molars with prismatic pattern resembling rootless teeth; dorsal border on infraorbital canal with shallow emargination
. . . . *Neotoma magister*

5b Total length less than 325 mm; supraorbital ridges prominent; frontal region not concave; molars with lophs or cusps; dorsal border of infraorbital canal deeply emarginate
. . . . 6

6a Tail usually shorter than head and body; fur very grizzled; no webbing between toes of hind feet; molars with lophs; upper cheek teeth with flattened S-shaped crowns
.... *Sigmodon hispidus*

6b Tail usually equal to, or longer than, the head and body; fur not grizzled; toes of hind feet webbed near base; molars with cusps; upper cheek teeth without S-shaped crowns
....................*Oryzomys palustris*

7a Dorsal pelage golden; posterior palatine foramina nearer to posterior edge of hard palate than to anterior palatine foramina
.... *Ochrotomys nuttalli*

7b Dorsal pelage whitish, grayish, or brownish; posterior palatine foramina about midway between posterior edge of hard palate and anterior palatine foramina
...................................8

8a Tail of adults usually distinctly bicolor; grayish dorsally with many black hairs; dorsal stripe usually indistinct or absent in adults
.... *Peromyscus maniculatus*

8b Tail of adults usually indistinctly bicolor; brownish dorsally with fewer black hairs; dorsal stripe usually well defined in adults
...................................9

9a Hind foot usually more than 22 mm; skull length more than 28 mm;
.... *Peromyscus gossypinus*

9b Hind foot usually less than 22 mm; skull length less than 26 mm;
.... *Peromyscus leucopus*

10a Size small; total length less than 200 mm; hind foot length less than 25 mm; length of skull less than 25 mm; supraorbital and temporal ridges absent; crown of first upper molar longer than combined crowns of second and third molars
........................*Mus musculus*

10b Size medium to large; total length more than 300 mm; hind foot length more than 25 mm; length of skull more than 30 mm; supraorbital and temporal ridges present; crown of first upper molar shorter than combined crowns of second and third molars
...................................11

11a Upper surface of skull with prominent supraorbital and temporal ridges that are nearly parallel; diastema slightly less than twice as long as cheek tooth row; tail shorter than head and body; females with 12 mammae
.... *Rattus norvegicus*

11b Upper surface of skull with prominent supraorbital and temporal ridges that flare posteriorly; diastema much less than twice as long as cheek tooth row; tail longer than head and body; females with 10 mammae
.... *Rattus rattus*

12a Size large; total length more than 200 mm; tail sparsely haired, laterally compressed; basal length of skull more than 50 mm
.... *Ondatra zibethicus*

12b Size small; total length less than 200 mm; tail well-haired, rounded; basal length of skull less than 50 mm
...................................13

13a Tail less than 25 mm
...................................14

13b Tail more than 25 mm
...................................15

14a Fur long, coarse; upper incisors broad, each with a faint longitudinal groove on anterior surface
.... *Synaptomys cooperi*

14b Fur soft, dense, velvety; upper incisors normal width; no longitudinal grooves
.... *Microtus pinetorum*

15a Palate ends posteriorly as a straight, transverse shelf; pelage usually reddish
.... *Clethrionomys gapperi*

15b Palate not ending in straight shelf; pelage dark brown to brownish-gray
...................................16

16a Yellowish colored nose; third upper molar with five to six triangles
. . . . *Microtus chrotorrhinus*

16b Nose not yellowish; third upper molar with four triangles
. . . . *Microtus pennsylvanicus*

Subfamily Sigmodontinae

Genus *Oryzomys*

Dentition: 1/1, 0/0, 0/0, 3/3 = 16

Marsh Rice Rat
Oryzomys palustris (Harlan)

Description. The marsh rice rat (Plate 45) is a slender, moderate-sized native rat. The rather coarse, moderately long fur is gray to brown with blackish hairs intermixed. The underparts and feet are whitish-gray and quite clearly delimited from the upperparts. The ears are small, inconspicuous, and well-haired. These mammals have a long, scaly, sparsely haired tail that may be much lighter below than above. The tail is usually equal to, or longer than, the head and body. The toes of the hind feet are joined by a web near their base. Females have eight mammae. Adult rice rats are usually between 225 and 300 mm in length, including a tail 100 to 175 mm long. Adults normally weigh between 40 and 85 g.

The skull possesses a short rostrum. The dorsal border of the infraorbital canal is deeply emarginate. Supraorbital and temporal ridges are prominent on the skull posterior to the eye socket. There is a pair of prominent openings in the hard palate behind the last molars. The upper molar teeth have two rows of tubercles on their cutting surfaces (Figure 85).

Distribution. This species ranges from eastern Texas (Wilkins, 1990) throughout most of the southeastern United States. It is found north to southeastern Missouri, southern Illinois, and Kentucky, and northward mainly along the Atlantic Coastal Plain to New Jersey and southeastern Pennsylvania.

Hall (1981) stated that the:

northern limit of range of this species seems to fluctuate, probably owing to fluctuation of population densities and is less precisely known than for most common North American mammals.

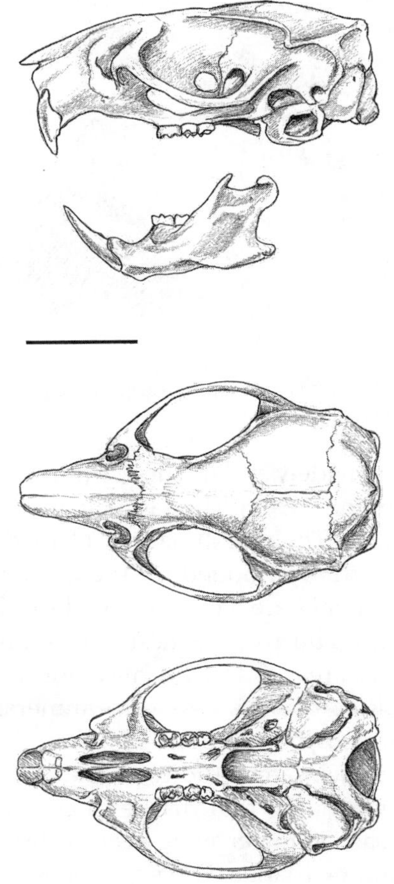

Figure 85. *Oryzomys palustris:* Left lateral view of skull and mandible, and dorsal and ventral view of skull. Scale bar = 10 mm.

This explains why maps depicting the range of this species by different authors are not in total agreement.

The rice rat is commonly distributed in Virginia east of a line from Westmoreland to Brunswick counties (Figure 86). It occurs on almost all of Virginia's barrier islands (Moncrief and Dueser, 1994).

Habitat. Rice rats inhabit wet, marshy fields and meadows, wooded swamps, and coastal salt marshes. Numerous specimens have been taken in dense honeysuckle near a salt marsh in Northampton County (CMNH). They will also live in drier areas as long as there is a heavy ground cover of grasses and sedges. On Assateague Island, Cranford and Maly (1990) reported it as most abundant in moist microhabitats and locally abundant in tidal creek areas.

Habits. Rice rats may be active at any time during the day and night, but they appear to

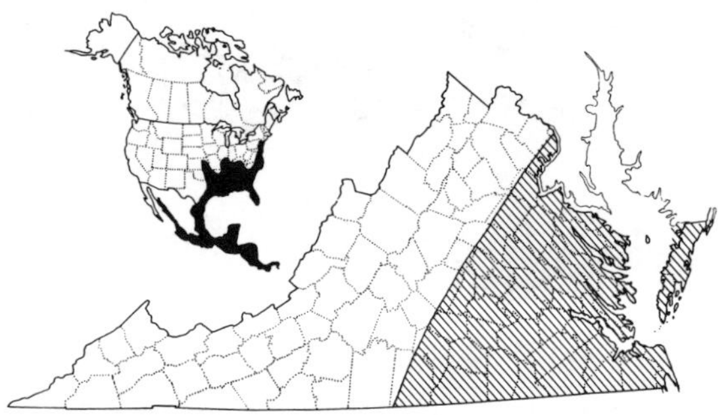

Figure 86. *Oryzomys palustris:* Range in Virginia and North America.

move more widely and frequently during darkness (Hamilton, 1946). They are active throughout the year. The marsh habitat of these rats may be partially flooded by the daily tides. Surface runways are 5 to 7.5 cm wide and lead from shallow burrows or nests to feeding areas. In wet areas, runways may not be well defined. Rice rats are strong swimmers, and when alarmed, they dive and swim rapidly and strongly underwater. Studies on the barrier islands have shown that marked rice rats can cross at least 50-meter-wide deep water channels separating islands (Forys and Dueser, 1993; Moncrief and Dueser, 1994). They are not especially sociable, and in captivity males and females will not share the same nest.

During daylight hours rice rats occupy either modified nests of the long-billed marsh wren or nests constructed entirely by the rats. Woven nests in marshy areas are usually constructed above the high-water level in clumps of reeds, cattails, and other vegetation. In Georgia, Sharp (1967) found that nests were "a meter or more above the surface of the marsh sediments near the tops of tall, dense stands of marsh grass along streamsides and on levees." The nest is between 25 and 45 cm in diameter and is loosely woven of shredded dry leaves and the finer parts of sedges and grasses. In drier localities it may be built on the ground under a tangled mass of weeds, brush, or a fallen log or at the end of a shallow burrow. Muskrat houses, both occupied and unoccupied, may occasionally be used as homesites.

Because of its usual habitat preference, this rodent rarely comes into direct conflict with man. In rice fields, pastures, or croplands, however, an abundant population of rice rats can be economically destructive. Because of their large numbers, they serve as an important source of food for many predators.

The home range of this species is between 0.23 and 0.37 ha (Negus, Gould, and Chipman, 1961; Birkenholz, 1963).

Food. Rice rats feed on green plants, the seeds of many grasses and sedges, fruits, berries, nuts, crustaceans, and other invertebrates. They have been recorded feeding on marsh grass, glasswort, gama grass, wild rye, and wild rice, as well as on small crustaceans and mollusks caught in tidal pools.

Several investigators have observed rice rats eating meat from various sources including muskrats, fish, mollusks, and young turtles. Kale (1965) observed predation on the eggs and young of long-billed marsh wrens in Georgia. Sharp (1967) recorded the food of 22 rice rats taken in salt marsh habitat in Georgia during the summer and early fall. Major food items consisted of rice-borer larvae (*Chilo* sp.) and small crabs. Incidental items included larval and adult flies and gnats, beetles, and some fibrous material and seeds of marsh grass. Sharp concluded that in the salt marsh ecosystem, this species is preferentially carnivorous, although plant foods may be utilized at certain times of the year.

In marshy areas, rice rats often bend over the vegetation to make a platform of dinner-plate size on which to feed (Hamilton, 1946). In captivity rice rats are reported to eat approximately one-quarter of their weight in food per day, or about twice their weight in food every week. Food hoarding behavior in captivity suggests that it occurs in the field (Dewsbury, 1970).

Reproduction and Development. Breeding in Virginia occurs from March to November (Dreelin and Rose, 1997). Gestation is approximately 23 days, and females breed again within a few hours after giving birth. Several litters, ranging from one to seven with an average of three to five young, are born annually. A female containing nine embryos was recorded from Lake Drummond by A. K. Fisher in 1895 (Handley, 1979a). On September 5 at Chincoteague, Hamilton (1946) took females containing seven and five embryos. Development of the young has been described by Hamilton (1946). Newborn have fine hair on their upperparts, their eyes are closed, and they weigh about 4 g. They are about 54 mm long at birth. Development is rapid, and both upper and lower incisors erupt on the fifth day. At about one week, the eyes open and the young, which are now completely furred, are able to run about. They are weaned in 11 to 13 days. They are capable of breeding at seven to eight weeks and are fully grown at four months.

Longevity. Most rice rats do not survive more than about nine months because they are subjected to heavy predation.

Parasites. The ticks *Ixodes cookei* and *Dermacentor variabilis* have been recorded on rice rats by Sonenshine and Turner (1988).

Predation. Owls, hawks, mink, weasels, raccoons, foxes, skunks, and snakes prey on these animals. Blem and Pagels (1973) and Jackson, Pagels, and Trumbo (1976) recorded this species from barn owl pellets in Northampton and Chesterfield counties in Virginia. A skull in the FMNH collection was recovered from an owl pellet at Kiptopeke in Northampton County.

Geographic Variation. *Oryzomys palustris palustris* (Harlan) is the only subspecies of rice rat that inhabits Virginia. Studies of allozymic variation between mainland and insular populations on the Eastern shore and adjacent barrier islands have revealed that rice rats are variable at 5 of 32 presumptive gene loci (Loxterman et al., 1994; Forys and Moncrief, 1994).

Location of Specimens. AMNH, CM, CMNH, CU, CUMZ, DMNH, EMU, FMNH, GMU, ISUVC, KU, LFCC, MVZ, NCSM, NVCC, ODU, RMWC, SUVM, UMMZ, USNM, VCU, VPISU, VPI-W.

Genus *Reithrodontomys*

Dentition: 1/1, 0/0, 0/0, 3/3 = 16

Eastern Harvest Mouse
Reithrodontomys humulis
Audubon and Bachman

Description. The eastern harvest mouse (Plate 46) is the smallest mouse inhabiting Virginia. The dorsal coloration is generally brown in the middle of the back shading to grayish-brown along the sides, while the belly is grayish-white. Individuals from Virginia's lower Piedmont region are grayer overall. The conspicuous ears are blackish-brown. The long, slender tail is sparsely haired and in coloration is similar to the back above and the belly below. The hind feet are long and narrow. Females possess six mammae. Adult eastern harvest mice are normally between 110 and 152 mm long, including a tail 47 to 73 mm long. Adults usually weigh between 7 and 14 g.

The skull of this species is smoothly rounded, moderately inflated, and without prominent ridges or processes. The zygomatic arches are slender and are normally parallel to the skull. The rostrum is short. Auditory bullae are present. A deep, conspicuous groove is present on the front surface of each curved upper incisor tooth, a feature that readily distinguishes the harvest mouse from the similar-appearing house mouse (Figure 87).

Distribution. The eastern harvest mouse is found in the southeastern United States from eastern Texas and eastern Oklahoma east to Florida and north to southern Ohio and Maryland.

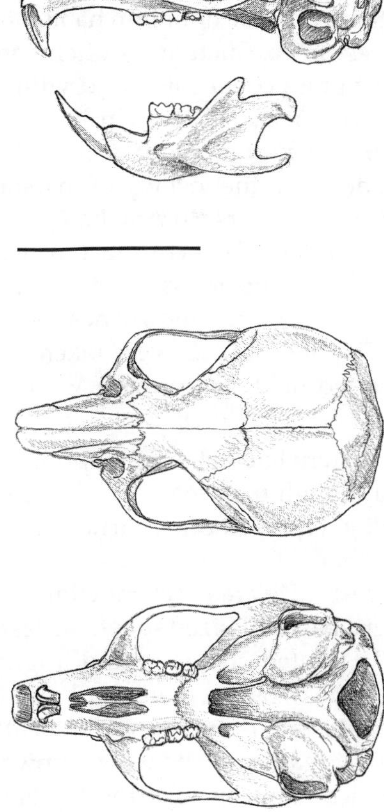

Figure 87. *Reithrodontomys humulis:* Left lateral view of skull and mandible, and dorsal and ventral view of skull. Scale bar = 10 mm.

Eastern harvest mice are probably nowhere near as abundant as other, more prolific, small rodents. In Virginia, this species exists in localized populations throughout the state (Figure 88).

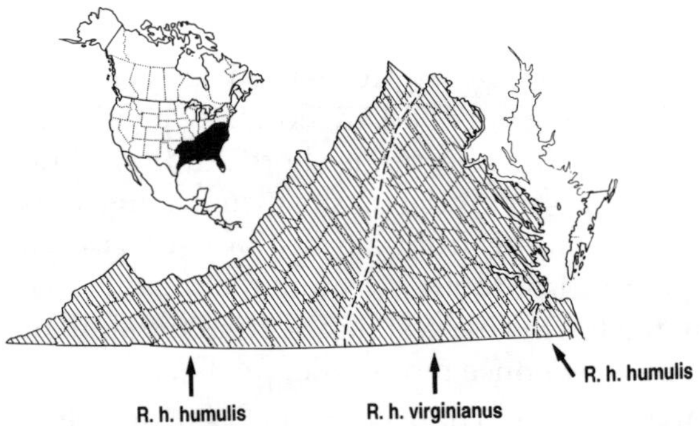

Figure 88. *Reithrodontomys humulis:* Range in Virginia and North America.

Habitat. Old fields and the brushy borders of cultivated land with grasses, broomsedge, and other herbaceous plants typical of early successional stages provide optimum habitat for eastern harvest mice. Such areas often consist of low, short grass cover interlaced with tangles of greenbrier or blackberry vines. Individuals may also be found along roadside ditches, in wet meadows, in the vicinity of marshes, and along stream borders. In Amelia County, Virginia, Lewis (1940) recorded harvest mice "where sphagnum moss formed an undergrowth to the sedges and rushes in standing water." Five individuals were taken in fallow and deserted fields in northern Virginia (Peacock and Peacock, 1961).

Habits. Eastern harvest mice are primarily nocturnal, although they may occasionally be active during daylight hours, particularly during cold weather.

Harvest mice are excellent climbers. They construct a baseball-sized spherical nest which is usually located above ground in grass, tall weeds, tangles of vines, or in a bird's nest. Some winter nests are in burrows or beneath logs. Vegetation is gathered and woven upward into a cup which is enclosed at the top and lined with plant fibers.

Average home range sizes in southeastern Virginia were 905 m^2 for males and 1,095 m^2 for females (Cawthorn and Rose, 1989). Howell (1954) recorded home ranges of 0.17 and 0.68 ha for two adult female harvest mice captured six and eight times in Tennessee. Dunaway (1968) did not calculate home range sizes but stated that some individuals trapped over periods of several months occupied relatively restricted areas, while other individuals shifted their activities to another part of the area or made occasional sallies outside of their ranges. He noted that territoriality did not seem well developed as the ranges of both sexes overlapped broadly during all seasons. Dunaway also noted that movements were more extensive during summer than during winter. Runways of other small rodents are used by harvest mice in their travels.

Harvest mice do not hibernate. They are somewhat gregarious. Dunaway (1968) reported a maximum density of 8.75 per ha. Cawthorn and Rose (1989) recorded a maximum density of 44.4 per ha during winter in southeastern Virginia. Jackson (1961) has commented on vocalization in *Reithrodontomys megalotis*: "It . . . has been heard to utter a series of rolling birdlike squeaks that could be considered a song." Calls have not been recorded from *Reithrodontomys humulis*.

Food. Harvest mice feed upon seeds of wild grasses and herbs, green vegetation, and some insects. During fall, seeds are cached in storage areas near the nest site. These small mice do not come into conflict with man since they feed mainly on native plants.

Reproduction and Development. In southeastern Virginia, *Reithrodontomys* has a breeding season extending from spring to early winter with a summer depression, and autumn breeding that produces a high winter density (Stankovich, 1984; Chandler, 1984; Cawthorn and Rose, 1989). From August to November, 82 percent of females were either pregnant or lactating (Chandler, 1984).

Hamilton (1943) stated that harvest mice begin breeding in March and that pregnant females had been taken in South Carolina as late as December. Dunaway (1968) noted that the breeding season in Tennessee extended approximately from late spring to late fall, although pregnant females were recorded on two occasions in January.

Following a gestation of approximately 21 to 24 days, the young are born in a woven grass nest. Litter sizes are usually between one and four, although up to eight have been reported. Average litter sizes of 2.2 (Layne, 1959) and 3.2 (Kaye, 1961; Dunaway, 1968) have been recorded during laboratory studies. Several litters are produced annually.

Growth and development of young eastern harvest mice have been studied by Layne (1959) and Kaye (1961). Newborn young are pink, have their eyes and ears sealed, and possess both vibrissae and sparse hairs scattered along the middle of the back. They weigh approximately 1 g. The ears unfold after one or two days, but the mice cannot hear until they are between 7 and 10 days of age. The eyes open between 7 and 12 days. The incisors usually appear at about one week, by which time the pelage exhibits the general juvenile color pattern of dark grayish-brown upperparts and grayish-white underparts. By the end of the second week, the juvenile pelage is well developed. Weaning occurs between two and four weeks, and sexual maturity is reached at two to three months. Female eastern harvest mice are highly solicitous of their young, and the males apparently aid in their care occasionally.

Longevity. Dunaway (1968) noted that the average life expectancy for this species was relatively long after the mice leave the nest. At six months about 28 percent of 88 mice were still present, and at 10 months 7 of 88 (8 percent) were still alive. One male remained on his study area for at least 463 days and one female for 398 days. Cawthorn and Rose (1989) reported one mouse surviving for at least 10 months.

Pelage Variations. Hooper (1952) noted that harvest mice molt at least twice before growing their adult pelage.

Parasites. The tick *Dermacentor variabilis* has been recorded from eastern harvest mice in Virginia by Sonenshine, Atwood, and Lamb (1966) and Sonenshine, Lamb, and Anastos (1965).

Predation. Harvest mice are probably preyed on by a variety of snakes, hawks, owls, and mammals. Jackson, Pagels, and Trumbo (1976) recorded this species in barn owl pellets in Chesterfield County.

Geographic Variation. The subspecies in Virginia is *Reithrodontomys humulis humulis* Audubon and Bachman. This subspecies has been identified in the western portion of the state as well as in the extreme southeastern corner. A variant inhabits most of the Piedmont and Coastal Plain regions of eastern Virginia.

Other Currently Recognized Subspecies. *Reithrodontomys humulis virginianus* A. H. Howell.

Location of Specimens. AMNH, BCV, CM, CU, CWM, DMNH, DWL, ISUVC, MVZ, NCSM, ODU, PWRC, UCM, UMMZ, USNM, VCU, VPISU, VPI-W.

Genus *Peromyscus*

Dentition: 1/1, 0/0, 0/0, 3/3 = 16

Deer Mouse
Peromyscus maniculatus Wagner

Description. The deer mouse (Plate 47) in Virginia is a medium-sized mouse with large eyes and moderately large ears. The overall dorsal coloration is grayish, and the belly is whitish. The distinctly bicolored tail is dark above and white below.

Two subspecies of deer mouse occur in Virginia. They are very different morphologically and ecologically. They can be best distinguished by the length of their tails. The tail of the woodland deer mouse, *Peromyscus maniculatus maniculatus,* is equal to or longer than its combined head and body length. The prairie deer mouse, *Peromyscus maniculatus bairdii,* has a much shorter tail, much less than half the total length. Both forms are similar to the white-footed mouse, *Peromyscus leucopus,* which is essentially intermediate in several characters between the two. The tail in the white-footed mouse, however, is less distinctly bicolored and is just slightly less than half the total length of the animal. The subspecies *bairdii* ranges between approximately 116 and 154 mm in total length, including a tail 40 to 58 mm long. The subspecies *maniculatus* ranges between approximately 155 and 220 mm in total length, including a tail 80 to 110 mm long. The white-footed mouse is between 140 and 205 mm in total length, including a tail 55 to 100 mm long.

The skull is rather short and compact with small auditory bullae. The skulls of *Peromyscus maniculatus* and *Peromyscus leucopus* are very similar. The anterior palatine foramina in *Peromyscus maniculatus maniculatus* are long, straight, and have parallel borders; those of the prairie deer mouse and the white-footed mouse are wider and have nonparallel lateral borders that bow out in the middle (Figure 89).

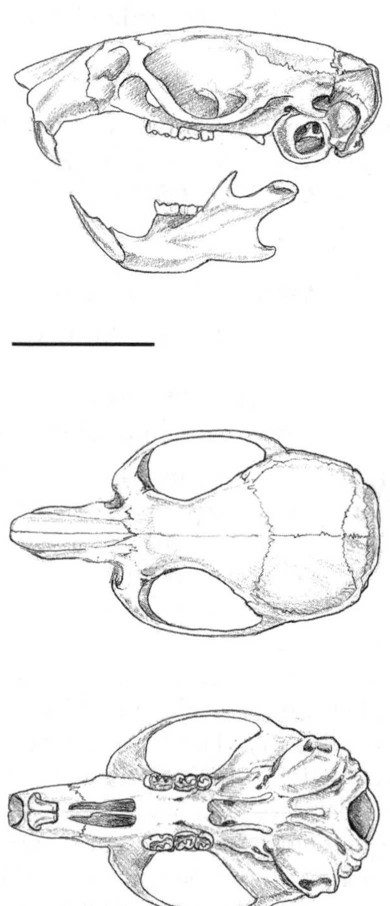

Figure 89. *Peromyscus maniculatus:* Left lateral view of skull and mandible, and dorsal and ventral view of skull. Scale bar = 10 mm.

Distribution. This species ranges throughout much of Alaska and Canada and is found throughout much of the United States except for most of the southeastern states.

In Virginia, the deer mouse is found only in the western and northern portions of the state (Figure 90). The prairie deer mouse was taken for the first time in Virginia in 1962 near Chantilly (Fairfax County) (Peacock and Peacock, 1962). It has also been recorded from Harrisonburg (Rockingham County), 9.7 km north of Warrenton (Fauquier County), Cedarville (Warren County), and 8.2 km southwest of Fairfield (Rockbridge County) (Pitts and Kirkland, Jr., 1987).

Habitat. The woodland deer mouse inhabiting the Appalachian Mountains is a forest-dwelling form and is most abundant in cool, moist situations. Together with the red-backed vole *(Clethrionomys gapperi),* these were the most abundant species found on the summit of Mount Rogers (Linzey, 1980). Kirkland (1975), however, recorded 56 percent of his specimens in non-forested habitats created by clearcutting. Although the deer mouse and the white-footed mouse may both occupy high-elevation habitat, studies in some areas such as Big Black Mountain (Barbour, 1951a) have shown that as the elevation decreases, the deer mouse becomes less abundant and the white-footed mouse becomes more numerous. The prairie deer mouse inhabits grasslands, open weedfields, fencerows, abandoned agricultural land, and even plowed areas (Whitaker, personal communication). In Virginia, this form has been taken "on barren ground surrounded by sparse vegetation; in moderately thick, seedy growth; along roadways; and on grazing land" (Peacock, 1967). The Rockbridge County specimen, the southernmost Virginia record, was taken among large rocks in "a tree line bordering a small grassy field adjacent to a small stream" (Pitts and Kirkland, Jr., 1987).

Habits. Deer mice are primarily nocturnal. They have good eyesight and keen senses of hearing, touch, and smell.

Nests of the woodland deer mouse may be located in trees, stumps, wood piles, or buildings. Wolff and Hurlbutt (1982) and Wolff and Durr (1986) reported differential use of nest sites in Giles County, Virginia. *Peromyscus*

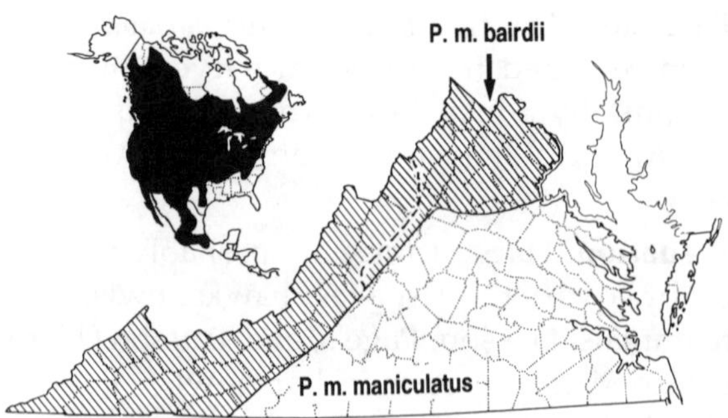

Figure 90. *Peromyscus maniculatus:* Range in Virginia and North America.

maniculatus preferred arboreal nesting sites high in large hollow trees during all seasons. *Peromyscus leucopus* was more variable in the use of ground and tree nest sites in summer but shifted to underground nests in winter. The nest of the prairie deer mouse is often in an underground tunnel or beneath boards on the surface of the ground.

Single use and multiple use burrows of *Peromyscus* were excavated, mapped, and measured in Giles County (Fortune and Cranford, 1994). Multiple use burrows had significantly larger entrances, more entrances, larger nest chamber sizes, longer total tunnel lengths, more tunnel direction changes, and more cached food types and volumes. Tunnel entrances were directed away from prevailing weather patterns.

Nests may be constructed of leaves, grass, shredded bark, moss, paper, cloth, or any other available material. Daily torpor has been noted in at least nine species of *Peromyscus,* including *Peromyscus maniculatus* (Tannenbaum and Pivorun, 1988). Torpor is a thermoregulatory mechanism that reduces metabolic expenditures during times of potential or actual energy stress. It is usually associated with low ambient temperatures and/or food shortages. Nestler (1989) demonstrated that animals undergoing daily torpor showed many of the same physiological characteristics, such as retention of carbon dioxide and respiratory acidosis, as animals preparing to enter hibernation.

Home range size is generally between about 0.4 and 1.2 ha. Home ranges were larger among males than females at Mountain Lake and they were larger at low densities than at high densities (Wolff, 1985c; 1986a). Mean home range size averaged 590 m^2. Population densities ranged from 2 to 19 per ha. During the breeding season, female deer mice may display territorial behavior. A definite homing ability for distances up to approximately 0.4 km is known for this species.

Food. Deer mice feed on a wide variety of items including various kinds of seeds, nuts, acorns, insects, and other invertebrates. Wolff et al. (1985) reported arthropods, fruit, nuts, green vegetation, and fungi eaten by deer mice in Giles County. The relative proportions of these diet items was arthropods (47 percent), fruit (15 percent), adult lepidopterans (10.2 percent), nuts and seeds (10.2 percent), green vegetation (8.6 percent), fungi (4.3 percent), and larval lepidopterans (2.4 percent). No significant difference existed between the diet of this species and *Peromyscus leucopus.* A study of the food habits of the woodland deer mouse in North Carolina and Tennessee revealed seeds, fruit, and vegetation as the principal food items with animal food (chiefly insects) constituting slightly less than 10 percent of the total food volume (Linzey and Linzey, 1973). Regardless of season or habitat, seeds comprised between 57 and 67 percent of the annual diet. Insects formed a larger portion of the diet in summer than in winter. Whitaker (1966) noted that 32.9 percent of the food eaten by the prairie deer mouse in Indiana was of animal origin. Stored food is located by smell (Howard, Marsh, and Cole, 1968).

Reproduction and Development. Wolff (1985) reported a bimodal breeding season in deer mice at Mountain Lake in Giles County. Breeding occurred between April and June and between September and October. The average litter size was 3.4.

Barbour (1951a) recorded pregnant female cloudland deer mice with two to four embryos from June 9 to August 18 and lactating females from June 16 through August 29 in Harlan County, Kentucky. Males in breeding condition were noted from June 9 through August 18. Females with five embryos have been recorded from Fairfax County, Virginia, on February 14 and September 16 (GMU). A lactating female was taken in Giles County, Virginia, on November 11. Kirkland and Linzey (1973) recorded 4.2 young per litter (range 1 to 7) for 33 litters from Cocke County, Tennessee. One pair of wild-caught mice produced 13 litters in slightly over a year (370 days) — 12 of these were born within a period of 313 days. Kirkland (1975) recorded a mean of 3.93 embryos (range 2 to 5) in 28 pregnant females from West Virginia. Pregnant females were taken as late as mid-October.

The average gestation for 22 litters in Tennessee was 28 to 29 days (Linzey, 1970). Newborn mice are pink, essentially hairless, and have their eyes and ears sealed. The ear canal opens at an average age of 11 days, the eyes open at an average age of 15 days, and the lower incisors erupt between six and seven days. Additional data on the growth and development of deer mice are given by Linzey (1970).

Blank et al. (1992) reported that female deer mice respond differentially to the inhibitory effects of a short photoperiod. Seventy-five percent showed significant reductions in body weight and reproductive tract weight when exposed to short photoperiods. The remaining 25 percent, however, showed no loss, indicating that populations are composed of subsets of individuals that differ in their reproductive response to short daylength.

Longevity. Deer mice in the wild rarely survive for more than 1.5 to 2 years, although captive deer mice have lived as long as eight years.

Pelage Variations. Immature deer mice are gray above and have a white belly and feet.

Parasites. The nematode *Capillaria hepatica* has been reported in deer mice from Virginia (Solomon and Handley, 1971). Hensley (1976b, 1978) recorded an unidentified botfly larva (probably *Cuterebra fontinella*) in 1 of 34 deer mice in western Virginia.

Predation. Deer mice are preyed upon by timber rattlesnakes *(Crotalus horridus)* (Solomon, 1974) as well as other snakes, hawks, owls, weasels, foxes, and bobcats. Skulls have been reported from barn owl pellets in Loudon County, Virginia. (GMU).

Geographic Variation. Two subspecies of deer mice occur in Virginia. *Peromyscus maniculatus maniculatus* Wagner occurs in the western portion of the state. *Peromyscus maniculatus bairdii* (Hoy and Kennicott) has been recorded in northern and western Virginia (Peacock and Peacock, 1962; Hensley, 1976b; Pitts and Kirkland, 1987).

Location of Specimens. AEL, AMNH, ASUMZ, AVL, BCV, CHAS, CM, CSULB, CU, CUC, DMNH, DWL, EKU, FSM, GMU, KU, LACM, LC, LFCC, LSUMZ, LU, MSB, NCSM, NVCC, RC, RMWC, RU, SUVM, UCONN, UGAMNH, UMMZ, USNM, VCU, VHCC, VPISU, VPI-W.

White-Footed Mouse
Peromyscus leucopus (Rafinesque)

Description. The white-footed mouse (Plate 48) is a medium-sized mouse with large eyes, long vibrissae, and moderately large ears. The dorsal pelage varies from reddish-brown to grayish-brown with the middorsal area being darker than the sides. Winter pelage is grayer. The belly and feet are white. The tail is slightly less than half the total length of the animal and it is usually indistinctly bicolor. Small internal cheek pouches are normally present. Females possess six mammae. Adult white-footed mice are usually between 140 and 205 mm long, including a tail 55 to 100 mm long. Adults weigh between 14 and 28 g.

The skull is relatively smooth. Auditory bullae and slender zygomatic arches are present. The anterior palatine foramina bow out near their middle. Except for its smaller size, the skull of this species is nearly identical to that of the cotton mouse (Figure 91).

Distribution. The white-footed mouse is found throughout most of the eastern and central United States, from southern Canada, Mon-

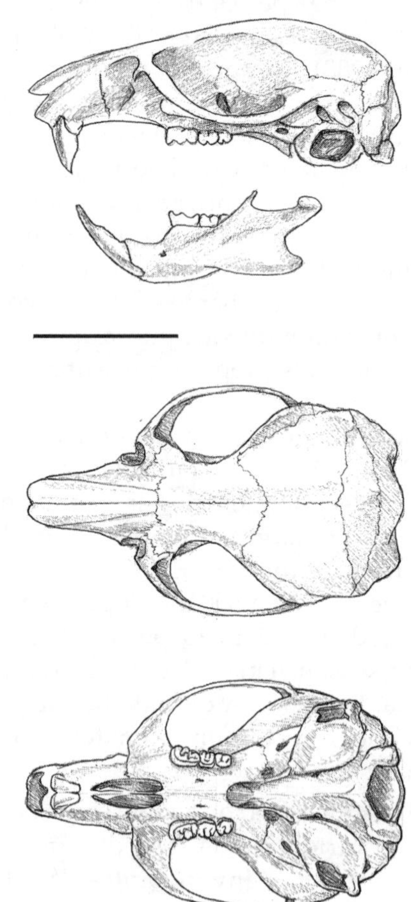

Figure 91. *Peromyscus leucopus:* Left lateral view of skull and mandible, and dorsal and ventral view of skull. Scale bar = 10 mm.

tana, Michigan, and Maine south to central South Carolina, central Georgia, central Alabama, and southwestern Mississippi. Its range extends westward to central Arizona and south through eastern Mexico and Yucatan.

It occurs statewide in Virginia (Figure 92). It is found on four of the barrier islands – Assateague, Wallops, Cedar, and Fishermans (Moncrief and Dueser, 1994).

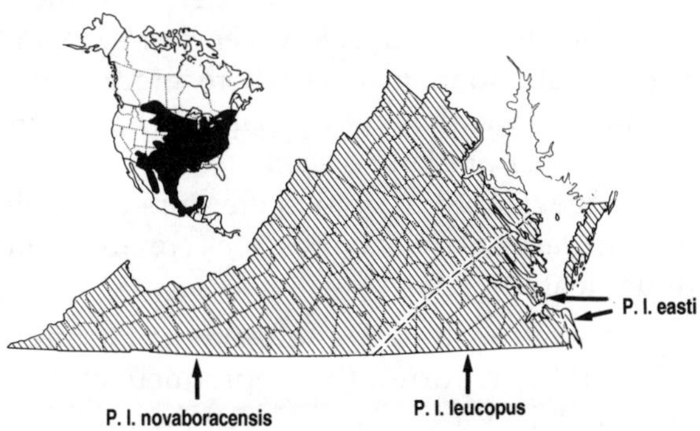

Figure 92. *Peromyscus leucopus:* Range in Virginia and North America.

Habitat. This mouse is found most commonly in brushy areas and in mixed or hardwood upland forests. Some individuals also inhabit riverbottom forests, but in some areas this habitat is occupied by the cotton mouse, *Peromyscus gossypinus.* According to McCarley (1963), white-footed mice are forced out of lowland areas as a result of competition with cotton mice. This premise is supported by the fact that in southern Illinois, where cotton mice do not occur, white-footed mice are more abundant in typical bottom woodlands (Layne, 1958). One Virginia variant lives among the thickets of myrtle behind the coastal sand dunes.

Habits. White-footed mice are primarily nocturnal and are active throughout the year, although they may become torpid for periods of several days under conditions of food deprivation and/or low temperature (Hill, 1975; Lynch et al., 1978). They are usually found in and around fallen logs, piles of rocks, stone walls, around buildings, and other such shelter.

The nest of this species may be in a hollow log or stump, in a hollow tree, in a ground burrow, in a deserted bird nest in a bush or low tree, or in a building. Nest sites located above ground are preferred. Using radiotelemetry at Mountain Lake, Wolff (1986a) located 43 nest sites in trees and 36 underground. Nests are constructed of leaves, grasses, moss, and shredded bark. Females may display territorial behavior during their breeding season, especially when densities are high. White-footed mice may be gregarious during winter, with as many as five animals huddling together in one nest (Wolff, 1986a). This behavior aids in their survival during cold weather.

Homing behavior is well developed in this species. A gradual decline in homing success occurs with increasing distance of displacement, although some individuals have returned to their original point of capture after having been displaced more than 1.6 km. Sight and olfaction are both probably used by these animals in finding their way back to their home area. August et al. (1989) presented data suggesting that this species has a magnetic sense and uses the geomagnetic field as a compass cue.

The home range of the white-footed mouse is generally between 0.1 and 0.6 ha and, as with most species, may vary widely in response to many different factors including habitat, breeding condition, population density, and food supply. Hensley (1978) reported reduced home ranges in botfly-infected animals. Home ranges were larger among males than females at Mountain Lake and, as usually is the case, they were larger at low densities than at high densities (Wolff, 1986a). Mean home range size from 1981 through 1983 was 634 m^2 for males and 511 m^2 for females. Population densities ranged from 6 to 38 per ha. Terman (1987) reported densities from 0.9 to 23 per ha.

A study of naturally-occurring island populations of these deer mice demonstrated that dispersal movements by young animals were accomplished by swimming (Sheppe, 1965). The longest swim recorded was 233 m by a mouse that returned to its home island after being moved to another site, tagged, and released.

White-footed mice are extremely clean and well-kempt. They have excellent senses of hearing, touch, and smell. Their eyesight is also good, particularly during the darker hours. They are adept climbers, using the tail to assist them in their travels above the ground.

White-footed mice of both sexes have been observed to move their front paws rapidly up and down against some resonant object, thus producing a "drumming" sound. This action usually occurs after the mice have been disturbed and is undertaken more often and under less provocation in the small, nervous, and easily excited species such as *Peromyscus leucopus* than in the larger, less excitable species of *Peromyscus*.

Food. White-footed mice are omnivorous, feeding primarily on seeds, fruits, berries, buds, insects, insect larvae, and other invertebrates such as spiders, snails, earthworms, millipedes, and centipedes. Wolff et al. (1985) recorded arthropods, fruit, nuts, green vegetation, and fungi in their diet in Giles County, Virginia. Frequency of occurrence was arthropods (44 percent), fruit (18 percent), green vegetation (9.8 percent), adult lepidopterans (9.5 percent), nuts and seeds (5.9 percent), fungi (4.9 percent), and larval lepidopterans (3.5 percent). No significant difference existed between the diet of this species and *Peromyscus maniculatus*. Lewis (1940) recorded these mice feeding extensively on the fruits of the coral berry *(Symphoricarpos orbiculatus)* during winter in Amelia County, Virginia. Calhoun (1941) calculated that 34 percent of the diet of this mouse in Tennessee was composed of animal foods.

Major summer food items recorded in North Carolina and Tennessee were insects (42.3 percent), fruit skins (17.5 percent), insect larvae (9.0 percent), and millipedes (5.9 percent). Seeds constituted only 2.2 percent of the total volume, while animal foods amounted to 51.4 percent (Linzey and Linzey, 1973). The marked contrast between the summer food habits of the cloudland deer mouse (seeds — 57.7 percent; animal food — 22.2 percent) and the white-footed mouse in this region may be ecologically significant since the two species overlap considerably in their habitat and altitudinal distribution.

Hamilton (1941) recorded the relative frequency of occurrence of food items between November and April in New York to be 72.8 percent arthropods, 43.9 percent nuts and seeds, and 20.5 percent green plant matter. Between May and October, the relative frequency was 71.0 percent arthropods, 52.3 percent fruit, 20.8 percent nuts and seeds, and 3.7 percent fungi. Whitaker (1963c) reported the summer diet in New York to consist of 51 percent nuts and seeds, 26.6 percent arthropods, and 15.3 percent green plant matter.

White-footed mice are normally not of great economic importance, although their consumption of insects and weed seeds is beneficial. Although a small amount of grain may be eaten, these mice prefer more cover than they find in a cultivated field and thus confine their feeding to the margins of the field that meet with undisturbed land. However, if these mammals are abundant in areas where reforestation is taking place, they may consume a considerable number of planted seeds.

Large quantities of food are stored in such hiding places as tree cavities, rock crevices, and under leaf litter.

Reproduction and Development. Terman (1986; 1993) reported that reproductive rates were high in March, April, September, and October and low in June on a study area in southeastern Virginia. Hawkins et al. (1986) reported an average litter size of 3.3 in Montgomery County.

At Mountain Lake in southwestern Virginia, Wolff and Lundy (1985) and Wolff (1985; 1986a) found a bimodal breeding season with peak activity in April through June and September through October with a midsummer breeding lull. Mice bred throughout the winter of 1985–1986. Average litter sizes during the five-year study ranged from 3.3 to 3.5 young per litter (range 1–6) and females averaged 1.4 litters per year. Most of the spring-born animals reached sexual maturity and bred in the fall, except when densities were high.

Cornish and Bradshaw (1978) reported a breeding season extending from February through October in West Virginia. Two periods of intensified breeding occurred, one in the early spring and one in late summer. Peak pregnancies were recorded during April and May and again during August.

A female containing five embryos was taken in Fairfax County, Virginia, on September 10 (GMU). Barbour (1951a; 1951b) recorded females with four and five embryos on July 22, August 18, and August 21 in West Virginia and Kentucky. Lactating females were recorded in March, June, July, and August. Males in breeding condition were taken from June 8 to August 26. In North Carolina, Brimley (1923) recorded pregnant females during January, March, April, July, and November.

Gestation is approximately 22 to 23 days, and females may breed again shortly after parturition. Gestation while the female is nursing a litter may be as long as 37 days (Svihla, 1932). Instances of paternal care have been noted by Horner (1947).

The development of young white-footed mice has been described by Svihla (1932). Newborn young are pink, toothless, lack visible hair, and have their eyes and ears closed. The ears unfold at about three days of age and the eyes open when the young mice are between four and five weeks of age. Females attain sexual maturity at approximately 46 days of age, although conception has been found to occur as early as 39 days (Clark, 1938). Female white-footed mice normally produce several litters a year, with one female having given birth to 26 litters during a two year period and another female having produced 14 litters in a 12 month period (Rood, 1966).

Post-weaning mortality is nearly constant, but autumn-born mice suffer higher mortality between 30 and 90 days after weaning than do spring-born mice (Schug et al., 1990; 1991). Autumn-born females have, on average, a longer lifetime than spring-born females. Both long- and short-lived females reproduced at the same rate. No difference in survival rate was found for males.

Among juveniles at Mountain Lake, none of the males and 7 of 23 (30 percent) females attained sexual maturity and bred within their maternal home ranges (Wolff and Lundy, 1985). Twenty-four percent (7 of 29) of adult females that bred in the spring bred again on the same grid in the fall. Four of the seven females moved the centers of their home ranges about 15 m (the approximate radius of a home range) after weaning their spring litters.

Longevity. Longevity in the white-footed mouse is about four to eight months in the wild, although a few individuals may survive two years or more. Captive white-footed mice have survived over five years.

Pelage Variations. Immature white-footed mice are gray above and have a white belly and feet. Gottschang (1956) described the molt from the gray juvenile pelage to the brown adult pelage. Molting begins between six and seven weeks and requires about three weeks before most mice attain their full adult coat. New fur first appears in front of, or above the hind leg and progresses forward along either side. The gray dorsal stripe is the last area to disappear.

Parasites and Disease. The following parasites have been reported from the white-footed mouse in Virginia by Jordan (1928); Shaftesbury (1934); Reynolds (1938); Moore (1949); Atwood et al. (1964; 1965); Sonenshine, Atwood, and Anastos (1965); Sonenshine, Atwood, and Lamb (1966); Bozeman, Shirai, Humphries, and Fuller (1967); Fox (1968); Solomon and Handley (1971); Hensley (1976a, 1976b, 1978); Jones (1978); Garrett and Sonenshine (1979); Holliman and Meade (1980); Sonenshine and Turner (1988); Eckerlin and Sawyer (1989); Painter and Eckerlin (1993); Hensley (1995); and Eckerlin (1997): **Bacteria** *(Rickettsia rickettsii);* **Protozoa** (protozoans) *(Acanthamoeba polyphaga);* **Nematoda** (roundworms) *(Capillaria hepatica, Trichinella spiralis);* **Trematoda** (flukes) *(Brachylaemus peromysci);* **Siphonaptera** (fleas) *(Ctenophthalmus pseudagyrtes, Epitedia wenmanni, Orchopeas leucopus = Ceratophyllus leucopus, Stenoponia americana = Stenoponia wetmorei);* **Acarina** (ticks) *(Amblyomma americanum, Amblyomma maculatum, Dermacentor variabilis, Ixodes angustus, Ixodes cookei, Ixodes dentatus, Ixodes scapularis);* and **Diptera** (flies) *(Cuterebra fontinella).*

The occurrence of kepone, a manmade chemical and environmental contaminant illegally released into the James River in the mid-1970s, was first recorded in tissues of this species by Terman and Huggett (1980). Kepone is an extremely stable, persistent, and bio-accumulative carcinogenic pesticide.

Predation. This species has been recorded from the stomach of a long-eared owl in Fairfax County, Virginia (Fisher, 1893). Many predators including snakes, other owls, hawks, weasels, foxes, bobcats, and domestic cats include these mice in their diet. Mitchell and Beck (1992) recorded this species from free-ranging domestic cats in New Kent and Henrico counties.

Geographic Variation. The subspecies in Virginia is *Peromyscus leucopus leucopus* (Rafinesque). Two variants have been identified in Virginia, but no primary isolating mechanisms exist. Dice (1940a) found no natural hybridization between this species and *Peromyscus* *gossypinus* in southeastern Virginia. Studies of allozymic variation in mainland and insular populations on the Eastern Shore and adjacent barrier islands has revealed that this species is variable at 7 of 32 presumptive gene loci (Loxterman et al., 1994).

Other Currently Recognized Subspecies. *Peromyscus leucopus easti* Paradiso; *Peromyscus leucopus noveboracensis* (Fischer).

Location of Specimens. AEL, AMNH, ANSP, ASUMZ, AVL, BCV, BRP, CAS, CHAS, CM, CMNH, CSULB, CU, CUMZ, CUC, DMNH, DWL, EHC, FSM, GMU, HSU, IOWA, ISUVC, KU, LACM, LC, LFCC, LSUMZ, MCZ, MMMN, MSB, MVZ, NCSM, NVCC, ODU, OU, RC, RMWC, SBC, SM, SUVM, UCONN, UGAMNH, UIMNH, UMMZ, USNM, VA, VCM, VCU, VMNH, VPISU, VPI-W, WL, YPM.

Cotton Mouse
Peromyscus gossypinus (LeConte)

Description. The cotton mouse (Plate 49) is very similar to the white-footed mouse. Its color ranges from dark sooty to tawny brown above and whitish below. The middorsal area is darker than the sides. The feet are white. The sparsely haired tail is less than half the total length and is usually indistinctly bicolor. Adult cotton mice can often be distinguished from white-footed mice by hind foot size. The white-footed mouse seldom has a hind foot longer than 23 mm (19–24 mm), while the hind foot in the cotton mouse is seldom shorter than 23 mm (22–26 mm). Cotton mice also possess large eyes and moderately large ears. Six mammae are present. Adult cotton mice are normally between 175 and 200 mm long, including a tail 70 to 90 mm long. They weigh between 28 and 56 g. Thus the cotton mouse differs from the white-footed mouse principally in its slightly larger size, its slightly darker color, and its larger hind foot.

The skull of this species is also similar to that of the white-footed mouse but averages slightly larger and is more robust (Figure 93).

Distribution. The cotton mouse is a species of the southeastern states. It is found from southeastern Virginia to southern Florida, west to southeastern Oklahoma and eastern Texas, and north to southern Illinois. Although found principally on the Coastal Plain, this species does extend into the Piedmont region and into the foothills of the mountains.

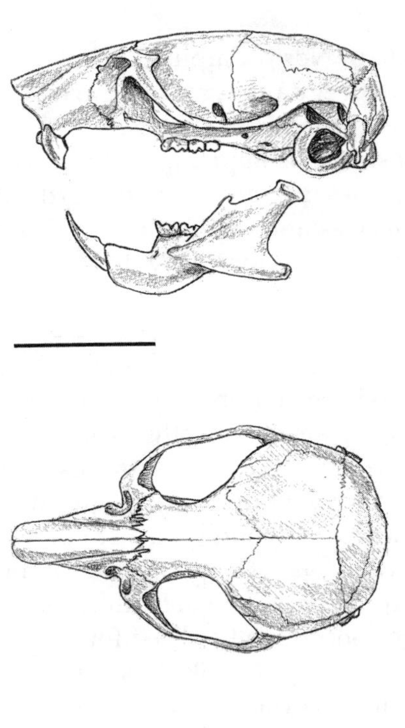

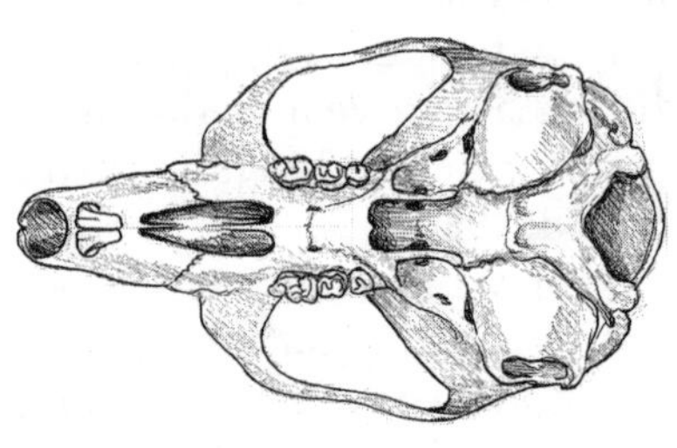

Figure 93. *Peromyscus gossypinus:* Left lateral view of skull and mandible, and dorsal and ventral view of skull. Scale bar = 10 mm.

In Virginia, the cotton mouse is found in localized populations in the southeastern portion of the state (Figure 94). Its status as one of Virginia's vulnerable mammals is presently undetermined due to lack of sufficient data (Handley, 1979b; 1991).

Habitat. Throughout most of their range, cotton mice prefer wooded low ground, floodplains of streams and rivers, timbered swampland, and brushy areas near water, whereas white-footed mice usually inhabit higher, drier ground, rocky ledges or bluffs, caves, and abandoned buildings. However, both species sometimes occupy the same habitat and have been taken on the same trap lines.

In Virginia, this species has been taken under a fallen tree root in greenbrier, honeysuckle, sweet bay, and black gum at the edge of swampy river-bottom woods (Ulmer, 1963).

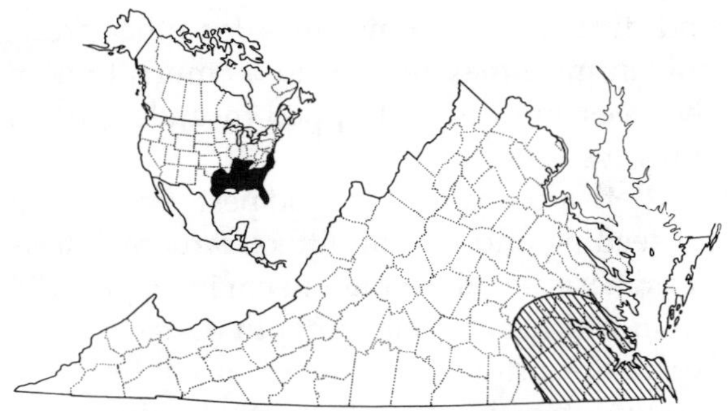

Figure 94. *Peromyscus gossypinus:* Range in Virginia and North America.

Jackson et al. (1976) found it abundant in periodically flooded timbered swampland.

Habits. Cotton mice, like white-footed mice, are nocturnal and are active throughout the year. Although primarily terrestrial, they have considerable climbing ability. In lowland areas, they are found most commonly in and around hollow trees, logs, stumps, piles of rocks, stone walls, and in buildings. Nests may be located within these structures or beneath the surface of the ground. The nest is generally constructed of grasses, leaves, shredded bark, and other similar materials that may be available.

Home ranges average between 0.6 and 0.8 ha. Many lowland areas inhabited by cotton mice are subject to periodic flooding. During flooding of short duration, these mice are reluctant to leave their home range and apparently live in trees until the water recedes.

Animals are apparently familiar with an area larger than the current home range as a result of dispersal, exploratory movements, and home range shifts. In extensive homing experiments, every individual of both sexes, when released in natural habitat, homed from distances up to 152 m, and at distances from 183 to 763 m, 78 percent of the males and 60 percent of the females returned. After being released, mice wandered at random until familiar territory was encountered and then were able to select a relatively direct pathway to the home range.

The senses of sight, hearing, and smell are well developed in this species. Drumming has been observed by Ivey (1949) and others.

Food. The food of cotton mice consists mainly of seeds, fruits, berries, nuts, insects, and other small invertebrates. A summer study in Tennessee revealed that 68 percent of their diet was composed of animal matter, especially beetles, lepidopterans, and spiders (Calhoun, 1941).

Reproduction and Development. Breeding in this species in Virginia probably begins in February and March and extends through the spring and summer. Gestation is approximately 23 days in a nonlactating female. Most births take place between 6 A.M. and noon (Pournelle, 1952). Litters range from one to seven (average = four). Newborn young are pink, toothless, and hairless except for fine vibrissae. Their eyes and ears are sealed. The pinnae of the ears unfold at about four days of age, and by one week the incisors have erupted. The eyes usually open when the young are 12 to 14 days old. Weaning occurs between three and four weeks. Male cotton mice may be sexually mature at 45 days of age, while the earliest fertile mating of a female cotton mouse occurred at 73 days of age (Pournelle, 1952).

Longevity. The average life span of a wild cotton mouse is approximately four to five months, with most surviving less than one year.

Predation. Cotton mice are taken by snakes, hawks, owls, skunks, weasels, foxes, and bobcats.

Geographic Variation. The subspecies inhabiting Virginia is *Peromyscus gossypinus gossypinus* (LeConte). *Peromyscus gossypinus* and *Peromyscus leucopus* are not well differentiated species. They are interfertile in the laboratory, but Dice (1940a) found no natural hybridization between them in southeastern Virginia.

Location of Specimens. AMNH, BCV, IOWA, ODU, UMMZ, USNM, VCU, VPISU.

Genus *Ochrotomys*

Dentition: 1/1, 0/0, 0/0, 3/3 = 16

Golden Mouse
Ochrotomys nuttalli (Harlan)

Description. The golden mouse (Plate 50) is one of the most beautiful and unique of the native mice inhabiting Virginia. It derives its common name from its bright russet and golden fur, which is dense and soft and covers its head, ears, back, and sides. The feet and underparts range from creamy white to cinnamon orange. The contrast between the back and belly is not as sharp as in the cotton mouse. The tail is pale golden brown above and creamy below. This species possesses several unique adaptations for its semiarboreal habits including a semiprehensile tail and feet that are smaller than in ground-dwelling mice of the same size. Females possess six mammae. Adult golden mice are normally between 140 and 200 mm in total length, including a tail 60 to 100 mm long. Adults weigh approximately 14 g.

The skull is relatively broad with an inflated braincase. Auditory bullae are present. The skull may be distinguished from *Peromyscus* because the posterior palatine foramina are nearer to the posterior edge of the hard palate than to the anterior palatine foramina. In *Peromyscus,* they are located approximately midway (Figure 95).

Distribution. The golden mouse is a species of the southeastern and southcentral United States. It ranges northward to central Virginia, Kentucky, and southern Illinois, westward to eastern Oklahoma and eastern Texas, and south to the Gulf of Mexico and central Florida.

Although infrequently seen, the golden mouse occurs throughout the southern half of Virginia (Figure 96). It is not rare, but it occurs in localized populations. It is abundant in the Dismal Swamp (Rose et al., 1990; Rose 1992).

Habitat. Golden mice are most often taken in lowland, heavily forested floodplains. They are semiarboreal and prefer areas of thick undergrowth, including vines such as greenbrier and honeysuckle. These mice may also be found in canebrakes, hammocks, moist thickets, along the brushy borders of fields, and occasionally in drier, upland situations.

Habits. The golden mouse is semiarboreal. I have observed golden mice climbing as high as 9 m above the ground. They run easily along limbs using their tails for balance, much as a tight-rope walker balances by shifting a pole from one side to the other. Whenever the animal pauses, its tail will immediately encircle a nearby vine or branch. The prehensile tail of the golden mouse cannot support the entire weight of the animal but is used mainly as a balancing and stabilizing organ.

The greenbrier vines that are almost always found in golden mouse habitat climb trees to considerable heights and serve as one of the main routes of travel, provide most of the nest sites, and produce fruits and seeds eaten by these mice. In the western portion of its range and during the summer in some other areas, golden mice may not spend as much time in the trees and can be trapped in underground runways.

Both arboreal and ground nests are utilized for feeding and rearing litters. Arboreal nests are spherical and average 14 cm in length, 11.4 cm in width, and 9 cm in depth (Linzey, 1968). Nests are often constructed in conifers, although other investigators and I have found them in maple and apple trees, mountain laurel, and blackberry patches. The nests are usually located either in forks of the trees or in greenbrier, honeysuckle, wild grapevines, or Spanish moss alongside the trees. Nest sites range from 0.5 to 8.2 m above the ground (Linzey, 1968).

The nests are usually composed of two distinct layers. The outer covering is mainly of leaves, deciduous or coniferous, or both. The inner nest chamber is constructed of finely shredded bark, grasses, and sometimes feathers. Seeds are found in most nests, varying from less than 1 to about 27 percent of the total weight of the nest (Linzey, 1968).

Not all golden mice construct arboreal nests. Some nests have been found in and under fallen logs and beneath stumps and rocks.

Golden mice often construct feeding platforms. They bring much of their food to these platforms and eat it there. These mice use their well-developed internal cheek pouches to transport seeds from one area to another. As the seeds are gathered, they are stuffed into the pouches, which gradually assume a lumpy appearance. When the golden mice return to their nest or feeding platform, they use their front feet to push the seeds out of the pouches. Careful dissection of feeding platforms can reveal much information about the dietary habits of these mice.

Home range size of the golden mouse cannot be directly compared to that of many other small mammals because the vertical component must be taken into consideration. Average home range sizes, calculated by a variety of methods, have ranged from 0.05 to 0.6 ha.

Golden mice spend the daylight hours in their nest and become active at dusk. They are among the most docile of all wild mice and are quite sociable, as many as eight having been found in the same nest. Population densities

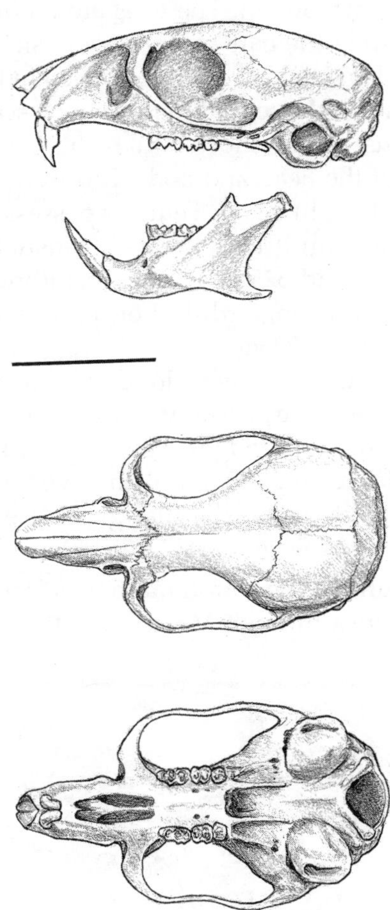

Figure 95. *Ochrotomys nuttalli:* Left lateral view of skull and mandible, and dorsal and ventral view of skull. Scale bar = 10 mm.

up to 8.9 mice per ha have been recorded.

Food. Golden mice are omnivorous. Greenbrier, cherry, sumac, and dogwood seeds form a large part of the diet, while fruits and nuts such as blackberries and acorns may constitute a considerable part of the food during certain seasons of the year (deRageot, 1964a; Linzey, 1968). Insect remains were found in approximately 70 percent of the golden mice that I examined in Tennessee and constituted a major food item.

Reproduction and Development. In Kentucky, Tennessee, and Virginia the breeding season extends from March to October with peaks occurring in late spring and early fall. On June 6, 1895, A. K. Fisher recorded a female with three or young in a nest 0.6 m above the ground in a bush in the Dismal Swamp (Handley, 1979a). Gestation is between 23 and 25 days. Litter size is from one to four with an average of 2.6 young per litter (Linzey and Linzey, 1967b). There is evidence that latitude and mean litter size are positively correlated in the golden mouse (Blus, 1966).

Growth and development has been studied (Linzey and Linzey, 1967b). At birth, golden mice are naked, pink, and blind and have their ears sealed. The ears become fully erect at about 1.8 days, but the young exhibit no reaction to sound until they are approximately 10 days. The first teeth, the lower incisors, begin to erupt at six days. The eyes of young golden mice open between 12 and 13 days. Weaning begins at approximately 17 to 18 days old, and is apparently complete by about three weeks. If the young are allowed to remain with their mother, they will continue to nurse for a longer period. Juvenile golden mice have dark golden fur, unlike the young of *Peromyscus*, which are gray until the first molt.

Longevity. McCarley (1958) recorded an average natural life span of approximately 6.5 months in Texas. An adult male lived in his study area for 19 months and was still alive when the study was discontinued. During my study of this species in Tennessee, 10 golden mice resided in the study area for eight months or longer. Two mice — a male and a female — were recorded in the study area for 366 and 365 days, respectively. Both animals were adult when first captured, and the male was still present at the conclusion of the study (Linzey, 1968). The longest recorded natural life span of a golden mouse is at least 2.5 years (Pearson, 1953).

In captivity 60 percent of the golden mice reaching adulthood survived longer than one year, 29 percent longer than two years, and 11 percent (17 animals) three years or longer. Of

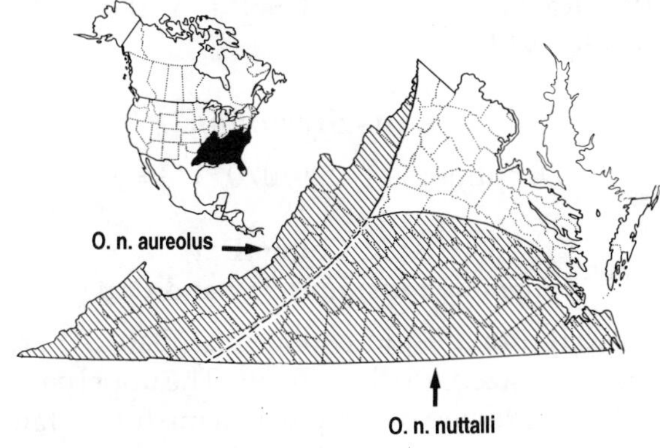

Figure 96. *Ochrotomys nuttalli:* Range in Virginia and North America.

these 17, five lived for six years or longer, and one, a female, lived for eight years, five months (Linzey and Packard, 1977). This is the longest life span recorded for any North American sigmodontine rodent.

Pelage Variations. The maturational and seasonal molts of the golden mouse have been studied in detail by Linzey and Linzey (1967a). The adult pelage is attained by a single maturational molt that begins on the ventral surface and spreads dorsally, meeting in the dorsal midline. It then proceeds anteriorly and posteriorly. Males begin molting at 36 days, females at 38 days. The average duration of the molt is between 25 and 29 days. Seasonal molts in the spring and fall are more irregular than the post-juvenile molt.

Parasites. The tick *Dermacentor variabilis* has been recorded from this species in the Dismal Swamp by Garrett and Sonenshine (1979).

Predation. No specific instances of predation upon golden mice have been recorded in Virginia. These mice are undoubtedly preyed on by snakes, owls, foxes, weasels, and skunks, even though their semiarboreal habits may make them less available to most of these predators than are the more terrestrial species of small mammals.

Geographic Variation. The subspecies in Virginia is *Ochrotomys nuttalli nuttalli* (Harlan). One geographic variant has been identified, but no primary isolating mechanism exists.

Other currently Recognized Subspecies. *Ochrotomys nuttalli aureolus* (Audubon and Bachman).

Location of Specimens. AMNH, BCV, CU, DMNH, GMU, ISUVC, MVZ, NCSM, ODU, RC, RMWC, UMMZ, USNM, VCU, VLM, VPISU, VPI-W.

Genus *Sigmodon*

Dentition: 1/1, 0/0, 0/0, 3/3 = 16

Hispid Cotton Rat
Sigmodon hispidus Say and Ord

Description. Hispid cotton rats (Plate 51) are medium-sized, stocky rodents. The upperparts of both sexes are covered with a mixture of tan, brown, and black fur which gives the animal a coarse, grizzled appearance. The underparts are usually whitish or grayish, and the feet are gray to dark brown. The eyes are moderately large, while the ears are relatively small and rounded and are partially concealed in the fur. The sparsely-haired tail has obvious scaly annulations and is shorter than the combined length of the head and body. It is dark above, grading to light below. Females possess 8 to 10 mammae. Adult cotton rats are usually between 225 and 325 mm long, including a tail 80 to 135 mm long. Adults normally weigh between 112 and 225 g.

The skull is relatively long and narrow and is characterized by a heavy rostrum and prominent supraorbital ridges. The cusps of the upper molar teeth exhibit a distinctive S-shaped pattern, a characteristic that gives rise to the generic name *Sigmodon* (Figure 97).

Distribution. The cotton rat ranges from Central America through Mexico and throughout

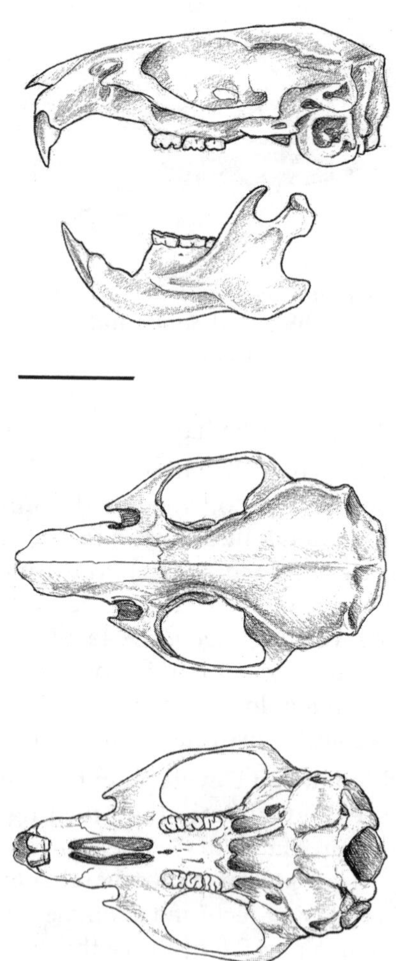

Figure 97. *Sigmodon hispidus:* Left lateral view of skull and mandible, and dorsal and ventral view of skull. Scale bar = 10 mm.

most of the southeastern United States north to southeastern Kentucky (Davis and Barbour, 1979) and southern Virginia. It is the most abundant rodent in most of this region. This species is apparently extending its range northward, perhaps in response to a warming trend in climate (Hall, 1958; Pagels and Adleman, 1971).

In Virginia, the cotton rat has been found in the southern portion of the state (Figure 98). It was first recorded from western Virginia in 1977 when six individuals were taken in Lee County (Davis and Barbour, 1979). Rose et al. (1990) recorded this species for the first time in the Dismal Swamp.

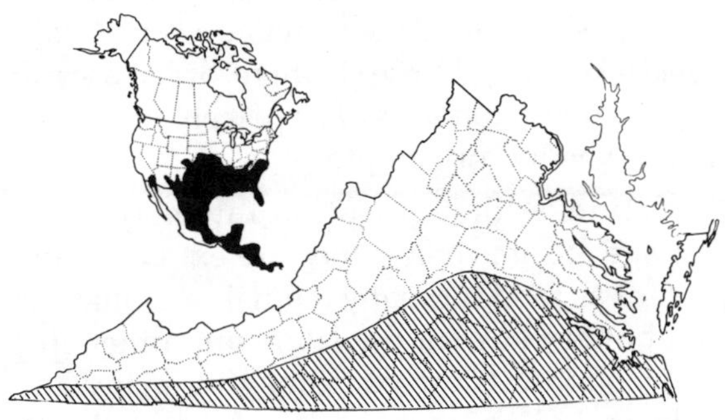

Figure 98. *Sigmodon hispidus:* Range in Virginia and North America.

Habitat. Dense grassy cover is an essential feature of good cotton rat habitat. Cotton rats are found in grassy fields, brushy pastures, ditches, marshes, and along the brushy or weed-grown borders of cultivated fields. Wright and Pagels (1977) reported on the climbing activity of this species, particularly in areas of honeysuckle.

Habits. Cotton rats are active all year, and at any hour of the day or night. Laboratory animals, however, exhibited the greatest amount of activity shortly after dark and at dawn (Calhoun, 1945). Decreased activity occurs during daylight in summer. Biotelemetric studies have revealed that most daily activity occurs from late afternoon to midnight (Roper, 1971). Also, heavy rain and extreme cold inhibited movements while light to moderate rain had little effect on activity. Kirksey et al. (1975) noted:

> *In Virginia,* Sigmodon *is diurnal most of the year but is often caught at night during severe winter weather (Pagels, unpublished), apparently foraging to support increased energy needs.*

These mammals make well-defined runways in the grass. Runways may be 7.5 to 10 cm wide and are kept shorn of new growth. Tunnels 6 to 10 cm below the surface of the ground join the surface runway system. Small piles of grasses and sedges are cut and placed at irregular intervals in the runways.

Nests are usually built beneath boards, logs, or rocks or in the ground at the end of a long but shallow tunnel. Nests are constructed of grass, fibers stripped from the stems of larger plants, and any other suitable material that may be available.

The average home range of this species is between 0.2 and 0.35 ha (Layne, 1974). Successful homing has been recorded from distances up to 1,500 m (Debusk and Kennerly, 1975).

Populations have been known to fluctuate greatly. During one such fluctuation in Texas, a seven-year drought followed by a year of high rainfall resulted in cotton rat populations as high as several hundred per acre (Davis, 1966). During another population explosion, Hamilton (1939) reported that the poisoning of 0.4 ha of sweet potatoes resulted in the destruction of over 500 cotton rats.

Destruction of quail eggs and eggs of other ground-nesting birds and competition for game foods has been noted. Schwartz and Schwartz (1959) stated:

> *In the southern United States these rats are considered important in relation to bobwhite quail. They compete with quail for food, and feed on quail eggs. However, occasional destruction of quail nests by these rats may have some beneficial aspects: it causes the hens to lay again and, because predation does not occur on all nests at one time, nest building is staggered throughout the breeding season. Thus, all nests are not vulnerable simultaneously to adverse weather or some other widespread agent of destruction.*

As a laboratory animal, the cotton rat has proved useful in research studies on poliomyelitis, typhus, tuberculosis, and diphtheria.

Food. Cotton rats feed mainly on the leaves, stems, roots, and seeds of grasses, sedges, and cultivated crops such as alfalfa, sweet potatoes, and various other truck crops. In feeding on tall plants, the rats sever the stems near the base and then cut them into sections. Other foods include the eggs and young of ground-nesting birds, insects, crayfish, fiddler crabs, and carrion. Cotton rats apparently do not practice food storage.

Reproduction and Development. In a study near Portsmouth, Rose (1986) and Rose and Mitchell (1990) reported no pregnant females from November through February. Thus, in Virginia the breeding season probably extends from February through September. Cotton rats are among the most prolific mammals with wild females producing three or four litters a year. In the laboratory, as many as nine litters a year have been produced by a single female.

Gestation requires about 27 days in this species, and three to eight hours after giving birth the female may breed again. Information on prenatal development of cotton rats has been presented by Keys (1966). Litter sizes range from 1 to 15 with a usual average of five to six young. Females containing four and five embryos have been recorded in Virginia by Lewis (1944) and Pagels and Adleman (1971). Rose and Mitchell (1990) reported an average litter size of 5.0 for southeastern Virginia. Small or young females carry fewer embryos than larger or older females. In addition, there is evidence that litter size is affected by latitude as well as by climate and season of the year (Goertz, 1965; Kilgore, 1970; Bowdre, 1971; Rose and Mitchell, 1990). A review of the literature concerning average litter size and litter size variation in *Sigmodon* has been presented by Goertz (1965).

The growth and development of young cotton rats has been described by Meyer and Meyer (1944). Newborn young are furred and are able to run about before their eyes open. At birth they are approximately 76 mm in length and weigh 6.5 g. The eyes usually open and the ears unfold within 18 to 36 hours following birth. The young venture from the nest at four to seven days of age, and are weaned between 15 and 25 days. Although some cotton rats may begin breeding when only 35 to 40 days old, most do not breed until they are about two months of age. Cotton rats are fully grown at five months.

Longevity. Few wild cotton rats may be expected to live more than six months; the oldest recorded one was 12 months old (Goertz, 1964). Provo (1957) found that only 13.2 percent of the cotton rats lived over six months, and the oldest animal in his study was 9.5 months old. Thus, in some populations, turnover may be virtually complete every six to nine months. Cotton rats have lived in captivity for five years and two months (Jones, 1982).

Parasites. The bacterium *Rickettsia rickettsii* has been isolated from this species in Virginia by Bozeman et al. (1967). Seidenberg et al. (1974) reported the cestodes *Choanotaenia nebraskensis, Hymenolepis diminuta, Raillietina bakeri,* and *Taenia taeniaeformis* and the nematodes *Longistriata adunca* and *Mastophorus muris.* Holliman and Meade (1980) recorded *Trichinella spiralis* from this species in Henrico County. Hopkins and Rose (1984) reported the nematode *Physaloptera hispida.* Hiller and Rose (1995) recorded ascarid worms in the stomachs of 23 percent of the animals taken in Portsmouth.

Predation. Although cotton rats may cause damage to some crops, they are extremely important as food for many animals and may act as a buffer between predators and other species. Cotton rats are consumed by many animals, including owls, hawks, foxes, bobcats, raccoons, weasels, mink, and many kinds of snakes.

Geographic Variation. The subspecies of cotton rat inhabiting Virginia is *Sigmodon hispidus hispidus* Say and Ord.

Location of Specimens. AV, BCV, CU, GMU, LU, ODU, UMMZ, USNM, VCU, VMNH, VPI-W.

Genus *Neotoma*

Dentition: 1/1, 0/0, 0/0, 3/3 = 16

Allegheny Woodrat
Neotoma magister Baird

Description. The Allegheny woodrat (Plate 52) is an attractive mammal. It looks like a big *Peromyscus* with its large eyes, long vibrissae, and soft, brownish-gray fur overlain with black-tipped hairs. A dark middorsal area is usually present. The throat, belly, and feet are whitish. The long, moderately well-haired tail is brownish above and white or gray below. The ears are relatively large and sparsely haired. Females possess four mammae. Adult woodrats attain lengths of 350 to 425 mm, including a tail 150 to 200 mm long. Adults generally weigh between 200 and 365 g.

The elongate skull has moderately developed supraorbital ridges and a slight interorbital constriction. Small, rounded auditory bullae are present. The top of the skull between the eye sockets is depressed, unlike the flattened condition found in the skulls of similar-appearing Norway and black rats. The molars have a prismatic pattern causing them to resemble rootless teeth. The dorsal border of the infraorbital canal is shallowly emarginate (Figure 99).

Distribution. Woodrats are restricted to Central and North America, with a number of species found in the western half of the continent. The Allegheny woodrat is found from northern Alabama and Georgia northward in the Appalachian Mountains to Connecticut. It ranges west to southern Indiana and Illinois.

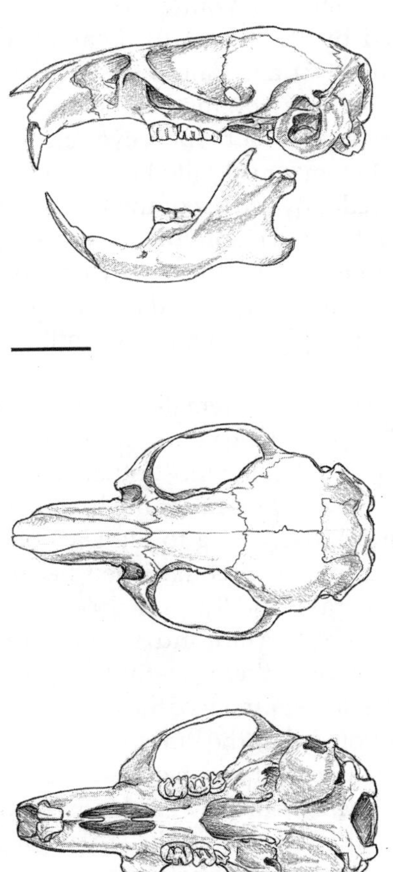

Figure 99. *Neotoma magister:* Left lateral view of skull and mandible, and dorsal and ventral view of skull. Scale bar = 10 mm.

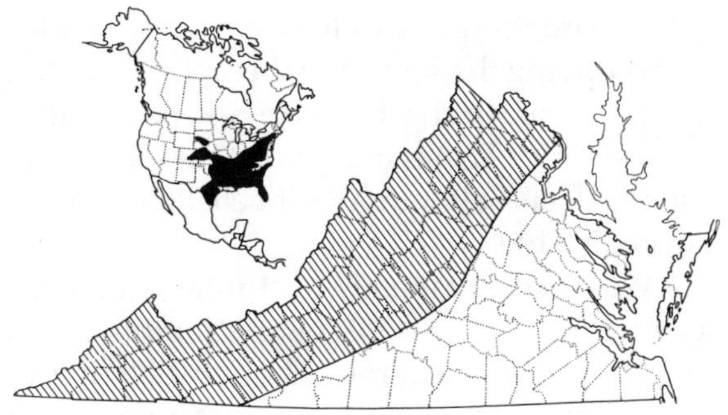

Figure 100. *Neotoma magister:* Range in Virginia and North America.

Originally, populations were classified as *Neotoma magister.* Later, *Neotoma magister* became a synonym of *Neotoma floridana.* On the basis of genetic and morphological differences, however, Hayes (1990), Hayes and Harrison (1992), and Hayes and Richmond (1993) concluded that *Neotoma floridana magister* was reproductively isolated from other taxa of woodrats and should be recognized as a distinct species using the biological species concept of Mayr (1942).

This species is found only in the northern and western portions of Virginia (Figure 100). It inhabits the cliffs and bluffs of river valleys as far east as Arlington County. The Northampton County specimens cited by Hayes and Richmond (1993) are in error (Hayes, personal communication, 1995; Fisher, personal communication, 1995).

Habitat. The Allegheny woodrat may be found in a variety of places including stream or gully banks, wooded bottomlands, swamps, caves, and cliffs. In rural areas woodrats frequently make their homes in outbuildings or abandoned structures.

Habits. Woodrats, also known as mountain rats and cave rats, are well known for their habit of collecting unusual objects such as nails, coins, spoons, bits of tin, colored glass, china, rags, bleached bones and skulls, eyeglasses, and false teeth. They exchange articles and will generally leave behind a few nuts, a pinecone, or a pebble in place of the object they have taken. Because of their habits, these rats are also referred to as packrats, particularly in the western states.

These mammals are primarily solitary, although some investigators have noted more or less colonial populations dwelling in localized habitat situations, as well as several individuals occupying the same nest. In captivity males, females, and young have been kept together successfully. These mammals are clean and usually docile, although their behavior remains unpredictable.

Woodrats are mainly nocturnal mammals, leaving their retreats just before sundown and returning before sunrise. Those rats living in caves, however, seem to be more active during the daylight hours. Woodrats are active throughout the year and do not hibernate.

These rats construct a football-sized nest of shredded bark and grasses. The "inner" nest may be surrounded by a conspicuous pile of sticks, twigs, and debris which may be up to 2.7 m in diameter and 1.2 to 1.5 m high. The shape, size, and construction of the houses vary according to the sites where they are located. Nests and houses are usually on the ground and may be located against the side of a tree; on, against, or beneath a fallen tree or tree stump; in buildings; in rock crevices; under overhanging ledges; or in dense brush. Woodrat nests in trees have been noted in areas that are inundated by water at certain times of the year (Neal, 1967). Well-defined trails lead to the nest. Arboreal nests in South Carolina have been found in tangles of grape and greenbrier vines up to a height of 4.5 m. Woodrats sometimes live in underground burrows.

Woodrat houses may have as many as 10 entrances. Rainey (1956) noted that occupied woodrat houses are frequently used as retreats by toads, lizards, snakes, opossums, shrews, cottontails, and deer mice.

The home range of woodrats is rarely more than 90 m across. Goertz (1970) recorded average home ranges between 0.17 and 0.26 ha. Woodrats released in woodland 183, 366, and 403 m from their point of capture returned to their home territory. Individuals released in pasture 0.8 kilometer away did not return (Lay and Baker, 1938). Movements of 0.8 to 1.2 km have been recorded by Wiley (1971).

"Drumming" has been observed in this species and serves as a warning or alarm note. The sound is produced by thumping the front or the hind feet. The rate and intensity of the thumping varies individually and also according to the degree of disturbance.

The senses of sight, smell, hearing, and touch are well developed in this species. Although generally silent, woodrats will utter loud squeaks when fighting or angry.

Food. Woodrats are mainly vegetarians, feeding on fruits, berries, nuts, seeds, bark, herbs, and grasses. A few insects may also be consumed. Food storage is usually begun in the fall of the year with the food normally stored in the upper portion of the house.

Reproduction and Development. The Allegheny woodrat breeds during the warmer months of the year and produces several litters annually. Barbour (1951a) recorded a male in breeding condition in July and a lactating female on August 24 in Harland County, Kentucky. Between 33 and 39 days following breeding, up to seven young are born. Small litters seem to be the norm, however, and most consist of two or three young. Females may breed again shortly after the birth of the litter.

Development of young woodrats has been described by Poole (1940), Pearson (1952), Hamilton (1953), and Rainey (1956). The young at birth are darkly pigmented on the back and have very sparse hair. Their eyes and ears are closed. Movement is limited to rolling and uncoordinated movements of the limbs. The pinnae of the ears have unfolded by one week and the eyes open during the third week. Weaning is usually between three and four weeks of age. Females probably do not breed until one year old.

When disturbed, female woodrats will exit from the nest with the young securely attached to the nipples. Unlike most other rodents, the incisor teeth are present at birth and serve to firmly attach the young to the teats of the female. This can be accomplished because the tips of the upper and lower incisors are spread apart so that a diamond-shaped space is formed between them. Hamilton (1953) discussed the development of the teeth in this species and noted that the curvature and separation of the tips of the incisors are lost by wear and that the incisor tips gradually straighten into the pattern of the adults. This straightening process takes place between 9 and 18 days of age.

Longevity. A male woodrat that was a 245 g adult when first captured survived for at least 1,352 days or a period of at least 45 months in the wild in Giles County (Mengak, 1997). A female that was a 230 g subadult when first captured survived for 1,318 days (44 months) at the same site. The estimated life span of the male was approximately 50 months; that of the female approximately 49 months.

Pelage Variations. Hovey (1882) noted: "In Counts Cave, 3 miles north of Luray, rats have been frequently caught that were perfectly white, and with large protruding eyes; evidently modified from outside varieties." This reference probably pertains to Allegheny woodrats.

Postjuvenile molting is discussed by Hamilton (1953) and Rainey (1956).

Parasites. The fleas *Ceratophyllus sexdentatus pennsylvanicus* and *Epitedia cavernicola* have been recorded from this species in Virginia by Jordan (1928), Holland and Benton (1968), and Fox (1968). Painter and Eckerlin (1987) reported a 50 percent flea infestation rate with an average of 3.2 fleas per animal. A botfly was present in the neck of a specimen taken in Shenandoah County, Virginia (GMU). Mengak and Terwilliger (1991) reported botfly infestations in five individuals from Shenandoah National Park and Castle Rock.

Predation. Potential predators of woodrats include various snakes, hawks, owls, raccoons, weasels, bobcats, skunks, and foxes. Bailey (1946) recorded a specimen taken by a timber rattlesnake in Giles County.

Location of Specimens. AMNH, ANSP, BRP, CHAS, CUC, DMNH, EKU, FSM, GMU, KU, LACM, LC, LFCC, LSUMZ, NVCC, OU, RMWC, UCLA, UCONN, UGAMNH, UMMZ, USNM, VHCC, VPISU, VPI-W.

Subfamily Arvicolinae

Genus *Clethrionomys*

Dentition: 1/1, 0/0, 0/0, 3/3 = 16

Southern Red-Backed Vole
Clethrionomys gapperi (Vigors)

Description. Red-backed voles (Plate 53) are small, moderately short-tailed mice. The dorsal pelage is reddish, the sides are grayish, and the belly is silvery. A wide reddish-brown dorsal stripe is frequently present. The medium-length tail is bicolor. Females possess eight mammae. Adult red-backed voles are generally between 120 and 165 mm long, including a tail 35 to 50 mm long. Adults weigh between 14 and 42 g.

The skull has a broad braincase and large auditory bullae. The palate ends posteriorly as a straight, transverse shelf (Figure 101).

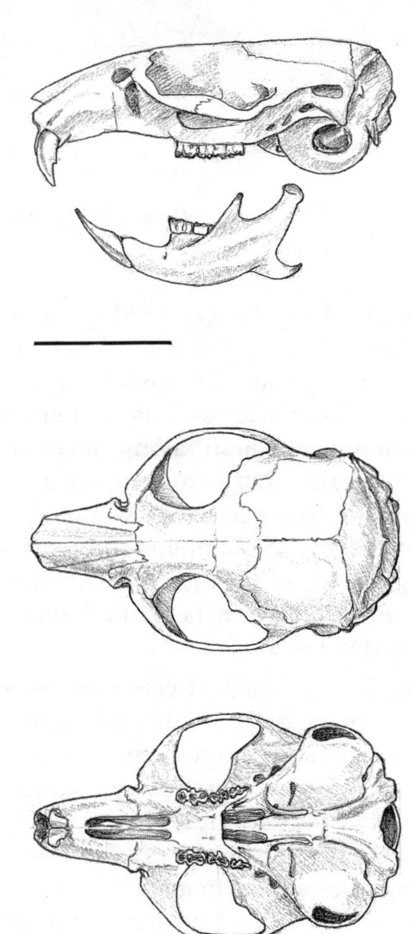

Figure 101. *Clethrionomys gapperi:* Left lateral view of skull and mandible, and dorsal and ventral view of skull. Scale bar = 10 mm.

Distribution. The red-backed vole occurs throughout most of Canada and the northern tier of the United States. The range extends south in the Appalachian Mountains to western North Carolina and in the Rocky Mountains to Arizona and New Mexico.

In Virginia, red-backed voles are found primarily in the western portion of the state (Figure 102).

Habitat. This vole is a northern species and is primarily an inhabitant of cool, damp areas in coniferous, deciduous, or mixed forests. Moss-

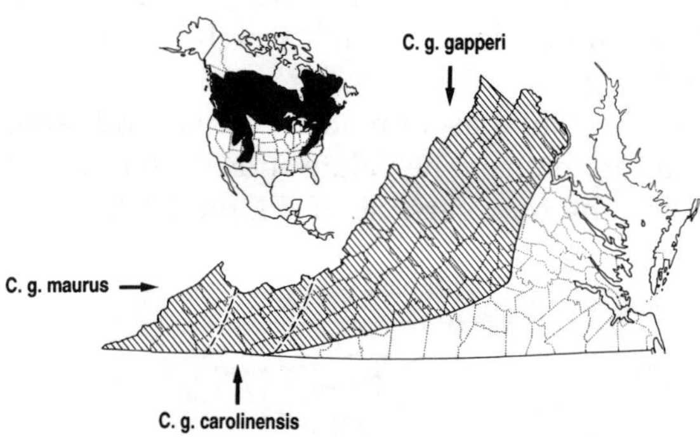

Figure 102. *Clethrionomys gapperi:* Range in Virginia and North America.

covered logs and rocks provide ideal habitat. I have taken this species from deep within the crevices among boulders on hillsides in southwestern Virginia as well as in a sphagnum-rhododendron marsh, along small boulder-strewn streams, and in a stump on a relatively dry hillside in a deciduous woodland. It was one of the two most abundant species taken during a study of the mammals on the summit of Mount Rogers for the United States Forest Service (Linzey, 1980c).

Habits. The red-backed vole may be active at any time of the day or night and during all seasons of the year. The nest consists of a grass-lined ball of dead leaves or grass and may be located beneath stumps, logs, or deep in the crevices between boulders. The home range encompasses approximately 0.16 ha.

Red-backed voles have been known to utter a trilling "song," and in some cases several voles join in, apparently answering one another.

Food. Food of the red-backed voles may consist of green vegetation, bark, fungi, seeds, nuts, and invertebrates.

Reproduction and Development. Red-backed vole litters are born from approximately March to October following a gestation of 17 to 19 days. Litter size may range from three to eight but normally is between four and six. A female taken in Giles County on September 12 contained five embryos (KU). Several litters are produced annually. A female with four embryos was recorded on June 14 on Whitetop Mountain in Grayson County (BRP). Barbour (1951a) recorded females with three to four embryos between June 8 and August 28 in Harlan County, Kentucky. Lactating females and males in breeding condition were noted during June and July.

Newborn voles are naked and blind. By four days of age, they are able to remain in an upright position most of the time. When eight days old, young voles are able to move about freely but awkwardly. The eyes open between the tenth and thirteenth day. Weaning occurs between 14 and 17 days of age (Benton, 1955b).

Longevity. Maximum longevity in red-backed voles is approximately 20 months (Manville, 1949).

Parasites. The nematode *Capillaria hepatica* has been reported in red-backed voles in Virginia (Solomon and Handley, 1971).

Predation. Snakes, hawks, owls, bobcats, foxes, and weasels can be expected to prey on red-backed voles. Barbour (1951a) recorded red-backed voles in four of eight timber rattlesnake stomachs from Harlan County, Kentucky.

Geographic Variation. The subspecies of red-backed vole that occurs in Virginia is *Clethrionomys gapperi gapperi* (Vigors). Two variants have been identified, but no primary isolating mechanisms exist.

Other Currently Recognized Subspecies. *Clethrionomys gapperi maurus* R. Kellogg.

Location of Specimens. AMNH, BCV, BRP, CHAS, CM, CU, CUC, DMNH, DWL, EKU, FSM, GMU, HSU, ISUVC, KU, LACM, LFCC, LSUMZ, NCSM, NVCC, RC, RMWC, RU, SUVM, UCLA, UGAMNH, UMMZ, USNM, VCU, VHCC, VPISU, VPI-W.

Genus *Microtus*

Dentition: 1/1, 0/0, 0/0, 3/3 = 16

Meadow Vole
Microtus pennsylvanicus (Ord)

Description. The meadow vole (Plate 54) is a moderate-sized, stout vole with small ears that are mostly hidden in the fur. The upperparts range from dark brown to brownish-gray, while the underparts are silvery-gray. The rather short, tail is usually less than half as long as the head and body combined and usually much more than twice the length of the hind foot. Females possess eight mammae. Adult meadow voles are generally between 125 and

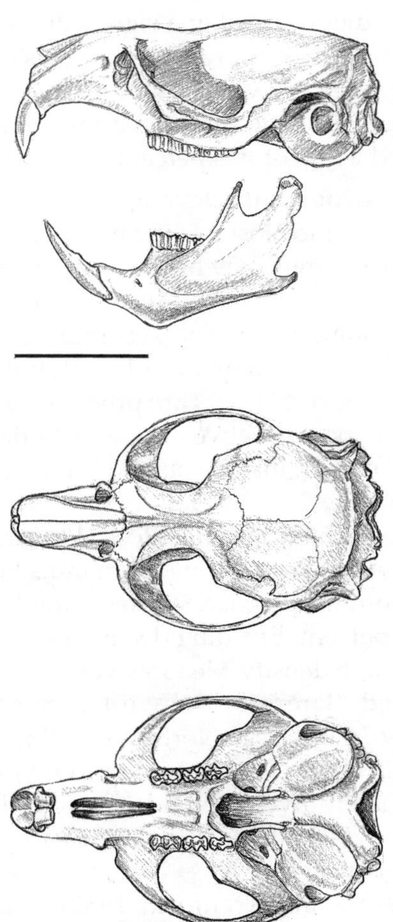

Figure 103. *Microtus pennsylvanicus:* Left lateral view of skull and mandible, and dorsal and ventral view of skull. Scale bar = 10 mm.

190 mm long, including a tail 38 to 63 mm long. Adults weigh between 28 and 70 g.

The skull possesses a short rostrum and a broad braincase. It differs from *Microtus chrotorrhinus* in that the incisive foramina are longer (usually greater than 5.0 mm) and they are constricted posteriorly (Kirkland and Jannett, 1982). The occlusal surface of the third upper molar consists of four triangles, whereas in *M. chrotorrhinus* it consists of five to six triangles (Figure 103).

Distribution. The meadow vole is a northern mammal and ranges throughout most of Alaska, Canada, and the northern conterminous United States. The range extends southeastward through Utah, New Mexico, northern Missouri, Kentucky, and eastern Tennessee to northern Georgia, South Carolina, and the westcentral coast of Florida (Nowak, 1990).

In Virginia, the meadow vole occurs statewide (Figure 104). Bailey (1946) believed this species to be "the most common mammal found in the United States east of the Mississippi River." Paradiso and Handley (1965) took 60 meadow voles from a line of 100 traps in one night on Assateague Island. They concluded that this was probably the most abundant mammal on the island.

Habitat. The meadow vole is primarily an open grassland species. It is found most often in old fields, orchards, and low moist areas near streams and lakes. In coastal areas this species is found in brackish and saltwater marshes. On Assateague Island, Paradiso and Handley (1965) recorded excellent trap success in tall grass and myrtle at a pond edge. Cranford and Maly (1990) reported that *Microtus* "tended to occupy microhabitats in which monocot vegetation and abundant ground cover occurred" on Assateague Island.

Habits. This vole is active both day and night during all seasons of the year. The most evident sign of its presence in an area is the surface runways that it constructs. These voles also have underground runway systems. Nests of dried grasses the size of a softball and completely roofed over may be constructed either above or below ground. Aboveground nests may be located in clumps of grass or beneath boards.

Van Vleck (1969) reported home ranges of between 0.01 and 0.35 ha in size. Madison (1980) recorded average daily ranges for males of 192 m^2 and, for females, 69 m^2. Adult females usually maintained a territory free of other females, while males overlapped considerably among themselves. Females are territorial with oscillations in their home range size dependent on their lactational state (McShea, 1989).

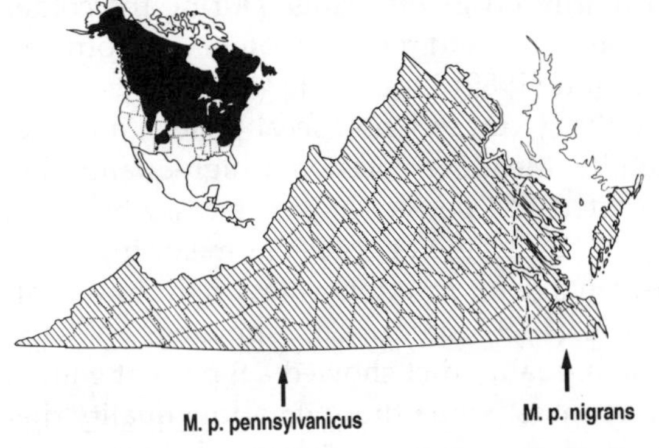

Figure 104. *Microtus pennsylvanicus:* Range in Virginia and North America.

Kratimeros and Rose (1991) reported a maximum density of 41 meadow voles per ha on Craney Island near Norfolk, while Cranford and Fortune (1994) reported peak densities of 125 per ha in Giles County. Annual population densities have been reported to be inversely related to the number of short-tailed shrews present (Eadie, 1952).

Successful homing has been recorded from distances up to 1,200 m (Robinson and Falls, 1965; Ostfeld and Manson, 1996). Fluharty et al. (1976) demonstrated that meadow voles use the sun for sun-compass orientation. Meadow vole populations fluctuate markedly at three-year to four-year intervals. At their peak some populations have reached an estimated 8,000 to 12,000 individuals per acre (Piper, 1909). In Virginia, Linduska (1942) recorded a cycle of approximately four years in Albemarle and Amelia counties. Peaks of abundance are followed by "crashes" or die-offs over a period of several months, which bring the population to an extreme low. A gradual buildup renews the cycle again. The reasons for these cycles have never been fully explained, but the effects of stress on the endocrine and reproductive systems appears to be a major factor.

These small mammals can cause considerable damage to orchards by eating the bark around the base of the trees. If a circle of bark completely around the tree is removed, the tree will have been effectively girdled, and it will die. Such damage is particularly extensive during the winter when snow is on the ground. The snow provides protective cover for the voles, which burrow through it and feast on the nutritious cambium layer of the bark.

Food. Food varies depending on the season of the year. During the warmer months voles feed primarily on green plants. During the colder months bark and roots are eaten. Cranford and Johnson (1989) investigated the effects of coprophagy (ingestion of fecal pellets) and diet quality. Meadow voles on a high-quality diet ingested 12.1 percent of their feces, which was significantly lower than the mean ingestion percentage for meadow voles on the low-quality diet (18.9 percent). Coprophagous voles fed a high quality diet showed a 9 percent gain in body mass, while those on a low quality diet showed a body-mass change of -1.6 percent. Prevention of coprophagy when fed a low-quality diet resulted in a significant decline of body mass. Noncoprophagous voles on a high quality diet showed a body-mass increase of 1.7 percent, while those on a low-quality diet showed a loss of -5.5 percent.

Reproduction and Development. The meadow vole is the most prolific mammal in North America. Litters may be born any time during the year. One female produced 17 litters in one year (Bailey, 1924). The gestation is 21 days. Litter size may range from 1 to 11, but usually is 3 to 5. Several litters are produced annually. Weaning occurs between 12 and 14 days after birth. Females may be able to breed when approximately 25 days old.

Near Charlottesville, Rose (1986) recorded pregnant females during all months but January. Monthly pregnancy rates varied from 40 to 100 percent. Breeding declined during periods of high density. Meadow voles were found to breed "late into the winter months" on Craney Island near Norfolk (Kratimeros and Rose, 1991). A nest containing four young approximately five days old was found on the Mackay Island National Wildlife Refuge (deRageot, 1992).

Pistole and Cranford (1982) found that growth and development was significantly affected by different photoperiods. Young and subadults maintained under a long photoperiod gained weight more rapidly and had significantly higher thyroid activity than did those under a short photoperiod.

McShea and Madison (1986, 1987) showed that spring-born female pups are heavier than males, whereas fall-born males are heavier than females. Nestling mortality showed a similar gender basis indicating possible maternal manipulation and selective allocation of energy by the mother under conditions of limited energy resources. Loss was greatest for the lightest pups and increased with increasing local density. Death may have occurred from inadequate nutrition or competition with larger siblings. On the other hand, the mother may selectively ignore, and possibly kill, the smallest pups (cull the litter) in order to increase the chances of survival of the larger pups.

Longevity. Although some meadow voles survive as long as 12 to 18 months in the wild, most live only three to six months. Rose and Dueser (1980) recorded average lifespans in Virginia ranging from 16.5 to 27.5 weeks. In most cases the average lifespan was greater for females than for males.

Parasites. The following parasites have been recorded from the meadow vole in Virginia by Keegan (1951); Gould and Miesse (1954); Spencer (1961); Atwood et al. (1964; 1965); Sonenshine, Lamb, and Anastos (1965); Sonenshine, Atwood, and Lamb (1966); Bozeman et al. (1967); Hensley (1976b, 1978); Fox (1968); Holliman and Meade (1980; Sonenshine and Turner (1988); and Painter and Eckerlin (1993): **Bacteria** *(Rickettsia rickettsii);* **Nematoda** (roundworms) *(Trichinella spiralis);* **Siphonaptera** (fleas) *(Ctenophthalmus pseudagyrtes);* **Acarina** (ticks) *(Dermacentor variabilis); Ixodes dentatus* **Acarina** (mites) *(Euhaemogamasus barberi);* and **Diptera** (flies) (Unidentified botfly larvae — probably *Cuterebra fontinella*).

Predation. Meadow voles are extremely important as food for carnivores. In many cases they undoubtedly act as a buffer between predators and game species. Snakes, hawks, owls, raccoons, foxes, bobcats, weasels, and mink are among the more significant predators. Madison (1976) recorded black racers *(Coluber constrictor)* and black rat snakes *(Elaphe obsoleta)* preying on these voles. Fisher (1893) recovered this species from a screech owl stomach in Falls Church, while Rageot (1957) recorded individuals from barred owl pellets in the Dismal Swamp. Blem and Pagels (1973), Jackson, Pagels, and Trumbo (1976), and Deibler (1988) found this species in barn owl pellets in Northampton, Chesterfield, and Prince William counties. Skulls have also been taken from barn owl pellets in Loudon County (GMU) and Northampton County (FMNH). Mitchell and Beck (1992) recorded the capture of these voles by free-ranging domestic cats in New Kent and Henrico counties.

Geographic Variation. The subspecies of meadow vole in Virginia is *Microtus pennsylvanicus pennsylvanicus* (Ord). One geographic variant has been identified in the southeastern portion of the state.

Other Currently Recognized Subspecies. *Microtus pennsylvanicus nigrans* Rhoads.

Location of Specimens. AEL, AMNH, ANSP, ASUMZ, AVL, BCV, BRP, CHAS, CM, CMNH, CSULB, CU, DMNH, DWL, EHC, FMNH, GMU, ISUVC, KU, LACM, LC, LFCC, LSUMZ, LU, MCZ, MMNH, MVZ, NVCC, ODU, RC, RMWC, RU, SUVM, UCM, UMMZ, USNM, VCU, VHCC, VMNH, VPISU, VPI-W, YPM.

Rock Vole
Microtus chrotorrhinus (Miller)

Description. The rock vole (Plate 55) is a medium-sized, brownish vole with the area from the nose to the eyes ranging from yellowish- to deep orange-rufous. The underparts are grayish white. Females possess eight mammae. Adult rock voles are between 140 and 175 mm long, including a tail 35 to 51 mm long. Adults weigh between 25 and 57 g.

The skull differs from *Microtus pennsylvanicus* in that the third upper molar possesses five to six triangles, whereas there are only four triangles in *Microtus pennsylvanicus.* The incisive foramina are shorter (usually less than 4.74 mm) and are not markedly tapered posteriorly (Kirkland and Jannett, 1982) (Figure 105).

Distribution. The rock vole ranges from Labrador west to northeastern Minnesota and south at higher elevations through New York and northeastern Pennsylvania. Isolated populations occur in the southern Appalachian Mountains.

The only Virginia specimen of this vole was taken on Allegheny Mountain in the Little Back Creek area in Bath County (Pagels, 1990). Fossils have been recovered from several caves in Bath and Augusta counties (Zakrzewski, 1985). The species has been classified as endangered in Virginia (Handley, 1991; Handley and Pagels, 1991) (Figure 106).

Habitat. Rock voles are found primarily among the mossy rocks and logs or in cool, moist talus areas at elevations above 915 m, although they have been found as low as 600 m in West Virginia. Individuals are often taken close to running water. The Bath County specimen was taken in mossy talus near a stream at an elevation of 1,036 m.

Habits. These voles utilize a network of runways beneath and between the rocks and boulders. They may be active any time of the day or night. In some areas they may be quite abundant, but they may be absent in other areas that appear as suitable. They are often found in association with the southern red-backed vole, *Clethrionomys gapperi.*

Food. The food of the rock vole includes small rootstocks, green grasses, fresh shoots, and berries (Hamilton, 1943). Blackberry seeds were found in the stomach of one individual from Tennessee (Linzey and Linzey, 1971). Whitaker and Martin (1977) recorded bunchberry comprising 47 percent of the food volume and green vegetation comprising 26 percent in New York, New Hampshire, Labrador, and Quebec.

Reproduction and Development. In Virginia, the rock vole probably breeds from early spring well into the fall. In Tennessee, a female with three nearly full-term embryos was recorded on March 13. Two of 13 females in West Virginia were reproductively active in October (Kirkland, 1977). Litter size in West Virginia averaged 2.8 (range 1 to 7) with the largest litters being produced in June. Females probably bear two or three litters annually.

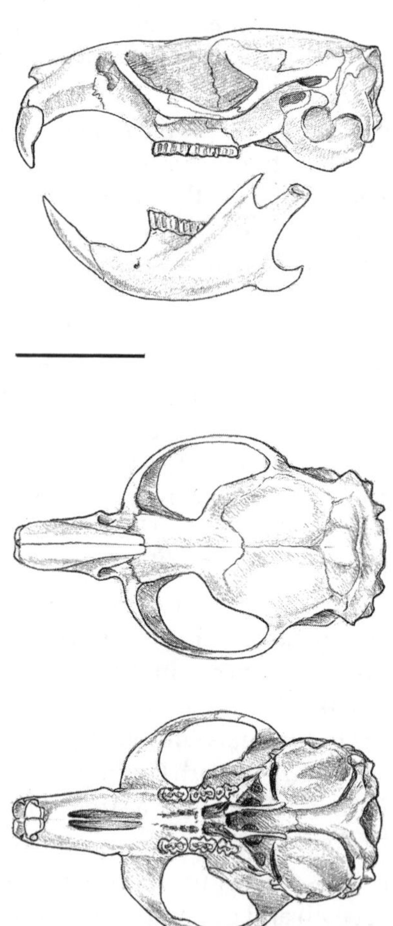

Figure 105. *Microtus chrotorrhinus:* Left lateral view of skull and mandible, and dorsal and ventral view of skull. Scale bar = 10 mm.

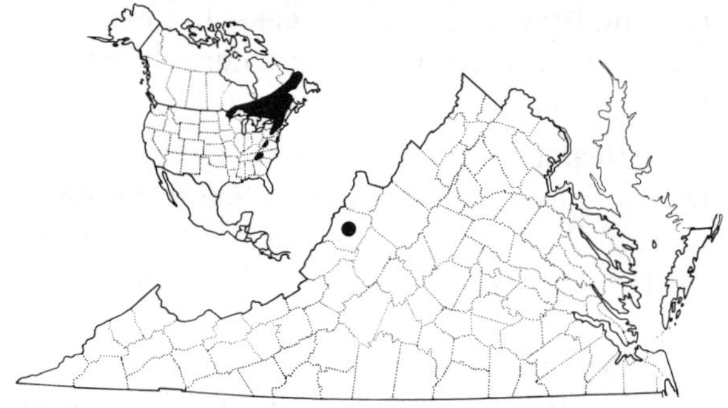

Figure 106. *Microtus chrotorrhinus:* Range in Virginia and North America.

Predation. Bobcats, rattlesnakes, and copperheads have been known to prey on rock voles (Linzey and Linzey, 1971; Linzey, 1995b).

Geographic Variation. The subspecies in Virginia is *Microtus chrotorrhinus carolinensis* Komarek.

Location of Specimen. VCU.

Woodland Vole
Microtus pinetorum (LeConte)

Description. The woodland vole (Plate 56) is a semifossorial rodent with a blunt nose and soft, molelike pelage. The fur is generally brownish above and grayish below. Black-tipped hairs are frequently present on the back and rump. It has a short, indistinctly bicolor tail which is only slightly longer than the small hind foot. Woodland voles have small, nearly concealed ears and small eyes. An additional adaptation for life below ground is the fact that its short fur lies flat against the body whether rubbed forward or backward, an obvious modification for traveling either way in tunnels. Females possess four mammae. Adult woodland voles are normally between 100 and 145 mm long, including a tail 18 to 20 mm long. Adults usually weigh between 21 and 56 g.

The skull is flat, short, and wide. Moderately inflated auditory bullae are present. The cheek teeth have the characteristic microtine pattern with folded enamel loops surrounding islands of dentine on the flat grinding surfaces. The third upper molar has two triangles (Figure 107).

Distribution. The woodland vole ranges throughout most of the eastern United States

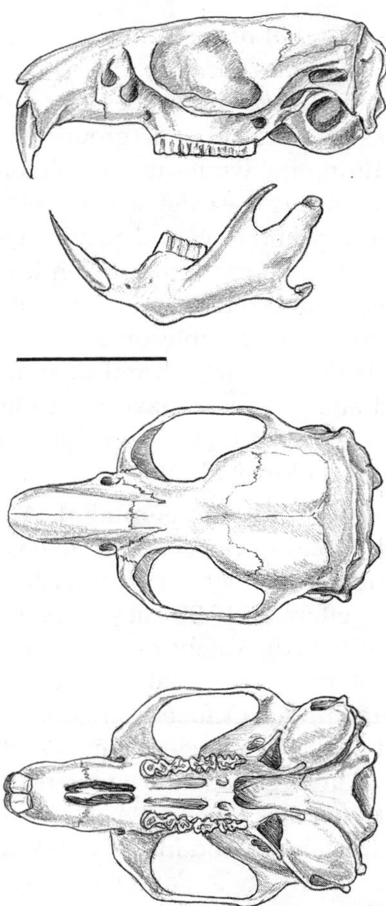

Figure 107. *Microtus pinetorum:* Left lateral view of skull and mandible, and dorsal and ventral view of skull. Scale bar = 10 mm.

from New Hampshire, Vermont, northern New York, Michigan, Wisconsin, and Ontario south to northern Florida, Alabama, southwestern Mississippi, and Louisiana. The range extends westward to central Texas, central Oklahoma, eastern Kansas, central Iowa, and southeastern Minnesota.

This species occurs throughout Virginia (Figure 108).

Habitat. The woodland vole's habitat is moist woodlands, but they often occur in orchards, fields, and in gardens. Light moist soil or deep humus combined with heavy ground cover is usually required in any of these areas for woodland voles to be present. Although it has been taken in swamps and marshes, it is most common in more upland areas.

Habits. Woodland voles appear to be somewhat more active during the night than during the day and they are active during all seasons and do not hibernate. They have a regular cycle of short periods of about an hour of activity and an hour of rest (Pearson, 1947). Movements above ground during daylight hours decrease during summer (Paul, 1970).

Woodland voles are excellent burrowers. Benton (1955a) recorded the following behavior:

> *As observed in captivity, the head and neck are used in a shovelling motion to loosen dirt, which is scratched out and pushed backward with the forefeet. The forefeet are used in a backward and sideward motion, both to loosen dirt and to sweep it back to the hind legs. A powerful sweep of the hind limbs then throws away the loosened dirt. When the burrowing has proceeded for a foot or so, the mouse turns around and pushes the accumulated debris out of the tunnel with his head, thus making the characteristic dirt piles.*

Woodland voles also make extensive use of both active and non-active mole burrow systems (Eadie, 1939).

Woodland vole burrows are constructed just beneath the leaf mold and usually descend only 7.5 to 10 cm. Occasionally tunnels may extend to a depth of 30 cm or more. In orchards, burrows often run along the roots of apple trees. The network of burrows often becomes quite complex around such trees. Hamilton (1938) noted that these voles often tunnel their way to fallen apples, where they burrow from beneath to feed on the fruit. I and others have also taken these rodents in shallow, exposed runways.

Nests are normally located in the underground burrow, although they may be under a stump, log, or other piece of debris. They are

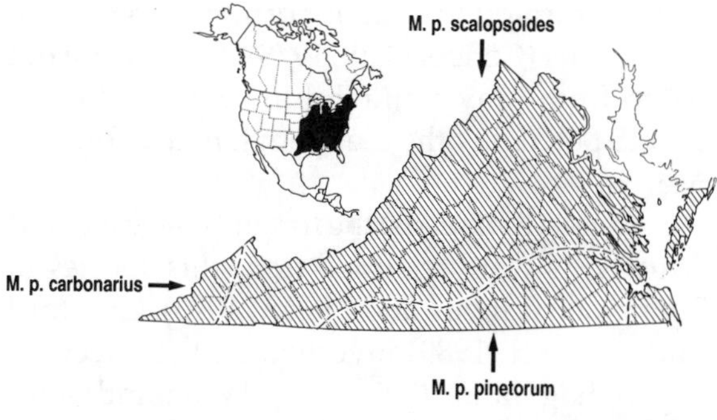

Figure 108. *Microtus pinetorum:* Range in Virginia and North America.

constructed of dead leaves, grasses, plant stems, and rootlets. Several exits usually lead from the nest.

Home range size is generally less than 90 m in diameter, although male mice have been known to range over 1.6 ha. Horsfall (1956) recorded a maximum home range of 0.1 ha in apple orchards in Virginia. Paul (1970) noted that home ranges overlapped broadly and several adult individuals were often taken at the same trap site, indicating that territoriality may not be highly developed in this species. Population density in orchards may be as high as 14 voles per ha (Smolen, 1981).

Benton (1955a) tested homing ability by releasing marked mice outside their home range. One individual returned a distance of 45 m in 24 hours, while another traveled 30 m and arrived at the home site within 12 hours.

Woodland vole populations vary from year to year. Hamilton (1938) and Benton (1955a) recorded populations of 200 to 300 voles per acre in New York. In some areas, population fluctuations tend to occur with some regularity in the form of cycles (Hamilton, 1938; Linduska, 1942). Paul (1970) has suggested that woodland voles in North Carolina never attain the high population densities found in northern areas.

The senses of hearing and touch are extremely well developed in these voles. Vocalizations include harsh chattering notes used during fights, as well as a "single or double note, reminiscent of the note of a wood thrush, [that] is used as an alarm note, and is often repeated rapidly in a low conversational tone" (Benton, 1955a).

Food. Woodland voles feed largely on roots, tubers, stems, bark, fruits, and seeds. Some insects may also be taken. In Virginia, forbs and grasses formed the major portion of the diet in all months (Cengel et al., 1978). Roots were not eaten from May through July, but constituted 7 to 15 percent of the diet from January through March.

Vegetation, seeds, the fungus *Endogone,* and fruit skins were recorded from this species in Tennessee (Linzey and Linzey, 1973). Cranford and Johnson (1989) investigated the effects of coprophagy and diet quality. Woodland voles on a high-quality diet ingested 15.2 percent of their feces. Prevention of coprophagy when fed a low-quality diet resulted in a significant decline in body mass.

In some areas quantities of fruits and rootstocks are stored in underground chambers for use during the winter months. In orchards these mice may cause extensive loss of trees by eating the bark and roots and girdling the trees, particularly when snow and fallen leaves are mounded around the bases. These voles have been particularly troublesome in the apple-growing regions of Virginia and adjacent states.

Lead and cadmium have been identified in the tissues of these voles in Virginia (Anderson, 1981; Scanlon et al., 1983).

Reproduction and Development. Although woodland voles have been reported as breeding throughout the year in Virginia and North Carolina (Jefferson, 1943; Lacy, 1948; Horsfall, 1963; Paul, 1970), Valentine and Kirkpatrick (1970) took pregnant females in Virginia only from April through October. Cengel et al. (1978) reported peak pregnancies from July through September in Virginia. Embryos were recorded in 7 of 13 females taken in August, in 7 of 9 taken in September, and in 3 of 16 taken in December and January in Patrick County (Jefferson, 1943). A female taken in Northampton County on March 14 contained two embryos. In the mountainous region of North Carolina most litters were born during the summer months, while in the warmer Piedmont area breeding declined markedly during the summer (Paul, 1970).

Gestation ranges from 20 to 24 days and is apparently not lengthened if the female is lactating (Kirkpatrick and Valentine, 1970). Average litter size in New York is 3.1 with a range from 1 to 6 (Schadler and Butterstein, 1979). In the south the usual litter consists of 1 to 3 young with an overall average of 2.0 to 2.2 (Jefferson, 1943; Horsfall, 1970; Paul, 1970). However, litters containing as many as seven young have been recorded. Females may breed immediately following the birth of the litter and produce up to four litters a year. Ovulation is not spontaneous but is induced by copulation (Kirkpatrick and Valentine, 1970).

Hamilton (1938), Paul (1970), and Hasbrouck and Kirkpatrick (1982) have described the development of young in this species. Newborn young are essentially hairless, lack teeth, and have their eyes and ears closed. The young cling tenaciously to the female's nipples, maintaining their grasp if she is frightened from the nest. The incisors erupt on the fifth or sixth day, the pinnae of the ears have unfolded by the eighth day, and the eyes open between 9 and 13 days of age. Young voles are weaned during their third week. Puberty occurs between 6 and 8 weeks in males and between 10 and 12 weeks in females (Schadler and Butterstein, 1979). Molting has been discussed by Hasbrouck and Kirkpatrick (1982). Neither photoperiod nor diet affected the age of molting to the adult pelage.

Derting and Cranford (1989) reported that short photoperiods had a stimulatory effect on growth between three and seven weeks of age. A short photoperiod stimulated body mass gains, the onset of molt, and the development of tertiary follicles, but it had few effects on reproductive organ masses. These responses differ markedly from those of many other microtine species, including *Microtus pennsylvanicus* (Pistole and Cranford, 1982).

Longevity. A wild individual woodland vole surviving for at least 18 months has been recorded by Gentry (1968).

Pelage variations. Molting in the woodland vole has been discussed by Benton (1955a).

Parasites. The louse *Pediculus* sp. and the tick *Dermacentor variabilis* have been recorded from woodland voles in Virginia by Lacy (1948), Sonenshine, Lamb, and Anastos (1965), and Sonenshine, Atwood, and Lamb (1966). Williams et al. (1978) reported the mite *Haemogamasus longitarsus.* Jones et al. (1982) reported that 6.7 percent of 105 voles were infected with the cestode *Taenia taeniaeformis.* Lochmiller et al. (1982) also recorded *Taenia taeniaformis* as well as the nematode *Capillaria gastrica.* The bacterium *Rickettsia rickettsii* has been isolated from woodland voles taken in King and Queen County, Virginia (Bozeman et al., 1967). The flea *Ctenophthalmus pseudagyrtes* was reported by Painter and Eckerlin (1993) from Westmoreland County.

Predation. Due to their semifossorial habits, woodland voles are not as susceptible to some predators as most other small mammals. Major predators may include snakes, owls, hawks, foxes, opossums, raccoons, mink, weasels, bobcats, and house cats. Rageot (1957) recorded individuals from barred owl pellets in the Dismal Swamp. Jackson, Pagels, and Trumbo (1976) found this species in barn owl pellets in Chesterfield County. Mitchell and Beck (1992) recorded the capture of woodland voles by free-ranging domestic cats in New Kent and Henrico counties. Barbour (1951a) recorded a woodland vole in the stomach of a black rat snake in Harland County, Kentucky.

Geographic Variation. Although three geographic variants of woodland vole have been identified in Virginia, the only subspecies inhabiting the state is *Microtus pinetorum pinetorum* (LeConte).

Other Currently Recognized Subspecies. *Microtus pinetorum carbonarius* (Handley); *Microtus pinetorum scalopsoides* (Audubon and Bachman).

Location of Specimens. AMNH, BCV, CAS, CM, CMNH, CU, CUC, DMNH, DWL, GMU, IOWA, ISU, LC, LFCC, LU, MVZ, NCSM, NVCC, ODU, RMWC, ROM, SUVM, UA, UCLA, UCM, UGAMNH, UMMZ, USNM, VCU, VPISU, VPI-W, YPM.

Genus *Synaptomys*

Dentition: 1/1, 0/0, 0/0, 3/3 = 16

Southern Bog Lemming
Synaptomys cooperi Baird

Description. The southern bog lemming (Plate 57) is a small, short-legged vole with a short tail about the length of the hind foot and broad heavy incisors with a groove on their outer surface. The upperparts are brownish-gray and the underparts grayish. The relatively massive head contains small ears that are nearly concealed by the fur. The tail is bicolor and less than 25 mm long. Females possess six to eight mammae. Adult southern bog lemmings usually range between about 100 and 138 mm in total length, including an 18 mm long tail. Adults weigh 14 to 42 g.

The upper incisors are very broad and possess a shallow longitudinal groove along their outer edge. The crowns of the molariform teeth are sharply angled along their inner and outer edges. The rostrum is short and thick. The supraorbital ridges fuse to form a median interorbital crest. The auditory bullae are large (Figure 109).

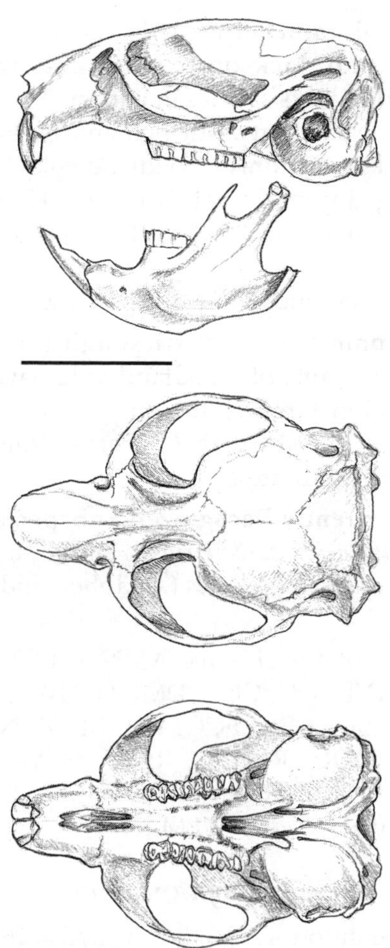

Figure 109. *Synaptomys cooperi:* Left lateral view of skull and mandible, and dorsal and ventral view of skull. Scale bar = 10 mm.

Distribution. The southern bog lemming ranges from New Brunswick and Nova Scotia south along the Atlantic Coast to Virginia and in the Appalachian Mountains to western North Carolina. It occurs westward to western Kansas, Nebraska, South Dakota, western Minnesota, and eastern Manitoba.

In Virginia, the range of the southern bog lemming is primarily west of the Blue Ridge (with two exceptions) (Figure 110). It appears to be uncommon throughout this portion of its range in Virginia, but this may be the result of ineffective trapping methods and insufficient fieldwork in appropriate habitat. An apparently disjunct population exists in the Dismal Swamp and vicinity in the extreme southeastern portion of Virginia and northeastern North Carolina. This latter population had not been seen since 1898 until several specimens were taken in North Carolina in the 1970s (Lee et al., 1982). The first Virginia specimens since 1898 were taken in April, 1980 (Rose, 1981). Subsequent trapping revealed this species to be abundant in both wet and dry habitats with densities up to 30 per ha (Handley, 1991).

Habitat. Bog lemmings have been taken in a variety of habitats in the Dismal Swamp ranging from wet boggy openings to dry young loblolly pine stands (Everton and Rose, 1982). I have taken this species along a river floodplain and in a dense growth of horsetail in western Virginia. In addition, populations inhabiting a relatively dry, old field area as well as a cedar and *Andropogon*-dominated area have been studied in southwestern Virginia (A. V. Linzey, 1981; 1984; Linzey and Cranford, 1984). Elsewhere in the southern Appalachians this species has been taken in pastures, grassy openings in woods, clearcuts, power line rights-of-way, and among mossy boulders in spruce forests (Linzey, 1983).

Habits. Bog lemmings are primarily nocturnal and are active during all months of the year (A. V. Linzey, 1980). Surface and underground runways are constructed. Nests may be built either above ground or in underground runways. A nest discovered by A. K. Fisher (1895) near the northwest corner of Lake Drummond was in a dry clump of grass and was composed of coarse fibers with a lining of finer material. Home ranges from 0.04 to 0.32 ha have been reported (Buckner, 1957; Connor, 1959; Getz, 1960). Population densities up to 51 per ha have been reported, although 4 to 12 per ha is prob-

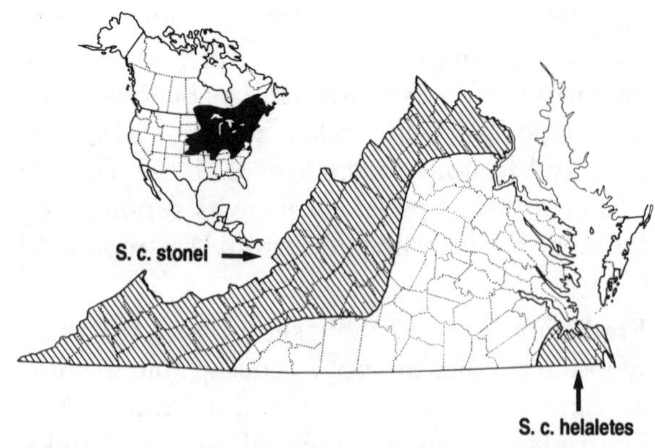

Figure 110. *Synaptomys cooperi:* Range in Virginia and North America.

ably more representative (A. V. Linzey, 1983).

Studies examining the coexistence of this species with *Microtus pennsylvanicus* in southwestern Virginia show that *Synaptomys* is found where ground cover is sparse and woody vegetation more abundant (A. V. Linzey, 1980; Linzey and Cranford, 1984). It differs in its daily activity rhythm from *Microtus*. Eighty-two percent of the individuals of *Synaptomys* were captured at night, whereas only 47 percent of the individual *Microtus* were captured during this same period. *Synaptomys* exhibited little seasonal variability with the percentage of nocturnal captures ranging from 75 to 100 percent. *Microtus* exhibited highest nocturnality between July and September (63 percent) and lowest between October and December (22 percent).

Food. Studies in Tennessee (Linzey and Linzey, 1973) and those by Eadie (1937) and Hamilton (1941) have shown that the food consists primarily of green vegetation but may be supplemented with fruits and fungi. In southwestern Virginia, major foods were broomsedge in summer and mosses in winter (Linzey, 1981). *Synaptomys* fed primarily on *Andropogon*, while *Microtus* ate considerable quantities of other monocots and dicots. Moss was always part of the diet of *Synaptomys*, but was only eaten by *Microtus* during the winter (A. V. Linzey, 1984). When *Microtus* were removed, the diet of *Synaptomys* diversified.

Reproduction and Development. Bog lemmings may breed in Virginia during any month of the year, although most breeding probably occurs during the warmer months. Bailey (1946) noted pregnant females from March 11 to October 7. A female containing four well-advanced embryos was taken in the Dismal Swamp on March 11 and a female with five embryos was recorded on October 24 in Augusta County (Stewart, 1943; Handley, 1979a). Females with embryos have also been recorded in Virginia on April 24 (4 embryos), April 30 (4), May 29 (3), July 17 (2), July 21 (3), July 23 (4), August 7 (4), August 15 (2), August 17 (4), August 18 (4), August 22 (3), September 15 (3), September 16 (3), September 23 (3), September 27 (3), October 2 (4, 4), December 30 (3), and December 31 (1). Pregnant bog lemmings have been taken in Kentucky during the period January 10 to March 21 (Barbour, 1956).

Gestation is 23 days, and several litters may be produced each year. A captive female gave birth to six litters and a total of 22 young during a 26 week period (Connor, 1959). The female mates again shortly after the birth of a litter. Litter size ranges from one to eight, although three or four is the usual size. Newborn bog lemmings are pink except for the light gray dorsum. They weigh approximately 4 g. They are well furred by seven days. The lower incisors erupt between six and eight days and the eyes open at 10 to 11 days of age. Weaning is completed by the end of the third week (A. V. Linzey, 1983).

Longevity. Connor (1959) reported wild individual bog lemmings surviving at least seven to eight months. A female captured as an adult lived two years and five months in captivity (A. V. Linzey, 1983).

Predation. Bog lemmings are probably preyed on to some extent by snakes, hawks, owls, foxes, bobcats, and weasels. Merriam (1892) recorded this species in pellets of a long-eared owl near Munson Hill, Virginia, while A. V. Linzey (1983) reported skulls from owl pellets in southwestern Virginia.

Geographic Variation. Two subspecies of the southern bog lemming — *Synaptomys cooperi cooperi* Baird and *Synaptomys cooperi helaletes* Merriam — inhabit Virginia.

Location of Specimens. AMNH, AVL, BCV, CM, CUC, DMNH, DWL, EMU, FMNH, FSM, ISU, MVZ, NVCC, ODU, PWRC, RMWC, UC, UCONN, UMMZ, USNM, VCU, VPISU, VPI-W.

Genus *Ondatra*

Dentition: 1/1, 0/0, 0/0, 3/3 = 16

Common Muskrat
Ondatra zibethicus (Linnaeus)

Description. The name "muskrat" (Plate 58) is derived from the musky odor and ratlike appearance of this large, semiaquatic rodent. It possesses dense, soft, glossy brown underfur overlaid with long, oily, reddish-brown or black guard hairs that enable the animal to shed water. The underparts of the body are whitish or pale brown. Muskrats also possess small ears and eyes, partially webbed hind feet, and a long, sparsely haired, laterally compressed, black tail that has a well-developed fringe of hairs on its underside. Along the edges of the hind feet and toes are rows of closely set, short, stiff hairs, generally called the swimming fringe, that aid the muskrat in swimming. The hind feet and tail act as efficient oars and rudder.

Concerning the musk glands, Perry (1982) stated:

> *Paired glands, which enlarge during the mating period, emit a musky yellowish secretion through openings within the foreskin of the penis. This secretion mixes with the urine and is deposited throughout the muskrat's territory on defecation posts, lodge bases, stations along travel routes, and at the actual time of mating. Females have similar glands that are not as active as those of males* (Schwartz and Schwartz, 1959).

The number of mammae in females apparently varies from 6 to 10, with 8 the most common number. Adult muskrats are usually between 545 and 640 mm long, including a tail 250 to 283 mm long. Adults generally weigh between 0.6 and 1.8 kg.

The angular skull has a long rostrum and heavy zygomatic arches. The postorbital processes are nearly right-angled and project into the orbit. Large auditory bullae are present. The cheek teeth are flat-surfaced, high crowned, and rootless with folded enamel loops surrounding the dentine. Orange enamel covers the front surface of the large incisor teeth. The lips close behind the incisor teeth allowing the muskrat to gnaw while submerged (Godin, 1977) (Figure 111).

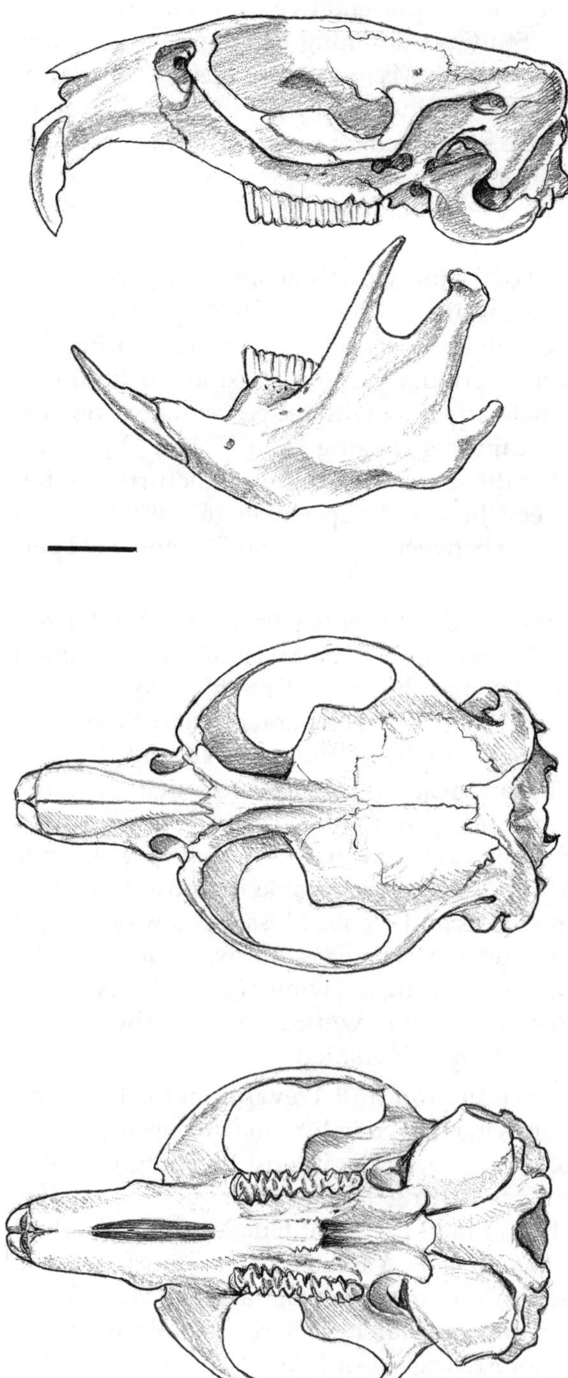

Figure 111. *Ondatra zibethicus:* Left lateral view of skull and mandible, and dorsal and ventral view of skull. Scale bar = 10 mm.

Distribution. The muskrat is distributed over most of North America north of Mexico, although it does not occur in Florida, along a strip of the Atlantic Coast in South Carolina and Georgia, and in most of California and Texas. The muskrat has been introduced into many areas where it did not occur naturally.

This species has been found throughout Virginia, although it is uncommon in most of the southwesternmost counties (Figure 112). In the Chesapeake Bay region, Wass (1972) noted that it was most common in the low salinity and freshwater marshes along the Rappahannock, Piankatank, Mattaponi, Pamunkey, and James rivers.

Comparative data on the fur catch in Virginia, including the muskrat, are presented in tables 2 and 3.

Habitat. Muskrats live in freshwater and saltwater marshes, swamps, and along the borders of ponds, lakes, and streams.

Habits. Muskrats are chiefly nocturnal but may be active at any hour of the day or night all seasons of the year. Evidence of muskrats consists of conspicuous houses, trails, and piles of cut sedges and cattails in a marsh.

Muskrats may construct houses of rushes, leaves, sticks, grasses, and mud. The size and height of the houses vary depending on the kind and amount of food present, the severity of the season, fluctuating water levels, and perhaps the number and individuality of the inhabitants. Houses range from 0.9 to 3 m in diameter at the base, rising 0.5 to 1.2 m above the water's surface. The walls vary in thickness from 10 to 30 cm. Muskrat houses are usually in water from 0.2 to 0.9 m in depth. There are one or more entrances per house, located 15 to 30 cm below the water level. One or more dry chambers, serve as living quarters. Other animals such as ants and other insects, snakes, turtles, lizards, frogs, and toads, use muskrat houses for sunning, as hibernation sites, or as incubation sites for eggs. Once muskrats leave the house, it deteriorates within a few months.

Where higher ground is available, such as in farm ponds, muskrats generally live in burrows, rather than in houses (Beshears and Haugen, 1953b). There was an average of two entrances per burrow, and the entrances opened at an average depth of 15 cm beneath the water. The entrances connected inside the dam and penetrated upward and into the dam an average distance of 1.5 m with an average rise in elevation of 0.76 m. The burrows led to a dry chamber which served as the living quarters. Muskrats can cause considerable damage to narrow dikes and dams. Beshears and Haugen asserted that the best assurance against such damage was to construct dams of well-packed, clay soil with tops at least 3.6 m across and slopes with a rise of 0.3 m or less for each 0.6 m of horizontal distance.

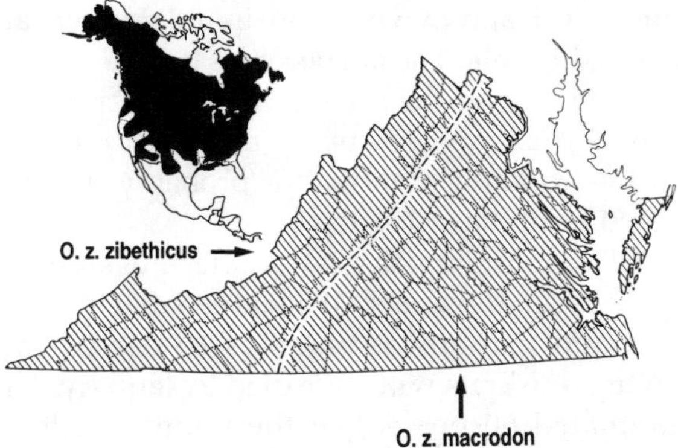

Figure 112. *Ondatra zibethicus:* Range in Virginia and North America.

Another type of structure used by muskrats has been referred to as a "feeding raft" (Svihla and Svihla, 1931). These rafts are used in areas where water levels are consistently high and consist of platforms of debris accumulated as the animals feed. The feeding platform may later be used for the basis of a house.

Muskrats are not especially sociable, although several adults may live in one house during the winter. In summer, a den is usually occupied by only one family.

Unmated males wander in the spring, but otherwise, muskrats usually remain in the same general location throughout the year (Perry, 1982). Movements between ponds and streams generally take place during spring and fall (Haugen, 1944; Shanks and Arthur, 1952). Dispersing young muskrats have been known to move up to 33.8 km, although most individuals tend to remain within 0.8 km of their birthplace (Errington and Errington, 1937; Errington, 1944; Takos, 1944). Homing is well developed. Of individuals released 500 to 2,000 m away, 57 percent returned; 3,000 m away, 31 percent returned; and 4,000 m away, 15 percent returned to their original home range (Mallach, 1972).

Muskrat fur normally sheds water, permitting buoyancy and allowing for quick drying. Spraying marsh areas with insecticides dissolved in fuel oil to control mosquitos can cause severe declines in muskrat populations. The oil apparently has a persistent and cumulative wetting effect on the fur, causing the animal to sink below the surface of the water and become thoroughly soaked.

The muskrat is an excellent swimmer and diver and can travel 55 m underwater without coming up for air. It can remain underwater up to 20 minutes (Irving, 1939; Errington, 1961) and can swim backwards or forward. In swimming the muskrat uses only its hind feet for propulsion, holding the forefeet motionless under the chest. The tail is used extensively when swimming underwater. The muskrat's sight, hearing, and sense of smell are poor, but it has an uncanny sense of direction.

The muskrat has been North America's most popular furbearer. Until recently, trappers were taking between 10 and 12 million muskrats every year. A total of 213,349 muskrat skins was reported by fur dealers in 1984–1985 in Virginia. The de-emphasis on trapping and furs, however, has created a drastic change. In 1990–1991 in Virginia, a total of 15,561 skins was reported. During 1979–1980, pelts in Virginia brought an average of $6.90 apiece. During 1990–1991, the average price was 95 cents. (Dennis Martin, personal communication). The processed fur is highly durable and in the past has been marketed under such names as River Mink, Water Mink, River Sable, Electric Seal, Plucked Beaver, Velvet Coney, and Hudson Seal. The carcasses have often been sold in eastern markets such as Baltimore, Washington, and Philadelphia as "marsh rabbit" and provide excellent eating.

Muskrats inhabiting the lower region of the Elizabeth River, a tributary of the James River near its confluence with the Chesapeake Bay, weigh less, have lower mean fat indexes, lower relative spleen weights, greater relative adrenal weights, and an increased incidence of disease and parasitism compared to muskrats inhabiting the less contaminated upper region of the Elizabeth River or Nansemond River (Halbrook et al., 1993). Concentrations of aluminum, cadmium, copper, nickel, zinc, and polyaromatic hydrocarbon compounds were greater in lower Elizabeth River muskrats than in upper Elizabeth River or Nansemond River muskrats. However, no significant differences in fecundity or density were observed among the regions studied.

Food. Muskrats are basically vegetarians and feed on the stems, leaves, and roots of many plants. At Maryland's Patuxent Wildlife Refuge, Llewellyn and Uhler (1952) recorded the more important native foods as burreed *(Sparganium americanum),* hairy arrowhead *(Sagittaria pubescens),* broadleaf arrowhead *(Sagittaria latifolia),* white water lily *(Nymphaea odorata),* common cattail *(Typha latifolia),* and water starwort *(Callitriche heterophylla).* Wass (1972) noted that the roots of Olney threesquare, cattails, and pickerel weed were preferred foods. Neves and Odom (1989) recorded this species feeding on mussels and Asiatic clams in the Holston and Clinch rivers in Virginia. They noted that muskrat predation "appears to be inhibiting the recovery of endangered mussel species."

In addition to vegetation, a muskrat's diet also consists of crayfish, other invertebrates, and occasionally a fish, frog, or turtle. Food is not stored.

In winter, when fresh food is scarce, muskrats will consume whatever is available. Winter foods may include hibernating animals, roots of aquatic plants, dried or rotting plant material, corncobs, and even their own houses and bedding. Svihla (1931a) reported that Louisiana muskrats consume one-third of their weight in food each day.

Reproduction and Development. Except during unusually cold winters, muskrats breed year-round (Wilson, 1954b). The period of greatest breeding activity is from mid-February to early May, with another smaller breeding peak in August and September. The period of heaviest production of young is from April 25 through May. Gestation varies from 25 to 30 days.

Most litters consist of three to five young. Average litter size of 206 sets of embryos in the North Carolina-Virginia study was 3.7 (range 1 to 6). Harris (1952) recorded an average of 3.9 embryos per female in Maryland. Several litters are produced each year. The female is usually bred again while she is still nursing.

Newborn muskrats have their eyes and ears closed, are sparsely haired, and have a round tail (Errington, 1939). They weigh approximately 21 g. The body is well haired by the end of the first week, and the eyes open between 14 and 16 days. Immediately before the eyes open, most of the young are able to swim and dive. The young are weaned in about one month and move to new living quarters at about this time. The tail becomes laterally compressed during the second month (Errington, 1963). Muskrats are approximately adult size in five to eight months but probably do not breed until the following year.

The mortality rate of young muskrats is quite high. Alexander (1956) noted that at least half and perhaps as many as 65 percent of young muskrats will have died by January. An estimated 60 percent of the young are lost through predation, disease, parasites, and fighting among themselves, particularly between different litters and age classes, before they reach a harvestable age (Beshears and Haugen, 1953a). Winter harvests are usually composed of approximately two-thirds young of the year and one-third adults.

Longevity. Schwartz and Schwartz (1959) noted that one tagged muskrat was known to have lived four years in the wild. Crandall (1964) reported a record of 5 years, 10 months in captivity.

Pelage Variations. The pelage of most muskrats is reddish-brown. However, black-and-tan as well as uniformly black muskrats have been recorded from Virginia marshes (Dozier, 1948a). An albino individual is in the VPI and SU mammal collection.

Perry (1982) noted that the muskrat is the most valuable fur animal in North America exceeding all other wild furbearers in number caught and overall pelt value. During the 1975–1976 season, over eight million muskrats were harvested in North America with a value of more than $29 million dollars (Perry, 1982).

Parasites. The tapeworm *Taenia taeniaformis* was recorded from 35.2 percent of 54 muskrats from Montgomery County, Virginia (Byrd, 1952b).

Predation. Important predators of muskrats include raccoons, marsh hawks, mink, and snakes. Young animals may also be taken by large predaceous fish, snapping turtles, owls, otters, and foxes. A skull was recovered from a raptor pellet in Fairfax County, Virginia (GMU).

Geographic Variation. The subspecies in Virginia is *Ondatra zibethicus zibethicus* (Linnaeus). Two geographic variants have been identified. A smaller form with darker pelage is found in the western third of the state, while a larger form inhabits the eastern two-thirds of Virginia.

Other Currently Recognized Subspecies. *Ondatra zibethicus macrodon* (Merriam).

Location of Specimens. AMNH, ANSP, BCV, CM, DMNH, GMU, LC, LFCC, LU, MCZ, MVZ, NCSM, NVCC, ODU, OU, RU, SUVM, TCWC, UCM, UMMZ, USNM, VCU, VPISU, VPI-W.

Subfamily Murinae

Genus *Rattus*

Dentition: 1/1, 0/0, 0/0, 3/3 =16

Black Rat
Rattus rattus (Linnaeus)

Description. The black rat (Plate 59) is a medium-sized, slender rat. It is more slender and has a shorter nose than the Norway rat. The fur is coarse. The ears are generally larger than those of the Norway rat and lack hair. The sparsely haired, scaly tail is longer than the head and body, usually being approximately 110 percent of the head and body length. The upperparts are brownish- or grayish-black and are usually darker than in the Norway rat, while the underparts are grayish-white, yellowish, or dark gray. Females possess 10 mammae. Adult black rats are usually between 325 and 425 mm in total length, including a tail 190 to 240 mm long. They usually weigh between 140 and 280 g.

The skull of this species has prominent ridges on the upper surface that flare posteriorly rather than being parallel as in the Norway rat. The skull of the black rat may also be distinguished from that of the Norway rat in that the diastema in the black rat is much less than twice as long as the cheek tooth row, whereas in the Norway rat it is slightly less than twice as long (Figure 113).

Distribution. The black rat is native to Asia Minor and the Orient (Walker, 1964). It is believed to have first arrived in North America about AD 1550 on the ships of the early European explorers. Captain John Smith (1612) noted that:

> *in searching our casked corne, wee found it halfe rotten, the rest is consumed with the many thousand rats (increased first from the ships) that we knewe not how to keepe that little wee had.*

Today, in North America, this species is found primarily around human habitations, mainly in coastal areas from Massachusetts to British Columbia and throughout much of Mexico. It is most abundant in the southeastern United States, particularly in seaports, although at most locations it is far outnumbered by the Norway rat. Ecke (1954) searched for but

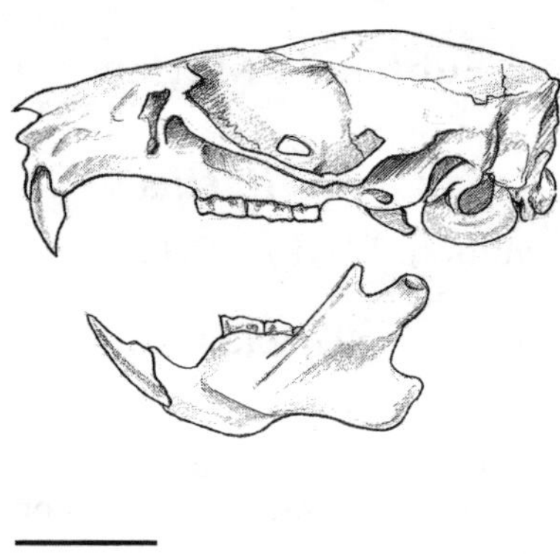

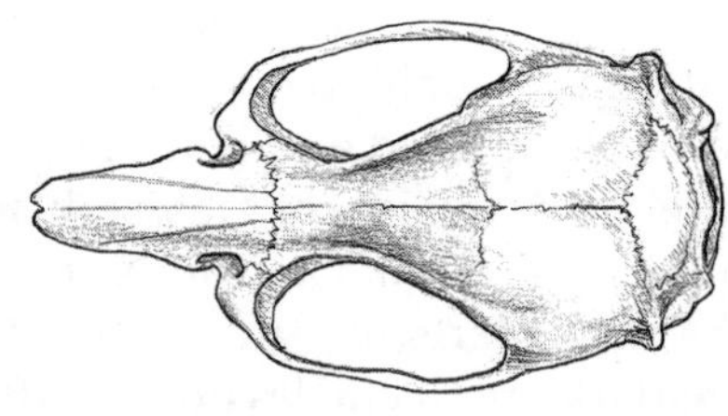

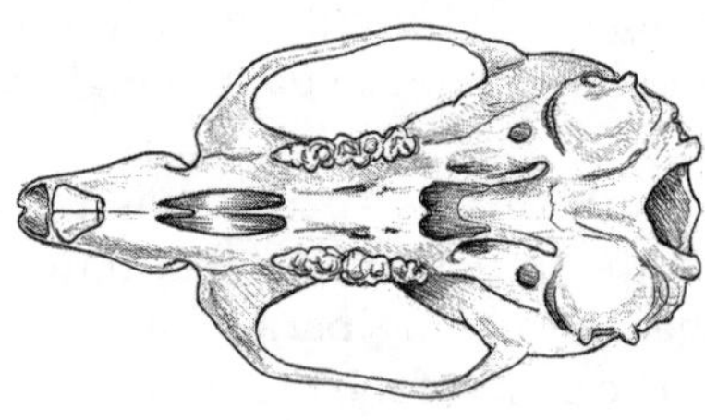

Figure 113. *Rattus rattus:* Left lateral view of skull and mandible, and dorsal and ventral view of skull. Scale bar = 10 mm.

did not find black rats living farther than 90 m from man-made structures in southwest Georgia. Feral populations have been known to exist in southern Florida (Worth, 1950a), southern Texas, and in Norfolk, Virginia (Hasseltine, 1929).

Regarding the black rat's distribution in Virginia, Handley and Gordon (1979e) stated:

> Rattus rattus *came to Virginia with the first English colonizers and spread with settlement to all parts of the state. After the introduction of* Rattus norvegicus *about 1775, black rat populations declined. The species is still found at widely scattered localities throughout the state, and it may even be locally common, but the remnant populations are isolated and irregularly distributed. Apparently the black rat today is absent from most of Virginia.*

Habitat. The black rat is a very agile climber and lives mostly in buildings. In areas where both Norway rats and black rats are present, the more aggressive Norway rat forces the black rat to live in the upper portions of buildings and in trees. Where Norway rats are absent, black rats will apparently burrow under buildings in the same manner as the former species (Milmore, 1943). In Florida, Worth (1950a) found that within the cities "Norway rats occupied wharves, warehouses, parks, dumps, embankments, and slum areas for the most part, while roof [black] rats were found in some warehouses and especially in the middle-and upper-class residential districts." The black rat is less of a burrower than the Norway rat, although it is occasionally found in fields.

Habits. Black rats are active throughout the year and do not hibernate. They are mainly nocturnal. Their sense of sight is poor and they are color blind, but their senses of smell, taste, touch, and hearing are excellent (Jackson, 1982). The black rat is less aggressive than the Norway rat and is driven out of certain areas by its larger relative. An example of this was the replacement of the roof rat by the Norway rat over a 1,610 km^2 area in southwest Georgia (Ecke, 1954).

Although only limited data are available concerning the home range of this species, it appears that individuals live in a very restricted area. Ecke (1955) reported that less than 1 percent of the marked rats were recaptured over 457 m from their original point of capture in Georgia. Only 12 percent of the marked rats had moved between buildings on the same farm. Stroud (1982) reported an average home range of 0.19 ha in California. Jackson (1982) noted an average home range radius of 50 m.

These rats, together with Norway rats, cause considerable damage by their despoliation of foodstuffs, their gnawing, and the fact that they harbor and carry a large number of diseases affecting both humans and other animals.

Food. Black rats are omnivorous and consume a wide variety of items. Their major food consists of garbage, grain, seeds, and meat. Insects and green vegetation may also be eaten.

Reproduction and Development. Black rats are prolific, but they produce smaller and fewer litters than the Norway rat. In Georgia, this species breeds throughout the year, with slight peaks in reproductive activity in March and August. After a gestation period of approximately 22 days, an average litter of about six young is born. It has been estimated that each adult female produces approximately 40 young per year.

Young black rats mature rapidly and are weaned when about three weeks old. They are able to reproduce at approximately three months of age.

Longevity. Worth (1950) recorded several individual black rats on his study area for a period of six months or more and one rat which he noted was "well over a year old." Captives have lived as long as four years and two months (Nowak, 1990).

Predation. Snakes, hawks, owls, and most carnivorous mammals are potential predators of black rats. Schwartz and Schwartz (1959) noted that the chief predator of the black rat in Missouri was the Norway rat.

Geographic Variation. The species occurring in Virginia is *Rattus rattus* Linnaeus. Many zoologists have considered the three color phases of this species to be distinct subspecies, namely *frugivorous* — brown back, white belly; *alexandrinus* — brown back, gray belly; and *rattus* — black back, dark gray belly. Caslick (1956) and Paradiso (1969) concluded, however, that these should be considered as color phases rather than distinct subspecies.

Location of Specimens. BCV, LFCC, RMWC, SNP, UMMZ, USNM, VPI-W.

Norway Rat
Rattus norvegicus (Berkenhout)

Description. The Norway rat (Plate 60), also known as the house rat or brown rat, is a moderately large, robust rat with coarse fur, large, nearly naked ears, and a long, sparsely haired, scaly tail. The tail is indistinctly bicolor and is approximately 80 percent of the head-body length. The upperparts are grayish or brownish and gradually shade into the underparts, which are grayish to soiled white. The feet are grayish to whitish. Females possess 12 mammae. Adult Norway rats are generally between 325 and 475 mm long, including a tail 150 to 215 mm long. They usually weigh between 280 and 335 g, although rats weighing 680 g have been recorded.

The upper surface of the skull has prominent ridges, which are more or less parallel (Figure 114). The cusps on the molar teeth are in three longitudinal rows and are quite distinct from those of the native sigmodontine rodents as discussed previously.

Distribution. The Norway rat is native to Japan and possibly the eastern mainland of Asia. It was not known in Europe until about 1553. However, it now has a cosmopolitan distribution and is found nearly everywhere humans have settled. It probably arrived in North America in ships about 1775 and has since spread over most of the continent (Silver, 1927b).

This species is common throughout Virginia.

Habitat. Norway rats are present wherever there is an abundance of food and shelter. This species is aggressive and extremely adaptable to a wide range of conditions. It is common in

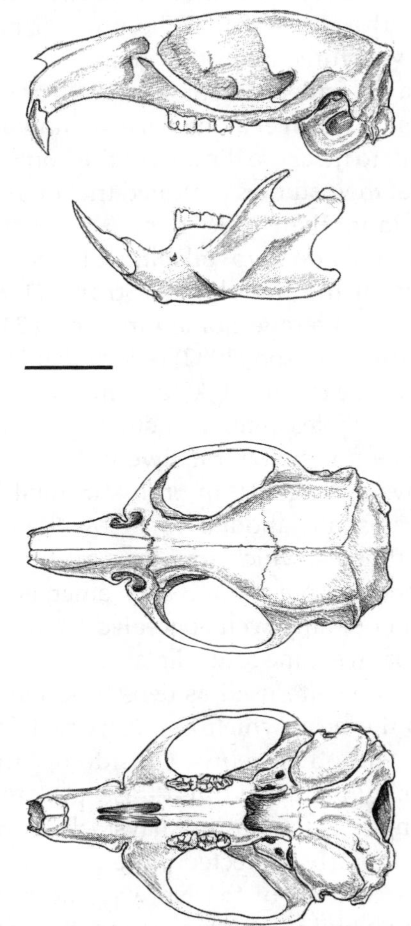

Figure 114. *Rattus norvegicus:* Left lateral view of skull and mandible, and dorsal and ventral view of skull. Scale bar = 10 mm.

towns and cities as well as in rural areas. Rats are usually associated with human habitations and may be found in and under buildings, in alleys, barnyards, fields, ditches, under feed stacks, in rubbish heaps, and in unsanitary dumps. They prefer places where they can burrow into the ground beneath protective shelter.

Habits. These rodents are mainly nocturnal and are active throughout the year. They commonly occur in colonies. Signs of their presence include gnawings, feces, and despoiled food. They are aggressive and often drive out native rats and mice. The Norway rat is more of a burrower and a less agile climber than the black rat. When the Norway rat extends its range into areas inhabited by the black rat, the latter species may be driven out by its larger, more aggressive relative.

Rat populations may build up to tremendous numbers under suitable conditions. During a poisoning program on a farm, Gunderson (1944) removed 1,147 individuals from a 1.2 ha area and estimated that the number actually killed was three times this many.

Davis, Emlen, and Stokes (1948) noted that because rats travel along narrow runways it is difficult to measure the area of the home range, but that their studies indicated that rats seldom travel more than 30 to 45 m. Movements depend mainly on the availability of food and the density of the population. Stroud (1982) recorded an average home range of 0.24 ha in California. Jackson (1982) reported an average home range radius of 30 to 50 m.

Where piles of trash or other debris are not available for shelter, rats live in burrows. Rat burrows average 0.9 m or less in total length and are usually about 0.3 m below the surface. These tunnels, which are 5 to 6 cm in diameter, have one or more entrances. An emergency exit, with an opening well concealed from view, is used for an escape route. Enlarged areas within the burrows are used as dens. Located in the den is the nest, which is constructed of rags, paper, and other debris. Outside of burrows, nests may be located in a trash pile, under a building or woodpile, in a haystack, or in some other similarly protected place.

The success of the Norway rat is largely due to its ability to adapt to many situations. These rats have adapted most successfully to human-altered habitats — buildings, dumps, and cultivated fields — rather than to native habitats. This is well illustrated by an observation of rats living in earthen banks bordering fish hatchery ponds. These rats, which quickly became accustomed to hatchery routine, synchronized their feeding time to correspond with the feeding of the fish. When food was thrown into the water, the rats entered the water and competed vigorously with the fish. They swam well and rapidly. Their sense of sight is poor, but their senses of smell, taste, touch, and hearing are excellent (Jackson, 1982).

The Norway rat is the most thoroughly disliked of rodents and has earned a reputation which all too often is transferred to our more attractive native rats. This introduced rat frequently lives under filthy conditions, harbors and carries diseases of humans and livestock, and is highly detrimental from an economic viewpoint. Hamilton (1947) noted that on farms rats eat incredible quantities of foodstuffs, destroy poultry, lay waste the stored fruits and vegetables, and riddle buildings with their sharp teeth. In cities, these rats destroy food and furniture and make extensive burrows under buildings. Measures to control the numbers of Norway rats in cities must include the reduction of food by better garbage sanitation and the elimination of living and breeding sites. Without such sanitation, only short-term reduction of numbers will be possible.

Perhaps the only redeeming feature of this species is that the common laboratory rat or white rat is an albino strain of this species, and it has proved extremely valuable in many fields of biological and medical research, including genetics, physiology, immunology, epidemiology, and pathology.

Barbour (1951a) noted that the natives in Harlan County, Kentucky (this county adjoins Virginia) "differentiated between *Rattus* and *Neotoma*: the former are referred to as 'gopher rats,' 'gophers,' or 'mine rats;' *Neotoma* are referred to as 'cliff rats' or 'woodrats.' The name 'mine rats' for *Rattus* apparently arose from the fact that the rats reportedly enter the numerous mines of the region and feed on scraps from the miners' lunch boxes."

Food. Norway rats are omnivorous and feed on grain, green vegetation, meat, eggs, nestling birds, insects, fruit, and garbage. A rat will eat a third of its weight in food in 24 hours and apparently prefers to feed shortly after dark and again in the early morning. Hamilton (1943) stated that an average 0.2 kg rat will eat or destroy two-thirds as much mash as will a hen and that a pair of rats will eat the equivalent of a 45-kg sack of mash or grain in a year. Rats need a great deal of water and apparently will gnaw through lead pipes to get moisture.

Reproduction and Development. Norway rats are among the most prolific of all mammals. When provided with abundant food and adequate shelter, they may breed all year. Storer and Davis (1953) recorded pregnancy peaks in May and September. Hamilton (1947) pointed out that temperature does not influence the number of young produced, since pregnant females in winter carried as many young as did females during other seasons of the year. The minimum gestation period is 22 days, although this is usually prolonged when a female is nursing previous young. Litters range in size from 6 to 22 young but usually consist of 7 to 9 young.

Newborn rats are blind, naked, and helpless. They grow rapidly, with the eyes opening between 14 and 17 days of age. The young are weaned when approximately three weeks old. Most rats breed for the first time when between three and four months old, although there is a record of an eight-week-old rat giving birth to 11 young (Hamilton, 1947). A single female may give birth to as many as 12 litters in a year.

Longevity. Although Hamilton (1943) noted that the normal life span of a wild Norway rat was thought to be about three years, Davis (1953b) reported that only 5 percent of the rats remained alive for 12 months on a Maryland farm.

Parasites and Disease. Rats *(Rattus norvegicus* and *Rattus rattus)* harbor and carry such devastating diseases as bubonic (black) plague, typhus, *Salmonella* (a common food poisoning), rabies, tularemia, trichinosis, rat-bite fever, Haverhill fever, and infectious jaundice. They played a prominent role in the spread of the plague, called "black death," which devastated Europe for half of the fourteenth century, killing one of every four humans. The great London plague of 1665 destroyed half the inhabitants of that city. In twenty years, plague killed nine million people in India. In the early 1900s, bubonic plague spread to the United States, where cases were reported in several cities on the Gulf Coast. Another rat-borne disease, murine typhus, resulted in many deaths in the southern United States during the 1940s. Incidence of murine typhus in humans has always been greatest in the Southeast, although campaigns against rats and their parasites over past decades have vastly reduced the prevalence of this disease. Rat-borne diseases are believed to have taken more human lives in the last fifteen centuries than all the wars and revolutions ever fought.

Histoplasmosis has been recorded in this species in Loudoun County by Emmons (1948; 1950); Emmons, Bell, and Olson (1947); Emmons and Ashburn (1948); and Emmons et al. (1955).

In a study of the port of Norfolk, Hasseltine (1929) recorded the fleas *Xenopsylla cheopis, Ceratophyllus fasciatus, Leptopsylla musculi, Ctenocephalus canis,* and *Echidnophaga gallinacea;* the louse *Polyplax spinulosa;* and the mites *Laelaps echidninus, Laelaps hawaiiensis, Liponyssus (Ornithonyssus) bacoti,* and *Veigaia* sp.

Jones (1978) and Jones et al. (1978a) recorded the tick *Dermacentor variabilis* and tularemia infection in this species from Fort Pickett. Hall and Turner (1976) recorded the northern fowl mite, *Ornithonyssus sylviarum,* from rats in Montgomery County, Virginia. Spatafora and Platt (1981; 1982) recorded the nematodes *Nippostrongylus brasiliensis* and *Heterakis spumosa* and the cestode *Vampirolepis (=Hymenolepis) nana.* Eckerlin and Sawyer (1989) recorded the protozoan *Acanthamoeba hatchetti.*

Predation. Snakes, owls, hawks, mink, weasels, cats, foxes, and other carnivores prey on these rodents. Blem and Pagels (1973); Jackson, Pagels, and Trumbo (1976); and Deibel (1988) recorded Norway rats from barn owl pellets in Northampton, Chesterfield, and Prince William counties. Encouragement, rather than elimination of these natural enemies, would result in the destruction of many more rats.

Geographic Variation. The only subspecies of Norway rat occurring in Virginia and North America is *Rattus norvegicus norvegicus* (Berkenhout).

Location of Specimens. ANSP, BCV, CM, CU, CUC, DMNH, GMU, ISUVC, LFCC, LSUMZ, LU, MCZ, NVCC, ODU, RU, SNP, UCM, UMMZ, USNM, VCU, VPISU, VPI-W.

Genus *Mus*

Dentition: 1/1, 0/0, 0/0, 3/3 = 16

House Mouse
Mus musculus Linnaeus

Description. The house mouse (Plate 61) is a small mouse with a long, slender, tapering tail. The tail is sparsely haired and scales are prominent. House mice are normally brownish-gray above and paler on the underparts. The tail is usually indistinctly bicolor, being darker above than below. Females have 10 mammae. Adult house mice are normally between 150 and 185 mm long, including a tail 74 to 100 mm long. Adults weigh between 14 and 28 g.

The skull is light and generally flat. The incisive foramina are long, usually extending back between the anterior molars. Cusps on the surface of the molar teeth are in three longitudinal rows. The crown of the first molar is elongated, being longer than the second and third molars combined. Ridges on the upper surface of the skull are absent or only slightly developed. Auditory bullae are present (Figure 115).

When captured in natural situations, the house mouse can be confused with native species, particularly the harvest mouse and *Peromyscus*. The combination of scantily haired tail, a gray belly, three rows of cusps on the molar teeth, and lack of grooves on the incisors will serve to distinguish this alien. *Mus* also has a strong musky odor. Both *Reithrodontomys* and *Peromyscus* have white bellies.

Distribution. The house mouse is native to Eurasia, but it now has a worldwide distribution because of accidental introductions. This species was not known in the United States until about the time of the American Revolution when it is believed to have arrived as a stowaway aboard transatlantic ships. It is believed originally to have been transported to the southern United States along shipping lanes from the Iberian peninsula (Schwarz and Schwarz, 1943). Jackson (1961) noted that because this highly adaptable species occupies a much more extensive habitat, it is about twice as abundant as the introduced Norway rat. Since it is often very common in cultivated fields, it is probably many times more abundant than *Rattus*.

This species is common throughout Virginia.

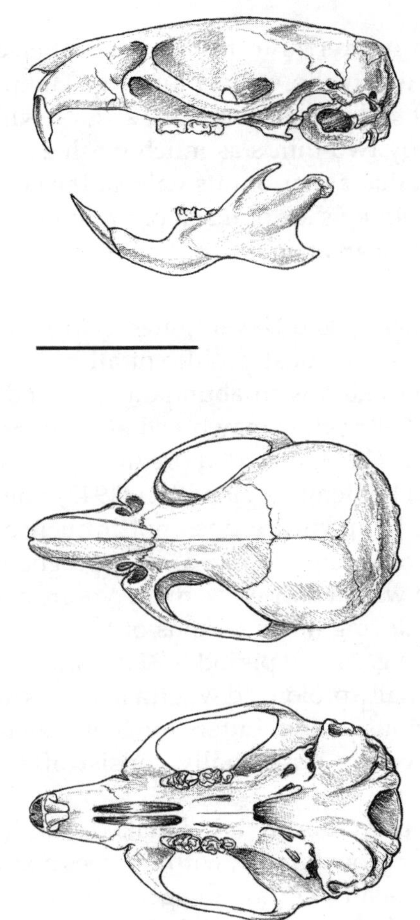

Figure 115. *Mus musculus:* Left lateral view of skull and mandible, and dorsal and ventral view of skull. Scale bar = 10 mm.

Habitat. House mice are usually associated with human habitations, but in many regions feral populations exist. It is often the most abundant mammal in cultivated fields. Individuals have been taken in fields, swamps, and salt marshes as well as in barns, houses, and other buildings. On Assateague Island, this species was abundant in the open habitat of the dune grassland and also occurred in shrub dominated habitats (Cranford and Maly, 1990). Over 77 percent of the 672 specimens of small mammals captured on Wallops Island were of this species (Kirkland and Fleming, 1990). Their principal habitat was primary dunes. Unlike the Norway rat, which is normally restricted to the basement and first floor of buildings, the house mouse may be found on every floor of tall buildings.

Habits. House mice tend to be nocturnal (Kirkland and Fleming, 1990), but they may be active day or night during every month of the year. They do not hibernate. Signs of their presence include gnawings and small, black droppings.

House mice make a variety of sounds including squeaks, calls, and even songs. Their voice has been described as birdlike in quality but weak, and their song as consisting of a series of pleasing musical chirps and twitters. Seton (1909) noted: "Out of the black darkness of a cupboard at midnight came a prolonged squeaking, trilling and churring, suggestive of a canary's song but of thinner and weaker quality. There could be no question that it was a 'singing mouse.' Many cases are on record." Other attributes include an ability to climb well and readily jump from high places. They are also good swimmers for short distances. Their sense of sight is poor and they are color blind, but their sense of smell, taste, touch, and hearing are excellent (Jackson, 1982).

An indoor nest may be concealed in a hole, in the woodwork, or beneath some sort of shelter. The nest may be composed of cloth, rags, paper, or any other soft material. Outdoor nests may be located in corn shocks, beneath debris, or in burrows of other animals. Where nesting sites and material are scarce, house mice have been reported to occupy communal nests. On Wallops Island released mice "frequently ran immediately to and entered burrows which they shared with ghost crabs" (Kirkland and Fleming, 1990).

Estimates of home range size for feral house mice range from about 395 to 1,220 m^2. Justice (1961) recorded the home ranges of two adult house mice for a 12-day period by use of smoked tracking boards. The home range of the male had a maximum length of 82 m, while that of the female was 101 m. Home ranges within buildings are smaller, with the animals generally traveling along walls and vertically in the walls. Brown (1953) recorded the average straight-line distance traveled by a male house mouse in a barn as 6 m and, by a female, 3.6 m.

Feral house mouse populations often fluctuate widely in size. Kirkland and Fleming (1990) reported estimated densities of 48.5 to 59.9 per ha on Wallops Island. Kratimeros and Rose (1991) reported a maximum density of 104 per ha on Craney Island near Norfolk. During an outbreak Pearson (1963) reported that areas normally sparsely inhabited by house mice supported populations of up to 300 mice per acre. A drastic decline in numbers followed this peak.

The house mouse is not colonial, although many individuals may often be found in a small area. Family units consisting of a male, one or more females, and their offspring may share a nest. Territoriality has been reported in this species by Crowcroft (1955) and Reimer and Petras (1967).

The familiar white or laboratory mouse widely used for research is an albino strain of the house mouse. Thus, this species has made valuable contributions to human society.

Food. These mice are omnivorous and feed on a wide range of items including grains, seeds, green vegetation, insects, other invertebrates, paste, and soap. Whitaker (1966) recorded the first extensive report on the foods of wild populations of this species in North America. Whitaker's study of 478 house mice revealed that 42 percent of the diet was composed of various types of seeds, especially those of wild grasses. Seeds of cultivated species including corn, wheat, sorghum, and soybeans comprised 22.9 percent of the diet. Of the animal foods, larval lepidopterans were a major food, comprising 15 percent of the total amount of food in the stomachs examined. Overall, animal foods comprised 24.1 percent of the food in the stomachs. Miscellaneous vegetation such as roots, stems, and green vegetation accounted for about 10 percent of the material. Its consumption of huge amounts of weed seeds and cutworms make this species almost entirely beneficial in cultivated areas. Most of the corn, wheat and sorghum seeds consumed were already on the ground.

Reproduction and Development. House mice are very prolific. They breed throughout the year in portions of their range and may have as many as 12 or 13 young per litter, although 4 to 7 is the average. Gestation is 18 to 20 days with an average of eight litters being produced annually. Smith (1954) reported that mice from food-handling establishments and residences had more embryos per litter (5.0 and 4.9, respectively) than those from other businesses and farm buildings (4.3 and 3.7, respectively). Strecker and Emlen (1953) found that confined mice on a limited food regime increased in number until limited by the food supply. At this point, the population ceased to grow and subsequently declined steadily due to a cessation of reproduction.

Newborn young are blind and naked and have their eyes and ears sealed. The eyes open at about 14 days of age. The young grow rapidly and are normally weaned by three weeks of age. Most individuals are sexually mature at two months, although some may begin breeding at five weeks.

Between 2 and 15 days, pups emit "wriggling" calls while pushing for the teats during suckling (Ehret and Bernecker, 1986). This low-frequency sound communication releases the maternal behavior and "attention" responses. Licking the pups is the most prominent maternal response, followed by changes of suckling position and nest building.

Longevity. Palmer (1954) reported that some captive house mice have lived six years, although the normal life span of this species is probably less than two years.

Pelage Variations. Molting in the house mouse has been discussed by Brechner and Kirkpatrick (1970).

Parasites and Disease. This species carries and transports many of the disease organisms discussed under the Norway and black rats. The tick *Dermacentor variabilis* and the mite *Myobia musculi* have been recorded in Virginia by Sonenshine, Atwood, and Lamb (1966); Sonenshine, Lamb, and Anastos (1965); and Ewing (1938). Smiley and Whitaker (1979) recorded the mite *Pygmephorus whitakeri.* Histoplasmosis has been recorded in this species in Loudoun County by Emmons (1948); Emmons, Bell, and Olson (1947); Emmons and Ashburn (1948); and Emmons et al. (1955). The bacterium *Leptospira ballum* has been recorded in Virginia by Yager et al. (1953). The external and internal parasites along with the bacterial, parasitical, and viral diseases of this species were summarized by Snell (1943).

Predation. Rageot (1957) recorded house mice in the stomach of a saw-whet owl in Princess Anne (Virginia Beach) County and in barred owl pellets on the western edge of the Dismal Swamp. These mice have also been recorded in long-eared and screech owl stomachs from Fairfax County and in a red-tailed hawk from Prince William County (Fisher, 1893). House mice were found in barn owl pellets in Chesterfield, Northampton, and Prince William counties by Jackson, Pagels, and Trumbo (1976); Blem and Pagels (1973); and Deibel (1988). Bobcats, feral cats, foxes, weasels, skunks, other hawks and owls, and snakes undoubtedly consume a considerable number of these mice.

Geographic Variation. The subspecies in Virginia is *Mus musculus musculus* Linnaeus.

Location of Specimens. AEL, AMNH, BCV, CAS, CM, CMNH, DMNH, EHC, GMU, ISUVC, LC, LFCC, LU, MCZ, MVZ, NCSM, NVCC, ODU, RMWC, SNP, SUVM, UCONN, UMMZ, USNM, VCU, VPISU, VPI-W.

Jumping Mice (Family Zapodidae)

Members of this family, which are found in parts of Europe, Asia, and North America, are commonly referred to as jumping mice. Jumping mice have long hind legs, large hind feet, and a tail that is considerably longer than the body. The infraorbital canal is large and oval. The upper incisors of North American forms are strongly curved and deeply grooved. Both upper and lower incisors are deep orange or yellow on their anterior surface.

On the basis of limb myology and cladistics, Stein (1990) and Stenbrot (1992) have proposed placing jumping mice in the subfamily Zapodinae within the family Dipodidae. Pending further study, these species are herein retained in the family Zapodidae (Jones et al., 1997).

Two genera of jumping mice inhabit North America. The genus *Zapus* includes the meadow jumping mice, while the genus *Napaeozapus* includes the woodland jumping mouse. Both genera are represented in Virginia.

Key to Species of Zapodidae

1a Total teeth 18; four upper molariform teeth on each side with the first small and peglike; tail usually lacks white tip
.... *Zapus hudsonius*

1b Total teeth 16; three upper molariform teeth on each side; tail usually ends in white tip
.... *Napaeozapus insignis*

Genus *Zapus*

Dentition: 1/1, 0/0, 1/0, 3/3 = 18

Meadow Jumping Mouse
Zapus hudsonius (Zimmermann)

Description. The meadow jumping mouse (Plate 62) is a medium-sized mouse with hind legs much longer than the forelegs and a long, tapering tail. The sparsely haired tail is longer than the body and is distinctly bicolor. The upperparts of the body are brownish-yellow mixed with black middorsally to form a dark stripe from the face to the base of the tail. The underparts are white or washed with yellowish, especially towards the sides. The ears are small and dark with a narrow, pale edge. Females possess eight mammae. Adult meadow jumping mice are between 185 and 225 mm long, including a tail 110 to 150 mm long. Adults weigh between 12 and 28 g.

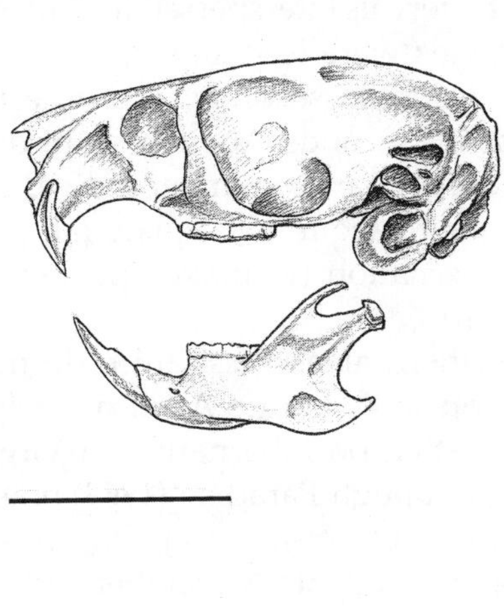

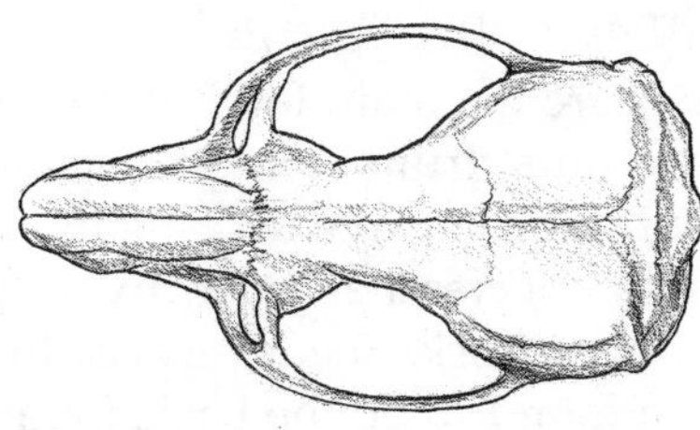

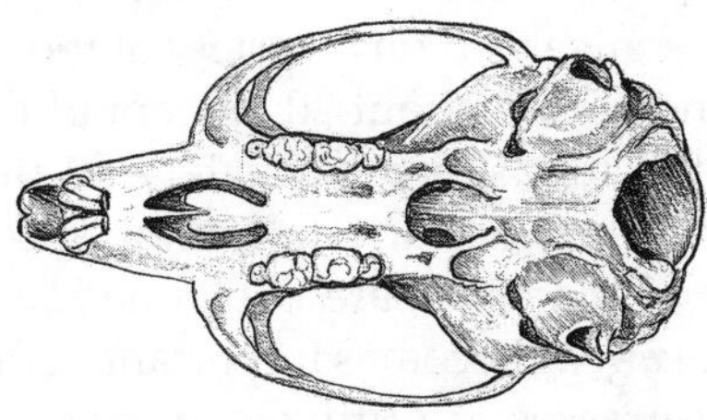

Figure 116. *Zapus hudsonius:* Left lateral view of skull and mandible, and dorsal and ventral view of skull. Scale bar = 10 mm.

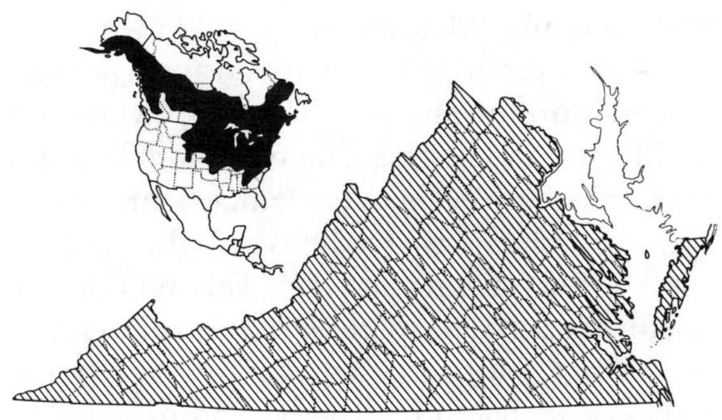

Figure 117. *Zapus hudsonius:* Range in Virginia and North America.

The skull is relatively light with a narrow braincase. Each of the two narrow upper incisors is curved and deeply grooved on its anterior surface. Both upper and lower incisors are orange on their anterior surfaces. A small, peglike premolar is present in the upper jaw, making a total of four upper cheek teeth. The only other North American jumping mouse (*Napaeozapus*) has only three upper cheek teeth. Relatively small auditory bullae are present (Figure 116).

Distribution. This species is found from Alaska across Canada, and south in the United States to northern Colorado, northeastern Oklahoma, eastern Alabama, and South Carolina. Within this range, jumping mice tend to be localized in their distribution and seldom are as abundant as some of our other small mammal species. However, populations may fluctuate considerably from year to year.

The meadow jumping mouse occurs statewide in Virginia (Figure 117). It is found on only one of the barrier islands, namely Assateague Island (Moncrief and Dueser, 1994).

Habitat. Meadow jumping mice prefer lush meadows and are often found near streams. Preferred habitats include wet meadows, bogs, grasslands, abandoned grassy fields, and forest glades.

Habits. Meadow jumping mice tend to be mainly nocturnal and rather solitary. Locomotion is normally by means of short hops of 2.5 to 15 cm, although when frightened they may leap a meter or more. The long tail serves as a balancing agent. They swim well and are also good climbers, as evidenced by the fact that Whitaker (1963a) observed jumping mice climbing grass stems to secure the seeds. Increased activity has been positively correlated with rainfall (Bider, 1968).

Active jumping mice have an average body temperature of about 37°C (99°F) (Morrison and Ryser, 1962). These investigators found a rhythmic daily cycle in the temperature of this species, with highest readings at night and lowest readings during the day. This reflects the nocturnal behavior pattern of this species.

Blair (1940) recorded the average home range of males to be 0.36 ha and of females, 0.38 ha. Quimby (1951) found at one locality, the average female home range was 0.16 ha, while that of males was 0.18 ha. On a second area he recorded an average home range of 1.1 ha for males and 0.64 ha for females. Both Quimby (1951) and Sheldon (1934) believed that jumping mice wander considerably, thus having a relatively unstable home range.

Jumping mice are normally silent, but several investigators have reported "suckling notes" in the young and squeaks and a drumming noise produced by vibrating the tail rapidly against a surface in adults (Whitaker, 1972).

Jumping mice do not make extensive use of burrows or runways other than the burrow leading directly to the nest or hibernation site. Few summer nests of this species have been found. They are usually located in a protected spot such as under some protecting object, in a hollow log or tree, or underground. Nests are of grasses, leaves, and wood pulp.

Meadow jumping mice are active only during the warmer months. They spend the winter in hibernation and hibernate as long or longer than most other mammals, but the period of dormancy is somewhat less in the southern states. The factor governing the onset of hibernation is not known, but it is apparently not temperature alone, as animals will hibernate in a heated room. Quimby (1951) speculated that the amount of body fat was a primary factor in determining the date of hibernation, and Neumann and Cade (1964) have presented evidence that "fattening" is influenced by day length. By fall these mice have become quite fat and are ready to enter into a prolonged period of true hibernation. Most put on about 6 g of fat (Whitaker, personal communication).

The hibernation period is normally spent in a lined burrow below the frost line, although some individuals have been found in nests of grass or leaves beneath logs and in coal-ash piles. Several jumping mice in North Carolina were found hibernating in separate compartments lined with dry leaves in a loose clay bank approximately 46 cm below ground level. An additional individual was found hibernating 10 to 15 cm below the surface of a clean road fill (Linzey and Linzey, 1968; Linzey, 1995a). Jumping mice have also been found hibernating in leaf nests within woodchuck burrows.

Dormant jumping mice normally curl into a ball with their nose and feet on their abdomen and their tail curled around their body. During this period their overall metabolism, temperature, heart rate, and breathing rate are greatly lowered. Waters and Stockley (1965) timed the breathing rate of a hibernating jumping mouse by observing the thoracic movements for 25 minutes. They recorded 29 intervals between thoracic movements with long and short intervals interspersed irregularly. Sixteen intervals were less than 5 seconds, four were from 6 to 15 seconds, and nine ranged from 63 to 141 seconds. About two-thirds of the population, primarily younger individuals not having time to acquire adequate fat, perishes during hibernation (Whitaker, personal communication).

In northern areas these mice do not normally reappear until late April or early May. No information on hibernation in Virginia is available, although Paradiso (1969) noted that in the vicinity of Washington, DC, these mice remain active well into November and emerge from hibernation in early April.

Food. Seeds are the main food of this species, but berries, nuts, fruits, and insects are also eaten. The most extensive investigation of the food of this species has been by Whitaker (1963a) in New York. Seeds, especially grass seeds, were found to be the basic food. Upon emerging from hibernation in late April and May, these mice feed on a variety of foods with seeds constituting about 20 percent of the diet and animal foods approximately 50 percent. During the summer and fall, more seeds and less animal materials are consumed, and the fungus *Endogone* becomes important in the diet. Different grasses are utilized in sequence as they progressively ripen. The more important seeds identified by Whitaker are *Phleum, Anthoxanthum, Poa, Cerastium, Rumex, Dactylus,*

Potentilla, Oxalis, Echinochloa, and *Ulmus.* The most important animal foods were larval lepidopterans and beetles. Whitaker presented evidence showing that the fungus *Endogone* was actively sought by jumping mice and was not solely ingested accidentally with other foods. The meadow jumping mouse does not store food.

Reproduction and Development. Jumping mice, other than the young of the previous year, breed soon after emerging from hibernation. Litters may be born from May to October, although most litters are produced during June and August (Whitaker, 1963a). Litter sizes range from three to seven with recorded averages of 3.5 to 5.7 young per litter. Gestation ranges from 17 to 21 days.

Development of meadow jumping mice has been described by Quimby (1951) and Whitaker (1963a). Newborn mice are pink, hairless except for minute vibrissae, and have their eyes and ears closed. The pinnae of the ears unfold during the first week. The incisors erupt during the second week, and the external auditory meatus opens during the third week. The hind feet, which are not disproportionately large at birth, grow rapidly, attaining nearly adult size by the fourth week. The eyes open and the juvenile pelage is replaced during the fourth week. The young mice are weaned at between four and five weeks.

Longevity. Several records of jumping mice surviving at least two years in the wild have been recorded by Quimby (1951) and Whitaker (1963a). A captive individual lived for five years (Jones, 1982).

Pelage Variations. Data on molting in meadow jumping mice have been presented by Quimby (1951), Krutzsch (1954), and Whitaker (1963a). The single annual molting spreads from anterior to posterior regions. There are no well defined molt lines. Pregnancy apparently does not interfere with molting since pregnant mice in advanced stages of molting have been recorded.

Predation. No specific instances of predation have been recorded in Virginia. Whitaker (1963a) summarized all available data concerning predation in this species. Major predators include owls, hawks, foxes, weasels, mink, house cats, and snakes.

Geographic Variation. The subspecies in Virginia is *Zapus hudsonius hudsonius* (Zimmermann).

Location of Specimens. BCV, BRP, CAS, CM, CUC, DMNH, GMU, HSU, ISU, ISUVC, LFCC, NVCC, SC, SNP, UMMZ, USNM, VCU, VPISU, VPI-W.

Genus *Napaeozapus*

Dentition: 1/1, 0/0, 0/0, 3/3 = 16

Woodland Jumping Mouse
Napaeozapus insignis (Miller)

Description. The woodland jumping mouse (Plate 63) is a medium-sized mouse with bright orange-brown sides and a dark, median dorsal band. The underparts are white. The front feet are small, but the hind feet are elongated. The bicolor tail is long (approximately 60 percent of the total length) and ends in a white tip (occasionally absent). The meadow jumping mouse normally does not have the tip on the tail white. Female woodland jumping mice possess eight mammae. Adults are usually between 210 and 250 mm in length, including a tail 125 to 150 mm long. Adults weigh between 21 and 28 g.

Napaeozapus has the incisors deeply grooved and the infraorbital canal is large as in *Zapus*. However, it has only three large upper molariform teeth, whereas *Zapus* has three large molariforms plus one small one (the premolar) (Figure 118).

Distribution. The woodland jumping mouse is found from Labrador, Quebec, and New Brunswick west to southeastern Manitoba and south in the Appalachian Mountains to eastern Kentucky and northern Georgia.

In Virginia this species is restricted to the area west of the Blue Ridge (Figure 119).

Habitat. The woodland jumping mouse inhabits the spruce-fir and hemlock-hardwood forests. Whitaker and Wrigley (1972) noted that in the southern part of the range many populations are isolated on mountain peaks and in cool moist coves. Areas of dense herbaceous growth in moist or mesic habitats are preferred. Individuals have also been taken in bogs and swamps. I have taken this species along the rhododendron-covered shores of mountain streams in numerous localities in Virginia, Ten-

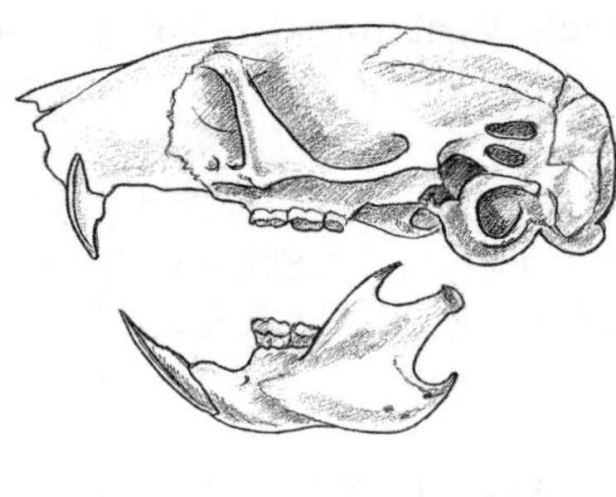

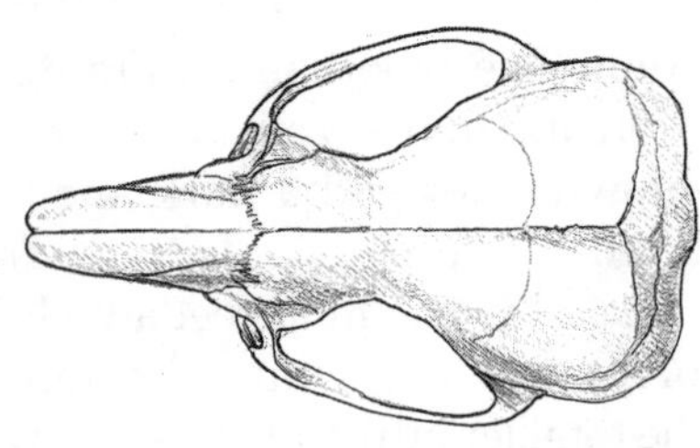

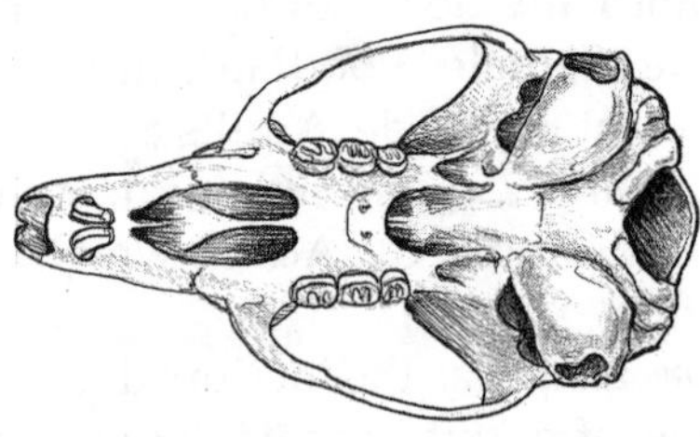

Figure 118. *Napaeozapus insignis:* Left lateral view of skull and mandible, and dorsal and ventral view of skull. Scale bar = 10 mm.

nessee, and North Carolina.

Habits. Woodland jumping mice are primarily nocturnal mammals. Locomotion is normally by means of short hops, although when frightened they may leap 2 or 3 meters. Home range size varies between 0.4 and 3.7 ha. They do not hesitate to enter water.

Nests are constructed of dry grasses and leaves and are usually located in brush piles or underground.

These mice hibernate from about October to May. This period is normally spent in a nest in a subterranean burrow. About two weeks before entering hibernation, jumping mice accumulate large fat reserves, amounting to as much as one-quarter of their body weight. Decreasing day length apparently stimulates fat deposition.

Food. Seeds, fungi, fruits, and insects constitute the primary food items. An examination of 103 stomachs of woodland jumping mice in New York revealed, by volume, the following items: subterranean fungi, 37 percent; seeds, 24 percent; fleshy fruits, 12 percent; lepidopterous larvae, 10 percent; miscellaneous vegetation, 8 percent; and beetles, 8 percent (Whitaker, 1963b). Major food items recorded in Tennessee were subterranean fungi, 40 percent; seeds, 30 percent; and fruit, 5 percent. Plant material formed approximately 76 percent of the total volume, while animal foods comprised 21.5 percent of the total food volume (Linzey and Linzey, 1973).

Reproduction and Development. The breeding season for woodland jumping mice in Virginia extends from May through August, with peaks appearing in June and August. One or two litters are produced annually. Gestation is approximately 29 days. Litter sizes range from two to seven with an average of four to five young. Barbour (1951a) recorded a female with four embryos on August 28, a lactating female on June 9, and males in breeding condition on June 9 and 10 in Harlan County, Kentucky, near the Virginia-Kentucky state line.

Newborn jumping mice are naked and pink and have their ears and eyes sealed. By the tenth day pigment spots are visible beneath the surface of the skin and the pinnae of the ears have unfolded. By the twelfth day the young can stand and take a few steps. By the fourteenth day the body is covered with fine hair, and by the eighteenth or nineteenth day the lower incisors have begun to erupt. The dorsal color pattern is developed by the twenty-sixth day at which time the eyes and the ear canals open. Weaning occurs at about

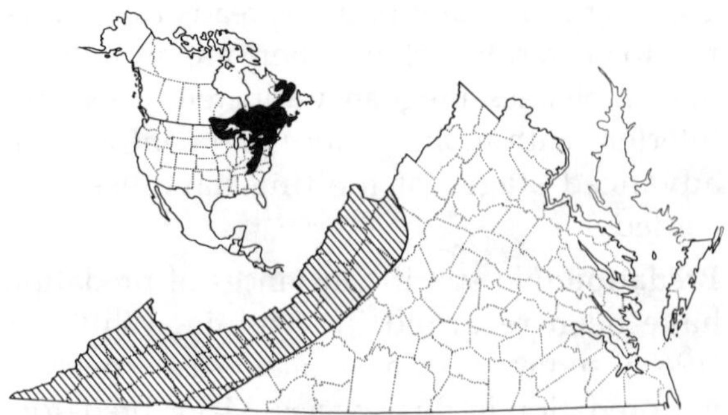

Figure 119. *Napaeozapus insignis:* Range in Virginia and North America.

five weeks of age (Layne and Hamilton, 1954).

Longevity. Nowak (1990) stated that many wild individuals live two, three, or even four years.

Pelage Variations. Molting in this species has been discussed by Wrigley (1972).

Predation. Major predators include snakes, owls, hawks, skunks, weasels, mink, bobcats, and domestic cats. In Virginia specimens have been discovered in the stomachs of a timber rattlesnake and a copperhead from the George Washington National Forest (Greenfield, 1938).

Geographic Variation. The subspecies in Virginia is *Napaeozapus insignis insignis* (Miller).

Location of Specimens. ASUMZ, BCV, CUC, DWL, EKU, HSU, LFCC, NVCC, RMWC, SNP, SUVM, UCONN, UIMNH, UMMZ, USNM, VCU, VPISU, VPI-W.

New World Porcupines (Family Erethizontidae)

This family contains moderately large, robust rodents with a body covered with hair and sharply pointed quills loosely attached to the skin. The short legs possess strong, curved claws. Four New World genera are included in this family, but only *Erethizon* once occurred in Virginia.

Genus *Erethizon*

Dentition: 1/1, 0/0, 1/1, 3/3 = 20

Porcupine [Extirpated]
Erethizon dorsatum (Linnaeus)

Description. The porcupine (Plate 64) is a moderately large, stout rodent with short legs and a relatively short, spiny, muscular tail. The dorsal surface of the body is covered not only with hair and underfur but by long quills. As many as 30,000 sharp, barbed quills may be present, some of which may be up to 7.6 cm long. No quills are present on the ventral surface of the body. The summer pelage is glossy brownish-black with a sprinkling of white hairs. The quills are yellowish-white with dark tips. During the winter the overall coloration is somewhat darker. Each front foot possesses four clawed toes, and each hind foot has five clawed toes. Adult porcupines range in total length from 645 to 1,030 mm, including a tail 145 to 300 mm long. Adults may weigh up to 18 kg.

A large infraorbital foramen is present on either side of the short, broad rostrum. The two rows of upper cheek teeth converge anteriorly toward the midline. The deeply pigmented incisors range from dull yellow to deep orange in color.

Distribution. The present range of the porcupine covers most of the forested portion of North America from Alaska and northern Canada south to southcentral Pennsylvania, Michigan, Minnesota, Texas, Arizona, California and northern Mexico. It is absent from the southeastern states, although it formerly occurred as far south as West Virginia and Tennessee in historic times (Parmalee and Guilday, 1966). Porcupine remains have also been recovered and identified from Indian sites dating from 6500 to 1000 B.C. in Tennessee and Alabama.

References to porcupines in Virginia are scarce. In 1739 John Clayton of Gloucester County noted the killing of two porcupines and stated that they were very scarce (Anonymous, 1899). Evans (1934) noted that a porcupine was involved in the discovery of Weyers Cave in Augusta County; however, Hovey (1882) and Kercheval (1925) noted that the animal involved was a woodchuck. Kercheval stated:

> *It seems that about the year 1804, one Bernard Weyer ranged these hills as a hunter. While pursuing his daily vocation, he found his match in a lawless groundhog, which not only eluded all his efforts, but eventually succeeded in carrying off the traps which had been set for his capture. Enraged at the loss of his traps he made an assault upon the domicil of the depredator, with spade and mattock.*

The original French version of the incident referred to the animal as a "porc-à-pic," which translates into "porcupine" or "hedgehog" (Bonfadini, 1894).

DeKay (1842) stated: "It is found in all the Northern States; in New York, Pennsylvania, the northern parts of Virginia, Kentucky, and through the western regions to the Rocky Mountains." Several years later Audubon and Bachman (1846) noted:

> *DeKay (Nat. Hist. of New York, p. 79) states, that it is found in the northern parts of Virginia and Kentucky. We however sought for it without success in the mountains of Virginia*

and could never hear of its existence in Kentucky.

In 1901 Elliot observed that the porcupine formerly "extended along the Alleghanies through Pennsylvania into Virginia and possibly to Kentucky."

As of 1978, occasional animals had been discovered as far south as western Maryland (Mansueti, 1950; Paradiso, 1969) and West Virginia (Goode, 1878; Brooks, 1911; Kellogg, 1937; McKeever, 1952). Thus, the porcupine was listed as extirpated in Virginia (Handley, 1979b). Feldhamer et al. (1981) and Lee (1987) have since provided additional records for Maryland.

A search of the mammal catalog in the Department of Fisheries and Wildlife mammal collection at Virginia Polytechnic Institute and State University, however, revealed data on a specimen taken at Pembroke in Giles County on June 23, 1952, by Dr. Henry Mosby. The animal's measurements were: total length – 756 mm, tail length – 220 mm, and hind foot length – 18 mm. The skin and skull were placed in the collection. However, neither could be located in December, 1992.

Concerning the extirpation of the porcupine, Handley (1979b) stated:

Why the porcupine has disappeared from the Southern Appalachians is not clear. Suitable food plants are present and human persecution cannot have been more severe than in the West, where it occurs much further south into Mexico. The sparcity of references to the porcupine in the Southern Appalachians in colonial times suggests that it was already uncommon or rare in the Southeast even at that early date.

Handley later (1991) stated:

Before the ink was dry on the 1978 account, raccoon hunters shot a porcupine weighing about 8 or 9 kg near the fire tower on Duncan Knob, Bath County, as was reported in a newspaper account with a photograph of the porcupine in the fall of 1978. Later, I learned that porcupine quills had been discovered in the late 1950s on Iron Mountain, Wythe County (G. G. Youngblood, pers. comm.). Then, in 1988, the dog of Jack Raybourne, Chief, Division of Game, Virginia Department of Game and Inland Fisheries, got a snout-full of porcupine quills in his backyard in the suburbs of Richmond!

I had thought that sporadic reports of porcupines in Virginia, West Virginia, and Maryland could be attributed to natural wandering from their normal range in Pennsylvania. However, it is at least as likely that porcupines might hitch rides on logging trucks, for example, heading south from Pennsylvania. Southern records in the past hundred years are interesting, but to date they have not represented resident populations or range extensions.

Geographic Variation. The subspecies formerly occurring in Virginia was *Erethizon dorsatum dorsatum* Linnaeus.

Location of Specimens. One specimen is recorded in the catalog of the Department of Fisheries and Wildlife at Virginia Polytechnic Institute and State University as being prepared for the mammal collection, but it could not be located in 1992. No other Virginia specimens are known to exist.

Nutria
(Family Myocastoridae)

The family Myocastoridae contains the nutria and hutias. These moderately large mammals may be terrestrial, fossorial, arboreal, or semiaquatic. Their native range includes southern South America and the West Indies. The current distribution of this family, due in part to human introductions, includes central and southern South America, the West Indies, and portions of North America and Europe. This family, together with other South American rodents and the New World porcupines (Family Erethizontidae), is classified in the rodent suborder Hystricomorpha and is characterized by having the infraorbital foramen greatly enlarged to allow for passage of the medial portion of the masseter (jaw) muscle. The angular region of the lower jaw normally has a prominent out-turned ridge for insertion of the masseter muscle.

Only one genus of these rodents, *Myocastor*, is found in Virginia.

Genus *Myocastor*

Dentition: 1/1, 0/0, 1/1, 3/3 = 20

Nutria
Myocastor coypus (Molina)

Description. Nutria (Plate 65) are large, robust, semiaquatic rodents whose fur varies in color from dark brown to yellowish-brown. The underparts are paler, and the tip of the muzzle and chin are white. Nutria have small ears and eyes, small front legs, and large hind legs. The toes of the forefeet are unwebbed, while those of the hind feet have a web joining the inner four toes but not the fifth outer toe. Large, sharp claws are present. The tail is round, scaly, and sparsely haired. The short round ears and the long whiskers around the mouth make the head appear broad and heavy. The lips close behind the incisors to allow the animal to gnaw while submerged. The nutria somewhat resembles a large muskrat or a small beaver but can easily be distinguished by the round tail (the muskrat's tail is vertically flattened; the beaver's tail is horizontally flattened). Females possess 8 mammae that are located high on the sides of the body, presumably an adaptation to give the young an opportunity to nurse while the mother is in the water. Adults are between 750 and 1,075 mm long, including a tail 300 to 450 mm long. Wild adults generally weigh between 4.5 and 9 kg.

The large, heavy skull possesses long incisive foramina and four large, broad, powerful, orange-red incisors. The color of the incisors is said to become deeper orange-red with age. The upper molars are extremely high-crowned. The paraoccipital process is greatly elongated, and its digital end is curved slightly anteriorly. Small postorbital processes are present (Figure 120).

Because the early Spaniards believed this mammal to be a form of European otter, they called it nutria, which means "otter" in Spanish. Other common names applied to this animal in the United states are coypu, coypus, nutria-rat, and South American beaver.

Distribution. Nutria are native to South America. The first nutria in North America were imported for fur farming in 1899 to Elizabeth Lake, California. During the next 30 years, some zoos and individuals imported additional nutria, but most of these were not successful

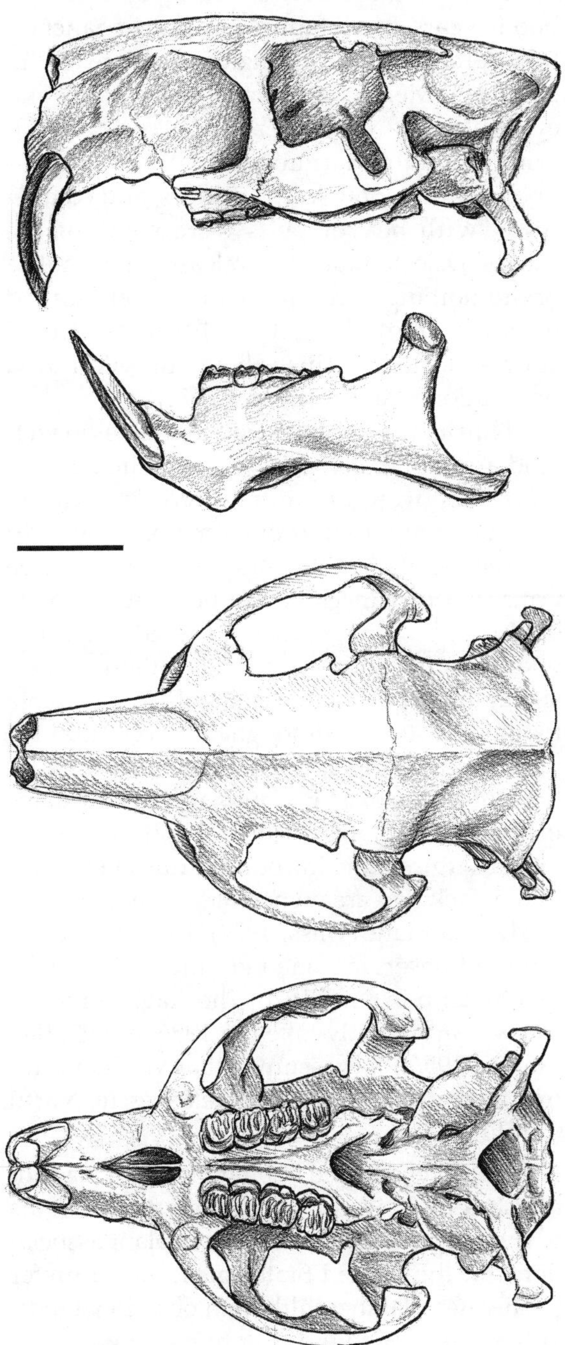

Figure 120. *Myocastor coypus:* Left lateral view of skull and mandible, and dorsal and ventral view of skull. Scale bar = 20 mm.

in reproducing and little information is available on their eventual fate. The first nutria to be born in North America were reported from C. R. Partik's fur farm in Lantier, Quebec, Canada, in 1927 and the La Forrest Fur Farm in Quebec, in 1931 (Ashbrook, 1948; Evans, 1970).

In the United States, the 1930s were the boom years for establishing nutria ranches; they sprang up in Washington, Oregon, Michigan, New Mexico, Louisiana, Ohio, Utah, and elsewhere. Shortly afterward, World War II came and nutria farming virtually collapsed – poor reproduction, low fur prices, and competition with beaver pelts were some of the causes. Dejected ranchers released their nutria or did nothing to recapture those that escaped because of inadequate holding facilities, storms, or floods. This is how our wild nutria populations started (Evans, 1970).

Nutria have established themselves in wetland areas in many parts of the United States. Since they were first introduced, wild nutria have been reported at one time or another in at least 40 of the 50 states and at least three Canadian provinces. Many populations have died out, but some nutria have adapted to a wide variety of conditions and continue to persist in areas previously claimed as unsuitable for their existence. Although they occur in small numbers in some of these areas, feral populations of nutria exist in approximately 15 states in the United States (Willner, 1982).

In Virginia, the introduced nutria is found in the Back Bay area where it has become relatively abundant (Wass, 1972). Meanley (1971) reported observing one individual in the Dismal Swamp in June 1970. The state's first nutria was apparently taken in 1956 in Back Bay (Snider, 1956). It is assumed that Virginia's nutria migrated from earlier releases in North Carolina.

Habitat. The original habitat of the nutria is in marshes and swamps and along the margins of rivers and lakes in freshwater plant associations. In the United States most nutria prefer freshwater marshes, although occasional individuals may be found near brackish water.

Habits. In general wild nutria are not wary animals and appear relatively docile. They sense danger primarily by hearing. They have relatively poor senses of sight and smell. In recent years, however, human activities have eliminated many fearless nutria. The wariest animals have been the most likely to survive and reproduce, passing on their wariness to their young.

Nutria may be active periodically throughout the day and night, although they are considered to be primarily nocturnal. Evans (1970) reported that in some areas during the winter they fed during the daylight hours, presumably prompted by hunger. When offered supplemental food during the winter, the nutrias resumed feeding only at night.

Nutria may rest and feed in open "beds" or "forms," or they may construct burrows wherever there is sloping ground — in banks, spoil areas, rolling marshland, or even muskrat houses or beaver lodges. Nutria also make extensive use of existing burrows abandoned by muskrats or other nutria. Most burrows are made in earth structures with a vertical or relatively sharp slope. Burrows are most common along banks with dense vegetation, shrubs, and trees and are quite rare in banks without vegetation. They are generally located along water courses.

A single nutria or a family group consisting of several generations may occupy a burrow. Burrows vary from simple, one-entrance, short tunnels to complex systems with several entrances on different levels, tunnels, and living chambers that are used during periods of fluctuating water levels. Tunnels normally extend from 1.2 to 1.8 m into the bank but may extend back as far as 45 m.

A nutria normally remains in the same general area throughout its life, living and feeding within about 180 m of the home burrow. However, Evans (1970) reported that nutria in agricultural areas dispersed an average maximum distance of almost 4.8 km. Several moved more than 56 km, and one individual traveled 83 km straight-line distance (equivalent to 120–150 km by water). Population density in Maryland ranged from 0.5 to 21.4 per ha (Willner et al., 1979).

The value of nutria is debatable. The fur is marketable and provides some income to trappers. Louisiana's nutria fur industry is the largest in the country, providing 95 percent of all nutria marketed (Table 8). Pelts are sold mostly for trim and lining, while the meat is sold primarily for mink and pet food. Comparative data on the wild fur catch in Virginia, including nutria, are presented in tables 2 and 3.

Although nutria do control some forms of aquatic and emergent vegetation, they may also damage anything they can eat, gnaw, and dig into. They dig into banks and eat and trample garden and field crops near the waters they inhabit. In some areas, nutria denude marshes so that tide and river waters erode established land areas, filling channels and established bays where duck hunters hunt. In other areas, nutria may compete with muskrats for food and cover.

In Louisiana, Evans (1970) found that muskrats preferred certain kinds of saltwater marshes, while nutria preferred freshwater marshes. In a few areas, however, both rodents inhabited the same marshland. While there was no serious physical competition, the burrowing and feeding activities of the nutria did destroy or damage muskrat houses. When nutria are removed from such an area, the muskrat population often skyrockets. Thus, even though nutria rarely injure muskrats physically, the nutrias' harassment and competition for food and territory are enough to keep the muskrat population from increasing at its normal potential.

Like many imported species, the nutria can be considered a mixed blessing. Because of its fur, the controversial mammal is of considerable worth in some areas. Elsewhere, however, its destructive tendencies often outweigh its good qualities.

Food. Nutria ordinarily feed entirely upon aquatic and semiaquatic vegetation. Atwood (1950) found no shell fragments, chitinous material, or other evidence of animal foods in Louisiana and concluded that nutria along the Gulf Coast were entirely vegetarian, a conclusion also drawn during food studies on Hatteras Island, North Carolina (Milne and Quay, 1966). Atwood noted that most of the coarse emergent plants and a few of the floating-leaved plants were utilized and that food was limited to the succulent and soft portions of the shoots and tubers. The most important food plants on Hatteras Island, North Carolina were *Typha latifolia, Typha angustifolia, Juncus roemerianus, Spartina alterniflora, Distichlis spicata, Nymphaea odorata, Zizania aquatica, Utricularia* spp., *Carex* spp., *Myriophyllum* spp., and *Potamogeton* spp. (Milne and Quay, 1967).

Atwood (1950) noted that most of the material cut for food is carried to feeding stations before being consumed. Large branches, planks, or logs are preferred for feeding stations, although shallow or exposed areas or dense stands of matted-down vegetation may also be used. Atwood found that the greatest use of feeding stations occurred during cold weather and the least use was during warm weather.

Nutria eat about 1.1 to 1.6 kg of food a day, consuming this total in numerous feedings rather than at one time. They normally feed by holding food items in their forepaws, either leaning forward while resting on their elbows or sitting in an upright position.

Under normal conditions, nutria keep down the growth of many plants but do not completely eliminate any of them. It is true that nutria do not control many of the underwater plants that fishermen find objectionable — coontail, bladderwort, algae, and some of the pondweeds — and they are usually of little aid against floating plants such as hyacinth, alligator weed, water lily, and water lotus. But nutria can be useful in helping control above-water plants such as cattails, rushes, and sedges, and by so doing create more usable water surface and open the way for plants more favored by waterfowl. In addition, nutria tend to avoid some of the better waterfowl foods such as smartweed and are not very interested in wild millet or bulrushes. They normally do not eat enough of such plants as Delta duck potato, duckweed, widgeon grass, and sago pondweed to seriously reduce the food supply for waterfowl.

Reproduction and Development. Nutria are prolific mammals and reportedly have young throughout the year in the United States. In South America there are two litters a year or sometimes five litters in two years. The gestation period is normally between 127 and 132 days and results in a litter of 1 to 11 young.

Of 71 adult female nutria taken near Mobile, Alabama, during February and March, 83 percent were pregnant or had recently given birth (Linzey, unpublished data). The number of embryos per female averaged 4.9 and ranged from one to eight. Average recorded number of embryos per pregnant female for other Gulf Coast nutria have ranged from 4.23 to 5.65 (Atwood, 1950; Adams, 1956; Harris, 1956). Evans (1970) reported an average litter size of approximately 4.5 young in southern Louisiana. Wilner et al. (1979) reported an average litter size of 3.96 (range 1–7) in Maryland. Litter size increases with age (Willner, 1982).

Newborn nutria are fully furred and have their eyes open. They have been observed swimming and feeding on vegetation within 24 hours after birth. Newborn nutria are between 30 and 32 cm long and normally weigh between 170 and 227 g. Most young are weaned in seven to eight weeks. The female apparently devotes little time to caring for the young and does not protect them from predators. Evans (1970) noted that young males born in early summer were sexually mature at four to six months of age, while those born in early winter did not mature until they were seven to eight months old. Females reached sexual maturity between four and seven months. The youngest reproductively mature female examined by Atwood was 3.8 months old. Physical maturity is reached at the age of 30 months.

Longevity. The average life expectancy of a wild nutria is approximately two years, although caged nutria have been known to live as long as 15 or 20 years (Evans, 1970). Gosling and Baker (1981) reviewed and corrected previously published longevity reports and presented longevity data for three male and three female captive nutria whose average age was 75.1 months (6.3 years) with a range from 70.3 to 80.6 months.

Predation. No specific instances of predation have been recorded in Virginia. Elsewhere, man, garfish, alligators, water moccasins, red-shouldered hawks, and cats have been observed preying on nutria.

Geographic Variation. Three subspecies of nutria are known in South America. Evans (1970) stated that those first introduced into the United States were brought from Argentina. However, those brought into this country in the 1930s were "very likely a mixture of races, since mixing to improve fur quality was well underway in Argentina and Europe at least a decade earlier." Evans stated:

> *In the United States, skulls similar to those of all three recognized races of nutria have been found. However, these types do not seem to be distributed geographically in any recognizable pattern, and in 1966 the United States National Museum reported that it was currently impossible to separate U.S. nutria into subspecies.*

Location of Specimens. VCU.

Whales, Dolphins, and Porpoises

The order Cetacea contains most of the fully aquatic mammals, the whales, narwhals, dolphins, and porpoises. They are characterized by a fusiform body that tapers gradually toward the tip of the tail. No cervical constriction is apparent. Unlike that of fish, the tail is flattened dorsoventrally and is expanded laterally into two pointed flukes. These mammals have large heads and reduced, flattened, paddlelike forelimbs. Hind limbs are absent. Vestiges of the pelvic girdle are embedded in the body wall but are not attached to the backbone. A median, dorsal fin is normally present, and like the flukes, it lacks bony support. The skin is almost devoid of hair except for bristles around the mouth in some forms. The eyes are small, the ear openings are minute, and the nostrils open separately or by a valvular aperture on the top of the head. This aperture, known as the blowhole, can be directly connected to the lungs so that the respiratory and alimentary tracts are separate. Pinnae are absent. The bones are spongy and have their cavities filled with oil. A thick subcutaneous layer of blubber is normally present.

Whales must come to the surface to breathe just like other swimming mammals. They can take great gulps of air and submerge for over one hour to depths up to 0.8 km with their lungs full of greatly compressed air. When a whale surfaces, it expels from its lungs the warm compressed air, which shoots out of the nostrils in the form of a jet. This air is warmer than the surrounding atmosphere and the moisture in it condenses into a cloudlike spray which can be seen for long distances.

Physiological adaptations of cetaceans to diving in their aquatic environment are truly remarkable. They can use a high percentage of inhaled oxygen because, in comparison with terrestrial mammals, cetaceans have a larger percentage of oxygen-storing erythrocytes and myoglobins. The arterial system is so constructed that the brain receives a normal blood supply, whereas there is a reduced supply to the muscles. Oxygen is conserved during dives by a reduction in heartbeat. A tolerance of high levels of carbon dioxide in the blood and tissues further extends the time of submergence. A number of rather complex modifications of the body allows these mammals to withstand the pressures associated with deep dives.

The order Cetacea is divided into two suborders. The suborder Odontoceti includes all of the toothed whales, such as the beaked whales, bottlenosed whales, sperm whales, narwhals, dolphins, killer whales, blackfish, and porpoises. These forms have an asymmetrical skull and a single blowhole. The suborder Mysticeti contains the baleen whales. These have no functional teeth but instead have plates of baleen suspended from the roofs of their mouths that form strainers for separating food from the water taken into the mouth. The skull is symmetrical, and a double blowhole is present. Mammals such as the gray whale, rorquals, humpback whale, blue whale, and right whale are members of this group. One

Figure 121. Delphinids recorded in the waters of Virginia. Scale bar = 1 m. Top to bottom: Striped Dolphin, *Stenella coeruleoalba;* Rough-Toothed Dolphin, *Steno bredanensis;* Bottle-Nosed Dolphin, *Tursiops truncatus;* Atlantic Spotted Dolphin, *Stenella frontalis;* Saddle-Backed Dolphin, *Delphinus delphis.*

Figure 122. Delphnids recorded in the waters of Virginia. Scale bar = 1 m. Top to bottom: Harbor Porpoise, *Phocoena phocoena;* Grampus, *Grampus griseus;* Long-Finned Pilot Whale, *Globicephala melaena;* Short-Finned Pilot Whale, *Globicephala macrorhynchus;* Atlantic White-Sided Dolphin, *Lagenorhynchus acutus.*

animal in this group, the blue whale, is the largest known mammal ever to inhabit the earth. Adults normally attain lengths of 21 to 26 m, although one individual has been recorded as long as 32.3 m. Their weight can range from 90 to 150 tons (Matthews, 1990).

Delphinids (Family Delphinidae)

The family Delphinidae consists of small to moderate-sized cetaceans with a notched tail. Most also have a well developed dorsal fin. The rostrum is as long as or longer than the cranial portion of the skull. Numerous teeth are present. At least two, and usually more, anterior cervical vertebrae are fused. No cervical constriction is apparent in well-fed adults.

Approximately 19 different kinds of porpoises and dolphins live in the coastal waters of the United States. Ten of these have been recorded in the waters of Virginia (Figures 121 and 122).

Key to Species of Delphinidae

1a Beak present
.... 2

1b Beak absent
.... 7

2a Beak indistinct; rostrum approximately same length as cranial portion of skull
.... *Lagenorhynchus acutus*

2b Beak distinct; rostrum longer than cranial portion of skull
.... 3

3a Beak set off from forehead by deep V-shaped groove; teeth smooth on sides
.... 4

3b Beak long, continuous with forehead, and not set off by distinct groove; teeth roughened on sides
.... *Steno bredanensis*

4a Upper parts of body grayish; usually less than 25 teeth per tooth row
.... *Tursiops truncatus*

4b Upper parts of body not grayish; usually more than 25 teeth per tooth row
.... 5

5a Alternating streaks of dark and light yellowish pigment on sides of body; palatal border of maxilla deeply grooved
.... *Delphinus delphis*

5b No yellowish streaks on sides of body; palatal border of maxilla ungrooved
.... 6

6a Grayish above, paler below; dark stripe from each eye to anus; dark stripe from each eye to pectoral fin
.... *Stenella coeruleoalba*

6b Dorsum dark with sprinkling of pale spots; belly pale with sprinkling of dark spots; stripes absent
.... *Stenella frontalis*

7a Snout pointed; teeth absent in upper jaw
.... *Grampus griseus*

7b Snout rounded; teeth present in both jaws
.... 8

8a Pectoral appendages approximately 20 percent of body length; color black with white markings on throat and belly
.... *Globicephala melaena*

8b Pectoral appendages less than 20 percent of body length; color black with no white markings
.... *Globicephala macrorhynchus*

Genus *Steno*

Dentition: 20/20 to 27/27

Rough-Toothed Dolphin
Steno bredanensis (Lesson)

Description. The dorsal surface of the rough-toothed dolphin (Figure 121), including the dorsal fin and the flippers, is purplish-black. The beak and underparts are pinkish-white. Yellowish-white spots or blotches are irregularly distributed on the sides of the body. The slender beak is long, narrow, and compressed from side to side. It is not set off from the forehead by a distinct step. Adults may reach 2.4 m in length.

Each tooth row in both upper and lower jaws contains 20 to 27 large conical teeth that are roughened and furrowed (Figure 123).

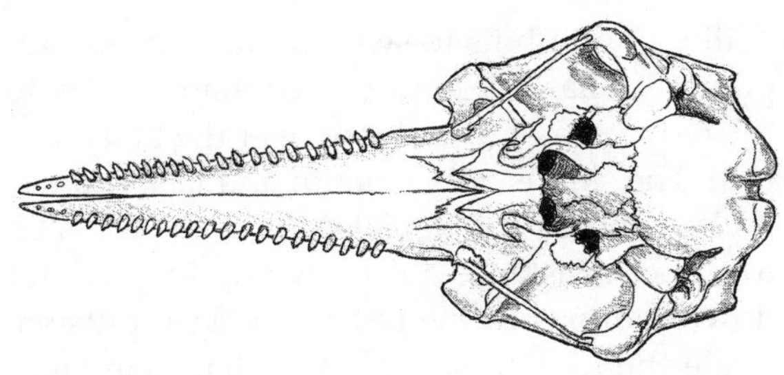

Figure 123. *Steno bredanensis:* Ventral view of skull. Scale bar = 10 cm.

Distribution. The rough-toothed dolphin inhabits the tropical and warm temperate waters of all oceans and adjoining seas (Nowak, 1991).

Two localities in Virginia have yielded specimens. During the 1800s two members of this species were found near Norfolk. In October, 1976, eight males and four females were taken near Sandbridge (Handley and Patton, 1947; Moore, 1953; Potter, 1979, 1991; personal communication, 1992).

Habits. These dolphins usually live in groups of less than 50 animals. They are easily trained and may be more intelligent than *Tursiops* (Nowak, 1991).

Food. Stomach contents have included fish and octopus (Nowak, 1991).

Longevity. Perrin and Reilly (1984) reported individuals with estimated ages up to 32 years.

Location of Specimens. USNM.

Genus *Tursiops*

Dentition: 20/20 to 28/28

Bottle-Nosed Dolphin
Tursiops truncatus (Montague)

Description. The upperparts, flukes, and flippers of the bottle-nosed dolphin (Figure 121) are purplish-gray to clear gray. The sides are light gray, and the underparts are whitish. The lower jaw and the edge of the upper lip are white with some mottling. Each tooth row consists of 20 to 28 large, conical teeth. The rostrum is long, tapering, and distinctly beaked. The digestive system has four compartments, somewhat similar to the complex stomach of ruminant animals. The first three compartments are for the holding and digesting of food. The fourth compartment corresponds to the duodenum, or first part of the small intestine (Lilly, 1961). The nostrils are united in a single blowhole near the top of the head. The opening of the blowhole is accomplished by muscle action, while closing is due to the natural elasticity of the surrounding tissues. Females possess two mammae. Adult bottle-nosed dolphins may reach lengths of 3.0 to 3.6 m. They normally weigh 150 to 200 kg.

Like other members of its suborder, the bottle-nosed dolphin has an asymmetrical skull with a single blowhole. The lower jaw protrudes beyond the upper jaw. When the dolphin rams a shark, its jaws are locked together by the interdigitated teeth. The bones of the forepart of the skull (maxillary and premaxillary), which are 3.5 to 4.0 cm thick, are able to withstand the shock of the ram.

Distribution. The bottle-nosed dolphin occurs "primarily in temperate and tropical waters of the Atlantic Ocean and adjoining seas" (Nowak, 1991). It is relatively common in both the Atlantic Ocean and the Gulf of Mexico.

This is the most commonly occurring marine mammal in Virginia waters. More than 475 records of strandings exist (Potter, 1991; personal communication, 1992; Swingle, personal communication, 1995). Among the localities are Assateague Island and Parramore Island, Accomack County; Cherrystone Point, Smiths Island, Fishermans Island, and Hog Island, Northampton County; Ocean View, City of Chesapeake; Kilmarnock, Lancaster County; Virginia Beach and Sandbridge, City of Virginia Beach; Bluff Point, Westmoreland County; and the cities of Hampton and Norfolk. Forty-two bottle-nosed dolphins washed ashore in 1994 alone (Anonymous, 1995). Paradiso and Handley (1965) noted that a female and her newborn calf were found on the ocean beach near the southern tip of Assateague Island. Wass (1972) noted that this dolphin is the only cetacean that enters the lower York River.

Habitat. These dolphins inhabit shallow coastal waters, low-salinity bays, and tidal river tributaries (Wilcox et al., 1998). This is the dolphin seen most frequently just beyond the breakwaters by visitors to bathing beaches.

Habits. These mammals generally travel in schools of from five or six to several hundred individuals. They are migratory throughout the northern parts of their range.

Tidal rhythm may be more important in

governing the daily activities of dolphins than darkness and light. They frequently enter brackish bays and creeks with the rising tide and usually leave as it falls. McBride and Hebb (1948) noted that this was presumably a response to the movements of the fish upon which they feed. Average home range has been estimated to be between 15 and 40 km^2 (Nowak, 1991). Caldwell (1955) reported a home range of 434,150 m^2 for an individual identifiable because of a damaged dorsal fin.

Aerial surveys conducted during July–October, 1980, and May–June, 1981, revealed an average density estimate of 0.159 dolphins per km^2 in the mouth of the Chesapeake Bay (Blaylock, 1988). Similar surveys along the southern Virginia coast and within 2 km of shore revealed an average density estimate of 3.4 dolphins per km^2. Average abundance in both areas combined was estimated at 340 dolphins. By relying upon the unique shape of dorsal fins, Blaylock (1988) resighted five of seven bottle-nosed dolphins a year later, a fact that suggests some individuals are seasonal residents.

Because of its tendency to occur in inshore waters, this species may be somewhat more vulnerable to storms than other species. Strandings, however, appear to be relatively infrequent and may be due to this animal's adaptation to shallow-water habitats. Other factors such as being shot or struck by boats, apparently kill more of these dolphins than strandings.

Bottle-nosed dolphins can dive to considerable depths. Neumann and Hull (1965–1966) reported circling a deep submersible Aluminaut at approximately 60 to 90 m, and echolocation sounds of dolphins were heard at close range at a depth of 183 m. Cadenat (1959) estimated that wild individuals of this species must dive to at least 198 m based on analysis of stomach contents of some members of this species. Under experimental conditions, a trained bottle-nosed dolphin has been down to a depth of 168 m (Ridgway, 1966).

Gunter (1954) noted that dolphins can be overtaken with outboard motorboats at a speed of 22 miles per hour, and a United States Department of the Interior Fisheries Center Leaflet (Anonymous, 1965a) stated that their maximum speed was about 35 miles per hour. The ability of dolphins to swim at high speeds apparently relates less to power than it does to the reduction of turbulence over the body surface. The skin is very smooth and lacks hair. It is also rubbery and flexible and can be adjusted to reduce resistance during swimming. Up and down motions of the tail provide propulsion, while the flippers are used for balancing and steering. Dolphins often leap well clear of the surface, then plunge in headfirst or fall on their side or back. Dolphins frequently swim just ahead of the bow of a ship, sometimes holding their position for miles. In the case of large vessels, they are "hitching a ride" on the compression wave caused by the forward motion of the ship.

Dolphins are highly intelligent mammals with extremely complex brains, and at times they display a degree of reasoning ability. Learning is rapid and requires relatively little repetition. They have been trained to retrieve balls and other thrown objects, raise flags, count, play bulb-horns, leap through hoops, and pull a boat or surfboard through the water while wearing a harness. They will engage in self-initiated play with feathers, pebbles, or other objects. They have also been trained to perform more serious functions such as carrying tools to divers and ferrying messages between undersea labs and surface facilities.

Dolphins use a variety of sounds to communicate with one another, including whistles, squeaks, clicks, barks, jaw claps, moaning, and wailing. The commonest sounds are a birdlike whistle and underwater clicks which have an ultrasonic component (Kellogg, Kohler, and Morris 1953). Individual variation in the whistle apparently provides a means by which one dolphin can identify other individuals. Most sounds are produced through the blowhole and are varied by changing the size of the blowhole and by placement of a movable tonguelike fold of skin (Lilly, 1961). Air sacs placed below the blowhole expel their contents through the blowhole. Some underwater sounds may be produced by the larynx. Dolphins are said to have the capacity to mimic human speech. As might be expected in such a vocal mammal, hearing is acute, and sounds ranging up to 153 kilocycles can be perceived by some individuals.

The remarkable intelligence and inventiveness of the bottle-nosed dolphin was demonstrated in Georgia in 1965 when two dolphins were observed cooperatively pushing waves into a muddy shore and stranding small fish (Hoese, 1971). The dolphins rushed up the bank and snatched the fish from the slippery mud before sliding back into the water. Usually the whole body of the dolphin, except the tail, came out of the water, but occasionally the whole body came completely out on land.

Extensive data concerning behavior in this species have been presented by McBride and Hebb (1948) and Caldwell, Caldwell, and Siebenaler (1965). Of particular interest is the manner in which a dolphin sleeps. The body usually floats near the surface, with the tail dangling somewhat and the head about 0.3 m below the surface. About every 30 seconds, the head is brought to the surface to breathe. The eyelids are closed during sleep but open several times a minute. Even during deep sleep, the eyes only remain closed for an average of 15 to 30 seconds.

The dolphin has no sense of smell, even though the ability to taste is apparently well developed. The eyes are adapted for vision both underwater and in air. However, a number of studies have demonstrated that dolphins avoid obstacles and locate food or other objects without the use of vision. This is accomplished by echolocation, or sonar. Blindfolded dolphins are able to navigate with no difficulty and can distinguish fish fragments from other similar-sized objects. During experiments on echolocation, the pulse rate varied from 16 pulses per second to 190 per second near the fish. Just before the dolphins seized the fish, the rate dropped to 26–50 per second. After the fish was taken, the rate rose briefly to as high as 416 per second. The sounds apparently emanated from the forehead region (Norris it al., 1961).

Reported instances of bottle-nosed dolphins coming to the aid of sick or injured individuals are numerous and have been summarized by Caldwell and Caldwell (1966). Siebenaler and Caldwell (1956) described one incident:

> *A one-stick charge of dynamite was exploded about three feet under the surface near a school of approximately 25* T. truncatus. *One partially stunned adult came to the surface and raced around the vessel in a wide arc, the animal exhibiting a 45° 'list.' Almost immediately two other adults came to the assistance of this injured companion. One came up from below on each side, and placing the upper lateral part of their heads (just behind the blowhole) approximately beneath the pectoral fins of the injured one, they buoyed it to the surface in an apparent effort to allow it to breathe while it remained partially stunned. Since the positions of the two assisting dolphins was such that they themselves could not breathe . . . , they had to swing away from their companion in order to surface and blow . . . . What seemed to be another assisting pair almost immediately resumed the support of the injured one . . . . the entire school remained nearby until the injured animal had recovered (several minutes), at which time they all left at a high speed.*

Food. The food of this species consists of 7 to 11 kg of fish a day. The fish consumed are primarily mackerel, herring, menhaden, and other gregarious species that are swallowed whole. However, they will feed on almost any species of fish. It is thought that digesting the fish also provides water, since most species of dolphins have no access to fresh water. Squid may form a portion of the diet (Evans, 1987).

Reproduction and Development. Mating and the birth of the young take place from February through May in the captive colony of dolphins at Marineland in Florida. However, the discovery of apparently recently born young in November, December, and January in Florida waters, the birth of young to two recently captured dolphins at the Miami Seaquarium in September, and the discovery of a newborn dolphin off the coast of England in July indicate that birth in wild bottle-nosed dolphin populations may occur outside this period (Moore, 1953; Tavolga and Essapian, 1957; Layne, 1965).

Details of the behavior of the bottle-nosed dolphin during mating, parturition, and rearing of the young have been provided by Tavolga and Essapian (1957). Pregnancy appears to last between 11 and 13 months. The single embryo is normally in the left horn of the uterus (Wislocki and Enders, 1941). Gunter (1942a) noted short hairs on the snouts of two embryos. Baby dolphins are normally born tail first which prevents drowning. Newborn calves are between 0.9 and 1.2 m long, weigh about 11 kg, are toothless, and have their eyes open. Whereas most female mammals bite the umbilical cord, the female dolphin snaps it within 10 cm of the body of her newborn young with a characteristic whirl of her body. The baby makes its way unaided to the surface. Some females have been observed swimming behind their newborn calves, pushing them to the surface so as to allow the calves to breathe. From the time of birth the calf can swim fast enough to keep up with adults swimming at a fairly high rate of speed.

McBride and Kritzler (1951) have noted:

> *During the first few weeks, when it surfaces to breathe, momentum throws its head clear at about a forty-five degree angle and the infant falls back with a light splash. It is not until it is a couple of months old that it acquires the smooth roll which characterizes the respiratory surfacing of the adult.*

Between two and four hours after birth, the baby nurses for the first time. The mother rolls over on one side and glides slowly during the few seconds while nursing takes place. During the first two weeks, nursing periods are spaced at intervals of 10 to 60 minutes, averaging about 26. During each period, the young dolphin may suckle only once or as many as nine times. It is believed that the milk is injected, rather than sucked, into the mouth and each suckling lasts, therefore, only a few seconds. As an adaptation to the animal's aquatic habitat, the mammae are located within two barely noticeable slits on either side of the female's genital opening. Although fish may first be eaten at about five months of age, the young may nurse for as long as 18 months. Females become sexually mature at four years of age and in captivity do not reproduce more than once every 2 years (McBride and Kritzler, 1951).

Mother dolphins are extremely solicitous and maintain constant vocal communication with their young. Sick, injured, and even dead young will be raised and carried at the surface by the female. The mother-young relationship may, in some instances, persist for several years.

Longevity. The lifespan of a dolphin is probably between 15 and 25 years. Specimens taken near Florida have lived at least 25 years (Nowak, 1991).

Predation and Disease. Fish such as sharks and barracudas are the only major predators, and even then, instances of dolphins being attacked and/or killed are rare and usually involve young animals. Most sharks usually steer clear of dolphins, for these powerful mammals can kill the menacing fish by butting then with their snouts.

From June, 1987, until May, 1988, an epizootic decimated the dolphin population along the east coast of the United States from New Jersey to Florida. Potter (1991) reviewed the course of the epizootic, the numbers of animals that died, the potential causative agents, and the long-term effects. Kuehl et al. (1991) reported that mid-Atlantic dolphins are contaminated with high concentrations of PCBs and PBBs, strong, immunosuppressive agents, toxic pesticides such as tech-chlordane, mirex, dieldrin, and DDE, and numerous other unidentified polychlorinated and polybrominated chemicals. The role of chemical residues in the mass mortality is currently being investigated. Based on histopathologic and immunocytochemical findings, Lipscomb et at. (1994) concluded that morbilliviral infection was the primary cause of the epizootic.

Location of Specimens. LSUMZ, USNM, VIMS.

Genus *Stenella*

Dentition: 30/30 to 52/52

Striped Dolphin
Stenella coeruleoalba (Meyen)

Description. The striped dolphin (Figure 121) is bluish-black above and grayish or whitish below. A narrow dark band is present on the side of the body and extends from the eye to the vent. Another dark band extends from the eye toward the flipper on each side. The eye is surrounded by dark pigment. The mouth region and the pectoral fins are also pigmented. Adult striped dolphins are normally between 1.8 and 2.4 m long. They may weigh up to about 120 kg.

Between 44 and 50 small, recurved teeth are present in each half of both upper and lower jaws.

For many years this species was classified as *Stenella styx* (Gray).

Distribution. The striped dolphin is found in the "tropical and temperate waters of the Atlantic, Indian, and Pacific oceans and adjoining seas" (Nowak, 1991).

Seventeen specimens have been recovered from Virginia's waters (Potter, 1991). Localities include Virginia Beach (December, 1938; November, 1978); Sandbridge (December, 1968; November, 1978; May, 1987; April, 1988); Chincoteague (April, 1977); Chincoteague Point (May, 1978); Chesapeake Beach (January, 1979); Newport News (April, 1979); Assateague Island (September, 1979; November, 1979; March, 1989); Wallops Island (July, 1981; October, 1981); Buckroe Beach (November, 1984); Smith Island (April, 1986; January, 1987); and Northampton County (May, 1990) (Barbour, 1943; Bailey, 1946; Potter, 1979, 1991, personal communication, 1992; Swingle, personal communication, 1995). Blaylock (1985) stated: "An extremely rare herd of striped dolphins was sighted near the mouth of the Chesapeake Bay in the 1960s."

Habits. These dolphins frequently travel in schools of up to several hundred individuals.

Food. This species feeds primarily on small fishes, squids, and crustaceans (Evans, 1987).

Reproduction. Females reportedly bear a single calf after a gestation period of 11 to 12 months. Sexual maturity in both sexes is reached at five to nine years of age, while physical maturity is attained at 14 to 17 years (Nowak, 1991).

Longevity. The estimated maximum age of the striped dolphin is 50 years (Nowak, 1991).

Location of Specimens. MCZ, USNM.

Atlantic Spotted Dolphin
Stenella frontalis (G. Cuvier)

Description. The Atlantic spotted dolphin (Figure 121) has a long, narrow, dark rostrum. The dark dorsum is sprinkled with pale spots, while the pale belly is sprinkled with dark spots. Adult spotted dolphins may reach a length of 2.1 m. They may weigh up to 120 kg.

Between 35 and 44 teeth are present in each half of both upper and lower jaws.

This species was formerly known as *Stenella plagiodon.*

Distribution. The Atlantic spotted dolphin inhabits the "tropical and warm temperate waters of the Atlantic Ocean and adjoining seas" (Nowak, 1991).

Seven individuals have been reported from Virginia (Potter, 1991; personal communication, 1992; Swingle, personal communication, 1995): one from Assateague Island (May 14, 1974); a male from False Cape (May 1, 1978); a female from Virginia Beach (April 2, 1981); one from Wachapreague Inlet (September 11, 1982); a female from Cedar Island (March 22, 1988; note correction of date from Potter, 1991); and a male from Sandbridge (September 19, 1989); and one from Norfolk (October, 1994).

Habits. The Atlantic spotted dolphin can swim at speeds of 22 to 28 km/hr (Nowak, 1991). Sounds produced by this dolphin have been identified as whistles and clicks (Caldwell, 1971; Caldwell et al., 1973). These dolphins may travel in schools ranging in size from 6 to 100 animals.

Food. This species feeds primarily on squid and small fishes (Evans, 1987).

Location of Specimens. USNM.

Genus *Delphinus*

Dentition: 47/47 to 65/65

Saddle-Backed Dolphin
Delphinus delphis Linnaeus

Description. In the saddle-backed dolphin (Figure 121), the dorsal surface of the body including the sickle-shaped dorsal fin, fluke, and narrow, pointed flippers are black. The underparts are white. The sides of the body possess undulating bands of gray, yellow, and white. Narrow dark stripes extend from dark eye rings to the base of the snout. A dark stripe extends forward on each side from the base of the flipper to the lower jaw. The beak is long and narrow and is set off from the head by a deep groove. Adult dolphins are between 1.8 and 2.4 m long and may weigh between 60 and 75 kg.

Each jaw contains 40 to 50 small conical teeth, each only about 2.5 mm in diameter (Figure 124).

Distribution. This species is found throughout the tropical and warm temperate oceans and adjoining seas of the world (Nowak, 1991).

Eleven records of saddle-backed dolphins have been recorded from Virginia (Potter, 1991).

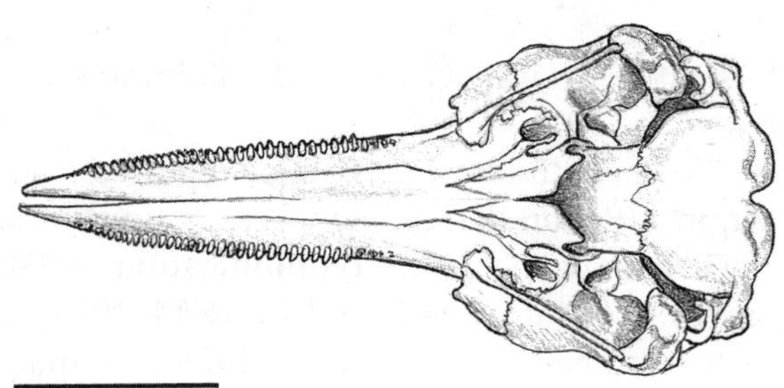

Figure 124. *Delphinus delphis:* Ventral view of skull. Scale bar = 10 cm.

Localities include Cobb Island, Northampton County (date unknown); Dam Neck Mills, City of Virginia Beach (date unknown); Parramore Island, Accomack County (three specimens – date unknown; January, 1976; April, 1986); Gwynn's Island, Mathews County (mother and young, May, 1931); Assateague Island, Accomack County (April, 1970; April, 1980; April, 1981; November, 1990); and Back Bay National Wildlife Refuge, City of Virginia Beach (May, 1977) (Bailey, 1946; Handley and Patton,l 1947; Potter, 1979; 1991; personal communication, 1992). In addition, color slides of a dolphin that washed ashore on Assateague Island in 1956 have been identified as this species (Paradiso and Handley, 1965; Wass, 1972).

Habits. These dolphins are primarily marine forms, but they have been known to ascend freshwater rivers for considerable distances. They are rapid swimmers; some individuals have been recorded at 40 km per hour.

Food. Food consists primarily of fishes and cephalopods from depths up to 280 m.

Reproduction and Development. A single calf is born from midwinter to summer following a gestation of 11 months. Newborn calves are between 760 and 940 mm long. The calves are weaned in four to five months. Females reach sexual maturity when three years old, males at four years.

Longevity. Saddle-backed dolphins are reported to live more than 20 years.

Geographic Variation. The saddle-backed dolphin, *Delphinus delphis* Linnaeus, is not divided into subspecies, although some authorities regard the northern Pacific population as a separate species.

Location of Specimens. USNM.

Genus *Lagenorhynchus*

Dentition: 22/22 to 46/46

Atlantic White-Sided Dolphin
Lagenorhynchus acutus (Gray)

Description. The Atlantic white-sided dolphin (Figure 122) has a blackish back and a whitish belly. A broad blaze is present on each side from the face to the tail. The upper portion of this pale area is white and the lower portion is yellowish. The flippers are black. A narrow black stripe extends from the flipper to the angle of the mouth. The head is short and blunt with an indistinct glossy black beak. Adult dolphins may reach 2.7 m in length. Adults may weigh up to 230 kg.

Each side of the upper and lower jaws contain 30 to 37 teeth (Figure 125).

Distribution. This species is normally found in the North Atlantic Ocean south to Cape Cod. However, in May, 1978, a female white-sided dolphin was found on Assateague Island (Potter, 1979). Testaverde and Mead (1980) record the date as May, 1977, an apparent error. Since that time, four additional specimens have been recorded from Parramore Island (April, 1980); Wachapreague (September, 1981); and Assateague Island (April, 1987; February, 1990) (Potter, 1991; personal communication, 1992).

Habits. These dolphins may travel in schools ranging from 6 to 1,000 or more individuals. Blaylock (1985) noted that in Virginia these dolphins normally occur well offshore between the Gulf Stream and the Labrador Current.

Food. Fishes such as herring, mackerel, and striped bass together with squid and crustaceans comprise the diet of this species (Evans,

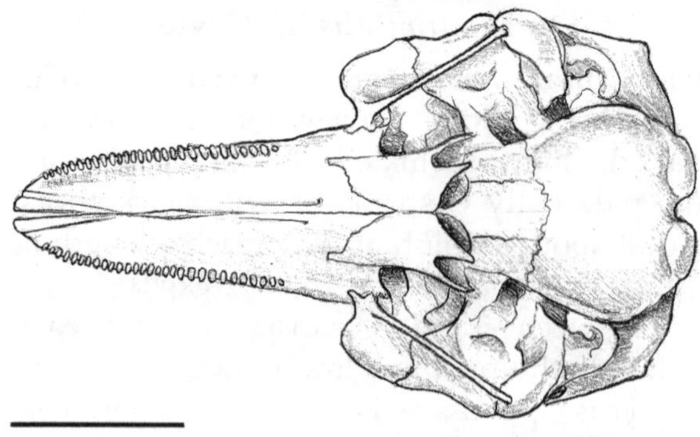

Figure 125. *Lagenorynchus acutus:* Ventral view of skull. Scale bar = 10 cm.

1987). Fish remains and squid beaks were found in the stomach of a specimen stranded on a Virginia beach (Blaylock, 1985).

Reproduction and Development. The gestation is thought to be about 10 months and calves are probably born in spring and early summer.

Location of Specimens. USNM.

Genus *Grampus*

Dentition: 0/3 to 0/7

Grampus (Risso's Dolphin)
Grampus griseus (Cuvier)

Description. The dorsal surface of the grampus (Figure 122) is gray anteriorly and black posteriorly. The dorsal fin, pectoral flippers, and fluke are black. The belly is light gray and gradually grades into the dorsal coloration. The grampus lacks a beak. Instead, the prominent, bulging forehead rises almost perpendicularly from the tip of the upper jaw. The sickle-shaped dorsal fin is high and is located about midway along the back. Males become increasingly scarred with age. Weights from 400 to 450 kg and lengths up to 4.3 m have been recorded.

Each side of the lower jaw may contain from three to seven teeth. Teeth are usually absent in the upper jaw (Figure 126).

Distribution. The grampus has been recorded from all oceans except those in the polar regions.

In Virginia five individuals have been recorded. Localities include Assateague Island (November, 1973; November, 1974; April, 1985), False Cape (April, 1989), and Northampton County (May, 1992), (Potter, 1979, 1991, personal communication, 1992; Swingle, personal communication, 1995).

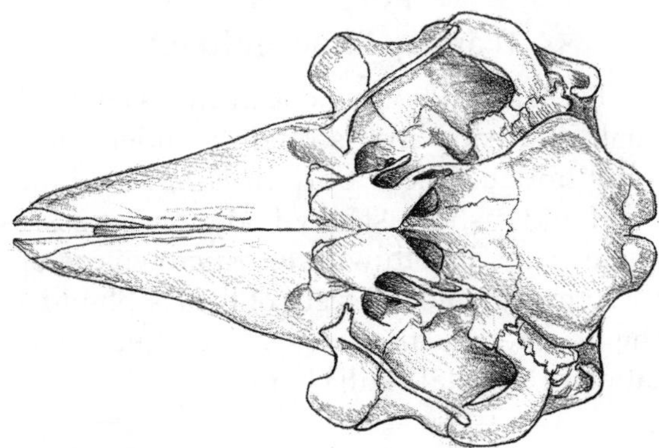

Figure 126. *Grampus griseus:* Ventral view of skull. Scale bar= 10 cm.

Habits. These mammals usually occur singly or in schools up to a dozen or so individuals. They are found offshore in Virginia waters near the outer continental shelf (Blaylock, 1985).

Food. Squid, octopus, and some fish are consumed by this species (Evans, 1987).

Reproduction. Females normally give birth to a single calf which may be 1.5 to 1.8 m in total length.

Location of Specimens. USNM.

Genus *Globicephala*

Dentition: 7/7 to 11/11

Long-Finned Pilot Whale
Globicephala melaena (Traill)

Description. Pilot whales are characterized by a high, bulging forehead that projects above the upper jaw. This bulging is caused by a cushion of fat located on the rostrum in front of the blowhole. The entire body is black except for a white area in the region of the throat. The dorsal fin is relatively large and is located forward of the middle of the body. The flippers are long and narrow. Long-finned pilot whales (Figure 122) reach lengths of 7.6 to 8.5 m. Adults usually weigh between 800 and 1,000 kg.

The anterior half of each upper and lower jaw contain from 7 to 11 small, conical, curved teeth.

Distribution. This species is found in the "cool temperate waters of the Southern Hemisphere and the North Atlantic" (Nowak, 1991).

Sixteen records exist for this species in Virginia waters: Dam Neck Mills near Cape Henry (March, 1887); Smith Island (July, 1935; May, 1985); Chincoteague Island (undated; February, 1937); Assateague Island (May, 1956; July, 1973; March, 1982; April, 1988); Wallops Island (March, 1986); False Cape (March, 1987); Cedar Island (April, 1987); Cedar Point (July, 1989); Virginia Beach (May 12, 1992); Accomack County, (July 7, 1992; October 16, 1992) (Bailey, 1946; Handley and Patton, 1947; Paradiso, 1958; Paradiso and Handley, 1965; Potter, 1979, 1991, personal communication, 1992; Swingle, personal communication, 1995).

Habits. These whales congregate in schools of 20 or more individuals. They primarily inhabit the waters near the edge of the continental shelf off Virginia (Blaylock, 1992).

Food. Squid form the major part of the diet, but octopus and fish are also consumed (Evans, 1987).

Reproduction and Development. Mating is presumably in April and May in the western Atlantic; calves are born in spring after a 15 to 16 month gestation. Newborn calves are approximately 1.8 m long. Calves are weaned at 22 months. Females become reproductively mature when six to seven years of age. Males begin breeding when about 12 years old.

Location of Specimens. GMU, USNM.

Short-Finned Pilot Whale
Globicephala macrorhynchus Gray

Description. The entirely black short-finned pilot whale also has a bulging forehead that projects above the upper jaw. The flippers are long and narrow. Adult short-finned pilot whales (Figure 122) are normally between 3.0 and 6.0 m long, although individuals up to 7.6 m have been recorded. Estimated weights of stranded animals have varied from about 45 kg for calves up to approximately 900 kg for adults.

The skull is broad and appears large and massive in proportion to the body. Each tooth row consists of seven to nine small, functional, conical, curved teeth that are confined to the anterior half of the jaw.

This species may also be known as *Globicephala sieboldii*.

Distribution. This species inhabits the "tropical and temperate waters of the Atlantic, Indian, and Pacific oceans and adjoining seas" (Nowak, 1991).

Eight specimens have been recorded from Virginia. A 15-foot-long male was recorded at Dam Neck Mills near Cape Henry in Virginia Beach in 1887 (True, 1889). Specimens have also been recorded from Cape Henry in Virginia Beach (date unknown); Parramore Island in Accomack County (undated; 1957); Virginia Beach (1953); Hampton (January, 1983); and Assateague Island (May, 1986) (Handley and Patton, 1947; Potter, 1979, 1991, personal communication, 1992). On March 4, 1994, a pilot whale stranded near Virginia Beach. Between February 26 and March 4, 1994, five additional short-finned pilot whales stranded at Corolla, North Carolina, just south of the Virginia state line (Swingle, personal communication, 1995).

Habitat. This species is found mainly in salt water of varying depths, although individuals have occasionally been observed in bays.

Habits. These mammals are found in schools, or gams, of considerable size, and seem to be migratory. They normally swim at a speed of approximately 8 km per hour. They are apparently normally nocturnal, although they rapidly become accustomed to daytime activity in captivity.

The short-finned pilot whale, or blackfish, is noted for following the leader into the beach and stranding while uttering bellowing and grunting noises.

Like dolphins, blackfish are highly vocal and sounds emitted include a high-pitched whistling, a smacking sound, a sound like a door being swung on rusty hinges, and a crying noise like the whine of a child.

This species has been recorded diving to a depth of 610 m (Nowak, 1991). They are extremely intelligent and have been used to retrieve objects as much as 500 m below the surface.

Food. Blackfish feed primarily on squid and fish.

Reproduction and Development. Bailey (1946) noted that single young are born at all seasons. A newborn short-finned pilot whale found off the coast of Massachusetts weighed at least 90 kg. The teeth had not yet erupted and the eyes appeared to be closed, although the lids seemed completely formed.

Location of Specimens. USNM.

Porpoises
(Family Phocoenidae)

The family Phocoenidae includes relatively small cetaceans and is often included in the Delphinidae. These porpoises have a blunt snout and a short, stocky body. They possess spade-shaped teeth with lobed crowns as opposed to the unlobed teeth of the Delphinidae. The phocoenids also possess a unique combination of skeletal skull characters.

Genus *Phocoena*

Dentition: 16/16 to 28/28

Harbor Porpoise
Phocoena phocoena (Linnaeus)

Description. The harbor porpoise (Figure 122) is a relatively short, stout cetacean. These mammals are usually blackish above and paler gray or whitish below. A dark line runs from the corner of the mouth to the flipper. A small, blunt, triangular dorsal fin is located approximately midway along the back. The flippers are moderately long and generally have tubercles on their anterior margins. Adults may reach 1.8 m in length and 45 to 55 kg in weight.

The skull contains 22 to 28 small, spade-shaped teeth on each side of the upper and lower jaws.

Distribution. This species is found primarily in the North Atlantic and North Pacific oceans, although occasional specimens individuals have been recorded along the coasts of several southeastern states.

In Virginia, 115 individuals have been recorded from the following localities: Metomkin Island (July, 1970); Norfolk (April, 1976); Virginia Beach (March, 1970; March, 1985; March, 1986; April, 1987; June, 1987; March, 1988; February, 1992; March, 1992; April, 1992; March-May 1993; April-May, 1994); Assateague Island (April, 1977; March, 1978; April, 1980; April, 1987; February, 1991); Lynnhaven Inlet (April, 1977; March, 1980); Chincoteague Island (January, 1979); Wallops Island (April, 1979); Sandbridge (March, 1984; March, 1985); York River (March, 1987); False Cape State Park (April, 1987); Back Bay National Wildlife Refuge (April, 1987); Harborton (May, 1988); Antipoison Creek (May, 1988); Camp Peary (March, 1989); Norfolk (May, 1994); Dam Neck Beach (March, 1991); and Accomack County (April-June, 1993; March-May, 1994) (Potter, 1979, 1991, personal communication, 1992; Swingle, personal communication, 1995). In 1994 alone, 47 harbor porpoises stranded in Virginia (Anonymous, 1995).

Habits. Harbor porpoises are usually found in groups of 2 to 10 individuals, although groups of about 100 have been reported. They spend the summer months near shore and the winter months in deeper waters. They generally swim just below the surface.

Food. Fish such as herring, mackerel, rock cod, sardines, and whiting form the bulk of the diet, although squid, eels, and crustaceans may also be eaten. Blaylock (1985) noted that the stomachs of stranded harbor porpoises in Virginia have contained bay anchovies and otoliths (earbones) of other small fishes. Gaskin et al. (1974) reviewed food habits studies of this species.

Reproduction. Breeding probably occurs during the summer, and a single calf is born after a gestation period of about 12 months. Newborn harbor porpoises are between 0.75 and 0.9 m long.

Location of Specimens. AMNH, USNM.

Beaked Whales
(Family Ziphiidae)

The family Ziphiidae includes medium-sized pelagic whales with a grooved throat and a single, median blowhole that is shaped like a half-moon. The single pair of grooves on the throat almost meet anteriorly but diverge posteriorly. The rostrum is elongated, and the single dorsal fin is located far posteriorly. Unlike other cetaceans, they usually lack the notch in the tail. Beaked whales vary from 4.5 to 12 m in total length. They weigh from 1,000 kg to over 11,000 kg (Nowak, 1991). Female adult beaked whales are generally larger than males.

These whales possess from two to seven fused cervical (neck) vertebrae. The general evolutionary trend in beaked whales has been to reduce or lose all the teeth in the upper jaw and most of the teeth in the lower except for one or two pairs at the front end that have become greatly enlarged. Some species retain small conical teeth in both jaws. In all North American species there are never more than four nor less than two functional teeth. These teeth are confined to the lower jaw.

Key to Species of Ziphiidae

1a Beak indistinct in larger individuals; distinct keel from dorsal fin to tail; dorsal fin tall and distinct; males with single tooth in each side of lower jaw conical, located near anterior end of mandible
.... *Ziphius cavirostris*

Figure 127. Beaked and sperm whales recorded in the waters of Virginia. Scale bar = 1 m. Top to bottom: Goose-Beaked Whale, *Ziphius cavirostris;* Dense-Beaked Whale, *Mesoplodon densirostris;* Gervais' Beaked Whale, *Mesoplodon europaeus;* Dwarf Sperm Whale, *Kogia simus;* Pygmy Sperm Whale, *Kogia breviceps;* Sperm Whale, *Physeter catodon.*

1b Beak distinct; no keel between dorsal fin and tail; dorsal fin small; males with single tooth in each side of lower jaw laterally flattened, pointed, and usually located near middle of mandible
. . . . 2

2a Prominent upward-curved lower jaw
. . . . *Mesoplodon densirostris*

2b Lower jaw not as above
. . . . 3

3a Body large (up to 6.7 m); laterally compressed; flukes without notch
. . . . *Mesoplodon europaeus*

3b Body smaller (up to 5.2 m); not laterally compressed; flukes sometimes slightly notched
. . . . *Mesoplodon mirus*

Genus *Ziphius*

Dentition: 0/2 to 0/4

Goose-Beaked Whale
Ziphius cavirostris Cuvier

Description. The goose-beaked whale (Figure 127) is usually dark grayish-black above and paler below. The face and anterior part of the body are often cream-colored.

The anterior end of each side of the lower jaw in males contains a single conical tooth which is directed upward and forward. These teeth are present in females but often do not erupt. Series of small nonfunctional teeth may be present in both upper and lower jaws (Figure 128). Adults may reach 7.5 to 8.5 m in length.

Distribution. This species is present in most of the oceans of the world.

Eight individuals have been recorded from Virginia (Potter, 1991). Localities include Parramore Island (date unknown); False Cape (August, 1944; April, 1978); Assawoman Island (January, 1980; January, 1981); and Seaford (January, 1986) (Potter, personal communication, 1992).

Habits. Few data are available concerning this species. These whales may be solitary, or individuals may travel in groups of 30 to 40 animals. They may remain submerged for at least half an hour.

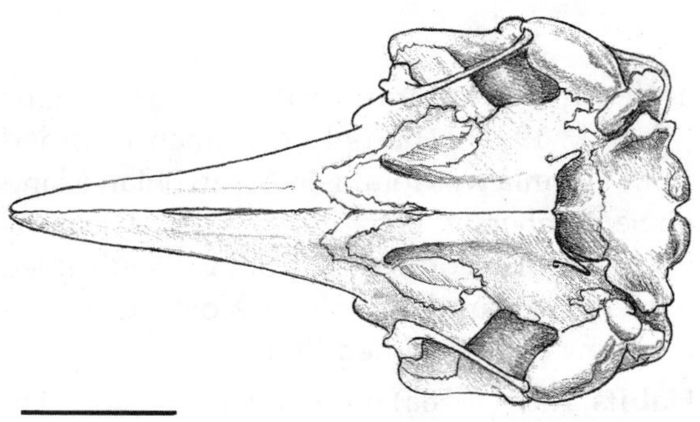

Figure 128. *Ziphius cavirostris:* Ventral view of skull. Scale bar = 20 cm.

Food. Squids may be a preferred food since one goose-beaked whale was found to have 1,304 squids in its stomach. Deepwater fish are also probably eaten.

Reproduction. The young are born after a gestation of about one year and at birth are approximately one-third the length of the mother.

Location of Specimens. USNM.

Dense-Beaked Whale
(Tropical Beaked Whale)
Mesoplodon densirostris (De Blainville)

Description. Dense-beaked whales (Figure 127) are almost completely black. They may have grayish or whitish patches on their ventral surface. Adults reach approximately 4.5 m in length. Hall (1981) used the generic name *Micropteron* instead of *Mesoplodon.*

The dense-beaked whale has a prominent upward-curved lower jaw. Near the middle of each side of the lower jaw are two laterally flattened, spade-shaped teeth. The teeth in *Mesoplodon densirostris* are "well exposed and extend above the upper jaw" (Nowak, 1991) (Figure 129).

Distribution. This species is found in tropical

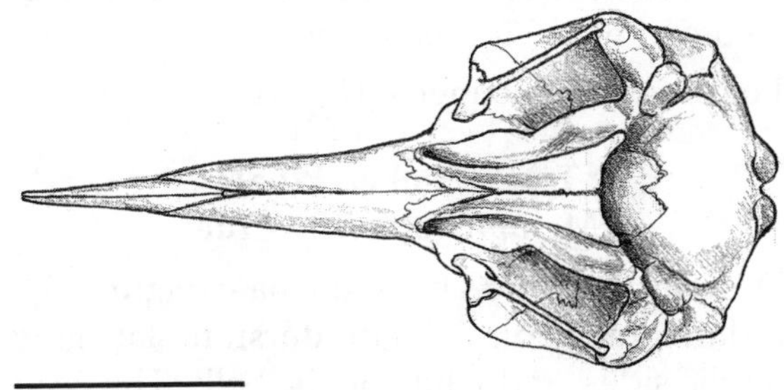

Figure 129. *Mesoplodon:* Ventral view of skull. Scale bar = 20 cm.

and warm temperate waters of all oceans (Nowak, 1991). The only specimen recorded from Virginia was found on Assawoman Island on September 30, 1973 (Potter, 1979). The nearest previous records were from Corson's Inlet, New Jersey, and Beaufort, North Carolina (Andrews, 1914; Ulmer, 1941).

Habits. Rice (1978a) observed a group of 10 to 12 of these whales dive. They did not resurfaced for more than 45 minutes.

Food. The food of this species includes squid, other cephalopods, and fish (Nowak, 1991).

Longevity. Maximum known longevity is 36 years (Mead, 1984).

Location of Specimens. USNM.

Gervais' Beaked Whale
Mesoplodon europaeus (Gervais)

Description. Gervais' beaked whales (Figure 127) are bluish black on the dorsum and paler on the belly. The body, which is laterally compressed, is higher than it is wide. The small head quickly tapers to a narrow beak.

Males possess two teeth, but unlike the goose-beaked whale, they are located 8 to 10 cm back from the tip of the lower jaw (Figure 129).

This is the largest member of the genus *Mesoplodon*. Adults may reach a length of 6.7 m and a weight of up to 2,700 kg.

Distribution. These whales are found in the western North Atlantic from New York to the West Indies (Nowak, 1991).

Only three individuals have been recorded from Virginia (Potter, 1991; Swingle, personal communication, 1995). A male was recorded from Wallops Island on July 10, 1985, and a female from Sandbridge on November 1, 1986. On December 13, 1992, a stranded whale was recorded near Virginia Beach.

Location of Specimens. USNM.

True's Beaked Whale
Mesoplodon mirus True

Description. True's beaked whale (Figure 130) is dark gray to black on the dorsum, slate gray on the sides, and white on the belly. The head is small and the beak is pronounced. These whales are similar to, but much smaller than *Ziphius cavirostris*.

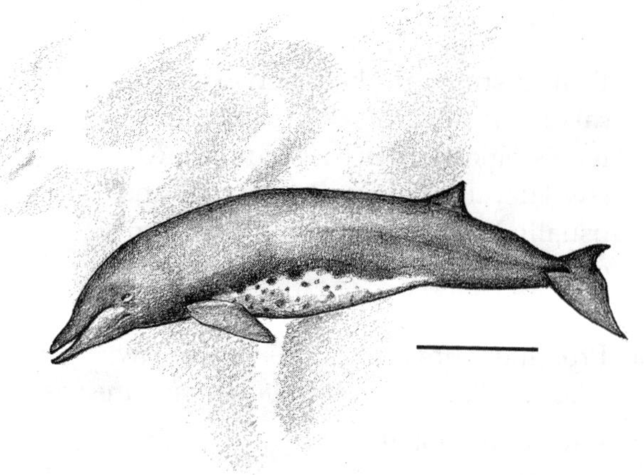

Figure 130. True's Beaked Whale, *Mesoplodon mirus*. Scale bar = 1 m.

The males of both species possess two teeth at the very tip of the lower jaw (Figure 129).

Adults are usually about 4.9 m in total length and weigh approximately 1,350 kg.

Distribution. True's beaked whale is found in temperate waters from Nova Scotia and Florida to the British Isles (Nowak, 1991).

Only one individual has been recorded from Virginia (Potter, 1991), a male from Assateague Island on March 11, 1977.

Location of Specimen. This record is from the Scientific Event Alert Network (SEAN) of the Smithsonian Institution.

Sperm Whales
(Family Physeteridae)

The family Physeteridae consists of three species, all of which have been recorded from Virginia. They range in size from the pygmy sperm whales, which may reach about 4.5 m in length, to the giant sperm whales, which may be 18 or 20 m long. The skull in the region of the nasal opening or blowhole is strongly asymmetrical because the single nasal opening is located to the left of the median line. Numerous teeth are present in the lower jaw. They are located in a groove rather than in distinct sockets. Functional teeth are absent from the upper jaw. A reservoir of clear oil is present in a hollow space above the cranium and rostrum.

Key to Species of Physeteridae

1a Size large; body length greater than 12 m; dorsal fin absent .... *Physeter catodon*

1b Size small; body length less than 12 m; dorsal fin present
. . . . 2

2a Total length less than 2.7 m; weight less than 300 kg
. . . . *Kogia simus*

2b Total length more than 2.7 m; weight more than 300 kg
. . . . *Kogia breviceps*

Genus *Kogia*

Dentition: 0/8 to 0/16

Pygmy Sperm Whale
Kogia breviceps (De Blainville)

Description. The pygmy sperm whale (Figure 127) is a small whale with a short head that comprises approximately one sixth of the total length. The lower jaw ends considerably short of the end of the snout. An oil producing gland known as a spermaceti organ is present in the head. The dark steel gray upper parts fade to gray on the sides and to dull white on the belly. A small dorsal fin is located just beyond the middle of the body. A bracket-shaped mark is present on each side of the head between the eyes and the flippers. The blowhole is located on the left side of the forehead. Adult pygmy sperm whales are between 2.7 and 3.4 m in total length (from tip of nose to notch in flukes) and usually weigh between 315 and 405 kg.

Each side of the lower jaw contains between 12 and 16 sharp, slender, curved teeth (Figure 131).

Distribution. This species is found in tropical and temperate oceans throughout the world (Nowak, 1991).

Thirty-two individuals have been recorded from Virginia (Potter, 1991). Localities include Dam Neck Mills (February, 1887); Parramore Island (December, 1970); Bavon Beach (April, 1974); Capahosic (October, 1975); Virginia Beach (December, 1975; January, 1978; December, 1979; May, 1981; January, 1982; April, 1987; September, 1994); Newport News (January, 1978); Metomkin Island (November, 1978); Smith Island (December, 1981); Fisherman's Island (July, 1983); Fort Story Army Base (September, 1983); Assateague Island (August, 1985; October, 1990); Hampton (September, 1985; February, 1994); Ship Shoal Island (October, 1985); Sandbridge (November, 1985); Dam Neck (November, 1985); Lynnhaven Inlet (September, 1989); Back Bay National Wildlife Refuge (September, 1989, September, 1997); Chincoteague (December, 1990) (Piers, 1923; Allen, 1941; Bailey, 1946; Handley and Patton, 1947; Potter, 1979, 1991, personal communication, 1992; Swingle, personal communication, 1995).

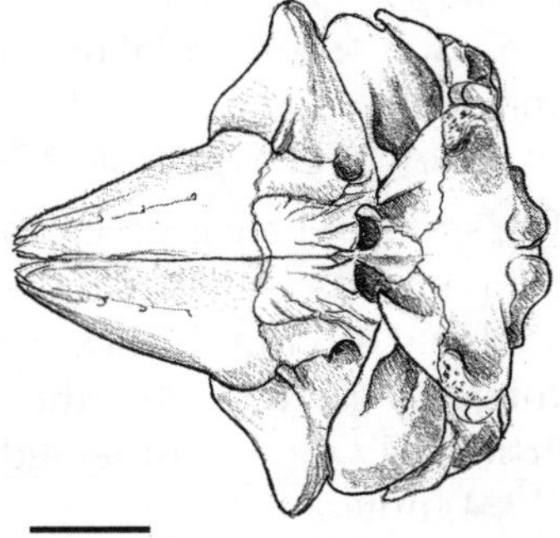

Figure 131. *Kogia:* Ventral view of skull. Scale bar = 10 cm.

Habits. These whales are normally solitary, but sometimes congregate in groups of three to five individuals.

Food. These whales are known to eat squid, octopus, fish, and crustaceans (Evans, 1987).

Reproduction. The female gives birth to a single young approximately 120 cm long after a gestation of over 11 months (Nowak, 1991).

Location of Specimens. USNM.

Dwarf Sperm Whale
Kogia simus (Owen)

Description. The dwarf sperm whale (Figure 127) closely resembles the pygmy sperm whale, and for many years the two were considered to be one species. Like the pygmy sperm whale, this species is dark steel gray above, gray on the sides, and whitish on the belly. The head is short and the lower jaw is small, narrow, and does not reach the end of the snout. The dorsal fin is located near the center of the back. The bracket-shaped mark is present on both sides of the head. The main distinguishing feature between this species and the pygmy sperm whale is size. Adult dwarf sperm whales range in total length from about 2.1 to 2.7 m and weigh between 135 and 180 kg.

The skull is asymmetrical and possesses a short broad rostrum. Each side of the lower jaw contains 8 to 11 sharp, slender curved teeth (Figure 131).

Distribution. This species occurs in tropical and temperate oceans throughout the world (Nowak, 1991).

Fourteen records of this species exist for Virginia (Potter, 1991; Swingle, personal communication, 1995). Localities include Cape Henry (April, 1939; April, 1940); Sandbridge (October, 1956); Assateague Island (May, 1978); Parramore Island (November, 1979); Chincoteague Inlet (July, 1980); Wallops Island (August, 1985; October, 1985); Virginia Beach (September, 1985; June, 1989); and Accomack County (October, 1990). The Cape Henry record consisted of a female and a calf as did the September, 1985 stranding at Virginia Beach (Allen, 1941; Barbour, 1943; Bailey, 1946; Handley and Patton, 1947; Blaylock, 1985; and Potter, 1979, 1991, personal communication, 1992).

Food. Squid, octopus, fish, crabs, and shrimp comprise the bulk of the diet.

Habits. Dwarf sperm whales may be either solitary or travel in small groups.

Reproduction and Development. A female recorded from Cape Henry on April 21 contained a large fetus. She was accompanied by a younger animal which was approximately 1.5 m long. The latter was probably a yearling born during the previous season and still nursing, since the adult was lactating abundantly (Allen, 1941).

Location of Specimens. USNM.

Genus *Physeter*

Dentition: 0/16 to 0/30

Sperm Whale
Physeter catodon Linnaeus

Description. The sperm whale (Figure 127) is the largest of the toothed whales, and it is the largest toothed mammal in the world (Nowak, 1991). The bluish-black upperparts gradually shade to silvery-gray or white below. The head is very large and rectangular when viewed in profile. It comprises approximately one-third of the total length. Most of the neck vertebrae are fused. The lower jaw is relatively small and narrow and ends well short of the end of the snout. The dorsal fin is absent and is replaced by a hump and a series of low ridges running along the posterior third of the dorsal surface. The pectoral appendages are quite small. Females possess two mammae located in deep, longitudinal slits on the ventral surface. Adult male sperm whales may reach 20 m in total length. They may weigh between 35,000 and 50,000 kg. Females weigh only about one-third as much (Nowak, 1991). Herman Melville's Moby Dick was an albino sperm whale.

Each side of the lower jaw contains 16 to 30 large, stout, conical teeth. The upper jaw contains numerous vestigial teeth buried in the gums (Figure 132). A spermaceti organ, or melon, is located above the broad flat rostrum. It may contain up to 1,900 liters of spermaceti or sperm oil (Nowak, 1991).

The sperm whale has been classified as *Physeter macrocephalus* by some authors.

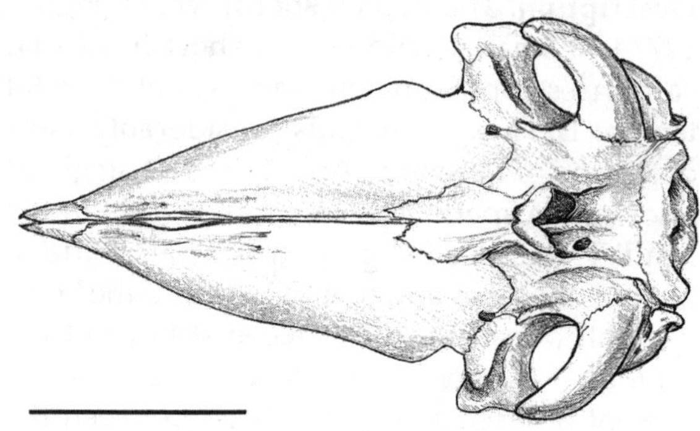

Figure 132. *Physeter catadon:* Ventral view of skull. Scale bar = 1 m.

Distribution. The sperm whale is found in all oceans of the world. Five individuals have been recorded from Virginia's waters. The first specimen was taken in December, 1891, from Green Run Inlet on Assateague Island on the Virginia-Maryland border (Paradiso and Handley, 1965). Other individuals have been found at Sandbridge on April 17, 1969; near Fisherman's Island on December 27, 1977; on Metomkin Island on January 20, 1979; and near Norfolk on June 23, 1982. Townsend (1935) recorded extensive sperm whaling operations off the east coast from New Jersey to Florida from 1761 to 1920.

Habits. The sperm whale is gregarious and often travels in groups of 100 or more. Blaylock (1985) stated that in Virginia these whales may be encountered near the 100-fathom line offshore, particularly near submerged canyons. Lowery (1974) noted:

> *The sperm whale family is a loose social group of about 30 individuals, which are part of the*

great school comprised of many families. The basic units, called harems by whale hunters, include young males and young females, pregnant cows, cows nursing calves, and an old bull, the harem master, who usually stations himself on the perimeter of the herd.

Sperm whales have been known to have become entangled in transoceanic cables at depths as great as 1,135 m. Dives may last an hour or more. Rice (1989b) recorded an 82-minute dive. After surfacing, the whale may blow as many as 60 or 70 times before making another descent. Lowery (1974) stated: "The spout is produced by the condensation of the moisture in the warm, stale air that is being exhaled, combined, according to some authorities, with a mucous foam from the sinuses."

The sperm whale is the only known cetacean to form a gummy material in its large intestine known as ambergris, a substance used in the manufacture of perfumes. When it first emerges from the whale's body, it has the consistency of thick grease, and after being exposed to the air it acquires a sweetish smell (Lowery, 1974).

Sperm whales produce a variety of sounds (Ellis, 1980). The most common are a series of low frequency clicklike pulses. Other sounds include groans, whistles, chirps, pings, squeaks, yelps, and wheezes. Underwater listening equipment can record these sounds from many kilometers away.

Food. The sperm whale consumes squid, octopus, and various kinds of fish including sharks and skates (Evans, 1987).

Reproduction and Development. Females mature between seven and nine years of age and a length of 8 to 9 m (Ohsumi, Kasuya, and Nishiwaki, 1963; Rice, 1989). They may breed either every two years or every five years. Those having a five-year reproductive cycle "mate in May of year I, give birth after a gestation period of 16 months in September of year II, nurse the calf for two years, or until September of year IV, rest for eight months, and are reimpregnated in May of year V" (Lowery, 1974). Sexual maturity in males is not complete until 18 to 21 years of age and a length of 11 to 12 m (Rice, 1989).

A newborn sperm whale calf is approximately 4.3 m long and weighs about 900 kg.

Longevity. Maximum longevity is "at least 60 to 70 years, judged by tooth layer counts" (Rice, 1989).

Location of Specimens. USNM.

Rorquals (Family Balaenopteridae)

The family Balaenopteridae consists of moderately large to large whales with numerous longitudinal grooves on the throat. One member of this family, the blue whale, is the largest known mammal. Some individuals exceed 30 m in total length. No functional teeth are present in adult balaenopterid whales although they may be present in some forms during embryonic development. Instead, plates of baleen are suspended from the roof of the mouth and form strainers for separating the food from the water taken into the mouth. Baleen is a horny material related to keratin and is similar to human fingernails. The inner portion of each plate of baleen is frayed out into bristlelike fibers which may be coarse or almost silky. These fibers serve to strain out the small organisms upon which these whales feed. A double blowhole and a dorsal fin are present.

Key to Species of Balaenopteridae

1a Flippers very long and narrow, approximately ¼ length of body; flippers scalloped with fleshy knobs along anterior border; dorsal fin low, humplike
.... *Megaptera novaeangliae*

1b Flippers shorter, less than ¼ length of body; flippers without fleshy knobs; dorsal fin not humplike
.... 2

2a Body length less than 10 m; broad white band on upper side of flippers
.... *Balaenoptera acutorostrata*

2b Body length more than 10 m; no white band on flippers
.... 3

3a Size medium; body length less than 15 m; rear margin of dorsal fin concave; flippers dark bluish-gray on both surfaces
.... *Balaenoptera edeni*

Figure 133. Baleen whales recorded in the waters of Virginia. Scale bar = 5 m. Top to bottom: Bryde's Whale, *Balaenoptera edeni;* Humpback Whale, *Megaptera novaeangliae;* Minke Whale, *Balaenoptera acutorostrata;* Fin Whale, *Balaenoptera physalus;* Black Right Whale, *Balaena glacialis.*

3b Size large; body length more than 15 m; rear margin of dorsal fin not concave; flippers not bluish-gray on both surfaces
.... *Balaenoptera physalus*

Genus *Balaenoptera*

Minke Whale
Balaenoptera acutorostrata Lacépède

Description. The minke whale (Figure 133), also known as the piked whale, little piked whale, and lesser rorqual, is the smallest of the baleen whales with adults reaching an average length of approximately 8.5 m. Females are larger than males. The upper surfaces are bluish-gray, and the undersurfaces are white. A broad white band is present on the dorsal surface of each flipper. The baleen plates, which number between 260 and 325 on each side of the upper jaw, range in length from 20 to 25 cm and in color from yellowish-white to pure white. The small dorsal fin has a curved tip and is located far back on the body.

The skull of the minke whale is illustrated in Figure 134.

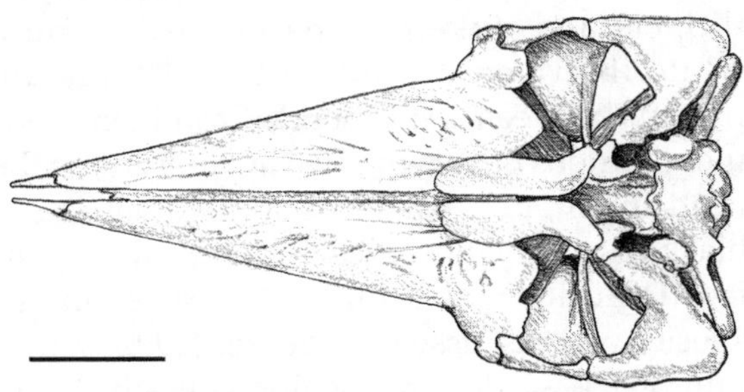

Figure 134. *Balaenoptera:* Ventral view of skull. Scale bar = 20 cm.

Distribution. Minke whales inhabit all oceans and adjoining seas (Nowak, 1991).

Six individuals have been found in Virginia waters. Single whales were taken at Onancock (July, 1977), Lynnhaven Inlet (September, 1978), Accomack County (June, 1994), and Hampton (July, 1994). Two minke whales were recorded in Virginia Beach during October, 1993 (Potter, 1979, 1991, personal communication, 1992; Swingle, personal communication, 1995).

Habits. Minke whales may occur singly or in small groups. They often enter bays and other inshore waters.

Food. Plankton, fish, and squid comprise the bulk of the diet.

Longevity. Maximum longevity in the minke whale has been estimated to be approximately 47 years (Haley, 1978).

Reproduction. Newborn calves have been recorded from November to January following a gestation of approximately 10 months. At birth, minke whales are about 2.7 m long.

Location of Specimens. USNM.

Bryde's Whale
Balaenoptera edeni Anderson

Description. Bryde's whale (Figure 133) is a slender, medium-sized rorqual. The dorsal surface is bluish-black with the underparts ranging from bluish-gray on the throat to white or yellowish-white posteriorly. Both surfaces of the flippers are dark bluish-gray. There are secondary ridges on either side of the central ridge of the head. They run from the tip of the snout to the side of the blowhole. There are approximately 40 to 50 throat grooves and 250 to 350 slate-gray baleen plates. Adults may reach lengths of 13 m.

The skull of Bryde's whale is illustrated in Figure 134.

Distribution. Bryde's whale is found in the "tropical and warm temperate waters of the Atlantic, Indian, and Pacific oceans and adjoining seas" (Nowak, 1991).

Only one specimen has been recorded from Virginia (Potter, 1991). It was found at Walnut Point, Northumberland County, in March 1923 (Miller, 1927). This specimen was originally identified as a sei whale *(Balaenoptera borealis)* until Mead (1977) reidentified it as *Balaenoptera edeni.*

Food. Crustaceans and fish are consumed by Bryde's whale (Evans, 1987).

Longevity. Some Bryde's whales have reached an estimated age of 72 years (Haley, 1978).

Reproduction. A single young is produced every other year after a gestation of approximately 12 months. Newborn calves are about 4 m long and weigh about 900 kg.

Location of Specimens. USNM.

Fin Whale
Balaenoptera physalus (Linnaeus)

Description. The large, flat-headed fin whale (Figure 133), also known as the finback whale and common rorqual, may reach a length of approximately 20 m or more and a weight of over 60 tons, making it the second largest of the whales. Females are slightly larger than males. The dorsal surfaces are brownish-gray, while the belly, inner sides of the flippers, and underside of the fluke are white. These whales have an unusual asymmetrical coloration in that the right side of the jaw and the right baleen plates are white, while those on the left are dark. Approximately 75 throat grooves are present between the flippers. Between 320 and 420 baleen plates, each approximately 0.9 m long, are present on each side of the upper jaw. Some are whitish and others are grayish blue.

The skull of the fin whale is illustrated in Figure 134.

Distribution. The fin whale is present in "all oceans and adjoining seas, but rare in tropical waters and pack ice" (Nowak, 1991).

This is the most common of the baleen whales in Virginia waters. Twenty specimens have been recorded: Mobjack Bay (August, 1858; May, 1866); Cobb Island (1880s; April, 1976); Chincoteague (June, 1927); Little Creek (April, 1947); Portsmouth (April, 1974; January, 1980; April, 1982); Assateague Island (May, 1955); Brandon Point (April, 1966); Sandbridge (February, 1973); Norfolk (February, 1976; January, 1983); Cedar Island (October, 1976); Hog Island (June, 1982); Newport News (October, 1987); Wallops Island (March, 1988); Eastville (September, 1988); and Virginia Beach (March, 1994) (Allen, 1869; Handley and Patton, 1947; Bailey, 1946, 1948; Paradiso and Handley, 1965; Wass, 1972; Potter, 1979, 1991, personal communication, 1992; Swingle, personal communication, 1995). The 1858 specimen from Mobjack Bay was originally recorded as a right whale *(Balaena glacialis)* (Cope, 1865a, 1869; Reynard, 1899; True, 1904; Bailey, 1946, 1948; Handley and Patton, 1947). The fin whale is currently listed by the United States Fish and Wildlife Service as endangered.

Habits. These whales are monogamous and may be found in pairs or groups up to 300 or more.

Food. Crustaceans and fishes comprise the bulk of the food of this species (Evans, 1987).

Reproduction and Development. Breeding is thought to occur during late fall and winter. Following a gestation of approximately 11 to 11.5 months, usually a single 6.5 m calf is born. By six months of age, the calf may be 12.2 to 13.4 m long. Sexual maturity is attained in 6 to 11 years. Females breed every two to three years.

Longevity. Haley (1978) estimated the age of some individuals at 114 years.

Location of Specimens. USNM.

Genus *Megaptera*

Humpback Whale
Megaptera novaeangliae (Borowski)

Description. The humpback whale (Figure 134) has a stout body and a moderate-sized, flattened head. The flippers are long, slender, and scalloped along their margins. They may be as much as a third of the total body length. Humpback whales are blackish above and grayish or whitish below. The throat is always white, while the belly and the undersurfaces of the flippers and fluke may be mottled or pure white. Between 21 and 36 throat folds are present between the flippers. Prominent nodules or knobs of varying size are present on the head and flippers. There are approximately 300 black baleen plates on each side of the upper jaw. The cellular structure of the baleen in this species was discussed by Pfeiffer (1992). Adult humpback whales are usually between 12 and 13 m in total length. They may weigh approximately 30,000 kg.

The skull of the humpback whale is illustrated in Figure 135.

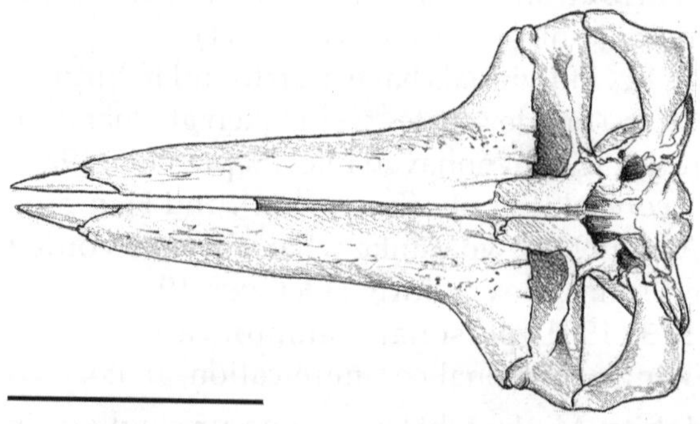

Figure 135. *Megaptera:* Ventral view of skull. Scale bar = 1 m.

Distribution. Humpback whales are found in all oceans and adjoining seas of the world (Rice, 1977).

Although Rhoads (1903) noted that this species had been taken on the coasts of Maine, Massachusetts, and Virginia, and Stone (1907) reported that this species "has been taken as far south as Virginia," the first documented specimen was not taken until 1972. Currently, 15 records exist for Virginia as follows: False Cape (July, 1972); Cape Henry (February, 1975; July, 1975); Wachapreague Inlet (September, 1978); Windmill Point (May, 1979); Cobb Island (February, 1986); Back Bay Wildlife Refuge (April, 1990); Rudee Inlet (April, 1990); Seashore State Park (May, 1990); Sandbridge (June, 1990); Big Island (November, 1990); Virginia Beach (February, 1992; October, 1992); and Dam Neck (June, 1995) (Potter, 1979, 1991, personal communication, 1992; Swingle, personal communication, 1995; Laerm et al., 1997). In addition, a vertebra was discovered near the southern tip of Assateague Island by C. F. Tessmer in June, 1959 (Paradiso and Handley, 1965).

The humpback whale is currently listed by the United States Fish and Wildlife Service as endangered.

Habits. Humpback whales are migratory. In the western North Atlantic, they spend the spring and summer in their polar feeding grounds off the coasts of the northeastern United States, Canada, Greenland, and Iceland after which they migrate to their subtropical and tropical winter breeding grounds in the Greater and Lesser Antilles. They may travel singly or in groups of a dozen or more. The observation of juvenile humpback whales in nearshore waters off the Virginia coast from January through March 1991 and 1992 indicates that some juveniles do not migrate to the breeding grounds but remain in nearshore waters to feed (Swingle et al. 1993). The presence of juveniles plus an increase in stranding frequencies in recent years may be indicative of an expanding humpback whale population in the North Atlantic. Humpback whales produce a wide variety of sounds, especially during their winter breeding season in the tropics.

Food. Shrimplike crustaceans (krill) comprise the main food of the humpback whale, but fish, cephalopods, and mollusks may also be consumed (Laerm et al., 1997).

Reproduction and Development. Mating occurs in winter immediately following the birth of a single 4.6 m long young. Gestation is between 11 and 12 months. Young humpback whales nurse approximately 11 months, by which time they are usually 8 to 9 m long. Sexual maturity occurs at the age of 8 to 12 years.

Location of Specimens. USNM.

Right Whales
(Family Balaenidae)

The family Balaenidae includes some of the largest baleen whales. They are heavy-bodied animals with thick blubber. The relatively large head accounts for about one-third of the total length of the body. The rostrum is narrow and greatly arched to contain the long baleen, while the lower jaw has a large, fleshy lip. There are no grooves on the throat. There is no dorsal fin. The short pectoral fin is broad and rounded. Long plates of baleen (2 to 3 m long) are suspended from each side of the upper part of the mouth. There may be 200 to 400 plates on each side of the jaw. The bristles of the baleen have an almost silky texture. The plates fold in the floor of the closed mouth and straighten when the mouth opens.

The large quantity of oil obtained from the blubber together with the great value of the fine silky baleen gave rise to the name right whales by early commercial whalers meaning these were the "right" whales to hunt.

This family consists of two species, only one of which has been recorded from Virginia.

Genus *Balaena*

Black Right Whale
Balaena glacialis (Borowski)

Description. The black right whale (Figure 133) is a large, heavy-bodied, blackish whale. The belly is also blackish, although irregular patches of white may be present in some individuals. These whales lack a dorsal fin and ventral throat grooves. Between 220 and 260 mostly dark plates of exceptionally long baleen are present on each side of the upper jaw. Each plate may be up to 2.4 m long. Knobby growths known as callosities are irregularly distributed around the blowholes, eyes, and on the nose, lips, and chin. Callosities are caused by small parasitic crustaceans known commonly as whale lice. The spout rises 2 to 3 m from the two blowholes. Since the blowholes are some distance apart, there are two columns that converge to form a V (Gilmore, 1978). Adult right whales are usually between 13 and 14 m in length (Banfield, 1974), and weigh approximately 20,000 to 25,000 kg.

The skull of the black right whale is illustrated in Figure 136.

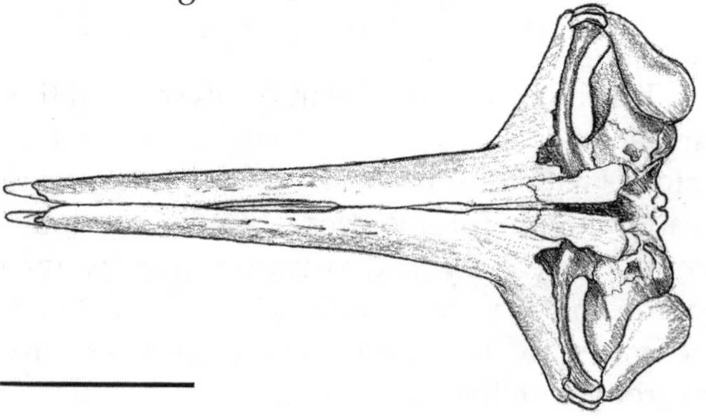

Figure 136. *Balaena:* Ventral view of skull. Scale bar = 1 m.

Distribution. Black right whales occur mainly in the temperate parts of the Atlantic, Indian, and Pacific oceans and adjoining seas (Nowak, 1991).

The only record of this species in Virginia waters was a sighting off Sandbridge on February 18, 1984 (Potter, 1991). A record of a right whale from Mobjack Bay in Gloucester County in 1858 (Handley and Patton, 1947) has been reidentified as a fin whale, *Balaenoptera physalus* (Potter, 1991).

It is believed that fewer than 100 right whales exist along the east coast of North America. They are listed by the United States as an endangered species (Webster et al., 1985).

Habits. Nowak (1991) noted that in the western Atlantic these migratory whales move into warmer waters during the winter and cooler waters during the summer. They are found from Cape Cod to Bermuda to the Gulf of Mexico from November to March. The major summer feeding grounds were in the vicinity of Newfoundland and in the Labrador Sea.

These slow swimming whales are usually found in small groups, although pods of 100 or more have been recorded (Banfield, 1974). Their habit of swimming slowly and migrating close to shore made them easy prey for early whalers.

Food. The diet of the black right whale consists primarily of small planktonic crustaceans (copepods) and small fish. The baleen strains organisms out of the water that flows into the mouth while the whale is swimming through the water with its mouth partially open.

Reproduction. Females give birth to a single young every two to five years during the winter in the western Atlantic. The young are weaned at 12 months. Sexual maturity is probably attained by 6 to 10 years of age.

Location of Specimens. No specimens from Virginia are known to exist in collections.

Carnivores

The order Carnivora includes the carnivores, the predatory or flesh-eating mammals. Carnivores are nearly worldwide in distribution and range in size from the 45-gram least weasel *(Mustela nivalis)* to the Alaskan brown bear *(Ursus arctos)*, which weighs up to 765 kg and is one of the largest land mammals in North America. These mammals vary widely in their habits. Some species of carnivores are regarded highly by humans as furbearers, while others are persecuted because of their predatory nature.

Members of the order Carnivora are recognized easily by the strong, conical, recurved canine tooth present on each side of the upper and lower jaws. Also, the last upper premolar and first lower molar act together in a shearing motion for cutting flesh and tendons. Known as the carnassial teeth, these specialized teeth are best developed in the cats and least modified in those species with more omnivorous diets. Other characteristic anatomical features include a skull with complete zygomatic arches, a large brain, and bones of the lower forelimb (radius and ulna) and hindlimb (tibia and fibula) that are unfused. Locomotion is digitigrade or plantigrade.

Two main evolutionary lines led to modern carnivores. One line (canoid) includes bears and weasels and ends with dogs, while the other line (feloid) ends with the cats. The order Carnivora comprises two living suborders. The suborder Fissipedia comprises land carnivores, while the suborder Pinnipedia includes the seals and sea lions. Some taxonomists place the seals in their own order (Pinnipedia). Nowak (1991) reviewed the taxonomic status of these groups.

Suborder Fissipedia
Land Carnivores

Dogs, Foxes, and Wolves
(Family Canidae)

The family Canidae includes the dogs, foxes, and wolves. Members of the Canidae occur throughout the world, although the dingo of Australia was probably brought there by early human inhabitants. Canids range in size from the tiny 1.3 kg desert fennec of the Old World to the gray wolf of North America, Europe, and Asia, which weighs up to 74 kg.

Canids have deep-chested, muscular bodies. The large ears are held erect, and the tail is long and bushy with a mane of stiff hairs on its upper side near the base. These hairs are associated with a sebaceous gland. The forefeet normally have five digits, while the hind feet have four. Only four toes show in each track, front and rear. The fifth toe on the front foot is a dew claw. Unlike those of a cat, a canid's claws are not retractile. Locomotion is digitigrade.

The skull has a long, narrow rostrum, and the auditory bullae are low. The teeth are those of a typical carnivore, with long, powerful canines and well-developed carnassials. It is sometimes difficult to distinguish the skull of a coyote from that of a domestic dog. The rostrum of the coyote skull is generally longer and narrower than that of a dog. According to Howard (1949), the length of the upper molar tooth row should be divided by the palatal width (between the premolars). If the molar tooth row is 3.1 or more times that of the palatal width, the specimen is a coyote, but if it is less than 2.7 times it is a dog. Hybrids, or coydogs, generally measure between 2.7 and 3.1

Three genera of canids — *Canis, Vulpes,* and *Urocyon* — occur in the United States, and all three are or have been represented in the fauna of Virginia.

Key to Species of Canidae

1a Skull more than 150 mm in total length; postorbital processes thickened and convex dorsally; tail less than half the length of head and body 2

1b Skull less than 150 mm in total length; postorbital processes thin, concave dorsally; tail more than half the length of head and body 4

2a Skull length less than 203 mm; total length less than 140 cm .... *Canis latrans*

2b Skull length more than 203 mm; total length more than 140 cm 3

3a Skull length greater than 250 mm .... *Canis lupus*

3b Skull length less than 250 mm .... *Canis rufus*

4a Temporal ridges forming U-shaped pattern; distinct step present on posteroventral portion of lower jaw; upper incisors without lobes; tail tip black .... *Urocyon cinereoargenteus*

4b Temporal ridges forming V-shaped pattern; lower jaw without step; upper incisors lobed; tail tip white .... *Vulpes vulpes*

Genus *Vulpes*

Dentition: 3/3, 1/1, 4/4, 2/3 = 42

Red Fox
Vulpes vulpes Linnaeus

Description. The red fox (Plate 66) is a medium-sized reddish canid with a long, round, bushy tail with a white tip. They have large, pointed, erect ears, and a sharp and elongate muzzle. The dorsal pelage is normally rusty-reddish to reddish-yellow intermixed with dark hairs in the middle of the back, while the fronts of the legs, feet, and backs of the ears are black, and the tail tip is white. The underparts are whitish or grayish-white. Three color phases have been reported: "cross" (pelage is mixed with gray and yellow, and gets its name from black cross formed by a line down the midback and another across the shoulders), "silver" (melanistic coat frosted with white), and "black" phases that are progressively darker. These color phases may occur in the same litter with normal reds. Five toes are present on the forefeet and four on the hind feet. The claws are nonretractile. Females possess eight mammae. Adult red foxes are generally between 90 and 107 cm long, including a tail 35 to 40 cm long. Adults normally weigh between 2.7 and 6.7 kg. Males are usually larger than females.

The skull of this species is relatively large and slender with a long, narrow rostrum. The temporal ridges converge posteriorly forming a V-shaped pattern. The top of the skull is depressed between the orbits. Prominent auditory bullae are present. The canine teeth are rather long and slender. The upper incisors are lobed (Figure 137).

Distribution. The range of this species extends from Alaska throughout all but the extreme north of Canada; south in the Cascade-Sierra Nevada chain to central California and in the Rocky Mountain chain to southern New Mexico; east of the plains, south to central Texas, southern Alabama, and western Florida.

Red foxes are not native to the southern states, but the manner in which they got there has never been definitely determined. Mansueti (1950) stated:

> *The* Centreville Record *claimed that the first fox-hunting in America took place in Queen Annes County [Maryland] about 1650, accord-*

ing to the Maryland Conservationist *(Vol. VII, No. 2). At that time the only fox hunted was the Eastern gray fox. A Captain of a tobacco schooner was instructed before 1650 to bring back eight pairs of red foxes, on his next trip to Liverpool. They arrived and were liberated along the Eastern Shore of Maryland. The way the foxes multiplied was "marvelous," according to the* Centreville Record *but they did not migrate into Virginia until the hard winter of 1679–80.*

William Byrd, writing during the 1730s, mentioned just the gray fox in Virginia along with the observation that the Virginia gray fox does not smell as bad as the European red fox. Beginning in the early 1800s the red fox began to be reported in the various journals, along with the gray fox, as a resident here in Virginia. Audubon and Bachman (1851) noted:

In the early history of our country the Red Fox was unknown south of Pennsylvania, that State being its Southern limit. In process of time it was found in the mountains of Virginia, where it has now become more abundant than the Gray Fox. A few years afterwards it appeared in the more elevated portions of North Carolina, then in the mountains of South Carolina, and finally in Georgia, where we have recently observed it.

Rhoads (1903) stated that

in earlier colonial times [the red fox] was unknown in the austral zone, its primitive distribution being greatly altered by its introduction into the austral habitat by fox-hunting man and by the altered environment of our lowlands. Owing to the importation of European Red-foxes into this country in early colonial times, our east American Red-fox is probably a mongrel species to that extent, claiming as we do that there was a specific difference between the two.

Other authors quote the Indians as saying that the red fox was not in the land before the coming of the white man (Bartram, cited by Kalm, 1770). Bailey (1896a) reported that it was first seen in Montgomery County, Maryland, between 1798 and 1802.

In view of these statements, said Rhoads (1903), *and of the fact that European Foxes had been introduced into New England, Pennsylvania and Virginia for sporting purposes by the middle of the 18th Century (1750), it looks quite likely that the Red-foxes mentioned by Kalm as being found in New Jersey and Pennsylvania in 1770 . . . and those described by Desmarest as coming from 'Virginia' in 1820, were pure descendants of the European Red-fox. In such a case* Vulpes fulvus, *of course, is a synonym of* Vulpes vulpes *(Linnaeus).*

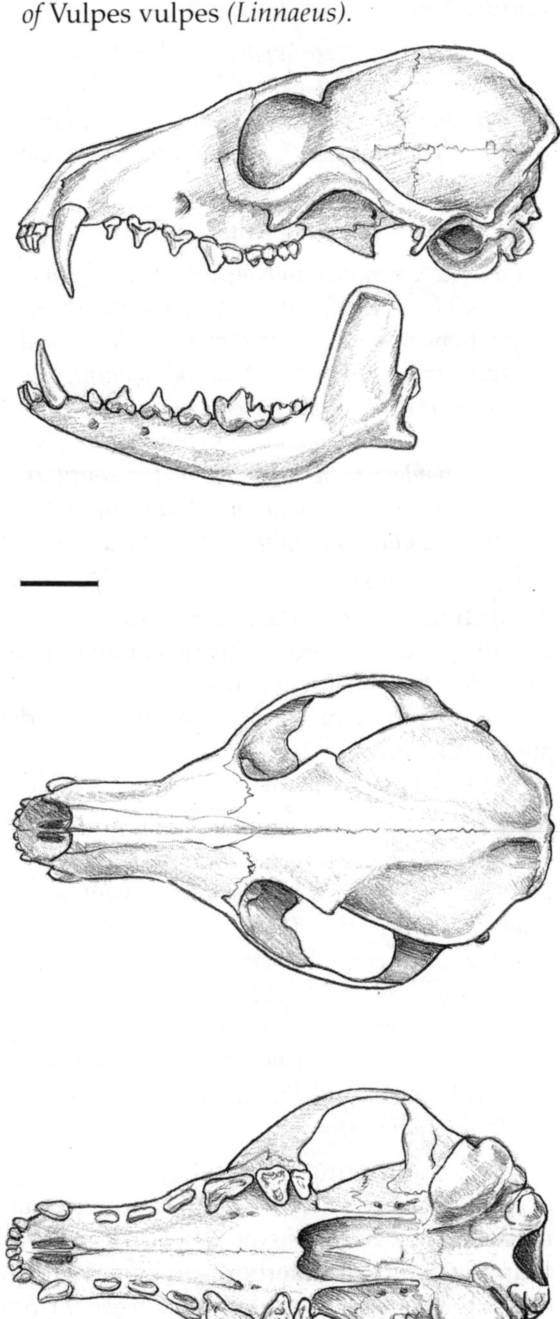

Figure 137. *Vulpes vulpes:* Left lateral view of skull and mandible, and dorsal and ventral view of skull. Scale bar = 20 mm.

Nelson (1918) stated that before the coming of the white man, red foxes originally ranged in America over nearly all the forested region from the northern limit of trees in Alaska and Canada south, east of the Great Plains, to Texas and also down the Rocky Mountains to middle New Mexico. He continued:

Originally they were apparently absent from the Atlantic and Gulf States from Maryland to Louisiana, but have since been introduced and become common south to Middle Georgia and Alabama.

Churcher (1959) concluded that:

a red fox was native to North America north of Lat. 40 N or 45 N, but was either scarce or absent from most of the unbroken mixed hardwood forests, where the gray fox was paramount. The European red fox was introduced into the eastern seaboard area about 1750, and either partially displaced the gray fox in the southern portion of the continent, or interbred with the scarce population of indigenous red fox to produce a hybrid population.

According to Schwartz and Schwartz (1959), opening of dense forests during colonial times provided habitat for red foxes, as well as for the animals they prey upon, and this caused a southward range extension.

Swink (1957) noted:

Further evidence has been recently presented from bone caves throughout the East, revealing a total absence of red fox remains in many caves which showed abundant gray fox remains as well as other common mammals. This evidence strongly supports the theory that red foxes, at least on the eastern seaboard, are doubtlessly a cross between our native red fox from the north central section and the European red fox, an introduction.

Other authorities attribute the occurrence of the red fox in various southern states to intentional releases of foxes by sportsmen. For example, Smith, Funderburg, and Quay (1960) noted that red foxes *(Vulpes fulva regalis)* from Minnesota, North Dakota, Iowa, and Nebraska were introduced in the mountains of North Carolina between 1953 and 1955.

Thus, it now seems to be generally recognized that the red fox of the Middle Atlantic states is a descendant of the English fox with perhaps some interbreeding occurring with the introduced form from the northern plains.

Mosby (1938) found red foxes present in all sections of the Virginia except the extreme southeastern counties. By 1948 red foxes were still either scarce or absent in the southeastern portion of the state. In 1950 Handley and Handley noted that the red fox was common throughout the upper portion of the James River Basin and that it "occurs in small numbers at least as far down the valley as Chesterfield and Charles City counties." Davis (1971) reported a complete absence of red foxes in the Dismal Swamp. In 1980 M. K. Garrett (personal communication), biologist at Great Dismal Swamp Wildlife Refuge, reported a few red foxes occurring in areas surrounding the swamp but none in the swamp itself (Figure 138).

Data on the red fox fur catch in Virginia are presented in tables 2 and 3.

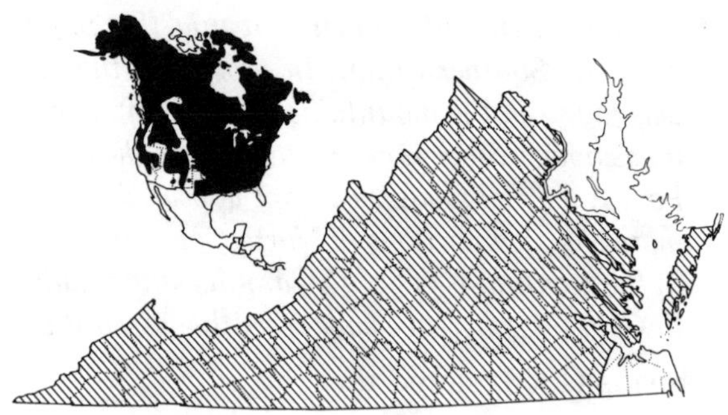

Figure 138. *Vulpes vulpes:* Range in Virginia and North America.

Habitat. The red fox inhabits broken, sparsely settled country. Farmland mixed with sparsely wooded areas, brushland, marshes, and streams provides ideal habitat. It also occupies borders and open areas in heavily forested regions. Red foxes occasionally wander into urban or suburban areas.

Habits. Red foxes are primarily nocturnal but may be active both day and night during all seasons. Daytime activity is often increased in winter, and activity patterns are governed by activity patterns of prey species. Red foxes do not hibernate. Unlike the gray fox, the red fox has no winter den and sleeps in the open.

Scott (1947) noted:

During the denning period the den serves as the principal hub of activity, and the theater of activity shifts in the direction of the move as the family is moved to successive dens. The rallying station serves as the hub when the young foxes leave the dens, and the theater of activity again shifts when new rallying stations are occupied. These theaters of activity appear to lose their identity as the family ties relax and dispersal gets under way.

In Europe and the United States, hunting the fox has been a favorite sport for hundreds of years. When pursued by a pack of hounds, a fox will lope along at about 9.6 km an hour. If the hounds get too close, it can speed up to 64 to 72 km an hour, but it cannot hold this pace for more than 1.6 km or so.

For its survival the fox depends not so much on speed as on artful maneuvers. The sagacity and cunning traits of this species are well known. One of its wiles for evading the hounds is to backtrack its own footsteps for some distance, then leap away to one side and make off in a new direction. Other ruses include running along the top of a rail fence or a stone wall and running through a shallow stream to make the hounds lose the scent. Foxes have hidden in chimneys and even in kitchen stoves as a last resort. The red fox is a past master at eluding its human or animal enemies, and it is usually only the young and inexperienced foxes that get caught by predators.

Red foxes have keen senses of sight, smell, and hearing. They will occasionally howl, although their normal vocalizations are much lower in tone. Playing frequently occurs among family groups. Curiosity is an outstanding trait, and red foxes have been known to follow people or to backtrack to see who is following them.

Red foxes develop social hierarchies among interacting individuals in areas where home ranges overlap. An individual establishes and maintains its rank in the "pecking order" by dominating others during physical and/or vocal combat. A rather vivid description of such an encounter is presented by Vincent (1958): "The ordinary method of combat is both a clamorous-vocal and a physical-contact battle. The two combatants come together, rise on their hind legs, and place their forepaws on the opponent's foreshoulders. With hind feet widely spaced, tails curved out and downward, ears flattened, mouths wide open, while holding each other at approximately a 45 degree angle, they attempt to push the opponent backward. While in the upright stance, both foxes have their mouths open wide with only an inch separating the two noses and two lower jaws. Sometimes both participants will snap their jaws and bob and weave their heads, while at other times the head is held almost stationary. From the human viewpoint, the fox backed farthest from the point of battle origin is the loser. Some animals soon turn and leave; others have held this upright position for three minutes. When one animal lowers his paws and turns away, the encounter ends with no immediate attempt toward renewal." Such combat is accompanied by screams that range from a "harsh, wheezing snort to a blatant scream." Although these interactions appear to be quite violent, an animal is rarely injured.

Ables (1969) reported home range sizes of 57.5 to 161.9 ha for 7 radio collared foxes in Wisconsin in mixed habitat. An adult male in less diverse habitat, however, had a home range of 5.1 km^2. Storm (1965) recorded an adult male home range 3.1 km long by 2.2 km wide.

Foxes may habitually travel the same route, producing well-worn trails. The adult female normally stays within one or two km of the den, although after the young have dispersed in the fall adult male red foxes may wander widely. Young red foxes may move considerable distances during dispersal, frequently traveling 24 to 40 km from the den site. A juvenile female tagged in Minnesota moved at least 203 km in 22 months (Longley, 1962). A juvenile male marked in Wisconsin was shot by a hunter in Indiana nine months later, having traveled a straight-line distance of 394 km (Ables, 1965).

Food. Red foxes are omnivorous and feed on a variety of animal and plant foods. Their feeding habits appear to be governed to a large extent by the relative availability of foods. When food is abundant, they may bury surplus meat in the ground or cover it with leaves and other debris.

A food habits study of 15 red foxes taken during January and February in Virginia revealed that rabbits and mice made up over half the food consumed (Nelson, 1933). Rabbits comprised 34 percent of the total food; mice, 18 percent; sheep, wool, and fat, 13 percent; and poultry, 12.5 percent. Other animal food consisted of gray squirrels, muskrats, quail, small nongame birds, and insects. Fruits and nuts were present in five stomachs and represented almost 14 percent of the entire food in the 15 stomachs. Beechnuts, persimmons, apples, corn, and peanuts were the most important vegetable foods.

A 15-month study of the red fox in Blacksburg yielded 549 scats for analysis (Swink, 1952). Among the 77 food items identified, the major food items and their percentages of frequency were: meadow mouse, 52 percent; cottontail, 34 percent; opossum, 9 percent; domestic chicken, 7 percent; striped skunk, 3.5 percent; and white-footed mouse, 3.5 percent.

An analysis of red fox scats collected from March through August in a muskrat marsh in Maryland revealed that field mice *(Microtus)* comprised a large proportion of food throughout the season (Heit, 1944). During June and July, however, muskrats were taken more frequently than mice. Cottontail rabbit remains were found frequently in early spring but failed to appear in scats collected after April. Birds formed a steady part of the diet throughout the season, with little change in frequency of occurrence. Insects and seeds were also identified.

An analysis of 56 scats collected between May and August on Assateague Island revealed the following percent frequency: mammals *(Sylvilagus floridanus, Microtus pennsylvanicus, Peromyscus leucopus)*, 87 percent; crustaceans, 65 percent; birds, 46 percent; insects, 32 percent; fish, 9 percent; and molluscs, 2 percent (Krim et al., 1990). Muskrat *(Ondatra zibethicus)* remains were found at fox excavations.

In the Saxis marshes on the seaside of the Eastern Shore the red fox actually lives in the marshes where it has been known to prey on muskrats (Wass, 1972).

People often believe that foxes are serious predators of ground-nesting birds such as quail, pheasants, and grouse. Food habits studies in Virginia and elsewhere do not bear this out. The fox must not be blamed for a scarcity of quail which may, in reality, be due to poor habitat.

Reproduction and Development. Mating in northern areas is usually in January and February (Sheldon, 1949). In Virginia, breeding activities are well under way by late February, perhaps nearly completed, and some data indicate that the breeding starts as early as the first week in January (Swink, 1957). Gestation is about 52 days. Litters average four to seven pups, usually born in late March or early April. Swink (1957) recorded an average of 4.4 young per litter for 13 litters near Blacksburg. The largest reported litter consisted of 17 pups in Michigan, all at the same stage of development and in poor condition (Holcomb, 1965).

Red fox pups are covered by a fine, silky, grayish-brown fur at birth. The eyes open at eight to nine days, and the pups begin to walk at three weeks. The ears become erect at four weeks. Pups attain their adult size in approximately six months (Samuel and Nelson, 1982) and disperse in September and October.

The den site is chosen with some care, and the excavated dirt is scattered so that no telltale mound is readily visible. Dens are often on wooded slopes and not infrequently in an open field. It is frequently in loose soil because foxes are not good diggers. A woodchuck burrow or a natural cavity may be enlarged for use. Woodchucks and red foxes have been known to coexist in the same burrow system.

The inside of the den is kept fairly clean, although the area surrounding the entrance may be littered with bones and leftover food. Although one family per den is probably the norm, communal denning is not infrequent in some areas.

A study of 73 red fox dens in Alabama revealed 43 in the ground, 25 in sawdust and slab piles, four in rocky ledges, and one under an abandoned barn (Pearson and Herbert, 1940). Dens generally had several entrances facing in different directions. Dens were found in areas ranging from dense woods along streams to extensive and open pastures on prairie land. The main entrance was frequently located on the side of a small ditch, gully, or stream bank. On Assateague Island, Krim et al. (1990) recorded the majority of dens in shrub succession and *Hudsonia* dune habitat, while woodland and dunegrass communities supported few dens. Active dens were 20 to 23 cm high and 22 to 25 cm wide.

Longevity. Wild foxes probably live two to four years. Tullar (1983) recorded one eight years and six months old in New York. It had been tagged as a pup and had moved 10 miles west of its original capture point. Mann (1930) reported a captive living for 10 years, while Flower (1931) reported a record of 12 years, 21 days.

Parasites and Disease. Swink (1952) recorded the following parasites from this species in Virginia: *Ctenocephalides felis* (cat flea), *Ctenocephalides canis* (dog flea), *Ixodes ricinus* (tick), and *Sarcoptes scabei* (mange mite). In 1948 a severe epidemic of mange occurred in red foxes in northern Virginia. The ticks *Amblyomma americanum, Dermacentor variabilis,* and *Ixodes cookei* have been recorded by Sonenshine and Stout (1971) and Sonenshine, Lamb, and Anastos (1965).

Rabies has been confirmed in this species in Virginia (see discussion under Gray Fox and tables 4, 5, and 6).

Geographic Variation. The red fox in Virginia and throughout most of the eastern United States should be classified as *Vulpes vulpes fulva* (Desmarest) (Paradiso, 1969).

Location of Specimens. BCV, CM, DMNH, GMU, LFCC, LU, NVCC, ODU, USNM, VCU, VHCC, VPISU, VPI-W.

Genus *Urocyon*

Dentition: 3/3, 1/1, 4/4, 2/3 = 42

Common Gray Fox
Urocyon cinereoargenteus (Schreber)

Description. The gray fox (Plate 67) is a medium-sized canid whose upperparts have a salt-and-pepper appearance resulting from alternating black and white bands on the guard hairs. The overall coloration is blackish-gray, with the darkest fur along the dorsal midline. The underparts are reddish-brown with areas of white fur on the throat, chest, and along the middle of the abdomen. The sexes are similar. The feet, legs, back of the ears, and sides of the neck are rusty-yellowish. The tail has a well-defined median black stripe and ends in a black tip. The pupil of the eye is elliptical, unlike the slitlike pupil of other foxes. Females possess six functional mammae. Adult gray foxes are 81 to 114 cm long, including a tail 28 to 43 cm long. Adults usually weigh between 3 and 6 kg.

The skull is moderately slender with a relatively short rostrum. The temporal ridges are far apart forming a U-shaped or lyre-shaped pattern and usually not uniting to form a sagittal crest. Prominent auditory bullae are present. A distinct step is present on the posteroventral portion of the mandible. Unlike the red fox, the upper incisors are simple and not lobed (Figure 139).

Distribution. The gray fox ranges from Central America through Mexico into the United States. It is found throughout the eastern United States and in the western states north to northwestern Oregon, central Nevada, and northern Colorado. These foxes were originally found in the western and southern states but have been continually expanding their range northward.

This species is common throughout Virginia (Figure 140). In 1612 Captain John Smith described the gray fox as being like "our silver-haired Conies, of small proportion, and not smelling like those of England." William Byrd, writing about 1730, said:

> *One has also foxes in this land. They are gray, but do not smell as bad as the European (variety), have reddish hair on their ears, and are unusually big, beautiful and always fat. When they are hunted, they take refuge in trees.*

W. B. Davis (1966) noted that in sections of Texas where coyotes formerly were numerous, the gray fox was scarce. After the elimination of the coyote, however, the gray fox has become abundant. He stated: "Perhaps the coyote tends to hold this fox in check under conditions where they both occupy the same area." If this is true, it will be interesting to see what changes are brought about in Virginia's gray fox population as the coyote continues expanding its range and becomes increasingly abundant in the state.

Data on the gray fox catch in Virginia are presented in tables 2 and 3.

Habitat. This is the common fox throughout the brushy and deciduous forest areas of the eastern, southern, and western United States. Rough, hilly terrain in the vicinity of streams and lakes is preferred. These foxes may also be found in heavily wooded swamps. Their preference for timber makes them less common on farmlands than the red fox.

Habits. The gray fox is more nocturnal than the red fox and is most active after sundown. Its bark, sometimes heard at nightfall, is short,

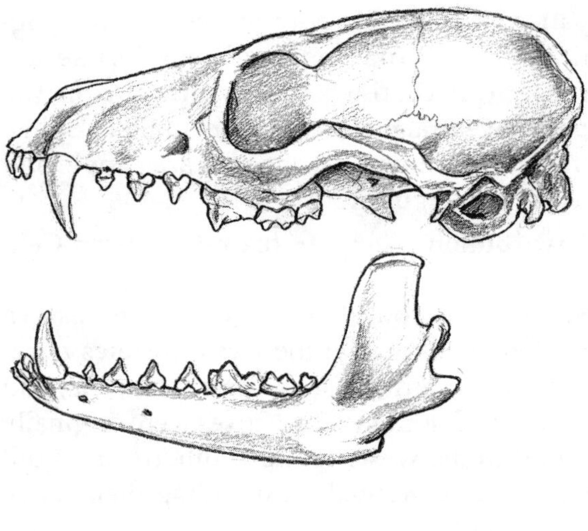

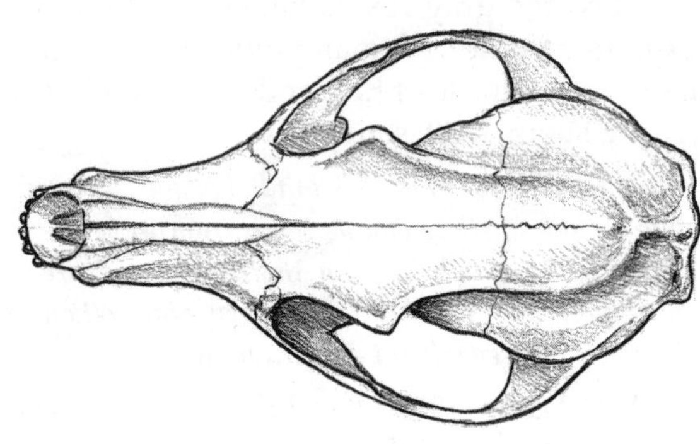

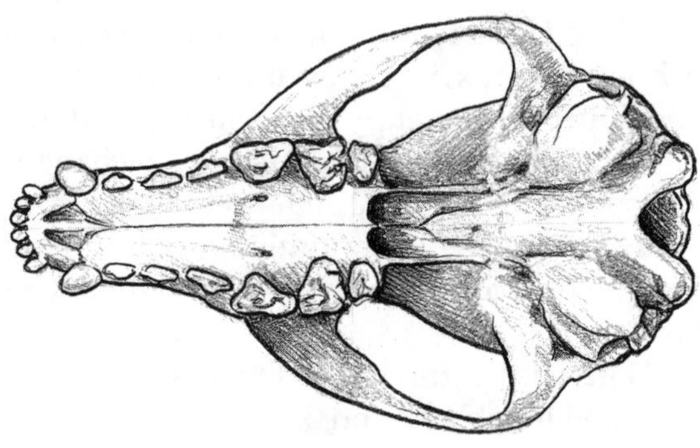

Figure 139. *Urocyon cinereoargenteus:* Left lateral view of skull and mandible, and dorsal and ventral view of skull. Scale bar = 20 mm.

harsh, and deep. Gray foxes are active both summer and winter.

While the red fox uses dens only when raising young, gray foxes apparently also use them for warmth during winter months. Gray fox dens are located in a variety of situations, but slab and scrap piles around abandoned sawmills seem to be preferred. Other dens have been located in hollow logs, under rocks, and in ground burrows. A gray fox has also been found denning 9.2 m above the ground in a large hollow oak (Davis, 1966). Unlike dens of the red fox, the majority of gray fox dens have only one entrance, with two entrances being the most found in any one den. Gray fox dens are usually located in more dense cover and are much less conspicuous than red fox dens.

Yearsley and Samuel (1980) reported an average home range of 97 ha for 3 males and 75 ha for a single female in West Virginia. Other radio-telemetry studies recorded home ranges of 4.27 km^2 for males and 3.67 km^2 for females in eastern Tennessee (Greenberg and Pelton, 1994), 136 and 107 ha for males and females in Illinois (Follmann, 1973) and 653 and 626 ha in Alabama (Nichelson and Hill, 1981).

One of the most interesting habits of the gray fox is its ability to climb trees. Because of this unusual behavior, the gray fox is commonly known as the "tree fox." Gray foxes will often seek refuge in a tree when being pursued, but they also climb trees at other times. Not only do they leap upon limbs of low trees and hop from branch to branch as they ascend, but they are fairly good climbers, hugging the trunk with their forelimbs and forcing themselves upward with their hind limbs. They may ascend 18 m above the ground (Fritzell and Haroldson, 1982). Audubon and Bachman (1846) stated:

> *We were unable to obtain any information in regard to the manner in which the Fox climbs trees, as he does not possess the retractile nails of the cat or the sharp claws of the squirrel, until we saw the animal in the act. At one time when we thus observed the Fox, he first leaped onto a low branch 4 or 5 feet from the ground, from*

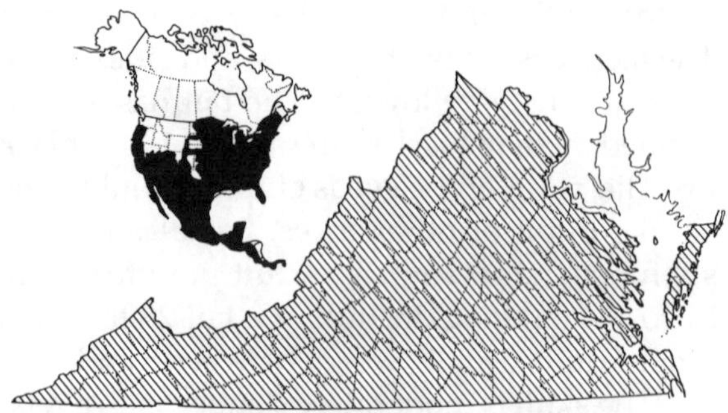

Figure 140. *Urocyon cinereoargenteus:* Range in Virginia and North America.

whence he made his way upward by leaping cautiously and rather awkwardly from branch to branch, till he attained a secure position in the largest fork of the tree, where he stopped. On another occasion, he ascended in the manner of a bear, but with far greater celerity, by clasping the stem of a small pine. We have since been informed that the Fox also climbs trees occasionally by the aid of his claws, in the manner of a raccoon or a cat.

The gray fox is more of a woodland species than the red fox and less frequently comes into contact with poultry and other domestic animals. It is a very good mouser, and its food habits show that it does not conflict much with human economic activities.

Food. Gray foxes are omnivorous. They feed primarily upon small mammals but also consume insects, birds and other vertebrates, nuts and fruits. Studies have suggested that gray foxes include a greater percentage of plant material in their diet than do red foxes (Hatfield, 1939; Scott, 1955). In some areas, plant foods (especially fruit) may be the primary food (Pils, 1965), while at other locales animal foods predominate. This suggests that availability strongly influences what foods are consumed.

A study of the winter food habits of 82 gray foxes taken from December to March in Virginia revealed that rabbits, mice, and native rats represented slightly over half of the food consumed (Nelson, 1933). Other animal food consisted of poultry, 8 percent; small nongame birds, 6 percent; and insects, 4 percent. In addition, gray squirrel, sheep (probably carrion), mourning dove, ruffed grouse, turtle, snake, and centipedes were recorded. Vegetable food consisting primarily of apples, beechnuts, corn, peanuts, grapes, hickory nuts, and persimmons were noted in 44 stomachs and represented over 22 percent of the total food.

Examination of 224 scats gathered during a three year study in Virginia revealed cottontail rabbits (*Sylvilagus* sp.), white-footed mice *(Peromyscus leucopus)*, arthropods, and fruit as major dietary items (Hensley, 1977). The stomach of an adult female in the Liberty University mammal collection contained 20 beetle larvae, five red centipedes, and one small bird.

A study in Maryland covering the period November through February revealed plant material comprising 30 percent of the diet and animal material 70 percent (Llewellyn and Uhler, 1952). Persimmon was the most important plant item. Rodents made up about half of the volume of the yearround food. Rabbits, birds, and insects constituted most of the remainder of the animal food.

Analyses of the stomachs of 24 Tennessee foxes collected from January to June found cottontails to be the primary food with arthropods and small mammals next in importance (Yoho and Henry, 1972).

Greenberg and Pelton (1991) examined fox scats from east Tennessee. No distinction was make between gray and red fox scats, although concurrent trapping indicated a population of 3:1, respectively. This study confirmed that foxes are opportunistic feeders and depend on seasonal food availability. It also indicated that vertebrate prey may only be taken in the absence of more easily obtainable plants and invertebrates. Vertebrate prey consisted primarily of rabbits and rodents and represented 67 percent of the dry weight of the January-April diet. Arthropods (predominantly 17-year locusts) comprised 96 percent of the May dry weight. Plant material (predominantly persimmons, cherry, blackberry, and squaw-root) made up 93 percent of the June to December diet.

Reproduction and Development. Gray foxes are seasonally monogamous, although occasionally some are polygamous. They breed from late February to early April in Virginia. Following a gestation of 51 to 63 days, an average of about four dark brown, blind pups are born in the den in a nest of leaves, grass, fur, and any other available material. They weigh from 85 to 113 g each. A female containing three embryos was recorded on March, 14, in Lynchburg, Virginia; another with four embryos was taken in Botetourt County, Virginia (date unknown).

The eyes open at about nine days of age. Both parents provide for and protect the pups, which are weaned between 8 and 10 weeks of age. Wood (1958) reported that juveniles reach adult weight at the age of five to six months. The young foxes normally remain with the female until fall, when they disband. Most gray foxes breed when nearly one year old, although some do not breed until their second year.

Longevity. Crandall (1964) recorded a captive animal that had lived for 10 years, 5 months, 18 days. Lord (1961a) estimated that the average longevity of a north Florida gray fox that survives to the stage of independence (about seven months) is about 18.5 months.

Parasites and Diseases. Gray foxes are subject to several diseases, the most prevalent of which are rabies and distemper. Rabies has been present for many years and has made some spectacular appearances, such as the outbreak in the Shenandoah Valley and in southwest Virginia beginning in 1954. The gray fox was the major carrier of rabies in Virginia for the period 1951–1976 and has caused considerable damage to livestock. It was the major source of human exposures to rabies for almost as many years.

Rabies, or hydrophobia, was first reported in the United States from Virginia in 1753 (Johnson, 1959; Steele, 1975). All warm-blooded animals are susceptible to rabies. The most commonly involved are skunks, raccoons, bats, and foxes. Table 4 presents data on cases of rabies in the United States, by category, for the period 1980–1993. During 1989, 34.5 percent of all rabies in the United States occurred in skunks, 32.1 percent in raccoons, 15 percent in bats, and 4.3 percent in foxes (Reid-Sanden et al., 1990).

In Virginia, gray foxes, red foxes, raccoons, and skunks are the main wildlife species carrying rabies (tables 5 and 6). Foxes are thought to be a permanent reservoir of rabies, although outbreaks occur only when the fox population is high. This allows easy contact between infected animals and susceptible animals. Carey (1982) noted that rabid foxes were most frequently encountered in localized areas in the mountains, valleys, and highlands of Virginia. He noted that

> *the localization of rabies is due, at least in part, to the effects of physiography on the density and contiguity of fox populations. . . .The Blue Ridge Mountains. . . . form the eastern boundary of the enzootic area. Major wind and water gaps in the Blue Ridge have provided portals for the occasional spread of rabies epizootics to fox populations east of the Blue Ridge.*

Early symptoms of rabies in foxes are loss of fear of humans and machines and roaming in daylight, often in farmyards and on highways. During this stage, they will sometimes attack human beings or dogs without provocation and then flee. There is a progressive loss of viciousness. In the final stage, there is paralysis, usually beginning with the jaw muscles.

Prior to the mid-1950s, rabies in Virginia was a disease found primarily in dogs. For example, in 1948 there were 158 confirmed cases of rabies — 131 in dogs and one in a fox. In 1954, 377 cases were confirmed with 187 (50 percent) involving foxes. In 1961, there were 190 laboratory-confirmed cases — 8 in dogs and 145 (76 percent) in foxes (Marx and Swink, 1963). In 1961, 24 percent of all fox rabies in the United States was reported from Virginia (Anonymous, 1961a). In 1970, 70 percent of reported cases were in wildlife species with foxes comprising 66 percent of the total. Foxes reached their highest percentage of laboratory-confirmed cases (88 percent) in 1975 (tables 2, 3 and 4).

Distemper can be disastrous to a fox population, but is usually local in scope and does very little to control foxes over a large area. Both rabies and canine distemper were reported by Davidson et al. (1992).

The bacterium *Histoplasma capsulatum* has been recorded by Emmons et al. (1955). The nematode *Physaloptera praeputialis* has been recorded from this species in Virginia by Chitwood (1931). Approximately eight tapeworms identified as *Taenia pisiformis* were found in the intestines of an adult female from Botetourt County, Virginia (LC). The ticks *Dermacentor variabilis, Amblyomma americanum, Ixodes cookei, Ixodes scapularis,* and *Ixodes texanus* have been recorded by Sonenshine, Lamb, and Anastos (1965) and Sonenshine and Stout (1971).

Predation. No specific instances of predation have been recorded from Virginia. Bobcats, large owls, and large hawks may prey on the pups if they are left unprotected. As in the red fox, the main enemies are humans, dogs, and automobiles.

Geographic Variation. The subspecies occurring throughout Virginia is *Urocyon cinereoargenteus cinereoargenteus* (Schreber).

Location of Specimens. ANSP, BCV, CM, CUC, GMU, LC, LFCC, LU, MCZ, NCSM, NVCC, ODU, SNP, UMMZ, USNM, VCU, VHCC, VLM, VPISU, VPI-W.

Genus *Canis*

Dentition: 3/3, 1/1, 4/4, 2/3 = 42

Coyote
Canis latrans Say

Description. The coyote (Plate 68) is a medium-sized canid. Its color varies, but it is usually a tawny gray or grizzled buff dorsally, with some of the guard hairs tipped with black. The sides are dull, and the throat and belly are white. In Virginia, however, approximately 25 percent of the coyotes are mostly black (Tomsa, personal communication, October, 1992). The fur is moderately long with rather coarse guard hairs. The feet, legs, and ears are more or less reddish. Females possess 10 mammae. Adults are usually between 112 and 137 cm long, including a tail 30 to 38 cm long. Adults normally weigh between 9 and 16 kg. In Tennessee, adult males averaged 14.1 kg and females 11.4 kg (Lydeard et al., 1986).

The skull is rather slender and elongate with a long, slender rostrum and moderately spreading zygomatic arches. The canine teeth are relatively long and narrow. The sagittal crest is well developed and prominent, particularly in adult males (Figure 141).

Distribution. The range of the coyote originally extended from Central America through Mexico, the western United States, and western Canada to Alaska. Its range in the United States has been expanding eastward as the forests have been cleared (Figure 142). Hamilton (1943) stated that coyotes were "generally common in northern Wisconsin and northern Michigan, western Illinois along the Mississippi River, and northern Indiana, and occurring sporadically from time to time in nearly every eastern state, from Maine to Florida." He noted that many of the coyotes reported or captured in the eastern states have been transported by tourists as prospective pets and have then either escaped or been released. In the southern states especially, coyotes have been released by fox hunters, who mistakenly have had coyote pups shipped to them instead of young foxes. Coyotes from Kansas are known to have been imported to Lincoln and Greenbrier counties in West Virginia. The Greenbrier specimens apparently were released (Taylor, Counts, and Mills, 1976). Hill et al. (1987) summarized reports of coyote liberations in the southeastern United States.

Young and Jackson (1951) showed the range of this species extending east to eastern Texas, western Arkansas, western Ohio, and southeastern Ontario. They mentioned that the coyote, "has been taken or recorded within the past two decades in . . . West Virginia, Virginia,

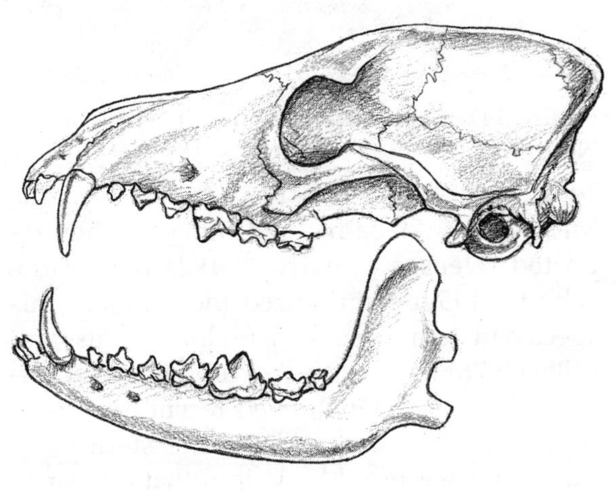

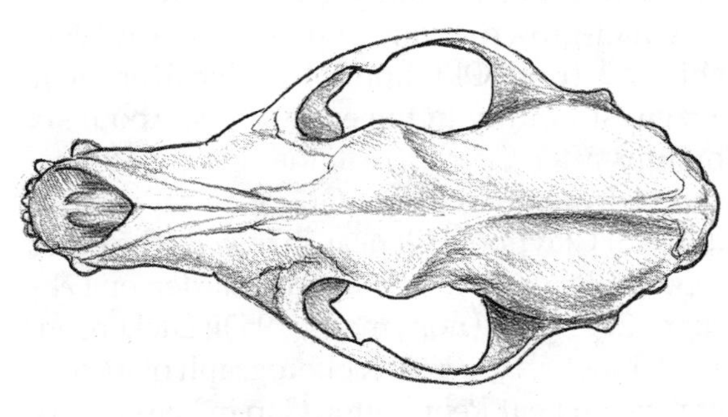

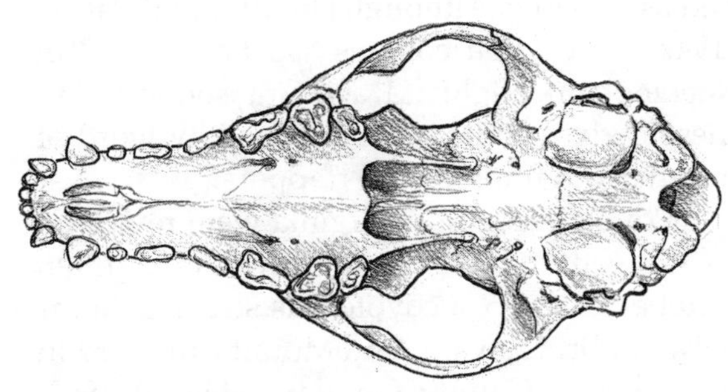

Figure 141. *Canis latrans:* Left lateral view of skull, and dorsal and ventral view of skull. Scale bar = 5 cm.

Figure 142. *Canis latrans:* Range in Virginia and North America.

Tennessee, North and South Carolina, Georgia, Mississippi, Alabama, and others." They reported releases as early as 1925 in Florida. Schultz (1955) summarized the status of this species in Tennessee, and Taylor, Counts, and Mills (1976) have done the same for West Virginia. Paradiso (1966) noted recent records of coyotes from eastern Arkansas, eastern Louisiana, and western Mississippi that appear to represent natural eastward range extensions. Bekoff (1977) showed the current range extending throughout the continental United States.

In 1950, what was possibly a coyote was killed in Augusta County (Anonymous, 1950e). Two half-grown coyote pups supposedly were shipped from Oklahoma to a location near Tazewell County in the early 1950s. About six months after their arrival, the two coyotes escaped from their cage. One was reportedly killed at Claypool Hill near Tazewell. The other reportedly was killed in Burkes Garden on February 22, 1952 (Anonymous, 1953i; Dickenson, 1953; Lineberry, 1968). A photograph of a "coyote" taken near Pennington Gap in Lee County appeared in *Virginia Wildlife* (Pilcher, 1971c). As far as is known, none of these animals was verified as a coyote. Although Handley and Patton (1947) stated that coyotes had been killed in Rockingham, Highland, and Grayson counties, these early records were obtained by word of mouth from hunters and trappers.

Coyote records in Virginia were reviewed by Carpenter (1971) and Nowak (1979). On October 25, 1965, a coyote was struck by a car between Bridgewater and Mount Crawford in Rockingham County. On November 20, 1965, a coyote was shot near Brownsburg in Rockbridge County (Allen, 1966a). On February 2, 1970, a 27-pound male coyote was shot near Mossy Creek in Augusta County. On February 28, 1970, another coyote was trapped in Augusta County. The skulls of three of these four specimens were verified as coyote skulls by John Paradiso of the United States National Museum (Paradiso, 1966; Carpenter, 1971). It is not known whether these animals represented a natural population whose range was extending into Virginia or whether they were released or had escaped.

During 1968 and 1969, a group of approximately eight animals, supposedly the result of the union of a female coyote and a dog, were hunted in Tazewell and Lee counties. Three reportedly were killed but their identification was never verified. A coyote-like animal was killed in Bath County in 1977 (Goodwin, 1979).

Since June, 1990, coyote control has been under the supervision of the Virginia Cooperative Coyote Damage Control Program of the United States Department of Agriculture. Tomsa (1992) reviewed historical data contained in records filed at the Animal Damage Control office in Blacksburg. Prior to 1983, eight coyotes were killed and identified in five counties. During the period 1983–1987, 53 coyotes were killed and identified in 10 counties. No records were available for 1988–1989. From June 1990 through June 1992, 71 coyotes were taken. Losses blamed on coyotes during this period amounted to 1,446 sheep, 35 goats, 28 calves, and 1 cow on 125 farms in 21 western Virginia counties. According to the Virginia Extension Service, there has been a 25 percent reduction in the number of sheep producers in Virginia since 1990 due to lower lamb prices as well as coyote predation. The number of sheep raised in the state has declined from 165,000 in 1990 to 99,000 in 1994. During this period, verified sheep kills by coyotes have ranged from 623 in 1992 to a low of 404 in 1993.

Habitat. Coyotes prefer open woodlands, woodland borders, prairies, and brushy areas.

Habits. Coyotes are mainly nocturnal, although they may be active during daylight hours. They are active both summer and winter. Members of a pair sometimes hunt cooperatively. The coyote has been known to play dead in order to capture birds. Its sense of sight, hearing, and smell are exceptionally acute.

Coyotes are the most vocal of all North American wild mammals. Their howling has long been a symbol of the Central Plains. A series of barks ending with a high-pitched howl may be emitted by single individuals and a number of animals will join together in a chorus. These calls may carry for several miles.

Coyotes do not travel in packs as do wolves. Rather, they travel separately or in family units and generally follow well-used runways or hunting routes. Coyotes are capable of attaining high rates of speed when chasing prey or eluding a pursuer. Running animals have been clocked at speeds up to 69 km per hour (Zimmerman, 1943; Cottam, 1945).

Coyotes may range extensively while searching for food. In a study involving animals from several western states, the distances traveled by coyotes between tagging and recovery averaged 22.9 km. The greatest distance moved was 185 km (Robinson and Grand, 1958). In Arkansas, coyote home range varied from 7.4 km^2 for immature females to 20.6 km^2 for adult males (Gipson and Sealander, 1972). The largest range was 30.2 km^2 for an adult male. Range boundaries of individual coyotes are marked by urine and feces. In Mississippi and Alabama, Sumner et al. (1984) reported an average female home range of 41.2 km^2 and an average male home range of 20.0 km^2. In western Tennessee, annual home ranges averaged 31 km^2 for males and 60 km^2 for females (Babb and Kennedy, 1988). Except during the breeding season, females consistently had larger home ranges than males. Greatest distances moved were approximately 70 km by an adult male and approximately 55 km by a yearling female.

The den is in a concealed place and is normally in a hole in the ground. The coyote may dig its own burrow but more frequently enlarges the burrow of a woodchuck, skunk, or fox. Rocky caverns may also be used as den sites. Some burrows may have two or three entrances. No nest material or lining is used in the enlarged nest chamber.

Coyotes are one of the most maligned mammals in the United States. Cattlemen and sheepmen claim they kill large numbers of calves, goats, and sheep. Although they may kill domestic animals at times, much of this damage is thought to have been done by wild dogs. Schwartz and Schwartz (1959) have noted that between 10 and 20 percent of the total food of the coyote probably constitute a financial loss to humans, while the rest is neutral or beneficial. Control should be directed toward troublesome individuals rather than resorting to large-scale poisoning campaigns that frequently destroy nontarget species.

Food. Coyotes feed primarily on small rodents and rabbits. Other food consists of carrion, other animals, and vegetable matter. Food not eaten immediately may be buried for future use. Sperry (1941) analyzed the stomachs of 8,339 coyotes from the western United States and recorded the following major food groups and their percentages by volume: rabbits, 32; carrion, 26; rodents, 17.5; domestic livestock (chiefly sheep and goats), 14; deer, 3.5; birds, 3; insects, 1; other animal matter (skunks, weasels, shrews, moles, snakes, lizards), 1; and vegetable matter, 2.

Limited information concerning food habits is available for the southeastern United States. Over half of the coyotes examined during a Louisiana food habits study had eaten rabbits and rodents (Wilson, 1967). Plant material occurred in 44 percent of the stomachs and was composed primarily of persimmons and watermelons. Other foods occurring with regular frequency included livestock, poultry and other birds, insects, and carrion. Cattle were an important food during the winter and probably were available to coyotes as a result of die-offs of weakened and diseased animals.

Smith and Kennedy (1983) recorded the following percent occurrences from 54 coyotes in western Tennessee: rodent 48.1; livestock 35.2; plant 27.8; rabbit 24.0; bird 16.7; insect 14.8; white-tailed deer 13.0; woodchuck 7.4; and reptile 3.7.

A larger study in Tennessee (262 digestive tracts) revealed rodents, persimmon *(Diospyros virginia)*, rabbit (*Sylvilagus* spp.), and white-tailed deer *(Odocoileus virginianus)* with the highest percentage occurrences (Lee and Kennedy, 1986). The most common rodents were cotton rat *(Sigmodon hispidus)*, deer mouse (*Peromyscus* spp.), and vole (*Microtus* spp.). There were no differences between sexes. The only significant variation among age classes was that juvenile animals ate more persimmons. The average percent occurrence of livestock was 16.7 percent. However, it was difficult to separate carrion from predator-killed animals.

Wooding et al. (1984) examined 211 scats and 100 stomachs from Alabama and Mississippi. The frequency of occurrence of major food items were rodents 43.1; fruit 38.6; rabbits 34.7; insects 29.9; white-tailed deer 28.0; and birds 22.5. Rabbits and rodents occurred most frequently in spring; rodents, insects, and birds in summer; fruit, primarily persimmons, in fall; and deer and rodents in winter. Livestock (cattle and hog) occurred in 24 percent of the stomachs and 4.3 percent of the scats.

The stomach contents of a coyote I examined in Mobile County, Alabama, in 1970 revealed: mammal remains, most if not all of which belonged to the cotton rat *(Sigmodon hispidus)*, 97 percent; vegetation, 2 percent; insect larvae, 1 percent (Linzey, 1970; 1971).

Reproduction and Development. In the western states, coyotes breed in late winter. Following a gestation of 60 to 64 days, the annual litter usually is born during April and May. The average litter consists of five to seven pups, although litters containing as many as 19 pups have been reported. However, some of these excessively large litters may have been the offspring of more than one female. Two studies in Tennessee have recorded average litter sizes of 5.8 (Lydeard et al., 1986) and 5.0 (range 1 to 12) (Kennedy et al., 1990).

The pups are furred at birth and have their eyes closed. They are able to walk at 8 to 10 days, and the eyes open between 10 and 12 days. They first leave the den when about three weeks old. Solid food regurgitated by the parents is provided to the pups as early as one month, although they are not completely weaned until they are more than three months old. The male feeds the female, and after weaning, food is brought to the pups by both parents. The young learn to hunt between two and three months of age. The family breaks up in early fall, when each pup seeks its own home site. Coyotes may begin breeding the year following their birth, although the percentage of yearlings that bear young varies with such conditions as severity of the winter and food availability. Coyotes may remain with the same mate for life, although some stay with a mate for only a few years, and others not more than a single year.

The coyote will breed with domestic dogs, and captive-born offspring of coyote-dog crosses have been described by Mengel (1971). Fertile offspring have been produced from crosses involving both male dogs and female coyotes and crosses involving female dogs and male coyotes. Such crosses occur in the wild, particularly where coyotes are scarce or where they have been introduced outside their normal range and cannot find mates of their own species. Such hybrids are commonly known as "coy-dogs" and have been reported in a number of eastern states. The percentage of such hybrids, however, is low. An interesting feature of coy-dog parental behavior is that the hybrid male, like the dog, does not assist in caring for the pups (Silver and Silver, 1969; Mengel, 1971). In the southwestern United States, as well as in some other areas, most wild coyote-like canids have been shown taxonomically to be coyotes and not coyote-dog hybrids (Smith and Kennedy, 1983; Lydeard et al., 1988).

Longevity. In the wild, few coyotes live more than six to eight years (Gier, 1968; Mathwig, 1976). Maximum ages known are 13.5 years (Nellis and Keith, 1976) and 14.5 years (Knowlton, 1972). A coyote lived 18.5 years in the National Zoological Park in Washington, DC (Mann, 1930).

Predation. Human hunting, trapping, and poisoning campaigns are the coyote's chief enemy. Most western states, at one time or another, have offered bounties for this animal. Some young may be taken by dogs or great horned owls.

Geographic Variation. The subspecies occurring in Virginia is *Canis latrans latrans* Say.

The word *coyote* comes from the Aztec word *Coyotyl* and means "barking dog" (Bekoff, 1977).

Location of Specimens. LFCC, LU, USNM.

Red Wolf [Extirpated]
Canis rufus (Bartram)

Description. The red wolf (Plate 69) is a small, slender, long-legged canid intermediate in size between the gray wolf and the coyote. It has been referred to as "rather greyhound-like in appearance, with long, somewhat spindly legs" (Young, 1946). The red wolf normally resembles the coyote in color but varies from grayish-brown to reddish-tawny to black. The underparts are whitish or buffy. The pelage is somewhat coarser than that of a coyote. Adults range

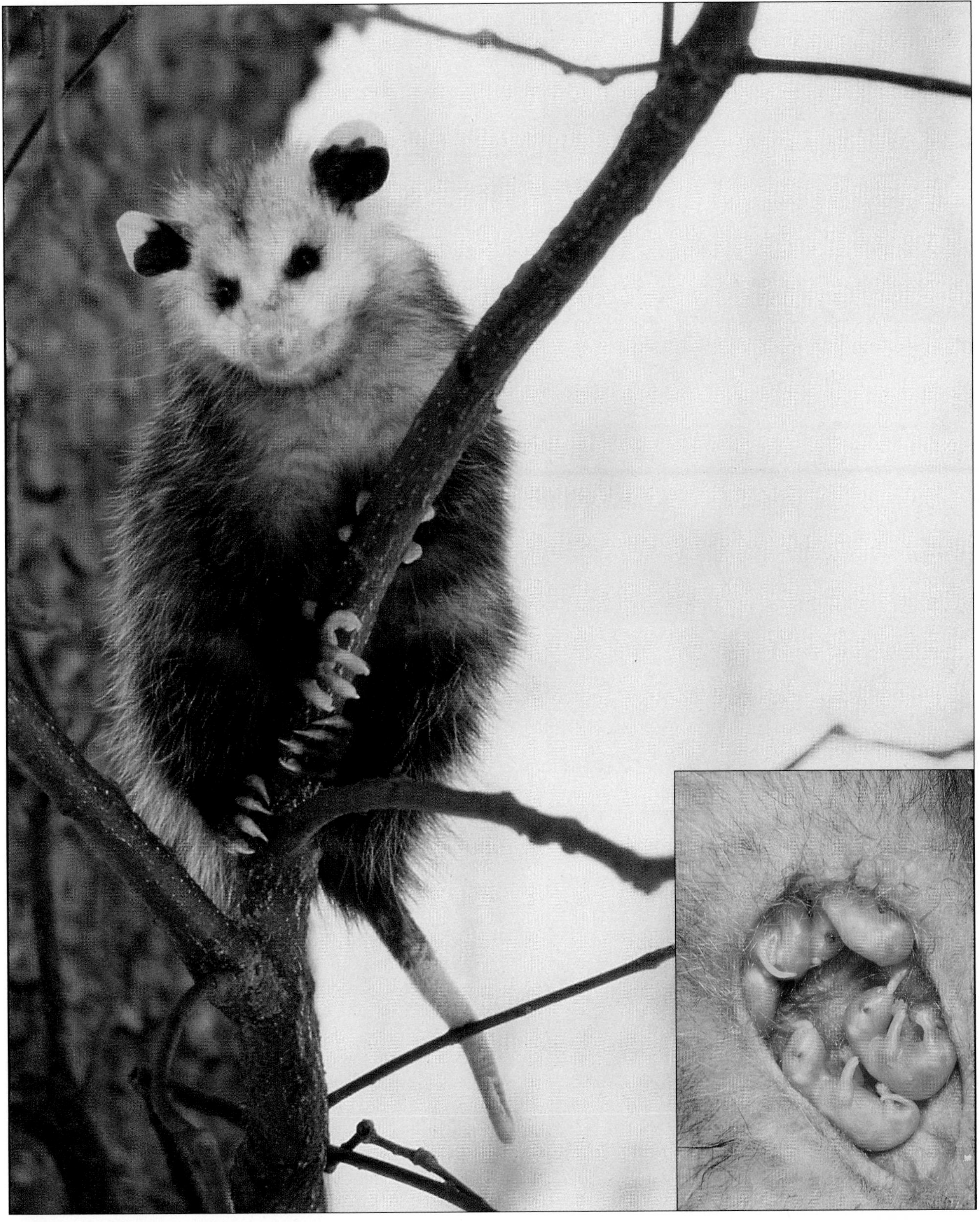

Plate 1. Virginia Opossum, *Didelphis virginiana*

Plate 2. Virginia Opossum suckling young.

Plate 3. Masked Shrew, *Sorex cinereus*

Plate 4. Southeastern Shrew, *Sorex longirostris*

Plate 5. Northern Water Shrew, *Sorex palustris*

Plate 6. Smoky Shrew, *Sorex fumeus*

Plate 7. Long-Tailed Shrew, *Sorex dispar*

Plate 8. Pygmy Shrew, *Sorex (Microsorex) hoyi*

Plate 9. Least Shrew, *Cryptotis parva*

Plate 10. Northern Short-Tailed Shrew, *Blarina brevicauda*

Plate 11. Southern Short-Tailed Shrew, *Blarina carolinensis*

Plate 12. Eastern Mole, *Scalopus aquaticus*

Plate 13. Hairy-Tailed Mole, *Parascalops breweri*

Plate 14. Star-Nosed Mole, *Condylura cristata*

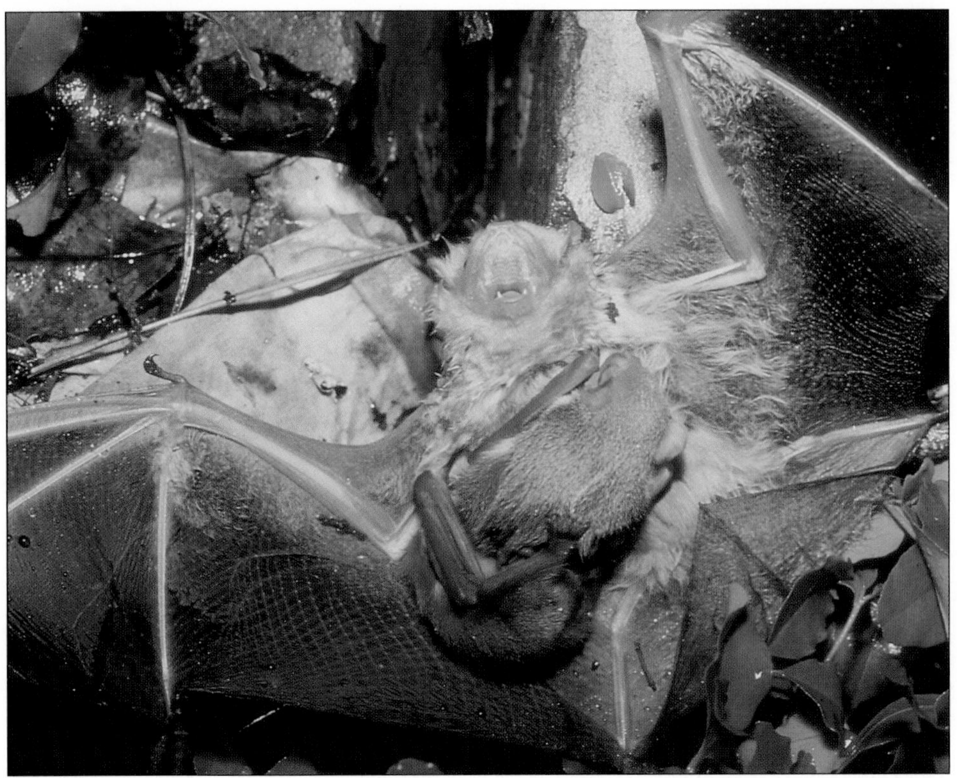

Plate 15. Female Red Bat nursing young.

Plate 16. Little Brown Myotis, *Myotis lucifugus*

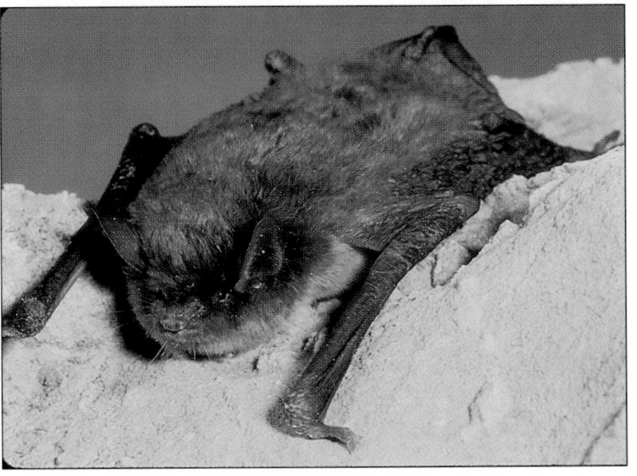

Plate 17. Southeastern Myotis, *Myotis austroriparius*

Plate 18. Gray Myotis, *Myotis grisescens*

Plate 19. Northern Myotis, *Myotis septentrionalis*

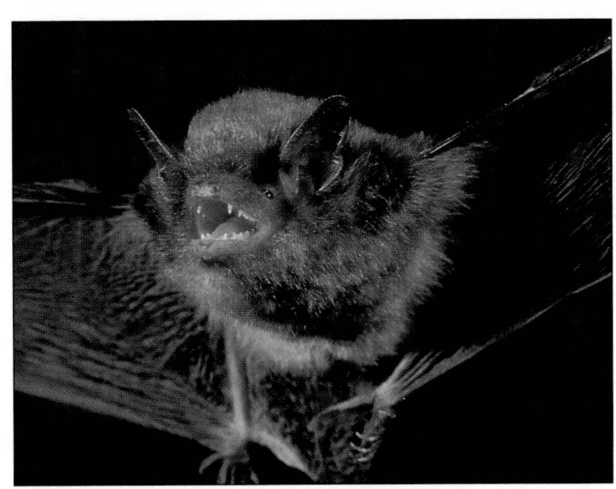

Plate 20. Indiana Myotis, *Myotis sodalis*

Plate 21. Eastern Small-Footed Myotis, *Myotis leibii*

Plate 22. Silver-Haired Bat, *Lasionycteris noctivagans*

Plate 23. Eastern Pipistrelle, *Pipistrellus subflavus*

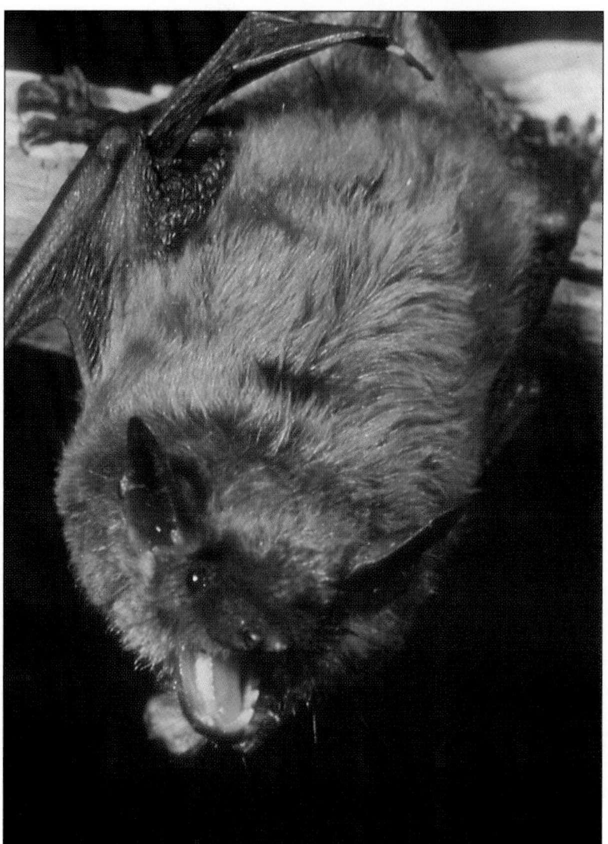

Plate 24. Big Brown Bat, *Eptesicus fuscus*

Plate 25. Evening Bat, *Nycticeius humeralis*

Plate 26. Eastern Red Bat, *Lasiurus borealis*

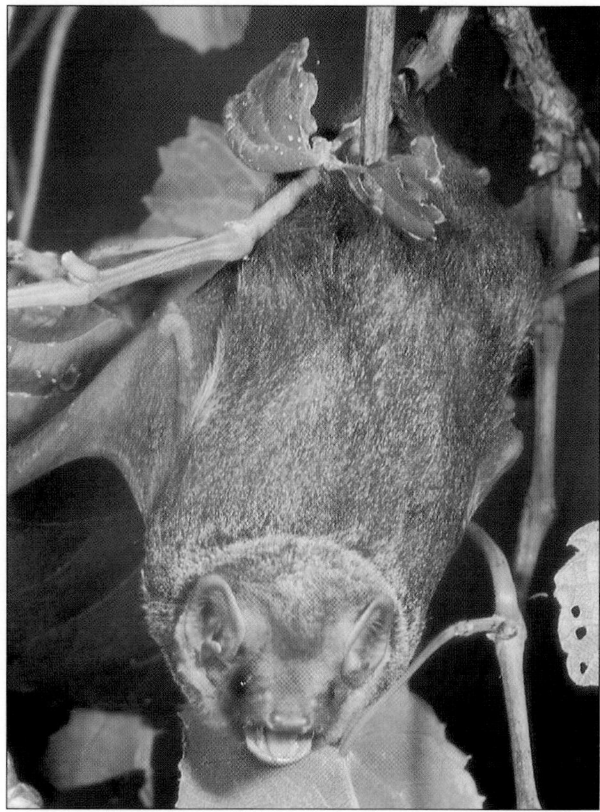

Plate 27. Seminole Bat, *Lasiurus seminolus*

Plate 28. Hoary Bat, *Lasiurus cinereus*

Plate 29. Northern Yellow Bat, *Lasiurus intermedius*

Plate 30. Townsend's (Western) Big-Eared Bat, *Corynorhinus townsendii*

Plate 31. Rafinesque's (Eastern) Big-Eared Bat, *Corynorhinus rafinesquii*

Plate 32. Marsh Rabbit, *Sylvilagus palustris*

Plate 33. Eastern Cottontail, *Sylvilagus floridanus*

Plate 34. Appalachian Cottontail, *Sylvilagus obscurus*

Plate 35. Snowshoe Hare, *Lepus americanus*

Plate 36. Black-Tailed Jackrabbit, *Lepus californicus*

Plate 37. Eastern Chipmunk, *Tamias striatus*

Plate 38. Woodchuck, *Marmota monax*

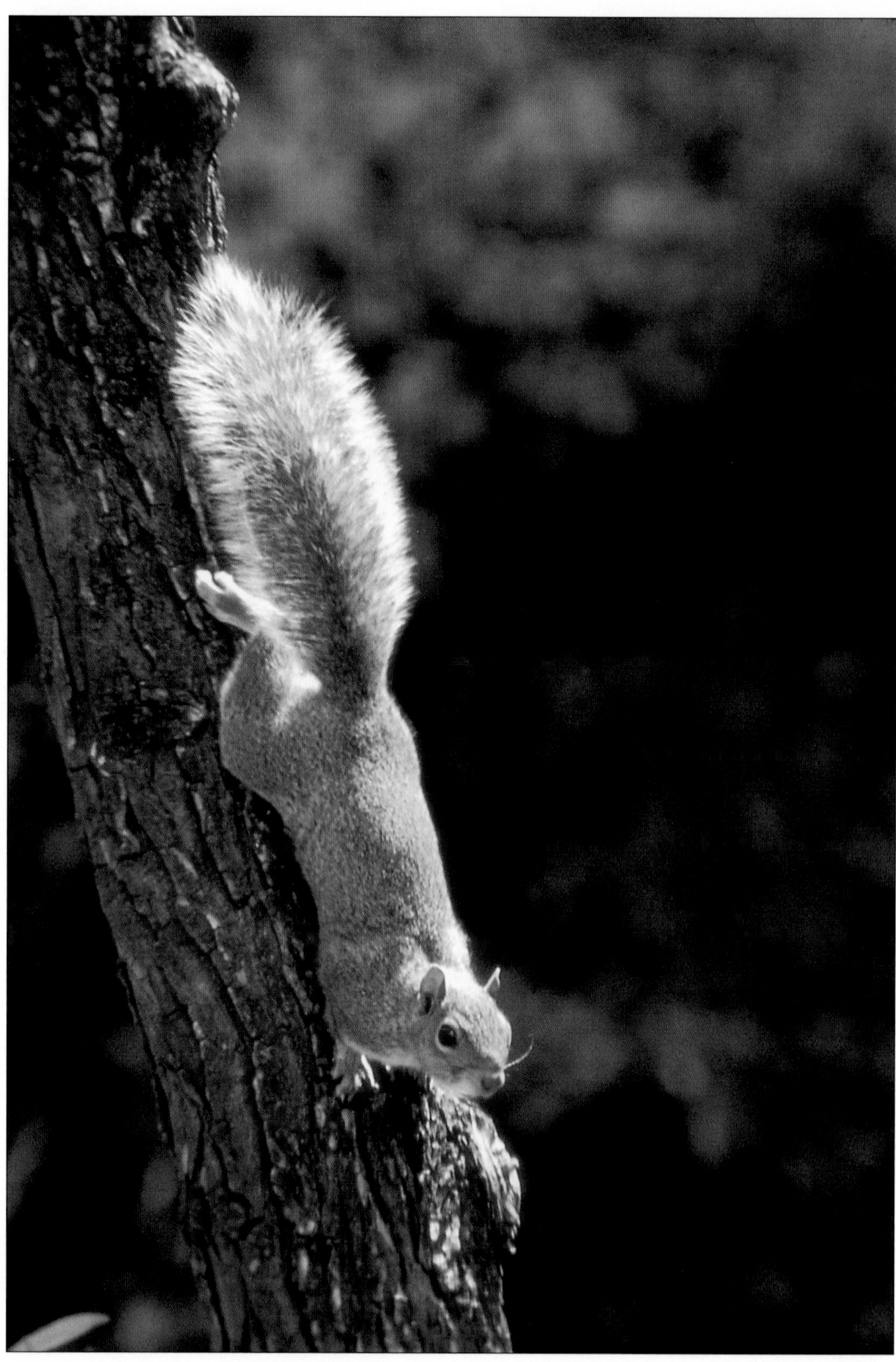

Plate 39. Eastern Gray Squirrel, *Sciurus carolinensis*

Plate 40. Eastern Fox Squirrel, *Sciurus niger*

Plate 41. Red Squirrel, *Tamiasciurus hudsonicus*

Plate 42. Southern Flying Squirrel, *Glaucomys volans*

Plate 43. Northern Flying Squirrel, *Glaucomys sabrinus*

Plate 44. American Beaver, *Castor canadensis*

Plate 45. Marsh Rice Rat, *Oryzomys palustris*

Plate 46. Eastern Harvest Mouse, *Reithrodontomys humulis*

Plate 47. Deer Mouse, *Peromyscus maniculatus*

Plate 48. White-Footed Mouse, *Peromyscus leucopus*

Plate 49. Cotton Mouse, *Peromyscus gossypinus*

Plate 50. Golden Mouse, *Ochrotomys nuttalli*

Plate 51. Hispid Cotton Rat, *Sigmodon hispidus*

Plate 52. Allegheny Woodrat, *Neotoma magister*

Plate 53. Southern Red-Backed Vole, *Clethrionomys gapperi*

Plate 54. Meadow Vole, *Microtus pennsylvanicus*

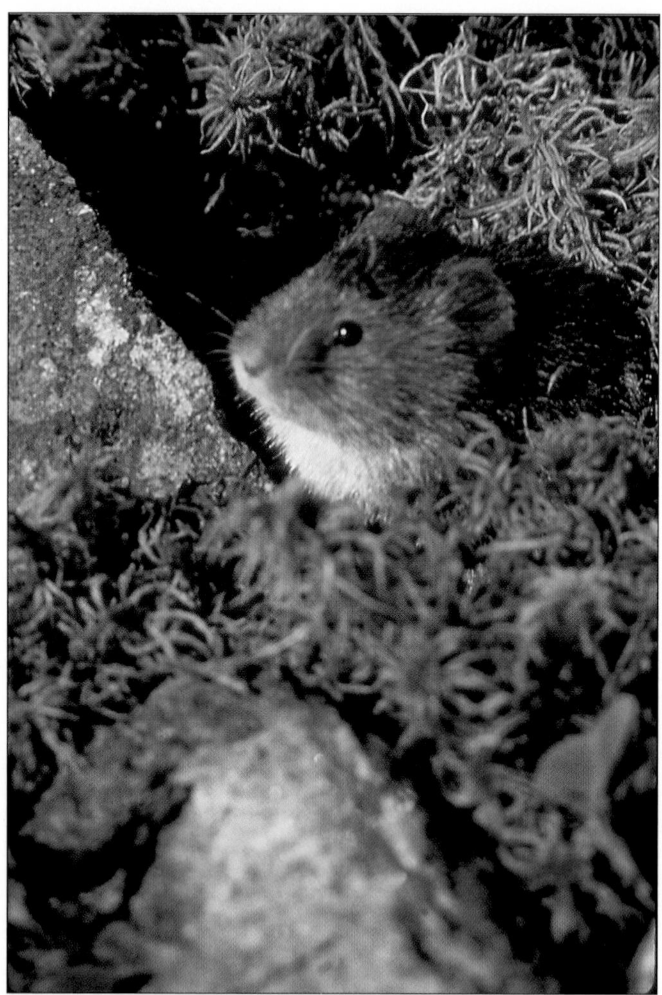

Plate 55. Rock Vole, *Microtus chrotorrhinus*

Plate 56. Woodland Vole, *Microtus pinetorum*

Plate 57. Southern Bog Lemming, *Synaptomys cooperi*

Plate 58. Common Muskrat, *Ondatra zibethicus*

Plate 59. Black Rat, *Rattus rattus*

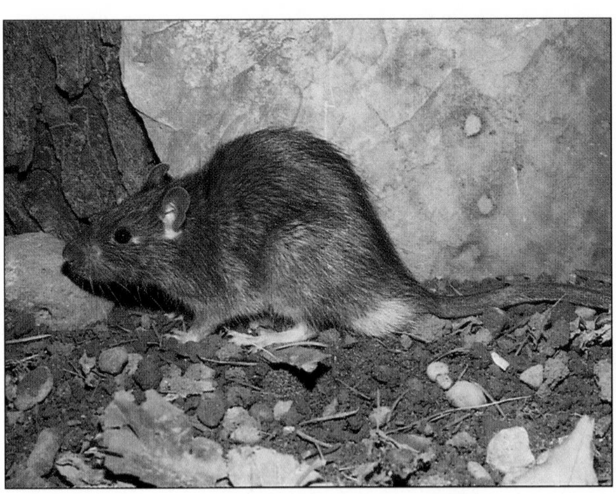

Plate 60. Norway Rat, *Rattus norvegicus*

Plate 61. House Mouse, *Mus musculus*

Plate 62. Meadow Jumping Mouse, *Zapus hudsonius*

Plate 63. Woodland Jumping Mouse, *Napaeozapus insignis*

Plate 64. Porcupine, *Erethizon dorsatum*

Plate 65. Nutria, *Myocastor coypus*

Plate 66. Red Fox, *Vulpes vulpes*

Plate 67. Common Gray Fox, *Urocyon cinereoargenteus*

Plate 68. Coyote, *Canis latrans*

Plate 69. Red Wolf, *Canis rufus*

Plate 70. Gray Wolf, *Canis lupus*

Plate 71. Black Bear, *Ursus americanus*

Plate 72. Common Raccoon, *Procyon lotor*

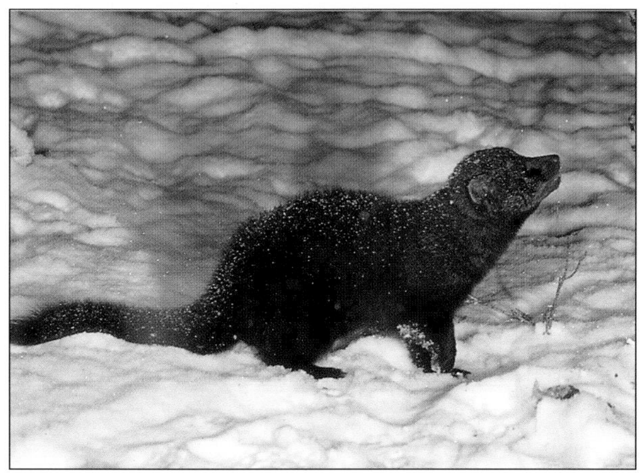

Plate 73. Fisher, *Martes pennanti*

Plate 74. Least Weasel, *Mustela nivalis*

Plate 75. Long-Tailed Weasel, *Mustela frenata*

Plate 76. Mink, *Mustela vison*

Plate 77. Northern River Otter, *Lutra canadensis*

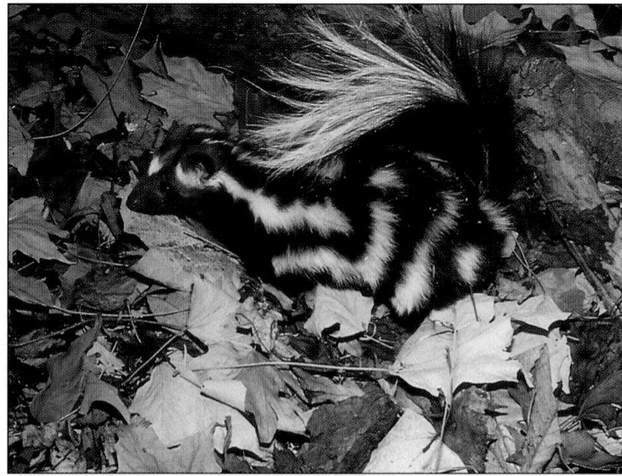

Plate 78. Eastern Spotted Skunk, *Spilogale putorius*

Plate 79. Striped Skunk, *Mephitis mephitis*

Plate 80. Mountain Lion, *Puma (Felis) concolor*

Plate 81. Bobcat, *Lynx rufus*

Plate 82. Harbor Seal, *Phoca vitulina*

Plate 83. Manatee, *Trichechus manatus*

Plate 84. Horse, *Equus caballus*

Plate 85. Pig, *Sus scrofa*

Plate 86. Sika Deer, *Cervus nippon*

Plate 87. Elk or Wapiti, *Cervus elaphus*

Plate 88. White-Tailed Deer, *Odocoileus virginianus*

Plate 89. American Bison, *Bison bison*

Plate 90. Cow, *Bos taurus*

Plate 91. Domestic Goat, *Capra hircus*

between 140 and 167 cm in total length, including a 33 to 43 cm tail. They weigh, on the average, between about 13 and 27 kg.

The skull of the red wolf is similar to that of the coyote. It is narrow and elongated, and the sagittal crest is usually well developed. The rostrum is long and slender, as are the canine teeth. The postorbital constriction is relatively narrow and elongated. Additional, more critical criteria have been utilized by Paradiso and Nowak (1972). Wayne and Gittleman (1995) presented evidence questioning whether the red wolf is a true species or a long-established hybrid of the gray wolf and coyote.

Distribution. The former distribution of this species encompassed most of the southeastern United States. Due to range expansion by the coyote *(Canis latrans)* and subsequent interbreeding with these and domestic dogs, the last wild populations of red wolves inhabiting the coastal area of southeastern Texas and southern Louisiana are probably not genetically pure.

In 1987, red wolves were reintroduced at the Alligator River National Wildlife Refuge in eastern North Carolina in order to reestablish a permanent population. During the next three years, a total of 31 red wolves were released on the Refuge, with 10 being released in September, 1990 (Smith, 1990). Several of these wolves have mated and produced litters. Four island propagation projects are currently operating in South Carolina, Mississippi, Florida, and North Carolina. Beginning in 1991, several pairs of red wolves have been released in the Great Smoky Mountains National Park in Tennessee. Whether or not these reintroductions will be successful in establishing permanent populations is not known at this time.

In western Virginia, the Explore Park and Mill Mountain Zoo plan to establish a breeding center for endangered North American species. Known officially as the American Center for Rare and Endangered Species (ACRES), the center's first project began in December, 1992, with the arrival of a male red wolf from the zoo in Wheeling, West Virginia (Yancey, 1992). A two-year-old female from the zoo in Tacoma, Washington arrived on February 5, 1993 (Yancey, 1993). No young were produced in 1993.

Nowak (1970) and Paradiso and Nowak (1972) included much of eastern and southern Virginia within the pre-1600 range of this species. Possibly some of the early accounts of wolves in Virginia could have been of the red wolf. For example, Purchas (1625) stated: "their Wolves are not bigger then our foxes."

Geographic Variation. The geographic variant most likely to have occurred in Virginia would have been *Canis rufus rufus* Audubon and Bachman.

Location of Specimens. No specimens from Virginia are known to exist in collections.

Gray Wolf [Extirpated]
Canis lupus Linnaeus

Description. The gray wolf (Plate 70) is a large canid possessing a long, bushy tail and large, erect ears. In general coloration, it resembles the coyote, but it is distinguished from the latter by its much larger size and heavier build. The dorsal color is usually grayish, consisting of a mixture of brown, gray, and black hairs. The underparts are whitish. Females possess 10 mammae. Adult gray wolves range from approximately 127 to 167 cm in total length, including a tail 28 to 45 cm long. Males stand 66 to 96 cm high at the shoulder and normally weigh between 27 and 45 kg. Females weigh approximately 25 percent less than males.

Distribution. The former range of this species was circumpolar, with gray wolves widely distributed in Eurasia and throughout most of North America south to southern Mexico. Outside of Alaska, however, only a few of these carnivores remain in the United States. Small populations exist in Isle Royale National Park and nearby areas bordering Lake Superior and in parts of the Rocky Mountain and Cascade-Sierra Nevada chains in the western part of the country.

The gray wolf formerly occurred throughout Virginia. Young and Goldman (1944) stated that wolves were common throughout most of Virginia, particularly in the mountains. They noted that the early records of attempts made by the settlers to extirpate wolves attested to the large number present. In addition, Virginia was the second colony to adopt a bounty for wolf control. This law was adopted by the Grand Assembly at Jamestown on September 4, 1632 (Green, 1940). In his *History of Norfolk*

County, Stewart (1902) stated:

Besides all these dangers to their own lives, the country was infested with wolves, which destroyed their domestic animals. The County Court on the 8th of October, 1639, took the matter in hand and resolved 'Whereas it doth appear that there are divers and many damages done unto cattle in this lower county of New Norfolk by the multitudes of wolves which do frequent the woods and plantations, it is therefore ordered that any person whatsoever within the aforesaid county shall kill any wolf and bring in the head to any officer in said county, the said person for every wolf so killed shall be paid by the sheriff fifty pounds of tobacco.' The price was afterward, in May, 1782, increased to 100 pounds net tobacco for every young wolf not exceeding six months of age, and 200 pounds for those over that age in Norfolk and other counties named in the act of the legislature, which was to be in force for three years — so for one hundred and fifty years the yearly levy accounts of the county have charges for wolves' heads.

Morton (1637) recorded that every Virginia colonial home kept "3 or 4 mongrel dogs to destroy vermin such as wolves." Colonel William Byrd stated in 1728: "This beast is not so untamable as the panther, but the Indians know how to gentle their whelps and use them about their cabans instead of dogs." Gray wolves were present in the District of Columbia as late as 1728 (McAtee, 1918).

According to Henderson (1920):

In the late autumn of 1761, Daniel Boone and Nathaniel Gist, the son of Washington's famous guide, who were both serving under Waddell, temporarily detached themselves from his command and led a small party on a 'long hunt' in the Valley of the Holston. While encamping near the site of Black's Fort, subsequently built, they were violently assailed by a pack of fierce wolves which they had considerable difficulty in beating off; and from this incident the locality became known as Wolf Hills (Now Abingdon, Virginia).

Handley (1979b) noted:

Wolves were found throughout the state when European colonists arrived, and most early accounts of Virginia mammals noted that they were abundant. Substantial bounties were paid for their extermination, and they were relentlessly hunted and trapped. Wolf populations dwindled as settlement advanced, and by the 1880s few wolves survived in Virginia.

The last two wolves were reportedly killed on Clinch Mountain in Tazewell County in the winter of 1909–1910 (Anonymous, 1949g). Wolves were last recorded in James City County in 1694, in Albemarle County in 1850, in Highland County in 1880, in Botetourt County in 1887, and in Bath County in 1890. Bailey (1946) recorded an account of the killing of a wolf in Powhatan County in 1901. Since all wolves in this portion of the state had undoubtedly been killed off many years earlier, this animal could have been a wanderer from farther west, an escapee from captivity, or some animal other than a wolf.

Geographic Variation. The geographic variant of gray wolf that formerly inhabited Virginia was *Canis lupus lycaon* Schreber.

Location of Specimens. No specimens from Virginia are known to exist in collections.

Bears (Family Ursidae)

The family Ursidae includes the largest living carnivores, the bears. They range in size from the 27 kg sun bear *(Helarctos)* to the 765 kg Alaska brown bear *(Ursus arctos)*. They inhabit the northern hemisphere and northern South America, living primarily in the temperate and tropical regions.

Bears have small eyes, small ears, and short tails. Five toes are present on each foot, and each has a nonretractile claw. The soles of the feet are not haired. Locomotion is plantigrade, and bears are able to walk short distances on the hind feet in an upright position. Auditory bullae are present but are only slightly inflated. Carnassial teeth are not developed, and three of the premolars in each jaw are rudimentary and may be lost. Most bears are omnivorous in their feeding habits, although the polar bear feeds mainly on seals and fish.

Among the carnivores, bears are most closely related to the dog and raccoon families. Only one genus of this family is represented in North America, and it includes four species: the black bear, grizzly bear, Alaskan brown bear, and the polar bear.

Genus *Ursus*

Dentition: 3/3, 1/1, 4/4, 2/3 = 42

Black Bear
Ursus americanus (Pallas)

Description. The black bear (Plate 71) is the only bear occuring in the eastern United States. It is a relatively large carnivore with rather short, stout legs and a very short tail that is practically concealed in the long, shaggy, black fur. In eastern North America black bears are predominantly glossy black with a brown muzzle, and they frequently have a small, white patch on the chest. The fur is longest and glossiest in fall; in summer the coat is ragged and dull due to wear and shedding.

Black bears have a long, brown muzzle with a straight facial profile, small eyes, and medium-sized, rounded, erect ears. The broad feet are completely plantigrade, and each foot possesses five clawed toes. The claws are long, strong, moderately curved, and nonretractile. Females possess six mammae. Adult black bears are generally between 1.4 and 1.8 m in total length and are 0.6 to 0.9 m high at the shoulder. Adults generally weigh between 90 and 180 kg although a few individuals weighing over 270 kg have been recorded. A bear killed in the Dismal Swamp in 1944 was estimated to weigh about 315 kg (Richards, 1953). Two bears killed in Nelson County, Virginia, during the 1956 hunting season weighed 286 and 288 kg. A large bear shot near Waynesboro in Augusta County, Virginia, in 1967 weighed 272 kg. A male in Lunenberg County in Virginia's piedmont weighed in at "well over 500 pounds" (230 kg) (Keyser, 1994). Males are, on the average, considerably larger than females.

The skull is large and somewhat elongate. The orbits are small. The lower jaw is short and moderately heavy. The three anterior premolars are rudimentary and are frequently absent, and the second premolar rarely is present in adults. This creates a diastema between the canines and the fourth premolar. The crowns of the molars are longer than broad and are adapted for crushing. The molars are progressively enlarged, with the last molar much larger than the one in front of it. Carnassial teeth are not highly developed and do not have a shearing function. Auditory bullae are present and slightly inflated (Figure 143).

Distribution. This species once ranged from Alaska across Canada and throughout the United States, but it has been extirpated in many parts of its former range. The present range includes the wilder areas of the north-

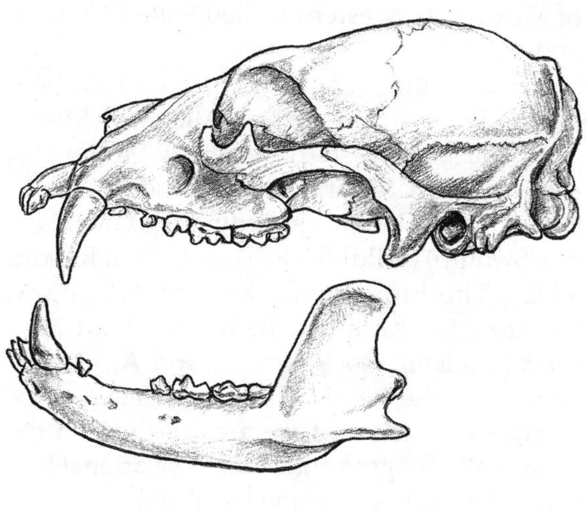

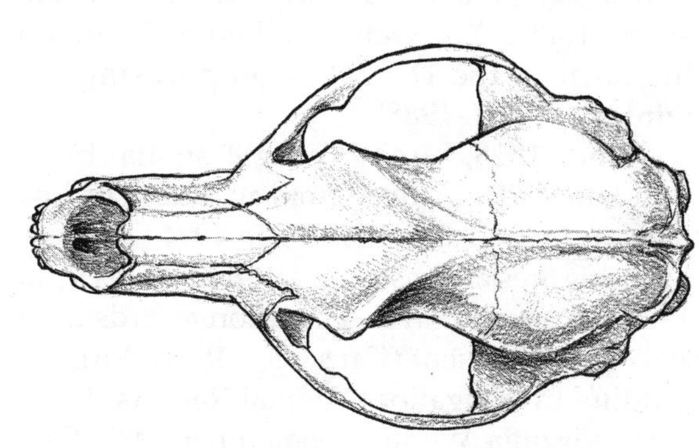

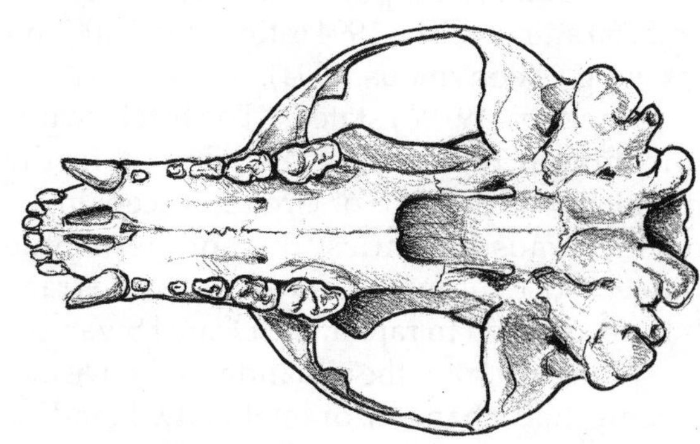

Figure 143. *Ursus americanus:* Left lateral view of skull, and dorsal and ventral view of skull. Scale bar = 5 cm.

eastern United States and Canada; the northern part of the Great Lakes states and western Ontario; the mountainous portions of New York, Pennsylvania, and the South Atlantic states; and the wild forested sections and timbered swamps of the Gulf and South Atlantic states, together with the mountainous regions of Mexico, the western United States, Canada, and Alaska.

Four primary populations of black bear exist in Virginia: the northern Allegheny Mountains, the southwestern Allegheny Mountains, the Shenandoah National Park, and the southeastern coastal plain (including the Great Dismal Swamp) (Wildlife Division Annual Report, 1992). The nine-county area of Alleghany, Rockbridge, Amherst, Bath, Highland, Augusta, Nelson, Rockingham, and Albemarle comprises the heart of Virginia's bear range (Figure 144). Most of the area lies within the George Washington and Jefferson National Forest and most has remained forested and uninhabited by humans. Black bears also inhabit the Dismal Swamp. Stewart (1902) noted that bears were abundant in the Dismal Swamp, and about 200 were killed each year. He stated that a Mr. Wallace killed 30 bears on his farm in the Dismal Swamp during the winter of 1887–1988.

Since 1928, Virginia's legal annual black bear harvest has ranged from an estimated low of 84 in 1943 to a high of 789 in 1994 (Table 9). These figures are based on estimated kills from 1928 to 1946 and on check station records from 1947 to the present (Carpenter, 1973); Virginia Wildlife Investigations Annual Reports, 1983–1988; Virginia Wildlife, September 1992; September, 1994). Richards (1953) estimated Virginia's black bear population at between 650 and 750 animals. The 1994 estimate is 3,500 and growing (Anonymous, 1994).

Handley (1979b) stated: "The black bear is uncommon but widely distributed in the mountainous portions of Virginia, except in the northernmost counties, the southern Blue Ridge, and in the far Southwest, where it is rare. It is uncommon to rare in the Dismal Swamp."

A decade later, the situation in the Dismal Swamp had changed dramatically. Handley (1991) stated:

> *Studies of Hellgren and Vaughan (1989) found that litter size, suspected modal age at primiparity, and interbirth interval of Dismal Swamp bears were indicative of good quality habitat. Their estimated density of 0.52 to 0.66 bears per km², corresponding to 286 to 368 bears in their 555 km² study area, is higher than any density found elsewhere in the southeastern United States. Not only does the Great Dismal Swamp National Wildlife Refuge support a healthy bear population within its boundaries, but it provides surplus bears that move out into surrounding areas with suitable habitat, as exemplified by the recent appearance of a sow and two cubs near Waverly, Sussex County, Virginia, about 60 km northwest of Great Dismal Swamp National Wildlife Refuge* (D. J. Schwab, pers. comm.).

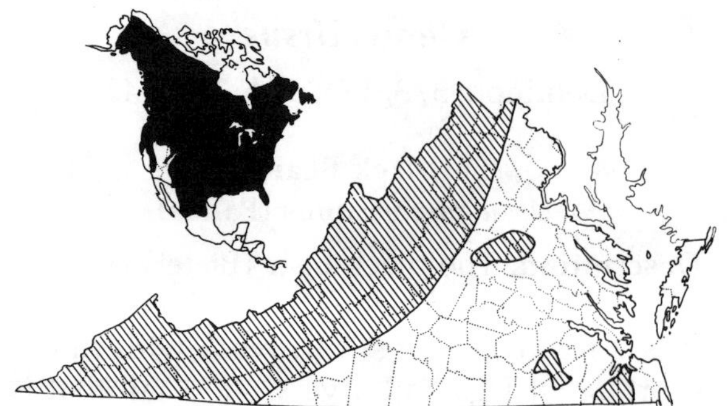

Figure 144. *Ursus americanus:* Range in Virginia and North America.

Data on the wild fur catch of the black bear in Virginia are presented in tables 2 and 3.

Habitat. In the eastern United States, black bears live primarily in heavily wooded forests and lowland swamps. Handley (1979b) noted:

> *Ideal upland habitat includes rugged areas with boulders, rock outcrops, ledges, and rock slides; thickets of mountain laurel and rhododendron; scrubby forest with numerous small openings; and no human habitations. Forest in upland bear range typically contains several species of oaks, pines, hickories, red maples, black gum, black birch, and wild cherries, and small openings with blueberries and blackberries. Ideal swamp habitat has myrtle thickets, cane brakes, tupelo, red maple, and tulip poplar, and adjacent uplands with dense thickets of* Smilax, *brambles, poison ivy, and sweet gum.*

Habits. Black bears are primarily solitary and nocturnal. They may occasionally be active during the day. In many sections of the country, bears are known to enter dormancy when cold weather approaches. They do not, however, exhibit many of the characteristics of true hibernation as exemplified by the woodchuck. Metabolism is reduced 50 to 60 percent, the heart rate drops from 40 to 50 beats per minute to 8 to 19 beats per minute, and respiration is slowed to 2 to 4 times per minute. The body temperature, however, is reduced only 7°C to 8°C (Svihla and Bowman, 1954; Pelton, 1982). A typical mammalian hibernator "reduces its body temperature, heart rate, and metabolism until body temperature is within 1°C of the ambient temperature" (Pelton, 1982). Whether or not an endogenous rhythm causes seasonal changes in bear physiology and behavior is unknown (Hellgren et al., 1989). In Virginia and other southern states, bears may bed down and remain inactive during short periods of extremely cold weather, while farther north the winter denning period often lasts from five to six months. In the Great Dismal Swamp, denning periods last (60 to 120 days) and up to 33 percent of the bears forage throughout the winter (Hellgren and Vaughan, 1987).

Results of physiological studies involving serum chemical and hematological values for Great Dismal Swamp black bears and for captive hibernating bears have been reported by Hellgren et al. (1989) and Hellgren et al. (1990).

Bears have no permanent summer home and sleep either in a tree or on the ground. During the winter in more northern areas, they make a bed of grass, leaves, twigs, and bark in a den located in a hollow tree, or in a slightly excavated hollow in the ground. In a study of denning ecology in the Great Dismal Swamp, Hellgren and Vaughan (1989) identified the following winter den types: 14 ground nests, 11 excavated ground cavities, 2 ground-level tree cavities, one above-ground-level tree cavity, and one stump den. Denning periods were among the shortest reported for black bears. Pregnant females entered dens earlier, emerged later, and denned longer than other age and sex groups.

Black bears have a well-defined home range. In such areas, they create well-worn pathways by repeatedly following the same route. The size of the home range varies due to sex, age, season, food availability, and population density. During short periods, most bears of both sexes stay in relatively small areas. Median range sizes of radio-collared bears in the Great Dismal Swamp were 21.4 km^2 for adult females, 33.1 km^2 for subadult females, and 79.0 km^2 for males (Hellgren and Vaughan, 1990). Radiotelemetry studies have revealed average home ranges of 61.0 km^2 and 16.9 km^2 for males and females on the Pisgah National Forest in North Carolina (Warburton and Powell, 1985), 42 km^2 and 15 km^2 for males and females in the Great Smoky Mountains National Park (Garshelis, 1978), and 196 km^2 and 38 km^2 for males and females in northeastern Pennsylvania (Alt et al., 1976). The home range size of adult male bears "is typically three to eight times larger than that of adult females" (Pelton, 1982). Home ranges often overlap extensively including core areas (areas of high-intensity use) (Hellgren and Vaughan, 1990; Horner and Powell, 1990). Neighboring bears often use areas of overlap for the same activities at the same time. Thus, the internal structure of home ranges, not just the outlines or total-area, needs to be analyzed in order to accurately depict black bear activities. Other eastern studies have revealed average movements of between 2.4 and 25.0 km over periods of 3 to 18 months (Chambers, 1959; Hewitt, Black, and Alsop, 1959; Knudsen, 1961). Maximum distances traveled ranged up to 74 km.

Black bears are able to return home after being transported many kilometers from their original capture point. The longest recorded translocation in which the bear returned home was a female that travelled 271 km (Harger, 1970). A study of navigation by translocated black bears was reported by Rogers (1987). Seventy-seven bears were translocated an average of 106 km (range 64 to 271 km). The 77 bears showed a highly significant preference for the home direction, and 34 of them reached home before they were shot, recaptured, or their radio-collars expired. Data indicated that neither random movements nor expanding search patterns were the basic mechanisms for homing and that ability to orient homeward did not depend upon familiarity with release areas.

In Virginia, a 2.5-year-old male was tagged at Big Levels in Augusta County and shot in Amelia County — a distance of 145 km. A male bear trapped in 1955 was moved from Big Levels to Vances Cove in Frederick County. It returned 156 km to its home range and was killed in 1958 (Anonymous, 1959g). The oldest tag return reported by Stickley (1961) was from a 1967 female, who carried her tag eight years and was killed only one km from where she was first captured.

Weekes (1970) recorded accounts of two bears that were transported 161 km from Sherando Lake in eastern Augusta County to Shenandoah County north of Columbia Furnace near the West Virginia line. During the hunting season the next year, both bears were killed within a radius of 29 km from where they had been trapped. These bears had to cross the Allegheny Mountains, the Shenandoah Valley, and US Route 11.

A bear that was released in Grayson County near Marion was killed by a hunter in Rappahannock two years later. It was one county away from the original capture site and had traveled over 400 km (Martin, 1995b).

Since 1988, the Virginia Department of Game and Inland Fisheries has relocated many bears to southwestern Virginia in an attempt to reestablish a viable bear population in that region of the state (Comly, 1993). As of September, 1994, 215 bears have been relocated (Martin, 1994). Most of these translocations have involved nuisance bears from areas near Shenandoah National Park.

Probably the most famous wandering bear in Virginia was a young female who was eventually named Rambling Rose. Rose had become a habitual and unwanted guest at picnics in Shenandoah National Park, and it was decided that for her own good she should be relocated. Rose was moved from her home territory in Augusta County to Sounding Knob in Highland County, a straight-line distance of approximately 97 km. Six days later she was back in the park. She was trapped again and taken to Mountain Lake in Giles County, approximately 209 km from her home territory. Rose returned again to the park and was caught 11 days later. She had crossed several interstate highways and other major highways and much open farmland on her journey. Finally, Rose was taken to the Dismal Swamp. She left immediately, went to North Carolina, and headed up the Roanoke River drainage on the way back to the mountains. Unfortunately, she was struck by a car and killed. It is estimated that Rambling Rose traveled at least 1,288 km during her summer journeys (Anonymous, 1979).

The Virginia Department of Game and Inland Fisheries has recently begun the most ambitious study of bears ever attempted in the state. The Alleghany Bear Study is a 5 to 8 year study designed to provide baseline data on reproduction, survival, movement, home range and sex ratios of the black bear population on the George Washington and Jefferson National Forest (Anonymous, 1994).

Eyesight in this species is not very good, but the senses of hearing and smell are excellent. Authorities agree that bears rely primarily on their keen sense of smell to locate food and detect intruders. Although normally silent, bears are capable of a wide variety of sounds. Black bears swim well, and unlike grizzly bears, they are expert tree climbers, particularly when young.

Black bears frequently scar the trunks of trees by gouging out chunks with their teeth or making deep scratches with their claws. It is generally believed that these marked trees serve as signposts to make bears aware of one another's presence and to mark the home range. Moore (1953) claimed bears use their smelling ability to determine the sex and species of animals that previously rubbed or clawed a tree.

Food. Although classified as carnivores, bears are essentially omnivorous and vary their diet with the season. In the spring, they feed on the tender leaves of plants and on the deciduous mast that has lain on the ground during the winter. During summer and autumn, their diet is governed by the availability of ripening fruits and nuts. A study of fall food habits in the George Washington National Forest revealed that fruits and nuts constituted the bulk of the diet (Cottam, Nelson, and Clarke, 1939). A five-year study in Virginia revealed that 62 percent of the fall and winter diet was composed of acorns. Blueberries, black gum, and greenbrier also were key foods, making up 17 percent of the winter food consumed (Stickley, 1957). Animal foods consist of ants, yellow jackets, bees and their honey, crickets, grasshoppers, fish, frogs, small rodents, rabbits, fawns, bird's eggs, and carrion of all kinds, including other bears.

In the Dismal Swamp, black bears also show a seasonal dietary pattern. In the spring, the diet consists of succulent herbaceous material. The diet changes to soft mast and corn in the summer. Early fall foods consisted of mast from gum and oak trees. Fruits of evergreen shrubs and vines dominated the late fall and winter diet. Animal foods comprised 3 percent of the annual diet (Hellgren and Vaughan, 1988). Nutritional values of seasonal diets were reported by Hellgren et al. (1989).

In searching for food, bears claw open rotten stumps and turn over logs and rocks. When they find a supply of extra food, they often cover it with debris and return to feed on it again. They have learned to like the foods of humans and may make themselves obnoxious and even dangerous around campsites and garbage disposal areas. "Outlaw" individuals occasionally become habituated to preying on domestic livestock.

Reproduction and Development. Black bears of both sexes do not usually become sexually mature until their third or fourth year. Most male bears are still immature at the height of the breeding season during the third year of life. Thus, first matings may take place when the bears are approximately 3.5 years old (Jackson, 1961; Erickson and Nellor, 1964; Raybourne, 1977). However, female black bears have been known to breed at 2.5 years of age, and there is a record of a 40.5 kg female giving birth to cubs (Stickley, 1957; Raybourne, 1977). In the Great Dismal Swamp, the youngest observed age of breeding from reproductive tracts or den observation was three years (Hellgren and Vaughan, 1989b).

A female's first litter usually consists of one young. In alternate years thereafter, she has other litters which generally contain two young, and sometimes three or four cubs. Rare cases have been reported of litters with five and even six young. Litter size frequencies are approximately as follows: single cubs, 7 to 15 percent; twin cubs, 40 to 50 percent; triplet cubs, 30 to 40 percent; and quadruplets, 5 to 10 percent (Erickson and Nellor, 1964). In a study of Virginia bears from 1958 to 1960 in Augusta, Rockbridge, and Alleghany counties, 39 female bears carried an average of 2.6 embryos or cubs per female (Stickley, 1961; 1963). Hellgren and Vaughan (1989b) recorded a mean litter size of 2.3 for 7 litters observed in dens in the Great Dismal Swamp. In Tennessee, the mean litter size for females with newborn cubs was 2.6. Mean litter size for females with yearlings was 2.2 (Eiler et al., 1989).

Mating in this species usually occurs in June or early July. Female black bears have seasonally constant estrus with ovulation induced after mating. The fertilized eggs start to develop but then enter a dormant stage in the uterus and do not become implanted there until fall. This process, known as delayed implantation, is also found in certain other mammals such as skunks and weasels. Because of this process, by early December the embryos are less than 19 mm long. The young are born in January or early February while the female is still denned, after a total gestation of 200 to 210 days. A detailed study of the breeding biology of the black bear has been presented by Erickson and Nellor (1964).

Information on the growth rate and early development of black bears has been presented by Schoonmaker (1938), Matson (1954), and Butterworth (1969). The newborn bear cub is smaller in proportion to the mother's size than any Virginia mammal except the opossum. At birth, the cub weighs 170 to 280 g and is about 230 mm long. The body is covered with fine black hair, and the eyes are closed. The eyes open between 25 and 30 days, while the upper incisors begin to cut through the gums when the cubs are between six and seven weeks old. At this time, they are about 300 mm long, weigh about 0.9 kg, and are well furred. In more northern areas, they leave the winter den with their mother in late March or April when they are two to three months old and weigh approximately 2.2 kg. They stay with her and continue to nurse throughout the summer, while she teaches them to feed and care for themselves. By fall, the cubs usually weigh between 18 and 23 kg. Cubs separated from the mother can be self-sufficient as early as 5.5 months of age. They normally stay with their mother through the winter and then separate. After the cubs leave their mother, they often live together through their second summer. Bears may reach maturity at three years, but full growth in size and weight is normally not attained until the sixth or seventh year. A study in Pennsylvania reported that a 10-month-old cub should weigh about 25 kg; yearlings about 45 kg; 2-year-olds about 70 kg; 3-year-olds about 93 kg; and 4-year-olds about 115 kg.

The female takes total responsibility for the care of the young and disciplines them very strictly. At a sign of danger, she may send them up a tree, and they are expected to remain there until she returns. However, when disturbed at the den, the female characteristically abandons both den and young (Svihla and Bowman,

1954).

Longevity. The life span of the wild black bear ordinarily does not exceed 12 to 15 years, although Erickson and Nellor (1964) recorded a wild bear with a known age of 24.4 years. Hellgren and Vaughan (1989b) recorded a 16-year-old male in the Great Dismal Swamp. A captive individual is known to have lived 25 years, 11 months, 6 days (Flower, 1931), and Burt and Grossenheider (1976) stated that black bears may live 30 years or more.

Parasites. The tick *Dermacentor variabilis* has been reported from this species in Virginia by Sonenshine, Lamb, and Anastos (1965).

In a study of endoparasites from the southeastern United States, bears from Virginia and West Virginia were grouped together in a "Northern mountain" region. Parasites recovered from these bears included: **Protozoa** (protozoans) *(Sarcocystis* sp.*)*; **Acanthocephala** (spiny-headed worms) *(Macracanthorhynchus ingens)*; and **Nematoda** (roundworms) (*Arthrocephalus lotoris, Baylisascaris transfuga, Capillaria putorii, Crenosoma* sp., *Cyathospirura* sp., *Gnathostoma* sp., *Gongylonema pulchrum, Molineus barbatus, Physaloptera* sp., *Strongyloides* sp.).

Predation. Adult black bears have practically no enemies besides man. Cubs may occasionally be killed by bobcats or cougars, and they are more susceptible than adults to being struck and killed by automobiles. Hellgren and Vaughan (1989b) reported intraspecific predation in the Great Dismal Swamp.

Geographic Variation. The subspecies occurring throughout Virginia is *Ursus americanus americanus* Pallas.

Location of Specimens. LFCC, LU, MCZ, MRNRA, NCSM, ODU, SNP, USNM, VCU, VHCC, VPISU, VPI-W.

Raccoons (Family Procyonidae)

The family Procyonidae consists of the raccoons, ringtails, coatis, kinkajous, olingos, and lesser pandas. All of the members of this family are partially arboreal, and most possess a moderately long, more or less bushy tail, ringed with alternating light and dark bands. These mammals have either plantigrade or semiplantigrade, pentadactyl feet with nonretractile or semiretractile claws. The skull possesses a rounded and well-inflated braincase and a short rostrum. Most procyonids, like the bears, have lost their highly specialized shearing cheek teeth and have developed lower-crowned, crushing teeth to accommodate their omnivorous diet.

Members of the family Procyonidae are found in temperate and tropical regions of North and South America and eastern Asia. Three genera occur in the United States, the ringtails *(Bassariscus)*, the raccoons *(Procyon)*, and the coatis *(Nasua)*. The lesser panda *(Ailurus)* is the Asiatic member of this family. The giant panda *(Ailuropoda)* was formerly classified in this family, but most authorities now include it in the family Ursidae with the bears. Only one genus, *Procyon*, inhabits Virginia.

Genus *Procyon*

Dentition: 3/3, 1/1, 4/4, 2/2 = 40

Common Raccoon
Procyon lotor (Linnaeus)

Description. The earliest reference to the common raccoon (Plate 72) found in the literature was by Captain John Smith (1612), who in describing the animals of Virginia said: "There is a beast they call *Aroughcun*, much like a badger, but useth to live on trees as Squirrels doe." Raccoons were described as "monkeys" by some of Virginia's early explorers. William Strachey (1612), for example, wrote: "The Rackoone I take to be a species of 'Monkey.'"

The raccoon is a medium-sized, heavily built, partially arboreal mammal with a white-bordered, black mask, which extends across the eyes and down onto the cheeks. This distinguishes the raccoon from all other Virginia mammals. Another familiar characteristic is the moderately long, well-haired tail alternately banded with five to seven blackish rings and terminating in a dark tip. The fur between the dark rings is a grizzled grayish or buff. The upperparts are generally a mixture of grizzled gray, brown, and black with the underfur dull grayish-brown. However, pelage color may range from light gray to almost black. The fur is long and loose. The underparts are dull grayish-brown, tinged with yellowish-gray or white. The sexes are similar. The head is broad with a pointed muzzle. The ears are prominent,

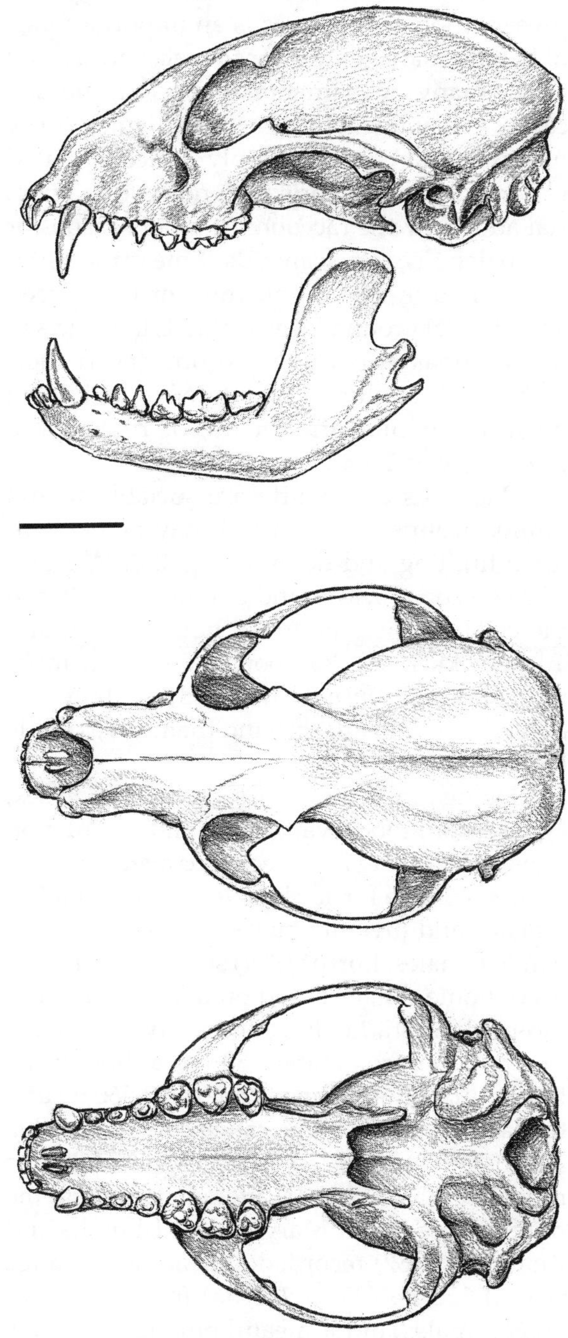

Figure 145. *Procyon lotor:* Left lateral view of skull, and dorsal and ventral view of skull. Scale bar = 20 mm.

erect, and somewhat pointed. The plantigrade feet have naked smooth soles and five very long digits, each of which possesses a nonretractile claw. The "hands" are well adapted for grasping and manipulating objects. Females possess six mammae. Adult raccoons are usually between 650 and 1,050 mm long, including a tail 190 to 300 mm long. Raccoons normally weigh between 4.5 and 9 kg, although some fat individuals have weighed as much as 25.4 and 28.3 kg (Wood, 1922; Scott, 1951). An 18 kg raccoon was killed near Fredericksburg in 1946 (Mosby, 1947). Raccoons stand 180 to 250 mm high at the shoulder, with being males somewhat larger than females.

The skull is broad, massive, and rounded with a broad rostrum and a broad, well-inflated braincase. Medium-sized auditory bullae are present. The zygomatic arches are widely flaring. Distinct postorbital processes and a sagittal crest are present (Figure 145).

Distribution. This species is found from Panama northward throughout Mexico and the United States to southern Canada.

Raccoons are among the most common and best known mammals and are found throughout Virginia (Figure 146). They are much more common in Tidewater Virginia, however, than in the western portion of the state. To increase the number of raccoons in western Virginia, in the 1940s the Commission of Game and Inland Fisheries purchased raccoons from other states and also livetrapped and moved them from eastern Virginia where they sometimes become too abundant.

Data on the wild fur catch in Virginia, including the raccoon, are presented in tables 2 and 3.

Habitat. Raccoons prefer moist areas and are found mainly in timbered swamps, river bottoms, along the banks of streams and lakes, and in the salt marshes along the coast. Forest, or at least groves of trees, are ordinarily a requirement. Barns, attics, and other buildings may be used when available.

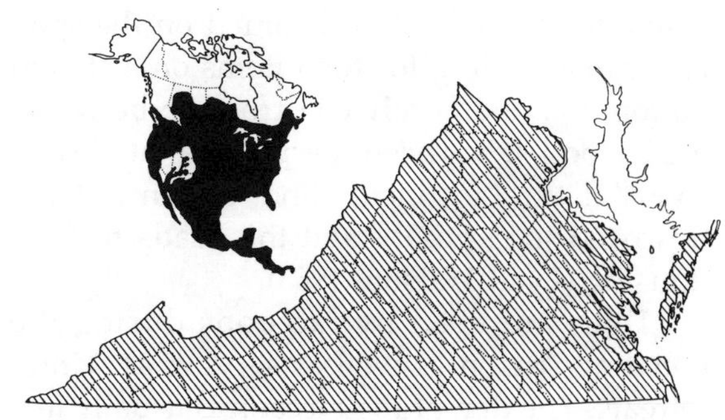

Figure 146. *Procyon lotor:* Range in Virginia and North America.

Habits. Raccoons are primarily nocturnal mammals, coming out of their dens shortly after dusk and remaining active until morning. Occasionally they may be observed during the daytime. Raccoons living in salt marshes are known to time their activity to the ebb and flow of the tides. Consequently, they are most active at low tide when crustaceans and mollusks are exposed and least active at high tide, almost without regard for the time of day. Although raccoons sleep for long periods during northern winters, they seldom den up or become inactive in Virginia except for short periods of several days during unusually cold and bitter weather. During such times, they will curl up and sleep a day or two, but as soon as the weather moderates, they will resume searching for food.

Raccoons swim well, but not far or often, preferring to wade in shallow water near shore. Although they are excellent climbers, often saving their lives by taking refuge in the trees, they spend most of their waking hours on the ground. They are able to descend trees either head-first or tail-first.

These mammals hear well, and their sense of sight is good, particularly in the dark. Their sense of smell is good but is not as well developed as their sense of touch, the latter being especially good in the forepaws and nose. Curiosity is a well-known behavioral trait, and raccoons tested in captivity have shown marked aptitudes for learning and problem solving.

The raccoon's habit of dousing its food in water before eating it is well known, hence its specific name, *lotor*, meaning "washer." Although captives often dip their food in water, this is by no means an invariable trait of wild raccoons. When they are feeding away from water, food is usually consumed on the spot. An animal feeling for food items on a stream bottom may be falsely construed to be washing its food. It has been speculated that the raccoons' natural instinct to find food in water is thwarted in captivity and this leads to food dousing (Lyall-Watson, 1963).

Dens are used by raccoons during the breeding season as well as serving as winter retreats. The den of the raccoon is usually in a hollow tree from 4.5 to 12 m above the ground, although dens may be made in fallen logs, old stumps, muskrat houses, deserted buildings, barn lofts, caves, and abandoned mines. The preservation of den trees is an important part of habitat management for the raccoon, as well as for many other mammal species. The den cavity is usually about 38 cm in diameter. The nest material consists simply of accumulated rotten wood and debris with no nesting material added by the raccoon. At other seasons or when den trees are scarce, daytime resting sites are located in ground burrows or in exposed situations at ground level. Animals living in salt marsh areas apparently do not desert their watery habitat during high tide but bed down on low flat platforms made of rushes and grasses (Ivey, 1948).

Raccoons apparently are sociable within family groups since several may be encountered hunting and denning together. A group of 23 raccoons was found denning together in the cellar of an abandoned house (Mech and Turkowski, 1966). Raccoons are not territorial in the normal sense of the word, but they will defend a certain area around themselves while feeding (Tevis, 1947).

Home range size varies depending on sex, age, season, food availability, and population density. Stuewer (1943) recorded average home ranges of 2.6 ha for adult males, 110 ha for adult females and juvenile males, and 45 ha for juvenile females. Lotze (1979) summarized studies of home ranges based on livetrapping. Radio-tracking studies have shown average home ranges of approximately 50 ha, although the largest male home range covered 2,560 ha and the largest female home range covered 806 ha. Sherfy (1980) recorded an average male home range of 285 ha and an average female home range of 165 ha in Maryland. Allsbrooks and Kennedy (1987) recorded a mean home range size of 172 ha (35 to 261 ha) for nine radio-tagged males and a mean home range of 118 ha (11 to 205 ha) for six adult females and one juvenile female in Tennessee.

That raccoons are capable of traveling long distances is shown by records of movements up to 265 km in length (Giles, 1943; Priewert, 1961; Lynch, 1967). Two ear-tagged raccoons that were released in southwest Virginia during the 1950s moved 12 and 33.8 km from their point of release. A third raccoon released in 1952 near Galax in Grayson County was captured in 1955 in Giles County, approximately 80 airline km from its release point (Anonymous, 1956e).

Several examples of high local populations densities have been recorded, including three to four per ha in Mississippi (Yeager, 1937), 42.5 per mi^2 in Illinois (Yeager and Rennels, 1943), and 100 taken from 42 ha in Missouri in 4.5 days in winter (Twichell and Dill, 1949). A mean density of 0.07 raccoons per 0.4 hectare or one raccoon per 5.9 ha has been reported in Virginia by Sonenshine and Winslow (1972).

Wood (1922) described the call of the raccoon as "a shrill tremulo cry, almost like a whistle, and on a still night (it) may be heard for a long distance." Although they growl in a deep voice when angry, their normal talk is a churring sound with many variations such as a rasping scream when suddenly and badly frightened, a loud purr to express pleasure, low repeated grunts that seem to indicate a warning to its offspring, and a hissing sound as a sort of a scolding cry.

Food. Raccoons are omnivorous and feed on a wide variety of plant and animal foods. The kind of food consumed is determined largely by availability. Wild fruits, berries, shellfish, crustaceans, fish, small mammals, reptiles, and birds are secured as opportunity offers.

A study of 520 raccoon stomachs and scats from Maryland revealed plant material representing 48 percent of the contents and animal material 52 percent (Llewellyn and Uhler, 1952). In summer, fall, and early winter plants provided the bulk of the diet. Chief plant foods included corn, wild grapes, wild black cherry, acorns, persimmon, pokeberries, and blackberries. Other plants were consumed sporadically or were prominent only for short seasons. The diet was practically devoid of plant materials during April and May. The animal portion of the diet was composed of over 100 species. The greatest volume of animal foods was taken in late winter and spring. Many animals depended largely on insects in late winter after most plant foods were depleted. In addition to insects, major animal foods consisted of crayfish, snails, amphibians, reptiles, fish, and rodents.

In another study in Maryland, plant material made up more than 80 percent of the dry weight of fall and winter food items, and approximately half of the spring and summer foods (Dunn, 1980). The predominant food item during fall seasons was corn. Animal material was important during the spring and summer, making up 31 and 51 percent of the total dry weight, respectively.

In Tennessee, persimmon, corn, insects, crayfish, pokeberry, and sugar hackberry were among the most important food items recorded (Tabatabai and Kennedy, 1988).

Raccoons readily capture fish from pools that become isolated because of receding water levels. Referring to some water holes near Lake Drummond in the Dismal Swamp in October, 1895, A. K. Fisher reported:

> *Judging from the tracks about these pools, as many as a dozen must have come every night to feed on the fish imprisoned therein. The heads of catfish, pike, eels, and perch were found in abundance under the bushes and along the edges where the raccoons had dropped them* (Goldman, 1950).

Wass (1972) noted that in the Chesapeake Bay region raccoons are the chief predators of young muskrats. A limited study of food habits of raccoons in southwestern Virginia in the 1950s revealed wild grapes, short-horned grasshoppers, huckleberries, acorns, beetles, and blackberries as the main food items (Kellner, 1954). Sonenshine and Winslow (1972) recorded beetles, blueberries, acorns, grass seeds, and corn from raccoons from two study areas in eastern Virginia. Raccoons have also been observed feeding on oysters and other bivalves.

Reproduction and Development. Mating usually takes place from mid-January to early March. Following a gestation of approximately 63 days, the single annual litter usually is born in April or May. Shaffer (1948) recorded litters born on April 19, May 2, and May 3 in Princess Anne County, Virginia, (now City of Virginia Beach). Litter sizes range from two to five. An examination of placental scars from 14 females revealed an average of 3.4 (range 3.3 to 3.7) in Virginia (McLaughlin, 1953). In a Maryland study, the breeding season extended from February to June with most births occurring in April. Mean litter size was 3.4 (Dunn, 1980). There is evidence that ovulation is not spontaneous but is induced by copulation (Llewellyn and Enders, 1954). Data on the growth rate of the raccoon fetus have been reported by Llewellyn (1953).

Bissonnette (1938) and Bissonnette and Csech (1937; 1939) have demonstrated that increasing day length is a factor determining the onset of breeding. It has also been suggested, however, that the precise timing of breeding may be modified by temperature immediately before the breeding season (Dorney, 1953; Sanderson, 1961).

The early development of young raccoons has been described by Hamilton (1936c) and Montgomery (1968). Newborn animals have blackish skin and are well covered with yellowish-gray fur. Indistinct darker areas show where the facial mask and tail rings will appear prominently later. Newborn raccoons normally weigh between 57 and 85 g. The blackish facial mask, made up of sparsely haired pigmented skin, is present at birth. It is fully haired when the young are about two weeks old. Similarly, pigmented skin marks the ultimate position of tail rings in the newborn animals. The tail rings are fully haired at three to four weeks. The eyes open when the young raccoons are between 18 and 23 days of age. The first milk teeth erupt at about one month, and permanent dentition is complete by 3.5 months (Montgomery, 1964). When 40 days old, they can eat some solid food, although weaning is not completed until the young are between three and four months old (Montgomery, 1969).

Male raccoons are polygamous and do not aid in caring for the young. The mother, however, is a devoted parent. She will move the young if the den is disturbed or if they outgrow it. Young being raised in den trees may be moved when they become quite active at seven to nine months of age. Like the female black bear, the mother raccoon may send her youngsters up a tree when danger threatens. She then relies on cleverness rather than speed in eluding the would-be attacker, and only when she knows no one is following her does she return to recover her family. The mother and young remain together into the late fall and often well into winter. The young raccoons gradually lose the instinct to follow, and ultimately they disperse widely, usually traveling and denning singly. Male raccoons attain sexual maturity at about 15 months of age, and both sexes usually attain adult weights at 15 months. Both males and females may either breed in their first year or wait until their second year.

Longevity. Haugen (1954) recorded a female raccoon that was shot 12 years and one month after it had been captured as a juvenile. The probable age of this animal was 12 years, 7 months. It was shot within 0.8 km of its original point of capture. A female raccoon fitted with a radio transmitter over 10 years earlier was trapped 2.5 km from where it was originally captured. Its estimated age was 11 years and 7 months (Cowan, 1985). Based on dental annuli Johnson (1970) and Lotze and Anderson (1979) estimated that some raccoons may live for 13 to 16 years in the wild. Palmer (1954) reported that zoo captives had lived 14 years. Jones (1982) reported a captive animal still living after 20 years and 7 months. While these examples reflect maximum longevity, the average life span of a raccoon in a stable population has been computed to be between 1.8 years (Sanderson, 1951; Dunn, 1980) and 3.1 years (Johnson, 1970).

Parasites and Disease. In the southeastern states, raccoons are known to carry at least 13 pathogens known to cause disease among humans (Bigler et al., 1975). These include canine distemper, rabies, leptospirosis, Chaga's disease, and tularemia. Meningitis and distemper have been recorded in Virginia (Virginia Wildlife Investigations Annual Report 1983–1984, pp. 99, 101, 108, 152). Jones et al. (1978a) recorded tularemia infections in four raccoons from Fort Pickett. In Virginia, the following parasites have been reported by Holloway (1956b; 1957a); Harkema and Miller (1964); Sonenshine, Lamb, and Anastos (1965); Sonenshine, Atwood, and Lamb (1966); Sonenshine and Levy (1971); Sonenshine and Stout (1971); Jacobson et al. (1976); Jones et al. (1978b); Garrett and Sonenshine (1979); Schaffer et al. (1981); Virginia Wildlife Investigations Annual Report 1983–1984, p. 107 and 1985–1986, p. 97; Sonenshine and Turner (1988); Snyder et al. (1989b); Hamir et al. (1993); and Eckerlin (1994): **Bacteria** *(Edwardsiella tarda)*; **Acanthocephala** (spiny-headed worms) *(Centrorhynchus* sp., *Macracanthorhynchus ingens)*; **Nematoda** (roundworms) *(Anthrocephalus lotoris, Baylisascaris procyonis, Capillaria aerophila, Capillaria plica, Capillaria procyonis, Capillaria putorii, Crenosoma goblei, Dracunculus insignis, Gnathostoma procyonis, Molineus barbatus, Physaloptera rara, Placoconus lotoris, Sellacotyle mustelae, Unci-*

naria stenocephala); **Trematoda** (flukes) *Apophallus venustus, Eurytrema procyonis, Parametorchis complexus, Phagicola angrense, Pharyngostomoides procyonis);* **Cestoda** (flukes) *(Atriotaenia procyonis, Mesocestoides variabilis);* and **Acarina** (ticks) *Amblyomma americanum, Dermacentor variabilis, Ixodes cookei, Ixodes dentatus, Ixodes texanus).*

In addition to the above, Schaffer et al. (1981) reported on a group of 20 raccoons from Hawkins and Union counties, Tennessee and Wise County, Virginia. The trematodes *Brachylaima virginianum, Metagonomoides oregonensis,* and *Metorchis conjunctus,* were recorded from this group.

Raccoons are an important vector of the rabies virus in the United States (Table 4). Beginning in 1990 and continuing to the present, raccoons have been the predominant species reported rabid in the United States (Krebs et al., 1995). During the period 1951–1980 in Virginia, only 29 confirmed cases of rabies were recorded in raccoons — an average of one case per year. Beginning in 1981, however, confirmed cases of rabies in raccoons have comprised no less than 56 percent of the total cases in both wild and domestic mammals (tables 5 and 6). Between 1981 and 1992, rabid raccoons comprised between 56 and 87 percent of the total cases (Torrence et al., 1992). The epidemic worked its way from Maryland into upper Accomack County on Virginia's Eastern Shore in 1994, and by 1996 the leading edge had moved south into Northampton County. The most likely cause of this epizootic of raccoon rabies is believed to be the release of infected raccoons transported from areas of major rabies outbreaks elsewhere in the southeastern United States (Smith et al., 1984; Bruggemann, 1992).

Pelage Variations. A dark-eyed, buff-colored raccoon was taken in Buckingham County, Virginia, in 1946 (Mosby, 1947). An erythristic individual in which the black facial mask, postauricular spots, dark bands on the tail, and dark tips of the hairs were light yellowish-brown was reported from Nelson County, by Goldman (1950). Albino raccoons were reported from Princess Anne County, (now City of Virginia Beach) by Shaffer (1948). The Pulaski County Sportsmen's Club released a light yellow raccoon with no mask and barely discernible rings on its tail (Anonymous, 1952). Pelage development in young raccoons has been discussed by Montgomery (1968).

Predation. Young raccoons have numerous enemies, including foxes, bobcats, hawks, owls, and snakes. Man and his dogs, however, are the raccoon's principal enemies.

Geographic Variation. *Procyon lotor lotor* (Linnaeus) is the subspecies that inhabits the entire state. *Procyon lotor maritimus* Dozier, which has been recorded from Saxis Island in Chesapeake Bay, has been considered a synonym of *Procyon lotor lotor* by Paradiso (1969) and Lotze and Anderson (1979).

Location of Specimens. AMNH, BCV, CM, DMNH, EHC, GMU, LFCC, LU, MCZ, NCSM, NVCC, ODU, SNP, SUVM, UMMZ, USNM, VCU, VHCC, VLM, VPISU, VPI-W.

Mustelids (Family Mustelidae)

The family Mustelidae contains a large, varied group of predatory mammals including the weasels, mink, ferrets, martens, fishers, wolverines, badgers, and otters. They range in size from the 45 g least weasel *(Mustela nivalis)* to the 30 kg sea otter *(Enhydra).* Members of this family may be terrestrial, fossorial, or semiaquatic. They have five well-clawed toes on each foot, with the feet plantigrade, semiplantigrade, or digitigrade. The limbs are short. Well-developed, paired anal scent glands are usually present. The skull generally has an elongate, flattened braincase and a short rostrum. All mustelids possess three incisors and one canine above and below. However, there is much variation in the molariform teeth. Carnassial teeth are well developed in most species, a reflection of their basically carnivorous diet. Delayed implantation of the embryo occurs in many species.

Mustelids occur throughout the world except for Australia, Madagascar, the Antarctic, and most oceanic islands. Seven genera of mustelids occur in the United States with three — *Martes* (fisher), *Mustela* (weasels and mink), and *Lontra* (river otter) — having been or currently being found in Virginia. Throughout history these animals have been valued for their fur.

Key to Species of Mustelidae

1a Skull flattened and broad; molariform teeth 5/5; feet broad and webbed
.... *Lontra (Lutra) canadensis*

1b Molariform teeth not 5/5; feet not broad and webbed
.... 2

2a Molariform teeth 5/6; last upper molar not dumbbell-shaped; total teeth 38; hind foot at least 75 mm long
.... *Martes pennanti*

2b Molariform teeth 4/5; last upper molar dumbbell-shaped; total teeth 34; hind foot less than 75 mm long
.... 3

3a Total length less than 175 mm; tail 25 percent or less of body length
.... *Mustela nivalis*

3b Total length more than 175 mm; tail more than 25 percent of body length
.... 4

4a Total length of skull less than 55 mm; auditory bullae longer than upper cheek tooth row; total length 400 mm or less; underparts buff or yellowish-white; tip of tail black; no white patch on chin or throat
.... *Mustela frenata*

4b Total length of skull more than 55 mm; auditory bullae about as long as upper cheek tooth row; total length more than 400 mm; underparts brown; tip of tail not black; white patch usually present on chin and throat
.... *Mustela vison*

Genus *Martes*

Dentition: 3/3, 1/1, 4/4, 1/2 = 38

Fisher [Extirpated; reintroduced]
Martes pennanti (Erxleben)

Description. The fisher (Plate 73) is a large weasel-like mustelid with low, rounded ears and bushy, tapering tail. The pelage is dark brown to nearly black. White-tipped hairs give the animal a frosted appearance. Many early accounts refer to this mammal as "black fox." Adult fishers are between 810 and 1,040 mm in total length, including a 330 to 400 mm tail. Females normally weigh between 1.3 and 3.2 kg, while males weigh between 2.7 and 5.4 kg.

Distribution. This furbearer is presently found across Canada and south into the New England states and New York. In the western United States it occurs south through western Montana and Idaho to Wyoming and south through the Cascade-Sierra Nevada chain to central California.

The former range of this species in the eastern United States extended south to Tennessee, North Carolina, Georgia, and northeastern Alabama. Allen (1876a) noted:

> *that early records show that both the fisher* (Mustela Pennanti) *and the marten* (Mustela Americana) *were common inhabitants of not only the whole of New England, but also of the Atlantic States generally as far southward as Virginia (excepting possibly a narrow belt along the seaboard), and even farther southward along the Alleghanies.*

Holder (1885) noted that it occurred "southwards, occasionally, on the mountains of Virginia."

The fisher has been classified as an endangered species in Virginia (Handley, 1979b; 1991). Handley (1979b) noted that formerly fishers were probably widespread in the mountains. He records an observation by Audubon and Bachman (1849) on Peters Mountain above Gray Sulphur Springs in Giles County, Virginia, and descriptions of what probably were fishers by residents of Middle Mountain in northwest Highland County, Virginia, before 1890. No other observations of fishers in Virginia were made until 1972 when Maurice Brooks reported one trapped on Allegheny Mountain in Highland County.

Since 1972 there have been only four other sightings in Virginia: near Harrisonburg in Rockingham County, in 1978; about 65 km northeast of Harrisonburg near Sperryville in Rappahannock County, in late November, 1981; on Allegheny Mountain in Highland County, in May, 1989; and in the Blue Hole area of Rockingham County, in December, 1989 (Handley, 1991). Handley attributes these most recent observations as stemming from introductions made in West Virginia in 1969. He noted that the West Virginia Department of Natural Resources introduced 15 fishers on

Canaan Mountain in Tucker County and eight at Cranberry Glades in Pocahontas County. Between 1969 and 1978, a total of 18 fishers had been taken in West Virginia and one in Maryland (Cottrell, 1978). The fishers are reproducing in West Virginia and the restocking appears to be successful. Any fishers presently in Virginia are probably wanderers from the West Virginia population.

Habitat. The fisher inhabits large, heavily wooded areas consisting of spruce, fir, or mixed hardwood trees. It also inhabits timbered northern bogs and swamps.

Habits. Fishers may be active at any hour of the day or night and during all seasons. They climb well and although they spend a considerable amount of time foraging and resting in trees, their activity is predominantly terrestrial (Powell, 1981). They are solitary animals except during the breeding season.

Dens are located primarily in hollow trees and in log piles. Occasionally, fishers will occupy crevices and spaces beneath large rocks and boulders. They do not burrow. Fishers can swim if necessary, but despite their name, they do not catch fish.

Fishers wander widely and may have a home range covering 15 to 35 km^2 (Powell, 1981).

Food. Squirrels, chipmunks, mice, woodchucks, rabbits, hares, and porcupines comprise the main food of fishers. Fruits and nuts may be eaten when available.

Reproduction and Development. Breeding usually occurs in early spring a few days after parturition. Following a gestation of approximately 352 days, a litter of one to five (average three) young are born. Within a week the female has mated again. The extremely long gestation is accounted for by the fact that fishers experience delayed implantation.

The eyes of young fishers open at about seven weeks of age. They remain in the den for about three months, after which they travel with the female until fall when the family breaks up.

Longevity. Fishers have lived 10 years in the wild and over 10 years in captivity (Powell, 1981).

Geographic Variation. The subspecies occurring in Virginia is *Martes pennanti pennanti* (Erxleben).

Location of Specimens. No specimens from Virginia are known to exist in collections.

American Marten [Not confirmed]
Martes americana (Turton)

Description. The marten is a slender-bodied arboreal weasel approximately the size of a small house cat. It is, however, longer and has a sharply pointed face. The dorsal coloration ranges from dark brown to pale buff, while the underparts are paler. A distinctive orange or yellow patch is present on the throat and chest. The fur is long and lustrous. The eyes and ears are relatively large, and the tail is bushy. Females have eight mammae. Adult martens are between 450 and 680 mm long including a tail that is about 150 mm long. They weigh 300 to 1,300 g.

Distribution. In 1585 Hariot noted:

> *We hope also of Marterne furres, and make no doubt by the relation of the people, but that in some places of the countrey there are store, although there were but two skinnes that came to our hand* (Tarbox, 1884).

The editor stated in a footnote that:

> *there were otters,* Lutra Canadensis, *and martens,* Mustela Americana, *in North Carolina; but these animals are far more abundant in colder regions, in the northern portions of America.*

Numerous authors have since listed the marten as having occurred south in the mountains to Virginia (Allen, 1876a; Anthony, 1928; Bailey, 1946; Brown, 1952; and others). Bailey (1946) noted that in the "Account Showing of the Quantity of Skins and Furs Imported Annually into the Kingdom from Virginia from Christmas 1698 to Christmas 1715," both martens and fishers were listed. Audubon and Bachman (1851–1854) stated that "we have sought for it in vain on the mountains of Virginia where notwithstanding, we think a straggler will occasionally make its appearance." Scharf (1882) said that marten occurred in western Maryland. Handley and Patton (1947) noted that although there is no record of any specific occurrence south of Pennsylvania, the marten might have occurred in the spruce forests that formerly covered eastern West Virginia and extended into the Virginia mountains. Mansueti (1950) stated that the marten had been completely extirpated from Maryland for at least 70 years and that its distribution was probably not widespread. Hagmeier (1957) has reviewed the distribution of the marten in North America.

Location of Specimens. No specimens from Virginia are known to exist.

Genus *Mustela*

Dentition: 3/3, 1/1, 3/3, 1/2 = 34

Least Weasel
Mustela nivalis Linnaeus

Description. The least weasel (Plate 74) has the distinction of being Virginia's smallest carnivore. These mammals are dark brown above and white on the chin, throat, chest, and belly. The short, totally brown tail comprises 25 percent or less of the body length and lacks a black tip. Females possess eight mammae. Adults are usually between 165 and 220 mm long, including a tail 25 to 45 mm long. Adults normally average about 45 g but may weigh between 25 and 65 g.

The skull (total length less than 32mm) is elongated with a smoothly rounded braincase. The frontal region is flat, and the rostrum is short. Postorbital processes and a weakly-developed sagittal crest are present. Zygomatic arches are slender, weak and moderately arched. Auditory bullae are large and flattened (Figure 147).

Distribution. The least weasel is primarily a northern species. It is found throughout most of Alaska and Canada south to British Columbia, Montana, Oklahoma, Kansas, Illinois, Indiana, Kentucky, and Pennsylvania and south in the Appalachian Mountains to Tennessee and North Carolina. It has been classified as status undetermined in Virginia (Handley, 1979b; 1991).

Handley (1991) recorded 13 specimens from Virginia. All were from the upper Piedmont and mountain counties — Montgomery, Bath, Giles, Roanoke, Augusta, Rockingham, Shenandoah, Fauquier, and Appomattox. Elevations range from 150 to 1,165 m (Figure 148). Hensley (personal communication, November, 1992) believes this species may be more abundant than records indicate since approximately 30 individuals have been recorded on or near the Bridgewater College campus in Rockingham County, Virginia during the past 25 years. McConnell (personal communication, 1995) recorded an individual from Yuma in Scott County in 1991.

Habitat. These weasels inhabit a variety of sites including old fields, hedgerows, and forested areas.

Habits. Least weasels are mainly active at night. Average home range size is about 0.8 hectare. Nests are usually underground and are lined with mouse fur. Occasionally nests may be found in holes in the walls of buildings and under corn shocks (Handley, 1979b).

The senses of smell, sight, and hearing are well developed. The range of hearing in the least weasel runs from less than 1 Khz to at least 61 Khz. It is unequalled among mammals in its sensitivity to low threshold sounds (Heffner and Heffner, 1985).

Vocalizations of this species have been analyzed by Huff and Price (1968) and Heidt and Huff (1970). Four basic vocalization have been

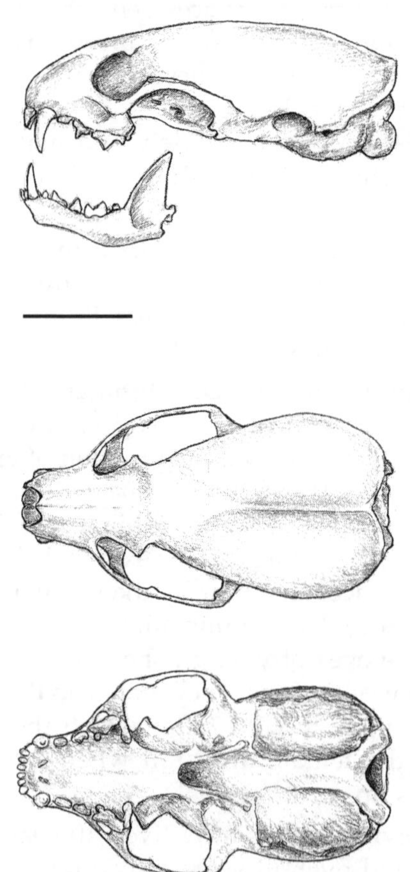

Figure 147. *Mustela nivalis:* Left lateral view of skull, and dorsal and ventral view of skull. Scale bar = 10 mm.

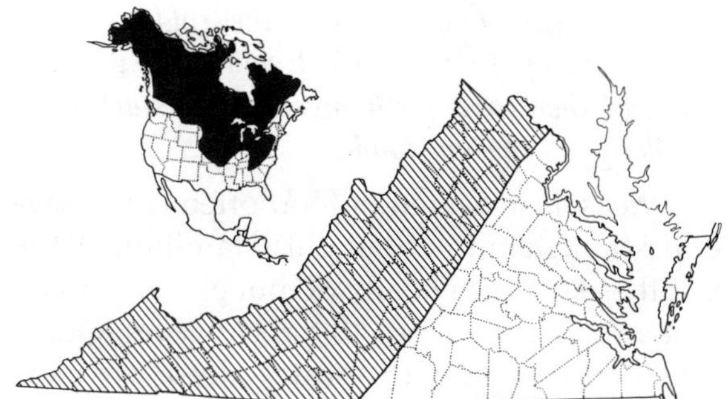

Figure 148. *Mustela nivalis:* Range in Virginia and North America.

described in adults — a chirp, hiss, trill, and squeal. At birth, newborn least weasels make high-pitched, short-bursted squeaking sounds. At the time the eyes open, the squeak is replaced by a chirp.

Food. These mammals are voracious feeders. Prey consists primarily of mice (*Microtus,* in particular), shrews, and insects. Prey species are usually killed by biting through the base of the skull. Excess food may be stored near its nest.

Reproduction and Development. The release of ova is induced by copulation (King, 1989). Litters of three to six young may be born during any month of the year following a gestation of 34 to 36 days. A female containing five embryos was recorded in Montgomery County, Virginia, on December 20 (VPI-W). Least weasels do not experience delayed implantation.

At four days of age young weasels are covered with fine white hair. The canines erupt at about 14 days, and the first brown hairs appear on the dorsum between the second and third week. By the fourth week, the dorsum is completely brown and the young are eating solid food. The eyes open between 26 and 29 days (Heidt et al., 1968). Young weasels are weaned when approximately six to seven weeks old.

Longevity. The record for a captive animal is 7 years, 9 months, and 16 days (Flower, 1931). There are no records of longevity in wild least weasels.

Predation. Snakes, owls, and house cats may prey upon least weasels. Handley (1949) recovered the skull and skeletal remains of a least weasel from a barn owl pellet taken near Blacksburg in Montgomery County, Virginia.

Geographic Variation. The subspecies in Virginia is *Mustela nivalis rixosa* Bangs.

Location of Specimens. BCV, LFCC, NVCC, SNP, USNM, VPISU, VPI-W.

Long-Tailed Weasel
Mustela frenata Lichtenstein

Description. The long-tailed weasel (Plate 75) is a fairly large weasel, brownish above and buff or yellowish-white below. The summer pelage is markedly darker brown than the buff-brown winter pelage. The tail has a distinct black tip. Females possess eight mammae. Adult long-tailed weasels in the eastern United States may attain a total length of 330 to 455 mm, including a tail 100 to 150 mm long. Adults normally weigh between 85 and 280 g. Males are considerably larger than females.

The skull is somewhat elongate and flattened with an evident sagittal crest and slender, weak zygomatic arches. The bony palate extends posteriorly beyond the molars. The last molar is dumbbell-shaped. Flattened, elongate auditory bullae are present (Figure 149).

Distribution. This species is found from southern Canada south through all of the United States, except the Sonoran Desert, and southward to northern Bolivia in South America. The long-tailed weasel is found throughout Virginia (Figure 150).

Data on the wild fur catch in Virginia, including weasels, are presented in tables 2 and 3.

Habitat. This weasel inhabits farmland as well as woodlands and swamps. Hedgerows and brushy field borders provide good habitat. Areas in the vicinity of water seem to be preferred.

Habits. Weasels are solitary. They are intensely active and alert at all seasons and may be seen at any hour. They are probably most active at night. Most of their time is spent on the ground, although they are able to climb trees.

Weasels are very quick, and their movements are difficult to follow. While they are running, the back is strongly arched at each bound and the tail is held straight out behind or at an angle. They have good powers of smell, sight, and hearing, and they are tireless hunters. A powerful and disagreeable musky odor is carried by all weasels and is liberated by excitement. To some persons it is more offensive

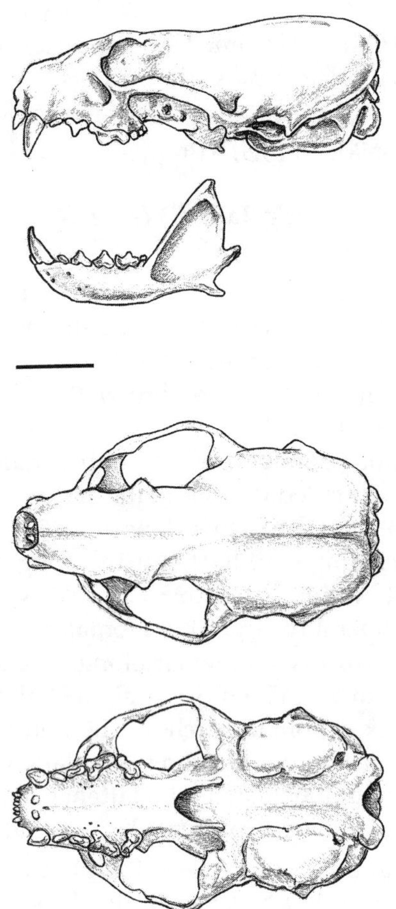

Figure 149. *Mustela frenata:* Left lateral view of skull, and dorsal and ventral view of skull. Scale bar = 10 mm.

than the musk of the skunk.

Weasels are very curious. The playfulness of a captive individual has been described by Moore (1945):

> *When its playground widened to include my table top, many more playthings became available. It pushed ink bottles about, rolled vials back and forth, wrestled with an electric extension cord, essayed to climb the goose-necked table lamp, jumped in and out of its cage, and wrestled with the large feet indecorously propped on the table. From one thing to another it dashed pausing and posing charmingly at the end of each short rush, a superb picture of grace and alertness. Attracted by my hand on the table the weasel nipped it gently and ran away, and then presently returned to sniff and nip and run again. This continued with the nip growing harder each time, eventually provoking a shout and a vigorous cuff which always missed the quick rascal. Lurking furtively behind objects at the far side of the table until the scolding tone went out of the voice which addressed it, the weasel then came forth once more to start another game of some kind.*

Weasels in search of food often cover several kilometers in one night (Hamilton 1943), but these travels usually do not encompass an area of more than 5 to 10 ha. However, Quick (1944) noted that in winter these weasels ranged over an area of 164 ha. They may travel up to about 5.6 km in a single night (Polderboer et al., 1941; Quick, 1944). DeVan (1982) recorded home ranges of 6 to 24 ha on Kentucky farmland for several radio-tagged adult males. The longest recorded movement of a weasel is of a tagged individual that moved 35 km in seven months (Burns, 1964).

Dens may be under the roots of a tree, in a hollow stump, in unused burrows of other animals, in sawmill slab piles, in crevices, in cliffs or rock piles, or occasionally in barns or other buildings. The nest consists of grasses, skins and fur of prey species, remnants of partially eaten mice and shrews, and droppings. Layers of grass placed over such debris at intervals gives the nest a layered appearance (Polderboer et al., 1941).

Food. Jackson (1961) stated that the long-tailed weasel was probably the most relentless, persistent, fearless, and rapacious of carnivores in the pursuit of its prey. Long-tailed weasels feed primarily on mice, rats, shrews, and moles, but they will also attack larger mammals such as squirrels and rabbits, and they eat a few birds, snakes, lizards, insects, and earthworms. Hamilton (1933) showed that more than 96 percent of the fall and winter foods consisted of small mammals, mainly mice. Barbour (1951a) recorded the remains of a smoky shrew *(Sorex*

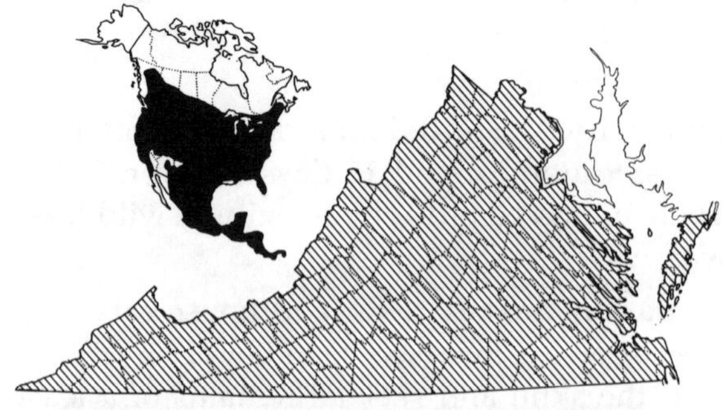

Figure 150. *Mustela frenata:* Range in Virginia and North America.

fumeus) in the stomach of one weasel and the remains of a nestling passerine bird in a weasel from Harland County, Kentucky. This species has also been known to feed on the big brown bat (Mumford, 1969).

The weasel usually bites the prey at the base of the skull, and then holds on firmly until the struggle is nearly over. Weasels often kill more than they can eat, storing the excess for future use. Weasels do not "suck the blood" of their victims, although they are known to lick the blood that comes from the wound. Weasels occasionally kill poultry, but their competence in controlling rats and mice makes them a valuable asset.

Reproduction and Development. Like the bear, long-tailed weasels have a prolonged gestation. The embryos do not become implanted in the wall of the uterus for many months. Thus, whereas breeding normally occurs in July or August, the young are not born until April or early May of the following year. The embryos are implanted only 21 to 28 days before the young are born (Wright, 1948). The average gestation is 279 days, although it may range from 205 to 337 days. Ovulation is induced by copulation (King, 1989).

There is a single annual litter, numbering from four to nine young born in a nest of fur, feathers, bones, and other remains of prey within the den. Sometimes leaves and dry grasses also included in the nesting material. The development of young long-tailed weasels has been described by Hamilton (1933). Newborn are blind and nearly naked except for some fine white hairs on the upper part of their body. They weigh about 3 g. At about three weeks, the canine and carnassial teeth have appeared and the young can eat small pieces of meat. The eyes open between 35 and 37 days, and weaning occurs at five to six weeks of age. The young are able to hunt by the time they are seven to eight weeks of age and are fully grown at 10 weeks. Both parents assist in caring for and bring food to the young.

Female long-tailed weasels may mate when only three to four months old. Males do not breed until their second summer (Wright, 1947).

Longevity. Some marked long-tailed weasels lived on a Colorado study area for up to three years (Svendsen, 1982). Captive individuals have lived at least five years (Palmer, 1954).

Pelage. Throughout a portion of its range, the long-tailed weasel undergoes a very interesting pelage change. From about the northern half of the United States northward, this animal changes in winter to a white or light brown coat except for its black tail tip. From southern Vermont to Maryland, west to northern Arizona, central California, and north into British Columbia some individuals turn white. South of this zone none of the weasels turn white in winter (Hamilton, 1933; Goodwin, 1935; Bissonnette and Bailey, 1944).

Parasites. The nematode *Trichinella spiralis* has been reported in this species from Mountain Lake in Giles County, Virginia (Solomon and Warner, 1969).

Predation. Weasels have numerous enemies, including snakes, hawks, owls, foxes, cats, and humans.

Geographic Variation. The subspecies in Virginia is *Mustela frenata frenata* Lichtenstein.

Location of Specimens. BCV, DMNH, GMU, LFCC, NVCC, SNP, UCM, UMMZ, USNM, VPISU, VPI-W.

Mink
Mustela vison Schreber

Description. The mink (Plate 76) is a large, almost uniformly dark brown, short-legged weasel. The underparts are only slightly paler than the back. Long, glistening guard hairs partially conceal the soft underfur. A white patch is usually present on the chin and may extend to the throat and chest. The somewhat bushy tail is less than half the length of the body. Males are considerably larger and heavier than females. Females possess eight mammae. Strong anal scent glands are present. Five toes are present on each foot and the hind feet may be slightly webbed. Adult mink are between 530 and 660 mm in total length, including a tail 175 to 225 mm long. They normally weigh between 0.5 and 1.4 kg.

The somewhat flattened skull has flattened, elongate auditory bullae. The rostrum is short and broad. The bony palate extends posteriorly beyond the last molars. The last molar in the upper jaw is dumbbell-shaped and is smaller than the tooth immediately anterior to it (Figure 151).

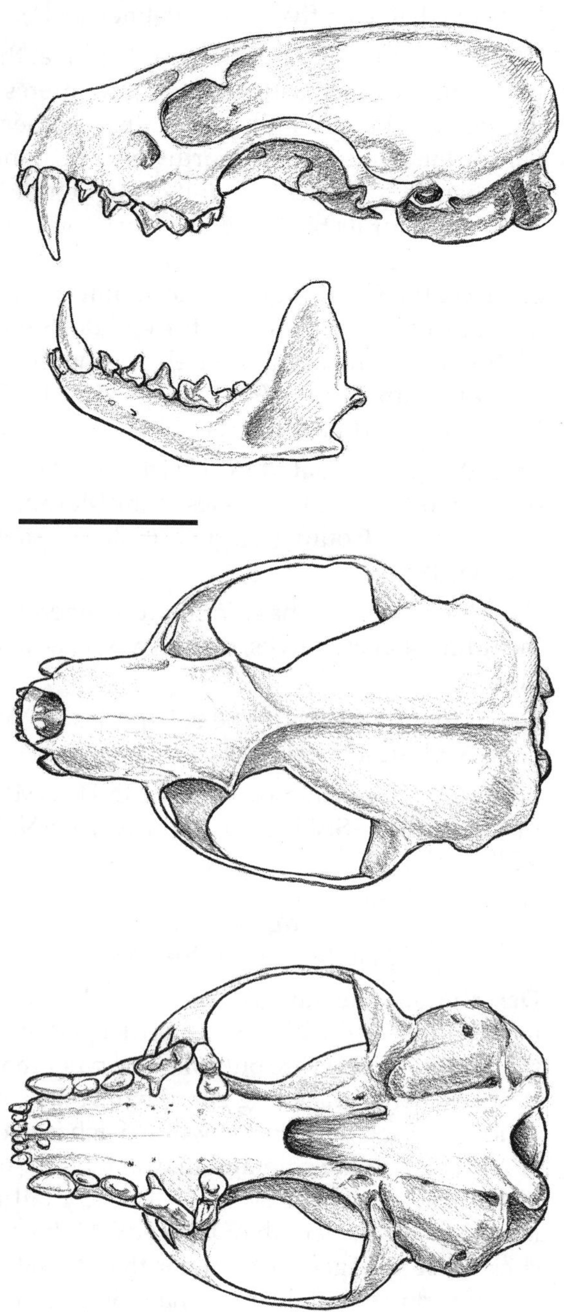

Figure 151. *Mustela vison:* Left lateral view of skull, and dorsal and ventral view of skull. Scale bar = 20 mm.

Distribution. Mink occur throughout Alaska and most of Canada, south throughout the eastern half of the United States to southern Florida and the Gulf Coast. They extend southward in the western United States to northern New Mexico, northern Nevada, and central California.

Mink are found throughout Virginia, ranging in abundance from scarce to relatively common (Figure 152). Shomon (1954) noted that it was present in almost every county but was most abundant in the Coastal Plain. Wass (1972) noted, however, that mink were scarce in all of the counties in the lower Chesapeake Bay region.

Data on the mink fur catch in Virginia are presented in tables 2 and 3.

Habitat. Mink are found mainly along the banks of streams, rivers, ponds, and lakes and in swamps and marshes. Forested, log-strewn, or brushy areas are preferred.

Habits. Mink are mainly nocturnal, semiaquatic mammals and seem to be most active around dawn and dusk. They are excellent swimmers and divers. Although they spend much time in the water, mink also travel much on land and on rare occasions climb small trees. Mink are active all year. They are normally solitary, except for family groups of mother and young.

The sense of smell is exceptionally well developed, while the senses of hearing and sight are moderately developed. Mink can hear ultrasound within frequencies emitted by potential rodent prey (Powell and Zielinski, 1989).

Males may range several kilometers along a stream. Marshall (1936) noted that females usually have a home range of 8 ha or less, while the male home range is much larger. Females normally confine their activities to 12 or 16 ha, while males may range over as much as 33 ha (Jackson, 1961). Jackson also noted that when food is scarce, the mink may travel as far as 24 to 29 km in one night. Hamilton (1943) noted that although the mink may wander extensively, it returns "with marked regularity to the various parts of its range."

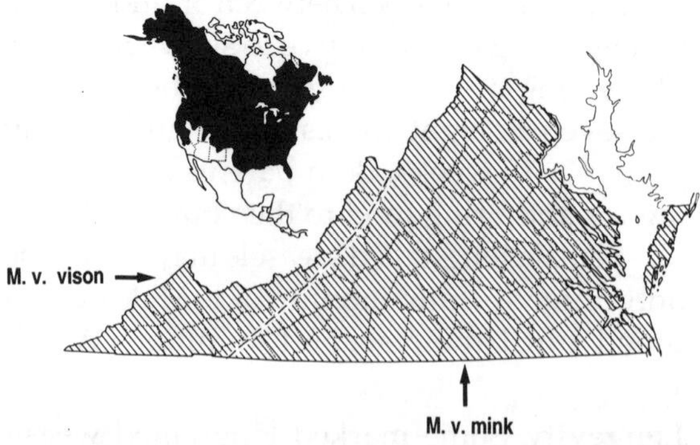

Figure 152. *Mustela vison:* Range in Virginia and North America.

The mink may dig its own burrow, or it may appropriate one made by some other animal such as a muskrat or rabbit. Dens may also be located under logs or debris, in rocks, or in muskrat houses.

When excited, mink discharge a powerful, acrid musk from the paired anal scent glands. Anthony (1928) paid tribute to the personality of a mink when he stated: "A trapped Mink is the triple distilled essence of fury and red-eyed rage."

Food. Mink feed primarily on mice, muskrats, rabbits, birds, frogs, fish, and crayfish. A male taken in Allegheny County, Virginia, in July had crayfish in its stomach. They are able to catch swimming fish. Two mink in Kentucky had been eating bats that were thought to have fallen from the ceiling of a cave (Goodpaster and Hoffmeister, 1950). Foods may be stored for future use. One den revealed the presence of 13 freshly killed muskrats, two mallard ducks, and one coot (Yeager, 1943).

The most extensive studies of the food habits of this species have been in the northern states (Dearborn, 1932; Hamilton, 1936a, 1940c, 1959; Sealander, 1943; Guilday, 1949; Grimm and Roberts, 1950; and Korschgen, 1958). A great variety of animal foods was eaten including field mice, muskrats, short-tailed shrews, cottontail rabbits, birds, snakes, frogs, salamanders, minnows, crayfish, and insects.

The only detailed food habits study in the South was by Wilson (1954a), who recorded the following percentages of frequency of foods from 335 stomachs and intestines from the coastal marshes of northeastern North Carolina: fish, 61 percent; mammals, 34 percent; birds, 18 percent; arthropods, 30 percent; amphibians, 13 percent; and reptiles, 5 percent.

Reproduction and Development. In northern areas, breeding normally occurs during February and March. Ovulation is induced by copulation. The single annual litter is produced in April or May after an average gestation of approximately 51 days (range 40 to 75 days) because of delayed implantation. Implantation occurs about 30 days before birth (Enders, 1952; Enders and Enders, 1963). Development of mink embryos has been described by Kissen and Price (1962). Litters may contain from three to 10 young, although the average is about four or five per litter. The young are born in a nest of feathers, fur, bones, grass, and plant fibers located in the den.

Limited data from these southeastern United States suggest a similar breeding season. In North Carolina, a female with six embryos and a female with three young were recorded on March 6 and May 17, respectively (Brimley, 1923). Young mink have been recorded in the Great Smoky Mountains National Park region of Tennessee and North Carolina in May, June, and July (Linzey and Linzey, 1968; Linzey, 1995a).

Newborn young have their eyes and ears sealed and are covered with fine, silvery-white hair (Svihla, 1931). Within two weeks, pale reddish-gray hair replaces the white hair. The teeth begin erupting between 16 and 21 days. The eyes open at about 37 days. Weaning is at about five weeks, and the young leave the den when six to eight weeks old. The young mink remain with the female until late summer or fall, at which time they disperse. Although the male may mate with several females, he usually stays with the last one and assists in caring for the young. Both males and females are capable of breeding during the breeding season following their birth.

A Maryland study found mean liver residues of polychlorinated biphenyls (PCBs) of 1.4 ppm for females and 1.5 ppm for males (O'Shea et al., 1981; Askins, 1982). These concentrations are comparable to those of experimental female ranch mink that showed reproductive failure. Other organochlorine compounds including DDT, DDE, dieldrin, oxychlordane, *trans*-Nonachlor, and heptachlor epoxide were present in low concentrations.

Mink in Virginia show little evidence of a major accumulation of heavy metals such as lead, cadmium, zinc, and copper (Ogle et al., 1985). Some metals such as cadmium are known to increase with age and significant concentrations were found in this study in which the majority of the animals were young of the year.

Longevity. Captive ranch mink have lived 10 years (Palmer, 1954), although the life span in the wild is probably closer to three or four years.

Pelage Variations. The process of molting in adult mink has been described by Bassett and Llewellyn (1949).

Parasites. The tick *Ixodes cookei* has been recorded from this species in Virginia by Sonenshine, Lamb, and Anastos (1965). Rabies has been confirmed in one animal from Fairfax County (Table 6).

Predation. Mink have few enemies other than humans and their traps. Occasionally, one may be attacked by a fox, bobcat, or great horned owl.

Geographic Variation. The subspecies occurring in Virginia is *Mustela vison vison* Schreber.

Other Currently Recognized Subspecies. *Mustela vison mink* Peale and Palisot de Beavois.

Location of Specimens. BCV, CM, CSULB, DMNH, GMU, LFCC, LU, SNP, SUVM, UMMZ, USNM, VHCC, VPISU, VPI-W.

Genus *Lontra (Lutra)*

Dentition: 3/3, 1/1, 4/3, 1/2 = 36

Northern River Otter
Lontra (Lutra) canadensis (Schreber)

Description. The northern river otter (Plate 77) is a lithe, long-bodied, short-legged mammal with a muscular body and a broad, flat head. The snout is broad and rounded, the ears are small, and the feet are webbed. Locomotion is digitigrade. A stout, tapering, muscular tail serves the otter as a rudder. The short, dense fur is brownish above and paler below when dry but appears to be almost black when wet. The chin and throat are grayish-white. The sexes are similar. Females possess four mammae. Adult males are usually between 950 and 1,250 mm in total length, including a tail 300 to 475 mm long. Adults are between 225 and 250 mm in height at the shoulder and generally weigh between 4.5 and 11.5 kg. Females are somewhat smaller than males.

The skull is broad and strongly flattened and can be distinguished from other carnivore skulls by the presence of five molariform teeth on each side of both upper and lower jaws. Auditory bullae are small and flattened. The carnassial teeth are large and well developed. The bony palate extends posteriorly beyond the last molars (Figure 153).

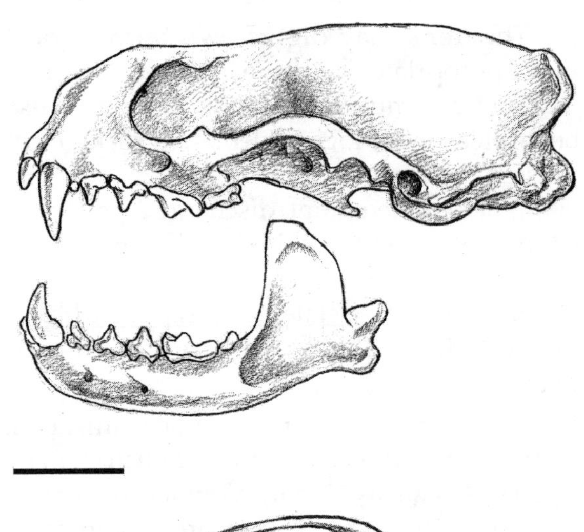

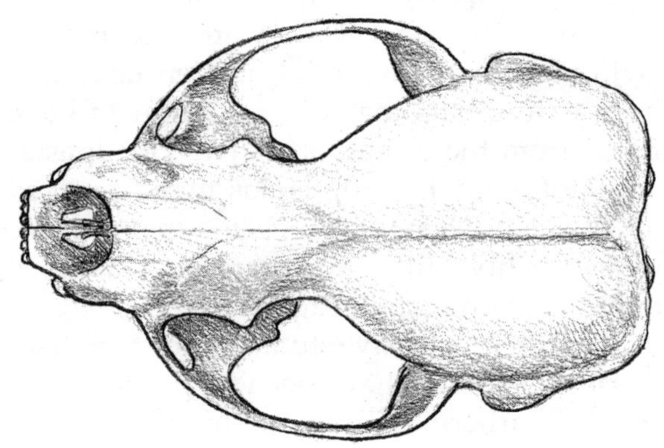

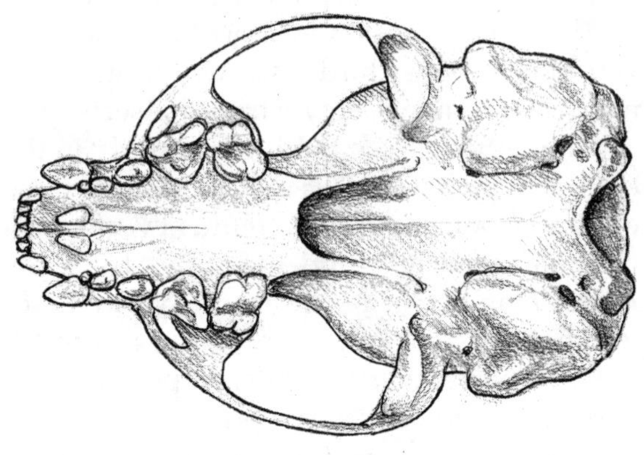

Figure 153. *Lontra (Lutra) canadensis:* Left lateral view of skull, and dorsal and ventral view of skull. Scale bar = 20 mm.

Distribution. The river otter ranges from Alaska and Canada throughout the United States except in the arid regions from central Texas west to southern Arizona, southern Nevada, and southern California.

The river otter was classified as an endangered species in Virginia in 1978 (Handley, 1979b), but its status has since been changed to special concern (Handley, 1991) (Figure 154). Handley (1979b) stated:

The river otter once was common throughout

Virginia. It still is fairly numerous in parts of the Coastal Plain and lower Piedmont, but is rare or extirpated in the remainder of the state.

Lewis (1940) noted that although the otter had been common along the Appomattox River and the larger creeks up to about 30 years ago (1910), it was now very rare. Paradiso (1969) noted that this species:

occurs on Assateague Island, where Jacob Valentine, former manager of the Chincoteague National Wildlife Refuge, told me that as many as seven were living in 1958. Most of these, however, were in the Virginia portion of the island, on the Refuge.

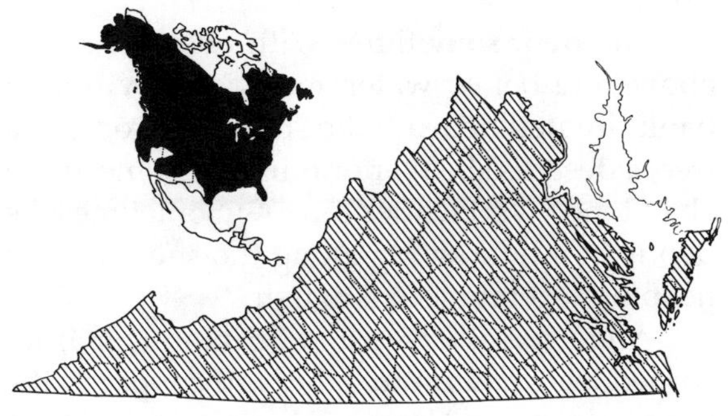

Figure 154. *Lontra (Lutra) canadensis:* Range in Virginia and North America.

Meanley (1971a) noted that otters were still common in the Dismal Swamp. Prior to 1978, only two recent records existed for western Virginia. In 1977 one otter was trapped in Frederick County. Also in 1977, tracks of three otters were observed in the snow in Wise County, (Downing, personal communication, 1978).

Regarding the gloomy forecast of the otter's status in Virginia in 1978, Handley (1991) stated:

That forecast, which lead to ranking the otter as endangered west of the Blue Ridge and in trouble in the eastern part of the state, has proved to be too pessimistic. Statistics compiled by the Virginia Department of Game and Inland Fisheries (1978) show that in the past decade otter populations have increased dramatically in the Coastal Plain and Piedmont and have improved west of the Blue Ridge . . . . In 1978 the Virginia Department of Game and Inland Fisheries closed the season on otter trapping west of the Blue Ridge. Since then, otters have been sighted with increasing frequency in western Virginia. . . . To supplement the natural immigration of otters into western Virginia, the Department of Game and Inland Fisheries has begun a program of restocking. In March 1988, the Department released 17 otters from Louisiana at sites on the Cowpasture River 1.6 km above Millboro Springs and 8.0 km below Millboro Springs in Bath County. The 17 otters consisted of eight females and nine males. Three were implanted with radio transmitters. One week after the release, 13 of the otters had survived (Martin, 1989). The otters still seem to be doing fine. They have scattered themselves out along the river north to Williamsville and south to the mouth of the Cowpasture, a distance of about 50 km of river. . . . With such a remarkable turnabout in the outlook for otter in Virginia, we feel confident in upgrading its status from endangered to special concern.

A total of 763 otters were tagged by Virginia Department of Game and Inland Fisheries personnel during the 1987–1988 trapping season. State law requires tagging of bobcat and otter pelts prior to sale by the trapper and hunter. A summary of otter tagging data for the period 1977–1988 is presented in table 2. A comparison of the wild fur catch from 1966–1993 from fur dealer reports is shown in Table 2. Virginia's total estimated otter fur value for 1992–1993 is given in Table 3.

In November, 1984, three native Virginia river otters were trapped and transported to West Virginia as part of a reintroduction program (Schreckengast, 1988). The three Virginia specimens were part of a total of 30 otters secured in Virginia, North Carolina and South Carolina. One of the Virginia otters died of pneumonia prior to release. The two remaining otters were released into the Little Kanawha River on December 6, 1984. Both were adult females.

Habitat. The river otter is found in swamps and marshes as well as along streams, rivers, and the borders of ponds and lakes. Although otters are generally found in fresh water, some do inhabit brackish areas.

Habits. Otters live together in family groups and are very sociable, gentle, and playful animals. Although often occupying regions close to man, they are seldom seen due to their secretive habits. Otters may be active day and night all seasons of the year.

River otters are the fastest mammals in lakes and rivers. They are excellent and graceful swimmers, moving in an undulating fashion, spending part of the time on top and part of the time underneath the water, or swimming with only the head above the surface. They are expert divers and have been recorded to a depth of 18 m (Scheffer, 1953). They can swim long distances beneath the surface, if the need arises, traveling for 0.4 km. They can remain submerged for several minutes without coming up for air. On the surface they can swim at least 9.5 km per hour. In spite of its short legs, the otter also moves readily on land, and on ice it expedites travel by sliding. On land an otter can run as fast as a man (Liers, 1951).

The otter is well adapted for life in the water, with its streamlined body, webbed feet, and long, tapering tail. The ears and nostrils can be closed to exclude water. The eyes are located near the top of the head, allowing the otter to see above water while it swims along nearly submerged. The dense, oily fur and heavy layer of body fat under the skin provide insulation. The senses of sight and hearing are less well developed than the sense of smell. The prominent facial whiskers are extremely sensitive to touch and can sense the movement of fish, even in murky water (Harris, 1968).

Tobogganing is a favorite sport of these good-natured animals. During winter, slides are made on steep slopes coated with ice and snow. During summer, a clay stream bank serves the same purpose. Taking turns, a family of otters will plunge down one after the other in quick succession with their legs turned backward. The water from their bodies greases the slide and heightens the fun. With a splash they land in the water; then they return to the top by a side path and start all over again.

Adult otters grunt, growl, and have a shrill chirp that sounds like a hiccup, a soft chuckle, and a variety of other noises. When frightened or angered, they scream and give forth a strong musk (Liers, 1951; Jackson, 1961).

Otters are continually on the move and may travel a 32 km circuit of connecting lakes and rivers in two or three weeks. They appear to travel more during the mating season than at any other time of the year (Wilson, 1959). They go from one place to another in fairly regular sequence, with part of the route often being overland. They remain for short periods where food is abundant. Home ranges change as bodies of water freeze or feeding and living conditions are altered. In the course of a year, an otter's home range may include as much as 80 to 160 km of shoreline (Liers, 1951; Schwartz and Schwartz, 1959). In areas where food is plentiful, a smaller home range may be adequate. From the birth of the young in the spring to the time of separation in the fall or winter, otters in North Carolina lived within an area of about 14.5 km^2 (Wilson, 1959). The home range of a mother tending her pups is seldom greater than a kilometer or so (Jackson, 1961).

The den, sometimes with entrances both above and below water, may be a cavity in a bank situated beneath the sprawling roots of a tree, a deserted beaver or muskrat home, or an abandoned woodchuck burrow. Sometimes the den is in a hollow log along the shore or in a heap of vegetation in a marsh.

Anderson-Bledsoe and Scanlon (1983) recorded lead, cadmium, zinc, and copper in the liver, kidneys, and bone of Virginia otters. Mean and median concentrations of these heavy metals were considered to be well below toxic concentrations.

Food. Otters are expert fishermen. Foods recorded from studies primarily in northern states include a variety of fish, crayfish, frogs, salamanders, turtles, snakes, earthworms, snails, and insects (Lagler and Ostenson, 1942; Stophlet, 1947; Liers, 1951; Ryder, 1955; Hamilton, 1961; Sheldon and Toll, 1964; Knudsen and Hale, 1968). Wass (1972) noted scats consisting entirely of blue crab skeletons in eastern Virginia. On occasion, otters also have been known to feed upon ducks and other water birds, hawks, snowshoe hares, muskrats, and young beavers. Some vegetation may be eaten, especially during the summer.

A fall and winter study of otter digestive tracts and scats in North Carolina revealed the following frequencies of occurrence: fish, 91 percent; crustaceans (crayfish, blue crab, and shrimp), 39 percent; insects (water beetles), 6 percent; amphibians (frogs), 6 percent; birds, 3 percent; muskrat, one percent; and clam, 1 percent. Forage fish such as carp, suckers, killifish, minnows, eels, shiners, mosquito fish, and bowfin comprised 57 percent of all fish taken (Wilson, 1954).

Much has been written on the supposed destructiveness of otters to trout, and without question they successfully pursue and capture these fish. Forage fish, however, apparently constitute effective buffers against otter predation for game and pan fish.

Reproduction and Development. Breeding occurs in the water, and the female usually remates not long after parturition. The male spends most of his time with one female, although he will mate with others. Gestation varies from 288 to 380 days, with implantation of the embryos being delayed for eight or more months until January or early February (Hamilton and Eadie, 1964). This variation in gestation is caused by the process known as delayed implantation where the embryo begins to develop but then development ceases for a variable period of time. Following implantation, development proceeds rapidly, and the young are usually born in March or April. A recently born otter was recorded from Nottaway County, Virginia, on March 24 (VPI-W). Wilson (1959) presented data from North Carolina indicating a somewhat earlier mating season with breeding starting in January and continuing into February and possibly into March.

Liers (1951) and Hamilton and Eadie (1964) described newborn otters, while Liers has discussed the growth and development of this species. The litter of one to four (usually two or 3) are born in a nest of dry vegetation within the den. Anderson and Scanlon (1981a) recorded mean corpora lutea in 24 females of 2.5 and a mean litter size for eight females of 2.8 embryos in Virginia. Wilson (1959) recorded an average of 2.9 young per litter. Newborn otters are blind, toothless, and covered with brownish-black fur that fades ventrally to a lighter, more grayish tone. The lips, cheeks, chin, and throat are also paler. They are between 250 and 280 mm in total length at birth.

When 7 to 10 days old, a pup raised by captive parents weighed 170 g, and 10 days later it weighed 0.45 kg. The eyes open between 21 and 35 days of age. When 10 to 12 weeks old, the pups come out of the den and play on land with their mother, who brings food, but they may not be weaned until considerably later. When the pups are about 14 weeks old, the mother introduces them to water and teaches them to swim. In some instances, the mother is said to take the pups on her back at first. When they have lost their fear of the water, the mother dives, returning to support them until the young are at last accomplished swimmers. The female usually will not allow the male to come near the pups until they are at least six months old, after which both parents assist in caring for the young. Meanley (1971) reported observing a pair with two pups, about two-thirds grown, in April in the Dismal Swamp. Mother and young remain together for about eight months, after which the young go their separate ways. Most otters breed for the first time when two years old (Liers, 1951; Hamilton and Eadie, 1964), although Liers (1958) reported a female breeding at the age of one year, three months. A captive female was still breeding at 17 years of age (Palmer, 1954).

Longevity. The normal life span of an otter is eight or nine years, but some individuals have been known to live at least 19 years (Palmer, 1954; Crandall, 1964; Walker, 1964).

Predation. Humans are the most important predators on the otter.

Parasites. The nematode *Gnathostoma miyazakii* was recorded in the kidneys of otters by Wheland et al. (1981). Rabies has been confirmed in one animal from Lancaster County (Table 6).

Geographic Variation. The subspecies occurring in Virginia is *Lontra (Lutra) canadensis lataxina* F. Cuvier.

Other Currently Recognized Subspecies. *Lontra (Lutra) canadensis canadensis* (Schreber).

Location of Specimens. CM, MCZ, NCSM, ODU, USNM, VPI-W.

Skunks and Stink Badgers (Family Mephitidae)

Skunks had been classified in the subfamily Mephitinae in the family Mustelidae for 150 years until Dragoo and Honeycutt (1997) provided convincing evidence from DNA studies that skunks (*Mephitis, Spilogale,* and *Conepatus*), as well as the Oriental stink badger *Mydaus*, should be placed in their own independent family — Mephitidae. These mammals have short limbs with five clawed toes on each foot. The claws are curved and nonretractile. A pair of well-developed anal scent glands are present. A short rostrum is present on the elongate and flattened skull. Carnassial teeth are well-developed.

Two members of this family — *Spilogale* (spotted skunk) and *Mephitis* (striped skunk) — occur in Virginia.

Key to Species of Mephitidae

1a Skull with flattened interorbital region; skull length less than 55 mm; infraorbital canal opening above anterior half of carnassial tooth; dorsal pelage with broken black and white stripes or spots; total length usually less than 550 mm; females with 10 mammae
.... *Spilogale putorius*

1b Skull with convex interorbital region; skull length more than 55 mm; infraorbital canal opening above posterior half of carnassial tooth; dorsal pelage usually with two continuous white stripes; total length more than 550 mm; females with 10–14 mammae
.... *Mephitis mephitis*

Genus *Spilogale*

Dentition: 3/3, 1/1, 3/3, 1/2 = 34

Eastern Spotted Skunk
Spilogale putorius Linnaeus

Description. The eastern spotted skunk (Plate 78) is the smaller of the two skunks occurring in Virginia. This relatively slender, short-legged skunk has long, soft, and silky fur. It is black with a white spot on the forehead, one white spot under each ear, and four to six dorsal and lateral white stripes that may be more or less broken and interrupted by black. White spots or crosswise patches are variously present on the rump. The proportions of black and white vary considerably, but there are no other mammals with a similar color pattern. The bushy tail is black but usually has a broad, white tip. Females have eight mammae. The claws on the forefeet are sharp, recurved, and about twice as long as those on the hind feet. The feet are plantigrade. Adult spotted skunks are usually between 450 and 600 mm long, including a tail 150 to 215 mm long. Adults stand approximately 150 mm high at the shoulder and weigh between 0.4 and 1.4 kg. Males are considerably heavier than females.

The skull is small and flattened with a weakly developed sagittal crest. Postorbital processes are present but are not well developed. The area above the eye sockets is nearly flat, in contrast to the convex shape of this region in the striped skunk. Auditory bullae are present and well inflated. The bony palate extends to or only slightly beyond the last molars. One squarish upper molar and two lower molars on each side distinguish the skull of the spotted skunk from all other carnivores except the striped skunk. The skull length is less than 55 mm in *Spilogale* and greater than 55 mm in *Mephitis.* Besides the differences in size and shape of the skull, the infraorbital canal opens above the anterior half of the carnassial tooth in the spotted skunk and over the posterior half in the striped skunk (Figure 155).

Distribution. The eastern spotted skunk ranges from northeastern Mexico through the Great Plains to the Canadian border and throughout the southeastern United States north to Pennsylvania.

In Virginia, this species inhabits the rock slides and rough forests west of the Blue Ridge Mountains (Figure 156).

Habitat. In Virginia, spotted skunks live in rock piles, rock slides, and crevices in cliffs in the mountain forests in the western portion of the state. In more southern portions of their range, however, they inhabit brushy and sparsely wooded areas and agricultural regions.

Habits. The spotted skunk rests or sleeps during the day and is active during the night. Its den may be in a hollow log, in a crevice among rocks, beneath a farm building, in lumber slab piles, or in a burrow in the ground. Crabb (1948) noted the three main requirements of a den site were darkness, protection against weather conditions, and protection against enemies. Spotted skunks are active throughout the winter in all parts of their range.

Spotted skunks range more widely summer than during winter (Crabb, 1948). During the winter most skunks never travel more than 0.8 km from their den. Activity is generally confined to an area of approximately 6.5 ha. During the spring and summer males travel widely, with some males recaptured at points 3.2 km

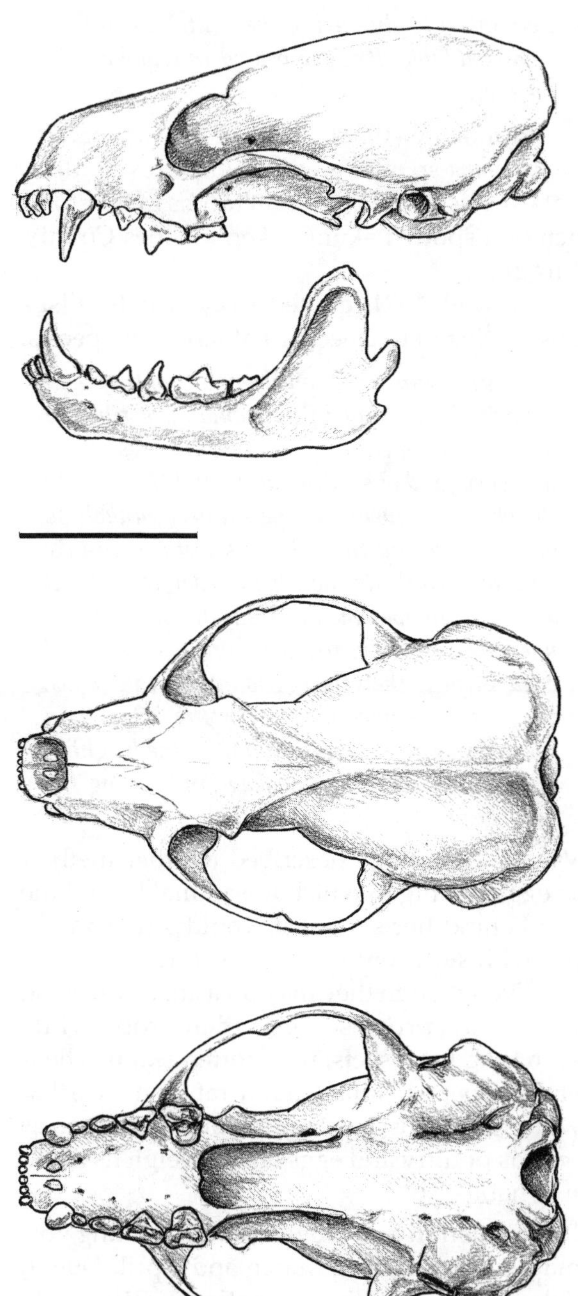

Figure 155. *Spilogale putorius:* Left lateral view of skull, and dorsal and ventral view of skull. Scale bar = 20 mm.

apart. The home range of females, however is much smaller.

Spotted skunks are more active, agile, and alert in every way than striped skunks. Unlike the striped skunk, spotted skunks are good climbers and have little difficulty climbing trees and fence posts or around rafters in buildings to escape danger. Normally, however, these skunks stay on the ground. The climbing ability of this species allows it to feed on somewhat different items than the striped skunk.

Frightened or angered skunks may stamp or pat their front feet in rapid succession on the floor or ground. This behavior may serve as a bluff or as a warning before the discharge of the scent.

The spotted skunk can also do a "handstand" on its front feet. The skunk upends itself, holds its tail in the air, and may walk up to several yards in this manner. In describing this behavior, Manaro (1961) stated:

> *My observations indicate that there is a fairly definite pattern of defensive behavior closely associated with the distance between the skunk and the approaching intruder. When a trapped animal is approached to within a distance of 8 to 15 feet, it begins a rapid series of handstands, each lasting between two and eight seconds. Reports of this distance vary from 12 feet (Howell, 1920) to 8 feet (Johnson, 1921) and the duration of each handstand from two (Johnson, 1921) to five seconds (Walter, 1930). Throughout the duration of the handstand, the hindlegs are spread laterally and the bristled tail is kept perpendicular to the ground. The animal advances and retreats on its forelegs only a few inches, apparently to maintain balance. When the observer comes to within about eight feet of a skunk, it immediately drops to all fours and assumes a horse-shoe-shaped stance with the anus and head directed towards the person. Frequently, skunks stamp their forefeet before, after, and in the case of one old male, during the handstand. Johnson (1921) reported that each handstand was accompanied by a musk discharge directed over the head of the skunk toward the intruder. I did not observe this action.*

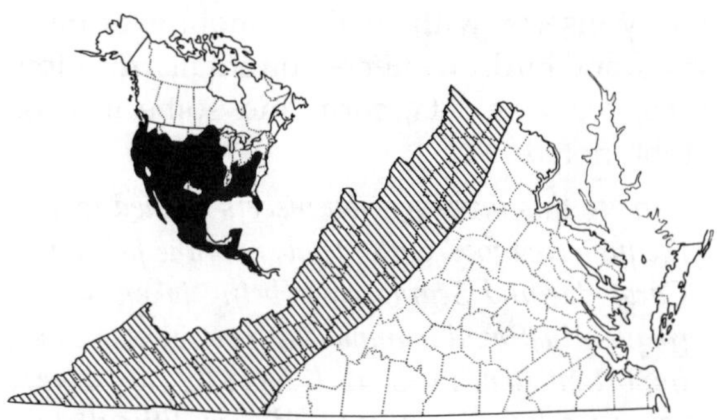

Figure 156. *Spilogale putorius:* Range in Virginia and North America.

Although the handstand serves primarily as a warning of anger and fear, it undoubtedly proves valuable as a bluff, and some skunks have even been observed doing it when playing among themselves.

The discharge of the spotted skunk consists of a few drops of fluid which may be sprayed a distance of 12 to 15 feet. The odor has been described as "quite different from that of the striped skunk, being sharper and more pungent" (Jackson, 1961) and as similar to "highly concentrated onion extract" (Manaro, 1961). Wood et al. (1991) identified three major volatile components of the anal sac secretion: (E)-2-butene-1-thiol, 3-methyl-1-butanethiol, and 2-phenylethanethiol. Spotted skunks lack the thioacetates found in striped skunk secretions.

Food. This skunk is omnivorous, with insects the most preferred food item. Many rodents are consumed, along with shrews, birds, eggs, amphibians, insects, other arthropods, carrion, fruit, and vegetable matter. Spotted skunks are excellent ratters and mousers. A spotted skunk in Virginia was observed killing a three-foot-long rattlesnake (Anonymous, 1940c).

Howell (1906) stated:

> *The food of the spotted skunks, judged by the records of 17 stomach examinations made by collectors of the Biological Survey, consists in large measure of insects, chiefly beetles and grasshoppers. These are supplemented by mice and other small mammals, lizards, salamanders, small birds, and crayfish. One stomach contained persimmons and several species of fungus.*

Crabb (1941) recorded the seasonal food habits of this species in Iowa: spring — native mice and insects; summer — predominantly insects, with smaller amounts of small mammals, fruits, birds, and birds' eggs; fall — predominantly insects, with smaller amounts of mice, fruits, and birds; winter — cottontails, meadow mice, Norway rats, corn, and some insects. Crabb noted:

> *During this investigation insects seemed to be the preferred food with members of the families Carabidae and Scarabaeidae being taken most frequently. Small mammals were a regular and important item in the diet. Norway rats were eaten freely when other food was difficult to obtain. Cottontail carrion and chicken carrion were taken freely during the winter when they were available. Birds appeared infrequently in the diet.*

Holloway (1958) recorded the salamander *Ambystoma* sp. along with millipedes, spiders, ants, beetles, true bugs, and moths in the stomach of a spotted skunk taken in Giles County, Virginia.

Howell (1921) quoted an early naturalist's description of the feeding habits of this species:

> *I will give some notes on the habits of the small striped skunk, and in particular describe the manner in which it disposes of the eggs which it is very fond of stealing at its nightly visits to the chicken house. . . . the skunk is unable to open the egg by the aid of its teeth or to take hold of it with its mouth in order to carry it away. It removes the egg from the nest, rolls it with the front paws to a place presenting a solid hard surface, then the egg is taken in its paws, the animal assumes an erect posture, lifts it from the ground, then lets it drop from the height of its body to insure its breakage in striking the hard ground.*

Van Gelder (1953) described another method of egg opening in which the animal kicked the egg behind her so that it would strike an object with sufficient force to crush it.

Even though they may occasionally feed on eggs and uproot some garden crops while searching for insects, the spotted skunk's beneficial aspects in killing many rats and mice that would otherwise destroy much stored grain as well as poultry and eggs far outweigh its negative habits.

Reproduction and Development. Mating normally occurs during March and April. Due to delayed implantation, gestation is 210 to 230 days with the blastocysts spending 180 to 200 days floating free in the uterus (Mead, 1968a, 1968b; Howard and Marsh, 1982).

The young number between two and six (usually four) and are born in a nest of grass or hay within the den. Young skunks are generally born during May or June, and in the southern portion of their range some females may have a second litter. A lactating female was recorded from Giles County, Virginia, on August 13 (VPI-W).

The growth and development of this species has been described by Crabb (1944). Newborn skunks have their eyes and ears closed and are covered with fine hair that shows the adult color pattern. At birth young spotted skunks are about 100 mm long and weigh about 9 g. At 24 days of age they elevated their tails in a warning fashion when frightened. The eyes open between 30 and 32 days, the teeth begin erupting at 35 days, and the first solid food is eaten at about 42 days of age. Release of musk was first noted when the young were 46 days old. Weaning takes place at about eight weeks of age, and the young may reach their full growth in slightly more than three months. Breeding occurs at one year.

Longevity. The longevity of this species under natural conditions is unknown, but a spotted skunk in captivity lived to be 9 years, 10 months old (Egoscue, Bittmenn, and Petrovich, 1970).

Parasites. The nematode *Trichinella spiralis* was recorded from 6 of 16 spotted skunks in Giles County, Virginia, (Solomon and Warner, 1969). Holloway (1956a; 1956b; 1956c; 1958) recorded the acanthocephalans *Centrorhynchus wardae* and *Echinopardalis macrurae* from this species at Mountain Lake in Giles County.

Predation. Barred and great horned owls, foxes, bobcats, and dogs kill some spotted skunks. Some are trapped for their fur, and others are killed by automobiles on the highway.

Geographic Variation. The subspecies in Virginia is *Spilogale putorius putorius* Linnaeus.

Location of Specimens. BCV, GMU, MCZ, OSU, PWRC, SNP, USNM, VPISU, VPI-W.

Genus *Mephitis*

Dentition: 3/3, 1/1, 3/3, 1/2 = 34

Striped Skunk
Mephitis mephitis (Schreber)

Description. The striped skunk (Plate 79) is a stout, short-legged mammal of about house-cat size, but with a relatively small head. The pelage is long, coarse, and oily. The body is black with a narrow white stripe running up the middle of the forehead and a broad white area on the nape of the neck that usually divides into a V at about the shoulders. The resulting two white stripes may continue to the base of the bushy tail. There is, however, much variation in the length and width of the stripes; some skunks have very broad, well-defined stripes, while in others the stripes are almost or completely lacking. The relatively small head possesses small, short, rounded ears, small eyes, and a pointed muzzle. The feet are semiplantigrade with long claws on the forefeet for digging. Two well-developed scent glands are present. Females possess 10 to 15 mammae and are smaller than males. Adult striped skunks are usually between 550 and 750 mm long, including a tail 175 to 300 mm long. Adults usually weigh between 1.3 and 4.5 kg.

The skull is long and relatively narrow between the orbits. Auditory bullae are present but are not greatly inflated. The upper molar is squarish in shape. The bony palate extends back to about the level of the posterior border of the upper molars (Figure 157).

Distribution. This species ranges from the southern Yukon and Northwest Territories in Canada south throughout the United States and into Mexico. The striped skunk is found throughout Virginia except in a few Tidewater counties (Anonymous, 1959l; Allen, 1965h) (Figure 158). Davis (1971) reported that there were no skunks in the Dismal Swamp.

Data on the wild fur catch in Virginia, including skunks, are presented in tables 2 and 3.

Habitat. Striped skunks prefer brushy and sparsely wooded areas and are most abundant in agricultural regions where the forest gives way to open lands and farm crops. Two-thirds of the captures recorded by Stout and Sonenshine (1974) in Virginia were in old fields and in areas of forested cover dominated by shrubs and tree seedlings.

Habits. Striped skunks are mainly nocturnal. Daylight hours are normally spent resting or sleeping in a hollow log, in wood piles, beneath an abandoned building, along a fence row, or in a burrow in the ground. A skunk may excavate its own burrow, or more commonly it will occupy an abandoned burrow previously constructed by some other mammal, usually a woodchuck. Such burrows may have up to five entrances and are usually 5 to 6 m long. The nest is composed of leaves. According to Schwartz and Schwartz (1959), leaves are gathered into a pile under the body and are shuffled along. They are either pushed into the den ahead of the animal, or the skunk backs into the opening and pulls the leaves inside with

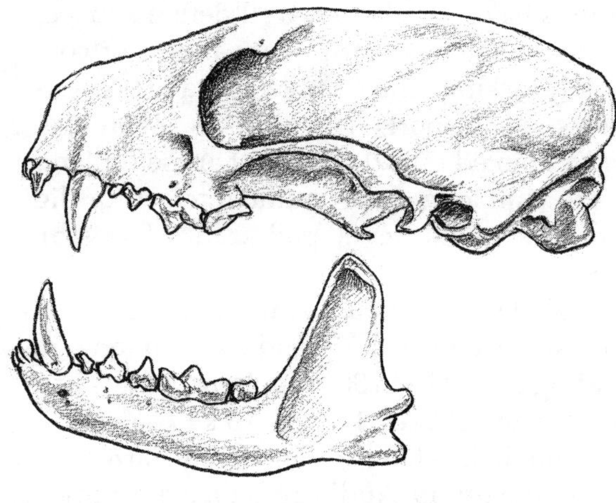

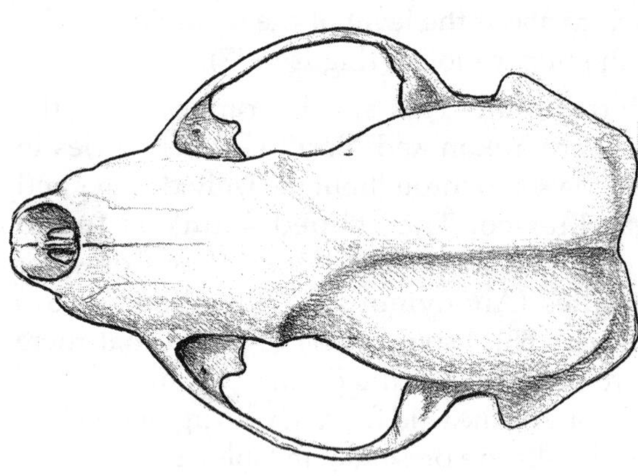

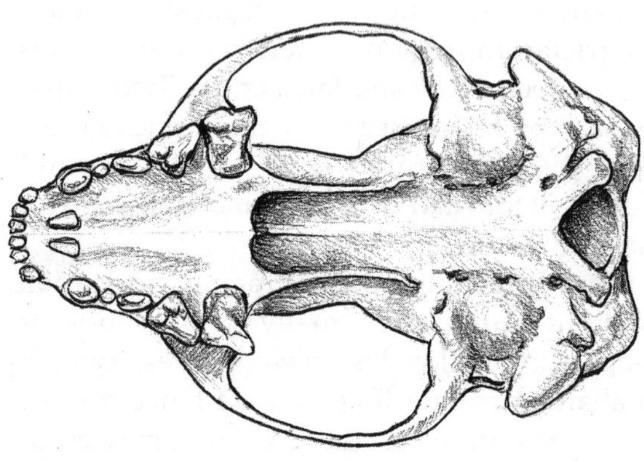

Figure 157. *Mephitis mephitis:* Left lateral view of skull, and dorsal and ventral view of skull. Scale bar = 20 mm.

its mouth.

Males are generally solitary during summer, but groups of several females and one or two males may occupy the same den during winter in more northern portions of their range. Striped skunks may become dormant for prolonged periods during severe winter weather, but they do not hibernate.

Striped skunks are deliberate, slow-moving creatures and seem to be rather confident of themselves. They are not good climbers. While skunks have an acute sense of touch, their other senses are said to be poorly developed. Vocalizations include squeals, growls, hisses, low churring, and twittering.

Home range size apparently varies considerably; it has been reported to range from 9.6 to 518 ha (Andrews and Ferris, 1966; Storm, 1972). It is not uncommon for several home ranges to overlap. Population densities ranging between one and 4.5 skunks per 41 ha (6.4 to 12.8 per km^2) were recorded in Hanover County, Virginia, by Stout and Sonenshine (1974).

Skunks possess two large musk glands embedded in a mass of muscle at the base of their tail that are always primed and ready to fire. When frightened or annoyed, the skunk contracts the muscles surrounding the glands, thus forcing the scent out in a fine, almost invisible spray. These glands discharge through a duct which normally occupies an internal position, but which is protruded from the anus when the animal is angered. Either one or both glands can be discharged simultaneously. The initial spray is the most powerful, but each adult animal is capable of four to six successive discharges, each accurate up to 3.5 to 4.5 m. The odor may carry 0.8 km or more.

The skunk generally releases its scent only as a last resort. When forced into a defensive position, the skunk will face its attacker, eyeing him, but with its body diagonal to the line

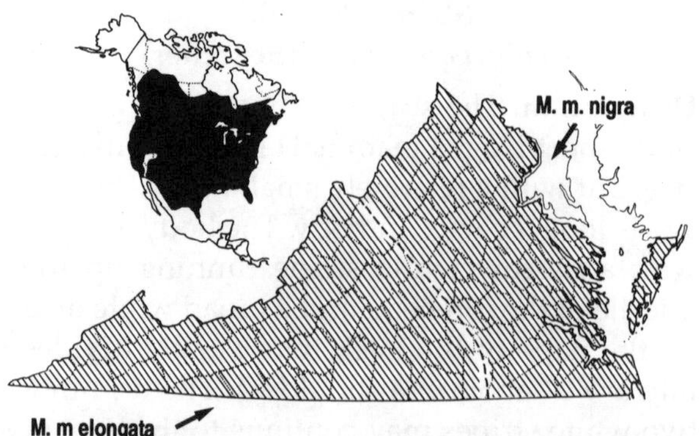

Figure 158. *Mephitis mephitis:* Range in Virginia and North America.

of sight, and its tail over its back. The skunk will growl its displeasure and stamp its front feet impatiently. If this is ineffective, the skunk will raise its tail as a final warning, but its discharge will be withheld as long as the very tip of the tail hangs limp. If the intruder persists, the tip of the tail goes up and the scent is discharged with accuracy at the head of the attacker.

At least seven major volatile components have been identified in the secretion of the striped skunk (Wood, 1990). The most abundant compound is (E)-2-butene-1-thiol and comprises 38 to 44 percent of the volatiles. Anal sac secretion is produced at the rate of about .33 liquid ounce per week. The fluid has a most distasteful and nauseating stench and produces intense smarting and burning if it comes in contact with the membranes of the eyes, nose, or mouth. It causes tears to flow freely and produces temporary blindness. The odor may not depart from clothing or animal fur for several weeks and returns if the clothing or fur becomes damp.

Skunk odor in clothing can be lessened by washing the clothes in a pail of water to which a cup of household ammonia has been added. An ammonia rinse or a tomato juice rubdown will remove most of the odor from a person's body. Also, a cloth or sponge saturated with turpentine and applied to the affected areas will immediately cause the odor to vanish.

Incongruous as it may seem, the oily yellow fluid produced by the skunk is used as a base for perfumes. After being extracted from the skunk, the fluid is refined, thus removing the disagreeable smell. The fluid that remains has a great capacity to fix and retain aromas. It is then blended with various scents to make fine perfumes.

Moseley (1977) stated:

The Indians ate skunk as a favorite food. They wore its fur after much airing and drying. Skunk oil was used for medicinal purposes. It was said to have great penetrating qualities which gave it importance in ointments. The Algonquins called the animal 'se-kaw-kawn' meaning 'where the skunk cabbages grow.' It was also known by other tribes as 'seganku.' Its generic name, 'Mephitis,' *is closer to the truth.* Mephitis *is defined as a bad-smelling vapor coming out of the earth, or a stench.*

Food. Striped skunks are omnivorous and feed on shrews, moles, bats, mice, chipmunks, and other small mammals, small birds, snakes, turtle eggs, frogs, fish, crayfish, insects and their larvae, carrion, corn, and berries (Howell, 1921; Sperry, 1933; Hamilton, 1936b; Kelker, 1937; Linzey and Linzey, 1968; Linzey, 1995a). During the summer, insects such as grasshoppers, crickets, beetles, and caterpillars; fruits; small mammals; and grains form the bulk of the skunk's food. A characteristic sign of the presence of a skunk is a series of small diggings 2.5 to 5 cm deep and 7 to 10 cm across. Such diggings are made while searching for insects and grubs and are made both by the claws and nose. During fall and winter, fruit, small mammals, carrion, grains and nuts, grasses, leaves, and buds are important. Occasionally they kill poultry or uproot plants in their search for insects.

During a three-year study, Kelker (1937) found that injurious insects ranged from less than 40 percent to 98 percent of all insect food consumed. Injurious insects predominated during the latter part of the summer.

W. B. Davis (1966) reported the following seasonal analyses from 79 striped skunks in Texas: Fall — insects, 76 percent; arachnids, 24 percent. Winter — insects, 52.3 percent; arachnids, 5.3 percent; reptiles, 1.6 percent; small mammals, 18.3 percent; vegetation, 22 percent; birds and millipedes making up the balance. Spring — insects, 96 percent; reptiles, 1.6 percent; small mammals, 2 percent; vegetation and small birds making up the balance. Summer — insects, 88 percent; arachnids, 4 percent; reptiles, 1.5 percent; small birds, 3.5 percent; centipedes, small mammals, and vegetation making up the balance.

A study in Maryland revealed a fall and winter diet consisting of 10 percent plant material and 90 percent animal material (Llewellyn and Uhler, 1952). Persimmon was the only plant found on a regular basis. Insects formed almost half of the total animal food and were most prominent in the fall. Beetles, grasshoppers, crickets, and true bugs were the main insect groups consumed. Other animal food consisted of rodents, rabbits, squirrels, birds, snakes, salamanders, millipedes, centipedes, and spiders.

On the basis of their food habits alone,

striped skunks are very beneficial. The occasional individual that habitually preys on hive bees can be excluded by elevating or fencing the hives.

Reproduction and Development. Striped skunks are polygamous and usually mate from late January through March. Most females normally produce a single annual litter, although two litters have been produced in one year in cases where the first litter did not survive. Following a gestation of 59 to 77 days, the litter of 3 to 10 (normally 4 to 7) young are born in a nest of dry leaves and grasses within the den. Stout and Sonenshine (1974) recorded two pregnant females in June in Hanover County, Virginia. Hamilton (1963) recorded an average of 5.8 embryos in 40 females in New York. Barbour (1951b) recorded litters of five and six young in early May in West Virginia. Reproduction behavior in the striped skunk has been described by Wight (1931).

Newborn young have their eyes and ears closed, well-developed claws, and a fine covering of hair in which the adult pattern is evident. Striped skunks weigh about 28 g at birth. The eyes open at 22 to 35 days, while the ears open between 24 and 27 days. The incisors erupt between 34 and 39 days. Young skunks nurse for six to seven weeks, after which they emerge from the den and begin following their mother on her nightly foraging trips. In this family parade, the mother leads and the little skunklets follow in a single file. The mother and young usually remain together until late summer, at which time they disband. The male does not assist in caring for the young. Young skunks begin breeding at one year of age (Stegeman, 1937; Verts, 1967).

Longevity. Striped skunks may live five to six years in the wild and have lived up to 10 years in captivity (Mann, 1930; Walker, 1964). Stout and Sonenshine (1974) recorded a female on their study area in Virginia for 48 months.

Predation. Because of its malodorous secretion, the striped skunk has few enemies. Its main predators are the great horned owl and the barred owl. In fact, it has been said that these owls feed so extensively on skunks that almost every one smells of skunk. Bobcats, foxes, and dogs also kill some skunks. Humans, with traps, take a large toll each year, and many are killed while crossing highways.

Parasites and Disease. The fungus *Histoplasma capsulatum* was recorded in 2 of 18 skunks from Virginia by Emmons et al. (1955). Jones et al. (1978a) recorded tularemia infection in one striped skunk from Fort Pickett. Sonenshine, Lamb, and Anastos (1965), Jones (1978), Sonenshine and Stout (1971), Sonenshine and Levy (1971), and Sonenshine, Atwood, and Lamb (1966) recorded the ticks *Dermacentor variabilis, Amblyomma americanum,* and *Ixodes cookei* from this species. In some portions of the country the striped skunk is a major carrier of rabies (see Table 4 in gray fox account). Although rabies has been found in Virginia skunks, the incidence is not nearly as high as in foxes. During the period 1951–1979 there were 52 laboratory-confirmed cases in skunks — an average of approximately two per year (Table 5). Beginning in 1980, however, a minimum of 20 confirmed cases have been recorded annually. This trend has continued through 1994.

Geographic Variation. The subspecies in Virginia is *Mephitis mephitis mephitis* (Schreber). Two geographic variants occur in the state. One form occurs north and east of a line running approximately between Brunswick and Highland counties; the other variant inhabits the remainder of the state.

Other Currently Recognized Subspecies. *Mephitis mephitis nigra* (Peale and Palisot de Beauvois); *Mephitis mephitis elongata* Bangs.

Location of Specimens. BCV, CM, CUC, DMNH, GMU, KU, LC, LFCC, LU, NVCC, SNP, UMMZ, USNM, VCU, VLM, VPISU.

Cats
(Family Felidae)

The family Felidae contains the cats, including the jaguar, ocelot, lion, bobcat, lynx, and domestic cat. These mammals are found throughout the world with the exception of Australia, Madagascar, and the Antarctic. Felids are carnivorous and have highly developed carnassial teeth. Other jaw teeth are reduced in both size and number with living forms having only one upper and one lower molar. The incisors are small, while the canines are large and recurved. Recurved horny projections on the tongue aid in grasping food. Five toes are present on each front foot and four toes on each hind foot. Claws are retractile. The foot posture is digitigrade.

The first toe on the front foot is high on the wrist and does not touch the ground when the cat is walking. The head is rounded and shortened, and the eyes have pupils that contract vertically. All felids have acute senses of sight, smell, and hearing. The young of our native cats are spotted at birth.

Two members of this family are native to Virginia, the mountain lion and the bobcat. In addition, domestic cats, both free-ranging and feral, occur statewide. Mitchell and Beck (1992) discussed predation by free-ranging domestic cats on native mammals. A medium-sized, short-tailed cat that is often confused with the bobcat is the lynx *(Lynx canadensis).* The lynx has prominent ear tufts, a ruff of long brown-tipped hairs on each side of the head, and a totally black tail tip. No verified records of the lynx exist for Virginia. Cope (1871), however, stated:

> *Like the red squirrel the Canada lynx extends to the southern limits of the Alleghany ranges, occupying the highest ground, though apparently not so restricted to the elevations as the first named. It is distinguished, by the name catamount, from the* Lynx rufus *which is called wild cat, and is well known to the hunters. It is known to be a northern species, being unknown in the wilds of the lower country of Virginia and North Carolina, where the* L. rufus *takes its place.*

Lee (1988) recorded the occurrence of *Lynx canadensis* in Garrett County, Maryland, prior to 1895.

Key to the Species of Felidae

1a Size large; tail long, at least 1/3 of total length; weight over 22.5 kg; total teeth 30; four upper molariform teeth
.... *Puma (Felis) concolor*

1b Size medium; tail short, less than 1/3 of total length; weight less than 22.5 kg; total teeth 28; three upper molariform teeth
.... *Lynx rufus*

Genus *Puma (Felis)*

Dentition: 3/3, 1/1, 3/2 or 2/2, 1/1 = 28 or 30

Mountain Lion
Puma (Felis) concolor Linnaeus

Description. The mountain lion (Plate 80), also known as the cougar, puma, panther, and painter, is the largest of the New World unspotted cats and, among cats, is exceeded in weight in the Americas only by the jaguar. Cougars have a long, lithe body; a long, cylindrical tail; small, rounded ears; long, sharp, retractile claws; and soft, rather short, fur. The dorsal part of the body is dull yellowish-brown or tawny, while the underparts vary from dull whitish to buff. The sides of the muzzle and the backs of the ears are black, while the upper lips, chin, and throat are white. The tail is well haired but not bushy, and except for its dark brown tip, it is the same color as the back. Females possess a total of eight mammae, although the most anterior pectoral pair are nonfunctional. Adults are between 1,800 and 2,700 mm in total length, including a tail 750 to 900 mm long. Adults stand between 660 and 790 mm high at the shoulder and weigh between 45 and 100 kg. Adult females are somewhat smaller than males.

The skull of this cat is short, broad, and rounded. The frontal region is high and arched. Well-developed carnassial teeth and auditory bullae are present (Figure 159).

Distribution. The mountain lion has the widest distribution of any species of native mammal in the Western Hemisphere, formerly ranging across southern Canada, throughout the United States, and south throughout South America to Patagonia. It is now extirpated from much of its range in the United States and some parts of South America. However, this large cat is still common locally from the Rocky Mountains westward, along the Mexican border in Texas, in southern Florida, and possibly from central Maine into Nova Scotia and New Brunswick.

The earliest record of the mountain lion in Virginia is found in Hariot's account of the new land (1588). The panther, or "Lyon," was encountered by the early settlers from the coastal areas to the mountains. Burnaby (1775) and McAtee (1918) allude to the occurrence of the mountain lion in the District of Columbia.

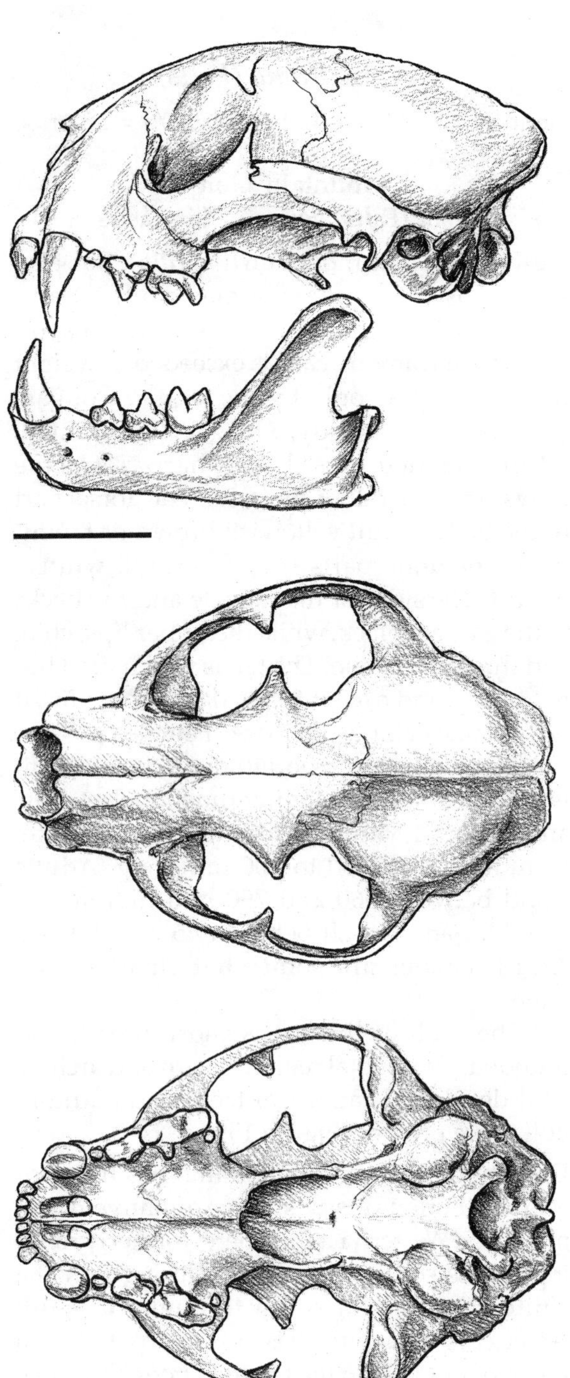

Figure 159. *Puma (Felis) concolor:* Left lateral view of skull, and dorsal and ventral view of skull. Scale bar = 5 cm.

Hallock (1880) listed it as still plentiful in the Dismal Swamp. As late as 1925, Stansbury (1925) still included the panther as part of the swamp's fauna.

As civilization advanced westward, however, these big cats gradually became fewer in number. Their decline has been attributed to two factors: bounty killing as an undesirable species and a decline in their major food supply, the white-tailed deer. The last known mountain lion in Virginia was killed in Washington County in 1882 (Denbigh, 1882) and in West Virginia in 1887.

During the next 75 to 80 years few mountain lion sightings were reported in the eastern United States. Although no specimens were preserved, there seems little doubt that cougars survived in the Great Smoky Mountains until about 1930 and in Pennsylvania until 1918 or beyond (Downing, 1981). The National Museum of Natural History has a kitten killed in Garrett County, Maryland, in the 1920s. During this time, however, extensive forested areas were gradually recovering from earlier logging operations. In addition, the establishment of national forests provided a measure of protection to many of these areas. Furthermore, the white-tailed deer was making a comeback from near extirpation in Virginia. Overhunting was the primary cause of the decline, particularly in western Virginia. Through the passage of game laws and restocking, the deer population had again become relatively abundant throughout the state by the 1960s.

In recent years the presence of these big cats has been reported from numerous areas in the eastern United States. Every year wildlife officials receive reports of persons who believe they have seen a cougar. In the majority of cases, these reports cannot be verified by a qualified observer, nor are any photographs, footprint casts, or the like presented as supporting evidence. Although many of these reports are quite interesting and provide descriptions of an animal resembling a cougar, they are not sufficient to establish its presence positively. The situation in Virginia is much the same, with numerous reported sightings. A few of these, however, have been by reliable observers, thus giving credence to the belief that a few cougars still roam the state.

The eastern subspecies of the mountain lion is listed as endangered throughout its range by the US Department of the Interior. The mountain lion has been afforded complete protection from hunting and trapping in Virginia since 1971, and has been classified as an endangered species in the state (Handley, 1979b; 1991).

Handley (1991) stated:

There most likely are mountain lions in western Virginia, but hard evidence is lacking. How many there are, where they are, whether they comprise an established breeding population, and whether they represent native Felis concolor couguar *or introduced, exotic subspecies are uncertain.*

In 1979, the author organized the Virginia Cougar Investigation. Over 2,000 posters have been distributed statewide to all state and national park and forestry offices, to all extension offices and to anyone seeking information about this cat. Posters are currently in place in many country stores and in shelters along the Appalachian Trail.

Between 1979 and 1994, a total of 279 reports of cougars in Virginia have been received. Of these, 124 (45 percent) have been considered reliable enough to warrant a colored pin on my large Virginia map (Figure 160). Mapped reports are grouped by years and their location is indicated by color-coded pins. Forty-eight percent of the mapped sightings were seen by more than one person. A majority of these reports have come from the Blue Ridge Mountains and areas to the west, although reported sightings have also been made in Amelia and Dinwiddie counties as well as in the Dismal Swamp.

During the period 1985–1989, 14 reports were mapped. From January, 1990 to April 1998, 19 reports were mapped.

Since 1979, numerous casts of track have been received. All but one are readily identifiable as dog tracks. The exception is a cement cast made in October, 1990, in Franklin County, Virginia. It shows some dog and some catlike characteristics.

I have three photographs of purported "cougars" in Virginia, but photo enhancement and forensic expert examination can still not make a positive identification. Hair samples and scats have been received and examined by experts, but without positive confirmation. Two covered deer kills have been examined but no evidence relating them to cougars could be found.

Reported sightings of cougars in Virginia appear to be concentrated in the Montgomery-Giles-Craig county area in the New River Valley and in the vicinity of the Peaks of Otter in Bedford and Botetourt counties. In June, 1990, a veteran US Forest Service technician was marking the boundary of a wilderness area near the Peaks of Otter when he reportedly observed a female cougar with two cubs sunning themselves and playing atop a large boulder. His closest approach to the animals was approximately 25 yards and his total observation time was approximately 25 minutes.

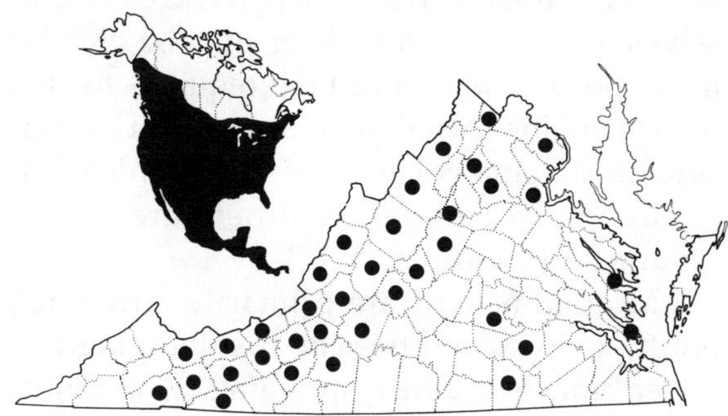

Figure 160. *Puma (Felis) concolor:* Range in Virginia and North America.

I am convinced that cougars are roaming certain areas of Virginia. Whether they are remnants of the original population that formerly inhabited the state or whether they have been introduced or escaped from captivity cannot be determined without additional supporting evidence. Two formerly captive mountain lions found in West Virginia in 1976 and two killed in North Carolina in the late 1980s are proof that some of the lions being seen are not necessarily natives. One of these animals, for example, had a tattoo in its ear; another had been feeding on domestic cat food. One of the lions had intestinal parasites similar to those found in domestic, not wild, cats.

Habitat. Mountain lions are now restricted mainly to mountains, hilly woodland, and southern swamps. Type of vegetation is not as important as a plentiful supply of deer and the absence of persecution by man.

Habits. Mountain lions are solitary animals and are mainly nocturnal, but may be active at any hour and at any season. They do not hibernate.

The mountain lion's shelter may be in a cave, a rocky cavern, under an overhanging ledge, in a crevice in a cliff, under an uprooted tree, or in dense vegetation. The home range is variable and depends on sex, age, food availability, and reproductive condition. Cats may regularly cover an area of 25 to 50 km^2 by means of "travelways" which may cross themselves at regular intervals or may be circular in shape. The length of time required for the mountain lion to make a round trip varies considerably. Some circuits may be completed in about two weeks, while others are longer (Young and Goldman, 1946).

Mountain lions are primarily terrestrial, but they do ascend trees by first jumping to a lower branch and then springing from branch to branch. They descend in the same manner. Mountain lions take to trees most often when they are being pursued. They generally avoid water if possible, but they can swim well if necessary.

Mountain lions emit a variety of sounds including low growls, a catlike mew, a hiss, a spit, a scream, and caterwauling (Young and Goldman, 1946). The mountain lion's scream has been likened to that of a woman or child in great distress, and Goldman (1939) commented that this animal "has a wild, weird scream-like cry not calculated to soothe the nerves of a night wayfarer on a lonely forest trail." Several investigators have compared the voice to that of an ordinary tomcat but greatly magnified.

Concerning the stalking of prey, Young and Goldman (1946) stated:

> *The puma relies upon its senses of smell and sight in its foraging. Its smell is keener than that of the bobcat, though less so than in either the wolf or the coyote. It can see its prey for a long distance, but unquestionably it does much of its silent, cautious stalking by the sense of smell alone, taking advantage of every cover until within striking distance of its victim. Its sense of hearing also is acute.*

Mountain lions will sometimes follow a man or other animal out of sheer curiosity, without any intent to attack.

Food. Mountain lions feed on many kinds of birds and mammals, including deer, rabbits, rodents, turkeys, and occasionally domestic animals. Deer are the preferred food. They have a habit of covering a kill with brush and returning to it for a second or third meal. Their presence should be encouraged since they assist in maintaining healthy herds and preventing overpopulation by culling mainly sick and lame animals.

Mountain lions do not have the endurance necessary to catch swift prey by running. Instead, they use their cushioned feet and their ability to conceal themselves to make a stealthy approach to within 10 m or so of their prey. At the appropriate moment, they pounce or spring onto the unsuspecting victim, gripping it firmly with their sharp claws and bringing it to the ground.

During his survey of the Virginia-North Carolina boundary line, Colonel William Byrd (Boyd, 1929) related:

> *The Indian kill'd a very fat Doe, and came across a Bear, which had been put to Death and was half devour'd by a Panther. The last of these Brutes reigns absolute Monarch of the Woods, and in the keenness of his hunger will venture to attack a Bear; tho' then 'tis ever by surprize, as all Beasts of the cat kind use to come upon their Prey.*
>
> *Their Play is to take the poor Bears napping, they being very drowsy Animals, and tho' they be exceedingly Strong, yet their Strength is heavy, while the Panthers are too Nimble and cunning to trust themselves within their Hugg.*
>
> *As formidable as this Beast is to his Fellow Brutes, he never has the confidence to venture upon a Man, but retires from him with great respect, if there be a way open for his Escape. However, it must be confesst, his Voice is a little contemptible for a Monarch of the Forrest, being not a great deal lowder nor more awful than the Mewing of a Household Cat.*

Reproduction and Development. Although mountain lions may breed throughout the year, mating is believed to be most common from December to March. Young mountain lions are generally born from April to September after a gestation of 82 to 96 days (Young and Goldman, 1946; Eaton and Verlander, 1977). Birth dates for five litters recorded in North America by Hall and Kelson (1959) were February, April, June, and July. Females with large embryos have also been reported in January, October, and December (Davis, 1966). The usual litter consists of two to three kittens, and litters may be spaced as far as two to three years apart. The young are born in the den, but no nest is constructed.

Newborn mountain lions are well furred, have their eyes closed, weigh about 400 g, and are between 200 and 300 mm long. The eyes open between 10 and 14 days, and the incisor teeth erupt between 10 and 20 days of age. Nursing normally continues for four to five weeks but may continue longer. By about six weeks of age, the young can consume fresh meat. By eight weeks they weigh about 4.5 kg, and at six months they weigh between 13 and 20 kg. Until approximately three months of age, young mountain lions have distinct black spots on their yellowish-brown coats and bands on their tails and legs. These markings fade rapidly but some may still be visible after 12 months. Young mountain lions remain with the female for an indefinite time, in some instances up to 18 to 24 months. Mountain lions are at least two, and probably three, years old when they begin breeding.

Longevity. The normal longevity of the mountain lion is probably near 12 years, although some captive animals have lived for 19 years (Young and Goldman, 1946; Ulmer, 1951).

Predation. Man is the mountain lion's main enemy.

Other Currently Recognized Subspecies. *Puma (Felis) concolor couguar* Kerr.

Location of Specimens. MCZ, USNM.

Genus *Lynx*

Dentition: 3/3, 1/1, 3/2 or 2/2, 1/1 = 28 or 30

Bobcat
Lynx rufus (Schreber)

Description. The bobcat (Plate 81) is a medium-sized, short-tailed member of the cat family. It has a short, broad face set off by a ruff of fur on the sides of the face extending from the ear down to the lower jaw. The prominent, pointed ears possess relatively short and inconspicuous ear tufts. The backs of the ears are blackish, and each has a centrally-located white spot. The dorsal pelage is brownish to pale yellowish interspersed with gray and consists of a mixture of tawny hairs tipped with black and white. The chin and underparts are whitish. Dark spots are usually present on the whitish belly. The tail is short with several blackish bars on the dorsal surface just in front of the tip. There are five toes on each front foot and four on each hind foot, all of which possess long, sharp, strongly recurved, retractile claws. Females possess six mammae. Adult bobcats are generally between 660 and 1,016 mm in total length, including a tail 100 to 165 mm long. Males normally weigh between 5.4 and 13.5 kg, while females weigh between 4 and 9 kg. An article in the Washington *Herald* dated November 5, 1920, recorded the killing of a large bobcat in the Dismal Swamp that measured 1,219 mm from its nose to the tips of the hind feet. An unusually large 14.4 kg specimen was taken in Smyth County, in 1942 (Cross, 1948), while Progulske (1955b) examined an 18 kg bobcat from Highland County, Virginia. An 18 kg specimen was reportedly taken in Floyd County, Virginia, in 1953 (Swink, 1959).

There has been much conjecture regarding the tufts of hair that occur on the bobcat's ears. Experiments seem to show that these hairs are an aid to the animal's hearing, acting as a sort of antenna in catching sound impulses. A cat with the tufts of hair clipped from each ear does not seem to respond to sounds as readily as does one with the ear tufts retained (Young, 1958).

The skull is short and rounded with well-developed carnassial teeth. Prominent postorbital processes and large, rounded auditory bullae are present (Figure 161).

Distribution. The bobcat formerly ranged from southern Canada throughout most of the United States south to central Mexico. It has, however, been extirpated from densely settled areas and from much of the central portion of the United States.

Two geographic variants occur in Virginia (Figure 162). One of these occurs in the Dismal Swamp and has been classified as status undetermined (Handley, 1991). Concerning this variant, Handley (1991) stated:

> *The bobcat is statewide in distribution: rare northward, uncommon in the southeastern part of the state, and common to abundant in the mountains. Populations are stable or increasing. Beyond its occurrence in the Dismal Swamp, the distribution of the subspecies* Felis rufus floridanus *in Virginia is undetermined.*

Although bobcats were fairly numerous during the colonial period, their range was greatly reduced as civilization pushed westward and timber cutting started. The number of these forest animals decreased steadily until the late 1930s. During the late twenties and early thirties, the national forests and the Shenandoah National Park were expanded and developed, and large land areas were protected from overcutting and uncontrolled burning, which allowed the natural habitat for bobcats to return very rapidly.

Progulske (1955b) noted that most of the bobcats in Virginia are located in the more rugged and secluded sections of the state. He stated:

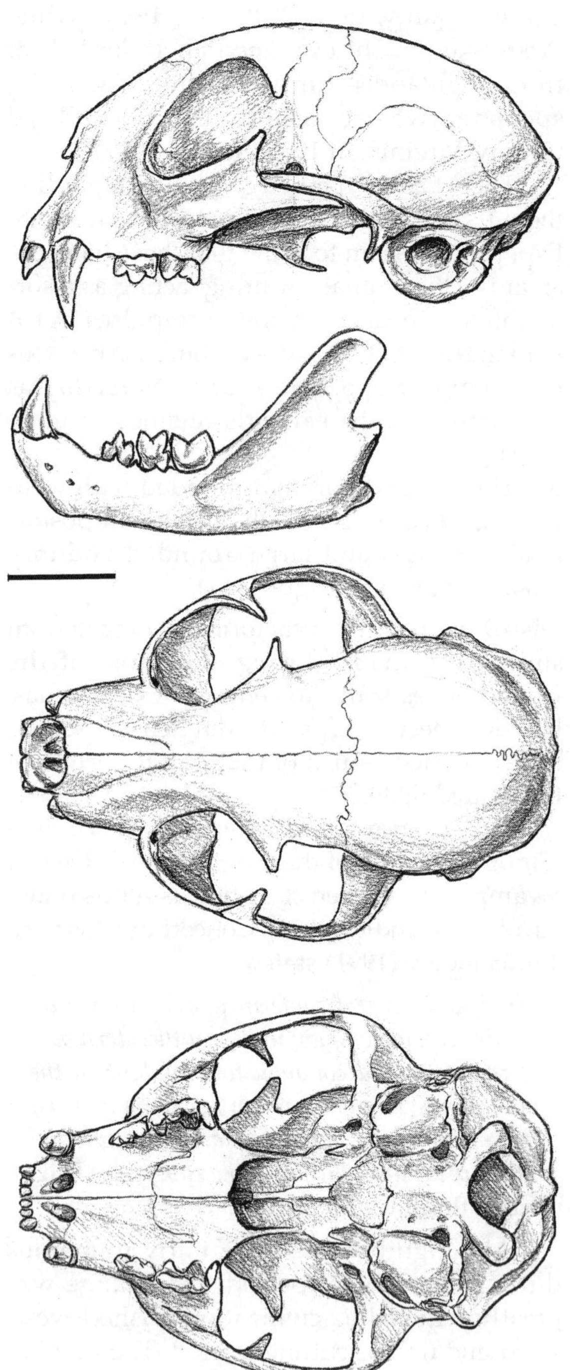

Figure 161. *Lynx rufus:* Left lateral view of skull, and dorsal and ventral view of skull. Scale bar = 20 mm

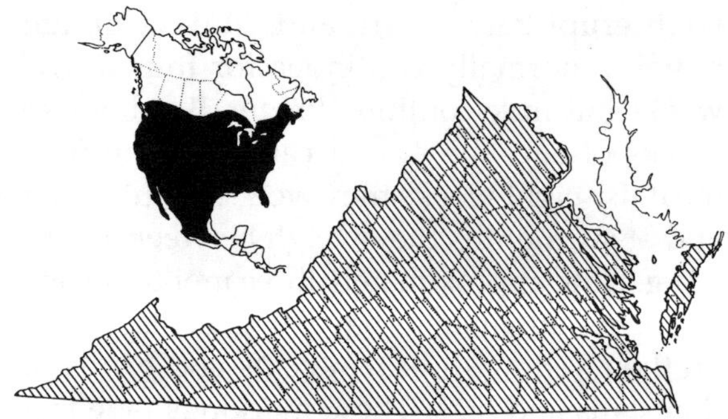

Figure 162. *Lynx rufus:* Range in Virginia and North America.

> *A few live in the Dismal Swamp in Nansemond and Norfolk counties. The Alleghany, Massanutten, and Blue Ridge Mountains seem to be the best 'cat territory. The Barbours Creek section of Craig County, Virginia, Poor Valley in Bland and Tazewell Counties, parts of Augusta County, Virginia, the Alleghany Mountain which runs through Highland, Bath, and Alleghany Counties, the Massanutten Range, and parts of Wise, Lee, and Scott Counties in southwest Virginia seem to hold the greatest bobcat concentrations.*

Bailey (1896a) reported bobcats to be very common in the Dismal Swamp. Progulske (1955b) estimated a population of approximately 2,500 bobcats in 40 Virginia counties.

The distribution and abundance of the bobcat changes with land use. Environmental changes resulting from agriculture and timber harvesting have opened up forested areas previously unsuitable for the bobcat, and its adaptability to such changes has allowed it to become the most numerous of the North American felids.

A total of 690 bobcats was tagged by Game Division personnel during 1987–1988. A summary of bobcat tagging data for 1977–1988 is presented in table 11.

Comparative data on the wild fur catch in Virginia, including the bobcat, are presented in tables 8 and 9.

Habitat. Bobcats are found in a variety of habitats ranging from forested mountainous regions and timbered swamps to the desert. In the southeastern United States the bobcat is found mainly in second-growth deciduous forests with much undergrowth interspersed with numerous clearings and swampy areas with grassy borders. River bottom swamps provide good habitat.

Habits. The bobcat is solitary and mainly nocturnal. It is active throughout the year. Because of its secretive nature, it is rarely observed. Although mainly terrestrial, it is a good tree climber and may spend considerable time resting on a limb. Young (1958) and others have noted that the bobcat dislikes water, but if forced into a lake or river, it can swim well. Young (1958) stated that the bobcat "will often outdistance dogs by its ability to leap out of deep water in bounding jumps similar to the bounding leaps of a deer." When not being pursued or molested, however, the bobcat will normally cross a stream at some natural bridge, such as a fallen log.

Like the mountain lion, male bobcats make "scrapes" along their trail routes. Bobcats use their hind feet to make small piles of leaves and sticks on which they urinate to warn other males that the territory is occupied.

Bobcats have excellent senses of sight, smell, and hearing. Schwartz and Schwartz (1959) noted:

> *In locating prey, a bobcat depends more upon its keen eyesight and hearing than its sense of smell. When stalking, it usually creeps stealthily along, then pounces on its prey; or it may crouch on a game trail or tree limb and await an unwary victim.*

Marshall and Jenkins (1966) stated that bobcats spend a great deal of time sitting, watching, and listening. When eluding pursuers, the bobcat will lay a difficult trail to follow rather than depend on speed (Pearson, 1954).

Bobcats are generally quiet, but at times they may growl, howl, meow, scream, hiss, and spit. They are especially vocal during the mating season. They have a highly developed sense of curiosity. Hamilton (1943) commented that they and their dens have a very strong odor.

The bobcat generally uses a permanent den only while raising its young. During the remainder of the year it uses a different "resting shelter" each day or every few days. Such shelters may be in thickets, beneath a fallen tree, inside a hollow snag, or in hollow logs on the ground.

The home range of a bobcat varies greatly. Kitchings and Story (1984) recorded an average home range size of 7,677 ha for two adult males in eastern Tennessee and 2,590 ha for three adult females. Kight (1962) estimated the home range to be between 0.4 and 1.6 km^2 in South Carolina. Marshall and Jenkins (1966) determined the movements of bobcats by radio-tracking and found that home ranges varied from 1.5 to 2.9 km^2 over periods of 41 to 74 days in South Carolina. The average distance traveled per day varied from 1.9 to 4.8 km. Using a minimum area method, Rucker et al. (1989) estimated a home range of 64.2 km^2 for a radio-collared adult male and 24.5 km^2 for three radio-collared adult females in Arkansas. Minimum density averaged one bobcat per 9.6 km^2. In eastern Kentucky radiotelemetry studies yielded an average male home range of 59.4 km^2 (range 14.5 to 133.3 km^2) and an average female home range of 4.7 km^2 (2.8 to 8.1 km^2) (Whitaker et al., 1987). Studies in other areas have shown that bobcats may cover an area up to 80 km in diameter (Sumner, 1931; Grinnell, Dixon, and Linsdale, 1937; Marston, 1942; Pollack, 1951; Robinson and Grand, 1958). According to Young (1958), the two most important factors that determine the home range of the bobcat are the available prey and the extent to which the bobcat is hunted.

Food. From analyses made throughout the United States, the main dietary items of the bobcat are rabbits and rodents (Hamilton, 1943; Davis, 1955; Progulske, 1955a; Young, 1958). Progulske's study in Virginia and North Carolina revealed the following percentages of frequency: cottontail 37.3; gray squirrel 24.8; deer 17.4; field mouse 11.1; unidentified bird 6.9; opossum 6.5; woodchuck 5.4; fox squirrel 3.4; various grasses 3.4; and chipmunk 3.0. Cottontail rabbits and gray squirrels, which comprised nearly 31 percent and 17 percent of the total volume of food, respectively, were the most important foods. Although deer comprised almost 12 percent of the total volume, it appeared to have been consumed more often as carrion rather than as freshly killed prey. However, once a bobcat learns to kill deer, they can often kill an animal up to 90 kg in size (Marston, 1942). Evidence indicates that bobcats jump onto the head of the deer, dig their claws into the base of its ears, and chew on the throat until the deer is killed (Downing, personal communication, December, 1992). Some bobcats undoubtedly are injured or even killed in such a struggle.

Handley (1979a) noted that the stomach of a bobcat taken on the shore of Lake Drummond on October 11, 1895, contained two bog lemmings *(Synaptomys)* and a song sparrow.

King et al. (1983) recorded the top eight winter food items in North Carolina by frequency of occurrence as rabbits, birds, cotton rats, white-tailed deer, small rodents, gray squirrels, raccoons, and opossums. Small numbers of reptiles, amphibians, fish, and insects were also identified.

Wild turkeys seem to be preyed on only where their range is subjected to periodic flooding causing them to seek higher elevations. If bobcats happen to be common in these areas, the turkeys are apt to be heavily preyed upon.

Bobcats cover uneaten prey for later use. Downing (personal communication, December, 1992) recorded a 31.4 kg deer being dragged to cover by a medium-sized bobcat.

Reproduction and Development. In Virginia, Progulske (1955b) reported that the breeding season starts around January 1, and extends into late May with some bobcats possibly even breeding during the summer. Ovulation is normally induced by copulation (Asdell, 1946). Most litters are born in April and May after a 50- to 70-day gestation. Some early breeding bobcats may produce a second litter later in the year (Duke, 1954). Two kittens approximately five weeks old were taken in Virginia on September 3 (Young, 1958). The average litter consists of two to three kittens but may range from one to five. Little or no nest is provided for the young, which are born in a dry, well-hidden, and inaccessible den. Young (1958) noted that den sites are most commonly observed under logs that are concealed by vines, in hollows of decomposing windfalls, in root depressions left by overturned trees, or in small natural rocky caves or recesses such as those found in limestone or eroded sandstone formations.

Newborn kittens have a mottled coat, have their eyes closed, are about 250 mm long, and weigh up to 340 g. The eyes open in 9 to 10 days, before the ears are fully erect. The young nurse for approximately two months, after which their diet is composed of meat. When the young are near weaning age, the male is allowed near them for the first time and may assist in obtaining food for them. By the fall of the year in which they are born, young bobcats will weigh 3.5 to 4.5 kg. The young stay with the female until fall or even later. Some females may mate when one year old (Pollack, 1950).

Longevity. Although little is known about the life span of bobcats in the wild, the average longevity is probably between six and eight years. Bobcats have been kept in captivity at the National Zoological Park in Washington, DC, for as long as 15 years, 10 months (Mann, 1930). A 13.7 kg male bobcat kept in a private zoo was said to be approximately 24 years, 6 months old at the time of its death (Carter, 1955).

Parasites and Diseases. The following internal and external parasites have been recorded from this species in Virginia by Progulske (1952a, 1952b); Klewer (1958); and Young (1958): **Acanthocephala** (spiny-headed worms) *(Onicola canis);* **Nematoda** (roundworms) *(Anafilaroides rostratus, Physaloptera praeputialis, Physaloptera rara, Spirura* sp., *Toxocara cati, Toxocara canis, Trichurus felis, Troglostrongylus wilsoni);* **Trematoda** (flukes) *(Paragonimus* sp.*);* **Cestoda** (tapeworms) *(Hydotigera macrocystis, Taenia krabbei, Taenia rileyi, Toxascaris leonina);* and **Siphonaptera** (fleas) *(Ctenocephalides felis).*

Rabies has been reported in bobcats in Virginia (Carey and McLean, 1978). Usually one or two laboratory-confirmed cases are reported each year (Table 5). Bobcats are also subject to distemper and cat enteritis, both of which are usually fatal.

Predation. Adult bobcats have relatively few enemies, although foxes and great horned owls may kill young. The mountain lion may kill an occasional individual, while coyotes have been observed to tree these mammals. Doe deer with fawns have been known to chase bobcats. Humans and dogs, however, are by far the most important predators.

Geographic Variation. The subspecies in Virginia is *Lynx rufus rufus* (Schreber). Two geographic variants may occur in the state. One form inhabits the southeastern portion of the state, while the other is found in the remainder of the state.

Other Currently Recognized Subspecies. *Lynx rufus floridanus* Rafinesque.

Location of Specimens. AMNH, ANSP, BCV, GMU, LU, LFCC, MCZ, NCSM, ROM, SNP, USNM, VHCC, VPISU, VPI-W.

Suborder Pinnipedia

Seals and Sea Lions (Family Phocidae and Family Otariidae)

Potter (1991) described the pinniped fauna of Virginia as follows:

> *Virginia's pinniped fauna consists primarily of stray harbor seals,* Phoca vitulina, *most of which are young of the year. Adult harbor seals are very uncommon at our latitude. Gray seals* Halichoerus grypus, *rare vagrants south of Massachusetts, occasionally may haul out on Virginia's beaches during severe winters. Two arctic or subarctic pinnipeds that have been reported as far south as Virginia are the hooded seal,* Cystophora cristata, *and the harp seal,* Pagophilus groenlandicus. *The presence of these species in temperate waters is extremely unusual and does not represent their normal distribution.*
>
> *The only sea lion reported in the western North Atlantic is the California sea lion,* Zalophus californianus. *The number of sightings of these feral exotics, native in the North Pacific, has decreased since the Marine Mammal Protection Act of 1972 regulated the taking and keeping of marine mammals. California sea lions probably are not reproducing in the North Atlantic and sightings of them represent individuals that were released or have escaped captivity.*

Wass (1972) noted that harbor seals (Plate 82) are frequently seen along the coast of Virginia. Blaylock (1985) stated: "Infrequently, small groups of harbor seals may be found near the islands of the Chesapeake Bay Bridge-Tunnel in spring and summer." Handley and Patton (1947) and Handley and Handley (1950) reported four individuals from the lower James River in James City and Warwick (now Newport News) counties and Chesapeake Bay off Back River in York County. In addition, Bailey (1946) cited records from Accomack County and from Richmond in Henrico County. Yearling seals are regular visitors to Virginia waters every winter, although adults usually do not move south of the New York-New Jersey area. Besides resting on the rock islands of the Chesapeake Bay Bridge-Tunnel, they have also been observed on piers and beaches.

Since January, 1991, 10 harbor seals have been recorded from the counties of Virginia Beach (January 1991; December, 1992; February, 1994; April, 1994), Suffolk (March, 1991), Charles City (January, 1992), Accomack (April, 1993), and Northampton (January, 1994). Since 1990, the Virginia Marine Science Museum Mammal Stranding Program has recorded only one gray seal (Accomack County, March, 1990) and one hooded seal (Accomack County, March, 1994).

A juvenile male hooded seal came ashore at Virginia Beach on February 27, 1996.

Sirenians

Living members of the order Sirenia include the manatees and dugongs, both of which are wholly aquatic herbivores. The skin covering the robust bodies of these mammals is sparsely covered by fine hairs. Forelimbs are paddle-shaped, and hind limbs are absent. The horizontally flattened tail is broad and rounded. The eyes are small, the nostrils are located on the upper surface of the snout, and ear pinnae are absent.

Manatees (Family Trichechidae)

Manatees are among the few living mammals that do not possess seven cervical (neck) vertebrae. They have only six. They also possess a unique dentition in which the two upper and lower incisors are rudimentary and are concealed beneath horny plates. These teeth are lost before maturity. Canine teeth are absent. Manatees possess a total of 11 upper and lower jaw teeth, but usually no more than 6 are present in each jaw at any one time. The teeth move forward and are replaced from behind. Thus, the anterior jaw teeth are lost before the posterior ones come into use. All of the teeth are similar in appearance. The skull consists of a relatively small braincase, a short, narrow rostrum, and massive zygomatic arches.

Genus *Trichechus*

Dentition: 2/2, 0/0, 6/6 to 11/11 = 16 to 26

Manatee
Trichechus manatus Harlan

Description. The manatee (Plate 83), a large aquatic mammal, has a uniform dull grayish spindle-shaped body. Algae and barnacles may be present on the skin. The head is broad, and the thick upper lip is cleft. Hairs are scattered over the body and stiff bristles are present around the muzzle. Nails are present on the dorsal surfaces of the forelimbs. Hind limbs are absent, but vestigial pelvic bones are present. Ear openings are minute, and external pinnae are absent. The tail is rounded and paddle-shaped. Females possess two mammae. Adult manatees reach lengths up to 3,900 mm and weigh up to 1,500 kg (Reynolds and Odell, 1991). The average adult is approximately 3,050 mm long and weighs about 500 kg.

The skull characteristics (Figure 163) are as described for the family.

Distribution. This species is found primarily from eastern Brazil to the West Indies and the Atlantic Coast of the southern United States. It has been found rarely in summer north to Virginia and North Carolina and along the coast of Texas.

Glover (1676), cited by McAtee (1950), provided a description of a possible early record of a manatee in the Rappahannock River about

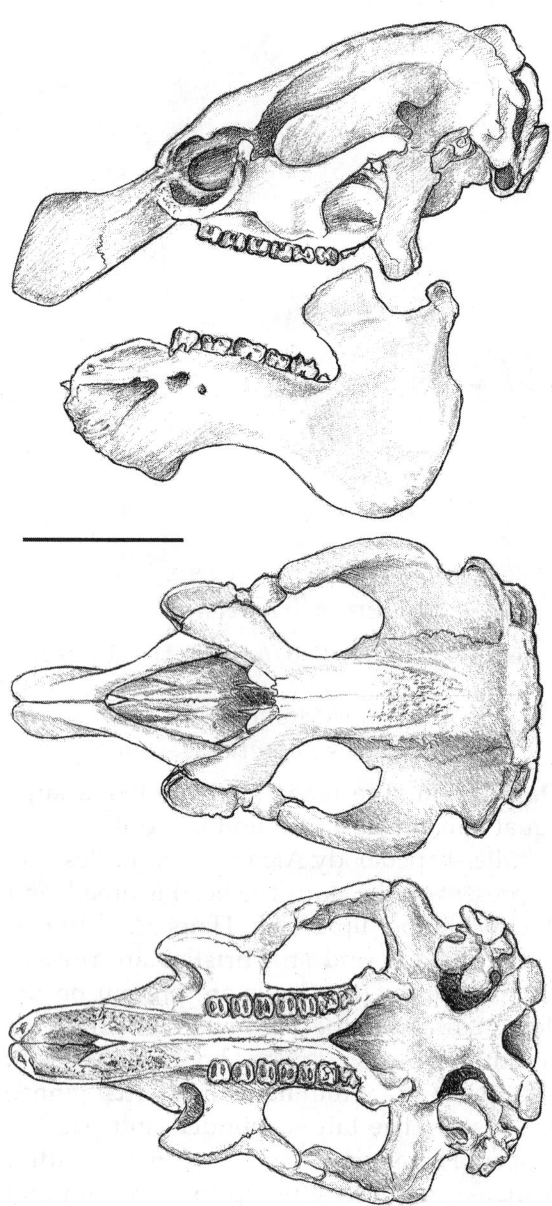

Figure 163. *Trichechus manatus:* Left lateral view of skull, and dorsal and ventral view of skull. Scale bar = 10 cm.

16 km from its mouth (Latitude 37° 38'). Glover stated:

> *And now it comes into my mind, I shall here insert an account of a very strange Fish or rather a Monster, which I happened to see in* Rapa-han-nock *River about a year before I came out of the Country; the manner of it was thus:*
>
> *As I was coming down the forementioned River in a Sloop bound for the Bay, it happened to prove calm; at which time we were three leagues short of the rivers mouth; the tide of ebb being then done, the sloop-man dropped his grap-line, and he and his boy took a little boat alone, in which time I took a small book out of my pocket and sate down at the stern of the vessel to read; but I had not read long before I heard a great rushing and slashing of the water, which caused me suddenly to look up, and about a half a stones cast from me appeared a most prodigious Creature, much resembling a man, only somewhat larger, standing right up in the water with his head, neck, shoulders, breast, and waste, to the cubits of his arms, above water; his skin was tawny, much like that of an* Indian; *the figure of his head was pyramidal, and slick, without hair; his eyes large and black, and so were his eye-brows; his mouth very wide, with a broad, black streak on the upper lip, which turned upwards at each end like mustachoes; his countenance was grim and terrible; his neck, shoulders, arms, breast and wast, were like unto the neck, arms, shoulders, breast and wast of a man; his hands, if he had any, were under water; he seemed to stand with his eyes fixed on me for some time, and afterward dived down, and a little after riseth at somewhat a farther distance, and turned his head towards me again, and then immediately falleth a little under water, and swimmeth away so near the top of the water, that I could discern him throw out his arms, and gather them in as a man doth when he swimmeth. At last he shoots with his head downwards, by which means he cast his tayl above the water, which exactly resembled the tayl of a fish with a broad fane at the end of it.*

The earliest verified manatee from Virginia was taken in 1908 off Ocean View. An article in *The Washington Post* dated September 23, 1908, stated:

> *A live sea cow, or manatee, weighing 1,500 pounds, was hauled ashore today at Ocean View in the seine of the J. H. Parkerson fishery. The fishermen succeeded in getting the manatee alive in a pen, where it is being kept as a curiosity.*

An article concerning this incident also appeared in *Forest and Stream* (Anonymous, 1908). It stated:

> *Fishermen at Ocean View, Virginia brought a manatee ashore in their seine last week and it*

will probably be sent to some museum, as it is a large, healthy specimen of the manatee usually found in Florida Waters.

No reports of manatees in Virginia's waters occurred for the next 70 years until August 27, 1978, when a manatee was sighted in Lynnhaven Bay in the City of Virginia Beach. Between 1978 and 1989, a total of seven additional individuals were recorded as follows: September 13, 1980, in Rich Creek, City of Hampton (sighting); October 23, 1980, at Buckroe Beach, City of Hampton (dead male); August-September, 1985, at Hampton, City of Hampton (sighting); August, 1987, at Hopewell, Prince George, Charles City and Chesterfield counties (sighting); June, 1988, at Smith Island, Northampton County (sighting); October 11–14, 1988, at Portsmouth, City of Portsmouth (sighting); and June-July, 1989, at Quinby Harbor and Upshur Bay in Accomack County (sighting). These records were obtained by Potter (1991).

On September 29, 1992, a manatee was observed swimming inside the Deep Creek Rock at Chesapeake (*Richmond Times-Dispatch,* September 30, 1992). During the summer of 1994 a male manatee was observed in Chesapeake Bay (Bay Journal, November, 1994). When it showed no signs of heading south as the weather grew cooler, it was captured by National Aquarium biologists, placed aboard a US Coast Guard C-130 transport plane and flown to Orlando where it was fitted with an electronic satellite transmitter and released. A padded belt at the base of the tail held a 1.2 m plastic strip. At the end of this strip was a 2.25 kg, 0.6 m casing that floated and held the transmitter. Readings could be obtained even when the animal was up to 1.8 m under water. During the summer of 1995, the same 3.4 m, 540 kg manatee departed from Jacksonville, Florida on June 15. By July 4, "Chessie" had entered Chesapeake Bay, having traveled 525 miles in 19 days (Anonymous, 1995a). Then he swam along the New Jersey coast to New England before returning to Florida (Reshetiloff, 1995). Never before had a manatee ever been observed so far north.

Blaylock (1985) noted that an autopsy of the specimen stranded at Buckroe Beach in 1980 showed that it died of starvation and, secondarily, pneumonia.

This species is endangered throughout its entire range, including Virginia. Handley (1991) classified the manatee as a vagrant.

Habitat. Manatees live in relatively shallow saltwater bays and in the fresh or brackish waters of sluggish coastal rivers.

Habits. Manatees may occur singly or in small groups. They can remain submerged for as long as 20 minutes but usually surface every 2 to 10 minutes to breathe, depending on how active they are. They are unable to tolerate water at temperatures less than 18°C (65°F) for long periods. They cannot survive in water where the temperature falls below 7.7°C (46°F).

Manatees usually swim between 1 and 3 m below the surface. Although they have been clocked at speeds up to 25 km/hr for short distances, their usual cruising speed is between 4 and 10 km/hr (Hartman, 1971). The deepest recorded dive is 10 m.

Manatees propel themselves forward by dorsoventral undulations of their tail. The tail is also used as a rudder for steering, banking, and rolling. The flippers are usually held loosely at the sides.

These mammals feed from six to eight hours daily, usually in sessions of two to four hours duration. Resting animals may remain suspended near the surface or near the bottom on the substrate.

Manatees produce a simple, squeaklike vocalization within the range of human hearing. No ultrasonic components have been identified (Schevitt and Watkins, 1965).

The presence of organochlorine pesticides, polychlorinated biphenyls, mercury, lead, cadmium, copper, iron, and selenium was investigated in Florida manatees by O'Shea et al. (1984). With the exception of copper, findings indicated that manatees were not excessively contaminated with the substances studied.

Food. Manatees are entirely herbivorous, grazing on a wide variety of aquatic vegetation including eelgrass, widgeon grass, turtle grass, lily pads, and water hyacinths. They may consume as much as 10 to 15 percent of their body weight in food each day (Odell, 1982).

Reproduction and Development. Females may give birth to a single calf during any month of the year after a gestation of at least 12 months (Reynolds and Odell, 1991). In

Florida, more births occur in spring and summer than at other times of the year. Newborn manatees weigh about 30 kg and are about 1,200 mm long. During their first few days of life, calves swim entirely with their flippers; only over a period of several weeks do they gradually learn to use their tail in swimming. Young manatees occasionally ride on their mother's back but more often swim beneath the mother's body.

The low reproductive rate results in only one calf being born every three years. Calves may remain with the female for more than a year after their birth. Calves are probably nursed for a year or longer, although the infant manatee begins to graze within days of its birth. Sexual maturity is probably attained between six and 10 years of age and a length of about 2.7 m (Reynolds and Odell, 1991).

Longevity. The life span of manatees in the wild is unknown but is estimated to be 40 to 50 years (Odell, 1982). A captive manatee at the Bradenton Museum in Florida is over 40 years old (Reynolds and Odell, 1991).

Predation. Man is the adult manatee's only enemy, most often inflicting mortal wounds with the propellers and keels of motor-driven boats. Some animals become entangled in ropes or are caught in fishing lines and nets. Dredging uproots or smothers with silt the bottom-growing plants on which manatees feed.

Geographic Variation. The subspecies in Virginia is *Trichechus manatus latirostris* (Harlan)

Location of Specimens. No specimens from Virginia are known to exist in collections.

Odd-Toed Ungulates

The order Perissodactyla, the odd-toed ungulates, is composed of the tapirs, rhinoceroses, and horses. These medium-sized to large mammals are adapted for running. The middle, or third, digit on each foot is larger than any of the others. The main axis of the foot lies directly over the third digit (mesaxonic). The facial part of the skull is usually long, the stomach is simple, the cecum is large, and a gallbladder is normally absent. A clavicle is also absent.

Only one family of Perissodactyla, Equidae, is found in North America.

Horses
(Family Equidae)

This family includes the zebras, asses, kiangs, and the true horses. The hind toes number three or fewer. Hooves are present. The ulna and fibula are incomplete; the metacarpals and metatarsals are fused. The premolars and molars have massive transversely ridged or complex crowns. The mammae are inguinal.

Genus *Equus*

Dentition: 3/3, 1/1, 3–4/3, 3/3 = 40–42

Horse
Equus caballus Linnaeus

Description. Horses (Plate 84) vary in color from black to white. They may be spotted or mottled. The skull is greatly elongated and the mandible is well developed. The ears are medium-sized and erect. The hair on the upper side of the neck is long and forms the mane. The tail is long. Adult horses may be 2,000 to 3,000 mm long with tail vertebrae 450 to 750 mm long. Adults weigh between 135 and 1,000 kg. Males are normally larger than females. This species has been domesticated, and selective breeding has resulted in body conformations suitable for racing, herding, plowing, etc.

The large skull has an elongated rostrum. Each eye socket is enclosed by a solid bony ring. The crowns of the premolars and molars are massive, quadrate, and transversely ridged (Figure 164).

Distribution. Two widely separated areas in Virginia — Assateague Island and Mount Rogers — are currently inhabited by semiwild, or free-roaming, bands of horses. The National Park Service oversees the northern (Maryland) herd of approximately 150 animals that range freely throughout the Maryland portion of Assateague Island. The southern (Virginia) herd is owned and managed by the Chincoteague, Virginia, Volunteer Fire Company. It consists of approximately 150 to 175 animals. The Maryland and Virginia herds have been separated since 1965.

The origin of the Assateague ponies is unclear. They may be descendants of ponies that originally escaped from early Spanish ships or ponies released in the late 1600s by early colonists. They have been known from Assateague for 250 years, but it is not known if this represents continuous habitation (Bixby, et al., 1994). There have been regular introductions, but few

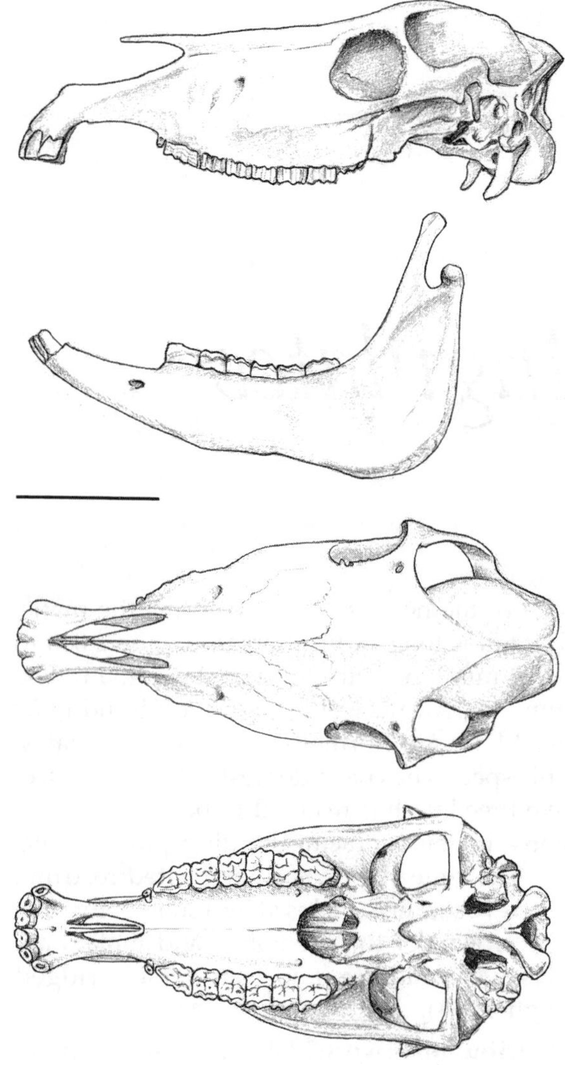

Figure 164. *Equus caballus:* Left lateral view of skull, and dorsal and ventral view of skull. Scale bar = 10 cm.

introduced animals survive. In 1978, 40 western mustangs were released on the Virginia portion of the island to infuse new blood into the small inbred herd. Within a year, most of the transplants had perished (Keiper, 1985).

Virginia's Assateague ponies live a completely free-roaming existence except for a period of about three days in July when most are rounded up and driven across the channel to Chincoteague. There approximately 80 percent of the foals are selectively culled and auctioned by members of the Chincoteague Volunteer Fire Department.

A small herd of 100 to 200 semiwild ponies inhabits the high country near Mount Rogers, particularly the Wilburn Ridge region. The grazing of these ponies serves to keep the high mountain pastures open. The National Forest Service permit allows 90 horses to graze on federal land. An additional 30 head are permitted on state park land. Bill Pugh, Hicks Pugh, and Morris Roberts put 32 or 33 ponies on Wilburn Ridge in the early 1970s (Bill Pugh, personal communication, August 28, 1992). The ponies were subsequently sold to the Wilburn Ridge Pony Association, members of which conduct spring and fall roundups, to brand new foals and cull the herd. Excess ponies are sold in the fall at Grayson Highlands State Park.

Habits. No formal study of the Wilburn Ridge ponies has been conducted. Most of our knowledge of feral horses in Virginia relates to the Assateague herd and particularly to those bands living on the Maryland end of the island.

The Assateague ponies roam the island in bands usually consisting of a stallion and several mares and foals. In Maryland, variation in harem band size is correlated with the number of sexually mature males in the population. Average harem size varies between 9 and 14 in Maryland, but in Virginia the harem bands average about 20 ponies per band.

Keiper (1990) stated: "Because the stallion is non-territorial and defends his harem rather than a distinct territory, the group is not restricted in its movement and can wander about to make use of the best available food from season to season."

Keiper (1985) noted that during daylight hours the Maryland ponies spend approximately 78 percent of the time grazing and 19 percent resting. At night approximately 54 percent of the time is spent grazing and 40 percent resting. Most grazing occurs after sunrise and in the late afternoon. Nocturnal activity patterns have been studied by Keiper and Keenan (1980).

During summer, ponies spend about 40 percent of their time in the salt marshes, 23 percent in the primary and secondary dunes, 22 percent in the grassy areas behind the dunes, 9 percent on the beach, 4 percent in the bay, and 2 percent on the mud flats (Keiper, 1985). In winter they utilize the dunes and inner dune areas to a greater extent and spend less time in the salt marshes. The movements of most of the Virginia ponies are restricted by fences, which prevent their grazing on the dunes and from using the beach. More than 80 percent of their time, both summer and winter, is spent in the marsh.

Average home range of harem bands on the northern unfenced Maryland portion of the island is 6.48 km^2, whereas average home range for the more restricted southern (Virginia) harem bands is 1.72 km^2.

Vocal, olfactory, tactile, and visual cues provide important means of communication between ponies. Vocal communication consists of short, high pitched squeals or screams, nickers, neighs, and whinnies.

Food. Approximately 80 percent of the diet of Maryland ponies consists of grass, primarily saltmarsh cordgrass. Other important grasses include American beach grass, American three-square rush, reed phragmites, and salt-meadow hay. Other foods consist of poison ivy and sandbur thorn balls. During the winter ponies browse on poison ivy stems, marsh elder shrubs, and bayberry (Keiper, 1985).

Reproduction and Development. Keiper (1990) reported that pony populations on the northern portion of Assateague Island (Maryland) more than doubled between 1975 and 1988 (45 to 152 animals). This represents an average increase of 8 percent per year.

Breeding occurs from March to September. A few females breed during their third summer when they are 24 to 26 months of age, but most do not begin breeding until they are three years old (Keiper, 1985).

Single foals are born from March to September after a gestation of probably 330 to 340 days as in domestic horses. Approximately half (52 percent) are born during May, 22 percent in June, 13 percent in April, and 10 percent in July (Keiper, 1985).

The foaling rate in Maryland was 54.4 percent and foal survival was 83.3 percent between 1975 and 1988. Mortality was estimated at about 5 percent. In Virginia, the foaling rate was 74 percent during 1975–1980.

The precocious foals have their eyes open at birth and are covered with hair. Foals stand and walk unsteadily at first, but within a few hours of their birth they are able to gallop a mile or more with their mothers (Keiper, 1985).

The sex ratio of the northern population is approximately 1 male to 2.4 females, while in the southern population it is 1 male to 6.4 females. The age structure of the two populations has been affected by human management, primarily the sale of colts. Approximately 60 percent of the Virginia herd is adult ponies, whereas less than 40 percent of the Maryland herd consists of adults (Keiper, 1985).

A vaccine made from pig ovaries has been used successfully to control wild horse populations (Kemp, 1988). In laboratory tests, the vaccinations have proven to be 90 percent effective and reversible. Fertility returns within a year. The vaccine has been successfully used to control the pony population in Maryland where a dart rifle is used to inject mares with the contraceptive drug.

Longevity. Most Assateague ponies live about 20 years, although one bought at the annual auction lived to be 35 (Keiper, 1985).

Parasites and Disease. In 1975, almost half of the Virginia herd tested positive for equine infectious anemia (EIA or swamp fever). The infected ponies were quarantined until 1978 when they were destroyed (Keiper, 1985). Equine encephalitis was also recorded in the Virginia herd in the mid-1970s, and outbreaks killed over 20 animals in Maryland during August and September, 1990–1991.

Location of Specimens. CM, CMHF, USNM.

Even-Toed Ungulates

The order Artiodactyla contains all of the even-toed hoofed ungulates. These mammals have paraxonic feet in which the axis of the foot passes between the third and fourth digits. The remaining digits are reduced or absent. The upper incisor teeth are reduced or absent. The canines are usually reduced or lost, although in some forms they are enlarged and tusklike. The molars may be low-crowned or high-crowned with crescents. The stomach may have up to four chambers.

This order is divided into three suborders on the basis of tooth structure. The suborder Suiformes is characterized by low-crowned teeth with low, rounded cusps (bunodont). Its members, which lack horns or antlers, include the pigs and hippopotamuses. The suborders Tylopoda (llamas and camels) and Ruminantia (deer, elk, caribou, moose, giraffe, pronghorn antelope, bison, sheep, goat, and others) have teeth in which the cusps are elongated longitudinally into crescents (selenodont). Horns or antlers are present in most of the latter group.

Pigs
(Family Suidae)

The members of this family have a head with an elongated, mobile snout. The nostrils open on the nearly naked, flat, oval terminal surface of the snout. The feet are narrow with four complete toes on each foot. Only the medial pair of toes reaches the ground, except when running, two dew claws also show in the track. The large upper canines grow outward and backward.

Only one representative of this family occurs in Virginia.

Genus *Sus*

Dentition: 3/3, 1/1, 4/4, 3/3 = 44

Pig
Sus scrofa Gray

Description. The appearance and morphological characteristics of free-roaming, or feral, pigs (Plate 85) are intermediate between those of domestic swine and the European wild boar. The degree of difference varies with the amount of crossbreeding and the length of time that the feral population has existed in the wild (Sweeney and Sweeney, 1982). The most common coloration is black, although black and white, black and brown, brown, and even all white individuals occur. The hairs are usually coarser and denser than those of domestic hogs. Females usually possess 12 mammae. Adult feral pigs range between approximately 1,000 and 1,950 mm in length, including a 150 to 300 mm tail. Individuals normally weigh between 31 and 150 kg.

The skull is elongated and laterally compressed. In the boar, both upper and lower canines are curved backward and outward, with the lower canines being aligned in front of the upper canines (Sweeney and Sweeney, 1982). In females, the canines are less developed. In both sexes, the canine teeth continue to grow throughout the life of the animal.

Concerning Virginia's feral pigs, Duncan and Schwab (1986) stated: "Back Bay pigs are smaller than domestic pigs and are comparable in size to their wild boar ancestors. Feral pigs in Virginia are thinner, appearing more streamlined in body shape, with longer and sharper tusks, and coarser coats than tame hogs. . . . Data from ten Back Bay hogs showed an average whole weight of 110 pounds with a range from 74.5 to 198 pounds. . . . The male hog is usually larger than the female, and both sexes usually increase in size through the second or third year of life. While Back Bay pigs closely resemble their tame counterparts, they have lost some characteristics of domestic pigs. Feral pigs at False Cape have straight tails and are usually jet black in coloration." Schwab (personal communication, December, 1992) reported that a recently-killed animal weighed 121.5 kg (270 lbs).

Distribution and Status. The presence of feral pigs in Virginia can be traced back to the English settlements on the lower James River in the early 1600s (Mayer and Brisbin, 1991). Due to a shortage of feed, the colonists permitted some of their domestic swine to roam freely throughout the area. Some of these animals became feral and their numbers increased. Towne and Wentworth (1950) noted that in 1627, wild pigs in that area of Virginia were "innumerable."

Feral or partially feral pigs have been present in the Dismal Swamp since the 1600s. These animals were branded and released in the swamp to feed, a common practice in the early 1700s (Wertenbaker, 1962). In March, 1728, William Byrd recorded free-ranging pigs in the Dismal Swamp (Boyd, 1929). During the early 1920s, Stansbury (1925) noted that the wild hog was considered a game species.

Panthers, wolves, wild cattle, wild hogs, and wild goats were reported in the swamp at one time or another. The panthers and wolves were the first to disappear many years ago. Up until a few years ago the others were found, but at present [1962] *none are found in the swamp* (Davis, 1971).

Handley (1979a) noted: "The fate of this animal [feral pig] in the Swamp, however, is uncertain. There seems to be no recent mention of it in the literature."

The current status and distribution of this species has been discussed by Mayer and Brisbin (1991). They stated:

The area of Princess Anne County around the Back Bay National Wildlife Refuge, Barbours Hill Game Management Area, and False Cape State Park had open range in the early 1920s and 1930s. Most, if not all, of the feral hogs now in these localities are descended from this early stock. When the refuge was established in 1938, all range stock were removed by their owners. Unclaimed animals remained to give rise to the present-day feral population (I. W. Ailes, personal communication; R. Duncan, personal communication). In the early 1960s, this population was estimated to be decreasing and to number fewer than 250 animals (Lewis et al., 1965). More recently, their numbers have increased, and this population was estimated to consist of approximately 1,000 animals in 1981 (I. W. Ailes, personal communication) and 400–500 animals in 1986 (Duncan and Schwab, 1986).

The presence of feral hogs in western Virginia has been reported (Anonymous, 1949; McKnight, 1964), but until recently no populations were known to exist (Mayer and Brisbin, 1991). Cochran (1995), however, verified populations in the Gatewood section of Pulaski County and the Mill Creek section of Wythe County. Some have been observed on national forest land. Field dressed weights ranging from 58 to 72 kg have been reported. An average of nine fetuses per sow were recorded.

An article in the *Roanoke Times and World-News* dated December 6, 1979, reported the escape of several wild boars from an estate near Leesburg. A similar escape in the mountains of North Carolina in 1920 led to a growing and expanding wild population of these mammals in North Carolina and Tennessee, where they are now considered a game species. Feral pigs are presently causing considerable damage to the vegetation, to amphibians, and to ground-nesting birds in the Great Smoky Mountains National Park (Linzey, 1995a).

Habitat. Virginia's feral hogs inhabit an area of barrier beach. Forested portions with pine and live oak support an understory of high-bush blueberry, cat briar, and poison ivy. The areas adjacent to the open beach consist of rolling sand hills that support live oak, black cherry, wax myrtle, and bayberry. The marshland consists primarily of cattails, black needlerush, and big cordgrass (Duncan and Schwab, 1986).

Habits. Feral hogs may be active at any time during the day or night. During the warmer months, they tend to be nocturnal in order to avoid the daytime heat. Movements are generally nomadic and are brought about by food availability. Hogs have keen senses of smell and hearing.

Food. Mast, roots, tubers, and the shoots of herbaceous vegetation constitute the primary foods. Fluctuations in food availability result in seasonal hog movements. In Virginia, live oak acorns are usually available from November through most of February and are a primary food (Duncan and Schwab, 1986). During this time, the hogs are concentrated in the upland areas and beaches. From April until late summer and early fall, the hogs are usually found in the freshwater marshes feeding on herbaceous vegetation.

Duncan and Schwab (1986) described the feeding habits as omnivorous and opportunistic. They stated: "Though preferring to be vegetarians, our hogs have been observed eating dead fish left on beaches by commercial fishermen, and hibernating frogs in large numbers."

Reproduction. Following a gestation of 112 to 114 days, a litter consisting usually of five to eight young is born in the spring, although litters of 1 to 12 have been reported (Sweeney and Sweeney, 1982). The nest usually consists of a shallow depression in the ground that may or may not contain bedding material. Although weaning occurs after about three to four months, piglets may remain with the mother for six months or longer. Males become sexually mature at five to six months of age and females at about 10 months.

Longevity. Nowak (1991) noted that average longevity in feral pigs is about 10 years, but some have lived as long as 27 years.

Parasites. Feral pigs are parasitized by lungworms, kidney worms, stomach worms, intestinal worms, and ticks (Duncan and Schwab, 1986).

Geographic Variation. The subspecies in Virginia is *Sus scrofa scrofa* Linnaeus.

Location of Specimens. USNM (domestic swine). No specimens of feral pigs from Virginia are known to exist in museum collections.

Deer
(Family Cervidae)

Deer, caribou, moose, and elk are all members of the family Cervidae. These animals, which are native throughout North America, most of South America, Europe, Asia, and northwest Africa, are best recognized by their antlers. These bony structures are present in most cervids but generally only on males. They occur in both sexes in caribou. Most cervids also have facial glands in pits in front of the eye and often glands on the legs and feet. Each foot has four digits; the two medial digits are well developed, but the two lateral digits are small and do not touch the ground except when running. Members of the Cervidae are ruminants, and the stomach has four chambers. Upper incisors are lacking. Canine teeth are absent or poorly developed in North American forms. The smallest member of this family is the antlerless musk deer of the Himalayas, which weighs about 10 kg; the North American moose, weighing 630 kg, is the largest.

Two representatives of this family — the native white-tailed deer and the introduced sika deer — occur in Virginia. A third member of this family, the elk or wapiti, formerly occurred in Virginia but is now extirpated.

Key to Species of Cervidae

1a Upper canine teeth absent
.... *Odocoileus virginianus*

1b Upper canine teeth present
.... 2

2a Size large; adult body length between 200 and 275 cm; males with large antlers two or three times the length of the head
.... *Cervus elaphus*

2b Size small; adult body length between 105 and 135 cm; males with small, straight antlers usually less than 20 cm long and with one or two short tines
.... *Cervus nippon*

Genus *Cervus*

Dentition: 0/3, 1/1, 3/3, 3/3 = 34

Sika Deer
Cervus nippon Temminck

Description. The body of a sika deer (Plate 86) is dark grayish-brown with faint white spotting. The ears are short and rounded. The small antlers are not curved as are those of white-tailed deer, but instead are straight with one or two short tines (one at the base and one near the tip) pointing forward. The antlers may reach a maximum length of 30 to 36 cm but usually are less than 20 cm long. The base of the antler beam is less than 2.5 cm in diameter. The small whitish tail is narrow and inconspicuous. A black-bordered rump patch containing white, erectile hairs is present. Adult sika deer are approximately 1,220 mm long and stand 760 to 915 mm high at the shoulder. They usually weigh between 40 and 80 kg. Keiper (1990) reported an average dressed weight of 18 male sika deer as 22.25 kg on the Maryland portion of Assateague Island, while 17 females averaged 19.39 kg.

The upper jaw bears a canine tooth on each side which protrudes 6 to 8 mm and is sometimes visible in the living animal when the mouth is closed (Figure 165).

Distribution. This Asian deer is native to Japan, Korea, and adjacent portions of China. *Sika* means "deer" in the Japanese language. Sika deer have been introduced and are thriving in several countries, including the United States. Free-ranging herds are currently found in Maryland, Virginia, Texas, Oklahoma, Kansas, and Wisconsin (Feldhamer, 1982).

The Maryland population originated in 1916 when four or five deer were released on James Island (Flyger and Warren, 1958). The population on Assateague Island is the result of the release of seven animals on the northern (Maryland) end of the island in the 1920s. Charles Law of Berlin, Maryland, purchased two males and three females in 1920. These were kept in an enclosure for several years, during which time one of the males died and three young were born. The deer were subsequently sold to a man who released them on Assateague Island (Flyger, 1960). They are now found throughout the southern (Virginia) portion of the island, in the Chincoteague National Wildlife Refuge, and several miles beyond the state line into Maryland (Handley, 1979b). In 1964, Flyger and Davis stated that this herd was in excess of 1,000 animals. From 1975 to 1977 the population held stable at about 700 animals (Badger, 1977). Keiper (1990) estimated the deer population in the portion of Maryland occupied by sikas to be composed of 75 percent sika deer and 25 percent white-tailed deer.

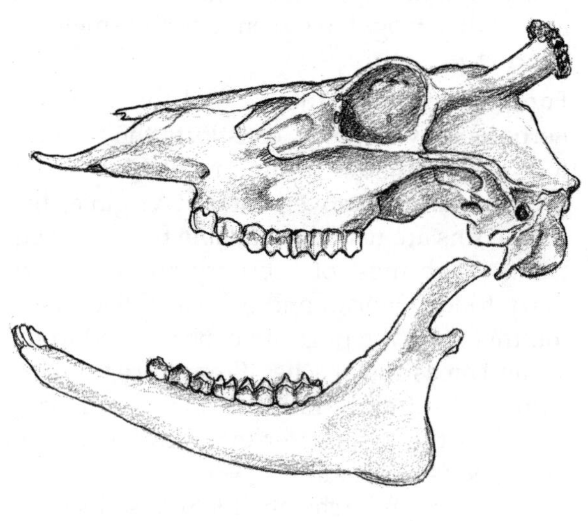

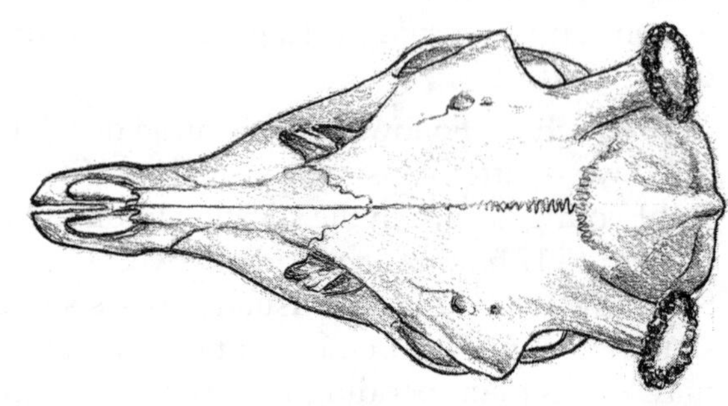

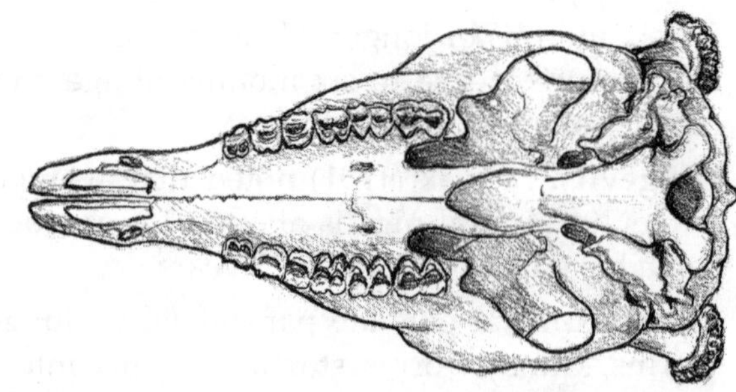

Figure 165. *Cervus nippon:* Left lateral view of skull, and dorsal and ventral view of skull. Scale bar = 5 cm.

In Virginia, this introduced species is found only on Assateague Island in Accomack County.

Habitat. Handley and Gordon (1979f) stated:

On Assateague Island the sika is found in the loblolly pine forests and in the open marshes, but it is most often encountered at the forest edge, in thickets of myrtle, greenbrier, and poison ivy.

Habits. On James Island, Maryland, sika deer are usually seen in groups varying in size from 6 to 60 animals (Flyger, 1960). Although they may be observed grazing during the day, they are primarily nocturnal. When disturbed, they run with bouncing, stiff-legged hops as though they have bed springs attached to their feet (Flyger and Warren, 1958). They take readily to water and can swim reasonably well. Feldhamer (1982) reported a home range of 73.5 hectares for a radio-collared female in Maryland and 151.0 hectares for a male.

Both sexes produce a birdlike chirp or whistle when startled. In addition, during the mating season, males reportedly utter loud screams at night (Flyger and Warren, 1958; Flyger, 1965).

Food. Studies on James Island in Maryland have revealed that sika deer feed on such plants as wax myrtle, grasses, red maple, red gum, loblolly pine, large-toothed aspen, pokeweed, and *Spartina patens* (Flyger and Warren, 1958; Christian et al., 1960). Greenbrier, honeysuckle, and poison ivy are also consumed. Major plants consumed on the Maryland portion of Assateague Island during the late fall included goldenrod, wax myrtle, cordgrass, dwarf sumac, and poison ivy (Keiper, 1990). On Assateague Island, deer frequently stand in 15 to 20 cm of water while grazing along marsh edges and in marshy glades.

Reproduction and Development. Sika deer on the Eastern Shore of Virginia and Maryland breed during October, November, and December. Feldhamer and Marcus (1994) reported that 94.5 percent of 54 adult females collected in late November and early December in Dorchester County, Maryland, had bred or ovulated. Following an eight-month gestation, a single young is born. Females generally produce their first fawn when they are two years old, although calves as young as five to six months of age in Maryland had bred or were in breeding condition (Mullan et al., 1988; Feldhamer and Marcus, 1994). On the Maryland portion of Assateague Island, Keiper (1990) reported that males comprised 42.8 percent of the population, females 41.8 percent, and fawns 15.4 percent.

Longevity. Ohtaishi (1978) reported a maximum longevity of 12 years in wild, unconfined deer and up to 25 years in captive deer. Crandall (1964) reported that a specimen in the National Zoological Park lived 25 years, 5 months.

Parasites and Disease. Shah et al. (1965) reported antibodies to *Myxovirus parainfluenza 3* in 1 of 12 deer in the Maryland-Virginia area.

Feldhamer (1982) stated:

In Maryland, a mass mortality of sika deer on James Island was initially attributed to pine oil poisoning and subsequent malnutrition (Hayes and Shotts, 1959). However, Christian et al. (1960) refuted this conclusion. Although they documented two diseases that occurred in members of the population (glomerulonephritis and inclusion hepatitis), they felt that these were effects rather than causes of population change. They attributed the mass mortality to "adreno-cortical-sympatho-adrenal, and other metabolic responses" that resulted from extremely high population densities and associated 'social strife'.

A comparative study of sika and white-tailed deer on the Chincoteague National Wildlife Refuge (Davidson and Crow, 1983) revealed that white-tailed deer harbored protozoan, helminth, and arthropod parasites whereas sika deer harbored only light infestations of ticks and chiggers. The ticks *Amblyomma americanum* and *Dermacentor variabilis* and the mite *Eutrombicula splendens* were recorded.

Geographic Variation. Handley and Gordon (1979f) stated that the subspecies inhabiting Virginia is undetermined but is probably *Cervus nippon nippon* Temminck.

Location of Specimens. GMU, USNM.

Elk (Wapiti) [Extirpated]
Cervus elaphus Erxleben

Description. The elk (Plate 87) is one of the largest members of the family Cervidae. The sides and back are grayish-brown, and the under-parts are blackish. The head, neck, and legs are dark brown. The rump and tail are buff-white. A dark brown mane is present on the neck. Females possess four mammae. The antlers usually possess at least five tines, with the brow tine forming an obtuse angle with the beam. Adult elk may reach a length of 270 to 300 cm and a height of between 120 and 150 cm. Females normally weigh between 225 and 270 kg, and some males may weigh as much as 450 kg.

Distribution. Elk originally ranged over much of the United States. Now, however, their range has been restricted mainly to scattered localities in the western half of the United States. The largest contiguous range exists in the Rocky Mountains south to northern New Mexico. Small, isolated, introduced populations exist in Pennsylvania, Michigan, and a number of other states.

When Virginia was first settled by Europeans, elk may have occurred throughout most of the state. In 1686, John Clayton referred to "Elke" which occurred "beyond the Inhabitants." Beverley noted in 1705 that it was necessary to travel inland to the "Frontier Plantations" or Piedmont area in order to find elk. In his *History of the Dividing Line,* Byrd stated in 1728:

> *Not far from our Quarters one of the men pickt up a pair of Elk's Horns, not very large, and discover'd the Track of the Elk that had Shed them. It was rare to find any Tokens of those Animals so far to the South, because they keep commonly to the Northward of 37 degrees, as the Buffaloes, for the most part, confine themselves to the Southward of that Latitude* (Boyd, 1929).

In 1739, another John Clayton, the botanist, reported that elk could only be found "among the mountains and desert parts of the country where there are as yet but few inhabitants." Elk were recorded near a lick in Tazewell County in 1768 and at the Great Lick near the present site of Roanoke (Cannaday, 1950). By 1781, Thomas Jefferson observed that "in Virginia the elk has abounded much, and [still] exists in smaller numbers." Cory (1912) noted that elk existed in western Virginia in 1847, and McAtee (1918) stated that elk persisted in Virginia until 1844. Baird (1859) recorded two elk killed in Clarke County, in October, 1854, and January, 1855. These specimens, apparently the last native elk known in Virginia, were cataloged in the US National Museum collection.

Wood (1943), Stras (1949), Cross (1950), McKenna (1962b), Halladay (1964), and Handley (1979b) have summarized the efforts to reintroduce elk in Virginia. Between 140 and 150 elk of the subspecies *Cervus elaphus nelsoni* from Yellowstone National Park were imported to Virginia in 1917. Approximately 25 to 30 animals died in transit or shortly after release. These elk were released in Bland, Botetourt, Cumberland, Giles, Montgomery, Princess Anne, Pulaski, Roanoke, Russell, Warren, and Washington counties. Although the releases in Cumberland County and Princess Anne County were unsuccessful, the elk in the mountains survived and reproduced. The first open hunting season on elk ran from December 15 through 31, 1920, with no hunting allowed on Sundays.

By 1922, Virginia's elk population was estimated at some 500 animals in the following counties: Bland (50), Botetourt (70), Craig (50), Giles (70), Roanoke (50), Russell (70), Washington (50), and Warren (30). The remainder were divided among Montgomery, Pulaski, and other unnamed counties. Crop damage by the elk increased.

The open season remained the last half of December during the 1920s but was shortened and changed to the first three days of December in 1930 with hunting allowed only in Bland, Craig, Giles, Montgomery, and Pulaski counties. In 1931, the season was changed to three days during the middle of November with hunting limited to bulls only in Botetourt, Bland, and Giles counties.

An additional 56 elk were imported from Yellowstone in 1935. Five animals died in transit. Of the remainder, 45 were released in the Sugar Hollow section of Giles County and six on national forest land in Botetourt County near Natural Bridge. By 1940, the Giles-Bland herd was estimated to contain approximately 100 animals and the Botetourt-Bedford herd approximately 25 animals.

The Giles-Bland herd ranged over Flat Top and Pearis mountains in northern Bland and southern Giles counties, a range of approximately 40,000 acres. The area is not good elk range; food habits studies revealed the herd's diet to be composed of only 26 percent grass, whereas grass makes up 60 percent of the food of elk on good ranges in western states (Baldwin and Patton, 1938).

Crop damage had become so great, especially in Giles and Bland counties, that in 1943 the season was extended to four days and elk of either sex could be killed legally in those two counties. The kill that year was 26 bulls and 20 cows, all taken in Giles County. Following three-day open seasons for bulls in 1944 and 1945, the elk season was closed for 10 years. It was reopened in Bedford County in 1956, but no kills were reported. By 1958 the Giles-Bland herd was estimated to number about 125 animals, while the Botetourt-Bedford population was estimated at 39 animals in 1963. Open seasons in 1958, 1959, and 1960 resulted in a kill of 20 bull elk, all in Giles County.

Handley (1979b) noted:

> *When the elk was reestablished in the Giles-Bland and Botetourt-Bedford ranges there were no white-tailed deer there. They had been Extirpated in the late 1800s. A total of 85 white-tailed deer were released in the Giles-Bland range in 1950–1956, and they thrived. Other releases had already established a deer population in the Botetourt-Bedford range. Later it was learned that these deer were infested with a nematode parasite,* Pneumostrongylus tenuis *which invades the lungs, brain, and spinal cord. In 1963, 85 percent of the deer checked in Giles and 78 percent of those checked in Botetourt carried this round worm. It is lethal to elk. The first evidence of it in the Giles-Bland elk was found in 1958, and in the Botetourt-Bedford elk in 1962. The herds were doomed. The last elk was seen in the Botetourt-Bedford range in 1970, and in the Giles-Bland range in 1974.*

Parasites. Lungworms *(Dictyocaulus)*, gulletworms *(Gongylonema)*, and organisms similar to *Leptospira* sp. were recorded in the Botetourt-Bedford herd (Halladay, 1964). The nematode *Pneumostrongylus tenuis* was also recorded.

Geographic Variation. The subspecies formerly inhabiting Virginia was *Cervus elaphus canadensis* Erxleben.

Location of Specimens. BRP, USNM, VPI-W.

Genus *Odocoileus*

Dentition: 0/3, 0/1, 3/3, 3/3 = 32

White-Tailed Deer
Odocoileus virginianus (Boddaert)

Description. The white-tailed deer (Plate 88) is the largest native herbivore currently inhabiting Virginia and the best known of the large game mammals of North America. One of its most familiar characteristics, and the one which provides its common name, is the white fur on the undersurface and edges of the tail. The back, sides, and limbs are generally reddish-brown during the summer, while the heavier winter coat is more somber and grayish. During all seasons the undersides and throat are white. Prominent glands are located at the inner corners of the eyes, the outside of the lower hind legs, the inner hind legs at the hocks, and between the toes. The leg glands secrete a musky substance which may be used in marking a trail. Males augment their glandular secretions at the hocks by urinating on these glands. Females possess four mammae. Adult deer are between 1,370 and 1,825 mm in total length, including a tail 150 to 300 mm long. They stand 760 to 1,065 mm high at the shoulder. Adult females usually weigh from 45 to 67 kg, while adult males may weigh from 56 to 113 kg, although some heavier individuals have occasionally been recorded.

With the exception of the reindeer and caribou, only male members of the family Cervidae normally possess antlers. Antlers are branched structures consisting of bone. They are shed annually and are regrown every year, arising from a projection on the frontal bone known as the pedicel. Bucks usually shed their antlers during late December, January, and February. The new antlers appear from two to six weeks after shedding and grow rapidly as the spring forage improves. During this period, the antlers are covered by a thin layer of finely haired skin. By late summer, they have attained their full size but are still in the "velvet." In September, the velvet loosens and is shed in pieces from the antlers, which are now hard and insensitive. The prongs of the antlers typically arise vertically from the main beam and generally are unbranched.

Although there is a general increase in the number of points in both antlers with an in-

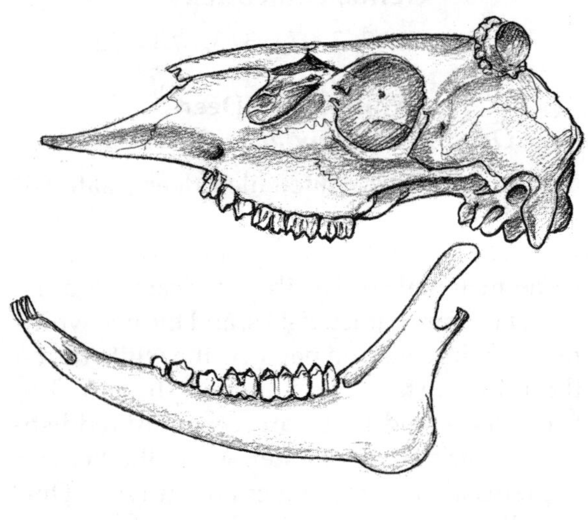

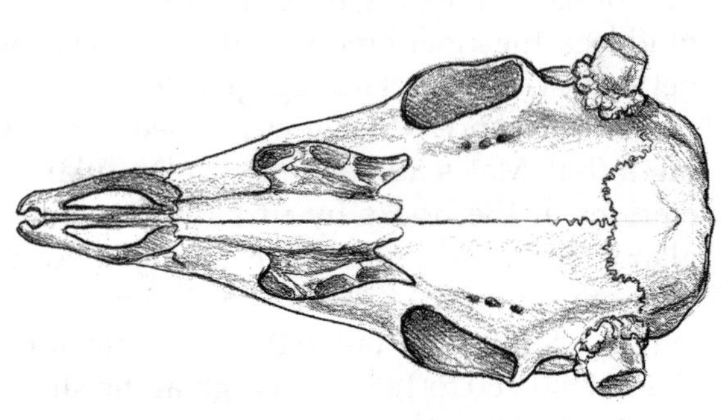

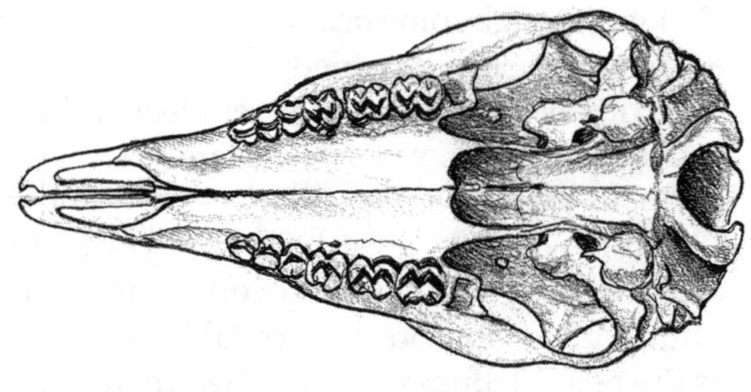

Figure 166. *Odocoileus virginianus:* Left lateral view of skull, and dorsal and ventral view of skull. Scale bar = 5 cm.

crease in age, neither the length of antlers nor the number of points can be used as a reliable indication of age. It is true that on a given deer the diameter of the antler near its base tends to enlarge with each new set of antlers. Antler beam diameters vary from place to place with the quality and quantity of forage available (Severinghaus et al., 1950). If the food browsed by deer is high in food values, i.e., calcium, phosphorus, and other minerals, antler growth will be rapid and well developed. If the food is less nutritious and low in essential minerals, antler growth will be slower and less developed.

The frequency of deer with a certain number of points on both antlers is often of interest to hunters. Records collected from Wisconsin, Michigan, Texas, and New York show that the most frequently encountered adult rack has eight points. Next to this is a 6 or 10 point rack. An even rather than an odd number of points is the more typical pattern of antler development. A rack with 11 or more points is found on about one buck in 20 to 70. One buck in about 300 to 400 has 13 or more points, one in about 1,000 to 1,300 has 15 or more points, and one buck in about 4,500 to 5,000 has 17 or more points (Severinghaus and Cheatum, 1956).

Auditory bullae are present but are only slightly inflated. Nevertheless, deer have a keen sense of hearing. Upper incisors and upper canines are both absent and are replaced by a pad of hard, thickened tissue (Figure 166).

Distribution. White-tailed deer are found from northern South America north through Mexico and the United States to southern Canada. They occur throughout the United States except in the arid portions of the West and Southwest. The population in the United States and Canada is currently estimated to be approximately 20 million animals.

White-tailed deer occur throughout Virginia (Figure 167). Although abundant during the Colonial period, this species declined with agricultural expansion and uncontrolled hunting — including hunting out-of-season, at night, and using dogs — reaching its lowest population in 1925 (Barick, 1951).

Uncontrolled hunting led to the near extir-

Figure 167. *Odocoileus virginianus:* Range in Virginia and North America.

pation of deer in western Virginia due to the fact that no extensive swamps or waterways were available as escape cover in the mountainous portions of the state. Areas now included in the cities of Norfolk and Suffolk and the counties of Surry, Highland, Bath, and Alleghany probably were never without a few deer. Although the native geographic variant continues to be present in a few areas of the state, most of the deer in Virginia today are a mixture of native, northern, and western white-tailed deer as a result of introductions made by the Commission of Game and Inland Fisheries (Woolley, 1946; Peery and Coggin, 1978).

The downward trend of the sizes of the deer herds was reversed by the passage in the late 1920s of the buck law, which permitted only male deer to be killed, prohibited the use of dogs in the mountainous sections, shortened the season, and authorized a restocking program undertaken by the Commission of Game and Inland Fisheries. Between 1930 and 1950, over 1,800 animals were imported from North Carolina, Pennsylvania, Florida, Michigan, Wisconsin, and other places (Engle, 1951; Peery and Coggin, 1978). Barick (1951) reported that Virginia had restocked 2,000 deer.

If given adequate protection during the breeding season, deer herds will increase approximately 30 percent each year. By 1950, Virginia reported a deer population of 64,000 with suitable range for a population of 190,000 deer (Barick, 1951).

Today, deer are once again abundant throughout the state. Harvest data for a period of 44 years from 1947 through the 1991–1994 hunting season is presented in Table 12. Comparative data on the wild fur catch in Virginia, including white-tailed deer, are presented in tables 7 and 8.

Habitat. The white-tailed deer is a creature of the woodlands. Instead of frequenting deep, dense stands of unbroken primeval forest, however, it chooses to live where dense woods and thickets alternate with open meadows and sunny forest glades. It also forages along forest margins and sometimes in orchards and farmland. Dense stands of mature conifers (except in winter in northern areas) and very extensive open areas are generally avoided.

The cutting of vast primeval forests and the subsequent springing up of second-growth vegetation have added much suitable habitat throughout the natural range of this animal. The abandonment of worked-out farms has provided the deer with excellent habitat and feeding grounds. White-tailed deer adapt so well to artificial landscapes, that they are found in considerable numbers on the edges of some large cities where they are often considered nuisances.

Variation in the growth and size of deer occurs mainly because of differences in the fertility of the soil and the availability of adequate nutritious food.

Habits. White-tailed deer are graceful, secretive, and alert. Although their sense of sight is good, they depend more upon their keen senses of hearing and smell for survival. At the approach of danger, the deer will silently move away, with head lowered and tail held down tight. The moment the deer starts to run, however, the white undersurface of the tail is held aloft – an unmistakable warning for other deer in the vicinity. A whistling snort is often heard as a startled deer bounds away.

Deer are mainly active in early morning and early evening, although some may remain abroad all night, particularly in areas where they are harried by man and during hunting seasons. Daylight hours are normally spent lying in concealing cover with most deer rarely moving about. Montgomery (1963) reported that deer in Pennsylvania spent the days in wooded areas but began to move into open fields one or more hours before sunset in winter and just before sunset in summer. He further noted that before bedding in the fields they grazed for about four hours after sunset in winter and for seven to eight hours after sunset in summer. Each time the deer bedded, it was for an average of one and one-half hours. They gradually moved back into the wooded areas as dawn approached.

White-tailed deer have no permanent or even semipermanent shelter or den. Each day they pick a different site on which to bed down. On sunny warm days, the deer will most likely select a shady site, while on cool or windy days the site will probably be sunny and protected. The presence or absence of insects also influences bed selection.

A radiotelemetry study of movements of deer in Shenandoah National Park revealed differing patterns according to season, sex, and habitat. Females monitored along the Skyline Drive had a mean range of 444 ha compared to 1,846 ha for males. Females in backcountry areas had a mean home range area of 879 ha compared to 1,586 for males (Scanlon and Vaughan, 1985).

Severinghaus and Cheatum (1956) stated:

> *The speed of the white-tailed deer has often been checked at 20 to 35 miles per hour. At 20 to 25 miles an hour it can continue for a long distance. Usually there is no need for prolonged exertion, for a swift bound and short burst of speed carries it away from most causes of alarm.*

The high-jumping abilities of this species are well known. High jumps of 2.6 m and running broad jumps of 9.1 m have been measured.

White-tailed deer are shy, secretive animals that normally gather in family groups composed of an adult doe, her young of the year, and her previous year's yearling does. Bucks are solitary in the fall, but congregate in large buck groups in spring and summer. In areas of heavy snowfall a number of families and other groups congregate in a restricted area called a "deer yard." In Shenandoah National Park, Scanlon and Vaughan (1983b) reported the largest group sizes in winter (mean 3.4, range of 1 to 28) and the smallest group sizes during late summer (mean 2.0, range of 1 to 10) and fawning (June-July, mean 1.7, range 1 to 9). Group size was largest at dusk (mean 2.7, range of 1 to 28) and smallest at dawn (mean 2.3, range 1 to 10) and during the day (mean 2.3, range 1 to 13).

Food. On most deer range in Virginia, a typical deer will eat between 2.25 and 4 kg of food per day. The white-tailed deer is selective and diverse in its feeding habits, keeping on the move and eating twigs or leaves here, acorns, mushrooms, or fruit there, and weeds or grasses elsewhere. Greenbrier, sourwood, sassafras, maple and oak sprouts, honeysuckle, and wild grape are regularly eaten. In the fall, deer are heavy mast feeders. Although twigs have been considered an important food in the southern United States in the past, several studies have shown that virtually all browsing of twigs takes place during the spring and summer when this part of the plant is growing rapidly and is succulent (Cushwa et al., 1970; Harlow and Hooper, 1972; Welch and Flyger, 1977; and others). In late fall on the northern (Maryland) portion of Assateague Island, major food items were pinweeds, wax myrtle, dwarf sumac, poison ivy, and goldenrod (Keiper, 1990).

An analysis of over 900 rumen samples from the Appalachian Mountain, Piedmont, and Coastal Plain provinces in the southeastern United States during the four seasons showed that deer select the same type of diet seasonally, although foraging in ecologically different areas (Harlow and Hooper, 1972). Hardened woody twigs had the lowest frequency of occurrence and lowest volume of all food categories. Green leaves of woody plants ranked highest in frequency of occurrence and volume. Mushrooms ranked third in frequency of occurrence and fifth in total volume. Forbs, grasses and sedges, mushrooms and other fungi, and dry leaves amounted to 35.9 percent of the annual volume of food, equaling the amount provided by green leaves of woody plants. Hardened twigs and buds comprised only 2.3 percent of the annual food volume.

Neither woody plants nor grasses contain as high a percentage of the essential nutrients in winter as they do in the spring. Lay (1957) found that most nutrients in 25 browse species dropped 50 percent from spring to winter. The nutrients in grasses dropped markedly from spring to winter, with the biggest drop coming after the first killing frost (Campbell and Cassady, 1954).

At times when deer populations build up to excessive numbers, available supplies of nutritious food may be virtually eliminated. Undernourished animals are susceptible to bronchial or other diseases, and a die-off results. Many deer in such areas die in winter with their stomachs more or less full of food having little nutritive value, rather than move to some less sheltered area having adequate sustaining food.

Reproduction and Development. In Virginia, the deer breeding season is usually in early to late November, depending on climatic variations in different parts of the state. Rutting bucks mark and defend territories and make scrapes advertising for does to breed. They viciously fight other bucks found in their territories. Gestation usually requires between 197 and 222 days, with the peak of fawning coming about six and one-half to seven months after that of breeding (Haugen and Davenport, 1950). Years of early mean birth dates in western Virginia were positively correlated with high rainfall the previous May and with a low fawn survival rate the previous summer (McGinnes and Downing, 1977). The birth of white-tailed deer fawns has been described by Michael (1964).

Fawns are reddish-brown with white dorsal spots. They are usually born during the latter part of May and the early part of June in Virginia. Each fawn weighs approximately 1.8 kg at birth.

The number of young born to each doe varies according to the mother's age and physical condition. Her firstborn is generally single; the second year she may have twins and sometimes triplets. Occasionally there are four, although this is rare for any deer. Females in poor condition due to an inadequate food supply will have fewer young than healthy females living in good habitat. A discussion of parturition and the behavior of fawns shortly after birth has been presented by Haugen and Speake (1957).

Fawns are capable of walking shortly after birth, but they travel very little during subsequent weeks. A study by Jackson, White, and Knowlton (1972) revealed that during their first two weeks of life fawns were active an average of 8 percent of the time. By one month of age, males were active about 16 percent of the time, and females were active about 12 percent of the time. The average number of daytime activity periods increased from two in fawns during the first week to five to six periods at one month of age. Most activity periods were less than 35 minutes long, but they increased in duration as the fawn became older. Two-hour activity periods were rare until fawns were more than one month old. Fawns were more active during midday hours in their first week of life, but they were most active in morning and evening thereafter.

During the first eight weeks following parturition, does associate very little with their fawns (Schwede et al., 1994). Except when the female is present and they are nursing, the fawns lie motionless and concealed by understory vegetation. Apparently, twin fawns rest in separate locations, a habit that reduces the possibility of predation on both young. Although they may begin sampling surrounding vegetation when a few days old, the fawns will not be weaned until three to four months of age. They remain spotted with white for four to five months. Female fawns may stay with the doe for two or more years, leaving for a brief period when the doe reaches the late stages of pregnancy and returning after the new fawn is able to travel. Buck fawns are likely to remain only one year, not returning after the new fawn is born (Severinghaus and Cheatum, 1956). Hawkins and Klimstra (1970) reported that the most common family group was an adult doe, her yearling daughter, and two fawns belonging to the older doe. The structure of family groups suggested that most groupings were matriarchal with three or even four generations present.

Some does are bred when six to eight months of age, but most do not breed until a year later.

A pilot study to test a birth control vaccine to slow population growth humanely was begun at the National Zoo research center in Front Royal in late 1992. The vaccine must be injected into the deer with a dart rifle. It is made up mainly of a protein that will be released slowly and which serves as a sperm receptor. The deer's body will produce antibodies against the foreign protein and these antibodies will also block the doe's sperm receptors as well, thus keeping the sperm from fertilizing its eggs. It is anticipated that one injection will stop egg fertilization for more than a year. This is the same vaccine that has been successfully used to control the wild pony population at Assateague Island National Seashore in Maryland.

Longevity. The white-tailed deer has a life expectancy of 15 to 20 years, but the life span seldom exceeds 10 years in the wild. A tagged deer brought from the Pisgah National Forest in North Carolina and released in Smyth County was retaken in 1950 and was at least 12 years old (Anonymous, 1951c). Tullar (1983) summarized longevity records including a 19 to 23 year old female from New York that was carrying an 80-day-old fetus. Tame or captive does have lived up to 20 years, and one had fawns at age 16 (Palmer, 1954). A doe may have as many as 31 fawns during the first 14 years of her life.

Pelage Variations. Partially white or piebald deer are not rare and are a great curiosity among hunters. Newspapers in almost every state show pictures and describe partially white deer that are shot every year. Several such deer have been reported in Virginia (Anonymous, 1956g, 1957d; Allen, 1965; Painter and Eckerlin, 1993). Several adult albino deer and twin albino fawns were reported at Fort Pickett (Anonymous, 1961i). A half white and half fawn-colored, short-legged deer was taken and photographed near Lightfoot in James City County (Anonymous, 1946a). These animals generally have long, shaggy hair like a goat and are all white except for brown on the tops of the shoulders. True albinos with pink eyes are quite rare. Bailey (1946) reported albino bucks from Surry and Bath counties. One such animal was taken along Stony Creek in Giles County (Miller, 1966). Another was observed and photographed near Charlottesville in 1976 (Murray, 1977b). A photograph of an albino with pink eyes appeared in *The Roanoke Times* (Anonymous, 1996b). A solid black buck was reportedly observed in James City County (Anonymous, 1949q). Piebald deer have numerous deformities and their fawns suffer much higher mortality rates than normal deer (McGinnes and Downing, 1969; Downing, personal communication, December, 1992).

Parasites and Disease. Several contagious diseases including septicemia and papillomas have occurred in Virginia's deer herds, but neither has reached epidemic proportions. In the mid-1930s, septicemia occurred in the deer herd on the George Washington National Forest but was confined to one local area. Infectious papillomas, or wartlike tumors, were found in several deer from James City County in 1946 (Woolley, 1946). An examination of 855 deer in 1952 from Bath, Augusta, and Shenandoah counties found one deer with papillomas, six with nose-bot larvae (*Cephenemyia* sp.), and a number with gullet worms *(Gongylonema pulchrum)*. Otherwise, the deer were in excellent physical condition (Richards, 1953). An examination of blood samples taken from 40 Virginia deer revealed no evidence of brucellosis or leptospirosis (Shotts, Greer, and Hayes, 1958). However, leptospiral antibodies were reported by Shotts and Hayes (1970). A study of Caroline County deer revealed a high incidence of the nematode *Gongylonema pulchrum* but no evidence of *Gongylonema verrucosum* or *Paramphistomum liorchis* (Prestwood, Smith, and Mahon, 1970).

A total of 309 deer heads from Shenandoah, Augusta, Bath, Rockbridge, Botetourt, Giles, and Craig counties were examined for the presence of *Pneumostrongylus tenuis* during November 1963 (Dudak, 1964; Dudak et al., 1965). A total of 73 percent of the deer examined were infected. Infection rates ranged from 100 percent infected in Bath County to 54 percent infected in Rockbridge County. Fifty percent of 30 lung specimens were infected. There appeared to be an equal likelihood of infection by *Pneumostrongylus* in deer of either sex less than eighteen months of age. Deer of either sex older than three and one-half years also had an equal likelihood of infection, but females between one and one-half and three and one-half were more likely to be infected and had a higher number of worms per infection than males. Heavier deer in the one and one-half to three and one-half year age group were also more likely to be infected. The authors stated that the deer-*Pneumostrongylus tenuis* relationship is a relatively stable and common association, with host populations seldom adversely affected by the parasites. Infected deer have also been confirmed from Caroline, Cumberland, James City, Norfolk, Nottoway, Prince George, Stafford, and Prince William counties (Prestwood and Smith, 1969).

Jones et al. (1978a) recorded tularemia infection in one animal from Fort Pickett. The ticks *Amblyomma americanum, Dermacentor albipictus,* and *Ixodes scapularis* have been recorded by Sonenshine, Lamb, and Anastos (1965); Jones (1978); Garrett and Sonenshine (1979); and Sonenshine and Turner (1988). Prestwood (1971) recorded the cestodes *Cysticercus tenuicollis (Taenia hydatigena)* and *Moniezia* spp. from this species in Virginia, while Payne, Maples, and Smith (1967) recorded the nematode *Oesophagostomum cervi* from 1 of 10 deer examined from the City of Chesapeake. The nematodes *Cooperia punctata, Dictyocaulus viviparus, Elaeophora schneideri, Nematodirus odocoilei, Oesophagostomum venulosum, Ostertagia dikmansi, Ostertagia mossi, Parelaphostrongylus andersoni, Setaria yehi, Skrjabinagia odocoilei,* and *Trichuris* sp. have been recorded by Prestwood et al.

(1971), Prestwood et al. (1973), Prestwood et al. (1974), Pursglove et al. (1976), Couvillion et al. (1985), and Virginia Wildlife Investigation Annual Report 1986–1987, p. 141. Trypanosomiasis was recorded by Kistner and Hanson (1969).

McKenney (1938) reported an outbreak of malignant edema and identified the causative organism as the bacterium *Clostridium septique*. The bacterium *Streptococcus faecalis* has been isolated from the liver of a deer from southwestern Virginia (Libke and Mosby, 1968). *Coccidia* sp. has been recorded from fawns in Montgomery County (Buckland et al., 1975). Dawson et al. (1994) reported the presence ofthe bacterium *Ehrlichia* spp. The protozoan *Babesia odocoilei* was recorded by Perry et al. (1985). Early September die-offs from epizootic hemorrhagic disease virus (EHD) occurred in Virginia in 1962, 1971, and 1974 with circumstantial evidence indicating similar die-offs occurring in the 1940s and 1950s (Prestwood et al., 1974; Peery and Coggin, 1978). Couvillion et al. (1981) summarized the history of hemorrhagic disease in the Southeast from 1971 through 1980. Hemorrhagic disease (HD) is attributable to bluetongue virus (BT). Stallknecht et al. (1991) recorded both EHD and BT. A possible case of paratuberculosis (Johne's disease), caused by *Mycobacterium paratuberculosis*, was reported by Libke and Walton (1975).

Davidson and Crow (1983) recorded the following parasites on five adult deer taken from the Chincoteague National Wildlife Refuge: Protozoa (*Sarcocystis odocoileocanis, Theileria cervi*, and *Trypanosoma cervi*); Cestoda (*Moniezia benedeni*); Nematoda (*Apteragia odocoilei, Dictyocaulus viviparus, Ostertagia dikmansi, Ostertagia mossi, Parelaphostrongylus tenuis*, Protostrongylid larvae, and *Setaria yehi*); and Acarina (*Amblyomma americanum, Eutrombicula splendens*, and *Tricholipeurus parallelus*).

The following helminths were recorded from five deer collected in Warren County in 1985 (Virginia Wildlife Investigations Annual Report 1986–1987 (pp. 108–111)): *Apteragia odocoilei, Dictyocaulus viviparus, Gongylonema pulchrum, Ostertagia dikmansi, Ostertagia mossi, Parelaphostrongylus tenuis*, Protostrongylid larvae, and *Taenia hydatigena*.

Serologic tests for antibodies to seven infectious disease agents also revealed evidence of exposure to bovine virus diarrhea (BVD) virus, infectious bovine rhinotracheitis virus, and parainfluenza-3 virus.

Predation. Deer have relatively few enemies. These include the mountain lion, bobcat, bear, coyote, dogs, and man. The domestic dog is undoubtedly the most important predator (Feldhamer, 1982). Many deer are struck and killed by motor vehicles.

In discussing the effects of hunters on the population dynamics of deer, Adams (1960) noted that man influences the population by being primarily sex selective (males) and secondarily age selective, while natural predators are just the reverse, being age selective first (very young or old) and secondarily sex selective. A study of the response of deer to being chased by hunting dogs has been presented by Sweeney, Marchinton, and Sweeney (1971).

Geographic Variation. The subspecies originally inhabiting Virginia was *Odocoileus virginianus virginianus* (Zimmermann). When Catesby sailed into the James River in 1712, he saw deer in large numbers. Later, he described those which he saw in tidewater Virginia and honored them by the specific name of *virginianus*. The importation of large numbers of deer from other states from 1930 to 1950 has made the genetic status of our current deer uncertain.

Location of Specimens. ANSP, CM, GMU, LFCC, LU, MCZ, ODU, SNP, UR, USNM, VCU, VHCC, VLM, VMNH, VPISU, VPI-W.

Bovids
(Family Bovidae)

The family Bovidae contains cattle, sheep, goats, bison, and African and Asian antelopes. Bovids of both sexes are characterized by the presence of hollow, unbranched horns. These horns are supported by bony cores and are not shed. Upper canine teeth are absent in both sexes. The lateral toes are reduced or totally absent, the ulna is reduced distally and is fused with the radius, and only a distal nodule remains as a vestige of the fibula. Bovids are ruminants, and the stomach has four chambers.

Bovids are native throughout much of North America, Eurasia, and Africa, and they have been introduced worldwide. The only member of this family which has occurred naturally in Virginia in historic time is the bison.

Genus *Bison*

Dentition: 0/3, 0/1, 3/3, 3/3 = 32

American Bison [Extirpated]
Bison bison (Linnaeus)

Description. Bison (Plate 89) are large herbivores with massive heads. Garretson (1938) stated:

> *The buffalo that ranged over the eastern states from Georgia to northern New York, being numerous in Pennsylvania, Maryland and Virginia, were said to be of a different type and much larger than those of the western plains. A good description of this animal is given by Henry W. Shoemaker as follows: '. . . the bison of Pennsylvania was a tremendous animal. . . he exceeded in size the buffaloes met with west of Ohio, Kentucky and Tennessee. In color the Pennsylvania bison was very dark, many of the old bulls being coal black, with grizzly white hairs around the nose and eyes. The hair was very short, with a tendency to crispness or curliness, especially at the joints. The hump, so conspicuous on the western bison was notable by its absence. . . . The legs were long, and fore and back legs evenly placed, the heavy front and meagre hindquarters of the western bison were not present, in other words the Pennsylvania bison was a beautifully proportioned beast. . . . The hair on the neck and shoulders was no longer than on other parts of the body, except with mature bulls, who carried a sort of mane or crest which reached its maximum length where the hump grows on the prairie buffalo. Both males and females wore beards but they were not heavy and consisted of tufts of straight, stiff black hair. The horns, which in mature specimens were very long, grew upwards, like the horns of Ayrshire cattle. Apparently the horns were much like those of* Bison bonasus *of Lithuania and Caucasus [the European bison].'*

Schorger (1944) presented evidence that the eastern bison was indistinguishable from the bison of the plains. The plains bison has a heavy head, a short neck, and shoulders that are high and humped. The long, woolly fur on the head, neck, shoulders, and front legs is blackish-brown; the fur on the body is short and brown. A beard is present on the chin. The tail is short and tufted at the tip.

Female bison possess four mammae. Adult bulls may be between 3,650 and 4,115 mm in total length, including a 600 mm tail. They are 1,675 to 1,825 mm high at the shoulder and weigh between 720 and 900 kg. Cows are approximately 2,700 mm long including a 600 mm tail, stand about 1,500 mm high at the shoulders, and weigh between 315 and 430 kg. Bison were the largest land mammals in North America in 1600.

Distribution. Bison formerly ranged through the plains of central North America from Mexico north into Canada and east as far as New York, Maryland, and Florida. These animals have been said to be the "most abundant game animal that civilized man ever beheld" (Cahalane, 1944). Today, bison exist only in zoological parks and in a few herds on refuges and preserves.

The earliest account of the discovery of bison east of the Alleghanies was recorded by the English navigator Sir Samuel Argall, who in 1612 sailed up the Potomac River as far as it was navigable, "about sixty-five leagues," and then marched for some distance into the country. Here, as he recorded:

> *I found great store of Cattle as big as Kine, of which, the Indians that were my guides, killed a couple, which wee found to be very good and wholesome meate, and are very easie to be killed, in regard they are heavy, slow, and not so wild as other beasts of the Wildernesse* (Purchas, 1625).

Goode (1896) mentioned that buffalo still abounded in the vicinity of Charlottesville at the time of Thomas Jefferson's birth, and that a calf captured in the Blue Ridge nearby was presented as a gift to the colonial governor in 1733. He further stated that:

> *a trail frequented by the buffalo herds crossed the Blue Ridge at Rockfish Gap, 24 miles west of Charlottesville, passed the Shenandoah at a ford near Staunton, and afterward over the next range by a passage still known as Buffalo Gap, into the beautiful valleys, then as at present called the Cow Pasture and the Calf Pasture.*

In 1728, William Byrd reported finding a three-year-old bull buffalo while surveying the southern boundary of the colony, about 155 miles from the coast (Boyd, 1929).

Roe (1970) noted that in 1701 the Huguenots who had settled near Manikintown (Manakin) on the James River, a few miles above Richmond, began domesticating buffalo. Hornaday (1889) stated:

> *It is also a matter of historical record that in 1786, or thereabouts, buffaloes were domesticated and bred in captivity in Virginia, and Albert Gallatin states that in some of the northwestern counties the mixed breed was quite common.*

Barton (1792) noted: "In the western parts of Virginia, etc. Bison-calves are sometimes met with in the farms of the remote settlers."

Salmon (1737) described the journey of Captain Henry Batt to the western portion of early Virginia:

> *They set out together from Appomattox, and in Seven Days March reached the Foot of the Mountains. The Mountains they first arriv'd at were not extraordinary high or steep, but after they had pass'd the first Ridge they encounter'd others that seemed to reach the Clouds, and were so perpendicular and full of Precipices, that sometimes in a whole Day's March they could not travel three miles in a direct Line. In other places they found large level Plains and fine Savanna's three or four miles wide, in which were an infinite quantity of Turkies, Deer, Elks, and Buffaloes, so gentle and undisturbed that they had no Fear at the Appearance of the Men, but would suffer them to come almost within reach of their Hands.*

In a letter dated March 31, 1739, John Clayton of Gloucester County wrote:

> *The bears, panthers, buffaloes and elks and wildcats are only to be found among the mountains and desert parts of the country where there are as yet few inhabitants, and the hunting there is very toilsome and sometimes dangerous.*

Buffalo were common in the Mount Rogers area of Virginia. In 1750 Dr. Thomas Walker led a surveying party through southwestern Virginia as far as Cumberland Gap. In his journal he stated: "We killed in the Journey 13 Buffaloes, 8 Elks, 53 Bears, 20 Deer, 4 Wild Geese, about 150 Turkeys, besides small Game. We might have killed three times as much meat, if we had wanted it." Even today in the Elk Garden area of Mount Rogers, the remains of a once huge buffalo wallow can be found being used by cattle that now graze the land.

Bison were apparently more numerous in Virginia than in any other of the Atlantic states. Garretson (1938) stated that the former abundance of buffalo is attested by the numbers of streams and other natural features that bear the prefix of "Buffalo." He noted that in Virginia east of the Alleghany Mountains there are four Buffalo Gaps, one Buffalo Run, one Buffalo River, two Buffalo Ridges, one Buffalo Hill, one Buffalo Branch, seven Buffalo Creeks, two Buffalo Springs, one Buffalo Station, one Buffalo Forge, one Buffalo Mills, and one Buffalo Ford. In addition, he stated:

> *In the 'Annals of Augusta County' it is stated that the buffalo roamed the Virginia hills and valleys and, in their migrations, made a well-defined trail between Rockfish Gap in the Blue Ridge and Buffalo Gap in the North Mountain, passing by the present site of Staunton.*

He also stated:

> *There is ample proof that bison were found in considerable numbers on the eastern slope of the Alleghany Mountains, and that they were gradually extending their range eastward and southward. It is reasonable to suppose that but for the advent of the white man they would in time, by continual advancing, have reached the Atlantic coast.*

The disappearance of the bison from the lands east of the Mississippi River was a slow and gradual process. They were never needlessly slaughtered as buffalo later were in the West. Instead, they became fewer and fewer as the American population expanded and people pressed into formerly unused lands. The last free-roaming buffalo east of the Mississippi was killed in the early 1830s, and the majority were gone well before that date (Rorabacher, 1970).

The last bison in this area are said to have been killed by Nathan Boone, a son of Daniel Boone, on the Kanawha River (West Virginia) about 1793, on the New River (Virginia or West Virginia), and near the Big Sandy River (Kentucky or West Virginia) in 1797 and 1798 (Coues, 1871). Roe (1970) noted that the last buffalo was killed in the Great Kanawha Valley, about 12 miles below Charleston, West Virginia, in 1815. Allen (1876b) dated their extirpation from Kentucky as about 1800 and from Tennessee between 1800 and 1810. Garretson (1938) stated that the bison was practically extinct east of the Mississippi River by 1820. Dunbar (1962) and Jakle (1968) provided additional notes on the presence of bison in Virginia and the Ohio valley and their disappearance.

Location of Specimens. No specimens from Virginia are known to exist in collections.

Genus *Bos*

Dentition: 0/4, 0/0, 3/3, 3/4 = 32

Cow
Bos taurus Linnaeus

Distribution. Feral cattle (Plate 90), resulting from straying animals, were reported in Virginia as early as 1694 by John Clayton. In the Dismal Swamp cattle would be branded and then turned loose to feed. Some would later be caught, but the others established feral populations. Reports of these feral animals stated that they were small, dark, and very wild. Herds were said to consist of 20 to 50 animals. They were as wary as the deer, and they ranged throughout the swamp (Shaler, 1890; Fisher, 1895; Dunn, 1907).

By the 1930s, Ariza (1932) and Davis (1934) stated that the feral cattle had disappeared. In 1953, Handley (1970a) was told by local residents that the organized attempts to eradicate the cattle had been unsuccessful. Davis (1971) stated that as of 1962 none were present in the swamp. The American Livestock Breeds Conservancy survey in 1990 noted that no cattle were present in the swamp. It noted that a few head were run in the swamp by an individual, but that they had been removed 10 to 12 years ago.

Location of Specimens. No feral Virginia specimens are known to exist in museum collections.

Genus *Capra*

Dentition: 0/4, 0/0, 3/4, 3/3 = 32

Goat
Capra hircus Linnaeus

Distribution. McKnight (1964) reported feral goats (Plate 91) on Assateague and Chincoteague islands, in the Shenandoah National Park, and near Big Stone Gap in Wise County, Virginia. Handley and Paradiso (1965) reported a herd numbering between 60 and 100 animals inhabiting the "old fields" area just south of the Virginia-Maryland boundary on Assateague Island. Wass (1972) noted that a herd on Watts Island had caused a browse line.

Davis (1971) noted that feral goats had been reported in the Dismal Swamp, but as of 1962 none were to be found. Hill (1973), however, stated that the swamp was inhabited by "some domesticated goats gone wild."

The American Livestock Breeds Conservancy survey in 1990 reported that goats were no longer present on Assateague and Chincoteague islands nor in Shenandoah National Park. They could obtain no information on, or even the location, of those reported from Wise County. Holleran (1996), however, reported feral goats still living on Giant Egging, a small island near Assateague.

Location of Specimens. No feral Virginia specimens are known to exist in museum collections.

Appendixes

Appendix I

Checklist of Mammals of Virginia

Order Didelphimorphia — American Opossums

Family Didelphidae — Opossums

Didelphis virginiana virginiana Kerr .... Virginia Opossum

Order Insectivora — Shrews and Moles

Family Soricidae — Shrews

Sorex cinereus cinereus Kerr. .... Masked Shrew
Sorex longirostris longirostris Bachman .... Southeastern Shrew
Sorex palustris punctulatus Hooper .... Northern Water Shrew
Sorex fumeus fumeus (Miller) .... Smoky Shrew
Sorex dispar dispar (Batchelder) .... Long-Tailed Shrew
Sorex (Microsorex) hoyi winnemana Preble .... Pygmy Shrew
Cryptotis parva parva (Say) .... Least Shrew
Blarina brevicauda brevicauda (Say) .... Northern Short-Tailed Shrew
Blarina carolinensis carolinensis (Bachman) .... Southern Short-Tailed Shrew

Family Talpidae — Moles

Scalopus aquaticus aquaticus (Linnaeus) .... Eastern Mole
Parascalops breweri (Bachman) .... Hairy-Tailed Mole
Condylura cristata cristata (Linnaeus) .... Star-Nosed Mole

Order Chiroptera — Bats

Family Vespertilionidae — Vespertilionid Bats

Myotis lucifugus lucifugus (LeConte) .... Little Brown Myotis
Myotis austroriparius austroriparius (Rhoads) .... Southeastern Myotis
Myotis grisescens A. H. Howell .... Gray Myotis
Myotis septentrionalis (Trouessart) .... Northern Myotis
Myotis sodalis Miller and Allen .... Indiana Myotis
Myotis leibii (Audubon and Bachman) .... Eastern Small-Footed Myotis
Lasionycteris noctivagans (LeConte) .... Silver-Haired Bat
Pipistrellus subflavus subflavus (F. Cuvier) .... Eastern Pipistrelle
Eptesicus fuscus fuscus (Palisot de Beauvois) .... Big Brown Bat
Nycticeius humeralis humeralis (Rafinesque) .... Evening Bat
Lasiurus borealis borealis (Müller) .... Eastern Red Bat

Lasiurus seminolus (Rhoads) .... Seminole Bat
Lasiurus cinereus cinereus (Palisot de Beauvois) .... Hoary Bat
Lasiurus intermedius floridanus (H. Allen) .... Northern Yellow Bat
Corynorhinus townsendii virginianus Handley .... Townsend's (Western) Big-Eared Bat
Corynorhinus rafinesquii rafinesquii (Lesson) .... Rafinesque's (Eastern) Big-Eared Bat

Order Lagomorpha — Lagomorphs

Family Leporidae — Hares and Rabbits

Sylvilagus palustris palustris (Bachman) .... Marsh Rabbit
Sylvilagus floridanus floridanus (Allen) .... Eastern Cottontail
Sylvilagus floridanus hitchensi Mearns .... Barrier Island Cottontail
Sylvilagus obscurus Chapman .... Appalachian Cottontail
Lepus americanus americanus Erxleben .... Snowshoe Hare
Lepus californicus californicus Gray .... Black-Tailed Jack Rabbit

Order Rodentia — Rodents

Family Sciuridae — Squirrels

Tamias striatus striatus (Linnaeus) .... Eastern Chipmunk
Marmota monax monax (Linnaeus) .... Woodchuck
Sciurus carolinensis carolinensis Gmelin .... Eastern Gray Squirrel
Sciurus niger niger Linnaeus .... Eastern Fox Squirrel
Tamiasciurus hudsonicus hudsonicus (Erxleben) .... Red Squirrel
Glaucomys volans volans (Linnaeus) .... Southern Flying Squirrel
Glaucomys sabrinus fuscus Miller .... Northern Flying Squirrel

Family Castoridae — Beavers

Castor canadensis canadensis Kuhl .... American Beaver

Family Muridae — Murid Rats and Mice

Oryzomys palustris palustris (Harlan) .... Marsh Rice Rat
Reithrodontomys humulis humulis Audubon and Bachman .... Eastern Harvest Mouse
Peromyscus maniculatus maniculatus Wagner .... Woodland Deer Mouse
Peromyscus maniculatus bairdii (Hoy and Kennicott) ... Prairie Deer Mouse
Peromyscus leucopus leucopus (Rafinesque) .... White-Footed Mouse
Peromyscus gossypinus gossypinus (LeConte) .... Cotton Mouse
Ochrotomys nuttalli nuttalli (Harlan) .... Golden Mouse
Sigmodon hispidus hispidus Say and Ord .... Hispid Cotton Rat
Neotoma magister Baird .... Allegheny Woodrat
Clethrionomys gapperi gapperi (Vigors) .... Southern Red-Backed Vole
Microtus pennsylvanicus pennsylvanicus (Ord) .... Meadow Vole
Microtus chrotorrhinus carolinensis Komarek .... Rock Vole
Microtus pinetorum pinetorum (LeConte) .... Woodland Vole
Synaptomys cooperi cooperi Baird .... Southern Bog Lemming
Synaptomys cooperi helaletes Merriam .... Dismal Swamp Southern Bog Lemming
Ondatra zibethicus zibethicus (Linnaeus) .... Common Muskrat
Rattus rattus (Linnaeus) .... Black Rat
Rattus norvegicus norvegicus (Berkenhout) .... Norway Rat
Mus musculus musculus Linnaeus .... House Mouse

Family Zapodidae — Jumping Mice

Zapus hudsonius hudsonius (Zimmermann) .... Meadow Jumping Mouse
Napaeozapus insignis insignis (Miller) .... Woodland Jumping Mouse

Family Erethizontidae — New World Porcupines
Erethizon dorsatum dorsatum Linnaeus (extirpated) .... Common Porcupine

Family Myocastoridae — Hutias and Nutria
Myocastor coypus (Molina) .... Nutria

Order Cetacea — Cetaceans

Family Delphinidae — Dolphins and Pilot Whales
Steno bredanensis (Lesson) .... Rough-Toothed Dolphin
Tursiops truncatus (Montague) .... Bottle-Nosed Dolphin
Stenella coeruleoalba (Meyen) .... Striped Dolphin
Stenella frontalis (G. Cuvier) .... Atlantic Spotted Dolphin
Delphinus delphis Linnaeus .... Saddle-Backed Dolphin
Lagenorhynchus acutus (Gray) .... Atlantic White-Sided Dolphin
Grampus griseus (Cuvier) .... Grampus
Globicephala melaena (Traill) .... Long-Finned Pilot Whale
Globicephala macrorhynchus Gray .... Short-finned Pilot Whale

Family Phocoenidae — Porpoises
Phocoena phocoena (Linnaeus) .... Harbor Porpoise

Family Ziphiidae — Beaked Whales
Ziphius cavirostris Cuvier .... Goose-Beaked Whale
Mesoplodon densirostris (De Blainville) .... Dense Beaked Whale
Mesoplodon europaeus (Gervais) .... Gervais' Beaked Whale
Mesoplodon mirus True .... True's Beaked Whale

Family Physeteridae — Sperm Whales
Kogia breviceps (De Blainville) .... Pygmy Sperm Whale
Kogia simus (Owen) .... Dwarf Sperm Whale
Physeter catodon Linnaeus .... Sperm Whale

Family Balaenopteridae — Rorquals
Balaenoptera acutorostrata Lacépède .... Minke Whale
Balaenoptera edeni Anderson .... Bryde's Whale
Balaenoptera physalus (Linnaeus) .... Fin Whale
Megaptera novaeangliae (Borowski) .... Humpback Whale

Family Balaenidae — Right Whales
Balaena glacialis (Borowski) .... Black Right Whale

Order Carnivora — Carnivores
Suborder Fissipedia — Land Carnivores

Family Canidae — Dogs and Foxes
Vulpes vulpes fulva (Desmarest) .... Red Fox
Urocyon cinereoargenteus cinereoargenteus (Schreber) ... Common Gray Fox
Canis latrans latrans Say .... Coyote
Canis rufus rufus(?) Audubon
and Bachman (extirpated) .... Red Wolf
Canis lupus lycaon Schreber (extirpated) .... Gray Wolf

Family Ursidae — Bears
Ursus americanus americanus Pallas .... Black Bear

Family Procyonidae — Raccoons
Procyon lotor lotor (Linnaeus) .... Common Raccoon

Family Mustelidae — Mustelids
Martes pennanti pennanti (Erxleben) (extirpated) ...... Fisher

Martes americana (Turton) (not confirmed) .... American Marten
Mustela nivalis rixosa Bangs .... Least Weasel
Mustela frenata frenata Lichtenstein .... Long-Tailed Weasel
Mustela vison vison Schreber .... Mink
Lontra (Lutra) canadensis lataxina F. Cuvier .... Northern River Otter

Family Mephitidae — Skunks

Spilogale putorius putorius Linnaeus .... Eastern Spotted Skunk
Mephitis mephitis mephitis (Schreber) .... Striped Skunk

Family Felidae — Cats

Puma (Felis) concolor Linnaeus .... Mountain Lion
Lynx rufus rufus (Schreber) .... Bobcat

Suborder Pinnipedia — Seals and Sea Lions

Family Phocidae — Hair Seals

Phoca vitulina Dekay .... Harbor Seal
Halichoerus grypus (Fabricius) .... Gray Seal
Cystophora cristata (Erxleben) .... Hooded Seal
Pagophilus groenlandicus (Erxleben) .... Harp Seal

Family Otariidae — Eared Seals

Zalophus californianus (Lesson) .... California Sea Lion

Order Sirenia — Manatees, Dugougs, and Sea Cows

Family Trichechidae — Manatees

Trichechus manatus latirostris (Harlan) .... Manatee

Order Perissodactyla — Odd-Toed Ungulates

Family Equidae — Horses

Equus caballus Linnaeus .... Horse

Order Artiodactyla — Even-Toed Ungulates

Family Suidae — Pigs

Sus scrofa scrofa Linnaeus .... Pig

Family Cervidae — Deer

Cervus nippon Temminck .... Sika Deer
Cervus elaphus canadensis Erxleben (extirpated) .... Elk or Wapiti
Odocoileus virginianus (Boddaert) .... White-Tailed Deer

Family Bovidae — Cattle and Antelopes

Bison bison (Linnaeus) (extirpated) .... Bison
Bos taurus Linnaeus .... Cattle
Capra hircus Linnaeus .... Domestic Goat

Appendix II

Mammals Whose Type Localities Are in Virginia

The following 14 species and subspecies of mammals are based on specimens taken in Virginia.

Opossum *(Didelphis virginiana).* Kerr, 1792. Type locality: Virginia.

Southeastern Shrew *(Sorex longirostris fisheri).* Merriam, 1895. Type locality: Lake Drummond, Dismal Swamp, Virginia.

Thompson's Pygmy Shrew *(Sorex hoyi winnemana).* Preble, 1910. Type locality: Bank of Potomac River near Stubblefield Falls, 4 miles below Great Falls of Potomac River, Fairfax County, Virginia.

Swamp Short-Tailed Shrew *(Blarina brevicauda telmalestes).* Merriam, 1895. Type locality: Lake Drummond, Dismal Swamp, Norfolk County, Virginia.

Star-nosed Mole *(Condylura cristata parva).* Paradiso, 1959. Type locality: 5 miles northwest of Stuart, Patrick County, Virginia.

Hitchen's Cottontail *(Sylvilagus floridanus hitchensi).* Mearns, 1911. Type locality: Smith's Island, Northampton County, Virginia.

Eastern Flying Squirrel *(Glaucomys volans volans)* (Linnaeus). Type locality: Fixed by Elliott (1901) as Virginia.

Eastern Harvest Mouse *(Reithrodontomys humulis virginianus).* A. H. Howell, 1940. Type locality: Amelia, Amelia County, Virginia.

Golden Mouse *(Ochrotomys nuttalli nuttalli)* (Harlan, 1832). Type locality: Norfolk, Norfolk County, Virginia.

Cotton Rat *(Sigmodon hispidus virginianus).* Gardner, 1946. Type locality: Triplet, 160 feet, Brunswick County, Virginia.

Bog Lemming *(Synaptomys cooperi helaletes).* Merriam, 1896. Type locality: Dismal Swamp, Norfolk County, Virginia.

Muskrat *(Ondatra zibethicus macrodon).* (Merriam, 1897). Type locality: Lake Drummond, Dismal Swamp, Norfolk County, Virginia.

Red Fox *(Vulpes vulpes fulva).* (Desmarest, 1820). Type locality: Virginia.

White-Tailed Deer *(Odocoileus virginianus virginianus).* (Zimmermann, 1780). Type locality: Virginia.

Appendix III
Glossary

Aestivation. A state of dormancy occurring during the summer; physiologically similar to hibernation.

Alar membrane. Wing membrane in bats.

Albino. An animal lacking normal pigmentation; characterized by having white fur and pink eyes.

Analogous. Having the same function.

Arboreal. Living in trees.

Aquatic. Living in the water.

Auditory (tympanic) bulla. A rounded, thin-walled, bony capsule enclosing the middle and inner ear of most mammals.

Bicornuate. Having two horns or extensions.

Bicuspid. A tooth having two cusps.

Bunodont. Teeth with low, rounded cusps.

Calcaneum. The heel bone.

Calcar. Cartilaginous spur arising from the heel of a bat to help support the interfemoral membrane; also found at the wrist of flying squirrels.

Canine. The tooth between the incisors and the premolars.

Carnassial. A shearing tooth of carnivores; the last upper premolar and first lower molar.

Carnivore. A mammal belonging to the order Carnivora; a meat-eater.

Carnivorous. Meat-eating.

Carrion. Dead or putrefying flesh; a carcass.

Caudad. Toward the tail or posterior part of the body.

Caudal. Of, pertaining to, near, [or toward] the tail or posterior part of the body.

Cerebellum. Dorsal expansion of anterior end of hindbrain; center of muscular control and coordination.

Cerebrum. Pair of dorsal lobes of the forebrain; each lobe known as a cerebral hemisphere; [function?].

Cervical. Pertaining to the neck.

Cheek teeth. Premolars and molars.

Chigger. Larval mite of the family Trombiculidae.

Chitin. A horny substance secreted by the upper layers of the skin and forming the hard outer covering of insects, crustaceans, etc.

Chorion. An extraembryonic membrane, primarily associated with gas exchange.

Clavicle. The bone normally connecting the scapula and sternum.

Cline. A character gradient.

Conifer. A cone-bearing tree.

Convergence. The tendency of taxa that are not closely related to evolve similar adaptations when subjected to similar environmental conditions.

Copulation. The act of uniting in sexual intercourse.

Corpus callosum. A broad, transverse sheet of nerve fibers connecting the cerebral hemispheres in higher mammals.

Cranium. Braincase.

Crepuscular. Active during periods surrounding dusk and dawn.

Cusp. One of the projections on the grinding surface of a tooth.

Delayed fertilization. A condition found in some bats where sperm are retained within the reproductive tract of the female, sometimes for several months, prior to ovulation and fertilization.

Delayed implantation. A condition found in some mammals where a fertilized egg will develop to the blastula stage, then lie quiescent, perhaps for months, before implantation and further development.

Deciduous. Shed at a certain stage of growth, such as teeth or antlers. In botany, the falling off or shedding of leaves at specific seasons; not evergreen.

Diastema. A distinct space or gap between two teeth.

Digitigrade. Type of foot in which only the toes touch the ground; entire weight of animal borne on "knuckles" (metacarpals and metatarsals).

Diphyodont. Having two sets of teeth, deciduous and permanent.

Disjunct. A population separated from the main range of a species.

Diurnal. Active during the daytime.

Duodenum. The anterior portion of the small intestine.

Ear ossicles. Three small bones – malleus, incus, stapes – found in the middle ear of mammals.

Echolocation. A guidance system in which the ear picks up sound waves bounced back from calls made by the animal itself.

Emargination. Notched margin or tip.

Emigrate. To move away from an area.

Epidermis. Outer layer of the skin.

Epipubic bone. One of a pair of bones extending forward from the anteroventral portion of the pelvic girdle in marsupials and monotremes; also called marsupial bones.

Erythrystic. Having excessive redness, particularly of the hair.

Erythrocyte. Red blood cell.

Estrus. The peak of the sexual cycle, culminating in ovulation.

Extirpation. The complete removal of a species from a locality where it once lived.

Extinction. The complete removal of all members of a species from the face of the earth.

Feces. Animal excrement.

Fenestrate. Having numerous openings, such as in the rostrum of the rabbit skull.

Feral. Wild; used to describe domestic animals that have reverted to a wild state.

Fibula. The smaller and more slender of the two bones in the hind limb.

Fluke. In cetaceans, one of the lobes of the taillike appendage. Also, a trematode parasite.

Forage. To search for food.

Foramen magnum. Large opening at the back of the skull through which the spinal cord passes.

Fossorial. Living in a burrow or hole in the ground.

Fusiform. Tapering from the middle toward each end; spindle-shaped.

Gait. The pattern of walking or stepping.

Gestation. The period of development of an embryo from conception until birth.

Gravid. Pregnant.

Guano. Bat feces.

Guard hairs. Long, outer, coarse hairs that protect the shorter, softer underfur.

Habitat. The specific area where a species or an individual animal usually lives.

Hallux. The innermost digit, or toe, of the hind limb.

Herbivore. Plant-eater.

Hermaphrodite. Having the characteristics of both sexes; bisexual.

Heterodont. Having teeth differentiated for various functions.

Hibernation. State of dormancy during the winter; characterized by the inhibition of physiological processes.

Home range. The area about its established home or nest that is traversed by an animal in its normal activities of food gathering, mating, and caring for its young.

Homing. The act of returning to familiar territory after having been displaced.

Homodont. Having essentially similar teeth in both upper and lower jaws.

Incisive foramen. One of a pair of openings in the anterior portion of the palate just behind the incisor teeth.

Incisors. Teeth in the front of the jaw adapted for cutting and/or gnawing.

Induced ovulation. Ovulation occurring immediately after, and as a result of, copulation.

Infraorbital canal (foramen). An opening in the skull in front of, and usually slightly below, the eye socket; may be enlarged into a canal.

Inguinal. In the groin region.

Innate. Inborn; not acquired or learned.

Insectivore. An insect-eating animal.

Insular. Having an island as its habitat.

Interfemoral membrane. A flight membrane of thin skin located between the hind limbs of bats; often involves the tail.

Invertebrate. An animal without a notochord or a vertebral column; insects, spiders, millipedes, etc.

Keel. A ridgelike part.

Lambdoidal crest. Ridge connecting the occipital and parietal bones of the skull.

Loph. A ridge formed by cusps of molar tooth.

Mammae. Milk glands; also known as mammary glands.

Masseter. Jaw muscle that raises the lower jaw.

Maxilla. One of a pair of bones in the upper jaw that bear the premolar and molar teeth.

Melanism. The development of dark coloring matter in the skin, hair, etc., due to extreme pigmentation; the opposite of albinism.

Metabolism. The aggregate of all chemical and physical processes constantly taking place in a living organism.

Migration. To move periodically and systematically from one region to another.

Molariform. Having the shape and appearance of molar teeth.

Molars. The set of grinding or cheek teeth located farthest back in the jaws; never preceded by milk teeth.

Molt. The shedding of hair in preparation for replacement by new growth.

Nocturnal. Active at night.

Occlude. To meet so that the corresponding cusps of the teeth of the upper and lower jaws fit closely together.

Olfactory. Pertaining to the sense of smell.

Omnivorous. Characterized by eating both animal and vegetable matter.

Palate. The bony roof of the mouth.

Palmate. Broad and flat, with fingerlike projections.

Paraoccipital process. A bony process on the posterior surface of the auditory bullae.

Parturition. Birth.

Pectoral girdle. The girdle of the anterior limbs.

Pelage. The coat of hair or characteristic covering of a mammal.

Pentadactyl. Having five fingers or toes.

Perineal. Referring to the region of the body at the posterior end of the trunk; the area surrounding the rectum.

Phalanx (plural: phalanges). One of the bones of a finger or toe.

Pinna. That portion of the ear projecting out beyond the head and serving to funnel sound waves into the ear canal.

Placenta. Tissues allowing for nourishment, exchange of respiratory gasses, and elimination of waste products between the developing embryo and the uterus of the mother.

Placental scar. Scar left on uterine wall after birth of young; marks site of attachment of embryo.

Plantigrade. Type of locomotion in which the entire sole and heel of the foot touches the ground, as in bears and man.

Postorbital process. A projection of the frontal bone directly behind the orbit.

Predator. An animal that kills another animal.

Prehensile. Adapted for grasping or coiling around and clinging to objects.

Premaxilla. The most anterior bone of the upper jaw; paired.

Premolars. Series of teeth on each side of jaw in front of true molars; distinguished from true molar teeth by having been preceded by milk teeth.

Preorbital region. Region in front of the eye.

Prey. Any animal seized by another for food.

Quadrupedal. An animal whose usual stance and locomotion makes use of four limbs.

Radiotelemetry. Using signals emanating from a radio transmitter attached to an animal to monitor its movements from a distant location.

Radius. The thicker and shorter bone of the forearm.

Retractile. Capable of being drawn back or in, as a cat's claws.

Rostrum. The preorbital part of the skull.

Sagittal crest. A median, raised ridge of bone on the braincase.

Scapular. Pertaining to the shoulder region.

Scat. Animal excrement.

Sebaceous gland. Oil-secreting gland in the skin.

Selenodont. Teeth in which the enamel of the crown is in the form of longitudinal crescents.

Senescence. Showing characteristics of old age.

Sternum. The breastbone.

Submaxillary gland. Small gland under the lower jaw; produces saliva.

Supraorbital process. A process of the frontal bone above the orbit, or eye socket.

Supraorbital ridge. Ridge situated above the orbit of the eye.

Tactile. Having the sense of touch.

Tarsus. The ankle.

Terrestrial. Living on the ground, as opposed to arboreal, aquatic, etc.

Territory. A defended area within the home range.

Tibia. The larger of the two bones in the hind limb.

Torpid. Dormant or inactive.

Tragus. Small, fleshy structure projecting upward inside front of ear of bat.

Truncate. Terminating abruptly as if the end were cut off.

Ulna. The narrower and longer bone of the forearm.

Ultrasonic. Sound waves above the range of human hearing.

Underfur. Thick, soft fur lying beneath the longer and coarser guard hairs.

Unguligrade. Type of locomotion employed by ungulates in which the entire weight of the animal is borne on the nails (hooves) of either one or two phalanges of each limb.

Unicuspid. A tooth with a single cusp. In shrews, applied to a row of three to five small teeth behind the enlarged pair of incisors.

Vibrissae. Stiff hairs growing from the region of the snout and often serving as organs of touch.

Viviparous. Term used to describe a species whose developing young become attached to the reproductive tract of the female and from which they receive oxygen and nourishment; young are born alive.

Zygomatic arch. An arch of bone forming the outside of each orbit, or eye socket.

Appendix IV
Credits for Color Plates

The author gratefully acknowledges the following persons and organizations for permitting the use of their color photographs in this volume. The numbers identify the color plates for which credit is given.

American Society of Mammalogists Slide Collection: 65

Roger W. Barbour: 5, 6, 7, 16, 17, 19, 24, 27, 29, 75

Christina M. Bird: 35

Richard E. Bird: Front cover, 33, 79, 81, 87, 88

Carolina Biological Supply Company, Inc.: 2

Kenneth L. Crowell: 55

L. Elliott: 53, 63

Thomas W. French: 4

General Biological Supply Company: 3, 76

Great Smoky Mountains National Park: 47, 69, 71

Harry Groot: 91

Graham C. Hickman: 14

Ken L. Jenkins: 72, 85

Ronald R. Keiper: 84, 86

John R. MacGregor: 15, 18, 20, 21, 22, 23, 25, 26, 30, 31, 48, 54, 60, 61, 62, 78

Sue Matthews, United States Fish and Wildlife Service: 82

David Mech, United States Fish and Wildlife Service: 70

Jon Nickles, United States Fish and Wildlife Service: 64

Donald L. Pattie: 74

Roger de Rageot: 32

Galen Rathburn, United States Fish and Wildlife Service: 83

Dave Shaffer, United States Fish and Wildlife Service: 67

Terry Shankle, North Carolina Wildlife Resources Commission: 40

R. Simpson: 8, 34, 37, 44, 51, 73, 77, 90

E. J. Taylor: 59

Ken Taylor, North Carolina Wildlife Resources Commission: 43

Tennessee Wildlife Resources Agency: 39, 42, 66, 68

R. Town, United States Fish and Wildlife Service: 58

G. L. Twiest: 38

United States Fish and Wildlife Service: 36

R. Wayne Van Devender: 9, 10, 11, 12, 13, 28, 45, 46, 49, 50, 52, 56, 57

Jerry O. Wolff: 41

Susan L. Woodward: 1, 89

J. Woody, United States Fish and Wildlife Service: 80

Appendix V
Tables

Table 1. Acronyms for mammal collections referenced in species accounts.

Acronym	Collection
AEL	Appalachian Environmental Laboratory, Frostburg State University, Frostburg, Maryland;
AMNH	American Museum of Natural History, New York, New York.
ANSP	Academy of Natural Sciences, Philadelphia, Pennsylvania.
ASU	Appalachian State University, Boone, North Carolina.
ASUMZ	Arkansas State University, State University, Arkansas.
AV	Averett College, Danville, Virginia.
AVL	Private collection of Alicia V. Linzey, Indiana, Pennsylvania.
BCV	Bridgewater College, Bridgewater, Virginia.
BRP	Blue Ridge Parkway, Luray, Virginia. (Currently housed at Western Carolina University, Cullowhee, North Carolina.)
CAS	California Academy of Sciences, San Francisco, California.
CHAS	Chicago Academy of Sciences, Chicago, Illinois.
CM	Carnegie Museum, Pittsburgh, Pennsylvania.
CMHF	Chincoteague Miniature Horse Farm, Chincoteague, Virginia.
CMNH	Cleveland Museum of Natural History, Cleveland, Ohio.
CSULB	California State University at Long Beach, Long Beach, California.
CU	Cornell University, Ithaca, New York.
CUC	Columbia Union College, Takoma Park, Maryland.
CUMZ	Museum of Zoology, Carleton University, Ottawa, Ontario.
CWM	College of William and Mary, Williamsburg, Virginia.
DMNH	Delaware Museum of Natural History, Wilmington, Delaware.
DWL	Private collection of Donald W. Linzey, Blacksburg, Virginia.
EHC	Emory and Henry College, Emory, Virginia.
EKU	Eastern Kentucky University, Richmond, Kentucky.
EMU	Eastern Michigan University, Ypsilanti, Michigan.
ETSU	East Tennessee State University, Johnson City, Tennessee.
FMNH	Field Museum of Natural History, Chicago, Illinois.
FSM	Florida Museum of Natural History, University of Florida, Gainesville, Florida.
GMU	George Mason University, Fairfax, Virginia.
GWNF	George Washington National Forest, Harrisonburg, Virginia.
HSU	Vertebrate Museum, Humboldt State University, Arcata, California.
IOWA	Museum of Natural History, University of Iowa, Iowa City, Iowa.
ISM	Illinois State Museum, Springfield, Illinois.
ISUVC	Indiana State University, Terre Haute, Indiana.
KU	Museum of Natural History, University of Kansas, Lawrence, Kansas.
LACM	Natural History Museum of Los Angeles County, Los Angeles, California.
LC	Lynchburg College, Lynchburg, Virginia.
LFCC	Lord Fairfax Community College, Middletown, Virginia.
LSUMZ	Museum of Zoology, Louisiana State University, Baton Rouge, Louisiana.
LU	Liberty University, Lynchburg, Virginia.
MCZ	Museum of Comparative Zoology, Harvard University, Cambridge, Massachusetts.
MMMN	Manitoba Museum of Man and Nature, Winnipeg, Manitoba.
MMNH	James F. Bell Museum of Natural History, University of Minnesota, Minneapolis, Minnesota.
MPH	Museum of the High Plains, Fort Hays State University, Hays, Kansas.
MRNRA	Mount Rogers National Recreation Area, Jefferson National Forest, Marion, Virginia.
MSB	Museum of Southwestern Biology, University of New Mexico, Albuquerque, New Mexico.

(Table 1, continued)

Abbreviation	Institution
MSUMZ	Museum of Zoology, Memphis State University, Memphis, Tennessee.
MVZ	Museum of Vertebrate Zoology, University of California, Berkeley, California.
NCSM	North Carolina State Museum of Natural History, Raleigh, North Carolina.
NVCC	Northern Virginia Community College, Annandale, Virginia.
ODU	Old Dominion University, Norfolk, Virginia.
OSU	Oklahoma State University, Stillwater, Oklahoma.
OU	Museum of Natural History, University of Oklahoma, Norman, Oklahoma.
PWRC	Patuxent Wildlife Research Center, Laurel, Maryland.
QM	Queensland Museum, Brisbane, Queensland, Australia.
RC	Roanoke College, Salem, Virginia.
RMWC	Randolph-Macon Woman's College, Lynchburg, Virginia.
ROM	Royal Ontario Museum, Toronto, Ontario.
RU	Radford University, Radford, Virginia.
SBC	Sweet Briar College, Sweet Briar, Virginia.
SM	Strecker Museum, Baylor University, Waco, Texas.
SNP	Shenandoah National Park, Luray, Virginia
SUVM	Shippensburg University, Shippensburg, Pennsylvania.
TCWC	Texas Cooperative Wildlife Collection, Texas A and M University, College Station, Texas.
TTU	Tennessee Technological University, Cookeville, Tennessee.
UA	University of Arizona, Tucson, Arizona.
UCLA	University of California at Los Angeles, Los Angeles, California.
UCM	University of Colorado Museum, University of Colorado, Boulder, Colorado.
UCONN	University of Connecticut, Storrs, Connecticut.
UGAMNH	Museum of Natural History, University of Georgia, Athens, Georgia.
UIMNH	Museum of Natural History, University of Illinois, Urbana, Illinois.
UMMZ	Museum of Zoology, University of Michigan, Ann Arbor, Michigan.
UR	University of Richmond, Richmond, Virginia.
USNM	National Museum of Natural History (formerly the United States National Museum), Washington, DC.
VCU	Virginia Commonwealth University, Richmond, Virginia.
VHCC	Virginia Highlands Community College, Abingdon, Virginia.
VIMS	Virginia Institute of Marine Science, Gloucester Point, Virginia.
VLM	Virginia Living Museum, Newport News, Virginia.
VMNH	Virginia Museum of Natural History, Martinsville, Virginia.
VPISU	Virginia Museum of Natural History at Virginia Tech, Virginia Polytechnic Institute and State University, Blacksburg, Virginia.
VPI-W	Department of Fisheries and Wildlife, Virginia Polytechnic Institute and State University, Blacksburg, Virginia.
WL	Washington and Lee University, Lexington, Virginia.
YPM	Peabody Museum of Natural History, Yale University, New Haven, Connecticut.

Table 2. Wild fur catch in Virginia, 1966–1993, from fur dealer reports (from trappers and hunters only).

Species	1966–67	1967–68	1968–69	1969–70	1970–71	1971–72	1972–73
Bear	-	22	15	14	8	19	10
Beaver	6,389	2,948	4,603	3,702	2,618	4,883	6,254
Bobcat	117	178	47	90	59	82	255
Deer	-	10,048	11,776	15,413	13,517	16,157	18,618
Fox, Gray	3,412	1,659	2,904	2,456	1,758	2,640	4,627
Fox, Red	-	1,023	1,401	1,368	1,102	1,687	4,101
Mink	3,716	2,437	3,421	2,597	1,899	2,146	3,685
Muskrat	184,807	120,471	209,818	177,844	128,991	146,905	200,543
Nutria	-	4	850	7	3337	-	-
Opossum	7,369	7,247	6,951	3,806	7,468	5,885	13,178
Otter	1,406	559	807	741	890	648	642
Raccoon	44,321	19,160	31,787	28,094	22,181	28,877	46,428
Skunk	4,129	2,092	1,827	1,674	547	249	1236
Weasel	248	152	87	113	45	62	242

Species	1973–74	1974–75	1975–76	1976–77	1977–78	1978–79	1979–80
Bear	16	23	24	27	8	8	9
Beaver	4,307	4,457	4,490	3,959	3,713	4,891	8,970
Bobcat	232	370	451	965	237	397	311
Deer	11,990	25,881	21,844	24,834	29,456	35,143	41,509
Fox, Gray	7,352	9,076	11,479	9,688	11,572	13,820	16,864
Fox, Red	2,771	3,077	3,734	4,164	4,991	6,244	7,782
Mink	2,883	3,965	5,072	3,417	2,787	2,488	3,890
Muskrat	163,678	172,118	191,206	145,177	141,921	141,409	167,803
Nutria	-	-	4,848	2,137	737	-	776
Opossum	21,760	34,789	25,034	22,802	18,161	21,832	35,483
Otter	602	661	594	550	815	784	947
Raccoon	39,019	50,699	70,418	54,671	63,472	75,014	87,678
Skunk	2,789	2,704	2,138	2,380	1,677	1,886	2,377
Weasel	260	224	138	128	103	141	134

Species	1980–81	1981–82	1982–83	1983–84	1984–85	1985–86	1986–87
Bear	9	32	14	10	53	7	13
Beaver	11,154	7,147	3,081	4,182	3,560	6,904	6,192
Bobcat	429	314	339	269	265	296	277
Deer	47,700	45,803	46,515	34,885	35,385	21,227	26,265
Fox, Gray	26,063	15,193	16,901	13,701	14,630	12,945	10,850
Fox, Red	11,038	8,854	9,136	7,319	9,527	6,470	6,459
Mink	5,835	3,053	2,480	2,604	2,333	2,208	2,238
Muskrat	213,349	110,809	82,038	95,037	98,312	71,634	64,579
Nutria	1,229	93	-	-	-	-	19
Opossum	40,261	18,274	18,841	10,852	9,854	7,308	8,761
Otter	1,192	757	419	649	610	709	733
Raccoon	118,950	85,657	85,987	74,917	68,990	62,260	69,678
Skunk	3,221	996	550	84	70	40	5
Weasel	239	65	100	16	16	6	9

(Table 2, continued)

Species	1987–88	1988–89	1989–90	1990–91	1991–92	1992–93
Bear	2	-	0	0	1	0
Beaver	4,728	-	1,798	2,222	3,887	1,677
Bobcat	263	-	44	16	46	41
Deer	22,789	**Data**	18,711	11,063	11,896	13,122
Fox, Gray	13,081	**Lost**	1,783	871	2,090	1,517
Fox, Red	5,319	-	913	971	1,376	812
Mink	1,646	-	400	391	647	382
Muskrat	63,464	-	13,080	15,734	21,961	10,380
Nutria	1,706	-	0	0	0	55
Opossum	5,714	-	680	385	1,369	619
Otter	785	-	182	140	436	267
Raccoon	65,065	-	9,125	4,256	5,254	4,918
Skunk	54	-	17	1	2	3
Weasel	12	-	0	0	0	0

Source: From Virginia Fur Harvest Status Report – 1993, Virginia Department of Game and Inland Fisheries, October 1994.

Table 3. Total value of fur purchased in Virginia, 1992–1993.

Species	Number of Pelts	Average Price	Total Value
Bear	0	$ 0.00	$ 0.00
Beaver	1,677	6.69	11,219.13
Bobcat	41	26.81	1,099.21
Deer	13,122	2.01	26,375.22
Gray Fox	1,517	7.75	11,756.75
Red Fox	812	9.07	7,364.84
Mink	382	11.35	4,335.70
Muskrat	10,380	1.46	15,154.80
Nutria	55	2.01	110.55
Opossum	619	1.35	835.65
Otter	267	24.99	6,672.33
Raccoon	4,918	3.33	16,376.94
Skunk	3	2.00	6.00
Weasel	0	0.00	0.00
Totals	**33,793**		**$ 101,307.12**

Source: Data compiled October, 1994, from Virginia Fur Harvest Status Report, Virginia Department of Game and Inland Fisheries.

Table 4. Cases of rabies in wild mammals in the United States, 1980–1993.

Year	Skunks	Foxes	Bats	Raccoons	Rodents and Lagomorphs	Other
1980	4096	213	726	394	6	86
1981	4480	196	858	481	10	102
1982	3088	222	975	1156	17	77
1983	2285	111	910	1906	21	61
1984	2082	139	1038	1820	29	65
1985	2507	181	830	1487	23	75
1986	2379	207	788	1576	15	70
1987	2033	119	629	1311	12	65
1988	1791	183	638	1463	25	74
1989	1657	207	720	1544	21	75
1993	7912	397	647	4311	57	166

Note: Data from Reid-Sanden et al., 1990; Krebs et al., 1994.

Table 5. Laboratory-confirmed cases of rabies in Virginia, 1951–1997.

YEAR	Total Cases Wild and Domestic	Fox	Bobcat	Raccoon	Bat	Squirrel	Skunk	Opossum	Rabbit	Deer	Groundhog	Rat	Other
1951	223	62=28%	-	-	-	-	-	-	1	-	-	1	-
1952	478	171=36%	2	1	-	-	-	-	-	1	-	1	-
1953	460	116=25%	5	2	-	-	2	-	-	-	-	-	-
1954	377	187=50%	4	1	-	-	-	-	-	-	-	-	-
1955	373	201=54%	5	2	-	-	-	-	-	-	-	-	-
1956	299	136=45%	4	-	-	-	1	-	-	-	1	-	-
1957	318	230=72%	1	-	-	-	-	-	-	1	-	-	-
1958	252	144=57%	3	2	-	2	2	-	-	-	-	-	-
1959	168	96=57%	1	-	2	-	3	-	-	-	-	-	-
1960	226	143=63%	3	-	-	2	1	-	-	-	-	-	-
1961	190	145=76%	2	-	-	1	1	-	-	-	-	-	-
1962	138	101=73%	3	-	2	-	-	-	1	-	1	-	-
1963	238	177=74%	1	2	4	-	1	-	-	-	-	-	-
1964	333	260=78%	1	-	2	-	1	-	-	-	-	-	-
1965	340	241=71%	2	2	3	-	-	-	-	-	-	-	-
1966	259	168=65%	2	-	3	-	1	-	-	-	-	-	-
1967	210	147=70%	-	-	4	-	3	-	-	1	-	-	-
1968	148	115=78%	-	-	9	-	-	-	-	-	-	-	-
1969	389	275=71%	4	2	4	1	10	2	4	-	-	-	-
1970	216	142=66%	2	1	2	-	5	-	-	-	-	-	-
1971	79	63=80%	-	-	1	-	3	-	-	-	-	-	-
1972	109	83=76%	-	-	17	-	2	-	-	-	-	-	-
1973	97	69=71%	-	-	13	-	3	-	-	-	-	-	-
1974	113	72=64%	-	-	16	-	3	-	-	-	-	-	-
1975	114	100=88%	1	-	5	-	2	-	-	-	-	-	-
1976	56	28=50%	-	-	23	-	1	-	-	-	-	-	-
1977	5	1	-	-	3	-	-	-	-	-	-	-	-
1978	14	-	-	3	8	-	3	-	-	-	-	-	-
1979	20	-	-	4	11	-	4	-	-	-	1	-	-
1980	35	1	-	7	6	-	20	-	-	-	-	-	-
1981	167	7	-	103=62%	8	-	45	-	-	-	-	-	-
1982	745	12	-	645=87%	9	-	59	-	-	-	6	-	-
1983	625	15	-	545=87%	17	-	33	-	-	-	6	-	-
1984	208	11	-	158=76%	11	-	22	-	-	-	1	-	-
1985	179	11	-	102=57%	16	-	43	-	-	-	1	-	-
1986	200	12	1	139=70%	2	-	38	-	-	-	-	-	-
1987	363	23	-	254=70%	6	-	57	-	-	-	1	-	a
1988	366	24	1	220=60%	11	-	89	-	-	-	2	-	-
1989	262	15	-	148=56%	14	-	58	3	-	-	1	-	a
1990	202	8	1	129=64%	6	-	42	-	-	-	-	-	-
1991	253	13	1	167=66%	8	-	51	-	-	-	2	-	-
1992	362	23	1	203=56%	12	-	77	-	-	-	1	-	b
1993	387	23	-	213=55%	12	-	94	-	-	-	6	-	c
1994	428	17	-	251=59%	9	-	105	1	-	-	5	-	c
1995	459	21	1	271=59%	8	1	114	-	-	-	3	-	c
1996	612	38	1	383=63%	17	1	124	1	-	-	6	-	b,c
1997	690	46	1	429=62%	22	-	142	1	-	-	5	-	b,c

[a] Beaver: 1987 (2), 1989 (1)

[b] Mink: 1992 (1), 1996 (1), 1997 (1)

[c] Otter: 1993 (1), 1994 (1), 1995 (1), 1996 (1), 1997 (1)

Notes: Data compiled from Virginia Department of Health, *Statistical Annual Reports*, 1951–1997, and Dr. Suzanne Jenkins, personal communication, 1994.

Table 6. Laboratory-confirmed rabies in Virginia mammals, by city or county, January 1961–April 1998.

County or City	Fox	Bobcat	Raccoon	Bat	Squirrel	Skunk	Opossum	Rabbit	Deer	Groundhog	Beaver
Accomack	3	-	67	-	-	-	-	-	-	-	-
Albemarle	93	-	45	10	-	29	-	-	-	-	-
Alexandria	1	-	111	9	-	1	-	-	-	-	-
Alleghany	26	2	12	1	-	8	-	-	-	-	-
Amelia[c]	-	-	10	1	-	2	-	-	-	-	-
Amherst	45	-	15	-	-	5	-	-	-	-	-
Appomatox	-	-	6	1	-	7	-	-	-	-	-
Arlington	4	-	94	4	-	-	1	-	-	1	-
Augusta	106	-	58	5	-	75	-	-	-	-	-
Bath	13	-	16	-	-	9	-	-	-	-	-
Bedford	194	-	23	4	-	13	-	-	-	-	-
Bland	17	-	1	-	-	-	-	1	-	-	-
Botetourt	75	-	8	3	-	16	-	-	-	-	-
Brunswick	-	-	2	-	-	1	-	-	-	-	-
Buchanan	2	-	-	-	-	-	-	-	-	-	-
Buckingham	-	-	4	-	-	9	-	-	-	-	-
Campbell	181	-	16	2	-	15	-	-	-	1	-
Caroline	21	-	17	-	-	9	1	-	-	-	-
Carroll	14	-	2	-	-	2	-	1	-	-	-
Charles City	1	-	4	-	-	1	-	-	-	-	-
Charlotte	1	-	4	-	-	7	-	-	-	-	-
Charlottesville	-	-	-	11	-	-	-	-	-	-	-
Chesapeake	1	-	17	2	-	-	-	-	-	-	-
Chesterfield	3	-	116	14	-	6	-	-	-	1	-
Clarke	27	1	37	1	-	2	-	-	-	-	-
Clifton Forge	-	-	1	-	-	-	-	-	-	-	-
Craig	4	2	4	-	-	1	-	-	-	-	-
Culpeper	23	-	36	-	-	11	-	-	-	-	-
Cumberland	-	1	15	-	-	4	-	-	-	-	-
Danville	-	-	1	-	-	-	-	-	-	-	-
Dickenson	2	-	-	-	-	-	-	-	-	-	-
Dinwiddie	-	-	15	-	-	4	-	-	-	-	-
Essex	6	-	27	-	-	2	-	-	-	-	-
Fairfax[a]	99	-	963	70	-	50	1	1	-	9	1
Fauquier	88	-	158	3	-	26	-	-	-	1	-
Floyd	17	-	18	-	-	4	-	-	-	1	-
Fluvanna	3	-	5	-	-	7	-	-	-	-	-
Franklin	7	-	20	1	-	14	-	-	-	-	-
Frederick	25	-	49	5	-	27	-	-	-	-	-
Fredericksburg	-	-	5	2	-	-	-	-	-	-	-
Giles	31	-	4	1	-	3	-	-	-	-	-
Gloucester	-	-	27	1	-	4	-	-	-	-	-

(Table 6, continued)

County or City	Fox	Bobcat	Raccoon	Bat	Squirrel	Skunk	Opossum	Rabbit	Deer	Groundhog	Beaver
Goochland	2	-	32	1	-	6	-	-	-	-	-
Grayson	19	-	16	-	-	7	-	-	-	-	-
Greene	3	-	14	-	-	3	-	-	-	1	-
Greensville	-	-	12	-	-	5	-	-	-	-	-
Halifax	3	-	19	1	-	8	-	-	-	-	-
Hanover	24	-	101	9	-	24	-	-	-	3	-
Henrico	8	-	63	10	-	8	-	-	-	1	-
Henry	1	-	9	-	-	1	-	-	-	-	-
Highland	6	1	9	-	-	7	-	-	-	-	-
Hopewell	-	-	15	2	-	-	-	-	-	-	-
Isle of Wight	-	-	20	-	-	-	-	-	-	-	-
James City[d]	4	-	15	1	-	11	-	-	-	-	-
King and Queen	5	-	13	-	-	2	-	-	-	-	-
King George	3	-	6	-	-	3	-	-	-	-	-
King William	6	-	19	-	-	5	-	-	-	1	-
Lancaster[b]	4	-	11	-	-	2	-	-	-	-	-
Lee	99	2	-	2	-	31	-	-	-	-	-
Loudoun	110	-	655	17	-	64	2	-	-	9	-
Louisa	19	-	54	1	-	23	-	-	-	-	-
Lunenburg	-	1	19	1	-	12	-	-	-	-	-
Lynchburg	1	-	10	2	-	6	-	-	-	1	-
Madison	15	-	23	-	-	18	-	-	-	-	-
Mathews	-	-	3	2	-	-	-	-	-	-	-
Mecklenburg	1	-	8	-	-	9	-	-	-	-	-
Middlesex	6	-	8	-	-	2	-	-	-	-	1
Montgomery	40	-	15	4	-	15	-	-	-	-	-
Nelson	74	-	19	2	-	18	-	-	-	-	-
New Kent	-	-	27	2	-	2	-	-	-	-	-
Newport News	-	-	38	1	-	3	-	-	-	-	-
Norfolk	2	-	7	-	-	1	-	-	-	-	-
Northampton	-	-	72	-	-	-	-	-	-	-	-
Northumberland[e]	3	-	10	-	-	2	-	-	-	-	-
Nottoway	1	-	29	-	-	8	-	-	-	-	-
Orange	10	-	53	-	-	6	-	-	-	2	-
Page	14	-	25	-	-	110	-	-	-	3	-
Patrick	11	-	17	1	-	3	-	-	-	-	-
Petersburg	1	-	8	5	-	-	-	-	-	-	-
Pittsylvania	3	-	32	-	-	13	-	-	-	-	-
Powhatan	1	-	19	1	-	5	-	-	-	-	-
Prince Edward	-	-	10	-	-	6	-	-	-	-	-
Prince George	2	-	47	5	-	2	-	-	-	-	-
Prince William	26	-	157	32	-	33	2	1	-	4	-
Pulaski	25	-	13	1	-	16	-	-	-	-	-
Rappahannock	17	-	17	-	-	7	-	-	-	-	-
Richmond	2	-	11	-	-	1	-	-	-	-	-

(Table 6, continued)

County or City	Fox	Bobcat	Raccoon	Bat	Squirrel	Skunk	Opossum	Rabbit	Deer	Groundhog	Beaver
Richmond City	2	-	34	6	-	-	-	-	-	-	-
Roanoke	28	2	5	2	-	2	-	-	-	-	-
Roanoke City	-	-	2	-	1	-	-	-	-	-	-
Rockbridge	71	1	17	5	-	14	-	-	-	-	-
Rockingham	128	-	66	2	-	100	-	-	-	-	-
Russell	72	4	1	-	-	27	-	-	-	-	-
Portsmouth	-	-	1	-	-	-	-	-	-	-	-
Scott	122	-	1	-	-	35	-	-	-	-	-
Shenandoah	34	-	84	4	-	63	-	-	-	1	1
Smyth	118	3	9	1	-	9	-	-	-	1	-
Southampton	1	-	8	2	-	2	-	-	-	-	-
Spotsylvania	17	-	42	4	-	29	-	-	-	1	-
Stafford	10	-	58	5	-	14	-	-	-	1	-
Suffolk	1	-	39	2	-	1	-	-	-	-	-
Surry	-	-	4	-	-	1	-	-	-	-	-
Sussex	-	-	16	1	-	2	-	-	-	-	-
Tazewell	67	1	9	1	1	5	-	-	-	-	-
Virginia Beach	2	-	63	4	-	-	-	-	-	1	-
Warren	25	-	63	2	-	12	-	-	-	-	-
Washington	195	2	-	2	-	62	-	1	1	-	-
Waynesboro	-	-	1	-	-	1	-	-	-	-	-
Westmoreland	4	-	12	-	-	1	-	-	-	-	-
Williamsburg	-	-	5	-	-	1	-	-	-	-	-
Wise	15	1	-	3	-	-	2	-	-	-	-
Wythe	68	-	12	-	1	6	-	1	-	1	-
York	1	-	28	-	-	-	-	-	-	-	-
Total	**2,685**	**24**	**4,391**	**300**	**3**	**1,269**	**9**	**6**	**1**	**43**	**3**

[a] Fairfax: 1 mink also.
[b] Lancaster: 1 otter also.
[c] Amelia: 1 otter also.
[d] James City: 1 mink also.
[e] Northumberland: 1 otter also.

Notes: Compiled from Virginia Department of Health, *Statistical Annual Reports*, 1951–1998, and Dr. Suzanne Jenkins, personal communication, 1994.

Table 7. Number of beavers tagged in Virginia, 1976–1987.

County	76 / 77	77 / 78	78 / 79	79 / 80	80 / 81	81 / 82	82 / 83	83 / 84	84 / 85	85 / 86	10 yr. avg	86 / 87
Accomack	-	-	-	-	-	-	-	-	-	-	-	-
Albemarle	10	39	13	89	105	4	57	48	48	56	47	40
Alleghany	19	46	33	40	61	31	47	17	28	15	34	54
Amelia	151	82	125	492	421	282	157	199	162	100	217	75
Amherst	7	13	2	6	10	14	8	4	10	55	13	42
Appomattox	32	5	7	67	100	47	13	44	78	74	47	36
Augusta	6	16	15	27	27	13	5	9	3	10	13	45
Bath	49	23	36	68	96	68	30	52	82	42	55	66
Bedford	9	13	7	17	26	11	3	3	7	25	12	5
Bland	7	5	4	27	14	10	8	10	19	13	12	18
Botetourt	7	16	11	11	31	4	7	14	7	2	11	16
Brunswick	17	136	33	241	430	311	159	112	118	82	164	83
Buchanan	-	-	1	16	-	-	1	-	-	-	2	-
Buckingham	27	56	55	162	211	74	46	58	102	109	90	65
Campbell	15	10	19	114	65	46	62	46	27	60	46	20
Caroline	625	694	669	1051	1035	226	377	443	468	958	655	564
Carroll	-	-	-	1	-	1	5	1	2	3	1	8
Charles City	53	29	12	140	237	280	38	61	30	40	92	81
Charlotte	128	181	96	611	297	183	272	133	173	163	224	158
Chesapeake	-	-	-	-	-	1	-	6	-	1	1	-
Chesterfield	82	139	200	305	262	138	207	84	88	131	164	106
Clarke	-	-	-	1	4	5	-	-	-	5	2	-
Craig	4	21	5	44	73	64	36	55	-	34	34	72
Culpeper	50	96	20	104	85	26	77	37	7	97	60	125
Cumberland	98	65	151	336	202	124	81	39	100	91	129	179
Dickenson	-	-	-	1	-	-	-	-	-	-	-	-
Dinwiddie	157	158	88	427	270	182	53	165	111	134	174	124
Essex	310	393	193	603	390	302	56	85	207	224	276	318
Fairfax	0	2	1	13	14	24	9	14	-	6	8	10
Fauquier	38	45	31	169	82	35	40	-	9	19	47	33
Floyd	14	5	5	23	4	27	13	4	17	4	12	26
Fluvanna	6	31	25	147	139	28	47	12	5	11	45	41
Franklin	3	3	7	6	5	3	5	5	12	5	5	16
Frederick	3	4	6	51	24	25	8	20	14	3	16	21
Giles	-	2	1	33	8	13	1	3	9	8	8	10
Gloucester	38	57	86	100	207	89	15	95	45	27	76	60
Goochland	109	74	53	232	161	53	109	26	40	161	102	62
Grayson	-	-	5	1	5	-	1	-	5	-	2	2
Greene	-	-	-	24	70	16	16	9	14	25	17	23
Greensville	48	59	74	70	135	33	26	104	18	15	58	35
Halifax	273	245	5	375	298	281	240	244	135	172	227	156
Hanover	195	349	289	377	409	282	73	112	146	265	250	376
Henrico	72	134	133	258	302	161	83	92	81	96	141	126
Henry	-	6	1	-	8	-	-	4	1	-	2	1
Highland	11	10	12	11	43	25	16	-	6	25	16	26
Isle of Wight	16	3	3	13	22	26	3	4	28	17	14	27
James City	20	73	55	82	75	61	47	48	52	34	55	53
King & Queen	338	225	306	475	340	317	121	206	299	312	294	537
King George	98	103	102	200	114	60	28	79	85	53	92	201
King William	221	300	181	166	293	368	129	161	80	343	224	344
Lancaster	53	10	6	18	6	1	10	-	3	2	11	36
Lee	-	-	-	-	-	-	-	-	-	-	-	-
Loudoun	8	3	3	47	47	17	8	-	2	21	16	27
Louisa	147	268	177	231	349	227	125	213	134	157	203	334
Lunenburg	34	32	19	98	74	5	59	61	122	74	58	82
Madison	26	60	44	176	90	24	18	45	37	30	55	98
Mathews	3	8	1	-	5	-	4	-	-	-	2	1
Mecklenburg	10	79	1	78	23	-	9	13	37	36	29	40
Middlesex	56	11	71	42	51	56	21	66	96	38	51	56
Montgomery	-	16	11	14	17	17	-	4	65	2	15	25
Nelson	24	9	14	31	22	-	52	9	14	29	20	10
New Kent	194	269	232	272	221	188	63	111	160	105	182	192
Northampton	-	-	-	-	-	-	-	-	-	-	-	-
Northumberland	27	44	54	42	8	15	15	29	27	17	28	37
Nottoway	89	36	111	290	355	163	88	97	68	150	145	46
Orange	89	206	143	173	263	143	274	64	70	45	147	132
Page	16	4	14	55	65	31	4	9	6	66	27	25
Patrick	-	1	-	4	1	3	-	-	-	7	2	-
Pittsylvania	40	59	52	127	113	70	46	58	44	64	67	69
Powhatan	96	62	29	446	128	82	27	58	44	85	106	81
Prince Edward	132	265	147	706	368	217	186	234	225	255	274	166
Prince George	49	32	5	131	115	84	65	35	39	49	60	16
Prince William	46	-	55	192	127	10	4	36	41	88	60	96
Pulaski	-	-	2	24	5	5	1	2	-	-	4	4
Rappahannock	26	23	11	26	44	18	3	11	12	1	18	18
Richmond	214	111	107	158	132	106	55	12	48	50	99	174
Roanoke	-	5	-	1	5	2	-	-	-	-	1	-
Rockbridge	12	7	18	38	45	12	6	11	3	2	15	19
Rockingham	3	16	-	13	20	29	16	8	17	14	14	35
Russell	-	-	-	9	1	-	-	9	4	-	2	2
Scott	-	-	-	-	-	-	-	-	6	-	1	1
Shenandoah	11	11	-	7	11	37	13	2	0	15	11	29
Smyth	1	2	-	12	8	9	3	1	-	1	4	7
Southampton	59	32	150	159	137	63	46	23	38	81	79	100
Spotsylvania	331	232	359	863	555	251	210	262	415	518	411	491
Stafford	11	142	217	395	330	203	118	106	235	373	213	172
Suffolk	-	1	-	2	3	-	8	9	2	1	3	44
Surry	2	8	12	21	20	26	8	-	1	1	10	9

(Table 7, continued)

County	76 / 77	77 / 78	78 / 79	79 / 80	80 / 81	81 / 82	82 / 83	83 / 84	84 / 85	85 / 86	10 yr. avg	86 / 87
Sussex	151	42	116	193	349	78	49	50	62	109	120	46
Tazewell	-	5	-	7	40	19	4	6	3	6	9	12
Virginia Beach	1	-	-	-	-	-	-	-	-	-	-	-
Warren	-	-	-	26	26	25	1	16	2	8	10	11
Warwick, Newport News & Hampton	1	-	8	-	23	-	2	-	-	-	3	-
Washington	-	6	6	20	3	5	7	-	-	-	5	18
Westmoreland	204	168	187	277	224	167	75	97	95	90	155	159
Wise	-	-	-	3	5	-	2	2	12	-	2	-
Wythe	-	-	2	6	1	-	-	-	2	-	1	6
York	14	3	6	1	20	29	6	-	-	1	8	7
Colvins Fur House, Gordonsville	-	-	-	-	282	-	-	-	-	-	28	-
Out of State	-	-	-	-	-	-	57	86	129	186	46	409
East of Blue Ridge	5,383	6,004	5,379	12,671	11,134	6,334	4,311	4,481	4,857	6,438	6,703	6861
West of Blue Ridge	163	220	187	590	642	477	235	254	312	278	339	558
Unknown	-	-	-	6	1	-	-	-	-	-	1	-
Statewide	5,546	6,224	5,566	13,267	12,059	6,811	4,603	4,821	5,298	6,902	7,117	7828

Note: Data from Commonwealth of Virginia, Commission of Game and Inland Fisheries.

Table 8. Nutria harvest records for Louisiana, 1973–1994.

Year	Number of Pelts	Approximate Price to Trapper	Value
1973–74	1,749,670	$5.25	$8,998,020.00
1974–75	1,502,617	$5.00	7,264,393.50
1975–76	1,525,506	$5.25	7,464,777.00
1976–77	1,890,853	$8.00	14,781,397.50
1977–78	1,714,083	$5.00	8,263,373.50
1978–79	1,145,084	$4.50	4,823,094.00
1979–80	1,300,822	$7.25	8,843,299.50
1980–81	1,207,050	$8.80	9,881,930.40
1981–82	961,471	$4.85	4,195,667.50
1982–83	730,731	$2.60	1,853,133.80
1983–84	881,551	$2.95	2,479,599.00
1984–85	1,214,600	$4.25	4,804,871.50
1985–86	761,948	$3.35	2,415,374.80
1986–87	986,014	$3.53	3,371,181.94
1987–88	617,646	$2.69	1,594,453.08
1988–89	223,222	$1.72	383,534.64
1989–90	292,760	$2.99	874,620.00
1990–91	134,196	$2.53	339,250.80
1991–92	240,229	$3.12	750,687.00
1992–93	129,545	$2.38	308,525.75
1993–94	215,968	$3.01	650,750.00

Note: Data from unpublished fur harvest statistics, Louisiana Department of Wildlife and Fisheries.

Table 9. Black bear harvest in Virginia, 1928–1998.

Year	Kill	Year	Kill	Year	Kill
1927–28	139	1951–52	327	1975–76	230
1928–29	292	1952–53	359	1976–77	217
1929–30	183	1953–54	275	1977–78	201
1930–31	245	1954–55	154	1978–79	218
1931–32	161	1955–56	135	1979–80	232
1932–33	145	1956–57	213	1980–81	432
1933–34	151	1957–58	272	1981–82	334
1934–35	110	1958–59	359	1982–83	365
1935–36	121	1959–60	208	1983–84	467
1936–37	116	1960–61	206	1984–85	472
1937–38	125	1961–62	339	1985–86	539
1938–39	105	1962–63	381	1986–87	564
1939–40	164	1963–64	259	1987–88	557
1940–41	133	1964–65	248	1988–89	579
1941–42	102	1965–66	122	1989–90	621
1942–43	84	1966–67	345	1990–91	327
1943–44	130	1967–68	342	1991–92	657
1944–45	149	1968–69	283	1992–93	483
1945–46	156	1969–70	326	1993–94	789
1946–47	163	1970–71	361	1994–95	518
1947–48	143	1971–72	145	1995–96	602
1948–49	147	1972–73	295	1996–97	602
1949–50	313	1973–74	214	1997–98	788
1950–51	148	1974–75	197		

Note: Estimates of the black bear harvest were made by game wardens from 1928 through 1946. Since 1947, all bears legally harvested have been tagged and registered at check stations.

Table 10. Number of otters tagged in Virginia, 1983–1994.

City or County	83 84	84 85	85 86	86 87	10 yr. Avg.	87 88	88 89	89 90	90 91	91 92	92 93	93 94
Accomack	21	18	15	18	27	12	4	-	-	-	5	-
Albemarle	2	6	5	2	2	6	3	2	-	2	-	-
Alleghany	-	-	-	-	-	-	-	-	-	3	-	-
Amelia	34	18	3	9	28	9	7	8	-	-	2	1
Amherst	4	3	2	7	2	3	1	4	2	4	-	-
Appomattox	3	10	4	4	5	8	4	2	1	1	-	4
Augusta	-	-	-	-	-	-	-	-	-	8	1	-
Bath	1	-	-	-	.1	-	-	-	-	2	8	-
Bedford	1	-	1	1	.4	-	-	-	-	2	-	-
Bland	-	-	-	-	-	-	-	-	-	-	-	-
Botetourt	-	-	-	-	-	-	-	-	-	-	-	-
Brunswick	15	30	13	26	22	34	18	21	5	19	-	11
Buchanan	-	-	-	-	-	-	-	-	-	-	-	4
Buckingham	1	10	2	7	6	7	1	-	7	5	-	7
Campbell	10	2	5	6	4	2	-	1	5	2	-	4
Caroline	22	49	55	38	43	32	38	21	11	45	29	38
Carroll	-	-	-	-	-	-	-	-	-	-	-	-
Charles City	11	1	7	16	12	2	4	-	5	3	11	-
Charlotte	14	16	17	31	20	4	23	12	3	19	-	19
Chesapeake	8	7	3	6	6	8	5	-	9	2	3	1
Chesterfield	16	15	33	10	25	16	25	1	5	1	-	-
Clarke	-	-	-	-	-	-	-	-	-	-	-	-
Craig	-	-	-	4	.4	-	-	-	-	-	-	-
Culpeper	3	-	3	-	2	15	1	-	1	2	-	-
Cumberland	6	28	8	12	12	14	10	7	-	18	-	3
Dickenson	-	-	-	-	-	-	-	-	-	-	-	-
Dinwiddie	16	10	10	14	16	6	-	5	-	9	-	17
Essex	23	20	9	31	32	24	20	2	-	-	5	-
Fairfax	-	-	-	-	.3	4	1	-	3	-	-	-
Fauquier	-	-	3	4	4	5	2	2	1	12	4	4
Floyd	-	-	-	-	-	-	-	-	-	-	-	-
Fluvanna	2	2	2	1	4	7	4	1	-	-	1	-
Franklin	-	-	1	1	.4	3	2	-	3	2	-	-
Frederick	-	-	1	1	.5	-	-	-	-	-	-	-
Giles	-	-	-	-	-	-	-	-	-	-	-	-
Gloucester	11	4	9	10	15	9	3	-	3	-	3	-
Goochland	9	2	4	3	6	-	1	7	1	-	-	16
Grayson	-	-	-	-	-	-	-	-	-	-	-	-
Greene	-	2	1	2	1	5	4	10	2	1	5	1
Greensville	8	25	5	11	17	22	2	-	-	7	-	-
Halifax	16	16	30	37	21	24	-	-	-	1	-	11
Hanover	11	22	27	26	23	3	9	32	-	5	21	25
Henrico	10	11	8	24	18	25	47	40	9	5	11	-
Henry	-	-	2	-	.2	-	-	-	-	-	-	-
Highland	-	-	-	-	-	-	-	-	1	3	-	-
Isle of Wight	2	6	12	15	11	11	18	2	4	-	10	1
James City	18	11	21	23	18	26	21	-	8	-	13	-
King & Queen	25	33	11	52	31	18	9	-	5	1	1	-
King George	12	8	3	7	9	5	11	-	-	-	-	-
King William	13	7	25	43	19	29	23	4	5	-	20	7

(Table 10, continued)

City or County	83 84	84 85	85 86	86 87	10 yr. Avg.	87 88	88 89	89 90	90 91	91 92	92 93	93 94
Lancaster	12	5	4	12	9	14	5	-	1	-	5	-
Lee	-	-	-	-	-	-	-	-	3	-	-	1
Loudoun	-	4	2	-	3	1	3	-	-	1	4	-
Louisa	5	7	9	18	15	6	4	5	-	2	8	2
Lunenburg	14	12	9	16	8	3	5	9	-	1	-	2
Madison	7	2	2	1	2	-	6	5	1	8	13	5
Mathews	2	1	-	4	6	5	1	-	-	-	-	-
Mecklenburg	4	4	8	6	5	2	5	4	1	-	-	-
Middlesex	28	27	13	10	19	34	16	-	19	-	27	-
Montgomery	-	13	-	-	1	-	-	-	-	-	-	-
Nelson	3	1	6	1	3	6	1	-	-	1	3	-
New Kent	24	17	26	28	22	29	9	-	19	2	4	-
Northampton	3	5	3	1	6	8	1	-	-	-	21	-
Northumberland	20	15	13	27	21	31	6	-	7	-	-	-
Nottoway	8	9	11	14	14	10	-	3	-	7	-	6
Orange	3	4	3	11	6	24	7	3	-	4	5	-
Page	-	-	-	5	1	-	-	-	-	-	-	-
Patrick	2	-	-	-	.2	1	-	-	-	-	3	-
Pittsylvania	2	6	11	10	6	11	6	2	1	1	-	-
Powhatan	6	4	10	12	14	23	3	5	-	-	-	6
Prince Edward	16	33	19	27	23	37	5	20	19	31	-	14
Prince George	13	10	5	7	8	7	-	-	10	-	4	-
Prince William	1	1	2	5	2	-	6	4	1	-	-	-
Pulaski	-	-	-	-	-	-	-	-	-	-	-	-
Rappahannock	1	3	-	1	2	-	-	-	-	-	1	1
Richmond	9	6	20	28	23	9	3	-	1	1	8	6
Roanoke	-	-	-	-	-	-	-	-	-	-	-	-
Rockbridge	-	-	-	-	-	-	1	2	-	3	2	-
Rockingham	-	-	-	-	-	-	-	-	-	-	26	-
Russell	-	-	-	-	-	-	-	-	-	-	-	-
Scott	-	-	-	-	-	-	-	-	-	4	-	-
Shenandoah	-	-	-	2	1	-	-	-	-	-	-	-
Smyth	-	-	-	-	-	-	-	-	-	-	-	-
Southampton	10	20	22	19	27	18	18	-	-	-	4	-
Spotsylvania	18	21	21	15	20	10	14	2	4	21	4	15
Stafford	3	16	29	11	14	12	4	1	-	2	1	-
Suffolk	14	7	14	15	12	20	10	-	-	-	9	6
Surry	1	-	1	4	4	-	-	-	3	-	10	-
Sussex	22	25	21	9	30	3	16	-	13	-	-	11
Tazewell	-	-	-	-	.2	-	-	1	-	-	-	-
Virginia Beach	9	5	15	17	21	13	8	2	2	-	2	1
Warren	-	-	-	-	-	5	-	-	-	-	-	-
Warwick, Newport News and Hampton	1	1	-	-	3	2	-	-	-	-	-	2
Washington	-	-	-	-	1	-	-	-	-	-	-	-
Westmoreland	26	30	22	20	33	17	8	-	-	-	1	-
Wise	-	-	-	-	-	-	-	-	-	-	1	6
Wythe	-	-	-	-	-	-	-	-	-	-	-	-
York	2	3	5	8	6	5	3	-	1	-	2	-

Source: Data compiled October, 1994, from Virginia Fur Harvest Status Report–1993, Virginia Department of Game and Inland Fisheries.

Table 11. Number of bobcats tagged in Virginia, 1983–1994.

City or County	83 84	84 85	85 86	86 87	10 yr. Avg.	87 88	88 89	89 90	90 91	91 92	92 93	93 94
Accomack	-	-	-	-	-	-	-	-	-	-	-	-
Albemarle	6	10	7	6	8	20	19	5	11	12	16	19
Alleghany	4	16	5	15	10	43	8	12	13	9	11	2
Amelia	-	-	1	6	1	5	7	8	1	1	3	18
Amherst	11	7	7	9	9	15	11	6	11	3	1	15
Appomattox	8	8	2	4	4	2	14	3	-	7	-	9
Augusta	6	12	11	23	15	32	12	9	15	6	14	13
Bath	5	6	24	22	11	26	18	10	15	10	13	14
Bedford	13	8	9	12	14	12	20	2	7	14	2	28
Bland	4	3	7	8	8	8	6	8	2	3	6	3
Botetourt	8	4	12	9	10	17	9	4	4	11	2	9
Brunswick	6	8	4	9	4	8	10	9	11	14	2	7
Buchanan	7	4	8	6	7	5	3	4	8	12	15	5
Buckingham	11	2	19	7	7	10	7	7	12	9	2	13
Campbell	3	6	1	2	2	1	1	2	2	6	1	1
Caroline	-	-	2	-	.3	-	-	-	10	-	-	85
Carroll	-	4	5	4	2	4	10	5	5	5	13	11
Charles City	-	-	-	-	.1	-	-	-	-	-	-	60
Charlotte	-	7	5	4	2	1	2	5	1	4	1	8
Chesapeake	-	4	3	1	2	1	5	-	3	1	7	8
Chesterfield	-	1	1	2	1	18	8	5	9	3	4	-
Clarke	1	-	-	-	.5	4	-	-	1	1	1	1
Craig	3	2	11	-	7	3	11	-	3	4	2	2
Culpeper	-	-	-	-	.2	2	1	-	1	-	-	48
Cumberland	-	1	3	1	3	4	3	13	14	15	1	15
Dickenson	2	2	1	6	2	-	-	-	3	2	4	-
Dinwiddie	2	1	5	4	1	11	3	5	-	13	1	14
Essex	-	-	-	1	.1	-	-	-	-	-	-	-
Fairfax	-	-	1	-	.1	-	-	-	3	-	1	1
Fauquier	-	-	9	7	4	9	14	5	6	2	5	13
Floyd	3	3	7	7	4	7	2	7	7	15	9	17
Fluvanna	-	-	-	-	.3	-	2	1	1	10	4	8
Franklin	6	4	5	4	4	9	5	1	-	4	-	3
Frederick	2	-	5	1	1	3	-	2	5	2	2	1
Giles	6	10	16	13	12	8	4	2	6	9	12	11
Gloucester	-	-	1	-	.1	-	-	-	-	-	-	-
Goochland	-	-	-	-	.1	8	3	-	3	1	5	10
Grayson	10	6	12	6	8	8	4	11	8	12	11	13
Greene	1	-	8	8	3	22	7	11	7	7	3	3
Greensville	3	-	-	7	1	4	10	-	-	3	5	25
Halifax	3	2	-	4	2	4	1	-	1	3	-	9
Hanover	-	-	1	-	.2	-	-	10	-	1	-	2
Henrico	-	-	-	-	-	1	10	10	10	4	-	-
Henry	-	1	-	2	.5	4	-	-	-	3	-	24
Highland	8	6	15	14	11	24	14	11	6	10	12	9
Isle of Wight	2	1	1	-	1	-	4	-	-	-	-	-
James City	-	-	-	-	-	-	-	-	-	-	-	-
King & Queen	-	-	-	-	-	-	-	-	-	-	-	-
King George	-	-	-	1	.1	-	-	-	-	-	-	-
King William	-	-	-	-	-	-	-	-	-	-	-	-
Lancaster	-	-	-	-	.7	-	-	-	-	-	-	-

(Table 11, continued)

City or County	83 84	84 85	85 86	86 87	10 yr. Avg.	87 88	88 89	89 90	90 91	91 92	92 93	93 94
Lee	6	15	19	22	11	42	7	10	-	5	4	1
Loudoun	1	-	5	1	2	2	3	2	6	13	7	1
Louisa	-	-	-	1	.1	-	-	1	-	-	-	36
Lunenburg	-	-	2	2	.8	4	3	1	3	2	2	9
Madison	4	17	9	7	6	10	12	2	3	3	4	1
Mathews	-	-	-	-	-	-	-	-	-	-	-	-
Mecklenburg	9	1	1	-	1	-	1	-	-	1	-	4
Middlesex	-	-	-	-	-	-	-	-	-	-	-	-
Montgomery	6	4	4	4	5	-	8	3	1	4	8	5
Nelson	15	10	16	20	12	42	16	10	4	8	1	11
New Kent	-	-	-	-	-	-	-	-	3	7	-	5
Northampton	-	-	-	-	-	-	-	-	-	-	-	-
Northumberland	-	-	-	-	-	-	-	-	-	-	-	12
Nottoway	-	-	1	1	.6	1	2	1	1	6	2	17
Orange	1	-	-	-	.4	-	3	-	-	-	-	-
Page	4	8	4	3	5	16	6	8	5	4	4	4
Patrick	4	5	3	4	5	10	5	7	6	8	-	4
Pittsylvania	1	1	5	8	2	3	1	-	1	4	3	7
Powhatan	-	1	1	2	.4	-	7	1	-	3	3	9
Prince Edward	5	3	2	4	2	10	6	10	4	12	1	8
Prince George	-	1	2	1	1	3	-	-	2	-	1	4
Prince William	-	2	-	1	.3	1	1	-	3	2	-	-
Pulaski	5	1	1	2	2	4	2	4	1	-	-	2
Rappahannock	4	4	3	10	4	6	7	2	3	5	6	5
Richmond	-	-	-	-	-	-	-	-	-	-	2	2
Roanoke	2	4	3	3	6	5	1	1	6	2	1	3
Rockbridge	14	13	17	8	16	37	8	4	6	2	2	3
Rockingham	2	21	21	18	11	26	12	11	17	9	6	6
Russell	6	3	3	7	6	10	5	2	3	14	8	7
Scott	11	13	8	7	9	9	10	3	1	3	10	12
Shenandoah	-	-	3	5	2	10	3	1	3	12	2	11
Smyth	10	4	9	8	7	7	4	3	5	7	6	-
Southampton	-	1	5	2	3	9	8	-	-	-	14	12
Spotsylvania	4	2	-	-	1	-	-	9	4	1	2	3
Stafford	2	1	-	1	.5	-	1	-	-	-	-	-
Suffolk	-	1	5	-	.9	4	3	-	-	-	1	-
Surry	-	-	3	1	1	1	-	-	1	-	2	1
Sussex	2	2	4	4	3	1	3	2	-	1	1	9
Tazewell	31	19	23	22	19	14	13	8	9	8	10	4
Virginia Beach	-	2	1	-	.8	4	-	-	-	-	2	-
Warren	1	-	1	3	4	6	4	3	7	3	-	-
Warwick, Newport News and Hampton	-	-	-	-	-	-	-	-	-	-	1	1
Washington	5	12	16	13	9	13	11	2	4	9	2	-
Westmoreland	-	-	-	-	-	-	-	-	-	-	-	1
Wise	13	25	14	16	16	14	3	1	6	7	16	1
Wythe	1	3	9	2	3	2	2	4	2	5	1	4
York	-	-	-	-	-	1	-	-	-	-	2	-
Statewide	**313**	**352**	**457**	**454**	**361**	**690**	**449**	**309**	**345**	**421**	**328**	**782**

Source: Data compiled October, 1994, from Virginia Fur Harvest Status Report - 1993, Virginia Department of Game and Inland Fisheries.

Table 12. **White-tailed deer harvest in Virginia, 1947–1997.**

Year	Harvest	Year	Harvest
1947–48	4,011	1972–73	48,775
1948–49	5,152	1973–74	60,798
1949–50	6,909	1974–75	61,989
1950–51	5,699	1975–76	63,443
1951–52	7,226	1976–77	63,671
1952–53	10,872	1977–78	67,059
1953–54	11,797	1978–79	72,545
1954–55	14,079	1979–80	69,940
1955–56	14,218	1980–81	75,208
1956–57	20,855	1981–82	78,388
1957–58	22,473	1982–83	88,745
1958–59	26,841	1983–84	85,807
1959–60	28,969	1984–85	84,432
1960–61	36,165	1985–86	101,412
1961–62	32,875	1986–87	121,760
1962–63	38,843	1987–88	119,309
1963–64	38,391	1988–89	114,562
1964–65	31,161	1989–90	135,094
1965–66	27,983	1990–91	160,411
1966–67	26,156	1991–92	179,344
1967–68	24,934	1992–93	200,446
1968–69	28,041	1993–94	201,122
1969–70	34,150	1994–95	209,373
1970–71	38,138	1995–96	218,476
1971–72	42,369	1996–97	207,560

Source: Data compiled by Virginia Commission of Game and Inland Fisheries.

Appendix VI
The Late Wisconsinan Mammalian Fauna of Virginia

Jerry N. McDonald,[1,2] *Ralph E. Eshelman,*[1,3] *Frederick Grady,*[1] *and David A. Hubbard, Jr.*[4]

The mammalian fauna that was in place in Virginia and its adjacent marine waters in AD 1600, on the eve of permanent colonization by western Europeans, was derived from the mammalian fauna that had occupied eastern North America and adjacent coastal waters during the Wisconsinan glaciation, ca. 90,000 to 10,000 years ago. Two thirds of the land mammals (68% of the genera) that are known to have been present in what is now Virginia during the Late Wisconsinan, ca. 25,000 to 10,000 years ago, are present in Virginia today. Twenty-two of the 65 genera present some 10,000 years ago have been lost from the fauna while 13 genera not present at the end of the Wisconsinan glaciation now occur within the Commonwealth, resulting in a mammalian fauna that is nearly (86%) as diverse at the generic level as that of 10,000 years ago albeit composed of a noticeably different generic mix. Where differences occur between the Late Wisconsinan and Historic/Modern faunas of Virginia, they can be attributed to one or more of the following processes. (1) Changes in the physical environment resulted in range changes. (2) Changes in the biological environment resulted in range changes. (3) Extinction terminated species. (4) Evolution created new species. (5) Different information exists in the zoological and paleontological records for different taxa, periods of time, and parts of the Commonwealth.

Here, we provide a list of mammals known in the Pleistocene local faunas of Virginia, a list of localities that have yielded these faunas, maps showing the distribution of Pleistocene occurrences in Virginia of mammalian genera, and a brief outline of the major patterns and processes that have characterized the transition from the Wisconsinan fauna to the Historic and Modern faunas of Virginia. The term Wisconsinan fauna is used herein to include genera and species of mammals represented in local faunas dating from ca. 90,000 years ago to ca. 9,000 years ago. This range of time begins with the approximate onset of the most recent major glacial phase of the Quaternary (the Wisconsinan, as applied to North America) and ends with the early part of the present interglacial phase (the Holocene) when the residual physical and biological elements of the glacial-age system were still present but waning as the emerging interglacial environment moved toward relative equilibrium. The term Historic fauna refers to the mammalian fauna of Virginia at about AD 1600, just before the European influence on Virginia's environment was initiated. Modern fauna refers to the mammalian fauna of Virginia today, that existing after

[1] Department of Paleobiology, National Museum of Natural History, Washington, DC

[2] Virginia Museum of Natural History, Martinsville, VA

[3] Eshelman and Associates, Lusby, MD

[4] Virginia Division of Mineral Resources, Charlottesville, VA

four centuries of Euro-American influence on the Commonwealth's environment and its component parts.

Many paleobiologists working with fossils of Quaternary age feel more comfortable and confident working at the level of genus than species when compiling inventories and comparing faunas. This is because all taxonomic groups are not equally well understood, the material available from any given local fauna or for any given taxon is often very limited in quality and quality, and there are diverging opinions among researchers as to the practice of assigning fossil specimens to any given taxon. Consequently, we base most of our considerations here on genera rather than species. We also use the most recently published taxonomic identification given for members of a local fauna. For example, in our compilation the Least Shrew is given as *Microsorex hoyi* whereas in the main body of this book the species is given as *Sorex hoyi*. *Neotoma floridana* and *Neotoma magister* are listed separately, even though they generally are considered conspecifics. Overall, we believe that this will prevent more confusion than it creates.

Changes in the physical and biological environment of eastern North America generally, or Virginia in particular, during the most recent glacial-interglacial cycle have been reviewed in Porter (1983), McDonald and Bird (1986), and Ruddiman and Wright (1987). Lists of mammalian taxa present in local faunas from eastern North America have been presented by Hibbard et al. (1965), Kurten and Anderson (1980), Lundelius et al. (1983), and Faunmap Working Group (1994). Reviews of Wisconsinan faunas known in Virginia have been presented recently by Eshelman and Grady (1986), McDonald (1986), and Hubbard and Grady (1997). Rose (1986c) reviewed the mammalian fauna as of ca. AD 1600. Overviews of human agency as an ecological force are presented in classic works by Marsh (1864), Thomas (1956), and Wagner (1960). Numerous opinions about, and case studies of, faunal extinctions during the Quaternary are presented in Martin and Klein (1984).

The Mammalian Fauna of Virginia

The Pleistocene fauna of Virginia included species representing 12 orders of mammals (Table A6-1). Among these, Edentata and Proboscidea are missing from the Historic/Modern faunas — *Megalonyx, Mammut, Mammuthus,* and *Dasypus bellus* are extinct. Sirenia, represented in the Historic/Modern fauna by *Trichechus manatus*, has not been recorded in the Wisconsinan fauna of Virginia. We have included Primates in our list of mammalian orders present in the Wisconsinan and Historic/Modern faunas because we believe it useful to view *Homo sapiens* as an integral member of the faunal community and a participant in the dynamics of ecosystems within which it is immersed.

Sixty-nine genera of mammals have been recorded for the Pleistocene fauna of Virginia (Table A6-2). The location of local faunas that constitute the Wisconsinan fauna are identified in Table A6-3 and located in Figure A6-1. Local faunas from which terrestrial mammals have been identified are presented in Figures A6-2 through A6-57. We consider this list of mammals and local faunas to be incomplete and expect that additional genera will be recognized in Virginia's Wisconsinan fauna as new local faunas are discovered and studied and as known local faunas are restudied in the light of newly-acquired information, analytical procedures, and philosophical perspectives.

Clearly, the known record attests to a former presence of the respective genera where their remains have been found, but the fossil record is subject to many biases and that fact needs to be kept in mind when evaluating the information that is available and presented here. The dynamics of erosion and deposition, and opportunities for the accumulation of skeletal and dental materials, vary widely from place to place. This variation results in differing accumulations of fossil-bearing deposits. Few local faunas are known, for example, from the Piedmont of Virginia — this is a region where erosion, not deposition, dominates, and there are few suitable sites that allow for the accumulation of deposits that could incorporate the remains of mammals. More local faunas are known from the sediment-rich Coastal Plain than from the Piedmont. Most of Virginia's local faunas, however, are known from the Appalachian Highlands, the mountainous western part of the Commonwealth where numerous caves and fissures have provided suitable environments for the accumulation and preservation of fossil-bearing deposits — especially sites that were used as owl roosts and carnivore dens. Another important bias influencing knowledge of Virginia's Wisconsinan fauna is the level and intensity of research interest in the subject. Fossils of Wisconsinan age have been known from Virginia since colonial time, but interest in the resource has been imbalanced temporally, geographically, and institutionally. Most local faunas known from Virginia have been collected during the twentieth century by the Carnegie Museum of Natural History and the National Museum of Natural History. Recently, the Virginia Museum of Natural History and the Virginia Division of Mineral Resources have taken active roles in locating and collecting fossil faunas in Virginia.

Changing Faunas

The known record of Wisconsinan and Historic/Modern faunas indicates that the composition of Virginia's mammalian community has been only modestly stable during the past ten or so millennia. Twenty-two genera have been deleted from the Wisconsinan fauna, 13 others have been added, and some have been both deleted and added. In addition, ranges of mammals within the Commonwealth have changed, as have population levels from ca. 9,000 years ago to ca. AD 1600, and from AD 1600 to the present (i.e., from the end of the Wisconsinan fauna to the onset of the Historic period, and then on to the time of the Modern fauna).

Changes in the physical environment of eastern North America is the most general of the readily recognizable causes for changes in the composition, distribution, and population levels of Virginia's faunas. As the earth passed from glacial to interglacial conditions, several changes in climatic parameters occurred. Generally, but not equally and not necessarily in precise synchrony, marine transgressions occurred as water-level in the oceans increased, mean temperatures increased, larger proportions of continental areas received greater amounts of precipitation, and patterns of seasonality changed. For Virginia, these changes translated into a warmer, more moist environment with less pronounced seasonal extremes of temperature and precipitation than had existed under the glacial climatic regime. Latitudinal and altitudinal shifts in biota occurred. At low and intermediate elevations, the dominantly-conifer forest and woodland vegetation of the glacial-age environment was generally replaced with a broadleaf-dominant forest. At higher elevations, where topographic relief was most pronounced, periglacial and boreal environments at highest elevations were replaced with hardy conifer and broadleaf forests as plant associations moved upslope in response to the less-limiting interglacial-age physical environment. Biotic communities associated with periglacial and boreal conditions were extinguished and left behind only relict populations of representative species, typically on higher elevations in western Virginia. Disappearance of periglacial conditions is the most parsimonious explanation for the extirpation of *Ochotona* and *Phenacomys* from Virginia. Species associated with the conifer-dominated forests and forest openings of higher and lower elevations (e.g., *Lepus americanus, Martes americana, Alces alces, Rangifer tarandus*) shifted northward or to higher elevations with the changing climate while others (e.g., *Myotis austroriparius, Oryzomys palustris, Sigmodon hispidus*), formerly found to the south of Virginia, shifted northward to extend their ranges into what is now the Commonwealth.

The late Wisconsinan was a time of major faunal extinction in North America (Martin and Klein, 1984), a wave of extinction that eliminated nearly two-thirds of North America's large-bodied mammalian genera. This wave eliminated several genera that were included in the Wisconsinan fauna of Virginia, including *Megalonyx, Castoroides, Arctodus, Mammut, Mammuthus, Equus, Tapirus, Mylohyus, Platygonus, Sangamona, Cervalces,* and *Bootherium*. In addition, the large-bodied species *Canis dirus* and *Panthera* or *Felis atrox* became extinct, as did the smaller-bodied *Dasypus bellus* and *Neofiber leonardi*. The presence of *Bison* in the Wisconsinan fauna of Virginia is uncertain, despite the fact that several fossil specimens have been assigned to the genus, but if it did occur in Virginia's Wisconsinan fauna, then the species of *Bison* that was present is also extinct.

Evolution is considered to be a continuous and continuing process, but there is substantial difference among proponents as to the mechanisms of evolution and the rate at which it works. The model that requires a long time to create a new species would have difficulty accommodating the evolution of one or more new species since the onset of the Holocene. Alternatively, the model that recognizes rapid evolution can accommodate the appearance of new species since the onset of the Holocene. *Bison bison,* present in the Historic fauna of Virginia, evolved during the Holocene about 5,000 to 4,000 years ago (McDonald, 1981). *Bison bison,* therefore, is a relatively new species, one that appeared after the Wisconsinan fauna had passed.

The role of human beings as important and influential ecological agents should not be underestimated. The long-established ability of *Homo sapiens* and its predecessors to modify environments — first with simple, then with increasingly complex tools; first in small numbers, then with ever-increasing numbers — has made important contributions to the history of biotic assemblages and dynamics. Direct harvest of plants and animals for use as food, clothing, shelter, and tools has influenced the number and viability of local populations of mammals, and sometimes entire species populations. Disruption of biotic communities, intentionally or unintentionally, other than by the direct harvest of resources, has had the net effect of simplifying the biotic composition of those communities. Overall, the diversity of the earth's biotic communities has been simplified by human actions. Humans have been present in Virginia for at least 14,000 years, probably longer, as documented at Saltville and Cactus Hill (McDonald, 1990; Hall, 1996; Wisner, 1996). Human hunting is considered one of the most likely reasons for the wave of extinctions that simplified North America's large mammal community at or near the end of the Wisconsinan glaciation (McDonald, 1984; Martin and Klein, 1984), and it is the explanation for these extinctions favored by two of us (JNM and REE). Prehistoric humans also modified Virginia's biotic communities in other ways, from inducing population-limiting stress upon some species of mammals (e.g., *Odocoileus virginianus*) to almost certainly improving habitat for others (e.g., *Peromyscus* spp., *Procyon lotor, Mephitis mephitis*). Euro-Americans accelerated the rate of environmental change and displaced a significant number of mammals in the Historic fauna, especially reducing or eliminating populations of large-bodied game, furbearing, and predatory species (e.g., *Castor canadensis, Lontra (Lutra) canadensis, Puma (Felis) concolor, Cervus elaphus, Bison bison*). At the same time, Euro-American culture brought exotic mammals to Virginia (e.g., in the genera *Mus, Rattus, Equus, Sus, Bos, Ovis, Capra*); attempted to reintroduce species that had been extirpated (e.g., in the genera *Cervus* and *Lepus*), and continues to add yet additional exotic species (e.g., *Lepus californicus, Myocastor coypus,* and *Cervus sika*). In summary, human agency has exerted conspicuous influence on the biogeography of Virginia — it has both simplified and diversified the mammalian faunas of Virginia while dramatically affecting the numbers and ranges of many species.

Lastly, as information continues to accumulate on the content of the Wisconsinan and Historic/Modern faunas, differences among these faunas and our levels of understanding them can be expected to change. Only recently did the first two records in Virginia of the short-faced bear, *Arctodus simus,* appear (Grady, 1995; Miller, 1998). Other large-bodied carnivores are suspected of having been present during the late Wisconsinan because of the overall dimensions of their ranges. *Symbos* and *Bootherium* were considered to be separate genera until they were recognized as male and female of the same species and synonymized as *Bootherium bombifrons* (McDonald and Ray, 1989). Both *Rangifer tarandus* and *Bootherium bombifrons* were considered boreal elements restricted to the Appalachian spine until investigation of coastal faunas revealed that their ranges had extended to lower elevations and latitudes than previously known (McDonald and Ray, 1993; McDonald, Ray, and Grady, 1996). A living population of *Microtus chrotorrhinus* was discovered in Virginia only recently (Handley and Pagels, 1991b), and the range of *Myotis austroriparius* has been known to extend into the Commonwealth for only a matter of months.

Table A6-1. Number of genera of mammals, by order, present in the Wisconsinan and Historic/ Modern faunas of Virginia.

Order	Wisconsinan Fauna	Historic/Modern Fauna
Marsupialia	1	1
Insectivora	7	6
Chiroptera	6	7
Primate	1	1
Edentata	2	0
Lagomorpha	3	2
Rodentia	20	22
Cetacea	1	15
Carnivora	14	17
Proboscidea	2	0
Sirenia	0	1
Perissodactyla	2	1
Artiodactyla	10	6
Totals	**69**	**79**

Note: The number of genera reported for the Historic/Modern fauna includes all genera known to have occurred in Virginia historically, including those considered to have been native as well as those that have been introduced by human agency during the past four hundred years. Wisconsinan data are from Eshelman and Grady (1986) and Grady (1996); Historic and Modern faunas data are from Linzey, this volume.

Table A6-2. Genera of mammals present in Virginia during the Late Pleistocene and Early Holocene, current status, and localities of record. (Numbers are keyed to sites in Table A6-3).

Marsupialia/Didelphimorphia			
Didelphis virginiana	Virginia Opossum	Present	36, 44, 46
Insectivora			
Sorex arcticus	Arctic Shrew	Extirpated	4, 11, 30, 43
Sorex cinereus	Masked Shrew	Present	3, 4, 11, 30, 43, 59
Sorex dispar	Long-Tailed Shrew	Present	4, 11, 30
Sorex fumeus	Smoky Shrew	Present	3, 4, 11, 30, 33, 43, 59
Sorex palustris	Water Shrew	Present	11, 30, 43
Sorex spp. indet.	Sorex Shrews		11, 24, 28, 30, 35, 47, 59
Microsorex hoyi	Pygmy Shrew	Present	11, 30, 35, 43, 47
Blarina brevicauda	N. Short-Tailed Shrew	Present	3, 4, 11, 20, 30, 33, 43, 59
Blarina spp. indet.	Blarina Shrews		17, 22, 24, 30, 35, 41, 47, 56, 73
Cryptotis parva	Least Shrew	Present	43
Soricid	Shrews		22, 39
Parascalops breweri	Hairy-Tailed Mole	Present	3, 4, 11, 17, 30, 33, 43, 59, 73
Scalopus aquaticus	Eastern Mole	Present	4, 11, 43
Scalopus spp. indet.	Scalopus Mole		30
Condylura cristata	Star-Nosed Mole	Present	3, 4, 11, 30, 33, 39, 43, 59
Chiroptera			
Myotis lucifugus or *Myotis sodalis*	Little Brown or Indiana Myotis	Present	4, 11, 30, 43

Myotis keenii	Keen's Bat	Present	4, 11, 30, 43
Myotis grisescens	Gray Bat	Present	4
Myotis leibii	E. Small-Footed Bat	Present	4, 11
Myotis spp. indet.	Myotis Bats		3, 4, 30, 33, 35, 54, 78, 81
Pipistrellus subflavus	Eastern Pipistrelle	Present	11, 33, 43, 59, 67, 78, 81
Pipistrellus spp. indet.	Pipistrelle Bats		4
Lasionycterus noctivagans	Silver-Haired Bat	Present	51
Eptesicus fuscus	Big Brown Bat	Present	3, 4, 11, 30, 33, 43
Eptesicus spp. indet.	Eptisicus Bats		30, 35, 43
Plecotus townsendii	W. Big-Eared Bat	Present	11
Plecotus spp. indet.	Plecotus Bats		4, 33
Lasiurus borealis	E. Red Bat	Present	11, 43
Chiropteran	Bats		6, 20, 22, 40, 47, 56
Primates			
Homo sapiens	Humans	Present[a]	53, 90, 91, 92
Edentata			
Megalonyx jeffersonii	Jefferson's Ground Sloth	Extinct	20, 37, 53
Dasypus bellus	Beautiful Armadillo	Extirpated /Extinct[b]	41
Lagomorpha			
Ochotona spp. indet.	Pikas		33
Sylvilagus transitionalis	New England Cottontail	Extirpated	11
Sylvilagus floridanus	Eastern Cottontail	Present	44, 46
Sylvilgus spp. indet.	Cottontails		43, 53, 54
Lepus americanus	Snowshoe Hare	Present	4, 11, 22, 43
Lepus spp. indet.	Hares		30
Leporid	Hares and Rabbits		3, 4, 17, 27, 28, 30, 35, 41, 43, 47, 48, 63, 73
Rodentia			
Tamias striatus	Eastern Chipmunk	Present	3, 4, 11, 20, 30, 33, 43, 54
Eutamias minimus	Least Chipmunk	Extirpated	11
Eutamias spp. indet.	Eutamias Chipmunks		4
Marmota monax	Woodchuck	Present	3, 4, 11, 20, 30, 33, 43, 44, 63
Marmota spp. indet.	Marmots		17, 24, 28, 35, 41, 76
Spermophilus tridecemlineatus	Thirteen-Lined Ground Squirrel	Extirpated	3, 4, 11, 30, 39, 43
Sciurus carolinensis	E. Gray Squirrel	Present	14, 33, 43
Sciurus spp. indet.	Sciurus Squirrels		3, 17, 30
Tamiasciurus hudsonicus	Red Squirrel	Present	3, 4, 11, 33, 43
Glaucomys volans	S. Flying Squirrel	Present	3, 4, 11, 17, 20, 30, 43
Glaucomys sabrinus	N. Flying Squirrel	Present	3, 4, 11, 30, 43
Glaucomys spp. indet.	Flying Squirrels		3, 11, 20, 28, 33, 47, 81
Sciurid	Squirrels		17, 22, 28, 35, 39, 41, 47, 48, 63, 73
Castor canadensis	Bever	Present	3, 17, 20, 22, 43, 46, 51
Castoroides ohioensis	Giant Beaver	Extinct	42, 43
Castorid	Beavers		47
Peromyscus maniculatus	Deer Mouse	Present	3, 4, 11, 43, 59
Peromyscus leucopus	White-Footed Mouse	Present	3, 4, 11, 30, 43

Peromyscus spp. indet.	Peromyscus Mice		3, 4, 17, 22, 24, 35, 43, 59, 63, 67, 73, 78, 81
Neotoma floridana[c]	Eastern Woodrat	Present[c]	3, 4, 11, 20, 30, 33, 43, 59, 67
Neotoma magister[c]	Allegheny Woodrat	Present	78, 81
Neotoma spp. indet.	Woodrats		4, 17, 22, 24, 28, 35, 39, 47, 48, 73, 76
Clethrionomys gapperi	S. Red-Backed Vole	Present	3, 4, 11, 17, 24, 30, 33, 35, 39, 41, 43, 47, 51, 59, 73, 78
Phenacomys intermedius	Heather Vole	Extirpated	3, 4, 11, 43, 59
Phenacomys spp. indet.	Phenacomys Voles		17, 30, 39, 41
Microtus pennsylvanicus	Meadow Vole	Present	3, 4, 11, 20, 24, 30, 33, 41, 43, 53, 59
Microtus chrotorrhinus	Rock Vole	Present	3, 4, 11, 24, 30, 33, 43
Microtus xanthognathus	Yellow-Cheeked Vole	Extirpated	3, 4, 11, 22, 28, 30, 43, 63
Microtus pinetorum	Woodland Vole	Present	3, 4, 11, 67
Microtus spp. indet.	Microtus Voles		3, 4, 17, 22, 24, 28, 30, 33, 35, 39, 41, 43, 47, 56, 59, 63
Neofiber leonardi	Round-Tailed Muskrat	Extirpated /Extinct[b]	59
Ondatra zibethicus	Muskrat	Present	3, 11, 43, 53, 59
Ondatra spp. indet.	Ondatra Muskrat		17, 22
Synaptomys cooperi	S. Bog Lemming	Present	3, 11, 17, 24, 30, 33, 35, 39, 41, 43, 47, 59
Synaptomys borealis	N. Bog Lemming	Extirpated	3, 4, 11, 24, 30, 33, 43, 59
Synaptomys spp. indet.	Bog Lemmings		28, 33, 35
Zapus hudsonius	Meadow Jumping Mouse	Present	11, 43, 59
Zapus spp. indet.	Zapus Jumping Mice		30, 33
Napaeozapus insignis	Woodland Jumping Mouse	Present	11, 24, 43, 59
Erethizon dorsatum	Porcupine	Present ?	11, 17, 30, 43, 59
Cetacea			
Eschrichtius glaucus	Gray Whale	Present	42
Cetacean	Whales and Porpoises		77
Carnivora			
Canis dirus	Dire Wolf	Extinct	11
Canis lupus	Gray Wolf	Extirpated	43, 51
Canis latrans	Coyote	Present	22
Canis spp. indet.	Canis Dogs		3, 22, 26, 40
Urocyon cinereoargenteus	Gray Fox	Present	51
Vulpes vulpes	Red Fox	Present	4
Vulpes spp. indet.	Vulpes Foxes		43
Canid	Dogs and Foxes		35, 47, 59
Arctodus simus	Short-Faced Bear	Extinct	78, 84
Ursus americanus	Black Bear	Present	3, 11, 22, 27, 43
Ursus spp. indet.	Ursus Bears		20, 26, 30, 38, 41, 44, 53, 55
Ursid	Bears		35, 40, 48
Procyon lotor	Raccoon	Present	3, 11, 17, 20, 30, 43, 45, 46, 54, 73
Martes americana	Marten	Extirpated	11, 17, 39, 43
Martes pennanti	Fisher	Present	3, 17, 43, 51
Mustela rixosa	Least Weasel	Present	3, 4, 11, 43
Mustela erminea	Ermine	Extirpated	11
Mustela frenata	Long-Tailed Weasel	Present	43

Mustela vison	Mink	Present	4, 11, 17, 43
Mustela spp. indet.	Mustela Weasels		11
Mephitis mephitis	Striped Skunk	Present	11, 43, 44, 46
Spilogale putorius	Eastern Spotted Skunk	Present	20, 51
Panthera sp. indet. or *Felis atrox*	Lion	Extinct	38, 40
Lynx spp. indet.	Lynx Cats		17, 39, 43
Odobenus rosmarus	Atlantic Walrus	Extirpated	42, 77
Halichoerus grypus	Gray Seal	Extirpated	77
Carnivoran	Carnivores		20, 77
Proboscidea			
Mammut americanum	American Mastodon	Extinct	1, 10, 14, 15, 18, 23, 31, 32, 53, 59, 65, 74, 79, 85, 86, 88, 89
Mammuthus primigenius	Woolly Mammoth	Extinct	14, 53, 81
Mammuthus spp. indet.	Mammoths	Extinct	14, 72
Perissodactyla			
Equus complicatus	Complex-Toothed Horse	Extinct	1, 20, 59
Equus fraternus	Brother Horse	Extinct	31
Equus spp. indet.	Horse		9, 18, 19, 20, 51, 53, 58, 60, 65, 73, 87
Tapirus veroensis	Vero Tapir	Extinct	59, 82, 83
Tapirus spp. indet.	Tapirs		20, 22, 38, 51, 73, 76
Artiodactyla			
Mylohyus nasutus	Long-Nosed Peccary	Extinct	59
Mylohyus spp. indet.	Mylohyus Peccary		3, 20, 22, 26, 43, 47, 51, 73
Platygonus compressus	Flat-Headed Peccary	Extinct	20, 31, 80, 81
Platygonus vetus	Leidy's Peccary	Extinct	68
Platygonus spp. indet.	Platygonus peccary		27, 45, 50, 56, 65
Cervus elaphus	Elk	Present	11, 59, 81
Cervus spp. indet.	Cervus Deer		17
Odocoileus virginianus	White-Tailed Deer	Present	4, 11, 20, 31, 40, 43, 53, 59
Odocoileus spp. indet.	Odocoileus Deer		17, 24, 35, 47, 73, 88
Sangamona spp. indet.	Fugitive Deer	Extinct	47, 76
Alces alces	Moose	Extirpated	59
Cervalces spp. indet.	Stag-Moose	Extinct	22, 53
Rangifer tarandus	Caribou	Extirpated	17, 24, 35, 53, 94
Bison spp. indet.	Bison		14, 20, 26, 31, 53, 59
Bootherium bombifrons	Harlan's Musk Ox	Extinct	14, 53, 59, 93

[a] Evidence of human agency at the indicated localities is based on the presence of tools, not skeletal or dental remains. Only the oldest or most well documented sites are reported here.

[b] The genus is extirpated in Virginia; the species is extinct.

[c] *Neotoma floridana* and *Neotoma magister* are considered synonyms.

Note: This table is based on Table 2 in Eshelman and Grady (1986), as modified by new information in Grady (1996); Hubbard and Grady (1997); McDonald and Ray (1993); McDonald, Ray, and Grady (1996); and Grady, Hubbard, and McDonald (unpublished data).

Table A6-3. Localities from which local faunas assigned to the Wisconsinan fauna have been collected in Virginia.

Locality	Depositional Environment	Assigned Age
1. Abingdon, Washington County	Salt Spring ?	Late Pleistocene
3. Back Creek Cave #1, Bath County	Rockshelter	Late Pleistocene
4. Back Creek Cave #2, Bath County	Rockshelter	Late Pleistocene/Early Holocene
9. Chesapeake City	Alluvium ?	Late Pleistocene
10. City Point, Prince George County	Alluvium ?	Late Pleistocene
11. Clarks Cave, Bath County	Cave	Late Pleistocene
14. Continental Shelf		Late Pleistocene
15. Covington, Alleghany County		Late Pleistocene
17. Darty Cave, Scott County	Cave	Late Pleistocene/Early Holocene
18. Deep Creek Pit, City of Chesapeake	Alluvium	Late Pleistocene[a]
19. Denniston, Halifax County		Late Pleistocene
20. Earlys Cave, Wythe County	Cave	Middle Pleistocene
22. Edinburg Fissure, Shenandoah County	Fissure	Late Pleistocene
23. Edom, Rockingham County		Late Pleistocene
24. Eggleston Fissure, Giles County	Fissure	Late Pleistocene
26. Fairview Beach, King George County		Pleistocene
27. Gardners Cave, Wythe County	Cave	Late Pleistocene
28. Gillespies Cliff Cave, Tazewell County	Cave	Late Pleistocene and Holocene
30. Holston Vista Cave, Washington County	Cave	Late Pleistocene/Holocene
31. Hot Run, Frederick County	Spring/Alluvium	Late Pleistocene[b]
32. Hot Springs, Bath County	Spring	Late Pleistocene
33. Jasper Saltpeter Cave, Lee County	Cave	Middle Pleistocene
35. Klotz Quarry Cave #5, Giles County	Cave	Late Pleistocene
36. Kumis, Roanoke County		Pleistocene ?
37. Lane Cave, Scott County	Cave	Late Pleistocene
38. Limeton, Warren County	Cave	Late Pleistocene/Early Holocene
39. Loop Creek Quarry Cave, Russell County	Cave	Late Pleistocene/Early Holocene
40. Luray Caverns, Page County	Cave	Pleistocene ?
41. Meadowview Cave, Washington County	Cave	Late Pleistocene
42. Metomkin and other islands, Accomack County	Coastal Sediments	Late Pleistocene
43. Natural Chimneys, Augusta County	Cave	Late Pleistocene
44. New Castle, Craig County		Pleistocene ?
45. New Quarry Cave, Smyth County	Cave	Late Pleistocene
46. Newport, Giles County		Late Pleistocene ?
47. Pembroke Railroad Cave #1, Giles County	Cave	Late Pleistocene
48. Pembroke Railroad Cave #2, Giles County	Cave	Late Pleistocene
50. Rass Hole, Highland County	Cave	Late Pleistocene/Holocene
51. Ripplemead Quarry, Giles County	Cave	Late Pleistocene/Holocene
53. Saltville, Smyth County	Fluvial/Lacustrine	Late Pleistocene[c]
54. Shenandoah Caverns, Shenandoah County	Cave	Pleistocene ?
55. Shires Saltpeter Cave, Craig County	Cave	Late Pleistocene/Holocene
56. Skyline Caverns, Warren County	Cave	Late Pleistocene
58. Staunton, Augusta County	Fissure	Late Pleistocene
59. Strait Canyon, Highland County	Fissure	Late Pleistocene[d]
60. Stratford Hall, Westmoreland County	Fluvial?	Late Pleistocene
63. Unknown, Clarke County	Cave?	Late Pleistocene
65. Unnamed Cave, Smyth County	Cave	Late Pleistocene
67. Varners Cave, Highland County	Cave	Pleistocene ?
68. Vickers Cave, Washington County	Cave	Middle Pleistocene ?

72. Warrenton, Fauquier County		Late Pleistocene
73. Will Fraleys Cave, Washington County	Cave	Late Pleistocene ?
74. Near Williamsburg, York County	Alluvial	Late Pleistocene
76. Winding Stairs Cave, Scott County	Cave	Late Pleistocene
77. Womack Pit, City of Virginia Beach	Coastal Sediments	Late Pleistocene
78. Island Ford Cave, Alleghany County	Cave	Late Pleistocene
79. Prince Albert Cave, Giles County	Cave	Late Pleistocene
80. Ruffners Cave #1, Page County	Cave	Late Pleistocene
81. Endless Caverns, Rockingham County	Cave	Late Pleistocene
82. Slip-Sliding-Away Cave, Scott County	Cave	Late Pleistocene
83. Lost Lake Cave, Scott County	Cave	Late Pleistocene
84. Unthanks Cave, Lee County	Cave	Late Pleistocene
85. Mumbauer Farm, Rockingham County	Cave	Late Pleistocene
86. Dortons Shop, Russell County	Karst	Late Pleistocene
87. Waterfall Cave, Smyth County	Cave	Late Pleistocene
88. Ratliff Reservoir Site, Russell County	Alluvium/ Colluvium	Late Pleistocene[e]
89. Chilhowie Trailer Park, Smyth County	Alluvium	Late Pleistocene
90. Flint Run Complex, Warren County	Alluvium	Late Pleistocene
91. Cactus Hill, Sussex County	Dune	Late Pleistocene
92. Williamson, Dinwiddie County	Dune	Late Pleistocene
93. Continental Shelf off Cape Charles	Submerged Surface	Late Pleistocene
94. Virginia Beach ?	Beach Sediments	Late Pleistocene[f]

[a] Radiocarbon dates on tusk of *Mammut americanum* yielded ages of 18,780±630 and 16,830 yr BP; wood located 0.3 m above tusk dated at >38,000 yr BP.

[b] Radiocarbon date on tooth of *Mammut* yielded age of 11,550±165 yr BP.

[c] Radiocarbon dates on plant and animal remains have yielded dates ranging from 27,000 to 10,050 yr BP for the Pleistocene deposits at this site.

[d] Radiocarbon date for this locality yielded age of 29,870 +1800/-1400 yr BP.

[e] Four radiocarbon dates bracketing the fossil-bearing deposits range from >44,000 to 29,100±300 yr BP.

[f] Radiocarbon date for *Rangifer* cranium yielded age of >36,830 yr BP.

Note: This table is based on Table 1 in Eshelman and Grady (1986). The numbers of localities as given in that table have been retained here for all sites through 77. Localities 78 through 94 are additions to the 1986 Eshelman and Grady list.

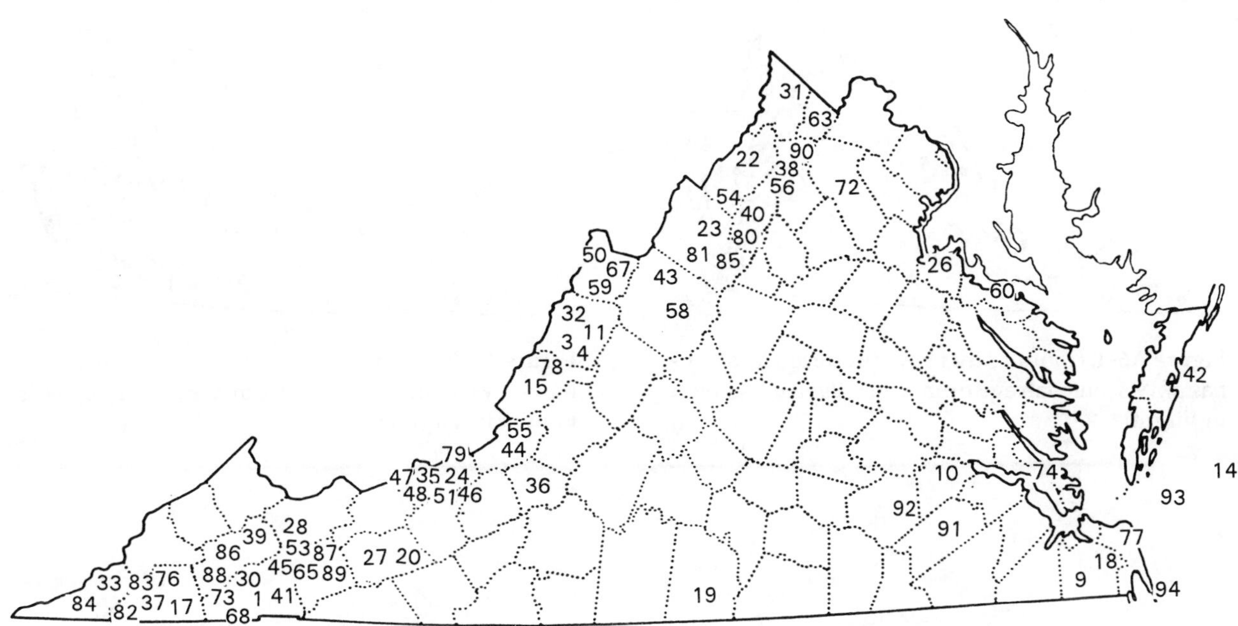

Figure A6-1. The location of sites, by county, that have produced the local faunas identified in Table A6-3. Numbers on the map correlate with those in Table A6-3.

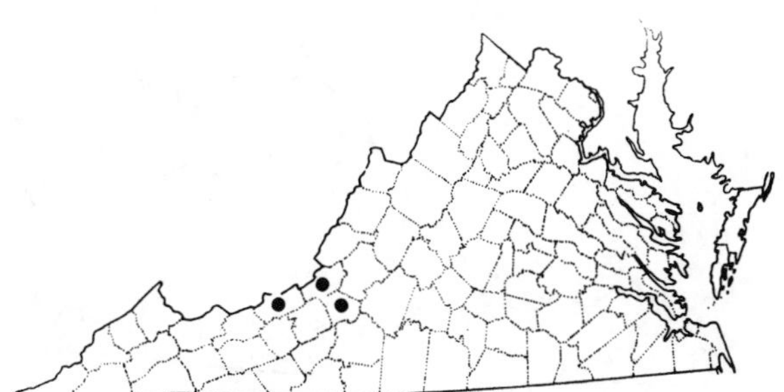

Figure A6-2. Counties that have produced local faunas of Wisconsinan age from which *Didelphis* is known in Virginia.

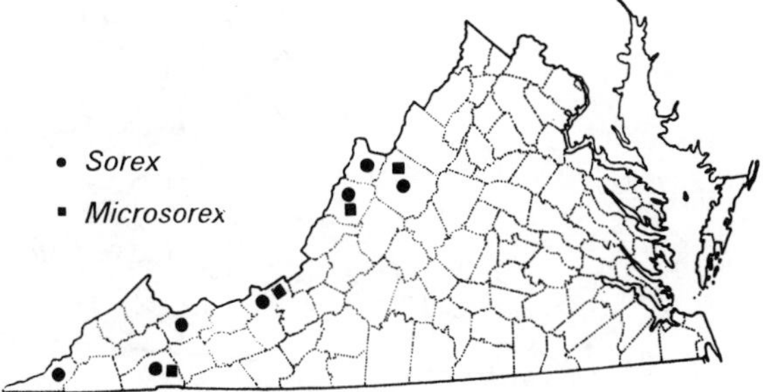

Figure A6-3. Counties that have produced local faunas of Wisconsinan age from which *Sorex* and *Microsorex* are known in Virginia.

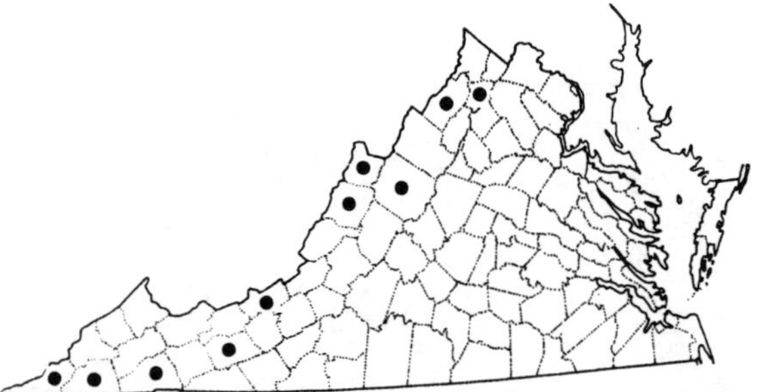

Figure A6-4. Counties that have produced local faunas of Wisconsinan age from which *Blarina* is known in Virginia.

Figure A6-7. Counties that have produced local faunas of Wisconsinan age from which *Scalopus* is known in Virginia.

Figure A6-5. County that has produced local faunas of Wisconsinan age from which *Cryptotis* is known in Virginia.

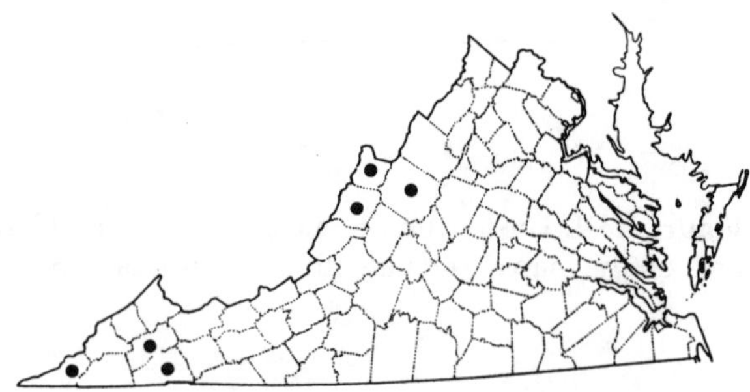

Figure A6-8. Counties that have produced local faunas of Wisconsinan age from which *Condylura* is known in Virginia.

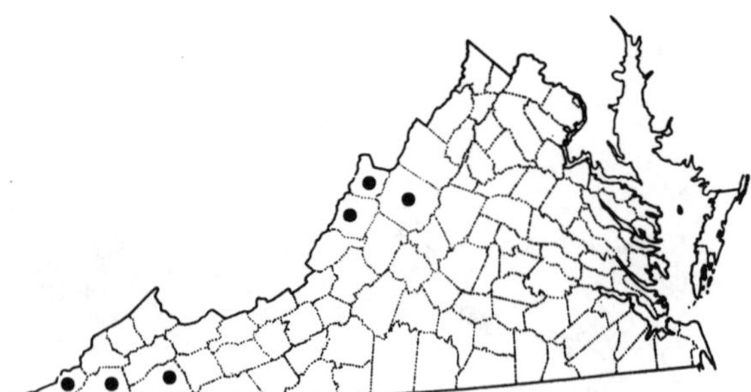

Figure A6-6. Counties that have produced local faunas of Wisconsinan age from which *Parascalops* is known in Virginia.

Figure A6-9. Counties that have produced local faunas of Wisconsinan age from which *Myotis* is known in Virginia.

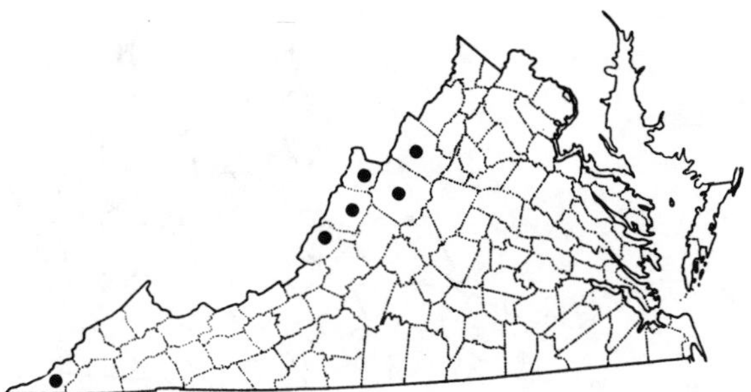

Figure A6-10. Counties that have produced local faunas of Wisconsinan age from which *Pipistrellus* is known in Virginia.

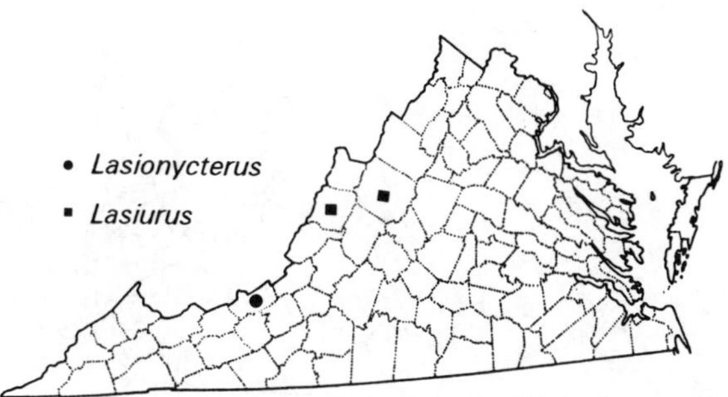

Figure A6-11. Counties that have produced local faunas of Wisconsinan age from which *Lasionycterus* and *Lasiurus* are known in Virginia.

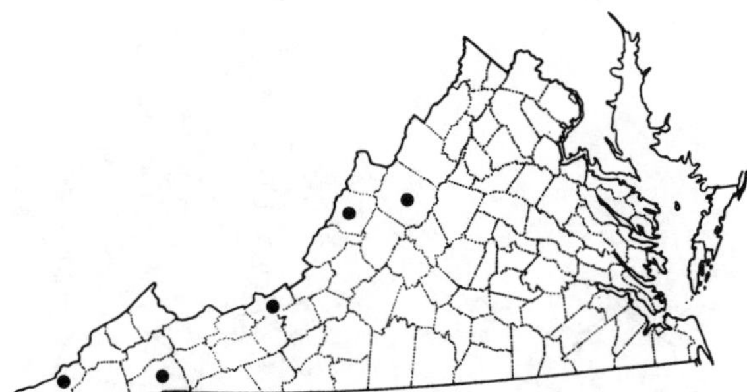

Figure A6-12. Counties that have produced local faunas of Wisconsinan age from which *Eptesicus* is known in Virginia.

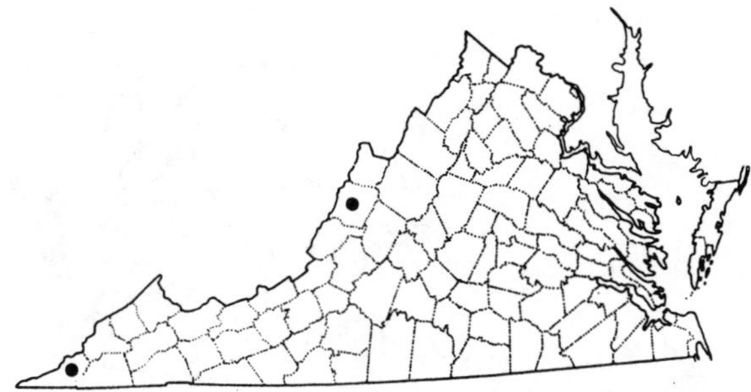

Figure A6-13. Counties that have produced local faunas of Wisconsinan age from which *Plecotus* is known in Virginia.

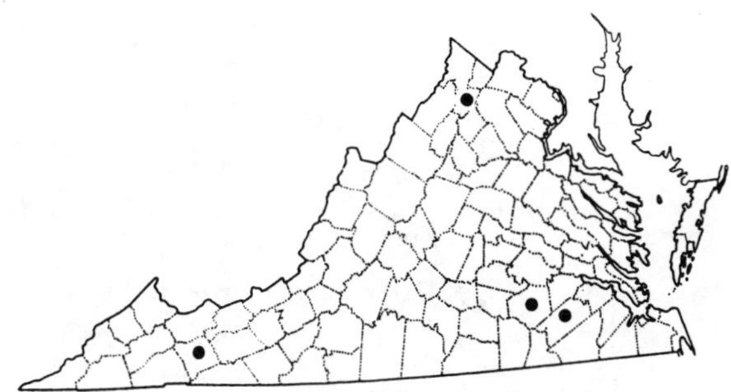

Figure A6-14. Counties that have produced local faunas of Wisconsinan age from which *Homo* is known in Virginia.

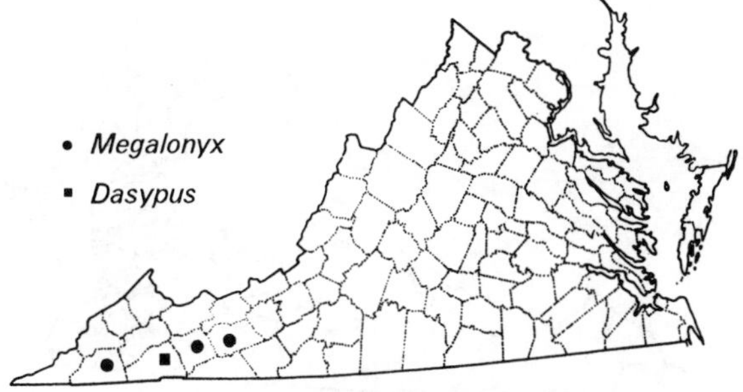

Figure A6-15. Counties that have produced local faunas of Wisconsinan age from which *Megalonyx* and *Dasypus* are known in Virginia.

Figure A6-16. County that has produced local faunas of Wisconsinan age from which *Ochotona* is known in Virginia.

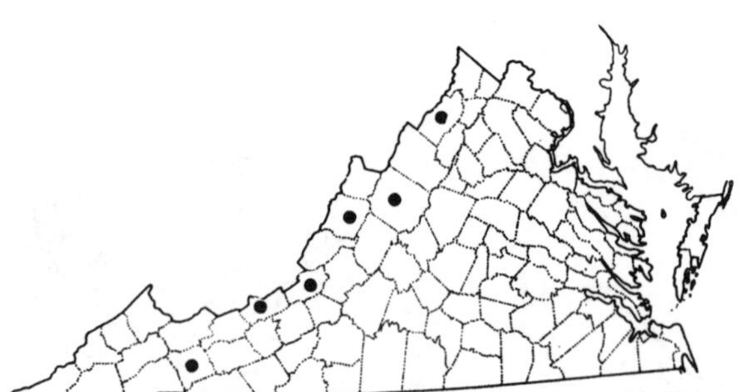

Figure A6-17. Counties that have produced local faunas of Wisconsinan age from which *Sylvilagus* is known in Virginia.

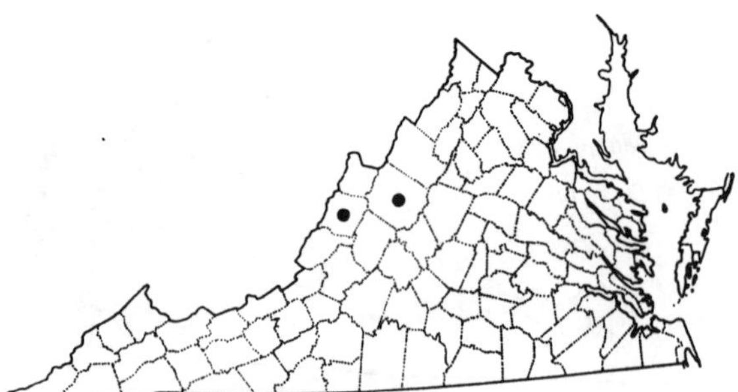

Figure A6-18. Counties that have produced local faunas of Wisconsinan age from which *Lepus* is known in Virginia.

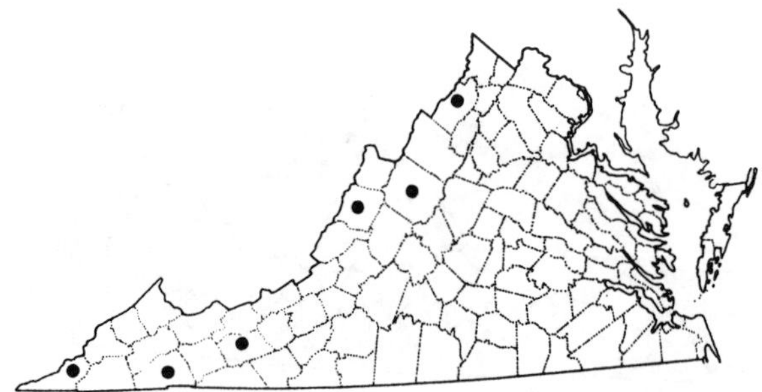

Figure A6-19. Counties that have produced local faunas of Wisconsinan age from which *Tamias* is known in Virginia.

Figure A6-20. County that has produced local faunas of Wisconsinan age from which *Eutamias* is known in Virginia.

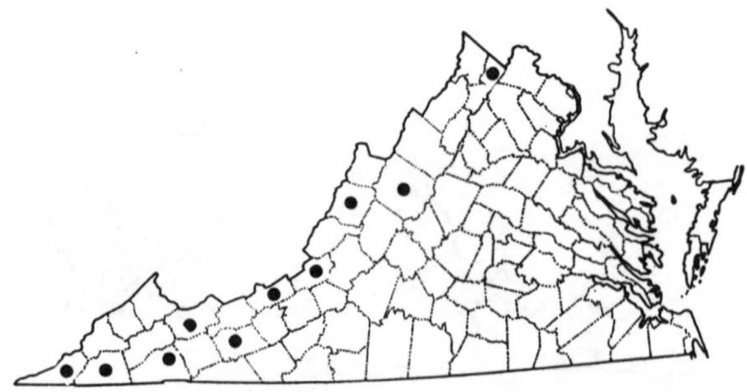

Figure A6-21. Counties that have produced local faunas of Wisconsinan age from which *Marmota* is known in Virginia.

Figure A6-22. Counties that have produced local faunas of Wisconsinan age from which *Spermophilus* is known in Virginia.

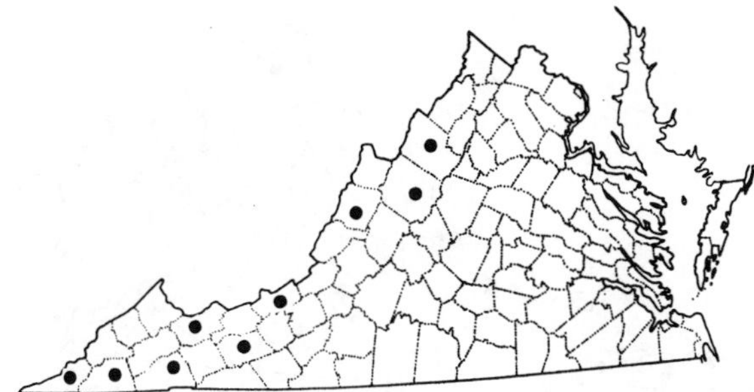

Figure A6-25. Counties that have produced local faunas of Wisconsinan age from which *Glaucomys* is known in Virginia.

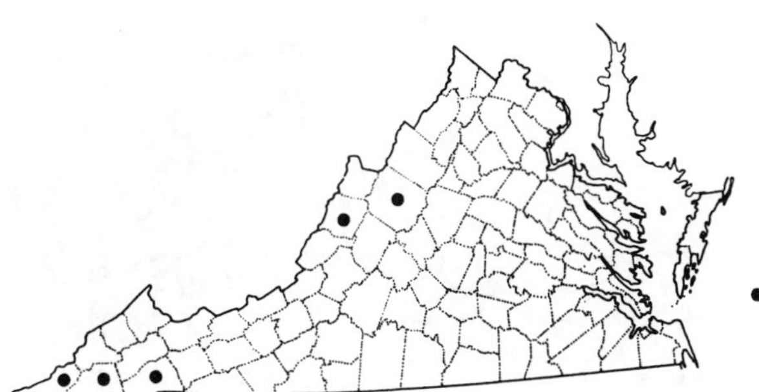

Figure A6-23. Counties that have produced local faunas of Wisconsinan age from which *Sciurus* is known in Virginia.

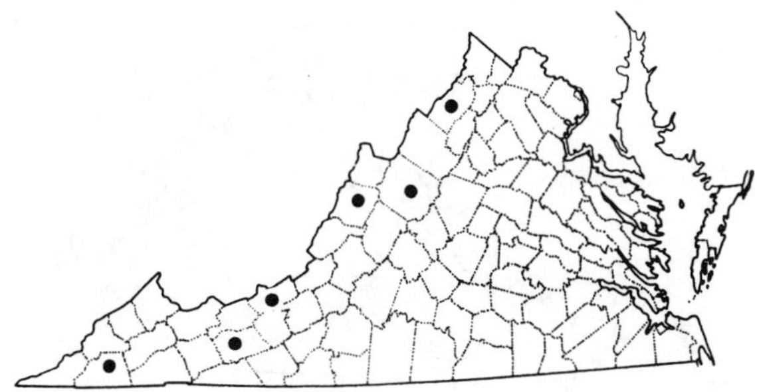

Figure A6-26. Counties that have produced local faunas of Wisconsinan age from which *Castor* is known in Virginia.

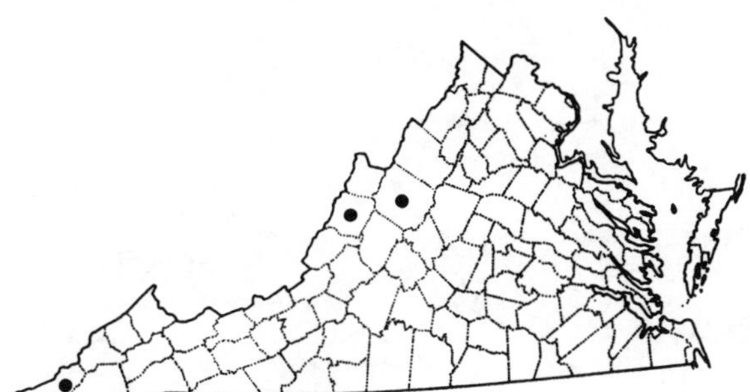

Figure A6-24. Counties that have produced local faunas of Wisconsinan age from which *Tamiasciurus* is known in Virginia.

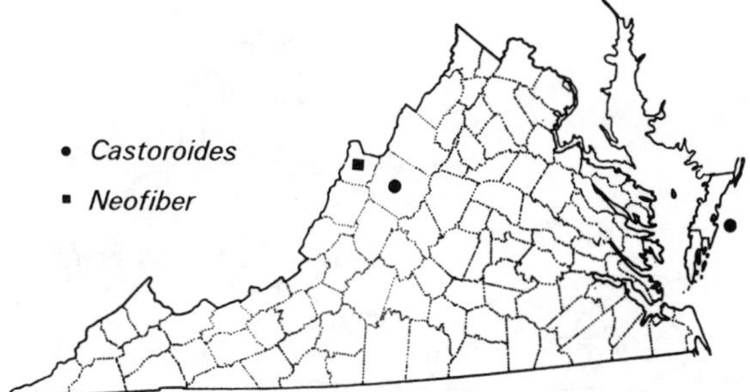

Figure A6-27. Counties that have produced local faunas of Wisconsinan age from which *Castoroides* and *Neofiber* are known in Virginia.

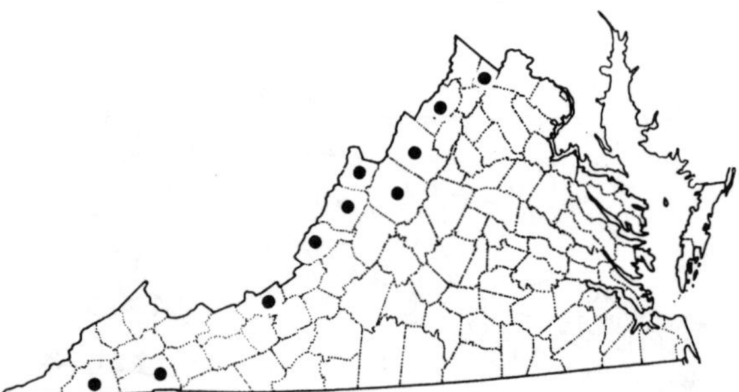

Figure A6-28. Counties that have produced local faunas of Wisconsinan age from which *Peromyscus* is known in Virginia.

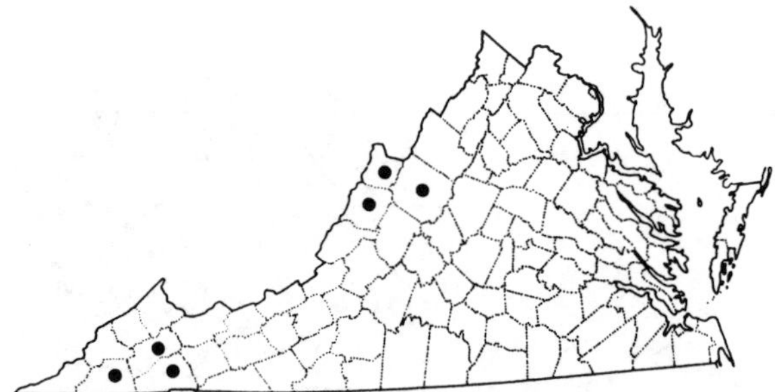

Figure A6-31. Counties that have produced local faunas of Wisconsinan age from which *Phenacomys* is known in Virginia.

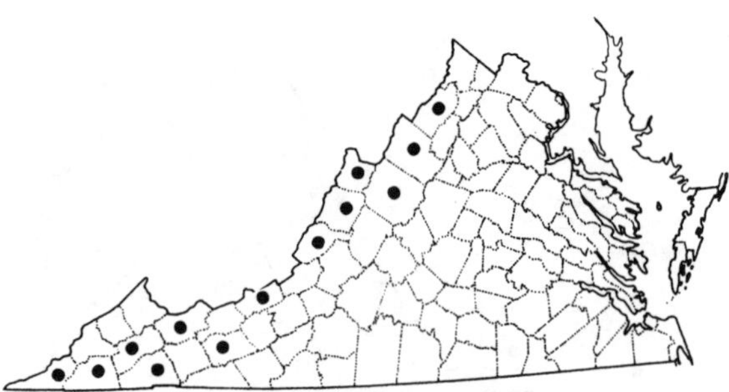

Figure A6-29. Counties that have produced local faunas of Wisconsinan age from which *Neotoma* is known in Virginia.

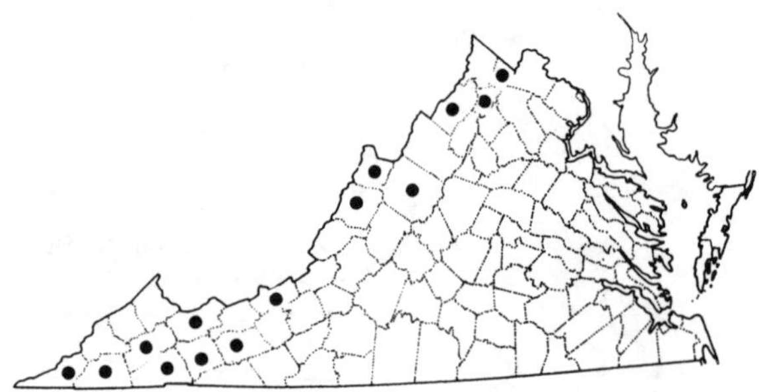

Figure A6-32. Counties that have produced local faunas of Wisconsinan age from which *Microtus* is known in Virginia.

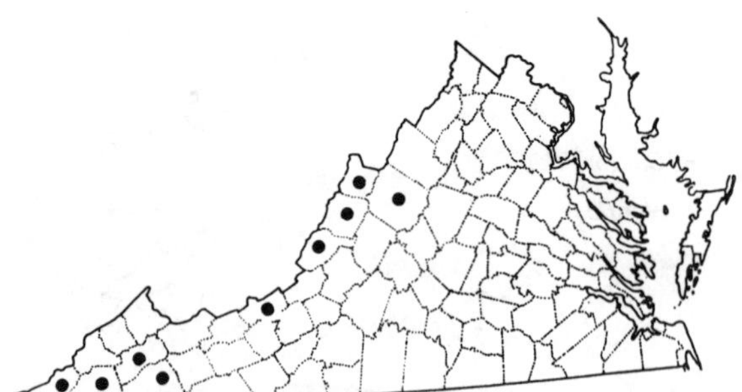

Figure A6-30. Counties that have produced local faunas of Wisconsinan age from which *Clethrionomys* is known in Virginia.

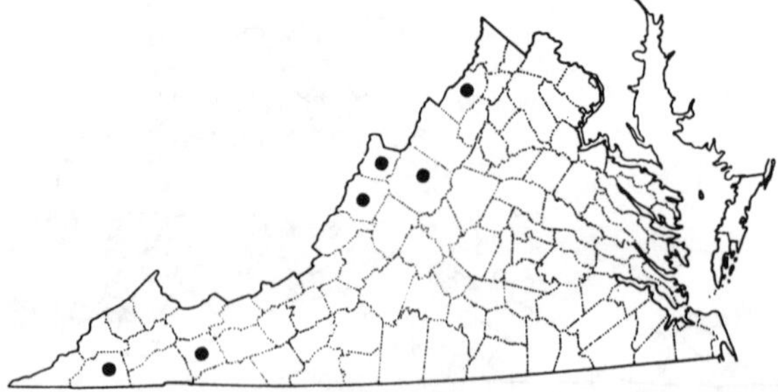

Figure A6-33. Counties that have produced local faunas of Wisconsinan age from which *Ondatra* is known in Virginia.

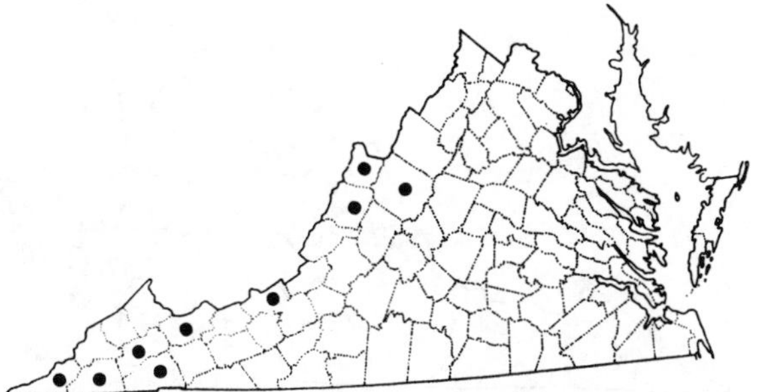

Figure A6-34. Counties that have produced local faunas of Wisconsinan age from which *Synaptomys* is known in Virginia.

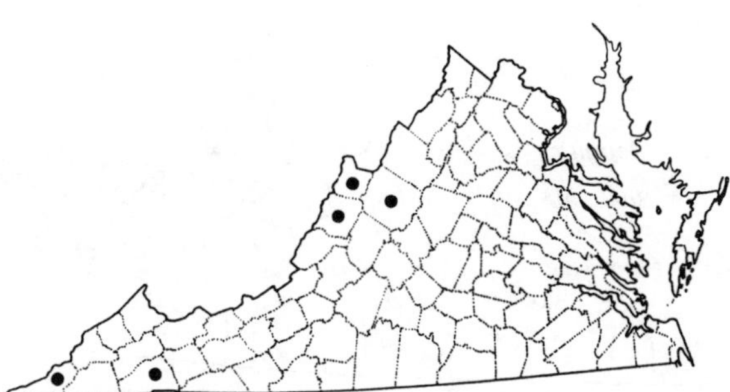

Figure A6-35. Counties that have produced local faunas of Wisconsinan age from which *Zapus* is known in Virginia.

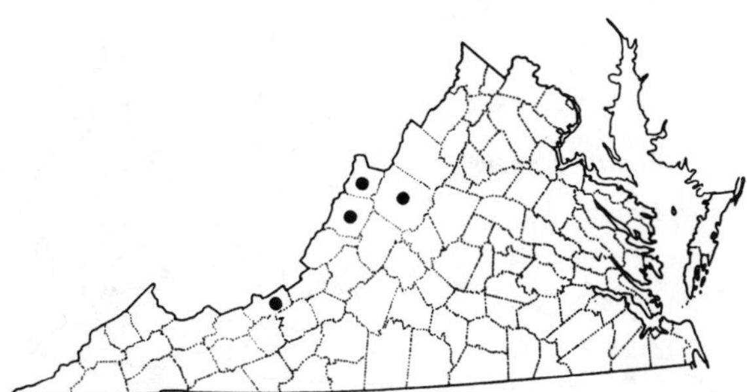

Figure A6-36. Counties that have produced local faunas of Wisconsinan age from which *Napaeozapus* is known in Virginia.

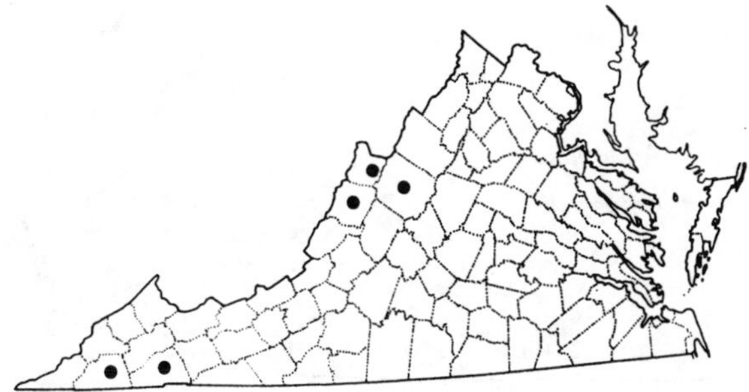

Figure A6-37. Counties that have produced local faunas of Wisconsinan age from which *Erethizon* is known in Virginia.

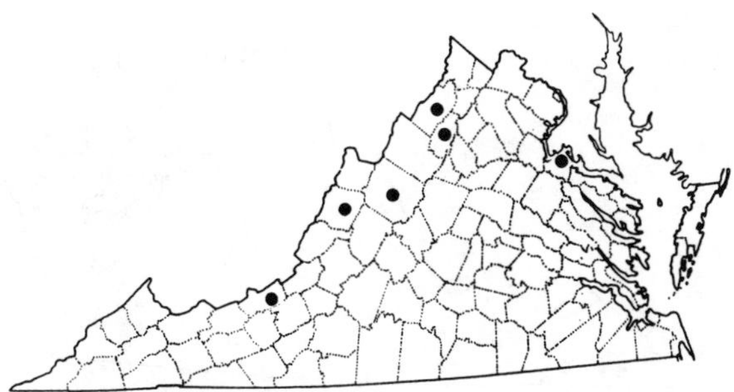

Figure A6-38. Counties that have produced local faunas of Wisconsinan age from which *Canis* is known in Virginia.

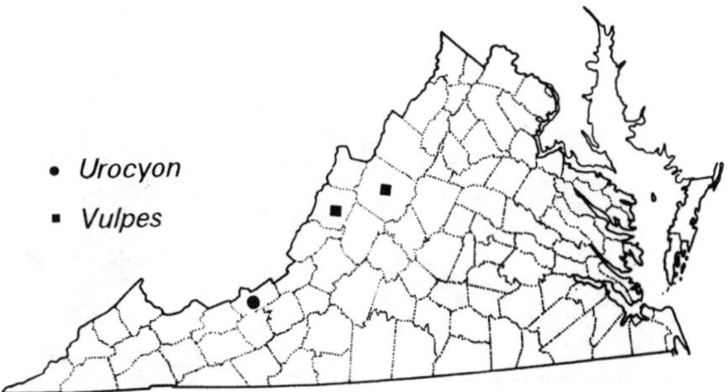

Figure A6-39. Counties that have produced local faunas of Wisconsinan age from which *Urocyon* and *Vulpes* are known in Virginia.

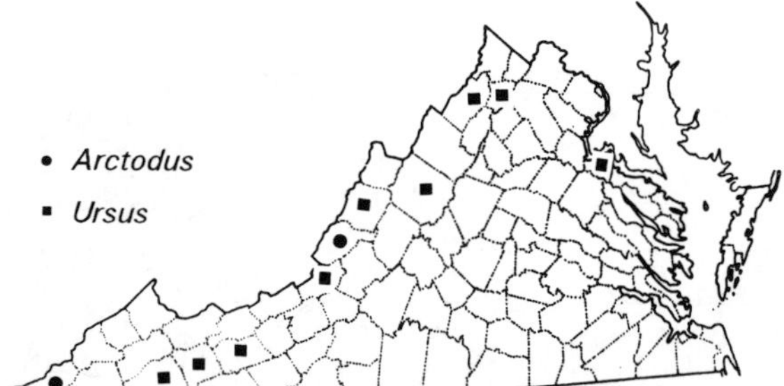

Figure A6-40. Counties that have produced local faunas of Wisconsinan age from which *Arctodus* and *Ursus* are known in Virginia.

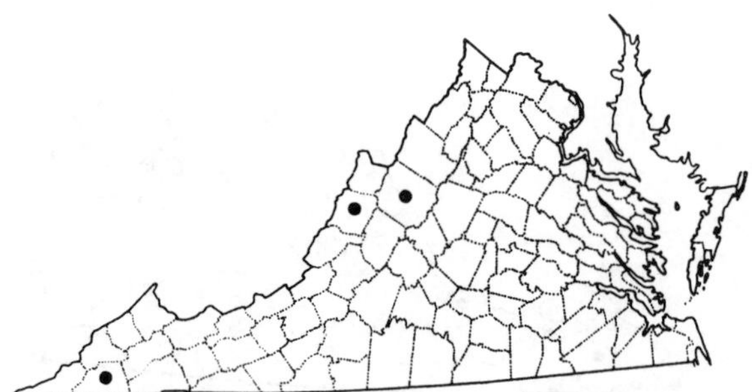

Figure A6-43. Counties that have produced local faunas of Wisconsinan age from which *Mustela* is known in Virginia.

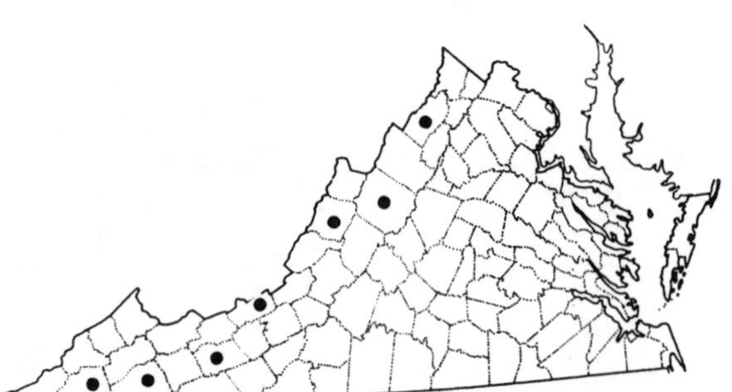

Figure A6-41. Counties that have produced local faunas of Wisconsinan age from which *Procyon* is known in Virginia.

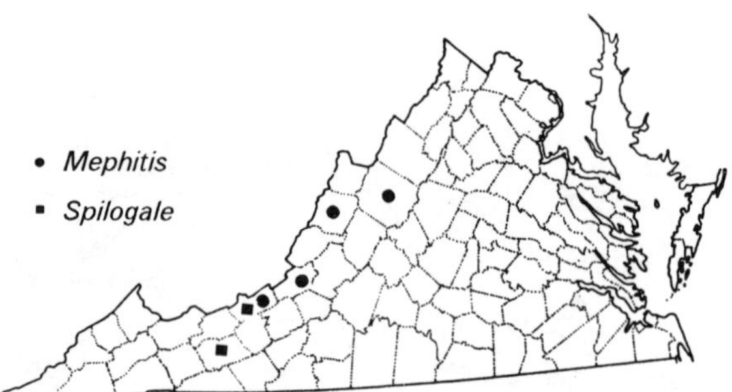

Figure A6-44. Counties that have produced local faunas of Wisconsinan age from which *Mephitis* and *Spilogale* are known in Virginia.

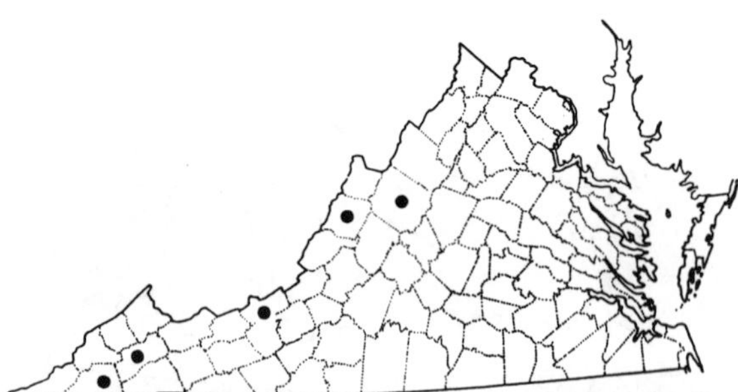

Figure A6-42. Counties that have produced local faunas of Wisconsinan age from which *Martes* is known in Virginia.

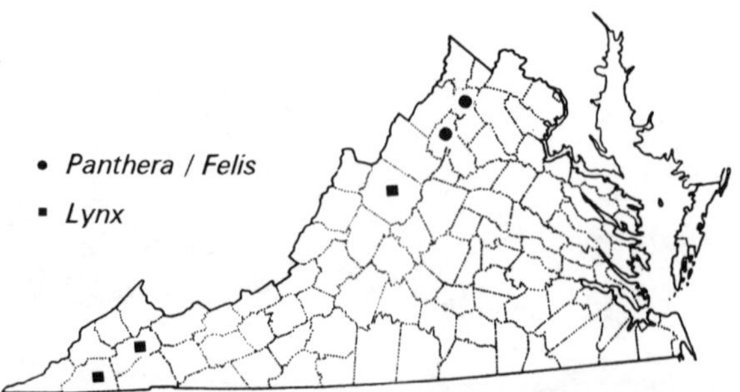

Figure A6-45. Counties that have produced local faunas of Wisconsinan age from which *Panthera* or *Felis* and *Lynx* are known in Virginia.

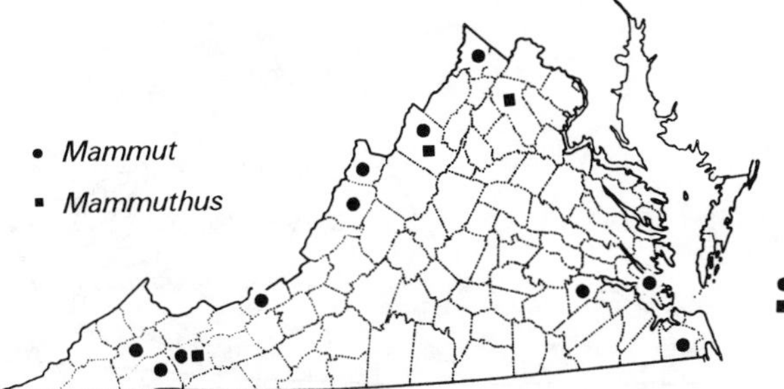

Figure A6-46. Counties that have produced local faunas of Wisconsinan age from which *Mammut* and *Mammuthus* are known in Virginia.

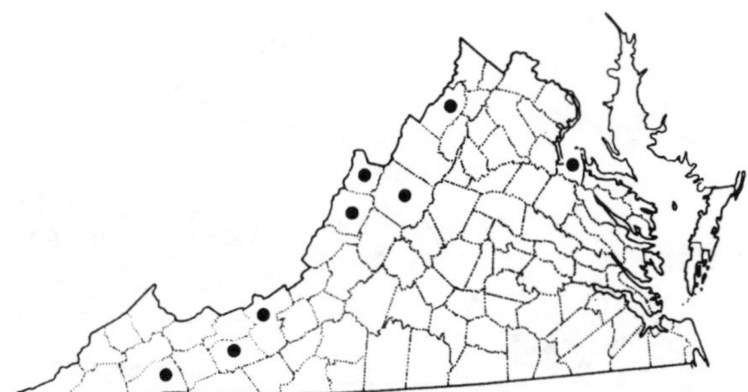

Figure A6-49. Counties that have produced local faunas of Wisconsinan age from which *Mylohyus* is known in Virginia.

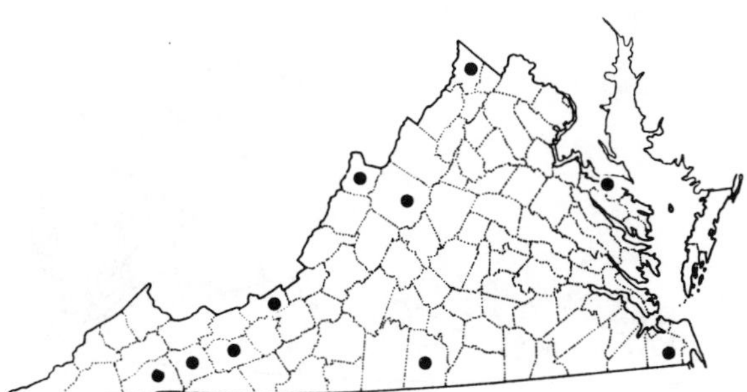

Figure A6-47. Counties that have produced local faunas of Wisconsinan age from which *Equus* is known in Virginia.

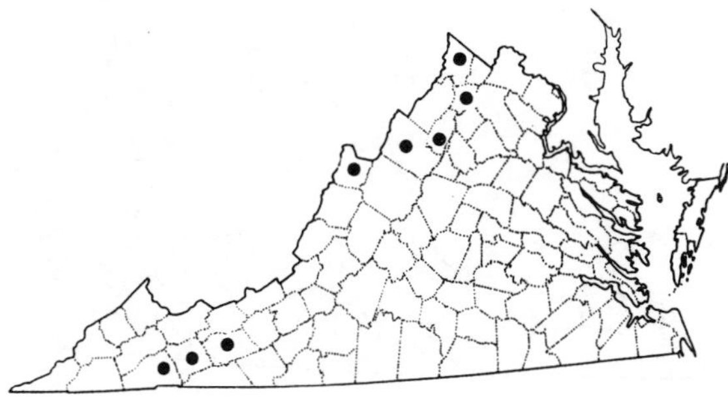

Figure A6-50. Counties that have produced local faunas of Wisconsinan age from which *Platygonus* is known in Virginia.

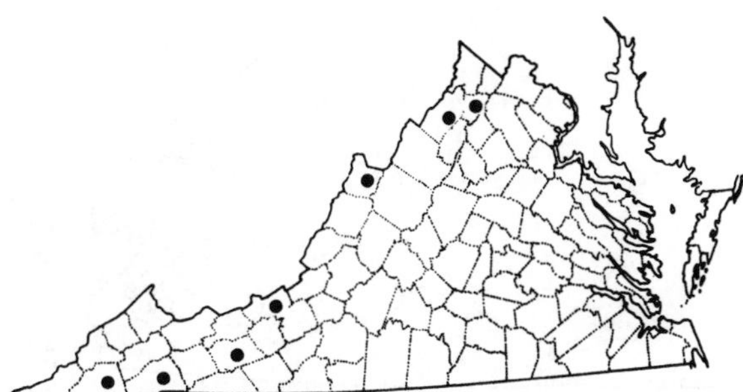

Figure A6-48. Counties that have produced local faunas of Wisconsinan age from which *Tapirus* is known in Virginia.

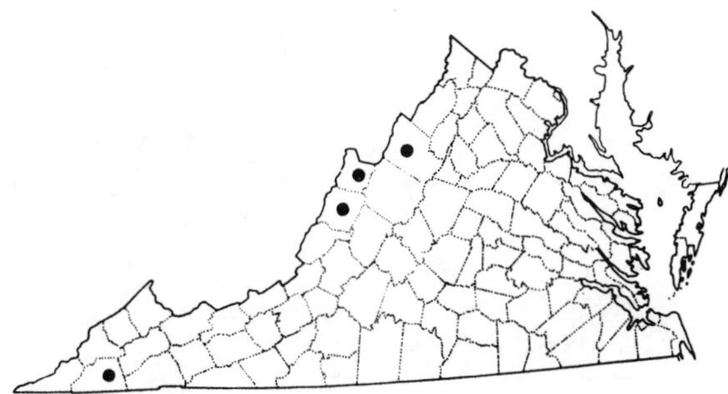

Figure A6-51. Counties that have produced local faunas of Wisconsinan age from which *Cervus* is known in Virginia.

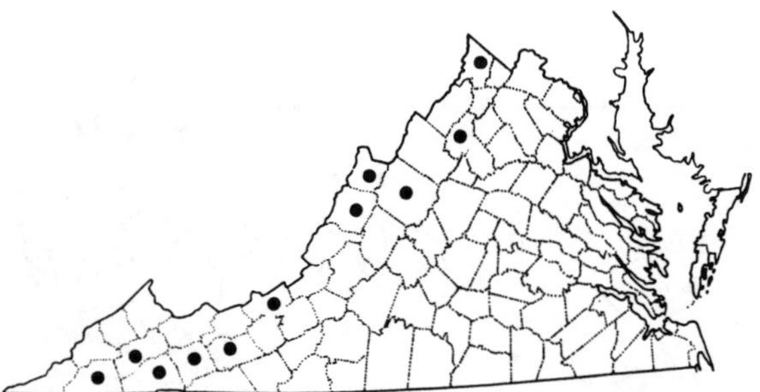

Figure A6-52. Counties that have produced local faunas of Wisconsinan age from which *Odocoileus* is known in Virginia.

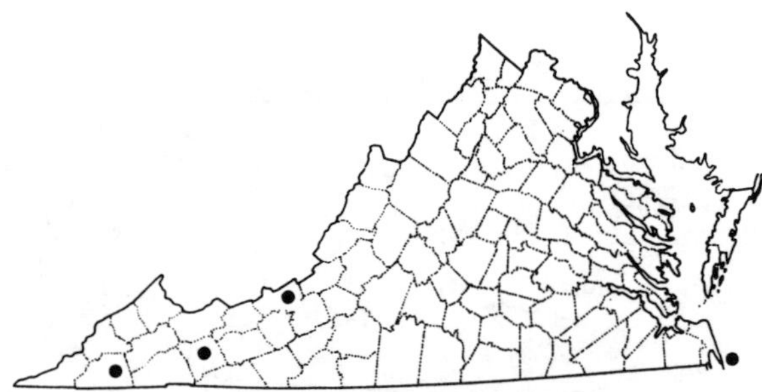

Figure A6-55. Counties that have produced local faunas of Wisconsinan age from which *Rangifer* is known in Virginia.

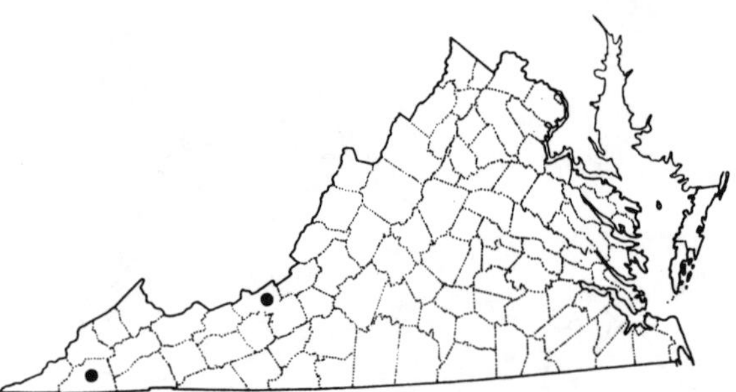

Figure A6-53. Counties that have produced local faunas of Wisconsinan age from which *Sangamona* is known in Virginia.

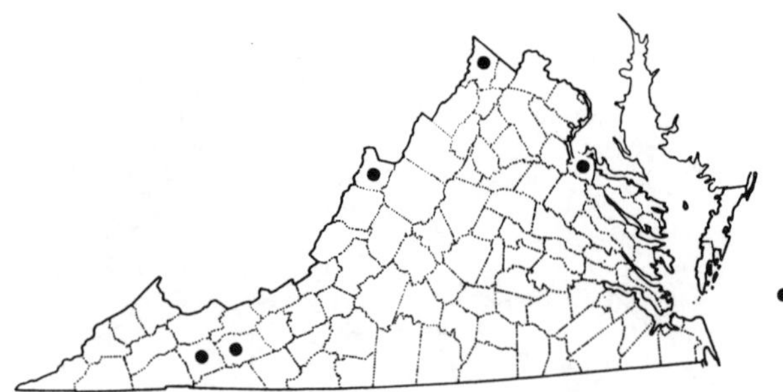

Figure A6-56. Counties that have produced local faunas of Wisconsinan age from which *Bison* is known in Virginia.

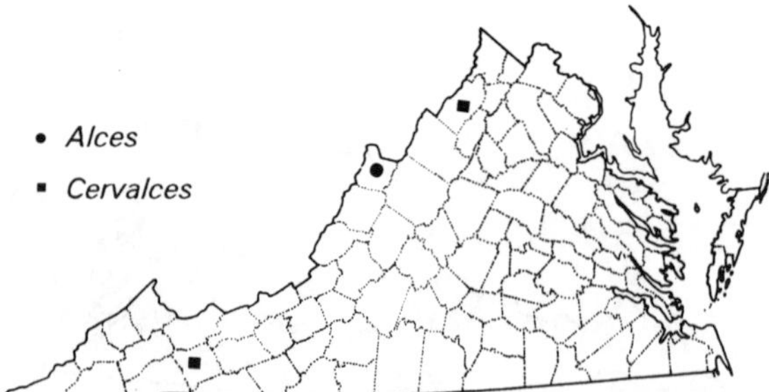

Figure A6-54. Counties that have produced local faunas of Wisconsinan age from which *Alces* and *Cervalces* are known in Virginia.

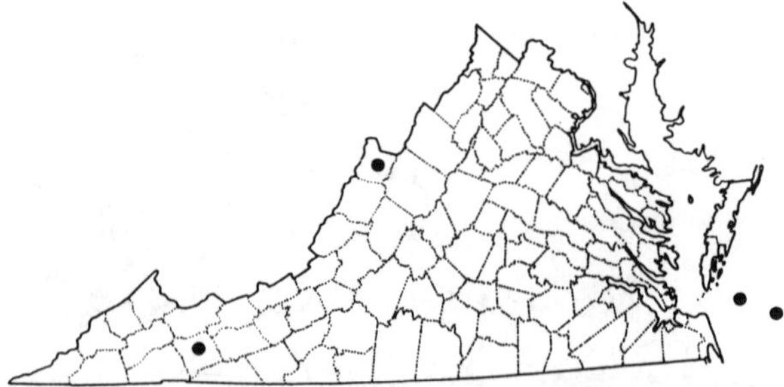

Figure A6-57. Counties that have produced local faunas of Wisconsinan age from which *Bootherium* is known in Virginia.

Literature Cited and Bibliography of Virginia Mammals

The following list of references serves two purposes: (1) it includes all references cited in the text and (2) all references preceded by an asterisk form a comprehensive bibliography of Virginia mammals. The bibliography of Virginia mammals contains 2,857 citations, including published articles dealing directly with Virginia mammals, articles using data from Virginia studies, and many unpublished theses and dissertations. Studies dealing entirely with laboratory-maintained colonies have, for the most part, been omitted. The bibliographic citations cover the period 1588 to the present and include many rare and difficult-to-locate references. Most of the citations included here have been examined during the course of this study in order to verify the citation and the data contained therein. In any effort of this magnitude, some references may inadvertently have been overlooked. The author requests that anyone with knowledge of such omissions please contact him with the necessary information so that the bibliography may be made more nearly complete.

---

*Abbott, H. G., and T. F. Quink. 1970. Ecology of eastern white pine seed caches made by small forest mammals. Ecology 51(2):271–278.

*Abbott, J. M. 1958. Death on the highway. Virginia Wildlife 19(6):16–17.

*Abler, W. A. 1974. Effects of energy and protein levels on attainment of puberty and steroid hormone production in captive female white-tailed deer. Master's thesis, Virginia Polytechnic Institute and State University, Blacksburg.

*Abler, W. A., D. E. Buckland, R. L. Kirkpatrick, and P. F. Scanlon. 1976. Plasma progestins and puberty in fawns as influenced by energy and protein. Journal of Wildlife Management 40(3):442–446.

Ables, E. D. 1965. An exceptional fox movement. Journal of Mammalogy 46(1):102.

Ables, E. D. 1969. Activity studies of red foxes in southern Wisconsin. Journal of Wildlife Management 33:145–153.

Adam, M. D., M. J. Lacki, and T. G. Barnes. 1994. Foraging areas and habitat use of the Virginia big-eared bat in Kentucky. Journal of Wildlife Management 58(3):462–469.

*Adams, C. C. 1926. The economic and social importance of animals in forestry, with special reference to wild life. Roosevelt Wild Life Bulletin 3(4):509–678.

*Adams, L. W., and A. D. Geis. 1983. Effects of roads on small mammals. Journal of Applied Ecology 20(2):403–415.

Adams, R. A. 1992. Stages of development and sequence of bone formation in the little brown bat, *Myotis lucifugus*. Journal of Mammalogy 73(1):160–167.

*Adams, W. H., Jr. 1956. The nutria in coastal Louisiana. Louisiana Academy of Sciences 19:28–41.

Adams, W. H., Jr. 1960. Population ecology of white-tailed deer in northeastern Alabama. Ecology 41(4):706–715.

*Adams, V. L., and R. K. Rose. 1990. The effect of 6-methoxybenzoxazolinone on reproductive condition in the hispid cotton rat, *Sigmodon hispidus*. Virginia Journal of Science 41(2):49. Abstract.

*Addy, C. E. 1940. Wildlife projects of the Virginia Agricultural Experiment Station, Virginia Wildlife 4(3):96–100.

*Addy, E. 1939. A weasel trails a rabbit. Journal of Mammalogy 20(3):382–373.

*Ahrens, C. 1968. Pouchy, the possum. Virginia Wildlife 29(9):10, 23.

*Ahrens, C. 1983. The woodchuck. Virginia Wildlife 44(2):32–33.

Aleksiuk, M. 1968. Scent-mound communication, territoriality, and population regulation in beaver (*Castor canadensis* Kuhl). Journal of Mammalogy 49(4):759–762.

Alexander, M. M. 1956. The muskrat in New York State. State University of New York, College of Forestry, Syracuse.

*Alicata, J. E. 1929. The occurrence of *Dirofilaria scapiceps* in rabbits. Journal of Parasitology 15:287.

Allen, A. A. 1921. Banding bats. Journal of Mammalogy 2(1):53–57.

*Allen, B. R. 1946. A word to the cottontail hunter. Virginia Wildlife 7(4):6–7.

*Allen, D., (editor). 1962a. Youth afield. Virginia Wildlife 23(2):23.

*Allen, D. 1962b. Youth afield. "Katie." Virginia Wildlife 23(5):22.

*Allen, D. 1962c. Youth afield. Virginia Wildlife 23(9):23.

*Allen, D. 1963. Youth afield. Virginia Wildlife 24(3):22–23.

*Allen, D. 1964a. Youth afield. Bland youth gets first deer. Virginia Wildlife 25(1):23.

*Allen, D. 1964b. Youth afield. Successful "Robin Hood." Virginia Wildlife 25(2):25.

*Allen, D. 1964c. Youth afield. Successful hunters. Virginia Wildlife 25(3):25.

*Allen, D. 1964d. Youth afield. Trapping hobby. Virginia Wildlife 25(4):24.

*Allen, D. 1965a. Youth afield. Dear with deer. Virginia Wildlife 26(2):25.

*Allen, D. 1965b. Eastern chipmunk *(Tamias striatus)*. Virginia Wildlife 26(4):16.

*Allen, D. 1965c. A good omen — bats. Virginia Wildlife 26(7):22.

*Allen, D. 1965d. The gray fox. Virginia Wildlife 26(11):12.

*Allen, D. 1965e. Jus' ramblin'. Virginia Wildlife 26(5):11.

*Allen, D. 1965f. "Pop goes the weasel." Virginia Wildlife 26(8):16.

*Allen, D. 1965g. Rarely waifs. Virginia Wildlife 26(5):14–15.

*Allen, D. 1965h. The striped skunk *(Mephitis mephitis)*. Virginia Wildlife 26(9):9.

*Allen, D. 1966a. Youth afield. Strange kill. Virginia Wildlife 27(4):24.

*Allen, D. 1966b. Youth afield. Hunter's prize. Virginia Wildlife 27(4):24.

Allen, D. L. 1943. Michigan fox squirrel management. Michigan Department of Conservation, Game Division Publication 100.

*Allen, E. G. 1938. The habits and life history of the eastern chipmunk, *Tamias striatus lysteri*. New York State Museum Bulletin no. 314.

*Allen, G. M. 1916. Bats of the genus *Corynorhinus*. Bulletin of the Museum of Comparative Zoology 60(9):331–358.

*Allen, G. M. 1923. Geographic distribution of certain New England mammals. American Naturalist 57(649):97–106.

*Allen, G. M. 1962. (1939). Bats. New York: Dover Publications.

*Allen, G. M. 1941. Pygmy sperm whale in the Atlantic. Publication 511, Field Museum of Natural History, Zoological Series, 27:17–36.

*Allen, G. M. 1972 (1942). Extinct and vanishing mammals of the Western Hemisphere with the marine species of all the oceans. American Commission for International Wild Life Protection, Special Publication no. 11. Reprinted by Cooper Square Publications, New York.

*Allen, H. 1864. Monograph of the bats of North America. Smithsonian Miscellaneous Publication 165.

*Allen, H. 1893. A monograph of the bats of North America. Bulletin of the United States National Museum no. 43.

*Allen, J. A. 1869. Catalogue of the mammals of Massachusetts: with a critical revision of the species. Bulletin of the Museum of Comparative Zoology 1(8):143–253.

*Allen, J. A. 1871. On the mammals and winter birds of east Florida, with an examination of certain assumed specific characters in birds, and a sketch of the bird-faunae of eastern North America. Part II. List of the mammals of East Florida, with annotations. Bulletin of the Harvard Museum of Comparative Zoology 2(3):168–185.

*Allen, J. A. 1874. On geographical variation in color among North American squirrels; with a list of the species and varieties of the American Sciuridae occurring north of Mexico. Proceedings of the Boston Society of Natural History 16:276–294.

*Allen, J. A. 1875. Synopsis of the American Leporidae. Proceedings of the Boston Society of Natural History 17:430–436.

*Allen, J. A. 1876a. The former range of some New England carnivorous mammals. American Naturalist 10:708–715.

*Allen, J. A. 1876b. The American bisons, living and extinct. Memoirs of the Museum of Comparative Zoology, Harvard 4(10):1–246. Also Memoirs of the Geological Survey, Kentucky 1(2):1–246.

*Allen, J. A. 1876c. The extirpation of the larger indigenous mammals of the United States. The Penn Monthly. October 1876: 794–806.

*Allen, J. A. 1880. History of North American pinnipeds. A monograph of the walruses, sea-lions, sea-bears, and seals of North America. Miscellaneous Publication 12, United States Geological and Geographical Survey of the Territories, United States Department of the Interior, Washington, DC.

*Allen, J. A. 1899. The North-American arboreal squirrels. American Naturalist 33(392):635–642.

*Allen, J. A. 1901. A preliminary study of the North American opossums of the genus *Didelphis*. Bulletin of the American Museum of Natural History 14:149–188.

Allsbrooks, D. W., and M. L. Kennedy. 1987. Movement patterns of raccoons *(Procyon lotor)* in western Tennessee. Journal of the Tennessee Academy of Science 62(1):15–19.

*Almy, G. 1978. A Massanutten buck. Virginia Wildlife 39(12):12–13.

*Almy, G. 1981. River bank quarry. The fox squirrel. Virginia Wildlife 42(1):20–22.

Alt, G. L., F. W. Alt and J. S. Lindzey. 1976. Home range and activity patterns of black bears in northeastern Pennsylvania. Transactions of the Northeast Section of the Wildlife Society 33:45–56.

Althoff, D. P., and G. L. Storm. 1989. Daytime spatial characteristics of cottontail rabbits in central Pennsylvania. Journal of Mammalogy 70(4):820–824.

*Alvord, C., and L. Bidgood. 1912. First explorations of the trans-Allegheny regions by the Virginians, 1650–1674. Cleveland: Arthur H. Clark.

*Bixby, D. E., C. J. Christman, C. J. Ehrman, & D. P. Sponenberg. 1994. Taking Stock: The North American Livestock Census. Blacksburg: The McDonald & Woodward Publishing Company.

*Amos, J. M. 1967. Year of the bears. Virginia Wildlife 28(8):19.

*Anburey, T. 1789. Travels through the interior parts of America. In a series of Letters. Vol. II. London.

*Anderson, D. 1979. Stone Mountain. Virginia Wildlife 40(5):10–12.

*Anderson, J. R. 1950. Rabies — a public health problem of increasing importance. Virginia Wildlife 11(8):18–22.

*Anderson, K. 1982. The river otter. Virginia Wildlife 43(12):34.

*Anderson, K. L. 1981. Population and reproduction characteristics of the river otter in Virginia and tissue concentrations of environmental contaminants. Master's thesis, Virginia Polytechnic Institute and State University, Blacksburg.

*Anderson, K. L., and P. F. Scanlon. 1981a. Organ weights of river otters. Virginia Journal of Science 32(3):86.

*Anderson, K. L., and P. F. Scanlon. 1981b. Reproduction and population characteristics of river otters in Virginia. Virginia Journal of Science 32(3):87.

*Anderson, K. L., and P. F. Scanlon. 1981c. Heavy metal concentrations in tissues of river otters from Virginia. Virginia Journal of Science 32(3):87.

*Anderson, K. L., F. A. Servello, and P. F. Scanlon. 1981. Heavy metal concentrations of tissues of pine voles from four Virginia orchards. Virginia Journal of Science 32(3): 87.

*Anderson-Bledsoe, K. L., and P. F. Scanlon. 1983. Heavy metal concentrations in tissues of Virginia river otters. Bulletin of Environmental Contamination and Toxicology 30(4):442–447.

*Anderson, R. M. 1946. Catalog of Canadian recent mammals. Bulletin of the National Museum of Canada 102.

*Anderson, S., J. K. Doutt, and J. S. Findley. 1963. Collections of mammals in North America. Journal of Mammalogy 44(4):471–500.

*Andrews, C. L., W. R. Davidson, and E. L. Provost. 1980. Endoparasites of selected population of cottontail rabbits *(Sylvilagus floridanus)* in the southeastern United States. Journal of Wildlife Diseases 16(3): 395–401.

*Andrews, C. L., R. R. Gerrish, and V. F. Nettles. 1980. Ectoparasites collected from eastern cottontails in the southeastern United States. Journal of Medical Entomology 17(5):479–480.

Andrews, R. C. 1914. Notice of a rare ziphioid whale, *Mesoplodon densirostris*, on the New Jersey Coast. Proceedings of the Philadelphia Academy of Science 66:437–440.

*Andrews, R. D., and D. H. Ferris. 1966. Relationships between movement patterns of wild animals and the distribution of leptospirosis. Journal of Wildlife Management 30(1):131–134.

*Annual Report Summary 1992. Nongame and Endangered Species Program. Virginia Department of Game and Inland Fisheries, Richmond.

*Anonymous. Undated. Rabies. United States Department of Health, Richmond, Va.

*Anonymous. 1837. Beavers of the Nottoway River. Ruffin's Farmer's Register 5(9):553–554.

*Anonymous. 1871. Fossil walrus. American Naturalist 5:316.

*Anonymous. 1875. Game bag and gun. Forest and Stream 5:42.

*Anonymous. 1876a. Furs and trapping. Forest and Stream 7(13):197.

*Anonymous. 1876b. The walrus formerly in South Carolina. American Naturalist 10:561.

*Anonymous. 1892. The Virginia Dismal Swamp. Scientific American 66:322.

*Anonymous. 1899. Virginia game, and field sports. Description of them by the botanist Clayton in 1739. Virginia Historical Magazine 7(2):172–174.

*Anonymous. 1900. The Dismal Swamp of Virginia. Scientific American 82:249–250.

*Anonymous. 1901. Some swamp experiences. Forest and Stream 57:286.

*Anonymous. 1908. A manatee in a net. Forest and Stream 71:532.

*Anonymous. 1920. Not so dismal after all. Literary Digest 64(6):88, 90.

*Anonymous. 1927. First game law of Old Dominion enacted in 1632, record shows. Game and Fish Conservationist 7(3):52.

*Anonymous. 1928a. Photograph of fawn from Bath County. Game and Fish Conservationist 7(6):158.

*Anonymous. 1928b. Photograph of two large bucks. Game and Fish Conservationist 8(2):47.

*Anonymous. 1929a. List black bear as game animal. Game and Fish Conservationist 8(5):119.

*Anonymous. 1929b. Photograph of lynx taken near Sperryville. Game and Fish Conservationist 9(2):33.

*Anonymous. 1929c. Photograph of two bobcats from Fort Lewis Mountain. Game and Fish Conservationist 9(3):72.

*Anonymous. 1930. Photograph of wild cat from Bath County, Virginia. Game and Fish Conservationist 9(6):121.

*Anonymous. 1931a. Photograph of raccoon killed by forest fire in the Dismal Swamp. Game and Fish Conservationist 11(3):71.

*Anonymous. 1931b. Photograph of wildcat from Fort Lewis Mountain Game Refuge. Game and Fish Conservationist 11(1):13.

*Anonymous. 1931c. 'Possum hunting in old Virginia. Game and Fish Conservationist 11(6):111.

*Anonymous. 1934. Do you know? Science News Letter 26(695):66.

*Anonymous. 1937a. Beaver thriving in nine counties. Virginia Wildlife 1(4):1.

*Anonymous. 1937b. Photograph of elk. Virginia Wildlife 1(4):1.

*Anonymous. 1938a. Tank provides squirrel deathtrap. Virginia Wildlife 1(10):8.

*Anonymous. 1938b. The national parks. Virginia Wildlife 1(12):4, 7.

*Anonymous. 1938c. Illegal kills mar elk season. Virginia Wildlife 2(3):8.

*Anonymous. 1938d. Deer vanquishes billygoat in one-sided death battle. Virginia Wildlife 2(3):8.

*Anonymous. 1938e. Virginia's wildlife future. American Wildlife 27(5):86–87, 94.

*Anonymous. 1938f. Questions and answers. Virginia Wildlife 1(12):8.

*Anonymous. 1939a. Fewer illegal deer killed last season. Virginia Wildlife 2(6):8.

*Anonymous. 1939b. Fat Bath County buck. Virginia Wildlife 2(6):8.

*Anonymous. 1939c. Big Levels wildlife refuge attracts national attention. Virginia Wildlife 2(5):8.

*Anonymous. 1939d. Beaver on increase. Virginia Wildlife 2(5):3.

*Anonymous. 1939e. Forest restocking program starts with large deer plantings. Virginia Wildlife 2(7):3.

*Anonymous. 1939f. The squirrel season. Virginia Wildlife 3(2):4.

*Anonymous. 1939g. Rockingham wants deer. Virginia Wildlife 3(4):2.

*Anonymous. 1940a. Ears or antlers? Virginia Wildlife 4(2):62–65.

*Anonymous. 1940b. A sportsman. Virginia Wildlife 4(1):39–40.

*Anonymous. 1940c. Spotted skunk battles rattlesnake. Virginia Wildlife 4(1):38.

*Anonymous. 1940d. The biological survey mammal collection. United States Department of the Interior, Bureau of Biological Survey Wildlife Leaflet BS–153.

*Anonymous. 1940e. The Biological survey collection. American Wildlife 29(2):59–60.

*Anonymous. 1940f. Beavers settle down. Virginia Wildlife 3(10):3.

*Anonymous. 1940g. Just what he wanted. Virginia Wildlife 4(2):81.

*Anonymous. 1941a. Gray squirrels. American Wildlife 30(2):85–86.

*Anonymous. 1941b. Abstract of fur laws, 1941–42. Wildlife Leaflet 199, United States Department of the Interior, Fish and Wildlife Service.

*Anonymous. 1941–42a. Young squirrels saved. Virginia Wildlife 5(1):31.

*Anonymous. 1941–42b. The heaviest deer. Virginia Wildlife 5(1):38.

*Anonymous. 1941–42c. Cat adopts squirrel. Virginia Wildlife 5(1):39.

*Anonymous. 1942a. The Biological Surveys mammal collection. Wildlife Leaflet 211, United States Department of the Interior, Fish and Wildlife Service.

*Anonymous. 1942b. The drumming log. Beaver. Virginia Wildlife 5(2):90.

*Anonymous. 1942c. Skunks are a nuisance — sometimes. Virginia Wildlife 6(1):38–39.

*Anonymous. 1946a. Freak deer. Virginia Wildlife 7(4):5.

*Anonymous. 1946b. Beaver transfer. Virginia Wildlife 7(4):4.

*Anonymous. 1946c. Replacement cost of game killed. Virginia Wildlife 7(6):9.

*Anonymous. 1946d. Swimming deer and dogs. Virginia Wildlife 7(2):18.

*Anonymous. 1946e. Virginia beaver management. Virginia Wildlife 7(2):23.

*Anonymous. 1946f. Virginia deer and bear trophies. Virginia Wildlife 7(2):3–4.

*Anonymous. 1947a. Bobcat subdued by farmer. Virginia Wildlife 8(12):26.

*Anonymous. 1947b. A spring tragedy. Virginia Wildlife 8(3):12–13.

*Anonymous. 1947c. Massive antlers. Virginia Wildlife 8(3):21.

*Anonymous. 1947d. Beaver cuttings. Virginia Wildlife 8(3):21–22.

*Anonymous. 1947e. Sheep killer taken on Whitetop. Virginia Wildlife 8(6):11.
*Anonymous. 1947f. Coon stocking news and views. Virginia Wildlife 8(7):12–13.
*Anonymous. 1948a. Animal tragedy. Virginia Wildlife 9(2):21.
*Anonymous. 1948b. Beagles and rabbits. Virginia Wildlife 9(2):20.
*Anonymous. 1948c. Bear increasing. Virginia Wildlife 9(2):20.
*Anonymous. 1948d. Cottontails doing well. Virginia Wildlife 9(3):22.
*Anonymous. 1948e. Deer drowns in Rappahannock River. Virginia Wildlife 9(12):25.
*Anonymous. 1948f. Deltaville group rescues deer. Virginia Wildlife 9(4):23.
*Anonymous. 1948g. Moles and shrews. Virginia Wildlife 9(9):9–10.
*Anonymous. 1948h. New electric deer fence. Virginia Wildlife 9(10):23.
*Anonymous. 1948i. Princess Anne County. Virginia Wildlife 9(3):15.
*Anonymous. 1948j. Puzzling wildlife episode. Virginia Wildlife 9(2):20.
*Anonymous. 1948k. Statewide deer antler and bear head contest. Virginia Wildlife 9(12):24.
*Anonymous. 1948l. Three jailed for killing deer. Virginia Wildlife 9(10):25.
*Anonymous. 1948m. The mountain lion in Virginia. Virginia Wildlife 9(1):21.
*Anonymous. 1949a. The white-tailed deer. Virginia Wildlife 10(1):7, 21.
*Anonymous. 1949b. The Virginia wildlife conservationgram. Virginia Wildlife 10(1): 13.
*Anonymous. 1949c. Big Thanksgiving day deer hunt in Essex County. Virginia Wildlife 10(1):23–24.
*Anonymous. 1949d. Squirrels fall hard. Virginia Wildlife 10(1):24.
*Anonymous. 1949e. Squirrel hunter drowned. Virginia Wildlife 10(1):25.
*Anonymous. 1949f. Hunter kills albino rabbit. Virginia Wildlife 10(1):25.
*Anonymous. 1949g. Wolves extirpated 50 years ago. Virginia Wildlife 10(1):26.
*Anonymous. 1949h. The groundhog and his shadow. Virginia Wildlife 10(2):8–9.
*Anonymous. 1949i. Maximum penalty for illegal deer kill. Virginia Wildlife 10(2):25.
*Anonymous. 1949j. Warden receives 51 'coons for distribution. Virginia Wildlife 10(4):25.
*Anonymous. 1949k. Otter trapped in Chesterfield County. Virginia Wildlife 10(4):25.
*Anonymous. 1949l. Free running dogs menace to deer. Virginia Wildlife 10(4):25.
*Anonymous. 1949m. Hunters caught spot-lighting deer. Virginia Wildlife 10(6):25.
*Anonymous. 1949n. Sheep-killing bear slain by Bland-County hunters. Virginia Wildlife 10(9):25–26.
*Anonymous. 1949o. Virginia Wildlife conservationgram. Virginia Wildlife 10(10):13.
*Anonymous. 1949p. Pig-killing bear slain. Virginia Wildlife 10(11):24.
*Anonymous. 1949q. Squirrel hunter sees black deer. Virginia Wildlife 10(11):25.
*Anonymous. 1949r. Poachers slay deer in Bath County before season opens. Virginia Wildlife 10(11):25.
*Anonymous. 1949s. Otter caught in beaver trap. Virginia Wildlife 10(11):25–26.
*Anonymous. 1949t. Solid white squirrel killed. Virginia Wildlife 10(11):26.
*Anonymous. 1949u. The wild razorback. Louisiana Conservationist 1(5):9.
*Anonymous. 1950a. Annual deer antler and bear head contest held. Virginia Wildlife 11(1):25.
*Anonymous. 1950b. Gentle deer. Virginia Wildlife 11(1):25–26.
*Anonymous. 1950c. Virginia wildlife conservationgram. Virginia Wildlife 11(2):13.
*Anonymous. 1950d. Nelson County hunter bags big bruin. Virginia Wildlife 11(2):24.
*Anonymous. 1950e. Wolf killed near Staunton. Virginia Wildlife 11(2):24–25.
*Anonymous. 1950f. Another albino squirrel bagged. Virginia Wildlife 11(2):25.
*Anonymous. 1950g. Buck or doe — which? Virginia Wildlife 11(3):24.
*Anonymous. 1950h. Sportsman's club releases jack rabbits. Virginia Wildlife 11(5):24.
*Anonymous. 1950i. Bear uses head to get in college. Virginia Wildlife 11(7):23.
*Anonymous. 1950j. Sheep killing bears cause trouble in Tazewell County. Virginia Wildlife 11(7):23.
*Anonymous. 1950k. Illegal killing of elk in Giles County costs farmer $250. Virginia Wildlife 11(7):24.
*Anonymous. 1950l. Game commission authorizes second bear hunt in Southwest. Virginia Wildlife 11(9):23.
*Anonymous. 1950m. Cow elk picks Blue Ridge Parkway for maternity ward. Virginia Wildlife 11(9):24.
*Anonymous. 1950n. Warden Bill's patrol. Virginia Wildlife 11(11):26.
*Anonymous. 1950o. Faded footprints. Virginia Wildlife 11(11):27.
*Anonymous. 1950p. Deer head with 26 points, western Virginia prize winner. Virginia Wildlife 11(12):27.
*Anonymous. 1951a. Winners receive prizes in statewide deer and bear contest. Virginia Wildlife 12(1):23.
*Anonymous. 1951b. Highland County warden gets tricky violator. Virginia Wildlife 12(1):24.
*Anonymous. 1951c. Virginia hunters bag long-lived specimens. Virginia Wildlife 12(2):13.
*Anonymous. 1951d. Two face doe killing charge in Augusta County. Virginia Wildlife 12(2):24.
*Anonymous. 1951e. Bear tree gap club active. Virginia Wildlife 12(8):23.
*Anonymous. 1951f. Skunk family stops traffic. Virginia Wildlife 12(8):24.
*Anonymous. 1951g. What every well-dressed fox should know. Virginia Wildlife 12(9):25.

*Anonymous. 1951h. Report on the dead deer situation. Virginia Wildlife 12(12):28.

*Anonymous. 1951i. Big cat falls prey to Richmonder. Virginia Wildlife 12(12):29.

*Anonymous. 1951j. A word of warning. Virginia Wildlife 12(12):29.

*Anonymous. 1951k. Note from a game warden. Virginia Wildlife 12(12):29.

*Anonymous. 1952a. Winners of state wide big game trophy contest. Virginia Wildlife 13(1):27.

*Anonymous. 1952b. Unusual kill and freeze. Virginia Wildlife 13(2):25.

*Anonymous. 1952c. Final tally on state's deer — bear — turkey kill received. Virginia Wildlife 13(3):13.

*Anonymous. 1952d. Squirrels have feelings too. Virginia Wildlife 13(3):24.

*Anonymous. 1952e. The case of the $4000 deer. Virginia Wildlife 13(4):24.

*Anonymous. 1952f. Warty deer found in New Kent County. Virginia Wildlife 13(4): 24.

*Anonymous. 1952g. Uncontrolled dogs menace wildlife. Virginia Wildlife 13(4):25.

*Anonymous. 1952h. The red fox *(Vulpes fulva)*. Virginia Wildlife 13(6):21.

*Anonymous. 1952i. The raccoon *(Procyon lotor)*. Virginia Wildlife 13(7):22.

*Anonymous. 1952j. Reward for meritorious service. Virginia Wildlife 13(10):23.

*Anonymous. 1952k. Pulaski club releases albino raccoon. Virginia Wildlife 13(10):23.

*Anonymous. 1952l. First deer released on new "deer breeding area." Virginia Wildlife 13(12):28.

*Anonymous. 1953a. Rabbit — $25.00 per pound. Virginia Wildlife 14(1):25.

*Anonymous. 1953b. "Back to the woods" for whitetails. Virginia Wildlife 14(1):25.

*Anonymous. 1953c. Illegal deer kill costs six nimrods $835.75. Virginia Wildlife 14(2):25.

*Anonymous. 1953d. You *can* increase wildlife on your land. Virginia Wildlife 14(3):20–22.

*Anonymous. 1953e. Maryland stocks deer, Virginia kills it. Virginia Wildlife 14(3):23.

*Anonymous. 1953f. Augusta County bear tally 105 for season. Virginia Wildlife 14(3):23.

*Anonymous. 1953g. Hog island muskrat harvest. Virginia Wildlife 14(4):23.

*Anonymous. 1953h. Rabid bobcat attacks timber worker. Virginia Wildlife 14(5):23.

*Anonymous. 1953i. Tazewell coyote believed introduced. Virginia Wildlife 14(5):23.

*Anonymous. 1953j. Albino woodchuck killed near Harrisonburg. Virginia Wildlife 14(6):24.

*Anonymous. 1953k. Radford arsenal deer doing well. Virginia Wildlife 14(8):26.

*Anonymous. 1953l. Deer mortality records sought for study. Virginia Wildlife 14(10): 26.

*Anonymous. 1953m. Hog island refuge. Virginia Wildlife 14(11):13–15.

*Anonymous. 1953n. Big Levels open to bow hunting. Virginia Wildlife 14(11):17.

*Anonymous. 1953o. The squirrel lost the bout. Virginia Wildlife 14(11):25.

*Anonymous. 1953p. Exceptional squirrel hunting luck. Virginia Wildlife 14(12):27.

*Anonymous. 1953q. No hunter's prize. Virginia Wildlife 14(12):27.

*Anonymous. 1954a. Big buck felled by "little stick." Virginia Wildlife 15(1):25.

*Anonymous. 1954b. Big game trophy contest. Virginia Wildlife 15(1):27.

*Anonymous. 1954c. Battle of the stags on Dry River. Virginia Wildlife 15(2):23.

*Anonymous. 1954d. Bigger bear kill west of Blue Ridge. Virginia Wildlife 15(3):13.

*Anonymous. 1954e. Twenty-five-point buck sets record. Virginia Wildlife 15(3):25.

*Anonymous. 1954f. No skunk after all. Virginia Wildlife 15(3):25.

*Anonymous. 1954g. Maimed Maryland deer bagged in Virginia. Virginia Wildlife 15(4):24.

*Anonymous. 1954h. Lucky shot from antique double barrelled shotgun bags 8-pointer. Virginia Wildlife 15(4):24.

*Anonymous. 1954i. More deer, bear, and turkeys in 1953–54. Virginia Wildlife 15(4):25.

*Anonymous. 1954j. Freak 45-point buck from James City County. Virginia Wildlife 15(7):24.

*Anonymous. 1954k. Another deer killed by dogs. Virginia Wildlife 15(7):24.

*Anonymous. 1954l. Virginia wildlife conservationgram. Virginia Wildlife 15(9):13.

*Anonymous. 1954m. Lunch at New River. Virginia Wildlife 15(9):25.

*Anonymous. 1954n. 'Coon shops in Charlotte Co. Virginia Wildlife 15(11):24.

*Anonymous. 1954o. A really remarkable rack. Virginia Wildlife 15(12):27.

*Anonymous. 1954p. Bear by the tail. Virginia Wildlife 15(12):28–29.

*Anonymous. 1954q. Virginia Dianas get their deer. Virginia Wildlife 15(12):29.

*Anonymous. 1955a. Reynard the hunter and the hunted. Virginia Wildlife 16(1):20–21.

*Anonymous. 1955b. Wildlife research shocks squirrels. Virginia Wildlife 16(1):26.

*Anonymous. 1955c. Squirrels rampant in Arlington. Virginia Wildlife 16(1):26.

*Anonymous. 1955d. Ninety-seven deer bagged during first two days in Warren. Virginia Wildlife 16(1):26.

*Anonymous. 1955e. Boy scouts try to do good deed for deer. Virginia Wildlife 16(2):26.

*Anonymous. 1955f. Big bobcat trapped in Massanutten Mountains. Virginia Wildlife 16(2):26.

*Anonymous. 1955g. Careful shooting pays dividends. Virginia Wildlife 16(3):24.

*Anonymous. 1955h. Virginia's deer, bear, and turkey kill for 1954–55. Virginia Wildlife 16(4):12.

*Anonymous. 1955i. Wildlife along the seashore. Virginia Wildlife 16(4):21–23.

*Anonymous. 1955j. Eleven was his lucky year. Virginia Wildlife 16(4):26.
*Anonymous. 1955k. Shenandoah, Bath, and Augusta counties were tops for hunters. Virginia Wildlife 16(5):13.
*Anonymous. 1955l. When a fellow needs a game warden. Virginia Wildlife 16(7):26.
*Anonymous. 1955m. The Dismal-No Business game management area. Virginia Wildlife 16(8):14–15.
*Anonymous. 1955n. 16 point buck winner west of Blue Ridge. Virginia Wildlife 16(9):24.
*Anonymous. 1955o. Raccoon on the loose at the game commission. Virginia Wildlife 16(11):26.
*Anonymous. 1955p. Deer on Blackbeard's and Hog islands. Virginia Wildlife 16(12):23.
*Anonymous. 1955q. Commission's better mousetrap catches deer. Virginia Wildlife 16(12):23.
*Anonymous. 1955r. Report on second Hog Island bowhunt. Virginia Wildlife 16(12):24.
*Anonymous. 1955s. Out of the past. Virginia Wildlife 16(4):16–17.
*Anonymous. 1956a. Bear with a homing instinct. Virginia Wildlife 17(1):13.
*Anonymous. 1956b. Eastern deer wins big game trophy contest. Virginia Wildlife 17(1):13.
*Anonymous. 1956c. Glimpses of the 1956 hunting season. Virginia Wildlife 17(1):14–15.
*Anonymous. 1956d. A rare bear in King William County. Virginia Wildlife 17(1):21.
*Anonymous. 1956e. A tagged raccoon reported. Virginia Wildlife 17(1):23.
*Anonymous. 1956f. A good season for bowhunters. Virginia Wildlife 17(1):24.
*Anonymous. 1956g. Albino deer killed in Nottoway County. Virginia Wildlife 17(2):25.
*Anonymous. 1956h. Notes on a homing bear. Virginia Wildlife 17(2):25.
*Anonymous. 1956i. Buck in velvet. Virginia Wildlife 17(2):26.
*Anonymous. 1956j. A believe it or not bear tale. Virginia Wildlife 17(3):26.
*Anonymous. 1956k. Nutria can become a nuisance. Virginia Wildlife 17(5):24.
*Anonymous. 1956l. Bright bunnies. Virginia Wildlife 17(8):24.
*Anonymous. 1956m. Highway no place for pedestrian deer. Virginia Wildlife 17(12):27.
*Anonymous. 1957a. Mathews County boasts aquatic deer. Virginia Wildlife 18(1):23.
*Anonymous. 1957b. Young lady expelled from St. Emma. Virginia Wildlife 18(1):25.
*Anonymous. 1957c. Field force notes. Virginia Wildlife 18(2):25.
*Anonymous. 1957d. Freak deer bagged in Southampton County. Virginia Wildlife 18(3):24.
*Anonymous. 1957e. National Museum identifies shrews. Virginia Wildlife 18(4):26.
*Anonymous. 1957f. 44 deer trapped in two weeks. Virginia Wildlife 18(5):24.
*Anonymous. 1957g. Bear stalks along Potomac. Virginia Wildlife 18(8):25.
*Anonymous. 1957h. Coon sings "Is I Blue?" Virginia Wildlife 18(8):25.
*Anonymous. 1957i. Game violators penalized. Virginia Wildlife 18(9):13.
*Anonymous. 1957j. Bow hunters take 22 deer at Hog Island. Virginia Wildlife 18(9):13.
*Anonymous. 1957k. 160-pound buck killed by dogs. Virginia Wildlife 18(9):24.
*Anonymous. 1957l. Bear gets canned. Virginia Wildlife 18(9):26.
*Anonymous. 1957m. Beaver colony in Orange County. Virginia Wildlife 18(9):26.
*Anonymous. 1957n. Bowhunter takes doe on opening day. Virginia Wildlife 18(9):27.
*Anonymous. 1957o. Deformed yearling doe killed by dogs. Virginia Wildlife 18(10):26.
*Anonymous. 1957p. The whitetail — most popular big-game animal in Virginia, the United States, and the world. Virginia Wildlife 18(11):6–8, 23.
*Anonymous. 1958a. New herd — nice deer. Virginia Wildlife 19(2):26.
*Anonymous. 1958b. The high cost of venison. Virginia Wildlife 19(3):12, 22.
*Anonymous. 1958c. Trespassing can be dangerous. Virginia Wildlife 19(3):23.
*Anonymous. 1958d. Rare hare. Virginia Wildlife 19(3):23.
*Anonymous. 1958e. New shrew found at Mountain Lake. Virginia Wildlife 19(3):25.
*Anonymous. 1958f. No light fine for dark hunting. Virginia Wildlife 19(4):23.
*Anonymous. 1958g. The story of the bears. Virginia Wildlife 19(4):23.
*Anonymous. 1958h. Saw too much for fox. Virginia Wildlife 19(6):26.
*Anonymous. 1958i. Virginia's 1958 elk season. Virginia Wildlife 19(9):13.
*Anonymous. 1958j. Bear tagging project highly successful. Virginia Wildlife 19(10):13.
*Anonymous. 1958k. Buck rescues fawn. Virginia Wildlife 19(1):25.
*Anonymous. 1959a. Public hunting land and the state circuit. Virginia Wildlife 20(1):14–15.
*Anonymous. 1959b. Four tagged bear reported. Virginia Wildlife 20(1):21.
*Anonymous. 1959c. Boonesville farmer kills 471-pound bear. Virginia Wildlife 20(1):26.
*Anonymous. 1959d. Virginia hunters take 272 bear during season. Virginia Wildlife 20(3):13.
*Anonymous. 1959e. Elk hunter. Virginia Wildlife 20(4):24.
*Anonymous. 1959f. Girl, 9, kills bear with one shot. Virginia Wildlife 20(4):24.
*Anonymous. 1959g. Story of bear's 97-mile hike told. Virginia Wildlife 20(4):26.
*Anonymous. 1959h. The drumming log. Virginia Wildlife 20(7):24.
*Anonymous. 1959i. A checklist of Virginia's mammals, birds, reptiles, and amphibians. Virginia Wildlife 20(9):13–16.

*Anonymous. 1959j. 13 bear tagged in research project. Virginia Wildlife 20(9):25.
*Anonymous. 1959k. Three-day Virginia elk season details announced. Virginia Wildlife 20(10):25.
*Anonymous. 1959l. Descriptions and life histories of Virginia's game and furbearing mammals. Virginia Wildlife 20(12):20–23.
*Anonymous. 1960a. Five elk bagged during Virginia's 1954 season. Virginia Wildlife 21(1):13.
*Anonymous. 1960b. Successful field trials held by the Virginia fox hunters association. Virginia Wildlife 21(1):23.
*Anonymous. 1960c. Commission field force notes. Virginia Wildlife 21(1):25.
*Anonymous. 1960d. Winter homes for wildlife. Virginia Wildlife 21(2):14–15.
*Anonymous. 1960e. Bear travel. Virginia Wildlife 21(2):24.
*Anonymous. 1960f. Young deer hunters. Virginia Wildlife 21(2):26.
*Anonymous. 1960g. The drumming log (picture). Virginia Wildlife 21(3):24–25.
*Anonymous. 1960h. Commission field force notes (picture). Virginia Wildlife 21(3):26.
*Anonymous. 1960i. The drumming log (picture). Virginia Wildlife 21(4):24–25.
*Anonymous. 1960j. The drumming log (picture). Virginia Wildlife 21(5):23.
*Anonymous. 1960k. Commission field force notes (picture). Virginia Wildlife 21(5):24–25.
*Anonymous. 1960l. Camp A. P. Hill game harvest high. Virginia Wildlife 21(7):24.
*Anonymous. 1960m. Commission field force notes (picture). Virginia Wildlife 21(7):24–25.
*Anonymous. 1960n. Fisherman kills rabid bobcat with stick. Virginia Wildlife 21(8):22–23.
*Anonymous. 1960o. S. E. Kitchen's 14 fox tails take 1st prize in Buckingham trapping. Virginia Wildlife 21(8):25.
*Anonymous. 1960p. Commission field force notes (picture). Virginia Wildlife 21(10):24–25.
*Anonymous. 1960q. Commission field force notes (picture). Virginia Wildlife 21(10):24–25.
*Anonymous. 1960r. Commission bear trappers tag a big one. Virginia Wildlife 21(11):11.
*Anonymous. 1960s. Young bowhunter bags 9-point buck. Virginia Wildlife 21(12):20.
*Anonymous. 1960t. Boy shoots squirrel with tusk. Virginia Wildlife 21(12):20.
*Anonymous. 1960u. The drumming log (picture). Virginia Wildlife 21(12):22–24.
*Anonymous. 1960v. Youths discover ancient whale on James. Virginia Wildlife 21(11):23.
*Anonymous. 1961a. Annual rabies surveillance report. United State Department of Health, Education, and Welfare, Public Health Service, Communicable Disease Center, Atlanta, Georgia.
*Anonymous. 1961b. Wise management of Giles-Bland game area pays off. Virginia Wildlife 22(1):17.
*Anonymous. 1961c. Winchester 11 year olds bag deer. Virginia Wildlife 22(1):21.
*Anonymous. 1961d. Heavy wildlife use of autumn olive noted in Virginia. Virginia Wildlife 22(1):22.
*Anonymous. 1961e. The drumming log (picture). Virginia Wildlife 22(1):23–26.
*Anonymous. 1961f. Western Virginia deer kill 18,225. Virginia Wildlife 22(2):13.
*Anonymous. 1961g. Covington youth kills bear. Virginia Wildlife 22(3):22.
*Anonymous. 1961h. Richmond boy bags big buck. Virginia Wildlife 22(3):22.
*Anonymous. 1961i. Albino deer at Camp Pickett. Virginia Wildlife 22(3):23.
*Anonymous. 1961j. Commission field force notes (picture). Virginia Wildlife 22(3):23–26.
*Anonymous. 1961k. State deer kill up 25 percent, 35 percent in east. Virginia Wildlife 22(4):13.
*Anonymous. 1961l. Virginia black bear kill down 42 percent. Virginia Wildlife 22(4):13.
*Anonymous. 1961m. The drumming log (picture). Virginia Wildlife 22(4):26.
*Anonymous. 1961n. Least weasel taken in Virginia. Virginia Wildlife 22(5):25.
*Anonymous. 1961o. Big game awards given at Bedford. Virginia Wildlife 22(6):25.
*Anonymous. 1961p. Three deer spotlighters sent to prison for killing deer out of season. Virginia Wildlife 22(6):25.
*Anonymous. 1961q. The drumming log (picture). Virginia Wildlife 22(6):25.
*Anonymous. 1961r. Lack of food limiting Dismal Swamp deer herd. Virginia Wildlife 22(7):13.
*Anonymous. 1961s. Game manager burned out. Virginia Wildlife 22(7):26.
*Anonymous. 1961t. "Bull and bear" and possum. Virginia Wildlife 22(12):23.
*Anonymous. 1961u. The drumming log (pictures). Virginia Wildlife 22(12):23.
*Anonymous. 1962a. The drumming log (pictures). Virginia Wildlife 23(1):24–25.
*Anonymous. 1962b. Parasites found in Virginia deer. Virginia Wildlife 23(3):9.
*Anonymous. 1962c. Highland County wildlife area slated for purchase. Virginia Wildlife 23(7):13.
*Anonymous. 1962d. Virginia's public hunting areas. Virginia Wildlife 23(11):16–17.
*Anonymous. 1963a. Either sex shooting boosts state deer kill. Virginia Wildlife 24(4):13.
*Anonymous. 1963b. Surry County bucks. Virginia Wildlife 24(4):25.
*Anonymous. 1963c. Powhatan wildlife management area. Virginia Wildlife 24(9):15–16.
*Anonymous. 1964a. Successful young hunters. Virginia Wildlife 25(4):25.
*Anonymous. 1964B. Virginia wildlife conservation-gram. Virginia Wildlife 25(5):13.
*Anonymous. 1965a. Dolphins and porpoises. United States Department of Interior, Fisheries Center Leaflet no. 1.
*Anonymous. 1965b. Tick fever. Virginia Wildlife 26(6):16–17.

*Anonymous. 1965c. Outlaw roundup on little creek. Virginia Wildlife 26(11):20.

*Anonymous. 1966. Animal-man diseases. Virginia Wildlife 27(5):18–22.

*Anonymous. 1967a. Hunters and hunting. Virginia Wildlife 28(3):23.

*Anonymous. 1967b. Virginia wildlife conservationgram. Virginia Wildlife 28(5):13.

*Anonymous. 1967c. Virginia wildlife conservationgram. Virginia Wildlife 28(6)13.

*Anonymous. 1967d. King cottontail. Virginia Wildlife 28(7):8.

*Anonymous. 1967e. Big game kill. Virginia Wildlife 28(10):15.

*Anonymous. 1968. Big game kill records by county. Virginia Wildlife 29(11):19.

*Anonymous. 1969a. Virginia big game kill records. Virginia Wildlife 30(11):15.

*Anonymous. 1969b. Opportunity: it's all yours. Don't miss it. Virginia Wildlife 30(12):6–7, 22.

*Anonymous. 1971a. Big eastern deer wins trophy contest. Virginia Wildlife 32(1):13.

*Anonymous. 1971b. Virginia wildlife conservationgram. Virginia Wildlife 32(3):13.

*Anonymous. 1971c. Mountain lions granted protection in Virginia. Virginia Wildlife 32(6):13.

*Anonymous. 1971d. Virginia big game kill records. Virginia Wildlife 32(11):15.

*Anonymous. 1972a. Western deer kill increase surprises experts. Virginia Wildlife 33(2):13.

*Anonymous. 1972b. Hunters bag 358 bears. Virginia Wildlife 33(3):13.

*Anonymous. 1972c. 350 acre gift expands Havens area. Virginia Wildlife 33(3):13.

*Anonymous. 1972d. 1971–72 big game harvest. Virginia Wildlife 33(10):20.

*Anonymous. 1972e. Western deer make clean sweep of state trophy contest. Virginia Wildlife 33(12):13.

*Anonymous. 1973. Snowshoe hare stocked in Virginia mountains. Virginia Wildlife 34(2):13.

*Anonymous. 1974a. The Dismal Swamp, for all to enjoy. Virginia Wildlife 35(4):19–20, 24.

*Anonymous. 1974b. Big game harvests. Virginia Wildlife 35(10):22.

*Anonymous. 1974c. Report on fox squirrels in Virginia. Unpublished management report. Virginia Commission of Game and Inland Fisheries, Richmond.

*Anonymous. 1975. The case of the acrobatic panhandler. Virginia Wildlife 36(2):18.

*Anonymous. 1976a. 1975–76 big game harvest roundup. Virginia Wildlife 37(3):12.

*Anonymous. 1976b. 1976 big game trophy winners. Virginia Wildlife 37(12):13.

*Anonymous. 1977. 1977 hunting season outlook. Virginia Wildlife 38(10):14.

*Anonymous. 1978. 1978 hunting season outlook. Virginia Wildlife 39(10):8.

*Anonymous. 1979a. Endangered species update. What is the status of Virginia's protected species?. Virginia Wildlife 40(6):24–25.

*Anonymous. 1979b. What to do with a wandering bear?. Virginia Wildlife 40(8):29.

*Anonymous. 1979c. Mammalian data manual. North Eastham, Massachusetts: JNL Publications.

*Anonymous. 1979d. Happy bee. Ranger Rick's Nature Magazine 13(9):15.

*Anonymous. 1979e. Endangered species update. Virginia Wildlife 40(6):24–25.

*Anonymous. 1979f. What to do with a wandering bear. Virginia Wildlife 40(8):29.

*Anonymous. 1979g. Statewide deer, bear, and turkey harvest. Virginia Wildlife 40(10):11.

*Anonymous. 1980. 1980 hunting outlook. Virginia Wildlife 41(10):21.

*Anonymous. 1981. 1981 hunting outlook. Virginia Wildlife 42(9):2b.

*Anonymous. 1983. All about antlers. Virginia Wildlife 44(11):32–33.

*Anonymous. 1984. Black bear status study. Virginia Commission of Game and Inland Fisheries Performance Report W-74-R-1. IA.

*Anonymous. 1989. Backtracking — into our history. Virginia Wildlife 50(1):1–34.

*Anonymous. 1994a. Virginia bear study begins on G W. Virginia Wildlife 55(9):30.

*Anonymous. 1994b. Manatee flown to warmer waters after summer in Bay. Bay Journal, November, 1994:12.

*Anonymous. 1995a. Manatee's wanderings monitored from space. Bay Journal 5(5):19.

*Anonymous, 1995b. Number of stranded dolphins, whales, seal spiraled in 1994. Bay Journal 5(2):11.

*Anonymous, 1996a. Blackwater bats. Virginia Chapter News, The Nature Conservancy. Fall/Winter, 1996:10

*Anonymous. 1996b. A rare find. The Roanoke Times:NRV Current:3.

*Anthony, H. E. 1928. Field book of North American mammals. New York: G. P. Putnam's Sons.

*Arber, E., (editor). 1884. Captain John Smith's works (1608–1631). Birmingham.

*Ariza, J. F. 1932. Dismal Swamp in legend and history. National Geographic Magazine 62:120–130.

Arlton, A. V. 1936. An ecological study of the mole. Journal of Mammalogy 17(4):349–371.

*Armstrong, C. W., (editor). 1991. Rabies prevention — United States, 1991. Virginia Epidemiology Bulletin 91(9):1–10.

Arner, D. H., J. Baker, D. Wesley, and B. Herring. 1969. An inventory and study of beaver impounded water in Mississippi. Proceedings of the 23rd Annual Conference of Southeastern Game and Fish Commissioners 23:110–128.

*Arnold, R. 1888. The Dismal Swamp and Lake Drummond. Norfolk, Virginia: Evening Telegram Print.

Asdell, S. A. 1946. Patterns of mammalian reproduction. Ithaca, New York: Comstock Press.

*Asdell, S. A. 1964. Patterns of mammalian reproduction. Ithaca, New York: University Press.

*Ash, E. C. 1972 (1927). Dogs: their history and development. 2 vols. New York: Benjamin Blom.

*Ashbrook, F. G. 1947a. Abstract of fur laws, 1947–48. United States Fish and Wildlife Service, Wildlife Leaflet 297.

*Ashbrook, F. G. 1947b. Annual fur catch of the United States. United States Fish and Wildlife Service, Wildlife Leaflet 298.

Ashbrook, F. G. 1948. Nutrias grow in United States. Journal of Wildlife Management 12(1):87–95.

*Ashbrook, F. G. 1952. Annual fur catch of the United States. United States Fish and Wildlife Service, Wildlife Leaflet 315.

*Ashbrook, F. G., and B. M. Arnold. 1927a. Fur bearing animals of the United States. Skunk. Little spotted skunk. The Fur Journal 1(1):38–42.

*Ashbrook, F. G., and B. M. Arnold. 1927b. Fur bearing animals of the United States. The opossum. The Fur Journal 1(3):28–29.

*Ashbrook, F. G., and F. L. Earnshaw. 1925. Law relating to fur animals for the season 1925–1926. United States Department of Agriculture, Farmers' Bulletin no. 1469.

*Ashbrook, F. G., and F. L. Earnshaw. 1926. Fur laws for the season 1926–27. United States Department of Agriculture, Farmers' Bulletin no. 1515.

*Ashbrook, F. G., and H. J. McMullen. 1925. A preliminary study of statistical data on fur resources and the fur trade. Pages 5–34. In: National Association of the Fur Industry Year Book.

Askins, G. R. 1982. Population characteristics of the wild mink in Maryland. Master's thesis, Frostburg State College.

Atwood, E. L. 1950. Life history studies of nutria, or coypu, in coastal Louisiana. Journal of Wildlife Management 14(3):249–265.

*Atwood, E. L., J. T. Lamb, and D. E. Sonenshine. 1964. The ecology of Rocky Mountain spotted fever in eastern United States with particular reference to Virginia. I. Epidemiology. Proceedings of the 18th Annual Conference of the Southeastern Association of Game and Fish Commissioners 18:110–119 [1967].

*Atwood, E. L., J. T. Lamb, and D. E. Sonenshine. 1965. A contribution to the epidemiology of Rocky Mountain spotted fever in the eastern United States. American Journal of Tropical Medicine and Hygiene 14(5):831–837.

*Audubon, J. J., and J. Bachman. 1839. Descriptions of new species of quadrupeds inhabiting New America. Journal of the Academy of Natural Sciences of Philadelphia 8(1):280–323.

*Audubon, J. J., and J. Bachman. 1841. Descriptions of new species of North American quadrupeds. Proceedings of the Academy of Natural Sciences of Philadelphia:92–103.

*Audubon, J. J., and J. Bachman. 1842. Descriptions of new species of quadrupeds inhabiting North America. Journal of the Academy of Natural Sciences of Philadelphia 8:280–323.

*Audubon, J. J., and J. Bachman. 1846–1854. The viviparous quadrupeds of North America. Volume 1: 383 pp. (1846); Volume 2: 334 pp. (1851); Volume 3: 384 pp. (1854).

*August, J. B. 1974a. A study of liberation of snowshoe hare on ancestral range in Virginia. Master's thesis, Virginia Polytechnic Institute and State University, Blacksburg.

*August, J. B. 1974b. The snowshoe hare in Virginia. Virginia Wildlife 35(9):16–17, 24.

*August, P. V., S. G. Ayvazian, and J. G. T. Anderson. 1989. Magnetic orientation in a small mammal, *Peromyscus leucopus.* Journal of Mammalogy 70(1):1–9.

*Averitt, J. W., and R. K. Rose. 1989. Seasonal dynamics of the anal gland of the hispid cotton rat, *(Sigmodon hispidus).* Virginia Journal of Science 40(2):54. Abstract.

*Avise, J. C., M. H. Smith, and R. K. Selander. 1979. Biochemical polymorphism and systematics in the genus *Peromyscus.* VII. Geographic differentiation in members of the *truei* and *maniculatus* species groups. Journal of Mammalogy 60(1):177–192.

Babb, J. G., and M. L. Kennedy. 1988. Home range of the coyote in western Tennessee. Proceedings of the Annual Conference of the Southeastern Association of Fish and Wildlife Agencies 42:443–447.

*Babin, M. J., and R. P. Eckerlin. 1994. Chromosomal comparisons in two populations of *Clethrionomys gapperi.* Virginia Journal of Science 45(2):55. Abstract

*Baccus, R., and J. O. Wolff. 1989. Genetic composition of fluctuating populations of *Peromyscus leucopus* and *Peromyscus maniculatus.* Journal of Mammalogy 70(3):592–602.

*Bachman, J. 1837a. Observations, on the different species of Hares (genus *Lepus*) inhabiting the United States and Canada. Journal of the Academy of Natural Sciences of Philadelphia 7:282–361.

*Bachman, J. 1837b. Some remarks on the genus *Sorex,* with a monograph of the North American species. Journal of the Academy of Natural Sciences of Philadelphia 7:362–402.

*Bachman, J. 1838. Monograph of the species of the genus *Sciurus* inhabiting North America. Proceedings of the Zoological Society of London. Part VI:85–103.

*Bachman, J. 1839. Abstract of a monograph of the genus *Sciurus* with descriptions of several new species and varieties. American Journal of Science and Arts 37:290–310. Also Charlesworth Magazine of Natural History:113–123, 154–162, 220–227, 330–337, 385–390.

*Badger, C. J. 1977. Little elk of Assateague. Virginia Wildlife 38(10):15–16.

*Badger, C. J. 1986. Elk of the islands. Virginia Wildlife 47(2):11–15.

*Baer, G. M., and D. B. Adams. 1970. Rabies in insectivorous bats in the United States, 1953–65. United States Public Health Reports 85(7):637–645.

Bailey, B. 1929. Mammals of Sherburne County, Minnesota. Journal of Mammalogy 10(2):153–164.

*Bailey, H. H. 1930. Correcting inaccurate ranges of certain Florida mammals and others of Virginia and

the Carolinas. Bulletin no. 5, Bailey Museum and Library of Natural History, Miami, Fla.

*Bailey, J. W. 1942. A check list of the Chordates of Virginia. Virginia Journal of Science 3(6):217.

*Bailey, J. W. 1946. The mammals of Virginia. Richmond, Virginia: Williams Printing Company.

*Bailey, J. W. 1948. The finback whale in Virginia waters. Journal of Mammalogy 29(2):183–184.

*Bailey, V. 1896a. List of mammals of the District of Columbia. Proceedings of the Biological Society of Washington 10:93–101.

*Bailey, V.1896b. Occurrence of the native wood rat at Washington, DC. Science 3(69):628.

*Bailey, V. 1900. Revision of American voles of the genus *Microtus.* North American Fauna 17.

*Bailey, V. 1913. The new subspecies of North American beavers. Proceedings of the Biological Society of Washington 26:191–194.

*Bailey, V. 1923. Mammals of the District of Columbia. Proceedings of the Biological Society of Washington 36:103–138.

*Bailey, V. 1924. Breeding, feeding and other life habits of meadow mice *(Microtus).* Journal of Agricultural Research 27(8):523–536.

*Bailey, V. 1926. Mammals of the vicinity of Washington. Journal of the Washington Academy of Science 16(16):441–445.

*Bailey, V. 1929. Government report of game survey in Bath and Highland Counties. Mammals. Game and Fish Conservationist 9(1):4–6.

*Bailey, V. 1931a. Deer studies in lowlands of Virginia. Game and Fish Conservationist 11(6):99–101, 104.

*Bailey, V. 1931b. Virginia black bears as game. Game and Fish Conservationist 11(6):110.

*Bailey, V. 1938a. Habits of lowly cottontail described by dean of wild life specialists. Virginia Wildlife 1(10):7.

*Bailey, V. 1938b. Naturalist explains habits of squirrels. Virginia Wildlife 1(12):7.

*Baird, S. F. 1857. Mammals. Pp. 1853–56. In: Reports of explorations and surveys, to ascertain the most practicable and economical route for a railroad from the Mississippi River to the Pacific Ocean. United States War Department, Washington. 8(1):1–757.

*Baird, S. F. 1859. Mammals of North America. Philadelphia: J. B. Lippincott and Company.

Bakeless, J. 1939. Master of the wilderness, Daniel Boone. New York: William Morrow and Company.

*Bakeless, J. E. 1961. The eyes of discovery. New York: Dover Publications.

*Baker, C. P. 1967. Beaver reported on lower Potomac. Atlantic Naturalist 22(2):126–127.

*Baker, J. 1990. Have you been in your woods lately? Virginia Wildlife 51(5):27–30.

Baker, W. W. 1965. A contribution to the knowledge of the distribution and movement of bats in north Georgia. Master's thesis, University of Georgia.

Bakken, A. 1959. Behavior of gray squirrels. Proceedings of the 13th Annual Conference of the Southeastern Association of Game and Fish Commissioners 13:393–407.

*Baldwin, J. T., Jr. 1969. The white squirrels of Chickahominy Park. Virginia Wildlife 30(4):8–9.

*Baldwin, W. P., and C. P. Patton. 1938. A preliminary study of the food habits of elk in Virginia. Transactions of the 3d North American Wildlife Conference:747–755.

Banfield, A. W. F. 1974. The mammals of Canada. Toronto: University of Toronto Press.

*Bangs, O. 1895. The geographical distribution of the eastern races of the cottontail (*Lepus sylvaticus* Bach.) with a description of a new subspecies and with notes on the distribution of the northern hare (*Lepus americanus* Erxl.) in the East. Proceedings of the Boston Society of Natural History 26:404–414.

*Bangs, O. 1896a. A review of the squirrels of eastern North America. Proceedings of the Biological Society of Washington 10:145–167.

*Bangs, O. 1896b. The skunks of the genus *Mephitis* of eastern United States. Proceedings of the Biological Society of Washington 10:139–144.

*Bangs, O. 1898a. The land mammals of peninsular Florida and the coast region of Georgia. Proceedings of the Boston Society of Natural History 28(7):157–235.

*Bangs, O. 1898b. The eastern races of the American varying hare, with description of a new subspecies from Nova Scotia. Proceedings of the Biological Society of Washington 12:77–82.

*Banker, M. E. 1994. Modeling white-tailed deer habitat quality and vegetation response to succession and management. Master's thesis, Virginia Polytechnic Institute and State University, Blacksburg.

*Baptiste, M. E. 1977. A survey of visitor knowledge, attitude, and judgement concerning black bears at Shenandoah National Park. Master's thesis, Virginia Polytechnic Institute and State University, Blacksburg.

*Baptiste, M. E., J. B. Whelan, and R. B. Frary. 1979. Visitor perception of black bear problems at Shenandoah National Park. Wildlife Society Bulletin 7(1):25–29.

*Barbehenn, K. R., and J. G. New. 1957. Possible natural intergradation between prairie and forest deer mice. Journal of Mammalogy 38(2):210–218.

*Barbour, P. L., (editor). 1969. The Jamestown voyages under the first charter 1606–1609. Cambridge: Hakluyt Society. Series III, no. 137:400–405.

*Barbour, R. W. 1951a. The mammals of Big Black Mountain, Harlan County, Kentucky. Journal of Mammalogy 32(1):100–110.

*Barbour, R. W. 1951b. Notes on mammals from West Virginia. Journal of Mammalogy 32(3):368–371.

*Barbour, R. W. 1956. *Synaptomys cooperi* in Kentucky, with description of a new subspecies. Journal of Mammalogy 37(3):413–416.

*Barbour, R. W., and W. H. Davis. 1969. Bats of America. Lexington: University Press of Kentucky.

Barbour, R. W., and W. H. Davis. 1974. Mammals of Kentucky. Lexington: University Press of Kentucky.

Barbour, R. W., W. H. Davis, and M. D. Hassell. 1966. The need of vision in homing by *Myotis sodalis*. Journal of Mammalogy 47(2):356–357.
*Barbour, T. 1943. Naturalists at large. Boston: Little Brown Company.
*Barbour, T., and G. M. Allen. 1922. The white-tailed deer of eastern United States. Journal of Mammalogy 3(2):65–78.
*Barco, S. 1995. Population patterns of bottlenose dolphins (*Tursiops truncatus*) in the nearshore waters of Virginia Beach, Virginia. Master's thesis, James Madison University, Harrisonburg.
*Barick, F. B. 1951. Deer restoration in the southeastern United States. Proceedings of the Annual Conference of the Southeastern Association of Game and Fish Commissioners 5:342–358.
*Barick, F. B. 1969a. Deer predation in North Carolina and other southeastern states. Pp. 25–31. In: White-tailed deer in the southern forest habitat. Proceedings of a symposium, Nacogdoches, Texas. 1969.
*Barick, F. B. 1969b. Deer predation in North Carolina and other southeastern states. Part I. Wildlife in North Carolina 33(7):7–10.
*Barick, F. B. 1969c. Deer predation in North Carolina and other southeastern states. Conclusion. Wildlife in North Carolina 33(8):4–6.
*Barkalow, F. S. 1962. Latitude related to reproduction in the cottontail rabbit. Journal of Wildlife Management 26(1):32–37.
*Barkalow, F. S. 1966. Rafinesque's big-eared bat. Wildlife in North Carolina 30(1):14–15.
Barkalow, F. S., Jr., and D. A. Adams. 1955. The seminole bat, *Lasiurus seminolus*, in North Carolina. Journal of Mammalogy 36(3):453–454.
Barkalow, F. S., and J. B. Funderburg, Jr. 1960. Probable breeding and additional records of the seminole bat in North Carolina. Journal of Mammalogy 41(3):394–395.
Barkalow, F. S., Jr. R. B. Hamilton, and R. F. Soots, Jr. 1970. The vital statistics of an unexploited gray squirrel population. Journal of Wildlife Management 34:489–500.
*Barkalow, F. S., and R. F. Soots, Jr. 1975. Life span and reproductive longevity of the gray squirrel, *Sciurus c. carolinensis* Gmelin. Journal of Mammalogy 56(2):522–524.
*Barnes, I. R. 1954. Paul Bartsch, Part 3. The Lebanon years. Atlantic Naturalist 9(3):116–126.
*Barnes, W. C. 1928. Rabbit fever or tularemia. Scientific Monthly 27:463–469.
*Barnosky, A. D. 1990. Evolution of dental traits since latest Pleistocene in meadow voles *(Microtus pennsylvanicus)* from Virginia. Paleobiology 16(3): 370–383.
*Barr, T. R. B. 1963. Infectious diseases in the opossum: a review. Journal of Wildlife Management 27(1):53–71.
*Barry, R. E., Jr., M.A. Botje, and L. B. Grantham. 1984. Vertical stratification of *Peromyscus leucopus* and *P. maniculatus* in southwestern Virginia. Journal of Mammalogy 65(1):145–148.
Bartenstein, S. 1981. Wintering wildlife. Virginia Wildlife 42(1):23.
*Bartenstein, S. 1982. Springtime for deer. Virginia Wildlife 43(5):24.
*Bartlett, T. 1972. Quantico's eager beavers. Virginia Wildlife 33(1):14–18.
*Barton, B. S. 1974 (1792). Notes on the animals of North America. Edited with introduction by K. B. Sterling. Natural Sciences in America Series. New York: Arno Press.
*Barton, B. S. 1823. Facts, observations, and conjectures, relative to the generation of the opossum of North America. In a letter from Professor Barton to Monsignor Roume, of Paris. Annals of Philosophy (later called the London, Edinburgh and Dublin Philosophy Magazine), n.s., 6:349–354.
*Bartram, W. 1973 (1792). Travels through North and South Carolina, Georgia, east and west Florida. London. Reprinted, Beehive Facsimile Press, Savannah, Georgia.
*Bartsch, P. 1901. A trip to the Dismal Swamp. Osprey 5:35–37, 55–56, 67–69.
*Bartsch, P. 1956. An interesting catch. Journal of Mammalogy 37(1):111.
*Bassett, B. 1987. The raccoon. Virginia Wildlife 48(7):34.
Bassett, C. F., and L. M. Llewellyn. 1949. The molting and fur growth pattern in the adult mink. American Midland Naturalist 42(3):751–756.
*Bassett, J. S., (editor). 1901. The writings of "Colonel William Byrd of Westover in Virginia Esqr." New York: Doubleday, Page and Company.
*Baumbarger, D. O. 1977. The status, regulations, and hunting and trapping pressures on foxes in Virginia. Master's thesis, Virginia Polytechnic Institute and State University, Blacksburg.
Beale, M. L. 1987. The computer cataloging of vertebrate study specimens. Virginia Journal of Science 38(2):76. Abstract.
*Beatty, R. C., and W. J. Mulloy, 1940. William Byrd's Natural History of Virginia. Richmond, Virginia: Dietz Press.
*Beaver, T. D., G. A. Feldhamer, and J. A. Chapman. 1982. Dental and cranial anomalies in the river otter (Carnivora: Mustelidae). Brimleyana no. 7:101–109.
*Beck, B. 1972. Roanoke River — beauty and disappointment. Virginia Wildlife 33(2):10–12.
*Becker, K. M., E. L. Spruill, and C. R. Terman. 1996. Pregnancy block in white-footed mice (*Peromyscus leucopus noveboracensis*): the role of lactation. Virginia Journal of Science 47(2):93. Abstract.
*Beebe, B. F. 1963. American lions and cats. New York: David McKay Company.
*Beeler, I. E., and T. J. O'Shea. 1988. Distribution and mortality of the West Indian manatee *(Trichechus manatus)* in the southeastern United States: a compilation and review of recent information. Volume 1: The Atlantic coast. Gainesville, Florida: National Ecology Research Center, Report no. 88–09.

Beer, J. R. 1955. Survival and movements of banded big brown bats. Journal of Mammalogy 36(2):242–248.

*Bekoff, M. 1977. *Canis latrans.* Mammalian Species no. 79.

*Bekoff, M. 1982. Coyote. Pp. 447–459. In: Chapman, J. A., and G. A. Feldhamer (editors), Wild mammals of North America. Baltimore: The Johns Hopkins University Press.

*Bell, J. F. 1970. Rocky Mountain spotted fever. Pp. 324–331. In: Davis, J. W., L. H. Karstad, and D. O. Trainer (editors), Infectious diseases of wild mammals. Ames: Iowa State University Press.

*Bell, J. F., and W. S. Chalgren. 1943. Some wildlife diseases in the eastern United States. Journal of Wildlife Management 7(3):270–278.

*Bell, J. M. 1913. Hunting the fleet-footed deer in Virginia. American Field 79(5):98.

*Bellig, R. A. 1962. A study of cottontail rabbit population dynamics in southeastern Virginia. Master's thesis, Virginia Polytechnic Institute and State University, Blacksburg.

*Belton, B. 1978. Walk on the wild side. Virginia Wildlife 39(11):18–19.

*Belwood, J. J. 1979. Feeding ecology of an Indiana bat community with emphasis on the endangered Indiana bat, *Myotis sodalis.* Master's thesis, University of Florida.

Bendel, P. R., and J. E. Gates. 1987. Home range and microhabitat partitioning of the southern flying squirrel *(Glaucomys volans).* Journal of Mammalogy 68(2):243–254.

*Beneski, J. T., Jr., and D. W. Stinson. 1987. *Sorex palustris.* Mammalian Species 296.

Benson, A. B. 1937. The America of 1750: Peter Kalm's travels in North America. The English version of 1770. 2 volumes, New York.

Benton, A. H. 1955a. Observations on the life history of the northern pine mouse. Journal of Mammalogy 36(1):52–62.

*Benton, A. H. 1955b. Notes on the behavioral development of captive red-backed mice. Journal of Mammalogy 36(4):566–567.

*Benton, A. H. 1980. Atlas of the fleas of eastern United States. Fredonia, New York: Marginal Media.

*Berkaw, M. N., and P. F. Scanlon. 1974. Seasonal variation in reproductive organs of male cottontail rabbits. Virginia Journal of Science 25(2):60. Abstract.

*Berry, E. W., and W. K. Gregory. 1906. *Prorosmarus alleni,* a new genus and species of walrus from the upper Miocene of Yorktown, Virginia. American Journal of Science 21(40):444–450.

*Berry, L. A. , E. D. Michael, and H. R. Sanderson. 1979. Effect of population density on captive gray squirrels. Transactions of the 35th Northeastern Fish and Wildlife Conference:53–59.

Beshears, W. W., Jr., and A. O. Haugen. 1953a. Muskrats in your farm pond. Alabama Conservationist 24:4–5, 22.

*Beshears, W. W., Jr., and A. O. Haugen. 1953b. Muskrats in relation to farm ponds. Journal of Wildlife Management 17(4):450–456.

*Best, T. L. 1996. *Lepus californicus.* Mammalian Species no 530:1-10.

*Best, T. L. and J. B. Jennings. 1997. *Myotis leibii.* Mammalian Species no. 547:1-6.

*Beverley, R. 1705. The history and present state of Virginia. L. B. Wright, (editor). 1947. Chapel Hill: University of North Carolina Press.

*Beverly, C. F. 1927. Game sanctuaries and game fish streams. Game and Fish Conservationist 7(2):35–36.

Bider, J. R. 1968. Animal activity in uncontrolled terrestrial communities as determined by a sand transect technique. Ecological Monographs 38:269–308.

Bigler, W. J., J. H. Jenkins, P. M. Cumbie, G. L. Hoff, and E. C. Prather. 1975. Wildlife and environmental health: raccoons as indicators of zoonoses and pollutants in southeastern United States. Journal of the American Veterinary Medical Association 167:592–597.

Birkenholz, D. E. 1963. Movement and displacement in the rice rat. Quarterly Journal of the Florida Academy of Science 26(3):269–274.

Bishop, S. C. 1947. Curious behavior of a hoary bat. Journal of Mammalogy 28(3,4):293–294, 409.

Bissonnette, T. H. 1938. Experimental control of sexual periodicity in animals and possible applications to wild life management. Journal of Wildlife Management 2(3):104–118.

Bissonnette, T. H., and E. E. Bailey. 1944. Experimental modification and control of molts and changes of coat-color in weasels by controlled lighting. Annals of the New York Academy of Science 45(6):221–260.

Bissonnette, T. H., and A. G. Csech. 1937. Modification of mammalian sexual cycles. VII — Fertile matings of raccoons in December instead of February induced by increasing daily periods of light. Proceedings of the Royal Society of London, series B., 122(827):246–254.

Bissonnette, T. H., and A. G. Csech. 1939. A third year of modified breeding behavior with raccoons. Ecology 20(2):156–162.

*Blackwell, S. A. 1928. An exciting chase. Game and Fish Conservationist 8(3):77.

*Blackwell, W. P. 1948. The status of the beaver in Virginia, 1947. Master's thesis, Virginia Polytechnic Institute and State University, Blacksburg.

*Blackwell, W. P. 1949. The beaver makes a comeback. Virginia Wildlife 10(1):19–20.

*Blair, C. W. 1979. Lead, cadmium, nickel, and zinc concentrations in small mammals and earthworms associated with highways of different traffic volumes. Master's thesis, Virginia Polytechnic Institute and State University, Blacksburg.

*Blair, C. W., A. L. Hiller, and P. F. Scanlon. 1977. Heavy metal concentrations in mammals associated with highways of different traffic densities. Virginia Journal of Science 28:61. Abstract.

*Blair, C. W., P. F. Scanlon, and A. L. Hiller. 1978. Lead, cadmium, nickel, and zinc levels in earthworms and mammals recovered near highways of different traffic volumes. Virginia Journal of Science 29(2):57. Abstract.

Blair, W. F. 1936. The Florida marsh rabbit. Journal of Mammalogy 17(3):197–207.

Blair, W. F. 1940. Home ranges and populations of the jumping mouse. American Midland Naturalist 23(1):244–250.

*Blair, W. F. 1968. Mammals. Pp. 453–562. In: Blair, W. F., A. P. Blair, P. Brodkorb, F. R. Cagle, and G. A. Moore. Vertebrates of the United States. 2d ed. New York: McGraw-Hill Book Company.

*Blaylock, R. A. 1984. The distribution and abundance of the bottlenose dolphin, *Tursiops truncatus*, in Virginia. Master's thesis, School of Marine Science, College of William and Mary.

*Blaylock, R. A. 1985. The marine mammals of Virginia. Virginia Institute of Marine Science Sea Grant Educational Series no. 35.

*Blaylock, R. A. 1986. The distribution and abundance of the bottlenose dolphin, *Tursiops truncatus* (Montagu 1821), in Virginia. Virginia Journal of Science 37(2):101. Abstract.

*Blaylock, R. A. 1988. Distribution and abundance of the bottlenose dolphin, *Tursiops truncatus* (Montagu, 1821), in Virginia. United States National Marine Fisheries Service Fisheries Bulletin 86(4):797–805.

*Blem, C. R., and J. F. Pagels. 1973. Feeding habits of an insular barn owl, *Tyto alba*. Virginia Journal of Science 24(4):212–214.

*Bliss, B. 1979. Habitat utilization by *Peromyscus leucopus* and *Blarina brevicauda* of an Appalachian forest in southwestern Virginia. Master's thesis, Virignia Polytechnic Institute and State University, Blacksburg.

*Bliss, B., A. R. Tipton, R. Lochmiller, and J. B. Whelan. 1978. Habitat utilization by *Peromyscus leucopus* and *Blarina brevicauda* of an Appalachian forest in southwestern Virginia. Virginia Journal of Science 29(2):57. Abstract.

*Bloch, C. P. and R. K. Rose. 1997. Population dynamics of *Oryzomys palustris* and *Microtus pennsylvanicus* in two Virginia tidal marshes. Virginia Journal of Science 48(2):79. Abstract.

Blus, L. J. 1966. Relationship between litter size and latitude in the golden mouse. Journal of Mammalogy 47(3):546–547.

Blus, L. J. 1978. Short-tailed shrews: toxicity and residue relationships of DDT, dieldrin, and endrin. Archives of Environmental Contamination and Toxicology 7:83–98.

*Blymyer, M. J. 1976a. A new elevation record for the New England cottontail *(Sylvilagus transitionalis)* in Virginia. Chesapeake Science 17(3):220–221.

*Blymyer, M. J. 1976b. Impact of clearcutting on indigenous mammals of southwest Virginia. Master's thesis, Virginia Polytechnic Institute and State University, Blacksburg.

*Blymyer, M. J. 1976c. Virginia's mountain cottontail. Virginia Wildlife 37(6):16.

*Blymyer, M. J., and H. S. Mosby. 1977. Deer utilization of clearcuts in southwestern Virginia. Southern Journal of Applied Forestry 1(3):10–13.

*Boddaert, P. 1784. Elenchus animalium. Sistens Quadrupedia huc usque nota, eorumque varietates. Roterdam: C. R. Hake. 1:1–174.

Bogan, M. A. 1972. Observations on parturition and development in the hoary bat, *Lasiurus cinereus*. Journal of Mammalogy 53(3):611–614.

Bogue, B. A., and T. L. Derting. 1991. Variation in microtine bioenergetic strategies and the adaptive capacity of the gut. Virginia Journal of Science 42(2):166. Abstract.

*Boldridge, J. R. 1970. Flattails and flat water. Virginia Wildlife 31(5):7, 22.

*Bole, B. P., Jr. and P. N. Moulthrop. 1942. The Ohio recent mammal collection in the Cleveland Museum of Natural History. Scientific Publications of the Cleveland Museum of Natural History 5(6):83–181.

*Bolton, C. O. 1979. The tale of Cold Duck. Virginia Wildlife 40(12):4–6.

*Bonfadini, R. 1894. Vita di Francesco Arese con documenti inediti. Torino-Roma: L. Roux E C.

*Bonwell, W. R., A. R. Tipton, J. B. Whelan, and T. L. Sharik. 1978. Response of understory vegetation and forest wildlife to commercial thinning. Virginia Journal of Science 29(2):57. Abstract.

*Booker, M. A. 1963. Bucks and antlers. Virginia Wildlife 24(1):16.

*Bookhout, T. A. 1964. The Allegheny spotted skunk in Maryland. Chesapeake Science 5(4):213–215.

*Boone and Crockett Club. 1964. Records of North American big game. New York: Holt, Rinehart and Winston.

*Boswell, H., III, and R. K. Rose. 1987. Small mammals and their habitats in the Dismal Swamp. Virginia Journal of Science 38(2):77. Abstract.

*Bourgeois, A., D. Kocka, and S. Klinger. 1995. Black bear habitat management in Virginia. Virginia Wildlife 56(9):10–14.

Bowdre, L. P. 1971. Litter size in *Sigmodon hispidus*. Southwestern Naturalist 16(1):126–128.

*Bowers, M. A. 1993. Influence of herbivorous mammals on an old-field plant community: years 1–4 after disturbance. Oikos 67(1):129–141.

*Bowers, M. A. 1995. Use of space and habitats by the eastern chipmunk, *Tamias striatus*. Journal of Mammalogy 76(1):12–21.

*Bowers, M. A., and A. Ellis. 1993. Load size variation in the eastern chipmunk, *Tamias striatus*: the importance of distance from burrow and canopy cover. Ethology 94(1):72–82.

*Bowers, M. A., J. L. Jefferson, and M. G. Kuebler. 1993. Variation in giving-up densities of foraging chipmunks *(Tamias striatus)* and squirrels *(Sciurus carolinensis)*. Oikos 66(2):229–236.

*Bowers, M. A., D. N. Welch, and T. G. Carr. 1990. Home range size adjustments by the eastern chipmunk, *Tamias striatus*, in response to natural and manipulated water availability. Canadian Journal of Zoology 68(9):2016–2020.

*Bowers, R. R. 1953. The free-running dog menace. Virginia Wildlife 14(10):5–7.

*Bowman, J. 1987. Virginia's whitetails. Disease. Virginia Wildlife 48(11):29–31.

*Bowman, J. 1989. Do you dial 911 for wildlife? Virginia Wildlife 50(8):26–28.

*Bowman, J. 1992. Steps to fewer deer tracks. Virginia Wildlife 53(1):9–13.

*Bowman, N. R., III. 1953. The relation of the skunk to game and burrow-using animals in Virginia. Master's thesis, Virginia Polytechnic Institute and State University, Blacksburg.

*Boyd, W. K., (editor). 1929. William Byrd's histories of the dividing line betwixt Virginia and North Carolina. North Carolina Historical Commission, Raleigh.

*Boyer, T. S., and C. R. Terman. 1992. A comparison of the level of female reproductive inhibition in white-footed mice *Peromyscus leucopus noveboracensis* from Michigan and Virginia. Virginia Journal of Science 43(2):228. Abstract.

*Boyer, T. S., and C. R. Terman. 1993. Comparing reproductive inhibition in female white-footed mice from Michigan and Virginia. Journal of Mammalogy 74(4):813–818.

*Bozeman, F. M., A. Shirai, J. W. Humphries, and H. S. Fuller. 1967. Ecology of Rocky Mountain spotted fever. II. Natural infection of wild mammals and birds in Virginia and Maryland. American Journal of Tropical Medicine and Hygiene 16(1):48–59.

Brack, V., Jr. 1985. The foraging ecology of some bats in Indiana. Proceedings of the Indiana Academy of Science 94:231–237.

Brack, V. 1988. The Indiana bat. Audubon Wildlife Report:609–622.

*Brack, V., and R. K. LaVal. 1985. Food habits of the Indiana bat in Missouri. Journal of Mammalogy 66(2):308–315.

*Bradley, E. L., and C. R. Terman. 1979. Ovulation in *Peromyscus maniculatus bairdi* under laboratory conditions. Journal of Mammalogy 60(3):543–549.

*Bradley, E. L., and C. R. Terman. 1981. Serum testosterone concentrations in male prairie deermice *(Peromyscus maniculatus bairdii)* from laboratory populations. Journal of Mammalogy 62(4):811–814.

*Brady, J. T. 1972. The behavior of displaced gray squirrels. Master's thesis, Virginia Polytechnic Institute and State University, Blacksburg.

*Bratton, P., Jr. 1978a. Treetop ramblers. Virginia Wildlife 39(10):4–5.

*Bratton, P., Jr. 1978b. Paradise lost. Virginia Wildlife 39(7):25–27.

*Bratton, P., Jr. 1978c. Peters Mountain. Virginia Wildlife 39(8):9–11.

*Bratton, P., Jr. 1979. The rivers of buffalo pastures. Virginia Wildlife 40(1):8–11.

*Bratton, P., Jr. and J. M. Price. 1975. Life in Laurel Fork. Virginia Wildlife 36(4):22–23.

*Braun, J. K., and M. L. Kennedy. 1983. Systematics of the genus *Blarina* in Tennessee and adjacent areas. Journal of Mammalogy 64(3):414–425.

*Bray, O. E., and V. G. Barnes, Jr. 1967. A literature review on black bear populations and activities. National Park Service and Colorado Cooperative Wildlife Research Unit Publication:1–34.

*Bray, R. S. 1939. *Sorex fontinalis* in Virginia. Journal of Mammalogy 20(1):102.

Brechner, R. E., and R. D. Kirkpatrick. 1970. Molt in two populations of the house mouse, *Mus musculus.* Proceedings of the Indiana Academy of Science 79:449–454.

*Breidling, F. E. 1980. An evaluation of small rodent populations in four Dismal Swamp plant communities. Master's thesis, Old Dominion University, Norfolk.

*Breidling, F. E., F. P. Day, Jr., and R. K. Rose. 1980. Evaluation of small rodent populations at four Dismal Swamp stands. Virginia Journal of Science 31(4):97. Abstract.

*Breidling, F. E., F. P. Day, Jr., and R. K. Rose. 1983. An evaluation of small rodents in four Dismal Swamp plant communities. Virginia Journal of Science 34(1):14–28.

*Brennan, T. M., and J. A. Cranford. 1985. Mowing effects on small mammal populations in a Blue Ridge Parkway vista. Virginia Journal of Science 36(2):105. Abstract.

Brenner, F. J. 1964. Reproduction of the beaver in Crawford County, Pennsylvania. Journal of Wildlife Management 28:743–747.

*Brenner, F. J. 1968. A three-year study of two breeding colonies of the big brown bat, *Eptesicus fuscus fuscus.* Journal of Mammalogy 49(4):775–778.

*Brigham, R. M., J. E. Cebek, and M. B. C. Hickey. 1989. Intraspecific variation in the echolocation calls of two species of insectivorous bats. Journal of Mammalogy 70(2):426–428.

*Brightman, T. 1975. Dismal Swamp deer hunt: a natural success. Virginia Wildlife 36(6):14–15.

*Brimley, C. S. 1905. A descriptive catalog of the mammals of North Carolina exclusive of the Cetacea. Journal of the Elisha Mitchell Scientific Society 21(1):1–32.

Brimley, C. S. 1923. Breeding dates of small mammals at Raleigh, North Carolina. Journal of Mammalogy 4(4):263–264.

*Brinkley, J. A. 1928. The Dismal Swamp of Virginia. Game and Fish Conservationist 8(2):48.

*Bristor, A., and J. Moore. 1975. Too many squirrels. Virginia Wildlife 36(5):16, 8.

Broadbooks, H. E. 1952. Nest and behavior of a short-tailed shrew, *Criptotis parva.* Journal of Mammalogy 33(2):241–243.

*Bromley, P. T., R. Lochmiller, and D. L. Chapman. 1979. Raccoon biology and management. Virginia Polytechnic Institute and State University Extension Publication 801.

Brooks, F. E. 1911. The mammals of West Virginia: Notes on the distribution and habits of all our known

native species. West Virginia State Board of Agriculture Report (Forestry) (1910) 20:9–30.
Brooks, F. E. 1923. Moles destroy wasps' nests. Journal of Mammalogy 4(2):183.
*Brooks, M. 1955. An isolated population of the Virginia varying hare. Journal of Wildlife Management 19:54–61.
*Brooks, M. 1957. Virginia's north country. Virginia Wildlife 18(2):5–7, 24.
*Brown, A. B. 1985. The bear necessities. Virginia Wildlife 46(7):26–29.
*Brown, G. H. 1952. Illustrated skull key to the recent land mammals of Virginia. Release no. 52–2, Virginia Cooperative Wildlife Research Unit, Blacksburg.
*Brown, G. H. 1957. An evaluation of the aldous browse measurement system and its application to the mountainous areas of Virginia. Master's thesis, Virginia Polytechnic Institute and State University, Blacksburg.
*Brown, I. 1966. Squirrels in the cedar. Virginia Wildlife 27(8):8.
*Brown, I. 1969. Rascals in the bean patch. Virginia Wildlife 30(5):12.
Brown L. G., and L. E. Yeager. 1945. Fox squirrels and gray squirrels in Illinois. Bulletin of the Illinois Natural History Survey 23(5):449–536.
Brown, M. K. 1979. Two old beavers from the Adirondacks. New York Fish and Game Journal 26:92.
Brown, R. Z. 1953. Social behavior, reproduction, and population changes in the house mouse (*Mus musculus* L.). Ecological Monographs 23:217–240.
*Bruce, J. A. 1937. *Sorex longirostris longirostris* in Augusta County, Virginia. Journal of Mammalogy 18(4):513–514.
*Bruce, P. A. 1924. History of Virginia. Volume I. Colonial period, 1607–1763. Chicago: American Historical Society.
*Bruggemann, E. P. 1992. Rabies in the mid-Atlantic states — should raccoons be vaccinated? Bioscience 42(9):694–699.
*Bryant, C. P., R. W. Young, and R. L. Kirkpatrick. 1978. Kepone residues in body tissues of raccoons collected along the James River, east of Hopewell, Virginia. Virginia Journal of Science 29(2):57. Abstract.
*Bryant, K. P. 1968. Letters. Wildlife hazards. Virginia Wildlife 29(4):3.
Buchler, E. R. 1975. Food transit time in *Myotis lucifugus* (Chiroptera: Vespertilionidae). Journal of Mammalogy 56(1):252–255.
*Buchler, E. R. 1976. The use of echolocation by the wandering shrew *(Sorex vagrans).* Animal Behaviour 24::858–873.
*Buckland, D. E. 1974. Blood urea nitrogen levels of white-tailed deer as an index of condition and nutritional intake. Master's thesis, Virginia Polytechnic Institute and State University, Blacksburg.
*Buckland, D. E., W. A. Abler, R. L. Kirkpatrick, and J. B. Whelan. 1975. Improved husbandry system for rearing fawns in captivity. Journal of Wildlife Management 39(1):211–214.
*Buckland, D. E., W. A. Abler, E. T. Reed, R. L. Kirkpatrick, and P. F. Scanlon. 1973. Breeding behavior of captive male white-tailed deer. Virginia Journal of Science 24:112. Abstract.
*Buckman, E. 1948. Shooting wildlife — camera style. Virginia Wildlife 9(3):14–15.
Buckner, C. H. 1957. Home range of *Synaptomys cooperi.* Journal of Mammalogy 38(1):132.
*Buffon's natural history of man, the globe, and of quadrupeds, with additions from Cuvier, Lacepede, and other eminent naturalists. 1885. Volume II. New York: John W. Lovell Company.
*Bullock, W. 1649. Virginia impartially examined. Printed by John Hammond, London.
*Bulmer, W., and P. King. 1992. Distribution of long-tailed shrews in northwestern Fairfax County. Virginia Journal of Science 43(2):229. Abstract.
*Burnaby, A. 1775. Travels through the middle settlements in North America in the years 1759 and 1760, with observations upon the state of the colonies. London: 3d ed. (Reprinted 1970 by Augustus M. Kelley, Publishers, New York.)
*Burnett, C. D., and T. H. Kunz. 1982. Growth rates and age estimation in *Eptesicus fuscus* and comparison with *Myotis lucifugus.* Journal of Mammalogy 63(1):33–41.
*Burnham, W. J. 1998. Chasing a ghost: has the mountain lion returned to the Blue Ridge? Blue Ridge Country 11(4):34–37.
Burns, J. J. 1964. Movements of a tagged weasel in Alaska. Murrelet 45(1):10.
*Burt, W. H. 1957. Mammals of the Great Lakes region. Ann Arbor: University of Michigan Press.
Burt, W. H., and R. P. Grossenheider. 1976. A field guide to the mammals. Boston: Houghton Mifflin Company.
*Burton. W. 1980. The creature from Eastern Bay. Chesapeake Bay Magazine, November.
Butterworth, B. B. 1969. Postnatal growth and development of *Ursus americanus.* Journal of Mammalogy 50(3):615–616.
*Byers, R. E. 1976. New compound (RH 787) for use in control of orchard voles. Journal of Wildlife Management 40(1):169–171.
Byers, R. E., and M. H. Merson. 1982. Current improvements in baiting pine and meadow voles. Proceedings of the Vertebrate Pest Conference 10:139–142.
*Byrd, M. A. 1951. The economic importance of the muskrat in Virginia, with particular emphasis on Montgomery, a mountainous county. Master's thesis, Virginia Polytechnic Institute and State University, Blacksburg.
*Byrd, M. A. 1952a. Sex and age ratios in the muskrat. Virginia Journal of Science 3:297. Abstract.
*Byrd, M. A. 1952b. High occurrence of *Taenia taeniaformis* in the muskrat. Virginia Journal of Science 3:298. Abstract.
*Byrd, M. A. 1953. Virginia's flying mammals — the bats. Virginia Wildlife 14(7):18–19, 22.
*Byrd, M. A. 1954. Ecological succession on abandoned farmland and its relationship to wildlife production

in Cumberland County, Virginia. Doctoral dissertation, Virginia Polytechnic Institute and State University, Blacksburg.

*Byrd, M. A. 1956. Relation of ecological succession to farm game in Cumberland County in the Virginia Piedmont. Journal of Wildlife Management 20:188–195.

Cadenat, J. 1959. Notes sur les Delphinides Ouest-Africains. VI. Le gros Dauphin gris *(Tursiops truncatus)* est-il capable de faire des plongees profondes. Bulletin of the Institute Franc Afrique Noire, series A, 21:1137–1143.

Cahalane, V. H. 1942. Caching and recovery of food by the western fox squirrel. Journal of Wildlife Management 6(4):338–352.

*Cahalane, V. H. 1944. Buffalo — wild or tame? American Forests, Oct. 1944:472–475.

*Cahalane, V. H. 1947. Mammals of North America. New York: Macmillan Company.

*Cahalane, V. H. 1948. The status of mammals in the United States National Park system, 1947. Journal of Mammalogy 29(3):247–259.

*Cahalane, V. H., (editor). 1967. The imperial collection of Audubon animals. Maplewood, New Jersey: Hammond.

Caldwell, D. K. 1955. Evidence of home range of an Atlantic bottlenose dolphin. Journal of Mammalogy 36(2):304–305.

Caldwell, D. K. 1961. The harbor seal in South Carolina. Journal of Mammalogy 42(3):425.

Caldwell, D. K., and M. C. Caldwell. 1971. Underwater pulsed sounds produced by captive spotted dolphins, *Stenella plagiodon*. Cetology 1:1–7.

*Caldwell, D. K., and M. C. Caldwell. 1989. Pygmy sperm whale *Kogia breviceps* (de Blainville, 1838): Dwarf sperm whale *Kogia simus* Owen, 1866. Pp. 235–260. In: Ridgeway, S. H., and S. R. Harrison (editors), Handbook of Marine Mammals. Volume 4. River dolphins and the larger toothed whales. New York: Academic Press.

Caldwell, M. C., and D. K. Caldwell. 1966. Epimeletic (care-giving) behavior in Cetacea. Pp. 755–789. In: Norris, K. S. (editor), Whales, Dolphins, and Porpoises. Berkeley: University of California Press.

Caldwell, M. C., D. K. Caldwell, and J. F. Miller. 1973. Statistical evidence for individual whistles in the spotted dolphin, *Stenella plagcidon*. Cetology 16:1–21.

*Caldwell, M. C., D. K. Caldwell, and J. B. Siebenaler. 1965. Observations on captive and wild Atlantic bottlenosed dolphins, *Tursiops truncatus*, in the northeastern Gulf of Mexico. Los Angeles County Museum Contributions in Science no. 91.

Calhoun, J. B. 1941. Distribution and food habits of mammals in the vicinity of the Reelfoot Lake Biological Station. Journal of the Tennessee Academy of Science 16:177–185, 207–225.

Calhoun, J. B. 1945. Diel activity rhythms of the rodents, *Microtus ochrogaster* and *Sigmodon hispidus hispidus*. Ecology 26(3):251–273.

*Calhoun, J. B. 1950. North American census of small mammals. Annual report of census made in 1949. Release no. 3. Roscoe B. Jackson Memorial Laboratory.

*Calhoun, J. B. 1951. North American census of small mammals. Annual Report of census made in 1950. Release no. 4. Roscoe B. Jackson Memorial Laboratory.

*Calhoun, J. B. 1956. Population dynamics of vertebrates. Compilations of research data. 1951. Annual report — North American census of small mammals. Release no. 5. Administrative Publication of the United States Department of Health, Education, and Welfare; National Institute of Mental Health.

*Calhoun, J. B., and A. A. Arata. 1957a. Population dynamics of vertebrates. Compilations of research data. 1952. Annual report — North American census of small mammals. Release no. 6. Administrative Publication of the United States Department of Health, Education, and Welfare; National Institute of Mental Health.

*Calhoun, J. B., and A. A. Arata. 1957b. Population dynamics of vertebrates. Compilations of research data. 1953. Annual report — North American census of small mammals. Release no. 7. Administrative Publication of the United States Department of Health, Education, and Welfare; National Institute of Mental Health.

*Calhoun, J. B., and A. A. Arata. 1957c. Population dynamics of vertebrates. Compilations of research data. 1954. Annual report — North American census of small mammals. Release no. 8. Administrative Publication of the United States Department of Health, Education, and Welfare; National Institute of Mental Health.

*Calhoun, J. B., and A. A. Arata. 1957d. Population dynamics of vertebrates. Compilations of research data. 1955 and 1956. Annual reports — North American census of small mammals and certain summaries for the years 1948 and 1956. Release no. 9. Administrative Publication of the United States Department of Health, Education, and Welfare; National Institute of Mental Health.

*Cameron, G. N., and S. R. Spencer. 1981. *Sigmodon hispidus*. Mammalian Species no. 158.

*Campbell, H. W. 1977. *Trichechus manatus* Linnaeus. Pp. 396–397. In: Cooper, J. E., S. S. Robinson, and J. B. Funderburg (editors), Endangered and Threatened Plants and Animals of North Carolina. Raleigh: North Carolina State Museum of Natural History.

Campbell, R. S., and J. T. Cassady. 1954. Moisture and protein forage on Louisiana forest ranges. Journal of Range Management 7(1):41–42.

*Cannaday, D. A. 1950. Trail blazers of southwest Virginia. Virginia Wildlife 11(2):10–12, 23.

*Cantner, D. E. 1957. Nature's busy sanitation crews. Virginia Wildlife 18(12):12–14, 26.

*Caras, R. A. 1967. North American mammals. Furbearing animals of the United States and Canada. New York: Meredith Press.

*Card, W. C. 1981. Nutritional influences on blood characteristics in white-tailed deer. Master's thesis, Virignia Polytechnic Institute and State University, Blacksburg.

*Carey, A. B. 1974. An analysis of an apparent rabies epizootic in Rockbridge County, Virginia. Master's thesis, Virginia Polytechnic Institute and State University, Blacksburg.

*Carey, A. B. 1982. The ecology of red foxes, gray foxes, and rabies in the eastern United States. Wildlife Society Bulletin 10:18–26.

*Carey, A. B., R. H. Giles, and R. G. McLean. 1978. The landscape epidemiology of rabies in Virginia. American Journal of Tropical Medicine and Hygiene 27(3):573–580.

*Carey, A. B., and R. G. McLean. 1978. Rabies antibody prevalence and virus tissue tropism in wild carnivores in Virginia. Journal of Wildlife Diseases 14(4):487–491.

*Carleton, M. D. 1989. Systematics and evolution. Pp. 7–141. In: Kirkland, G. L., Jr., and J. N. Layne (editors), Advances in the study of *Peromyscus* (Rodentia). Lubbock: Texas Tech University Press.

*Carlile, D. W. 1979. The effects of forest thinning on the food-based carrying capacity of a mixed oak forest for white-tailed deer in the ridge and valley province of Virginia. Master's thesis, Virginia Polytechnic Institute and State University, Blacksburg.

*Carlile, D. W., A. R. Tipton, J. B. Whelan, and T. L. Sharik. 1978. Changes in productivity of food for white-tailed deer and wild turkey following a forest thinning operation in the Ridge and Valley province of Virginia. Virginia Journal of Science 29(2):58. Abstract.

*Carlile, D. W., J. B. Whelan, T. L. Sharik, and A. R. Tipton. 1977. The effects of a commercial thinning operation on the quality and quantity of white-tailed deer forage in mixed-oak forests of the Ridge and Valley province of Virginia. Virginia Journal of Science 28(2):62. Abstract.

*Carlile, D. W., J. B. Whelan, and A. R. Tipton. 1977. Use of a mixed-oak forest in the Ridge and Valley province of Virginia by white-tailed deer following a spring fire. Virginia Journal of Science 28(2):62. Abstract.

*Carlson, C. E. 1964. A red fox fatality by self-entrapment. Journal of Mammalogy 45(2):318–319.

*Carney, D. W. 1985. Population dynamics and denning ecology of black bears in Shenandoah National Park, Virginia. Master's thesis, Virginia Polytechnic Institute and State University, Blacksburg.

*Carney, D. W., and M. R. Vaughan. 1987. Survival of introduced black bear cubs in Shenandoah National Park, Virginia. International Conference of Bear Research Management 7:83–85.

*Carney, W. P., P. W. Schilling, A. E. McKee, B. S. Holderman, and J. A. Stunkard. 1970. *Eurytrema procyonis*, a pancreatic fluke of North American carnivores. Journal of Wildlife Diseases 6(4):422–429.

*Carpenter, M. 1956. Reddish Knob — Roadway to the sky. Virginia Wildlife 17(5):19–20.

*Carpenter, M. 1966. Methods of repelling deer in gardens, orchards, and fields in Virginia. Proceedings of the 23rd Annual Conference of Southeastern Game and Fish Commissioners 23:233–235.

*Carpenter, M. 1968. Vital statistics of a deer herd. Virginia Wildlife 29(5):8–9.

*Carpenter, M. 1969. Late returns from black bear tagging study. Virginia Wildlife 30(10):6–7.

*Carpenter, M. 1970. Operation bear trap. Virginia Wildlife 31(3):6–7.

*Carpenter, M. 1971. Some recent coyote records in Virginia. Virginia Wildlife 32(6):14–15.

*Carpenter, M. 1972. The big Powhatan buck. Virginia Wildlife 33(10);20.

*Carpenter, M. 1973. The black bear in Virginia. Richmond: Virginia Commission of Game and Inland Fisheries.

*Carpenter, M. 1975. Some facts about Shenandoah County deer. Virginia Wildlife 36(11):20.

*Carroll, R. P. 1929. Survey of Cedar Creek in the Natural Bridge estate. Game and Fish Conservationist 9(3):53–56.

*Carson, K. A., J. L. Cole, and R. K. Rose. 1994. Ultrastructure of the olfactory epithelium of the short-tailed shrew, *Blarina brevicauda.* Pages 211–216. In: Merritt, J. F., G. L. Kirkland, Jr., and R. K. Rose (editors). Advances in the biology of shrews. Special Publication Number 18, Carnegie Museum of Natural History, Pittsburgh.

*Carter, J. L. 1979. Swimming as a determinate to immigration for two small mammals in coastal Virginia. Master's thesis, Old Dominion University, Norfolk.

*Carter, J. L., and J. F. Merritt. 1981. Evaluation of swimming ability as a means of island invasion by small mammals in coastal Virginia. Annals of the Carnegie Museum 50(2):31–46.

*Carter, R. 1968. The courage of wildlife. Virginia Wildlife 29(9):11, 22.

Carter, T. D. 1955. Remarkable age attained by a bobcat. Journal of Mammalogy 36(2):290.

Caslick, J. W. 1956. Color phases of the roof rat, *Rattus rattus.* Journal of Mammalogy 37(2):255–257.

Casteel, D. A. 1966. Nest building, parturition, and copulation in the cottontail rabbit. American Midland Naturalist 75(1):160–167.

Casteel, D. A. 1967. Timing of ovulation and implantation in the cottontail rabbit. Journal of Wildlife Management 31(1):194–197.

Catesby, M. 1974 (1754). The natural history of Carolina, Florida, and the Bahama Islands. Savannah, Georgia: Beehive Press.

*Catlin, D. 1986. The winter sleepers. Virginia Wildlife 47(2):4–7.

*Caturano, S. L., R. L. Kirkpatrick, and M. H. Merson. 1978. Preliminary studies of digestibility of grass and forb diets by pine voles. Virginia Journal of Science 29(2):58. Abstract.

*Cawthorn, J. M., and R. K. Rose. 1989. The population ecology of the eastern harvest mouse *(Reithro-*

dontomys humulis) in southeastern Virginia. American Midland Naturalist 122(1):1–10.

*Cengel, D. J. 1975. Seasonal comparison of food habitat patterns and reproductive attainment of the pine vole in two northern Virginia orchards. Master's thesis, Virginia Polytechnic Institute and State University, Blacksburg.

*Cengel, D. J., and R. L. Kirkpatrick. 1974a. Pine vole reproduction in two orchard habitats. Virginia Journal of Science 25(2):61. Abstract.

*Cengel, D. J., and R. L. Kirkpatrick. 1974b. Seasonal variation of body fat levels in pine voles. Virginia Journal of Science 25(2):62. Abstract.

*Cengel, D. J., J. E. Estep, and R. L Kirkpatrick. 1978. Pine vole reproduction in relation to food habits and body fat. Journal of Wildlife Management 42(4):822–833.

*Centers for Disease Control. Rabies surveillance report, March and April, 1973. Lawrenceville, Georgia: United States Department of Health, Education and Welfare.

*Centers for Disease Control. 1983. Update: raccoon rabies — mid-Atlantic states. Morbidity and Mortality Weekly Report 32:97–98.

*Centers for Disease Control. 1985. Rabies surveillance annual summary, 1984. Atlanta: Centers for Disease Control.

Chamberlain, A. F. 1963. American Indian legends and beliefs about the squirrel and the chipmunk. Journal of American Folklore 9(32):48–50.

Chambers, R. E. 1959. Job completion report. Pittman-Robertson Investigations Project W-36-R.

*Chandler, M. C. 1984. Life history aspects of *Reithrodontomys humulis* in southeastern Virginia. Master's thesis, Old Dominion University.

*Chandler, M. C., and R. K. Rose. 1984. Life history parameters of the eastern harvest mouse in southeastern Virginia. Virginia Journal of Science 35(2):80.

*Chapman, J. A. 1975. *Sylvilagus transitionalis.* Mammalian Species no. 55.

*Chapman, J. A., K. L. Cramer, N. J. Dippenaar, and T. J. Robinson. 1992. Systematics and biogeography of the New England cottontail, *Sylvilagus transitionalis* (Bangs, 1895), with the description of a new species from the Appalachian Mountains. Proceedings of the Biological Society of Washington 105(4):841–866.

Chapman, J. A., and G. A. Feldhamer (editors), 1982. Wild mammals of North America. Baltimore: The Johns Hopkins University Press.

Chapman, J. A., A. L. Harman, and D. E. Samuel. 1977. Reproductive and physiological cycles in the cottontail complex in western Maryland and nearby West Virginia. Wildlife Monographs 56:1–73.

*Chapman, J. A., J. G. Hockman, and W. R. Edwards. 1982. Cottontails. Pp. 83–123. In: Chapman, J. A., and G. A. Feldhamer (editors), Wild mammals of North America. Baltimore: The Johns Hopkins University Press.

*Chapman, J. A., J. G. Hockman, and M. M. Ojeda C. 1980. *Sylvilagus floridanus.* Mammalian Species no. 136.

Chapman, J. A., J. C. Lanning, G. R. Willner, and D. Pursley. 1980. Embryonic development and resorption in feral nutria *(Myocastor coypus)* from Maryland. Mammalia 44(3):371–379.

Chapman, J. A., and R. P. Morgan. 1973. Systematic status of the cottontail complex in western Maryland and nearby West Virginia. Wildlife Monographs 36:1–54.

*Chapman, J. A., and J. L. Paradiso. 1972. First records of the New England cottontail *(Sylvilagus transitionalis)* from Maryland. Chesapeake Science 13(2):148–149.

Chapman, J. A., and J. R. Stauffer, Jr. 1981. The status and distribution of the New England cottontail. Pp. 973–983. In: Myers, K., and C.D. MacInnes (editors), Proceedings of the World Lagomorph Conference. Guelph, Ontario. August 1979.

*Chapman, J. A., and G. R. Willner. 1981. *Sylvilagus palustris.* Mammalian Species no. 153.

*Charlton, E. R., Jr. 1976. Just lion around. Virginia Wildlife 37(5):23.

*Chasseur. 1875. The Nottoway region. Forest and Stream 5(16):242.

*Chickering, J. W., Jr. 1873. The flora of the Dismal Swamp. American Naturalist 7:521–524.

*Chitwood, B. G. 1931. *Physaloptera praeputialis* from *Urocyon* sp., in Virginia and *Lynx rufus,* Nevada. Journal of Parasitology 18:53.

Choate, J. R. 1970. Systematics and zoogeography of middle American shrews of the genus *Cryptotis.* University of Kansas Publications, Museum of Natural History 19:195–317.

*Choate, J. R., and H. H. Genoways. 1975. Collections of recent mammals in North America. Journal of Mammalogy 56(2):452–502.

*Christian, J. J., V. Flyger, and D. E. Davis. 1960. Factors in the mass mortality of a herd of sika deer, *Cervus nippon.* Chesapeake Science 1:79–95.

*Church, J. 1805. A cabinet of quadrupeds with historical and scientific descriptions. 2 vols. Printed for Darton and Harvey: London.

*Church M. L. 1925. *Mustela allegheniensis* in North Carolina. Journal of Mammalogy 6(4):281.

*Churcher, C. S. 1959. The specific status of the New World red fox. Journal of Mammalogy 40(4):513–520.

*Clapp, R. B., J. S. Weske, and T. C. Clapp. 1976. Establishment of the black-tailed jackrabbit on the Virginia Eastern Shore. Journal of Mammalogy 57(1):180–181.

*Clark, A. H. 1925. Animals of land and sea. New York: D. Van Nostrand Company.

*Clark, A. H. 1939. Some Pleistocene mammals from Warren County, Virginia. Science 88(2273):82. Also, The Raven 10(4, 5):6–7.

*Clark, B. K., B. S. Clark, and D. M. Leslie, Jr. 1990. Endangered Ozark big-eared bat eaten by eastern woodrat. Prairie Naturalist 22(4):273–274.

Clark, D. R., Jr. 1978. Uptake of dietary PCB by pregnant big brown bats *(Eptesicus fuscus)* and their fetuses. Bulletin of Environmental Contamination and Toxicology 19:707–714.

Clark, D. R., Jr. 1979. Lead concentrations: bats vs. terrestrial small mammals collected near a major highway. Environmental Science and Technology 13(3):338–341.

Clark, D. R., Jr. 1981. Bats and environmental contaminants: a review. United States Department of the Interior, Fish and Wildlife Service Special Scientific Report — Wildlife no. 235, Washington DC.

Clark, D. R., Jr. 1986. Toxicity of methyl parathion to bats: mortality and coordination loss. Environmental Toxicology and Chemistry 5:191–195.

Clark, D. R., Jr. 1987. Orthene toxicity to little brown bats *(Myotis lucifugus):* acetylcholinesterase inhibition, coordination loss, and mortality. Environmental Toxicology and Chemistry 6:705–708.

Clark, D. R., Jr. 1988. How sensitive are bats to insecticides? Wildlife Society Bulletin 16:399–403.

*Clark, D. R., Jr., and C. M. Bunck. 1991. Trends in North American small mammals found in common barn-owl *(Tyto alba)* dietary studies. Canadian Journal of Zoology 69:3093–3102.

Clark, D. R., Jr., C. M. Bunck, and E. Cromartie. 1983. Year and age effects on residues of dieldrin and heptachlor in dead gray bats, Franklin County, Missouri -1976, 1977, and 1978. Environmental Toxicology and Chemistry 2:387–393.

Clark, D. R., Jr., R. L. Clawson, and C. J. Stafford. 1983. Gray bats killed by dieldrin at two additional Missouri caves: aquatic macroinvertebrates found dead. Bulletin of Environmental Contamination and Toxicology 30:214–218.

Clark, D. R., Jr., and A. Krynitsky. 1978. Organochlorine residues and reproduction in the little brown bat, Laurel, Maryland — June 1976. Pesticides Monitoring Journal 12(3):113–116.

Clark, D. R., Jr., and T. G. Lamont. 1976a. Organochlorine residues and reproduction in the big brown bat. Journal of Wildlife Management 40(2):249–254.

Clark, D. R., Jr., and T. G. Lamont. 1976b. Organochlorine residues in females and nursing young of the big brown bat *(Eptesicus Fuscus).* Bulletin of Environmental Contamination and Toxicology 15(1):1–8.

*Clark, D. R., Jr., R. K. LaVal, and D. M. Swineford. 1978. Dieldrin-induced mortality in an endangered species, the gray bat *(Myotis grisescens).* Science 199:1357–1359.

Clark, D. R., Jr., and R. M. Prouty. 1976. Organochlorine residues in three bat species from four localities in Maryland and West Virginia, 1973. Pesticides Monitoring Journal 10(2):44–53.

Clark, D. R., Jr., and R. M. Prouty. 1984. Disposition of dietary dieldrin in the little brown bat and correlation of skin levels with body burden. Bulletin of Environmental Contamination and Toxicology 33:177–183.

Clark, F. H. 1938. Age of sexual maturity in mice of the genus *Peromyscus.* Journal of Mammalogy 19(2):230–234.

*Clark, G. 1968. Letters. Wildlife hazards. Virginia Wildlife 29(4):3.

*Clark, M. K. (editor). 1987. Endangered, threatened, and rare fauna of North Carolina. Occasional Papers of the North Carolina Biological Survey, 1987–3.

*Clark, M. K., and D. S. Lee. 1987. Big-eared bat, *Plecotus townsendii,* in western North Carolina. Brimleyana no. 13:137–140.

*Clark, M. K., M. S. Mitchell, and K. S. Karriker. 1993. Notes on the geographical and ecological distribution of relict populations of *Synaptomys cooperi* (Rodentia: Arvicolidae) from eastern North Carolina. Brimleyana 19:155–167.

*Clarke, S. 1670. Plantations of the English in America. London.

Clawson, R. L., and D. R. Clark, Jr., 1989. Pesticide contamination of endangered gray bats and their food base in Boone County, Missouri, 1982. Bulletin of Environmental Contamination and Toxicology 42(3): 431–437.

*Clayton, J. 1693. II. A continuation of Mr. John Clayton's account of Virginia. Of the earth and soyl. Philosophical Transactions of the Royal Society of London 17(205):941–948.

*Clayton, J. 1694. III. A continuation of Mr. John Clayton's account of Virginia. On the beasts and serpents of Virginia. Philosophical Transactions of the Royal Society of London 18(210):121–135.

*Clements, R. J. 1973. Raccoon movements as an indicator of transplant stocking effectiveness and socioeconomic aspects of raccoon hunting. Master's thesis, Virginia Polytechnic Institute and State University, Blacksburg.

*Clifford, C. M., G. Anastos, and A. Eibl. 1961. The larval ixodid ticks of the eastern United States (Acarina: Ixodidae). Miscellaneous Publications, Entomological Society of America 2(3):213–237.

*Clifford, R. 1967. A memorable 'coon hunt. Virginia Wildlife 28(2):10–11.

Clifford, R. C. 1967. Interesting facts about wildlife. Virginia Wildlife 28(6):7.

*Clifford, R. C. 1968. Only old bonehead knows (and he isn't telling). Virginia Wildlife 29(2):10–11.

*Clifton, E. E. 1962. A bear with a bow. Virginia Wildlife 23(10):11, 16.

*Cline, G. A. 1988. Habitat relationships of bobwhite quail and cottontail rabbits on agricultural lands in Halifax County, Virignia. Master's thesis, Virginia Polytechnic Institute and State University, Blacksburg.

*Clinton, D. 1815. Introductory discourse, delivered before the Literary and Philosophical Society of New-York, on the Fourth of May, 1814. New York: David Longworth. Included *in* Contributions to the history of American natural history. Introduction K. B. Sterling. New York: Arno Press.

*Coale, C. B. 1878. The life and adventures of Wilburn Waters, the famous hunter and trapper of White Top Mountain; embracing early history of southwestern Virginia. Richmond: G. W. Gary and Company. (Reprinted 1976 by Commonwealth Press, Radford, Virginia.)

*Cochran, A. R. 1946. Forests and game. Virginia Wildlife 7(1):7–8, 10.

*Cochran, B. 1970. Rabbits are no. 1 in his book. Virginia Wildlife 31(11):4–5.

*Cochran, B. 1971. Squirrels: no. 1 game target. Virginia Wildlife 32(9):4–5.

*Cochran, B. 1990. Trophy tales. Virginia Wildlife 51(8):21–25.

*Cochran, B. 1995. Hog wild. The Roanoke Times, December 25, 1995:B6.

*Cocking, D., R. Hayes, M. L. King, M. J. Rohrer, R. Thomas, and D. Ward. 1991. Compartmentalization of mercury in biotic components of terrestrial flood plain ecosystems adjacent to the South River at Waynesboro, Va. Water, Air and Soil Pollution 57–58:159–170.

*Cockrum, E. L. 1952. Mammals of Kansas. University of Kansas Publications, Museum of Natural History 7(1):1–303.

*Cockrum, E. L. 1955. Reproduction in North American bats. Transactions of the Kansas Academy of Science 58:487–511.

Cockrum, E. L. 1956. Homing, movements, and longevity of bats. Journal of Mammalogy 37(1):48–57.

*Coe, R. J. 1974. The causes of bias in white-tailed deer kill data. Master's thesis, Virginia Polytechnic Institute and State University, Blacksburg.

*Coe, R. J., R. L. Downing, and B. S. McGinnes. 1980. Sex and age bias in hunter-killed white-tailed deer. Journal of Wildlife Management 44(1):245–249.

*Coffey, W. 1971. Outdoors. Bristol *Herald Courier,* March 7, 1971: 8c.

*Coggin, J. L. 1954. A wildlife survey of Patrick County, Virginia. Master's thesis, Virginia Polytechnic Institute and State University, Blacksburg.

*Coggin, J. L. 1955a. Along forest waterways. Virginia Wildlife 16(9):16–18.

*Coggin, J. L. 1955b. Winter and wildlife. Virginia Wildlife 12(2):5–7, 19.

*Coggin, J. L. 1956a. Fascination abounds in the flora and fauna of high altitude country. Virginia Wildlife 17(2):8–10.

*Coggin, J. L. 1956b. Meadows of Dan. Virginia Wildlife 17(6):21–23.

*Coggin, J. L. 1957. Opossum hunt, mountain style. Virginia Wildlife 18(1):16–17.

*Coggin, J. L. 1971. A look at the 1970 deer season (west). Virginia Wildlife 32(4):10–11.

*Coggin, J. L. 1973. Gray squirrel nesting study. Virginia Wildlife 34(4):18–19.

*Coggin, J. L. 1974. Report on fox squirrels in Virginia. Virginia Commission of Game and Inland Fisheries, Richmond.

*Coggin, J. L. 1975. Collecting and interpreting harvest facts. Virginia Wildlife 36(10):18–20.

*Coggin, J. L. 1980a. The bobcat. Virginia Wildlife 41(1):23.

*Coggin, J. L. 1980b. Sly as a fox. Virginia Wildlife 41(2):23.

*Coggin, J. L. 1980c. The raccoon. Virginia Wildlife 41(3):24.

*Coggin, J. 1987. Virginia's whitetails. Research. Virginia Wildlife 48(11):20–23.

*Coleman, S. 1979. The gray squirrel. Virginia Wildlife 40(11):23.

Coles, R. W. 1970. Pharyngeal and lingual adaptations in the beaver. Journal of Mammalogy 51(2):424–425.

*Collins, J. M. 1973. Some aspects of reproduction and age structures in the black bear in North Carolina. Proceedings of the 27th Annual Conference of Southeastern Game and Fish Commissioners 27:163–170.

*Comer, J. A., W. R. Davidson, A. K. Prestwood, and V. F. Nettles. 1991. An update on the distribution of *Parelaphostrongylus tenuis* in the southeastern United States. Journal of Wildlife Diseases 27(2):348–354.

*Comly, L. M. 1993. Survival, reproduction, and movements of translocated nuisance black bears in Virginia. Master's thesis, Virginia Polytechnic Institute and State University, Blacksburg.

Conaway, C. H. 1952. Life history of the water shrew *(Sorex palustris navigator).* American Midland Naturalist 48(1):219–248.

Conaway, C. H. 1958. Maintenance, reproduction, and growth of the least shrew in captivity. Journal of Mammalogy 39(4):507–512.

Conaway, C. H. 1959. The reproductive cycle of the eastern mole. Journal of Mammalogy 40(2):180–194.

*Conaway, C. H., and D. W. Pfitzer. 1952. *Sorex palustris* and *Sorex dispar* from the Great Smoky Mountains National Park. Journal of Mammalogy 33(1):106–108.

Conley, D. W. 1980. The taxonomic and biochemical relationships of the opossum in eastern North America. Master's thesis, Frostburg State University.

*Conlogue, G. J., J. A. Odgen, and W. J. Foreyt. 1980. Pediculosis and severe heartworm infection in a harbor seal. Veterinary Medicine Small Animal Clinic 75(7):1184–1187.

*Conner, P. F. 1960. The small mammals of Otsego and Schoharie counties, New York. New York State Museum of Science Service Bulletin 382:1–84.

*Conners, J. A. 1988. Shenandoah National Park: An interpretive guide. Blacksburg, Virginia: The McDonald & Woodward Publishing Company.

Connor, P. F. 1959. The bog lemming *Synaptomys cooperi* in southern New Jersey. Publications of the Museum, Michigan State University, Biological Series 1:161–248.

Conrad, L. G. 1961. Distribution and speciation problems concerning the long-eared bat, *Plecotus townsendii virginianus.* D. C. Speleograph 17:49–52.

*Conrad, L. G. 1964. Bat banding in Virginia and West Virginia. Bulletin of the National Speleological Society 26(2):61.

Constantine, D. G. 1967. Rabies transmission by air in bat caves. Public Health Service Publication no. 1617.

*Cook, D. B. and S. B. Robeson. 1945. Varying hare and forest succession. Ecology 26(4):406–410.

*Cooke, J. A., and C. R. Terman. 1975. The influence of displacement distance and vision on the homing behavior of the white-footed mouse *(Peromyscus* *feucopus [sic] noveboracensis).* Virginia Journal of Science 26(2):53.

*Cooke, J. A., and C. R. Terman. 1977. Influence of displacement distance and vision on homing behavior of the white-footed mouse *(Peromyscus leucopus noveboracensis).* Journal of Mammalogy 58(1):58–66.

*Cooley, P. 1980. Beaver basics. Virginia Wildlife 41(1):9–11.

*Cooley, R. A., and G. M. Kohls. 1945. The genus *Ixodes* in North America. National Institutes of Health Bulletin no. 184.

*Cooper, J. E. 1960. Collective notes on cave-associated vertebrates. Baltimore Grotto News 3(10):152–158.

*Cooper, J. E. 1961. Cave records for the salamander *Plethodon richmondi richmondi* Pope, with notes on additional cave-associated species. Herpetologica 17(4):250–255.

*Cope, E. D. 1865a. Note on a species of whale occurring on the coasts of the United States. Proceedings of the Academy of Natural Sciences of Philadelphia:168–169.

*Cope, E. D. 1865b. Note on a species of hunchback whale. Proceedings of the Academy of Natural Sciences of Philadelphia:178–181.

*Cope, E. D. 1866a. [Description of the cranium of a blackfish from Delaware Bay, and note on a whale from Mobjack Bay, Virginia.] Proceedings of the Academy of Natural Sciences of Philadelphia:7–8.

*Cope, E. D. 1866b. Third contribution to the history of the Balaenidae and Delphinidae. Proceedings of the Academy of Natural Sciences of Philadelphia:293–300.

*Cope, E. D. 1867a. Specimens of four extinct species of Mammalia. Proceedings of the Academy of Natural Sciences of Philadelphia:131–132.

*Cope, E. D. 1867b. Remarks on the contents of caves of southwestern Virginia. Proceedings of the Academy of Natural Sciences of Philadelphia:137–138.

*Cope, E. D. 1867c. An addition to the vertebrate fauna of the Miocene period, with a synopsis of the extinct Cetacea of the United States. Proceedings of the Academy of Natural Sciences of Philadelphia:138.

*Cope, E. D. 1868. Observations on the living inhabitants of caves in southwestern Virginia. Proceedings of the Academy of Natural Sciences of Philadelphia:85–86.

*Cope, E. D. 1869. Synopsis of the extinct Mammalia of the cave formations in the United States. Proceedings of the American Philosophical Society 11:171–192.

*Cope, E. D. 1871. Observations on the fauna of the southern Alleghanies. American Naturalist 4:392–402.

Cope, J. B., and S. R. Humphrey. 1967. Homing experiments with the evening bat, *Nycticeius humeralis.* Journal of Mammalogy 48(1):136.

Cope, J. B., and S. R. Humphrey. 1977. Spring and autumn swarming behavior in the Indiana bat, *Myotis sodalis.* Journal of Mammalogy 58(1):93–95.

*Copenhaver, E. H. 1938. About game in Virginia. Virginia Wildlife 1(10):3.

*Cordes, C. L., and F. S. Barkalow, Jr. 1972. Home range and dispersal in a North Carolina gray squirrel population. Proceedings of the 26th Annual Conference of the Southeastern Association of Game and Fish Commissioners 26:124–135.

Cornish, L. M., and W. N. Bradshaw. 1978. Patterns in twelve reproductive parameters for the white-footed mouse *(Peromyscus leucopus).* Journal of Mammalogy 59(4):731–739.

*Cornwell, G. W. 1966. Cottontails. Virginia Wildlife 27(6):16.

*Cory, C. B. 1912. The mammals of Illinois and Wisconsin. Museum of Natural History Publication 153. Zoological series 11.

*Cosgrove, G. E., L. C. Satterfield, and V. F. Nettles. 1981. Neoplasia. Pp. 62–71. In: Davidson, W. R., F. A. Hayes, V. F. Nettles, and F. E. Kellogg (editors), Diseases and parasites of white-tailed deer. Miscellaneous Publication no. 7, Tall Timbers Research Station, Tallahassee, Florida.

*Cothran, A. 1961. Hunting Virginia's elk. Virginia Wildlife 22(11):18–19.

Cottam, C. 1945. Speed and endurance of the coyote. Journal of Mammalogy 26(1):94.

*Cottam, C., A. L. Nelson, and T. E. Clarke. 1939. Notes on early winter food habits of the black bear in George Washington National Forest. Journal of Mammalogy 20(3):310–314.

Cottrell, W. 1978. The fisher *(Martes pennanti)* in Maryland. Journal of Mammalogy 59(4):886.

*Couch, C. R. and J. F. Pagels. 1996. Temporal variation in shrew assemblages: a pitfall removal study. Virginia Journal of Science 47(2):150. Abstract.

*Coues, E. 1871. Former eastward range of the buffalo. American Naturalist 5:719–720.

*Coues, E. 1876. Some account, critical, descriptive, and historical, of *Zapus hudsonius.* Bulletin of the United States Geological Survey of the Territories, series 2(1):253–262.

*Coues, E. 1877. Fur-bearing animals: a monograph of North American Mustelidae. United States Department of the Interior Miscellaneous Publication no. 8.

*Coues, E., and J. A. Allen. 1877. Monographs of North American Rodentia. I–XI. Report of the United States Geological Survey of the Territories 11:1–1091.

*Couvillion, C. E. 1981. A comparison of summer and fall abomasal parasite counts (APC) of southeastern white-tailed deer. Master's thesis, University of Georgia, Athens.

*Couvillion, C. E., C. B. Crow, and W. R. Davidson. 1982. An evaluation of hunter-killed white-tailed deer for abomasal parasite count (APC) studies. Proceeding of the 36th Annual Conference of the Southeastern Association of Fish and Wildlife Agencies 36:427–435.

*Couvillion, C. E., W. R. Davidson, and V. F. Nettles. 1985. Distribution of *Elaeophora schneideri* in white-tailed deer in the southeastern United States, 1962–1983. Journal of Wildlife Diseases 21(4):451–453.

*Couvillion, C. E., V. F. Nettles, W. R. Davidson, J. E. Pearson, and G. A. Gustafson. 1981. Hemorrhagic disease among white-tailed deer in the Southeast from 1971 through 1980. Proceedings of the Annual Meeting of the United States Animal Health Association 85:522–537.

Cowan, W. F. 1985. Longevity record for a wild raccoon, *Procyon lotor,* in Manitoba. Canadian Field-Naturalist 99(1):115.

*Cowles, C. J. 1974. Ovarian and uterine changes of gray squirrels as affected by season, age, reproductive state, and exogenous hormones. Master's thesis, Virginia Polytechnic Institute and State University, Blacksburg.

*Cowles, C. J., R. L. Kirkpatrick, and J. O. Newel. 1974. Adrenal weights of gray squirrels as affected by season, sex, and age. Virginia Journal of Science 25(2):62. Abstract.

*Cowles, C. J., R. L. Kirkpatrick, and J. O. Newel. 1977. Ovarian follicular changes in gray squirrels as affected by season, age, and reproductive state. Journal of Mammalogy 58(1):67–73.

*Cowles, C. J., R. L. Kirkpatrick, and P. F. Scanlon. 1978. A comparison of microscopic to macroscopic counts of luteal glands in the gray squirrel. Virginia Journal of Science 29(2):59. Abstract.

*Coyle, J. F. 1981. Some effects of picnickers on a gray squirrel population. Virginia Journal of Science 32(3):89. Abstract.

Crabb, W. D. 1941. Food habits of the prairie spotted skunk in southeastern Iowa. Journal of Mammalogy 22(4):349–364.

Crabb, W. D. 1944. Growth, development, and seasonal weights of spotted skunks. Journal of Mammalogy 25(3):213–221.

Crabb, W. D. 1948. The ecology and management of the prairie spotted skunk in Iowa. Ecological Monographs 18:201–232.

*Crable, A. 1982. The whitetail in Virginia. Virginia Wildlife 43(11):4–7.

Crandall, L. S. 1964. The management of wild mammals in captivity. Chicago: The University of Chicago Press.

*Cranford, J. A. 1984. Prey biased killing behavior of least weasels *(Mustela nivalis).* Virginia Journal of Science 35(2):81. Abstract.

*Cranford, J. A. 1985. Differential effects of 6-MBOA on reproduction in small mammals. Virginia Journal of Science 36(2):107. Abstract.

*Cranford, J. A. 1986. Stimulation of small mammal reproduction in the field with 6-MBOA. Virginia Journal of Science 37(2):61. Abstract.

*Cranford, J. A. 1989a. The mouse that hops like a kangaroo. The Virginia Explorer 5(8):5–7.

*Cranford, J. A. 1989b. Hibernation in the eastern chipmunk *(Tamias striatus):* age and sex specific differences. Virginia Journal of Science 40(2):55. Abstract.

*Cranford, J. A. 1990. Winter sleep. The Virginia Explorer 6(2):4–8.

*Cranford, J. A. 1991. Eastern chipmunk *(Tamias striatus)* nests, activity, and food hoarding. Virginia Journal of Science 42(2):168. Abstract.

*Cranford, J. A. 1993a. Mammalian pest species in urban and suburban environments. Virginia Journal of Science 44(2):110. Abstract.

*Cranford, J. A., and T. L. Derting. 1983. Intra and interspecific behavior of *Microtus pennsylvanicus* and *Microtus pinetorum.* Behavioral Ecology and Sociobiology 13(1):7–11.

*Cranford, J. A., T. L. Derting, and D. H. Pistole. 1980. Demographic patterns of *Microtus pennsylvanicus* populations in old field communities. Virginia Journal of Science 31(4):98. Abstract.

*Cranford, J. A., and D. S. Fortune. 1994a. Small mammal population dynamics at Mt. Lake Biological Station. Virginia Journal of Science 45(2):57. Abstract.

*Cranford, J. A., and D. S. Fortune. 1994b. Mexican free-tailed bats at Mt. Lake Biological Station! Virginia Journal of Science 45(2):111. Abstract.

*Cranford, J. A., and E. O. Johnson. 1989. Effects of coprophagy and diet quality on two microtine rodents *(Microtus pennsylvanicus* and *Microtus pinetorum).* Journal of Mammalogy 70(3):494–502.

*Cranford, J. A., and M. S. Maly. 1986. Habitat associations among small mammals in an oldfield community on Butt Mountain, Virginia. Virginia Journal of Science 37(3):172–176.

*Cranford, J. A., and M. S. Maly. 1988. Small mammal associations on Chincoteague National Wildlife Refuge, Assateague Island, Virginia. Virginia Journal of Science 39(2):111. Abstract.

*Cranford, J. A., and M. S. Maly. 1990. Small mammal population densities and habitat associations on Chincoteague National Wildlife Refuge, Assateague Island, Virginia. Virginia Journal of Science 41(4A): 321–329.

*Cranford, J. A., and D. Tomblin. 1993b. Habitat preferance shifts in *Peromyscus leucopus* (white-footed mice) when infected with bot fly larva. Virginia Journal of Science 44(2):110. Abstract.

*Cranford, J. A., and J. O. Wolff. 1986. Stimulation of reproduction in *Peromyscus leucopus* and *Peromyscus maniculatus* with 6-MBOA in the field. Virginia Journal of Science 37(4):240–247.

*Crawford, H. S. 1976. Woody plants selected by beavers in the Appalachian Ridge and Valley Province. United States Department of Agriculture Forest Service Research Paper no. 346, Northeastern Forest Experiment Station.

*Crawford, H. S., J. B. Whelan, R. F. Harlow, and J. E. Skeen. 1975. Deer range potential in selective and clearcut oak-pine stands in southwestern Virginia. United States Forest Service Research Paper SE-134:1–12.

Crichton, E. G., P. H. Krutzsch, and M. Chvapil. 1982. Studies on prolonged spermatozoa survival in Chiroptera -II. The role of zinc in the spermatozoa storage phenomenon. Comparative Biochemistry and Physiology 71A(1):71–77.

*Cross, G. H. 1974. Woodchuck control. Virginia Polytechnic Institution and State University Cooperative Extension Service Publication MT no. 6G Wildlife (revised).

*Cross, G. H. 1976. Moles and their control. Virginia Polytechnic Institution and State University Cooperative Extension Service Publication MT no. 4G Wildlife.

*Cross, R. H., Jr. 1942. A study of the habits and management of the gray squirrel in Virginia (continued). Master's thesis, Virginia Polytechnic Institute, Blacksburg.

*Cross, R. H., Jr. 1946. The gray squirrel. Virginia Wildlife 7(2):14, 20.

*Cross, R. H., Jr. 1947. Cottontail rabbits. Virginia Wildlife 8(4):6–8.

*Cross, R. H., Jr. 1948. The bobcat. Virginia Wildlife 9(3):19–20.

*Cross, R. H., Jr. 1949. Squirrels in September? Virginia Wildlife 10(9):8–9.

*Cross, R. H., Jr. 1950. Virginia's elk herds. Virginia Wildlife 11(6):10–11, 22.

*Cross, R. H., Jr. 1959. Virginia's deer, bear, and turkey kill for 1958–59. Virginia Wildlife 20(5):13.

*Cross, R. H., Jr. 1960. Virginia's deer, bear, and turkey kill for 1959–60. Virginia Wildlife 21(4):11.

*Cross, R. H., Jr. 1962. Virginia's deer, bear, and turkey kill for 1961–62. Virginia Wildlife 23(5):12.

*Cross, R. H., Jr. 1972. Responding to the challenge. Virginia Wildlife 33(3):9–11.

Crowcroft, P. 1955. Territoriality in wild house mice, *Mus musculus* L. Journal of Mammalogy 36(2):299–301.

*Crum, J. M., R. Fayer, and A. K. Prestwood. 1981. *Sarcocystis* spp. in white-tailed deer I. Definitive and intermediate host spectrum with a description of *Sarcocystis odocoileocanis* n. sp. Journal of Wildlife Diseases 17(4):567–579.

*Crum, J. M., V. F. Nettles, and W. R. Davidson. 1978. Studies on endoparasites of the black bear *(Ursus americanus)* in the southeastern United States. Journal of Wildlife Diseases 14(2):178–186.

*Crum, J. M., and A. K. Prestwood. 1977. Transmission of *Sarcocystis leporum* from a cottontail rabbit to domestic cats. Journal of Wildlife Diseases 13(2):174–175.

*Crum, J. M., and A. K. Prestwood. 1982. Prevalence and distribution of *Sarcocystis* spp. among white-tailed deer of the southeastern United States. Journal of Wildlife Diseases 18(2):195–203.

*Currier, M. J. P. 1983. *Felis concolor.* Mammalian Species no. 200.

*Curtis, J. M. 1983a. The white-footed deer mouse. Virginia Wildlife 44(1):4–5.

*Curtis, J. M. 1983b. The little brown bat. Virginia Wildlife 44(8):23.

*Curtis, R. L., Jr. 1971. Climatic factors influencing hunter sightings of deer on the Broad Run research area. Master's thesis, Virginia Polytechnic Institute and State University, Blacksburg.

*Curtis, R. L., Jr., H. S. Mosby, and C. T. Cushwa. 1973. The influence of weather on hunter-deer contacts in western Virginia. Proceedings of the 26th Annual Conference of the Southeastern Association of Game and Fish Commissioners 26:282–285.

Cushwa, C. T., R. L. Downing, R. F. Harlow, and D. F. Urbston. 1970. The importance of woody twig ends to deer in the Southeast. United States Department of Agriculture Forest Service Research Paper SE-67, Southeastern Forest Experiment Station, Asheville, North Carolina.

*Cutler, M. R. 1960a. Public hunting and fishing areas in western Virginia. Virginia Wildlife 21(11):16–19.

*Cutler, M. R. 1960b. Public hunting and fishing areas in tidewater Virginia. Virginia Wildlife 21(12):8–9.

*Cuvier, G. 1827. The animal kingdom arranged in conformity with its organization. V. A synopsis of the species of the class Mammalia. London. 392 pp. Reprinted 1840.

*Dalby, P. L., and D. O. Straney. 1975. The relative effectiveness of two sizes of Sherman live traps in capturing *Peromyscus.* Virginia Journal of Science 26(2):53. Abstract.

*Dalby, P. L., and D. O. Straney. 1976. The relative effectiveness of two sizes of Sherman live traps. Acta Theriologica 21(23):311–313.

*Dale, C. K. 1949. Ecology and wildlife potentialities of the Rocky Knob area in Floyd and Patrick counties, Virginia. Master's thesis, Virginia Polytechnic Institute and State University, Blacksburg.

*Dale, P. H. 1967. Letters. Virginia Wildlife 28(6):3.

*Dale, S. 1736. A letter from Samuel Dale, M. L. to Sir Hans Sloane, Bart. President of the Royal Society, containing the descriptions of the moose-deer of New England, and a sort of stag in Virginia; with some remarks relating to Mr. Ray's description of the flying squirrel of America. Philosophical Transactions 39(444):384–389.

*Dalke, P. D. 1937. A preliminary report of the New England cottontail studies. Transactions of the 2d North American Wildlife Conference 2:542–548.

Dalke, P. D. 1942. The cottontail rabbit in Connecticut. Connecticut Geology and Natural History Survey Bulletin 65:1–97.

*Dalton, V. M. 1983. Activity patterns of a maternity colony of *Plecotus townsendii virginianus.* Bat Research News 24:56–57.

*Dalton, V. M. 1987. Distribution, abundance, and status of bats hibernating in caves in Virginia. Virginia Journal of Science 38(4):369–379.

*Dalton, V. M, V. Brack, Jr., and P. M. McTeer. 1986. Food habits of the big-eared bat, *Plecotus townsendii virginianus,* in Virginia. Virginia Journal of Science 37(4):248–254.

*Dalton, V. M., and C. O. Handley, Jr. 1991a. Gray myotis. Pp. 567–569. In: Terwilliger, K. (coordinator), Virginia's endangered species. Blacksburg: The McDonald & Woodward Publishing Company.

*Dalton, V. M., and C. O. Handley, Jr. 1991b. Western big-eared bat. Pp. 573–575. In: Terwilliger, K. (coordinator), Virginia's endangered species. Blacksburg: The McDonald & Woodward Publishing Company.

*Dalton, V. M., and C. O. Handley, Jr. 1991c. Social myotis. Pp. 569–570. In: Terwilliger, K. (coordinator), Virginia's endangered species. Blacksburg: The McDonald & Woodward Publishing Company.

*Daniel, F. L. 1978. The fall and winter food habits of the black bear *(Ursus americanus)* in the Great Dismal Swamp of Virginia. Master's thesis, Old Dominion University, Norfolk.

*Davenport, L. B., Jr. 1951. The economic importance of the black bear in Virginia. Master's thesis, Virginia Polytechnic Institute and State University, Blacksburg.

*Davenport, L. B., Jr. 1953. Agricultural depredation by the black bear in Virginia. Journal of Wildlife Management 17(3):331–340.

*Davey, S. P. 1954. Outlook on deer. Virginia Wildlife 15(11):8–9.

*Davey, S. P. 1955a. The white-tailed deer in Virginia. Education Leaflet no. 14. Virginia Commission of Game and Inland Fisheries.

*Davey, S. P. 1955b. The white-tailed deer in Virginia. Virginia Wildlife 16(8):18–20.

*Davey, S. P. 1955c. A report on the glades deer. Virginia Wildlife 16(9):5–7, 22.

*Davey, S. P. 1956a. Fertility and rearing success measurements of Virginia's deer herds. Proceedings of the 10th Annual Conference of the Southeastern Association of Game and Fish Commissioners 10:47–51.

*Davey, S. P. 1956b. Good dividends in deer anticipated. Virginia Wildlife 17(9):8–9.

*Davey, S. P. 1957. Results of the 1956 deer season west of the Blue Ridge. Virginia Wildlife 18(2):18–19.

*Davey, S. P. 1959. The past, present, and future of Virginia's deer management program. Virginia Wildlife 20(8):5–7.

*Davey, S. P., and J. F. Rodgers. 1961. Deer harvests from a Virginia military area. Virginia Wildlife 22(12):12.

*Davidson, W. R. 1976. Endoparasites of selected populations of gray squirrels *(Sciurus carolinensis)* in the southeastern United States. Proceedings of the Helminthological Society of Washington 43(2):211–217.

*Davidson, W. R., and J. P. Calpin. 1976. *Hepatozoon griseisciuri* infection in gray squirrels of the southeastern United States. Journal of Wildlife Diseases 12(1):72–76.

*Davidson, W. R., and C. B. Crow. 1983. Parasites, diseases, and health status of sympatric populations of sika deer and white-tailed deer in Maryland and Virginia. Journal of Wildlife Diseases 19(4):345–348.

*Davidson, W. R., C. B. Crow, J. M. Crum, and R. R. Gerrish. 1983. Observations on *Theileria cervi* and *Trypanosoma cervi* in white-tailed deer *(Odocoileus virginianus)* from the southeastern United States. Proceedings of the Helminthological Society of Washington 50(1):165–169.

*Davidson, W. R., V. F. Nettles, L. E. Hayes, E. W. Howerth, and C. E. Couvillion. 1992. Diseases diagnosed in gray foxes *(Urocyon cinereoargenteus)* from the southeastern United States. Journal of Wildlife Diseases 28(1):28–33.

*Davidson, W. R., and A. K. Prestwood. 1979. *Apteragia pursglovei* sp.n. (Trichostrongyloidea: Trichostrongylidae) from the white-tailed deer *(Odocoileus virginianus).* Journal of Parasitology 65:280–284.

*Davis, D. E. 1953. Studies on rabbits and spotted fever. Transactions of the 18th North American Wildlife Conference :188–190.

Davis, D. E. 1966. The moult of woodchucks *(Marmota monax).* Mammalia 30:640–644.

Davis, D. E., J. T. Emlen, Jr., and A. W. Stokes. 1948. Studies on home range in the brown rat. Journal of Mammalogy 29(3):207–225.

Davis, D. W. 1969. The behavior and population dynamics of the red squirrel, *Tamiasciurus hudsonicus,* in Saskatchewan. Ph.D. dissertation, University of Arkansas, Fayetteville.

*Davis, H. J. 1971. The Great Dismal Swamp: Its history, folklore, and science. Murfreesboro, North Carolina: Johnson Publishing Company.

*Davis, J. 1945. The Shenandoah. New York: Farrar and Rinehart.

Davis, J. R. 1955. Food habits of the bobcat in Alabama. Master's thesis, Auburn University, Auburn, Alabama.

*Davis, L. S. 1967. Dynamic programming for deer management planning. Journal of Wildlife Management 31(4):667–679.

*Davis, M. 1934. "Great Dismal" pictures. South Atlantic Quarterly 33:171–184.

Davis, R. 1966. Homing performance and homing ability in bats. Ecological Monographs 36:201–237.

Davis, R. 1970. Carrying of young by flying female North American bats. American Midland Naturalist 83(1):186–196.

Davis, R., and E. L. Cockrum. 1963. "Malfunction" of homing ability in bats. Journal of Mammalogy 44(1):131–132.

Davis, R. B., C. F. Herreid II, and H. L. Short. 1962. Mexican free-tailed bats in Texas. Ecological Monographs 32(4):311–346.

Davis, W. B. 1966. The mammals of Texas. Bulletin no. 41, Texas Parks and Wildlife Department, Austin.

Davis, W. H. 1959. Disproportionate sex ratios in hibernating bats. Journal of Mammalogy 40(1):16–19.

*Davis, W. H. 1959. Taxonomy of the eastern pipistrel. Journal of Mammalogy 40(4):521–531.

*Davis, W. H. 1966. Population dynamics of the bat *Pipistrellus subflavus.* Journal of Mammalogy 47(3):383–396.

Davis, W. H., and R. W. Barbour. 1970. Homing in blinded bats *(Myotis sodalis).* Journal of Mammalogy 51(1):182–184.

*Davis, W. H., and R. W. Barbour. 1979. Distributional records of some Kentucky mammals. Transactions of the Kentucky Academy of Sciences 40(3–4):111.

*Davis, W. H., R. W. Barbour, and M. D. Hassell. 1968. Colonial behavior of *Eptesicus fuscus*. Journal of Mammalogy 49(1):44–50.

Davis, W. H., and J. W. Hardin. 1967. Homing in *Lasionycteris noctivagans*. Journal of Mammalogy 48(2):323.

Davis, W. H., and C. L. Rippy. 1968. Distribution of *Myotis lucifugus* and *Myotis austroriparius* in the southeastern United States. Journal of Mammalogy 49(1):113–117.

Dawe, A. R., W. A. Spurrier, and J. A. Armour. 1970. Summer hibernation induced by cryogenically preserved blood "trigger." Science 168:497–498.

*Dawson, J. E., J. E. Childs, K. L. Biggie, C. Moore, D. Stallknecht, J. Shaddock, J. Bouseman, E. Hofmeister, and J. G. Olson. 1994. White-tailed deer as a potential reservoir of *Ehrlichia* spp. Journal of Wildlife Diseases 30(2):162–168.

*Dean, G. W. 1930. Fires and wild life in the Dismal Swamp. Game and Fish Conservationist 10(4):94–95.

*Deans, B. 1979. Impressions of Assateague. Virginia Wildlife 40(12):26–28.

*Dearborn, N. 1932. Foods of some predatory fur-bearing animals in Michigan. University of Michigan School of Forestry and Conservation Bulletin no. 1.

*Dearborn, N. 1946. Miscellaneous notes. Journal of Mammalogy 27(2):178.

Debusk, J., and T. E. Kennerly, Jr. 1975. Homing in the cotton rat, *Sigmodon hispidus* Say and Ord. American Midland Naturalist 93:149–157.

*Decker, A. M. 1977. Elk garden field. Virginia Wildlife 38(4):26.

*Decker, E. 1978. Exotics. Pp. 249–256. In: Schmidt, J. L., and D. L. Gilbert (editors) Big game of North America. Harrisburg, Pennsylvania: Stackpole Books.

*DeGarmo, W. R. 1941. A study in forest wildlife relationships. Master's thesis, Virginia Polytechnic Institute and State University, Blacksburg.

*Deibler, S. R. 1988. Prey species of barn owls in northern Virginia by pellet analysis. Virginia Journal of Science 39(2):112. Abstract.

*DeKay, J. E. 1842. Zoology of New York, or the New York fauna. In: DaKay, J. E., The natural history of New York. Part I. Zoology. Albany: D. Appleton and Company.

*DeLaBarre, C. F. 1941. Planned conservation education in the public schools. Virginia Wildlife 4(3):115–119.

*DeLaBarre, C. F. 1946. Cooperative wildlife management in Virginia. Transactions of the 11th North American Wildlife Conference:313–322.

Delcourt, H. R., and P. A. Delcourt. 1986. Late Quaternary vegetational change in the central Atlantic states. Pp. 23–35. In. McDonald, J. N., and S. O. Bird (editors), The Quaternary of Virginia — A Symposium Volume. Charlottesville: Virginia Department of Mines, Minerals and Energy.

*Delzell, D. E. 1970. The Dismal Swamp — its natural history. Living Wilderness 34:29–33.

*Denbigh. 1882. Wolves in Virginia. Forest and Stream 18(10):189.

*Dennis, J. 1973. The vanishing Delmarva squirrel. National Parks and Conservation Magazine 47(10): 10–11.

*Dennis, J. V. 1988. The great cypress swamps. Baton Rouge: Louisiana State University Press.

*DeRageot, R. 1992. Osbervations on the mammals of Mackay Island National Wildlife Refuge, Virginia and North Carolina. Banisteria 1:11–13.

*DeRageot, R. H. 1964a. The golden mouse. Virginia Wildlife 25(2):10–11.

*DeRageot, R. H. 1964b. The strange semi-tropical world of the salamanders. Virginia Wildlife 25(4):12, 17–18.

*Derowitsch, D. C., and V. M. Tipton. 1984. Techniques for observing a summer colony of bats; use of video equipment. Virginia Journal of Science 35(2):90. Abstract.

*Derting, T. L. 1989a. Prey selection and foraging characteristics of least weasels *(Mustela nivalis)* in the laboratory. American Midland Naturalist 122(2):394–400.

*Derting, T. L. 1989b. Metabolism and food availability as regulators of production in juvenile cotton rats. Ecology 70(3):587–595.

*Derting, T. L. 1997. Subspecific variation in life-history traits of hispid cotton rats (*Sigmodon hispidus*). Journal of Mammalogy 78(2):613-625.

*Derting, T. L., and B. A. Bogue. 1993. Responses of the gut to moderate energy demands in a small herbivore *(Microtus pennsylvanicus)*. Journal of Mammalogy 74(1):59–68.

*Derting, T. L., and J. A. Cranford. 1982. Development and sexual maturation in pine voles *(Microtus pinetorum)*. Virginia Journal of Science 33(3):102. Abstract.

*Derting, T. L., and J. A. Cranford. 1989. Influence of photoperiod on postnatal growth, sexual development, and reproduction in a semifossorial microtine, *Microtus pinetorum*. Canadian Journal of Zoology 67(4):937–941.

*Derting, T. L., and P. A. McClure. 1989. Intraspecific variation in metabolic rate and its relationship with productivity in the cotton rat, *Sigmodon hispidus*. Journal of Mammalogy 70(3):520–531.

*Desch, C. E., and W. B. Nitting. 1974. *Demodex odocoilei* sp. Nov. from the white-tailed deer, *Odocoileus virginianus*. Canadian Journal of Zoology 52:785–789.

*Desmarest, M. A. G. 1820. Mammalogie ou description des espèces de mammifères. Volume 1. Paris:. Chez Mme Veuve Agasse.

DeVan, R. 1982. The ecology and life history of the longtailed weasel *(Mustela frenata)*. Doctoral dissertation, University of Cincinnati.

*Dew, E. M., K. A. Carson, and R. K. Rose. 1998. Seasonal changes in brown fat and pelage in southern short-tailed shrews. Journal of Mammalogy 79(1): 271-278.

Dewsberry, D. A. 1970. Food hoarding in rice rats and cotton rats. Psychological Reports 26:174.

*Dice, L. R. 1940a. Relationships between the woodmouse and the cotton-mouse in eastern Virginia. Journal of Mammalogy 21(1):14–22.

*Dice, L. R. 1940b. The relation of genetics to geographical distribution and speciation; Speciation. II. Speciation in *Peromyscus.* American Naturalist 74(753):289–298.

*Dice, L. R. 1968. Speciation. Pp. 75–97. In: King, J. A. (editor), Biology of *Peromyscus.* Special Publication no. 2. American Society of Mammalogists.

*Dickenson, L. L. 1953. The elusive killer of Burkes Garden. Virginia Wildlife 14(10):16–17, 23.

*Dickerson, L. M. 1928. Observations on parturition in the opossum *Didelphys virginiana.* Science 68(1753):111–112.

*Dickerson, L. M. 1930. A new variety of *Harmostomum opisthotrias* from the North American opossum, *Didelphys virginiana,* with a discussion of its possible bearing on the origin of its host. Parasitology 22:37–46.

*Diersing, V. E. 1980. Systematics and evolution of the pygmy shrews (subgenus *Microsorex*) of North America. Journal of Mammalogy 61(1):76–101.

*Dimmick, R. W. 1973. Zinc phosphide and prolin for controlling prairie voles in Virginia pine plantations. Proceedings of the 26th Annual Conference of the Southeastern Association of Game and Fish Commissioners 26:293–295.

*Dixon, K. R. 1982. Mountain lion. Pp. 711–727. In: Chapman, J. A., and G. A. Feldhamer (editors), Wild mammals of North America. Baltimore: The Johns Hopkins University Press.

*Dobson, G. E. 1882–83. A monograph of the Insectivora, systematic and anatomical. London: J. van Voorst.

*Doebel, J. H. 1967a. Home range and activity of the gray squirrel in a southwest Virginia woodlot. Master's thesis, Virginia Polytechnic Institute and State University, Blacksburg.

*Doebel, J. H. 1967b. A note on denning habits of the gray squirrel. Virginia Wildlife 28(8):6.

*Doebel, J. H. 1967c. Radiotracking Mr. Bushytail. Virginia Wildlife 28(3):4–5.

*Doebel, J. H., and B. S. McGinnes. 1974. Home range and activity of a gray squirrel population. Journal of Wildlife Management 38(4):860–867.

*Dolan, J. D. 1996. Distribution of small mammal species in managed pine plantations. Virginia Journal of Science 47(2):94. Abstract.

*Dolan, J. D. and R. K. Rose. 1997. Attributes of small mammal communities in intensively managed pine plantations. Virginia Journal of Science 48(2):81. Abstract.

*Dolan, P. G., and D. C. Carter. 1977. *Glaucomys volans.* Mammalian Species no. 78.

*Dolnack, G. E., Jr. 1973. Wild tails of Virginia. Virginia Wildlife 34(12):21.

Don, B. A. C. 1983. Home range characteristics and correlates in tree squirrels. Mammal Review 13:123–132.

Donohoe, R. W., and R. O. Beal. 1972. Squirrel behavior determined by radiotelemetry. Ohio Department of Natural Resources, Fish and Wildlife Report 2:1–20.

*Dooley, J. L., Jr., and R. D. Dueser. 1990. An experimental examination of nest-site segregation by two *Peromyscus* species. Ecology 71(2):788–796.

Doremus, H. M. 1965. Heart rate, temperature, and respiration rate of the short-tailed shrew in captivity. Journal of Mammalogy 46(3):424–425.

Dorney, R. S. 1953. Some unusual juvenile raccoon weights. Journal of Mammalogy 34(1):122–123.

Doutt, J. K., C. A. Heppenstall, and J. E. Guilday. 1973. Mammals of Pennsylvania. Third edition. Harrisburg: Pennsylvania Game Commission.

*Dow, S. A. 1958. Interstate traffic of fish, wild birds, and mammals report. Proceedings of the 12th Annual Conference of the Southeastern Association of Game and Fish Commissioners 12:327–330.

*Downing, R. L. 1981. The current status of the cougar in the southern Appalachian. Proceedings of Nongame and Endangered Wildlife Symposium, Athens, Georgia. August 13–14, 1981. pp. 142–151.

*Downing, R. L., and B. S. McGinnes. 1969. Capturing and marking white-tailed deer fawns. Journal of Wildlife Management 33(3):711–714.

*Downing, R. L., and B. S. McGinnes. 1976. Movement patterns of white-tailed deer in a Virginia enclosure. Proceedings of the 29th Annual Conference of the Southeastern Association of Game and Fish Commissioners 29:454–459.

*Downing, R. L., B. S. McGinnes, R. L. Petcher, and J. L. Sandt. 1969. Seasonal changes in movements of white-tailed deer. Pp. 19–24. In: White-tailed deer in the southern forest habitat. Proceedings of a Symposium 1969. Nacogdoches, Texas.

*Downing, R. L., E. D. Michael, and R. J. Poux, Jr. 1977. Accuracy of sex and age ratio counts of white-tailed deer. Journal of Wildlife Management 41(4):709–714.

*Downs, J. 1966. This is Hawfield. Virginia Wildlife 27(10):14–15.

*Doyle, W. E. 1881. History of the buffalo. American Naturalist 15:119–124.

*Dozier, H. L. 1948a. Color mutations in the muskrat *(Ondatra z. macrodon)* and their inheritance. Journal of Mammalogy 29(4):393–405.

*Dozier, H. L. 1948b. A new eastern marsh-inhabiting race of raccoon. Journal of Mammalogy 29(3):286–290.

Dragoo, J. W. and R. L. Honeycutt. 1997. Systematics of mustelid-like carnivores. Journal of Mammalogy 78(2):426-443.

*Dreelin, E. A. and R. K. Rose. 1997. Annual reproductive cycle of *Oryzomys palustris* in a Virginia tidal marsh. Virginia Journal of Science 48(2):81. Abstract.

*Drinkwater, R. B. 1982. A study of the recognition and utilization of *Mytilus* as a food source by *Rattus norvegicus.* Virginia Journal of Science 33(3):103. Abstract.

*Drinkwater, R. B. 1983. The status and dynamics of the bobcat population in Virginia. Master's thesis,

Virginia Polytechnic Institute and State University, Blacksburg.

*Drinkwater, R. B., and B. S. McGinnes. 1981. A brief view of the age distribution and recent reproductive potential of Virginia bobcats. Virginia Journal of Science 32(3):91. Abstract.

*Drinkwater, R. B., and B. S. McGinnes. 1982. Preliminary analyses of a field technique for age determination of bobcats. Virginia Journal of Science 33(3):103. Abstract.

*Drowne, T. P. 1900. A trip to Fauquier Co., Virginia; with notes on the specimens obtained. The Museum 6(3):38–45.

*Dubey, J. P., A. N. Hamir, C. A. Hanlon and C. E. Rupprecht. 1992. Prevalence of *Toxoplasma gondii* infection in raccoons. Journal of the American Veterinary Medical Association 200(4):534–536.

*DuBrock, C. W. 1980. An analysis of Virginia black bear population dynamics. Master's thesis, Virginia Polytechnic Institute and State University, Blacksburg.

*DuBrock, C. W., A. R. Tipton, and J. W. Raybourne. 1981. Population dynamics of black bears in Virginia. Transactions of the Northeastern Section of the Wildlife Society 38:107.

*DuBrock, C. W., A. R. Tipton, and J. B. Whelan. 1978. Evaluation of a bear hunters survey and its implications on black bear management in Virginia. Proceedings of the 32d Annual Conference of the Southeastern Association of Fish and Wildlife Agencies 32:202–207.

*Dudak, D. 1964. The incidence and degree of infection of *Pneumostrongylus tenuis* in the white-tailed deer of western Virginia. Master's thesis, Virginia Polytechnic Institute and State University, Blacksburg.

*Dudak, D., G. W. Cornwell, R. B. Holliman, and B. S. McGinnes. 1965. The incidence and degree of infection of *Pneumostrongylus tenuis* in the white-tailed deer of western Virginia. Proceedings of the 19th Annual Conference of the Southeastern Association of Game and Fish Commissioners 19:128–141.

*Dudderar, G. R. 1967. A survey of the food habits of the gray squirrel *(Sciurus carolinensis)* in Montgomery County, Virginia. Master's thesis, Virginia Polytechnic Institute and State University, Blacksburg.

*Dudderar, G. R., and J. R. Beck. 1973. Rats and their control. Virginia Polytechnic Institute and State University Extension Division Publication 272.

*Dueser, R. D. 1987. Status of the endangered Delmarva peninsula fox squirrel in Virginia. Virginia Journal of Science 38(2):79. Abstract.

*Dueser, R. D. 1988. Mammals of the Virginia barrier islands. Virginia Journal of Science 39(2):112. Abstract.

*Dueser, R. D. 1990. Absence of habitat differences between coexisting species of woodland *Peromyscus.* Bulletin of the Ecological Society of America 71(2) (Supplement):142.

Dueser, R. D., and W. C. Brown. 1980. Ecological correlates of insular rodent diversity. Ecology 6(1):50–56.

*Dueser, R. D., W. C. Brown, G. S. Hogue, C. McCaffrey, S. A. McCuskey, and G. J. Hennessey. 1979. Mammals on the Virginia barrier islands. Journal of Mammalogy 60(2):425–429.

*Dueser, R. D., W. C. Brown, S. A. McCuskey, and G. S. Hogue. 1976. Vertebrate zoogeography of the Virginia Coast Preserve. Pp. 439–518. In: Virginia Coast Preserve Study, Ecosystem Description. 1976. Arlington: The Nature Conservancy.

*Dueser, R. D., J. L. Dooley, Jr., and G. J. Taylor. 1988. Habitat structure, forest composition and landscape dimensions as components of habitat suitability for the Delmarva fox squirrel. United States Forest Service General Technical Report RM-166:414–421.

*Dueser, R. D., and C. O. Handley, Jr. 1991. Fox Squirrel. Pp. 585–589. In: Terwilliger, K. (coordinator). Virginia's endangered species. Blacksburg: The McDonald & Woodward Publishing Company.

*Dueser, R. D., and J. H. Porter. 1979. Biogeography of mammals on the Virginia barrier islands. Virginia Journal of Science 30(2):47. Abstract.

*Dueser, R. D., and J. H. Porter. 1986. Habitat use by insular small mammals: relative effects of competition and habitat structure. Ecology 67(1):195–201.

*Dueser, R. D., and K. Terwilliger. 1987. Status of the Delmarva fox squirrel *(Sciurus niger cinereus)* in Virginia. Virginia Journal of Science 38(4):380–388.

*Dueser, R. D., G. D. Therres, and G. J. Taylor. 1988. Translocation histones for the endangered Delmarva fox squirrel in Maryland: guidelines for implementing a conservation strategy. Transactions of the Northeast Section of the Wildlife Society 45:78.

*Dueser, R. D., M. L. Wilson, and R. K. Rose. 1981. Attributes of dispersing meadow voles in open-grid populations. Acta Theriologica 26(8):139–162.

Duke, K. L. 1954. Reproduction in the bobcat. Anatomical Record 120(3):816–817.

Dunaway, P. B. 1968. Life history and populational aspects of the eastern harvest mouse. American Midland Naturalist 79(1):48–67.

*Dunbar, G.S. 1962. Some notes on bison in early Virginia. Virginia Place-Name Society, Occasional Papers no. 1, January 30. Charlottesville.

*Duncan, B. 1987. Virginia's whitetails. Management. Virginia Wildlife 48(11):4–9.

*Duncan, B. 1996. Shed antlers: nature's lost and found. Virginia Wildlife 57(3):10–14.

*Duncan, B., and D. Schwab. 1986. Virginia's Bay of Pigs. Virginia Wildlife 47(8):16–21.

*Duncan, P. M., (editor). 1883. Cassell's Natural History. 6 volumes. New York:. Cassell Petter and Galpin.

Dunford, C. 1970. Behavioral aspects of spatial organization in the chipmunk, *Tamias striatus.* Behaviour 36(3):215–231.

Dunford, C. 1972. Summer activity of eastern chipmunks. Journal of Mammalogy 53(1):176–180.

*Dunn, J. B. 1907. The history of Nansemond County, Virginia. Suffolk, Virginia: Nansemond Company.

Dunn, J. P. 1980. Reproduction, physiological responses, age structure and food habits of the raccoon in Maryland. Master's thesis, Frostburg State College.

*Dunn, J. P., J. A. Chapman, and R. E. Marsh. 1982. Jackrabbits. Pp. 124–145. In: Chapman, J. A., and G. A. Feldhamer (editors), Wild mammals of North America. Baltimore: The Johns Hopkins University Press.

*Durloo, R. S. 1966. Midsummer in the marshes. Virginia Wildlife 27(9):9.

*Dutton, H. J., II. 1987. An assessment of the nurtitional status and habitat quality of a southwestern Virginia deer herd. Master's thesis, Virginia Polytechnic Institute and State University, Blacksburg.

*Dutton, H. J., J. L. Waldon, and P. T. Bromley. 1987. Categorization and seasonal periodicity of terrestrial vertebrate pest control inquiries in Virginia. Proceedings of the Eastern Wildlife Damage Control Conference 3:83–88.

Eadie, W. R. 1937. The Cooper lemming mouse in southern New Hampshire. Journal of Mammalogy 18(1):102–103.

*Eadie, W. R. 1939. A contribution to the biology of *Parascalops breweri*. Journal of Mammalogy 20(2): 150–173.

Eadie, W. R. 1944. The short-tailed shrew and field mouse predation. Journal of Mammalogy 25:359–364.

Eadie, W. R. 1952. Shrew predation and vole populations on a localized area. Journal of Mammalogy 33(2):185–189.

Eadie, W. R., and W. J. Hamilton, Jr. 1956. Notes on reproduction in the star-nosed mole. Journal of Mammalogy 37(2):223–231.

*Earles, M. G. 1972. Old rag revisited. Virginia Wildlife 33(4):18–19.

*Early, G., and T. P. McKenzie. 1991. The Northeast regional marine mammal stranding network. Pp. 63–68. In: Reynolds, J. E. III, and D. K. Odell (editors), Marine mammal strandings in the United States. Proceedings of the Second Marine Mammal Stranding Workshop. Miami, Florida. December 3–5, 1987. NOAA Technical Report NMFS 98.

*Earnshaw, F. L., and F. A. Grimes. 1929. Fur laws for the season 1929–1930. United States Department of Agriculture Farmer's Bulletin no. 1618.

*East, B. 1979. Cougar comeback in the East. American Forests 85:21, 54–59.

Easterla, D. A. 1968. Parturition of Keen's Myotis in southwestern Missouri. Journal of Mammalogy 49(4):770.

Easterla, D. A., and L. C. Watkins. 1969. Pregnant *Myotis sodalis* in northwestern Missouri. Journal of Mammalogy 50(2):372–373.

*Eastman, C. R. 1915. Early portrayals of the opossum. American Naturalist 49(586):585–594.

*Eaton, R. L., and K. A. Verlander. 1977. Reproduction in the puma: biology, behavior, and ontogeny. Pp. 45–70. In: Eaton, R. L. (editor), The world's cats. Volume 3, Number 3. Seattle: Carnivore Research Institute, Burke Museum, University of Washington.

*Eaton, W. P. 1910. The real Dismal Swamp. Harper's Monthly Magazine 122:18–30.

*Echternach, J. L. 1981. The food habits of beavers in southeastern Virginia. Virginia Journal of Science 32(3):91. Abstract.

*Echternach, J. L., Jr. 1982. Food habits and ecology of beavers in southeastern Virginia. Master's thesis, Old Dominion University, Norfolk, Virginia.

*Echternach, J. L., and R. K. Rose. 1987. Use of woody vegetation by beavers in southeastern Virginia. Virginia Journal of Science 38(3)226–232.

Ecke, D. H. 1954. An invasion of Norway rats in southwest Georgia. Journal of Mammalogy 35(4):521–525.

Ecke, D. H. 1955. The reproductive cycle of the Mearns cottontail in Illinois. American Midland Naturalist 53(2):294–311.

*Eckerlin, R. P. 1983. Parasites of the opossum, *Didelphis virginiana*, in northern Virginia. Virginia Journal of Science 34(3):120. Abstract.

*Eckerlin, R. P. 1985. Parasites of suburban gray squirrels, *Sciurus carolinensis*, in northern Virginia. Virginia Journal of Science 36(2):107. Abstract.

*Eckerlin, R. P. 1988. The rare fluke *Urotrematulum attenulatum* Macy, 1933 from the silver-haired bat, *Lasionycteris noctivagans*, in Virginia. Virginia Journal of Science 39(2):113. Abstract.

*Eckerlin, R. P. 1992. The homogonic life cycle of *Strongyloides robustus*, an intestinal parasite of squirrels. Virginia Journal of Science 43(2):229. Abstract.

*Eckerlin, R. P. 1993a. Parasites of surburban cottontails. Virginia Journal of Science 44(2):110. Abstract.

*Eckerlin, R. P. 1993b. Helminth parasites from two populations of the Delmarva fox squirrel *(Sciurus niger cinereus)* in Maryland and Virginia. Pp. 53–56. In: Moncrief, N. D., et al. (editors). Proceedings of the Second Symposium on Southeastern Fox Squirrels, *Sciurus niger*. Virginia Museum of Natural History Special Publication no. 1.

*Eckerlin, R. P. 1994. Prevalence and geographic distribution of the raccoon nematode, *Baylisascaris procyonis*. Virginia Journal of Science 45(2):57. Abstract.

*Eckerlin, R. P. 1997. Ticks of the Dismal Swamp of Virginia. Virginia Journal of Science 48(2):82. Abstract.

*Eckerlin, R. P., and H. F. Painter. 1986. Species composition of flea populations of southern flying squirrels, *Glaucomys volans*, from different elevations in Virginia. Virginia Journal of Science 37(2):62. Abstract.

*Eckerlin, R. P., and H. F. Painter, 1991. Leptinidae (Coleoptera) in Virginia. Virginia Journal of Science 42:169.

*Eckerlin, R. P., and H. F. Painter. 1994. The sucking lice (Insecta: Anoplura) of Virginia sciurids. Virginia Journal of Science 45(2):105 Abstract.

*Eckerlin, R. P. and H. F. Painter. 1995. First record of *Tamiophila grandis* (Insecta: Siphonaptera) from Virginia. Banisteria no. 6:24–25.

*Eckerlin, R. P., and T. K. Sawyer. 1989. Survey for *Acanthamoeba* in the Potomac basin. Virginia Journal of Science 40(2):56. Abstract.

*Edmonds, M. G. 1970. Bear acquaintance. Virginia Wildlife 31(7):16–18.

*Edwards, J. W., P. A. Tappe, and N. D. Moncrief (compilers). 1990. Proceedings of the First Symposium on Southeastern Fox Squirrels, *Sciurus niger*. Virginia Museum of Natural History, Martinsville.

Egoscue, H. J., J. G. Bittmenn, and J. A. Petrovich. 1970. Some fecundity and longevity records for captive small mammals. Journal of Mammalogy 51(3):622–623.

Ehret, G., and C. Bernecker. 1986. Low-frequency sound communication by mouse pups *(Mus musculus):* wriggling calls release maternal behaviour. Animal Behaviour 34(3):821–830.

*Eike, D. R. 1969. An unusual hunt. Virginia Wildlife 30(3):11.

*Eiler, J. H., W. G. Wathen, and M. R. Pelton. 1989. Reproduction in black bears in the southern Appalachian Mountains. Journal of Wildlife Management 53(2):353–360.

*Elkins, D. 1979. Open house for raccoons. Virginia Wildlife 40(2):6–7.

*Elkins, P. 1971. Remembering in the rain. Virginia Wildlife 32(4):7.

*Elkins, P. 1974. Virginia's loneliest river. Virginia Wildlife 35(9):7–9.

*Ellerman, J. R. 1940. The families and genera of living rodents . . . . British Museum (Natural History), London. 2 volumes.

*Elliott, C. (editor). 1942. Fading trails. The story of endangered American wildlife. New York: Macmillan Company.

*Elliot, D. G. 1901a. A synopsis of the mammals of North America and the adjacent seas. Field Columbian Museum Publication 45. 2(1):1–471.

*Elliot, D. G. 1901b. A list of the land and sea mammals of North America north of Mexico. Supplement to the synopsis. Field Columbian Museum Publication 57. 2(2):473–522.

*Ellis, R. 1980. The book of whales. New York: Alfred A. Knopf.

*Ellis, R. W. 1976. The impact of steam alteration on wildlife along tributaries of the Roanoke River, Charlotte County, Virginia. Master's thesis, Virginia Polytechnic Institute and State University, Blacksburg.

*Ellis, R. W., and J. B. Whelan. 1979. Impact of stream channelization on riparian small mammal and bird populations in Piedmont Virginia. Transactions of the 35th Northeastern Fish and Wildlife Conference:92–104.

*Ellzey, M. G. 1885. The fox as a tree climber. Forest and Stream 25(13):245.

*Emmons, C. W. 1948. Histoplasmosis in wild rats. United States Public Health Reports 63:1416–1422.

*Emmons, C. W. 1949. Histoplasmosis in animals. Transactions of the New York Academy of Science, Series II, 11:248–254.

*Emmons, C. W. 1950. Histoplasmosis: animal reservoirs and other sources in nature of the pathogenic fungus, *Histoplasma*. American Journal of Public Health 40(4):436–440.

*Emmons, C. W., and L. L. Ashburn. 1948. Histoplasmosis in wild rats. Occurrence and histopathology. Public Health Reports 63:1416–1422.

*Emmons, C. W. , J. A. Bell, and B. J. Olson. 1947. Naturally occurring histoplasmosis in *Mus musculus* and *Rattus norvegicus*. United States Public Health Reports 62:1642–1646.

*Emmons, C. W., D. A. Rowley, B. J. Olson, C. F. T. Mattern, J. A. Bell, E. Powell, and E. A. Marcey. 1955. Histoplasmosis. Proved occurrence of inapparent infection in dogs, cats, and other animals. American Journal of Hygiene 61(1):40–44.

Enders, R. K. 1952. Reproduction in the mink *(Mustela vison)*. Proceedings of the American Philosophical Society 96(6):691–755.

Enders, R. K., and A. C. Enders. 1963. Morphology of the female reproductive tract during delayed implantation in the mink. Pp. 129–140. In: Enders, A. C. (editor), Delayed implantation. Chicago: University of Chicago Press.

Engel, J. M., et. al. 1975. Recovery plan for the Indiana bat. Report to Director, United States Fish and Wildlife Service. Unpublished.

*Engle, J. W., Jr. 1949a. An investigation of conditions influencing the pattern of overpopulated deer areas in Virginia. Master's thesis, Virginia Polytechnic Institute and State University, Blacksburg.

*Engle, J. W., Jr. 1949b. The whitetail makes a comeback! Virginia Wildlife 10(12):18–20.

*Engle, J. W., Jr. 1950. The present status and estimated distribution of the white-tailed deer in Virginia. Virginia Journal of Science 1(2):347. Abstract.

*Engle, J. W., Jr. 1951. Problems of deer herd management. Virginia Wildlife 12(5):22–24.

*Engle, J. W., Jr. 1954a. The beaver in Virginia. Educational Leaflet no. 3. Virginia Commission of Game and Inland Fisheries.

*Engle, J. W., Jr. 1954b. Present status of the beaver in Virginia 15(4):16–17.

*Engle, J. W., Jr. 1962a. Highland wildlife management area. Virginia Wildlife 23(11):16.

*Engle, J. W., Jr. 1962b. Observations on the growth and wildlife utilization of autumn olive *(Elaegnus umbellata)* on the George Washington National Forest, Virginia. Proceedings of the 16th Annual Conference of the Southeastern Association of Game and Fish Commissioners 16:32–34.

*Engle, J. W., Jr. 1963a. An analysis of the deer–bear damage stamp funds in Virginia. Proceedings of the 17th Annual Conference of the Southeastern Association of Game and Fish Commissioners 17:100–107. (1965).

*Engle, J. W., Jr. 1963b. Welcome to Little North Mountain. Virginia Wildlife 24(11):14–15.

*Engle, J. W., Jr. 1971. Hare hunt. Virginia Wildlife 32(4):20–21.

*Engle, J. W., Jr., and P. J. Hanlon. 1952. Knowledge gained at the Big Levels managed hunt. Virginia Wildlife 13(5):10–13.

*English, E. I., and M. A. Bowers. 1994. Vegetational gradients and proximity to woodchuck *(Marmota monax)* burrows in an old field. Journal of Mammalogy 75(3):775–780.

*Enright, J. B. 1962. Geographical distribution of bat rabies in the United States, 1953–60. American Journal of Public Health 52:484–488.

*Environmental Research Group, Georgia State University. 1974. Economic survey of wildlife recreation: Detailed analysis for Virginia. Georgia State University, Atlanta.

*Environmental Research Group, Georgia State University. 1974. Economic survey of wildlife recreation: Executive summary for Virginia. Georgia State University, Atlanta.

*Erdle, S. Y., and J. F. Pagels. 1991. Further observations on distribution and habitat of *Sorex longirostris fisheri*. Virginia Department of Conservation and Recreation, Natural Heritage Technical Report 91–2.

*Erdle, S. Y. and J. F. Pagels. 1995. Observations on *Sorex longirostris* (Mammalia: Sorcidae) and associates in eastern portions of the historical Great Dismal Swamp. Banisteria no. 6:17–23.

*Erickson, A. B. 1944. Helminths of Minnesota Canidae in relation to food habits, and a host list and key to the species reported from North America. American Midland Naturalist 32(2):358–372.

*Erickson, A. B. 1947. Helminth parasites of rabbits of the genus *Sylvilagus*. Journal of Wildlife Management 11(3):255–263.

Erickson, A. W., and J. Nellor. 1964. Breeding biology of the black bear. Pp. 5–45. In: Erickson, A. W., J. Nellor, and G. A. Petrides (editors), The black bear in Michigan. Michigan State University Agricultural Experiment Station Research Bulletin 4.

*Ernst, C. H. 1975. Skull key to adult land mammals of Delaware, Maryland, and Virginia. Chesapeake Science 16(3):198–204.

*Ernst, C. H. 1977. Skull key to adult mammals of Delaware, Maryland, and Virginia. II. Marine mammals. Chesapeake Science 18(1):84–87.

*Ernst, C. H. 1994. Noteworthy mammal records from northern Virginia. The Maryland Naturalist 38(3–4):1–2.

Errington, P. L. 1939. Observations on young muskrats in Iowa. Journal of Mammalogy 20(4):465–478.

Errington, P. L. 1944. Additional studies on tagged young muskrats. Journal of Wildlife Management 8(4):300–306.

Errington, P. L. 1961. Muskrats and marsh management. Harrisburg, Pennsylvania: Stackpole Company.

Errington, P. L. 1963. Muskrat populations. Ames: Iowa State University Press.

Errington, P. L., and C. S. Errington. 1937. Experimental tagging of young muskrats for purposes of study. Journal of Wildlife Management 1(1):49–61.

*Eshelman, R. E., and F. Grady. 1986. Quaternary vertebrate localities of Virginia and their avian and mammalian fauna. Pp. 43–70. In. McDonald, J. N., and S. O. Bird (editors), The Quaternary of Virginia — A Symposium Volume. Charlottesville: Virginia Department of Mines, Minerals and Energy.

Essapian, F. S. 1963. Observations on abnormalities of parturition in captive bottle-nosed dolphins, *Tursiops truncatus*, and concurrent behavior of other porpoises. Journal of Mammalogy 44(3):405–414.

*Estep, J. E. 1975. Seasonal variation in body fat and food habits of pine voles from two Virginia orchards. Master's thesis, Virginia Polytechnic Institute and State University, Blacksburg.

*Estep, J. E., D. J. Cengel, R. E. Noffsinger, and R. L. Kirkpatrick. 1975. Food habits of pine voles in two Virginia apple orchards. Virginia Journal of Science 26(2):54. Abstract.

*Evans, A. 1934. Arese, Francesco. A trip to the prairies and in the interior of North America [1837–1838]. Translated by A. Evans. New York: Harbor Press.

*Evans, C. 1983. Beavers. Virginia Wildlife 44(5):21.

*Evans, C. S. 1987. Demographic features of rabid and rabies suspect bats in Virginia. Master's thesis, Virginia Commonwealth University.

*Evans, C. S., and J. F. Pagels. 1986. Virginia bats and nontraditional collecting: what can they tell us about life histories? Virginia Journal of Science 37(2):63. Abstract.

*Evans, C. S., and J. F. Pagels. 1987. Demographic features of rabid and rabies suspect bats in Virginia. Virginia Journal of Science 38(2):80. Abstract.

*Evans, J. 1970. About nutria and their control. Resource Publication no. 86, Bureau of Sport Fisheries and Wildlife, Denver.

*Evans, P. G. H. 1987. The natural history of whales and dolphins. New York: Facts on File Publications.

Evans, R. D., K. C. Sadler, C. H. Conaway, and T. S. Baskett. 1965. Regional comparisons of cottontail reproduction in Missouri. American Midland Naturalist 74(1):176–184.

*Everton, R. K. 1985. The relationship between habitat structure and small mammal communities in southeastern Virginia and northeastern North Carolina. Master's thesis, Old Dominion University.

*Everton, R. K., and R. K. Rose. 1981. The habitats of the southern bog lemming, *Synaptomys cooperi*, in the Great Dismal Swamp. Virginia Journal of Science 32(3):91. Abstract.

*Everton, R. K., and R. K. Rose. 1982. The southern bog lemming, *Synaptomys cooperi*, in the Dismal Swamp. Virginia Journal of Science 33(3):105. Abstract.

*Ewan, J., and N. Ewan. 1970. John Banister and his natural history of Virginia, 1678–1692. Urbana: University of Illinois.

*Ewing, H. E. 1925. New parasitic mites of the genus *Laelaps*. Proceedings of the Entomological Society of Washington 27(1):1–7.

*Ewing, H. E. 1931. Some factors affecting the distribution of and variation in North American ectoparasites. American Naturalist 65(699):360–369.

*Ewing, H. E. 1938. North American mites of the subfamily Myobiinae, new subfamily (Arachnida). Proceedings of the Entomological Society of Washington 40(7):180–197.

*Fain, A., and K. Hyland. 1974. The Listrophoroid mites in North America. II. — The family Listrophoridae Megnin and Trovessart (Acarina: Sorcoptiformes) (1). Entomologie 50(1):1–69.

*Fanney, B. B. 1953. When Jamestown was a colony. Virginia Wildlife 14(8):16–17, 23.

*Farb, P. 1966. The land and wildlife of North America. New York: Time.

*Farrell, C. E. 1956. Chiggers of the genus *Euschongastia* (Acarina: Trombiculidae) in North America. Proceedings of the United States National Museum 106 (3364):85–235.

Faunmap Working Group. 1994. Faunmap: A database documenting Late Quaternary distributions of mammal species in the United States. Illinois State Museum Scientific Papers 25. (Faunmap Home Page is accessed at *http//www.museum.state.il.us/research/faunmap*.)

Fay, F. H. 1954. Quantitative experiments on the food consumption of *Parascalops breweri*. Journal of Mammalogy 35(1):107–109.

*Fearnow, T. C. 1947. Forest wildlife in the postwar era. Virginia Wildlife 8(1):17–19.

*Fearnow, T. C. 1985. Wildlife management on the Virginia national forests. Proceedings of the Annual Conference of the Southeastern Association of Game and Fish Commissioners 1–6:199–202.

*Federal Register. 1993. Volume 58, number 64. U.S. Government Printing Office, Washington, DC. Pp. 17,789–17,791.

*Feldhamer, G. A. 1980. *Cervus nippon*. Mammalian Species no. 128.

*Feldhamer, G. A. 1982. Sika deer. Pp. 1114–1123. In: Chapman, J. A., and G. A. Feldhamer (editors), Wild mammals of North America. Baltimore: The Johns Hopkins University Press.

Feldhamer, G. A., D. R. Gillespie, and W. B. Taliaferro. 1981. Recent record of a porcupine in western Maryland. Proceedings of the Pennsylvania Academy of Science 55:199.

*Felix, A. C. III, T. L. Sharik, and B. S. McGinnes. 1986. Effects of pine conversion on food plants of northern bobwhite quail, eastern wild turkey, and white-tailed deer in the Virginia piedmont. Southern Journal of Applied Forestry 10(1):47–52.

*Fenneman, N. M. 1938. Physiography of the eastern United States. New York: McGraw-Hill Book Company.

*Fenton, M. B. 1970. Population studies of *Myotis lucifugus* (Chiroptera: Vespertilionidae). Life Sciences Contributions, Royal Ontario Museum 77:1–34.

*Fenton, M. B., and R. M. R. Barclay. 1980. *Myotis lucifugus*. Mammalian Species no. 142.

*Fenton, M. B., and G. P. Bell. 1981. Recognition of insectivorous bats by their echolocation calls. Journal of Mammalogy 62(2):233–243.

*Ferguson, H. L. 1976a. The impact of stream alteration on wildlife along tributaries of the Roanoke River, Charlotte County, Virginia. Master's thesis, Virginia Polytechnic Institute and State University, Blacksburg.

*Ferguson, J. D. and J. F. Pagels. 1997. Tail lability in the smoky shrew (*Sorex fumeus*). Virginia Journal of Science 48(2):151. Abstract.

*Ferguson, H. L. 1976b. Beaver. Virginia Wildlife 37(9):4–5.

Ferron, J., and J. P. Ovellet. 1991. PHysical and behavioral postnatal development of woodchucks *(Marmota monax)*. Canadian journal of Zoology 69(4): 1040–1047.

*Fies, M. 1984. A different kind of rabbit. Virginia Wildlife 45(10):7–9.

*Fies, M. 1986. Night gliders. Virginia Wildlife 47(12):23–25.

*Fies, M. 1990a. Bigfoot. Virginia Wildlife 51(2):8–11.

*Fies, M. 1990b. The numbers game — small game population management. Virginia Wildlife 51(5):4–10.

*Fies, M. 1992. Wanted: Dead or Alive? Virginia Wildlife 53(1):4–8.

*Fies, M. L. 1991a. Snowshoe hare. Pp. 576–578. In: Terwilliger, K. (coordinator). Virginia's endangered species. Blacksburg: The McDonald & Woodward Publishing Company.

*Fies, M. L. 1991b. Eastern cottontail. Pp. 578–580. In: Terwilliger, K. (coordinator). Virginia's endangered species. Blacksburg: The McDonald & Woodward Publishing Company.

*Fies, M. L. 1992. Survival and movements of relocated snowshoe hares *(Lepus americanus)* in western Virginia. Virginia Journal of Science 43(2):230. Abstract.

*Fies, M. L. 1993. Fox squirrels *(Sciurus niger)* in Virginia: a review of historical records and information from recent population surveys. Pp. 37–49. In: Moncrief, N. D., et al. (editors). Proceedings of the Second Symposium on Southeastern Fox Squirrels, *Sciurus niger*. Virginia Museum of Natural History Special Publication no. 1.

*Fies, M. L., and J. Coggin. 1985. New England cottontail investigations. Final report. Virginia Wildlife Investigations. Annual Report, July 1, 1984 — June 30, 1985. Virginia Commission of Game and Inland Fisheries.

*Fies, M. L., and J. L. Coggin. 1985. New information on the distribution and status of the New England cottontail in Virginia. Transactions of the Northeastern Section of the Wildlife Society 42:185–192.

*Fies, M. L., and C. O. Handley, Jr. 1991. Marsh rabbit. Pp. 580–582. In: Terwilliger, K. (coordinator). Virginia's endangered species. Blacksburg: The McDonald & Woodward Publishing Company.

*Fies, M. L., D. D. Martin, and G. T. Blank, Jr. 1987. Movements and rates of return of translocated black bears in Virginia. International Conference on Bear Research and Management 7:369–372.

*Fies, M. L., and J. F. Pagels. 1987. Preliminary results from a northern flying squirrel nest box study in Virginia. Virginia Journal of Science 38(2):80. Abstract.

*Fies, M. L., and J. F. Pagels. 1988. Northern flying squirrel investigations. Pp. 75–80. In: Virginia Wildlife Investigations. Annual Progress Report 1987–88. Virginia Department of Game and Inland Fisheries.

*Fies, M. L., and J. F. Pagels. 1991. Northern flying squirrel. Pp. 583–584. In: Terwilliger, K., (coordinator). Virginia's endangered species. Blacksburg: The McDonald & Woodward Publishing Company.

Findley, J. S., and J. K. Jones, Jr. 1956. Molt of the short-tailed shrew, *Blarina brevicauda*. American Midland Naturalist 56(1):246–249.

Findley, J. S., and C. Jones. 1964. Seasonal distribution of the hoary bat. Journal of Mammalogy 45(3):461–470.

*Firestone, L., and W. Morse. 1976. A guidebook to Virginia's favorite islands — Chincoteague and Assateague. Richmond: Good Life Publishers.

*Fischman, H. R. 1976. Consideration of an association between geographic distribution of caves and occurrence of rabies in foxes. Journal of the American Veterinary Medical Association 169(11):1207–1213.

*Fischman, H. R., and G. S. Young. 1976. An association between the occurrence of fox rabies and the presence of caves. American Journal of Epidemiology 104(6):593–601.

*Fishbein, D. B., A. J. Belotto, R. E. Pacer, J. S. Smith, W. G. Winkler, S. R. Jenkins, and K. M. Porter. 1986. Rabies in rodents and lagomorphs in the United States, 1971–1984: increased cases in the woodchuck *(Marmota monax)* in mid-Atlantic states. Journal of Wildlife Diseases 22(2):151–155.

*Fishel, S., and K. McCravy. 1988. Marsh rabbit project report. Project no. W-74-R-S-1. Virginia Wildlife Investigations. Annual Progress Report 1987–88. Virginia Department of Game and Inland Fisheries.

*Fisher, A. K. 1893. The hawks and owls of the United States in their relation to agriculture. Bulletin no. 3. Division of Ornithology and Mammalogy, United States Department of Agriculture, Washington, DC.

*Fisher, A. K. 1895. The Dismal Swamp and its occupants. Scientific American 73:220.

*Fisher, R. D. 1969. Aggressive behavior in the golden mouse *Ochrotomys nuttalli*. Master's thesis, Virginia Polytechnic Institute and State University, Blacksburg.

*Fitch, J. H. 1966. Weight loss and temperature response in three species of bats in Marshall County, Kansas. Search 6:17–24.

*Fitch, J. H., and K. A. Shump, Jr. 1979. *Myotis keenii*. Mammalian Species no. 121:1–3.

*Fitzgerald, V. J., and J. O. Wolff. 1988. Behavioral responses of escaping *Peromyscus leucopus* to wet and dry substrata. Journal of Mammalogy 69(4):825–828.

*Fitzgerald, W. R. 1966. More than just the fishing. Virginia Wildlife 27(6):18.

*Flakne, J. T. 1970. Virginia's Mason Neck. Atlantic Naturalist 25(2):59–64.

*Fleet, H. 1871. A brief journal of a voyage made in the bark "Warwick" to Virginia and other parts of the continent of America. Pp. 221–237. In: Neill, E. D. (editor), The English colonization of America during the seventeenth century. London.

*Fleisher, S. 1985. Activitatsmuter von Weisswedelhirschen *(Odocoileus virginianus)* wahrend der Brunft. Master's thesis, University of Bielefeld, Germany.

Flower, S. S. 1931. Contributions to our knowledge of the duration of life in vertebrate animals. 5. Mammals. Proceedings of the Zoological Society of London 101:145–234.

Fluharty, S. L., D. H. Taylor, and G. W. Barrett. 1976. Sun-compass orientation in the meadow vole, *Microtus pennsylvanicus*. Journal of Mammalogy 57(1):1–9.

Flyger, V. 1959. A comparison of methods for estimating squirrel populations. Journal of Wildlife Management 23:220–223.

Flyger, V. 1960. Movements and home range of the gray squirrel, *Sciurus carolinensis*, in two Maryland woodlots. Ecology 41:365–369.

*Flyger, V. 1960. Sika deer on islands in Maryland and Virginia. Journal of Mammalogy 41(4):140.

*Flyger, V. 1965. Virginia's newest big game animal. Virginia Wildlife 26(2):8–9.

*Flyger, V. 1969. The 1968 squirrel "migration" in the eastern United States. Contribution no. 379, Natural Resources Institute, University of Maryland.

*Flyger, V., and N. W. Davis. 1964. Distribution of sika deer *Cervus nippon* in Maryland and Virginia in 1962. Chesapeake Science 5(4):212–213.

*Flyger, V., and J. E. Gates. 1982. Fox and gray squirrels. Pp. 209–229. In: Chapman, J. A., and G. A. Feldhamer (editors), Wild mammals of North America. Baltimore: The Johns Hopkins University Press.

*Flyger, V., and L. W. Lustig. 1977. The potential for reestablishing fox squirrels in portions of their former range in the northeastern states. Transactions of the Northeastern Section of the Wildlife Society 33:13–17.

Flyger, V., and D. A. Smith. 1980. A comparison of Delmarva fox squirrel and gray squirrel habits and home range. Transactions of the Northeastern Section of the Wildlife Society 37:19–22.

Flyger, V., and J. Warren. 1958. Sika deer in Maryland — an additional big game animal or a possible pest. Proceedings of the 12th Annual Conference of the Southeastern Association of Game and Fish Commissioners 12:209–211.

*Fodor, B. 1970. The wolf in the southeastern United States: A bibliography. Bibliography series no. 19.

Office of Library Services, United States Department of the Interior, Washington, DC.

*Fogl, J. G. 1972. A new method of aging gray squirrels *(Sciurus carolinensis)* by use of cementum annuli. Master's thesis, Virginia Polytechnic Institute and State University, Blacksburg.

*Fogl, J. G., and H. S. Mosby. 1978. Aging gray squirrels by cementum annuli in razor-sectioned teeth. Journal of Wildlife Management 42(2):444–448.

Follmann, E. H. 1973. Comparative ecology and behavior of red and gray foxes. Doctoral dissertation, Southern Illinois University.

*Force, P. (editor). 1836–46. Tracts and other papers relating principally to the origin, settlement, and progress of the colonies in North America from the discovery of the country to the year 1776. Washington, D. C. 4 volumes.

*Ford, L. J., and R. K. Rose. 1984. A small mammal community dominated by *Synaptomys cooperi* and *Microtus pinetorum.* Virginia Journal of Science 35(2):82. Abstract.

*Foreman, G. (editor). 1968. Adventure on Red River: Report on the exploration of the headwaters of the Red River by Captain Randolph B. Marcy and Captain G. B. McClellan. Norman: University of Oklahoma Press.

*Formanowicz, D. R., Jr., P. J. Bradley, and E. D. Brodie, Jr. 1989. Food hoarding by the least shrew *(Cryptotis parva):* intersexual and prey type effects. American Midland Naturalist 122(1):26–33.

*Forster, J. R. 1771. A catalogue of the animals of North America. London: B. White.

*Forster, J. R. 1772. Account of several quadrupeds from Hudson's Bay. Philosophical Transactions 62:370–381.

*Fortenbery, A., and J. A. Cranford. 1985. Energy savings resulting from huddling behavior in *Peromyscus.* Virginia Journal of Science 36(2):108. Abstract.

*Fortenbery, D. K. 1959a. Evaluation of rabbit management methods by live trapping. Virginia Journal of Science 10(2):262. Abstract.

*Fortenbery, D. K. 1959b. An evaluation of some rabbit management procedures as applied in southeastern Virginia. Master's thesis, Virginia Polytechnic Institute and State University, Blacksburg.

*Fortune, D. S., and J. A. Cranford, 1994. Burrow use and burrow structure of *Peromyscus* species at Mt. Lake Biological Station. Virginia Journal of Science 45(2):58. Abstract.

*Forys, E. A., and R. D. Dueser. 1990. The effect of immigration on island colonization and population persistence of *Oryzomys palustris* on the barrier islands of Virginia. Virginia Journal of Science 41(2):54. Abstract.

*Forys, E. A., and R. D. Dueser, 1993. Inter-island movements of rice rats *(Oryzomys palustris).* American Midland Naturalist 130 (2): 408–412.

*Forys, E. A., and N. D. Moncrief. 1994. Gene flow among island populations of marsh rice rats *(Oryzomys palustris).* Virginia Journal of Science 45(1):3–11.

*Foster, B. C. 1906. Where are the deer? Forest and Stream 66:996.

Fouch, W. R. 1958. Longevity records for the fox squirrel. Journal of Mammalogy 39(1):154–155.

*Fox, I. 1968. Fleas of eastern United States. New York: Hafner Publishing Company.

*Freeland, E. D. 1948. Shenandoah National Park. Virginia Wildlife 9(9):17–20.

*Freer, R. S., and F. T. Hanenkrat. 1980. The central Blue Ridge. Part III: The fauna of the Blue Ridge. Virginia Wildlife 41(9):16–20.

*French, T. W. 1976. The first record of the southeastern shrew, *Sorex longirostris,* in West Virginia. Proceedings of the West Virginia Academy of Science 48:120–122.

*French, T. W. 1980a. *Sorex longirostris.* Mammalian Species no. 143.

*French, T. W. 1980b. Natural history of the southeastern shrew, *Sorex longirostris.* Bachman. American Midland Naturalist 104:13–31.

*French, T. W. 1981. Notes on the distribution and taxonomy of short-tailed shrews (genus *Blarina*) in the Southeast. Brimleyana no. 6:101–110.

*French, T. W. 1984. Dietary overlap of *Sorex longirostris* and *Sorex cinereus* in hardwood floodplain habitats in Vigo County, Indiana. American Midland Naturalist 111(1):41–46.

*Freund, F. R. 1954. Insects and wildlife. Virginia Wildlife 15(5):18–19, 21.

*Friedman, H. 1967. Colour vision in the Virginia opossum. Nature 213(5078):835–836.

*Fritzell, E. K., and K. J. Haroldson. 1982. *Urocyon cinereoargenteus.* Mammalian Species no. 189.

*Frost, N. 1946. The American elk. Pp. 40–43. In: Gallery of North American game. New York: Outdoor Life.

*Frum, W. G. 1948. *Corynorhinus macrotis,* big-eared bat, in West Virginia. Journal of Mammalogy 29(4):418.

*Fujita, M. S., and T. H. Kunz. 1984. *Pipistrellus subflavus.* Mammalian Species no. 228.

*Fulgham, T. 1981. The muskrat. Virginia Wildlife 42(12):7–8.

*Funderburg, J. B. 1961. Erythristic raccoons from North Carolina. Journal of Mammalogy 42(2):270–271.

*Funderburg, J. B. 1974. A preliminary ecological survey of the Mattaponi-Polecat Creek Swamp in Caroline County, Virginia. Bulletin of the Maryland Herpetological Society 10(3):73–76.

*G. W. B. 1878. Glorious old Gloucester, Virginia. Forest and Stream 11:33–34.

Gabrielson, G. W., and E. N. Smith. 1985. Physiological responses associated with feigned death in the American opossum. Acta Physiologica Scandinavica 123(4):393–398.

*Gabrielson, I. N. 1960. Wildlife and agriculture in Virginia. Virginia Wildlife 21(2):4–6.

*Gallatin, A. 1836. A synopsis of the Indian tribes within the United States east of the Rocky Mountains, and in the British and Russian possessions in

North America. Transactions and Collections of the American Antiquarian Society 2:1–422.

*Gardner, A. L. 1982. Virginia opossum. Pp. 3–36. In: Chapman, J. A., and G. A. Feldhamer (editors), Wild mammals of North America. Baltimore: The Johns Hopkins University Press.

*Gardner, M., C. 1946. A new cotton rat from Virginia. Proceedings of the Biological Society of Washington 59:137.

*Garner, N. P., and M. R. Vaughan. 1987. Black bears' use of abandoned homesites in Shenandoah National Park. International Conference on Bear Research and Management 7:151–157.

*Garner, N. P., and M. R. Vaughan. 1989. Black bear-human interactions in Shenandoah National Park, Virginia. Pp. 155–161. In: Bromley, M. (editor), Bear-People Conflicts: Proceedings of a Symposium on Management Strategies. 1989.

*Garretson, M. S. 1938. The American bison. New York: New York Zoological Society.

*Garrett, M. K., and D. F. Sonenshine. 1979. The ecology of the two dominant tick species in relation to the Dismal Swamp National Wildlife Refuge in Virginia. Pp. 222–243. In: Kirk, P. W., Jr. (editor), The Great Dismal Swamp. Charlottesville: University Press of Virginia.

Garshelis, D. L. 1978. Movement, ecology and activity behavior of black bears in the Great Smoky Mountains National Park. Master's thesis, University of Tennessee.

*Garshelis, D. L., and E. C. Hellgren. 1994. Variation in reproductive biology of male black bears. Journal of Mammalogy 75(1):175–188.

Gaskin, D. E., P. W. Arnold, and B. A. Blair. 1974. *Phocoena phocoena*. Mammalian Species no. 42.

*Gaston, G. R. 1979. Exploring the eerie depths. Virginia Wildlife 40(10):16–19.

Gates, W. H. 1937. Notes on the big brown bat. Journal of Mammalogy 18(1):97–98.

*Gaudette, M. T. 1986. Modeling winter habitat for white-tailed deer in southwestern Virginia. Master's thesis, Virginia Polytechnic Institute and State University, Blacksburg.

*Gaudette, M. T., and D. F. Stauffer. 1988. Assessing habitat of white-tailed deer in southwestern Virginia. Wildlife Society Bulletin 16(3):284–290.

*Gavitt, J. D. 1973. Disturbance effect of free-running dogs on deer reproduction. Master's thesis, Virginia Polytechnic Institute and State University, Blacksburg.

*Gavitt, J. D., R. L. Downing, and B. S. McGinnes. 1975. Effect of dogs on deer reproduction in Virginia. Proceedings of the 28th Annual Conference of the Southeastern Association of Game and Fish Commissioners 28:532–539.

*Genoways, H. H., J. R. Choate, E. F. Pembleton, I. F. Greenbaum, and J. W. Bickham. 1976. Systematists, other users, and uses of North American collections of recent mammals. Museology, Texas Tech University. no. 3.

Gentry, J. B. 1968. Dynamics of an enclosed population of pine mice, *Microtus pinetorum*. Research in Population Ecology 10(1):21–30.

*Gentry, W. 1971. Rare kill in Fluvanna. Virginia Wildlife 32(11):21.

*George, S. B. 1988. Systematics, historical biogeography, and evolution of the genus *Sorex*. Journal of Mammalogy 69(3):443–461.

*George, S. B., J. R. Choate, and H. H. Genoways. 1986. *Blarina brevicauda*. Mammalian Species no. 261.

*George, S. B., H. H. Genoways, J. R. Choate, and R. J. Baker. 1982. Karyotypic relationships within the short-tailed shrews, genus *Blarina*. Journal of Mammalogy 63(4):639–645.

*Gerardi, M. H., and J. E. Fisher. 1975. The effects of an interstate highway upon movement patterns of small rodents. Virginia Journal of Science 26(2):55. Abstract.

*Getz, L. L. 1960. Home ranges of the bog lemming. Journal of Mammalogy 41(3):404–405.

*Getz, L. L. 1989. A 14-year study of *Blarina brevicauda* populations in east-central Illinois. Journal of Mammalogy 70(1):58–66.

Giacolone-Madden, J. R. 1976. The behavioral ecology of the southern flying squirrel, *Glaucomys volans*, Long Island, New York. Doctoral dissertation, City University of New York.

*Gibson, D. 1979. Birds and bats. Virginia Wildlife 40(2):30.

*Gibson, D. F. 1980. Clinical and physiological assessment of xylazine hydrochloride (Rompun) applications in captive white-tailed deer with emphasis on handling stress. Master's thesis, Virginia Polytechnic Institute and State University, Blacksburg.

*Gidley, J. W., and C. L. Gazin. 1933. New Mammalia in the Pleistocene fauna from Cumberland Cave. Journal of Mammalogy 14(4):343–357.

*Gidley, J. W., and C. L. Gazin. 1938. The Pleistocene vertebrate fauna from Cumberland Cave, Maryland. Bulletin of the United States National Museum 171.

Gier, H. T. 1968. Coyotes in Kansas. Kansas State University Agriculture Experiment Station Bulletin no. 393.

*Gilchrist, C. P. 1964. The controversial Mr. Beaver. Virginia Wildlife 25(1):8–9.

*Gildea, L., Jr. 1961. The burnt hammock bear. Virginia Wildlife 22(11):9–10.

Giles, L. W. 1943. Evidences of raccoon mobility obtained by tagging. Journal of Wildlife Management 7(2):235.

*Giles, R. H., Jr. 1959. About bats. Virginia Wildlife 20(10):20–21.

*Giles, R. H., Jr. 1960. Salt as a game management tool. Virginia Wildlife 21(8):16–17.

*Giles, R. H., Jr. 1974. An earring for Elmer. Virginia Wildlife 35(10):18.

*Giles, R. H., Jr., and A. B. Carey. 1973. Notes on rabies in Virginia. Virginia Wildlife 34(7):8.

*Giles, R. H., Jr., and J. V. Gwynn. 1962. The Alleghany County, Virginia, deer herd. Virginia Journal of Science 13(1):1–16.

*Gill, T. N., and E. Coues. 1877. Material for a bibliography of North American mammals. Pp. 951–1081 (Appendix B). In: Coues, E., and J. A. Allen (editors), Monographs of North American Rodentia. Report of the United States Geological Survey of the Territories. Volume 11.

*Gill, W. 1981. Manatee found in Chesapeake Bay Virginia. Endangered Species Technical Bulletin. Department of the Interior, United States Fish and Wildlife Service Endangered Species Program, Washington, DC. 6(1):6–7.

*Gillam, H. (editor). 1962a. The drumming log. Virginia Wildlife 23(3):23–24.

*Gillam, H. (editor). 1962b. The drumming log. Virginia Wildlife 23(6):23–24.

*Gillam, H. (editor). 1962c. The drumming log. Virginia Wildlife 23(8):25.

*Gillam, H. (editor). 1962d. The drumming log. Virginia Wildlife 23(9):24–25.

*Gillam, H. (editor). 1963a. The drumming log. Virginia Wildlife 24(1):22.

*Gillam, H. (editor). 1963b. The drumming log. Virginia Wildlife 24(8):24.

*Gillam, H. (editor). 1963c. Bowhunter's buck from Gathright. Virginia Wildlife 24(12):24.

*Gillam, H. (editor). 1964a. New record whitetail tops trophy contest. Virginia Wildlife 25(1):14–15.

*Gillam, H. (editor). 1964b. Deadly duel. Virginia Wildlife 25(1):24.

*Gillam, H. (editor). 1964c. Dog victim recovers nicely. Virginia Wildlife 25(1):24.

*Gillam, H. (editor). 1964d. Nice Fauquier buck. Virginia Wildlife 25(2):24.

*Gillam, H. (editor). 1964e. Wheelchair no handicap to outdoor fan. Virginia Wildlife 25(2):24.

*Gillam, H. (editor). 1964f. Freak deer bagged in state. Virginia Wildlife 25(3):24.

*Gillam, H. (editor). 1964g. Big racks from Fluvanna. Virginia Wildlife 25(4):23.

*Gillam, H. (editor). 1964h. Big bear. Virginia Wildlife 25(4):23.

*Gillam, H. (editor). 1965a. Nice trophy heads typify contest. Virginia Wildlife 26(1):14–15.

*Gillam, H. (editor). 1965b. Bowman's bear. Virginia Wildlife 26(1):24.

*Gillam, H. (editor). 1965c. Archer scores bullseye on running deer. Virginia Wildlife 26(1):24.

*Gillam, H. (editor). 1965d. Sika deer again for Assateague. Virginia Wildlife 26(7):24.

*Gillam, H. (editor). 1966a. Archery wounds not fatal. Virginia Wildlife 27(1):24.

*Gillam, H. (editor). 1966b. Rack roundup. Virginia Wildlife 27(2):6–7.

*Gillam, H. (editor). 1966c. Sika buck. Virginia Wildlife 27(9):24.

*Gillam, H. (editor). 1967a. Western deer again tops trophy contest. Virginia Wildlife 28(1):25.

*Gillam, H. (editor). 1967b. Old-timer bags first buck. Virginia Wildlife 28(2):24.

*Gillam, H. (editor). 1967c. Duel to the death. Virginia Wildlife 28(2):24.

*Gillam, H. (editor). 1967d. Freak buck. Virginia Wildlife 28(3):21.

*Gillam, H. (editor). 1967e. Minister bags trophy buck. Virginia Wildlife 28(4):24.

*Gillam, H. (editor). 1967f. Spotsylvania buck. Virginia Wildlife 28(6):24.

*Gillam, H. (editor). 1968a. Fox catch from suburbs indicates high numbers. Virginia Wildlife 29(5):24.

*Gillam, H. (editor). 1968b. The ugly game of spotlighting. Virginia Wildlife 29(6):24.

*Gillam, H. (editor). 1969. Big game trophy show. Virginia Wildlife 30(12):21.

*Gillam, H. (editor). 1970a. Big Spotsylvania rack. Virginia Wildlife 31(3):24.

*Gillam, H. (editor). 1970b. Handsome Chesterfield buck. Virginia Wildlife 31(3):24.

*Gillam, H. (editor). 1971a. A tale that bears retelling. Virginia Wildlife 32(2):24.

*Gillam, H. (editor). 1971b. The drumming log. Virginia Wildlife 32(4):24.

*Gillam, H. (editor). 1971c. Giant Brunswick buck. Virginia Wildlife 32(5):24.

*Gillam, H. (editor). 1971d. Old pitchfork brought to bag. Virginia Wildlife 32(6):24.

*Gillam, H. (editor). 1971e. Tremendous buck. Virginia Wildlife 32(9):24.

*Gillam, H. (editor). 1972a. Trapper makes surprise catch. Virginia Wildlife 33(1):24.

*Gillam, H. (editor). 1972b. The drumming log. Virginia Wildlife 33(2):24.

*Gillam, H. (editor). 1972c. Thoughtless slaughter. Virginia Wildlife 33(3):22.

*Gillam, H. (editor). 1972d. The drumming log. Virginia Wildlife 33(8):23.

*Gillam, H. (editor). 1977. More wildlife on your property. Virginia Commission of Game and Inland Fisheries, Richmond.

*Gillam, H. L. 1983. The shrews — a pictorial essay on these voracious little mammals. Virginia Wildlife 44(1):16–19.

*Gillam, H. L. 1984. The small rodents. Virginia Wildlife 45(2):10–13.

Gillette, L. N. 1980. Movement patterns of radio-tagged opossums in Wisconsin. American Midland Naturalist 104(1):1–12.

*Gilley, S. 1982. The Delmarva fox squirrel: making a comeback? Virginia Wildlife 43(12):24–25.

*Gilley, M. S. 1987. The role of education in Virginia's nongame program. Proceedings of the Southeastern Nongame Endangered Wildlife Symposium 3:242–244.

*Gilmore, R. M. 1946. Mammals in archeological collections from southwestern Pennsylvania. Journal of Mammalogy 27(3):227–234.

Gilmore, R. M. 1978. Right whale. Pp. 62–69. In: Haley, D. (editor), Marine mammals of eastern North Pacific and Arctic waters. Seattle: Pacific Search Press.

*Gilmore, R. M., and J. E. Gates. 1985. Habitat use by the southern flying squirrel at a hemlock-northern hardwood ecotone. Journal of Wildlife Management 49(3):703–710.

Gipson, P. S., and J. A. Sealander. 1972. Home range and activity of the coyote *(Canis latrans frustror)* in Arkansas. Proceedings of the 26th Annual Conference of the Southeastern Association of Game and Fish Commissioners 26:82–95.

*Givens, L. S. 1938. A preliminary ecological survey to determine the potentialities of the Mountain Lake region for wildlife production. Master's thesis, Virginia Polytechnic Institute and State University, Blacksburg.

*Glenn, H. 1927. Bruin, the modern "Dread Scott" of the Dismal Swamp. Game and Fish Conservationist 7(3):51–52.

*Glover, T. 1676. An account of Virginia, its scituation, temperature, productions, inhabitants, and their manner of planting and ordering tobacco. Philosophical Transactions of the Royal Society of London 11(126):625–626.

*Godfrey, C. 1995. Black bears: my first choice in research. Virginia Wildlife 56(9):31.

*Godin. A. J. 1977. Wild mammals of New England. Baltimore: The Johns Hopkins University Press.

*Godin, A. J. 1982. Striped and hooded skunks. Pp. 674–687. In: Chapman, J. A., and G. A. Feldhamer (editors), Wild mammals of North America. Baltimore: The Johns Hopkins University Press.

*Godman, J. D. 1826–28. American Natural History. Part I. Mastology. 3 volumes. Philadelphia: H. C. Carey and I Lea. (Reprinted 1974 by Arno Press, New York.)

*Godman, J. D. 1846. American Natural History. 3d ed. 2 volumes. Philadelphia: Uriah Hunt and Son.

*Goertz, J. W. 1964. The influence of habitat quality upon the density of cotton rat populations. Ecological Monographs 34(4):359–381.

Goertz, J. W. 1965. Reproductive variation in cotton rats. American Midland Naturalist 74(2):329–340.

Goertz, J. W. 1970. An ecological study of *Neotoma floridana* in Oklahoma. Journal of Mammalogy 51(1):94–104.

*Goldman, E. A. 1910. Revision of the wood rats of the genus *Neotoma.* North American Fauna 31.

*Goldman, E. A. 1918. The rice rats of North America (genus *Oryzomys*). North American Fauna 43.

*Goldman, E. A. 1939. North American big game. Pp. 407–414. In: A book of the Boone and Crockett Club. New York: Charles Scribner's Sons.

*Goldman, E. A. 1944. Status of *Peromyscus nuttalli aureolus*. Journal of Mammalogy 25(4):414.

*Goldman, E. A. 1950. Raccoons of North and Middle American. North American Fauna 60.

*Goldsmith, C. D. 1976. Lead levels in soil, vegetation, and animals associated with highways of various traffic densities. Master's thesis, Virginia Polytechnic Institute and State University, Blacksburg.

*Goldsmith, C. D., Jr., M. N. Berkaw, and P. F. Scanlon. 1974. Body weight-organ weight relationships in cottontail rabbits. Virginia Journal of Science 25(2):63. Abstract.

*Goldsmith, C. D., Jr., and P. F. Scanlon. 1977. Lead levels in small mammals and selected invertebrates associated with highways of different traffic densities. Bulletin of Environmental and Contamination Toxicology 17(3):311–316.

*Golley, F. B. 1962. Mammals of Georgia. Athens: University of Georgia Press.

*Gooch, B. 1969. Hunters' longest season. Virginia Wildlife 30(10):4–5, 20.

*Gooch, B. 1970. Hunt and harvest the surplus. Virginia Wildlife 31(12):8–9.

*Gooch, B. 1980. Habitat and harvest produce deer. Virginia Wildlife 41(2):31.

*Gooch, B. 1989. There's no tougher sport. Virginia Wildlife 50(2):26–29.

*Gooch, B. 1989. Welcoming the bears home. Virginia Wildlife 50(12):4–7.

*Gooch, Bob. 1991. Squirrels of the season. Virginia Wildlife 52(10):13–16.

*Goode, G. B. 1878. The occurrence of the Canada porcupine in West Virginia. Smithsonian Miscellaneous Collections 19(1):264–265. (Proceedings of the United States National Museum 1:264–265.

*Goode, G. B. 1886. The beginnings of natural history in America. Annual presidential address delivered at the sixth anniversary meeting of the Biological Society of Washington, February 6, 1886. Pp. 355–406. In: Annual Report of the Board of Regents Smithsonian Institution for Year Ending June 30, 1897. Washington, DC. (1901). Also in Sterling, K. B. 1974. Contributions to the history of American natural history. New York: Arno Press. 1974.

*Goode, G. B. 1896. Albemarle in Revolutionary days. National Geographic Magazine 7(8):271–281.

*Goode, G. B. 1901. The beginnings of American science. Annual Report of the Board of Regents Smithsonian Institution for Year Ending June 30, 1897:407–466.

Goodpaster, W. W., and D. F. Hoffmeister. 1950. Bats as prey for mink in Kentucky cave. Journal of Mammalogy 31(4):457.

*Goodpaster, W. W., and D. F. Hoffmeister. 1954. Life history of the golden mouse *Peromyscus nuttalli,* in Kentucky. Journal of Mammalogy 35(1):16–27.

*Goodrich, J. M., and J. Berger, 1994. Winter recreation and hibernating black bears. Biological Conservation 67(2):105–110.

*Goodrich, S. G. 1859 (1861). Illustrated natural history of the animal kingdom. Volume I. New York: Derby and Jackson.

*Goodwin, G. G. 1935. The mammals of Connecticut. Hartford.

*Goodwin, G. G. 1954. Southern records for Arctic mammals and a northern record for Alfaro's rice rat. Journal of Mammalogy 35(2):258.

*Goodwin, S. 1979. The phantom of River Bend farm. Virginia Wildlife 40(3):4–6.

*Gosling, L. M., and S. J. Baker. 1981. Coypu *(Myocastor coypus)* potential longevity. Journal of Zoology (London) 197(2):285–289.

*Gottmann, J. 1955. Virginia at mid-century. New York: Henry Holt Company.

Gottschang, J. L. 1956. Juvenile molt in *Peromyscus leucopus noveboracensis*. Journal of Mammalogy 37(4):516–520.

*Gould, D. J., and M. L. Miesse. 1954. Recovery of a *Rickettsia* of the spotted fever group from *Microtus pennsylvanicus* from Virginia. Proceedings of the Society for Experimental Biology and Medicine 85:558–561.

Gould, E. 1955. The feeding efficiency of insectivorous bats. Journal of Mammalogy 36(3):399–407.

Gould, E. 1969. Communication in three genera of shrews (Soricidae): *Suncus, Blarina,* and *Cryptotis*. Communications in Behavioral Biology, Part A. 3(1):11–31.

Gould, E., W. McShea, and T. Grand. 1993. Function of the star in the star-nosed mole, *Condylura cristata*. Journal of Mammalogy 74(1):108–116.

Gould, E., N. C. Negus, and A. Novick. 1964. Evidence for echolocation in shrews. Journal of Experimental Zoology 156(1):19–38.

*Gouveia, M. E. B. 1978. Don't eat the garbage. Virginia Wildlife 39(6):10–11.

*Grady, F. 1995. The first record of *Arctodus simus* from Virginia. Program 1995, National Speleological Society Convention, Blacksburg Virginia, p. 38. Abstract.

*Graf, R. L. 1973. Methods for delineating wildlife and other environmental management regions. Master's thesis, Virginia Polytechnic Institute and State University, Blacksburg.

*Graf, R. L., and R. H. Giles, Jr. 1974. A technique for delineating optimum deer management regions. Proceedings of the 28th Annual Conference of the Southeastern Association of Game and Fish Commissioners 28:581–586.

*Graham, J. 1978. Underground weather forecaster. Virginia Wildlife 39(2):24–25.

*Graham, R. W., and H. A. Semken. 1976. Paleoecological significance of the short-tailed shrew *(Blarina),* with a systematic discussion of *Blarina ozarkensis*. Journal of Mammalogy 57(3):433–449.

*Gram, W. D., H. W. Heath, H. A. Wichman, and G. R. Lynch. 1982. Geographic variation in *Peromyscus leucopus:* short-day induced reproductive regression and spontaneous recrudescense. Biology of Reproduction 27(2):369–373.

*Graves, S., J. Maldonado, and J. O. Wolff. 1988. Use of ground and arboreal microhabitats by *Peromyscus leucopus* and *Peromyscus maniculatus*. Canadian Journal of Zoology 66(1):277–278.

*Green, D. D. 1940. Controlling predatory animals. American Wildlife 29(1):35–40.

*Green, K. 1978. Backpacking the skyline. Virginia Wildlife 39(3):18–20.

*Green, W. 1969. Camp Pickett's eager beavers. Virginia Wildlife 30(6):20–21.

*Greenberg, C. H., and M. R. Pelton. 1991. Food habits of gray foxes *(Urocyon cinereoargenteus)* and red foxes *(Vulpes)* in east Tennessee. Journal of the Tennessee Academy of Science 66(2):79–84.

Greenberg, C. H. and M. R. Pelton. 1994. Home range and activity patterns by gray foxes *Urocyon cinereoargenteus* (Carnivora: Canidae), in east Tennessee. Brimleyana 21:131–140.

*Greenfield, R. 1938. *Napaeozapus insignis* in Virginia. Journal of Mammalogy 19(2):254.

Greenhall, A. M. 1973. Indiana bat: a cave-dweller in trouble. National Parks and Conservation Magazine 47(8):14–17.

Griffin, D. R. 1940. Migrations of New England bats. Bulletin of the Museum of Comparative Zoology, Harvard University 86:216–247.

Griffin, D. R. 1953. Bat sounds under natural conditions, with evidence for echolocation of insect prey. Journal of Experimental Zoology 123(3):435–466.

Griffin, D. R. 1958. More about bat "radar." Scientific American 199(1):40–44.

Griffin, D. R. 1970. Migrations and homing of bats. Pp. 233–265. In: Wimsatt, W. A. (editor), Biology of bats. New York: Academic Press.

Griffin, D. R., J. H. Friend, and F. A. Webster. 1965. Target discrimination by the echolocation of bats. Journal of Experimental Zoology 158(2):155–168.

Griffin, D. R., and H. B. Hitchcock. 1965. Probable 24-year longevity records for *Myotis lucifugus*. Journal of Mammalogy 46(2):332.

Griffin, D. R., F. A. Webster, and C. R. Michael. 1960. The echolocation of flying insects by bats. Animal Behaviour 8:141–154.

*Griffith, L. A., and J. E. Gates. 1985. Food habits of cave-dwelling bats in the central Appalachians. Journal of Mammalogy 66(3):451–460.

Grimes, F. G. 1935a. Abstract of fur laws, 1935–36. United States Department of Agriculture, Bureau of Biological Survey, Wildlife Research and Management Leaflet BS-23.

*Grimes, F. G. 1935b. Bounties paid by states. United States Department of Agriculture, Bureau of Biological Survey, Wildlife Research and Management Leaflet BS-24.

Grimes, F. G. 1936. Abstract of fur laws, 1936–37. United States Department of Agriculture, Bureau of Biological Survey, Wildlife Research and Management Leaflet BS-68.

*Grimes, F. G. 1937. Abstract of fur laws, 1937–38. United States Department of Agriculture, Bureau of Biological Survey, Wildlife Research and Management Leaflet BS-97.

*Grimes, F. G. 1938. Abstract of fur laws, 1938–39. United States Department of Agriculture, Bureau of Biological Survey, Wildlife Research and Management Leaflet BS-118.

*Grimes, F. G. 1939. Abstract of fur laws, 1939–40. Wildlife Leaflet 147, United States Department of the Interior, Fish and Wildlife Service.

*Grimes, F. G. 1940. Abstract of fur laws, 1940–41. Wildlife Leaflet 174, United States Department of the Interior, Fish and Wildlife Service.

Grimm, W. C., and H. A. Roberts. 1950. Mammal survey of southwestern Pennsylvania. Pittman-

Robertson Project 24-R, Pennsylvania Game Commission, Harrisburg.
Grimm, W. C., and R. Whitebread. 1952. Mammal survey of northeastern Pennsylvania. Pennsylvania Game Commission, Harrisburg.
Grinnell, J., J. S. Dixon, and J. M. Linsdale. 1937. Furbearing mammals of California. Their natural history, systematic status, and relations to man. 2 volumes. Berkeley: University of California Press.
Grizzell, R. A., Jr. 1955. A study of the southern woodchuck, *Marmota monax monax*. American Midland Naturalist 53(2):257–293.
*Guerrero, R. 1994. *Sciurodendrium gardneri,* new species (Nematoda: Trichostrongyloidea: Heligmonellidae), a parasite of *Sciurus carolinensis* Gmelin. 1788 (Mammalia: Sciuridae), with comments on the biogeography of *Sciurodendrum* Durette-desset. 1971. Proceedings of the Biological Society of Washington 107(1):179–184.
*Guggisberg, C. A. W. 1975. Wild cats of the world. New York: Taplinger Publishing Company.
Guilday, J. E. 1949. Winter food of Pennsylvania mink. Pennsylvania Game News 20(19):12, 32.
*Guilday, J. E. 1958. The prehistoric distribution of the opossum. Journal of Mammalogy 39(1):39–43.
*Guilday, J. E. 1962. The Pleistocene local fauna of the Natural Chimneys, Augusta County, Virginia. Annals of the Carnegie Museum 36:87–122.
*Guilday, J. E. 1968. Grizzly bears from eastern North America. American Midland Naturalist 79(1):247–250.
*Guilday, J. E. 1971. The Pleistocene history of the Appalachian mammal fauna. Pp. 233–262. In: Holt, P. C. (editor), The distributional history of the biota of the southern Appalachians. Part III. Vertebrates. Blacksburg: Virginia Polytechnic Institute and State University.
*Guilday, J. E., and H. W. Hamilton. 1966. The late Pleistocene small mammals of Eagle Cave, Pendleton County, West Virginia. Annals of the Carnegie Museum 44:45–58.
*Guilday, J. E., and H. W. Hamilton. 1978. Ecological significance of displaced boreal mammals in West Virginia caves. Journal of Mammalogy 59(1):176–181.
*Guilday, J. E., H. W. Hamilton, and P. W. Parmalee. 1975. Caribou (*Rangifer tarandus* L.) from the Pleistocene of Tennessee. Journal of the Tennessee Academy of Science 50:109–112.
*Guilday, J. E., P. W. Parmalee, and H. W. Hamilton. 1977. The Clark's Cave bone deposit and the late Pleistocene paleoecology of the central Appalachian Mountains of Virginia. Bulletin of the Carnegie Museum of Natural History no. 2:1–87.
Gunderson. H. 1944. Notes on a heavy Norway rat population. Journal of Mammalogy 25(3):307–308.
Gunter, G. 1942a. Contributions to the natural history of the bottle-nose dolphin, *Tursiops truncatus* (Montague), on the Texas coast, with particular reference to food habits. Journal of Mammalogy 23(3):267–276.
*Gunter, G. 1942b. Further miscellaneous notes on American manatees. Journal of Mammalogy 23(1): 89–90.
*Gunter, G. 1954. Mammals of the Gulf of Mexico. United States Fish and Wildlife Service Fishery Bulletin 89. Volume 55:543–551.
Gurnell, J. 1987. The natural history of squirrels. New York: Facts on File Publications.
*Gutheim, F. A. 1949. The Potomac. New York: Rinehart and Company.
*Guthrie, D. R. 1965a. Fear-stress in the gray squirrel *(Sciurus carolinensis).* Master's thesis, Virginia Polytechnic Institute and State University, Blacksburg.
*Guthrie, D. R. 1965b. Some physiological changes associated with fatal fear-stress in the gray squirrel. Virginia Journal of Science 16(4):338. Abstract.
*Guthrie, D. R., H. S. Mosby, and J. C. Osborne. 1966. Hematological values for the eastern gray squirrel *(Sciurus carolinensis).* Canadian Journal of Zoology 44:323–327.
*Guthrie, D. R., J. C. Osborne, and H. S. Mosby. 1967. Physiological changes associated with shock in confined gray squirrels. Journal of Wildlife Management 31(1):102–108.
Guthrie, M. J. 1933. Notes on the seasonal movements and habits of some cave bats. Journal of Mammalogy 14(1):1–19.
*Guthrie, W. A. 1964a. An investigation of sampling methodology of winter browse. Master's thesis, Virginia Polytechnic Institute and State University, Blacksburg.
*Guthrie, W. A. 1964b. Sampling methodology of winter deer browse. Virginia Journal of Science 15(4):289. Abstract.
*Guthrie, W. A. 1966a. Squirrels: when should we hunt them? Virginia Wildlife 27(5):14–15.
*Guthrie, W. A. 1966b. Brunswick co-op area pays off. Virginia Wildlife 27(9):6–7.
*Guthrie, W. A. 1968a. Arcadia wildlife management unit. Virginia Wildlife 29(8):4–5.
*Guthrie, W. A. 1968b. Wildlife management on the Blacksburg ranger district. Virginia Wildlife 29(9):7, 20.
*Guthrie, W. A. 1968c. Wildlife management on the New Castle ranger district. Virginia Wildlife 29(10):8.
*Guthrie, W. A. 1974. Scram or stay put? Virginia Wildlife 35(10):12.
*Gwathmey, J. H. 1951. The Mattaponi. Virginia Wildlife 12(2):18–20.
*Gwathmey, J. H. 1952. Opportunities for hunting in Virginia. Virginia Wildlife 13(11):5–7.
*Gwynn, J. 1987. Deer herd health check. Virginia Wildlife 48(11):28.
*Gwynn, J. V. 1958. How it fared west of the Blue Ridge. Virginia Wildlife 19(3):10–11.
*Gwynn, J. V. 1963. Big game harvest. Virginia Wildlife 24(11):8.
*Gwynn, J. V. 1964. Big game forecast. Virginia Wildlife 25(11):8–9.
*Gwynn, J. V. 1965a. Western deer herd report. Virginia Wildlife 26(1):16–17.

*Gwynn, J. V. 1965b. Sportsman: we can give you sustained yield deer herd management (if you want it). Virginia Wildlife 26(11):4–6, 22.

*Gwynn, J. V. 1976. The Virginia deer management program 1946–1976. Paper read at 12th Northeast Deer Study Group meeting, Chicopee, Massachusetts, August 31-September 2, 1976.

*Gwynn, J. V., J. E. Thornton, and H. A. Trumbo. 1966. The western deer season — 1965. Virginia Wildlife 27(2):4–5, 22.

*Hagmeier, E. M. 1957. Distribution of marten and fisher in North America. Canadian Field-Naturalist 70(4):149–168.

*Hahn, W. L. 1908. The mammals of Indiana. Pp. 417–663. In: 33d Annual Report,Indiana Department of Geology and Natural Resources.

*Hakim, S. A. 1993. Seasonal range and habitat selection by white-tailed deer in northwestern Virginia. Doctoral dissertation, University of Montana, Missoula.

*Halbrook, R. S. 1990. Muskrat population in Virginia's Elizabeth River: influence of environmental contaminants. Doctoral dissertation, Virginia Polytechnic Institute and State University, Blacksburg.

*Halbrook, R. S., R. L. Kirkpatrick, P. F. Scanlon, M. R. Vaughan, and H. P. Veit. 1993. Muskrat populations in Virginia's Elizabeth River: physiological condition and accumulation of environmental contaminants. Archives of Environmental Contamination and Toxicology 25(4):438–445.

*Hale, E. E. 1860. Original documents from the state-paper office, London, and the British museum; illustrating the history of Sir Walter Raleigh's first American colony, and the colony at Jamestown. Archeologia Americana 4:21–24.

*Hale, J. P. 1931. Trans-Allegheny pioneers. Historical sketches of the first white settlers west of the Alleghenies 1748 and after. 2d edition. Charleston, West Virginia: Kanawha Valley Publishing Company.

Haley, D. (editor). 1978. Marine mammals of eastern North Pacific and Arctic waters. Seattle: Pacific Search Press.

*Haley, W. D. (editor). 1860. Phillip's Washington described. New York: Rudd and Carleton.

Hall, D. A. 1996. Simple tools, hearth found beneath Clovis horizon: S. E. Virginia site yields 15,000-year-old date. Mammoth Trumpet 11 (4): 1, 14–18.

*Hall, E. R. 1951. A synopsis of the North American lagomorpha. University of Kansas Publications, Museum of Natural History 5(10):119–202.

*Hall, E. R. 1958. Introduction, Part II. Pp. 371–373. In: Hubbs, C. L. (editor), Zoogeography. American Association for the Advancement of Science Publication 51.

*Hall, E. R. 1981. The mammals of North America. Volumes 1 and 2. New York: John Wiley and Sons.

*Hall, E. R., and E. L. Cockrum. 1953. A synopsis of the North American microtine rodents. University of Kansas Publications, Museum of Natural History 5(27):373–498.

*Hall. E. R., and J. K. Jones, Jr. 1961. North American yellow bats, "Dasypterus", and a list of the named kinds of the genus *Lasiurus* Gray. University of Kansas Publications, Museum of Natural History 14:73–98.

*Hall, H. F., III. 1978. The ecology of rabies in northeastern Tennessee. Doctoral dissertation, University of Tennessee, Knoxville.

*Hall, J. S. 1962. A life history and taxonomic study of the Indiana bat, *Myotis sodalis*. Reading Public Museum and Art Gallery, no. 12. Reading, Pennsylvania.

Hall, J. S., R. J. Cloutier, and D. R. Griffin. 1957. Longevity records and notes on tooth wear of bats. Journal of Mammalogy 38(3):407–409.

Hall, J. S., and W. H. Davis. 1958. A record of homing in the big brown bat. Journal of Mammalogy 39(2):292.

*Hall, J. S., and N. Wilson. 1966. Seasonal populations and movements of the gray bat in the Kentucky area. American Midland Naturalist 75(2):317–324.

*Hall, P. K. 1968. Wildlife in a Virginia suburb. Virginia Wildlife 29(6):22–23.

*Hall, R. D., and E. C. Turner, Jr. 1976. The northern fowl mite (Acarina: Macromyssidae) collected from rats in a chicken house. Journal of Medical Entomology 13(2):222–223.

*Halladay, O. J. 1964. An ecological study of the elk in Bedford and Botetourt counties, Virginia. Master's thesis, University of Michigan, Ann Arbor.

*Hallberg, G. R., H. A. Semken, and L. C. Davis. 1974. Quaternary records of *Microtus xanthognathus* (Leach), the yellow-cheeked vole, from northwestern Arkansas and southwestern Iowa. Journal of Mammalogy 55(3):640–645.

*Hallett, J. G. 1978. *Parascalops breweri*. Mammalian Species no. 98.

*Hallett, J. G., M. A. O'Connell, G. D. Sanders, and J. Seidensticker. 1991. Comparison of population estimators for medium-sized mammals. Journal of Wildlife Management 55(1):81–93.

*Hallock, C. 1877. The sportsman's gazetteer and general guide; game animals, birds, and fishes of North America; their habits and various methods of capture. New York: Forest and Stream Publishing Company.

*Hallock, C. 1880. The sportsman's gazetteer and general guide. 5th edition. New York: Forest and Stream Publishing Company.

*Halls, L. K. 1978. White-tailed deer. Pp. 42–65. In: Schmidt, J. L., and D. L. Gilbert (editors), Big game of North America. Harrisburg, Pennsylvania: Stackpole Books.

*Halls, L. K. 1984. White-tailed deer. Ecology and management. Harrisburg, Pennsylvania: Stackpole Books.

*Hamilton, R. B. 1969. September squirrels? Virginia Wildlife 30(1):8–9.

Hamilton, W. J., Jr. 1929. Breeding habits of the short-tailed shrew, *Blarina brevicauda*. Journal of Mammalogy 10(2):125–134.

Hamilton, W. J., Jr. 1930. Notes on the mammals of Breathitt County, Kentucky. Journal of Mammalogy 11(3):306–311.

Hamilton, W. J., Jr. 1931. Habits of the star-nosed mole, *Condylura cristata*. Journal of Mammalogy 12(4):345–355.

Hamilton, W. J., Jr. 1933. The weasels of New York. Their natural history and economic status. American Midland Naturalist 14(4):289–344.

*Hamilton, W. J., Jr. 1934. The life history of the rufescent woodchuck, *Marmota monax rufescens* Howell. Annals of the Carnegie Museum 28:85–178.

*Hamilton, W. J., Jr. 1935. Field-mouse and rabbit control in New York orchards. Cornell Extension Bulletin 338.

Hamilton, W. J., Jr. 1936a. Food habits of the mink in New York. Journal of Mammalogy 17(2):169.

Hamilton, W. J., Jr. 1936b. Seasonal food of skunks in New York. Journal of Mammalogy 17(3)240–246.

*Hamilton, W. J., Jr. 1936c. The food and breeding habits of the raccoon. Ohio Journal of Science 36(3):131–140.

*Hamilton, W. J., Jr. 1937. The value of predatory mammals. Bulletin of the New York Zoological Society 40(2):39–45.

Hamilton, W. J., Jr. 1938. Life history notes on the northern pine mouse. Journal of Mammalogy 19(2):163–170.

*Hamilton, W. J., Jr. 1939. American mammals. Their lives, habits, and economic relations. New York: McGraw-Hill Book Company.

*Hamilton, W. J., Jr. 1940a. The biology of the smoky shrew (*Sorex fumeus fumeus* Miller). Zoologica 25:473–492.

*Hamilton, W. J., Jr. 1940b. The molt of *Blarina brevicauda*. Journal of Mammalogy 21(4):457–458.

Hamilton, W. J., Jr. 1940c. Summer food of minks and raccoons on the Montezuma marsh, New York. Journal of Wildlife Management 4(1):80–84.

Hamilton, W. J., Jr. 1941. The food of small forest mammals in eastern United States. Journal of Mammalogy 22(3):250–263.

*Hamilton, W. J., Jr. 1943. Mammals of eastern United States. New York: Cornell University Press.

*Hamilton, W. J., Jr. 1944. The biology of the little short-tailed shrew, *Cryptotis parva*. Journal of Mammalogy 25(1):1–7.

*Hamilton, W. J., Jr. 1946. Habits of the swamp rice rat, *Oryzomys palustris palustris* (Harlan). American Midland Naturalist 36(3):730–736.

*Hamilton, W. J., Jr. 1947. Rats and their control. Cornell Extension Bulletin 353.

Hamilton, W. J., Jr. 1953. Reproduction and young of the Florida wood rat, *Neotoma f. floridana* (Ord). Journal of Mammalogy 34(2):180–189.

Hamilton, W. J., Jr. 1959. Foods of mink in New York. New York Fish and Game Journal 6(1):77–85.

Hamilton, W. J., Jr. 1961. Late fall, winter, and early spring foods of 141 otters from New York. New York Fish and Game Journal 8:106–109.

Hamilton, W. J., Jr. 1963. Reproduction of the striped skunk in New York. Journal of Mammalogy 44(1): 123–124.

*Hamilton, W. J., Jr., and W. R. Eadie. 1964. Reproduction in the otter, *Lutra canadensis*. Journal of Mammalogy 45(2):242–252.

*Hamilton, W. J., Jr., and J. O. Whitaker, Jr. 1979. Mammals of the eastern United States. 2d edition. Ithaca, New York: Comstock Publishing Associates.

*Hamir, A. N., D. E. Snyder, C. A. Hanlon, and C. E. Rupprecht. 1993. A trematode (*Phagicola* sp.) — induced mesenteric lymphadenitis and enteritis in raccoons *(Procyon lotor)*. Veterinary Pathology 30(4): 373–376.

*Hamnett, W. L., and D. C. Thornton. 1953. Tar Heel wildlife. Raleigh: North Carolina Wildlife Resources Commission.

*Hamor, R. 1615. A true discourse on the present state of Virginia. till June 18, 1614. London. Reprinted 1860 by J. Munsell, Albany.

*Handley, C. O. 1931. The effect of the recent drouth on wild life in Virginia. Game and Fish Conservationist 11(2):40–41, 44.

*Handley, C. O., Jr. 1948. Habitat of the golden mouse in Virginia. Journal of Mammalogy 29(3):298–299.

*Handley, C. O., Jr. 1949. Least weasel, prey of barn owl. Journal of Mammalogy 30(4):431.

*Handley, C. O., Jr. 1953a. A new flying squirrel from the southern Appalachian Mountains. Proceedings of the Biological Society of Washington 66:191–194.

*Handley, C. O., Jr. 1953b. Abnormal coloration in the pine mouse *(Pitymys pinetorum)*. Journal of Mammalogy 34(2):262–263.

*Handley, C. O., Jr. 1955. New bats of the genus *Corynorhinus*. Journal of the Washington Academy of Sciences 45(5):147–149.

*Handley, C. O., Jr. 1956. The shrew *Sorex dispar* in Virginia. Journal of Mammalogy 37(3):435.

*Handley, C. O., Jr. 1959. A revision of American bats of the genera *Euderma* and *Plecotus*. Proceedings of the United States National Museum 110:95–246.

*Handley, C. O., Jr. 1966. A synopsis of the genus *Kogia* (pygmy sperm whales). Pp. 62–69. In: Norris, K. S. (editor), Whales, dolphins, and porpoises. Berkeley: University of California Press.

*Handley, C. O., Jr. 1971. Appalachian mammalian geography — recent epoch. Pp. 263–303. In: Holt, P. C. (editor), The distributional history of the biota of the southern Appalachians. Part III. Vertebrates. Blacksburg: Virginia Polytechnic Institute and State University.

*Handley, C. O., Jr. 1979a. Mammals of the Dismal Swamp: a historical account. Pp. 297–357. In: Kirk, P. W., Jr. (editor), The Great Dismal Swamp. Charlottesville: University Press of Virginia.

*Handley, C. O., Jr. 1979b. Mammals. Pp. 483–621. In: Linzey, D. W. (editor), Proceedings of the symposium on endangered and threatened plants and animals of Virginia. Blacksburg: Virginia Polytechnic Institute and State University.

*Handley, C. O., Jr. 1982. Deletion of *Sorex cinereus fontinalis* from taxa known to occur in Virginia. Journal of Mammalogy 63(2):319.

*Handley, C. O., Jr. 1991a. Terrestrial mammals of Virginia: trends in distribution and diversity. Virginia Journal of Science 42(2):171. Abstract.

*Handley, C. O., Jr. 1991b. Mammals. Pp. 539–616. In: Terwilliger, K., coordinator. Virginia's endangered species. Blacksburg: The McDonald & Woodward Publishing Company.

*Handley, C. O., Jr. 1992. Terrestrial mammals of Virginia: trends in distribution and diversity. Virginia Journal of Science 43(1B):157–169.

*Handley, C. O., Jr. 1997. Mammals found in Virginia. Pp. 261–263. In: D. W. Johnston (compiler). A Birder's Guide to Virginia. American Birding Association, Inc.

*Handley, C. O., Jr., and L. K. Gordon. 1979a. *Sylvilagus palustris*. Pp. 550–552. In: Linzey, D. W. (editor), Proceedings of the symposium on endangered and threatened plants and animals of Virginia. Blacksburg: Virginia Polytechnic Institute and State University.

*Handley, C. O., Jr., and L. K. Gordon. 1979b. *Sylvilagus floridanus*. Pp. 566–567. In: Linzey, D. W. (editor), Proceedings of the symposium on endangered and threatened plants and animals of Virginia. Blacksburg: Virginia Polytechnic Institute and State University.

*Handley, C. O., Jr., and L. K. Gordon. 1979c. *Sylvilagus transitionalis*. Pp. 567–571. In: Linzey, D. W. (editor), Proceedings of the symposium on endangered and threatened plants and animals of Virginia. Blacksburg: Virginia Polytechnic Institute and State University.

*Handley, C. O., Jr., and L. K. Gordon. 1979d. *Sciurus niger*. Pp. 507–513. In: Linzey, D. W. (editor), Proceedings of the symposium on endangered and threatened plants and animals of Virginia. Blacksburg: Virginia Polytechnic Institute and State University.

*Handley, C. O., Jr., and L. K. Gordon. 1979e. *Rattus rattus*. Pp. 516–518. In: Linzey, D. W. (editor), Proceedings of the symposium on endangered and threatened plants and animals of Virginia. Blacksburg: Virginia Polytechnic Institute and State University.

*Handley, C. O., Jr., and L. K. Gordon. 1979f. *Cervus nippon*. Pp. 561–565. In: Linzey, D. W. (editor), Proceedings of the symposium on endangered and threatened plants and animals of Virginia. Blacksburg: Virginia Polytechnic Institute and State University.

*Handley, C. O., Jr., and L. K. Gordon. 1979g. *Condylura cristata parva*. Pp. 537–540. In: Linzey, D. W. (editor), Proceedings of the symposium on endangered and threatened plants and animals of Virginia. Blacksburg: Virginia Polytechnic Institute and State University.

*Handley, C. O., Jr., and L. K. Gordon. 1979h. *Lutra canadensis*. Pp. 522–526. In: Linzey, D. W. (editor), Proceedings of the symposium on endangered and threatened plants and animals of Virginia. Blacksburg: Virginia Polytechnic Institute and State University.

*Handley, C. O., Jr., and L. K. Gordon. 1979i. *Felis concolor*. Pp. 527–532. In: Linzey, D. W. (editor), Proceedings of the symposium on endangered and threatened plants and animals of Virginia. Blacksburg: Virginia Polytechnic Institute and State University.

*Handley, C. O. Jr., and L. K. Gordon. 1979j. *Ursus americanus*. Pp. 552–558. In: Linzey, D. W. (editor), Proceedings of the symposium on endangered and threatened plants and animals of Virginia. Blacksburg: Virginia Polytechnic Institute and State University.

*Handley, C. O. Jr., and L. K. Gordon. 1979k. *Peromyscus gossypinus*. Pp. 572–573. In: Linzey, D. W. (editor), Proceedings of the symposium on endangered and threatened plants and animals of Virginia. Blacksburg: Virginia Polytechnic Institute and State University.

*Handley, C. O. Jr., and L. K. Gordon. 1979l. *Microtus chrotorrhinus*. Pp. 574–576. In: Linzey, D. W. (editor), Proceedings of the symposium on endangered and threatened plants and animals of Virginia. Blacksburg: Virginia Polytechnic Institute and State University.

*Handley, C. O. Jr., and L. K. Gordon. 1979m. *Synaptomys cooperi*. Pp. 577–580. In: Linzey, D. W. (editor), Proceedings of the symposium on endangered and threatened plants and animals of Virginia. Blacksburg: Virginia Polytechnic Institute and State University.

*Handley, C. O., Jr., and C. O. Handley, Sr. 1950. Mammals. Pp. 235–276. In: Virginia Academy of Sciences. The James River Basin — Past, Present, and Future. Richmond: Virginia Academy of Sciences.

*Handley, C. O., Jr., and E. K. V. Kalko. 1993. A short history of pitfall trapping in America, with a review of methods currently used for small mammals. Virginia Journal of Science 44(1):19–26.

*Handley, C. O., Jr., and J. F. Pagels. 1991a. Star-nosed mole. Pp. 565–567. In: Terwilliger, K., (coordinator). Virginia's endangered species. Blacksburg: The McDonald & Woodward Publishing Company.

*Handley, C. O., Jr., and J. F. Pagels. 1991b. Rock vole. Pp. 589–591. In: Terwilliger, K., (coordinator). Virginia's endangered species. Blacksburg: The McDonald & Woodward Publishing Company.

*Handley, C. O., Jr., J. F. Pagels, and R. H. deRageot. 1979. *Microsorex hoyi*. Pp 545–547. In: Linzey, D. W. (editor), Proceedings of the symposium on endangered and threatened plants and animals of Virginia. Blacksburg: Virginia Polytechnic Institute and State University.

*Handley, C. O., Jr., and J. Paradiso. 1965. Checklist of mammals of Assateague Island. Chesapeake Science 6(3):167–177.

*Handley, C. O., Jr., and C. P. Patton. 1947. Wild mammals of Virginia. Richmond: Commission of Game and Inland Fisheries.

*Handley, C. O., Jr., and D. Schwab. 1991. Eastern big-eared bat. Pp. 571–573. In: Terwilliger, K., coordinator. Virginia's endangered species. Blacksburg: The McDonald & Woodward Publishing Company.

*Handley, C. O., Jr., G. Tipton, and A. Tipton. 1979a. *Plecotus rafinesquii*. Pp. 548–549. In: Linzey, D. W. (editor), Proceedings of the symposium on endangered and threatened plants and animals of Virginia. Blacksburg: Virginia Polytechnic Institute and State University.

*Handley, C. O., Jr., G. Tipton, and A. Tipton. 1979b. *Plecotus townsendii*. Pp. 497–500. In: Linzey, D. W. (editor), Proceedings of the symposium on endangered and threatened plants and animals of Virginia. Blacksburg: Virginia Polytechnic Institute and State University.

*Handley, C. O., Jr., and M. Varn. 1994. Identification of the Carolinian shrews of Bachman 1837. Pp. 393–406. In: Merritt, J. F., G. L. Kirkland, Jr, and R. K. Rose (editors). Advances in the biology of shrews. Special Publication number 18, Carnegie Museum of Natural History, Pittsburgh.

*Hanenkrat, F. T. 1978. Vampire. Virginia Wildlife 39(1):12–14.

*Hanlon, C. L., D. E. Hayes, A. N. Hamir, D. E. Snyder, S. Jenkins, C. P. Hable, and C. E. Rupprecht. 1989. Proposed field evaluation of a rabies recombinant vaccine for raccoons *(Procyon lotor)*: site selection, target species characteristics and placebo baiting trials. Journal of Wildlife Diseases 25(4):555–567.

Hansen, R. M., and J. T. Flinders. 1969. Food habits of North American hares. Colorado State University Range Science Department Science Series 31.

*Hanson, J. C. 1966. Some physiological characteristics of wild, cage-stressed, and shockcomatose gray squirrels. Master's thesis, Virginia Polytechnic Institute and State University, Blacksburg.

*Hariot, T. 1588. A briefe and true report of the new found land of Virginia. London: Privately published.

*Hariot, T. 1903 (1588). A brief and true report of the new found land of Virginia. Reproduced in facsimile from the first edition of 1588. Introduction by Luther S. Livingston. New York: Dodd, Mead Company.

*Harkema, R. 1936. The parasites of some North Carolina rodents. Ecological Monographs 6:153–232.

*Harkema, R., and G. C. Miller. 1964. Helminth parasites of the raccoon, *Procyon lotor*, in the southeastern United States. Journal of Parasitology 50(1):60–66.

*Harlan, R. 1825. Fauna Americana; being a description of the mammiferous animals inhabiting North America, etc. Philadelphia: A. Finley.

Harger, E. M. 1970. A study of homing behavior of black bears. Master's thesis, Northern Michigan University, Marquette.

*Harlan, R. 1832. Description of a new species of quadruped of the genus *Arvicola (A. nuttalli)*. Monthly American Journal of Geology and Natural Science, Philadelphia 1:446.

*Harlow, R. F. 1961. Characteristics and status of Florida black bear. Transactions of the 26th North American Wildlife Conference 26:481–495.

*Harlow, R. F. 1971. Foods of white-tailed deer in the Southeast based on rumen analysis. Master's thesis, Virginia Polytechnic Institute and State University, Blacksburg.

*Harlow, R. F. 1990. Food habits of southern flying squirrels *(Glaucomys volans)* collected from red-cockaded woodpecker *(Picoides borealis)* colonies in South Carolina. American Midland Naturalist 124(1):187–191.

*Harlow, R. F., and R. G. Hooper. 1972. Forages eaten by deer in the Southeast. Proceedings of the 25th Annual Conference of the Southeastern Association of Game and Fish Commissioners 25:18–46.

Harney, B. A., and R. D. Dueser. 1987. Vertical structure of activity of two *Peromyscus* species: an experimental analysis. Ecology 68(4):1084–1091.

*Harper, F. 1927. Mammals of the Okefinokee Swamp region of Georgia. Proceedings of the Boston Society of Natural History 38(7):191–396.

Harris, C. J. 1968. Otters, a study of the recent Lutrinae. London: Weidenfeld and Nicholson.

Harris, M. J. 1956. The nutria as a wild fur mammal in Louisiana. Transactions of the 21st North American Wildlife Conference 21:474–486.

*Harris, M. J., T. H. J. Huisman, and F. A. Hayes. 1973. Geographic distribution of hemoglobin variants in the wild deer. Journal of Mammalogy 54(1):270–274.

*Harrison, G. H. 1958. Trapping bear facts. Virginia Wildlife 19(12):10–13.

*Harrison, G. H. 1960. Virginia . . . where the buffalo roamed. Virginia Wildlife 21(9):8.

*Harrison, G. H. 1960. On top of old . . . Mount Rogers — highest point in Virginia. Virginia Wildlife 21(8):14–15.

*Hart, L. A. 1970. Structure of the gastric mucosa as related to feeding habits in selected species of New World bats. Doctoral dissertation, Virginia Polytechnic Institute and State University, Blacksburg.

*Hartman, C. G. 1952. Possums. Austin: University of Texas Press.

Hartman, D. S. 1971. Behavior and ecology of the Florida manatee, *Trichechus manatus latirostris* (Harlan), at Crystal River, Citrus County. Doctoral dissertation, Cornell University, Ithaca.

*Hartman, G. D., and J. L. Gottschang. 1983. Notes on sex determination, neonates, and behavior of the eastern mole, *Scalopus aquaticus*. Journal of Mammalogy 64(3):539–540.

Harvey, M. J. 1967. Home range, movements, and diel activity of the eastern mole, *Scalopus aquaticus*. Doctoral dissertation, University of Kentucky, Lexington.

Harvey, M. J. 1976. Home range, movements, and diel activity of the eastern mole, *Scalopus aquaticus*. American Midland Naturalist 95:436–445.

*Harvey, M. J. 1976. Endangered Chiroptera of the southeastern United States. Proceedings of the 29th

Annual Conference of the Southeastern Association of Game and Fish Commissioners 29:429–433.

*Harvey, M. J. 1978. Status of the endangered big-eared bat, *Plecotus townsendii virginianus,* in Kentucky. Journal of the Tennessee Academy of Science 53(2):73.

*Harvey, M. J. 1992. Bats of the eastern United States. Little Rock: Arkansas Game and Fish Commission.

*Hasbrouck, J. J., and R. L. Kirkpatrick. 1982. Molting in pine voles as affected by age, sex, nutrition and photoperiod. Virginia Journal of Science 33(3):108. Abstract.

*Hasbrouck, J. J., F. A. Servello, and R. L. Kirkpatrick. 1986. Influence of photoperiod and nutrition on pine vole reproduction. American Midland Naturalist 116(2):246–255.

*Hasbrouck, J. J., and A. R. Tipton. 1982. Analysis of spatial dynamics of the pine vole *(Microtus pinetorum).* Virginia Journal of Science 33(3):109.

Hassell, M. D., and M. J. Harvey. 1965. Differential homing in *Myotis sodalis.* American Midland Naturalist 74(2):501–503.

*Hasseltine, H. E. 1929. Rat-flea survey of the port of Norfolk, Va. Public Health Report 44(11):579–589.

*Hatcher, C. L. 1975. Go in the back way. Virginia Wildlife 36(12):19–20.

Hatfield, D. M. 1939. Winter food habits of foxes in Minnesota. Journal of Mammalogy 20(2):202–206.

*Hatt, R. T. 1929. The red squirrel: its life history and habits. Roosevelt Wildlife Annals 2(1):1–146.

Hatt, R. T. 1944. A large beaver-felled tree. Journal of Mammalogy 25(3):313.

Haugen, A. O. 1942. Home range of the cottontail rabbit. Ecology 23(3):354–367.

Haugen, A. O. 1944. Highway mortality of wildlife in southern Michigan. Journal of Mammalogy 25(2): 177–184.

Haugen, A. O., and L. A. Davenport. 1950. Breeding records of whitetail deer in the upper peninsula of Michigan. Journal of Wildlife Management 14(3): 290–295.

Haugen, A. O., and D. W. Speake. 1957. Parturition and early reactions of white-tailed deer fawns. Journal of Mammalogy 38(3):420–421.

Haugen, O. L. 1954. Longevity of the raccoon in the wild. Journal of Mammalogy 35(3):439.

*Hawkins, L. K., and J. A. Cranford. 1986. Factors influencing female reproduction in two species of *Peromyscus* in Virginia. Virginia Journal of Science 37(2):67. Abstract.

*Hawkins, L. K., J. A. Cranford, and T. L. Derting. 1986. Factors influencing female reproduction in two species of *Peromyscus* in Virginia. Virginia Journal of Science 37(4):221–229.

Hawkins, R. E., and W. D. Klimstra. 1970. A preliminary study of the social organization of white-tailed deer. Journal of Wildlife Management 34(2):407–419.

*Hay, O. P. 1921. Descriptions of some Pleistocene vertebrates found in the United States. Proceedings of the United States National Museum 58(2328):83–146.

*Hay, O. P. 1923. The Pleistocene of North America and its vertebrated animals from the states east of the Mississippi River and from the Canadian provinces east of Longitude 95 . Carnegie Institute, Washington, D. C. Publication 322.

*Hay, O. P. 1929–30. Second bibliography and catalogue of the fossil vertebrata of North America. Volumes I and II. Carnegie Institute, Washington, D. C.

*Haycox Photoramic. 1964. The western on the eastern shore. Virginia Wildlife 25(7):14–15.

*Hayes, F. A., W. T. Gerard, E. B. Shotts, and G. L. Dills. 1960. Further serologic studies of brucellosis in white-tailed deer of the southeastern United States. Journal of the American Veterinary Medical Association 137(3):190–191.

Hayes, F. A., and E. B. Shotts. 1959. Pine oil poisoning in sika deer. Southeastern Veterinarian 10:34–39.

*Hayes, J. P. 1990. Biogeographic, systematic, and conservation implications of geographic variation in woodrats of the eastern United States. Ph.D. dissertation, Cornell University, Ithaca, New York.

*Hayes, J. P. and R. G. Harrison. 1992. Variation in mitochondrial DNA and the biogeographic history of woodrats *(Neotoma)* in the eastern United States. Systematic Biology 41:331–344.

*Hayes, J. P., and M. E. Richmond. 1993. Clinal variation and morphology of woodrats *(Neotoma)* of the eastern United States. Journal of Mammalogy 74(1):204–216.

*Hayes, R., P. T. Nielsen and W. D. Cocking. 1986. Terrestrial bioaccumulation of mercury in small mammals and invertebrates on the South River flood plain, Waynesboro, Virginia. International Congress on Ecology 4:175.

*Hays, W. J. 1871. Notes on the range of some of the animals in America at the time of the arrival of the white men. American Naturalist 5(7):387–392.

*Headlee, A. S. 1952. The parade of Virginia wildlife 1,000,000 years ago. Virginia Wildlife 13(6):14–16, 23.

*Heard, L. P. 1963. Notes on cottontail rabbit studies in Mississippi. Proceedings of the 17th Annual Conference of the Southeastern Association of Game and Fish Commissioners 17:85–92.

*Hebbard, C. B. 1963. Letters. Caught in the act. Virginia Wildlife 24(11):3.

Heffner, R. S., and H. E. Heffner. 1985. Hearing in mammals: the least weasel. Journal of Mammalogy 66(4):745–755.

Heidt, G. A., and J. N. Huff. 1970. Ontogeny of vocalization in the least weasel. Journal of Mammalogy 51(2):385–386.

Heidt, G. A., M. K. Petersen, and G. L. Kirkland, Jr. 1968. Mating behavior and development of least weasels *(Mustela nivalis)* in captivity. Journal of Mammalogy 49(3):413–419.

*Heiner, A. B. 1967. The creek named Sarah. Virginia Wildlife 28(4):10–11.

Heit, W. S. 1944. Food habits of red foxes of the Maryland marshes. Journal of Mammalogy 25(1):55–58.

*Hellgren, E. C. 1988. Ecology and physiology of a black bear *(Ursus americanus)* population in Great Dismal Swamp and reproductive physiology in the captive female black bear. Doctoral dissertation, Virginia Polytechnic Institute and State University, Blacksburg.

*Hellgren, E. C., D. W. Carney, N. P. Garner, and M. R. Vaughan. 1988. Use of breakaway cotton spacers on radio collars. Wildlife Society Bulletin 16(2):216–218.

*Hellgren, E. C. and D. S. Maehr. 1992. Habitat fragmentation and black bears in the eastern United States. Eastern Workshop Black Bear Research and Management 11:154–165.

*Hellgren, E. C., and M. R. Vaughan. 1987. Home range and movements of winter-active black bears in the Great Dismal Swamp of Virginia and North Carolina. Pp. 227–234. In: Zager, P. (editor), Bears: their biology and management. Seventh International Conference on Bear Research and Management, Williamsburg, Virginia.

*Hellgren, E. C., and M. R. Vaughan. 1988. Seasonal food habits of black bears in Great Dismal Swamp, Virginia-North Carolina. Proceedings of the 42nd Annual Conference of the Southeastern Association of Fish and Wildlife Agencies 42:295–305.

*Hellgren, E. C., and M. R. Vaughan. 1989a. Denning ecology of black bears in a southeastern wetland. Journal of Wildlife Management 53(2):347–353.

*Hellgren, E. C., and M. R. Vaughan. 1989b. Demographic analysis of a black bear population in the Great Dismal Swamp. Journal of Wildlife Management 53(4):969–977.

*Hellgren, E. C., and M. R. Vaughan. 1989c. Rectal temperatures of immobilized, snare-trapped black bears in Great Dismal Swamp. Journal of Wildlife Diseases 25(3):440–443.

*Hellgren, E. C., and M. R. Vaughan. 1990. Range dynamics of black bears in Great Dismal Swamp, Virginia-North Carolina. Proceedings of the 44th Annual Conference of the Southeastern Association of Game and Fish Commissioners 44:268–278.

*Hellgren, E. C. and M. R. Vaughn. 1994a. External morphometrics of black bears, *Ursus americanus* (Carnivora: Ursidae), in the Great Dismal Swamp of Virginia and North Carolina. Brimleyana 21:141–149.

*Hellgren, E. C. and M. R. Vaughn. 1994b. Conservation and management of isolated black bear populations in the southeastern coastal plain of the United States. Proceedings of the 48th Annual Conference of the Southeastern Association of Fish and Wildlife Agencies 48:276–285.

*Hellgren, E. C., M. R. Vaughan, F. C. Gwazdauskas, B. Williams, P. F. Scanlon, and R. L. Kirkpatrick. 1991. Endocrine and electrophoretic profiles during pregnancy and nonpregnancy in captive female black bears. Canadian Journal of Zoology 69(4):892–898.

*Hellgren, E. C., M. R. Vaughan, and R. L. Kirkpatrick. 1989. Seasonal patterns in physiology and nutrition of black bears in Great Dismal Swamp, Virginia-North Carolina. Canadian Journal of Zoology 67(8):1837–1850.

*Hellgren, E. C., M. R. Vaughan, R. L. Kirkpatrick, and P. F. Scanlon. 1990. Serial changes in metabolic correlates of hibernation in female black bears. Journal of Mammalogy 71(3):291–300.

*Hellgren, E. C., M. R. Vaughan, and D. F. Stauffer. 1991. Macrohabitat use by black bears in a southeastern wetland. Journal of Wildlife Management 55(3):442–448.

*Henderson, A. 1920. The conquest of the old Southwest; the romantic story of the early pioneers into Virginia, the Carolinas, Tennessee, and Kentucky, 1740–1790. New York: The Century Company.

*Henderson, C. 1950. The Shenandoah. Virginia Wildlife 11(12):8–9, 26.

*Henn, A. W. 1912. The range of size in the vertebrates. American Naturalist 46(543):157–162.

*Hensley, M. S. 1976a. Influence of cuterebrid infestation upon select population parameters in wood mice. Virginia Journal of Science 27(2):44. Abstract.

*Hensley, M. S. 1976b. Prevalence of cuterebrid parasitism among woodmice in Virginia. Journal of Wildlife Diseases 12:172–179.

*Hensley, M. S. 1977a. Vulnerability of botfly-infested woodmice to predation by foxes. Virginia Journal of Science 28(2):63. Abstract.

*Hensley, M. S. 1977b. Food habits of gray foxes as revealed by fecal analysis. Virginia Journal of Science 28(2):63. Abstract.

*Hensley, M. S. 1978. An analysis of the effects of cuterebrid parasitism on population dynamics of *Peromyscus leucopus*. Doctoral dissertation, University of Tennessee, Knoxville.

*Hensley, M. S. 1995. Coevolutionary implications of breeding cessation in *Cuterebra*-infested *Peromyscus* populations. Virginia Journal of Science 46(2):94. Abstract.

*Hensley, M. S., and J. E. Fisher. 1975. The effect of fox control on rodent populations. Virginia Journal of Science 26(2):56. Abstract.

*Hensley, M. S., and J. E. Fisher. 1976. Effects of intensive gray fox control on population dynamics of rodents and sympatric carnivores. Proceedings of the 29th Annual Conference of the Southeastern Association of Game and Fish Commissioners 29:694–705.

*Herman, C. M., and J. R. Reilly. 1955. Skin tumors on squirrels. Journal of Wildlife Management 19(3):402–403.

*Herold, D. G., and B. C. McCary. 1957. Early Virginia Indians' hunting and trapping methods. Virginia Wildlife 18(7):10–11.

*Herring, T. G. 1958. A rebel yell saved the day. Virginia Wildlife 19(12):16.

*Herrman, A. 1673. Map of Virginia and Maryland. London. Privately published.

*Hershkovitz, P. 1948. The technical name of the Virginia deer with a list of the South American forms. Proceedings of the Biological Society of Washington 61:41–48.

*Herschkovitz, P. 1966. Catalog of living whales. United States National Museum Bulletin 246:1–259.

*Hertel, L. A., and D. W. Duszynski. 1987. Coccidian parasites (Apicomplexa: Eimeriidae) from insectivores. III. Seven new species in shrews (Soricidae:

Soricinae) from Canada, Japan, and the United States. Journal of Parasitology 73(1):172–183.

*Hesselton, W. T., and R. M. Hesselton. 1982. White-tailed deer. Pp. 878–901. In: Chapman, J. A., and G. A. Feldhamer (editors), Wild mammals of North America. Baltimore: The Johns Hopkins University Press.

*Heuser, C. H., and C. G. Hartman. 1928. Some old and forgotten observations upon the breeding habits of the opossum. Journal of Mammalogy 9(1):61–62.

Hewitt, O. H., H. C. Black, and R. G. Alsop. 1959. Home range and movement of the black bear in New York. Federal Aid in Wildlife Restoration Project 4-89-R. Mimeographed.

Hibbard, C. W., J. E. Guilday, C. E. Ray, D. E. Savage, and D. W. Taylor. 1965. Quaternary mammals of North America. Pp. 509–525. In: Wright, H. E., Jr., and D. D. Frey (editors), The Quaternary of the United States. Princeton: Princeton University Press.

*Hibler, C. P., and A. K. Prestwood. 1981. Filarial nematodes of white-tailed deer. Pp. 351–362. In: Davidson, W. R., F. A. Hayes, V. F. Nettles, and F. E. Kellogg (editors), Diseases and parasites of white-tailed deer. Miscellaneous Publication no. 7, tall Timber Research Station, Tallahassee, Florida.

*Hickey, M. B. C., and M. B. Fenton. 1990. Foraging by red bats *(Lasiurus borealis)*; do intraspecific chases mean territoriality. Canadian Journal of Zoology 68(12):2477–2482.

*Hicks, J. 1956. The beaver in Bath County. Virginia Wildlife 17(4):18–19, 23.

*Higgins, J. 1995. Survival of the harvested bear population. Virginia Wildlife 56(9):29.

*Hill, D. 1973. The great Swamp's brightened future: anything but dismal. Commonwealth 40:19–24, 48–52.

Hill, E. P. 1967. Homing by a cottontail rabbit. Journal of Mammalogy 48(4):648.

Hill, E. P. 1968. Notes on the life history of the swamp rabbit in Alabama. Proceedings of the 21st Annual Conference of the Southeastern Association of Game and Fish Commissioners 21:117–123.

*Hill, E. P. 1972. The cottontail rabbit in Alabama. Auburn University Agricultural Experiment Station Bulletin 440.

*Hill, E. P., P. W. Sumner, and J. B. Wooding. 1987. Human influences on range expansion of coyotes in the Southeast. Wildlife Society Bulletin 15(4):521–524.

Hill, R. W. 1975. Daily torpor in *Peromyscus leucopus* on an adequate diet. Comparative Biochemistry and Physiology 51A:413–423.

*Hiller, B. and R. K. Rose. 1995. Infestation rates and biomasses of a stomach ascarid in a population of *Sigmodon hispidus*, the hispid cotton rat of southeastern Virginia. Virginia Journal of Science 46(2):94. Abstract.

*Hisey, W. E., Jr. 1961. Bushy-tail serenade. Virginia Wildlife 22(10):6–7.

Hitchcock, H. B. 1965. Twenty-three years of bat-banding in Ontario and Quebec. Canadian Field Naturalist 79:4–14.

Hitchcock, H. B. and K. Reynolds. 1942. Homing experiments with the little brown bat, *Myotis lucifugus lucifugus* (LeConte). Journal of Mammalogy 23(3): 258–267.

*Hoar, A. R. 1980. A methodology for mapping probable ranges of endangered terrestrial mammals within selected areas of Virginia. Master's thesis, Virginia Polytechnic Institute and State University, Blacksburg.

*Hobson, C. S. Bat records from southeastern Virginia including a new resident species, *Myotis austroriparius* (Chiroptera: Vespertilionidae). Brimleyana. (in press)

*Hobson, C. S. and J. N. Holland. 1995. Post-hibernation movement and foraging habitat of a male Indiana bat, *Myotis sodalis* (Chiroptera:Vespertilionidae), in western Virginia. Brimleyana 23:95–101.

Hodgson, J. R. 1986. The occurrence of small mammals in the diets of largemouth bass *(Micropterus salmoides)*. Jack-Pine Warbler 64(3–4):39–40.

Hoese, H. D. 1971. Dolphin feeding out of water in a salt marsh. Journal of Mammalogy 52(1):222–223.

*Hoffman, R. L. 1979. Physical and environmental geography of Virginia. Pp. 17–29. In: Linzey, D. W. (editor), Proceedings of a symposium on endangered and threatened plants and animals of Virginia. Blacksburg: Virginia Polytechnic Institute and State University.

*Hoffmann, R. S., and J. W. Koeppl. 1985. Zoogeography. Pp. 84–115. In: Tamarin, R. H. (editor), Biology of New World *Microtus*. The American Society of Mammalogists Special Publication Number 8.

*Hoffmeister, D. F., and C. O. Mohr. 1972. Fieldbook of Illinois mammals. New York: Dover Publications.

*Hoge, G. W. 1964. Discovering the Machodoc. Virginia Wildlife 25(5):16.

Holcomb, L. C. 1965. Large litter size of red fox. Journal of Mammalogy 46(3):53a.

*Holder, J. B. 1885. Animate creation; popular edition of "Our living world," a natural history by the Rev. J. G. Wood. Revised and adapted to American zoology by Joseph B. Holder. 3 volumes. New York: Selmar Hess.

*Holdsworth, R. P. 1953. West Augusta twice visited. Virginia Wildlife 14(9):20–21.

*Holland, C. 1997. Stress-induced thermogenesis in wild and domestic house mice (*Mus musculus*). Virginia Journal of Science 48(2):84. Abstract.

*Holland, C. G. (editor). 1952. The description of Virginia by Captain John Smith (1608–1631). Bulletin of the Archeological Society of Virginia 6(3):1–16.

*Holland, C. G. 1964. Old bones and the biologist. Virginia Wildlife 25(12):12, 19.

*Holland, G. P., and A. H. Benton. 1968. Siphonaptera from Pennsylvania mammals. American Midland Naturalist 80(1):252–261.

Holler, N. R., and C. H. Conaway. 1979. Reproduction of the marsh rabbit *(Sylvilagus palustris)* in south Florida. Journal of Mammalogy 60(4):769–777.

*Holleran, P. 1996. Chincoteague's wild horses. Virginia Explorer 12(3):9–12.

*Holliman, R. B. 1966. A *Trypanosoma lewisi*-like organism from the rabbit, *Sylvilagus floridanus,* in Virginia. Journal of Parasitology 52(3):622.

*Holliman, R. B., and B. J. Meade. 1980. Native trichinosis in wild rodents in Henrico County, Virginia. Journal of Wildlife Diseases 16(2):205–207.

Holling, C. S. 1958. Sensory stimuli involved in the location and selection of sawfly cocoons by small mammals. Canadian Journal of Zoology 36(5):633–653.

*Hollister, N. 1911a. Remarks on the long-tailed shrews of the eastern United States, with description of a new species. Proceedings of the United States National Museum 40:377–381.

*Hollister, N. 1911b. A systematic synopsis of the muskrats. North American Fauna 32:1–47.

*Hollister, N. 1913. A synopsis of the American minks. Proceedings of the United States National Museum 44:471–480.

*Holloran, R. L. 1976. Computing deer seasons. Virginia Wildlife 37(10):14–15.

*Holloran, R. L. 1978. A white-tailed deer harvest data-analysis and information system for Virginia. Master's thesis, Virginia Polytechnic Institute and State University, Blacksburg.

*Holloway, H. L. 1956a. A new species of the acanthocephalan genus *Centrorhynchus* from *Spilogale putorius.* American Society of Biologists Bulletin 3(1):10.

*Holloway, H. L. 1956b. The Acanthocephala of Mountain Lake mammals. Virginia Journal of Science 7:285. Abstract.

*Holloway, H. L. 1956c. Notes on the helminths of mammals in the Mountain Lake region. Doctoral dissertation, University of Virginia, Charlottesville.

*Holloway, H. L. 1957. *Sorex dispar* at Mountain Lake, Virginia. Journal of Mammalogy 38(3):406.

*Holloway, H. L. 1958. Notes on the helminths of mammals in the Mountain Lake region. Part III. The genus *Centrorhynchus* in North America, with the description of a new species. Virginia Journal of Science 9(2):221–232.

*Holloway, H. L. 1959. Notes on the helminths of mammals in the Mountain Lake region. V. The helminths of rabbits. Virginia Journal of Science 10(2):261. Abstract.

*Holloway, H. L. 1966. Helminths of rabbits and opossums at Mountain Lake, Virginia. Bulletin of the Wildlife Disease Association 2:38–39.

*Holloway, H. L., and J. L. Dowler. 1963. The helminths of opossums in western Virginia. Virginia Journal of Science 14(4):203.

*Holmes, D. J. 1991. Social behavior in captive Virginia opossums, *Didelphis virginiana.* Journal of Mammalogy 72(2):402–410.

*Holmgren, V. C. 1973. R is for raccoon. Virginia Wildlife 34(6):12.

*Holsinger, J. R. 1964. The gray myotis in Virginia. Journal of Mammalogy 45(1):151–152.

*Holzenbein, S. 1990. Integration of maturing white-tailed deer *(Odocoileus virginianus)* into the adult population. Ph. D. dissertation. University of Georgia, Athens.

*Holzenbein, S., and R. L. Marchinton. 1992a. Emigration and mortality in orphaned male white-tailed deer. Journal of Wildlife Management 56(1):147–153.

*Holzenbein, S., and R. L. Marchinton. 1992b. Spatial integration of maturing-male white-tailed deer into the adult population. Journal of Mammalogy 73(2):326–334.

*Homo. 1881. Game bag and gun. The Shenandoah Valley. Forest and Stream 17(19):370.

*Hooper, E. T. 1942. The water shrew *(Sorex palustris)* of the southern Allegheny mountains. Occasional Paper, University of Michigan Museum of Zoology 463:1–4.

*Hooper, E. T. 1943. Geographic variation in harvest mice of the species *Reithrodontomys humulis.* Occasional Paper, University of Michigan Museum of Zoology 477:1–19.

*Hooper, E. T. 1952. A systematic review of the harvest mice (genus *Reithrodontomys*) of Latin America. Miscellaneous Publication, Museum of Zoology, University of Michigan 77:1–255.

*Hooper, E. T. 1968. Classification. Pages 27–74. In: King, J. A. (editor). Biology of *Peromyscus* (Rodentia). Special Publication no. 2, The American Society of Mammalogists.

*Hooper, E. T., and E. R. Cady. 1941. Notes on certain mammals of the mountains of southwestern Virginia. Journal of Mammalogy 22(3):323–325.

*Hopkins, P. A., and R. K. Rose. 1984. Reproduction in tidewater cotton rats. Virginia Journal of Science 35(2):82. Abstract.

*Hornaday, W. T. 1889. The extermination of the American bison, with a sketch of its discovery and life history. United States National Museum Annual Report for 1887. Part II. Pp. 367–548.

*Hornaday, W. T. 1913. Popular official guide to the New York zoological park. 12th ed. New York: New York Zoological Society.

*Hornaday, W. T. 1913. Our vanishing wild life. New York: New York Zoological Society.

*Hornaday, W. T. 1914. The American natural history. New York: Charles Scribner's Sons.

Horner, B. E. 1947. Paternal care of young mice of the genus *Peromyscus.* Journal of Mammalogy 28(1):31–36.

*Horner, B. E. 1954. Arboreal adaptations of *Peromyscus,* with special reference to use of the tail. Contributions of the Laboratory of Vertebrate Biology, University of Michigan no. 61.

Horner, M. A., and R. A. Powell. 1990. Internal structure of home ranges of black bears and analyses of home-range overlap. Journal of Mammalogy 71(3):402–410.

*Horsfall, F., Jr. 1951. Estimation of orchard mouse populations by trapping. Abstract of paper read before the Southern Association of Agricultural Workers. Mimeographed.

*Horsfall, F., Jr. 1953. Mouse control in Virginia orchards. Virginia Agricultural Experiment Station Bulletin 465:1–26.

*Horsfall, F., Jr. 1956a. Pine mouse control with ground-sprayed endrin. Proceedings of the American Society of Horticultural Science 67:68–74.

*Horsfall, F., Jr. 1956b. Rodenticidal effect on pine mice of endrin used as a ground spray. Science 123:61.

*Horsfall, F., Jr. 1963. Observations on fluctuating pregnancy rate of pine mice and mouse feed potential in Virginia orchards. Proceedings of the American Society of Horticultural Science 83:276–279.

*Horsfall, F., Jr. 1964. Diversification of cover as an aid to ground spray control of pine mice. Paper presented at Cumberland-Shenandoah Fruit Workers Conference.

*Horsfall, F., Jr., R. E. Webb, and R. E. Byers. 1973. How to successfully meet pine voles on their terms. Virginia Fruit 61:3–15.

*Horsley, B. D. 1991. Blue jay captures bat. Chat 55(2):30–31.

*Hostetter, D. R. 1939. Chipmunks and birds. Journal of Mammalogy 20(1):107–108.

*Hostetter, J. H. 1939. Rockbridge County notes. Virginia Wildlife 3(2):4–5.

Hougart, B. 1975. Activity patterns of radio-tracked gray squirrels. Master's thesis, University of Maryland, College Park.

*Hovey, H. C. 1882. Celebrated American caverns, especially Mammoth, Wyandot, and Luray. Cincinnati: R. Clarke and Company.

Howard, W. E. 1949. A means to distinguish skulls of coyotes and domestic dogs. Journal of Mammalogy 30(2):169–171.

*Howard, W. E., and R. E. Marsh. 1982. Spotted and hog-nosed skunks. Pp. 664–673. In: Chapman, J. A., and G. A. Feldhamer (editors), Wild mammals of North America. Baltimore: The Johns Hopkins University Press.

*Howard, W. E., R. E. Marsh, and R. E. Cole. 1968. Food detection by deer mice using olfactory rather than visual cues. Animal Behaviour 16(1):13–17.

*Howdyshell, V. 1963. Al's story and mine. Virginia Wildlife 24(12):8–9.

*Howell, A. B. 1927. Revision of the American lemming mice (genus *Synaptomys*). North American Fauna 50.

*Howell, A. H. 1901. Revision of the skunks of the genus *Chincha.* North American Fauna 20.

*Howell, A. H. 1906. Revision of the skunks of the genus *Spilogale.* North American Fauna 26.

*Howell, A. H. 1908. Notes on diurnal migrations of bats. Proceedings of the Biological Society of Washington 21:35–38.

*Howell, A. H. 1909. Notes on the distribution of certain mammals in the southeastern United States. Proceedings of the Biological Society of Washington 22:55–68.

*Howell, A. H. 1914. Revision of the American harvest mice (genus *Reithrodontomys*). North American Fauna 36.

*Howell, A. H. 1915. Revision of the American marmots. North American Fauna 37.

*Howell, A. H. 1918. Revision of the American flying squirrels. North American Fauna 44.

*Howell, A. H. 1921. A biological survey of Alabama. North American Fauna 45.

*Howell, A. H. 1925. Preliminary descriptions of five new chipmunks from North America. Journal of Mammalogy 6(1):51–54.

*Howell, A. H. 1929. Revision of the American chipmunks (genera *Tamias* and *Eutamias*). North American Fauna 52.

*Howell, A. H. 1939. Description of a new subspecies of the golden mouse. Journal of Mammalogy 20(4):498.

*Howell, A. H. 1940. A new race of the harvest mouse *(Reithrodontomys)* from Virginia. Journal of Mammalogy 21(3):346.

Howell, J. C. 1954. Populations and home ranges of small mammals on an overgrown field. Journal of Mammalogy 35(2):177–186.

*Howle, T. P. 1915. Beaver in the James River. Forest and Stream. April, 1915:229.

*Hubbard, D. A., Jr., and F. Grady. 1997. Vertebrate paleontological cave resources in Virginia, USA. Proceedings of the 12th International Congress of Speleology, 1997, Switzerland, 3:175–177.

*Hubbard, D. R. 1985. A descriptive epidemiological study of raccoon rabies in a rural environment. Journal of Wildlife Diseases 21(2):105–110.

*Huber, W. W. 1949. Dot and Dash. Virginia Wildlife 10(10):11–12, 18.

*Huff, C. P., Jr. 1962. Mr. Groundhog — the prognosticator. Virginia Wildlife 23(2):12.

Huff, J. N., and E. O. Price. 1968. Vocalizations of the least weasel, *Mustela nivalis.* Journal of Mammalogy 49(3):548–550.

*Hugo, N. 1986a. The opossum. Virginia Wildlife 47(8):34.

*Hugo, N. 1986b. A housing shortage. Virginia Wildlife 47(12):4–8.

*Hugo, N. 1987. A catamount tale. Virginia Wildlife 48(2):8–13.

*Hugo, N. 1988a. The river otter. Virginia Wildlife 49(5):34.

*Hugo, N. 1988b. The weasel. Virginia Wildlife 49(7):34.

*Huisman, T. H. J., A. M. Dozy, and M. H. Blunt. 1968. The hemoglobin heterogeneity of the Virginia white-tailed deer: a possible genetic explanation. Archives of Biochemistry and Biophysics 127:711–717.

*Hulbert, A. B. 1903. Historic highways of America. Volume VI: 53. Boone's wilderness road. Cleveland: Arthur H. Clark.

Humphrey, S. R. 1971. Population ecology of the little brown bat, *Myotis lucifugus,* in Indiana and north-central Kentucky. Doctoral dissertation, Oklahoma State University, Stillwater.

*Humphrey, S. R. 1975. Nursery roosts and community diversity of Nearctic bats. Journal of Mammalogy 56(2):321–346.

*Humphrey, S. R. 1978. Status, winter habitat, and management of the endangered Indiana bat, *Myotis sodalis*. Florida Scientist 41(2):65–76.

*Humphrey, S. R., and J. B. Cope. 1968. Records of migration of the evening bat, *Nycticeius humeralis*. Journal of Mammalogy 49(2):329.

Humphrey, S. R., and J. B. Cope. 1976. Population ecology of the little brown bat, *Myotis lucifugus*, in Indiana and north-central Kentucky. American Society of Mammalogists Special Publication no 4.

Humphrey, S. R., A. R. Richter, and J. B. Cope. 1977. Summer habitat and ecology of the endangered Indiana bat, *Myotis sodalis*. Journal of Mammalogy 58(3):334–346.

*Hundley, L. R. 1953. The estimation of populations of some game species. Master's thesis, Virginia Polytechnic Institute and State University, Blacksburg.

*Hundley, L. R. 1959. Available nutrients in selected deer-browse species growing on different soils. Journal of Wildlife Management 23(1):81–90.

Hungerford, K. E. and N. G. Wilder. 1941. Observations on the homing behavior of the gray squirrel *(Sciurus carolinensis)*. Journal of Wildlife Management 5:458–460.

*Hunsaker, D., II. 1977. The biology of marsupials. New York: Academic Press.

*Hunter, A. 1876. The Dismal Swamp. Forest and Stream 5(23):353–354.

*Hunter, A. 1881. Through the Dismal Swamp. Potter's American Monthly 17:1–15.

*Hunter, A. 1895. The Great Dismal Swamp. Outing 27:70–76.

*Husar, S. L. 1978. *Trichechus manatus*. Mammalian Species no. 93.

*Hutchinson, D. 1990. A helping hand. Virginia Wildlife 51(6):18–23.

Innes, S. and D. M. Lavigne. 1979. Comparative energetics of coat colour polymorphs in the eastern gray squirrel, *Sciurus carolinensis*. Canadian Journal of Zoology 57:585–592.

Irving, L. 1937. The respiration of beavers. Journal of Cellular and Comparative Physiology 9(3):437–451.

Irving, L. 1939. Respiration in diving mammals . Physiological Review 19(1):112–134.

Irving, L., and M. D. Orr. 1935. Diving habits of the beaver. Science 82(2137):569.

*Ittner, M. 1954. Live-trapping beaver for the Commission is no picnic. Virginia Wildlife 15(6):16–17, 19.

Ivey, R. D. 1948. The raccoon in the salt marshes of northeastern Florida. Journal of Mammalogy 29(3):290–291.

Ivey, R. D. 1949. Life history notes on three mice from the Florida east coast. Journal of Mammalogy 30(2):157–162.

*Izor, R. J. 1979. Winter range of the silver-haired bat. Journal of Mammalogy 60(3):641–643.

*Jackson, H. H. T. 1915. A review of the American moles. North American Fauna 38.

*Jackson. H. H. T. 1928. A taxonomic review of the American long-tailed shrews (genera *Sorex* and *Microsorex*). North American Fauna 51.

*Jackson, H. H. T. 1961. Mammals of Wisconsin. Madison: University of Wisconsin Press.

*Jackson, H. W. 1944. A preliminary check list of the cave fauna of southwest Virginia. Bulletin of the National Speleological Society 6:56–57.

*Jackson, H. W. 1948. Wildlife underground. Virginia Wildlife 9(10):5–7, 26.

Jackson, R. M., M. White, and F. F. Knowlton. 1972. Activity patterns of young white-tailed deer fawns in south Texas. Ecology 53(2):262–270.

*Jackson, R. S., J. F. Pagels, and D. N. Trumbo. 1976. The mammals of Presquile, Chesterfield County, Virginia. Virginia Journal of Science 27(1):20–23.

Jackson, W. B. 1982. Norway rat and allies. Pp. 1077–1088. In: Chapman, J. A., and G. A. Feldhamer (editors), Wild mammals of North America. Baltimore: The Johns Hopkins University Press.

*Jackson, W. B., J. E. Brooks, A. M. Bowerman, and D. E. Kaukeinen. 1973. Anticoagulant resistance in Norway rats in United States cities. Pest Control 41(4):56–58, 60–64, 81.

*Jackson, W. B., J. E. Brooks, A. M. Bowerman, and D. E. Kaukeinen. 1975. Anticoagulant resistance in Norway rats as found in United States cities. Pest Control 43(4):12, 14–16; 43(5):14, 16, 18, 20, 22–24.

*Jacobs, J. 1990. The recovery planning process and the endangered Delmarva fox squirrel. Page 5. In: Edwards, J. W. et al. (editors). First Symposium on Southeastern Fox Squirrels. Virginia Museum of Natural History. Abstract.

*Jacobson, H. A. 1973. Pathological and physiological relationships of parasitic disease in a select cottontail rabbit population. Master's thesis, Virginia Polytechnic Institute and State University, Blacksburg.

*Jacobson, H. A. 1974. Of grizzly bears and mink. Virginia Wildlife 35(2):5, 20.

*Jacobson, H. A. 1975. Where have all the rabbits gone? Virginia Wildlife 36(8):9.

*Jacobson, H. A. 1976. Investigation of a major reduction in hunter harvest of the cottontail rabbit in southeastern Virginia. Doctoral dissertation, Virginia Polytechnic Institute and State University.

*Jacobson, H. A., D. P. Kibbe, and R. L. Kirkpatrick. 1975. Ectopic fetuses in two cottontail rabbits. Journal of Wildlife Diseases 11:540–542.

*Jacobson, H. A., and R. L. Kirkpatrick. 1973a. The use of insecticide-generating collars for the investigation of parasitic disease in wildlife populations. Proceedings of the 27th Annual Conference of the Southeastern Association of Game and Fish Commissioners 27:344–345.

*Jacobson, H. A., and R. L. Kirkpatrick. 1973b. Influence of insecticide-generating collars and antihelminth drug treatment on parasites of cottontail rabbits. Virginia Journal of Science 24(1):124.

*Jacobson, H. A., and R. L. Kirkpatrick. 1974. Effects of parasitism on selected physiological measurements of the cottontail rabbit. Journal of Wildlife Diseases 10:384–391.

*Jacobson, H. A., R. L. Kirkpatrick, H. E. Burkhart, and J. W. Davis. 1978. Hematologic comparisons of shot and live trapped cottontail rabbits. Journal of Wildlife Diseases 14(1):82–88.

*Jacobson, H. A., R. L. Kirkpatrick, and R. B. Holliman. 1974. Emaciation and enteritis of cottontail rabbits infected with *Hasstilesia tricolor* and observations on a fluke to fluke attachment phenomenon. Journal of Wildlife Diseases 10:111–114.

*Jacobson, H. A., R. L. Kirkpatrick, and B. S. McGinnes. 1975. Tularemia: its possible role in regulation of cottontail rabbit populations in Virginia. Virginia Journal of Science 26(2):56. Abstract.

*Jacobson, H. A., R. L. Kirkpatrick, and B. S. McGinnes. 1978. Disease and physiologic characteristics of two cottontail populations in Virginia. Wildlife Monograph 60:1–53.

*Jacobson, H. A., and B. S. McGinnes. 1975. Botfly *(Cuterebra buccata)* parasitism of the cottontail rabbit in Virginia. Virginia Journal of Science 26(2):56. Abstract.

*Jacobson, H. A., B. S. McGinnes, and E. P. Catts. 1978. Bot fly myiasis of the cottontail rabbit, *Sylvilagus floridanus mallurus* in Virginia with some biology of the parasite, *Cuterebra buccata.* Journal of Wildlife Diseases 14(1):56–66.

*Jacobson, H. A., P. F. Scanlon, V F. Nettles, and W. R. Davidson. 1976. Epizootiology of an outbreak of cerebrospinal nematodiasis in cottontail rabbits and woodchucks. Journal of Wildlife Diseases 12:357–360.

Jakle, J. A. 1968. The American bison and the human occupance of the Ohio Valley. Proceedings of the American Philosophical Society 112:299–305.

*James, S. V. 1968. Otto the otter. Virginia Wildlife 29(3):5.

*Jefferson, R. N. 1943. Notes on the pine mice. Virginia Fruit 31(5):10, 12, 14.

*Jefferson, T. 1782. Notes on the state of Virginia. Paris: Privately printed.

*Jefferson, T. 1797. A memoir on the discovery of certain bones of a quadruped of the clawed kind in the western parts of Virginia. Transactions of the American Philosophical Society 4:246–260.

*Jenkins, J. T. 1921. A history of the whale fisheries. London: Kennikat Press.

*Jenkins, S. 1984. Mid-Atlantic raccoon rabies outbreak. Rabies Information Exchange, Public Health Service, Centers for Disease Control, United States no. 9:47–59.

*Jenkins, S. 1994. Bats and the risk of rabies. Epidemiology Bulletin 94(6):2.

*Jenkins, S. H., and P. E. Busher. 1979. *Castor canadensis.* Mammalian Species no. 120:1–8.

*Jenkins, S. R., B. D. Perry, and W. G. Winkler. 1988. Ecology and epidemiology of raccoon rabies. Reviews of Infectious Diseases, 10, Supplement 4:S620–S625.

*Jenkins, S. R., and W. G. Winkler. 1987. Descriptive epidemiology from an epizootic of raccoon rabies in the middle Atlantic states, 1982–1983. American Journal of Epidemiology 126(3):429–437.

*Jenney, E. W., F. A. Hayes, and C. L. Brown. 1970. Survey for vesicular stomatitis virus neutralizing antibodies in serums of white-tailed deer *Odocoileus virginianus* of the southeastern United States. Journal of Wildlife Diseases 6(4):488–493.

Jennings, W. L. 1958. The ecological distribution of bats in Florida. Doctoral dissertation thesis, University of Florida, Gainesville.

Jensen, I. M. 1983. Metabolic rates of the hairy-tailed mole, *Parascalops breweri* (Bachman, 1842). Journal of Mammalogy 64(3):453–462.

Jensen, I. M. 1986. Foraging strategies of the mole (*Parascalops breweri* Bachman, 1842). I. The distribution of prey. Canadian Journal of Zoology 64(8): 1727–1733.

*Johenning, L. 1931. A North Mountain outlaw. Game and Fish Conservationist 10(6):115.

Johnson, A. S. 1970. Biology of the raccoon (*Procyon lotor varius* Nelson) in Alabama. Auburn University Agricultural Station Bulletin 402.

Johnson, C. E. 1921. The "hand-stand" habit of the spotted skunk. Journal of Mammalogy 2(2):87–89.

*Johnson, D. H. 1950. *Myotis subulatus leibii* in Virginia. Journal of Mammalogy 31(2):197.

*Johnson, G. B. 1938a. Surry County's big buck. Virginia Wildlife 1(11):2–3.

*Johnson, G. B. 1938b. The private life of a Virginia fox. Virginia Wildlife 2(2):2–3.

*Johnson, G. B. 1938c. Still-hunting the black bear. Virginia Wildlife 1(10):6.

*Johnson, G. B. 1939. The deer of the United States. Virginia Wildlife 3(3):2, 7.

*Johnson, G. B. 1940. An eastern Virginia deer hunt. Virginia Wildlife 4(2):71–72.

*Johnson, G. B. 1942. The beaver. Virginia Wildlife 6(1):28–34.

*Johnson, G. B. 1947. The whales. Virginia Wildlife 8(10):6–8.

*Johnson, G. B. 1953. Virginia deer antlers grow big. Virginia Wildlife 14(4):10–1.

*Johnson, H. N. 1959. Rabies. Pp. 405–431. In: Rivers, T. M., and F. L. Horsfall, Jr. (editors), Viral and rickettsial infections of man. 3d edition. Philadelphia: J. B. Lippincott Company.

*Johnson, M. S. 1926. Activity and distribution of certain wild mice in relation to biotic communities. Journal of Mammalogy 7(4):245–277.

*Johnson, P. B. 1933. Accidents to bats. Journal of Mammalogy 14(2):156–157.

*Johnson, P. G. 1973. James Patton and the Appalachian colonists. Verona, Virginia: McClure Press.

*Johnston, D. E. 1906. A history of Middle New River settlements and contiguous territory. Huntington, West Virginia: Standard Printing and Publishing Company.

*Johnston, D.W. 1997. Some important Virginia specimens in the National Institution for the Promotion of Science. Banisteria 10:9–13.

Jones, C. 1967. Growth, development, and wing loading in the evening bat, *Nycticeius humeralis* (Rafinesque). Journal of Mammalogy 48(1):1–19.

*Jones, C. 1977. *Plecotus rafinesquii.* Mammalian Species no. 69.

Jones, C. and R. W. Manning. 1989. *Myotis austroriparius.* Mammalian Species no. 332.

Jones, C., R. S. Hoffmann, D. W. Rice, M. D. Engstrom, R.D. Bradley, D. J. Schmidly, C. A. Jones, and R. J. Baker. 1997. Revised checklist of North American mammals north of Mexico, 1997. Museum of Texas Tech University Occasional Papers no. 173:1–19.

*Jones, C. A., S. R. Humphrey, T. M. Padgett, R. K. Rose, and J. F. Pagels. 1991. Geographic variation and taxonomy of the southeastern shrew *(Sorex longirostris).* Journal of Mammalogy 72(2):263–272.

*Jones, C. S., and J. F. Pagels. 1979. The distribution of the southeastern shrew, *Sorex longirostris,* in Virginia. Virginia Journal of Science 30(2):48. Abstract.

*Jones, E. J. 1978. Some diseases and parasites affecting cottontail rabbits in Virginia. Master's thesis, Virginia Polytechnic Institute and State University, Blacksburg.

*Jones, E. J., J. J. Hasbrouck, and F. A. Servello. 1982. Relationship of *Taenia taeniaeformis* strobilocerci and body and reproductive organ weights in pine voles. Virginia Journal of Science 33(3):110. Abstract.

*Jones, E. J., B.S. McGinnes, and R. L. Kirkpatrick. 1978a. A survey for tularemia in Piedmont Virginia. Virginia Journal of Science 29(2):62. Abstract.

*Jones, E. J., B. S. McGinnes, and R. L. Kirkpatrick. 1978b. The distribution of *Baylisascaris procyonis* in Virginia. Virginia Journal of Science 29(2):62. Abstract.

*Jones, E. J., and A. R. Tipton. 1978. Age structure of a cottontail rabbit population in Piedmont Virginia. Virginia Journal of Science 29(2):62. Abstract.

Jones, E. N. 1990. Effects on forage availability on home range and population density of *Microtus pennsylvanicus.* Journal of Mammalogy 71(3):382–389.

*Jones, G. S. and M. K. Klimkiewicz. 1971. Mammals of Mason Neck. Atlantic Naturalist 26(3):108–114.

*Jones, G. W. 1939. An unusual woodchuck refuge. Journal of Mammalogy 20(4):504–505.

*Jones, J. C. 1954. Rabies in Virginia and its relation to wildlife. Virginia Wildlife 15(4):8–10, 12.

*Jones, J. C. 1955. The status of rabies in the middle Atlantic states of Virginia, West Virginia, Maryland, Delaware, and the District of Columbia for the fiscal year 1953–1954. Maryland Conservationist 32(4):6–11.

Jones, J. K., Jr., R. S. Hoffmann, D. W. Rice, C. Jones, R. J. Baker, and M. D. Engstrom. 1992. Revised checklist of North American mammals north of Mexico, 1991. Occasional Papers, The Museum, Texas Tech University no. 146.

Jones, M. L. 1982. Longevity of captive mammals. Zoological Garten 52:113–128.

*Jones, S. C., III. 1993. Surveys for bottlenose dolphins in lower Chesapeake Bay, 1992. Virginia Journal of Science 44(2):111. Abstract

*Jones, T. D. 1969a. Br'er rabbit and the country boy. Virginia Wildlife 30(3):12.

*Jones, T. D. 1969b. A visit to the dismal swamp. Virginia Wildlife 30(7):8–9.

*Jonkel, C. 1978. Black, brown (grizzly), and polar bears. Pp. 226–248. In: Schmidt, J. L., and D. L. Gilbert (editors), Big game of North America. Harrisburg, Pennsylvania: Stackpole Books.

*Jordan, D. S. 1888. A manual of the vertebrate animals of the northern United States. 5th ed. Chicago: A. C. McClung and Company.

*Jordan, D. S. 1929. Manual of the vertebrate animals of the northeastern United States. 13th ed. New York: World Book Company.

*Jordan, K. 1928. Siphonaptera collected during a visit to the eastern United States of North America in 1927. Novitates Zoologicae 34:178–188.

Junge, J. A., and R. S. Hoffman. 1981. An annotated key to the long-tailed shrews (genus *Sorex*) of the United States and Canada, with notes on Middle American *Sorex.* Occasional Papers, Museum of Natural History, University of Kansas, 94:1–48.

*Jurney, R. C., S. S. Obenshain, E. Shulkcum, H. C. Porter, E. F. Henry, J. R. Moore, R. E. O'Brien, and R. C. Jurney, Jr. 1945. Soil survey — Washington County, Virginia. Series 1937, no. 14. United States Department of Agriculture, Bureau of Plant Industry, Soils, and Agricultural Engineering, Washington, DC.

Justice, K. E. 1961. A new method for measuring home ranges of small mammals. Journal of Mammalogy 42(4):462–470.

Kale, H. W., II. 1965. Ecology and bioenergetics of the long-billed marsh wren *Telmatodytes palustris griseus* (Brewster) in Georgia salt marshes. Publications of the Nuttall Ornithological Club 5:1–142.

*Kalko, E. K. V., and C. O. Handley, Jr. 1993. Comparative studies of small mammal populations with transects of snap traps and pitfall arrays in southwest Virginia. Virginia Journal of Science 44(1):3–18.

*Kalm, P. 1772. Travels into North America. 2 volumes. London.

*Kaminsky, M. A., and R. H. Giles, Jr. 1975. An analysis of deer spotlighting in Virginia. Proceedings of the 28th Annual Conference of the Southeastern Association of Game and Fish Commissioners 28:729–740.

*Kasbohm, J. W. 1994. Response of black bears to gypsy moth infestation in Shenandoah National Park, Virginia. Doctoral dissertation, Virginia Polytechnic Institute and State University, Blacksburg.

*Kasbohm, J. W., D. A. Miller, and M. R. Vaughan. 1994. Taxonomy of black bears in the southeastern United States. Annual Report, United States Fish and Wildlife Service. 24 pp.

*Kasbohm, J. W., M. R. Vaughan, and J. G. Kraus. 1994. Black bear harvest and nuisance behavior in response to gypsy moth infestation. Proceedings of the

48th Annual Conference of the Southeastern Association of Fish and Wildlife Agencies 48:261–269.

*Kaufman, D. W., and G. A. Kaufman. 1989. Population biology. Pp. 233–270. In: Kirkland, G. L., Jr., and J. N. Layne (editors), Advances in the study of *Peromyscus* (Rodentia). Lubbock: Texas Tech University Press.

*Kaufmann, J. H. 1982. Raccoon and allies. Pp. 567–585. In: Chapman, J. A., and G. A. Feldhamer (editors), Wild mammals of North America. Baltimore: The Johns Hopkins University Press.

Kaye, S. V. 1961. Laboratory life history of the eastern harvest mouse. American Midland Naturalist 66:439–451.

*Keefe, J. F. 1967. The world of the opossum. Philadelphia: J. B. Lippincott Company.

*Keegan, H. L. 1951. The mites of the subfamily Haemogamasinae (Acari:Laelaptidae). Proceedings of the United States National Museum 101(3275): 203–268.

Keen, R., and H. B. Hitchcock. 1980. Survival and longevity of the little brown bat *(Myotis lucifugus)* in southeastern Ontario. Journal of Mammalogy 61(1):1–7.

*Keiper, R. R. 1976a. Social organization of feral ponies. Proceedings of the Pennsylvania Academy of Science 50(1):69–70.

*Keiper, R. R. 1976b. Interactions between cattle egrets and feral ponies. Proceedings of the Pennsylvania Academy of Science 50(1):89–90.

*Keiper, R. R. 1977. Observations on the nocturnal behavior of feral ponies. Proceedings of the Pennsylvania Academy of Science 51(1):57–58.

*Keiper, R. R. 1979. The behavior, ecology, and social organization of the feral ponies of Assateague Island. Proceedings of the First Conference on Scientific Research in the National Parks, United States National Park Service Transactions and Proceedings Series no. 5. Volume I. p. 369–371.

*Keiper, R. R. 1985. The Assateague ponies. Centreville, Maryland: Tidewater Publishers.

Keiper, R. R. 1988. Biology of large grazing mammals on the Virginia barrier islands. Virginia Journal of Science 39(2):166. Abstract.

Keiper, R. R. 1990. Biology of large grazing mammals on the Virginia barrier islands. Virginia Journal of Science 41(4A):352–363.

Keiper, R. R., and J. Berger. 1982. Refuge-seeking and pest avoidance by feral horses in desert and island environments. Applied Animal Ecology 9(2):111–120.

*Keiper, R. R., and K. Houpt. 1984. Reproduction in feral horses: an eight-year study. American Journal of Veterinary Research 45:991–995.

*Keiper, R. R., and M. A. Keenan. 1980. Nocturnal activity patterns of feral ponies. Journal of Mammalogy 61(1):116–118.

Kelker, G. H. 1937. Insect food of skunks. Journal of Mammalogy 18(2):164–170.

*Keller, B. L. 1985. Reproductive patterns. Pp. 725–778. In: Tamarin, R. H. (editor), Biology of New World *Microtus*. American Society of Mammalogists Special Publication no. 8.

*Kellner, W. C. 1953. Factors influencing the raccoon and its management in southwestern Virginia. Master's thesis, Virginia Polytechnic Institute and State University, Blacksburg.

*Kellner, W. C. 1954. The raccoon in southwestern Virginia. Virginia Wildlife 15(1):16–17, 21.

*Kellner, W. C. 1955a. Ringtail — cutup of the woodlands. Virginia Wildlife 16(3):9–10.

*Kellner, W. C. 1955b. The gray squirrel in Virginia. Virginia Wildlife 16(7):22–24.

*Kellner, W. C. 1955c. The Dismal-No Business area of Giles and Bland counties. Virginia Wildlife 16(8):10–12.

*Kellner, W. C. 1955d. Ringtail — cutup of the woodlands. Educational Leaflet no. 8:1–4. Virginia Commission of Game and Inland Fisheries, Richmond.

*Kellner, W. C. 1955e. The gray squirrel in Virginia. Educational Leaflet no. 13:1–4. Virginia Commission of Game and Inland Fisheries, Richmond.

Kellogg, R. 1937. Annotated list of West Virginia mammals. Proceedings of the United States National Museum 84:443–479.

*Kellogg, R. 1939a. A new red-backed mouse from Kentucky and Virginia. Proceedings of the Biological Society of Washington 52:37–40.

*Kellogg, R. 1939b. Annotated list of Tennessee mammals. Proceedings of the United States National Museum 86:245–303.

*Kellogg, R. 1956. What and where are the whitetails? Pp. 31–55. In: Taylor, W. P. (editor), The deer of North America. Harrisburg, Pennsylvania: The Stackpole Company.

*Kellogg, R. 1965. Fossil marine mammals from the Miocene Calvert formation of Maryland and Virginia. United States National Museum Bulletin 247, Parts 1 and 2.

Kellogg, W. N., R. Kohler, and H. N. Morris. 1953. Porpoise sounds as sonar signals. Science 117(3036):239–243.

Kennedy, M. L., J. G. Babb, R. M. Lee III, and C. Lydeard. 1990. Average litter size of the coyote in Tennessee. Journal of the Tennessee Academy of Science 65:61–62.

Kennedy, M. L., and T. L. Best. 1972. Flight speed of the gray bat, *Myotis grisescens*. American Midland Naturalist 88(1):254–255.

*Kenney, J. E., M. T. Mengak, and J. Holland. 1994. Status and distribution of the Allegheny woodrat in Virginia with notes on ecology. Virginia Journal of Science 45(2):59. Abstract.

*Kenyon, I., and G. Norman. 1990. All in the family. Virginia Wildlife 51(5):11–18.

*Kercheval, S. 1925. (1850). A history of the Valley of Virginia. 4th ed. Revised and extended by the author, and new notes added by the editor. Strasburg, Virginia: Shenandoah Publishing House.

*Kerns, T. 1985. Mink tales. Virginia Wildlife 46(1):22–25.

*Kerpez, T. A. 1994. Effects of group selection and clearcut openings on wildlife in Appalachian hardwood forests. Doctoral dessertation, Virginia Polytechnic Institute and State University, Blacksburg.

*Kerr, R. 1792. The animal kingdom, or zoological system, of the celebrated Sir Charles Linnaeus; Class I. Mammalia: containing a complete systematic description, arrangement, and nomenclature, of all the known species and varieties of the Mammalia, or animals which give suck to their young; being a translation of that part of the Systema Naturae, as lately published, with great improvements, by Professor Gmelin of Goettingen. Printed for J. Murray and R. Faulder, London.

*Kesteloo, L. G. 1948. So *this* is deer hunting! Virginia Wildlife 9(2):6–8.

*Kesteloo, L. G. 1963. Archery at Hog Island. Virginia Wildlife 24(1):14–15.

Keys, C. E. 1966. The development of the cotton rat, *Sigmodon hispidus texianus,* through the first nine and one half days of gestation. I. Ovarian stages and ovulation. Journal of the Alabama Academy of Science 37(1):3–7.

*Keyser, P. 1994. Guess who's coming to dinner? Virginia Wildlife 55(11):3–7.

*Keyser, P. 1995. Home sweet home. Virginia Wildlife 56(11):10–17.

*Kibbe, D. P. 1969. The effects of nutrition on the reproductive physiology of captive cottontail rabbits, *Sylvilagus floridanus* (Allen). Master's thesis, Virginia Polytechnic Institute and State University, Blacksburg.

*Kibbe, D. P., and R. L. Kirkpatrick. 1971. Systematic evaluation of late summer breeding in juvenile cottontails, *Sylvilagus floridanus.* Journal of Mammalogy 52(2):465–467.

Kight, J. 1962. An ecology study of the bobcat, *Lynx rufus* (Schreber) in west-central South Carolina. Master's thesis, University of Georgia, Athens.

*Kilgore, D. L., Jr. 1970. The effects of northward dispersal on growth rate of young, size of young at birth, and litter size in *Sigmodon hispidus.* American Midland Naturalist 84(2):510–520.

*Kilpatrick, J. 1944. The Virginia sportsman — return of the night hunters. Virginia Wildlife 7(3):14–15, 21.

*Kiltie, R. A. 1989. Wildfire and the evolution of dorsal melanism in fox squirrels, *Sciurus niger.* Journal of Mammalogy 70(4):726–739.

King, A. M., R. A. Lancia, S. D. Miller, D. K. Woodward, and J. D. Hair. 1983. Winter food habits of bobcats in North Carolina. Brimleyana 9:111–122.

King, C. 1989. The natural history of weasels and stoats. Ithaca, New York: Comstock Publishing Associates.

*King, H. 1953. The $4000 deer. Virginia Wildlife 14(4):20–21.

*King, J. A. 1968. Biology of *Peromyscus.* American Society of Mammalogists Special Publication no. 2.

*King, J. E. 1964. Seals of the world. London: British Museum (Natural History).

*Kingsley, J. S. (editor) 1884. The standard natural history. V. Mammals. Boston: S. E. Cassino and Company.

*Kingsley, J. S., and E. Breck. 1894. Nature's wonderland, or short talks on natural history for young and old. 4 volumes. New York: F. R. Niglutsch.

*Kingston, N. 1981. Protozoan Parasites. Pp. 193–236. In: Davidson, W. R., F. A. Hayes, V. F. Nettles, and F. E. Kellogg. Diseases and parasites of white-tailed deer. Miscellaneous Publication no. 7, Tall Timbers Research Station, Tallahassee, Florida.

*Kinlaw, A. 1995. *Spilogale putorius.* Mammalian Species no. 511:1-7.

Kirkland, G. L., Jr. 1975a. Notes on the cloudland deer mouse *(Peromyscus maniculatus nubiterrae)* in West Virginia. Proceedings of the West Virginia Academy of Science 47:74–79.

*Kirkland, G. L., Jr. 1975b. Taxonomy and geographic distribution of *Peromyscus maniculatus nubiterrae* Rhoads (Mammalia: Rodentia. Annals of the Carnegie Museum 45(10):213–229.

*Kirkland, G. L., Jr. 1977. The rock vole, *Microtus chrotorrhinus* (Miller) (Mammalia: Rodentia) in West Virginia. Annals of the Carnegie Museum 46:45–53.

*Kirkland, G. L., Jr. 1981. *Sorex dispar* and *Sorex gaspensis.* Mammalian Species no. 155.

*Kirkland, G. L., Jr. and T. V. Fleming. 1988. Ecology of feral house mice *(Mus musculus)* on Wallops Island, Virginia. Virginia Journal of Science 39(2):116. Abstract.

*Kirkland, G. L., Jr. and T. V. Fleming. 1990. Ecology of feral house mice *(Mus musculus)* on Wallops Island, Virginia. Virginia Journal of Science 41(4A): 330–339.

*Kirkland, G. L., Jr. and F. J. Jannett, Jr. 1982. *Microtus chrotorrhinus.* Mammalian Species no. 180.

*Kirkland, G. L., Jr. and A. V. Linzey. 1973. Observations on the breeding of the deer mouse, *Peromyscus maniculatus nubiterrae.* Journal of Mammalogy 54(1):254–255.

*Kirkland, G. L., Jr. and H. M. VanDeusen. 1979. The shrews of the *Sorex dispar* group: *Sorex dispar* Batchelder and *Sorex gaspensis* Anthony and Goodwin. American Museum Novitates no. 2675:1–21.

*Kirkpatrick, J. F., B. L. Laley, S. E. Shideler, J. F. Roser, and J. W. Turner, Jr. 1993. Non-instrumented immunoassay field tests for pregnancy detection in free-roaming feral horses. Journal of Wildlife Management 57(1):168–173.

*Kirkpatrick, J. F., and J. W. Turner, Jr. 1991a. Changes in herd stallions among feral horse bands and the absence of forced copulation and induced abortion. Behavioral Ecology and Sociobiology 29(3):217–219.

*Kirkpatrick, J. F., and J. W. Turner, Jr. 1991b. Compensatory reproduction in feral horses. Journal of Wildlife Management 55(4):649–652.

*Kirkpatrick, R. L. 1975. Ovarian follicular and related characteristics of white-tailed deer as influenced by season and age in the Southeast. Proceedings of the 28th Annual Conference of the Southeastern Association of Game and Fish Commissioners 28:587–594.

*Kirkpatrick, R. L., and D. M. Baldwin. 1974. Population density and reproduction in penned cottontail rabbits. Journal of Wildlife Management 38(3):482–487.

*Kirkpatrick, R. L., D. E. Buckland, W. A. Abler, P. F. Scanlon, J. B. Whelan, and H. E. Burkhart. 1975. Energy and protein influences on blood urea nitrogen levels in white-tailed deer fawns. Journal of Wildlife Management 39(4):692–698.

*Kirkpatrick, R. L., J. L. Coggin, H. S. Mosby, and J. O. Newell. 1976. Parturition times and litter sizes of gray squirrels in Virginia. Proceedings of the 30th Annual Conference of the Southeastern Association of Fish and Wildlife Agencies 30:541–545.

*Kirkpatrick, R. L., J. P. Fontenot, and R. F. Harlow. 1969. Seasonal changes in rumen chemical components as related to forages consumed by white-tailed deer of the Southeast. Transactions of the 34th North American Wildlife and Natural Resources Conference 34:229–238.

*Kirkpatrick, R. L., and D. P. Kibbe. 1971. Nutritive restriction and reproductive characteristics of captive cottontail rabbits. Journal of Wildlife Management 35(2):332–338.

*Kirkpatrick, R. L., and P. F Scanlon. 1984. Care of captive whitetails. Pp. 687–696. In: Halls, L. K. (editor), White-tailed Deer: Ecology and Management. Harrisburg: Stackpole Company.

*Kirkpatrick, R. L., and G. L. Valentine. 1970. Reproduction in captive pine voles, *Microtus pinetorum.* Journal of Mammalogy 51(4):779–785.

*Kirksey, E. R. 1973. The relation of metabolism and temperature selection to various acclimation temperatures in the cotton rat *(Sigmodon hispidus).* Master's thesis, Virginia Commonwealth University, Richmond.

*Kirksey, E. R., J. F. Pagels, and C. R. Blem. 1975. The role of the tail in temperature regulation of the cotton rat, *Sigmodon hispidus.* Comparative Biochemistry and Physiology. A. Comparative Physiology 52(4):707–711.

Kissen, A. T., and J. W. Price. 1962. Studies on the embryology of the mink. Journal of Morphology 110(1):105–119.

*Kistner, T. P., and W. L. Hanson. 1969. Trypanosomiasis in white-tailed deer. Journal of Wildlife Diseases 5(4):398–399.

Kitchings, J. T., and J. D. Story. 1984. Movements and dispersal of bobcats in east Tennessee. Journal of Wildlife Management 48(3):957–961.

*Klewer, H. L. 1958. The incidence of helminth lung parasites of *Lynx rufus rufus* (Schreber) and the life cycle of *Anafilaroides rostratus* Gerichter, 1949. Journal of Parasitology 44(1):29.

*Klimkiewicz, M. K. 1970. Autumn migration flyway one — Mason Neck. Atlantic Naturalist 25(4):160–164.

Klugh, A. B. 1927. Ecology of the red squirrel. Journal of Mammalogy 8:1–32.

Knowlton, F. F. 1972. Preliminary interpretations of coyote population mechanics with some management implications. Journal of Wildlife Management 36:369–382.

Knudsen, G. J. 1961. We learn about bears. Wisconsin Conservation Bulletin 26(6):13–15.

Knudsen, G. J., and J. B. Hale. 1968. Food habits of otters in the Great Lakes region. Journal of Wildlife Management 32(1):89–93.

*Knuth, C. 1976. Game and fish research. Virginia Wildlife 37(8):8–13.

*Knuth, C. 1978. Game and furbearing mammals of Virginia. Virginia Wildlife 39(9):16–19.

*Knuth, C. S. 1986. Ol' musquash. Virginia Wildlife 47(2):22–24.

*Knuth, S. 1988. Deer management in Virginia: it only gets better. Virginia Wildlife 49(9):26–28.

*Kohls, G. M. 1940. Siphonaptera. A study of the species infesting wild hares and rabbits of North America north of Mexico. National Institutes of Health Bulletin no. 175.

*Kokel, R. W. 1992. Virginia's other squirrel. Virginia Wildlife 53(10):22–26.

*Koopman, K. F. 1965. A northern record of the yellow bat. Journal of Mammalogy 46(4):695.

*Kopf, V. 1987. Progress report on state species ranking activities. Virginia Journal of Science 38(2):82. Abstract.

*Kopf, V. E. 1983. the relationship between foor intake and thyroid hormone concentrations in white-tailed deer. Doctoral dissertation, Virginia Polytechnic Institute and State University, Blacksburg.

*Kopf, V. E., D. L. Drawe, P. F. Scanlon, and F. C. Gwazdauskas. 1982. Comparison of thyroid hormone concentrations in blood of white-tailed deer from Virginia and Texas. Virginia Journal of Science 33(3):114. Abstract.

*Kopf, V. E., P. F. Scanlon, R. L. Kirkpatrick and F. C. Gwazdauskas. 1982. Thyroid hormone concentrations in blood of pregnant white-tailed deer. Virginia Journal of Science 33(3):114. Abstract.

*Koprowski, J. L. 1994a. *Sciurus niger.* Mammalian Species no 479:1–9. The American Society of Mammalogists.

*Koprowski, J. L. 1994b. *Sciurus carolinensis.* Mammalian Species no. 480:1–9. The American Society of Mammalogists.

Koprowski, J. L., J. L. Roseberry, and W. D. Klimstra. 1988. Longevity records for the fox squirrel. Journal of Mammalogy 69(2):383–384.

Korschgen, L. J. 1958. December food habits of mink in Missouri. Journal of Mammalogy 39(4):521–527.

*Kratimenos, G. E., and R. K. Rose. 1991. Population dynamics of house mice and meadow voles on a dredge disposal site. Virginia Journal of Science 42(2):172. Abstract.

*Krebs, J. W., R. C. Holman, U. Hines, T. W. Strine, E. J. Mandel, and J. E. Childs. 1992. Rabies surveillance in the United States during 1991. Journal of the American Veterinary Medical Association 201(12): 1836–1848.

*Krebs, J. W., T. W. Strine, and J. E. Childs. 1993. Rabies surveillance in the United States during 1992. Journal of the American Veterinary Medicine Association 203(12):1718-1731.

*Krebs, J. W., T. W. Strine, J. S. Smith, C. E. Rupprecht, and J. E. Childs. 1994. Rabies surveillance in the United States during 1993. Journal of the American Veterinary Medical Association 205(12):1695–1709.

*Krebs, J. W., M. L. Wilson, and J. E. Childs. 1995. Rabies — epidemiology, prevention, and future research. Journal of Mammalogy 76(3):681–694.

*Kreitzer, J. F. 1967. Mother knows best. Virginia Wildlife 28(5):21–22.

Krim, P. M. 1988. Den site characteristics and food habits of the red-fox *(Vulpes vulpes)* on Assateague Island. Virginia Journal of Science 39(2):116. Abstract.

*Krim, P. M., T. L. Bashore, and G. L. Kirkland, Jr. 1990. Den site characteristics and food habits of the red fox (*Vulpes vulpes*) on Assateague Island, Maryland. Virginia Journal of Science 41(4A):340–351.

Krohne, D. T., J. F. Merritt, S. H. Vessey, and J. O. Wolff. 1988. Comparative demography of forest *Peromyscus.* Canadian Journal of Zoology 66(10):2170–2176.

Krosch, H. F. 1973. Some effects of the bite of the short-tailed shrew, *Blarina brevicauda.* Journal of the Minnesota Academy of Science 39:21.

*Krug, A. S. 1960. Evaluation of intensified rabbit management procedures on public hunting areas in southcentral Virginia. Master's thesis, Virginia Polytechnic Institute and State University, Blacksburg.

*Kuehl, D. W., R. Haebler, and C. Potter, 1991. chemical residues in dolphins from the U.S. Atlantic coast including Atlantic bottlenose obtained during the 1987/88 mass mortality. Chemosphere 22(11):1071–1084.

*Kruper, J. H., and T. L. Derting. 1991. Small mammal occurrence and habitat associations in a suburban environment. Virginia Journal of Science 42(2):216. Abstract.

*Krutzsch, P. H. 1954. North American jumping mice (genus *Zapus*). University of Kansas Publication, Museum of Natural History 7(4):349–472.

*Krutzsch, P. H. 1966. Remarks on silver-haired and Leib's bats in eastern United States. Journal of Mammalogy 47(1):121.

*Krutzsch, P. H., and E. G. Crichton. 1986. Reproduction of the male eastern pipistrelle, *Pipistrellus subflavus,* in the north-eastern United States. Journal of Reproduction and Fertility 76(1):91–104.

Kunz, T. H. 1974. Reproduction, growth, and mortality of the vespertilionid bat, *Eptesicus fuscus,* in Kansas. Journal of Mammalogy 55(1):1–13.

*Kunz, T. H. 1982. *Lasionycteris noctivagans.* Mammalian Species no. 172.

Kunz, T. H. (editor). 1982. Ecology of bats. New York: Plenum Press.

Kunz, T. H., and E. L. P. Anthony. 1982. Age estimation and post-natal growth in the bat *Myotis lucifugus.* Journal of Mammalogy 63(1):23–32.

*Kunz, T. H., and R. A. Martin. 1982. *Plecotus townsendii.* Mammalian Species no. 175.

*Kurta, A., and R. H. Baker. 1990. *Eptesicus fuscus.* Mammalian Species no. 356.

*Kurta, A., and M. E. Stewart. 1990. Parturition in the silver-haired bat, *Lasionycteris noctivagans,* with a description of the neonates. Canadian Field-Naturalist 104(4):598–600.

*Kurtén, B., and E. Anderson. 1980. Pleistocene mammals of North America. New York: Columbia University Press.

*Lackey, J. A., D. G. Huckaby, and B. G. Ormiston. 1985. *Peromyscus leucopus.* Mammalian Species no. 247.

*Lacki, M. J., M. D. Adam, and L. G. Shoemaker. 1994. Observations on seasonal cycle, population patterns and roost selection in summer colonies of *Plecotus townsendii virginianus* in Kentucky. American Midland Naturalist 131:34–42.

Lacki, M. J., L. S. Burford, and J. O. Whitaker, Jr. 1995. Food habits of gray bats in Kentucky. Journal of Mammalogy 76(4):1256–1259.

*Lacy, B. R. 1948. The acceptability and palatability of certain feeds, diluents, and poisons to *Pitymys, Microtus,* and *Peromyscus.* Master's thesis, Virginia Polytechnic Institute and State University, Blacksburg.

*Laerm, J., M. A. Menzel, and J. L. Boone. 1997. Mensural discrimination of *Sorex longirostris* and *Sorex cinereus* (Insectivora: Soricidae) in the southeastern United States. Brimleyana 24:15-27.

*Laerm, J., F. Wenzel, J. E. Craddock, D. Weinand, J. McGurk, M. J. Harris, G. A. Early, J. G. Mead, C. W. Potter, and N. B. Barros. 1997. New prey species for northwestern Atlantic humpback whales. Marine Mammal Science 13(4):705–711.

*Laerm, J., C. H. Wharton, and W. M. Ford. 1995. First record of the water shrew, *Sorex palustris* Richardson (Insectivora: Soricidae), in Georgia with comments on its distribution and status in the southern Appalachians. Brimleyana 22:47–51.

*Laerm, J., C. H. Wharton, and W. M. Ford. 1997. The rock shrew, *Sorex dispar* (Insectivora: Soricidae), in Georgia with comments on its conservation status in the southern Appalachians. Brimleyana 24:1-5.

Lagler, K. F., and B. T. Ostenson. 1942. Early spring food of the otter in Michigan. Journal of Wildlife Management 6(3):244–254.

Lair, H. 1985. Length of gestation in the red squirrel, *Tamiasciurus hudsonicus.* Journal of Mammalogy 66(4):809–810.

*Lambert, E. 1971. The year the wild ones won. Virginia Wildlife 32(9):6–7, 23.

*Lantz, D. E. 1907. An economic study of field mice. United States Department of Agriculture, Biological Survey Bulletin no. 31.

*Lantz, D. E. 1908. The rabbit as a farm and orchard pest. United States Department of Agriculture Yearbook for 1907:329–342.

*Lantz, D. E. 1910a. The muskrat. United States Department of Agriculture Farmers' Bulletin no. 396.

*Lantz, D. E. 1910b. Raising deer and other large game animals in the United States. United States Department of Agriculture Farmers' Bulletin no. 36.

*Lantz, D. E. 1914. Economic value of North American skunks. United States Department of Agriculture Farmers' Bulletin no. 587.

*Lantz, D. E. 1916a. Cottontail rabbits in relation to trees and farm crops. United States Department of Agriculture Farmers' Bulletin no. 702.

*Lantz, D. E. 1916b. Laws relating to fur-bearing animals, 1915. United States Department of Agriculture Farmers' Bulletin no. 706.

*Lantz, D. E. 1916c. Laws relating to fur-bearing animals, 1916. United States Department of Agriculture Farmers' Bulletin no. 783.

*Lantz, D. E. 1917. The muskrat as a fur bearer. United States Department of Agriculture Farmers' Bulletin no. 869.

*Lantz, D. E. 1918. The control of mice in Virginia orchards. Virginia State Horticultural Society Report 22:151–161.

*Lariviere, S. and M. Pasitschniak-Arts. 1996. *Vulpes vulpes*. Mammalian Species no 537:1-11.

*Lariviere, S. and L. R. Walton. 1997. *Lynx rufus*. Mammalian Species no. 563:1-8

*Larson, B. J. 1990a. Population viability analysis for the endangered Delmarva fox squirrel. Pp. 3–4. In: Edwards, J. W. et al. (editors). First Symposium on Southeastern Fox Squirrels. Virginia Museum of Natural History. Abstract.

*Larson, B. J. 1990b. Habitat utilization, population dynamics and long-term viability in an insular population of Delmarva fox squirrels *(Sciurus niger cinereus)*. Master's thesis, University of Virginia, Charlottesville.

*Larson, B. J., and R. D. Dueser. 1990. Habitat utilization in an insular population of Delmarva fox squirrels *(Sciurus niger cinereus)*. Virginia Journal of Science 41(2):56. Abstract.

Larson, J. S. 1967. Age structure and sexual maturity within a western Maryland beaver *(Castor canadensis)* population. Journal of Mammalogy 48(3):408–413.

*Latham, R. M., and C. R. Studholme. 1947. Spotted skunk in Pennsylvania. Journal of Mammalogy 28(4):409.

*Lauer, D. M., and D. E. Sonenshine. 1978. Bionomics of the squirrel flea, *Orchopeas howardi* (Siphonaptera: Ceratophyllidae), in laboratory and field colonies of the southern flying squirrel, *Glaucomys volans*, using radiolabeling techniques. Journal of Medical Entomology 15(1):1–10.

LaVal, R. K., R. L. Clawson, M. L. LaVal, and W. Caire. 1977. Foraging behavior and nocturnal activity patterns of Missouri bats, with emphasis on the endangered species *Myotis grisescens* and *Myotis sodalis*. Journal of Mammalogy 58:592–599.

LaVal, R. K., and M. L. LaVal. 1980. Ecological studies and management of Missouri bats, with emphasis on cave-dwelling species. Missouri Department of Conservation, Terrestrial Series 8:1–53.

Lay, D. W. 1957. Browse quality and the effects of prescribed burning in southern pine forests. Journal of Forestry 55:342–347.

Lay, D. W., and R. H. Baker. 1938. Notes on the home range and ecology of the Atwater wood rat. Journal of Mammalogy 19(4):418–423.

*Layne, J. N. 1958. Notes on mammals of southern Illinois. American Midland Naturalist 60(1):219–254.

Layne, J. N. 1959. Growth and development of the eastern harvest mouse, *Reithrodontomys humulis*. Bulletin of the Florida State Museum 4(2):61–82.

*Layne, J. N. 1965. Observation on marine mammals in Florida waters. Bulletin of the Florida State Museum 9(4):131–181.

Layne, J. N. 1967. Evidence for the use of vision in diurnal orientation of the bat *Myotis austroriparius*. Animal Behaviour 15(4):409–415.

Layne, J. N. 1974. Ecology of small mammals in flatwoods habitat in north-central Florida, with emphasis on the cotton rat *(Sigmodon hispidus)*. American Museum Novitates 2544:1–48.

Layne, J. N., and W. J. Hamilton, Jr. 1954. The young of the woodland jumping mouse, *Napaeozapus insignis insignis* (Miller). American Midland Naturalist 52:242–247.

*Lederer, J. 1672. The discoveries of John Lederer in three several marches from Virginia, to the West of Carolina, and other parts of the continent: begun in March 1669, and ended in September 1670. Printed by J. C. for S. Heyrich, London.

Lee, D., J. Funderburg, and M. Clark. 1982. A distributional survey of North Carolina mammals. Occasional Papers of the North Carolina Biological Survey 1982–10:1–70.

Lee, D. S. 1987. The star-nosed mole on the Delmarva Peninsula: zoogeographic and systematic problems of a boreal species in the South. Maryland Naturalist 31(2):44–57.

*Lee, D. S. 1988. Wm. H. Fisher's *Mammals of Maryland:* a previously unknown early compilation of the state's fauna. Maryland Naturalist 32(1–2):9–37.

*Lee, D. S. and M. K. Clark. 1993. A second record of the southern bog lemming, *Synaptomys cooperi*, from the Delmarva Peninsula. The Maryland Naturalist 37(1–2):29–35.

*Lee, D. S., and J. B. Funderburg. 1977a. *Lepus americanus virginianus* Harlan. Pp. 405. In: Cooper, J. E., S. S. Robinson, and J. B. Funderburg (editors), Endangered and threatened plants and animals of North Carolina. Raleigh: North Carolina State Museum of Natural History.

*Lee, D. S., and J. B. Funderburg. 1977b. *Microtus pennsylvanicus nigrans* Rhoads. Pp. 406. In: Cooper, J. E., S. S. Robinson, and J. B. Funderburg (editors), Endangered and threatened plants and animals of North Carolina. Raleigh: North Carolina State Museum of Natural History.

*Lee, D. S., and J. B. Funderburg. 1977c. *Sciurus niger* (subspecies) Linnaeus. Pp. 405. In: Cooper, J. E., S. S. Robinson, and J. B. Funderburg (editors), Endangered and threatened plants and animals of North

Carolina. Raleigh: North Carolina State Museum of Natural History.

*Lee, D. S., and J. B. Funderburg. 1977d. *Sorex longirostris fisheri* Merriam. Pp. 403. In: Cooper, J. E., S. S. Robinson, and J. B. Funderburg (editors), Endangered and threatened plants and animals of North Carolina. Raleigh: North Carolina State Museum of Natural History.

*Lee, D. S., and J. B. Funderburg. 1982. Marmots. Pp. 176–191. In: Chapman, J. A., and G. A. Feldhamer (editors), Wild mammals of North America. Baltimore: The Johns Hopkins University Press.

Lee, D. S., J. B. Funderburg, and M. Clark. 1982. A distributional survey of North Carolina mammals. Occasional papers of the North Carolina Biological Survey 1982–10. North Carolina State Museum, Raleigh.

*Lee, J. M., and R. H. Giles, Jr. 1972. Furry political plum. Virginia Wildlife 33(3):6–7.

Lee, R. M., III and M. L. Kennedy. 1986. Food habits of the coyote in Tennessee. Proceedings of the 40th Annual Conference of the Southeastern Association of Fish and Wildlife Agencies 40:364–372.

*Leffler, J., and K. Terwilliger. 1991. Performance Report: Endangered bat investigations. Pp. 14–18. In: Nongame and Endangered Species Investigations Annual Report, 1990–1991. Virginia Department of Game and Inland Fisheries, Richmond.

*Leffler, J. W., R. Powers, C. Hobson, R. Reynolds, G. Nussbaum, J. Holland, and K. Terwilliger. 1993. Bat investigations annual report. Pp. 55–71. In: Terwilliger, K. (editor). Virginia Nongame and Endangered Wildlife Investigations. Virginia Department of Game and Inland Fisheries, Richmond.

*Legrand, A. A. 1958. Fox hunting along the shores of Buggs Island Lake. Virginia Wildlife 19(12):22–23.

*Leidy, J. 1851. Description of *Balaena palaeatlantica* and *Balaena prisca,* Leidy, based on fragments of fossil bones from the Miocene Formation of Virginia. Proceedings of the Academy of Natural Sciences of Philadelphia 5:308–309.

*Leidy, J. 1852. Remarks on a fossil Delphinus *(D. conradi)* from the Miocene of Virginia. Proceedings of the Academy of Natural Sciences of Philadelphia 6:35.

*Leidy, J. 1853. The ancient fauna of Nebraska: or a description of remains of extinct Mammalia and Chelonia from the Mauvaises Terres of Nebraska. Smithsonian Contributions to Knowledge 6(7):1–126.

*Leidy, J. 1856a. Notice of some remains of extinct vertebrated animals. Proceedings of the Academy of Natural Sciences of Philadelphia 8:163–165.

*Leidy, J. 1856b. Notices of remains of extinct vertebrated animals discovered by Professor E. Emmons. Proceedings of the Academy of Natural Sciences of Philadelphia 8:255–256.

*Leidy, J. 1857. Notice of remains of the walrus discovered on the coast of the United States. Transactions of the American Philosophical Society 11:83–86.

*Leitch, M. 1949. Deer in combat. Virginia Wildlife 10(6):18–20.

*Lenker, D. K. 1973. A study of spermatozoan reserves of male white-tailed deer and of the reproductive physiology of fawns. Master's thesis, Virginia Polytechnic Institute and State University, Blacksburg.

*Lenker, D. K., and P. F. Scanlon. 1974. Gonad activity of male and female fawns of the white-tailed deer. Proceedings of the 27th Annual Conference of the Southeastern Association of Game and Fish Commissioners 27:295.

*Lewis, C. R. 1969. Letters. Locked antlers. Virginia Wildlife 30(2):3.

*Lewis, J. B. 1927. A mink fight. Journal of Mammalogy 8(4):308.

*Lewis, J. B. 1928. Wild life of the Dismal Swamp. Game and Fish Conservationist 8(4):95–98.

*Lewis, J. B. 1929. Opossum in captivity. Journal of Mammalogy 10(2):167–168.

*Lewis, J. B. 1937. List of mammals observed in Amelia, Brunswick, and Norfolk counties. 6 pp. Typescript. (In Virginia Cooperative Wildlife Research Unit library.)

*Lewis, J. B. 1939. Naturalist writes of Dismal Swamp. Virginia Wildlife 2(7):2.

*Lewis, J. B. 1940. Mammals of Amelia County, Virginia. Journal of Mammalogy 21(4):422–428.

*Lewis, J. B. 1941. Porcupine in Virginia. Journal of Mammalogy 22(4):452.

*Lewis, J. B. 1943. Notes on the Bachman shrew. Journal of Mammalogy 24(1):97–98.

*Lewis, J. B. 1944. Cotton rat in lower Piedmont Virginia. Journal of Mammalogy 25(2):195–196.

*Lewis, J. B. 1945a. Mammals of the Seward Forest (Va.) and adjacent territory, 1940–1944. 9 pp. Typewritten.

*Lewis, J. B. 1945b. Frugivorous rat in Virginia. Journal of Mammalogy 26(3):309.

*Lewis, J. C. 1966. The fox rabies control program in Tennessee, 1965–1966. Transactions of the 31st North American Wildlife Conference 31:269–280.

*Lewis, J. C. 1975. Control of rabies among terrestrial wildlife by population reduction. Pp. 243–259. In: Baer, G. M. (editor), The natural history of rabies. Volume II. New York: Academic Press.

*Lewis, J. C., R. Murray, and G. Matschke. 1965. Hog subcommittee report to the chairman of the forest game committee. Southeastern Section of the Wildlife Society.

*Lewis, M. G. 1939. Deer on refuge prefer peach twigs above other browse. Virginia Wildlife 3(3):3.

Libby, W. L. 1957. Observations on beaver movements in Alaska. Journal of Mammalogy 38(2):269.

*Libke, K. G., and H. S. Mosby. 1968. Stress-induced hemopericardium (cardiac tamponade) in a deer. Journal of the American Veterinary Medical Association 153(7):813–815.

*Libke, K. G., and A. M. Walton. 1975. Presumptive paratuberculosis in a Virginia white-tailed deer. Journal of Wildlife Diseases 11(4):552–553.

*Lichtenfels, J. R. 1970. Two new species of *Pterygodermatites* (Paucipectines) Quentin, 1969 (Nematoda: Rictulariidae) with a key to the species from North American rodents. Proceedings of the Helminthological Society of Washington 37:94–101.

Liers, E. E. 1951. Notes on the river otter (*Lutra canadensis*). Journal of Mammalogy 32(1):1–9.

Liers, E. E. 1958. Early breeding in the river otter. Journal of Mammalogy 39(3):438–439.

Lilly, J. C. 1961. Man and dolphin. Garden City, New York: Doubleday and Company.

*Linden, E. 1993. Beware of rabies. Time Magazine 142(8):58–59.

*Linduska, J. P. 1942. Cycles of Virginia voles. Journal of Mammalogy 23(2):210.

Linduska, J. P. 1947. Longevity of some Michigan farm game mammals. Journal of Mammalogy 28(2):126–129.

*Lineberry, M. 1968. Varmint in the garden. Virginia Wildlife 29(2):6–7, 21–22.

Link, V. B. 1955. A history of plague in the United States of America. United States Public Health Monograph no. 26.

*Linnaei, C. 1956. (1758). Systema naturae. 10th ed. Volume I. British Museum (Natural History), London.

*Linscombe, G., N. Kinler, and R. J. Aulerich. 1982. Mink. Pp. 629–643. In: Chapman, J. A., and G. A. Feldhamer (editors), Wild mammals of North America. Baltimore: The Johns Hopkins University Press.

*Lint, J. B. 1974. Effect of a supplemental food supply on the reproductive attainment of the gray squirrel *(Sciurus carolinensis)*. Master's thesis, Virginia Polytechnic Institute and State University, Blacksburg.

*Lint, J. B., and H. S. Mosby. 1974. Effect of a supplemental food supply on the reproductive attainment of the gray squirrel *(Sciurus carolinensis)*. Virginia Journal of Science 25(2):66. Abstract.

*Linzey, A. 1980. Daily activity rhythms in *Synaptomys cooperi* and *Microtus pennsylvanicus*. Virginia Journal of Science 31(4):101. Abstract.

*Linzey, A. V. 1970. Postnatal growth and development of *Permyscus maniculatus nubiterrae*. Journal of Mammalogy 51(1):152–155.

*Linzey, A. V. 1981. Patterns of coexistence in *Microtus pennsylvanicus* and *Synaptomys cooperi*. Doctoral dissertation, Virginia Polytechnic Institute and State University, Blacksburg.

*Linzey, A. V. 1983. *Synaptomys cooperi*. Mammalian Species no. 210. American Society of Mammalogists.

*Linzey, A. V. 1984. Patterns of coexistence in *Synaptomys cooperi* and *Microtus pennsylvanicus*. Ecology 65(2):1984.

*Linzey, A. V., and J. A. Cranford. 1984. Habitat selection in the southern bog lemming, *Synaptomys cooperi*, and the meadow vole, *Microtus pennsylvanicus*, in Virginia. Canadian Field-Naturalist 98(4):463–469.

*Linzey, A. V., and D. W. Linzey, 1971. Mammals of Great Smoky Mountains National Park. Knoxville: University of Tennessee Press.

*Linzey, D. W. 1968. An ecological study of the golden mouse, *Ochrotomys nuttalli*, in the Great Smoky Mountains National Park. American Midland Naturalist 79(2):320–345.

Linzey, D. W. 1970. Mammals of Mobile and Baldwin counties, Alabama. Journal of the Alabama Academy of Science 41(2):64–99.

Linzey, D. W. 1971. Animal harvested in south Alabama probably coyote-red wolf hybrid. Alabama Conservation 41(6):6–7.

*Linzey, D. W. (editor) 1979. Proceedings of the symposium on endangered and threatened plants and animals of Virginia. Blacksburg: Virginia Polytechnic Institute and State University.

*Linzey, D. W. 1980a. Wanted: Alive! A grass-roots effort is underway to identify and save Virginia's endangered species. Virginia Wildlife 41(1):6–8.

*Linzey, D. W. 1980b. Terrestrial vertebrates. Pp. 258–320 and 439–457. In: A preliminary environmental analysis of a potential site for an Appalachian Power Company pumped storage hydroelectric facility. Brumley Gap FERC Project Number 2812. Volume 1: Ecological Component Report. Blacksburg: Virginia Polytechnic Institute and State University.

*Linzey, D. W. 1980c. Endangered and threatened mammals in the Mount Rogers National Recreation Area. Unpublished final report to United States Forest Service.

*Linzey, D. W. 1983a. Status and distribution of the northern water shrew *(Sorex palustris)* and two subspecies of northern flying squirrel (*Glaucomys sabrinus coloratus* and *Glaucomys sabrinus fuscus*). Final Report to United States Fish and Wildlife Service. Contract no. 14–16–0005–79–068.

Linzey, D. W. 1983b. Distribution and status of the northern flying squirrel and the northern water shrew in the southern Appalachians. United States Park Service Annual Scientific Research Meeting 9:13.

*Linzey, D. W. 1984. Distribution and status of the northern flying squirrel and the northern water shrew in the southern Appalachians. United States Park Service Research Resource Management Report SER-71: 193–200.

Linzey, D. W. 1984. A multitude of monikers. Virginia Wildlife 45(2):24–25.

*Linzey, D. W. 1987. Southern flying squirrel. The Virginia Explorer 3(3):4–5.

*Linzey, D. W. 1987. Mammoths and mastodons. The Virginia Explorer 3(4):9–11.

*Linzey, D. W. 1989. Cougars in the New River region? Proceedings of the New River Symposium, National Park Service. April, 1989:39–44 .

*Linzey, D. W. 1989. The mountain lion in Virginia. The Virginia Explorer 5(4):12–14.

*Linzey, D. W. 1991. Cougars in the New River region? An update. Proceedings of the New River Symposium, National Park Service. April, 1991:80–83.

Linzey, D. W. 1995a. Mammals of the Great Smoky Mountains National Park. Journal of the Elisha Mitchell Scientific Society 111(1):1–81.

*Linzey, D. W. 1995b. Mammals of Great Smoky Mountains National Park. Blacksburg: The McDonald & Woodward Publishing Company.

Linzey, D. W., and A. V. Linzey. 1967a. Maturational and seasonal molts in the golden mouse, *Ochrotomys nuttalli*. Journal of Mammalogy. 48(2):236–241.

Linzey, D. W., and A. V. Linzey. 1967b. Growth and development of the golden mouse, *Ochrotomys nuttalli nutalli*. Journal of Mammalogy 48(3):445–458.

*Linzey, D. W., and A. V. Linzey. 1968. Mammals of the Great Smoky Mountains National Park. Journal of the Elisha Mitchell Scientific Society 84(3):384–414.

Linzey, D. W., and A. V. Linzey. 1973. Notes on food of small mammals from Great Smoky Mountains National Park, Tennessee-North Carolina. Journal of the Elisha Mitchell Scientific Society 89(1–2):6–14.

*Linzey, D. W., and A. V. Linzey. 1979. Growth and development of the southern flying squirrel *(Glaucomys volans volans)*. Journal of Mammalogy 60(3):615–620.

*Linzey, D. W., and R. L. Packard. 1977. *Ochrotomys nuttalli*. Mammalian Species no. 75:1–6.

*Lipford, M. L., G. D. Rouse, and C.A. Clampitt. 1987. The Virginia natural heritage program: monitoring rare species and exemplary communities. Virginia Journal of Science 38(4):389–398.

*Lipscomb, T. P., F. Y. Schulman, D. Moffett, and S. Kennedy. 1994. Morbilliviral disease in Atlantic bottlenose dolphins *(Tursiops truncatus)* from the 1987–1988 epizootic. Journal of Wildlife Diseases 30(4):567–571.

*Little, H. A. 1951. An evaluation of Virginia's farm game program. Master's thesis, Virginia Polytechnic Institute and State University, Blacksburg.

*Llewellyn, L. M. 1942. Notes on the Alleghenian least weasel in Virginia. Journal of Mammalogy. 23(4): 439–441.

*Llewellyn, L. M. 1943. A determination of the species and subspecies of the rabbits if the genus *Sylvilagus* and their distribution in Virginia. Master's thesis, Virginia Polytechnic Institute and State University, Blacksburg.

Llewellyn, L. M. 1953. Growth rate of the raccoon fetus. Journal of Wildlife Management 17(3):320–321.

Llewellyn, L. M., and F. H. Dale. 1964. Notes on the ecology of the opossum in Maryland. Journal of Mammalogy 45(1):113–122.

*Llewellyn, L. M., and R. K. Enders. 1954. Ovulation in the raccoon. Journal of Mammalogy 35(3):440.

*Llewellyn, L. M., and C. O. Handley. 1945. The cottontail rabbits of Virginia. Journal of Mammalogy 26(4):379–390.

*Llewellyn, L. M., and F. M. Uhler. 1952. The foods of fur animals of the Patuxent Research Refuge, Maryland. American Midland Naturalist. 48(1)193–203.

Lloyd, J. E. 1972. Vocalization in *Marmota monax*. Journal of Mammalogy 53(1):214–216.

*Lochmiller, R. L. 1979. Bioenergetics and nutrition of the pine vole *(Microtus pinetorum)* in two Virginia apple orchards. Master's thesis, Virginia Polytechnic Institute and State University, Blacksburg.

*Lochmiller, R. L., E. J. Jones, J. B. Whelan, and R. L. Kirkpatrick. 1982. The occurrence of *Taenia taeniaeformis* Strobilocerci in *Microtus pinetorum*. Journal of Parasitology 68(5):975–976.

*Lochmiller, R. L., R. M. Robinson, and R. L. Kirkpatrick. 1982. Infection of *Microtus pinetorum* with the nematode *Capillaria gastrica* (Baylis, 1926) Baylis, 1931. Proceedings of the Helminthological Society of Washington 49(2):321–323.

*Lochmiller, R. L.,II, R. J. Kendall, P. F. Scanlon, and R. L. Kirkpatrick. 1979. Lead concentrations in pine voles trapped from two Virginia orchards. Virginia Journal of Science 30(2):50. Abstract.

*Lochmiller, R. L., R. L. Kirkpatrick, and J. B. Whelan. 1979a. Seasonal variations in food availability for two *Microtus pinetorum* populations from southwest Virginia apple orchards. Virginia Journal of Science 30(2):50. Abstract.

*Lochmiller, R. L., R. L. Kirkpatrick, and J. B. Whelan. 1979b. Digestibility of apple, forb and laboratory chow diets by *Microtus pinetorum*. Virginia Journal of Science 30(2):50. Abstract.

*Lochmiller, R. L., J. B. Whelan, and R. L. Kirkpatrick. 1982. Energetic cost of lactation in *Microtus pinetorum*. Journal of Mammalogy. 63(3):475–481.

*Lochmiller, R. L., J. B. Whelan, and R. L. Kirkpatrick. 1983. Seasonal energy requirements of adult pine voles, *Microtus pinetorum*. Journal of Mammalogy. 64(2):345–350.

*Loeb, S. C., and N. D. Moncrief. 1993. The biology of fox squirrels *(Sciurus niger)* in the Southeast: a review. Pp. 1–19. In: Moncrief, N. D., et al. (editors). Proceedings of the Second Symposium on Southeastern Fox Squirrels, *Sciurus niger*. Virginia Museum of Natural History Special Publication no. 1.

*Long, C. A. 1971. Taxonomic revision of the mammalian genus *Microsorex* Coues. Transactions of the Kansas Academy of Science 74(2):181–196.

*Long, C. A. 1972. Notes on habitat preference and reproduction in pigmy shrews, *Microsorex*. Canadian Field-Naturalist. 86:155–160.

*Long, C. A. 1974. *Microsorex hoyi* and *Microsorex thompsoni*. Mammalian Species no. 33.

*Long, N. A. 1959. Queen Creek — a daughter of the York. Virginia Wildlife 20(1):23.

*Longhurst, W. M. 1957. The effectiveness of hunting in controlling big-game populations in North America. Transactions of the 22d North American Wildlife Conference 22:544–569.

Longley, W. H. 1962. Movements of red fox. Journal of Mammalogy 43(1):107.

Lord, R. D., Jr. 1960. Litter size and latitude in North American mammals. American Midland Naturalist 64(2):488–499.

Lord, R. D., Jr. 1961a. A population study of the gray fox. American Midland Naturalist 66(1):87–109.

Lord, R. D., Jr. 1961b. Potential life span of cottontails. Journal of Mammalogy 42(1):99.

Lotze, J. -H. 1979. The raccoon *(Procyon lotor)* on St. Catherines Island, Georgia. 4. Comparisons of home ranges determined by livetrapping and radio-tracking. American Museum Novitates no. 2664:1–25

*Lotze, J. H., and S. Anderson. 1979. *Procyon lotor.* Mammalian Species no. 119.

*Lovelace, T. S. 1950. Faulkland: mecca for wildlife. Virginia Wildlife 11(5):21–23.

*Lovett, R. 1972. Letters. Virginia Wildlife 33(4):3.

*Lowe, D. W., J. R. Matthews, and C. J. Moseley (editors) 1990. The official world wildlife fund guide to endangered species of North America. 2 volumes. Washington, D. C.: Beacham Publishing, Incorporated.

*Lowery, G. H., Jr. 1974. The mammals of Louisiana and its adjacent waters. Baton Rouge: Louisiana State University Press.

*Lowman, G. E. 1975. A survey of endangered, threatened, rare, status undetermined, peripheral, and unique mammals of the southeastern national forests and grasslands. United States Forest Service, Atlanta.

*Loxterman, J. L., N. D. Moncrief, R. D. Dueser, and J. F. Pagels. 1994. Allozymic variation in mainland and insular populations of *Oryzomys palustris* and *Peromyscus leucopus.* Virginia Journal of Science 45(2):106. Abstract.

*Loxterman, J. L., N. D. Moncrief, R. D. Dueser, C. R. Carlson, and J. F. Pagels. 1998. Dispersal abilities and genetic population structure of insular and mainland *Oryzomys palustris* and *Peromyscus leucopus.* Journal of Mammalogy 79(1):66-77.

Luckens, M. M., and W. H. Davis. 1964. Bats: sensitivity to DDT. Science 146:948.

Luckens, M. M., and W. H. Davis. 1965. Toxicity of dieldrin and endrin in bats. Nature 207:879–880.

*Lucker, J. T. 1943. A new trichostrongylid nematode from the stomachs of American squirrels. Journal of the Washington Academy of Science 33:75–79.

*Ludlam, K. 1954. Skyline at night. Virginia Wildlife 15(8):8–9.

*Ludwick, R. L. 1966. Energy metabolism of the eastern gray squirrel. Master's thesis, Virginia Polytechnic Institute and State University, Blacksburg.

*Ludwick, R. L., J. P. Fontenot, and H. S. Mosby. 1969. Energy metabolism of the eastern gray squirrel. Journal of Wildlife Management 33:569–575.

Lundelius, E. L., Jr., R. W. Graham, E. Anderson, J. E. Guilday, J. A. Holman, D. W. Steadman, and S. D. Webb. 1983. Terrestrial vertebrate faunas. Pp. 311–353. In: Porter, S. C. (editor), Late-Quaternary Environments of the United States. Volume 1 — The Late Pleistocene.

*Lustig, L. W., and V. Flyger. 1976. Observations and suggested management practices for the endangered Delmarva fox squirrel. Proceedings of the 29th Annual Conference of the Southeastern Association of Game and Fish Commissioners 29:433–440.

*Lyall-Watson, M. 1963. Critical re-examination of food "washing" behavior in the raccoon (*Procyon lotor* Linn.). Proceedings of the Zoological Society of London 141(2):371–393.

Lydeard, C., M. L. Kennedy, and E. P. Hill. 1988. Taxonomic assessment of coyotes and domestic dogs in the southeastern United States. Proceedings of the Annual Conference of the Southeastern Association of Fish and Wildlife Agencies 42:513–519.

Lydeard, C., R. M. Lee, III, and M. L. Kennedy. 1986. Population characteristics of the coyote *(Canis latrans)* in Tennessee. Journal of the Tennessee Academy of Science 61(2):40–41. Abstract.

*Lydekker, R. 1898. The deer of all lands. London: Rowland Ward, Limited.

*Lyell, C. 1845. Travels in North America in the years 1841–1842: with geological observations on the United States, Canada, and Nova Scotia. 2 volumes. London: J. Murray.

Lynch G. M. 1967. Long-range movement of a raccoon in Manitoba. Journal of Mammalogy 48(4):659–660.

Lynch, G. R., F. D. Vogt, and H. R. Smith. 1978. Seasonal study of spontaneous daily torpor in the white-footed mouse, *Peromyscus leucopus.* Physiological Zoology 51:289–299.

*Lyne, R. C. 1950. An old Virginia rabbit hunt. Virginia Wildlife 11(2):20–22.

*Lyon, L. A., and P. F. Scanlon. 1985. Population structure and behavior of white-tailed deer groups using soybean fields. Virginia Journal of Science 36(2):89. Abstract.

*Lyon, L. A., and P. F. Scanlon. 1985. Evaluating reports of deer damage to crops: implications for wildlife research and management programs. Proceedings of the Eastern Wildlife Damage Control Conference 2:224–231.

*Lyon, L. A., and P. F. Scanlon. 1987. Use of soybean fields in eastern Virginia by white-tailed deer. Proceedings of the Eastern Wildlife Damage Control Conference 3:108–117.

*Lyon, L. A., and P. F. Scanlon. 1987. Perceptions and management preferences of game wardens and extension agents towards deer damage to soybeans. Proceedings of the Eastern Wildlife Damage Control Conference 3:132–139.

*Lyon, M. W., Jr. 1904. Classification of the hares and their allies. Smithsonian Miscellaneous Collection 45(1456):321–447.

*Lyon, M. W. 1936. Mammals of Indiana. American Midland Naturalist 17:1–384.

*Lyon, M. W., and W. H. Osgood. 1909. Catalogue of the type-specimens of mammals in the United States National Museum, including the Biological Survey collection. United States National Museum Bulletin 62.

*Maben, J. W. 1966. Letters. Kills white rabbit. Virginia Wildlife 27(2):3.

*Mabry, M. L., and C. R. Terman. 1994. Social influences on reproductive maturation in female white-footed mice (Peromyscus leucopus noveboracensis). Virginia Journal of Science 45(2):60. Abstract.

*MacPherson, S. L. 1984. The nutritional ecology of pine voles and meadow voles. Master's thesis, Virginia Polytechnic Institute and State University, Blacksburg.

*MacPherson, S. L. 1990. An apple a day keeps the pine vole — here to stay. Virginia Wildlife 51(1):24–25.

*MacPherson, S. L., and R. L. Kirkpatrick. 1984. The effect of winter food supplementation on body condition and reproduction of pine voles in an apple orchard. Virginia Journal of Science 35(2):84. Abstract.

*MacPherson, S. L., F. A. Servello, and R. L. Kirkpatrick. 1984. Digestibilities of pine vole diets in different orchard habitat types. Virginia Journal of Science 35(2):85. Abstract.

Madden, J. R. 1974. Female territoriality in a Suffolk County, Long Island, population of *Glaucomys volans*. Journal of Mammalogy 55(3):647–652.

*Madison, D. M. 1976. Behavioral and sociochemical susceptibility of meadow voles *(Microtus pennsylvanicus)* to snake predators. American Midland Naturalist 100(1):23–28.

*Madison, D. M. 1977. Movements and habitat use among interacting *Peromyscus leucopus* as revealed by radiotelemetry. Canadian Field-Naturalist 91(3):273–281.

*Madison, D. M. 1978. Movements and habitat among *Peromyscus leucopus* as revealed by radiotelemetry. Canadian Field-Naturalist 91(3)273–281.

*Madison, D. M. 1978. Movements as indicators of reproductive events among female meadow voles as revealed by radiotelemetry. Journal of Mammalogy 59(4):835–843.

*Madison, D. M. 1980. Space use and social structure in meadow voles, *Microtus pennsylvanicus*. Behavioral Ecology and Sociobiology 7(1):65–71.

*Madison, D. M. 1985. Activity rhythms and spacing. Pp. 373–419. In: Tamarin, R. H. (editor), Biology of New World *Microtus*. American Society of Mammalogists Special Publication no. 8.

Majors, E. 1955. Population and life history studies of the cottontail rabbit in Lee and Tallapoosa counties, Alabama. Master's thesis, Auburn University, Auburn.

Mallach, N. 1972. Translokationsversuche mit besamratten (*Ondatra zibethica* L.). Anzeiger fuer Schaedlingskunke, Pflanzenschutz, Umweltschutz 45:40–44.

*Mallory, F. F., and R. A. Dieterich. 1985. Laboratory management and pathology. Pp. 647–684. In: Tamarin, R. H. (editor). Biology of New World *Microtus*. The American Society of Mammalogists Special Publication no. 8.

*Maly, M. S., and J. A. Cranford. 1984. Home range instability and overlap in rice rats. Virginia Journal of Science 35(2):85. Abstract.

*Maly, M. S., and J. A. Cranford. 1985. Relative capture efficiency of large and small Sherman live traps. Acta Theriologica 30(8):165–167.

*Mammalian Data Manual. 1979. Endangered, vulnerable, rare mammals of the United States. North Eastham, Massachusetts. JNL Publications.

Manaro, A. J. 1961. Observations on the behavior of the spotted skunk in Florida. Quarterly Journal of the Florida Academy of Sciences 24(1):59–63.

*Manlove, M. N., R. Baccus, M. R. Pelton, M. H. Smith, and D. Graber. 1980. Biochemical variation in the black bear. Bear Biology Association Conference Series 3:37–41.

*Mann, H. 1952. The first hundred years of conservation in "Ould Virginia.". Virginia Wildlife 8(4):10–12.

Mann W. M. 1930. Wild animals in and out of the zoo. Smithsonian Science Series 6.

Manski, D. A., L. W. VanDruff, and V. Flyger. 1981. Activities of gray squirrels and people in a downtown Washington, D. C. park: management implications. Transactions of the North American Wildlife and Natural Resources Conference 46:439–454.

*Mansueti, R. 1950. Extinct and vanishing mammals of Maryland and District of Columbia. Maryland Naturalist 20:1–48.

*Mansueti, R. 1952. Comments on the fox squirrels of Maryland. Maryland Naturalist 22(3–4):30–41.

*Mansueti, R., and V. F. Flyger. 1952. Long-tailed shrew *(Sorex dispar)* in Maryland. Journal of Mammalogy 33(2):250.

Manville, R. H. 1949. A study of small mammal populations in northern Michigan. Miscellaneous Publications, Museum of Zoology, University of Michigan 73.

*Manville, R. H. 1956. The mammals of Shenandoah National Park. Shenandoah National Historical Association Bulletin no. 2.

*Manville, R. H., and P. G. Favour, Jr. 1960. Southern distribution of the Atlantic walrus. Journal of Mammalogy 41(4):499–503.

*Manville, R. H., and J. J. Wilson. 1970. Fossil walrus from Virginia waters. Journal of Mammalogy 51(4):810–811.

*March, J. A., Jr., and R. K. Rose. 1995. The population dynamics of *Oryzomys palustris*, the marsh rice rat, from eastern shore tidal marshes. Virginia Journal of Science 46(2):94. Abstract.

Marsden, H. M., and N. R. Holler. 1964. Social behavior in confined populations of the cottontail and the swamp rabbit. Wildlife Monograph no. 13.

Marsh, G. P. 1864. Man and Nature; or, Physical Geography as Modified by Human Action. New York: Scribners.

*Marshall, A. D., and J. H. Jenkins. 1966. Movements and home ranges of bobcats as determined by radio-tracking in the upper coastal plain of west-central South Carolina. Proceedings of the 20th Annual Conference of the Southeastern Association of Game and Fish Commissioners 20:206–214.

Marshall, L. G., J. A. Case, and M. O. Woodburne. 1990. Phylegenetic relationships of the families of marsupials. Pp. 433–505. In: Genoways, H. H. (editor),

Current mammalogy. Volume 2. New York: Plenum Press.
Marshall, W. H. 1936. A study of the winter activities of the mink. Journal of Mammalogy 17(4):382–392.
Marston, M. A. 1942. Winter relations of bobcats to white-tailed deer in Maine. Journal of Wildlife Management 6(4):328–337.
*Martin, D. 1989. Otters, otters, and, more otters? Virginia Wildlife 50(6):16–21.
*Martin, D. 1989. Virginia otter research. The Virginia Explorer 5(10):7–9.
*Martin, D. 1991. Sly fox. Virginia Wildlife 52(1):4–7.
*Martin, D. 1994. Black bear. Virginia Wildlife 55(9):17–18.
*Martin, D. 1995a. A history of black bear in Virginia. Virginia Wildlife 56(9):4–7.
*Martin, D. 1995b. Problem black bears. Virginia Wildlife 56(9):15–19.
*Martin, D. 1995c. Virginia's black bear harvest. Virginia Wildlife 56(9):20–21.
*Martin, D. and G. Blank, Jr. 1986. A trickster on the horizon. Virginia Wildlife 47(11):17–21.
*Martin, D., and G. T. Blank Jr. 1986. The gentle bruin. Virginia Wildlife 47(12):12–21.
Martin, I. G. 1981. Venom of the short-tailed shrew *(Blarina brevicauda)* as in insect immobilizing agent. Journal of Mammalogy 62(1):189–192.
*Martin, J. H. (editor) 1987. Proceedings of a symposium: species of special concern in Virginia. Virginia Journal of Science 38(4)265–412.
Martin, P. S., and R. G. Klein (editors). 1984. Quaternary extinctions: a prehistoric revolution. Tucson: University of Arizona Press.
*Martin, R. A. 1968. Late Pleistocene distribution of *Microtus pennsylvanicus*. Journal of Mammalogy 49(2):265–271.
*Martin, R. A. 1972. Synopsis of late Pliocene and Pleistocene bats of North America and the Antilles. American Midland Naturalist 87:326–335.
*Martin, S. M. 1989. Habitat: It's not as simple as it looks. Virginia Wildlife 50(3):24–27.
*Martin, T. M. 1968. Points-a-plenty. Virginia Wildlife 29(2):18..
*Martone, J. C. 1969. Letters. Trapped doe. Virginia Wildlife 30(12):3.
*Marx, M. B., and F. N. Swink, Jr. 1963. The Virginia predator rabies control program — 1961–1962. Journal of the American Veterinary Medical Association 143(1):170–177.
Matson, J. R. 1954. Observations on the dormant phase of a female black bear. Journal of Mammalogy 35(1):28–35.
*Matter, S. F., J. F. Zawacki, and M. A. Bowers. 1996. Habitat fragmentation and the perceived and actual risk of predation. Virginia Journal of Science 47(1):19–27.
*Matthew, K. K. 1989. Eye of newt, tale of bat... The Virginia Explorer 5(10):4–6.
*Maurice, S. 1951. Lumberjacks of the animal kingdom. Virginia Wildlife 12(8):11–12.
*Maxwell, G. 1967. Seals of the world. Boston: Houghton Mifflin Company.
*Mayer, J. J., and I. L. Brisbin, Jr. 1990. Wild pigs in the United States. Athens: The University of Georgia Press.
Maynard, C. J. 1889. Singular effects produced by the bite of a short-tailed shrew, *Blarina brevicauda*. Contributions in Science 1:57–59.
*MacClintock, D. 1970. Squirrels of North America. New York: Van Nostrand Reinhold Company.
*McAtee, W. L. 1918. A sketch of the natural history of the District of Columbia together with an indexed edition of the United States Geological Survey's 1917 map of Washington and vicinity. Bulletin of the Biological Society of Washington 1:1–142.
*McAtee W. L. 1950. Possible early record of a manatee in Virginia. Journal of Mammalogy 31(1):98–99.
*McBee, K., and J. W. Bickham. 1990. Mammals as bioindicators of environmental toxicity. Pp. 37–88. In: Genoways, H. H. (editor), Current mammalogy. Volume 2. New York: Plenum Press.
McBride, A. F., and D. O. Hebb. 1948. Behavior of the captive bottle-nose dolphin, *Tursiops truncatus*. Journal of Comparative and Physiological Psychology 41(2):111–123.
McBride, A. F., and H. Kritzler. 1951. Observations on pregnancy, parturition, and postnatal behavior in the bottle-nose dolphin. Journal of Mammalogy 32(3): 251–266.
*McBride, J. E. 1981. Electrophoretic investigation of genetic characteristics in the pine vole. Master's thesis, Virginia Polytechnic Institute and State University, Blacksburg.
*McBride, J. E., R. L. Kirkpatrick, J. J. Ney, and A. R. Tipton. 1981. Genetic investigation of endrin resistance in pine voles using starch-gel electrophoresis. Virginia Journal of Science 32(3):95. Abstract.
McCabe, R. A. 1947. Homing of flying squirrels. Journal of Mammalogy 28(4):404.
*McCarley, W. H. 1954. The ecological distribution of the *Peromyscus leucopus* species group in eastern Texas. Ecology 35(3):375–379.
*McCarley, W. H. 1958. Ecology, behavior, and population dynamics of *Peromyscus nuttalli* in eastern Texas. Texas Journal of Science 10:147–171.
*McCarley, W. H. 1963. Distributional relationships of sympatric populations of *Peromyscus leucopus* and *Peromyscus gossypinus*. Ecology 44(4):784–788.
*McClung, R. M. 1969. Lost wild America. New York: William Morrow and Company.
*McCord, C. M., and J. E. Cardoza. 1982. Bobcat and lynx. Pp.728–766. In: Chapman, J. A., and G. A. Feldhamer (editors), Wild mammals of North America. Baltimore: The Johns Hopkins University Press.
*McCravy, K., and R. K. Rose. 1987. The status of the marsh rabbit in Virginia. Virginia Journal of Science 38(2):83. Abstract.
*McCravy, K. W., and R. K. Rose. 1989. The analysis of internal and external features of reproduction in

small mammals. Virginia Journal of Science 40(2):57. Abstract.

*McCravy, K. W., and R. K. Rose. 1990. An analysis of external features as predictors of reproductive status in small mammals. Virginia Journal of Science 41(2):56. Abstract.

*McCravy, K. W., and R. K. Rose. 1992. An analysis of external features as predictors of reproductive status in small mammals. Journal of Mammalogy 73(1):151–159.

McDonald, J. N. 1982. North American bison: their classification and evolution. Berkeley: University of California Press.

McDonald, J. N. 1984. The reordered North American selection regime and late Quaternary megafaunal extinctions. Pp. 404–439. In: Martin, P. S., and R. G. Klein (editors), Quaternary extinctions: a prehistoric revolution. Tucson: Univeristy of Arizona Press.

*McDonald, J. N. 1986. On the status of Quaternary vertebrate paleontology and zooarcheology in Virginia. Pp. 89–104. In. McDonald, J. N., and S. O. Bird (editors), The Quaternary of Virginia — a symposium volume. Charlottesville: Virginia Department of Mines, Minerals and Energy.

*McDonald, J. N. 1990. Temporal overlap of now-extinct megafauna and paleo-Indians at Saltville, Virginia, USA. In. Myler, E. A. (editor), Abstracts of the sixth international conference, International Council for Archaeozoology. Abstract.

*McDonald, J. N. 1992. Saltville. A window on the Ice Age of southwestern Virginia. Virginia Explorer 8(1):8–15.

McDonald, J. N., and S. O. Bird (editors). 1986. The Quaternary of Virginia — a symposium volume. Charlottesville: Virginia Department of Mines, Minerals and Energy.

*McDonald, J. N., and C. E. Ray. 1989. The autochthonous North American musk oxen *Bootherium, Symbos,* and *Gidleya* (Mammalia: Artiodactyla: Bovidae). Smithsonian Contributions to Paleobiology 66.

*McDonald, J. N., and C. E. Ray. 1993. Records of musk oxen from the Atlantic coastal plain of North America. The Mosasaur 5: 1–18.

*McDonald, J. N., C. E. Ray, and F. Grady. 1996. Pleistocene caribou *(Rangifer tarandus)* in the eastern United States: new records and range extensions. Pp. 406-430. In: Stewart, Kathlyn M., and K. L. Seymour (editors), Palaeoecology and palaeoenvironments of late Cenozoic mammals: tributes to the career of C. S. (Rufus) Churcher. Toronto: University of Toronto Press.

*McElroy, D. J. and R. K. Rose. 1987. The effect of burning on small mammal populations in a longleaf/loblolly pine association. Virginia Journal of Science 38(2):84. Abstract.

*McEwan, B. 1980. Misty blue mountains. Virginia Wildlife 41(1):25–26.

*McGavock, A. M. 1967. Letters. Virginia Wildlife 28(1):3.

*McGill, W. M. 1933. Caverns of Virginia. Virginia Geological Survey Bulletin 35:1–187.

*McGinnes, B. S. 1957. A study of tularemia in a native population of wild rabbits in an enclosure. Virginia Journal of Science 8(2):303. Abstract.

*McGinnes, B. S. 1958. Some factors influencing the cottontail rabbit in southwestern Virginia. Doctoral dissertation, Virginia Polytechnic Institute and State University, Blacksburg.

*McGinnes, B. S. 1959. Incidence and causes of tularemia in humans in Virginia. Virginia Journal of Science 10(2):262. Abstract.

*McGinnes, B. S. 1960. An archer's ringside report of buck's battle. Virginia Wildlife 21(11):12.

*McGinnes, B. S. 1963. Letters. Woodchuck oddity. Virginia Wildlife 24(11):27.

*McGinnes, B. S. 1964a. Depletion of a cottontail rabbit population attributed to tularemia. Wildlife Disease (Microcard)34. Card 1.

*McGinnes, B. S. 1964b. Parasites of cottontail rabbits in southwestern Virginia. Wildlife Disease (Microcard)35:1–11.

*McGinnes, B. S. 1969. How size and distribution of cutting units affect food and cover of deer. Pp. 66–70. In: Proceedings of a symposium on white-tailed deer in southern forest habitat. Nacogdoches, Texas: Stephen F. Austin State College.

*McGinnes, B. S., and R. L. Downing. 1969. Fawn mortality in a confined Virginia deer herd. Proceedings of the 23d Annual Conference of the Southeastern Association of Game and Fish Commissioners 23:188–191.

*McGinnes, B. S., and R. L. Downing. 1972. Variation in peaks of fawning in Virginia. Proceedings of the 26th Annual Conference of the Southeastern Association of Game and Fish Commissioners 26:22–27.

*McGinnes, B. S., and R. L. Downing. 1977. Factors affecting the peak of white-tailed deer fawning in Virginia. Journal of Wildlife Management 41(4):715–719.

*McGinnes, B. S., J. S. Lindzey, G. W. Wood, and G. R. Dudderar, compilers. 1969. A partial bibliography of the cottontail rabbits. Virginia Polytechnic Institute Extension Division Publication MT-83.

*McGinnes, B. S., and J. H. Reeves. 1958. Deer jaws from excavated Indian sites let us compare Indian-killed deer with modern deer. Virginia Wildlife 19(12):8–9.

*McInteer, J. 1963. Wild fur. Virginia Wildlife 24(1):11–12.

*McInteer, J. 1964. Hunters ask: What happened to the rabbit? Virginia Wildlife 25(6):9–10,22.

McKeever, S. 1952. A survey of West Virginia mammals. West Virginia Conservation Commission, Pittman-Robertson Project 22-TC. Mimeographed.

*McKeever, S. 1958. Goosebeak whale from North Carolina. Journal of Mammalogy 39(3):440.

*McKenna, G. 1960. Squirrel hunting in Virginia. Virginia Wildlife 21(10):6–7,12.

*McKenna, G. 1962a. Deer hunting in western Virginia. Virginia Wildlife 23(11):10–11.

*McKenna, G. 1962b. Elk in Virginia. Virginia Wildlife 23(10):6–7.

*McKenney, F. D. 1938. Malignant edema in deer. Transactions of the 3d. North American Wildlife Conference:886–889.

*McKinny, T. D. 1969. Activity of acetylcholinesterase in brains of male cottontail rabbits. Journal of Wildlife Management 33(2):418–420.

*McKinny, T. D. 1970. Behavioral interactions in grouped male cottontails. Journal of Mammalogy 51(2):402–403.

*McKinny, T. D., D. M. Baldwin, and R. H. Giles. 1970. Effects of differential grouping in adrenal catecholamines in the cottontail rabbit. Physiological Zoology 43(1):55–59.

*McKinny, T. D., and R. L. Kirkpatrick. 1970. Brain weight and activity of acetylcholinesterase in differentially grouped cottontail rabbits. Journal of Mammalogy 51(2):389–391.

*McKnight, T. 1964. Feral livestock in Anglo-America. University of California Publications in Geography no. 16.

*McLaughlin, J. H. 1953. Factors influencing the raccoon and its management in southwestern Virginia. Master's thesis, Virginia Polytechnic Institute and State University, Blacksburg.

*McLaughlin, J. H. 1960. Why not stock more elk in Virginia? Virginia Wildlife 21(3):20–21.

*McLean, R.G. 1970. Wildlife rabies in the United States: recent history and currents concepts. Journal of Wildlife Diseases 6(4):229–235.

*McLean, R. G. 1975. Raccoon rabies. Pp. 53–77. In: Baer, G. M. (editor), The natural history of rabies. Vol.II New York: Academic Press.

*McManus, J. J. 1974. *Didelphis virginiana*. Mammalian Species no. 40.

McShea, W. J. 1986. Social organization and spacing of a fossorial insectivore *(Condylura cristata)*. American Zoologist 26(4):97A. Abstract.

McShea, W. J. 1989. Reproductive synchrony and home range size in a territorial microtine. Oikos 56(2):182–186.

*McShea, W. J. 1990a. Social tolerance and proximate mechanisms of dispersal among winter groups of meadow voles, *Microtus pennsylvanicus*. Animal Behaviour 39(2):346–351.

*McShea, W. J. 1990b. Interrelationships of mast crops, white-tailed deer, and their mast consumers. Virginia Journal of Science 41(2):56. Abstract.

*McShea, W. J., and A. B. Gilles. 1992. A comparison of traps and fluorescent powder to describe foraging for mast by *Peromycus leucopus*. Journal of Mammalogy 73(1):218–222.

McShea, W. J., and D. M. Madison. 1986. Sex ratio shifts within litters of meadow voles *(Microtus pennsylvanicus)*. Behavioral Ecology and Sociobiology 18(6):431–436.

*McShea, W. J., and D. M. Madison. 1987. Partial mortality in nesting meadow voles, *Microtus pennsylvanicus*. Animal Behaviour 35(4):1253–1255.

*McShea, W. J., and J. Rappole. 1991. White-tailed deer as keystone species within forest habitats in Virginia. Virginia Journal of Science 42(2):173. Abstract.

*McShea, W. J., and J. H. Rappole. 1992. White-tailed deer as a keystone species within forest habitats of Virginia. Virginia Journal of Science 43(1B):177–186.

*McShea, W. J., and G. Schwede. 1993. Variable acorn crops: responses of white-tailed deer and other mast consumers. Journal of Mammalogy 74(4):999–1006.

*McShea, W. J., C. Wemmer, and M. Stuwe. 1993. Conflict of interests: a public hunt at the National Zoo's Conservation and Research Center. Wildlife Society Bulletin 21(4):492–497.

*Mead, C. P. 1948. A new wildlife era: what the sportsman's money is buying on the Virginia national forests. Virginia Wildlife 9(1):16–18.

*Mead, J. G. 1977. Records of sei and Bryde's whales from the Atlantic coast of the United States, the Gulf of Mexico, and the Caribbean. Reports of the International Whaling Commission, Special Issue 1:113–116.

*Mead, J. G. 1979. An analysis of cetacean strandings along the eastern coast of the United States. United States Marine Mammal Commission Report no. MMC-77/13:54–68.

Mead, J. G. 1984. Survey of reproductive data for the beaked whales *(Ziphiidae)*. Pp. 91–96. In: Perrin, W. F., R. L. Brownell, Jr. and D. P. DeMaster (editors), Reproduction in whales, dolphins and porpoises. Report of the International Whaling Commission, Special Issue no. 6.

*Mead, J. G. 1989. Beaked whales of the genus *Mesoplodon*. Pp. 349–430. In: Ridgeway, S. H., and S. H. Harrison (editors), Handbook of marine mammals. Vol.4. River dolphins and the larger toothed whales. New York: Academic Press.

*Mead, J. G., and C. W. Potter. 1990. Natural history of bottlenose dolphins along the central Atlantic coast of the United States. Pp. 165–195. In: Leatherwood, S., and R. R. Reeves (editors), The bottlenose dolphin. New York: Academic Press.

*Mead, J. G. and C. W. Potter. 1995. Recognizing two populations of the bottlenose dolphin *(Tursiops truncatus)* off the Atlantic coast of North America. Morphologic and ecologic considerations. IBI Reports no. 5:31–44.

*Mead, R. A. 1968a. Reproduction in western forms of the spotted skunk (genus *Spilogale*). Journal of Mammology 49(3):373–390.

Mead, R. A. 1968b. Reproduction in eastern forms of the spotted skunk (genus *Spilogale*). Journal of Zoology 156(1):119–136.

*Meade, B. J. 1977. Experimental trichinosis in wild rodents. Master's thesis, Virginia Polytechnic Institute and State University, Blacksburg.

*Meagher. M. 1986. *Bison bison*. Mammalian Species no. 266.

*Meagher, M. M. 1978. Bison. Pp. 122–133. In: Schmidt, J. L., and D. L. Gilbert (editors), Big game of North America. Harrisburg, Pennsylvania: Stackpole Books.

*Meanley, B. 1971a. Great Dismal Swamp mammals. Atlantic Naturalist 26(1):17–18.

*Meanley, B. 1971b. The Dismal Swamp — its flora and fauna. Living Wilderness 34:34–37.

*Meanley, B. 1973. The Great Dismal Swamp. Washington, DC: Audubon Nature Society of the Central Atlantic States.

*Mearns, E. A. 1907. Mammals of the Mexican boundary of the United States. Bulletin of the United States National Museum 56, part 1:155–361.

*Mearns, E. A. 1911. A description of a new rabbit from islands off the coast of Virginia. Proceedings of the United States National Museum 39(1784):227–228.

*Mearns, L. Z. 1897. On the occurrence of the genus *Reithrodontomys* in Virginia. American Naturalist 31:160–161.

*Mech, L. D. 1974. *Canis lupus*. Mammalian Species no. 37.

*Mech, L. D., and F. J. Turkowski. 1966. Twenty-three raccoons in one winter den. Journal of Mammalogy 47(3):529–530.

*Mechler, J. L., III. 1970. Factors influencing the white-tailed deer harvest in Virginia, 1947–1967. Master's thesis, Virginia Polytechnic Institute and State University, Blacksburg.

*Mehta, J. N. 1986. White-tailed deer density and habitat relationships. Master's thesis, Virginia Polytechnic Institute and State University, Blacksburg.

*Mellace, D. R. 1973. Hormonal induction of ovulation in captive gray squirrels *(Sciiurus carolinensis)*. Master's thesis, Virginia Polytechnic Institute and State University, Blacksburg.

*Mellace, D. R., R. L. Kirkpatrick, and P. F. Scanlon. 1974. Reproductive examination of gray squirrels by laparotomy. Proceedings of the 27th Annual Conference of the Southeastern Association of Game and Fish Commissioners 27:342–343.

*Mengak, M. T. 1997. New field records for longevity in Allegheny woodrats (*Neotoma magister*). Banisteria 10:27-28.

*Mengak, M. T., and A. R. Tipton. 1978. Comparison of small mammal occurrence in one and four year old pine plantations. Virginia Journal of Science 29(2):65. Abstract.

*Mengak, M. T., and K. Terwilliger. 1991. Performance report. Woodrat studies. Pp. 111–125. In: Nongame and endangered species investigations annual report. 1990–1991. EW-2-3. Virginia Department of Game and Inland Fisheries, Richmond. Mengel, R. M. 1971. A study of dog-coyote hybrids and implications concerning hybridization in *Canis*. Journal of Mammalogy 52(2):316–336.

*Mercer, H. C. 1894. Cave exploration in the eastern United States. University of Pennsylvania Department of Archaeology.

*Merriam, C. H. 1892. The occurrence of Cooper's lemming mouse *(Synaptomys cooperi)* in the Atlantic states. Proceedings of the Biological Society of Washington 7:175–177.

*Merriam, C. H. 1895a. Revision of the shrews of the American genera *Blarina* and *Notiosorex*. North American Fauna 10:5–34.

*Merriam, C. H. 1895b. Synopsis of the American shrews of the genus *Sorex*. North American Fauna 10:57–100.

*Merriam, C. H. 1896. Revision of the lemmings of the genus *Synaptomys*, with descriptions of new species. Proceedings of the Biological Society of Washington 10:55–64.

*Merriam, C. H. 1897. Description of a new muskrat from the Dismal Swamp, Virginia. Proceedings of the Biological Society of Washington 11:143.

*Merriam, C. H. 1900. Preliminary revision of the North American red foxes. Proceedings of the Washington Academy of Science 2:661–667.

*Merriam, C. H. 1901. Synopsis of the rice rats (genus *Oryzomys*) of the United States and Mexico. Proceedings of the Washington Academy Science 3:273–295.

Merriam, H. G. 1963. An unusual fox:woodchuck relationship. Journal of Mammalogy 44(1):115–116.

*Merritt, J. F. 1981. *Clethrionomys gapperi*. Mammalian Species no. 146.

*Merson, M. H. 1975. Reproductive characteristics and hormone levels of white-footed mice after dietary exposure to a polychlorinated biphenyl. Master's thesis, Virginia Polytechnic Institute and State University, Blacksburg.

*Merson, M. H. 1979. Influence of restricted feed intake on the reproductive characteristics, energetics, and body composition of two species of rodents. Master's thesis, Virginia Polytechnic Institute and State University, Blacksburg.

*Merson, M. H., C. J. Cowles, and R. L. Kirkpatrick. 1978. Characteristics of captive gray squirrels exposed to cold and food deprivation. Journal of Wildlife Management 42(1):202–205.

*Merson, M. H., and R. L. Kirkpatrick. 1976. Reproductive performance of captive white-footed mice fed a PCB. Bulletin of Environmental Contamination and Toxicology 16(4):392–396.

*Merson, M. H., R. L. Kirkpatrick, P. F. Scanlon, and F. C. Gwazdauskas. 1983. Influence of restricted food intake on reproductive characteristics and carcass fat of male white-footed mice. Journal of Mammalogy 64(2):353–355.

Mertz, G. 1984. Sound: wildlife survival tool. Virginia Wildlife 45(5):17–20.

*Millar, J. S. 1989. Reproduction and development. Pp. 169–232. In: Kirkland, G. L., Jr., and J. N. Layne (editors), Advances in the study of *Peromyscus* (Rodentia). Lubbock: Texas Tech University Press.

Meyer, B. J., and R. K. Meyer. 1944. Growth and reproduction of the cotton rat, *Sigmodon hispidus hispidus*, under laboratory conditions. Journal of Mammalogy 25(2):107–129.

Michael, E. D. 1964. Birth of white-tailed deer fawns. Journal of Wildlife Management 28(1):171–173.

*Miller, A. 1998. Conservancy's cave yields bear bones find. Nature Conservancy Virginia Chapter News, Spring: 6.

*Miller, D. H. 1964. Pygmy shrew in Vermont. Journal of Mammalogy 45(4):651–652.

Miller, D. R. 1987. The decoy deer sting operation. Proceedings of the 13th Annual Conference of the Southeastern Association of Fish and Wildlife Agencies 41:474–476.

*Miller, E. J., and P. T. Bromley. 1989. Wildlife management on conservation reserve program land: the farmer's view. Transactions of the North American Wildlife and Natural Resources Conference 54:377–381.

*Miller, G. S., Jr. 1895. The long-tailed shrews of the eastern United States. North American Fauna 10:35–56.

*Miller, G. S., Jr. 1896. Genera and subgenera of voles and lemmings. North American Fauna 12.

*Miller, G. S., Jr. 1897a. Revision of the North American bats of the family Vespertiliondae. North American Fauna 13.

*Miller, G. S., Jr. 1897b. Notes on the mammals of Ontario. Proceedings of the Boston Society of Natural History 28:1–44.

*Miller, G. S., Jr. 1898. An instance of local temperature control of the distribution of mammals. Science, n.s., 8(201):615–618.

*Miller, G. S., Jr. 1899. Preliminary list of the mammals of New York. Bulletin of the New York State Museum 6(29):273–390.

*Miller, G. S., Jr. 1900. Key to the land mammals of northeastern North America. Bulletin of the New York State Museum 8:59–160.

*Miller, G. S., Jr. 1912. List of North American land mammals in the United States National Museum, 1911. United States National Museum Bulletin 79.

*Miller, G. S., Jr. 1924. List of North American recent mammals, 1923. United States National Museum Bulletin 128.

*Miller, G. S., Jr. 1927. A pollack whale on the coast of Virginia . Proceedings of the Biological Society of Washington 40:111–112.

*Miller, G. S., Jr. and G. M. Allen. 1928. The American bats of the genera *Myotis* and *Pizonyx*. Bulletin of the United States National Museum 144:1–218.

*Miller, G. S., Jr. and R. Kellogg. 1955. List of North American recent mammals. United States National Museum Bulletin 205.

*Miller, G. S., Jr., and J. A. G. Rehn. 1901. Systematic results of the study of North American land mammals to the close of the year 1900. Proceedings of the Boston Society of Natural History 30:1–352.

*Miller, H. L. 1966. Letters. Albino deer. Virginia Wildlife 27(2):27.

*Miller, P. S. 1994. Living with bats. Bats 12(1):13–16.

Milmore, B. K. 1943. Harborage of *Rattus rattus alexandrinus*. United States Public Health Reports 58(41):1507–1509.

Milne, R. C., and T. L. Quay. 1966. The foods and feeding habits of the nutria on Hatteras Island, North Carolina. Proceedings of the 20th Annual Conference of the Southeastern Association of Game and Fish Commissioners 20:112–123.

*Mirarchi, R. E. 1975. Seasonal variation in reproductive organs, hormone levels, and antler development of male white-tailed deer. Master's thesis, Virginia Polytechnic Institute and State University, Blacksburg.

*Mirarchi, R. E., B. E. Howland, P. F. Scanlon, R. L. Kirkpatrick, and L. M. Sanford. 1978. Seasonal variation in plasma LH, FSH, prolactin, and testosterone concentrations in adult male white-tailed deer. Canadian Journal of Zoology 56(1):121–127.

*Mirarchi, R. E., M. D. Russel, P. F. Scanlon, and R. L. Kirkpatrick. 1975. Antler shedding times for white-tailed deer in different regions of Virginia. Virginia Journal of Science 26(2):58. Abstract.

*Mirarchi, R. E., P. F. Scanlon, and R. L. Kirkpatrick. 1974. Monthly gonadal changes in male white-tailed deer. Virginia Journal of Science 25(2):67. Abstract.

*Mirarchi, R. E., P. F. Scanlon, and R. L. Kirkpatrick. 1977. Annual changes in spermatozoan production and associated organs of white-tailed deer. Journal of Wildlife Management 41(1):92–99.

*Mirarchi, R. E., P. F. Scanlon, and R. L. Kirkpatrick, and C. B. Schreck. 1977. Androgen levels and antler development in captive and wild white-tailed deer. Journal of Wildlife Management 41(2):178–183.

*Mitchell, J. 1748. Dissertatio brevis de Principus botanicorum et zoologorum, deque nova stabiliendo naturae rerum congruo cum appendice aliquot generum plantarum recens conditorum et in Virginia observatorum. Nuremburg.

*Mitchell, J. C., and R. A. Beck. 1991. Free-ranging domestic cat predation on vertebrates in rural and urban Virginia. Virginia Journal of Science 42(2):174. Abstract.

*Mitchell, J. C., and R. A. Beck. 1992. Free-ranging domestic cat predation on native vertebrates in rural and urban Virginia. Virginia Journal of Science 43(1B):197–207.

*Mitchell, J. C., S. Y. Erdle, and J. F. Pagels. 1993. Evaluation of capture techniques for amphibian, reptile, and small mammal communities in saturated forested wetlands. Wetlands 13(2):130–136.

Mitchell, P. C. 1911. On longevity and relative viability in mammals and birds; with a note on the theory of longevity. Proceedings of the Zoological Society of London:425–548.

*Mitchell, S. L., J. A. Smith, and W. Cooper. 1828. Discovery of a fossil walrus in Virginia. Report of Messrs. Mitchell, J. A. Smith, and Cooper, on a fossil skull sent to Dr. Mitchell by Mr. Cropper, of Accomoc County, Virginia. Annals of the Lyceum of Natural History of New York:271–272.

*Mohr, C. E. 1933. Observations on the young of cave-dwelling bats. Journal of Mammalogy 14(1):49–53.

*Mohr, C. E. 1953. A survey of bat banding in North America, 1932–1951. The American Caver 14:3–13.

Mohr, C. E. 1972. The status of the threatened species of cave dwelling bats. National Speleological Society Bulletin 34(2):33–47.

*Moncrief, N. D. 1989. Effects of barriers to gene flow on the population genetics of mammals. Virginia Journal of Science 41(2):57. Abstract.

*Moncrief, N. D., and R. D. Dueser. 1991. Genetic variation within and among populations of Delmarva fox squirrels *(Sciurus niger cinereus)*. Final report. United States Fish and Wildlife Service, Region 5.

*Moncrief, N. D. 1993. Allozymic variation in populations of the gray squirrel, *Sciurus carolinensis*, from eastern North America. Virginia Journal of Science 44(2):111. Abstract.

*Moncrief, N. D. and J. M. Anderson. 1997. White-belted coloration in a northern short-tailed shrew (*Blarina brevicauda*). American Midland Naturalist 137(2):397-400.

*Moncrief, N. D. and R. D. Dueser. 1992. Genetic variation in eastern fox squirrels, including populations of the endangered Delmarva fox squirrel *(Sciurus niger cinereus)*. Virginia Journal of Science 43(2):231. Abstract.

*Moncrief, N. D., and R. D. Dueser. 1994. Island hoppers. Virginia Explorer 10(4):14–19.

*Moncrief, N. D., J. W. Edwards, and P. A. Tappe (editors). 1993. Proceedings of the Second Symposium on Southeastern Fox Squirrels, *Sciurus niger*. Virginia Museum of Natural History Special Publication 1.

*Moncrief, N. D., W. D. Webster, B. E. Gurshaw, and R. K. Rose. 1996. Geographic variation in North Carolina and Virginia populations of the southeastern shrew, *Sorex longirostris*, including the federally threatened *S. l. fisheri*. Virginia Journal of Science 47(2):96. Abstract.

*Monson, G. 1971. Springfield phenology. Atlantic Naturalist 26(2):65–70.

*Montali, R. J., P. C. Mann, and J. Seidensticker. 1981. Rabies in raccoons — Virginia. Morbidity and Mortality Weekly Report 30:353–355.

Montgomery, G. G. 1963. Nocturnal movements and activity rhythms of white-tailed deer. Journal of Wildlife Management 27(3):422–427.

Montgomery, G. G. 1964. Tooth eruption in pre-weaned raccoons. Journal of Wildlife Management 28(3):582–584.

Montgomery, G. G. 1968. Pelage development of young raccoons. Journal of Mammalogy 49(1):142–145.

Montgomery, G. G. 1969. Weaning of captive raccoons. Journal of Wildlife Management 33(1):154–159.

*Montgomery, S. D. 1973. Energy dynamics of a woodlot gray squirrel population. Master's thesis, Virginia Polytechnic Institute and State University, Blacksburg.

*Montgomery, S. D., F. B. Whelan, and H. S. Mosby. 1975. Bioenergetics of a woodlot population of gray squirrels. Journal of Wildlife Management 39(4):709–717.

*Montz, W. E., Jr. 1983. Effects of organophosphate insecticides on aspects of reproduction and survival in small mammals. Doctoral dissertation, Virginia Polytechnic Institute and State University, Blacksburg.

*Montz, W. E., Jr., W. C. Card, and R. L. Kirkpatrick. 1981. Effects of nutrition and PCB exposure on selected blood characteristics of raccoons and opossums. Virginia Journal of Science 32(3):96. Abstract.

*Montz, W. E., Jr., P. F. Scanlon, J. A. Cranford, and R. L. Kirkpatrick. 1983. Small mammal trapping in "no-till" soybean fields. Virginia Journal of Science 34(3);129. Abstract.

*Montz, W. E., Jr., P. F. Scanlon, and R. L. Kirkpatrick. 1983. Effects of field application on the anti-cholinesterase insecticide methomyl on brain acetylcholinesterase activities in wild *Mus musculus*. Bulletin of Environmental and Contamination Toxiology 31(2):158–163.

Moore, C. B. 1953. Bears. Pp. 55–82. In: Ways of mammals. New York: The Ronald Press Company.

Moore, J. C. 1943. A contribution to the natural history of the Florida short-tailed shrew. Proceedings of the Florida Academy of Science 6:155–166.

Moore, J. C. 1945. Life history notes on the Florida weasel. Proceedings of the Florida Academy of Science 7(4):247–263.

Moore, J. C. 1947. Nests of the Florida flying squirrel. American Midland Naturalist 38(1):248–252.

*Moore, J. C. 1949. Notes on the shrew, *Sorex cinereus*, in the southern Appalachians. Ecology 30(2):234–237.

*Moore, J. C. 1951. The range of the Florida manatee. Quarterly Journal of the Florida Academy of Science 14:1–19.

*Moore, J. C. 1953. Distribution of marine mammals to Florida waters. American Midland Naturalist 49(1):117–158.

*Moore, J. C. 1956. Variation in the fox squirrel in Florida. American Midland Naturalist 55(1):41–65.

*Moore, J. C. 1957. The natural history of the fox squirrel, *Sciurus niger shermani*. Bulletin of the American Museum of Natural History 113(1):1–71.

*Moore, J. C. 1959. Relationships among living squirrels of the Sciurinae. Bulletin of the American Museum of Natural History 118(4):155–206.

*Moore, L. W. 1940. The orchard mouse situation in Virginia. Virginia Fruit 28(1):69–72.

*Moore, W. G., and R. H. Folk, III. 1978. Crop damage by white-tailed deer in the Southeast. Proceedings of the 32d Annual Conference of the Southeastern Association of Fish and Wildlife Agencies 32:263–268.

*Morgan, A. H. 1939. Field book of animals in winter. New York: G. P. Putman's Sons.

*Morgan, L. H. 1868. The American beaver and his works. Philadelphia: J. B. Lippencott and Company.

*Morgan, J. V. 1959. The Dragon canoe cruising trail. Virginia Wildlife 20(6):20–21.

*Moro, M. H., J. T. Horman, H. R. Fischman, J. K. Grigor and E. Israel. 1991. The epidemiology of rodent and lagomorph rabies in Maryland, 1981 to 1986. Journal of Wildlife Diseases 27(3):452–456.

Morrison, P., and F. A. Ryser. 1962. Metabolism and body temperature in a small hibernator, the meadow

jumping mouse, *Zapus hudsonius*. Journal of Cell Physiology 60:169–180.
Morton, T. 1637. New England Canaan or New Canaan. Amsterdam: J. F. Stam.
*Mosby, H. S. 1947. Virginia animals everyone should know: the raccoon. Virginia Wildlife 8(2):8–9,20.
*Mosby, H. S. 1948. The foxes of Virginia — a controversial subject. Virginia Wildlife 9(5):8–10.
*Mosby, H. S. 1950. Cooperative wildlife management on the Virginia state forests. Journal of Forestry 48(10):700–702.
*Mosby, H. S. 1953. A brief report on the 1952 Big Levels refuge hunt. Virginia Wildlife 14(3):18–19.
*Mosby, H. S. 1968a. Letters. Seeks black squirrel records. Virginia Wildlife 29(2):3.
*Mosby, H. S. 1968b. The squirrel hunting dilemma. Virginia Wildlife 29(9):5,21.
*Mosby, H. S. 1969. The influence of hunting on the population dynamics of a woodlot gray squirrel population. Journal of Wildlife Management 33(1):59–73.
*Mosby, H. S. 1972. A "wonder" drug from deer? Virginia Wildlife 33(9):17–18.
*Mosby, H. S., R. L. Kirkpatrick, and J. O. Newell. 1977. Seasonal vulnerability of gray squirrels to hunting. Journal of Wildlife Management 41(2):284–289.
*Moseley, K. W. 1961. Wildlife and our old farmhouse. Virginia Wildlife 22(2):8–9.
*Moseley, K. W. 1965a. The outraged skunk and other characters. Virginia Wildlife 26(7):6–7.
*Moseley, K. W. 1965b. Squirrels on an old rail fence. Virginia Wildlife 26(1):6–7.
*Moseley, K. W. 1968. Survival. Incredible and audacious. Virginia Wildlife 29(6):20–21.
*Moseley, K. W. 1969a. Happenings. Virginia Wildlife 30(8):9–10.
*Moseley, K. W. 1969b. Happy hunting. Virginia Wildlife 30(10):11, 18–19.
*Moseley, K. W. 1969c. Skylarkers of the night. Virginia Wildlife 30(4):21–22.
*Moseley, K. W. 1971. Home — is a place to stay. Virginia Wildlife 32(4):16–17.
*Moseley, K. W. 1972. Bread line of possums. Virginia Wildlife 33(2):18–19.
*Moseley, K. W. 1977. Scat skunk. Virginia Wildlife 38(5):10–11.
Mueller, H. C. 1968. The role of vision in vespertilionid bats. American Midland Naturalist 79:524–525.
Mueller, H. C., and J. T. Emlen, Jr., 1957. Homing in bats. Science 126(3268):307–308.
*Mullan, J. M., G. A. Feldhamer, and D. Morton. 1988. Reproductive characteristics of female sika deer in Maryland and Virginia. Journal of Mammalogy 69(2):388–389.
*Mumaw, D. K. 1965. Evaluation of prescribed burning in relation to available deer browse. Master's thesis, Virginia Polytechnic Institute and State University, Blacksburg.
Mumford, R. E. 1969. Long-tailed weasel preys on big brown bats. Journal of Mammalogy 50(2):360.
Mumford, R. E. 1973. Natural history of the red bat *(Lasiurus borealis)* in Indiana. Periodical Biology 75:155–158.
*Muncy, R. J. 1954. The status of the white-tailed deer in Bath County, Virginia. Master's thesis, Virginia Polytechnic Institute and State University, Blacksburg.
*Munford, G. L. 1960. The Wakefield community hunt club. Virginia Wildlife 21(12):17–18.
*Murie, O. J. 1951. The elk of North America. Harrisburg, Pennsylvania: The Stackpole Company, and Washington, DC: Wildlife Management Institute.
*Murphy, W. F. 1973. Induction of ovulation in the cottontail rabbit. Master's thesis, Virginia Polytechnic Institute and State University, Blacksburg.
*Murphy, W. F., P. F. Scanlon, and R. L. Kirkpatrick. 1974. Examination of ovaries in living cottontail rabbits by laparotomy. Proceedings of the 27th Annual Conference of the Southeastern Association of Game and Fish Commissioners 27:343–344.
*Murray, E. 1977a. Summer at the Mountain Lake Biological Station. Virginia Wildlife 38(4):9–10, 16.
*Murray. E. 1977b. White deer: a surprising common phenomenon. Virginia Wildlife 38(12):20–21.
*Murray, E. 1978. Area in crisis: Back Bay. Virginia Wildlife 39(2):26–28.
*Murray. J. J. 1933. Black bears in Virginia. Raven 4(2):9.
*Murray, J. J. 1948. The Great Dismal Swamp. Raven 19(3–4):14–26.
*Murrill, W. A. 1927. American wildcats. Forest and Stream 97:476–478, 504.
*Muul, I. 1968. Behavioral and physiological influences on the distribution of the flying squirrel, *Glaucomys volans.* Miscellaneous Publications, Museum of Zoology, University of Michigan no. 134.
Muul, I. 1969. Mating behavior, gestation period, and development of *Glaucomys sabrinus.* Journal of Mammalogy 50(1):121.
Muul. I. 1970. Intra- and inter-familial behavior of *Glaucomys volans* (Rodentia) following parturition. Journal of Animal Behaviour 18(1):20–25.
*Myers, D. 1967. Woodchucks — the hard way. Virginia Wildlife 28(9):19.
*Myers, E. 1971. Bowhunting the white-tail. Virginia Wildlife 32(10):4–6.
*Myers, E. 1972. The whitetail deer. Virginia Wildlife 33(2):4–5.
*Myers, E. 1975. Bobcat. Virginia Wildlife 36(8):6–7.
*Myers, H. 1961. Nature's home for sportsmen. Philpott Reservoir. Virginia Wildlife 22(1):16–17.
*Nagorsen, D. 1985. *Kogia simus.* Mammalian Species no. 239.
*Neal, W. A. 1967. A study of the ecology of the woodrat in the hardwood forests of the lower Mississippi River basin. Master's thesis, Louisiana State University, Baton Rouge.
*Needham, K. 1995. A day in the life of radio telemetry from the ground. Virginia Wildlife 56(9):30.
*Neely, R. A. 1966. The influence of saturation stocking and cover manipulation on the cottontail rabbit

(Sylvilagus floridanus). Master's thesis, Virginia Polytechnic Institute and State University, Blacksburg.

*Negus, N. C., E. Gould, and R. K. Chipman. 1961 Ecology of the rice rat, *Oryzomys palustris* (Harlan), on Breton Island, Gulf of Mexico, with a critique of the social stress theory. Tulane Studies in Zoology 8:93–123.

Nellis, C. H., and L. B. Keith. 1976. Population dynamics of coyotes in central Alberta. Journal of Wildlife Management 40(3):389–399.

*Nelson, A. L. 1933. A preliminary report on the winter food of Virginia foxes. Journal of Mammalogy 14(1):40–43.

*Nelson, E. W. 1909. The rabbits of North America. North American Fauna 29.

*Nelson, E. W. 1916. The larger North American mammals. National Geographic Magazine 30:385–472.

*Nelson, E. W. 1917. The rat pest. National Geographic Magazine 32(1):1–23.

*Nelson, E. W. 1918. Smaller mammals of North America. National Geographic Magazine 33:371–493.

*Nelson, F. P. 1950. Factors limiting cottontail rabbits on representative areas of Virginia. Master's thesis, Virginia Polytechnic Institute and State University, Blacksburg.

*Nelson, T. R. 1955. Ramsey's Draft. Virginia Wildlife 16(5):21–23.

*Nesbitt, W. H., and J. S. Parker. 1977. North American big game. Washington, DC: The Boone and Crockett Club.

Nestler, J. R. 1989. Metabolic regulation during daily torpor in *Peromyscus maniculatus.* American Zoologist 29(4):5A.

*Nettles, V. F., J. L. Corn, G. A. Erickson, and D. A. Jessup. 1989. A survey of wild swine in the United States for evidence of hog cholera. Journal of Wildlife Diseases 25(1):61–65.

*Nettles, V. F., W. R. Davidson, S. K. Fisk, and H. A. Jacobson. 1975. An epizootic of cerebrospinal nematodiasis in cottontail rabbits. Journal of the American Veterinary Medical Association 167:600–602.

*Nettles, V. F., W. R. Davidson, and D. E. Stallknecht. 1992. Surveillance for hemorrhagic disease in white-tailed deer and other wild ruminants, 1980–1989. Proceedings of the Southeastern Association of Fish and Wildlife Agencies 46:138–146.

*Nettles, V. F., and G.. L. Doster. 1976. Nasal bots of white-tailed deer in the southeastern United States. Proceedings of the 29th Annual Conference of the Southeastern Association of Game and Fish Commissioners 29:651–655.

*Neves, R. J., and M. C. Odom. 1989. Muskrat predation on endangered freshwater mussels in Virginia. Journal of Wildlife Management 53(4):934–941.

Neumann, A. C., and E. W. S. Hull. 1965–66. Editor takes a dive half-mile down to the floor of the gulf stream. Geo-Marine Technology 2:16–27.

Neumann, R., and T. J. Cade. 1964. Photoperiodic influence on the hibernation of jumping mice. Ecology 45(2):382–384.

*Newcombe, C. L. 1930. An ecological study of the Allegheny cliff rat *(Neotoma pennsylvanica stone).* Journal of Mammalogy 11(2):204–211.

*Newell J. O. 1968. Seasonal reproduction in the female gray squirrel *Sciurus carolinensis.* Virginia Journal of Science 19(3):181. Abstract.

*Newman, W. C. 1951. The antlers of the whitetail. Virginia Wildlife 12(11):16–17.

*Newsom, J. D. 1969. History of deer and their habitat in the South. Pp. 1–7. In: White-tailed deer in the southern forest habitat. Proceedings of a Symposium, Nacogdoches, Texas: Stephen F. Austin State College.

*Newsom, W. M. 1926. Whitetailed deer. New York: C. Scribner and Sons.

Nichelson [sic], W. S., and E. P. Hill. 1981 An ecological study of the gray fox in eastcentral Alabama. Cooperative Wildlife Project Final Report, Project Number W-44–5.

*Nichols, B. E., J. L. Sandt, and G. A. Whitaker. 1977. Delmarva's wildlife work group's procedure for habitat analysis. Proceedings of the 31st Annual Conference of the Southeastern Association of Fish and Wildlife Agencies 31:8–17.

*Nichols, D. G. 1938. Notes on American house mice. Journal of Mammalogy 19(2):253.

*Nichols, D. G. 1944. Further considerations of American house mice. Journal of Mammalogy 25(1):82–84.

*Noffsinger, R. E. 1976. Seasonal variation in the natality, mortality, and nutrition of the pine vole in two orchard types. Master's thesis, Virginia Polytechnic Institute and State University, Blacksburg.

*Noffsinger, R. E., R. L. Kirkpatrick, and J. E. Estep. 1975. Population characteristics and densities of the pine vole in a maintained and an abandoned orchard. Virginia Journal of Science 26(2):59. Abstract.

*Nongame Summary EW-2–2, 1989/90. Virginia Department of Game and Inland Fisheries, Richmond.

Norris, K. S., J. H. Prescott, P. V. Asa-Dorian, and P. Perkins. 1961. An experimental demonstration of echo-location behavior in the porpoise, *Tursiops truncatus* (Montagu). Biological Bulletin 120(2):163–176.

Novakowski, N. S. 1969. The influence of vocalization on the behavior of beaver, *Castor canadensis* Kuhl. American Midland Naturalist 81(1):198–204.

*Nowak, R. M. 1970. Report on the red wolf. Defenders of Wildlife News 45(1):82–94.

*Nowak, R. M. 1977. Proposal for endangered status and critical habitat for the Virginia big-eared bat. Federal Register 42:61290–61292. December 2, 1977.

*Nowak, R. M. 1979a. North American Quaternary *Canis.* Monograph of the Museum of Natural History, University of Kansas no. 6.

*Nowak, R. M. 1979b. Reproposal of critical habitat for the Virginia big-eared bat. Federal Register 44(170): 51144–51145.

*Nowak, R. M. 1984. Endangered and threatened wildlife and plants; proposed endangered status for two kinds of northern flying squirrel. Federal Register 49(226):45880–45884.

*Nowak, R. M. 1991. Walker's Mammals of the World. 5th. ed. 2 vol. Baltimore: The Johns Hopkins University Press.

*Obaugh, W. 1968. Nature's Rip Van Winkles. Virginia Wildlife 29(12):8.

*Obaugh, W. 1969a. Former Virginian. Virginia Wildlife 30(9):18.

*Obaugh, W. 1969b. Two thousand mile footpath. Virginia Wildlife 30(4):22–23.

*Obaugh, W. 1970. An ancient inhabitant. Virginia Wildlife 31(3):21–22.

*Obaugh, W. 1971a. Panther stories. Virginia Wildlife 32(7):16–18.

*Obaugh, W. 1971b. Dogs and deer. Virginia Wildlife 32(8):22.

*Odell, D. K. 1982. West Indian manatee. Pp. 828–837. In: Chapman, J. A., and G. A. Feldhamer (editors), Wild mammals of North America. Baltimore: The Johns Hopkins University Press.

*Odum, E. P. 1944a. Notes on small mammal populations at Mountain Lake, Virginia. Journal of Mammalogy 25(4):408–410.

*Odum, E. P. 1944b. *Sorex longirostris* at Mountain Lake, Virginia. Journal of Mammalogy 25(2):196.

*Odum, E. P. 1944c. Water consumption of certain mice in relation to habitat selection. Journal of Mammalogy 25(4):404–405.

Odum, E. P. 1949. Small mammals of the Highlands (North Carolina) Plateau. Journal of Mammalogy 30(2):179–192.

Odum, E. P. 1955. An eleven year history of a *Sigmodon* population. Journal of Mammalogy 36(3):368–378.

*Oelschlaeger, A., P. F. Scanlon, M. N. Berkaw, R. L. Kirkpatrick, and F. C. Gwazdauskas. 1978. Annual variation in circulating testosterone levels in cottontail rabbits. Virginia Journal of Science 29(2):67. Abstract.

Office of Endangered Species and International Activities. 1973. Threatened wildlife of the United States. Washington, D. C.: United States Government Printing Office.

*Ogburn, C. 1974. The return of the cougar. Washington Post, October 31, 1974.

*Ogden, J. L. 1970. A tale of two bears. Virginia Wildlife 31(12):20.

*Ogle, M. 1984. Heavy metal concentration, aging techniques and population characteristics of mink in Virginia with a review of the literature on delayed implantation in the mink. Master's thesis, Virginia Polytechnic Institute and State University, Blacksburg.

*Ogle, M. C. 1984. Heavy metal concentration, aging techniques and population characteristics of mink in Virginia with a review of literature on delayed implantation in the mink. Master's thesis, Virginia Polytechnic Institute and State University, Blacksburg.

*Ogle, M. C., P. F. Scanlon, A. G. Clark, and J. V. Gwynn. 1990. A system for determining age of mink. Transactions of the 19th International Union of Game Biologists Congress, Trondhiem, Norway. September, 1989. 19(1):342–347.

*Ogle, M. C., P. F. Scanlon, and R. L. Kirkpatrick. 1984. Heavy metal concentrations in Virginia mink. Virginia Journal of Science 35(2):87. Abstract.

*Ogle, M. C., P. F. Scanlon, R. L. Kirkpatrick, and A. G. Clark. 1984. Aging techniques and population characteristics of Virginia mink. Virginia Journal of Science 35(2):86. Abstract.

*Ogle, M. C., P. F. Scanlon, R. L. Kirkpatrick, and J. V. Gwynn. 1985. Heavy metal concentrations in tissues of mink in Virginia. Bulletin of Environmental Contamination and Toxicology 35(1):29–37.

*Ohsumi, S., T. Kasuya, and M. Nishiwaki. 1963. Accumulation rate of dentinal growth layers in the maxillary tooth of the sperm whale. Scientific Reports, Whales Research Institute (Tokyo) 17:15–35.

*Olbricht, G. 1990. Streifgebiete und Aktivitatsmuster von Weisswedelhirschen *(Odocoileus virginianus)* wahrend des Fruschtfalles. Master's thesis, Freie University, Berlin, Germany.

*Oleyar, C. M. 1969. Evaluation of a technique employing the chemosterilant diethylstilbestrol for suppressing reproduction of wild foxes in Virginia. Master's thesis, Virginia Polytechnic Institute and State University, Blacksburg.

*Oleyar, C. M. and B. S. McGinnes. 1974. Field evaluation of diethylstilbestrol for suppressing reproduction in wild foxes. Journal of Wildlife Management 38(1):101–106.

*Olmstead, D. L. 1970. Effect of certain environmental factors on white-tailed deer productivity in the eastern United States and Texas. Master's thesis, University of Connecticut, Storrs.

*Olsen, J. 1962. The cursed Swamp. Sports Illustrated 17(22):68–82.

*Olsen, S. 1990. The importance of white-tailed deer in Virginia prehistory. The Virginia Explorer 6(5):10.

*Olson, B. J., J. A. Bell, and C. W. Emmons. 1947. Studies on histoplasmosis in a rural community. American Journal of Public Health 37:441–449.

*Orgain, J. R., Jr. 1967. A stretched out deer. Virginia Wildlife 28(2):21.

*Ormond, C. 1961. Bear! Harrisburg, Pennsylvania: The Stackpole Company.

*Orr, R. T. 1950. Unusual behavior and occurrence of a hoary bat. Journal of Mammalogy 31(4):456–457.

*Osgood, W. H. 1907. Some unrecognized and misapplied names of American mammals. Proceedings of the Biological Society of Washington 20:43–52.

*Osgood, W. H. 1909. Revision of the mice of the American genus *Peromyscus.* North American Fauna 28.

O'Shea, T. J., J. E. Kaiser, G. R. Askins and J. A Chapman. 1981. Polychlorinated biphenyls in a wild mink population. Pp. 1746–1751. In: Chapman, J. A., and D. Pursley (editors), Proceedings of the Worldwide Furbearer Conference, Frostburg State College. August 1980.

O'Shea, T. J., J. F. Moore, and H. I. Kochman. 1984. Contaminant concentrations in manatees in Florida. Journal of Wildlife Management 48(3):741–748.

Ostfeld, R. S. and R. H. Manson. 1996. Long-distance homing in meadow voles, *Microtus pennsylvanicus*. Journal of Mammalogy 77(3):870–873.

*Otto, R. A. 1976. Horizontal starch gel electrophoresis as a technique for examining gray squirrel population genetics. Master's thesis, Virginia Polytechnic Institute and State University, Blacksburg.

*Otto, R. A., and J. E. Estep. 1977. The eastern chipmunk. Virginia Wildlife 38(6):4–6.

Ouellet, J.-P., and J. Ferron. 1988. Scent-marking behavior by woodchucks *(Marmota monax)*. Journal of Mammalogy 69(2):365–368.

*Owen, F. R. 1968. Rabbit habits. Virginia Wildlife 29(7):20–21.

*Owen, J. G. 1984. *Sorex fumeus*. Mammalian Species no. 215.

*Owen, R. 1861. John Hunter: essays and observations on natural history, anatomy, physiology, psychology, and geology. Vol. 2. London: John Van Voorst.

*Owens, F. R. 1966. Bird feeders are for BIRDS, Sammy! Virginia Wildlife 27(1):12.

*Pack, J. C. 1966. Influence of the social hierarchy on gray squirrel behavior. Master's thesis, Virginia Polytechnic Institute and State University, Blacksburg.

*Pack, J. C. 1967. Squirrel society. Virginia Wildlife 28(1):8.

*Pack, J. C., H. S. Mosby, and P. B. Siegel. 1967. Influence of social hierarchy on gray squirrel behavior. Journal of Wildlife Management 31(4):720–728.

*Packard, F. M. 1972. Beavers in Fairfax County. Atlantic Naturalist 21(1):3–4.

*Packard, R. L. 1969. Taxonomic review of the golden mouse *Ochrotomys nuttalli*. Miscellaneous Publications, Museum of Natural History, University of Kansas 51:373–406.

*Padgett, T. M. 1987. The first record of the seminole bat, *Lasiurus seminolus*, (Chiroptera:Vespertilionidae) from Virginia. Virginia Journal of Science 38(3):253.

*Padgett, T. M. 1989. A range extension of the marsh rabbit, *Sylvilagus palustris*, from southeastern Virginia. Virginia Journal of Science 40(3):177.

*Padgett, T. M. 1991. The identification, distribution, and status of the threatened Dismal Swamp shrew *(Sorex longirostris fisheri)*. Master's thesis, Old Dominion University, Norfolk, Virginia.

*Padgett, T. M., R. K. Everton and R. K. Rose. 1987. The identification of the threatened southeastern shrew, *Sorex longirostris fisheri*, using multivariate statistical techniques. Virginia Journal of Science 38(2):85. Abstract.

*Padgett, T. M., R. K. Everton and R. K. Rose. 1987. The identification of the threatened southeastern shrew using multivariate statistical techniques. Virginia Journal of Science 38(4):351–357.

*Padgett, T. M., and R. K. Rose. 1984. Bats of the Dismal Swamp region. Virginia Journal of Science 35(2):87. Abstract.

*Padgett, T. M., and R. K. Rose. 1991. Bats (Chiroptera:Vespertilionidae) of the Great Dismal Swamp of Virginia and North Carolina. Brimleyana 17:17–26.

*Padgett, T. M. and R. K. Rose. 1994. The pygmy shrew, *Sorex hoyi winnemana* (Insectivora: Soricidae), from the coastal plain of North Carolina. Brimleyana 21:87–90.

*Pagels, J. 1986. The meadow vole. Virginia Wildlife 47(7):34.

*Pagels, J. 1987a. A deadly trap. Virginia Wildlife 48(10):24–27.

*Pagels, J. 1987b. The eastern woodrat. Virginia Wildlife 48(10):34–35.

*Pagels, J. 1988a. The fisher. Virginia Wildlife 49(2):34–35.

*Pagels, J. 1988b. The chipmunk. Virginia Wildlife 49(6):34.

*Pagels, J. 1988c. The bobcat. Virginia Wildlife 49(10):34.

*Pagels, J. 1989a. The muskrat. Virginia Wildlife 50(7):34.

*Pagels, J. 1989b. The gray fox. Virginia Wildlife 50(10):34–35.

*Pagels, J. 1989c. Of mice and men and other mammals. Virginia Wildlife 50(12):16–21.

*Pagels, J. 1990a. The striped skunk. Virginia Wildlife 51(4):34.

*Pagels, J. 1990b. The woodchuck. Virginia Wildlife 51(7):34–35.

*Pagels, J. 1990c. Tail tales. Virginia Wildlife 51(11):4–8.

*Pagels, J. 1992a. Virginia's wildlife. The cotton rat. Virginia Wildlife 53(6):27.

*Pagels, J. 1992b. The star-nosed mole. Virginia Wildlife 53(9):34.

*Pagels, J. 1993. The long-tailed weasel. Virginia Wildlife 54(7):20–21.

*Pagels, J. F. 1977a. Observations on the distribution and habitat requirements of the hispid cotton rat, *Sigmodon hispidus*, in Virginia. Virginia Journal of Science 28(2):66. Abstract.

*Pagels, J. F. 1977b. Distribution and habitat of cotton rat *(Sigmodon hispidus)* in central Virginia. Virginia Journal of Science 28(3):133–135.

*Pagels, J. F. 1979. The changing scene. Pp. 603–609. In: Linzey, D. W. (editor), Proceedings of the Symposium on Endangered and Threatened Plants and Animals of Virginia. Blacksburg: Virginia Polytechnic Institute and State University.

*Pagels, J. F. 1982. Relative abundance of mammals in seven habitats of the Piedmont of North Carolina and Virginia. Virginia Journal of Science 33(3):117. Abstract.

*Pagels, J. F. 1984. The shrews of Virginia: a progress report. Virginia Journal of Science 35(2):87. Abstract.

*Pagels, J. F. 1985. The shrews of Virginia. Final report. Virginia Department of Game and Inland Fisheries, Richmond.

*Pagels, J. F. 1986a. The earth shifters. Virginia Wildlife 47(5):21–24.

*Pagels, J. F. 1986b. The eastern pipistrelle. Virginia Wildlife 47(10):34–35.

*Pagels, J. F. 1986c. The white-footed mouse. Virginia Wildlife 47(12):34–35.

*Pagels, J. F. 1987a. The pygmy shrew, rock shrew and water shrew: Virginia's rarest shrews (Mammalia: Soricidae). Virginia Journal of Science 38(2):85. Abstract.

*Pagels, J. F. 1987b. The pygmy shrew, rock shrew and water shrew: Virginia's rarest shrews (Mammalia: Soricidae). Virginia Journal of Science 38(4):364–368.

*Pagels, J. F. 1990. First record of the rock vole, *Microtus chrotorrhinus* (Miller) (Rodentia: Cricetidae), in Virginia. Brimleyana no. 16:1–3.

*Pagels, J. F. 1991. A high elevation record for the least shrew, *Cryptotis parva* (Say). Virginia Journal of Science 42(3):361–362.

*Pagels, J. F. 1994. Leaf-carrying with the tail in the Virginia opossum, *Didelphis virginiana*. Banisteria 7:55–56.

*Pagels, J. F., and R. G. Adleman. 1971. A note on the cotton rat in central Virginia. Virginia Journal of Science 22(4):195.

*Pagels, J. F., and C. R. Blem. 1973. Metabolized energy of the big brown bat *Eptesicus fuscus* (Chiroptera). Comparative Biochemistry and Physiology A, 45:497–501.

*Pagels, J. F., R. P. Eckerlin, J. R. Baker and M. L. Fies. 1990. New records of the distribution and the intestinal parasites of the endangered northern flying squirrel, *Glaucomys sabrinus* (Mammalia: Sciuridae) in Virginia. Brimleyana 16:73–78.

*Pagels, J. F., and S. Y. Erdle. 1990. Demographic features of shrews in two contrasting habitats. Virginia Journal of Science 41(2):57. Abstract.

*Pagels, J. F., S. Y. Erdle, K. L. Uthus and J. C. Mitchell. 1991. Small mammal diversity in hardwood forest and clearcut habitats in the Virginia Piedmont. Virginia Journal of Science 42(2):175. Abstract.

*Pagels, J. F., S. Y. Erdle, K. L. Uthus, and J. C. Mitchell. 1992. Small mammal diversity in forested and clear cut habitats in the Virginia Piedmont. Virginia Journal of Science 43(1B):171–176.

*Pagels, J. F., M. L. Fies, and R. Glasgow. 1991. Appalachian water shrew recovery plan. Virginia Department of Game and Inland Fisheries, Richmond.

*Pagels, J. F., and T. W. French. 1987. Discarded bottles as a source of small mammal distribution data. American Midland Naturalist 118(1):217–219.

*Pagels, J. F., and M. W. Goehle. 1977. Laboratory interactions of the hispid cotton rat, *Sigmodon hispidus*, and the eastern meadow vole, *Microtus pennsylvanicus*. Virginia Journal of Science 28(2):66. Abstract.

*Pagels, J. F., and C. O. Handley, Jr. 1989. Distribution of the southeastern shrew, *Sorex longirostris* Bachman, in western Virginia. Brimleyana 15:123–131.

*Pagels, J. F., and C. O. Handley, Jr. 1991. Water shrew. Pp. 564–565. In: Terwilliger, K., (coordinator), Virginia's endangered species. Blacksburg: The McDonald & Woodward Publishing Company.

*Pagels, J. F., C. S. Jones and C. O. Handley, Jr. 1982. Northern limits of the southeastern shrew, *Sorex longirostris* Bachman (Insectivora: Soricidae), on the Atlantic Coast of the United States. Brimleyana 8:51–59.

*Pagels, J. F., R. Reynolds, and K. Terwilliger. 1991. Performance Report. Northern flying squirrel and water shrew investigation. Pp. 24–38. In: Nongame and endangered species investigations annual report, 1990–1991. EW-2-3. Virginia Department of Game and Inland Fisheries, Richmond.

*Pagels, J. F., S. C. Rinehart, J. C. Mitchell, K. A. Buhlmann, and C. A. Pague. 1994. Mammal biodiversity and community structure in five forested habitats on Shenandoah Mountain, Virginia. Virginia Journal of Science 45(2):108. Abstract.

*Pagels, J. F., L. A. Smock, and S. H. Sklarew. 1996. The water shrew, *Sorex palustris*, and its habitat in Virginia. Virginia Journal of Science 47(2):154. Abstract.

*Pagels, J. F., and C. M. Tate. 1975. Small mammals of the Paddy Knob-Little Back Creek area of Bath Co., Virginia. Virginia Journal of Science 26(2):59. Abstract.

*Pagels, J. F., and C. M. Tate. 1976. Shrews (Insectivora: Soricidae) of the Paddy Knob-Little Back Creek area of western Virginia. Virginia Journal of Science 27(4):202–203.

*Pagels, J. F., K. L. Uthus, and H. E. Duval. 1994. The masked shrew, *Sorex cinereus*, in a relictual habitat of the southern Appalachian Mountains. Pp. 103–109. In: Merritt, J. F., G. L. Kirkland, Jr., and R. K. Rose (editors). Advances in the biology of shrews. Special Publication 18, Carnegie Museum of Natural History, Pittsburgh.

*Pague, C. A., and K. A. Buhlmann. 1991. Rare animals of Back Bay, Virginia Beach, Virginia. Pp. 148–158. In: Marshall, H. G., and M. D. Norman (editors), Proceedings of the Back bay Ecological Symposium. Norfolk: Old Dominion University.

*Pague, C. A., J. C. Mitchell, D. A. Young and K. A. Buhlmann. 1990. Species composition and seasonal surface activity of terrestrial vertebrates in five northern Virginia piedmont natural communities. Virginia Journal of Science 41(2):58. Abstract.

*Painter, H. F., and R. P. Eckerlin. 1982. Fleas from mammals of Fairfax County, Virginia. Virginia Journal of Science 33(3):117. Abstract.

*Painter, H. F., and R. P. Eckerlin. 1984. Seasonal variations in species composition of siphonapteran parasite populations on southern flying squirrels. Virginia Journal of Science 35(2):88. Abstract.

*Painter, H. F., and R. P. Eckerlin. 1985. The status of the dog flea, *Ctenocephalides canis*, in Virginia. Virginia Journal of Science 36(2):114. Abstract.

*Painter, H. F., and R. P. Eckerlin. 1987. The value of nest examination in the study of flea populations. Virginia Journal of Science 38(2):86. Abstract.

*Painter, H. F., and R. P. Eckerlin. 1989. Boreal fleas of the southern Appalachians. Virginia Journal of Science 40(2):57. Abstract.

*Painter, H. F., and R. P. Eckerlin. 1990. Progress report on establishment of a baseline siphonapteran inventory for Virginia. Virginia Journal of Science 41(2):58. Abstract..

*Palmer, E. L., and H. S. Fowler. 1975. Fieldbook of natural history. 2d edition. New York: McGraw-Hill Book Company.

Palmer, R. S. 1954. The mammal guide. Garden City, New York: Doubleday and Company.

*Palmer, T. S. 1912. Chronology and index of the more important events in American game protection, 1776–1911. United States Department of Agriculture, Biological Survey Bulletin 41.

*Palmer, T. S. 1922. Game as a national resource. United States Department of Agriculture Bulletin 1049.

Panuska, J. A., and N. J. Wade. 1956. The burrow of *Tamias striatus.* Journal of Mammalogy 37:23–31.

*Paradiso, J. L. 1958. The common blackfish in Virginia coastal waters. Journal of Mammalogy 39(3):440–441.

*Paradiso, J. L. 1959. A new star-nosed mole *(Condylura)* from the southeastern United States. Proceedings of the Biological Society of Washington 72:103–108.

*Paradiso, J. L. 1960. Size variation in the rice rat. Journal of Mammalogy 41(4):516–517.

*Paradiso, J. L. 1960. A new white-footed mouse *(Peromyscus leucopus)* from southeastern Virginia. Proceedings of the Biological Society of Washington 73:21–23.

*Paradiso, J. L. 1966. Letters. Virginia coyotes identified. Virginia Wildlife 27(6):3,26.

*Paradiso, J. L. 1969. Mammals of Maryland. North American Fauna 66.

Paradiso, J. L., and A. M. Greenhall. 1967. Longevity records for American bats. American Midland Naturalist 78(1):251–252.

*Paradiso, J. L., and C. O. Handley, Jr. 1965. Checklist of mammals of Assateague Island. Chesapeake Science 6(3):167–171.

*Paradiso, J. L., and R. M. Nowak. 1972. *Canis rufus.* Mammalian Species no. 22.

*Paradiso, J. L., and R. M. Nowak. 1982. Wolves. Pp. 460–474. In: Chapman, J. A., and G. A. Feldhamer (editors), Wild mammals of North America. Baltimore: The Johns Hopkins University Press.

*Parker, J. C. 1968. Parasites of the gray squirrel in Virginia. Journal of Parasitology 54(3):633–634.

*Parker, J. C. 1971. Protozoan, helminth, and arthropod parasites of the gray squirrel in southwestern Virginia. Doctoral dissertation, Virginia Polytechnic Institute and State University, Blacksburg.

*Parker, J. C., and R. B. Holliman. 1971a. Notes on *Gongylonema pulchrum* Molin, 1857 (Nematoda: Spiruridae) in the gray squirrel in southwestern Virginia. Journal of Parasitology 57(3):629.

*Parker, J. C., and R. B. Holliman. 1972. A method for determining ectoparasite densities on gray squirrels. Journal of Wildlife Management 36(4):1227–1234.

*Parker, R. L. 1975. Rabies in skunks. Pp. 41–51. In: Baer, G. M. (editor), The natural history of rabies. Volume II. New York: Academic Press.

*Parker, R. R., J. Bell, C. Frederick, S. William, F. B. Thrailkill, and M. T. McKee. 1952. The recovery of strains of Rocky Mountain spotted fever and tularemia from ticks of the eastern United States. Journal of Infectious Diseases 91:231–237.

Parmalee, P. W., and J. E. Guilday. 1966. A recent record of porcupine from Tennessee. Journal of the Tennessee Academy of Sciences 41(3):81–82.

Parsons, H. J., D. A. Smith, and R. F. Whittam. 1986. Maternity colonies of silver-haired bats, *Lasionycteris noctivagans,* in Ontario and Saskatchewan. Journal of Mammalogy 67(3):598–600.

*Parsons, L. M., and C. R. Terman. 1976. The influence of vision and olfaction on the homing ability of the white-footed mouse *(Peromyscus leucopus noveboracensis).* Virginia Journal of Science 27(2):48. Abstract.

*Parsons, L. M., and C. R. Terman. 1978. Influence of vision and olfaction on the homing ability of the white-footed mouse *(Peromyscus leucopus noveboracensis).* Journal of Mammalogy 59(4):761.

*Paschal, J. E., J. H. Richardson, and D. E. Sonenshine. 1972. A simulated model of a white-footed mouse *(Peromyscus leucopus)* population in a part of the great Dismal Swamp. Virginia Journal of Science 23(3):114. Abstract.

*Paschal, J. E., D. E. Sonenshine, and J. H. Richardson. 1979. A simulation model of a *Peromyscus leucopus* population in an area of the Dismal Swamp. Pp. 277–296. In: Kirk, P. W., Jr. (editor), The Great Dismal Swamp. Charlottesville: University Press of Virginia.

*Paterson, R. L. 1984. High incidence of plant material and small mammals in the autumn diet of turkey vultures in Virginia. Wilson Bulletin 96(3):467–469.

Patterson, A. P., and J. W. Hardin. 1969. Flight speeds of five species of vespertilionid bats. Journal of Mammalogy 50(1):152–153.

*Patterson, J. B. 1974. Panther sighting recalled. Virginia Wildlife 36(2):3.

*Patton, C. P. 1938a. Animals. Richmond, Virginia: Times-Dispatch, October 30, 1938:6.

*Patton, C. P. 1938b. A preliminary distributional list of the mammals of Virginia. Master's thesis, Virginia Polytechnic Institute and State University, Blacksburg.

*Patton, C. P. 1939. Distribution notes on certain Virginia mammals. Journal of Mammalogy 20(1):75–77.

*Patton, C. P. 1941. The eastern cotton rat in Virginia. Journal of Mammalogy 22(1):91.

*Patton, T. H. 1963. Fossil remains of southern bog lemming in Pleistocene deposits of Texas. Journal of Mammalogy 44(2):275–277.

*Paul, J. R. 1965. *Blarina telmalestes* in North Carolina. Journal of Mammalogy 46(3):496.

*Paul, J. R. 1970. The pine vole in North Carolina. Reports of Investigations, no. 20. Illinois State Museum.

*Pauley, R. 1974. Madness after dark. Virginia Wildlife 35(1):4–6.

*Payne, J. L. 1987. Habitat variation among montane island populations of the flying squirrel, *Glaucomys sabrinus*, in the southern Appalachian mountains. Master's thesis, Virginia Commonwealth University, Richmond.

*Payne, J. L., D. R. Young and J. F. Pagels. 1989. Plant community characteristics associated with the endangered northern flying squirrel, *Glaucomys sabrinus*, in the southern Appalachians. American Midland Naturalist 121(2):285–292.

*Payne, N. F. 1964a. The influence of hunting on rabbit populations in southeastern Virginia. Master's thesis, Virginia Polytechnic Institute and State University, Blacksburg.

*Payne, N. F. 1964b. The influence of hunting on rabbit populations in southeastern Virginia. Virginia Journal of Science 15(4):296.

*Payne, N. F. 1975. Range extension of the marsh rabbit in Virginia. Chesapeake Science 16(1):77–78.

*Payne, N. F., B. S. McGinnis and H. S. Mosby. 1987. Capture rates of cottontails, opossums, and other wildlife in unbaited wooden box traps. Virginia Journal of Science 38(1):23–26.

*Payne, R. L., W. P. Maples, and J. F. Smith. 1967. The occurrence of *Oesophagostomum cervi* Mertts, 1948, in white-tailed deer *(Odocoileus virginianus)* of the southeastern United States. Journal of Parasitology 53(4):691.

*Peacock, R., and D. Peacock. 1961. The harvest mouse in northern Virginia. Journal of Mammalogy 42(4):543–544.

*Peacock, D. B. 1967. Some notes on Virginia and North Carolina mammals. Journal of the Washington Academy of Science 57:242–244.

*Peacock, D. B., and R. Peacock. 1962. *Peromyscus maniculatus bairdii* in Virginia. Journal of Mammalogy 43(1):98.

Pearson, A. M., and J. E. Herbert. 1940. Sly B'rer fox has many entrances to his den. Alabama Conservation 1(2):9.

Pearson, O. P. 1942. On the cause and nature of a poisonous action produced by the bite of a shrew *(Blarina brevicauda)*. Journal of Mammalogy 23(2): 159–166.

*Pearson, O. P. 1944. Reproduction in the shrew (*Blarina brevicauda* Say). American Journal of Anatomy 75:39–93.

Pearson, O. P. 1947. The rate of metabolism of some small mammals. Ecology 28(2):127–145.

Pearson, O. P. 1956. A toxic substance from the salivary glands of a mammal (short-tailed shrew). Pp. 55–58. In: Buckley, E. E. (editor), Venoms. Washington, D. C.: American Association for the Advancement of Science.

Pearson, O. P. 1963. History of two local outbreaks of feral house mice. Ecology 44(3):540–549.

Pearson, P. G. 1952. Observations concerning the life history and ecology of the woodrat, *Neotoma floridana floridana* (Ord). Journal of Mammalogy 33(4):459–463.

Pearson, P. G. 1953. A field study of *Peromyscus* populations in Gulf Hammock, Florida. Ecology 34(1): 199–207.

Pearson, P. G. 1954. Mammals of Gulf Hammock, Levy County, Florida. American Midland Naturalist 51(2):468–480.

*Peden, W. (editor), 1955 (1787). Notes on the State of Virginia. Chapel Hill: University of North Carolina Press..

*Peery, C. H. 1948. Breeding potentialities of the gray squirrel at Blacksburg, Virginia. Master's thesis, Virginia Polytechnic Institute and State University, Blacksburg.

*Peery, C. H. 1949. Poor Valley — rich in wildlife. Virginia Wildlife 10(10):19–21.

*Peery, C. H. 1953. A look at southwest Virginia's deer herd. Virginia Wildlife 14(12):20–21.

*Peery, C. H. 1963. We are in business on Clinch Mountain. Virginia Wildlife 24(6):10–11.

*Peery, C. H. 1968. The economics of Virginia's deer transplantation program. Proceedings of the 22d Annual Conference of the Southeastern Association of Game and Fish Commissioners 22:142–144.

*Peery, C. H. 1969. Odd adventures out-of-doors. Virginia Wildlife 30(2):19.

*Peery, C. H. 1970. Deer take the high road. Virginia Wildlife 31(9):8.

*Peery, C. H., and J. Coggin. 1978. Virginia's white-tailed deer. Richmond: Virginia Commission of Game and Inland Fisheries.

*Pelton, M. R. 1982. Black bear. Pp. 504–514. In: Chapman, J. A., and G. A. Feldhamer (editors), Wild mammals of North America. Baltimore: The Johns Hopkins University Press.

*Pelton, M. R., and R. G. Nichols. 1972. Status of the black bear *(Ursus americanus)* in the Southeast. Pp. 18–23. In: Miller, R. (editor), Proceedings of the 1972 Black Bear Conference. Delmar: New York State Department of Environmental Conservation.

*Pelton, M. R., and R. H. Conley, chairmen. 1974. Second eastern workshop on black bear management and research. Project W-46-R, Tennessee Wildlife Resources Agency and University of Tennessee, Knoxville.

Pelton, M. R., and E. E. Provost. 1972. Onset of breeding and breeding synchrony by Georgia cottontails. Journal of Wildlife Management 36:544–549.

*Percy, A. 1950. The Appalachian Trail in Virginia. Virginia Wildlife 11(5):5–7.

*Perdue, W. M. 1963. The bear and I. Virginia Wildlife 24(12):16–17.

Perrin, W. F., and S. B. Reilly. 1984. Reproductive parameters of dolphins and small whales of the family Delphinidae. Pp. 97–133. In: Perrin, W. F., R. L. Brownell, Jr., and D. P. DeMaster (editors), Reproduction in whales, dolphins and porpoises. Report of the International Whaling Commission, Special Issue no. 6.

*Perry, B. D., N. Garner, S. R. Jenkins, K. McCloskey, and D. H. Johnston. 1989. A study of techniques for the distribution of oral rabies vaccine to wild raccoon populations. Journal of Wildlife Diseases 25(2):206–217.

*Perry, B. D., D. K. Nichols, and E. S. Cullom. 1985. *Babesia odocoilei* Emerson and Wright, 1970 in white-tailed deer, *Odocoileus virginianus* (Zimmermann), in Virginia. Journal of Wildlife Diseases 21(2):149–152.

*Perry, H. R., Jr. 1982. Muskrats. Pp. 282–325. In: Chapman, J. A., and G. A. Feldhamer (editors), Wild mammals of North America. Baltimore: The Johns Hopkins University Press.

*Perry, M. C. 1970. Studies of deer-related dog activity in Virginia. Master's thesis, Virginia Polytechnic Institute and State University, Blacksburg.

*Perry, M. C. 1971a. Spring fawn hunt. Virginia Wildlife 32(5):6–7.

*Perry, M. C. 1971b. University maternity ward. Virginia Wildlife 32(6):18–19.

*Perry, M. C., and R. H. Giles, Jr. 1970. Studies of deer-related dog activity in Virginia. Proceedings of the 24th Annual Conference of the Southeastern Association of Game and Fish Commissioners 24:64–73.

*Perry, M. C., and R. H. Giles, Jr. 1971. Free running dogs. Virginia Wildlife 32(5):17–19.

*Petcher, R. L. 1967. A population study of a confined deer herd. Master's thesis, Virginia Polytechnic Institute and State University, Blacksburg.

*Petersen, K. E., and T. L. Yates. 1980. *Condylura cristata.* Mammalian Species no. 129.

*Peterson, R. L., and S. C. Downing. 1952. Notes on the bobcats *(Lynx rufus)* of eastern North America with the description of a new race. Contributions of the Royal Ontario Museum of Zoology and Palaeontology 33:1–23.

*Petrides, G. A. 1944. A gall insect food of the gray squirrel. Journal of Mammalogy 25(4):410.

Petrides, G. A. 1949. Sex and age determination in the opossum. Journal of Mammalogy 30(4):364–378.

*Pettis, J. P. 1978. The influence of temperature and season on heat production and heart rates of adult gray squirrels. Master's thesis, Virginia Polytechnic Institute and State University, Blacksburg.

*Pettis, J. P., and C. J. Cowles. 1978. Gray squirrel. Endangered species model. Virginia Wildlife 39(2):4–5.

*Pfeiffer, C. J. 1992. Cellular structure of terminal baleen in various mysticete species. Aquatic Mammalogy 18(3):67–73.

*Phelps, C. F. 1947a. The big five upland game animals in Virginia. Virginia Wildlife 8(2):12–14, 17.

*Phelps, C. F. 1947b. The beaver. Virginia Wildlife 8(9):5–6, 20.

*Phelps, C. F. 1950. Captive game. Virginia Wildlife 11(7):10–12.

*Phelps, C. F. 1951. A report on the 1950–51 deer season. Virginia Wildlife 12(3):12.

*Phelps, C. F. 1952. A report on the 1951–52 deer, bear and turkey kill. Virginia Wildlife 13(4):18–20.

*Phelps, C. F. 1953. A report: The 1952–53 deer, bear and turkey kill. Virginia Wildlife 14(4):22,26.

*Phelps, C. F. 1954. Deer, bear, and turkey kill for 1953–54. Virginia Wildlife 15(4):13.

*Phelps, C. F. 1956. Virginia's deer, bear and turkey kill for 1955–56. Virginia Wildlife 17(4):13.

*Phelps, C. F. 1957. Virginia's deer, bear and turkey kill for 1956–57. Virginia Wildlife 18(5):21.

*Phelps, C. F. 1958. Virginia's deer herd increasing. Virginia Wildlife 19(5):20–21.

*Phelps, C. F. 1964a. An appraisal of Virginia's wildlife resources. Virginia Wildlife 25(6):4–5, 20–21.

*Phelps, C. F. 1964b. Wildlife management on Virginia military areas. Virginia Wildlife 25(8):4–5, 20–21.

Phillips, G. L. 1966. Ecology of the big brown bat (Chiroptera: Vespertilionidae) in northeastern Kansas. American Midland Naturalist 75(1):168–198.

Pianka, E. R. 1976. Natural selection of optimal reproductive tactics. American Zoologist 16:775–784.

*Pierce, G. W., and D. R. Griffin. 1938. Experimental determination of supersonic notes emitted by bats. Journal of Mammalogy 19(4):454–455.

*Pierce, R. M. 1979. Seasonal feeding habits of the river otter *(Lutra canadensis)* in ditches of the Great Dismal Swamp. Master's thesis, Old Dominion University, Norfolk.

*Piers, H. 1923. Accidental occurrence of the pygmy sperm whale *(Kogia breviceps)* on the coast of Nova Scotia: an extension of its known range; with remarks on the probability of the former presence in these waters of the true sperm whale *(Physeter macrocephalus).* Proceedings and Transactions of the Nova Scotian Institute of Science, Halifax 15:95–114.

*Pilcher, A. (editor), 1967. Youth afield (picture). Virginia Wildlife 28(1):23.

*Pilcher, A. (editor), 1968. Hunter bags bobcat. Virginia Wildlife 29(4):23.

*Pilcher, A. (editor), 1969a. Youth afield. Virginia Wildlife 30(2):25.

*Pilcher, A. (editor), 1969b. Fox trophy for a deer hunter. Virginia Wildlife 30(3):23.

*Pilcher, A. (editor), 1969c. Youth afield. Virginia Wildlife 30(7):25.

*Pilcher, A. (editor), 1970a. Bullpasture buck. Virginia Wildlife 31(3):25.

*Pilcher, A. (editor), 1970b. Novices and veteran report hunting success. Virginia Wildlife 31(5):25.

*Pilcher, A. (editor), 1971a. Youth afield. Virginia Wildlife 32(4):25.

*Pilcher, A. (editor), 1971b. Pretty rack. Virginia Wildlife 32(5):25.

*Pilcher, A. (editor), 1971c. Coyotes cause consternation. Virginia Wildlife 32(7):25.

*Pilcher, A. (editor), 1971d. After-school trapline yield. Virginia Wildlife 32(7):25.

*Pilcher, A. (editor), 1972. Youth afield. Virginia Wildlife 33(4):25.

*Pilcher, A. (editor), 1973. Hunting season a real success. Virginia Wildlife 34(2):25.

Pils, C. M. 1965. Late fall and early winter foods of the gray fox *(Urocyon cinereoargenteus)* in southern Illi-

nois. Master's thesis, Southern Illinois University, Carbondale.
*Pinkerton, J. 1819. A general collection of the best and most interesting voyages and travels in all parts of the world. 12 volumes.
Piper, D. 1909. The Nevada mouse plague of 1907–1908. United States Department of Agriculture Farmer's Bulletin no. 352.
*Pistole, D. H., and J. A. Cranford. 1982. Photoperiodic effects on growth in *Microtus pennsylvanicus.* Journal of Mammalogy 63(4):547–553.
*Pitts, R. M., and G. L. Kirkland, Jr. 1987. A record of the prairie deer mouse *(Peromyscus maniculatus bairdii)* from Rockbridge County, Virginia. Proceedings of the Pennsylvania Academy of Science 61(2):205.
Pitts, T. D. 1991. Reproduction of southern flying squirrels *(Glaucomys volans)* in Weakley County, Tennessee. Journal of the Tennessee Academy of Science 66(2):71. Abstract.
Polderboer, E. B., L. W. Kuhn, and G. O. Hendrickson. 1941. Winter and spring habits of weasels in central Iowa. Journal of Wildlife Management 5(1):115–119.
Pollack, E. M. 1950. Breeding habits of the bobcat in northeastern United States. Journal of Mammalogy 31(3):327–330.
Pollack, E. M. 1951. Observations on New England bobcats. Journal of Mammalogy 32(3):356–358.
*Poole, A. J., and V. S. Schantz. 1942. Catalog of the type specimens of mammals in the United States National Museum, including the Biological Surveys collection. United States National Museum Bulletin 178.
*Poole, E. L. 1932. A survey of the mammals of Berks County, Pennsylvania. Reading Public Museum and Art Gallery Bulletin 13.
*Poole, E. L. 1940. A life history sketch of the Allegheny woodrat. Journal of Mammalogy 21(3):249–270.
*Poole, E. L. 1943. *Synaptomys cooperi stonei* from the eastern shore of Maryland. Journal of Mammalogy 24(1):103.
*Poole, E. L. 1944. The technical names of the northeastern fox squirrels. Journal of Mammalogy 25(3):315–317.
*Poole, E. L. 1949. A second Pennsylvania specimen of *Lasiurus seminolus* (Rhoads). Journal of Mammalogy 30(1):80.
*Pope, R. E. 1965. Letters. Biggest groundhog. Virginia Wildlife 26(6):3.
*Porter, J. H. 1988. Mice in motion:dispersal in two species of *Peromyscus.* Doctoral dissertation, University of Virginia, Charlottesville.
Porter, J. H., and R. D. Dueser. 1982. Niche overlap and competition in an insular small mammal fauna: a test of the niche overlap hypothesis. Oikos 39(2):228–236.
Porter, J. H., and R. D. Dueser. 1986. A test for suppression of body growth and sexual maturity in small male meadow voles *(Microtus pennsylvanicus)* in field enclosures. American Midland Naturalist 115(1):181–190.
Porter, J. H., and R. D. Dueser. 1988. Mice in motion: immigration and social resistance in *Peromyscus* populations. Bulletin of the Ecological Society of America Supplement 69(2):263–264.
*Porter, J. H., and R. D. Dueser. 1989. A comparison of methods for measuring small-mammal dispersal by use of a Monte-Carlo simulation model. Journal of Mammalogy 70(4):783–793.
Porter, S. C. (editor). 1983. Late-Quaternary Environments of the United States: Volume I — The Late Pleistocene. Minneapolis: University of Minnesota Press.
*Porterfield, T. R. 1970. Effects of season and plane of nutrition upon serum lipids and protein of white-tailed deer. Master's thesis, Virginia Polytechnic Institute and State University, Blacksburg.
*Potkay, S. 1970. Diseases of the opossum *(Didelphis marsupialis):* a review. Laboratory Animal Care 20(3):502–511.
*Potter, C. W. 1979. The marine fauna. Pp. 595–602. In: Linzey, D. W. (editor), Proceedings of the Symposium on Endangered and Threatened Plants and Animals of Virginia. Virginia Polytechnic Institute and State University, Blacksburg.
*Potter, C. W. 1991. Marine mammals. Pp. 603–607. In: Terwilliger, K. (coordinator). Virginia's endangered species. Blacksburg: The McDonald & Woodward Publishing Company.
*Poughkeepsie, H. E. 1875. Editorial. Forest and Stream 5(11):167.
Pournelle, G. H. 1952. Reproduction and early post-natal development of the cotton mouse, *Peromyscus gossypinus gossypinus.* Journal of Mammalogy 33(1):1–20.
*Poussin, C., and J. A. Simmons. 1982. Low-frequency hearing sensitivity in the echolocating bat, *Eptesicus fuscus.* Journal of the Acoustical Society of America 72(2):340–342.
*Poux, R. J., Jr. 1972. Deer behavior as it effects sex and age ratio counts. Master's thesis, Virginia Polytechnic Institute and State University, Blacksburg.
*Powell, B. H. 1976. Improved techniques for marking, night-viewing, and aging white-tailed deer, *Odocoileus virginianus.* Master's thesis, Old Dominion University, Norfolk.
*Powell, R. A. 1981. *Martes pennanti.* Mammalian Species no. 156.
*Powell, R. A., and W. J. Zielinski. 1989. Mink response to ultrasound in the range emitted by prey. Journal of Mammalogy 70(3):637–638.
*Pratt, H. D., B. F. Bjornson, and K. S. Littig. 1977. Control of domestic rats and mice. United States Department of Health, Education and Welfare Publication no. 77–8141.
*Pratt, H. S. 1935. A manual of land and fresh water vertebrate animals of the United States (exclusive of birds). 2d edition. Philadelphia: P. Blakiston's Son and Company.
*Preble, E. A. 1899. Revision of the jumping mice of the genus *Zapus.* North American Fauna 15.

*Preble, E. A. 1910. A new *Microsorex* from the vicinity of Washington, D. C. Proceedings of the Biological Society of Washington 23:101–102.

*Prestwood, A. K. 1971. Cestodes of white-tailed deer *(Odocoileus virginianus)* in the southeastern United States. Journal of Parasitology 57(6):1292.

*Prestwood, A. K., F. A. Hayes, J. H. Eve, and J. F. Smith. 1973. Abomasal helminths of white-tailed deer in southeastern United States, Texas, and the Virgin Islands. Journal of the American Veterinary Medical Association 163(6):556–561.

*Prestwood, A. K., T. P. Kistner, F. E. Kellogg, and F. A. Hayes. 1974. The 1971 outbreak of hemorrhagic disease among white-tailed deer of the southeastern United States. Journal of Wildlife Diseases 10(3):217–224.

*Prestwood, A. K., V. F. Nettles, and F. E. Kellogg. 1974. Distribution of muscleworm, *Parelaphostrongylus andersoni,* among white-tailed deer of the southeastern United States. Journal of Wildlife Diseases 10(4):404–409.

*Prestwood, A. K., and T. R. Ridgeway. 1972. Elaeophorosis in white-tailed deer of the southeastern U.S.A.: case report and distribution. Journal of Wildlife Diseases 8(3):233–236.

*Prestwood, A. K., and J. F. Smith. 1969. Distribution of meningeal worm *(Pneumostrongylus tenuis)* in deer in the southeastern United States. Journal of Parasitology 55(4):720–725.

*Prestwood, A. K., J. F. Smith, and J. Brown. 1971. Lungworms in white-tailed deer of the southeastern United States. Journal of Wildlife Diseases 7(2):149–154.

*Prestwood, A. K., J. F. Smith, and W. E. Mahan. 1970. Geographic distribution of *Gongylonema pulchrum, Gongylonema verrucosum,* and *Paramphistomum liorchis* in white-tailed deer of the southeastern United States. Journal of Parasitology 56(1):123–127.

*Price, E. W. 1928. Two new nematode worms from rodents. Proceedings of the United States National Museum 74(2749):1–5.

*Price, J. 1976. Mountain Lake: a feeling of wilderness. Virginia Wildlife 37(6):10–11, 24.

*Price, S. 1975. Whitetail. Virginia Wildlife 36(5):17–18.

*Priest, W. I. 1929. A hunting trip in Loudoun County. Game and Fish Conservationist 8(6):139.

Priewert, F. W. 1961. Record of an extensive movement by a raccoon. Journal of Mammalogy 42(1):113.

Pringle, L. P. 1960. A study of the biology and ecology of the New England cottontail, *Sylvilagus transitionalis.* Progress report. Proceedings of the Northeast Section of the Wildlife Society, Annual Conference, Providence, Rhode Island. Mimeographed.

*Prior, E. T. 1969. A study of rabies incidence in western Virginia. Master's thesis, Virginia Polytechnic Institute and State University, Blacksburg.

*Prior, E. T., and R. H. Giles, Jr. 1974. A study of rabies in southwestern Virginia. Virginia Wildlife 35(7):21.

*Progulske, D. R. 1952a. Parasites and diseases — a probable check on bobcat populations. Virginia Journal of Science 3(2):296–297. Abstract.

*Progulske, D. R. 1952b. The bobcat and its relation to prey species in Virginia. Master's thesis, Virginia Polytechnic Institute and State University, Blacksburg.

*Progulske, D. R. 1955a. Game animals utilized as food by the bobcat in the southern Appalachians. Journal of Wildlife Management 19(2):249–253.

*Progulske, D. R. 1955b. How serious is the bobcat in Virginia? Virginia Wildlife 16(5):18–20.

Provo, M. M. 1957. The annual cycle of the cotton rat, *Sigmodon hispidus* (Say and Ord). 51 pages. Typescript, in files at University of Georgia.

*Pupek, D. 1997. Big-eared bat bounces back. Endangered Species Bulletin 22(3):12-13.

*Purchas, S. 1625. His pilgrimes. Volume IV, page 1765.

*Pursglove, S. R., A. K. Prestwood, V. F. Nettles, and F. A. Hayes. 1976. Intestinal nematodes of white-tailed deer in southeastern United States. Journal of the American Veterinary Medical Association 169(9): 896–900.

*Puscheck, L. 1987. Tularemia in Virginia. Epidemiology Bulletin 87(9):1-3.

Quick, H. F. 1944. Habits and economics of the New York weasel in Michigan. Journal of Wildlife Management 8(1):71–78.

*Quigley, B. 1996. Slaughter hungering panthers are seldom seen, but often discussed. Virginia Explorer 12(2):19–21.

*Quillen, J. H., Jr. 1959a. Deer density and distribution in relation to natural and management modified environmental factors. Master's thesis, Virginia Polytechnic Institute and State University, Blacksburg.

*Quillen, J. H., Jr. 1959b. Effect of forestry practices and wildlife management on abundance and distribution of deer. Virginia Journal of Science 10(2):262. Abstract.

Quimby, D. C. 1951. The life history and ecology of the jumping mouse, *Zapus hudsonius.* Ecological Monographs 21:61–95.

*Quinn, D. B. (editor), 1967. George Percy — observations gathered out of "A Discourse of the Plantation of the Southern Colony in Virginia by the English, 1606." Charlottesville: University Press of Virginia.

*Quinn, I. T. 1953. The battle for wildlife. Virginia Wildlife 14(12):10–12.

*Quisenberry, J. 1939. The value of wildlife to Augusta County. Virginia Wildlife 2(11):7.

*Quortrup, E. R. 1946. Tumors of deer. Virginia Wildlife 7(1):15, 18.

*R. F. B. 1878. The mountainous region of Virginia. Forest and Stream 11(2):33. August 15, 1878.

*R. M. C. 1961. The T. M. Gathright wildlife management area. Virginia Wildlife 22(12):16.

Rabinowitz, A. R., and M. D. Tuttle. 1982. A test of the validity of two currently used methods of determining bat prey preferences. Acta Theriologica 27:283–293.

*Rageot, R. H. 1955. A new northernmost record of the yellow bat, *Dasypterus floridanus*. Journal of Mammalogy 36(3):456.

*Rageot, R. H. 1957. Predation on small mammals in the Dismal Swamp, Virginia. Journal of Mammalogy 38(2):281.

Rainey, D. G. 1956. Eastern woodrat, *Neotoma floridana:* life history and ecology. University of Kansas Publication, Museum of Natural History 8(10):535–646.

*Ralls, K., and P. H. Harvey. 1985. Geographic variation in size and sexual dimorphism of North American weasels. Biological Journal of the Linnean Society 25(2):119–167.

*Ramer, G. A. 1971. Wasted wildlife. Virginia Wildlife 32(7):3.

*Randolph, M. J. 1964. The sly ones. Virginia Wildlife 25(6):6–8.

*Rathbun, G. B., R. K. Bonde, and D. Clay. 1982. The status of the West Indian manatee on the Atlantic coast north of Florida. Pp. 152–165. In: Odom, R. R., and J. W. Guthrie (editors), Proceedings of the Symposium on Nongame and Endangered Wildlife, Georgia Department of Natural Resources, Game and Fish Division, Technical Bulletin W15.

Rawley, E. 1954. Additional evidence provided on beaver longevity. Utah Fish and Game Bulletin 10(7):2, 5, 6.

*Ray, C. E., B. N. Cooper, and W. S. Benninghoff. 1967. Fossil mammals and pollen in a late Pleistocene deposit at Saltville, Virginia. Journal of Paleontology 41(3):608–622.

*Raybourne, J. W. 1972. Operation black bear. Virginia Wildlife 33(12):6–7.

*Raybourne, J. W. 1974. In search of the bear facts. Virginia Wildlife 35(6):20–21.

*Raybourne, J. W. 1977. A study of black bear populations in Virginia. Transactions of the Northeast Section of the Wildlife Society 33:71–81.

*Raybourne, J. W., and J. E. Thornton. 1973. Doe deer and apple pie. Virginia Wildlife 34(1):4–5.

*Rayburn, E. B. 1972. A measure of the natural potential of land for supporting deer populations. Master's thesis, Virginia Polytechnic Institute and State University, Blacksburg.

*Redd, J. B., Jr. 1956a. Live trapping as a technique of estimating rabbit abundance. Virginia Journal of Science 7(2):284. Abstract.

*Redd, J. B., Jr. 1956b. Abundance and distribution of the cottontail rabbit as affected by land use. Master's thesis, Virginia Polytechnic Institute and State University, Blacksburg.

*Redd, J. B., Jr. 1956c. A closer look at the cottontail rabbit. Virginia Wildlife 17(12):18–19, 25.

*Redd, J. B., Jr. 1957. What about the San Juan rabbit? Virginia Wildlife 18(4):18–20.

*Redington, B. C. 1970 (1971). Studies on the morphology and taxonomy of *Haemogamasus reidi* Ewing, 1925 (Acari: Mesostigmata). Acarologia 12(4):643–667.

*Reed, E. T. 1974. Effects of fall orphaning on white-tailed deer fawns. Master's thesis, Virginia Polytechnic Institute and State University, Blacksburg.

*Reed, E. T., B. S. McGinnes, and B. N. Reed. 1974. Parturition site in relation to subsequent home range of white-tailed deer fawns. Virginia Journal of Science 25(2):68. Abstract.

*Reeves, J. H., Jr. 1958. Precolonial game conditions in Virginia. Virginia Journal of Science 9(2):390–391. Abstract.

*Reeves, J. H., Jr. 1960. The history and development of wildlife conservation in Virginia: a critical review. Doctoral dissertation, Virginia Polytechnic Institute and State University, Blacksburg..

*Reich, L. M. 1981. *Microtus pennsylvanicus*. Mammalian Species no. 159.

Reidinger, R. F., Jr. 1972. Factors influencing Arizona bat population levels. Doctoral dissertation, University of Arizona, Tucson.

*Reid-Sanden, F. L., J. G. Dobbins, J. S. Smith, and D. B. Fishbein. 1990. Rabies surveillance in the United States during 1989. Journal of the American Veterinary Medical Association 197(12):1571–1583.

*Reilly, V. 1958. Virginia meets the rabid fox problem. Virginia Wildlife 19(2):22–24.

Reimer, J. D., and M. L. Petras. 1967. Breeding structure of the house mouse, *Mus musculus*, in a population cage. Journal of Mammalogy 48(1):88–99.

*Repine, J. 1969. Mr. Ringtail. Virginia Wildlife 30(1):21.

*Report of the American Bison Society, 1927–1928–1929–1930. 1931. New York: American Bison Society.

*Reshetiloff, K. 1995. Endangered Florida manatee returns to mid-Atlantic region. Bay Journal 5(6):16,13.

*Reshetiloff, K. 1997. Let's not leave Delmarva fox squirrel out on a limb. Bay Journal 7(9):24, 23.

*Reynard. 1889. Capturing a whale. American Field 31(9):196–198.

*Reynolds, B. D. 1938. *Brachylaemus peromysci* n. sp. (Trematoda) from the deer mouse. Journal of Parasitology 24(3):245–248.

*Reynolds, H. W., R. D. Glaholt, and A. W. L. Hawley. 1982. Bison. Pp. 972–1007. In: Chapman, J. A., and G. A. Feldhamer (editors), Wild mammals of North America. Baltimore: The Johns Hopkins University Press.

*Reynolds, J. E., III and D. K. Odell. 1991. Manatees and dugongs. New York: Facts on File.

*Reynolds, R. J., and M. Fies. 1993. Some demographic features of northern flying squirrels *(Glaucomys sabrinus)* in Virginia. Virginia Journal of Science 44(2):113. Abstract.

*Rhoads, S. N. 1894. A contribution to the life history of the Allegheny cave rat, *Neotoma magister* Baird. Proceedings of the Philadelphia Academy of Natural Sciences:213–221.

*Rhoads, S. N. 1903. The mammals of Pennsylvania and New Jersey. Philadelphia: privately published.

*Rhoads, S. N. and R. T. Young. 1897. Notes on a collection of small mammals from northeastern North

Carolina. Proceedings of the Philadelphia Academy of Natural Sciences:303–312.

*Rhoads, S. 1972. Letters. Virginia Wildlife 33(4):3.

*Rhoads, S. 1979. Scouting for whitetails. Virginia Wildlife 40(10):20–21.

Rice, D. W. 1957. Life history and ecology of *Myotis austroriparius* in Florida. Journal of Mammalogy 38(1):15–32.

Rice, D. W. 1977. A list of the marine mammals of the world. 3rd edition. United States National Marine Fisheries Service, NOAA Technical Report, NMFS SSRF-711.

Rice, D. W. 1978. Beaked whales. Pp. 88–95. In: Haley, D. (editor), Marine mammals of eastern North Pacific and Arctic waters. Seattle: Pacific Search Press.

Rice, D. W. 1989. Sperm whale. Pp. 177–233. In: Ridgway, S. H., and S. R. Harrison (editors), Handbook of marine mammals. Volume 4. River dolphins and the larger toothed whales. New York: Academic Press.

*Richards, E. V. 1950. Wasted wildlife. Virginia Wildlife 11(4):16–17, 22.

*Richards, E. V. 1951. The Massanutten Mountains. Virginia Wildlife 12(12):10–11, 20.

*Richards, E. V. 1953a. Highlights of Virginia's 1952 deer study. Virginia Wildlife 14(10):18–19, 22.

*Richards, E. V. 1953b. Virginia's black bear — good or bad? Virginia Wildlife 16–17, 21, 23.

*Richards, E. V. 1955. Whitetails at North River. Virginia Wildlife 16(7):20–21.

*Richards, E. V. 1956. More forest game. Virginia Wildlife 17(1):16–18.

*Richards, E. V. 1957. Some bear facts. Virginia Wildlife 18(3):8–10.

*Richards, E. V. 1968. Should we manage the black bear? Virginia Wildlife 29(3):8–9.

*Richardson, J. 1829. Fauna boreali Americana: or the zoology of the northern parts of British America:.... London: John Murray.

*Richardson, J. I. 1973. A confirmed occurrence of the rough-toothed dolphin *(Steno bredanensis)* on the Atlantic coast of the United States. Journal of Mammalogy 54(1):275.

*Richmond, N. D., and W. C. Grimm. 1950. Ecology and distribution of the shrew *Sorex dispar* in Pennsylvania. Ecology 31:279–282.

*Ridgway, S. H. 1966. Studies on diving depth and duration in *Tursiops truncatus.* Proceedings of the 3d Annual Conference on Biological Sonar and Diving Mammals:151–158.

Ritzler-Old, C., and T. L. Derting. 1990. *Microtus pennsylvanicus* and *M. pinetorum* densities and differential responsiveness to a terrestrial predator model. Virginia Journal of Science 41(2):59. Abstract.

*Robertson, A. W. 1928. Some hunting experiences and observations. Game and Fish Conservationist 8(4):85–87.

*Robertson, A. W. 1929. The attitude of colonial Virginia toward wild life conservation. Game and Fish Conservationist 9(3):50–51.

*Robertson, A. W. 1931. Survey of wild life conservation in Virginia. Game and Fish Conservationist 10(6):105–106, 120.

*Robertson, J. T. 1931. Building up the Virginia deer herd. Game and Fish Conservationist 11(4):75–77, 82.

*Robinson, D. E., and E. D. Brodie, Jr. 1982. Food hoarding behavior in the short-tailed shrew *Blarina brevicauda.* American Midland Naturalist 108(2):369–375.

*Robinson, S. S., and D. S. Lee. 1980. Recent range expansion of the groundhog, *Marmota monax,* in the Southeast (Mammalia: Rodentia). Brimleyana 3:43–48.

*Robinson, W. 1923. Woodchucks and chipmunks. Journal of Mammalogy 4(4):256–257.

Robinson, W. B., and E. F. Grand. 1958. Comparative movements of bobcats and coyotes as disclosed by tagging. Journal of Wildlife Management 22(2):117–122.

Robinson, W. L., and J. B. Falls. 1965. A study of homing of meadow mice. American Midland Naturalist 73:188–224.

*Roe, F. G. 1970. The North American buffalo. A critical study of the species in its wild state. 2d edition. Toronto: University of Toronto Press.

*Rogers, C. 1964. The fox and the fish. Virginia Wildlife 25(5):10.

Rogers, L. L. 1987. Navigation by adult black bears. Journal of Mammalogy 68(1):185–188.

*Rolston, H., III. 1968. Mystery and majesty in Washington County. Virginia Wildlife 29(11):6–7, 22–23.

Rongstad, O. J. 1969. Gross prenatal development of cottontail rabbits. Journal of Wildlife Management 33(1):164–168.

Rood, J. P. 1966. Observations on the reproduction of *Peromyscus* in captivity. American Midland Naturalist 76(2):496–503.

*Roosevelt, T. 1893. The wilderness hunter. New York: G. P. Putnam's Sons.

*Roosevelt, T., T. S. Van Dyke, D. G. Elliot, and A. J. Stone. 1902. The deer family. New York: Macmillan Company.

*Roper, L. J. 1948. Tularemia spells rabbit fever. Virginia Wildlife 9(12):10–11.

Roper, R. A. 1971. The application of biotelemetry to field studies of the cotton rat. Doctoral dissertation, Auburn University, Auburn, Alabama.

*Rorabacher, J. A. 1970. The American buffalo in transition: a historical and economic survey of the bison in America. Saint Cloud, Minnesota: North Star Press.

*Rose, R. K. 1979. Levels of wounding in the meadow vole, *Microtus pennsylvanicus.* Journal of Mammalogy 60(1):37–45.

*Rose, R. K. 1981a. *Synaptomys* not extinct in the Dismal Swamp. Journal of Mammalogy 62(4):844–845.

*Rose, R. K. 1981b. Dismal Swamp mammals — past. Virginia Journal of Science 32(3):97. Abstract.

*Rose, R. K. 1981c. Small mammals in openings in Virginia's Dismal Swamp. Brimleyana 6:45–50.

*Rose, R. K. 1982. The southeastern shrew, *Sorex longirostris,* in the Dismal Swamp. Virginia Journal of Science 33(3):118. Abstract.

*Rose, R. K. 1983. A study of two rare mammals endemic to the Virginia/North Carolina Dismal Swamp. Final Report 14–16–0005–81–003, on file with the United States Fish and Wildlife Service.

*Rose, R. K. 1986a. Reproductive strategies of Virginia meadow voles, cotton rats, and harvest mice. Virginia Journal of Science 37(2):71. Abstract.

*Rose, R. K. 1986b. Reproductive strategies of meadow voles, hispid cotton rats, and eastern harvest mice in Virginia. Virginia Journal of Science 37(4):230–239.

*Rose, R. K. 1986c. Late prehistoric and protohistoric large mammal zoogeography of Virginia. Pp. 79–88. In: McDonald, J. N., and S. O. Bird (editors), The Quaternary of Virginia — a symposium volume. Virginia Division of Mineral Resources Publication 75.

*Rose, R. K. l989. The status and distribution of three small mammals endemic to the Great Dismal Swamp of Virginia and North Carolina. Virginia Journal of Science 40(2):58. Abstract.

*Rose, R. K. 1991. The effects of habitat fragmentation and loss on Dismal Swamp mammals. Virginia Journal of Science 42(2):175. Abstract.

*Rose, R. K. 1992. The effects of habitat fragmentation and loss on Dismal Swamp mammals. Virginia Journal of Science 43 (1B):187–196.

*Rose, R. K., and R. D. Dueser. 1978. Patterns of seasonal body growth in temperate meadow voles (*Microtus pennsylvanicus:* Rodentia). Congress Theriologica Internationale 2:45.

*Rose, R. K., and R. D. Dueser. 1980. Lifespan of Virginia meadow voles. Journal of Mammalogy 61(4):760–763.

*Rose, R. K., R. K. Everton, and T. M. Padgett. 1987. The status and distribution of the threatened Dismal Swamp southeastern shrew. Virginia Journal of Science 38(2):87. Abstract.

*Rose, R. K., R. K. Everton, and T. M. Padgett. 1987. Distribution and current status of the threatened Dismal Swamp southeastern shrew, *Sorex longirostris fisheri.* Virginia Journal of Science 38(4):358–363.

*Rose, R. K., R. K. Everton, J. F. Stankovich, and J. W. Walke. 1990. Small mammals in the Great Dismal Swamp of Virginia and North Carolina. Brimleyana 16:87–10l.

*Rose, R. K., and W. D. Hueston. 1978. Wound healing in meadow voles. Journal of Mammalogy 59(1):186–188.

*Rose, R. K., and M. H. Mitchell. 1990. Reproduction in the hispid cotton rat, *Sigmodon hispidus* Say and Ord (Rodentia: Muridae), in southeastern Virginia. Brimleyana 16:43–59.

*Rose, R. K., and T. M. Padgett. 1991. Southeastern Shrew. Pp. 562–564.In: Terwilliger, K., (coordinator). Virginia's endangered species. Blacksburg: The McDonald & Woodward Publishing Company.

*Rose, R. K. and D. H. Thomas. 1995. The small mammal community in forested wetlands of southeastern Virginia as revealed by pitfall trapping studies. Virginia Journal of Science 46(2):97. Abstract.

*Rose, R. K., and J. W. Walke. 1988. Seasonal use of nest boxes by *Peromyscus* and *Ochrotomys* in the Dismal Swamp of Virginia. American Midland Naturalist 120(2):258–267.

*Rose, R. K., and J. Winchell. 1994. Evaluation of the gross anatomy and seasonal changes in a perineal gland in the hispid cotton rat, *Sigmodon hispidus.* Virginia Journal of Science 45(2):62. Abstract.

*Roseberry, T. 1989. Old-timer tricks. Virginia Wildlife 50(10):12–15.

*Ross, A. 1967. Ecological aspects of the food habits of insectivorous bats. Proceedings of the Western Foundation of Vertebrate Zoology 1(4):205–263.

*Rowley, M. A. 1986. The role of terrestrial gastropods in transmission of the meningeal worm *Parelaphostrongylus tenuis* at the National Zoological Park's conservation and research center. Master's thesis, Virginia Commonwealth University, Richmond.

*Rowley, M. A., E. S. Loker, J. F. Pagels, and R. J. Montali. 1987. Terrestrial gastropod hosts of *Parelaphostrongylus tenuis* at the National Zoological Park's Conservation and Research Center, Virginia. Journal of Parasitology 73:1084–1089.

*Ruckel, S. W. 1975. Field evaluation of diethylstilbestrol as a chemosterilant for woodchucks. Master's thesis, Virginia Polytechnic Institute and State University, Blacksburg.

*Ruckel, S. W., P. F. Scanlon, and R. L. Kirkpatrick. 1976. Reproductive characteristics of woodchucks in southwest Virginia. Virginia Journal of Science 27(2):49. Abstract.

*Ruckel, S. W., P. F. Scanlon, R. L. Kirkpatrick, and M. D. Russell. 1976. Influence of season on reproductive characteristics of woodchucks in Virginia. Proceedings of the 30th Annual Conference of the Southeastern Association of Fish and Wildlife Agencies 30:386–391.

Rucker, R. A., M. L. Kennedy, G. A. Heidt, and M. J. Harvey. 1989. Population density, movements, and habitat use of bobcats in Arkansas. The Southwestern Naturalist 34(1):10l–108.

*Rudis, V. A., and J. B. Tansey. 1995. Regional assessment of remote forests and black bear habitat from forest resource surveys. Journal of Wildlife Management 59(1):170–180.

Ruddiman, W. F., and H. E. Wright, Jr. (editors). 1987. The Geology of North America. Volume K-3: North America and Adjacent Oceans During the Last Deglaciation. Denver: Geological Society of America.

*Rudnick, A. 1960. A revision of the mites of the family Spinturnicidae (Acarina). University of California Publications in Entomology 17(2):157–284.

*Rue, L. L., III. 1964. The world of the beaver. Philadelphia: J. B. Lippincott Company.

*Ruedas, L. A., R. C. Dowler, and E. Aita. 1989. Chromosomal variation in the New England cottontail, *Sylvilagus transitionalis.* Journal of Mammalogy 70(4):860–864.

*Ruffin, E. 1837. Observations made during an excursion to the Dismal Swamp. Petersburg (Va.) Farmers' Register 4:513–521.

*Ruggiero, L. F. 1972. Comparison of *in vivo* and *in vitro* dry matter digestion in the white-tailed deer. II. Estimation of fecal output using chromic oxide. Master's thesis, Virginia Polytechnic Institute and State University, Blacksburg.

*Ruggiero, L. F., and D. Ruggiero. 1972. Wildlife campus. Virginia Wildlife 33(8):14–15.

*Ruggiero, L. F., and J. B. Whelan. 1976. A comparison of in vitro and in vivo feed digestibility by white-tailed deer. Journal of Range Management 29(1):82–83.

*Rumsey, R. M. 1968. Letters. Eye-opener. Virginia Wildlife 29(10):3.

*Russ, W. P. 1973. The rare and endangered terrestrial vertebrates of Virginia. Master's thesis, Virginia Polytechnic Institute and State University, Blacksburg.

*Russ, W. P. 1974. Endangered vertebrates of Virginia. Virginia Wildlife 35(9):13–15, 18.

*Russell, J. F. 1967a. Return of the squirrels. Virginia Wildlife 28(6):11.

*Russell, J. F. 1967b. Bird watcher's dividend. Virginia Wildlife 28(8):18.

*Russell, J. F. 1970. The groundhog that came to dinner. Virginia Wildlife 31(2):23.

*Russell, M. D. 1977. Testosterone levels, size characteristics and antler cycles in fawn and yearling white-tailed deer. Master's thesis, Virginia Polytechnic Institute and State University, Blacksburg.

*Russell, M. D., J. A. Wesson, III, R. L. Kirkpatrick, and P. F. Scanlon. 1975. Seasonal and age differences in male reproductive organ weights of white-tailed deer. Virginia Journal of Science 26(2):60. Abstract.

Rust, C. C. 1966. Notes on the star-nosed mole *(Condylura cristata)*. Journal of Mammalogy 47(3): 538.

*Rutherfoord, J. T. 1961. Hickory Lodge. Virginia Wildlife 22(12):16–19.

Ryan, J. M. 1986. Dietary overlap in sympatric populations of pygmy shrews, *Sorex hoyi,* and masked shrews, *Sorex cinereus,* in Michigan. Canadian Field-Naturalist 100(2):225–228.

Ryder, R. A. 1955. Fish predation by the otter in Michigan. Journal of Wildlife Management 19(4):497–498.

Rysgaard, G. N. 1942. A study of the cave bats of Minnesota with especial reference to the large brown bat, *Eptesicus fuscus fuscus* (Beauvois). American Midland Naturalist 28(1):245–267.

*S. B. 1892. Game bag and gun, Nottoway County. Forest and Stream 39:205.

*S. P. L. 1898. A bet and a rabbit chase. Recreation, November, 1898:363.

*Saari, S. 1974. Nature's engineers. Virginia Wildlife 35(2):19–20.

*Saari, S. 1977. Outfoxed. Virginia Wildlife 38(3):6–8.

*Sadler, W. W. 1975. How to hunt . . . old browns. Virginia Wildlife 36(7):25–26.

*Salmon, T. 1736–38. Modern history: or, The present state of all nations. Describing their respective situations, persons, habits, buildings, manners, laws and customs, religion and policy, arts and sciences, trades, manufactures, and husbandry, plants, animals and minerals. Volume 3, Chapter IV. Of the Virginian animals. Pages 339–374. London.

Sample, B. E., and R. C. Whitmore. 1993. Food habits of the endangered Virginia big-eared bat in West Virginia. Journal of Mammalogy 4(2):428–435.

*Samuel, D. E., and B. B. Nelson. 1982. Foxes. Pp. 475–490. In: Chapman, J. A., and G. A. Feldhamer (editors), Wild mammals of North America. Baltimore: The Johns Hopkins University Press.

*Sanders, O. T., Jr. 1971. Sulfur content of deer hair. Master's thesis, Virginia Polytechnic Institute and State University, Blacksburg.

*Sanders, O. T., Jr., and R. L. Kirkpatrick. 1977. Reproductive characteristics and corticoid levels of female white-footed mice fed *ad Libitum* and restricted diets containing a polychlorinated biphenyl. Environmental Research 13:358–363.

Sanderson, G. C. 1951. Breeding habits and a history of the Missouri raccoon population from 1941 to 1948. Transactions of the 16th North American Wildlife Conference:445–461.

Sanderson, G. C. 1961. The reproductive cycle and related phenomena in the raccoon. Doctoral dissertation, University of Illinois, Urbana.

*Sandt, J. L. 1969. The influence of a clearcut area on a confined deer herd in a predominately grassland habitat. Master's thesis, Virginia Polytechnic Institute and State University, Blacksburg.

*Sawyer, S. L. 1983. Homing and ecology in the southern flying squirrel, *Glaucomys volans,* in southeastern Virginia. Master's thesis, Old Dominion University, Norfolk.

*Sawyer, S., and R. K. Rose. 1984. Homing and ecology in the southern flying squirrel, *Glaucomys volans.* Virginia Journal of Science 35(2):88. Abstract.

*Sawyer, S. L., and R. K. Rose. 1985. Homing in and ecology of the southern flying squirrel *Glaucomys volans* in southeastern Virginia. American Midland Naturalist 113(2):238–244.

*Saylor, L. W. 1938. Hairy-tailed mole in Virginia. Journal of Mammalogy 19(2):247.

*Scammon, C. M. 1869. On the cetaceans of the western coast of North America. Proceedings of the Philadelphia Academy of Natural Science:13–63.

Scanlon, J. J., and T. L. Sharik. 1986. Forage energy for white-tailed deer in loblolly pine plantations. Journal of Wildlife Management 50(2):301–306.

*Scanlon, J. J., and M. R. Vaughan. 1983a. Social and spatial ecology of white-tailed deer in Shenandoah National Park, Virginia. Shenandoah National Park Research Paper.

*Scanlon, J. J., and M. R. Vaughan. 1983b. Social grouping of white-tailed deer in Shenandoah National Park, Virginia. Proceedings of the 37th Annual Conference of the Southeastern Association of Fish and Wildlife Agencies 37:146–160.

*Scanlon, J. J., and M. R. Vaughan. 1985a. Relationship between injection point of succinylcholine chloride and time to immobilization for white-tailed deer. Transactions of the Northeast Section of the Wildlife Society 42:219.

*Scanlon, J. J., and M. R. Vaughan. 1985b. Movements of white-tailed deer in Shenandoah National Park, Virginia. Proceedings of the 39th Annual Conference of the Southeastern Association of Fish and Wildlife Agencies 39:396–402.

*Scanlon, P. F. 1974. Abnormalities of mandibles and of limbs in white tailed deer from Virginia. Proceedings of the 27th Annual Conference of the Southeastern Association of Game and Fish Commissioners 27:301–302.

*Scanlon, P. F. 1980. Ecological implications of heavy metal contamination of roadside habitats. Proceedings of the 33rd Annual Conference of the Southeastern Association of Fish and Wildlife Agencies 33:136–145.

*Scanlon, P. F. 1981. Fawning time. Virginia Wildlife 62(5):4–5.

*Scanlon, P. F. 1987. Patterns of embryonic loss in white-tailed deer. Transactions of the 18th Congress of the International Union of Game Biologists Supplement 18:8.

*Scanlon, P. F., R. E. Byers, and M. B. Moss. 1987. Protection of apple trees from mule deer browsing by a soap. Virginia Journal of Science 38(2):63. Abstract.

*Scanlon, P. F., R. J. Kendall, R. L. Lochmiller, II, and R. L. Kirkpatrick. 1983. Lead concentrations in pine voles from two Virginia orchards. Environmental Pollution (Series B) 6:157–160.

*Scanlon, P. F., R. E. Mirarchi, and R. L. Kirkpatrick. 1974. Timing of velvet shedding and antler casting by white-tailed deer in Virginia. Virginia Journal of Science 25(2):68. Abstract.

*Scanlon, P. F., R. E. Mirarchi, and E. T. Reed. 1974. Immobilization of white-tailed deer with succinylcholine chloride. Virginia Journal of Science 25(2):68. Abstract.

*Scanlon, P. F., R. E. Mirarchi, and J. A. Wesson, III. 1977. Aggression toward immobilized white-tailed deer by other deer and elk. Wildlife Society Bulletin 5(4):193–194.

*Scanlon, P. F., A. Oelschlaeger, M. N. Berkaw, R. L. Kirkpatrick, and F. C. Gwazdauskas. 1981. Seasonal influences on reproductive and endocrine characteristics of male cottontail rabbits. Pp. 204–209. In: Myers, K., and C. D. MacInnes (editors), Proceedings of the World Lagomorph Conference, Guelph, Ontario. August, 1979.

Schadler, M. H., and G. M. Butterstein. 1979. Reproduction in the pine vole, *Microtus pinetorum.* Journal of Mammalogy 60(4):841–844.

*Schaffer, G. D., W. R. Davidson, V. F. Nettles, and E. A. Rollor, III. 1981. Helminth parasites of translocated raccoons *(Procyon lotor)* in the southeastern United States. Journal of Wildlife Diseases 17(2):217–227.

Scharf, J. T. 1882. History of western Maryland . . . . 2 volumes. Philadelphia: L. H. Everts.

Scheffer, T. H. 1909. Investigation of the mole. Transactions of the Kansas Academy of Science 23:119–131.

*Scheffer, T. H. 1922. American moles as agricultural pests and fur producers. Farmer's Bulletin no. 1247.

Scheffer, V. B. 1953. Otters diving to a depth of sixty feet. Journal of Mammalogy 34(2):255.

*Scheffer, V. B. 1969. Seals, sea lions, and walruses. A review of the Pinnipedia. Stanford, California: Stanford University Press.

Schevill, W. E., and W. A. Watkins. 1965. Underwater calls of *Trichechus* (manatee) Nature 205:373–374.

*Schiavone, M.V., P. F. Scanlon, and L. M. Borrero-Yu. 1997. Fluoride contents of Virginia white-tailed deer in relation to fluoride related tooth lesions. Virginia Journal of Science 48(2):119. Abstract.

Schmeltz, L. L., and J. O. Whitaker, Jr. 1977. Use of woodchuck burrows by woodchucks and other mammals. Transactions of the Kentucky Academy of Science 38(1–2):79–82.

Schoonmaker, W. J. 1938. Notes on the black bear in New York State. Journal of Mammalogy 19(4):501–502.

*Schorger, A. W. 1944. The validity of *Bison bison pennsylvanicus.* Journal of Mammalogy 25(3):313–315.

Schowalter, D. B., L. D. Harder, and B. H. Treichel. 1978. Age composition of some vespertilionid bats as determined by dental annuli. Canadian Journal of Zoology 56:355–358.

*Schreckengast, G. E. 1988. River otter reintroductions in West Virginia. Master's thesis, West Virginia University, Morgantown.

Schug, M. D., S. H. Vessey, and A. I. Korytko. 1990. Seasonal survivorship and its effects on longevity in a population of white-footed mice *(Peromyscus leucopus).* Ohio Journal of Science 90(2):1.

Schug, M. D., S. H. Vessey, and A. I. Korytko. 1991. Longevity and survival in a population of white-footed mice *(Peromyscus leucopus).* Journal of Mammalogy 72(2):360–366.

Schultz, V. 1955. Status of the coyote and related forms in Tennessee. Journal of the Tennessee Academy of Science 30(1):44–46.

*Schultz, V., and M. A. Byrd. 1957. An analysis of covariance of cottontail rabbit population data. Journal of Wildlife Management 21(3):315–319.

*Schwab, D. 1986. Study of simulated deer browse on soybeans and observations of white-tailed deer usage of soybean fields in southeastern Virginia. Paper presented to North Eastern Deer Study Group. . In: Virginia Wildlife Investigations Annual Report, July 1, 1985–June 30, 1986:154–172.

*Schwab, D. 1987. Virginia's whitetails. Damage. Virginia Wildlife 48(11):24–27.

*Schwab, D. 1990. Swampwitches. Virginia Wildlife 51(3):13–14.

*Schwab, D., and M. Fies. 1990. Relocation of the southern fox squirrel *(Sciurus niger niger)* in southeastern

Virginia. Page 1. In: Edwards, J. W. et al. (editors). First Symposium on Southeastern Fox Squirrels. Virginia Museum of Natural History. Abstract.

*Schwartz, A. 1956. A new subspecies of the longtail shrew (*Sorex dispar* Batchelder) from the southern Appalachian mountains. Journal of the Elisha Mitchell Scientific Society 72:24–30.

*Schwartz, A., and E. P. Odum. 1957. The woodrats of the eastern United States. Journal of Mammalogy 38(2):197–206.

*Schwartz, B. 1928. The occurrence of larval tapeworms in the liver, spleen, kidneys, omentum and heart of a squirrel *(Sciurus carolinensis)*. Journal of Parasitology 15:67.

*Schwartz, C. W., and E. R. Schwartz. 1981. The wild mammals of Missouri. 2d edition. Columbia: University of Missouri Press.

Schwarz, E., and H. K. Schwarz. 1943. The wild and commensal stocks of the house mouse, *Mus musculus* Linnaeus. Journal of Mammalogy 24(1):59–72.

*Schwede, G. 1991. Some behavioral aspects of the fawning season in white-tailed deer *(Odocoileus virginianus)*. Ph.D. dissertation, University of Bielefeld, Germany.

*Schwede, G., H. Hendrichs, and C. Wemmer. 1994a. Early mother-young relations in white-tailed deer. Journal of Mammalogy 75(2):438–445.

*Schwede, G., H. Hendrichs, and C. Wemmer. 1994b. Sibling relations in young white-tailed deer fawns *Odocoileus virginianus*. Mammalia 58(2):175–181.

*Schwede, G., and S. Holzenbein. 1991. Aspects of sparring in white-tailed deer. Applied Animal Behaviour Science 29(1–4):506–507. Abstract.

*Schwede, G., S. Holzenbein, and H. Hendrichs. 1990. Sparring in white-tailed deer *(Odocoileus virginianus)*. Zeitschrift fur Saugetierkunde 55(5):331–339.

*Scott, D. E. 1983. Habitat utilization by two small mammal species: what is the role of competition? Master's thesis, University of Virginia, Charlottesville.

*Scott, D. E., and R. D. Dueser, 1992. Habitat use by insular populations of *Mus* and *Peromyscus:* What is the role of competition? Journal of Animal Ecology 61(2):329–338.

Scott, T. G. 1947. Comparative analysis of red fox feeding trends on two central Iowa areas. Iowa Agricultural Experiment Station Research Bulletin 353:426–487.

Scott, T. G. 1955. Dietary patterns of red and gray foxes. Ecology 36(2):366–367.

Scott, T. G., and W. D. Klimstra. 1955. Red foxes and a declining prey population. Southern Illinois University Monograph Series no. 1.

*Scott, W. E. 1951. Wisconsin's first prairie spotted skunk, and other notes. Journal of Mammalogy 32(3):363.

*Scully, F. 1981. The shrew. Virginia Wildlife 42(10):25.

Sealander, J. A. 1943. Winter food habits of mink in southern Michigan. Journal of Wildlife Management 7(4):411–417.

Sealander, J. A., and H. Young. 1955. Preliminary observations on the cave bats of Arkansas. Proceedings of the Arkansas Academy of Science 7:21–31.

*Seidenberg, A. J., P. C. Kelly, E. R. Lubin, and J. D. Buffington. 1974. Helminths of the cotton rat in southern Virginia, with comments on the sex ratios of parasitic nematode populations. American Midland Naturalist 92(2):320–326.

*Seidensticker, J. 1983. Management of white-tailed deer at the National Zoological Park's Conservation and Research Center. International Zoological Yearbook 23:234–236.

*Seidensticker, J., A. J. T. Johnsingh, R. Ross, G. Sanders, and M. B. Webb. 1988. Raccoons and rabies in Appalachian mountain hollows. National Geographic Research 4(3):359–370.

*Seneca, E. D. 1961. Deer distribution, usage and population on the Broad Run management area, Craig County, Virginia. Master's thesis, Virginia Polytechnic Institute and State University, Blacksburg.

*Sentell, S. W., and W. C. Compton. 1987. Evidence for sensory awareness in death-feigning opossums *(Didelphis Marsupialis)*. Virginia Journal of Science 38(3):200–203.

*Serabian, E. A. and J. A. Cranford. 1997. Testosterone, dominance, and spatial relationships of *Peromyscus leucopus* in relation to breeding seasons. Virginia Journal of Science 48(2):90. Abstract.

*Servello, F. A. 1981. Nutritional ecology of the pine vole in relation to apple tree root damage. Master's thesis, Virginia Polytechnic Institute and State University, Blacksburg.

*Seton, E. T. 1909. Life-histories of northern animals. 2 volumes. New York: Charles Scribner's Sons.

Seton, E. T. 1920. Migrations of the gray squirrel *(Sciurus carolinensis)*. Journal of Mammalogy 1(2):53–58.

*Seton, E. T. 1929. Lives of game animals. 4 volumes. New York: Doubleday, Doran and Company. (Reprinted 1953 by Charles T. Branford Company, Boston.)

*Severinghaus, C. W., and E. L. Cheatum. 1956. Life and times of the white-tailed deer. Pp. 57–186. In: Taylor, W. P. (editor), The deer of North America. Harrisburg, Pennsylvania: The Stackpole Company.

Severinghaus, C. W., H. F. Maguire, R. A. Cookingham, and J. E. Tanck. 1950. Variations by age class in the antler beam diameters of white-tailed deer related to range conditions. Transactions of the 15th North American Wildlife Conference:551–570.

Shadle, A. R. 1954. Sizes of wood cuttings handled by beavers. American Midland Naturalist 52(2):510–512.

*Shaffer, C. H. 1948a. A study of raccoons in Princess Anne County, Virginia. Master's thesis, Virginia Polytechnic Institute and State University, Blacksburg.

*Shaffer, C. H. 1948b. The opossum. Virginia Wildlife 9(1):19–20.

*Shaffer, C. H. 1952. Wildlife waterloos. Virginia Wildlife 13(8):16–17, 20.

*Shaffer, C. H. 1970. Wildlife in the James River Basin. Virginia Wildlife 31(8):10–11, 21.

*Shaffer, C. H. 1975. Giving Nature a push: the role of live-trapping in wildlife management programs. Virginia Wildlife 36(2):19–20.

*Shaffer, K. 1974. A simple solution to deer damage. Virginia Wildlife 35(5):22.

*Shaftesbury, A. D. 1934. The Siphonaptera (fleas) of North Carolina with special reference to sex ratio. Journal of the Elisha Mitchell Scientific Society 49:247–263.

*Shah, K. V., G. B. Schaller, V. Flyger, and C. M. Sherman. 1965. Antibodies to *Myxovirus parainfluenza 3* in sera of wild deer. Bulletin of the Wildlife Disease Association l:31–32.

*Shaler, N. S. 1890a. General account of the fresh-water morasses of the United States, with a description of the Dismal Swamp district of Virginia and North Carolina. United States Geological Survey Annual Report 10:255–339.

*Shaler, N. S, 1890b. Fresh-water morasses of the United States. U.S. Geological Survey Annual Report, X:313–339.

*Shanholtz, M. I. 1952. The truth about rabies. Virginia Wildlife 8(4):5–7, 13.

*Shank, R. 1986. Cultivating wildlife. Virginia Wildlife 47(3):4–8.

Shanks, C. E., and G. C. Arthur. 1952. Muskrat movements and population dynamics in Missouri farm ponds and streams. Journal of Wildlife Management 16(2):138–148.

Sharp, H. F., Jr. 1967. Food ecology of the rice rat, *Oryzomys palustris* (Harlan), in a Georgia salt marsh. Journal of Mammalogy 48(4):557–563.

Sharp, W. M. 1958. Aging gray squirrels by use of tail-pelage characteristics. Journal of Wildlife Management 22(1):29–34.

*Shaver, D. H. 1940. Corky: a pet woodchuck. Virginia Wildlife 3(9):6.

*Sheffield, S. R. and H. H. Thomas. 1997. *Mustela frenata*. Mammalian Species no. 570:1-9.

Sheldon, C. 1934. Studies on the life histories of *Zapus* and *Napaeozapus* in Nova Scotia. Journal of Mammalogy 15(4):290–300.

*Sheldon, H. L. 1959. Wildlife operations on Camp A. P. Hill. Virginia Wildlife 20(4):16–17, 11.

*Sheldon, H. L. 1961. The Ward-Rue wildlife management area. Virginia Wildlife 22(11):7.

Sheldon, W. G. 1949. Reproductive behavior of foxes in New York State. Journal of Mammalogy 30(3):236–246.

Sheldon, W. G. 1953. Returns on banded red and gray foxes in New York State. Journal of Mammalogy 34(1):125.

Sheldon, W. G., and W. G. Toll. 1964. Feeding habits of the river otter in a reservoir in central Massachusetts. Journal of Mammalogy 45(3):449–455.

*Shelton, N. 1975. The nature of Shenandoah. Natural History Series, National Park Service, Washington, D. C..

*Shepherd, V. 1986. Beavers — loved or dammed? Virginia Wildlife 47(7):22–26.

*Shepherd, V. 1989a. Backtracking to the unspoiled days. 1600–1915. Virginia Wildlife 50(1):4–11.

*Shepherd, V. 1989b. Backtracking to the troubled times. 1916–1936. Virginia Wildlife 50(1):12–19.

*Shepherd, V. 1989c. Backtracking to the challenge of restoration. 1937–1970s. Virginia Wildlife 50(1):20–27.

*Shepherd, V. 1989d. Backtracking and looking forward . . . 1980s? Virginia Wildlife 50(1):28–34.

*Sheppe, W. 1965. Dispersal by swimming in *Peromyscus leucopus*. Journal of Mammalogy 46(2): 336–337.

*Sherfy, F. C. 1980. Home range, habitat use, and density of the raccoon in Maryland. Master's thesis, Frostburg State College, Frostburg, Maryland.

Sherman, H. B. 1939. Notes on the food of some Florida bats. Journal of Mammalogy 20(1):103–104.

Sherman, H. B. 1945. The Florida yellow bat, *Dasypterus floridanus*. Proceedings of the Florida Academy of Science 7(2–3):193–197.

*Shields, A. R. 1961. A bit of Canada in southwestern Virginia. Virginia Wildlife 22(5):4–5, 11.

*Shimmel, A. G. 1969. Pop goes the weasel. Virginia Wildlife 30(5):10–11.

*Shipley, D. D. 1941. A study of the habits and management of the gray squirrel in southwest Virginia. Master's thesis, Virginia Polytechnic Institute and State University, Blacksburg.

*Shirai, A., M. F. Bozeman, S. Perri, J. W. Humphries, and H. S. Fuller. 1961. Ecology of Rocky Mountain spotted fever. I. *Rickettsia rickettsii* recovered from a cottontail rabbit from Virginia. Proceedings of the Society for Experimental Biology and Medicine 107(1):211–214.

*Shires, C. 1963. The milkman goes a-trapping. Virginia Wildlife 24(12):14–15.

*Shoemaker, D. J. 1979. Nutritional ecology of cottontail rabbits from two Virginia locations. Master's thesis, Virginia Polytechnic Institute and State University, Blacksburg.

*Shoemaker, D. J., R. L. Kirkpatrick, and B. S. McGinnes. 1978. Seasonal food habits of cottontail rabbits in two areas of Virginia. Virginia Journal of Science 29(2):69. Abstract.

*Shomon, J. J. 1947. The Great Dismal Swamp. Virginia Wildlife 8(9):3–4.

*Shomon, J. J. 1949. Lute, the otter. Virginia Wildlife 10(12):16–17, 23.

*Shomon, J. J. 1953. Animal tracks — and how to know them. Virginia Wildlife 14(12):15–18.

*Shomon, J. J. 1954. *Mustela* — tireless marauder of the marshes. Virginia Wildlife 15(3):8–9.

*Shomon, J. J. 1955. Hunting in Virginia. Virginia Wildlife 16(12):18–19.

*Shomon, J. J. 1956. Million dollar rat. Virginia Wildlife 17(12):7–9, 26.

Short, H. L. 1961. Fall breeding activity of a young shrew. Journal of Mammalogy 42(1):95.

*Shorten, M. 1951. Some aspects of the biology of the grey squirrel *(Sciurus carolinensis)* in Great Britain. Proceedings of the Zoological Society of London 121(2):427–459.

*Shortridge, R. 1966. The bear who came to dinner. Virginia Wildlife 27(10):4–6.

*Shotts, E. B. 1981. Leptospirosis. Pp. 138–147. In: Davidson, W. R., F. A. Hayes, V. F. Nettles, and F. E. Kellogg (editors), Diseases and parasites of white-tailed deer. Miscellaneous Publication no. 7, Tall Timbers Research Station, Tallahassee, Florida.

*Shotts, E. B., W. E. Greer, and F. A. Hayes. 1958a. A preliminary survey of the incidence of brucellosis and leptospirosis among white-tailed deer *(Odocoileus virginianus)* of the Southeast. Journal of the American Veterinary Medical Association 133(7): 359–361.

*Shotts, E. B., W. E. Greer, and F. A. Hayes. 1958b. A preliminary survey of the incidence of brucellosis and leptospirosis among white-tailed deer *(Odocoileus virginianus)* of the Southeast. Proceedings of the 12th Annual Conference of the Southeastern Association of Game and Fish Commissioners 12:206–208.

*Shotts, E. B., Jr. and F. A. Hayes. 1970. Leptospiral antibodies in white-tailed deer of the southeastern United States. Journal of Wildlife Diseases 6(4):295–298.

*Shumaker, D. 1984. The night stalkers. Virginia Wildlife 45(12):8–11.

*Shump, K. A., Jr., and A. V. Shump. 1982a. *Lasiurus borealis*. Mammalian Species no. 183.

*Shump, K. A., Jr., and A. V. Shump. 1982b. *Lasiurus cinereus*. Mammalian Species no. 185.

Siebenaler, J. B., and D. K. Caldwell. 1956. Cooperation among adult dolphins. Journal of Mammalogy 37(1):126–128.

Siegler, H. R. 1956. Immature water shrews found in a beaver lodge. Journal of Mammalogy 37(2):277–278.

*Sikes, R. K., and E. S. Tierkel. 1960. Wildlife rabies studies in the southeast. 65th Annual Proceedings of the United States Livestock Sanitary Association.

*Sikes, R. S., and M. L. Kennedy. 1992. Morphologic variation of the bobcat *(Felis rufus)* in the eastern United States and its American Midland Naturalist 128:313–324.

*Sileo, L., Jr. 1966. Fertility analyses of the ranges of the white-tailed deer in the eastern United States. Master's thesis, University of Connecticut, Storrs.

*Silver, H., and W. T. Silver. 1969. Growth and behavior of the coyote-like canid of northern New England with observation on canid hybrids. Wildlife Society Monograph 17:1–41.

*Silver, J. 1927a. Mouse control in field and orchard. United States Department of Agriculture Farmer's Bulletin no. 1397.

Silver, J. 1927b. The introduction and spread of house rats in the United States. Journal of Mammalogy 8(1):58–60.

*Silver, J. 1930. Wildcat control campaign in western Virginia. Game and Fish Conservationist 9(6):157.

Simmons, J. A., D. J. Howell, and N. Suga. 1975. Information content of bat sonar echoes. American Scientist 63:204–215.

*Simpson, G. G. 1943. The beginnings of vertebrate paleontology in North America. Proceedings of the American Philosophical Society 86(1):130–188.

*Sims, J. 1987. Virginia's whitetails. Habitat. Virginia Wildlife 48(11):10–13.

*Sipe, T. W. and C. R. Terman. 1996. The role of female positional choice in pregnancy block (the Bruce Effect) in prairie deermice (*Peromyscus maniculatus bairdii*). Virginia Journal of Science 47(2):98. Abstract.

*Skeen, J. E. 1971. Indices of stress in crowded populations of house mice and white mice. Master's thesis, Virginia Polytechnic Institute and State University, Blacksburg.

*Skeen, J. E. 1975. The relationship of certain ruminoreticular and blood variables to the nutritional status of white-tailed deer. Doctoral dissertation, Virginia Polytechnic Institute and State University, Blacksburg.

*Skewes, O. H. 1953. A canoe trip on the Rappahannock River. Virginia Wildlife 14(6):8–10, 20.

*Skinner, H. 1980. Of trappers and skins. Virginia Wildlife 41(1):13–15.

*Skinner, H. E., Jr. 1978. Sanctuary near the crowds. Virginia Wildlife 39(7):10–12.

*Slaughter, D. 1982. Bambi revisited. Virginia Wildlife 43(5):17–19.

*Slaughter, H., and D. Slaughter. 1982. The ponies of Assateague. Virginia Wildlife 43(7):25–28.

*Slaughter, M. D. 1934. The wild mammals of Virginia. Master's thesis, University of Richmond, Richmond.

*Small, H. B. 1864. The animals of North America. Series l. Mammalia. Montreal: Printed by J. Lovell.

*Smart, C. W. 1970. A computer model of wildlife rabies epizootics and an analysis of incidence patterns. Master's thesis, Virginia Polytechnic Institute and State University, Blacksburg.

*Smart, C. W., R. H. Giles, Jr., and D. C. Guynn, Jr. 1973. Weight tape for white-tailed deer in Virginia. Journal of Wildlife Management 37(4):553–555.

*Smiley, R. L., and J. O. Whitaker, Jr. 1979. Mites of the genus Pygmephorus (Acari: Pygmephoridae) on small mammals in North America. Acta Zoologica Achdemiae Scientiarum Hangaricae 25(3–4):383–408.

Smith, C. C. 1965. Interspecific competition in the genus of tree squirrels, *Tamiasciurus*. Ph. D. dissertation, University of Washington, Seattle.

Smith, C. C. 1978. Structure and function of the vocalizations of tree squirrels *(Tamiasciurus)*. Journal of Mammalogy 59(4):793–808.

*Smith, C. R., J. Giles, M. E. Richmond, J. Nagel, and D. W. Yambert. 1974. The mammals of northeastern Tennessee. Journal of the Tennessee Academy of Science 49(3):88–94.

*Smith, E. R., J. B. Funderburg, Jr., and T. L. Quay. 1960. A checklist of North Carolina mammals. Raleigh: North Carolina Wildlife Research Commission.

Smith, E., and W. Goodpaster. 1958. Homing in nonmigratory bats. Science 127(3299):644.

Smith, E., and K. Hale. 1953. A homing record in the bat, *Myotis lucifugus lucifugus*. Journal of Mammalogy 43(1):122.

*Smith, F. R. 1938. Muskrat investigations in Dorchester County, Md. 1930–34. United States Department of Agriculture Circular no. 474.

*Smith, J. 1612. A map of Virginia with a description of the countrey, the commodities, people, government and religion. Printed by Joseph Barnes, Oxford, England.

*Smith, J. 1624. The generall historie of Virginia, New England and the Summer Isles. M. Sparkes, London.

*Smith, J. S., J. W. Sumner, L. F. Roumillat, G. M. Baer, and W. G. Winkler. 1984. Antigenic characteristics of isolates associated with a new epizootic of raccoon rabies in the United States. Journal of Infectious Diseases 149:769–774.

Smith, L. 1941. Observations on the nest building behavior of the opossum. Journal of Mammalogy 22(2):201–202.

Smith, N. B., and F. S. Barkalow, Jr. 1967. Precocious breeding in the gray squirrel. Journal of Mammalogy 48(2):328–330.

Smith, R. 1990. Red wolf: three years into the reintroduction. American Association of Zoological Parks and Aquariums 1990 Annual Conference Proceedings:498–502.

Smith, R. A., and M. L. Kennedy. 1983. Food habits of the coyote *(Canis latrans)* in western Tennessee. Journal of the Tennessee Academy of Science 58(1–2):27–28.

Smith, R. A., and M. L. Kennedy. 1983. Taxonomic status of the coyote in Tennessee. Proceedings of the 37th Annual Conference of the Southeastern Association of Fish and Wildlife Agencies 37:219–227.

*Smith, T. T. 1958. Prince William Forest Park. Virginia Wildlife 19(9):16–18.

*Smith, W. P. 1991. *Odocoileus virginianus*. Mammalian Species no. 388:1–13.

Smith, W. W. 1954. Reproduction in the house mouse, *Mus musculus* L., in Mississippi. Journal of Mammalogy 35(4):509–515.

*Smolen, M. J. 1981. *Microtus pinetorum*. Mammalian Species no. 147.

*Smyth, T. 1946. *Synaptomys cooperi* in southwestern Virginia. Journal of Mammalogy 27(3):277.

Snell, G. D. (editor), 1943. Biology of the laboratory mouse. Philadelphia: Blakiston Company.

*Snider, B. 1956. The thing. Virginia Wildlife 17(3):12.

*Snyder, D. E., A. N. Hamir, C. A. Hanlon, and C. E. Rupprecht. 1989a. *Dirofilaria immitis* in a raccoon *(Procyon lotor)*. Journal of Wildlife Diseases 25(1): 130–131.

*Snyder, D. E., A. N. Hamir, C. A. Hanlon, and C. E. Rupprecht. 1989b. *Phagicola angrense* (Digenea: Heterophyidae) as a cause of enteritis in a raccoon *(Procyon lotor)*. Journal of Wildlife Diseases 25(2): 273–275.

*Snyder, D. E., A. N. Hamir, C. A. Hanlon, and C. E. Rupprecht. 1991. Lung lesions in an opossum *(Didelphis virginiana)* associated with *Capillaria didelphis*. Journal of Wildlife Diseases 27(1):175–177.

*Snyder, D. P. 1982. *Tamias striatus*. Mammalian Species no. 168.

Snyder, R. L., D. E. Davis, and J. J. Christian. 1961. Seasonal changes in the weights of woodchucks. Journal of Mammalogy 42(3):297–312.

Sollberger, D. E. 1940. Notes on the life history of the small eastern flying squirrel. Journal of Mammalogy 21(3):282–293.

Sollberger, D. E. 1943. Notes on the breeding habits of the eastern flying squirrel *(Glaucomys volans volans)*. Journal of Mammalogy 24(2):163–173.

*Solomon, G. B. 1974. Probable role of the timber rattlesnake, *Crotalus horridus*, in the release of *Capillaria hepatica* (Nematoda) eggs from small mammals. Virginia Journal of Science 25(4):182–184.

*Solomon, G. B., and C. O. Handley, Jr. 1971. *Capillaria hepatica* (Bancroft, 1893) in Appalachian mammals. Journal of Parasitology 57(5):1142–1144.

*Solomon, G. B., and G. S. Warner. 1969. *Trichinella spiralis* in mammals at Mountain Lake, Virginia. Journal of Parasitology 55(4):730–732.

*Sonenshine, D. E. 1972. The ecology of the American dog tick, *Dermacentor variabilis*, in a study area in Virginia. Part I. Studies on population dynamics using radioecological methods. Annals of the Entomological Society of America 65:1164–1175.

*Sonenshine, D. E. 1990. Ecology of Rocky Mountain spotted fever in Virginia and Maryland. Virginia Journal of Science 41(3):167–168.

*Sonenshine, D. E., E. L. Atwood, and J. T. Lamb, Jr. 1966. The ecology of ticks transmitting Rocky Mountain spotted fever in a study area in Virginia. Annals of the Entomological Society of America 59(6):1234–1262.

*Sonenshine, D. E., D. G. Cerretani, and G. Enlow. 1973. Improved methods for capturing wild flying squirrels. Journal of Wildlife Management 37(4):588–590.

*Sonenshine, D. E., and G. M. Clark. 1968. Field trials on radioisotope tagging of ticks. Journal of Medical Entomology 5(2):229–235.

*Sonenshine, D. E., J. T. Lamb, Jr., and G. Anastos. 1965. The distribution, hosts, and seasonal history of Virginia ticks. Virginia Journal of Science 16(1):26–91.

*Sonenshine, D. E., and D. M. Lauer. 1976. Radioecological studies of the squirrel flea *Orchopeas howardi* in laboratory and field colonies of the southern flying squirrel, *Glaucomys volans*. Virginia Journal of Science 27(2):50. Abstract.

*Sonenshine, D. E., D. M. Lauer, T. C. Walker, and B. L. Elisberg. 1979. The ecology of *Glaucomys volans* (Linnaeus, 1758) in Virginia. Acta Theriologica 24(26):363–377.

*Sonenshine, D. E., and G. F. Levy. 1971. The ecology of the lone star tick *(Amblyomma americanum)* in two contrasting habitats in Virginia (Acarina: Ixodidae). Journal of Medical Entomology 8(6):623–635.

*Sonenshine, D. E., and G. F. Levy. 1981. Vegetative associations affecting *Glaucomys volans* in central Virginia. Acta Theriologica 26(23):359–371.

*Sonenshine, D. E., and J. Stout. 1970. A contribution to the ecology of ticks infesting wild birds and rabbits in the Virginia-North Carolina Piedmont (Acarina: Ixodidae). Journal of Medical Entomology 7(6):645–654.

*Sonenshine, D. E., and J. Stout. 1971. Ticks infesting medium-sized wild mammals in two forest localities in Virginia (Acarina: Ixodidae). Journal of Medical Entomology 8(3):217–227.

*Sonenshine, D. E., and R. Turner. 1988. Lyme disease in Virginia and North Carolina wildlife. Pp. 197–204. In: Virginia Wildlife Investigations, July l, 1987–June 30, 1988. Virginia Department of Game and Inland Fisheries.

*Sonenshine, D. E., and E. L. Winslow. 1972. Contrasts in distribution of raccoons in two Virginia localities. Journal of Wildlife Management 36:838–847.

*Sowell, A. L. and R. K. Rose. 1995. Distribution of marsh rice rats *(Oryzomys palustris)* and meadow voles *(Microtus pennsylvanicus)* in a tidal marsh on the eastern shore of Virginia. Virginia Journal of Science 46(2):99. Abstract.

*Spatafora, G. A., and T. R. Platt. 1981. A survey of the helminth parasites of rats, *Rattus norvegicus,* from Maymont Park, Richmond, Virginia. Virginia Journal of Science 32(3):98. Abstract.

*Spatafora, G. A., and T. R. Platt. 1982. Survey of the helminth parasites of the rat, *Rattus norvegicus,* from Maymont Park, Richmond, Virginia. Virginia Journal of Science 33(2):3–6.

*Speck, F. G. 1928. Chapters on the ethnology of the Powhatan tribes of Virginia. Indian Notes and Monographs l:5. Lancaster, Pennsylvania: Lancaster Press.

*Speck, F. G., R. B. Hassrick, and E. S. Carpenter. 1946. Rappahannock taking devices: traps, hunting, and fishing. Joint Publications, University of Pennsylvania Museum and Philadelphia Anthropological Society no. l.

*Speck, F. G., and C. E. Schaeffer. 1950. The deer and the rabbit hunting drive in Virginia and the southeast. Southern Indian Studies 2(1):3–20.

*Speers, R. T. 1950. The mountain "boomer." Virginia Wildlife 11(2):16–17, 26.

*Speers, R. T. 1951a. Virginia's eastern shore. Virginia Wildlife 12(4):18–19, 23.

*Speers, R. T. 1951b. Skunks of Virginia. Virginia Wildlife 12(1):16–18.

*Spencer, D. A. 1939. Electrical recording of the activities of small mammals. Journal of Mammalogy 20(4):479–489.

*Spencer, F. J. 1961. Tick-borne disease in Virginia, 1949–1958. An ecological note. American Journal of Tropical Medicine and Hygiene 10:220–222.

Sperry, C. C. 1933. Opossum and skunk eat bats. Journal of Mammalogy 14(2):152–153.

Sperry, C. E. 1941. Food habits of the coyote. United States Fish and Wildlife Service, Wildlife Research Bulletin 4.

*Spiers, J. K. 1973. A microscopic key to the hairs of Virginia land mammals. Master's thesis, Virginia Polytechnic Institute and State University, Blacksburg.

*Spiers, J. K. 1974. When a mammal leaves its fingerprints. Virginia Wildlife 35(2):14–15.

*Squires, W. H. T. 1928. The days of yester-year in colony and commonwealth. Portsmouth, Virginia: Printcraft Press.

*Stains, H. J. 1956. The raccoon in Kansas; natural history, management, and economic importance. University of Kansas Museum of Natural History Miscellaneous Publication no. 10.

*Stalling, D. T. 1997. *Reithrodontomys humulis.* Mammalian Species no. 565:1-6.

*Stallknecht, D. E., J. L. Blue, E. A. Rollor, III, V. F. Nettles, W. R. Davidson, and J. E. Pearson. 1991. Precipitating antibodies to epizootic hemorrhagic disease and bluetongue viruses in white-tailed deer in the southeastern United States. Journal of Wildlife Diseases 27(2):238–247.

*Stallknecht, D. E., and G. A. Erickson. 1986. Antibodies to vesicular stomatitis New Jersey type virus in a population of white-tailed deer. Journal of Wildlife Diseases 22(2):250–254.

*Stallknecht, D. E., V. F. Nettles, G. A. Erickson, and D. A. Jessup. 1986. Antibodies to vesicular stomatitis virus in populations of feral swine in the United States. Journal of Wildlife Diseases 22(3):320–325.

*Stankavich, J. F. 1984. Demographic analysis and microhabitat relationships of a small mammal community in clearings of the Great Dismal Swamp. Master's thesis, Old Dominion University, Norfolk.

*Stankavich, J. F., and R. K. Rose. 1981. Small mammals of the Dismal Swamp. Virginia Journal of Science 32(3):98. Abstract.

*Stankavich, J. F., and R. K. Rose. 1982. Community structure in small mammals of the Dismal Swamp. Virginia Journal of Science 33(3):119. Abstract.

*Stansbury, C. F. 1907. In the Great Dismal Swamp. Eclectic Magazine 148(1):3–17.

*Stansbury, C. F. 1925. The lake of the Great Dismal. New York: Albert and Charles Boni.

Stapanian, M. A. and C. C. Smith. 1984. Density-dependent survival of scatterhoarded nuts: an experimental approach. Ecology 65:1387–1396.

*Steele, J. H. 1967. Canine and wildlife rabies in the United States. Bulletin of Pathology 8(9):264–265.

*Steele, J. H. 1975. History of rabies. Pp. l–29. In: Baer, G. M. (editor), The natural history of rabies. Volume I. New York: Academic Press.

Stegeman, L. C. 1937. Notes on young skunks in captivity. Journal of Mammalogy 18(2):194–202.

Stein, B. R. 1990. Limb myology and phylogenetic relationships in the superfamily Dipodoidea (birch mice, jumping mice, and jerboas). Z. zool. Syst. Evolut.-forsch 28:299–314.

Stenbrot, G. I. 1992. Cladistic approach to the analysis of phylogenetic relationships among dipodoid rodents. Sbornik trudov Zoologicheskogo muzeia 29:176–201.

*Steirly, C. C. 1956. Walrus tusk on Parramore Island. Virginia Wildlife 17(1):12.

*Stewart, R. E. 1943. The lemming mouse in Shenandoah Mountains, Virginia. Journal of Mammalogy 24(1):104.

*Stewart, W. H. (editor), 1902. History of Norfolk County, Virginia, and representative citizens. Chicago: Biographical Publishing Company.

*Stickley, A. R., Jr. 1956. An investigation of factors affecting the bear kill in Virginia. Virginia Journal of Science 7(2):284. Abstract.

*Stickley, A. R., Jr. 1957a. The status and characteristics of the black bear in Virginia. Master's thesis, Virginia Polytechnic Institute and State University, Blacksburg.

*Stickley, A. R., Jr. 1957b. Black bear cub growth study and its implications on management. Virginia Journal of Science 8(2):303–304. Abstract.

*Stickley, A. R., Jr. 1959a. How's the black bear doing? Virginia Wildlife 20(11):18–19.

*Stickley, A. R., Jr. 1959b. Operation bear cub. Virginia Wildlife 20(2):16–17.

*Stickley, A. R., Jr. 1961. A black bear tagging study in Virginia. Proceedings of the 15th Annual Conference of the Southeastern Association of Game and Fish Commissioners 15:43–52.

*Stickley, A. R., Jr. 1963. Dividends from bear trapping. Virginia Wildlife 24(2):7–9.

*Stiles, C. W. 1897. A revision of the adult tapeworms of hares and rabbits. Proceedings of the United States National Museum 19(1105):145–235.

*Stiteler, W. M., Jr. and P. A. Shrauder. 1964. Production and deer utilization of woody browse on the Jefferson National Forest, Virginia. Proceedings of the 18th Annual Conference of the Southeastern Association of Game and Fish Commissioners 18:21–30.

*Stockle, A. W., G. L. Doster, and W. R. Davidson. 1978. Endogenous fat as an indicator of physical condition of southeastern white-tailed deer. Proceedings of the 32d Annual Conference of the Southeastern Association of Fish and Wildlife Agencies 32:269–279.

*Stone, W. 1907 (1908). Part II. The mammals of New Jersey. Pp. 33–110. In: Annual Report of the New Jersey State Museum, Trenton, N.J..

*Stone, W., and W. E. Cram. 1904. American animals. A popular guide to the mammals of North America north of Mexico, with intimate biographies of the more familiar species. New York: Doubleday, Page and Company.

Stones, R. C., and L. P. Branick. 1969. Use of hearing in homing by two species of *Myotis* bats. Journal of Mammalogy 50(1):157–160..

Stophlet, J. J. 1947. Florida otters eat large terrapin. Journal of Mammalogy 28(2):183.

Storer, T. I., and D. E. Davis. 1953. Studies on rat reproduction in San Francisco. Journal of Mammalogy 34(3):365–373.

Storm, G. L. 1965. Movements and activities of foxes as determined by radio tracking. Journal of Wildlife Management 29(1):1–12.

*Storm, G. L. 1972. Daytime retreats and movements of skunks on farmlands in Illinois. Journal of Wildlife Management 36(1):31–45.

*Stout, J. 1967. An additional record of the *Sorex longirostris* from eastern Virginia. Chesapeake Science 8(4):264.

*Stout, I. J., and D. E. Sonenshine. 1974a. Ecology of an opossum population in Virginia, 1963–69. Acta Theriologica 19(15):235–245.

*Stout, I. J., and D. E. Sonenshine. 1974b. A striped skunk population in Virginia, 1963–1969. Chesapeake Science 15(3):140–145.

*Strachey, W. 1849. The historie of travaile into Virginia Brittannia during 1610–12 by William Strachey, Gent, London. London: The Hakluyt Society.

*Strachey, W. 1964. A voyage to Virginia in 1609. Edited by L. B. Wright. Charlottesville: University Press of Virginia.

*Strandtmann, R. W. 1949. The blood-sucking mites of the genus *Haemolaelaps* (Acarina: Laelaptidae) in the United States. Journal of Parasitology 35(4):325–352.

*Stras, B. W. 1949. The history and organization of the Commission of Game and Inland Fisheries. Part II. Virginia Wildlife 10(8):5–7, 12, 19.

Strecker, R. L., and J. T. Emlen, Jr. 1953. Regulatory mechanisms in house-mouse populations: the effect of limited food supply on a confined population. Ecology 34(2):375–385.

*Streitmatter, R. 1978. Wild forever. Virginia Wildlife 39(1):6–8.

*Strode, D. D., and W. J. Cloward. 1969. The goals of the southern national forests in white-tailed deer management. Pp. 85–87. In: Proceedings of a Symposium on White-tailed Deer in Southern Forest Habitat. Nacogdoches, Texas: Stephen F. Austin State College.

*Strohlein, D. A., C. B. Crow, and W. R. Davidson. 1988. Distribution of *Spiculopteragia pursglovei* and *S. odocoilei* (Nematoda: Trichostrongyloidea) from white-tailed deer *(Odocoileus virginianus)* in the southeastern United States. Journal of Parasitology 74(2):347–349.

*Strother, D. H. (Porte Crayon). 1856. The Dismal Swamp. Harper's New Monthly Magazine 13:441–455.

Stroud, D. C. 1982. Population dynamics of *Rattus rattus* and *R. norvegicus* in a riparian habitat. Journal of Mammalogy 63(1):151–154.

Stuewer, F. W. 1943. Raccoons: their habits and management in Michigan. Ecological Monographs 13:203–257.

*Stüwe, M. 1984/85. Aspects of structure and reproduction of white-tailed deer populations, *Odocoileus virginianus*, in Venezuela and Virginia. Saeugetierkundliche Mitteilungen 32(2):137–141.

*Stüwe, M. 1986a. Behavior and ecology of a white-tailed deer population *(Odocoileus virginianus)* at high density. Ph.D. dissertation, University of Bielefeld, Germany.

*Stüwe, M. 1986b. Flight order and its development in white-tailed deer. Journal of Wildlife Management 50(4):699–701.

*Stüwe, M. and Ch. Wemmer. 1985. The population dynamics of an enclosed, unhunted whitetailed deer *(Odocoileus virginianus)* population. Zeitschrift fuer Jagdwissenschaft 31(4):221–229.

*Sullivan, J. A. 1973a. Effects of social interaction on the reproductive tracts of male white-footed mice *(Peromyscus leucopus)*. Master's thesis, Virginia Polytechnic Institute and State University, Blacksburg.

*Sullivan, J. A. 1973b. Serendipity and the pump box *Peromyscus*. Virginia Wildlife 34(12):10.

*Summers, L. P. 1966 (1903). History of southwest Virginia, 1746–1786, Washington County, 1777–1870. Baltimore: Genealogical Publishing Company.

*Summers, L. P. 1929. Annals of southwest Virginia, 1769–1800. Abingdon, Virginia: L. P. Summers.

*Sumner, E. L., Jr. 1931. An outline of the habits of the bobcat with some directions for trapping. California Fish and Game 17:251–254.

Sumner, P. W., E. P. Hill, and J. B. Wooding. 1984. Activity and movements of coyotes in Mississippi and Alabama. Proceedings of the 38th Annual Conference of the Southeastern Association of Fish and Wildlife Agencies 38:174–181.

*Sutton, H. 1955. A filthy bogg. Saturday Review of Literature 38:38–39.

*Sutton, M. 1984. Rabies. Just the facts. Virginia Wildlife 45(6):8–9.

*Svendsen, G. E. 1982. Weasels. Pp. 613–628. In: Chapman, J. A., and G. A. Feldhamer (editors), Wild mammals of North America. Baltimore: The Johns Hopkins University Press.

Svihla, A. 1931a. The field biologist's report. Pp. 278–287. In: Arthur, S. C. (compiler), The fur animals of Louisiana. Louisiana Department of Conservation Bulletin 18 (revised).

Svihla, A. 1931b. Habits of the Louisiana mink *(Mustela vison vulgivagus)*. Journal of Mammalogy 12(4):366–368.

Svihla, A. 1932. A comparative life history study of the mice of the genus *Peromyscus*. Miscellaneous Publication no. 24, Museum of Zoology, University of Michigan.

Svihla, A., and H. S. Bowman. 1954. Hibernation in the American black bear. American Midland Naturalist 52(1):248–252.

Svihla, A., and R. D. Svihla. 1931. The Louisiana muskrat. Journal of Mammalogy 12(1):12–28.

*Swanton, J. R. 1946. The Indians of the southeastern United States. Smithsonian Institution Bureau of American Ethology Bulletin 137.

*Sweeney, J. M., and J. R. Sweeney. 1982. Feral hog. Pp. 1099–1113. In: Chapman, J. A., and G. A. Feldhamer (editors), Wild mammals of North America. Baltimore: The Johns Hopkins University Press.

*Sweeney, J. R., R. L. Marchinton, and J. M. Sweeney. 1971. Responses of radio-monitored white-tailed deer chased by hunting dogs. Journal of Wildlife Management 35(4):707–716.

*Sweet, J. C., Jr. 1950. An evaluation of the deer and grouse management practices on the Jefferson National Forest, Virginia. Master's thesis, Virginia Polytechnic Institute and State University, Blacksburg.

*Swift, J. R., P. F. Scanlon, M. G. Babler, and R. W. Rexroad. 1995. Patterns in occurrences of deer-vehicle collisions. Virginia Journal of Science 46(2):126. Abstract.

*Swift, L. W. 1954. Canoeing in the Washington area. Virginia Wildlife 15(11):20–21.

*Swingle, W. M., S. G. Barco, T. D. Pitchford, W. A. McLellan and A. D. Pabst. 1993. Appearance of juvenile humpback whales feeding in the nearshore waters of Virginia. Marine Mammal Science 9(3):309–315.

*Swink, F. N., Jr. 1952a. Effects of the red fox on other game. Virginia Wildlife 13(10):20–22.

*Swink, F. N., Jr. 1952b. The effect of red fox populations on other game species. Virginia Journal of Science 3(2):297. Abstract.

*Swink, F. N., Jr. 1952c. The effects of red fox populations on other game species. Master's thesis, Virginia Polytechnic Institute and State University, Blacksburg.

*Swink, F. N., Jr. 1956. Rabies and wildlife. Virginia Wildlife 17(7):5–7.

*Swink, F. N., Jr. 1957. Red foxes — facts and fancies. Virginia Wildlife 18(8):5–7, 22.

*Swink, F. N., Jr. 1958. The gray ghost of southern woodlands. Virginia Wildlife 19(9):10–12.

*Swink, F. N., Jr. 1959. Bobcats. Virginia Wildlife 20(6):16–17.

*Switzer, R., translator. 1969. Chateaubriand's travels in America. Lexington: University of Kentucky Press.

Tabatabai, F. R., and M. L. Kennedy. 1988. Food habits of the raccoon *(Procyon lotor)* in Tennessee. Journal of the Tennessee Academy of Science 63(4):89–94.

*Taitt, M. J., and C. J. Krebs. 1985. Population dynamics and cycles. Pp. 567–620. In: Tamarin, R. J. (editor), Biology of New World *Microtus*. American Society of Mammalogists Special Publication no. 8.

Takos, M. J. 1944. Summer movements of banded muskrats. Journal of Wildlife Management 8(4):307–311.

Tannenbaum, M. G., and E. B. Pivorun. 1988. Seasonal study of daily torpor in southeastern *Peromyscus maniculatus* and *Peromyscus leucopus* from mountains and foothills. Physiological Zoology 61(1):10–16.

*Tate, C. M. 1977. Distribution and systematic relationship of two forms of the short-tailed shrew (Soricidae: *Blarina*) in central Virginia. Master's thesis, Virginia Commonwealth University, Richmond.

*Tate, C. M., J. F. Pagels, and C. O. Handley, Jr. 1980. Distribution and systematic relationship of two kinds of short-tailed shrews (Soricidae: *Blarina*) in south-central Virginia. Proceedings of the Biological Society of Washington 93(1):50–60.

Tavolga, M. C., and F. S. Essapian. 1957. The behavior of the bottle-nosed dolphin *(Tursiops truncatus):* mating, pregnancy, parturition and mother-infant behavior. Zoologica 42(1):11–31.

*Taylor, G. J. 1974 (1973). Present status and habitat survey of the Delmarva fox squirrel *(Sciurus niger cinereus)* with a discussion of reasons for its decline. Proceedings of the 27th Annual Conference of the Southeastern Association of Game and Fish Commissioners 27:278–289.

Taylor, G. J. 1976. Range determination and habitat description of the Delmarva fox squirrel in Maryland. Master's thesis, University of Maryland, College Park.

*Taylor, G. J., and V. Flyger. 1974. Distribution of the Delmarva fox squirrel *(Sciurus niger cinereus)* in Maryland. Chesapeake Science 15(1):59–60.

*Taylor, J. W. 1958. Rare plants and animals survive in Lebanon sanctuary. Virginia Wildlife 19(11):22–23.

*Taylor, J. W. 1974a. The Dismal Swamp lemming mouse. Virginia Wildlife 35(5):27.

*Taylor, J. W. 1974b. The Delmarva fox squirrel. Virginia Wildlife 35(6):22.

*Taylor, J. W. 1974c. Rafinesque's big-eared bat. Virginia Wildlife 35(8):27.

*Taylor, J. W. 1974d. Northern flying squirrel. Virginia Wildlife 35(11):27.

*Taylor, J. W. 1974e. The eastern panther. Virginia Wildlife 35(12):24.

Taylor, R. W., C. L. Counts, III, and S. B. Mills. 1976. Occurrence and distribution of the coyote, *Canis latrans* Say, in West Virginia. Proceedings of the West Virginia Academy of Science 48:73–77.

*Taylor, W. H. 1963a. Weston refuge. Virginia Wildlife 24(3):16.

*Taylor, W. H. 1963b. Game harvest and hunter use Camp A. P. Hill, Bowling Green, Virginia. Proceedings of the 17th Annual Conference of the Southeastern Association of Game and Fish Commissioners 17:168–172.

*Taylor, W. H. 1967a. The Quantico story. Proceedings of the 21st Annual Conference of the Southeastern Association of Game and Fish Commissioners 21:97–103.

*Taylor, W. H. 1967b. The Quantico conservation story. Virginia Wildlife 28(8):10–11, 20–21.

*Taylor, W. H. 1968a. Rabbits behind a fence. Virginia Wildlife 29(2):4–5.

*Taylor, W. H. 1968b. Old paddletail never quits. Virginia Wildlife 29(12):6–7.

*Taylor, W. H. 1971. Counting deer. Virginia Wildlife 32(6):9–10.

*Taylor, W. H. 1977. A progress report on APC technique in Virginia. Proceedings of the Joint Northeast-Southeast Deer Study Group Meeting, Virginia Commission of Game and Inland Fisheries, Pittman-Robertson Project W-40R:74–79.

Tefft, B. C., and J. A. Chapman. 1983. Growth and development of nestling New England cottontails, *Sylvilagus transitionalis.* Acta Theriologica 28(19):317–320.

Terman, C. R. 1966. Population fluctuations of *Peromyscus maniculatus* and other small mammals as revealed by the North American Census of Small Mammals. American Midland Naturalist 76:419–426.

*Terman, C. R. 1968. Population dynamics. Pp. 412–450. In: King, J. A. (editor), Biology of *Peromyscus.* Special Publication no. 2, The American Society of Mammalogists.

*Terman, C. R. 1986. Demographic characteristics of white-footed mice *(Peromyscus leucopus noveboracensis)* in natural populations during a three year period. Virginia Journal of Science 37(2):73. Abstract.

*Terman, C. R. 1987a. Studies of natural populations of *Peromyscus leucopus noveboracensis:* variations in density and reproductive characteristics. Virginia Journal of Science 38(2):88. Abstract.

*Terman, C. R. 1987b. Intrinsic behavioral and physiological differences among laboratory populations of prairie deermice. American Zoologist 27(3):853–866.

*Terman, C. R. 1988. Reproductive characteristics of laboratory maintained *Peromyscus.* Virginia Journal of Science 39(2):123. Abstract.

*Terman, C. R. 1990. Female induced reproductive inhibition of female white-footed mice *(Peromyscus leucopus noveboracensis):* variability of response by Virginia mice. Virginia Journal of Science 41(2):61. Abstract.

*Terman, C. R. 1991. Reduction of reproduction at varying densities in natural populations of white-footed mice *(Peromyscus leucopus noveboracensis).* Virginia Journal of Science 42(2):178. Abstract.

*Terman, C. R. 1992a. Reproductive inhibition in female white-footed mice from Virginia. Journal of Mammalogy 73(2):443–448.

*Terman, C. R. 1992b. Internal hermaphroditism in a white-footed mouse *(Peromyscus leucopus noveboracensis).* Virginia Journal of Science 43(2):233. Abstract.

*Terman, C. R. 1992c. Hermaphroditism in a white-footed mouse *(Peromyscus leucopus noveboracensis).* American Midland Naturalist 128(2):411–415.

*Terman, C. R. 1992d. Mid-summer suppression of reproduction in a wild population of white-footed mice *(Peromyscus leucopus noveboracensis)* is not prevented by supplemental food. Virginia Journal of Science 43(2):233. Abstract.

*Terman, C. R. 1992e. Midsummer inhibition of reproduction in a wild population of white-footed mice *(Peromysous leucopus noveboracensis)* is not prevented by supplemental food. Bulletin of the Ecological Society of America 73(2)suppl:364.

*Terman, C. R. 1993a. Mid-summer reproductive inhibition in a wild population of white-footed mice: an examination of density influences. Virginia Journal of Science 44(2):114.Abstract.

*Terman, C. R. 1993b. Studies of natural populations of white-footed mice: reduction of reproduction at varying densities. Journal of Mammalogy 74(3):678–687.

*Terman, C. R. 1994. Reproductive recovery of wild white-footed mice in the laboratory. Virginia Journal of Science 45(2):63. Abstract.

*Terman, C. R. 1995. Nest box use by wild populations of white-footed mice *(Peromyscus leucopus noveboracensis)* in eastern Virginia. Virginia Journal of Science 46(2):99. Abstract.

*Terman, C. R. 1996. Nest box use by wild populations of white-footed mice *(Peromyscus leucopus noveboracensis)* in Virginia. Virginia Journal of Science 47(1):3–7.

*Terman, C. R. 1998. Early-summer reproductive curtailment in wild white-footed mice and reproductive recovery in the laboratory. Journal of Mammalogy 79(1):320-325.

*Terman, C. R., N. J. Anderson, and R. H. Mann. 1989. A further examination of reproductive performance in the laboratory by white-footed mice *(Peromyscus leucopus noveboracensis)* captured in the wild. Virginia Journal of Science 40(2):61. Abstract.

*Terman, C. R., and R. J. Huggett. 1980. Occurrence of kepone in white-footed mice *(Peromyscus leucopus noveboracensis)* on Jamestown Island, Virginia. Virginia Journal of Science 31(4):102.

*Terman, C. R., and J. F. Sassaman. 1967. Sex ratio in deer mouse populations. Journal of Mammalogy 48(4):589–597.

*Terrill, T. H., V. G. Allen, J. P. Fontenot, J. A. Cranford, and J. G. Foster. 1991. Influence of flooded soil on chemical composition of annual ryegrass and digestibility by meadow voles. Virginia Journal of Science 42(1):101–111.

*Terwilliger, K. 1985. Are the big silvers gone? Virginia Wildlife 46(6):11–13.

*Terwilliger, K. (coordinator). 1991a. Virginia's endangered species. Blacksburg: The McDonald & Woodward Publishing Company.

*Terwilliger, K. 1991b. Performance Report: Delmarva fox squirrel investigations. Pp. 10–13. In: Nongame and Endangered Species Investigations Annual Report, 1990–1991. Virginia Department of Game and Inland Fisheries, Richmond.

*Terwilliger, K. and J. Musik. 1995. Management plan for sea turtles and marine mammals in Virginia. Final Report: National Oceanic and Atmospheric Administration, Washington, D. C.

*Terwilliger, K. and J. R. Tate (coordinators). 1995. A guide to endangered and threatened species in Virginia. Blacksburg: The McDonald & Woodward Publishing Company.

*Testaverde, S. A. and J. G. Mead. 1980. Southern distribution of the Atlantic whitesided dolphin, *Lagenorhynchus acutus,* in the western North Atlantic. United States National Marine Fisheries Service, Fisheries Bulletin 78(1):167–169.

Tevis, L., Jr. 1947. Summer activities of California raccoons. Journal of Mammalogy 28(4):323–332.

Tevis, L., Jr. 1950. Summer behavior of a family of beavers in New York State. Journal of Mammalogy 31(1):40–65.

The Nature Conservancy. 1996. Virginia scientists discover rare bat on Conservancy preserve. http://www.tnc.org. October, 1996.

Thomas, D. W., M. Dorais, and J. Bergeron. 1990. Winter energy budgets and cost of arousals for hibernating little brown bats, *Myotis lucifugus.* Journal of Mammalogy 71(3):475–479.

Thomas, K. R. 1974. Burrow systems of the eastern chipmunk (*Tamias striatus pipilans* Lowery) in Louisiana. Journal of Mammalogy 55(2):454–459.

*Thomas, O. 1911. The mammals of the tenth edition of Linnaeus; an attempt to fix the types of the genera and the exact bases and localities of the species. Proceedings of the Zoological Society of London:120–158.

Thomas, W. L. (editor). 1956. Man's Role in Changing the Face of the Earth. 2 Volumes. Chicago: The University of Chicago Press.

*Thompson, J. A. 1971. Responses of several stressed mouse populations to endotoxin challenge. Master's thesis, Virginia Polytechnic Institute and State University, Blacksburg.

*Thompson, J. H. 1948. The hills of Joppa ring again. Virginia Wildlife 9(1):14–15, 22.

*Thompson, R. C. 1949. For real sport give me the bow. Virginia Wildlife 10(1):8–9,11.

*Thompson, R. L. 1962. An investigation of some techniques for measuring availability of oak mast and deer browse. Master's thesis, Virginia Polytechnic Institute and State University, Blacksburg.

*Thompson, W., E. Lilleleht, and C. R. Terman. 1986. Observations of raccoon *(Procyon lotor)* predatory behavior on white-footed mice *(Peromyscus leucopus).* Virginia Journal of Science 37(2):73. Abstract.

*Thomson, C. E. 1982. *Myotis sodalis.* Mammalian Species no. 163.

*Thornton, J. E. 1940. An ecological study of forest clearings on the Big Levels Game Refuge. Master's thesis, Virginia Polytechnic Institute and State University, Blacksburg.

*Thornton, J. E. 1947. The black bear. Virginia Wildlife 8(3):6–7, 9, 20.

*Thornton, J. E. 1954a. The cottontail rabbit in Virginia. Virginia Wildlife 15(7):18–20.

*Thornton, J. E. 1954b. The cottontail rabbit in Virginia. Educational Leaflet no. 4. Virginia Commission of Game and Inland Fisheries.

*Thornton, J. E. 1955. An old man remembers... Virginia Wildlife 16(11):8–9, 17, 22.

*Thornton, J. E. 1958. Water holes for wildlife. Virginia Wildlife 19(2):20–21.

*Thornton, J. E. 1960. The management of upland game on public lands in Virginia. Proceedings of the 14th Annual Conference of the Southeastern Association of Game and Fish Commissioners 14:78–84.

*Thornton, J. E. 1968. The northwestern Virginia deer herd . . . Where does it go from here? Virginia Wildlife 29(4):10, 20–21.

*Thornton, J. E. 1970. Northwestern Virginia's 1969 deer harvest. Virginia Wildlife 31(7):22.

*Thornton, J. E. 1977. Rappahannock Wildlife Management Area. Virginia Wildlife 38(1):23–25.

*Thornton, J. E. and R. E. Elliott. 1960. Watersheds and wildlife. Virginia Wildlife 21(7):8–9, 12.

*Thornton, N. 1975. G. Richard Thompson Wildlife Management Area. Virginia Wildlife 36(7):8.

*Thornton, W. M. 1896. Spottswood's expedition of 1716. National Geographic Magazine 7(8):265–269.

Thwaites, R. G. 1916. Daniel Boone. New York: D. Appleton and Company.

*Tinkle, D. W., and W. W. Milstead. 1960. Sex ratios and population density in hibernating *Myotis*. American Midland Naturalist 63(2):327–334.

*Tipton, G., A. Tipton, and C. O. Handley, Jr. 1979a. *Myotis grisescens*. Pp. 492–494. In: Linzey, D. W. (editor), Proceedings of the Symposium on Endangered and Threatened Plants and Animals of Virginia. Blacksburg: Virginia Polytechnic Institute and State University.

*Tipton, G., A. Tipton, and C. O. Handley, Jr. 1979b. *Myotis sodalis*. Pp. 494–497. In: Linzey, D. W. (editor), Proceedings of the Symposium on Endangered and Threatened Plants and Animals of Virginia. Blacksburg: Virginia Polytechnic Institute and State University.

*Tipton, V. 1984. Going bats. Virginia Wildlife 45(6):30–31.

*Tipton, V. M. 1984. Evidence of movement of a maternity colony of *Plecotus townsendii virginianus* throughout the summer. Virginia Journal of Science 35(2):90. Abstract.

*Tipton, V. M., and V. Brack, Jr. 1986. Food habits of the bat, *Plecotus townsendii virginianus*, in Virginia. Virginia Journal of Science 37(2):74. Abstract.

Tomasi, T. E. 1979. Echolocation by the short-tailed shrew *Blarina brevicauda*. Journal of Mammalogy 60(4):751–759.

*Tomblin, D. C., and J. A. Cranford. 1993. Effects of gypsy moth defoliation on small mammals. Virginia Journal of Science 44(2):115. Abstract.

*Tomblin, D. C., and J. A. Cranford. 1994. Sex and age class habitat discrimination by *Peromyscus* spp. at different stages of gypsy moth disturbance. Virginia Journal of Science 45(2):64. Abstract.

Tomkins, I. R. 1935. The marsh rabbit: an incomplete life history. Journal of Mammalogy 16(3):201–205.

Tomkins, I. R. 1955. The distribution of the marsh rabbit in Georgia. Journal of Mammalogy 36(1):144–145.

*Tomsa, T. 1992. Synopsis of coyote depredation problems and damage control efforts in Virginia. United States Department of Agriculture, Animal Damage Control Office, Blacksburg. Mimeographed.

*Torrence, M. E. 1990. A log-linear model for predicting risk factors for rabies positivity in raccoons in Virginia. Doctoral dissertation, Virginia Polytechnic Institute and State University, Blacksburg.

*Torrence, M. E., S. R. Jenkins, and L. T. Glickman. 1992. Epidemiology of raccoon rabies in Virginia, 1984 to 1989. Journal of Wildlife Diseases 28(3):369–376.

*Toweill, D. E., and J. E. Tabor. 1982. River otter. Pp. 688–703. In: Chapman, J. A., and G. A. Feldhamer (editors), Wild mammals of North America. Baltimore: The Johns Hopkins University Press.

*Towne, C. W., and E. N. Wentworth. 1950. Pigs from cave to cornbelt. Norman: University of Oklahoma Press.

*Townsend, C. H. 1935. The distribution of certain whales as shown by logbook records of American whaleships. Zoologica 19(1):1–50.

*Townsend, V. R. 1994. The availability of small mammal prey for foraging pit vipers. Virginia Journal of Science 45(2):65. Abstract.

*Trapp, G. R., and D. L. Hallberg. 1983. Ecology of the gray fox *(Urocyon cinereoargenteus)*: a review. Pp. 164–178. In: Fox, M. W. (editor), The wild canids. Malabar, Florida: Robert E. Krieger Publishing Company, Incorporated.

*Troubetzkoy, D. 1954. Why the groundhog has his day. Virginia Wildlife 15(2):20–22.

*Troubetzkoy, U. 1961. The Great Dismal Swamp. Virginia Cavalcade 10:19–27.

*Troubetzkoy, U. 1967a. Seasons in Dismal Swamp — spring. Virginia Wildlife 28(6):17–20.

*Troubetzkoy, U. 1967b. Seasons in Dismal Swamp — summer. Virginia Wildlife 28(8):4–5, 22–23.

*Troubetzkoy, U. 1967c. Seasons in Dismal Swamp — autumn. Virginia Wildlife 28(10):6–8, 17.

*Troubetzkoy, U. 1968. Seasons in Dismal Swamp — winter. Virginia Wildlife 29(3):6–7, 19–22.

*Troubetzkoy, U. 1976. A look at Virginia — 1607 . . . . Virginia Wildlife 37(7):9–13.

*True, F. W. 1884. Catalogue of the aquatic mammals exhibited by the United States National Museum. Washington, D. C.: Government Printing Office.

*True, F. W. 1885. A provisional list of the mammals of North and Central America, and the West Indian Islands. United States National Museum Proceedings (1884) 7:587–611.

*True, F. W. 1889. A review of the family Delphinidae. United States National Museum Bulletin 36.

*True, F. W. 1891. The puma or American lion: *Felis concolor* of Linnaeus. Report of the United States National Museum 1889:591–608.

*True, F. W. 1896. A revision of the American moles. Proceedings of the United States National Museum 19(1101):1–111.

*True, F. W. 1903. First record of the Pollack whale *(Balaenoptera borealis)* in the western North Atlantic. Science 17(421):150.

*True, F. W. 1904. The whalebone whales of the western North Atlantic. Smithsonian Contributions to Knowledge 33.

Tryon, C. A., and D. P. Snyder. 1973. Biology of the eastern chipmunk, *Tamias striatus*: life tables, age distributions, and trends in population numbers. Journal of Mammalogy 54(1):145–168.

Tullar, B. F., Jr. 1983a. An unusually long-lived red fox. New York Fish and Game Journal 30(2):227.

Tullar, B. F., Jr. 1983b. A long-lived white-tailed deer. New York Fish and Game Journal 30(1):119.

*Tumlison, R., and M. E. Douglas. 1992. Parsimony analysis and the phylogeny of the plecotine bats (Chiroptera: Vespertilionidae). Journal of Mammalogy 73(2):276–285.

*Tuttle, M. D. 1976. Population ecology of the gray bat *(Myotis grisescens):* philopatry, timing and patterns of movement, weight loss during migration, and seasonal adaptive strategies. Occasional Papers of the Museum of Natural History, University of Kansas 54.

Tuttle, M. D. 1988. America's neighborhood bats. Austin: University of Texas Press.

Tuttle, M. D., and P. B. Robertson. 1969. The gray bat, *Myotis grisescens,* east of the Appalachians. Journal of Mammalogy 50(2):370.

*Tuttle, M. D., and D. E. Stevenson. 1977. An analysis of migration as a mortality factor in the gray bat based on public recoveries of banded bats. American Midland Naturalist 97(1):235–240.

*Twente, J. W., Jr. 1955. Some aspects of habitat selection and other behavior of cavern-dwelling bats. Ecology 36(4):706–732.

Twichell, A. R. 1939. Notes on the southern woodchuck in Missouri. Journal of Mammalogy 20(1):71–74.

Twichell, A. R., and H. H. Dill. 1949. One hundred raccoons from one hundred and two acres. Journal of Mammalogy 30(2):130–133.

*Tyler, L. G. (editor), 1907. Narratives of early Virginia, 1606–1625. New York: Charles Scribner's Sons.

*Tyson, E. 1698. Carigueya, seu Marsupialie Americanum, or The anatomy of an opossum, etc. Philosophical Transactions 20(239):105–164.

*Uhlig, H. G. 1955a. The gray squirrel, its life history, ecology, and population characteristics in West Virginia. Final Report, Pittman-Robertson Project 31-R, Conservation Commission of West Virginia, Charleston.

Uhlig, H. G. 1955b. The determination of age of nestling and sub-adult gray squirrels in West Virginia. Journal of Wildlife Management 19(4):479–483.

Uhlig, H. G. 1956. A theory on leaf nests built by gray squirrels on Seneca State Forest, West Virginia. Journal of Wildlife Management 20(3):263–266.

Ulmer, F. A., Jr. 1941. *Mesoplodon mirus* in New Jersey, with additional notes on the New Jersey *M. densirostris,* and a list and key to the ziphioid whales of the Atlantic coast of North America. Proceedings of the Philadelphia Academy of Natural Sciences 93:107–122.

Ulmer, F. A., Jr. 1951. Cats — great and small. America's First Zoo 3(2):4–6.

*Ulmer, F. A., Jr. 1963. Northward extension of the range of the cotton mouse in Virginia. Journal of Mammalogy 44(2):273–274.

*United States Congress. 1989. First session on the conclusions of the clinical investigation of the 1987–88 mass mortality of the bottlenose dolphins along the United States central and south Atlantic coasts. Subcommittee on Oversight and Investigations, Committee on Merchant Marine and Fisheries, House of Representatives, 101st Congress, first session. Serial number 101–20:1–302. United States Government Printing Office, Washington, DC.

*United States Fish and Wildlife Service. 1937–79. Big-game inventories of the United States. Wildlife Leaflets, United States Department of the Interior.

*United States Fish and Wildlife Service. 1939–79. Annual fur catch of the United States. Wildlife Leaflets, United States Department of the Interior.

*United States Fish and Wildlife Service. 1965–78. Wildlife research — problems, programs, progress. Washington, D. C.

*United States Fish and Wildlife Service. 1989. Endangered and threatened wildlife and plants. United States Government Printing Office, Washington, D. C.

*United States Fish and Wildlife Service. 1992. Delmarva fox squirrel *(Sciurus niger cinereus)* recovery plan, second revision. Technical/Agency Draft. Newton Corner, Massachusetts.

*Urban, V. K. 1988. Home range, habitat utilization, and activity of the endangered northern flying squirrel. Master's thesis, West Virginia University, Morgantown.

*Urbston, D. F. 1968. A comparison of several techniques for aging white-tailed deer. Master's thesis, Virginia Polytechnic Institute and State University, Blacksburg.

*Valentine, G. L. 1968a. Laboratory breeding in the pine vole. Virginia Journal of Science 19(3):183. Abstract.

*Valentine, G. L. 1968b. A field survey and laboratory experiments on the reproductive physiology of the pine vole *Pitymys pinetorum* (LeConte). Master's thesis, Virginia Polytechnic Institute and State University, Blacksburg.

*Valentine, G. L., and R. L. Kirkpatrick. 1970. Seasonal changes in reproductive and related organs in the pine vole, *Microtus pinetorum* in southwestern Virginia. Journal of Mammalogy 51(3):553–560.

*Vance, J. 1985. Raising a stink. Virginia Wildlife 46(7):3–6.

*van Doren, M. (editor), 1928. The travels of William Bartram. New York: Dover Publications.

VanGelder, R. G. 1952. The spotted skunks *(Spilogale)* of eastern United States. Master's thesis, University of Illinois, Urbana.

VanGelder, R. G. 1953. The egg-opening technique of a spotted skunk. Journal of Mammalogy 34(2):255–256.

*VanGelder, R. G. 1959. A taxonomic revision of the spotted skunks (genus *Spilogale*). Bulletin of the American Museum of Natural History 117:229–392.

Van Vleck, D. B. 1965. The anatomy of the nasal rays of *Condylura cristata.* Journal of Mammalogy 46(2):248–253.

*Van Wormer, J. 1966. The world of the black bear. Philadelphia: J. B. Lippincott Company.

*Van Zyll de Jong, C. G. 1972. A systematic review of the Nearctic and Neotropical river otters (genus *Lutra,* Mustelidae, Carnivora). Royal Ontario Museum, Life Science Contribution 80:1–104.

*Vashon, A. 1995. Natural history of the black bear. Virginia Wildlife 56(9):7–9.

*Vaughan, M. R. 1995. Black bear research in Virginia. Virginia Wildlife 56(9):22–28.

*Vaughan, M. R., and P. F. Scanlon. 1990. The extent and management of damage by black bears. Transactions of the 19th International Union of Game Biologists Congress, Trondheim, Norway 19(2):581–591. September, 1989.

Venters, H. D., W. R. Hoffert, J. E. Scatterday, and A. V. Hardy. 1954. Rabies in bats in Florida. American Journal of Public Health 44(2):182–185.

*Verts, B. J. 1967. The biology of the striped skunk. Urbana: University of Illinois Press.

*Villarejo, M. 1982a. The unpopular 'possum. Virginia Wildlife 43(2):4–5.

*Villarejo, M. 1982b. The flying squirrel. Virginia Wildlife 43(11):24–25.

*Vincent, R. E. 1958. Observations of red fox behavior. Ecology 39(4):755–757.

*Virginia Commission on the Conservation of Caves. 1979. Report of the Virginia Commission on the Conservation of Caves to the governor and the General Assembly of Virginia. House Document no. 5.

*Virginia Cooperative Wildlife Research Unit. 1940–79. Quarterly progress reports.

*Virginia Department of Health. 1951–92. Statistical annual reports.

*Virginia Department of Health. Division of Epidemiology. Animal rabies by species and county, 1975–92. Richmond, Virginia.

*Virginia Wildlife Investigations. Annual Reports. July l, 1983 to June 30, 1988. Federal Aid in Wildlife Restoration Projects W-74-R-2 to W-74-R-6. Virginia Department of Game and Inland Fisheries, Richmond.

Vispo, C. R. 1988. An observation of a wild group of masked shrews, *Sorex cinereus*. Canadian Field-Naturalist 102(4):731–733.

*Vogelsang, R. W. 1977. Blood urea nitrogen, serum cholesterol and progestins as affected by nutritional intake, pregnancy and the estrous cycle in white-tailed deer. Master's thesis, Virginia Polytechnic Institute and State University, Blacksburg.

*Wade-Smith, J., and B. J. Verts. 1982. *Mephitis mephitis*. Mammalian Species no. 173.

Wagner, P. J. 1960. The Human Use of the Earth: An Examination of the Interaction Between Man and His Physical Environment. New York: The Free Press.

*Walke, J. W. 1984. Effects of supplemental food and flooding on arboreal activity in Dismal Swamp small mammals. Virginia Journal of Science 35(2):91. Abstract.

*Walke, J. W. 1984. Activity levels of arboreal rodents *Peromyscus* and *Ochrotomys* evaluated with nest cans in seasonally flooded forests. Master's thesis, Old Dominion University, Norfolk.

*Walke, J. W., and R. K. Rose. 1982. The effect of supplemental food on arboreal small mammals in the Dismal Swamp. Virginia Journal of Science 33(3):122. Abstract.

Walker, E. P. 1954. Shrews is shrews. Nature Magazine 47:125–128.

*Walker, E. P. 1964. Mammals of the world. 3 volumes. Baltimore: The Johns Hopkins University Press.

*Walker, M. L., and W. W. Becklund. 1970. Checklist of the internal and external parasites of deer, *Odocoileus hemionus* and *O. virginianus*, in the United States and Canada. Special Publication no. 1. Index Catalogue of Medical and Veterinary Zoology, US Government Printing Office, Washington, DC.

*Walley, H. D., and W. L. Jarvis. 1971. Longevity record for *Pipistrellus subflavus*. Transactions of the Illinois Academy of Science 64(3):305.

*Walls, M. L. 1974. A dynamic white-tailed deer population simulator and lessons from its use. Master's thesis, Virginia Polytechnic Institute and State University, Blacksburg.

*Walls, M. 1987. Virginia's whitetails. Trophy deer. Virginia Wildlife 48(11):14–17.

*Walters, E. E. 1967. Spotting the spotlighter. Virginia Wildlife 28(1):9.

*Wang, K., P. Payne, and V. Thayer (compilers). 1994. Coastal stock(s) of Atlantic bottlenose dolphin: status review and management. United States Department of Commerce, NOAA Technical Memorandum NMFS-OPR-4, Washington, D. C.

Warburton, G. S., and R. A. Powell. 1985. Movements of black bears on the Pisgah National Forest. Proceedings of the 39th Annual Conference of the Southeastern Association of Fish and Wildlife Agencies 39:351–361.

*Warren, E. 1990. Noah's ark in Virginia. Virginia Explorer 6(7):10–13.

*Warren, R. J. 1976a. Influence of dietary Mirex and nutritive restrictions on cottontail rabbit reproductive physiology. Master's thesis, Virginia Polytechnic Institute and State University, Blacksburg.

*Warren, R. J. 1976b. How many rabbits? Virginia Wildlife 37(9):27.

*Warren, R. J. 1979. Physiological indices for the assessment of nutritional status in white-tailed deer. Doctoral dissertation, Virginia Polytechnic Institute and State University, Blacksburg.

*Warren, R. J., and R. L. Kirkpatrick. 1976. Influence of mirex ingestion on cottontail eye lens weights. Journal of Wildlife Management 40(4):797–799.

*Warren, R. J., and R. L. Kirkpatrick. 1978. Indices of nutritional status in cottontail rabbits fed controlled diets. Journal of Wildlife Management 42(1):154–158.

*Warren, R. J., and R. L. Kirkpatrick. 1982. Evaluating nutritional status of white-tailed deer using fat indices. Proceedings of the 36th Annual Conference of the Southeastern Association of Fish and Wildlife Agencies 36:463–472.

*Warren, R. J., R. L. Kirkpatrick, and F. C. Gwazdauskas. 1978. Serum progestins during gestation in the cottontail rabbit. Virginia Journal of Science 29(2):70. Abstract.

*Warren, R. J., R. L. Kirkpatrick, A. Oelschlaeger, P. F. Scanlon, and F. C. Gwazdauskas. 1981. Dietary and seasonal influences on nutritional indices of adult male white-tailed deer. Journal of Wildlife Management 45:926–936.

*Warren, R. J., R. L. Kirkpatrick and R. W. Young. 1978. Barbituate-induced sleeping times, liver weights, and reproduction of cottontail rabbits after mirex ingestion. Bulletin of Environmental Contamination and Toxicology 0007–4861:223–228.

*Warren, R. J., R. W. Vogelsang, R. L. Kirkpatrick, and P. F. Scanlon. 1978. Reproductive behaviour of captive white-tailed deer. Animal Behaviour 26:179–183.

*Wass, M. L. (compiler). 1972. A check list of the biota of lower Chesapeake Bay. Special Scientific Report no. 65, Virginia Institute of Marine Science, Gloucester Point, Virginia.

Waters, J. H., and B. H. Stockley. 1965. Hibernating meadow jumping mouse on Nantucket Island, Massachusetts. Journal of Mammalogy 46(1):67–76.

*Watkins, G. K. 1994. White-tailed deer *(Odocoileus virginianus)* in an urban park in southeastern Virginia. Virginia Journal of Science 45(2):153. Abstract.

Watkins, L. C. 1969. Observations on the distribution and natural history of the evening bat *(Nycticeius humeralis)* in northwestern Missouri and adjacent Iowa. Transactions of the Kansas Academy of Science 72:330–336.

*Watkins, L. C. 1972. *Nycticeius humeralis.* Mammalian Species no. 23.

*Watkins, T. D. 1957. Hunting, fishing and recreation in Chesterfield. Virginia Wildlife 18(8):12, 24.

*Watson, A. M. and R. K. Rose. 1997. The annual reproductive cycle of the meadow vole in a Virginia salt marsh. Virginia Journal of Science 48(2):91. Abstract.

*Watson, E. A. 1901. Some notes on deer at Nimrod Hall, Bath County. American Field 56(22):453.

*Watson, S. 1953. Headwaters of the Potomac. Virginia Wildlife 14(11):10–12.

*Wayne, R. K. and J. L. Gittleman. 1995. The problematic red wolf. Scientific American 273:36–39.

*Webb, R. E., and F. Horsfall, Jr. 1967. Endrin resistance in the pine mouse. Science 156:1762.

*Webster, W. D. 1989. The natural history of two rare mammals (rock shrew, *Sorex dispar,* and rock vole, *Microtus chrotorrhinus*) in North Carolina. Final Report to North Carolina Wildlife Resources Commission, Wilmington, North Carolina.

*Webster, W. D., J. K. Jones, Jr., and R. J. Baker. 1980. *Lasiurus intermedius.* Mammalian Species no. 132.

*Webster, W. D., J. F. Parnell, and W. C. Biggs, Jr. 1985. Mammals of the Carolinas, Virginia, and Maryland. Chapel Hill: University of North Carolina Press.

*Weekes, B. 1970a. Foxy Reynard is fair game for absentee hunter, the trapper. Virginia Wildlife 31(2):9–11.

*Weekes, B. 1970b. Mink and muskrat: fur out of winter's barrenness. Virginia Wildlife 31(3):17–18.

*Weekes, B. 1970c. Let's give the black bear a break. Virginia Wildlife 31(9):9–10.

*Weekes, B. 1970d. Hunting coon. Virginia Wildlife 31(11):6–7, 21–22.

*Weekes, B. 1970e. The deer hunter: what makes him do his thing. Virginia Wildlife 31(12):6–7, 19.

*Weekes, B. 1971. 'Possum! Virginia Wildlife 32(11):19–20.

*Weekes, B. 1972. Squirrel man. Virginia Wildlife 33(11):9–11.

*Weekes, B. 1977. Hunting and the gray squirrel population. Virginia Wildlife 38(5):7–9.

*Weekes, W. D. 1974. A 15-year research summary and hunting harvest data evaluation of the Broad Run Management Area. Master's thesis, Virginia Polytechnic Institute and State University, Blacksburg.

*Weekes, W. D. 1977. The sun grows antlers. Virginia Wildlife 38(5):17–18, 34.

*Weekes, W. D., and B. S. McGinnes. 1976. The white-tailed deer at Broad Run. Virginia Wildlife 37(2):16–17.

*Weigl, P. D. 1969. The distribution of the flying squirrels *Glaucomys volans* and *G. sabrinus:* an evaluation of the competitive exclusion idea. Doctoral dissertation, Duke University, Durham.

Weigl, P. D. 1974. Study of the northern flying squirrel, *Glaucomys sabrinus,* by temperature telemetry. American Midland Naturalist 92(2):482–486.

*Weigl, P. D. 1977. *Glaucomys sabrinus coloratus* Handley. Northern flying squirrel. Pp. 398–400. In: Cooper, J. E., S. S. Robinson, and J. B. Funderburg (editors), Endangered and Threatened Plants and Animals of North Carolina. Raleigh: North Carolina State Museum of Natural History.

*Weigl, P. D. 1978. Resource overlap, interspecific interactions and the distribution of the flying squirrels, *Glaucomys volans* and *G. sabrinus.* American Midland Naturalist 100(1):83–96.

*Weigl, P. D., T. W. Knowles, and A. C. Boynton. 1992. The distribution and ecology of the northern flying squirrel, *Glaucomys sabrinus coloratus,* in the Southern Appalachians. Unpublished final report submitted to United States Fish and Wildlife Service.

*Weigl, P. D., M. A. Steele, L. J. Sherman, J. C. Ha, and T. S. Sharpe. 1989. The ecology of the fox squirrel *(Sciurus niger)* in North Carolina: implications for survival in the Southeast. Bulletin of the Tall Timbers Research Station 24:1–93.

*Welch, J. L., and V. Flyger. 1977. Seasonal feeding habits of white-tailed deer in southern Maryland. Proceedings of the 31st Annual Conference of the Southeastern Association of Fish and Wildlife Agencies 31:159–166.

*Wells-Gosling, N., and L. R. Heaney. 1984. *Glaucomys sabrinus.* Mammalian Species no. 229.

*Wemmer, C., and M. Stüwe. 1985. Reducing deer populations in large enclosures through drives. Wildlife Society Bulletin 13:245–248.

*Wertenbaker, T. J. 1962. Norfolk: historic southern port. Durham: Duke University Press.

*Wertheim, R. F. 1969. Responses of pine voles and white mice to crowding and to bacterial endotoxin.

Master's thesis, Virginia Polytechnic Institute and State University, Blacksburg.

*Wertheim, R. F., and R. F. Giles, Jr. 1971. Effects of bacterial endotoxin and crowding on pine voles and white mice. Journal of Mammalogy 52(1):238–242.

*Wesson, J. A., III. 1975. A deer in hand. Virginia Wildlife 36(8):14–15.

*Wesson, J. A., III. 1976. Influence of physical restraint and restraint-facilitating drugs on blood measurements of white-tailed deer and other selected mammals. Master's thesis, Virginia Polytechnic Institute and State University, Blacksburg.

*Wesson, J. A., III, P. F. Scanlon, R. L. Kirkpatrick, and H. S. Mosby. 1979. Influence of chemical immobilization and physical restraint on packed cell volume, total protein, glucose, and blood urea nitrogen in blood of white-tailed deer. Canadian Journal of Zoology 56:756–767.

*Wesson, J. A., III, P. F. Scanlon, and R. E. Mirarchi. 1975. Immobilization of white-tailed deer with succinylcholine chloride: success rate, reactions of deer and some physiological effects. Proceedings of the 28th Annual Conference of the Southeastern Association of Game and Fish Commissioners 28:500–506.

*West, W. R. 1951. Abnormal tooth development in the groundhog, *Marmota monax monax*. Virginia Journal of Science 2(2):310. Abstract.

*Wetmore, A. 1923. The wood rat in Maryland. Journal of Mammalogy 4(3):187–188.

*Wetmore, A. 1933. The red bat in the Washington region in winter. Journal of Mammalogy 14(2):157–158.

*Wetmore, A. 1936. Hibernation of the brown bat. Journal of Mammalogy 17(2):130–131.

*Wetmore, A. 1952. The gray fox attracted by a crow call. Journal of Mammalogy 33(2):244–245.

*Wetzel, R. M. 1955. Speciation and dispersal of the southern bog lemming, *Synaptomys cooperi* (Baird). Journal of Mammalogy 36(1):1–20.

*Whelan, J. B. 1962. The correlation between available deer browse, forest cover type, and forest site. Master's thesis, Virginia Polytechnic Institute and State University, Blacksburg.

*Whelan, J. B., R. F. Harlow, and H. S. Crawford. 1971. Selectivity, quality, and *in vitro* digestibility of deer foods: a tentative model. Transactions of the 28th Northeast Fish and Wildlife Conference 28:67–81.

*Wheland, J., K. L. Anderson, and P. F. Scanlon. 1981. Frequency of *Gnathostoma miyazakii,* in kidneys of river otters in Virginia. Virginia Journal of Science 32(3):99. Abstract.

Whitaker, J., R. B. Frederick, and T. L. Edwards. 1987. Home-range size and overlap of eastern Kentucky bobcats. Proceedings of the 41st Annual Conference of the Southeastern Association of Fish and Wildlife Agencies 41:417–423.

*Whitaker, J. O., Jr. 1963a. A study of the meadow jumping mouse, *Zapus hudsonius* (Zimmermann), in central New York. Ecological Monographs 33(3):215–254.

Whitaker, J. O., Jr. 1963b. Food, habitat and parasites of the woodland jumping mouse in central New York. Journal of Mammalogy 44(3):316–321.

Whitaker, J. O., Jr. 1963c. Food of 120 *Peromyscus leucopus* from Ithaca, New York. Journal of Mammalogy 44(3):418–419.

Whitaker, J. O., Jr. 1966. Food of *Mus musculus, Peromyscus maniculatus bairdii* and *Peromyscus leucopus* in Vigo County, Indiana. Journal of Mammalogy 47(3):473–486.

Whitaker, J. O., Jr. 1967. Hoary bat apparently hibernating in Indiana. Journal of Mammalogy 48(4):663.

Whitaker, J. O., Jr. 1970. The biological subspecies: an adjunct to the biological species. The Biologist 52(1):12–15.

Whitaker, J. O., Jr. 1972a. *Zapus hudsonius*. Mammalian Species no. 11.

*Whitaker, J. O., Jr. 1972b. Food habits of bats from Indiana. Canadian Journal of Zoology 50(6):877–883.

*Whitaker, J. O., Jr. 1974. *Cryptotis parva*. Mammalian Species no. 43.

*Whitaker, J. O., Jr. 1987. Keys to the vertebrates of the eastern United States excluding birds. Second edition. Edina, Minnesota: Alpha Editions, Burgess International Group, Incorporated.

Whitaker, J. O., Jr., and P. Clem. 1992. Food of the evening bat *Nycticeius humeralis* from Indiana. American Midland Naturalist 127:211–214.

Whitaker, J. O., Jr., and W. W. Cudmore. 1987. Food and ectoparasites of shrews of south central Indiana with emphasis on *Sorex fumeus* and *Sorex hoyi.* Proceedings of the Indiana Academy of Science 96:543–552.

Whitaker, J. O., Jr., and S. L. Gummer. 1992. Hibernation of the big brown bat, *Eptesicus fuscus,* in buildings. Journal of Mammalogy 73(2):312–316.

*Whitaker, J. O., Jr., and W. J. Hamilton, Jr. 1998. Mammals of the eastern United States. 3rd edition. Ithaca, New York: Cornell University Press.

Whitaker, J. O., Jr., G. D. Hartman, and R. Hein. 1994. Food and ectoparasites of the southern short-tailed shrew, *Blarina carolinensis* (Mammalia: Soricidae), from South Carolina. Brimleyana 21:97–105.

*Whitaker, J. O., Jr., G. S. Jones, and D. D. Pascal, Jr. 1975. Notes on mammals of the Fires Creek area, Nantahala Mountains, North Carolina, including their ectoparasites. Journal of the Elisha Mitchell Scientific Society 91:13–17.

Whitaker, J. O., Jr., and R. E. Mumford. 1972. Food and ectoparasites of Indiana shrews. Journal of Mammalogy 53(2):329–335.

*Whitaker, Jr., J. O., R. K. Rose, and T. M. Padgett. 1997. Food of the red bat *Lasiurus borealis* in winter in the Great Dismal Swamp, North Carolina and Virginia. American Midland Naturalist 137(2):408-411.

*Whitaker, J. O., Jr., and N. Wilson. 1974. Host distribution lists of mites (Acari), parasitic and phoretic in the hair of wild mammals of North America, North of Mexico. American Midland Naturalist 91:1–67.

*Whitaker, J. O., Jr., and R. E. Wrigley. 1972. *Napaeozapus insignis.* Mammalian Species no. 14o. 14.

*White, C. P. 1982. Endangered threatened wildlife of the Chesapeake Bay region: Delaware, Maryland, and Virginia. Maryland: Tidewater Publications.

*White, M., 1974. Museum studies ice age deposits in Bath County cave. Virginia Wildlife 35(5):23.

*White, M. 1975. Recovery team for endangered squirrel. Virginia Wildlife 36(11):23.

*White, M. 1976. Drumming log. Virginia Wildlife 37(11):29.

*White, M. 1983. Bats in your belfry? Virginia Wildlife 44(3):4–6.

*Whitehead, G. K. 1972. Deer of the world. London: Constable and Company.

*Whitehead, T. 1893. Virginia: a hand-book giving its history, climate, and mineral wealth; its educational, agricultural and industrial advantages. Richmond: Everett Waddey Company.

*Whitlock, S. C. 1939. The prevalence of disease and parasites in whitetail deer. Transactions of the 4th North American Wildlife Conference 4:244–249.

*Whitney, C., G. B. Grinnell, and O. Wister. 1904. Musk-ox, bison, sheep and goat. New York: Macmillan Company.

*Whitney, L. F., and A. B. Underwood. 1952. The raccoon. Orange, Connecticut: Practical Science Publishing Company.

*Wiesner, L. O., Jr. 1973. Evaluation of various artificial cover structures for increasing rabbit numbers. Master's thesis, Virginia Polytechnic Institute and State University, Blacksburg.

Wight, H. M. 1931. Reproduction in the eastern skunk *(Mephitis mephitis nigra).* Journal of Mammalogy 12(1):42–47.

*Wigington, J. 1976. Bison in Virginia? Virginia Wildlife 37(7):6.

*Wilcox, S. W. 1976. Deer production in the United States 1969–1973. Tempe: Arizona State University.

*Wilcox, T. F., S. G. Barco, and W. M. Swingle. 1998. Distribution of the Atlantic bottlenose dolphin (*Tursiops truncatus*) in the Chesapeake Bay drainage in Virginia. Brimleyana no. 11:33–37.

*"Wildfowl Will." 1920. Weight of foxes. Forest and Stream 90(9):502–503.

*Wildlife Division Annual Report. 1992. Virginia Department of Game and Inland Fisheries, Richmond.

*Wiley, D. N., R. A. Asmutis, T. D. Pitchford, and D. P. Gannon. 1995. Stranding and mortality of humpback whales, *Megaptera novaeangliae*, in the mid-Atlantic and southeast United States, 1985–1992. Fishery Bulletin, U.S. 93:196–205.

Wiley, R. W. 1971. Activity periods and movements of the eastern woodrat. Southwestern Naturalist 16(1):43–54.

*Wiley, R. W. 1980. *Neotoma floridana.* Mammalian Species no. 139.

Wilkins, K. T. 1990. Range extension and county records for two species of rodents in Texas. Texas Journal of Science 42(2):199–200.

*Willard-Mack, C. L., and C. R. Terman. 1981. Kepone levels of selected terrestrial animal species from the Jamestown Island area. Virginia Journal of Science 32(3):100. Abstract.

*Willey, C. R. 1959. Wild animals as insect control agents. Virginia Wildlife 20(4):5–6.

Williams, C. E., and A. L. Caskey. 1965. Soil fertility and cottontail fecundity in southeastern Missouri. American Midland Naturalist 74(1):211–224.

*Williams, G. L., R. L. Smiley, and B. C. Redington. 1978. A taxonomic study of the genus *Haemogamasus* in North America, with descriptions of two new species (Acari: Mesostigmata, Laelaptidae). International Journal of Acarology 4(3):235–273.

*Williamson, J., J. Morgan, and G. Spiegal. 1991. The coyote problem in the New River valley of Virginia. Proceedings of the new River Symposium 1991:70–79.

*Williamson, J. F., Jr. 1983. The bears of Shenandoah. Virginia Wildlife 44(2):14–16.

*Williamson, J. F., Jr., A. R. Tipton, R. M. Keel, Jr., and J. B. Whelan. 1980. Assessment of black bear habitat suitability in the Great Dismal Swamp. Transactions of the Northeast Section of the Wildlife Society 38:120–132.

*Willner, G. R. 1982. Nutria. Pp. 1059–1076. In: Chapman, J. A., and G. A. Feldhamer (editors), Wild mammals of North America. Baltimore: The Johns Hopkins University Press.

*Wilson, E. W. 1959. The bear in early America. Virginia Wildlife 20(1):20–21.

*Wilson, E. W. 1961. Hunting in early Virginia. Virginia Wildlife 22(12):6–7.

*Wilson, G. 1932. Smyth County history and traditions. Kingsport, Tennessee: Kingsport Press.

*Wilson, J. H. 1967. A test for homing in the gray squirrel. Master's thesis, Virginia Polytechnic Institute and State University, Blacksburg.

*Wilson, K. A. 1954a. The role of mink and otter as muskrat predators in northeastern North Carolina. Journal of Wildlife Management 18(2):199–207.

*Wilson, K. A. 1954b. Litter production of coastal North Carolina muskrats. Proceedings of the 8th Annual Conference of the Southeastern Association of Game and Fish Commissioners 8:13–19.

*Wilson, K. A. 1959. The otter in North Carolina. Proceedings of the 13th Annual Conference of the Southeastern Association of Game and Fish Commissioners 13:267–277.

*Wilson, S. 1982. Parent-young contact in prairie and meadow voles. Journal of Mammalogy 63(2):300–305.

Wilson, W. C. 1967. Food habits of the coyote, *Canis latrans,* in Louisiana. Master's thesis, Louisiana State University, Baton Rouge.

Wimsatt, W. A. 1960. An analysis of parturition in Chiroptera, including new observations on *Myotis l. lucifugus.* Journal of Mammalogy 41(2):183–200.

Wimsatt, W. A. 1969. Some interrelations of reproduction and hibernation in mammals. Pp. 511–549. In:

Woolhouse, H. W. (editor), Dormancy and survival. New York: Academic Press.

*Winkler, W. G. 1975. Fox rabies. Pp. 3–22. In: Baer, G. M. (editor), The natural history of rabies. Volume II. New York: Academic Press.

*Winkler, W. G. 1984. Current status of rabies in the United States. Pp. 17–28. In: Winkler, W. G. (editor), Rabies concepts for medical professionals. Miami, Florida: Merieux Institute, Incorporated.

*Winkler, W. G., and K. Bögel. 1992. Control of rabies in wildlife. Scientific American 266(6):86–92.

*Winkler, W. G., J. S. Shaddock, and C. Bowman. 1985. Rabies virus in salivary glands of raccoons *(Procyon lotor).* Journal of Wildlife Diseases 21(3):297–298.

*Winslow, E. L., and D. E. Sonenshine. 1971. Trap manifested behavior and distribution of raccoons in two natural areas of Virginia as related to available foods. Virginia Journal of Science 22(3):103. Abstract.

Wislocki, G. B., and R. K. Enders. 1941. The placentation of the bottle-nosed porpoise *(Tursiops truncatus).* American Journal of Anatomy 68:97–125.

*Wisner, G. 1996. Saltville site has evidence of 14,000-year-old feasts: Radiocarbon dates in high-resolution context. Mammoth Trumpet 11 (4): 1, 18–20.

*Wodenoth, R. 1649. A perfect description of Virginia: being a full and true revelation of the present state of the plantation, their health, peace and plenty; the number of people, with their abundance of cattel, fowl, fish, etc. London: Printed at the Star under Peter Church in Cornhill.

*Wolfe, J. L. 1982 *Oryzomys palustris.* Mammalian Species no. 176.

*Wolfe, J. L., and A. V. Linzey. 1977. *Peromyscus gossypinus.* Mammalian Species no. 70. American Society of Mammalogists.

*Wolff, J. O. 1984. Proximate causation for intra- and interspecific territoriality in *Peromyscus leucopus* and *P. maniculatus.* Virginia Journal of Science 35(2):92. Abstract.

*Wolff, J. O. 1985a. Maternal aggression as a deterrent to infanticide in *Peromyscus leucopus* and *P. maniculatus.* Animal Behavior 33(1):117–123.

*Wolff, J. O. 1985b. Comparative population ecology of *Peromyscus leucopus* and *Peromyscus maniculatus.* Canadian Journal of Zoology 63(1):1548–1555.

*Wolff, J. O. 1985c. The effects of density, food, and interspecific interference on home range size in *Peromyscus leucopus* and *Peromyscus maniculatus.* Canadian Journal of Zoology 63(11):2657–2662.

*Wolff, J. O. 1986a. Life history strategies of white-footed mice *(Peromyscus leucopus).* Virginia Journal of Science 37(2):75. Abstract.

*Wolff, J. O. 1986b. Life history strategies of white-footed mice *(Peromyscus leucopus).* Virginia Journal of Science 37(4):208–220.

*Wolff, J. O. 1986c. The effects of food on midsummer demography of white-footed mice, *Peromyscus leucopus.* Canadian Journal of Zoology 64(4):855–858.

*Wolff, J. O. 1986d. Infanticide in white-footed mice, *Peromyscus leucopus.* Animal Behavior 34(5):1568.

*Wolff, J. O. 1986e. Getting along in Appalachia. Natural History 95:44–48.

*Wolff, J. O. 1989. Social behavior. Pp. 271–291. In: Kirkland, G. L., Jr., and J. N. Layne (editors), Advances in the study of *Peromyscus* (Rodentia). Lubbock: Texas Tech University Press.

*Wolff, J. O. 1992. Parents suppress reproduction and stimulate dispersal in opposite-sex juvenile white-footed mice. Nature (London) 359(6394):409–410.

*Wolff, J. O. 1993. Does the "Chitty effect" occur in *Peromyscus?* Journal of Mammalogy 74(4):846–851.

*Wolff, J. O. 1994. Reproductive success of solitarily and communally nesting white-footed mice and deer mice. Behavioral Ecology 5(2):206–209.

*Wolff, J. O., and D. M. Cicirello. 1989. Field evidence for sexual selection and resource competition infanticide in white-footed mice. Animal Behavior 38(4):637–642.

*Wolff, J. O., and R. D. Dueser. 1983. Competition between *Peromyscus leucopus* and *P. maniculatus.* Virginia Journal of Science 34(3):137. Abstract.

*Wolff, J. O., and R. D. Dueser. 1986. Noncompetitive coexistence between *Peromyscus* species and *Clethrionomys gapperi.* Canadian Field-Naturalist 100(2):186–191.

*Wolff, J. O., R. D. Dueser, and K. S. Berry. 1985. Food habits of sympatric *Peromyscus leucopus* and *Peromyscus maniculatus.* Journal of Mammalogy 66(4):795–798.

*Wolff, J. O., and D. S. Durr. 1986. Winter nesting behavior of *Peromyscus leucopus* and *Peromyscus maniculatus.* Journal of Mammalogy 67(2):409–412.

*Wolff, J. O., M. H. Freeberg, and R. D. Dueser. 1983. Interspecific territoriality in two sympatric species of *Peromyscus* (Rodentia: Cricetidae). Behavioral Ecology and Sociobiology 12(3):237–242.

*Wolff, J. O., and B. Hurlbutt. 1982. Day refuges of *Peromyscus leucopus* and *Peromyscus maniculatus.* Journal of Mammalogy 63(4):666–668.

*Wolff, J. O., and K. I. Lundy. 1985a. Intra-familial dispersion patterns in white-footed mice, *Peromyscus leucopus.* Virginia Journal of Science 36(2):116. Abstract.

*Wolff, J. O., and K. I. Lundy. 1985b. Intra-familial dispersion patterns in white-footed mice, *Peromyscus leucopus.* Behavioral Ecology and Sociobiology 17(4):381–384.

*Wolff, J. O., K. I. Lundy, and R. Baccus. 1988. Dispersal, inbreeding avoidance and reproductive success in white-footed mice. Animal Behavior 36(2):456–465.

*Wolff, J. O., and C. VanCleef. 1983. Species recognition and behavioral isolation in *Peromyscus leucopus* and *P. maniculatus.* Virginia Journal of Science 34(3):137. Abstract.

*Womack, J. C. 1960. Letters. Fawn, fish and friends. Virginia Wildlife 21(7):3.

Wood, J. E. 1958. Age structure and productivity of a gray fox population. Journal of Mammalogy 39(1):74–86.

Wood, N. A. 1922. The mammals of Washtenaw County, Michigan. Occasional Papers of the Museum of Zoology, University of Michigan no. 123.

*Wood, R. K. 1939. Virginia elk hunting grows in popularity. Virginia Wildlife 3(3):3.

*Wood, R. K. 1940a. On winter trails of the American elk. Richmond, Virginia, Times Dispatch. February 4, 1940:4.

*Wood, R. K. 1940b. Elk in Virginia. Virginia Journal of Science 1(2):217–218.

*Wood, R. K. 1940c. Ears or antlers? Virginia Wildlife 4(2):62–65.

*Wood, R. K. 1943. The elk in Virginia. Master's thesis, Virginia Polytechnic Institute and State University, Blacksburg.

Wood, W. F. 1990. New components in defensive secretion of the striped skunk, *Mephitis mephitis.* Journal of Chemical Ecology 16(6):2057–2065.

Wood, W. F., C. G. Morgan, and A. Miller. 1991. Volatile components in defensive spray of the spotted skunk, *Spilogale putorius.* Journal of Chemical Ecology 17(7):1415–1420.

*Woodfin, M. 1932. William Byrd and the Royal Society. Virginia Magazine of History and Biography 40(1):23–34; (2):111–113.

*Wooding, J. B., J. A. Cox, and M. R. Pelton. 1994. Distribution of black bears in the southeastern coastal plain. Proceedings of the 48th Annual Conference of the Southeastern Association of Fish and Wildlife Agencies 48:270–275.

Wooding, J. B., E. P. Hill, and P. W. Sumner. 1984. Coyote food habits in Mississippi and Alabama. Proceedings of the 38th Annual Conference of the Southeastern Association of Fish and Wildlife Agencies 38:182–188.

*Woods, C. A., L. Contreas, G. Willner-Chapman, and H. P. Widden, 1992. *Myocastor coypus.* Mammalian Species no. 398:1–8.

*Woodside, A. M. 1943. Orchard mouse control. Virginia Fruit 31:111–115.

*Woodside, A. M., R. N. Jefferson, R. C. Moore, and E. H. Glass. 1942. Control of field mice in apple orchards. Virginia Polytechnic Institute Experiment Station Bulletin 344.

*Woodson, D. L. 1975. Behavior of yearling white-tailed deer orphaned as fawns. Master's thesis, Virginia Polytechnic Institute and State University, Blacksburg.

*Woodson, D. L., B. S. McGinnes, and R. L. Downing. 1975. Behavior of yearling white-tailed deer orphaned as fawns. Virginia Journal of Science 26(2):61. Abstract.

*Woodson, D. L., E. T. Reed, R. L. Downing, and B. S. McGinnes. 1980. Effect of fall orphaning on white-tailed deer fawns and yearlings. Journal of Wildlife Management 44(1):249–252.

*Woodward, S. L., and R. L. Hoffman. 1991. The nature of Virginia. Pp. 23–48. In: Terwilliger, K. (coordinator). Virginia's Endangered Species. Blacksburg: The McDonald & Woodward Publishing Company.

*Woolley, D. J. 1940. The survival of restocked deer in Virginia. Master's thesis, Virginia Polytechnic Institute and State University, Blacksburg.

*Woolley, D. J. 1946. The white-tailed deer. Virginia Wildlife 7(5):6–7, 16.

*Woolley, D. J. 1947. The muskrat. Virginia Wildlife 8(11):6–8.

*Worley, O. 1967. Deer opener is dear to hunters. Virginia Wildlife 28(11):8, 17.

*Worley, O. 1968. A season to remember. Virginia Wildlife 29(3):4.

*Worley, O. 1970a. Home-made caller fools toms. Virginia Wildlife 31(4):7, 16.

*Worley, O. 1970b. This hunter-angler is a real "equal." Virginia Wildlife 31(11):10–11.

*Woronecki, P. P. 1961. Evaluation of some cottontail rabbit management procedures as applied in Piedmont Virginia. Master's thesis, Virginia Polytechnic Institute and State University, Blacksburg.

Worth, C. B. 1950. Field and laboratory observations on roof rats, *Rattus rattus* (Linnaeus), in Florida. Journal of Mammalogy 31(3):293–304.

*Wright, D. E. 1977. Geographic and seasonal variation in the tail and body measurements of the hispid cotton rat, *Sigmodon hispidus.* Master's thesis, Virginia Commonwealth University, Richmond.

*Wright, D. E., and J. F. Pagels. 1975. Scansoriality in the cotton rat, *Sigmodon hispidus.* Virginia Journal of Science 26(2):61. Abstract.

*Wright, D. E., and J. F. Pagels. 1977. Climbing activity in the hispid cotton rat, *Sigmodon hispidus,* and the eastern meadow vole, *Microtus pennsylvanicus.* Chesapeake Science 18(1):87–89.

*Wright, H. E., and D. G. Frey (editors), 1965. The Quaternary of the United States. Princeton, New Jersey: Princeton University Press.

Wright, P. L. 1947. The sexual cycle of the male long-tailed weasel *(Mustela frenata).* Journal of Mammalogy 28(4):343–352.

Wright, P. L. 1948. Breeding habits of captive long-tailed weasels *(Mustela frenata).* American Midland Naturalist 39(2):338–344.

*Wright, S. L. and R. K. Rose. 1995. The diet of *Oryzomys palustris* based on stomach content analysis. Virginia Journal of Science 46(2):100. Abstract.

*Wrigley, R. E. 1972. Systematics and biology of the woodland jumping mouse, *Napaeozapus insignis.* Illinois Biological Monograph 47. Urbana: University of Illinois Press.

*Wyman, J. 1850. Notice of remains of vertebrated animals found at Richmond, Virginia. American Journal of Science 10(21):228–235.

*Wyman, J. 1857. Fossil bones of seals found beneath the city of Richmond, were exhibited. Proceedings of the Boston Society of Natural History 3:241.

*Yager, R. H., W. S. Gochenour, Jr., A. D. Alexander, and P. W. Wetmore. 1953. Natural occurrence of *Leptospira ballum* in rural house mice and in an opossum. Proceedings of the Society of Experimental Biology and Medicine 84(3):589–590.

*Yancey, D. 1992. Pet project gets a name. Roanoke Times and World News, July 15, 1992:B3.

*Yancey, D. 1993. Love match isn't a howling success. Roanoke Times and World News.

Yates, T. 1978. The systematics and evolution of North American moles (Insectivora: Talpidae). Doctoral dissertation, Texas Technological University.

*Yates, T. L., W. R. Barber, and D. M. Armstrong. 1987. Survey of North American collections of Recent mammals. Journal of Mammalogy 68(2), supplement:1–76.

Yates, T. L., and I. F. Greenbaum. 1982. Biochemical systematics of North American moles (Insectivora: Talpidae). Journal of Mammalogy 63(3):368–374.

*Yates, T. L., and R. J. Pedersen. 1982. Moles. Pp. 37–51. In: Chapman, J. A., and G. A. Feldhamer (editors), Wild mammals of North America. Baltimore: The Johns Hopkins University Press.

*Yates, T. L., and D. J. Schmidly. 1978. *Scalopus aquaticus.* Mammalian Species no. 105.

Yeager, L. E. 1937. Naturally sustained yield in a farm fur crop in Mississippi. Journal of Wildlife Management 1(1):28–36.

*Yeager, L. E. 1941. A contribution toward a bibliography on North American fur animals. Biological Notes no. 16. Urbana: Illinois Natural History Survey.

Yeager, L. E. 1943. Storing of muskrats and other foods by minks. Journal of Mammalogy 24(1):100–101.

Yeager, L. E., and R. G. Rennels. 1943. Fur yield and autumn foods of the raccoon in Illinois river bottom lands. Journal of Wildlife Management 7(1):45–60.

Yearsley, E. F., and D. E. Samuel. 1980. Use of reclaimed surface mines by foxes in West Virginia. Journal of Wildlife Management 44:729–734.

*Yeatter, R. E., and D. H. Thompson. 1952. Tularemia, weather and rabbit populations. Illinois Natural History Survey Bulletin 25(6):351–382.

Yerger, R. W. 1953. Home range, territoriality, and populations of the chipmunk in central New York. Journal of Mammalogy 34(4):448–458.

Yerger, R. W. 1955. Life history notes on the eastern chipmunk, *Tamias striatus lysteri* (Richardson), in central New York. American Midland Naturalist 53(2):312–323.

*Yocum, S. M. 1988. Effects of low level lead and cadmium on reproduction in *Peromyscus leucopus* and a study of lead concentrations in small mammals from old orchards. Master's thesis, Virginia Polytechnic Institute and State University, Blacksburg.

*Yocum, S. M., P. F. Scanlon, M. Moss, and W. E. Montz, Jr. 1986. Reproductive characteristics of a captive colony of *Peromyscus leucopus.* Virginia Journal of Science 37(2):76. Abstract.

Yoho, N. S., and V. G. Henry. 1972. Foods of the gray fox *(Urocyon cinereoargenteus)* on European wild hog *(Sus scrofa)* range in east Tennessee. Journal of the Tennessee Academy of Science 47(2):77–79.

*Young, S. P. 1946. The wolf in North American history. Caldwell, Idaho: Caxton Printers.

*Young, S. P. 1956. The deer, the Indians and the American pioneers. Pp. 1–27. In: Taylor, W. P. (editor), The deer of North America. Harrisburg, Pennsylvania: The Stackpole Company.

*Young, S. P. 1958. The bobcat of North America. Harrisburg, Pennsylvania: The Stackpole Company.

*Young, S. P., and E. A. Goldman. 1944. The wolves of North America. New York: Dover Publications.

*Young, S. P., and E. A. Goldman. 1946. The puma, mysterious American cat. Washington, D. C.: American Wildlife Institute.

*Young, S. P., and H. H. T. Jackson. 1951. The clever coyote. Harrisburg, Pennsylvania: The Stackpole Company and Washington, D. C.: Wildlife Management Institute.

*Zadnik, A. K. and M. T. Mengak. 1996. Habits and mating behavior of captive Allegheny woodrats *(Neotoma magister).* Virginia Journal of Science 47(2):98. Abstract.

*Zakrzewski, R. J. 1985. The fossil record. Pp. 1–51. In: Tamarin, R. H. (editor), Biology of New World *Microtus.* American Society of Mammalogists Special Publication no. 8.

*Zepp, R. L., Jr. 1974. The effects of a PCB and a restricted diet and their interaction on cottontail rabbit reproductive characteristics. Master's thesis, Virginia Polytechnic Institute and State University, Blacksburg.

*Zepp, R. L., and R. L. Kirkpatrick. 1974. Diurnal variation of plasma corticoid levels in captive cottontail rabbits. Virginia Journal of Science 25(2):71. Abstract.

*Zepp, R. L., Jr., and R. L. Kirkpatrick. 1976. Reproduction in cottontails fed diets containing a PCB. Journal of Wildlife Management 40(3):491–495.

*Zepp, R. L., Jr., O. T. Sanders, and R. L. Kirkpatrick. 1974. Reduction of pentobarbital-induced sleeping times in PCB-treated cottontail rabbits. Bulletin of Environmental Contamination and Toxicology 12(5):518–521.

Zimmerman, R. S. 1943. A coyote's speed and endurance. Journal of Mammalogy 24(3):400.

*Zimmerman, T. E., and A. A. Dugdale. 1971. Bear Tolley — great hunter of long ago. Virginia Wildlife 32(1):4–5, 20.

Zinn, T. L. and S. H. Humphrey. 1983. Seasonal food resources and prey selection of the southeastern brown bat *(Myotis austroriparius)* in Florida. Florida Scientist 44:81–90.

Index